PAN	Polyarteritis nodosa	**PSS**	Progressive systemic sclerosis	
P and P	Prothrombin and preconvertin time	**PT**	Prothrombin time	
PCO	Polycystic ovarian disease	**PTH**	Parathyroid hormone	
PCO_2	Partial pressure of carbon dioxide	**PTT**	Partial prothrombin time	
PCP	*Pneumocystis carinii* pneumonia	**Q**	Pulmonary perfusion	
		RA	Rheumatoid arthritis	
PDGF	Platelet-dependent growth factor	**RAS**	Renin-angiotensin system (consider context)	
PET	Positron emission tomography	**RAS**	Reticular activating system (consider context)	
PF-3	Platelet factor 3	**RBC**	Red blood cell	
PGE	Prostaglandin E	**RDN**	Respiratory disease of the newborn	
PGE_2	Prostaglandin E_2	**RDS**	Respiratory distress syndrome	
PGI_2	Prostaglandin I_2			
PHP	Pseudohypoparathyroidism	**RF**	Rheumatic fever (consider context)	
PID	Pelvic inflammatory disease			
PKD	Polycystic kidney disease	**RF**	Rheumatoid factor (consider context)	
PKU	Phenylketonuria			
PMN	Polymorphonuclear (leukocyte)	**RHD**	Rheumatic heart disease	
		RNA	Ribonucleic acid	
PMS	Premenstrual syndrome	**RS**	Reed-Sternberg cell	
PN	Pyelonephritis	**RV**	Residual volume	
PNH	Paroxysmal nocturnal hemoglobinuria	**SA**	Sacroiliac joint	
		SAA	Serum amyloid-associated protein	
PNS	Peripheral nervous system			
PO_2	Partial pressure of oxygen	**SAP**	Systemic arterial pressure	
PRCA	Pure red cell aplasia	**SCID**	Severe combined immunodeficiency disease	

SGOT	Serum glutamic oxaloacetic transaminase
SIADH	Syndrome of inappropriate ADH secretion
SL	Semilunar
SLE	Systemic lupus erythematosus
SPECT	Single photon emission computerized tomography
SSPE	Subacute sclerosing panencephalitis
SV	Stroke volume
T1, T2, etc.	First, second thoracic vertebrae, etc.
T_3	Triiodothyronine
T_4	Thyroxine
TAF	Tumor angiogenesis factor
TBG	Thyroxine-binding globulin
TBW	Total body water
T_C	Cytotoxic T cell
TC-II	Transcobalamin II
TENS	Transcutaneous electrical nerve stimulation
TF	Tissue factor
T_H	Helper T cell
THA	Tetrahydroaminoacridine
THP	Tissue hydrostatic pressure
TLC	Total lung capacity
TNF	Tumor necrosis factor

TOP	Tissue osmotic pressure
t-PA	Tissue plasminogen activator
TRAb	TSH receptor antibody
TRH	Thyrotropin-releasing hormone
T_S	Suppressor T cell
TSA	Tumor-associated antigens
TSAb	Thyroid-stimulating antibody
TSF	Thrombocytosis-stimulating factor
TSH	Thyroid-stimulating hormone
TSI	Thyroid-stimulating immunoglobulin
TT	Thrombin time
TTP	Thrombotic thrombocytopenic purpura
TxA_2	Thromboxane A_2
UC	Ulcerative colitis
UCB	Unconjugated bilirubin
V	Pulmonary ventilation
VC	Vital capacity
VLDL	Very-low-density lipoprotein
vWF	Von Willebrand's factor
WBC	White blood cell

Essentials of Pathophysiology

Concepts and Applications for Health Care Professionals

Essentials of Pathophysiology

Concepts and Applications for Health Care Professionals

Thomas J. Nowak
British Columbia Institute of Technology

A. Gordon Handford
British Columbia Institute of Technology

In Consultation with
Geraldine M. Whitelegg, M.D.
Paul M. Zulver, M.A., B.M., B.Ch., (Oxon.)

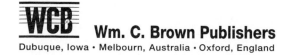
Wm. C. Brown Publishers
Dubuque, Iowa • Melbourn, Australia • Oxford, England

Book Team

Editor *Colin H. Wheatley*
Developmental Editor *Jane E. DeShaw*
Production Editor *Cathy Ford Smith*
Designer *Eric Engelby*
Art Editor *Jodi Wagner*
Photo Editor *Rose Deluhery*
Permissions Coordinator *Karen Dorman*

Wm. C. Brown Publishers

A Division of Wm. C. Brown Communications, Inc.

Vice President and General Manager *Beverly Kolz*
Vice President, Publisher *Kevin Kane*
Vice President, Director of Sales and Marketing *Virginia S. Moffat*
National Sales Manager *Douglas J. DiNardo*
Marketing Manager *Patrick Reidy*
Advertising Manager *Janelle Keeffer*
Director of Production *Colleen A. Yonda*
Publishing Services Manager *Karen J. Slaght*
Permissions/Records Manager *Connie Allendorf*

Wm. C. Brown Communications, Inc.

President and Chief Executive Officer *G. Franklin Lewis*
Corporate Senior Vice President, President of WCB Manufacturing *Roger Meyer*
Corporate Senior Vice President and Chief Financial Officer *Robert Chesterman*

Copyedited by Emily Arulpragasam

The credits section for this book begins on page 655 and
is considered an extension of the copyright page.

Illustrations provided by Diphrent Strokes and WCBC Illustration
Department.

Printed in the United States of America by Wm. C. Brown Communications, Inc.,
2460 Kerper Boulevard, Dubuque, IA 52001

10 9 8 7 6 5 4 3 2 1

To my parents, my wife Maryanna, and my children Allison, Christopher, and Andrea. If not for you, for whom?
T.J.N.

To my family and friends.
A.G.H.

Brief Contents

Preface xv
acknowledgements xvi
notes to the reader xvii

Contents

x   Contents

Preface

This text provides an introduction to the essential concepts of pathophysiology for those in training as allied health care professionals. These are the nonphysicians who provide the basis for diagnosis, therapy, and care in various health care settings. The text's writing grew out of the difficulty we encountered in seeking a pathophysiology text that could meet our students' needs without overwhelming them with irrelevant or distracting detail. A further problem was that texts of the appropriate level often included too many specifics of clinical practice. These too often interfere with the students' view of the foundation concepts.

In answer to these difficulties, we have produced a focused treatment of the essential concepts of pathophysiology at a level appropriate to most students' needs. It also avoids undue emphasis on the clinical specifics of any one specialty, presenting the fundamental "whys" and de-emphasizing the clinical "how to's." The result is a text that provides a better fit with today's crowded curricula. We have simplified the content without diluting it.

Recognizing the substantial variations in level among the various health care training programs, we have sought to provide sufficient information to minimize any deficiencies.

On the other hand, some of the material may be seen as a bit too deep on first exposure; it is included because it may well prove useful at some later point in the curriculum or after entry to practice. We hope that the text will retain a place in the graduate's professional reference library.

This text stands alone as an instructional resource, but we have sought to extend its effectiveness by integrating its traditional typeset components with contemporary laserdisc technology. This aim is achieved by the placement of barcodes on the printed page. The barcodes are keyed to a laserdisc collection of thousands of pathology images contained on the laserdisc entitled *A Slice of Life*. For those with access to a laserdisc player, monitor, and barcode reader in a library, learning center, or classroom, a given conceptual point made on the printed page can be instantly reinforced by a relevant full-color image. This approach allows visual learning support that text production costs make prohibitive. The result is a powerfully integrated learning system that sustains student interest, enhances motivation, and provides additional scope for the creative instructor's classroom and laboratory activities.

Acknowledgements

The names on the title page of this book do not accurately reflect the many who have played a direct or indirect part in bringing this project to completion. We are pleased to acknowledge the contributions of the following.

The Department of Pathology in the University of British Columbia's Faculty of Medicine, and in particular, Dr. W. Chase for access to the specimens in the Boyd Museum and the preparation of many of the photographs which augment the text.

The BCIT Department of Medical Radiography Technology, for access to its collection of medical radiographs.

The BCIT Department of Medical Laboratory Technology, for use of its facilities and histological slide collection.

Ken Kajiwara, for his photographic skill and experience, delivered far beyond the degree indicated by the numbers on the invoice.

Dr. John H. Emes, Ph.D., for his gracious contribution to the text's graphics.

Our medical consultants, Dr. Geraldine Whitelegg and Dr. Paul Zulver, whose patience and guidance were invaluable assets in focusing our efforts.

Our families, who accepted, with good grace, the necessity of too frequently having to take second place to "The Book."

We are also indebted to the manuscript reviewers whose knowledge and objective appraisal kept us to the straight and narrow:

Reviewers

John Dziak
Community College of Allegheny County

Lois S. Ellis
Indiana Wesleyan University

Louis A. Giacinti
Milwaukee Area Technical College

Larry E. Hibbert
Ricks College

Larry S. Johns
Camosun College

Lori Kashuba
University of Alberta Hospitals School of Nursing

Holly J. Morris
Lehigh County Community College

William L. Teitjen
Georgia Southwestern College

James K. VanArsdel
Chapman University

T.J.N.
A.G.H.

Notes to the Reader

To promote a clear understanding of the essentials of pathophysiology, the information in this text is presented in a logical progression of conceptual development. A core of foundation material is treated in the introduction and first six chapters, which constitute part I. Part II then goes on to explore the patterns of disease in the body's major organ systems. Each chapter in part II provides a review of those aspects of normal anatomy and physiology required for an understanding of the pathophysiology that follows. If you are fresh from your anatomy and physiology preparation, you may well forgo these, but many students will find them useful and conveniently placed.

The demands of individual curricula will, of course, dictate the sequence of topics in a given course of study, but where possible, we strongly recommend that you follow the chapter sequence as it stands. We feel that it provides a logically unfolding conceptual framework that fosters better understanding and increases the ease with which this information can be transferred to your clinical experiences.

We have placed great emphasis on the visual components of the text. Photographs have been selected to establish certain points, and where appropriate, these are reinforced with details of the history behind the image to provide greater impact. In many cases, we employ carefully executed line art to emphasize key elements and to de-emphasize the potentially confusing nonessentials that can make a specimen or microscopic field very difficult to interpret. Finally, because of their usefulness and popularity, we have made extensive use of flow charts. These not only crystallize the essence of pathogenesis for many students, they also provide a convenient means of study and review.

Throughout the text, special interest content is highlighted with icons to indicate the focus of the material:

Research   Clinical applications

General interest   Extra detail

Some instructors may leave these for you to pursue as your interests dictate, or may use them as a stimulus to classroom discussions or to further exploration in term papers or class presentations.

A case study is provided at the end of each chapter. This provides some "real world" reference that reinforces the information in the chapter, at the same time illustrating that the development and treatment of disease are often not as straightforward or tidy as one might hope. They also serve as reminders that not all health care is provided in large metropolitan medical centers. In addition, the case studies provide an insight into the way in which the various imaging, diagnostic laboratory, and nursing fields combine to address a given patient's situation—a perspective easily lost amid the details and restricted focus of day-to-day activity in one's particular field.

Because the training of health care professionals involves a significant amount of clinical exposure, we include some references to diagnostic procedures and therapy. Our goal is not to provide specific instruction in these areas, but rather to show how their clinical relevance logically emerges from the principles of pathophysiology. Also, linking clinical situations to their underlying pathophysiology provides for more meaningful learning and better retention.

To promote easier recognition of the essentials, at the end of each chapter we list its key concepts, referenced to relevant text pages. These might be thought of as representing the trunk and main branches of the pathophysiological tree, with the twigs and leaves seen as specific matters of detail. The different specialty fields in which health care professionals practice, by their different emphases, may require a different mix of these details, but the key concepts form the core that is common to all.

At each chapter's end we also present a selection of review activities. These are intended to stimulate a more positive and effective interaction with the subject matter as a means of enhancing understanding and retention. An active approach is far more effective than repeatedly rereading the same pages or pursuing other, similarly passive and inefficient study practices. Once you become familiar with this approach and experience its benefits, you should be able to generate similar review activities on your own. We are confident that more effective and enjoyable learning experiences will result.

This text can be used like any other, but if you have access to a library, learning center, or classroom equipped with a barcode laserdisc system and the laserdisc *A Slice of Life,* it has an added dimension. As you read, the text indicates points at which a barcode on the page should be scanned. The barcode sends an image to the screen that illustrates the point made in the text. In this way, many more images can be made available than could possibly be included in the text. Another approach is to read the text first, and then to return to the barcoded images to review and reinforce the text content, verifying understanding and retention. You may develop other uses for these readily accessible images, such as class presentations. Whatever your learning style, this added capability of the text gives you the potential to develop new and creative learning activities.

Finally, a word about our text's logo. We selected Leonardo daVinci's famous drawing, which depicts the human figure's proportion and balance, as representative of the state of health and well being. Although subject to disruption by the various disease processes described in the text, it is the restoration of this state toward which the efforts of health care professionals are directed. Our best wishes for your studies in pursuit of this goal!

Part One

Foundation Concepts of Pathophysiology

Introduction

Objection, evasion, distrust, and irony are signs of health.
Everything absolute belongs to pathology.

Friedrich Wilhelm Nietzche
Beyond Good and Evil

Before we proceed to study the specifics of pathophysiology, it will be useful to establish a core of fundamentals. These provide the context in which all subsequent text material is presented and introduce some essential terminology that is widely used by health care professionals.

First, let us distinguish between the terms **pathology** and **pathophysiology.** While both terms refer to the study of disease, pathology is a broader term dealing with all aspects of disease. In practice, it is usually used in the context of the work of physicians or pathologists who are concerned not only with disease generally, but often with the details of the gross and microscopic characteristics of diseased organs or tissues. By contrast, the focus of pathophysiology is the abnormal functioning of diseased organs with application to diagnostic procedures and patient care. Of course, the two terms have large areas in common, and the distinction between them is more of emphasis than of essential difference. The health care professionals for whom this book is intended will find that pathophysiology is the more useful focus.

DISEASE AND ETIOLOGY

We consider that we are healthy when our physical and mental capacities can be fully utilized. When these are impaired, we say that disease is present. Broadly speaking, a disruption of the homeostatic balance required for optimal cellular function underlies the loss of functional capacity. This disruption at the cellular level will, sooner or later, be expressed at the somatic (whole body) level, and be recognized as disease.

The cause of a disease is called its etiological agent, or its **etiology.** Strictly speaking, etiology is the study of disease causation, but common usage equates the terms etiology and cause. For example, you might hear that some types of liver disease have a viral etiology, while others are caused by blockage of the bile ducts. When etiology is unknown, the disease is said to be **idiopathic.**

Considered broadly, there are three categories of etiology. Diseases are described as genetic, congenital, or acquired. In disease with a **genetic** etiology, an individual's genes are responsible for some structural or functional defect. A normal gene may mutate (change) and become defective, but more often, defective genes are passed from parents to their offspring. In **congenital** disease, the genetic information is intact, but other factors in the embryo's intrauterine environment interfere with normal development. Cysticfibrosis is a genetic disease, whereas fetal alcohol syndrome is the result of a mother's alcohol intake, which produces congenital abnormalities in a genetically normal infant. The third, and largest, category of etiology is **acquired** disease. In these conditions, genes and development are normal, but other factors, encountered later, produce the disease. Examples are tuberculosis, emphysema, or acquired immune deficiency syndrome (AIDS).

SIGNS, SYMPTOMS, AND PATHOGENESIS

When indications of illness arise, the sufferer may seek medical assistance. Medical personnel will respond by assessing the patient's description of the nature and timing of the abnormalities (the **medical history**), and then perform an examination. The patient may describe sensations of abnormality such as pain or **malaise,** the generalized feeling of illness or loss of well-being. These are known as **symptoms** because they reflect the patient's subjective experiences; no one else can feel the patient's pain or experience the malaise. On the other hand, a **sign** can be detected by an observer, for example, elevated body temperature in fever, or an altered pulse rate. Consider the situation of a patient's abdominal pain, a symptom experienced only by the patient, and abdominal tenderness, a sign. An observer can't feel the pain, but can easily see the patient's exaggerated response to abdominal pressure.

The characteristic combination of signs and symptoms associated with a particular disease is called a **syndrome.** Some syndromes are so closely linked to a specific disease that the term is used in naming it. Examples include Down's syndrome, a genetic abnormality, adult respiratory distress syndrome (ARDS), fetal alcohol syndrome, and AIDS.

In assessing a patient's signs and symptoms, conclusions can often be drawn about the pattern of development of the disease: its **pathogenesis.** A typical pathogenetic sequence involves some initial damage that produces certain effects, which in turn produce other effects, and so on as the disease progresses. Each stage of the development may produce characteristic signs and symptoms. Another aspect of pathogenesis is the time over which a disease develops. **Acute** conditions have a more rapid onset, develop quickly, and are usually of short duration. By contrast, a **chronic** disease is typically of longer duration, often lasting months or even years. Note, however, that in some chronic diseases the onset is abrupt, while in others the onset is more **insidious,** that is, with seemingly minor changes that don't arouse immediate concern.

The somatic distribution of damage in a particular disease may also be considered as an element of its pathogenesis. If damage is described as **local,** it is confined to one region of the body. In **systemic** disease, the effects are felt more widely. For example, a cancer's early growth might

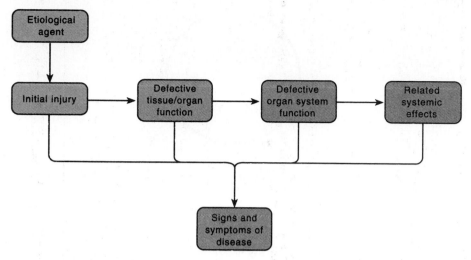

Figure 1.1   The principal elements of disease pathogenesis.

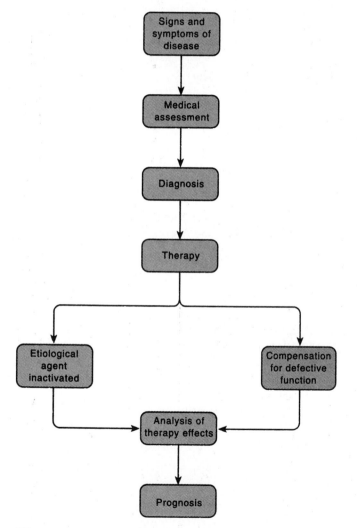

Figure 1.2   Medical intervention in disease.

be localized within the lung, but later in the course of the disease systemic effects result from its spread to other organs. Within a diseased organ, damage is said to be **focal** when limited to one or more distinct sites. If more uniformly distributed, damage is said to be **diffuse**. Figure 1.1 summarizes the principal elements of pathogenesis.

DIAGNOSIS, THERAPY, AND PROGNOSIS

Analysis of an array of signs and symptoms, coupled with a consideration of pathogenesis, often leads to a **diagnosis,** the identification of the patient's specific disease. Once the diagnosis is established, **therapy** can proceed. Therapy is the treatment of disease with the aim of achieving a cure, or at least reducing the patient's signs and symptoms to a level where some near-normal functional capacity can be restored. For example, antibiotic therapy may completely destroy infecting organisms to effect a quick cure. By contrast, in certain heart diseases, one drug might be used to stabilize the heart's rhythm and another to promote loss of excessive body fluid. In this way they make the heart better able to pump efficiently, even though the underlying cause of the problem can't be corrected.

An assessment of the body's responses to therapy, knowledge of a disease's pathogenesis, and clinical experience can all combine to provide the basis for **prognosis.** This is the prediction of a particular disease's outcome (fig. 1.2). Typically, early diagnosis and treatment of cancer is associated with a good prognosis. The prognosis is less good if there is delay in its identification and treatment.

With this background in basic concepts and terminology, we can turn to the study of cell injury. For those in need of a brief review of normal cytology, we start with a section on the normal cell.

Chapter One

Cell Injury

*We do not die wholly at our deaths: we have moldered away
long before.*

William Hazlitt
On the Feeling of Immortality in Youth

I n this chapter's analysis of the causes and mechanisms of cell injury, we often make reference to the normal cell, contrasting it with an injured or otherwise abnormal cell. For this reason, a brief review of normal cell structure and function follows. If your background is up to date, you may want to move directly to the discussion of cell injury. If you do, remember that the review material is here for reference if you need it.

THE NORMAL CELL

In the same way that body structure and function are based on the cell, cellular structure and function are based on subunits of the cell. At the subcellular level, specific cell structures called **organelles** perform the various tasks that contribute to the cell's overall functioning.

The general and specialized functions of the cell are the result of its organization at the chemical level. When left to themselves, atoms and molecules tend toward random patterns of organization. Cells can counter this process, and the ability to do so is critical in the distinction between the living and the nonliving.

The Plasma Membrane

The **cell membrane,** or **plasma membrane,** is composed of phospholipid, cholesterol, glycolipid, protein, and glycoprotein. It is important to the cell in three ways. First, it defines the size and shape of the cell and acts as a container for all its components. Second, the membrane is able to influence the passage of various substances between the cell and its environment. The membrane is described as **selectively permeable,** because some molecules, water for instance, pass freely through it's pores, whereas others, sodium ion for example, are quite restricted in their transmembrane movement. This property of the plasma membrane is especially significant because the cell depends on transmembrane movement for the uptake of nutrients and the outward passage of cell products and wastes (fig. 1.1, *top*). When the cell must expend energy to move molecules against a concentration gradient, the process is described as **active transport.** Because of the energy expenditure, the active transport systems that effect ion movement are known as **ion pumps.**

The properties of the cell membrane also provide for the larger-scale movement of material into or out of the cell. For inward movement (**endocytosis),** a region of the membrane first sags in and then pinches off, forming a vacuole within the cytoplasm. **Phagocytosis** is the type of endocytosis involved in the uptake of particulate matter, while fluids, and the molecules they contain, enter the cell by **pinocytosis.** The process is reversed in **exocytosis,** where cytoplasmic vacuoles merge with the membrane, passing their contents to the cell's exterior (fig. 1.1, *bottom*).

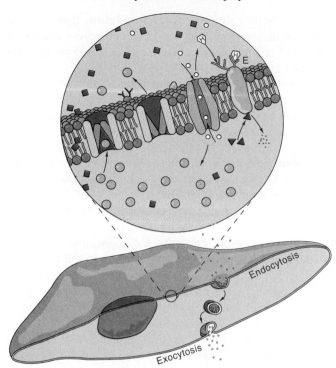

Figure 1.1   *Top:* Magnified endothelial cell membrane, showing lipid-soluble molecules (small squares) passing through membrane by dissolving in membrane lipid. Larger circles represent transport via specific transport systems, while smaller circles move through pores. Binding of hormone (H) at reactive site (E) triggers degradation of intracellular molecule. *Bottom:* Endocytosis and exocytosis.

The third function of the cell membrane derives from the fact that it provides the surface at which the cell interacts with its environment. Factors outside the cell can influence its activities by affecting membrane permeability or cellular metabolism. Such influence depends on the binding of specially structured control chemicals to correspondingly structured **reactive sites** (receptors) in the plasma membrane (fig. 1.1, *top*). These receptors are often formed by the carbohydrate component of membrane glycoprotein. This mechanism is the basis of most hormone-cell interactions, synaptic transmission between neurons, and much of the immune response. Binding at membrane reactive sites also provides for the uptake of specific molecules in some endocytosis.

The Mitochondrion

Many of the molecules entering the cell through its membrane serve as energy sources. Most cellular activity is driven by energy that the cell must extract from these energy-rich molecules. Glucose is the most common such molecule. Once glucose is inside the cell, enzymes break the six-carbon molecule into two three-carbon units.

The organelle called the **mitochondrion,** then extracts much of their energy. ▮ The process involves a series of chemical changes that release the energy in small, easily handled amounts. The energy that is released is captured and stored in adenosine triphosphate (ATP). In ATP the energy is present in the form of chemical bond energy, which is readily available for transfer to various other metabolic pathways as needed.

ATP is produced in the mitochondrion as a product of the **citric acid cycle,** which is also known as the **Krebs cycle.** It involves a sequence of energy-yielding chemical transformations that produce carbon dioxide (CO_2). Complete energy extraction requires that the Krebs cycle reactions be linked to other reaction systems that work with it, releasing energy, consuming oxygen, and producing water. The inhalation of oxygen-rich air and the exhalation of CO_2-rich air reflect, at the somatic level, energy metabolism occurring at the cellular level. Because the mitochondrial reactions require oxygen, the energy metabolism of the mitochondrion is called **aerobic.**

The significance of the mitochondria as the sites of energy metabolism lies in their enzymes. Most enzymes specific to the energy-releasing reactions are found within the mitochondria. Depending on a cell's energy requirements, its cytoplasm may contain a few hundred or as many as thousands of mitochondria. Each of these is composed of two lipoprotein membranes (fig. 1.2, *top*). The outer, limiting membrane provides the characteristic elongated shape of the mitochondrion. The inner membrane is less regular and is thrown into a series of folds, each called a **crista.** The cristae provide a large membrane surface that can support enzymes as dictated by the requirements of the reaction sequences. Thus the mitochondrion not only houses the enzymes but organizes them as well (fig. 1.2, *bottom*).

Much mitochondrial ATP production is used to drive the large amount of synthetic activity carried on by the cell. Formation of cell constituents is required for normal growth and reproduction and for the replacement of damaged organelles. Cells must also be able to synthesize the wide variety of enzymes needed for their membrane functions, energy metabolism, and the synthesis of cell parts and secretions. Because cell organelles are rich in protein, and because enzymes are made of protein as well, much cell activity is devoted to protein synthesis.

Granular Endoplasmic Reticulum

Protein synthesis occurs in the **cytoplasm.** This is the fluid of the cell, which consists of the cell water, its solutes, and the organelles. The physical characteristics of the cytoplasm shift between fluid and gel states as required. The cytoplasm contains an extensive membrane complex called the **endoplasmic reticulum** (ER). ER is normally present

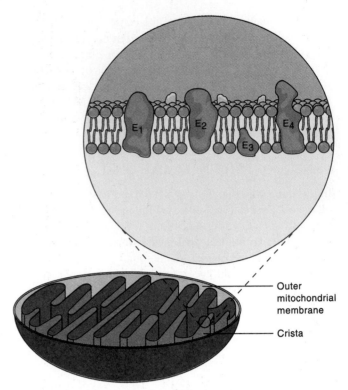

Figure 1.2   Section through a mitochondrion with a portion of one of its cristae magnified to show the linear sequence of four representative enzymes. Held in this sequence, they function more effectively in the stepwise catalytic conversions that are involved in energy metabolism.

in the cytoplasm in two different configurations. One consists of long, parallel arrays of flattened membrane sacs called **cisternae.** The cisternae are interconnected and may have small, rounded masses called **ribosomes** associated with their cytoplasmic surfaces. The presence of ribosomes in this form of ER is indicated in the name **granular endoplasmic reticulum** (GER). The term rough ER is also used (fig. 1.3).

In supporting ribosomes, GER contributes to the synthesis of protein, since protein is formed on the surface of the ribosomes. After it is formed, newly synthesized protein may pass to the interior of the GER, for storage and possible modification, until needed. This occurs not only for protein that is to be moved out of the cell for external use but also for protein that is to be incorporated into cell membranes. Soluble protein that is to be used directly within the cytoplasm is synthesized on the surfaces of free ribosomes, those not associated with the GER.

The Golgi Complex

Before secretion takes place, the GER passes its newly synthesized product to another organelle in the cytoplasm called the **Golgi complex.** This organelle consists of a

Figure 1.3   Granular endoplasmic reticulum (GER). Note the ribosomes at the surface and the interconnections among the cisternae.

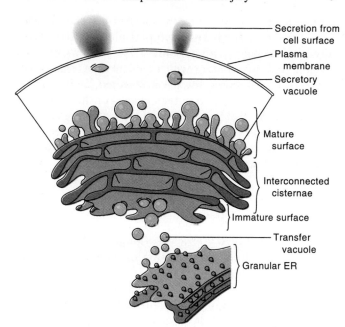

Figure 1.4   The Golgi complex. Cell product received from the GER is stored and/or modified prior to delivery to the plasma membrane for release.

stacked cluster of membranous cisternae. **2** Small pieces of GER membrane, containing newly synthesized protein, pinch off from the GER and join the Golgi complex. On receiving the protein, the Golgi complex stores it until it is needed (fig. 1.4). Often **carbohydrate** or lipid is added to the stored protein to form a fully functional product. When the product is required, small sacs called **vesicles,** containing the newly formed secretion, separate from the Golgi complex and move to the plasma membrane. They merge with it and pass the product to the exterior of the cell. The product is now available to function in the vicinity of the producer cell or at some distant point to which the blood delivers it.

Agranular Endoplasmic Reticulum

The second ER configuration involves smaller, tubular cisternae, which are less uniformly arranged. They lack ribosomes at their membrane surfaces and are therefore described as agranular. The membranes of this **agranular endoplasmic reticulum** (AER) function in detoxification (fig. 1.5), a process in which the enzymes of the AER chemically change substances that threaten the cell by their presence in its cytoplasm. This chemical alteration usually eliminates the potential for damage presented by the foreign substance. Cells are normally exposed to many such potentially damaging agents in the course of their normal activities. AER cisternae also contain enzymes that function in the formation of the major lipid forms: phospholipid, triglyceride, and steroid. For example, a cell secreting steroid hormones would contain significant amounts of AER.

Figure 1.5   Agranular endoplasmic reticulum (AER). Note the lack of ribosomes and the tubular cisternae.

The Lysosome

Another of the cytoplasmic organelles is the **lysosome.** It is found freely distributed in the cytoplasm and consists of a membrane vesicle containing more than thirty different enzymes, which are capable of degrading most macromolecules. For this reason, lysosome membranes must have chemical properties that can resist the activities of the enzymes they contain. In the absence of this resistance, the enzymes would degrade the lysosome membrane and escape to destroy the cell of which they are a part. As foreign material enters the cell, some of the plasma membrane encloses it within a cytoplasmic bubble called a **digestive vacuole** or **phagosome.** Lysosomes move to the vacuole and, by merging with its membrane, empty their enzymes into it. Next, the pH is lowered, activating the enzymes. They then destroy the contents of the vacuole by digesting them (fig. 1.6). When cell organelles are damaged or are no longer required, they are eliminated by a similar process. The vacuole involved is then called an **autophagosome,** because the cell is digesting part of itself.

The Nucleus

The functioning of the various cell organelles is smoothly coordinated and highly efficient. Complex control mechanisms provide internal regulation of their function. The source of this control is found in the cell's **nucleus.** Separated by a two-layered membrane from the cytoplasm, the nucleoplasm contains protein and long filaments of deoxyribonucleic acid (DNA) called **chromosomes.** DNA structure incorporates a coding system that contains the information needed for producing the enzymes on which cellular metabolism depends. Thus all cell function depends on the chromosomes.

Later in this chapter we will see how injury to cells affects the functioning of organelles. First, however, it will be useful to analyze the causes of cell injury.

CAUSES OF CELL INJURY

In analyzing and classifying the causes of cell injury, it is common to identify a fairly large number of causes. For example, in one classification, hypoxia, chemicals, physical agents, infectious agents, immune injury, genetic defects, nutritional imbalances, and aging are cited as the causes of cell injury. Other systems might have five or seven categories. Such approaches may be useful in providing the background needed for diagnosis, therapy, or day-to-day care in a particular disease. However, strictly speaking, there are only three essential means whereby a cell can be injured. From the perspective of the cell's functional needs, injury is the result of (1) the lack of a substance necessary to the cell—a **deficiency,** (2) the presence of a substance that interferes with cell function—poisoning or **intoxication,** or (3) the loss of the cell's structural integrity—physical injury, also called **trauma.**

Deficiency

The life processes of the cell derive from its complex metabolism, presenting a great variety of specific chemical requirements as well as a general need for an energy supply. Any lack of these interferes with cell function and can therefore cause injury. The most common causes of death in Western societies, heart attack and stroke, are caused by oxygen and nutrient deficiencies in critical organs. Starvation involves a lack of dietary energy sources and of

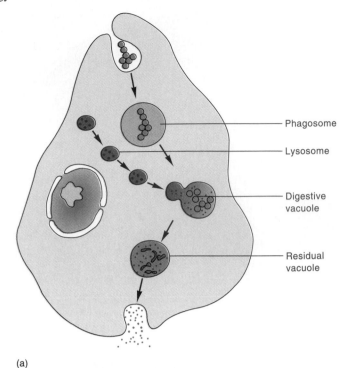

Phagosome

Lysosome

Digestive vacuole

Residual vacuole

(a)

(b)

Figure 1.6 (*a*) The role of the lysosome. Bacteria are destroyed by lysosomal enzymes after fusion of lysosome and phagosome. The resulting debris is expelled by exocytosis. (*b*) Phagocytic cell.

many molecules with specific roles in metabolism. In many cases, diets are ample and even excessive in providing energy sources, but for lack of a specific nutrient, cell injury may still occur. For example, a dietary deficiency of thiamin, one of the B vitamins, causes damage to nervous tissue because the vitamin is required for the normal carbohydrate metabolism of the tissue. A lack in the diet is called a **primary nutrient deficiency;** a **secondary nutrient deficiency** arises when substances that are present in the diet cannot be absorbed.

Genetic defects can also cause injurious deficiencies in cells. Many substances in the cell's metabolic pathways are

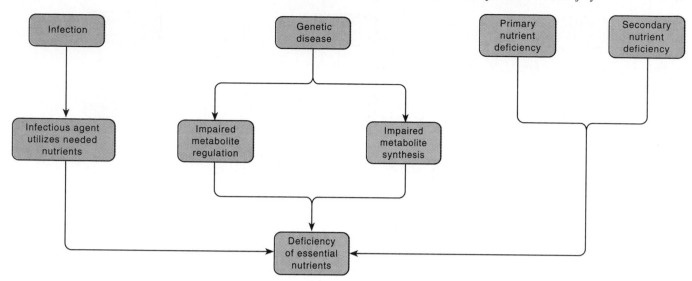

Figure 1.7   Factors that may produce a deficiency of essential nutrients.

synthesized on the basis of information encoded in the genes that are present in the chromosomes. As chromosomes are damaged, production of metabolic intermediates declines and cell function is compromised by the resulting deficiency. Another problem can arise from inadequate genetic control of metabolism. We noted earlier the dependence of cellular metabolism on enzymes that control these complex reactions. It follows that even if adequate amounts of **precursors** (starting forms) and intermediates are available, improper regulation due to lack of controlling enzymes will disrupt cellular function (fig. 1.7).

Remember that our discussion is focused on injury to the cell that suffers the deficiency. In pernicious anemia, a secondary nutrient deficiency arises because gastric mucosal cells cannot synthesize the substance (intrinsic factor) that is needed for the absorption of Vitamin B_{12}. The stomach cells, which cannot produce the intrinsic factor, do not directly suffer for its lack. But without absorption of the vitamin, the marrow's rate of red cell production falls, and all body cells are threatened with a deficiency of oxygen. Another example is viral action, which can cause systemic deficiencies. Following infection of a cell, the virus causes the cell to construct new virus particles, which are then released from the infected cell. Although the cell can survive for some time in this way, it is reasonable to assume that the viruses are utilizing cell metabolites that would otherwise be available for use in the production of substances needed in other parts of the body, e.g., neurotransmitters or hormones.

Intoxication

The second mechanism of cell injury is poisoning. Many substances will interfere with normal function when present within cells. Such injurious substances are called **toxins,** and they are said to produce an intoxication. Toxins may originate outside the cell or they may arise internally. Toxins of external origin are called **exogenous** and can be characterized as being of biological or nonbiological origin.

Biological toxins are produced by living organisms, most commonly by microorganisms. As agents of **infection,** they gain access to body tissues and release injurious substances. The most common sources of biological toxins are bacteria, but other microorganisms, for example, fungi or protozoa, can also produce toxins.

Nonbiological exogenous toxins are injurious chemicals that originate outside the body. Their damaging effect may be the result of exposure to a substance that is not well tolerated, as when carbon tetrachloride (CCl_4) fumes are inhaled. Alternatively, safe levels of a normally used substance may be exceeded. This case is seen in accidental or suicidal overdoses of therapeutic drugs—barbiturate intoxication, for example.

Injurious substances that arise inside the cell are called **endogenous** toxins. They may be formed in several ways (fig. 1.8). One way involves a chromosomal defect that causes a toxic substance to be produced. For example, an abnormal chromosome defect might result in the lack of an enzyme. For its lack, some metabolic intermediate that is normally consumed in the reaction sequence might instead build up to toxic levels. On the other hand, if the intermediate is not itself toxic, its elevated level might activate an alternative metabolic pathway, the products of which are themselves toxic. An example of the latter case is phenylketonuria (PKU). In this condition, toxic phenylketones formed via such an alternative pathway interfere with normal neurological development.

Ionizing radiation, the type associated with X-rays and radioactivity, provides a second means of endogenous toxin production. Ionizing radiation is high-energy radiation that can interact with cell components to produce toxic chemical fragments called free radicals. Free radicals have

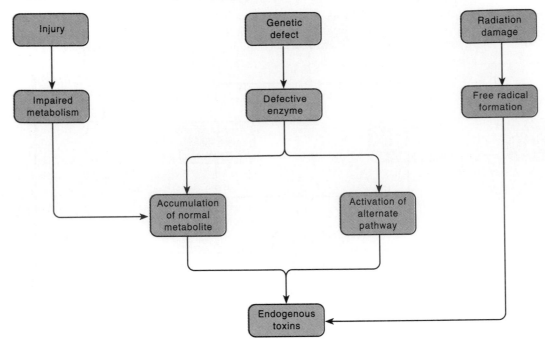

Figure 1.8   Sources of endogenous toxins.

the ability to interact vigorously with other chemical constituents of the cell, disrupting them and interfering with normal functions. Membrane lipids, cell proteins (including enzymes), and DNA are particularly susceptible to free-radical damage.

A third way in which endogenous toxins can arise involves the accumulation of metabolic by-products to toxic levels. Many substances produced by cells are not normally toxic—CO_2 and bilirubin, for example. If they are not removed from the cell, however, their levels rise and damage can result. Note that cell injury from such a build-up of normally tolerated substances is secondary to the problem that has interfered with their normal removal.

Trauma

Trauma is physical injury. Many different agents are able to cause injury by physical disruption of cells. In some cases the physical damage is so great that the cell's integrity is completely lost as its membranes rupture and its contents are dispersed.

Trauma can be caused by physical agents. One is extreme cold, or **hypothermia,** which injures cells as a result of ice crystal formation in the water of the cytoplasm. This kind of damage is typical in frostbite. On the other hand, extreme heat, or **hyperthermia,** damages cells by disrupting and coagulating proteins. Such denaturation of protein is characteristic of burns. Serious injury to the cell results, since both its structural material and its metabolic

enzymes are involved. Burns can result from direct or near contact with a hot object or from exposure to the sun's radiation. Electric currents also cause burning because, as electricity flows through tissue, substantial amounts of heat are produced.

Ionizing radiation is another physical agent that injures by burning when doses are high. At low doses, it also causes damage by disrupting the cell's nucleic acids. One of these, DNA, is highly susceptible to breakage by ionizing radiation. The effects can be serious, especially when the chromosomes of the reproductive cells are involved, because spermatozoa or ova with altered chromosomes can give rise to defects in fetal development.

Mechanical pressure is another source of traumatic injury. In the face of increased pressure, cells are physically overwhelmed and can't maintain their structural integrity. Thus pressure applied to a body surface, the pressure of a rapidly expanding tumor, or that of an abnormally bulging artery can subject adjacent cells to traumatic injury. Sound of high intensity can also cause injury, because loud noises generate high pressures in the fluids of the delicate inner ear.

Physical injury may arise from the action of microorganisms. We noted earlier that some bacteria use toxins to damage cells, but bacteria can also cause physical damage in the infection process. Potent enzymes released by bacteria can break up the connective tissues that support the host's cells, as well as disrupting the cells themselves. Many viral infections commonly involve trauma. As viruses multiply within cells, they cause rupture of the

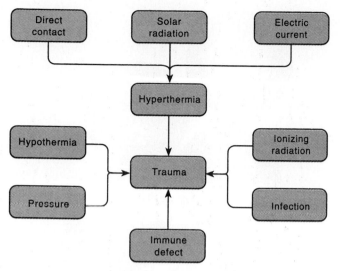

Figure 1.9   Factors in the etiology of cell trauma.

cell membrane, which releases them to infect other cells. Some larger microorganisms, like the protozoa, can attack individual cells. For example, in malaria, a form of the infecting agent (genus *Plasmodium*) that is intermediate in the life cycle causes damage by entering and then rupturing red blood cells. **3**

The immune system normally works to protect us, but sometimes its responses actually cause immune injury. In these cases, antigen-antibody interactions at cell surfaces lead to physical disruption of the cell membrane. An example involves viruses. After entering the cell, a virus can trigger production of many new viruses. The newly formed viruses are released from the cell without damaging it. But in the process, some viral protein becomes incorporated into the plasma membrane. This allows specialized cells of the immune system to recognize the viral protein as foreign and to attack the cell by binding to the viral proteins. The result is membrane trauma and cell death.

Other viruses, the agent of hepatitis B, for example, activate another immune response, which results in the formation of channels or pores in the cell membrane. These, in effect, destroy the barrier and selective permeability functions of the membrane, and the cell's integrity is lost as movement through its membrane becomes unrestricted.

The factors that can produce traumatic damage are summarized in figure 1.9.

CELL INJURY: EFFECTS AND RESPONSES

The effects of cell injury depend on a subtle interplay between structure and function. A structurally damaged organelle may function improperly, or altered function

may arise first and then give rise to structural changes. Although changes in both structure and function are usually involved in cell injury, it is often quite difficult to pinpoint the initial change, because the first identifiable disruption may be several steps removed from the original disturbance. It is also important to note that the effects of injury, and the cell's responses to it, are determined not only by the nature of the causative agent, but also by the intensity, the duration, and the number of exposures to it. The pulmonary effects of low-level exposure to an irritant inhaled over many months may produce the cough and chronic breathing difficulties seen in many coal miners, while a single exposure lasting only a few minutes may be life-threatening, as in an attack of legionnaire's disease. **4**

Reversible Changes: Functional

Cell and Tissue Accumulations

Much injury directly or indirectly disrupts the cell's energy metabolism or its protein synthesis capability. As a result, various substances accumulate within the cell. Water is one such substance.

Hydropic Change When damage reduces cellular energy production, membrane ion pumps, which are fueled by ATP, fail to eject sodium ions from the cell. Normally, leakage of sodium ions (Na^{++}) into the cytoplasm is countered by the membrane pumps, but without adequate ATP, sodium ions accumulate inside the cell. The rise in their concentration increases the osmotic pressure, and water inflow follows (fig. 1.10). The water that enters the cell by osmosis is sequestered within vacuoles, and as many such "water bubbles" accumulate in the cytoplasm, the cell swells. **5** Accumulating water also causes swelling of the ER, Golgi complex, and mitochondria. The vacuoles cause the cell's optical properties to change and the cytoplasm appears paler. This condition is known as **cloudy swelling.** When vacuolation is pronounced, the term **hydropic change** or **hydropic degeneration** is used (fig. 1.11). In this more severe condition, rupture of the cell may result.

Fatty Change Another type of intracellular accumulation is **fatty change,** in which cell injury causes fat to accumulate within the cell. First small fat droplets and then larger masses form until the cell becomes swollen. Cytoplasm and nucleus are subjected to potentially damaging pressure as they are pushed to the periphery of the cell (fig. 1.12). As cells enlarge, so does the entire organ, which in extreme cases can triple in size (see fig. 14.16). With increasing severity of injury, the accumulated fat may cause rupture of cells, which is followed by the coalescence of fat from adjacent cells to form fatty deposits within the

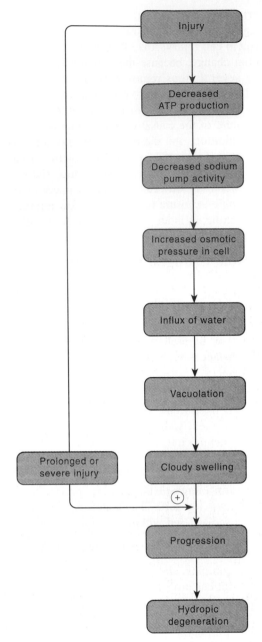

Figure 1.10   Pathogenesis of hydropic degeneration.

(a)

(b)

Figure 1.11   Cloudy swelling. (*a*) Normal microscopic appearance of four representative renal tubules in cross section. (*b*) Appearance after exposure to an injurious toxin. The individual cells are swollen and pale because of the presence of water-filled cytoplasmic vacuoles. As its cells enlarge, the entire kidney appears swollen.

damaged organ. Kidney, heart, and liver **6** commonly demonstrate this response to injury. Anoxia (abnormally low oxygen in the tissue) and intoxications—especially in the case of alcoholic liver damage—are typical causes of fatty change.

   Tissues susceptible to fatty degeneration are those that utilize fat as an energy source or those involved in the synthesis of lipids. Studies of liver function indicate that free fatty acids (FFAs) reach the liver from fat stores throughout the body. Within the liver the FFAs may be

(a)   (b)

Figure 1.12   Fatty change. (*a*) Liver damage from alcohol abuse. Compare normal cells at lower left with fat-filled, damaged cells indicated by arrow. (*b*) Cardiac muscle cells damaged by chronic oxygen deficiency. Darkly stained fat fills vacuoles in the cytoplasm of the injured cells (arrow).

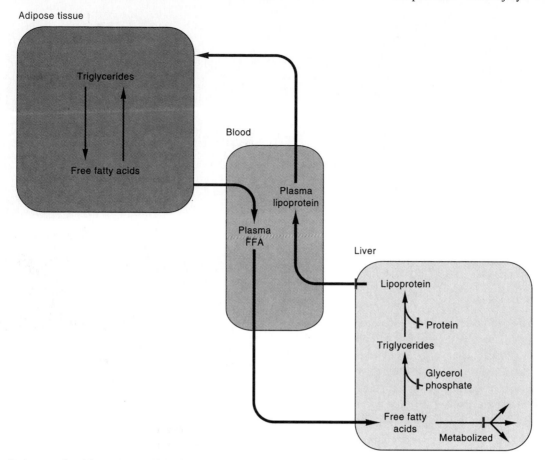

Figure 1.13   Pathogenesis of fatty change in the liver. In liver, free fatty acids (FFA) that are not metabolized are converted to triglyceride and combined with protein. The resulting lipoprotein is returned to adipose tissue stores. Only lipoprotein can be cleared from the cell. The bars indicate the points at which injury can interfere with the process to cause fat accumulation.

metabolized to various products, for example, cholesterol or phospholipid, or they may be used in energy metabolism. However, most are combined with glycerol phosphate to form triglycerides. These, in turn, are used to form lipoprotein by combination with protein that the hepatocyte (liver cell) has produced. The lipoprotein is then passed to the exterior of the cell, where it is taken up by the blood, which returns it to adipose tissue. It is significant that hepatocyte membrane transport systems can export lipid only in the form of lipoprotein. When injured, the hepatocyte may have difficulty coping with the continually arriving FFAs. It may be unable to metabolize them adequately or it may be unable to form triglyceride or to produce lipoprotein. Finally, it may not be able to clear lipoprotein from its cytoplasm by passing it to the exterior. Whatever the specific derangement, the result will be a build-up of fat within the cytoplasm (fig. 1.13).

Residual Bodies   The intracellular accumulation of **residual bodies** is related to the cell's capacity to cope with potentially threatening bacteria or to deal with damaged organelles. Residual bodies are derived from phagosomes whose contents are not expelled, but instead are retained

when lysosome numbers are inadequate to complete digestion or when damaged cell structures are resistant to lysosomal enzyme attack. The term **lipofuscin granule** is applied to residual bodies that contain undigested cell membrane lipids (fig. 1.14). These dark-staining bodies are most often found in neurons, liver, and myocardium. **7** As more and more accumulate with increasing age, they can be interpreted as an indication of the cell's history of injury (fig. 1.15).

Hyaline Change   In typical light microscope sections of damaged tissue, a pink-staining, glasslike substance may be seen in or between cells. **8** This material is called **hyaline,** and the condition in which it is present is referred to as **hyaline change** or **hyalinization.** The material deposited is usually protein and may be found in damaged arterioles, renal tubules, damaged liver cells, and neurons. In some cells infected with viruses, newly formed viral particles appear as hyaline. Generally, the presence of hyaline serves as a nonspecific indicator of cell injury.

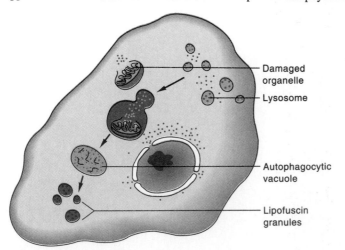

Figure 1.14   Formation of lipofuscin granules.

Adaptive Responses

Injury to the cell is often reversible, because the cell has an array of adaptive responses that help it to cope with injury or adverse conditions. These can be used when needed and can be deactivated when the situation returns to normal. The following discussion describes the principal adaptive mechanisms that enable the cell to cope with injury. Note that different cell types vary in their ability to utilize them.

Alternative Metabolism In confronting unfavorable conditions, a cell can employ alternative metabolic pathways that allow it to adjust to them. For example, in conditions of hypoxia (oxygen deficiency), the major energy production pathway of the cell is threatened. This is because its most efficient yield of ATP depends on the oxygen-dependent metabolic pathway called **oxidative phosphorylation.** Many tissues can adapt to hypoxia by relying on an anaerobic (without oxygen) energy metabolism: glycolysis. If normal oxygen levels are restored, the cells can revert to their normal aerobic energy metabolism.

Similarly, should the supply of the body's principal energy source, glucose, be interrupted, many cells can turn to fat or protein as a fuel. The breakdown of these materials can produce enough energy to sustain cell activities until glucose levels return to normal.

Altered Size Size changes are another adaptive capability exhibited by cells. **Hypertrophy** is the process of cell and organ enlargement that occurs in response to increased demands. Gland cells that enlarge in response to greater tropic hormone stimulation, nephron tubule cells that grow larger to cope with the extra workload resulting from toxic kidney damage, and myocardial cells that increase in size and strength when required to pump through a narrowed heart valve **9** are examples of adaptive hypertrophy.

The other size adaptation is **atrophy,** or shrinking. Various factors that reduce demand on a cell or decrease its normal input stimuli can produce shrinking. The most common cause is reduced workload, which produces the condi-

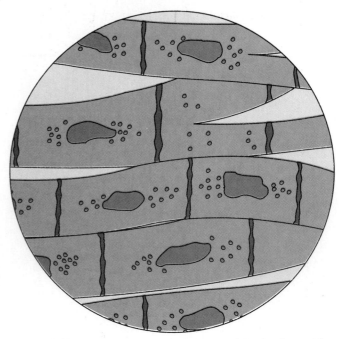

Figure 1.15   Diagrammatic representation of lipofuscin granules in cardiac muscle tissue of an elderly person. These residual bodies are evidence of the cells' ability to adapt to the many challenges that confronted them over many years.

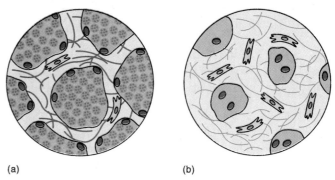

(a)   (b)

Figure 1.16   Atrophy. (*a*) Normal skeletal muscle fibers in cross section, showing the myofibrils so tightly packed in the sarcoplasm that the cell's multiple nuclei are forced to the periphery. (*b*) Polio blocks nerve stimulation to muscle, and atrophy results. Note the shrinkage and loss of myofibrillar organization.

tion of **disuse atrophy.** Patients confined to bed for a prolonged period lose muscle and skeletal mass as a result of reduced loading. The cell benefits because the reduction in size lowers its energy and other metabolic requirements and allows it to function more efficiently until demand increases. However, patients can suffer fatigue and possible bone fractures if they resume normal activities before an adequate hypertrophy response can restore their strength.

Inadequate neurological or hormonal stimulus can also induce atrophy. The loss of strength and muscle mass seen in poliomyelitis **10** **11** is associated with significant muscle atrophy that is due to loss of nervous stimulus (fig. 1.16). Another example is the atrophy of the thyroid gland

Heat Stress Proteins

When exposed to a wide variety of adverse conditions, e.g., anoxia, toxins, elevated temperature, or trauma, cells respond with the production of **stress proteins.** Because they were initially discovered in experiments that used heat to stress cells, they were called **heat stress** or **heat shock** proteins (hsp's). Although there is much to be learned about their adaptive role in injured cells, they seem to help cells to cope with life-threatening conditions. For example, heat or free-radical damage to cell proteins causes them to unfold (denature). This change is followed by their clumping together to form insoluble tangles of protein that accumulate in the cytoplasm, interfering with cell structure and function. The hsp's that form in response to the adverse condition can help in at least three ways. One is by binding to the damaged proteins in a way that makes it easier for enzymes to destroy them before they can form clumps. Another is by stabilizing the proteins long enough to enable them to refold and become functional once again. Third, the denatured proteins, with stabilizing hsp's bound to them, are more easily passed through the cell membrane, a change allowing them to be expelled before they can form clumps (see box fig. 1.1).

There are more than thirty recognized hsp's. Continuing research indicates that they have potential relevance to a wide variety of diagnostic or preventive procedures. For example, when produced following injury, hsp's are picked up by the blood. Their presence in a blood sample therefore provides an early indication of cell injury that could enable some preventive response or more prompt therapeutic intervention.

Although the pattern is not yet clearly established, certain cell types may produce only certain hsp's. This difference, if confirmed, would allow greater diagnostic accuracy at an earlier stage, before more grossly detectable signs and symptoms develop. Another potential application is the possibility of preadapting cells to an anticipated stress, such as surgery. Experiments have shown that a mild stress triggers hsp production. Perhaps if a patient's temperature were intentionally raised prior to surgery, the hsp's produced in response to the heat stress would increase the patient's ability to cope with the stress of surgery.

Another possible application of hsp's is in the field of environmental pollution. Since certain toxins, including heavy metals, induce hsp production, their presence in the body could indicate exposure to pollutants that had yet to cause enough damage to produce more obvious signs and symptoms.

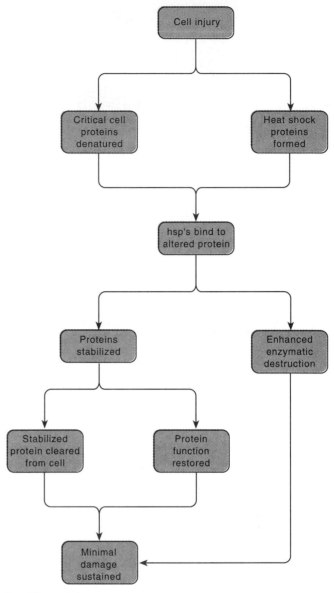

Box Figure 1.1   The role of heat shock proteins in enabling cells to cope with damage.

---

that follows a decline in the level of its regulating hormone TSH (thyroid-stimulating hormone). **12**

Organelle Changes By altering its complement of organelles, a cell is better able to respond to unfavorable conditions. The liver, for example, employs enzyme systems associated with its agranular endoplasmic reticulum to degrade toxic chemicals. When levels of such a substance rise, the liver responds by producing more AER, matching its detoxification capacity to the increased demand. Similarly, when a cell faces a sustained increase in energy demand, it can form more mitochondria to boost ATP production. Note that these adaptations are seen only when

Nowok # 21265701 pat berendes

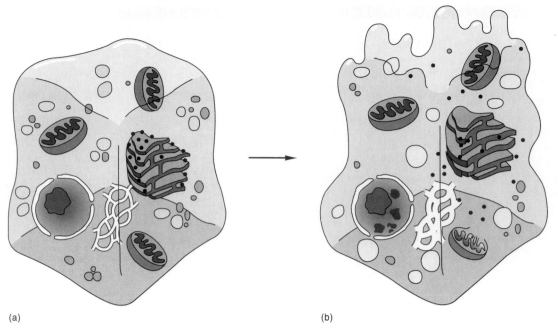

(a)   (b)

Figure 1.17   (*a*) A normal cell and (*b*) an injured cell. In the injured cell, note the blebs in the plasma membrane, swollen and distorted mitochondria and ER, ribosomes lost from ER surfaces, vacuolated cytoplasm, and nuclear clumping.

altered conditions persist over an extended period. They do not come into play in response to short-term changes.

Reversible Changes: Structural

Depending on the nature and duration of injury, cells suffering damage exhibit various structural alterations. The plasma membrane is quick to show effects. For example, it may become stretched and distorted, producing cytoplasmic bulges called **blebs,** which project from the surface of the cell. In some cases, the membrane may exhibit focal coiling, producing forms that resemble the whorled pattern seen in the myelin formation. Such membrane abnormalities are called **myelin figures. 13** In other cases damage may cause specialized membrane structures, such as microvilli or desmosomes, to become distorted and functionally compromised.

In the earlier discussion of cloudy swelling, we noted that an injured cell may enlarge as the result of osmotic water inflow. Injury-related changes in organelle membranes also allow water to leak into the organelles, causing them to become enlarged and distorted. This change is seen in the Golgi complex, ER, and mitochondria. Swollen mitochondria may also develop densely stained regions within their internal matrix, and as GER cisternae swell, ribosomes are lost from their surfaces. Ribosomes can be seen dispersed in the cytoplasm of an injured cell, but when conditions are restored, they can reaggregate at ER membrane surfaces.

In reversible injury, the nuclear structure remains essentially unchanged, although the nucleolus may show some loss of organization. If injury is severe, some clumping of the nuclear material may be seen (fig. 1.17).

Irreversible Injury and Necrosis

Structural Changes

The severely injured cell, which cannot recover its normal functions, shows structural changes that are more extreme than those seen in the reversibly injured cell. The plasma membrane exhibits more extreme distortions, accompanied by varying degrees of increased permeability. The latter change allows a more rapid inflow of sodium, calcium, and water. Gaps in the membrane also allow escape of vital cell constituents. In extreme cases, the cell membrane ruptures and its contents spill into the exterior. Mitochondrial and ER membranes undergo similar breakdown. The mitochondria may greatly enlarge and exhibit bizarre structural distortions, often developing focal deposits of calcium in their interior. The ER often develops myelin figures. In severe irreversible injury, ER cisternae may also rupture and disperse in the cytoplasm.

The irreversibly injured cell also has fewer lysosomes. This is because lysosomal membranes lose their stability when severely injured. Normally, these membranes isolate their potent lysosomal enzymes from the cytoplasm, but in irreversibly injured cells, the less stable membranes break open, releasing their destructive contents and reducing the number of lysosomes.

The single most significant indicator of irreversible cell injury is an altered nucleus. Housing the vital chromosomes, the nucleus must remain intact and functional if the cell is to have any chance of recovery. Following cell death, in some cases the nucleus seems to fade and melt into the cytoplasm. This condition is called **karyolysis 14** (fig. 1.18). In other cases, the nucleus may shrink

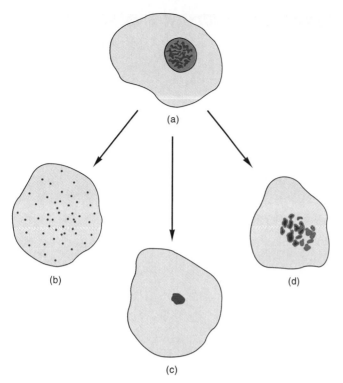

Figure 1.18 (*a*) A representative normal cell, with translucent cytoplasm and with a nucleus showing typical chromatin staining. The nature and intensity of injury produce different nuclear effects in necrosis: (*b*) karyolysis, (*c*) pyknosis, and (*d*) karyorrhexis.

and condense (**pyknosis**), **15** or it may break up into densely staining fragments that disperse in the cytoplasm (**karyorrhexis**). **16**

Mechanisms of Irreversible Injury

In irreversible injury, a small number of derangements have widespread and devastating effects. One of these is damage to cell membrane, both the plasma membrane and those forming the cellular organelles. When membranes are damaged, their permeability and cytoplasm organizing functions are compromised. The result is severe swelling from sodium influx, loss of cytoplasmic constituents to the cell's exterior, and a large flow of calcium into the cell. High levels of intracellular calcium denature protein, thus interfering with enzyme functions, and the excessive calcium ions interact with various other ions to disrupt the electrolyte balance within the cell. Damaged mitochondrial membranes mean a decline in ATP production. As we noted earlier, when energy levels fall, cells can respond by switching to glycolysis for ATP production. However, this anaerobic energy metabolism produces high levels of acid products. These lower the pH, a change that triggers the activation and release of lysosomal enzymes that can degrade important cytoplasmic and nuclear structures.

Cell Death

Depending on the nature and intensity of injury, its timing, and the innate resistance of the cell, different cells may respond in different ways when exposed to the same injurious agent. They may adapt within a normal range of wear and tear. They may be reversibly injured and recover, or they may be permanently affected and forced to function at a less than normal level. In the extreme case, injury can result in cell death.

These concepts are presented in figure 1.19. The vertical axis represents the cell's level of functional capacity, with the normal range indicated by shading. Time is represented by the horizontal axis. During the life of the cell, various injuries occur. Minor, well-tolerated injuries represent a normal wear-and-tear level of demand to which the cell can adapt and still maintain normal function. Cell activities are not significantly affected by these physiological stressors. For example, the hepatocyte can adapt to a chronic, low-level intoxication by producing more AER.

Figure 1.19 also shows a later, more severe injury that significantly affects cellular function, and indicates three possible outcomes of exposure to such an injurious stressor. In one (curve A), the cell overcomes the effect of the injury and returns to a normal functional level. Another possibility (curve B) is that the cell recovers, but not at its normal functional level; the injury effects are nonreversible. Curve C shows the third possible outcome. The functional capacity of the cell has fallen to a level below which no recovery is possible (dashed line in the figure), and cell death results. But notice that the cell death need not be immediate. Even though the cell has dropped beyond the critical point of no return, some time may pass before the loss of functional capacity is complete. Also note that the "point of no return" is a theoretical point not clinically definable or detectable by laboratory or other tests. Therapeutic intervention seeks to interrupt the decline in functional capacity. The timing and effectiveness of the intervention determines whether partial or complete function is restored. These possibilities are represented by curves C´ and C´´.

The condition of cell death is called **necrosis.** It is accompanied by substantial changes in the cell and in the tissue of which it is a part. The contents of the cell are broken down by its endogenous enzymes and by the enzymes of phagocytic cells that arrive at the scene to assist the process. The resulting debris is removed, and healing of the tissue usually follows.

The cell enzymes involved are primarily those of the lysosomes. When, and only when, a cell suffers a lethal injury, lysosomes release their enzymes into the cytoplasm, and these initiate the chemical breakdown of cell constituents. Note that this event is nothing like the cell's using its lysosomes in some suicidal impulse. Lysosomal enzymes are released only after the point of lethal injury.

Free Radicals

Current research is uncovering the important role of free radicals as a major factor in cell membrane damage. The phospholipid core of the membrane is highly sensitive to damage by free radicals; the process is known as **lipid peroxidation.** Free radicals can be produced by ionizing radiation or as the products of metabolism of exogenous chemicals, such as the trichloromethyl radical that is formed in liver from carbon tetrachloride. They can also be produced by reactions that release hydroxyl radicals (— OH) or the molecular-oxygen free radical called **superoxide.** The superoxide and hydroxyl radicals are known as **activated oxygen species.**

An important aspect of free-radical formation is **self-propagation** or **autocatalysis.** This means that the formation of one free radical leads to its interaction with other molecules, not only causing damage but producing a new free radical, which can then repeat the cycle, to produce a self-catalyzing chain reaction. In this way a single event forming only one free radical can produce far-reaching effects (box fig. 1.2a). On the other hand, the cell is not completely at the mercy of free radicals. Some reaction chains may be interrupted when free radicals interact to produce stable forms. Various specific enzymes promote such reactions and serve as a valuable mechanism that limits free-radical formation. Other substances may take up (scavenge) free radicals to interrupt the chain sequences. Vitamin E is an example of such a scavenger molecule derived from the diet. Substances that oppose the effects of oxygen free radicals are called **antioxidants** (box fig. 1.2b).

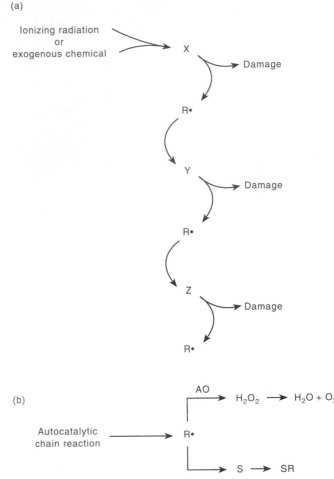

Box Figure 1.2 (a) An autocatalytic chain reaction produces damage to critical cell constituents X, Y and Z, while generating a new free radical, R• at each step. (b) The cell's antioxidants, AO, or scavenger molecules, S, interact with free radicals to produce stable forms, terminating the chain reaction.

The cell is, in effect, already dying, and the lysosomes are simply speeding the breakdown and removal of nonfunctional tissue from the scene.

Microscopic study of necrotic tissue usually reveals two forms of necrosis: **coagulation necrosis** and **liquefaction necrosis.** If chemical factors in the necrotic tissue cause the cellular and extracellular proteins to coagulate, the result is a firm and relatively intact region of necrosis in which the essentials of normal tissue architecture are retained (fig. 1.20). This is coagulation necrosis,

17 typically seen in anoxic and toxic injury to most tissues except those of the brain. After a few days the coagulated region breaks down and the resulting debris is cleared by phagocytes.

In brain tissues, the lack of extracellular proteins such as collagen results in a much shorter period of coagulation. By the time the tissue is observed, a more liquid region of dead cells, tissue fluid, and phagocytic cells has formed. This is the condition described as liquefaction necrosis. Nervous tissue injured by anoxia or bacterial toxins most often exhibits this form of necrosis. **18**

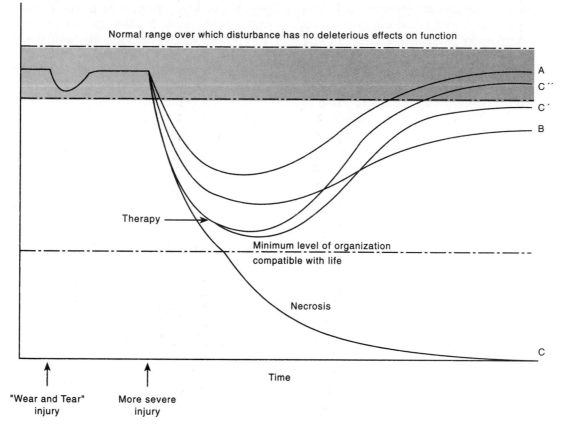

Figure 1.19   Changes in functional capacity in response to injury. Therapeutic intervention may fully or partially restore function, but if it is ineffective, cell death may be unavoidable. See text.

(a)   (b)

Figure 1.20   Coagulation necrosis. (a) A section of kidney, showing the normal arrangement of tubules, ducts, vessels, and supporting connective tissue. (b) Oxygen deprivation has caused cell death, but the tissue's essential organization is retained.

In certain cases, coagulation necrosis may produce unusual characteristic features. **Caseous necrosis** is an example that is often seen in tuberculosis. In this infection, the necrotic tissue has a pale yellow, granular, cheeselike appearance. [19] (The word "caseous" comes from the Latin for cheese.)

Gangrene, or gangrenous necrosis, is another form of coagulation necrosis. It is characterized by the presence of noxious products of anaerobic bacterial metabolism. If these organisms, which can thrive without oxygen, gain access to an area of damage caused by reduced blood flow **(ischemia),** they can proliferate in the oxygen-deprived necrotic tissue. This process is often referred to as **putrefaction.** In some cases, foul-smelling gases are produced. If the enzymes of invading phagocytic cells break down the necrotic debris and produce some liquefaction, the descriptive term **wet gangrene** [20] is applied. More typically, coagulation is sustained, and the condition is called **dry gangrene.** [21]

Calcification At sites of necrosis, regardless of type, calcium deposition often occurs. This is especially the case in persistent injury or where damage effects are slow to develop. Initially the calcium crystals that form are tiny, but progressive deposition produces larger masses that can lead to significant rigidity and brittleness in the affected tissue. The process, called **dystrophic calcification,** often serves to indicate necrosis and little else. In some cases, however, calcification can produce its own complications—for example, in heart valves whose calcified leaflets cannot fully open or close, or in calcified arteries that lose their elasticity.

Metastatic calcification also involves calcium salt deposition but differs from dystrophic calcification in two ways: (1) it occurs in otherwise normal, as opposed to necrotic, tissue, and (2) the deposition is a consequence of an excessive systemic calcium level, or **hypercalcemia.** Although generally widespread, calcium deposits are most often found in lung, kidney, blood vessels, and the mucous membrane of the stomach. If severe, metastatic calcification may interfere with lung or kidney function, but generally its consequences are minimal.

TISSUE VULNERABILITY TO INJURY

Because the various cells of the body have different characteristics, they differ in their vulnerability to injury. Consider the following examples.

Ischemia

Central nervous system (CNS) neurons are highly sensitive to ischemia because they have a high metabolic rate and are dependent on glucose as their only energy source. Thus the brain can tolerate loss of blood supply for only a few minutes before a lack of ATP permanently injures its neurons. This type of cell injury is the underlying cause of **stroke,** which kills millions of people every year. In contrast, kidney or liver cells are less sensitive to ischemia. At body temperature, these tissues can tolerate up to 60 minutes of interrupted blood flow without permanent damage. By cooling the kidney to lower its metabolic rate and thereby reduce its energy demand, this time can be extended up to 10 hours. This tolerance is a significant factor in being able to transplant a kidney from a healthy donor to a patient whose kidneys are damaged beyond saving. Even more tolerant of ischemia are fibroblasts. These connective tissue cells can tolerate ischemia for prolonged periods, far longer than neurons or kidney and liver cells. This proves valuable when fibroblasts must form scar tissue at injury sites, where oxygen levels remain low until new blood vessels can form.

CCl_4 Intoxication

Carbon tetrachloride (CCl_4), an exogenous toxin that causes liver damage after it is inhaled, provides another example of differential cell vulnerability to injury. From the respiratory passages, CCl_4 enters the blood and ultimately reaches the liver. **22** Although the lining of the res-

piratory passages, lung tissue, and blood cells are all exposed to the CCl_4, it causes greatest damage in the much more susceptible hepatocytes. The breakdown of CCl_4 by liver cells produces a toxic free radical. Because the other tissues can't break down CCl_4, they are little affected by their exposure to it.

Ionizing Radiation

When the body is exposed to ionizing radiation, many different tissues are damaged. As we noted earlier, DNA is especially sensitive to high-energy radiation damage. In particular, actively dividing cells that are undergoing DNA replication are susceptible to injury from this source. For this reason, areas of rapid mitosis, such as red bone marrow and gastrointestinal mucous membranes, show the greatest disruption of function after exposure to radiation. Such disruption underlies the problems of nausea, diarrhea, gastrointestinal hemorrhage, hair loss, and bone marrow effects typically associated with radiation exposure.

Viral Infection

A last example of differential vulnerability is viral infection. Viruses enter and then disrupt cells from within. However, most viruses can't simply enter any cell they happen to contact. A specific interaction between the virus and the host cell is involved, so that each virus can infect only a specific type of cell. A particular case of extreme specificity is seen in the polio virus, which infects neurons in the gray matter of the spinal cord. The virus attacks only the cells of the anterior horns, which supply stimulation to skeletal muscle. **23** Several other types of neurons are immediately adjacent but they are not affected. The specificity of viral attack seems to be based on the fact that the susceptible cell has membrane surface receptors to which the viral particle can bind. This binding is the critical step that allows the virus to enter the cell. Tissues lacking specific receptors provide no easy access to the cell's interior and so are much less vulnerable to attack.

DETERMINATION AND MONITORING OF CELL INJURY

We have seen that cells are subject to injury and that in response they undergo certain changes in their function and structure. As we noted in the introduction, successful outcome of a particular medical problem requires that the problem be correctly identified so that appropriate therapy can be undertaken. In other words, one needs to know not just that something is wrong, but the precise nature of the defect. The problem is to determine which of the many body cells have been injured, and to what degree. There are

Diagnosis is often complicated by the fact that a given pattern of signs and symptoms may be associated with more than one disease. In such cases, serum enzyme levels can sometimes be used to differentiate among several possibilities. The following example illustrates the principle. Several different liver diseases produce an accumulation of bile pigments that discolors the skin and whites of the eyes—the condition called jaundice. The diagnostic challenge is to identify which disease is responsible for a given patient's jaundice. The problem can be solved because different types of liver cell damage lead to different levels of release into the blood of the enzyme alkaline phosphatase. Box figure 1.3 shows that in liver damage caused by bile duct obstruction (obstructive jaundice), the enzyme is present at almost five times its normal level. But it is present at only twice the normal level in cirrhosis or viral hepatitis. Now consider the case of viral hepatitis, in which the damage releases over fifteen times the normal level of serum glutamic oxaloacetic transaminase (SGOT). If such high levels of SGOT occur, it is easy to exclude obstruction or cirrhosis as contributing to the patient's jaundice, because in these conditions, SGOT doesn't usually exceed four times normal.

Box Figure 1.3   Different liver diseases produce varying patterns of enzyme loss to the blood. Assessing serum levels of appropriate enzymes is a valuable diagnostic aid.

four common approaches to this problem: assessments of functional loss, detection of cell constituents released from injured cells, monitoring of electrical activity, and direct tissue examination.

Functional Loss

The loss of mobility suffered from a leg fracture is obvious. Functional deterioration of internal organs may not be so easily apparent, but it can be assessed in various ways. These usually reveal subtle changes in the body fluids, which reflect the functional deterioration. For example, the liver normally removes the pigment bilirubin from the blood and excretes it into the bile. Thus, the finding of elevated plasma levels of bilirubin may indicate functional deterioration of liver cells. Similarly, hydrogen ion (H^+) is normally excreted by the kidney. When the kidney suffers damage, its excretion of H^+ is likely to be reduced. A clue to this functional loss appears in a decrease in the concentration of H^+ in the urine. In another case, alterations from the normal values of oxygen and carbon dioxide in the blood can be a sign of functional decline in the respiratory system.

Release of Cell Constituents

A second means of determining cell injury is based on the release of cell constituents by injured cells. Normally, substances confined to the cell's interior, such as potassium ions (K^+) and cell enzymes, leak to the exterior at a slow, steady rate, establishing a normal plasma level. Injury-related permeability changes or complete cell rupture allows them to reach the blood in larger quantities. High plasma levels of these substances can therefore be taken as indications of cell injury.

Because potassium ions are much more concentrated in the cell than in its exterior, a rising level of plasma potassium indicates widespread tissue damage. For example, elevated plasma potassium is a typical result of hemolysis, which involves the rupture of red blood cells.

(a)

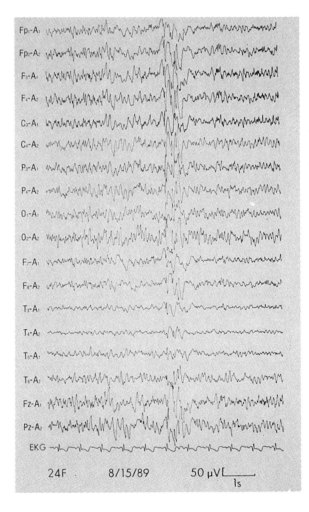

(b)

Figure 1.21   (a) Electrical monitoring of the heart activity, shown beside an electrocardiogram (ECG) that indicates an unusually rapid heart rate. (b) The scalp placement of electrodes used for monitoring brain activity. The accompanying electroencephalogram (EEG) is one that indicates seizure activity.

The other substances that may also escape through ruptured or damaged membranes are intracellular enzymes, for example, creatine phosphokinase (CPK). This enzyme is abundant in skeletal and cardiac muscle and in the brain. In the necrosis that follows a heart attack or stroke, the tissues release CPK. Thus a high plasma level of CPK can initally indicate, or later confirm, that skeletal, cardiac, or brain tissue damage has occurred. Similarly, an increased plasma level of the enzyme gamma-glutamyl transferase (GGT) is an indication of liver damage, because large quantities of this enzyme are normally present in hepatocytes.

High liver enzyme levels do not necessarily indicate liver damage; instead they may signal a high rate of production of detoxification enzymes in response to the threat of some poison. On the other hand, a decline in plasma enzymes is not a good sign either. It may be that so much tissue damage has already occurred that in the remaining cells, normal enzyme leakage is insufficient to maintain even the normally low plasma level.

Tumor cells tend to overproduce their intracellular enzymes. For example, the cells of prostate gland cancer, upon spreading to other body sites, produce large amounts of the enzyme acid phosphatase. Without this indication of its activity, the presence of the tumor might go undetected for a dangerously long time.

In a few cases an enzyme is present in significant quantities in only one tissue. When the plasma level of that enzyme is increased, the finding points directly to the site of the damage. An example is the enzyme alcohol dehydrogenase, produced only in the liver.

Electrical Activity

A third approach to assessing cell injury involves the monitoring of electrical activity to detect changes from the normal. The effects of much of the electrical activity in the interior of the body can be detected at its surface by specialized electronic equipment, which can then visually display the results. Any change from the normal electrical pattern can be interpreted in terms of altered functioning. This approach is used most commonly in studying the heart, for which the **electrocardiogram** (ECG or EKG) is used (fig. 1.21a). Similarly, the electrical activity of the brain can be displayed in an **electroencephalogram** (EEG) to assess seizure activity (fig. 1.21b) or to monitor a patient in a coma. Electrical activity associated with muscular contraction is displayed in the **electromyogram** (EMG), which can yield useful information regarding muscle weakness or paralysis. The conduction times of the action potentials that elicit muscle contraction responses can also indicate abnormality. If conduction times increase, the reason may be neuron injury or defective synaptic transmission.

Biopsy

A fourth means of determining cell injury is direct microscopic examination of the tissue in which damage is suspected. A small portion of tissue is removed from the body in a minor surgical procedure called a **biopsy.** The tissue is then prepared for microscope study. Biopsies are also often done to study tissue organization and cell characteristics. The goal is to determine whether a tumor may be present or, if present, whether it is a benign or more threatening malignant tumor.

Case Study

A 54-year-old man came to his general practitioner for a physical examination. He was found to be in good health overall, but the physician thought he detected alcohol on the man's breath. This particularly concerned him because the patient had a history of alcoholism, although he had abstained from drinking for the past three years. In response the physician's general question on his continuing to avoid alcohol, the man denied any alcohol use.

As part of the patient's general blood analysis, the physician requested that the serum level of gamma-glutamyl transferase (GGT) be measured. The blood tests confirmed the general good health of the patient, but GGT was clearly elevated above normal. With this evidence, and no indication of liver damage, the doctor called the patient in for a consultation, during which the patient admitted his recent return to drinking in response to work-related stresses. He agreed to enter and follow through with a medically supervised alcohol rehabilitation program.

Commentary

In this all-too-common situation, the outcome may well be a positive one. Too often the alcoholic denies excessive drinking and strongly resists efforts to interrupt it.

Because the elevation of serum GGT is a sensitive indicator of alcohol abuse, it is often used in establishing the presence of covert drinking. In the case of this enzyme, a high serum level is due, not to its release from damaged liver cells, but rather to the high cellular levels formed in response to high alcohol intake. The physician's evidence of drinking, which could not be refuted, effectively undercut any inclination to denial and may have been a factor in the agreement to enter the rehabilitation program. There is also a good chance that the serum GGT would be used in the patient's rehabilitation program to monitor alcohol abstinence.

Key Concepts

1. Although many different agents or mechanisms may be involved in causing cell injury, from the cellular perspective injury is essentially the result of (1) a deficiency of a necessary metabolite, (2) the presence of a toxic substance, or (3) disruption of the physical integrity of the cell (pp. 10–13).

2. The intensity, duration, and number of exposures to an etiological agent determine the degree of cell injury, but the resulting signs and symptoms may reflect effects that are several steps removed from the initial biochemical disturbance (p. 13).

3. A common, reversible effect of cell injury is the abnormal intracellular accumulation of certain substances, most often water, fat, or proteins of various types (pp. 13–15).

4. Cells may adapt to injury by temporarily altering their size, their mix of cytoplasmic organelles, or their metabolism in order to cope better with unfavorable conditions (pp. 16–18).

5. Injured cells may demonstrate reversible structural changes, most often involving membrane malformations, swelling and distortion of cellular organelles, and the disaggregation of ribosomes from endoplasmic reticulum surfaces (p. 18).

6. Severe injury can irreversibly damage cells, producing more extreme intracellular changes such as pronounced disruption or rupture of cytoplasmic structures, loss of cell constituents through damaged membranes, the release of lysosomal contents, and nuclear degeneration (pp. 18–19).

7. Many variables combine to determine the outcome of cell injury, which may be (1) relatively mild and reversible damage, (2) more severe damage, with some lingering functional deficit, or (3) cell death. Therapeutic intervention can often improve the outcome (pp. 18–22).

8. The features that are characteristic of coagulation necrosis, liquefaction necrosis, caseous necrosis, or gangrene reflect differences in combined effects of lysosomal enzymes on extracellular proteins, peculiarities of the necrotic debris, and the action of bacterial products (if infection is involved) (pp. 20–22).

9. Variations in tissue characteristics determine the observed differences in their susceptibility to injury (p. 22).

10. Cell injury can be assessed by direct and indirect analysis of altered function, by detection of cell constituents or abnormal enzyme levels in the plasma or urine, by monitoring of electrical activity, or by examination of a tissue sample (pp. 22–25).

REVIEW ACTIVITIES

1. Look back to figure 1.7. Be certain that you know the difference between primary and secondary nutrient deficiency and that you could give an example of how an infectious agent might contribute to the deficiency problem.

2. Lay out a flow chart that indicates clearly the pathogenesis of fatty change. Start with: "FFAs enter cell" and end with "lipid accumulation." Check back in the text to verify that you've got the whole story.

3. In figure 1.17, without consulting the legend, for each organelle in (a), identify how it has changed in the postinjury state (b). Check page 18 for verification.

4. Complete the table on the right by providing information on the body fluid or region analyzed in diagnosis and on a possible cause of an abnormal value of the variable. Pages 22 to 25 may be worth consulting if blanks remain after your initial attempt.

Abnormal Variable	Fluid/Region Assessed	Possible Problem
Bilirubin		
CO_2		
K^+		
CPK		
H^+		
O_2		
EEG		

5. Look back to the case study at the end of the chapter. In the commentary, note that the GGT level was elevated not because of damage, but in response to a potentially injurious agent. Is this a useful adaptive response? Is it a specific example of the general case described on page 23? Would you expect a liver biopsy (if one were done) to reveal increased AER in the patient's hepatocytes? Would the liver cells be different sometime after a successful rehabilitation program? Is the GGT increase a reversible or irreversible adaptation?

Chapter Two

Inflammation

...people in good health were all of a sudden attacked by violent heats in the head, and redness and inflammation in the eyes, the inward parts, such as the throat or the tongue, becoming bloody...

Thucydides
The Peloponnesian Wars

Injury to the body or a breach of its defensive barriers triggers a versatile, localized response called **acute inflammation.** The response involves a dramatic increase in blood flow to the injury site, which causes it to become red and warm. Local swelling also occurs, as a result of the movement of fluid and cells to the intercellular spaces, and the site becomes painful. These signs and symptoms were recorded as early as 2,000 years ago by the Roman physician Celsus. For this reason, they are often referred to by the original Latin terms **rubor** (redness), **calor** (heat), **tumor** (swelling), and **dolor** (pain). Later the Greeks (Galen) added a fifth classic sign: loss of function (**functio laesa**). You may still come across these terms in modern medical literature and practice. Because acute inflammation arises in response to many types of injury, it is very common. All those conditions whose names end in the suffix "itis," e.g., dermatitis, meningitis, pericarditis, are inflammatory conditions.

Before moving to the study of inflammation, you may find it useful to review the following information on normal vascularized connective tissue and the formation of tissue fluid.

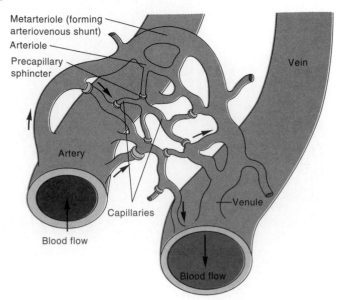

Figure 2.1   The relationship of artery, arteriole, capillaries, venules, and veins in the microcirculation. Metarterioles can shunt blood past the tissue when the precapillary sphincters, which regulate blood flow through the tissue, are closed.

NORMAL VASCULARIZED CONNECTIVE TISSUE

The inflammatory response is focused in the vascularized connective tissue present throughout the body. The vessels that participate in the response are the capillaries and the post-capillary venules (fig. 2.1). **Capillaries** are short (1–2 mm) tubes formed of flattened endothelial cells supported by a basement membrane on their tissue surfaces. The basement membrane is composed of collagen fiber bundles embedded in a gel of **proteoglycans,** compounds that contain protein and sugar.

Functionally, the capillaries are significant because they provide for the exchange of oxygen, nutrients, and wastes between the blood and tissue spaces. Flow through a network of capillaries is controlled by groups of smooth muscle cells located in the walls of the smallest arterioles, the vessels that supply the capillaries. These smooth muscle sphincters can alter their degree of constriction, allowing more or less blood to perfuse the capillaries as demand changes. For this reason, they are known as **precapillary sphincters.** Beyond a bed of interconnected capillaries lie the vessels that drain them, the **post-capillary venules.** These venules have somewhat thicker walls than capillaries, because smooth muscle and some protective connective tissue are also present.

Normal vascular permeability is determined by the cells of the capillary endothelium. These flattened cells fit tightly together like tiles as they line the vessel lumen. Where two adjacent endothelial cells meet, forming an **endothelial junction,** their edges overlap and a thin layer of intercellular substance (glycoprotein) fills the gap. Most substances entering the tissue must pass through the endothelial cells either by diffusion or in transfer vesicles. Open channels formed by temporary merging of vesicles may contribute to the process (fig. 2.2).

Surrounding the vessels in vascular connective tissue is a complex consisting of the **extracellular matrix** (ECM) and the various cells and fibers contained within it. The extracellular matrix consists largely of proteoglycans. These provide anchorage for the collagen and elastic fibers present in connective tissues, as well as for capillaries, whose basement membranes bind to proteoglycans. **Fibroblasts** in connective tissues are the cells that produce the proteins of the extracellular matrix and many of its fibers. Macrophages (a kind of phagocytic cell) may be present to engulf any debris formed by normal tissue wear and tear. Mast cells, which have various roles in mediating inflammation, are also typically scattered through the extracellular matrix of a connective tissue.

The formation of tissue fluid and its return to the blood depends on the balance of pressure across the capillary wall. Because **blood hydrostatic pressure (BHP),** the fluid pressure of blood confined within vessels, is high near the arterial end of the capillary, fluid is forced out of the vessel to form **tissue fluid.** A slight **tissue osmotic pressure** (TOP), which derives from the abundance of solute molecules in the interstitial spaces, assists this outward flow. Near the venous end of the capillary, blood hydrostatic pressure is lower, but the osmotic attraction of the blood for water, called **blood osmotic pressure** (BOP), is higher because the loss of fluid to the tissue spaces concentrates the plasma proteins. As well, fluids driven into the interstitium are confined within its spaces, producing a tissue hydrostatic pressure (THP) that adds to blood osmotic

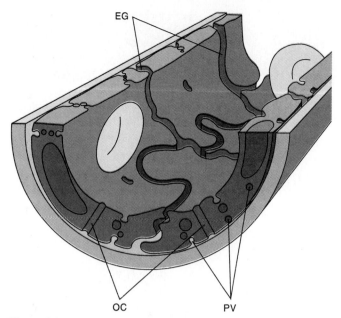

Figure 2.2   The capillary endothelium in vascular permeability. EG: The endothelial gap between adjacent cells. PV: Pinocytotic vesicles carrying fluid between the blood and tissue spaces. OC: Open channels formed by the merging of pinocytic vesicles. Broken lines indicate that the channel lies below the plane of the section.

Blood hydrostatic pressure   Tissue osmotic pressure   Tissue hydrostatic pressure   Blood osmotic pressure

Figure 2.3   Tissue fluid formation, showing the pressures across the capillary wall that contribute to the formation of tissue fluid and its return to the plasma. Shading indicates the pressures whose contribution is minor.

pressure. Together, blood osmotic pressure and tissue hydrostatic pressure force the fluid back into the capillary to complete the exchange (fig. 2.3). Because the pressures that produce tissue fluid are slightly greater than those that return it to the blood, some excess extracellular fluid results. This is normally drained off by the lymph capillaries and returned to the venous circulation.

ACUTE INFLAMMATION

The acute inflammatory response has two distinct components. One is its vascular component, which consists of an increased blood flow to the damaged tissue and an increase in capillary and venule permeability. This component leads to the redness and warmth that are so often observed at the

Increased flow without increased permeability, such as occurs in an active muscle, moves more fluid to the tissues, but this fluid simply represents an increase in volume and not a change in the nature of the fluid. Such a fluid is called a transudate. It has relatively little protein, and has a specific gravity of 1.012 or less. The exudate that forms with increased permeability is rich in proteins and cells, and has a specific gravity of 1.020 or greater.

site of injury, and to the swelling that follows as fluid increasingly moves to the tissue spaces.

The second component is cellular. Large numbers of specialized leukocytes (white blood cells) move to the tissue spaces, where they inactivate certain disease agents (e.g., bacteria) and remove debris. This movement of fluid, suspended substances, and cells is called **exudate** formation and depends on both the increased blood flow through the capillary bed and the increased permeability of the vasculature.

The Formation of Exudate: Vascular Factors

Hyperemia and Stasis

In response to injury, blood flow changes at the scene occur almost immediately. After an initial fleeting constriction, arterioles and precapillary sphincters supplying the damaged tissue dilate. This change has the effect of reducing vascular resistance, and blood flow to the area increases greatly. The increased blood flow is called **hyperemia.** Shortly after hyperemia develops, capillaries and venules dilate as well. This response is largely a passive yielding to the increased blood pressure caused by the large volume of blood entering these vessels from their dilated supply arterioles (fig. 2.4).

An immediate consequence of hyperemia is an increase in blood hydrostatic pressure. As a result, blood osmotic pressure is overwhelmed and tissue fluid formation increases along the entire length of the capillary. This increase in tissue fluid is the principal factor in the swelling associated with acute inflammation. Inflammatory exudate may also contribute to the pain of inflammation by increasing the pressure and tension applied to nerve endings in the inflamed tissue. The throbbing nature of some inflammatory pain results from arterial pressure pulses that are transmitted to the swollen tissues, alternately increasing and decreasing the pain-causing pressure.

The locally increased blood pressure of hyperemia also promotes the movement of fluid from the blood to the tissue spaces. The loss of fluid from the blood has the effect of increasing the viscosity of the blood and slowing its rate of flow. Sometimes the flow becomes so slow that

Figure 2.4   In inflammation, arteriolar dilation allows increased blood flow, which causes passive dilation of the capillaries and venules.

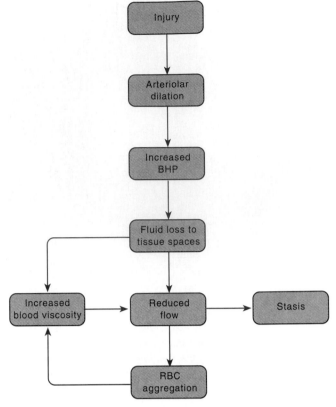

Figure 2.5   Blood flow in the microcirculation following injury. Loss of fluid to exudate formation can greatly reduce the rate of flow, even to the point of complete stoppage, or stasis.

movement in the capillaries and venules stops. This condition is called **stasis**. Stasis in the venules tends to elevate capillary blood pressure, contributing to exudate formation by increasing the movement of fluid out of the blood into the interstitium (fig. 2.5). The process is greatly increased by the second aspect of the vascular inflammatory response, increased vascular permeability.

Changes in vascular permeability result from changes at the endothelial junctions of venules. Following injury, endothelial cells contract slightly, so that the cell margins pull away from adjacent cells and the normally narrow gaps become wider. As a result, fluid moves much more readily from the vessel, especially because capillary blood hydrostatic pressure has risen. The newly widened gaps also allow larger proteins to escape to the tissue spaces (fig. 2.6). This change increases the tissue osmotic pressure (TOP), which favors exudate formation by further drawing fluid from the blood. Little or no fluid normally leaves the blood from venules. Injury causes permeability increases in these vessels and leads to a further increase in exudate formation in injured tissues.

Mild to moderate injury and severe injury differ in the patterns of permeability change they produce. Mild to moderate injury elicits a two-phase permeability change: first, a rapid and brief (up to 30 minutes) increase in permeability of venules, then a second increase that develops more slowly (hours) and is sustained longer (several hours up to

days). Severe injury damages or destroys endothelial cells; it allows exudation to begin immediately and to persist for one to several days. In such cases, red blood cells may also enter the interstitium.

Having considered the formation of a fluid exudate in acute inflammation, you may well ask, What good comes from the accumulation of fluid and plasma proteins at an injury site? We can identify four benefits. One is dilution of toxins. The accumulating fluid dilutes any harmful substances at the scene, reducing the further damage they might do. A second benefit is the increased pain caused by the swelling. The pain forces limits on use of the affected part and thus may prevent additional injury. The third benefit is the presence, at the injury site, of antibodies that would be retained in the blood without a change in vascular permeability. In the tissue spaces they can act against disease-causing microorganisms. A fourth beneficial effect of the fluid exudate is its content of proteins, which foster the phagocytosis of microorganisms, cellular debris, and various other particles associated with tissue damage. The mechanics of phagocytosis are described in some detail in a later section.

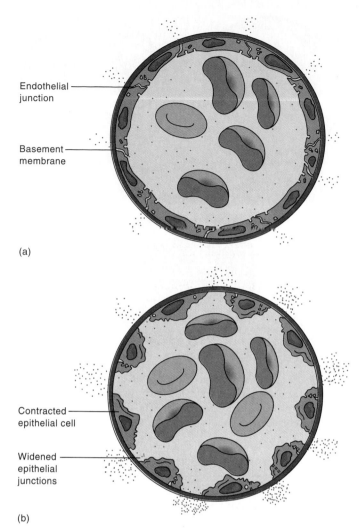

Endothelial junction

Basement membrane

(a)

Contracted epithelial cell

Widened epithelial junctions

(b)

Figure 2.6   Permeability changes in acute inflammation. Compare the normal movement of fluid through the vessel in region A with the flow typical of acute inflammation in region B, where the widened endothelial junctions allow more fluid to escape to the tissue spaces.

Descriptive Classification

Acute inflammations can be classified on the basis of differences in the nature of their fluid exudates. These differences are linked to the severity of injury. This means that a single descriptive term provides information about both the intensity of injury and the nature of the tissue's response. **Serous inflammation** is the response to a mild injury in which only fluid is allowed to escape to the interstices (another term for intercellular spaces). In such cases the endothelial cells contract only slightly, so that more fluid escapes but protein is retained. The watery fluid seen in the blistering of mildly burned skin is an example of a serous

inflammation. **1** At inflamed mucous membrane surfaces, e.g., in mild upper respiratory infections, fluid exudate also contains mucus.

Increased levels of tissue damage cause increased permeability, allowing protein molecules, notably fibrinogen, to leave the blood. In the tissues the fibrinogen is converted to strands of fibrin, which cause the fluid to coagulate. The affected tissue will have masses of gelled exudate covering its surface. Such a fibrinous exudate may be seen in various forms of pericarditis **2** or in the pleurae in pneumonia.

More severe injury, causing greater necrosis or involving a more potent toxin or irritant, causes a **purulent** or **suppurative inflammation.** Here the exudate contains large numbers of leukocytes called neutrophils, which accumulate at the scene of damage. These cells, both living and dead, along with the necrotic debris and fluid exudate, form the thick, white or greenish fluid called **pus, 3** which is common to many acute inflammations. Diffuse suppurative inflammation is called **cellulitis.** An **abscess,** on the other hand, is a localized accumulation of pus that develops at a focus when an agent of injury cannot be quickly neutralized. **4** When the inflammatory response finally removes the threat, a fluid-filled sac called a **cyst** may remain. Ultimately the cyst may diminish as the fluid is resorbed or replaced by connective tissue. In extreme cases a subsurface abscess can enlarge and spread. As tissue becomes necrotic, many cell constituents are released into the abscess. This change increases the osmotic attraction for water from surrounding tissues into the pus-filled area. The result is physical pressure that tends to expand the abscess along lines of least resistance, into the surrounding tissues.

Where injury is of great intensity, capillary damage allows the escape of blood to the tissue. This **hemorrhagic inflammation 5** is characterized by the presence of large numbers of erythrocytes (red blood cells) in the interstices. Thus there is an increase in the amount of debris that must ultimately be removed to allow healing to restore the tissue.

The descriptions we have just given indicate general characteristics. Since injury will vary in the nature and intensity of damage it may cause, more than one of the various types of acute inflammation will often be represented in any particular case.

The Formation of Exudate: Cellular Factors

The outpouring of large numbers of white blood cells from the blood is called **leukocyte emigration.** Normally, about half of the leukocytes in the blood move with the flowing plasma. Others move more slowly, rolling along the surface of the endothelium that lines the lumen of the vessels.

1 43772   **2** 18719   **3** 10067

4 10781   **5** 39908

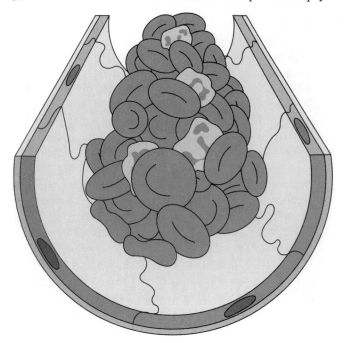

Figure 2.7   Axial flow of blood. The formed elements cluster around the long axis of the vessel to form a central column which is surrounded by the plasma.

Figure 2.8   Margination and pavementing of leukocytes. (*a*) Slowing blood flow allows margination as leukocytes move to the margins of the central column. (*b*) Margination is well advanced, allowing contact with endothelium. (*c*) Pavementing.

Occasionally these rolling cells will pass from the blood to the tissue spaces, where most survive for only a day or so. The majority of the circulating leukocytes are neutrophils, and it is the neutrophils that have this short tissue life span. Monocytes, by contrast, may live in the tissue for years. Leukocytes lost from the blood in this way are replaced from bone marrow and lymphoid tissue. During an inflammatory response, the emigration of leukocytes is greatly increased, an effect due in part to changes in the normal pattern of blood flow.

Margination

Blood flowing at normal rates demonstrates the phenomenon of **axial flow.** This means that the moving blood distributes itself in the vessel so that its formed elements (erythrocytes, leukocytes, platelets) move in a central column parallel to the long axis of the vessel. The largest of the formed elements, the leukocytes, are nearest to the center, with the smaller red cells and platelets forming the outer layers. Plasma surrounds this column of formed elements and flows smoothly along the endothelial lining of the vessel. (fig. 2.7).

As fluid is lost and flow rate decreases in an inflamed tissue, the central column of formed elements enlarges so that its borders move nearer to the endothelium. In addition, the loss of plasma to the tissues causes erythrocytes to aggregate. These clumps of cells now constitute the largest units in the column of formed elements, and as such they assume a more central location within it. In consequence,

the leukocytes are forced to assume peripheral positions at the margins of the column, near the vascular endothelium (fig. 2.8 *a,b*). The phenomenon is called **margination.**

Pavementing and Adhesion

As a result of margination, leukocytes are much more likely to contact endothelium. In injured vascular tissue, they are able to adhere to the endothelial surface and resist being moved by the flowing plasma. As they adhere along the surface they flatten to suggest the appearance of paving stones; hence this phenomenon is called **pavementing** of leukocytes (fig. 2.8*c*). **6**

The mechanism involved in pavementing derives from the effects of injury on the vascular endothelium. When damaged, the venule endothelium becomes sticky, because specific adhesion molecules on the luminal surface of the endothelial cells are exposed. Leukocyte membrane receptors can readily bind to the sticky surface (fig. 2.9).

Endothelial stickiness increases with severity of injury and thus provides an automatically graded emigration response. More severe injury produces greater endothelial change and thus greater leukocyte pavementing.

The importance of leukocyte pavementing is that it provides for the transition of leukocytes from a state of motion to a state of attachment to the venule endothelium at an injury site. This is the essential step that precedes their leaving the blood for the tissue spaces.

Figure 2.9   Pavementing of leukocytes at an injury site (circled area). Only in the injured area are endothelial leukocyte receptors exposed to allow adherence to the surface of the postcapillary venules. No cells can stick to the endothelial surfaces outside the injured area.

Emigration and Diapedesis

The emigration of leukocytes from the blood to the tissue spaces occurs in stages. After initially adhering to the endothelial surface, they start to slide along the surface in an amebalike fashion. This movement continues until an endothelial junction is reached. There, the leukocyte forms a slender extension of its cytoplasm, which it insinuates into the gap between the cells. Probably by physical pressure, but perhaps by enzymatic or other chemical means, the gap is widened just enough for the leukocyte to squeeze past the endothelium. After a pause the cell continues by traversing the basement membrane and the rest of the wall, finally reaching the tissue space (fig. 2.10). **7** The process takes about ten minutes. Other leukocytes will often follow at the point where a given junction has been "eased" by the passage of the first leukocyte. During the inflammatory response, emigration occurs at the endothelial gaps of postcapillary venules. Emigration is not seen in capillaries or in the arterial system.

Sometimes the active process of emigration is called **diapedesis,** but the use of this term should be limited to describing the passive movement of red cells that may occur at the same site. In such cases, blood hydrostatic pressure forces red blood cells into the tissue spaces, particularly where there has been extensive endothelial damage. These cells then die, releasing hemoglobin, which is converted to hemosiderin. Macrophages stained with hemosiderin at the site of inflammation bear witness to red blood cell extravasation (i.e., movement out of the vessel into tissue interstices).

Two types of leukocyte are dominant in the acute inflammatory response. The earliest cells arriving at the scene of injury are the neutrophils. On reaching the tissue

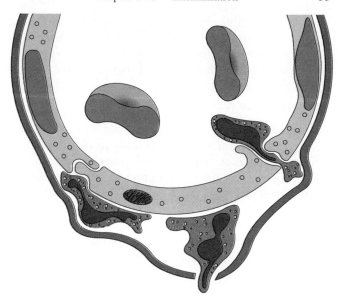

Figure 2.10   Leucocyte emigration. One polymorphonuclear cell (neutrophil) is shown emigrating via an endothelial gap. A second cell, at lower left, pauses after leaving the lumen. At lower right, a third cell passes through the basement membrane to reach the tissue spaces.

spaces they are often described as **polymorphonuclear cells** (PMNs) because of their multilobed nuclei. (Strictly, the term PMN also includes leukocytes called eosinophils and basophils.) A later phase of emigration delivers larger numbers of leukocytes to the tissue spaces. These cells, lacking segmentation in their nuclei, are called **mononuclear** cells or monocytes. In the tissue spaces, they are called **macrophages,** because of their large size and phagocytic capability.

Over the period of an acute inflammatory response, PMNs are initially the most numerous leukocytes on the scene. Their numbers then decline and macrophage numbers increase until, later in the response, the mononuclear cell dominates in the area of injury. There are four principal reasons for this observed pattern. One is the much greater number of neutrophils in circulation, as compared with monocytes; there are more of them available to emigrate. Second, outside the bloodstream the polymorphonuclear leukocytes survive for only a short time, often only a matter of hours (up to 48). This pattern may be related to the lower pH and higher temperature of damaged tissue. In contrast, the macrophage can survive for much longer periods and hence will outlive polymorphonuclear leukocytes at the scene. A third factor is the difference in agents that attract macrophages into the tissue (chemotactic agents) and further agents that keep them resident at the site. Chemotactic agents that attract both neutrophils and monocytes predominate early, while those selective to monocytes persist. Fourth, there is evidence that macrophages can replicate within the tissue. This may be an unusual event, but it has been documented. Experimental evidence indicates that peak polymorphonuclear leukocyte levels are reached at about 6–12 hours after injury. These levels decline 12–24 hours postinjury as mononuclear cell numbers simultaneously increase to reach a maximum after about five days.

Phagocytosis

As we have seen, one aspect of exudate formation is the delivery of great numbers of phagocytes to the site of inflammation. In the tissue spaces, particles such as dysfunctional cells, infectious agents (fungi or bacteria), immune complexes, or the debris that results from tissue damage are phagocytized. Removal of the injurious agent is an obvious advantage. Less obviously, the phagocytosis of debris is beneficial in removing material that might be subject to bacterial action, causing putrefaction.

Effective phagocytic activity involves several steps. Once in the tissue a phagocyte must become activated and move to the immediate vicinity of its target; then it must recognize and attach to it. Finally, it must engulf and destroy the target by releasing enzymes and other toxic substances that it has produced and stored in its lysosomes. These are required to kill the pathogen and/or break down the target molecules. The following discussion describes the events of phagocytosis in more detail.

Chemotaxis

When a phagocyte enters an inflamed tissue and encoun-ters an increased concentration of some chemical attractant, a **chemotactic agent,** it exhibits **chemotaxis.** This is a directed migration of the leukocyte toward regions of increasingly high concentrations of the agent (see fig. 2.11). The process of chemotaxis is based on the presence of specific receptors for the chemotactic agent on the surface of the leukocyte. The binding of the agent to the receptors triggers a complex chain of biochemical events whose net effects change the cell into a larger, more active phagocyte with high levels of destructive agents stored in its intracellular granules. In this state the cell is said to be activated. Binding also mobilizes and directs the phagocyte's movement.

Recognition and Attachment

Although phagocytosis of "naked" particles may occur (e.g., latex beads are engulfed by neutrophils in a test tube), it tends to be a slow and inefficient process. **Opsonization** greatly enhances phagocytosis. Opsonins are substances from the plasma that have particular affinity for the surface features of foreign particles. Leukocytes are able to respond to opsonins because they display leukocyte binding sites. Once an opsonin-coated particle is bound to the surface receptors of the phagocyte, the particle is readily engulfed.

Figure 2.11   The initial random movements of a phagocytic cell are altered when it encounters chemotactic agents. Its movement becomes focused, moving up the concentration gradient to the source of the agent.

Engulfment and Destruction

Binding of a particle to the phagocyte membrane elicits the next step, engulfment (fig. 2.12). In this step, the phagocyte membrane flows around the particle to enclose it in a cytoplasmic phagosome. Granular-appearing lysosomes that contain destructive agents then merge with the phagosome membrane, thereby bringing their contents into contact with the particle. As lysosomes merge with the phagosomes their numbers within the phagocyte are reduced and the phagocyte is said to have *degranulated.*

If a particle is too large to be easily engulfed, for example, a multicellular parasite or a long asbestos fiber, there may be regurgitation of the granule contents into the tissue spaces. The same thing may happen when immune complexes are deposited on an exposed basement membrane, as occurs in certain immune-mediated diseases of the kidney and lung. The leukocyte attempting to engulf this flat surface experiences "frustrated phagocytosis," and releases toxic and degradative substances that damage the basement membrane and the surrounding cells and matrix.

The killing of microorganisms, the destruction or inactivation of toxic agents, and the degradation of macromolecules are the specialized tasks of phagocytes. Although some of the specifics differ, many basic mechanisms are shared between neutrophils and macrophages, and this discussion will not differentiate between them. Killing is accomplished by two broad classes of mechanisms: **oxygen-independent** and **oxygen-dependent.** Oxygen-independent mechanisms involve the release of preformed substances that damage bacterial cell walls, disrupt bacterial replication, and produce a low pH, which may be directly toxic and may indirectly aid the function of other

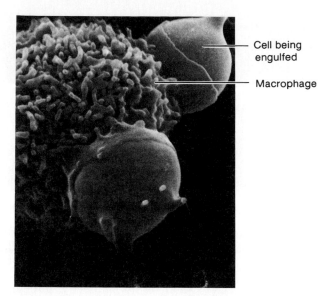

Figure 2.12 This large phagocytic cell is simultaneously engulfing two cells that are no longer functional (about × 5600).

enzymes. As well as killing, phagocyte enzymes can digest bacteria and tissue debris, an action that promotes healing. Elastase, a proteolytic enzyme that breaks down elastin, and collagenase, an enzyme that degrades collagen, are examples of lysosomal enzymes active in removing intercellular debris. (In sterile inflammation such as occurs in a burn, the removal of damaged tissue is the principal role of phagocytes.) Oxygen-dependent killing is accomplished by the creation and release of two particularly reactive oxygen metabolites: hypochlorous acid (HOCl, the same substance used to disinfect swimming pools) and the hydroxyl radical (fig. 2.13). The action of toxic radicals was described in chapter 1. Another term for these substances is oxygen free radicals.

In the case of regurgitation or frustrated phagocytosis, the destructive capacity of oxygen free radicals can be turned on the host tissues. When these effects are combined with those of oxygen-independent processes, the enzymes, toxins, and inflammatory mediators, the potential for damage is clear.

Bacterial Defenses

Bacteria have evolved a variety of defenses against phagocytosis. Some bacteria produce exotoxins that kill leukocytes or inhibit chemotaxis. Some produce a slimy coat to which opsonins have difficulty binding. Some forestall phagocyte binding by shedding substances that bind opsonins so that they cannot attach to the bacterium. And some have tough capsules or can produce cytotoxins to protect them against destruction if they are engulfed.

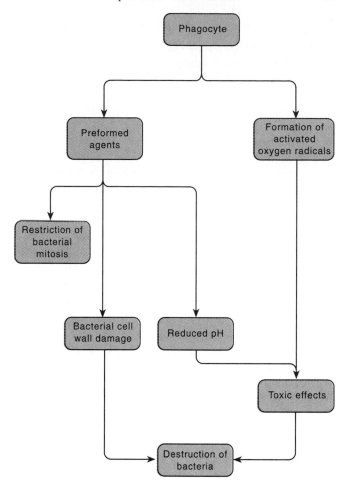

Figure 2.13 Mechanisms underlying the destruction of bacteria by phagocytes at an injury site.

There are some endogenous sources of free radicals. The electron transport chain that is linked to ATP synthesis in mitochondria constantly leaks electrons that generate toxic free radicals. Some enzymes are directly oxidative, for example, xanthine oxidase, which is formed in hypoxic conditions. It is apparently responsible for the damage that occurs in an ischemic tissue when its blood supply is restored. In such **reperfusion injury,** the tissue survives the initial anoxia but is damaged by the production of radicals when oxygen becomes available again. Use of the antioxidant allopurinol has sometimes been effective in treating reperfusion injury.

Defects in Leukocyte Function

Effective phagocyte function depends on a chain of events that begins with margination and pavementing and culminates in removal of the injurious agent, healing, and return to the preinjury state. Defects at any point in the chain will impair host defenses. A number of conditions can produce such defects.

Certain leukocyte defects are associated with chronic or recurrent infections, often involving bacteria with low infection potential. An example is **chronic granulomatous disease of childhood,** a rare genetic defect in phagocyte killing that is due to impaired production of oxygen free radicals. Affected children develop persistent and widespread suppurating infections and often die at an early age. In another rare genetic disease, **Chediak-Higashi syndrome,** there are defects in both phagocyte motility and degranulation, often leading to early death. In a more common example, diabetics suffer defects in phagocytosis that are derived from circulatory problems secondary to changes in their blood vessels. These problems prevent inflammatory cells from being effectively delivered to the site of inflammation. Leukemias may prevent mobilization of leukocytes from the bone marrow, and other diseases may affect opsonization or formation of chemotactic factors. In some diseases (e.g., arteriosclerosis, malnutrition), the formation of an adequate exudate is compromised, and finally, many drugs (e.g., steroids, morphine, tetracycline, chloramphenicol) also interfere with phagocyte function.

Chemical Mediation of Inflammation

To this point in our consideration of acute inflammation, we have been content to examine the particulars of its vascular and cellular components. We can now address the question; What causes these events to occur? More specifically, what triggers the dilation and permeability changes that occur, what activates phagocytic cells, and further, how are these responses linked to the injury that induces them? The answer, in essence, is the process of chemical mediation. That is, injury initially causes certain chemical substances to be produced or released at the site of injury, and these substances then bring about, directly or indirectly, the assortment of specific changes we group under the term acute inflammation.

A variety of different triggering events, often called **initiators,** produce essentially the same vascular and cellular responses; for this reason, acute inflammation is said to be **nonspecific.** Traumatic injury, substances released from infective agents, immune complex deposition, and other factors (table 2.1) all induce essentially the same response.

Table 2.1   Factors that Can Act as Initiators in the Chemical Mediation of the Inflammatory Response

Substances released from injured cells
Direct stimulus to mast cells (trauma, cold)
Microbial products
Exposure of basement membrane or connective tissue components
Complement activation
Deposition of antigen/antibody complexes
Disruption of vascular integrity

Initiators achieve their results indirectly, through a larger number (and the list is growing) of **chemical mediators** that work directly to elicit the vascular and cellular events that make up the inflammatory response. A given initiator often activates several mediators, whose effects may overlap and intertwine, but which ultimately achieve a response that focuses inflammation on the injurious or potentially injurious agents. Although many and complex, mediator systems can be classed as cell-derived or plasma-derived.

Cell-Derived Mediators

Mast cells, **8** widely distributed in vascular connective tissue, inflammatory cells—neutrophils and macrophages—and platelets are the principal sources of the cell-derived mediators of inflammation. In response to an initiator, these cells and platelets release preformed mediators that are stored in cytoplasmic granules. In other cases, the initiator triggers an activation sequence that produces newly formed mediators. In either case, the various vascular and cellular components of inflammation are then produced by the action of the mediators. Some important cell-derived mediators are presented in figure 2.14. Histamine contributes to early vasodilation and permeability increases, while other mast-cell mediators are chemotactic for neutrophils. The preformed mediators of the mast cell are stored in cytoplasmic vesicles that cause the cells to have a granular appearance. For this reason, mediator release is described as **degranulation, 9** a term that we encountered in a different context in the loss of lysosomes in a phagocyte.

Once at the scene of damage, phagocytes and mast cells produce various mediators categorized as **leukotrienes** and **prostaglandins.** Leukotrienes and pros-

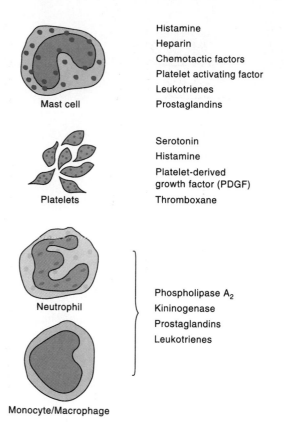

Figure 2.14   Cellular sources of selected inflammatory mediators. Note that leukotrienes and prostaglandins are produced from arachidonic acid derived from the source cell's plasma membrane phospholipids.

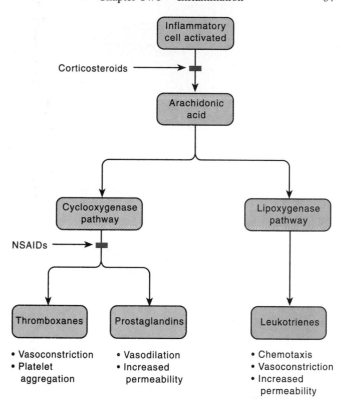

Figure 2.15   The formation of arachidonic acid and some of the inflammatory roles of its principal derivatives. Also indicated are the sites of blocking action by corticosteroids and nonsteroidal anti-inflammatory agents (NSAIDs).

taglandins are derived from a common lipid precursor called **arachidonic acid.** It is formed from the phospholipids of the cell membrane when an initiator triggers formation of an activation enzyme system. Figure 2.15 presents this concept, identifies some of the specific mediators of both groups, and indicates some of their principal contributions to inflammation. There are many different leukotrienes and prostaglandins, each with a particular and perhaps contradictory mediation role. We present only the ones that are best understood.

The two pathways that diverge from arachidonic acid are the **lipoxygenase pathway** (producing leukotrienes) and the **cyclooxygenase pathway** (producing prostaglandins). Some anti-inflammatory therapy uses a class of drugs called **nonsteroidal anti-inflammatory drugs** (NSAIDs). These selectively block the cyclooxygenase pathway (fig. 2.15). The term nonsteroidal is useful in distinguishing them from the corticosteroid-related agents, which also have anti-inflammatory effects. These act by blocking the formation of arachidonic acid and,

therefore, the inflammatory mediators that derive from it. For this reason, corticosteroids have a broader action. We will consider other aspects of therapy in inflammation, in particular why it should be necessary at all, in a later section of this chapter.

Some mediators, for example, **platelet-derived growth factor** (PDGF), or **thromboxanes,** play more important roles in other responses that may be related to inflammation (healing, in this case). Blood coagulation is another example that has been well studied. We will deal with those processes, and the chemical mediators relevant to them, in chapters 4 and 7.

Plasma-Derived Mediators

Most plasma-derived mediators of inflammation are formed at the end of a sequence of activation steps called a **cascade.** In essence, a number of inactive proteins circulate in the plasma. Following an initial activation event, one of these proteins is activated. It is then able to activate a

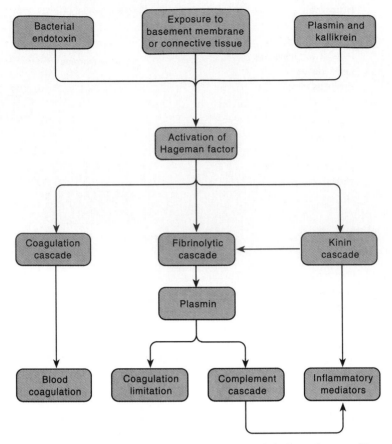

Figure 2.16   Four cascades with a role in coping with injury are related through their dependence on Hageman factor.

second protein, which in turn activates a third, and so on. There are four interrelated cascades—the blood coagulation cascade, the kinin cascade, the fibrinolytic cascade, and the complement cascade (fig. 2.16). All four can be directly or indirectly triggered by the presence of the active form of a circulating protein known as **Hageman factor** (also called clotting factor XII).

The coagulation and fibrinolytic cascades function in inflammation and blood loss prevention, and the complement cascade is linked both to inflammation and to the immune system. In other words, only the kinin cascade seems to restrict its role to mediating inflammation. More detail on the coagulation and fibrinolytic cascades is presented in chapter 7.

The kinin cascade is significant in that one of its components, **bradykinin,** is a contributing factor to the pain of inflammation. Other factors, noted earlier, are the tension and pressure produced by the accumulation of inflammatory exudate at the damage site. Lowered pH and potassium released from damaged cells also play a role.

The complement system consists of over twenty circulating proteins. Their sequential activation produces a complex of five proteins called the **membrane attack complex** (MAC), which can destroy invading microorganisms by punching holes in their membranes. Beyond this,

various of the activated intermediate complement proteins act as mediators of inflammation, with specific roles in promoting dilation, permeability, chemotaxis, phagocytosis, and histamine release, as well as enhancing the kinin cascade. Activation of the complement cascade may be triggered by microorganism surfaces and by antibody in conjunction with its defensive role of the immune system (see chapter 5).

The chemical mediators that produce acute inflammation tend to be formed or released in a rapid, dramatic fashion and thereby orchestrate an appropriately aggressive response to injury. In the same manner, the concentration of these mediators drops suddenly after a time, ending the acute inflammation. This drop results from a combination of the following: mediator release is exhausted or terminated, cascades are triggered that reverse the mediating cascades, anti-inflammatory, antioxidant, and antiproteolytic agents are delivered to the site of former injury. The result is a quenching of the acute inflammation that is analogous to the processes that limit coagulation of blood. It also sets the stage for the healing process.

The plasma-derived mediator that is not formed by a cascade is **antibody.** This key element of the immune system may be the initiator that activates the complement cascade. Its role in triggering the release of cell-derived mediators in allergy disorders is described in chapter 5.

Systemic Effects of Acute Inflammation

Most of us are only too familiar with some of the systemic effects of inflammation: fever, loss of appetite, increase in very deep sleep, perhaps a rapid weight loss, and residual weakness. We may have experienced the reaction of our lymphatic system to infection. Perhaps our axillary or neck lymph nodes were swollen and sore to the touch (the condition called **lymphadenitis**). If the inflammation was related to a localized bacterial infection, we may have noted reddened streaks moving slowly proximally as lymph vessels in an inflamed state (**lymphangitis**) attempted to cope with a spreading infection. The thin, loose-walled capillaries of the lymph system aid in draining off the exudate (edema fluid) formed in an inflammation, but can pass bacteria into the blood, producing **bacteremia,** and thereby spread the infection.

Some systemic effects are less readily observable. **Leukocytosis** is a two- to threefold increase of circulating leukocytes (up to 30,000/mm^3). This change is rapid and involves both the release of stored neutrophils, largely from the lung capillaries and bone marrow, and an increase in leukocyte production by red bone marrow. The latter is in response to "colony stimulating factors" released from activated macrophages and T lymphocytes. (For more about T lymphocytes, see chapter 5.) Laboratory blood tests not only indicate the presence of leukocytosis but can differentiate among the various white cell types. These **differential white cell counts** are useful in diagnosis. For example, bacterial infection and ischemic damage produce elevated neutrophil counts (**neutrophilia**). On the other hand, viral infections stimulate **lymphocytosis** (an increase in the number of lymphocytes), while allergic reactions or parasitic infections produce a relatively greater rise in eosinophils (**eosinophilia**).

Therapeutic Modification of Acute Inflammation

This section describes the rationale for limiting inflammation and the essential concepts of anti-inflammation therapy. It may seem strange to consider limiting the inflammatory response when we've just identified its beneficial role in dealing with the agents that produce tissue damage. However, even though acute inflammation accomplishes this task, there are some problems associated with excessive or inappropriate inflammation.

The first of these is pain, a benefit to some degree in signaling the fact of tissue damage and in limiting use of an injured tissue. But when pain is intense and prolonged, it can present significant problems to the patient. Second, sometimes swelling is so great that it impairs function, perhaps by limiting joint mobility or obstructing some anatomical passage. An example of the latter case would be acute pancreatitis, where the swollen pancreas can compress the common bile duct. Remember also that swelling can pro-

 Another set of changes that can be revealed by laboratory testing is a rise in what have been collectively called **acute phase proteins** (also called acute phase reactants). They include fibrinogen, α_1-proteinase inhibitor, C-reactive protein, and SAA (serum amyloid associated) protein. While some information on the roles played by three of these proteins is available, the function of the SAA protein in inflammation remains a mystery, despite the fact that it can be measured at 500–1,000-fold increased concentrations in acute inflammation. Generally, only C-reactive protein will be assessed to confirm a suspected inflammatory process.

duce pain as tissue pressures impinge upon nerve endings and pain-producing mediators accumulate. So when swelling is excessive, excessive pain may also be present. A third problem arising out of the acute inflammatory response is tissue damage. A good example is a type of glomerulonephritis in which immune complexes are present in renal basement membranes. These complexes are chemotactic for neutrophils, which move to the scene and attempt to engulf them, but this event promotes frustrated phagocytosis and the release of substances that damage the basement membrane, leading in many cases to the threat of renal failure. The overall situation is summarized in figure 2.17.

You can see, then, that the inflammatory response has the potential to further complicate the patient's problems rather than reducing them. For this reason, therapy to limit the inflammatory response may be necessary. The challenge, of course, is to apply therapy in such a way as to limit inflammation, thus preventing excessive pain and tissue damage, while allowing a sufficient response to deal effectively with the problem. We will now consider some specific ways of modifying the inflammatory response. Broadly, there are both physical approaches and those that use therapeutic drugs.

Temperature

It has long been recognized that temperature manipulation is effective in coping with excessive inflammation. Application of cold to the damaged area causes a reduction of swelling. This effect is probably due to a vasoconstriction reflex in arterioles to prevent heat loss. Of course, at the scene of damage, the reduced blood flow has the effect of reducing formation of fluid exudate and swelling is relieved. The opposite situation, heat application, is also helpful in that an elevated temperature favors phagocytosis. In this context, you can understand the logic of temperature therapy in typical muscle and connective tissue injury. Cold is applied early, to limit swelling; then later, when

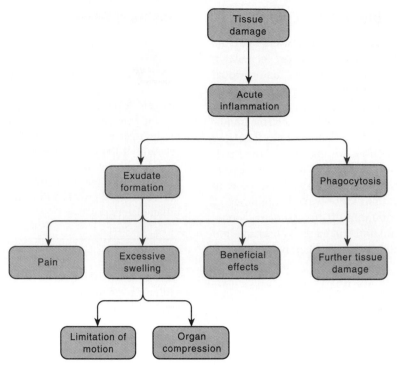

Figure 2.17   The rationale for therapeutically limiting inflammation is based on its excessive or inappropriate effects. Therapy seeks to minimize these without limiting the beneficial aspects of inflammation.

phagocytes have accumulated at the scene, heat is applied to stimulate phagocytosis. One of the beneficial effects of fever, which is often associated with inflammation, may be the enhancement of phagocytosis that occurs as body temperature rises. Note that heat application is one of the few methods of enhancing a beneficial aspect of inflammation. Most often, suppression of an excessive response is the basis for therapy.

Elevation and Pressure

Another physical approach to dealing with an excessive inflammatory response is aimed at limiting swelling. In the case of damage involving the limbs, elevation is often successful in promoting drainage to reduce swelling. More importantly, blood flow is slowed, since the blood must oppose gravity in flowing to an elevated point, so fluid exudate formation, and therefore swelling, can be conveniently reduced. In some cases, constricting wrappings may be applied to the inflamed area. These will prevent exudate formation by increasing the pressure in the tissues so that fluid is prevented from leaving the blood vessels. The higher tissue fluid pressures also promote lymphatic drainage.

Drug Therapy

In addition to altering the physical conditions described above, a major approach to anti-inflammatory therapy is directed at the chemical mediation system that underlies it.

A variety of chemicals called **antihistamines** block the action of histamine at its blood vessel receptors. We have already mentioned the roles of nonsteroidal anti-inflammatory agents and corticosteroids, but a few further comments are appropriate. By blocking cyclooxygenase activity, agents like ibuprofen and acetylsalicylic acid (ASA, more commonly known as aspirin) block prostaglandin synthesis and thereby remove an important inflammatory mediator. To the extent that they successfully suppress the inflammation, they also bring pain relief by blocking the formation of pain mediators like bradykinin and prostaglandins, and suppressing K^+ and acid stimuli.

Steroid therapy has broad anti-inflammation effects because it interferes with the release of arachidonic acid from inflammatory cells. As a result, prostaglandin synthesis is reduced, and vasodilation and swelling are suppressed. And since arachidonic acid is the precursor of the leukotrienes, their vascular and cellular stimuli are also limited. The net effect is to reduce swelling and minimize damage from phagocytic cells. Another beneficial steroid effect involves lysosomes. By stabilizing lysosomal membranes, steroids can limit the release of enzymes and thereby reduce damage at the scene of inflammation. The anti-inflammatory effects of corticosteroids can be quite potent. For example, after injection into an inflamed joint, vessel permeability is so reduced that normal joint fluid production declines. This decline can result in exquisite pain, but it is relatively short-lived, lasting perhaps a few days, until fluid levels rise enough to allow normal joint movement.

Table 2.2   Selected Agents Typically Involved in Chronic Inflammation

Inflammatory Agent	Disease
Microorganisms	
Mycobacterium tuberculosis	Tuberculosis
Mycobacterium leprae	Leprosy
Listeria species	Listeriosis
Treponema pallidum	Syphilis
Brucella species	Brucellosis
Foreign Bodies	
Asbestos	Asbestosis
Silica	Silicosis
Beryllium	Berylliosis
Various organic dusts	Specific to the agent

Before leaving this section, let us note two potential complications of anti-inflammation therapy. One involves healing. Since some anti-inflammatory drugs, steroids for example, interfere with healing, incautious use can extend and complicate tissue restoration. A second problem has to do with infection. In damping the acute inflammatory response, we limit a major defense against infection. This means that therapy can induce a greater susceptibility to infection at the same time as it seeks to reduce inflammatory damage or other problems arising from an excessive inflammatory response.

CHRONIC INFLAMMATION

Description

In some cases, when the acute inflammatory response is unable to remove or neutralize an injurious agent, the response is modified to forms called subacute or chronic. The distinctions between these are not well defined, but general guidelines indicate that the term **subacute** applies in inflammations lasting beyond one week. After six weeks' duration the term **chronic** is applied. It is not unusual for a chronic response to last many months, even years. However, more than duration differentiates these responses. The nature of the response also changes. As the inflammatory process continues, fluid exudate diminishes in significance and the cellular response assumes dominance; whatever the nature of the inciting agent, the chronic response is dominated by a massive build-up of cells in the affected tissue. These cells are primarily macrophages and lymphocytes (cells normally involved in mediating immune system responses). The transition between the subacute and

the chronic patterns is variable and hence not easily identified, so our consideration will emphasize the chronic inflammatory response.

In chronic inflammation there is, in essence, a standoff between the attack of the injurious agent and the counterattack mounted by the defenses of the host. The agent and the host are just capable of resisting each other's attacks, but neither is strong enough to overwhelm the other. The agents involved are typically of low invasive ability. They are unable to penetrate deeply into or spread rapidly throughout the body of the host. Such agents might be certain bacteria, fungi, or larger parasites. Some are organisms that can shelter from the immune system by living, at least part of the time, within macrophages. Some of the microorganisms involved in chronic inflammation are listed in table 2.2. Foreign bodies that are insoluble in the body's fluids, although nonliving, can also elicit a chronic inflammatory response (table 2.2). Because talc powder, composed of magnesium silicate, used to be used to dust surgical gloves, it sometimes made its way into surgical wounds, stimulating a chronic foreign-body response. Intravenous drug abusers may use talc to carry or dilute a drug and thereby introduce it into the body. The talc tends to be trapped in the capillaries of the lung and can initiate a chronic inflammation there.

Regardless of the specific nature of the inciting agent, its presence in the tissues promotes a long-term conflict with the phagocytic cells of the host. This conflict typically proceeds at the expense of normal tissues. Their heavy infiltration by inflammatory cells progressively interferes with normal function. When the process continues over months and years, function deteriorates as tissue is destroyed, accumulating inflammatory cells replace functional tissues, and scarring develops. This deterioration can ultimately lead to somatic death—ironically, an ultimate victory for the biological agent at the expense of the host on which it depends.

Pathogenesis

Chronic inflammation is initiated by a typical acute response. However, the response is unable to eliminate the injurious agent or resolve the effects of injury. As we have seen, by the later stages of acute inflammation, macrophages are the dominant leukocytes at the scene, with some lymphocytes now present as well. In chronic inflammation, the highly active macrophages are also unable to remove the agent, and it persists in spite of their efforts at phagocytosis.

The long-term presence of the irritant may allow its antigenic properties to stimulate the host immune response. In the case of inert, nonbiological irritants (e.g., asbestos particles), products of damaged tissue may provide the stimulus. In any case, stimulation of the immune system leads to activation of its lymphocytes, which respond by releasing substances called **lymphokines.** These have

Figure 2.18   Action of migration inhibition factor (MIF).
(*a*) Phagocytes introduced to the surface of a growth medium
move out from the point of introduction. (*b*) When the medium
contains MIF, their migration is greatly suppressed.

Figure 2.19   (*a*) Diagram of a granuloma and its principal
components. (*b*) Close-up of a multinucleated giant cell (arrow) at
the center of a long-standing granuloma.

various specific effects on macrophages that contribute to the chronic inflammatory response. This situation is in con-trast to acute inflammation, where chemical inflammatory media-tors are responsible for neutrophil activation. The predomi-nant cells of chronic inflammation, the macrophages, are under the more direct control of a subpopulation of lympho-cytes called T_H cells (helper T cells). T_H cells and mac-rophages establish an interaction whereby the macrophages inform the lymphocytes as to the immune nature of the inflammatory initiator. The T_H lymphocytes then release sub-stances that activate macrophages (MAF—macrophage-activating factor) and keep them at the site of inflammation (MIF—migration inhibition factor), where their efforts can be best focused (fig. 2.18). Another contrast with acute inflam-mation concerns the sequencing of healing. In acute inflam-mation, the initial response is usually effective and healing follows. In chronic inflammation, inflammatory and repair processes occur at the same time so that neither is effective.

Classification

Two patterns of chronic inflammation can be distinguished. In one, called **nonspecific chronic inflammation,** a diffuse accumulation of macrophages and lymphocytes develops at the site of injury. **10** Most chronic inflammations are of this type. A less common but distinctive form of the process is seen in the second pattern of chronic inflammation, **granulomatous inflammation.** This condition is char-acterized by a focal response that leads to the formation of a specific lesion, the **granuloma** **11** (fig. 2.19). This roughly spherical mass is formed by hundreds of trans-formed macrophages called **epithelioid cells.** These have more cytoplasm than typical macrophages and are heavily granulated. They are surrounded by lymphocytes and fibroblasts. There may also be a central mass of necrotic tissue that has been "walled off," often containing the inju-rious agent. Also present in many instances are very large,

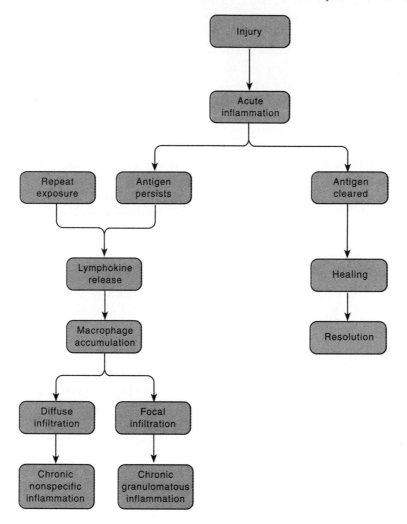

Figure 2.20   Essential pathogenesis of chronic inflammation.

multinucleated cells. These are formed by the merging of macrophages or the coalescence of several (a dozen would not be unusual) to form very large cells with phagocytic capabilities. They are descriptively termed **multinucleated giant cells.** 12

Typically, foreign-body granulomas are centered on the particle involved. Granulomas that arise in an allergic reaction to persistent bacterial, viral, or fungal agents tend to develop a necrotic center as they get larger. Those that develop with an intracellular bacterium (e.g., tuberculosis, syphilis, leprosy) show the characteristic pattern of necrosis referred to earlier as caseous necrosis. In this case the center of the granuloma produces a crumbly, cheeselike breakdown product (hence the term caseous). 13

Figure 2.20 provides an overview of the mechanisms underlying chronic inflammation. Here, immune-mediated processes are emphasized, although, as we have already noted, nonimmunogenic stimuli are often involved. The emphasis here is on the central role of the lymphocyte in mediating the response.

Sarcoidosis is a granulomatous disease that is relatively uncommon, but that can have devastating consequences for about 20% of its victims. Its small, scattered, noncaseating granulomas can affect the eye, liver, skin, lymph node, lungs, spleen, or bone marrow. Sarcoidosis typically affects young people (20–35) and is ten times more common in blacks than whites, while it is very rare in Orientals. Its cause is unknown.

Case Study

A 25-year-old construction worker came to a general practitioner because of a painful, red swelling over his patella, which had been bothering him in his work for the past three days. Nothing in his medical history seemed likely to be a contributing factor, other than that he had recently been camping and had been badly bitten by mosquitos.

The examination revealed an area of 5 cm diameter that was swollen, red, and hot, with a central accumulation of pus. The lesion was strongly suggestive of a mosquito bite that had become infected, forming a large boil.

The boil was incised and drained, and a sample of pus was sent for laboratory culture and sensitivity studies to determine the organism involved and its antibiotic sensitivities. Pending results of these studies, Cloxicillin was prescribed on the assumption that *Staphylococcus aureus* was likely to be found. A dressing was applied to the patient's knee. Two days later, lab results confirmed that cloxicillin-sensitive *Staph. aureus* was involved.

Over the following months the patient suffered recurring boils, which were presenting problems in his work. Blood sugar tests were done and found to be normal. A nasal culture revealed *Staph. aureus* to be resident in the nasal passages. An appropriate course of antibiotic therapy was instituted to eradicate the staph organisms and the patient has had no further problems with recurring boils.

Commentary

This is a situation in which resident nasal organisms provide a source of reinfection, which in this case those relatively easily dealt with.

Because draining a boil is usually adequate, prescribing an antibiotic is normally not necessary. However, in this case, several factors indicated that antibiotic therapy was prudent: the size of the lesion and its location, where it was subject to bending of the knee and friction from clothing, the risk of further irritation on the job site, and the physician's assessment of the patient's inadequate hygiene.

The blood sugar test was done in the face of recurring boils to determine whether an early diabetes mellitus condition might be contributing to the ease with which organisms were becoming established. In diabetics, elevated glucose levels provide a nutrient medium for infecting organisms at the same time as a compromised circulation limits the ability to cope with infection. Fortunately, no diabetes was present and the situation was resolved with relative ease.

Key Concepts

1. The cardinal signs of inflammation are redness, heat, swelling, pain, and loss of function (p. 28).

2. Increases in blood pressure and capillary permeability associated with the inflammatory response lead to accumulation of fluid exudate and phagocytic cells at the site of injury (pp. 28–29).

3. The type of exudate formed is related to the nature of the injury and affects the pattern of healing (pp. 29–30).

4. Changes in vascular flow and the stickiness of postcapillary venules ensure the delivery of appropriate numbers of leukocytes to the site of injury (pp. 30–34).

5. An initial wave of neutrophils is followed by a later wave of monocytes capable of being focused by the lymphocytes, thereby staging the cellular response to injury (pp. 31–32).

6. The destruction of pathogens and the removal of debris are accomplished by phagocytic cells, which enter the tissue, become activated, move toward the target, recognize and attach to it, and then engulf and destroy it (pp. 34–35).

7. A variety of cell-derived and plasma-derived chemical mediators orchestrate, maintain, and then quench the acute inflammatory response (pp. 36–38).

8. Cold or heat, elevation and pressure, antihistamines, corticosteroids, and nonsteroidal anti-inflammatory agents can be used to control excessive or inappropriate acute inflammation (pp. 39–40).

9. Chronic inflammation develops when some persistent infection or foreign substance stimulates a lymphocyte-mediated accumulation of activated macrophages (pp. 41–43).

REVIEW ACTIVITIES

1. Diagram the sequence of events that starts with cell injury and leads to increased vascular permeability.

2. Explain how phagocytosis, chemotaxis, emigration, pavementing, and margination are related.

3. Describe the role of four types of chemical mediators thought to contribute to acute inflammation.

4. Construct a table relating a type of acute inflammation with its corresponding exudate characteristics.

5. Sketch a flow chart that traces the development of a granuloma.

6. List four methods of suppressing the inflammatory response and indicate the mechanism that operates in each case.

7. Corticosteroids and NSAIDs act to quench the production of certain delayed mediators. Get as fanciful as you like and invent a new way of controlling the acute inflammatory response (remember this is purely theoretical). Is there anything else you could do to knock out a chronic inflammatory response, other than treating the tissue with corticosteroids or NSAIDs?

Chapter Three

Fever

So when a raging fever burns
We shift from side to side by turns;
An 'tis poor relief we gain,
To change the place to keep the pain.

Isaac Watts
Some Thoughts of God and Death

I nflammation is often accompanied by elevation of the body temperature above its normal range. This condition is known as **fever** or **pyrexia.** The association of fever with disease, especially infection, has been recognized for hundreds of years. Indeed, many infectious diseases are named fevers (e.g., typhoid fever, rheumatic fever, cat-scratch fever) because fever dominates the clinical pattern of the disease. Rather than a defect in the system that regulates body temperature, fever represents an upward adjustment of the temperature level that the system seeks to establish and maintain. This point is better appreciated in the context of normal thermal regulation.

NORMAL THERMOREGULATION

At rest, normal oral temperature varies within a surprisingly narrow range of values whose average is about 36.7° C. Temperatures normally do not vary more than 0.5° C (1°F) from this value. A similar range is observed for rectal temperature, with its average values elevated about 0.5° C above oral, while the average axilla's (armpit) temperature is about 0.5° C lower than oral temperature. Body temperature varies throughout the day, with lowest temperatures in the early morning and highest around 10 P.M. (table 3.1). The normal body temperature value most often used is 37° C (98.6° F).

Body temperature is closely regulated because temperature changes can significantly affect cellular functions. Since most cell enzymes function optimally in the normal body temperature range, a common metabolic standard is established throughout the body. Alterations of temperature for a sustained period can have damaging effects and may even be fatal. For example, a cranial temperature of 40.5° C (105° F) will disturb brain function, producing bewilderment and confusion. A sustained body temperature of 41° C (106° F) is all that is necessary for many other tissues to suffer damage. With an increase to 43° C (109° F) for only a few hours, somatic death usually follows. Similarly, if body temperature falls below normal, it can affect enzyme function and slow metabolism to the point that damage results.

Maintenance of a given body temperature is achieved by balancing heat production against heat loss. Heat is produced by all cells in the course of normal metabolism, because cellular energy conversions are considerably less than 100% efficient. This means that energy in the form of heat is constantly produced and released from living tissues. The amount of heat will vary with normal fluctuations of metabolic activity related to each tissue's characteristic functions. For example, at rest, the liver has a higher metabolic rate than does skeletal muscle, and so it pro-duces more heat. During exercise, however, muscle heat production rises dramatically, and when activity diminishes, temperature declines to normal levels.

Table 3.1	Daily Temperature Fluctuation: Average Rectal Temperatures of a Group of Adults Taken at Intervals over 24 Hours

Time	Temperature (° C)
Midnight	36.85
0200	36.73
0400	36.60
0800	36.65
Noon	37.00
1600	37.20
2000	37.15
2200	37.10

Heat loss is achieved primarily by the delivery of heat energy to the surface of the body, where any excess can be lost to the environment. The delivery is accomplished by the blood, which picks up heat as it passes throughout the body and then carries it to the skin.

Mechanisms of Heat Loss

The skin is well suited to temperature regulation, because it has a large surface area from which heat can be lost. Heat loss is accomplished by four mechanisms: radiation, evaporation, conduction, and convection. In loss by **radiation,** heat energy moves directly away from the warm skin surface. When you place a hand near a red-hot cooking element, you feel heat without actually touching the element, because of energy radiating from it.

In **evaporation,** water at the skin surface is converted from a liquid to a vapor state. The process consumes heat energy from the surrounding skin, causing body temperature to fall. The water that evaporates is secreted by the skin's sweat glands. It is moved to the surface by contraction of smooth muscle in the ducts that drain the glands. The openings of these ducts at the surface are called **pores.** Heat loss by evaporation from pulmonary surfaces occurs, but is not nearly as significant in humans as it is in some animals, whose panting is an important means of increasing heat loss.

Conduction is a third means of losing heat. It involves direct transfer of heat by physical contact between the body and a cooler surrounding medium. In humans this situation arises most typically when the body is immersed in water. Immersion is often used therapeutically to reduce fever. When heat is carried away by movement of the air or water surrounding the body, the mechanism is called **convection.**

The mechanisms just described work automatically. But active behavioral responses can increase heat loss. For example, moving to a cooler location promotes heat loss, as does increasing skin surface exposure by rolling up shirt sleeves or wearing shorts rather than full-length slacks. Similarly, loosening the clothing promotes air flow to increase evaporation and convection losses.

Mechanisms of Heat Production

As we noted earlier, heat is constantly being produced by cellular metabolism and must continually be lost to prevent overheating. On the other hand, if body temperature should fall, additional heat production is required. Like heat loss, heat production comes about by a physiological reflex and various appropriate behavioral responses.

The heat production reflex is shivering. Shivering entails a pattern of rapidly alternating skeletal muscle contractions that produce no skeletal motion. It does, however, increase the amount of heat liberated by the contracting muscle. The muscle converts chemical energy in its fuel molecules, principally glucose, to the mechanical energy needed for the contraction. As this occurs, heat energy is released because of the inefficiency of the conversion process. Heat production behaviors also include conscious patterns of motions that also utilize muscle contractions to produce heat, such as arm waving or jumping in place.

Regulation of Heat Loss

At rest, metabolic heat production is relatively constant. Variations in the metabolic rate are not used as a means of regulating temperature. Instead, heat loss mechanisms are modified to achieve the required body temperature. Body temperature increases stimulate more heat loss, whereas temperature decreases below the normal range cause heat loss mechanisms to be inhibited. In other words, the system functions by allowing either more or less heat loss to the environment as required. At extremes of temperature, reflex shivering or behavioral responses are brought into play. Behavioral heat conservation measures include adding insulating layers of clothing or blankets and reducing the body surface area by curling into the fetal position or clenching the hands. Heat loss occurs at the skin's surface and depends primarily on two easily altered mechanisms.

One involves heat loss at the skin's surface, based on the transfer of heat from the blood. Dermal blood vessels are so arranged that, depending on the pattern of arteriolar constriction, blood can be distributed to vessels that are either nearer the surface or farther from it. When blood is moved near the surface, more heat is lost. When blood is

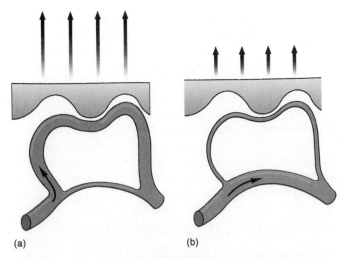

Figure 3.1   Heat loss and dermal blood flow. (*a*) Blood moving near the skin's surface loses body heat. (*b*) Heat loss is reduced when more blood is diverted from the surface.

moved farther from the surface, less heat is lost (fig. 3.1). No new heat is produced, but temperature is maintained by cutting losses.

The second mechanism used to regulate heat loss involves sweat production at the skin's surface. Changes in sweat production cause greater or lesser heat loss. The skin usually feels dry because perspiration fluid is quickly evaporated from it after reaching the surface. When temperature rises, production rates exceed evaporation rates, and fluid accumulates.

Having considered the sources of heat and the mechanisms of heat loss, let us now take a closer look at the responses of the tissues involved. What are the factors that determine the appropriate response in the tissues that affect heat loss and heat production? In other words, what controls and coordinates the blood vessels, sweat glands, shivering, and the various behavioral responses, so that temperature is maintained at the desired level?

Negative Feedback Control of Body Temperature

A control system is a collection of components that function to maintain some variable at a particular value. Control systems are used extensively in engineering applications, and they function in biological control as well. To maintain control of a variable such as temperature, the control system must have one or more components that can respond to bring about changes in the variable (fig. 3.2). These responding tissues are called **effectors.** In a physiological control system there is often more than one effector, and each of them must receive controlling input information. This information will stimulate them to increase or decrease their particular response. Control of the effectors

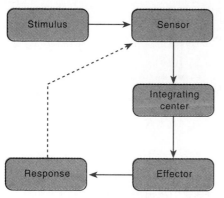

Figure 3.2 Essential elements and interrelationships of a negative feedback control system.

is achieved by a second control system component called an **integrator** or **integrating center** (IC). It is here that control "decisions" are reached on the basis of information regarding body temperature. This information is sent to the integrating center by specialized receptors called **sensors,** which are sensitive to changes in temperature. The system maintains the particular variable close to a certain value called the system's **set point.**

As body temperature changes, sensors alter their output to the integrating center, which then compares the information with its set point. If the difference between the two values falls outside an acceptable range, the integrating center institutes a corrective response by the system's effectors. The response tends to restore the set point value and therefore decrease the stimulus to the sensors. Because the system's response is monitored and acted upon in further corrective action, this type of control system is said to operate according to the principle of feedback. Since the corrective response is always in a direction opposite to the direction of change from the set point, such control is said to be **negative feedback control.** Thus if temperature is too high, the negative feedback system will cause it to be lowered; if too low, the system will raise it. In this way correction for changes from the set point is always achieved.

In humans, the major temperature regulation effectors are dermal arterioles, sweat glands, and the skeletal muscles involved in both shivering and the various temperature-related behavioral responses. All of these receive controlling input from the **thermoregulation center** in the hypothalamus, which functions as integrating center. Temperature information is detected in all parts of the body by sensors called **thermoreceptors.** From these, the temperature information is relayed to the hypothalamus for analysis. Some neurons in the hypothalamus are also directly sensitive to temperature. These provide an important contribution to the process, since they directly monitor levels of heat in the blood that flows through the brain. Normal human thermoregulation is summarized in figure 3.3.

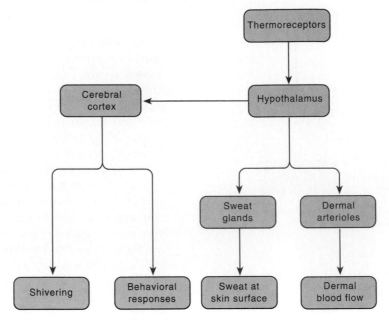

Figure 3.3   Principal mechanisms of human thermoregulation.

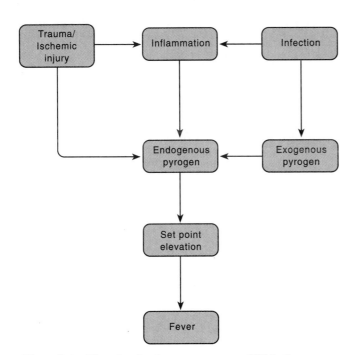

Figure 3.4   The role of endogenous pyrogen (EP) in the pathogenesis of fever.

the functional LPS can cause "injection fevers." These were a common complication of the administration of intravenous fluids, particularly in the early days when less was known of the mechanisms underlying fever. They can be prevented if fluids are prepared in sterile conditions and then specifically treated to remove LPS. While humans are exquisitely sensitive to LPS, a wide range of other organisms and substances can act as exogenous pyrogens, including viruses, bacteria, fungi, and a wide range of antigenic

or toxic substances. Many therapeutic agents, either because of excess dosage (e.g., aspirin, atropine, chlorpromazine) or a particular patient sensitivity (e.g., cimetidine, ibuprofen, bleomycin, penicillins) may be pyrogenic. Aspirin is interesting in this context since it is commonly used as an antipyretic agent.

Endogenous Pyrogens

As we have seen, an exogenous pyrogen generates fever through its capacity to stimulate the production and release of endogenous pyrogens (EPs). These are substances produced in an inflammatory response that act on receptors in the hypothalamus to cause an upward alteration of its temperature set point. The clinically relevant sources of EPs that have been identified include PMNs, lymphocytes, and especially macrophages. The EPs include IL-1 (interleukin 1), TNF (tumor necrosis factor), INF-α (interferon alpha), and a recently implicated substance called macrophage inflammatory protein-1 (MIP-1). The best characterized are IL-1 and TNF. IL-1 is produced by a wide number of cells in response to injury or inflammatory activation, and especially by activated macrophages, which appear to be the principal source of IL-1 in its role as an endogenous pyrogen. Certainly, the fever spikes noted in bacteremia are best explained by EP production related to the activation of free monocytes and macrophages resident in the liver, spleen, and other tissues.

Essentially, then, endogenous pyrogens are produced and released by the body's phagocytic cells. In response to pyrogenic stimuli, these cells produce and release EPs. A notable exception exists in certain malignant tumors. The nonphagocytic cells of these tumors (e.g., leukemia and

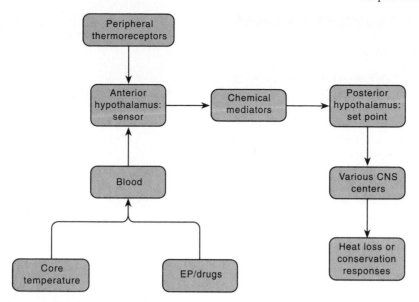

Figure 3.5   Hypothalamic processing in thermoregulation.

Hodgkin's disease) are able to release EPs. This mechanism may explain the fever commonly seen in some tumor patients, but other mechanisms may well be involved.

EPs are released only after a delay that follows the initial stimulation of phagocytic cells. This lag period lasts about one hour, after which body temperature starts to increase. Release of EPs after stimulation can continue for up to 15 hours. EPs are potent; only minute amounts are required to initiate pyrexia.

There is still work to do in clarifying hypothalamic temperature regulation mechanisms. A thermosensitive nucleus (the preoptic nucleus) in the anterior hypothalamus receives stimulatory inputs from warm and cold receptors in the skin, the body core, and the hypothalamus itself, as well as being the site of action of at least some EPs. This combined sensor/thermostat puts out a signal to the posterior hypothalamus, which appears to contain the system's set point (fig. 3.5). The posterior hypothalamus gets constant feedback about surface and core temperature, detects deviations from set point, and then adjusts output to cortical, hypothalamic, and brain stem centers that can generate an appropriate corrective response.

Temperature-related intrahypothalamic signaling depends on several intermediary steps involving prostaglandin E (PGE), monoamines (particularly serotonin), cAMP (cyclic adenosine monophosphate), and perhaps cGMP (cyclic guanosine monophosphate). IL-1, TNF, and IFN-α all act through a pathway mediated by prostaglandin synthesis. In fact, increased prostaglandin levels in the blood (which might be associated with inflammation) trigger a set point rise in the same way that serotonin or cAMP injected into the hypothalamus does. (Previously, this observation led to the erroneous idea that PGE was an endogenous pyrogen.) Substances that inter-fere with prostaglandin synthesis (e.g., nonsteroidal anti-inflammatory agents) act as antipyretics. That is why ASA and acetaminophen are commonly used to reduce set point and thereby control fever.

The Role of Fever

Fever is a common response to infectious, toxic, or immunologic diseases among warm-blooded animals. Even cold-blooded creatures like lizards and snakes "treat" infection by lying in the sun and raising their body temperatures. If this response or mammalian fever is experimentally interfered with, the result is increased disease and death rates. Recent *in vitro* studies that allow control of other factors have shown that temperatures typical of fever enhance many aspects of immune function and phagocytosis. Conversely, some bacteria and viruses have been shown to reproduce more slowly when temperature is elevated. In experiments with AIDS patients, when the temperature of the blood was raised by circulating and heating it outside the body, there were decreases in indicators of infection. It also appears that, in certain bacteria, temperature elevation interferes with the uptake of iron that they require for proliferation.

Taken together, these seemingly small individual gains from a rise in temperature seem to provide a significant overall benefit. Thus the idea that fever is "bad" and that it should always be reduced is oversimplified. In many cases a moderate degree of fever may enhance the patient's defensive responses, providing more real benefit than would be gained by limiting the fever to provide a bit of comfort. On the other hand, modern interventions like antibiotics tend to offset the argument. Since antibiotics are

Febrile Seizures

Certain young children can respond to fever with convulsions, much to the horror of their parents. For the vast majority these **febrile seizures** are quite benign. Of children who have experienced a fever-associated convulsion, about 35% will have a second (or more), and most of these will occur within a year. Of those children experiencing febrile seizures who are neurologically normal, perhaps 1% will go on to develop epilepsy. On the other hand, children with neurological abnormalities stand an increased chance of both febrile seizures and subsequent epilepsy. Those children who develop convulsions at lower temperature thresholds (38° C) tend to be more at risk. At one time, chronic anticonvulsant therapy (usually with phenobarbital) was recommended for any child who had two febrile seizures. Now such intervention is restricted to those children with neurological abnormalities, those with prolonged seizures, or those with a family history of seizure disorders. The simple administration of acetaminophen is usually very effective in controlling fevers and associated seizures.

Figure 3.6   Pharmaceutical intervention in fever.

available to counteract the potential negative effects of fever suppression, there is no reason to sacrifice the comfort that antipyretic agents offer.

Harmful Effects of Fever

There are very few situations in which fever is actually dangerous. One of these arises in patients with compromised cardiac function. Fever results from increases in both heat retention and production. As well, warmer tissues increase their metabolic rate during a fever. This change is reflected in a 13% increase in oxygen consumption (and cardiac output) per degree C rise in temperature. In high fevers, this can amount to a large increase in cardiac workload, a situation poorly tolerated by a person with heart disease.

Normally, fever peaks at a maximum of about 40.5° C (105° F) following resetting of the hypothalamic set point. This maximum assumes a healthy, functioning hypothalamus. In cases of head injury, that compromises hypothalamic functioning, fever can climb to dangerous levels, perhaps requiring emergency application of cooling blankets, ice baths, or even iced gastric washing and cold intravenous fluids. Such dramatic intervention is necessary in part because of the harmful accelerating effect that fever has on the formation of extracellular fluids in the brain, which can raise cranial pressure.

Fever can also pose a threat during pregnancy. There is evidence that an excessive body core temperature, **hyperthermia,** either from fever or other causes like saunas or heat, may be harmful to the fetus.

Generally, any patient with hyperpyrexia—fever over 41° C (106° F)—requires emergency medical care.

Antipyretic Therapy

The decision to treat a fever is made after determining its cause. Failure to identify and treat the underlying pathology will, at best, result in only temporary relief and, at worst, mask a progressive disease. Sometimes health care professionals must deal with fevers of unknown origin (FUO). In these cases, the fever continues for at least two weeks while routine diagnostics fail to determine a cause. Careful follow-up eventually identifies the agent in perhaps 85% of cases. Infections (35–40%), malignant tumors (20%), and collagen-vascular diseases, often autoimmune (15%), are the most common.

When the decision to treat is made, the common antipyretic agent is either aspirin (**acetylsalicylic acid, ASA**) or acetaminophen. These create their effects by inhibiting prostaglandin production in the hypothalamus (fig. 3.6), which has the effect of blocking set point elevation and maintaining the set point at nearer normal levels. Note that ASA and most antipyretics reduce the set point only in febrile conditions, probably because it is only in those cases that prostaglandins are the intervening signal. When the same agents are used for their pain suppression effects in nonfebrile patients, no prostaglandins are involved, so no temperature reduction occurs. When fever is the result of damage to the hypothalamus, antipyretic agents are less effective, or ineffective, because the focus of their action is unresponsive to them.

Earlier, we referred to more aggressive physical antipyretic approaches, e.g., ice baths. With these therapies there is often a parallel administration of antipyretic drugs to offset the body's attempts to maintain temperature at the altered set point. This might include administering other agents to reduce shivering.

Elevated brain temperature is poorly tolerated and produces intense discomfort and irritability. A cool hand or cloth on the forehead, a welcome cooling breeze—all of us know how comforting these can be during a fever. There is good evidence that these are something more than simply local comforts. Cooling applied to the forehead can reduce brain temperatures and ease discomfort seven times more effectively than cooling applied to other body surfaces.

The key to this cooling efficiency lies in the arrangement of some of the cerebral blood vessels. Most of the blood drained from the forehead, and from the triangle around the nose, passes to a complex of veins at the base of the brain called the cavernous sinus. Cooling the blood from these areas, either by breathing cooled air or cooling the forehead, significantly reduces the temperature of the blood perfusing the brain. This is because the internal carotid arteries, which provide 70% of the brain's blood, pass through the cavernous sinus on their way to the circle of Willis. This means that blood that has been cooled at forehead and face, and is traveling away from the brain via the cavernous sinus, surrounds warm arterial blood in the internal carotids. This arrangement allows heat to pass to the cooler venous blood, efficiently reducing brain temperature.

Blood and brain temperature reductions of 1–2° C have been experimentally achieved by cooling the forehead. This is sufficient to cool the brain below core body temperature and provide a significant sense of relief. The brain cooling occurs without affecting the hypothalamic center responsible for fever, because the blood supply to the hypothalamus is delivered by the vertebral arteries, which lack the heat exchange arrangement of the internal carotids.

Case Study

A 10-year-old girl complained of vague periumbilical pain, intermittent nausea, and appetite loss. Her parents had measured her temperature and found it fluctuating between normal and 38.5° over a period of five days. The family physician then saw her, and found her temperature to be 37.5°. Her pharyngeal tonsils were slightly enlarged, with no evidence of pus. No neck or other lymph node enlargement was detected, nor were there any signs or symptoms that suggested an abdominal abnormality. The physician ordered blood counts and a urinalysis, and suggested to the parents that the problem was probably a mild viral infection that would soon pass. The laboratory results were normal, supporting the doctor's assessment.

A week later the parents and child returned. They reported that little had changed: temperatures remained intermittently elevated, the child ate poorly, and she had added generalized joint pains to her list of complaints. Examination revealed that nothing had changed and that all joints appeared normal, providing little basis for diagnostic insights. Further laboratory tests were ordered: another blood count, as well as a throat culture and determination of the erythrocyte sedimentation rate (ESR). These were again normal, except for a markedly elevated ESR, supporting the tentative diagnosis of infection. The parents were advised to monitor the situation and administer acetaminophen to reduce the fever and joint pain.

After five more days without improvement, the child's abdominal pain intensified and a skin rash developed over her buttocks and legs. Alarmed and frustrated with the inability of their family doctor to solve the problem, they took the child to the hospital emergency room. Examination there revealed a temperature of 38.0°, normal joints, and diffuse abdominal tenderness. The character of the rash suggested that it was linked to the seepage of blood from small vessels into the skin. A series of lab tests, including cell and platelet counts, an ESR, and a urinalysis were ordered and the parents were advised to continue acetaminophen, pending the results of the tests.

Test results indicated all blood counts to be normal with an elevated ESR. From the pattern and duration of the child's signs and symptoms, a diagnosis of Henoch-Schonlein purpura was finally made. This was suggested by the persistently elevated ESR amid an array of otherwise normal results.

Commentary
In this case, fever of unknown origin and various other signs and symptoms persisted for three weeks before the nature of the disease fully emerged. The natural anticipation that some typical childhood infection was at fault was the reason for the initial examination of the child's tonsils. The absence of any localizing signs in the abdomen indicated that acute appendicitis or other specific abdominal problems were probably not involved.

The ESR is the time it takes for red cells to settle out of a blood sample. Increased times are taken to be caused by a higher plasma fibrinogen content, which makes the plasma more viscous. This is apparently part of a generalized response to stress, such as an infection.

Henoch-Schonlein purpura is relatively rare and seems to involve a defect of the immune system that produces a generalized vasculitis. This irritation and inflammation of the blood vessel linings gives rise to patchy blood loss into the skin (purpura), as well as into the abdomen and joints. The laboratory findings don't point specifically to the disease, but are primarily used to exclude other possible diagnoses. For example, platelet counts were needed to eliminate the possibility of a bone marrow defect, which would reduce platelet numbers and impair blood clotting.

The mild form of this relatively rare disease is usually self-limiting and typically resolves in a few weeks.

Key Concepts

1. Long recognized as linked to disease, fever is not an abnormality of thermoregulation but is rather an upward adjustment of its set point (p. 47).

2. The skin's blood flow and sweat gland activity can be altered to cause loss of heat by way of radiation, conduction, and evaporation or to foster heat retention (p. 47).

3. Negative feedback control serves as the integrating principle in the operation of the thermoregulatory system's sensors, integrator, and effectors (p. 48).

4. Pyrogens induce fever by elevating the temperature set point of the thermoregulation center in the hypothalamus (p. 49).

5. Various exogenous pyrogens (including components of infectious agents) trigger phagocytic cells to release a variety of endogenous pyrogens (pp. 49–51).

6. Fever seems to enhance host capacities to resist infection or better cope with other forms of injury (p. 51).

7. Extreme or prolonged fever may result from long-standing injury or from a damaged hypothalamus, posing particular risk to heart and brain (p. 52).

8. Commonly used antipyretic agents work by suppressing the production or action of the chemical mediators that upwardly adjust the temperature set point in the hypothalamus (p. 52).

REVIEW ACTIVITIES

1. Analyze the data in table 3.1 to verify that it corresponds to the statement on page 47 regarding oral temperature variation. Does it?

2. On figure 3.3, using a light pencil, add "Increased Body Temperature" at the top, draw an arrow to "Thermoreceptors" and then add up or down arrows to indicate more or less sweat at the skin surface, more or less dermal surface blood, or more or less shivering. Now repeat with a red pencil with "Decreased Body Temperature" at the top, another line to "Thermoreceptors," and more arrows. Do the directions your arrows point reflect the information on pages 48 to 49? If not, think it over and make appropriate modifications.

3. Lay out a flow chart that relates an EP and its source, prostaglandins, set point change, and the effects of ASA. Have your chart start with an infection and build up a fever. Then indicate how therapeutic intervention might restore normal temperature.

4. Convince yourself that you know how an antipyretic agent like acetaminophen can lower body temperature, and why it works only in fever but not when temperature is normal. A small collection of brief written phrases will be more convincing than a few vague thoughts.

Chapter Four

Healing

What wound did ever heal but by degrees?

William Shakespeare
Othello

In response to tissue destruction, the body has a remarkable ability to replace lost tissue, restoring structure, strength, and sometimes function. This restoration process is called **healing,** and it allows us to confront with greater confidence the rather hazardous world in which we live. In coping with injury and its immediate effects, the acute inflammatory response provides a transition between injury and healing. Inflammatory exudate provides an appropriate medium in which healing can occur, and phagocytosis clears the area of injurious agents and debris that would prevent or delay healing. Thus inflammation and healing are closely related, and there is considerable overlap between the two responses following injury.

COMPONENTS OF THE HEALING PROCESS

The healing process provides for the replacement of lost tissue through the proliferation of adjacent undamaged tissue. Most organs of the body are formed of characteristic functional cells, the **parenchyma,** which are bound together and supported by connective tissue, the **stroma.** Healing takes one of two forms. When tissue is replaced from parenchyma, the process is called **regeneration.** When fibrous scar tissue fills the gap left by the loss of damaged tissue, it is called **repair.** Because the replacement tissue must have a blood supply, the formation of new vascular channels is an important aspect of healing. Since much injury occurs at body surfaces, either internal or external, it is also important that the protective epithelium be reestablished at damaged surfaces. Now let us consider these four major components of healing—regeneration, repair, revascularization, and reepithelialization—in more detail.

Regeneration

Cells lost through injury may be replaced by cell division (**mitosis**) of the adjacent uninjured parenchymal cells. The process continues until the volume of newly formed tissue approximates the volume of tissue that was lost to injury. The new tissue assumes normal functions, and for this reason regeneration offers the ideal response to tissue loss. However, not all tissues of the body possess the same degree of regenerative capacity. In terms of their regeneration pattern, there are three types of tissue: labile, stable, and permanent.

The cells of **labile** tissues must divide continually to replace cells that are constantly being depleted by normal processes. For example, red bone marrow, lymphoid tissues, and some epithelial tissues divide steadily throughout life. In these tissues, regeneration involves accelerating the normal mitotic rate to replace tissue lost through injury.

Stable tissues are those whose cells do not normally divide beyond adolescence, when normal development is

The differing regeneration capacities of the body tissues have significant implications for medical therapy. For example, much surgical intervention is possible because an incision in the skin or gastrointestinal mucosae is quickly followed by regeneration of the surface. Bone marrow or blood can be donated to someone in need because the tissue surrendered by the donor will soon be replaced. On the other hand, therapy aimed at central nervous system damage can't overcome the essential inability of neurons to regenerate, and will therefore be much less effective.

complete. These cells are able to function throughout life, so that high mitosis rates are not normally required. However, stable tissues can increase their mitosis rate when damaged tissue must be replaced. Many glands consist of stable tissue, with the liver demonstrating an especially well-developed regenerative capacity. Certain cells of connective tissues, such as fibroblasts and osteoblasts, are also stable. Regeneration in these tissues usually proceeds in an orderly fashion as newly formed cells organize according to a pattern dictated by the remaining undamaged stroma. This pattern of regeneration occurs, for example, in toxic or anoxic injury, to which the parenchymal cells are more sensitive than those of the stroma. When the stroma is also disrupted, regeneration is affected. In the absence of a normal stromal architecture to provide an organizing framework, the pattern of regeneration may be disordered. The resulting abnormal tissue configuration can lead to functional deficiency. Regeneration, therefore, can produce a tissue with nearly normal functions or one with some degree of functional loss. In either case, restoration of function is the significant factor in healing by regeneration.

For a sense of perspective on the distinction between labile and stable tissues, consider their relative rates of mitosis in adults. In a labile tissue, the number of actively dividing cells exceeds 1.5% of the total number of its cells. By contrast, in a stable tissue, fewer than 1.5% of the cells are undergoing a division at any given time.

The third pattern of regeneration is demonstrated in tissues that are termed **permanent.** Soon after birth such tissues lose all mitotic ability, never to regain it. This means that loss of permanent tissue usually results in functional loss. The most common permanent tissues are nervous tissue and cardiac and skeletal muscle. When cells are destroyed, muscle and some other permanent tissues can increase the size of the remaining cells (hypertrophy) to compensate for loss of function. Because the remaining cells cannot reproduce, loss of permanent tissue is followed by scarring. Table 4.1 summarizes some key aspects of the regeneration process.

1 15199

2 29272

3 20719

4 14875

Table 4.1   Some Essential Features of the Three Regeneration Categories

Tissue Class	% Cells in Mitosis	Representative Examples
Labile	>1.5	Epithelium, red marrow
Stable	<1.5	Gland, fibroblasts
Permanent	0	Neurons, skeletal and cardiac muscle

Repair

Healing by repair is the process of laying down fibrous connective tissue to restore the strength and structural integrity of damaged tissues that cannot regenerate. Strong, collagen-rich replacement tissue forms a **scar** by the process of **fibrosis.**

The principal event of fibrosis is the formation of collagen fibers. The **fibroblast** is the cell specialized for this task. It is normally present in the connective tissues of the organ's stroma. Fibroblasts are quite resistant to damage and hence are likely to survive at the scene of injury to initiate repair by fibrosis. In addition, migration of fibroblasts from adjacent areas and their mitotic division both contribute to the steady increase in the number of fibroblasts available for collagen formation at the scene of damage. **5**

The formation of collagen starts with the secretion of its fundamental subunit, procollagen. Outside the cell, procollagen molecules are enzymatically altered so that they can link together, end to end, forming long filaments of collagen. These join together to form thicker collagen fibers, which in turn group together to form a collagen fiber bundle. The process can be compared to the production of a thick, strong rope from tiny and individually weak strands of plant fibers or nylon.

Newly formed collagen is quite weak until about five days postinjury. Strength rapidly increases after this, as the fibers cross-link within collagen fiber bundles. Cross-linking occurs by means of chemical bonds that form between adjacent fibers. The resulting bundles have great **tensile strength,** the ability to resist being pulled apart. The tensile strength of collagen is greater than that of most plastics and approaches that of cast iron. After its formation, collagen steadily increases in strength as cross-links between fibers continue to develop. The increase in strength continues even after new collagen production stops (fig. 4.1). As strength in individual collagen fiber bundles is increasing, the scar's strength also develops as a result of a change in the orientation of the bundles within the repair tissue. In response to the tensions and pressures existing at the injury site, the bundles realign along lines of stress to provide additional strength even though no additional collagen has been formed.

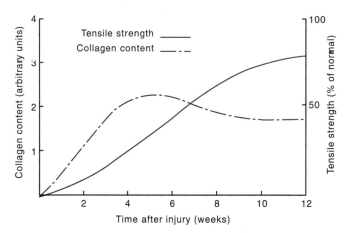

Figure 4.1   Development of tensile strength in a healing skin wound. After collagen synthesis stops, strength continues to increase because of cross-linking between collagen fibers.

Collagen formation occurs in the fluid medium formed by the exudate of the acute inflammatory response. This fluid is modified to become the **ground substance,** or **matrix,** which is the intercellular material of the scar tissue. The fluid first assumes a loosely gelled, semisolid consistency and is then modified as fibroblasts secrete mucopolysaccharide into it. Beyond merely providing a fluid medium in which fibrosis can occur, the intercellular matrix directly interacts with fibroblasts and collagen fibers to promote the process. The ultimate development of a strong and well-anchored scar is related as much to adequate matrix deposition as to the formation of collagen fibers. Figure 4.2 summarizes the essentials of collagen formation and strength development in scar tissue.

When tissue damage occurs, blood usually escapes from disrupted vessels to flood the area. Plasma fibrinogen is converted to fibrin, forming a mesh that entraps blood cells and tissue debris. This gelled mass is called a **clot.** It must be removed before healing can be completed. The elimination of the clot by phagocytosis and its replacement by scar tissue are together known as **organization.** The same term is applied to the removal of necrotic debris and its replacement by fibrous connective tissue. For example, since cardiac muscle tissue is permanent, a necrotic region of myocardium will be organized by macrophages and fibroblasts to form scar tissue (fig. 4.3). **6**

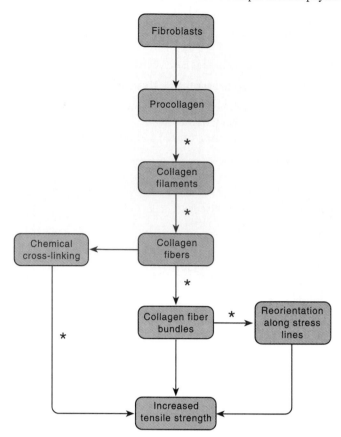

Figure 4.2 Collagen formation and the development of tensile strength in scar tissue. An asterisk denotes dependence on interactions with the intercellular matrix.

Revascularization

Whether regeneration or repair provides the replacement tissue, blood supply to the area must be restored. Initially, blood is required to supply the specialized activities related to healing (e.g., phagocytosis, mitosis, and collagen synthesis). After formation, the replacement tissue must be provided with a blood supply to meet its normal maintenance requirements. The production of new blood vessels to supply and drain the site of damage is called **revascularization** or **angiogenesis.** It occurs in the loosely gelled, protein-rich exudate that forms at the damage site. As new blood vessels develop, the exudate takes on a characteristic pink and granular appearance under magnification. For this reason it is called **granulation tissue** (fig. 4.4). The process of scarring that we described in the last section is actually dependent on the organization of granulation tissue.

Granulation tissue does not in itself provide strength to a healing wound. Rather, it is an intermediate tissue in which fibrosis and the completion of revascularization are favored, and in which macrophages complete the clearing of debris and fibrin from the wound site.

In revascularization, new capillaries are formed from intact vessels adjacent to the wound site. Endothelial cells from these vessels migrate into the damaged area and undergo mitosis to form endothelial buds, or cords,

Figure 4.3 Organization following ischemic damage to myocardium. (*a*) A microscopic view of normal myocardial tissue. (*b*) Following prolonged reduction of blood flow, the damaged myocardium has been organized. A few surviving muscle fibers remain scattered in the fibrous scar tissue.

Figure 4.4 Granulation tissue, consisting of newly formed vessels in recently gelled exudate. Clear spaces are the lumina of these vessels, in which red cells can be seen.
T. J. Nowak

projecting from the parent vessel. Figure 4.5 illustrates the development of new vessels from these early buds. An elongating bud may loop back to reestablish contact with its parent vessel. When this happens, a lumen forms within the bud and merges with the parent vessel to form a continuous new blood channel. Similarly, buds from different parent vessels may meet, fusing to form a new blood channel between the previously isolated parent vessels. In some cases an elongating cord may advance some distance without contacting another vessel or bud. If it extends beyond the point of obtaining adequate nutrient supply from its parent vessel, the cord may degenerate. The resulting cellular debris will be cleared by macrophages still at work in the granulation tissue matrix.

Lumen formation in an advancing vascular bud involves enlargement, mitosis, and vacuolation of its endothelial cells. As they migrate into an injury site, the cells enlarge and then divide. The resulting daughter cells develop cytoplasmic vacuoles that progressively enlarge

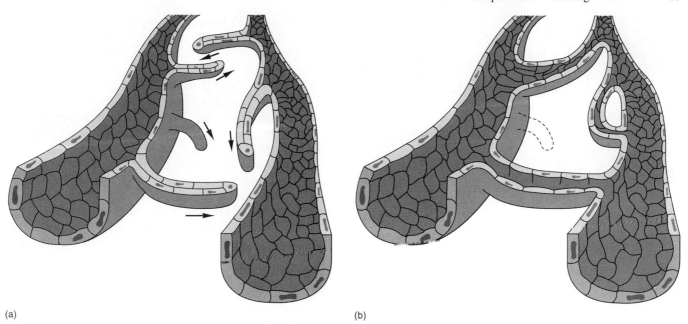

(a)   (b)

Figure 4.5   Revascularization. (*a*) Endothelial buds form from undamaged endothelia. (*b*) Three new channels have formed while an isolated bud degenerates.

and then merge with the vacuoles of adjacent cells. With continued fusion of adjacent vacuoles in the advancing cord, the new lumen is formed (fig. 4.6).

Once formed, the new blood vessels slowly undergo a series of changes. They differentiate and become rearranged to form a pattern of vessel distribution that more nearly approximates that of normal tissues. Some of the newly formed capillaries acquire the wall structure and flow patterns of arterioles, whereas others are modified to become venules. This means, in effect, that from a common starting structure, an endothelial tube, the different vessel walls are built up from inside out. Of course, some of the initially formed vessels become mature capillaries, but note that at the outset they are leaky and highly permeable, so that much fluid and even intact red blood cells can escape from them. The continued swelling seen at an injury site, even after the inflammatory response has faded, is explained by the higher permeability of the newly formed vessels of the healing wound.

As the process of revascularization continues, lymphatic drainage is reestablished along with blood supply, although this process starts later and is slower than the formation of new blood vessels. New lymphatic capillaries form in the same way as blood capillaries and ultimately differentiate to form larger lymphatics as necessary. Although the underlying mechanism is unclear, it is interesting that the new endothelial buds of blood capillaries never link up with those originating from a lymphatic vessel.

Final changes in blood vessel distribution involve an overall reduction in vessel numbers, and hence flow, in the healing tissue. The healing region has an initially higher metabolic demand, which is due to the activity levels of

(a)   (b)

(c)

(d)

Figure 4.6   Mechanism of revascularization. (*a*) Bud arises from normal endothelium adjacent to damage site. (*b*) Cells divide, enlarge, and develop vacuoles in their cytoplasm. (*c*) Vacuoles merge to form the lumen of the new vessel. The new channel extends by merging with another advancing bud. (*d*) The new vessel.

Figure 4.7 Reepithelialization. (*a*) Damaged epithelium. (*b*) Newly formed cells migrate across wound surface. (*c*) On contact, migrating cells alter their plane of division. (*d*) The restored epithelium.

cells involved in phagocytosis, fibrosis, and cell division. With healing completed, these activities decline and vascular supply is correspondingly reduced. It is for this reason that newly formed scar tissue has a pink appearance whereas an older scar, with its reduced vascular supply, is more pale.

Revascularization of a wound also involves new growth of vasomotor neurons in the months following vessel formation. These provide nervous control of vascular function.

Reepithelialization

In healing it is important to reestablish the protective epithelium that covers body and organ surfaces. This replacement of lost surface lining is called **reepithelialization.** It is possible because epithelial tissues are labile and hence readily able to supply replacement cells by mitosis.

In reepithelialization at a wound edge (fig. 4.7), a zone of active mitosis develops a short distance from the damaged edge. Newly produced cells, and those originally at the edge of the damaged area, move away from the edge

onto the denuded surface. This motion is not the ameboid motion normally used by phagocytes. Instead it involves a characteristic ruffling of the membrane on the advancing side of the cell, which seems to draw the cell over the surface. In most cases, cell migration occurs on the surface of organizing granulation tissue. In the case of an **abrasion** (scraping injury) of the skin, where only the epidermis is lost, sliding of epithelial cells occurs at the surface of the underlying dermis, which has remained intact.

Epithelial migration continues, with the cells secreting a new basement membrane as they proceed. When the sheets of cells advancing from opposite wound edges meet, they become anchored to the basement membrane and alter their plane of division. Newly formed daughter cells are now moved up, away from the wound surface, rather than along it (fig. 4.7*b*,*c*). Differentiation accompanies these divisions to replace the specialized cell types that were lost. **7** In skin injuries where parts of hair follicles and sweat glands remain intact, they serve as points from which new epithelial growth can spread. Mitosis in these structures provides new cells that migrate away from the follicle or gland to contribute to restoration of the epithelial surface. Note, however, that damaged follicles and skin glands cannot regenerate to form functional replacements.

In reepithelialization and revascularization, new functional replacement tissue is produced by mitosis of undamaged cells. Thus these two processes are, strictly speaking, special cases of regeneration. We have considered them separately in the context of their special relevance to the healing process.

WOUND HEALING: THE SKIN

Wounds of the skin are the most common type seen by medical personnel. For this reason, and because of their ready accessibility, the healing of skin wounds has been intensively studied. They provide an excellent example of how the various aspects of healing contribute to the restoration of structure and function after an injury. Depending on the nature of the wound, healing is said to be either primary or secondary.

Primary Healing

Primary healing, or **healing by first intention,** is the term used to describe healing of an **incision,** or severing wound of the skin. In such a wound the damage is minimal and the wound edges are closely apposed. This is the type of wound resulting from a surgical incision, where surgical closures, sutures, for example, secure the wound edges, or from a cut in the skin where there are no stresses that might cause separation of the wound edges.

After an incision, bleeding into the narrow gap between the tissue surfaces is quickly followed by clot formation (fig. 4.8*a*). **8** The clot serves not only to limit

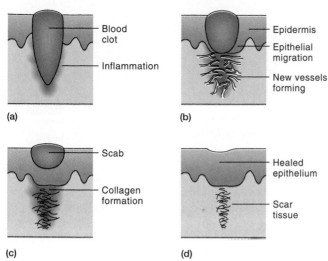

(a)

(b)

(c)

(d)

Figure 4.8 Primary healing. (*a*) Incised wound filled by blood clot. (*b*) Reepithelialization and revascularization are under way. (*c*) Collagen formation builds strength. (*d*) Healing is complete. Note lack of pigment above scar.

Figure 4.9 Skin scar. The pale line of the scar can be seen at the site of an old skin wound.

The index finger of the senior author showing a 19-year-old scar. Note the paleness due to the underlaying scar tissue and lack of pigment in the replacement epithelium. The scar's shape matches that of a serrated knife edge that was clumsily driven through the skin while cutting a banana. The senior author is 19-years-older, but probably not much wiser. T. J. Nowak

further blood loss but also to seal the wound from dehydration and invasion by infective microorganisms. It also provides early stabilization of the wound as its fibers bind to elements of the intercellular matrix adjacent to the wound. Once the clot has formed, its surface dries and, together with some tissue debris, produces a scab. **9** As in any injury, the acute inflammatory response forms a fluid exudate and delivers numerous inflammatory cells to the scene of the incision. The phagocytes quickly go to work removing tissue debris. They also disrupt and digest the clot by releasing enzymes into it. In this process, hemoglobin released from entrapped red cells is broken down to yield pigments that contribute to the early discoloration sometimes seen at the wound site.

By two to three days after injury, granulation tissue is present and both fibroblast activity and revascularization are well under way (fig. 4.8*b, c*). New blood channels form as previously described, and blood supply to the wound is restored. The blood provides nutrients to the fibroblasts, which are secreting new matrix and procollagen. Initially formed collagen fibers assume a vertical orientation at the margins of the wound, but by the sixth postinjury day, responding to normal skin stresses, they align horizontally to bridge the gap and join to the adjacent undamaged dermis, thus binding the opposite sides of the wound together. After six to eight days, the wound is usually strong enough to allow removal of surgical stitches. Collagen continues to form and increases in strength as a dermal scar is formed.

As these events proceed in the dermis, new epithelium forms at the surface of the wound to restore the epidermis. As the migrating cells slide across the wound gap, they liberate enzymes that aid in loosening the clot, which presents an obstacle to their passage. When the opposing sheets of cells meet, after about two days, they differentiate

to restore the epidermis that was lost. The newly formed epidermis now completely separates the healing dermis from the overlying scab. Resumption of keratin formation causes loosening of the scab so that it can be easily lost from the newly restored surface (fig. 4.8*d*). It is important to leave the scab in place until it loosens in this way. Premature scab removal can disrupt both dermis and epidermis, causing new damage and delaying healing.

As epidermal regeneration proceeds, pigment-producing cells (melanocytes) are not replaced. Their lack contributes to the lighter color of the epidermis overlying the scar. As we indicated earlier, reduced blood supply in the underlying mature scar tissue also contributes to its paler than normal appearance (fig. 4.9).

By the second postinjury week, inflammatory swelling and phagocytic cell numbers are reduced. Organization of granulation tissue is complete and vascularity is greatly reduced. Fibroblasts continue to proliferate and collagen bundle formation proceeds, producing an increasingly dense and pale scar mass spanning the original incision site.

The strength of fully healed skin, although adequate, never reaches its preinjury level. When the supporting sutures are removed, usually after five to seven days, skin strength is only about 10% of normal. A rapid increase in strength follows over the next two to four weeks as new collagen fibers continue to be laid down. By two months, strength is about one-third of normal, and continued collagen cross-linking yields further increases, to about 70–80% of normal, after three months. This is the maximum strength that the scar will achieve.

8168

(a)

(b)

(c)

(d)

Figure 4.10   Secondary healing. (*a*) Blood clot fills wound. (*b*) Granulation tissue fills gap and reepithelialization starts. (*c*) Granulation tissue is organized. (*d*) Healing is complete.

Secondary Healing

Secondary healing, or **healing by second intention** (fig. 4.10), is seen in wounds whose edges are not closely apposed. Such wounds are common in skin and in the mucous membranes of the gastrointestinal tract; a duodenal ulcer is an example. **10** These wounds are larger than incised wounds, have more debris that must be removed,

(a)   (b)

Figure 4.11   Reduction of wound size by wound contraction. (*a*) Initial wound. (*b*) Wound after contraction.

and involve a larger gap to be filled by replacement tissue. For these reasons secondary healing takes longer than primary healing. The same mechanisms that operate in primary healing are involved, with two additional distinguishing characteristics. One of these characteristics is the much larger quantity of granulation tissue that must form to fill the wound gaps. The second is **wound contraction.**

In secondary healing, soon after granulation tissue forms, the wound edges draw in toward the center. This contraction reduces both the size of the gap that the granulation tissue must fill and the area that new epithelium must re-cover (fig. 4.11). The mechanism underlying wound contraction depends on a specialized cell found only at secondary healing sites. It is called a **myofibroblast** because it exhibits contractile capability while resembling a fibroblast. The origin of myofibroblasts is unclear, but they may be derived from **pericytes.** These are cells, resembling smooth muscle cells, that associate with the outer surfaces of capillaries.

Myofibroblasts function by first anchoring themselves to other cells or fibrous structures at the margins of the wound. They then slowly contract, drawing in the edges to reduce the size of the wound. The process is initiated two or three days postinjury and can continue for weeks, ultimately reducing the size of the wound by 70% or more.

The original shape of a wound is often quite different from its final scar because of a peculiarity of the wound contraction process. The myofibroblasts seem to align themselves so that they contract in a direction at right angles to the wound's margin, i.e., toward the geometric center of the wound. As contraction proceeds, near edges meet first, then those further apart come together, with the furthest points on the edges joining last. The specific scar configurations that derive from various original wound shapes are shown in figure 4.12*a.* Note that in the case of a circular wound, as the contraction process draws in the edges, a point is reached where the myofibroblasts can no longer overcome the resistance offered by the crowding of wound edge structures. For this reason, compared to other shapes, a circular wound leaves more surface for reepithelialization to restore. The underlying wound contraction mechanism that produces differently shaped scars is illustrated in figure 4.12*b, c.*

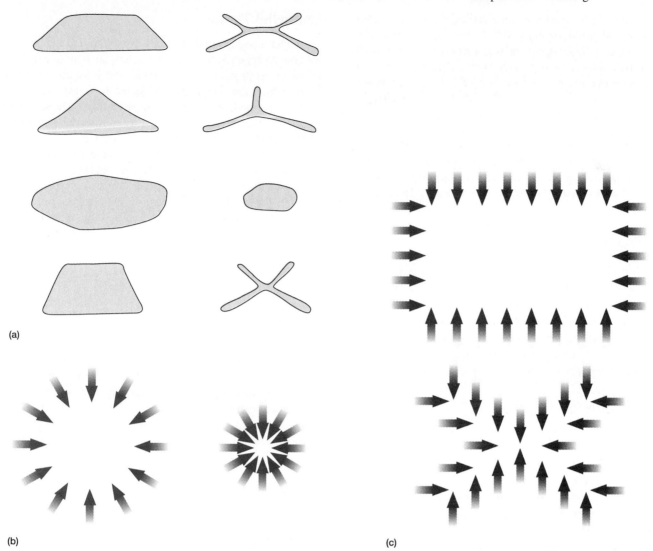

Figure 4.12 Wound contraction. (*a*) The shape of the scar is determined by the movement of the wound's edges toward its center. (*b*) A circular wound doesn't fully close because of crowding as the edge nears the center. (*c*) In comparison with (*b*), this rectangular wound will have a smaller scar, since the edges are able to draw in more closely.

HEALING: THE MAJOR TISSUES

Connective Tissues

Because of their comparatively limited blood supply, healing in the connective tissues tends to be a prolonged process. Faced with such delayed healing, an injured individual often becomes impatient and should be cautioned against prematurely stressing the healing tissue.

Bone

Osseous tissue has well-developed powers of regeneration. When bone is fractured, new bone tissue is formed and eventually restores the original structure and strength at the point of damage. After the edges of the fractured bone are properly positioned (**reduced**) and movement is restricted by a splint or cast, the healing of the bone proceeds in three stages.

Immediately after a bone fracture, there is bleeding into the gap between the bone ends and, when the periosteum is torn, into the surrounding muscle mass. The first stage of healing involves the early removal of blood clots, bone fragments, and other tissue debris. As phagocytic cells clear the area, granulation tissue forms and becomes organized. Its capillaries develop from undamaged vessels in adjacent tissues. Also in this initial stage of healing, **osteoblasts** (bone-forming cells) held in reserve in the periosteum and endosteum are activated. They migrate to the fracture site to initiate the second stage of the process.

Osteoblasts start to form deposits of cartilage in the organized granulation tissue early in the second stage of bone healing. The resulting fibrocartilaginous mass spans the break and provides early stabilization of the fracture. This tissue is called **osteoid** or **soft callus.** It is soon ossified by osteoblasts to form a loosely organized mass of woven bone that resembles cancellous bone (spongy bone). This **hard callus** [11] is structurally weak and, because its production is excessive, there is local enlargement at the fracture site.

The third stage involves the restructuring of the hard callus to restore the characteristic architecture of normal bone. The restructuring is accomplished jointly by osteoblasts and **osteoclasts** (bone-dissolving cells). These cells build up and break down the hard callus, modeling the bone to finally restore its normal structure. [12] Restoration of the overlying periosteum accompanies that of the bone (fig. 4.13).

The first stage of healing occurs in the four to five days following fracture. The second stage follows over the next three weeks, with final remodeling sometimes continuing over many months or even years. During this extended period of remodeling, the bone is strong enough to accommodate normal loading stresses and there is no indication of the subtle changes in bone structure that continue.

Tendon/Ligament

Regeneration of tendon and ligament is usually successful in injuries where relatively regular edges can be closely approximated and tightly sutured. Fibroblasts can then produce densely packed collagen bundles that span the damage site to restore tensile strength. If the edges of the damaged tissue are not held tightly together, or if a crushing injury produces irregular, roughened surfaces, scar tissue forms in the intervening spaces. The result is a weaker union with less tensile strength and reduced functional capacity.

Cartilage

When damaged, cartilage heals by fibrous repair. Scar tissue is supplied by fibroblasts from the protective sheet of perichondrium that covers cartilage surfaces. The scarring that follows cartilage damage can produce some loss of function, a persistent complication for those who suffer athletic and fitness-related injuries.

Adipose Tissue

Although the cells of adipose tissue cannot themselves undergo mitosis, their precursor cells are widely distributed and these cells are able to differentiate to produce new replacement tissue.

Epithelial Tissue

As we have seen, some epithelia are labile and hence readily able to regenerate. This characteristic is of great value in restoring protection at external and internal body surfaces, which are frequently subjected to injury. As previously described, epithelial cells reestablish the covering over a damaged surface by gliding across the gap in the tissue. This process occurs not only in the skin, but in the extensive mucous membranes, vascular endothelial linings, and many other epithelial surfaces within the body. An exception is the epithelium of respiratory surfaces in the adult. [13] In these tissues, regeneration can take place if the damage to the epithelium is superficial, but not if the basement membrane and underlying intercellular matrix are disrupted. In the latter case, proliferating fibroblasts repair the damage by forming scar tissue (fig. 4.14).

Glandular Tissue

Most of the body's glands are formed of stable tissue. When they are damaged, the lost cells are readily replaced by new growth of functional tissue. The liver is notable in having prodigious powers of regeneration. Animal experiments indicate complete restoration of lost tissue when as much as 90% of the liver is surgically removed. Similar levels of regeneration are likely in humans. When tissue damage is extensive, however, the arrangement of the newly regenerated tissue may vary somewhat from the normal, causing some functional loss. In the kidney, cells of the nephron tubule are able to regenerate if damaged. However, no replacement of glomerular or Bowman's capsule cells is possible. When nephrons are lost, the remaining tubules compensate by hypertrophy.

In liver and kidney, severing injury sustained over an extended period can destroy both parenchymal cells and their supporting stroma. In such cases, the lost tissue is replaced by a smaller volume of dense scar tissue. The contracted scar masses draw inward, producing a pattern of irregular surface depressions. The characteristic appearance of the kidney in chronic glomerulonephritis and that of the liver in hepatic cirrhosis [14] are good examples (fig. 4.15).

There are some exceptions to the usual pattern of regeneration in glandular tissue. The parathyroid glands possess only minimal regenerative capacity. Similarly, tissues of the adrenal medulla and the posterior pituitary gland are unable to produce new functional cells when damaged. This lack seems related to their derivation from nervous tissue, which is permanent.

[11] 7029

[12] 14666

[13] 14917

[14] 46285

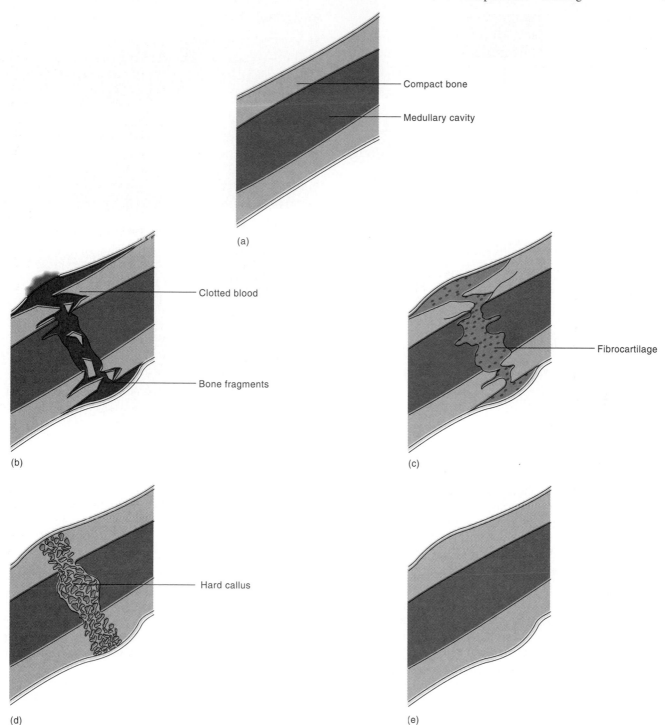

Figure 4.13   Bone healing. (*a*) Cross section through the intact bone. (*b*) Following the fracture, clotted blood and bone fragments are cleared by phagocytes. (*c*) and (*d*) Formation of the transitional hard callus, which is modeled by osteoblasts and osteoclasts to yield the fully restored bone (*e*).

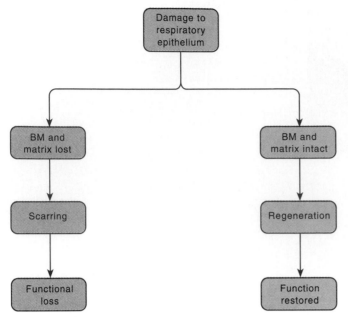

Figure 4.14   Healing of respiratory epithelium depends on the status of the basement membrane (BM) and the underlying intercellular matrix.

Nervous Tissue

Since nervous tissue is permanent tissue, no mitosis of neurons is possible after birth. In nervous tissue, damaged cells are replaced by **gliosis**—the proliferation of nonconducting **neuroglia.** **15** These cells are abundant in nervous tissue and provide support, phagocytosis, and repair functions that blood cells and fibroblasts perform in other tissues. In the central nervous system, if cell bodies remain intact, some initial regeneration of axons may occur. But after 10–14 days the proliferating glial cells form a scarlike mass that blocks any further growth of the damaged axons. Thus no function can be restored by axon regeneration.

In the peripheral nervous system, when only part of a myelinated neuron process is lost through damage, the lost portion can regenerate if the supporting connective tissue and **Schwann cells** are intact along the original path of the neuron process. This is often the case, because the Schwann cell is more resistant to injury than is the neuron process. After injury, the process distal to the point of injury degenerates, and the resulting debris is removed by macrophages (fig. 4.16*a*). Regeneration replaces any Schwann cells lost at the injury site (fig. 4.16*b*). Next, a tuft of newly formed sprouts grows out from the end of the remaining neuron process (fig. 4.16*c*). One of these finds its way into the tube of connective tissue and continues to grow along the tube until it reaches the point served by the original process (fig. 4.16*d*). The remaining sprouts are lost, and myelination of the newly regenerated process proceeds. This pattern of regeneration is relatively slow and may take weeks to complete. It cannot replace any

Figure 4.15   Long-term damage followed by scarring has produced the roughened surface of this kidney, a characteristic of chronic glomerulonephritis.

specialized sensory receptors at the ends of sensory neuron dendrites. The result is some loss of sensation even though motor function is restored.

When a nerve's connective tissue is lost through injury, so that it can't provide guidance for the regenerating neuron process, damaged neurons are unlikely to be replaced.

Muscle Tissue

Skeletal muscle and cardiac muscle are also permanent tissues. When they are lost, healing is accomplished through fibrous repair. As we have seen, this process implies loss of function, in this case a decline in the contractile strength of the injured muscle. However, muscle tissue possesses a highly developed compensation capability. Its cells can increase in size and contractile strength. This hypertrophy results in an increased muscle mass in response to demand. **16** Weight lifters produce no new cells as their training proceeds; rather, existing cells hypertrophy. Not only can skeletal muscle and the muscle of the heart restore their

(a) At injury

(b) Ellipsoids   3 days later

(c) One week later

(d) Two weeks later

(e) Reinnervation and Remyelination

Figure 4.16   Regeneration of a neuron process. (*a*) Damaged axon. (*b*) Debris is cleared by phagocytosis and undamaged Schwann cells proliferate. (*c*) Axon buds emerge from stump of axon. (*d*) A single bud extends along the cylinder of Schwann cells that reestablish the myelin sheath. Other buds have degenerated. (*e*) Regeneration complete.

strength to reach preinjury levels, but they can increase their strength to levels higher than any previously achieved. Therefore, a patient whose heart has been damaged need not become an invalid. Full recovery is possible if hypertrophy is cautiously induced by presenting the myocardium with gradually increasing demands.

Like neurons, muscle fibers can regenerate a portion of their structure under certain circumstances. In the case of damage from a crushing injury, the muscle's stroma

remains largely intact. Supporting sheaths of connective tissue remain to act as guides for the growth of the end of the damaged muscle fiber. On the other hand, when a severing injury cuts through the supporting stroma, the muscle fibers draw back from the point of injury, and with loss of stromal guidance the potential for regeneration is lost.

In the case of smooth muscle tissue, there are indications that some regeneration does occur. Mitotic capability is quite limited, however, and fibrous repair is most common. A notable exception is the wall of the uterus, which has the capacity for significant cell division. During pregnancy, some cells enlarge while others undergo mitosis to produce new tissue. Of course, this is a normal response, which anticipates the extra strength required for delivery of an infant, not a response to injury.

COMPLICATIONS OF HEALING

The healing process occasionally goes astray, so that healing is inadequate, is delayed, or has undesirable consequences. The following are the most common complications of healing.

Contracture

When damage is extensive, newly formed collagen demonstrates an exaggerated contraction as it matures. This process is called **contracture.** It can be so pronounced that serious distortion can result. For example, in widespread skin burns, contracture can cause substantial disfiguration (fig. 4.17). The change from normal appearance can have significant psychological impact, especially when the face is involved. Contracture may also limit mobility. For example, contracture following burns of the skin of the neck may limit motion of the head. When the skin of the hand is involved, the motion of wrist and finger joints can be restricted.

In repair of damage to the walls of tubular organs, contracture of scar tissue presents another type of problem. As contracture proceeds, it causes a narrowing or **stricture** in the lumen of the organ. The consequences can be serious, because normal motion of the organ contents is slowed or even stopped (stasis). **17** In the intestine a stoppage can lead to infection, which can in turn lead to perforation of the wall and the rapid spread of infection throughout the abdomen. Stricture of the ureter will also predispose to infection, which can affect the kidney, and stricture of the Fallopian tube can lead to sterility. Stricture is also a common complication of venereal disease.

Adhesions

Another type of complication can arise as exudate is organized at certain sites. In particular, repair of serous membranes may

Contracture
following burn

Figure 4.17 Following a skin burn, contracture may produce distortion of body contours and may also restrict motion of joints.

Figure 4.18 Adhesions. Arrows at left show free intestinal surfaces, which allow movement without restriction. Arrow at right shows adhesion binding intestinal surfaces and restricting normal movements.
These adhesions developed in the bowel of an elderly woman following rupture of her diseased colon. She had been convalescing in hospital for a fractured hip, when a weak point in her colon ruptured, causing the peritonitis that led to her death. The adhesions had formed as the irritated peritoneal sheets were undergoing repair, but extensive damage to various abdominal structures overwhelmed her weakened defenses and she died.

involve organization of inflammatory exudate between serous membranes adjacent to the site of damage. The resulting repair produces a firm union of the two membranes, which normally move freely against one another. Such joining of serous membranes is called an **adhesion.** The major effect of adhesions is the restriction of movement in structures that must move freely. **18** In injury or surgical intervention involving the heart, lungs, or most abdominal organs, the possibility of developing adhesions is always present. After abdominal or thoracic surgery, it is relatively common for a patient to be readmitted to the hospital because of problems related to adhesions (fig 4.18).

Dehiscence

Dehiscence is the breaking open of a healing wound. The essential cause is pressure applied to the healing tissues, which interferes with the development of normal strength. The abdominal wall is the most common site of dehiscent wounds because of the relatively high pressure in the abdomen. **19** Paroxysms (acute, violent episodes) of coughing, vomiting, or diarrhea can greatly raise abdominal pressure and increase the chances that the wound will burst.

Dehiscence presents two principal risks. One is the exposure of the abdominal contents to infection as the

wound breaks open. The second is that a loop of intestine will be squeezed into the open wound, so that its blood supply is threatened by compression of its blood vessels. Loss of blood supply may be followed by gangrenous necrosis. **20** The displacement of an organ from its normal body cavity position is called **herniation.** Dehiscence following abdominal surgery may produce an incisional hernia.

Keloids

Keloids are irregular masses of scar tissue that protrude from the surface of the skin. **21** They result from the overproduction of dermal collagen during healing. Keloids usually arise on the upper body and are seen more frequently in blacks and Orientals. If disfiguring, they may be surgically removed, but they have a tendency to recur after removal (fig. 4.19).

Keloid formation may be due to excessive release of a particular growth factor known to promote fibroblast proliferation. This factor, TGF-β (transforming growth factor beta), is secreted by macrophages and platelets at the scene of damage. Even the secretion of normal amounts of TGF-β may produce keloids in individuals who are highly sensitive to its effects.

Proud Flesh

The overproduction of granulation tissue is called **proud flesh.** It presents a problem in that the excess of tissue can

18   40680   **19**   24557   **20**   40301

20   17646

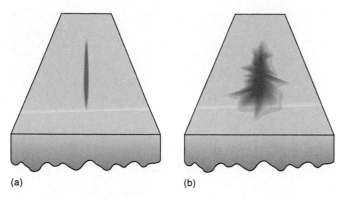

Figure 4.19   Keloid formation. (*a*) A section of skin in which an incision is healing normally. (*b*) The irregular piling up of excessive scar tissue forms the keloid.

protrude from the wound to interfere with reepithelialization. This condition, sometimes also known as exuberant granulations, may arise if a wound becomes infected.

Suture Complications

Minor punctures of the skin heal quickly and with minimal scar tissue formation. Thus puncture scars from therapeutic injections or from tissue biopsies tend to be of little consequence. However, in healing of a surgical incision, a minor complication can arise because of the stitching used to secure the wound edges. At the surface, where the suture material enters the skin, the epithelium is interrupted. This condition stimulates epithelial mitosis and migration, but the cells cannot spread across the intervening suture material. Instead, they migrate into the dermis along the suture channel. Later, when the stitches are removed, most of the new epithelium is carried off with the suture material and the surface regenerates normally. In some cases, however, keratin from the epithelium, which is normally restricted to the surface of the skin, is sealed within the suture tract deep in the dermis. Its presence causes a prolonged and exaggerated inflammatory response, which delays healing and causes increased scar tissue formation.

Therapy

Some therapy can have an inhibitory effect on healing. For example, anticancer therapy using radiation or chemicals, or both, suppresses tumor cell division, but can also suppress the mitosis needed for normal healing. Various anti-inflammatory drugs or immune system suppressants interfere with processes important to healing, such as protein synthesis, wound contraction, and reepithelialization. Corticosteroid preparations used to limit inflammation can also interfere with healing. However, these effects seem limited to the first two postinjury days. After this early healing period, corticosteroid inhibition of healing is minimal.

REQUIREMENTS FOR HEALING

Clearance of Debris

For optimal healing to occur, the scene of damage must be cleared of debris, tissue remnants, pus, and any extraneous matter, e.g., bullet fragments. Inability to remove such material will increase the likelihood of infection and delay and complicate the healing process.

Immobility

Movement near wound edges delays or prevents healing because it prevents the joining of tissues across the damaged area. For example, consider what happens with bone fractures that have not been immobilized. In this case, constant motion prevents normal calcification, so that a fibrocartilaginous mass resembling osteoid is formed and maintained. This condition is called **fibrous union.** Obviously, the replacement tissue in this case is much weaker than the original tissue. Immobility is also especially important in tendon and nerve regeneration, where accurate alignment of newly forming structures is critical.

Blood Supply

Adequate blood circulation is required for the delivery of oxygen and nutrients to the area that must be healed. Many of the healing problems so commonly seen in the elderly are the result of age-related circulation deficiencies. For example, even with adequate immobilization, fibrous union often occurs in the healing of hip fractures of older persons. In diabetics, even trivial peripheral skin injuries may heal poorly because of the inadequate blood supply caused by the disease.

Nutrients

Specific nutrient requirements for healing are relatively few. Although much new protein is synthesized during healing, dietary protein deficiency will depress the healing response only if prolonged. The amino acid methionine is required for normal healing. This might seem surprising in that this amino acid does not occur in collagen. It is, however, required for the production of the mucopolysaccharide used in forming new extracellular matrix. Zinc is also required for normal healing, but its function is not clearly understood. Possibly it contributes to those characteristics of the matrix that make it an optimal environment for collagen formation.

In forming collagen, vitamin C (**ascorbic acid**) is required for the conversion of an amino acid in the production of procollagen. Without this conversion step, fibroblasts cannot secrete procollagen. Another essential nutrient is

Table 4.2	Factors that Stimulate or Inhibit Various Components of the Healing Process

Name	Standard Designation
Epidermal growth factor	EGF
Platelet-derived growth factor	PDGF
Transforming growth factor	TGFα, TGFβ*
Fibroblast growth factor	FGF
Alpha-interferon	α-interferon*
Interleukin 1	IL-1
Tumor necrosis factor	TNF

*Inhibition is the dominant effect.

copper. It is a component of the enzyme that facilitates the cross-linking upon which collagen fiber bundles depend for added strength. Deficiencies of either vitamin C or copper will result in the formation of weakened scars.

CONTROL AND REGULATION OF HEALING

The processes that contribute to normal healing are closely regulated. When injury occurs, cells begin to divide to form replacement tissue. When sufficient tissue is formed, cell division stops. Regeneration in the liver is a good example. Some factors initiate mitosis when cells are lost. The process continues only until adequate replacement tissue is formed and then stops. New growth is orderly, and is limited to the replacement of lost tissue only. When the process is not orderly and well controlled, excess tissue is produced, with potentially serious consequences. This situation is described more fully in chapter 5, in the discussion of tumors.

There is much about the control of the healing process that is not well understood, but an array of chemical control factors is being carefully studied. These can be identified in the plasma and at healing sites. They have the ability to promote and inhibit many of the processes known to be involved in healing. Generally, two broad categories are recognized: **growth factors,** which promote growth, and **growth inhibitors,** with the opposite effect. These widely distributed substances regulate the processes vital to normal healing: migration of fibroblasts and epithelial cells, new blood vessel formation, mitosis, and collagen formation. The principal growth factors are listed in table 4.2.

Some aspects of healing depend on cell interactions with the extracellular matrix. Surface receptors on fibroblasts, and on other cells involved in healing, are specific for various of the elements that form the complex intercel-

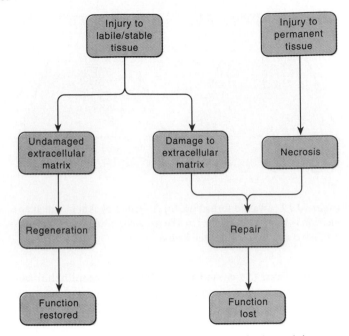

Figure 4.20   Role of the extracellular matrix in determining functional loss.

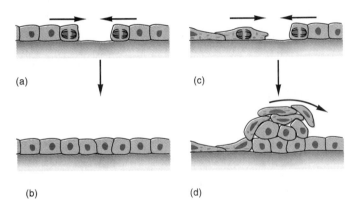

Figure 4.21   Contact inhibition. (*a*) Similar cells reproduce and move over surface. (*b*) When they come into contact, mitosis stops. (*c*) Different cell types approach each other. (*d*) When these come into contact, no inhibition results.

lular material. Interactions with the matrix affect cell proliferation and migration, as well as differentiation. Thus, rather than being an inert filler, the extracellular matrix has a specific role in regulating regeneration and repair. This is the likely explanation for the scarring that follows the destruction of the extracellular matrix in stable tissues. Although remaining cells are able to undergo mitosis, they fail to do so for lack of regulatory input from extracellular matrix interactions. Healing then proceeds by repair. When the extracellular matrix is undamaged, regeneration proceeds normally (fig. 4.20).

Study of the factors that control healing has the potential for great therapeutic benefit. For example, knowledge of the factors that stimulate the healing process would speed the recovery of burn victims and could reduce the length of postsurgical hospitalization. Several preparations containing various tissue growth factors are currently being studied to assess their therapeutic potential.

Physical contact between cells is also a factor in regulating the mitosis of reepithelialization. When dividing cells contact each other, mitosis stops. This phenomenon, called **contact inhibition** (fig. 4.21), can be demonstrated by cells grown in laboratory cultures. On surfaces, cells starting from two points will divide and migrate until the two sheets of cells meet. Following contact, their mitosis rate drops markedly. Note, however, that this response occurs only when the advancing sheets of cells are of the same tissue. Contact with other tissues or nonliving barriers does not affect the mitosis rate.

Case Study

A 27-year-old woman came to her general practitioner because of mild but persistent pain in her lower abdomen. A pelvic examination revealed a mildly purulent cervical discharge. Samples for culture were obtained. She was otherwise healthy, and no indications of other problems were evident. The woman was sexually active, not using birth control pills, and was not pregnant. When the culture results were returned, they indicated the presence of *Chlamydia trachomatis,* and the physician recalled the patient to begin therapy.

She could not at first be reached, but returned ten days later, explaining she had been forced to leave town on short notice to attend a business meeting for another manager who had been in an auto accident. She was concerned because while away she had developed a fever and her lower abdominal discomfort had worsened. These problems had no sooner subsided than another emerged. For the previous three days she had been experiencing more pronounced pain in her right upper abdominal quadrant. She explained that it was especially severe when taking a deep breath. On examination, her right upper quadrant was quite tender but she seemed otherwise normal. She had no other complaints, and verified that her upper quadrant pain wasn't aggravated by fatty meals. She was admitted for an exploratory laparoscopy, and tetracycline antibiotic therapy was started.

The exploration of the abdomen revealed some postinflammatory adhesions at the openings of the right Fallopian tube. Also present were elongated strands of fibrous adhesions joining the abdominal wall and the surface of the liver. These were surgically cleared, as were the adhesions at the Fallopian tubes.

Recovery from the procedure was uneventful. The patient was released with instructions to return for monitoring over the next three weeks. She was advised that the adhesions at the opening of the Fallopian tube might reduce the chances of her becoming pregnant. She was also advised to discuss the situation with her sexual partners and to encourage them to get treatment, because they were the likely source of her infection, and, since infected males are typically asymptomatic, they were likely to be unaware of their infectious state.

Commentary

Many cases of salpingitis (inflammation of the Fallopian tubes) arise as the result of infection that is sexually transmitted, often producing only mild symptoms. *Chlamydia trachomatis* is increasingly involved, but tetracycline therapy is quite effective in dealing with this organism. The less common complication seen in this case is the spread of the organisms, by blood, lymph, or over connecting peritoneal surfaces, to reach the peritoneal capsule of the liver. The resulting inflammation produces a condition known as **perihepatitis,** or the **Fitzhugh-Curtis syndrome.** The irritated liver capsule initially develops a fibrinous surface exudate, which later forms characteristic "violin string" adhesions to the anterior abdominal wall, producing pain as respiratory or other motion applies tension to the liver surface.

The low probability that a gall bladder problem was causing abdominal pain in a woman of this young age, and the possibility that other potentially more serious problems could involve similar signs and symptoms, made the laparoscopy decision a sound one. The fact that this patient was not using birth control pills was a factor to consider in the context of the increased incidence of gall bladder problems in users of the "pill."

The antibiotic therapy was successful and the fact that only one Fallopian tube had been involved decreased the chance that fertility had been impaired.

Key Concepts

1. Following injury and the inflammatory response, the healing process replaces lost tissue (p. 56).

2. Healing involves four components that combine to restore lost parenchyma, replace stroma, reestablish blood supply and surface integrity (p. 56).

3. The ability of the healing process to restore function in the face of tissue loss is determined by the differing regenerative capacities of the body tissues (p. 56).

4. Scarring is the result of the repair process, which employs fibroblasts to lay down high-tensile-strength collagen as a strong replacement tissue (p. 57).

5. The healing process, and the replacement tissue it forms, are both dependent on the prompt restoration of blood supply via revascularization, which forms new flow channels that are derived from undamaged vessels adjacent to the injury site (pp. 58–60).

6. Damage at internal and external surfaces is restored by mitosis of undamaged cells at the wound edges (p. 60).

7. Primary and secondary healing are different patterns of wound healing, which are elicited as a function of wound size and the distance between the wound's opposite edges (pp. 60–62).

8. Patterns of healing among the various tissues and organs differ on the basis of several factors such as tissue regenerative capacity, basement membrane restoration, and the status of the intercellular matrix (pp. 63–67).

9. Healing may be complicated by various derangements that limit normal motion of joints or internal organs, interfere with the healing process itself, allow a wound to reopen, or produce significant skin irregularities (pp. 67–69).

10. For healing to proceed optimally, various physical, vascular, and nutrient requirements must be met (p. 69).

11. The precise control required for the initiation, orderly development, and appropriate cessation of the healing response is provided by a complex of closely interrelated chemical mediators and interactions with the intercellular matrix (pp. 69–70).

REVIEW ACTIVITIES

1. Link the following scrambled elements in a flow chart that reflects the sequence of events in revascularization. Pages 58–60 should be your guide.

   Bud degenerates

   Arteriole formation

   Lumen formation

   Advancing buds contact

   Differentiation of new capillaries

   New capillaries formed

   Buds emerge from intact vessels

   Lymphatic vessel formation

   Venule formation

   No bud contact

2. Study figure 24.2. Make a rough sketch or tracing to show what the damaged skin in the diagram would look like after completion of healing. Which skin structures will you leave out of your sketch? Pages 62–63 have the answer if you need it.

3. Locate a few of your own skin scars. Study the shape of each and relate it to the original wound shape. (Don't forget your scalp. Hair can hide some fascinating scars.) Analyze how wound contraction produced the transition from the original to the

final shape. A water-soluble marker pen might be useful in marking the original wound edges and tracing their movements. Check with a friend so that you can verify each other's assessments. Figures 4.11 and 4.12 may be helpful in this exercise.

4. Be certain that you understand the use of the term organization in the context of healing. To help, jot down its essential definition and then list how it applies to scarring, primary healing, and adhesion formation. If unsure, check pages 57, 58, 62, and 67.

5. In the section on how therapy can interfere with healing (p. 69), note the references to the effects of corticosteroids and NSAIDs. Now locate the flow chart in chapter 2 that indicates specific points at which those therapeutic agents produce their effect.

6. Two of the key concepts in this chapter make reference to the role of the intercellular matrix in healing. Find three flow charts in this chapter that specifically refer to this role (you may need to consult the legend to identify one of them). Reflect on the content of the flow charts.

Chapter Five

Diseases of Immunity

Half the secret of resistance is cleanliness, the other half is dirtiness.

Anonymous

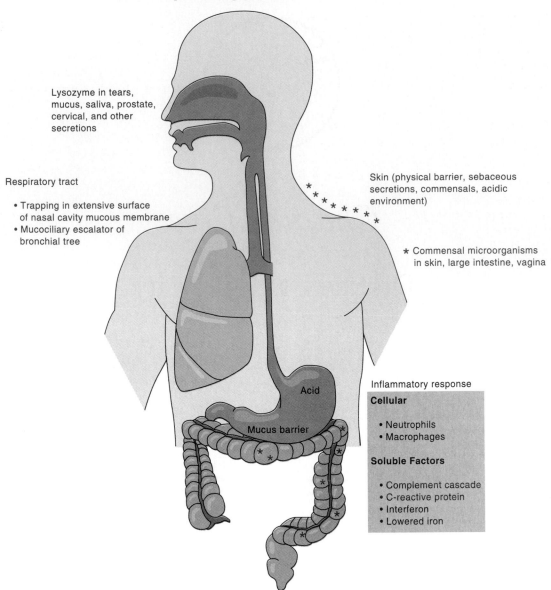

Lysozyme in tears,
mucus, saliva, prostate,
cervical, and other
secretions

Respiratory tract

• Trapping in extensive surface
  of nasal cavity mucous membrane
• Mucociliary escalator of
  bronchial tree

Skin (physical barrier, sebaceous
secretions, commensals, acidic
environment)

★ Commensal microorganisms
  in skin, large intestine, vagina

Acid

Mucus barrier

Inflammatory response

Cellular

• Neutrophils
• Macrophages

Soluble Factors

• Complement cascade
• C-reactive protein
• Interferon
• Lowered iron

Figure 5.1   Summary of mechanisms of nonspecific defense.

IMMUNITY

A casual glance at a magazine or a few hours of TV would convince a visitor from another planet that North Americans are obsessed with sterilizing, deodorizing, sanitizing—in a word, cleanliness. Indeed, basic modern sanitation preserves us from many of the plagues that carried away one-third of the population of medieval Europe. The defensive mechanisms described in chapters 2 and 3 (and outlined in figure 5.1 and table 5.1) are assailed by many of the microorganisms to which we are exposed. It makes sense that the more times these defenses are breached, the more likely we are to be colonized by one of these invading microorganisms. Figure 5.1 and table 5.1 concentrate on antimicrobial defense mechanisms that are always in place or that can be rapidly mobilized, and that require no previous contact with a specific microorganism to be effective in neutralizing it. They are often collectively termed natural defenses or **innate** or **nonspecific immunity.** (The Latin term "immunitas" means "freedom from public service." It was a special honor bestowed upon highly regarded individuals, exempting them from the usual burdens of citizenship in Rome like taxes and military service.) In this scheme we have included so-called barrier defenses that are

Table 5.1	Essential Elements of Nonspecific Defenses

Physical Barriers

Skin
Mucous membranes: GI, respiratory, genitourinary tracts
Mucociliary blanket of respiratory passages
Surface flushing: tears, urine, GI contents

Antibacterial Agents

Acidity of stomach, skin, urinary tract, vagina
Various secretions, e.g., lysozyme in tears
Rapidity of pH change in GI tract

Commensal Microorganisms

Growth provides an environment that is inhospitable to competing, potentially pathogenic, organisms

Ongoing Phagocytosis

Phagocytic cells routinely destroy threatening organisms

Inflammatory Response

Destruction and phagocytosis by neutrophils, macrophages, and natural killer cells
Direct and indirect pathogen destruction by the complement cascade
Promotion of phagocytosis by C-reactive protein
Resistance to viral infection mediated by interferon

Fever

Temperature elevation enhances phagocytosis
Inhibition of mitosis by iron depletion

designed to block, inactivate, or destroy pathogens (disease producers) before they can enter the body. So, in terms of "cleanliness," barriers prevent entry of organisms, and complement, neutrophils, macrophages, etc., clean up any that breach the barriers.

In contrast to our innate defenses against infection, there is another kind of resistance that is acquired after birth. It is here that dirtiness has its place. A population's lack of exposure to a microorganism might make first contact devastating. A clear example is the experience of native North Americans, whose first contact with measles and smallpox came with the European explorers, traders, and settlers. This example tells us several things about acquired immunity. First, it is specific: Native Americans coped quite effectively with the spectrum of diseases with which they had experience before contact with Europeans. They were probably, by and large, healthier than the tattered sailors who gladly left their ships to come ashore and mingle, but they were devastated by the diseases that the sailors carried, because they'd had no previous exposure to them. The specific nature of their vulnerability implies the second feature of acquired immunity. It is the immune system's capacity to recognize a microorganism. A third feature is the system's more effective response to second and subsequent exposures to the same pathogen. This demonstrates learning, and the long-term retention of the improved response demonstrates memory. Finally, our immune system is able to discriminate between foreign substances and those that make up our own body, and to direct its attack only against intruders. It can even detect and attack abnormal cells of the body such as tumor cells or those harboring viruses. These four processes (recognition, learning, memory, and self-discrimination) are characteristic of **acquired immunity,** also called **adaptive** or **specific immunity.** The components of this system normally work effectively in direct attack on invading pathogens or in collaboration with the components of nonspecific immunity to ensure the ultimate survival of the individual.

Fundamentals of Specific Immunity

Some writers restrict their use of the term immunity to the topic that follows, preferring the term **nonspecific defenses** to **nonspecific immunity.** In practice there is no neat boundary between the two. Survival would be impossible without nonspecific defenses but, as is demonstrated in AIDS, paralysis of acquired immunity is also incompatible with life. The basic function of specific immunity is to focus and reinforce nonspecific defenses. Its capacity to discriminate "self" from "nonself" adds some potent weapons to our defensive arsenal.

T Lymphocytes, B Lymphocytes, Antibodies, and Third Population Cells

Lymphocytes, the cells that mediate specific immunity, **1** fall into three distinct populations: T lymphocytes, B lymphocytes, and the so-called third population cells.

T Lymphocytes **T lymphocytes** are cells produced in the bone marrow or thymus. Wherever they originate, they migrate to the thymus, where they mature (the T is for thymus). T-cell surfaces are studded with molecules called **T-cell receptors,** which are the key to their function in the immune system. T lymphocytes are able to "recognize" the molecular aspects of a wide variety of foreign substances, particularly the surface features of microorganisms, because their receptor shapes match, allowing them to bind together. Each distinct population of T cells—and there are probably a million different populations or **clones** possible

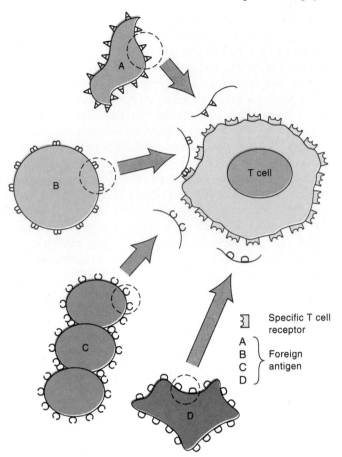

Figure 5.2   Schematic interaction between T-cell surface receptors and the molecular features of a foreign substance (in this case, parts of the surface proteins of an invading microorganism). Note that this particular T cell binds only to B surface antigen. Lack of a match to A, C, and D means no binding can occur. Binding is critical because this "recognition" triggers an immune response to the microbe.

Specific T cell receptor

A
B   Foreign
C   antigen
D

in a human being—bears a unique T-cell receptor. It is this receptor that interacts with ("recognizes") the foreign substance (fig. 5.2). The general shape of all T-cell receptors is the same, but fine details of structure make them different for each clone. These fine structural differences determine the shape and the distribution of electrical charges on the recognition site and thereby the shape and characteristics of the substance with which it will bind.

Anything the specific immune system is able to recognize and to which it responds is called an immunogen or antigen (for antibody generator—antibodies will be discussed shortly). Only parts of a microbe are antigenic (immunogenic), and within the antigen there may be different regions with which a T-cell receptor can bind. These specific regions are called **antigenic determinants** or **epitopes.** Our immune system has the capacity to recognize over a million epitopes. This enormous variety of recognition codes means that sometimes we will produce a response to something harmless (the basis of allergies). At other times we may confuse nonself-antigens with self-antigens (part of the basis of autoimmune diseases).

As we noted, T cells are capable of generating a wide variety of receptor molecules (many more than the million-plus we normally produce). The genetic processes that lead to this diversity are thought to be fairly random. Presumably there are occasions when receptors to self-antigens are produced along with receptors to foreign antigens. After all, we have a lot in common at the molecular level with the pathogens that invade us. To cope with this situation, as T cells mature and display their clonal receptors in the thymus, those cells that have receptors for self-antigens are eliminated or suppressed. In this way, we develop an immune system that attacks only foreign antigens while accepting (tolerating) those recognized as self-antigens. This feature, known as **self-tolerance,** works well enough to make autoimmune disease the exception rather than the rule.

B Lymphocytes The T-cell receptor is very closely related to the antibody. Antibodies are produced by a class of cells called **B lymphocytes.** These cells arise in the red bone marrow. In birds, the animal in which B-cell maturation was first described, B lymphocytes migrate to a region of the cloaca (a common intestinal and urogenital duct) called the bursa of Fabricius; the B comes from bursa. In humans, maturation proceeds in the bone marrow. Much of what we have said about T-cell receptors holds here as well, including the deletion or suppression of any emerging B cells that are specific to self-antigens. The surface of a particular B lymphocyte is dotted with copies of the antibody it produces. Through these a mature B lymphocyte can react to a specific epitope. Its response is to produce antibodies that have affinity with that epitope. To understand why this might be helpful we should look at the structure and function of antibodies.

Antibodies Antibodies are Y-shaped protein molecules that provide a flexible means of linking our relatively limited repertoire of defenses to the host of invaders that threaten us (fig. 5.3). They are a remarkably simple solution to the problem of defending against a large variety of specific pathogens without developing undue complexity. Part of the secret is in the Fab portion of the antibody. Fab stands for **antigen-binding fragment,** and the end part of the structure is analogous to the T-cell receptor binding site. Through the Fab the immune system can attach to and mark any of a million-plus foreign epitopes. It can also attach to and neutralize toxic substances produced by microorganisms. Through the Fc (for **crystallizable fragment**) component, which forms the stalk of the Y, the immune system gets a single, common handle on all this diversity. The antibody response to an antigenic stimulus

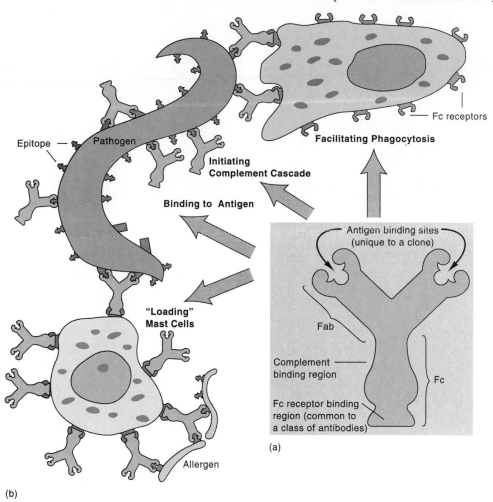

Epitope — / Pathogen

Initiating
Complement Cascade

Binding to Antigen

Facilitating Phagocytosis

Fc receptors

Antigen binding sites
(unique to a clone)

Fab

Complement
binding region

Fc

Fc receptor binding
region (common to
a class of antibodies)

(a)

"Loading"
Mast Cells

Allergen

(b)

Figure 5.3   (*a*) Schematic of the structure of an antibody molecule, identifying the variable antigen binding regions (Fab) and the common stalk (Fc), which mediates the interaction of the antibody with components of the nonspecific defenses. (*b*) Antibody binding has a wide range of effects. Complement deposition damages microorganisms directly and produces products that enhance inflammation. Along with antibody, complement enhances phagocytosis. Binding of antibody to mast cells "loads" (sensitizes) them.

will be the production of masses of antigen-specific antibody that can bind to the antigen.

Macrophages, PMNs, and eosinophils have Fc receptors on their membranes. These allow them to carry surface antibody to tissues where invading organisms are present. When the antigens of the infecting agent bind the membrane antibody, phagocytosis and cytotoxicity of antibody-labeled pathogens follow (fig. 5.2). Binding of the Fc region by platelets, mast cells, and complement is an initiating factor in the release of various of the mediators of inflammation described in chapter 2.

There is more to the subject of antibodies than appears in the simple diagram of figure 5.2, but for our purposes only a brief review of this topic is needed. There are five classes of antibodies. Two have relevance to antibody labeling of bacteria. In a normal immune response

an activated clone of B cells first produces **IgM** class (for immunoglobulin M) antibodies and then shifts its production to **IgG** class antibodies (this is called class switching). IgM antibodies have a different shape (actually five Y's in a wheel), but the Fab binding site is exactly the same (fig. 5.4). IgG is the principal immunoglobulin circulating in the blood. A third class of antibody, **IgE,** is mainly involved in antigen triggering of mast cells and is of clinical significance in allergies and in parasitic worm (helminth) infestations. **IgA** is the secreted antibody and is found in saliva, breast milk, and respiratory and genitourinary tract secretions. **IgD** seems to serve as an antigen receptor on lymphocyte membranes. These five types of antibody form a first line of protection along with the nonspecific defenses. Collectively, antibodies used to be called gamma-globulins. Figure 5.5 pictures a routine, normal pattern of

Figure 5.4   Schematic representation of the structure of an IgM antibody. Essentially it consists of five IgG-type units joined at the Fc regions.

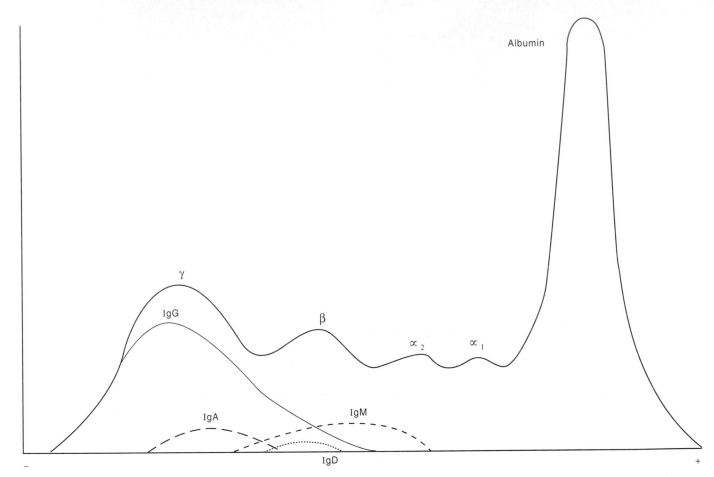

Figure 5.5   Graph of plasma electrophoresis, showing the relative location of four immunoglobulins. IgE is in too low a concentration to be evident. Plasma proteins migrate in a charged field in a way that depends on their size and charge. The peaks have been arbitrarily named α_1, α_2, β, and γ. IgG contributes the bulk of protein in the γ peak. For this reason, in the past the immunoglobulins have been called "gammaglobulins."

serum electrophoresis that indicates the location of the antibody classes relative to the other major plasma proteins.

Third Population Cells The **third population** cells, also called **non-T, non-B,** or **null cells,** are large granular lymphocytes. **2** They are capable of two distinct patterns of cell-killing activity. The first, **antibody-dependent cellu-**

lar cytotoxicity (ADCC), is important in some forms of autoimmune disease. Lymphocytes that employ this pattern have numerous Fc receptors; they attach to a cell that has been covered with an antibody and kill it. Such lymphocytes are sometimes called **K cells (killer cells). Natural killer** (NK) cytotoxic activity is quite different. It seems to be important in the control of tumor development, since

Figure 5.6   (*a*) The Fc receptors of K cells enable them to bind and destroy antibody (ABY) coated target cells. This feature is called antibody-dependent cytotoxicity (ADCC). Natural killer (NK) cells can interact with target cells whose surfaces are altered. The target cell is destroyed as a result. (*b*) Natural killer cells engaging and killing a tumor cell.

Monoclonal Antibodies: A Breakthrough in Research and Therapy

Because antigens are often complex, composed of perhaps several different epitopes, the stimulation of the B-cell population is comparably complex. Several different resting B-cell types are activated to produce several different antibodies; that is, the normal antigenic response is polyclonal. On the other hand, all the descendants of a single B-cell produce the same antibody with affinity for the same epitope, a so-called monoclonal antibody. Say we are interested in labeling a particular epitope because that epitope is unique to a line of cells we are studying and we wish to identify those cells among a complex culture. We could produce a monoclonal antibody (Mab) to that epitope, label it in some way we could detect, expose the culture to the labeled antibody, and simply pick out our target cells. Alternatively, we could use a Mab to identify the cellular distribution of a particular protein.

Monoclonal antibodies can be used therapeutically in a wide variety of ways: to carry bound toxins exclusively to a tumor cell that displays a unique antigen, to block a receptor-mediated process, or to neutralize some substance, released by cells in the body, that is causing disease. Today the production of Mab has become routine technology.

NK cells can recognize a cell that is becoming abnormal, then engage and kill it (see fig. 5.6). In both ADCC and NK cytotoxicity, the target cell membrane forms blebs and ruptures, while the DNA fractures.

Lymphoid Tissue

The primary lymphoid tissues (red bone marrow and thymus) house the lymphoid stem cells, which produce immature T and B cells. After the selective deletion of any self-antigen-reactive lymphocytes that may arise, these T and B cells move out to the secondary lymphoid tissues, which include the lymph nodes, spleen, tonsils, and Peyer's patches in the intestines. Lymphocytes from the primary lymphoid tissues leave the bloodstream from the postcapillary venules in the secondary lymphoid tissues and take up temporary residence. They can then leave the secondary lymphoid tissues in the draining lymph to reenter the blood circulation and begin another circuit of lymphocyte traffic (fig. 5.7*a*).

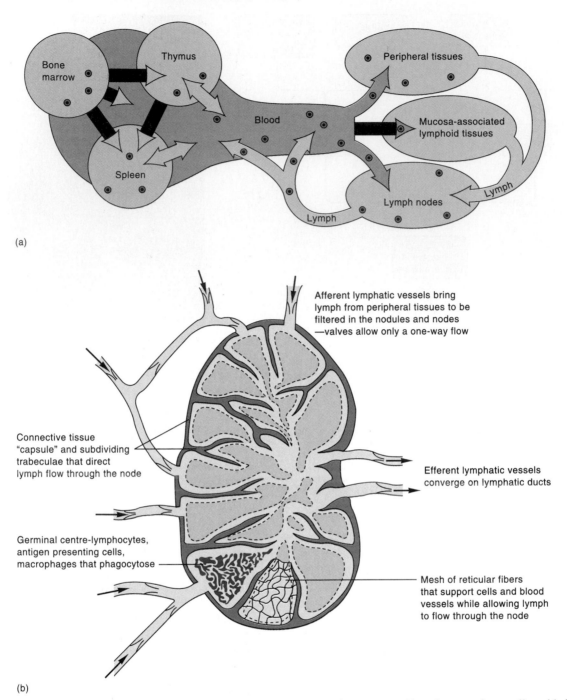

(a)

(b)

Figure 5.7   (*a*) Course of "lymphocyte traffic." Arrows indicate the direction of movement of lymphocytes. Stem cells reside in bone marrow and produce immature lymphocytes that migrate to the thymus and spleen to mature and replicate. Migration into lymphoid tissues is facilitated by the presence of specialized regions of postcapillary venules. Inflammation greatly enhances immigration into peripheral tissues. (*b*) Lymph node. Afferent lymphatic vessels bring lymph from peripheral tissues to be filtered in the nodules and nodes. Valves in the lymph vessels impose a one-way flow. (*c*) Major concentrations of lymphoid tissue, principal drainage routes, and major lymphatic vessels.

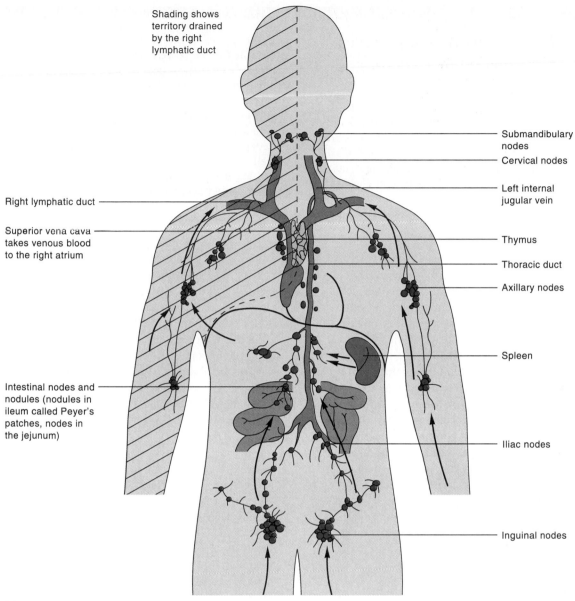

Shading shows territory drained by the right lymphatic duct

Right lymphatic duct

Superior vena cava takes venous blood to the right atrium

Intestinal nodes and nodules (nodules in ileum called Peyer's patches, nodes in the jejunum)

Submandibulary nodes

Cervical nodes

Left internal jugular vein

Thymus

Thoracic duct

Axillary nodes

Spleen

Iliac nodes

Inguinal nodes

(c)

Lymphokine-Activated Killer Cells and Cancer Therapy

ADCC and NK cytoxicity are of great interest as a mode of cancer therapy and are the modes of choice in the treatment of renal cell adenocarcinoma and malignant melanoma. Lymphocytes are isolated from the patient's bloodstream and cultured in a medium with concentrations of a stimulatory substance (a lymphokine) called interleukin 2 (IL-2), which is normally released by activated T cells. The culture produces large granular lymphocytes that exhibit greatly enhanced antitumor activity. When these **lymphokine-activated killer (LAK) cells** are reintroduced to the patient's bloodstream, they appear to seek out and destroy or weaken developing tumor cells. The initial promise of LAK cells appears to be limited to a fairly narrow range of tumor types, but NK cells may be important in ongoing tumor surveillance, which eliminates individual aberrant cells as they arise. Perhaps 20% of tumors arise from the inclusion of viral DNA (called viral oncogenes), and these may be the target of NK activity. People whose immune system is compromised are more subject to these tumors, perhaps because of decreased immune tumor surveillance.

This constant migration serves two purposes. First, the lymphoid tissues are strategically located to encounter antigen shortly after it violates the body's outer defenses. In figure 5.7c, note the concentrations of nodes where the limbs join the trunk, as well as the masses of lymphoid tissue that are associated with the mouth and gut. Lymphocytes are placed in these locations where they are most likely to encounter potentially harmful microorganisms that have breached skin or mucosal barriers. Second, recall that perhaps a million unique clones exist. Estimates are that we possess about a million-million lymphocytes. However, only perhaps 500,000 of those cells are in a given clone, and fewer still are also able to respond to antigen in a way that will produce adaptive immunity. As well, the cells involved in immunity must be in close proximity to others of their clone to cooperate in the development of a full response. This requirement reduces the chances that a given cell will encounter antigens. Lymphocyte traffic increases the odds dramatically.

The Immune Response

We have talked of antigens as though they were drifting about ready to bump into a lymphocyte. Although this can happen, the usual circumstance is that the nonspecific defenses, often in the guise of a macrophage, have engaged and destroyed at least one of the invading hoard of pathogens. The phagocytosed organism is "processed" and elements of it, the antigens, are then displayed on the surface of the macrophage, which presents them to T cells. (This process makes the macrophage an antigen-presenting cell, of which we will learn later.) Of the multitude of T cells, one will have a T-cell receptor that corresponds to an epitope of the antigen, and this receptive T cell is central to the immune response. It is therefore called a **helper T cell** (or T_H cell). The process of matching the epitope to the T_H cell is called **clonal selection.** Once selected, the T_H cell mediates the several components of the immune response.

The first component is clonal expansion; the responsive T_H cell proliferates, producing an expanded clone of similarly antigen-responsive T_H cells, as well as some inactive T_H cells that are retained as memory cells so that future encounters with the same antigen will result in a faster, stronger response (fig. 5.8). Other T cells respond to the T_H cell with activation and proliferation. One type is the **suppressor T cell (T_S)**, which balances the action of T_H by muting the response in the absence of continued antigenic stimulation. **Cytotoxic T cells (T_C)** are able to identify and kill virus- or parasite-infected cells. It is possible to discriminate between T_H and T_S/T_C cells in that T_H cells display a protein on their surface called CD4 that cooperates with the T-cell receptor in antigen presentation. Therefore T_H cells are also referred to as T_4 cells. Both T_S and T_C cells have a different surface molecule, called CD8, and are thereby designated T_8 cells.

While T_S and T_C cells are being stimulated, T_H cells also foster the development of an antibody response (called the humoral response) in B cells with the same specificity. After presentation of antigen by macrophages in the presence of activated T_H cells, the B cells undergo clonal expansion with retention of a pool of memory B cells. B cells that actively secrete antibody (at a rate of perhaps 2000 antibodies per second for their 5–7-day life) are called **plasma cells.** All of this cellular proliferation will swell the lymph nodes in which it occurs, a phenomenon most of us have experienced as swollen, perhaps tender lymph nodes in our throats or armpits. Figure 5.9 illustrates the principal elements of the balanced T cell (cellular) and antibody (humoral) response just described. In actual circumstances, usually one or the other response is dominant.

The first antibody response to an antigen takes about a week to mobilize. IgM production is followed by class switching to IgG, which peaks at about 12 days and then tapers off. Compared with this primary antigen "challenge," the second and subsequent challenges produce a faster rise in antibody production, which is retained at

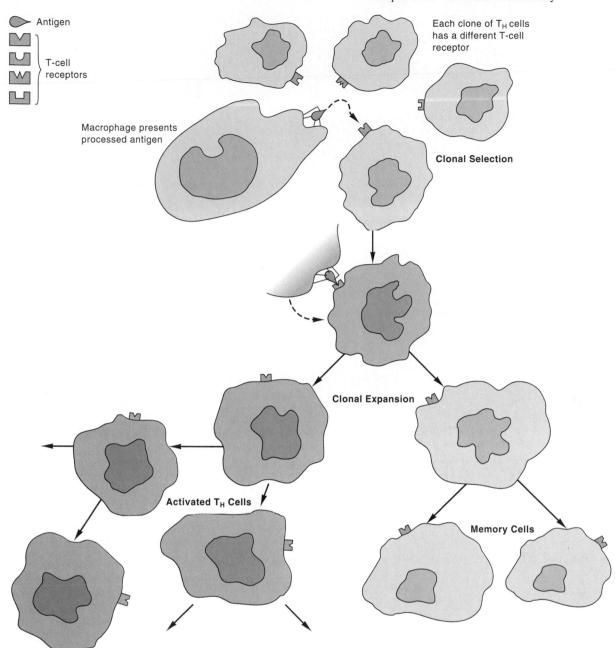

Antigen

T-cell
receptors

Each clone of T$_H$ cells
has a different T-cell
receptor

Macrophage presents
processed antigen

Clonal Selection

Clonal Expansion

Activated T$_H$ Cells

Memory Cells

Figure 5.8   In clonal selection, an antigen-presenting cell interacts with an antigen-responsive helper T cell, (T$_H$). Activation and proliferation of the responsive clone results in clonal expansion, producing many activated T$_H$ cells and a reserve of memory T cells.

higher levels for a longer time. As well, the secondary response is predominantly IgG and the individual antibodies have a higher affinity for antigen (fig. 5.10). The effect is that both the specific immune response and the nonspecific defenses it supports are stronger and more effective.

Communication between the cells involved in the immune response is mediated by factors called **cytokines** (literally, cell movers). Most cytokines act on cells in the immediate vicinity of the secreting cell or even on themselves, but some—for example, interleukin 1, which we encountered as a mediator of fever in chapter 3—act on distant target organs. Research on the cytokines has progressed like the investigations by the proverbial blind men who touch and describe an elephant, each perceiving an entirely different phenomenon. The result was a welter of names that were based on what the discoverer initially thought the function of a factor to be. Recently, at least for those factors originally thought to be produced by active

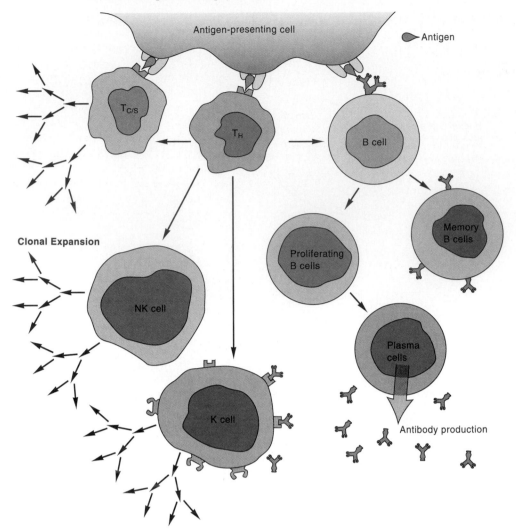

Figure 5.9   When sensitized T_H cells act upon sensitized cytotoxic/suppressor T cells ($T_{C/S}$), sensitized B cells, and nearby K and NK cells, the result is clonal expansion, antibody production, and the retention of a pool of memory B cells.

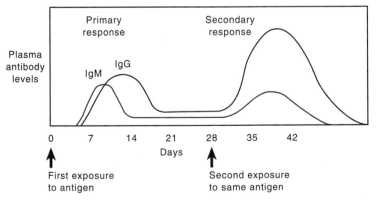

Figure 5.10   Comparison of primary and secondary antibody responses. The second exposure to a specific antigen produces a more rapid, extensive, and prolonged antibody production. IgG can permeate tissues more readily and binds to antigen with greater affinity.

!! *Economy of Size and Delayed Response*

Reflect for a moment on the significance of memory cells and the secondary response. The alternative approach to the problem of coping quickly with a threatening antigenic challenge would be to produce and hold the responsive T- and B-cell clones in reserve. An analogy might be the musculoskeletal system, in which our peak strength greatly exceeds the ordinary demands of activities like walking and breathing, in order to cope with the extraordinary challenge of running for a bus. To match our equivalent muscle mass the lymphoid tissues, which collectively account for about 2% of our body weight, would have to weigh perhaps 100 times as much, with an attendant increase in food requirements. So the trade-off for this incredible economy of size is the 5–7-day lagtime for clonal expansion of antigen-specific memory T- and B-cell lines. Of course, while we suffer for a week with our cold or flu, it may be difficult to derive comfort from the fact that, by and large, our immune system can take credit for our survival!

Table 5.2	The Principal Cytokines

Cytokine	Source	Principal Effects
Interleukin 1 (IL-1)	Antigen-presenting cells	Immune response activation, enhancement of inflammation
Interleukin 2 (IL-2)	Helper T cells	Immune response activation, some tumor therapy applications
Interleukins 3–11	Various cells	Of this group, IL-4 is perhaps the most important in mediating a broad array of immune and chronic inflammatory responses
Interferon (IFN)	Various cells: leukocytes, fibroblasts, epithelia	Direct inhibition of viral replication, promotion of the destruction of virally infected cells
Tumor necrosis factor (TNF)	Macrophages, T cells	Antiviral/antiparasite action, tumor cytotoxicity, enhanced phagocytosis, some cancer side effects
Colony-stimulating factor (CSF)	Various cells	Division and differentiation of hemopoietic stem cells

These are water-soluble molecules that typically exert their effects on adjacent cells in mediating their various contributions to body defenses.

leukocytes (the interleukins), such names have been replaced by numbers based on order of discovery.

Table 5.2 presents a selected list of cytokines for reference. For our purposes IL-1 is important. Besides being an endogenous pyrogen, it is released by the antigen-presenting cell at the same time as it presents processed antigen to the T_H cell. These two stimuli (IL-1 and appropriate antigen) are necessary to activate the T_H cell, which responds by producing IL-2. This interleukin then acts on adjacent T and B cells of the same clone, stimulates the T_H cell itself, and is responsible for clonal expansion. (We have already described how IL-2 is used to stimulate the proliferation of NK cells into LAK cells.) IL-4 (B-cell growth factor) and IL-6 (B-cell differentiation factor) are also released by T_H cells to foster clonal expansion of B and T cells. Figure 5.11 diagrams these interactions and figure 5.12 presents an overview of this section. We will now look at some of the ways an understanding of normal immune function can be used to avoid disease.

THERAPEUTIC APPLICATIONS OF IMMUNITY

Immunization

Immunization is the prophylactic (preventive) technique of artificially inducing an immune response. [3] The technique seeks to stimulate the immune system without exposing the body to an infection. The means is most commonly a preparation of the antigenic components of a microorganism, or of its toxins. This preparation is called a **vaccine.**

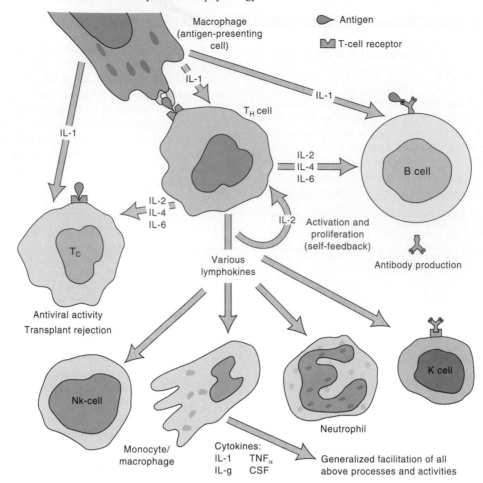

Figure 5.11   Interactions between activated T_H cell and other effectors of specific and nonspecific immunity. The role of specific cytokines is noted.

Failure to Immunize

Recently there has been concern because a routine immunization has been too effective! Following the introduction of the Salk vaccine against the crippling and potentially fatal disease poliomyelitis in the 1950s, a generation of children grew up for whom polio was just a scary memory. But memory fades and so did full compliance with public health expectations of routine immunization. In the late 1980s, sporadic cases of polio were showing up in unimmunized children.

It is interesting to note that the technique of vaccination was developed well before the essentials of immune function were understood. In 1796 the British physician Edward Jenner took advantage of the antigenic similarity between the relatively harmless cowpox virus and the deadly smallpox virus to invent vaccination. Smallpox was declared eradicated worldwide in 1979. Vaccines have been developed for a wide range of both viral and bacterial infections (table 5.3).

Vaccines may include killed microorganisms, attenuated (weakened) microorganisms, or inactivated microbial toxins. The basic principle of a vaccine is that it is harmless, while still containing antigenic material that can induce a primary antibody response with the long-term retention provided by memory T and B cells. Subsequent encounters with the same antigenic determinants will elicit a brisk and usually effective secondary immune response.

An interesting variant of vaccination occurs with the treatment of suspected rabies infection, where the immunization vaccine is given *after* the primary infection. Rabies has a long (at least two weeks) and variable incubation period, and once symptoms are displayed the disease is almost invariably fatal. Between infection and disease there is a window during which repeated inoculation of attenuated rabies virus triggers an immune response that copes with the incipient infection. Previously a course of 14–21 injections was required, but recent improvements in techniques have reduced the number to 4–6.

The Use of Antisera

The immunity induced by vaccination is called **active** because it is indistinguishable from a normal primary immune response; it requires the full participation of the

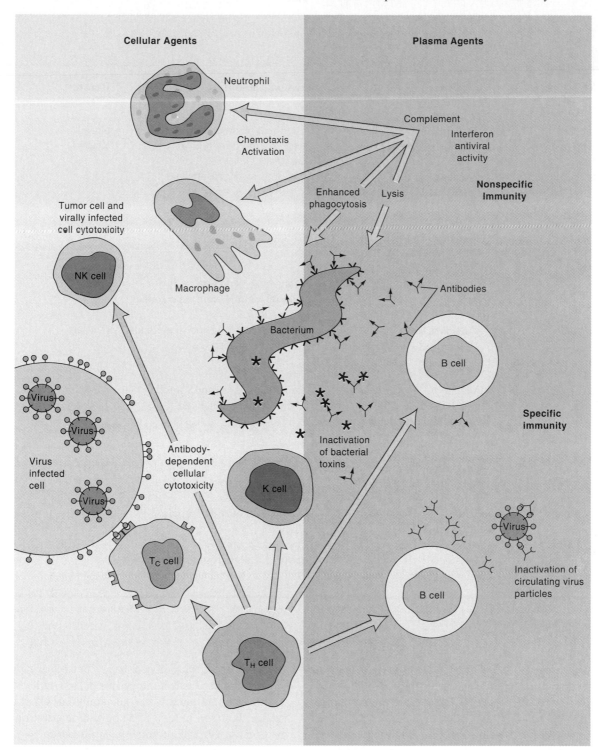

Figure 5.12   Overview of nonspecific and specific immunity.

immune system. **Passive** immunity, by contrast, is protection that is imported in the form of ready-made antibodies from outside the system. Characteristically, this immunity lasts only a short while (weeks or months). Natural passive immunity is transferred to a fetus with the already formed maternal antibodies that are transported across the placental barrier to the infant. In breast milk, antibody transfer continues this passive support of the very young infant's relatively incompetent immune system. Artificial passive immunity is conferred by the transfer of antibodies from a sensitized host (in the past often a horse, but increasingly monoclonal antibodies are used) to a nonimmune recipient so that those antibodies can interfere with or interrupt a pathological process already underway. The serum

Table 5.3   A Selection of Vaccines Commonly Used against Viral and Bacterial Diseases in Humans

Disease	Vaccine	Recommendation	Booster
Viral Diseases			
Hepatitis B	Viral antigen	High-risk medical personnel	None
Influenza	Inactivated virus	Chronically ill individuals and those over 65	Yearly
Measles	Attenuated viruses (combined MMR vaccine)	Children 15–19 months old	None
Mumps			
Rubella			
Poliomyelitis	Attenuated or inactivated virus (oral poliomyelitis vaccine [OPV])	Children 2–3 years old	Adults as needed
Rabies	Inactivated virus	Individuals in contact with wildlife, animal control personnel, veterinarians	None
Yellow fever	Attenuated virus	Military personnel and individuals traveling to endemic areas	10 years
Bacterial Disease			
Cholera	Fraction of *Vibrio cholerae*	Individuals in endemic areas	6 months
Diphtheria	Diphtheria toxoid, killed	Children 2–3 months old	10 years
Pertussis	*Bordetella pertussis,* tetanus toxoid (DPT vaccine)		
Tetanus			
Haemophilus influenza	Polysaccharide-protein conjugate	Children under 5 years of age	None
Plague	Fraction of *Yersinia pestis*	Individuals in contact with rodents in endemic areas	Yearly
Pneumococcal pneumonia	Purified *S. pneumoniae* polysaccharide	Adults over 50 with chronic disease	None
Tuberculosis	*Mycobacterium bovis* BCG (attenuated)	Individuals exposed to TB for prolonged periods of time	3–4 years
Typhoid fever	Killed *Salmonella typhi*	Individuals in endemic area	3–4 years

injected for this purpose is rich in the antibody of interest and is called an **antiserum.** The term continues to be used with artificially produced antibodies that are not carried in serum.

Antisera can be used in different circumstances. In suspected rabies infection, for example, rabies antiserum is used to infiltrate the wound and neutralize the virus before it can enter tissues and replicate. In another approach, antiserum is introduced into the bloodstream of infected individuals before they have developed an immune response to neutralize virulent pathogens. In effect, the antiserum buys time for activation of the immune system. A third application of antisera is in the neutralization of bacterial toxins. For example, improperly preserved food may host a bacterium (*Clostridium botulinum*) that produces a dangerous poison called botulinum toxin. Antibotulinum toxin antiserum will effectively neutralize the toxin before it can have a devastating effect on neuromuscular and nervous system function.

The fourth application is interesting in that it is intended to prevent a normal immune response rather than to support a weak or absent one. If a pregnant woman who is negative for the Rh factor on her red blood cells (about 15% of women) carries a fetus who inherited Rh factor from an Rh-positive father, she is at risk of becoming exposed to her fetus's Rh-positive blood and developing an immune response to it. This is of little consequence to her directly, since she encounters only tiny amounts of

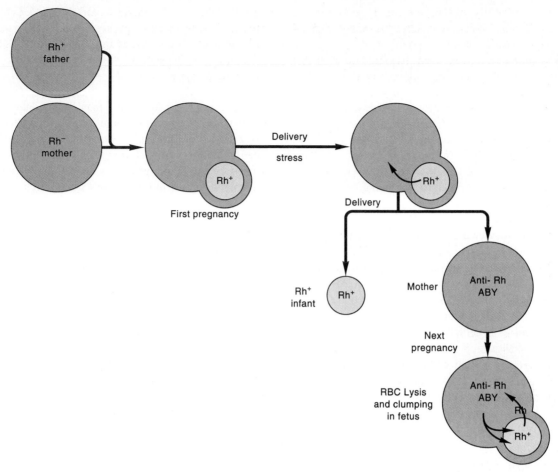

Figure 5.13 The immunology of erythroblastosis fetalis. Delivery stresses allow the Rh antigens of a Rh$^+$ fetus to cross to its Rh$^-$ mother. Anti-Rh antibody production follows the delivery. In the second and subsequent pregnancies with an Rh$^+$ fetus, the antibody can cross to the fetus, causing potentially serious damage.

Rh-positive RBCs. The situation for the fetus is different. The most usual circumstance is that the original antigen exposure occurs during labor with the first child, when its Rh antigens are more likely to gain access to the maternal circulation. Even a minute transfer of fetal RBCs mobilizes maternal antibody production. During a following pregnancy these antibodies cross the placenta, attach to fetal red blood cells, and induce lysis of RBCs or their clumping followed by destruction in the liver. The resultant anemia and jaundice in the infant, called **erythroblastosis fetalis** or **hemolytic disease of newborns** (fig. 5.13), is potentially fatal.

In current medical management, routine maternal blood tests detect pregnancies that pose such risks. Within 48 hours of delivery (or at any other point that fetal blood transfer is suspected), anti-Rh antibodies are administered to the mother in the form of **RhoGAM antiserum.** These bind to fetal RBCs in the mother and tag them for phagocytosis in the liver or spleen. By preventing immune sensitization in the mother, this approach, where used, has virtually eliminated the risk of erythroblastosis fetalis.

IMMUNE-MEDIATED TISSUE INJURY

We now turn to diseases of immunity, beginning with conditions that have as their basis "too much immunity." We will deal with four broad patterns of immune-mediated injury called hypersensitivity reactions (which includes allergies) and then discuss a therapeutic intervention that is made problematic by the normal functioning of the immune system: transplantation.

Hypersensitivity Reactions

Our skin and intestine and our respiratory and other mucosal barriers are richly supplied with mast cells that are studded with IgE antibodies. In these locations, mast cells are ideally situated to detect the entry of parasitic worms (helminthic infections), **4** which shed antigen as part of their attempt to confuse the host immune system. If all goes according to *our* schedule, these parasitic antigens bind to IgE on mast cells, causing the cells to degranulate and triggering a localized inflammatory response. Some of the mediators released by activated mast cells attract eosinophils, which are specially adapted to engage and kill the threatening parasitic worms.

Western sanitation and personal hygiene are such that most of you reading this book have never been made ill by parasitic worms. However, about 15% of you will be familiar with the misery of "pollen season." The same system that improves the chances of survival against parasitic infection sets certain individuals up for allergies; that is, an inherently harmless antigen (allergen) activates a bothersome and potentially fatal **anaphylaxis.** The Greek roots here are *ana*-(without) and-*phylaxis* (watching or guarding) and the term implies a dramatic reaction that occurs without warning. **Immediate hypersensitivity** or **anaphylactic (type I) hypersensitivity** are terms applied to this pattern of immune system response, in which the cure (immune response) is worse than the disease. There are three other broad patterns of hypersensitivity in which immune system overactivity causes tissue damage: antibody-dependent cytotoxicity (type II), immune-complex-mediated hypersensitivity (type III), and cell-mediated, delayed-type hypersensitivity (type IV). Figure 5.14 presents the key features. Because these reactions are central to many diseases of immunity and are significant in other disorders, we will discuss each in a little more detail. Note, however, that we describe them separately for convenience only. Seldom does one pattern occur in complete isolation from others.

Type I: Immediate Hypersensitivity (Anaphylaxis)

In this pattern of hypersensitivity, the first exposure to antigen, which may be through the skin or at a mucosal surface, produces no noticeable reaction. Nevertheless, antigen-presenting cells have captured and processed the allergen and presented it to B and T cells, and cell production of the corresponding IgE antibodies has been launched. The IgE antibodies bind to the Fc receptors on local mast cells and spill over into the circulation to bind on mast cells throughout the body. They are now primed for the next contact with the allergen (this sensitization can last for months). When the next exposure occurs, allergen binds to the Fab, cross-linking adjacent antibodies and causing mast cell degranulation and mediator release (fig. 5.14a). The immediate (5–30 minutes) response is' largely due to the release of preformed histamine. It consists of an increase in vascular permeability as well as the constriction of bronchial muscles and a narrowing of airways. Histamine also stimulates increased secretion from nasal, bronchial, and gastric glands. Other specific reactions are associated with the degranulation of mast cells in the skin (**hives**), the eye (**conjunctivitis**), and the mucous membranes of the nasal cavity (**rhinitis**). This early reaction can be over in an hour. Other mediators—those responsible for the cellular infiltration and tissue damage that accompany more extensive allergic reactions—take longer to be released or to act.

They include chemotactic factors for eosinophils and neutrophils, leukotrienes, prostaglandins, platelet-activating factor, and protein-digesting enzymes. These mediators account for the second wave or late phase reaction of immediate hypersensitivity, which occurs in two to eight hours and may last for two or three days (fig. 5.15). The symptoms of the first wave may be subdued if the person has been taking antihistamines. On the other hand, epinephrine (a beta-adrenergic compound) can block mast cell degranulation by interfering with ability of the mast cell to respond. Another approach is the use of corticosteroids and nonsteroidal anti-inflammatory agents that block the synthesis of leukotrienes and prostaglandins, and thereby the late phase reaction, while leaving the early phase unaffected.

Localized anaphylaxis can take many forms: allergic asthma, hay fever, eczema, urticaria (hives). The name **atopy** is sometimes applied to this constellation of symptoms in individuals with a family history of allergies. Although these people tend to have elevated plasma IgE levels, only with atopic eczema is there any good correlation between allergic symptoms and measured IgE. Allergy sufferers also tend to have both an inherited general hyper-responsiveness and an inherited antigen-specific response. Lowered numbers and depressed activity of suppressor T cells play an important role. Even with a genetic predisposition, however, the allergy tends to develop only after repeated exposure to low doses of allergen presented (usually) at a mucosal barrier.

One way to control an allergy is to avoid the allergen, whether in foods, the droppings of dust mites in house dust, animal dander, etc. It will also be helpful (though difficult) to avoid exposure to environmental pollutants. Sulfur dioxide, nitrogen oxides, fly ash, and diesel fumes can make the mucosa more permeable and thereby worsen ordinary allergic reactions. Instead of avoidance, the physician may try injections of the same allergen, in low and increasing doses, to reduce sensitivity. Injection tends to increase IgG, which acts as a blocking antibody, removing antigen from tissue fluids before it can interact with mast cells.

Unfortunately, desensitization procedures are not risk-free. Sometimes they trigger a generalized or systemic anaphylaxis. In this case, widespread mast cell degranulation with histamine release can result in profound circulatory shock as fluids pool in the capillary bed and are lost from the vascular compartment; other symptoms are also present (fig. 5.16). Systemic anaphylaxis can also be brought on by drugs (e.g., penicillin or sulfonamides), insect venoms (e.g., bees, wasps, **5** or foods (e.g., peanuts, seafoods). Whatever the triggering allergen, the pattern is the same. Within minutes the person experiences pruritus (intense itching), urticaria, erythema (red rash), wheezing, and dyspnea (labored breathing). The larynx swells, and there may be vomiting, cramps, and diarrhea. In the worst case, laryngospasm may lead to suffocation and death. To counter the

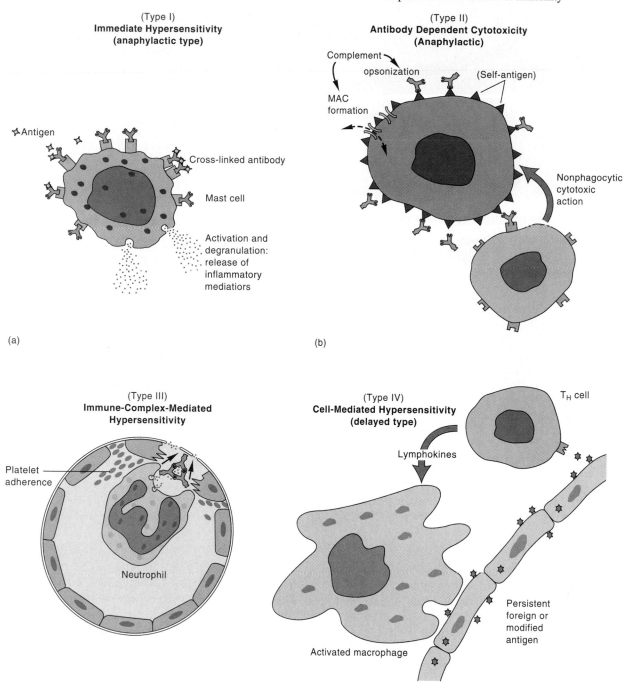

Figure 5.14   Overview of hypersensitivity reactions.

reaction, histamine competitors (e.g., epinephrine or isoproterenol) and antihistamines are administered parenterally (by injection). Systemic anaphylaxis is mediated by IgG as well as IgE antibodies. The term anaphylactoid is applied to conditions that are clinically identical to anaphylaxis but are due to the direct action of chemicals or drugs on mast cells, causing degranulation without the mediation of IgE. In these cases, usually large amounts of drugs are involved and the reaction is dose-related.

Type II: Antibody-Dependent Cytotoxicity

This pattern of hypersensitivity is triggered when antibodies attach to the surface of individual cells, such as red blood cells, or to cells or surfaces associated with a solid tissue, like the glomerular basement membrane of the kidney (fig. 5.14b). The antibody acts as an anchor and activator for K cells that then engage in antibody-dependent cellular cytotoxicity (ADCC). As well, antibody Fc

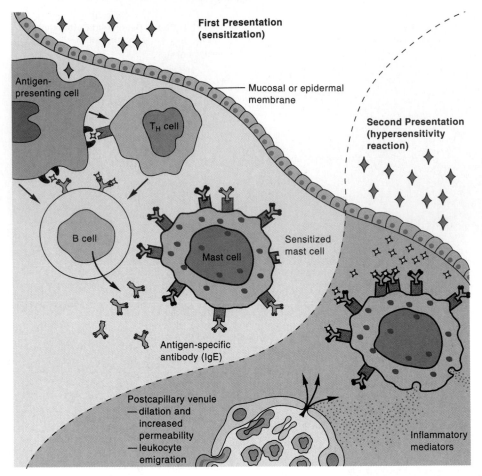

Figure 5.15   Immediate hypersensitivity. First contact with antigen results in plasma cell production of antigen-specific IgE antibody. This binds to the Fc receptors on mucosal, dermal, or perivascular mast cells, thus arming them (sensitizing them to antigen). The second and subsequent contacts result in mast cell degranulation and synthesis of secondary mediators.

components assist in the phagocytic activity of other cells whose surfaces bear Fc receptors (neutrophils and macrophages). Antibody attachment to a cell surface forms a favored site for the precipitation of complement—an event leading to activation of the complement cascade. As we noted in chapter 2, this cascade is associated with assembly of a membrane attack complex (MAC) and lysis of cell membranes, with chemotaxis of neutrophils, eosinophils, and macrophages, with activation of phagocytic cells and their release of mediators, and with facilitation of phagocytosis through opsonization.

From this brief summary of the usually beneficial effects of antibody binding, you can see how potent a weapon antibodies might be when turned against our own cells. There are several different diseases in which this takes place (table 5.4). Some of these are genuine autoimmune disorders in which errant or uncontrolled plasma cells produce antibodies against self-antigens (e.g., myasthenia gravis or Goodpasture's syndrome). Some involve

drugs combining with antibody. The complexes thus formed then attach to adjacent tissues, cuing the cytotoxic mechanisms just described. Since the tissues themselves are not involved in initiating the reaction, this has been called the "innocent bystander" mechanism.

Type III: Immune-Complex-Mediated Hypersensitivity

Immune complexes are simply aggregations of antigen and their corresponding antibodies. When there is a good match between the concentration of antigen and the antibody produced to deal with it, such as occurs in a healthy immune response to infection, large complexes are formed and carried in the bloodstream (many attached to red blood cells). These are quickly removed in the liver and spleen, and the infective organism is thereby neutralized. When antigen is in excess, as it might be in lungs subjected to continuous inhalation of antigenic dust, or when antibody is in excess, as in autoimmune disease, smaller complexes are

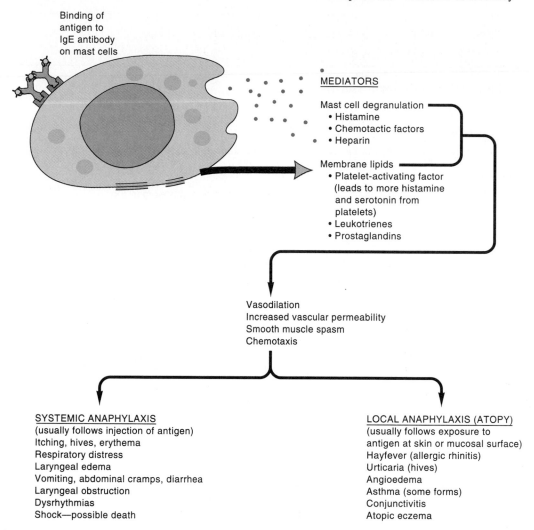

Figure 5.16   Symptoms associated with immediate hypersensitivity. Systemic anaphylaxis and local anaphylaxis both result from antigen activation of sensitized mast cells.

formed. It is these that produce the damage in immune-complex-mediated hypersensitivity. When they deposit in blood vessel walls, the small complexes mediate the formation of microthrombi and cause endothelial damage (fig. 5.14c). The deposition in vessel walls also triggers a variety of inflammatory processes involving complement activation, vasodilation, increased permeability, phagocyte chemotaxis, and frustrated phagocytosis followed by basement membrane damage.

Where the antibody is specific to a tissue, as it is in arthritis, deposition tends to occur in that tissue. In the case of a large burden of exogenous antigen, as occurs in various inhalation diseases called pneumonoconioses, the area of exposure (the lung) tends to be the area of deposition. Table 5.5 presents some of the disorders that principally involve the type III mechanism; figure 5.17 summarizes the relevant pathophysiology.

Type IV: Cell-Mediated, Delayed-Type Hypersensitivity

This is the principal mechanism of damage in tuberculosis, contact dermatitis, many fungal, viral, and parasitic infections, and acute and chronic transplant rejection. The mediating cells are cytotoxic T cells, activated macrophages, K cells (ADCC), and also NK cells. Helper T cells orchestrate the attack against a resistant, largely intracellular bacterium (in tuberculosis and leprosy), against a persistent immune complex (in contact dermatitis), or against foreign tissue (in transplantation) (fig. 5.14d). Antigen presentation and T_H sensitization are prerequisites. In the tuberculin test for TB and in contact dermatitis, subsequent exposure to the antigen activates responsive T_H cells, which produce a variety of cytokines. These attract and mobilize "angry" macrophages, which attempt relatively indiscriminate

Table 5.4   Diseases in Which Type II Hypersensitivity (Antibody-Dependent Cytotoxicity) Plays a Major Role

Antiglomerular Basement Membrane Nephritis

Antibodies to glomerular basement membrane can severely damage the kidney and threaten renal failure.

Goodpasture's Syndrome

Characterized by pulmonary hemorrhages combined with glomerular damage caused by cross-reacting antibodies.

Transfusion Reactions

Cells of an incompatible donor are destroyed by complement-dependent lysis and opsonization.

Erythroblastosis Fetalis

Maternal antibodies cross the placenta to destroy the cells of her Rh^+ fetus via complement-mediated processes.

Autoimmune Hemolytic Anemia; Agranulocytosis; Thrombocytopenia

Self-reactive antibodies attack a population of cells via complement-dependent mechanisms.

Drug-Related Anemias

Complexing of a therapeutic drug and red cell antigens induces immune-mediated hemolysis and indirect organ damage.

Graft Rejection

Foreign tissue destruction by immune-mediated cellular attack on antibody-coated cells: antibody-dependent cellular toxicity (ADCC).

Myasthenia Gravis

Autoimmune destruction of acetylcholine receptors in muscle produces greatly weakened muscular responses.

Grave's Disease

Antibodies that bind to thyroid gland receptors induce excessive thyroxine secretion and hyperthyroid effects.

---

phagocytosis and, along with lymphocytes and fluid, form an exudate that peaks at about 48–72 hours (hence, delayed). In contact dermatitis **6** the antigen, perhaps nickel, rubber, or poison oak or ivy, is usually deposited superficially in the epidermis, whereas in the tuberculin test, the inoculant, derived from the tubercle bacillus, is introduced into the dermis and the infiltrate is largely dermal. Figure 5.18 provides an overview of type IV hypersensitivity.

The Major Histocompatibility Complex

Surveillance for intruding microorganisms that have evaded nonspecific defenses may be based on either of two strategies. The first involves the production of molecules that recognize or have an affinity for parts of other molecules that are not normally encountered in the body. The antibodies and T-cell receptors that we have discussed are examples of this approach. In essence it involves the recognition of "foreignness": this substance is nonhuman, it is potentially dangerous and must be destroyed. This is an excellent strategy—none of us would have survived to adulthood without it—but it has a significant flaw, similar to one that human spies exploit. A microorganism skilled in

Table 5.5   Disorders That Result from Immune-Complex-Mediated (Type III) Hypersensitivity

Serum Sickness

Damage from frustrated phagocytosis of immune complexes deposited in capillaries following large transfusions of foreign serum, e.g., horse antidiphtheria serum.

Immune Complex Glomerulonephritis

Damage to the glomerulus following deposition of immune complexes which may form as a result of certain viral or bacterial infections.

Neurological Disorders; Skin Rashes

Immune complex deposition in various brain or nerve sites or the skin.

Rheumatoid Arthritis

Local production and deposition of antibodies against the synovial membrane elicit type III hypersensitivity responses leading to joint inflammation and damage.

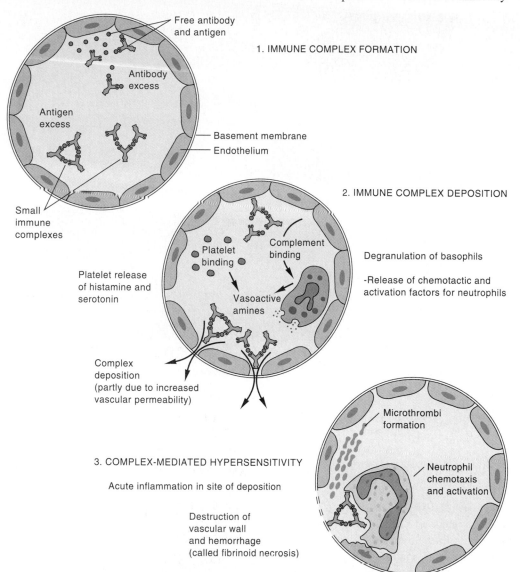

1. IMMUNE COMPLEX FORMATION

Free antibody and antigen

Antibody excess

Antigen excess

Basement membrane

Endothelium

Small immune complexes

2. IMMUNE COMPLEX DEPOSITION

Platelet binding

Complement binding

Degranulation of basophils

-Release of chemotactic and activation factors for neutrophils

Platelet release of histamine and serotonin

Vasoactive amines

Complex deposition (partly due to increased vascular permeability)

Microthrombi formation

Neutrophil chemotaxis and activation

3. COMPLEX-MEDIATED HYPERSENSITIVITY

Acute inflammation in site of deposition

Destruction of vascular wall and hemorrhage (called fibrinoid necrosis)

Figure 5.17   Summary of steps involved in immune-complex-mediated hypersensitivity (type III). The vessels involved may be specialized, as are those in the glomerulus or the choroid plexus, or deposition may reflect hemodynamic factors, as in the accumulation of complexes on the heart valves.

the art of disguise, which displayed surface features that closely resembled the surface features of human cells, could escape detection. Such a perfect pathogen could sweep through the human population in a devastating plague.

Fortunately, there is no such thing as a typical human cell. As we all know from hearing about the problems of transplant rejection or about campaigns to find suitable bone marrow donors, human cells (in fact those of most animals) have features that are virtually unique to each individual. This opens the possibility of a second strategy for immune defenses: the recognition of "nonself." This strategy is utilized when our immune system identifies and attacks a virally infected cell. In becoming a factory for

viral production, the cell has been altered, allowing it to be discriminated from normal "self" and killed. The immune system has the capacity to recognize the individual's unique cell surface features. This cell surface protein "fingerprint" is determined by a region on chromosome 6 called the **major histocompatibility complex (MHC).** The membrane protein products of the MHC genes are involved in the rejection (or acceptance) of transplanted tissues, hence the term histocompatibility. In the transplantation of cells producing elements of the immune system, e.g., bone marrow, a very close match is crucial, so the antigens on the surface of leukocytes are carefully characterized or "typed" in the process of selecting a donor. This practice has given rise to the term **HLA (human leukocyte**

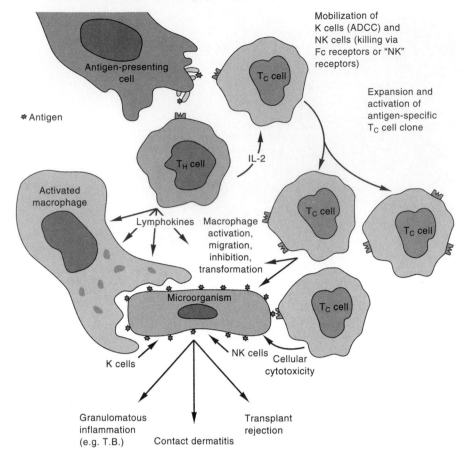

Figure 5.18   Cell-mediated, delayed-type hypersensitivity (type IV).

antigens), which is essentially interchangeable with the term MHC. Typing the leukocyte antigens will indirectly identify the antigens found on other tissues, so this approach is also used for kidney and other transplants. Note in passing that while the MHC is a major determinant of transplant success, many other factors play important roles—for example, ABO and other blood group compatibility, age, previous transfusions, further disease, and the response to and tolerance of immunosuppressive drugs.

MHC Class I and Class II: Antiviral Activity Disease Susceptibility, APC, Tissue Typing

Two MHC subtypes have been identified. The MHC class I surface proteins function as the essential self marker. The MHC class II antigens are less widespread, playing recognition and communication roles among cells of the immune system. We will present just the highlights of these functions.

Antiviral Activity Cytotoxic T cells (T_C) play a crucial role in our resistance against viruses. Viruses are intracellular parasites unable to reproduce without the assistance of a cell. They enter a cell by first attaching to surface molecules that the cell developed for quite other purposes. Once

inside, the virus is hidden from immune detection and can, using the metabolic machinery of the cell, assemble new virus particles that can exit the cell to infect other cells. The shedding of virus particles may kill the host cell. Fortunately, antigenic elements of the virus are usually displayed on the surface of an infected cell. T_C cells can detect these viral antigens but require that the antigen be associated with an MHC class I molecule. This association is interpreted by the T_C cell to mean that although this cell is "self," it is infected and must be destroyed. It then attacks and kills the cell and its viral contents (fig. 5.19).

Disease Susceptibility Certain diseases are more common in individuals bearing certain HLA antigens or patterns of antigens. The increase in relative risk of developing the disease varies (see table 5.6). These findings argue for a direct or indirect role of immune system function in many very significant diseases, a topic that we will discuss later. As well, the intensity of immune responses appears to be based on MHC. This is good news for the person who "never gets a cold" but a great burden for the hay fever victim, both of whom display strong immune responses.

Antigen-Presenting Cells As we described earlier, before the immune system can mount a response, antigen must be presented to T_H (helper T) cells. You may also recall that

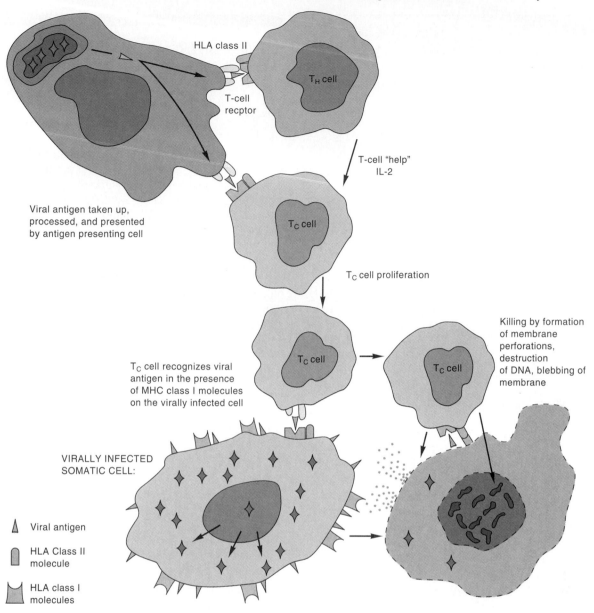

Figure 5.19   Antiviral activity of cytotoxic T lymphocytes (T$_C$ cells).

only T cells from a specific clone will recognize a particular antigen. The cells that process and display antigens for T$_H$ cells are known as **antigen-presenting cells** (APCs). The dominant APCs are probably cells of the monocyte/macrophage cell line: macrophages in tissues, monocytes in the blood, Kupffer cells in the liver, resident macrophages in the spleen and lymph nodes, and microglia in the brain. The term also applies to various nonphagocytic cells (for example, dendritic cells) in the skin, lymphoid tissue, and other tissues; and both B and T cells can function as APCs. These cells can interact with microorganisms shortly after they enter the body and process their antigenic components so they are capable of stimulating T$_H$ cells. They then enter the lymph drainage, move to the appropriate

part of the lymph node, and select and interact with the T$_H$ cells. This last step is effected through the association of the antigen with an MHC class II molecule. These are only expressed on APCs and are the essential recognition factor between APC and T$_H$ cells. Therefore, T$_H$ recognition of antigen is said to be class II restricted.

Tissue Transplantation

Tissue matching and the development of selective immune suppression have led to dramatic improvements in the success of transplant therapy. The following sections deal with some general issues in transplant rejection and some approaches that seek to improve graft survival.

Table 5.6	Selected HLA Antigens and Their Associated Diseases	

Disease	HLA Allele	Risk Increase
Rheumatoid arthritis	DR4	5.8x
Dermatitis herpetiformis	DR3	56.4x
Chronic active hepatitis (autoimmune)	DR3	13.9x
Celiac disease	DR3	10.8x
Sjögren's disease	DR3	9.7x
Addison's disease (adrenal)	DR3	6.3x
Type I diabetes mellitus	DR3/4	14.3x
Goodpasture's syndrome	DR2	13.1x
Ankylosing spondylitis	B27	84.4x
Myasthenia gravis	B8	4.4x

x represents risk in the normal population. The risk of contracting the disease is greater when the antigen is present, but note that in no case is the disease certain to develop. These data hold for those of European Caucasian extraction.

Data derived from Roitt, I., *Essential Immunology*, Seventh Ed., Blackwell Scientific Publications, London, 1991.

Transplant Rejection

Tissues vary in their tendency to generate an immune-mediated rejection, whatever their particular HLA match (fig. 5.20). One factor involved is the density of the dendritic cells present: both skin and bone marrow are rich in these APCs and are better able to mount a vigorous reaction. A second factor is the variation in the expression of the class II MHC. Some tissues (e.g., liver and kidney) produce relatively little antigen and thereby generate milder reactions. In the case of the liver, its large volume of tissue can act like a sponge for the antibody, causing its distribution in low concentrations throughout.

Very rapid (hyperacute) rejection can occur if an individual has had previous contact with specific foreign tissue antigens, usually by transfusion or previous transplantation. In such a sensitized individual, it may be only minutes before preformed antibodies initiate complement-mediated destruction of the transplanted tissue. As a result, a transplanted kidney, for example, rather than being firm, pink, and producing ample urine would be soft and pale, and would produce only drops of bloody urine. The antibodies appear to attach to the vascular endothelium, **7** triggering complement deposition, neutrophil infiltration, platelet and fibrin adhesion, and the formation of thrombi in the arterioles **8** and glomerular and peritubular capillaries. In the more usual transplant rejection problem, where there is some degree of MHC incompatibility, the reaction takes longer to develop.

MHC: Tissue Typing

The MHC occupies a significant part (1/3000th) of our entire genetic endowment (the human genome). The varied combination of alternate alleles gives rise to a great deal of variability from individual to individual in HLA type, in excess of perhaps one million! On average, you would have to test over 50,000 people from the general population before encountering a workable HLA match (range 1/450 for a common match, 1/750,000 for a rare match). Of course, the odds are greatly improved in related individuals and identical twins, who have identical or very closely similar HLA.

In practice, MHC antigens are not randomly distributed and selected in the population. Certain genes are more commonly found associated with each other, and certain constellations of HLA antigens are more common in specific racial groups. This pattern sometimes helps focus the search.

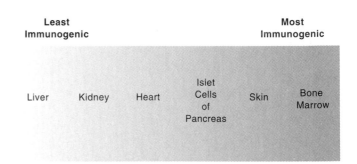

Figure 5.20   Tissues vary in their tendency to generate immune-mediated rejection.

Although the mechanism of rejection probably varies with the nature of the tissue and the degree of incompatibility, all the mechanisms require that the host T_H cells (helper T cells) come into contact with the graft tissue's MHC antigens. This contact is probably mediated by the dendritic cells of the graft tissue itself. These cells can interact directly with host T_H cells via their class II molecules or can process graft antigen and then present it to T_H cells in association with class II molecules. Either method will strongly activate T_H cells.

At this point, three different possibilities exist. In the first, antigen-specific T_H cells stimulate the activation and proliferation of appropriate T_C cells, which then mount a focused attack on the transplant tissue. In the second, responsive antigen-specific T_H cells move to the graft site, where they release lymphokines. These recruit monocyte/macrophages and T_C cells to the graft site and

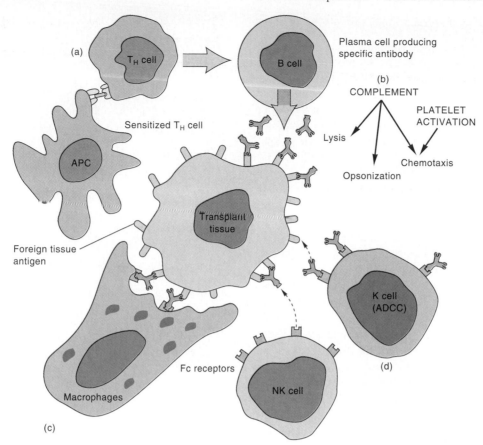

Figure 5.21   Overview of mechanisms of graft rejection. (*a*) Antigen-presenting cells facilitate T-cell sensitization, which enhances complement deposition and platelet aggregation (*b*) and, in turn, phagocytosis. Antibody binding makes possible antibody-dependent cellular cytotoxicity (*c*). NK cells attack the transplant tissue (*d*) while sensitized and activated T cells mobilize a chronic attack on the graft tissue.

maintain them at the scene while they destroy the tissue. (You may recognize this as a delayed-type hypersensitivity reaction.) As well as these direct cell-mediated mechanisms of graft rejection, there is a third mechanism in which antibodies play a role. The responsive T_H cell interacts with the appropriate B cell clone, producing a shower of antibodies to the implanted tissue's MHC antigens. These can trigger either complement-mediated graft damage or antibody-mediated cellular cytotoxicity. The latter is accomplished by K or killer cells.

Antibodies generated by MHC incompatibility can produce an acute rejection, either hours or days after transplantation or much later, when immunosuppressant therapy is terminated. Fortunately, HLA cross-matching has largely eliminated this pattern of rejection. There still remains the risk of chronic rejection, which is typically cell-mediated. It can be prevented only by very close cross-matching or continued immunosuppression. Sometimes purging the graft tissue of potential APCs, for example by infusing the donor

kidney with cytotoxic drugs or by subjecting skin grafts to ultraviolet light, enhances transplant acceptance.

Bone marrow transplantation presents a special rejection problem. In this case the graft is being done because there is a serious defect in the person's own bone marrow, for example leukemia or perhaps radiation damage that has reduced the numbers of blood-producing cells. Preliminary to the injection of donor bone marrow, the patient's bone marrow is destroyed, in order to remove the offending tumor cell lines in the case of leukemia. If the donor marrow contains mature competent T_H cells, these can set up an assault on the patient's cells because the donor T_H cells recognize the host tissue as foreign. This potentially fatal rejection of the host cells by the donor tissue is called **graft-versus-host** disease. It typically affects the host liver, skin, and GI mucosa. Close MHC matching and selective T-cell depletion of donor marrow are often effective in preventing this major problem. Figure 5.21 presents an overview of the mechanisms of graft rejection.

Improving Graft Survival

The goals for improving graft acceptance and survival are to avoid T_H cell sensitization and to suppress the response of any sensitized T_H cells that already exist. As we have just seen, the first goal is approached by careful tissue matching and by using cytotoxic agents to clean the donor organ of resident APCs. The pool of previously sensitized T_H cells can be reduced by administering cytotoxic or specific anti-T-cell agents, e.g., antithymocyte globulin (ATG) or antilymphocyte globulin (ALG), to the recipient.

Drugs are also routinely used to suppress the immune response to transplanted tissue. Corticosteroids (e.g., prednisone) have potent anti-inflammatory and immunosuppressant effects. By blocking the metabolic pathways that produce long-acting inflammatory mediators, they dramatically mute or reverse the rejection reaction.

Other drugs have a more focused effect. The commonly used immunosuppressant drug cyclosporine A (CSA) blocks the production of interleukin 2 (IL-2) in a T_H cell. As a result, the T_H cell can't communicate with itself; that is, the IL-2 can't feed signals back to the T_H cell and so the cell does not proliferate. Thus there is blockage of the stimulation of related B cells (suppression of antibody production) and cytotoxic T cells (suppression of T_C-mediated graft rejection). Cyclophosphamide, another immunosuppressant drug, has its effect through a quite different route. It interferes with the normal cycling of surface receptors, limiting T_H and B-cell responses to activation and proliferation signals. Figure 5.22 summarizes the approaches to improving graft survival.

Although corticosteroids, cyclosporine A, and cyclophosphamide greatly improve graft survival rates by suppressing a major protective response, they share the unfortunate side effect of making a person more vulnerable to infection. If the recipient develops an infection that is unresponsive to antibiotics, the immunosuppressant drugs must be discontinued, which means that the graft may be rejected.

IMMUNE DEFICIENCY SYNDROMES

Just as an immune system that functions too intensely can create problems, one that functions poorly can impair our capacity to deal effectively with infection. Much of our understanding of basic immune system function has been derived from observing the disease states that occur when one or more components of the immune system are congenitally absent or malfunctioning, usually through a genetic abnormality. These primary immunodeficiencies—B-cell deficiencies, T-cell deficiencies, combined B- and T-cell deficiencies, defects in phagocytosis or cytotoxicity, deficiencies in complement components—have provided "experiments in nature" from which scientists have drawn conclusions about the contribution of specific immune system components. The following discussion is organized in

RECIPIENT FACTORS

Matching of HLA-B and DR

Resolution of destructive lifestyle practices

Compliance with therapy

Purging recipient of sensitized T_H cells

DONOR FACTORS

Healthy organ

Harvesting and storage appropriate to specific tissue

Purging donor organ of resident APCs

DRUGS TO SUPPRESS IMMUNE RESPONSE

Corticosteroids (anti-inflammatory and immune suppressant)

Cyclosporine (blocks production of IL-2)

Cyclophosphamide (interference with receptor recycling)

Figure 5.22   Strategies used to improve graft survival.

terms of such components. However, as you can now appreciate, normal function depends on an interaction among them. As we will see, immune deficiency diseases often produce widespread and complex effects.

Primary Immune Deficiencies

Primary immune deficiencies are often genetically determined. They usually become apparent from recurrent or persistent infections suffered by infants beyond six months of age. This pattern suggests that the passive immunity conferred on an infant by the mother has not been replaced by normal active immune responses. Treatment of these individuals must take into account their extreme vulnerability to infection; for example, a child may have to live in a completely isolated environment. Vaccines may present an infection risk despite the fact that the virus has been attenuated. Even blood transfusions may be the cause of graft-versus-host disease, because the donor T cells are not resisted in their attack on what is, to them, foreign tissue.

B-Cell Deficiencies

In very general terms, B-cell deficiencies result in recurrent or overwhelming infections by viruses that are normally neutralized by antibody (e.g., the virus that causes rubella) or by bacteria that can resist phagocytosis unless they are well opsonized by antibody (e.g., *staphylococcus* or the *Haemophilus influenzae* responsible for meningitis in very young children). The B-cell deficit produces lowered or absent gammaglobulin levels (**hypogammaglobulinemia**). In **Bruton's agammaglobulinemia** the antibody levels are variable and may be profoundly depressed. This is an X-linked disease and therefore affects primarily males. The lymphoid tissues, with the exception of the thymus, are poorly developed. These are presumably the bursa-equivalent tissues, and their absence interferes with the maturation of the pre-B cells produced in bone marrow in normal numbers. T-cell numbers and function are normal, as is their coping with most viral and fungal infections. For unknown reasons, many individuals with Bruton's agammaglobulinemia develop autoimmune connective tissue diseases like rheumatoid arthritis and systemic lupus erythematosus.

T-Cell Deficiencies

In general, T-cell deficiencies result in chronic or recurrent infections with viruses (recall that T_C cells destroy virally infected cells) and yeasts/fungi (like *Candida* and *Histoplasma*) or intracellular bacteria (like the mycobacterium responsible for tuberculosis). Such deficiencies are one characteristic of the **DiGeorge syndrome.** This disorder is accompanied by various nonimmune abnormalities, in varying degrees. They include small jaw and cheeks, turned-down mouth, partial or complete absence of parathyroids, and heart defects. Because these structures all derive from associated embryonic structures they point, together with the absent or incomplete thymus, to a common developmental problem occurring about the seventh week of gestation. Depending on the particular developmental deficits, the newborn may face immediate, life-threatening disorders that derive from an interrupted aortic arch or hypocalcemia from impaired parathyroid hormone secretion. The failure of normal thymus development, which, like the other defects, may be due to viral infection, trauma, or perhaps a blood clot, leads to a profound T-cell deficit. The thymic hypoplasia is sometimes treated by transplantation of fetal thymic tissue. If blood products are given, they need to be irradiated to prevent donor T cells from engrafting and producing graft-versus-host disease.

In some cases of T-cell deficiency, people lack a specific clone of T cells, and therefore they cannot recognize and respond to the antigen specific to that T-cell receptor. Such is the case in **chronic mucocutaneous candidiasis.** 9, 10 People with this disorder suffer mild to severe *Candida* infections of the mucous membranes and skin without mounting an effective immune response because their T-cells don't recognize this antigen. The candidiasis may appear as thrush, an infection of the tongue or oral cavity involving ulcers and white spots. The vagina is also commonly colonized, and the esophagus is a less common but very serious target. The consequences of T_H cell deficiency are shown in figure 5.23.

Gene Therapy for SCID

In the spring of 1991 the first results were announced for new and exciting therapy. A little girl with the ADA deficiency form of SCID had responded well and was maintaining adequate lymphocyte counts and producing functional immune responses. In the treatment, doctors had separated circulating lymphocytes from her blood and had introduced a functional ADA gene into them by infecting them with an ADA-bearing virus; then they had expanded the isolated lymphocyte pool by treating it with interleukin 2 to promote proliferation, and finally they had reintroduced these cells to her body. If it were possible to isolate lymphocyte stem cells and treat them in this way, a permanent cure could be achieved. Very active research proceeds in this and other directions. This is the first example of effective human gene therapy and holds great promise.

Severe Combined Immunodeficiency Disease (SCID)

As the name implies, SCID is a very serious disorder of both T-cell and immunoglobulin production and function. It is inherited, either through autosomal recessive or X-linked transmission, and is typically a common (T and B) stem cell disorder. Without a successful bone marrow transplant, children with SCID succumb to opportunistic infections during their first year of life. The microorganisms involved include those that affect the AIDS patient: *Pneumocystis carinii, Candida, Pseudomonas,* cytomegalovirus, and the virus that causes herpes simplex. Marrow transplantation may fail, either because of NK-cell-mediated rejection or because of fatal graft-versus-host disease. About half the children with the autosomal recessive pattern of transmission lack an enzyme in their red and white blood cells called ADA (adenosine deaminase). Its absence leads to the accumulation of substances toxic to lymphocytes.

Table 5.7 summarizes the features of the disorders we have been discussing. It also gives information about several other primary immune deficiency diseases. These are quite rare, often genetic, disorders whose signs and symptoms are related to the lack of a particular component of the immune system.

Secondary Immune Deficiencies

The thymus achieves its peak size during adolescence, the time during which we contact and establish immunity against a wide variety of pathogens. After that it gradually atrophies, and by middle age it is only a fraction of its former size. Although the number of circulating T cells doesn't drop significantly, the capacity to mount a T-cell-mediated immune response does decrease with increasing age. (For example, there is a reduction in delayed-type

40349   40350

Table 5.7   Key Features of Selected Immunodeficiency States

Deficiency/Disease	Comments
B Cells	
Bruton's agammaglobulinemia (or Bruton's panhypogam-maglobulinemia)	Recurrent pyogenic (pus-forming) infections at 5 to 6 mo of age No B cells in peripheral blood X-linked genetics; more boys affected IgG levels variable, others absent Lack of "bursa-equivalent tissue"
Isolated IgA deficiency	Most common immunodeficiency condition (other than AIDS) Absence of secretory IgA Some may have more GI, pulmonary, and urogenital infections Transfusion may induce severe anaphylaxis
Acquired hypogammaglobulinemia (common variable immunodeficiency)	Depressed antibody levels Recurrent pyogenic infections from 15–35 yr Higher incidence of autoimmune disease
T Cells	
DiGeorge syndrome	Extreme T-cell deficit Associated with facial abnormalities, parathyroid and cardiac defects Chronic /recurrent viral, yeast, fungal, bacterial infections
Chronic mucocutaneous candidiasis	Chronic mild/severe *Candida* infections: thrush, vaginal, and esophageal infections
B and T Cells	
Severe combined immunodeficiency disease (SCID)	Genetic defect causing inadequate B/T-cell production Early onset (6 mo) Chronic/recurrent viral fungal infections Susceptible to graft-versus-host disease
Wiskott-Aldrich syndrome	X-linked; mostly boys affected Severe eczema, thrombocytopenia, allergies, recurrent infections
Ataxia-telangiectasia	Autosomal recessive inheritance Cerebellar degeneration (ataxia) and telangiectasia (small vessel dilation) Decreased antibody production and T-helper activity

hypersensitivity reactions in the tuberculin test.) At the same time, there is an increase in the levels of circulating autoantibodies. These are self-reactive antibodies and are involved in a variety of autoimmune diseases, to be described in some detail at the end of this chapter. Thus there are age-related trends in immune system function that may be associated with impaired immunity and the development of autoimmune disorders.

Diet can also affect immune function. Those subjected to severe caloric or protein malnutrition, particularly children, suffer impaired T-cell, complement, and neutrophil function. They are therefore particularly vulnerable to bacteria that require opsonization and phagocytosis or T-cell-mediated cellular immunity. Selective deficiencies can also lead to impaired immunity. For example, a zinc deficiency, which might be caused by a failure to absorb

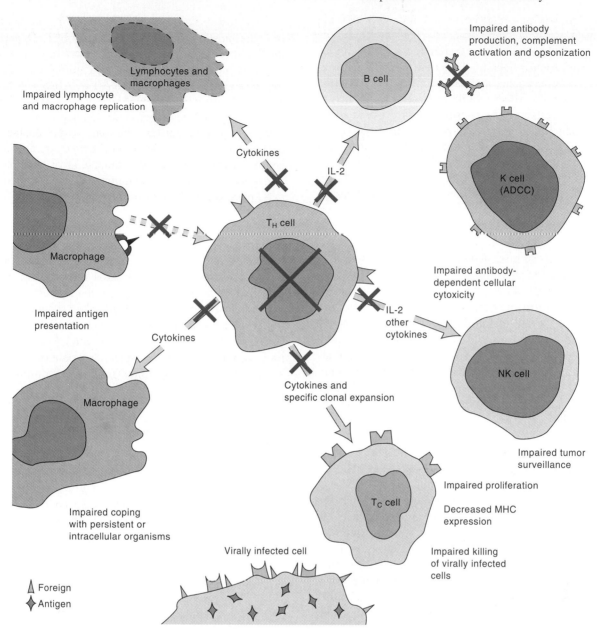

Figure 5.23   Summary of the impact of drastically reduced T_H cell numbers.

zinc, by zinc loss through diarrhea, by severe burns, or by renal disease, can severely impair both T-and B-cell function.

Besides opening the barrier to infection that the skin usually provides, extensive burns can lead to both a generalized suppression of immune function and focal, antigen-specific immune suppression. Complement levels are depressed and neutrophil chemotaxis and cytotoxicity are reduced, so that the burn victim is more vulnerable to infection by bacteria that are difficult to engulf without opsonization (e.g., *Haemophylus influenzae* or *Staphylococcus*).

Impaired immunity can be secondary to a number of other disorders. For example, diabetes mellitus produces vascular changes and impaired leukocyte function, which together reduce both inflammatory and specific immune responses and contribute to the recurrent and prolonged infections characteristic of that disease. Malignancies of bone marrow (leukemia and myeloproliferative disorders) and lymphoid tissues (lymphoma) can suppress immune function, as can certain infections (e.g., congenital rubella, cytomegalovirus, tuberculosis, coccidiomycosis).

Deficiencies may also be associated with medical treatments (iatrogenic deficiencies). The most obvious example has been mentioned: infections associated with the use of immunosuppressant drugs in transplantation. Chemotherapeutic agents and radiation used for treating cancer differentially affect rapidly replicating cells such as blood-forming cells in bone marrow and lymphoid tissues. Besides producing a generally lowered white blood cell count, tumor suppression therapy can paralyze both T- and B-cell responses to a specific pathogen by blocking clonal expansion. Other drugs (e.g., some anticonvulsants, antimicrobials, tranquilizers, or analgesics) are directly toxic or produce immune-mediated effects on mature lymphocytes. Depression of immune function is a potential side effect that must be monitored routinely with many medications. In the same vein, surgery and anaesthesia can depress T- and B-cell function and induce severe lymphocyte deficiency for up to a month.

The correlation between presumably stressful life events (divorce, death of family member, promotion, job loss, etc.) and the incidence of disease (including infection) was noted twenty years ago. Stress appears to reactivate latent viral infections and may have a role in making individuals more vulnerable to new infection. There is evidence for interaction between the neuroendocrine and immune systems: many lymphoid tissues are innervated, and immune system cells can both produce and respond to agents with neuroendocrine activity (e.g., endorphins, ACTH, TSH, interleukin 1). Corticosteroids produced during stress reactions depress macrophage production of interleukin 1, and this change could interfere with antigen presentation and initiation of the immune response. As well, corticosteroids can have the effect of depressing IL-2 production by helper T cells, thereby affecting the primary immune response and subsequent sensitization. The interactions in stress are complex and only partially understood. From what is known, stress could be the basis of either immune system hyperactivity or hypofunction. For vulnerable individuals, stress may play an important role in immune-mediated illness (e.g., autoimmune disease) or immune deficiency.

Acquired Immune Deficiency Syndrome (AIDS)

A decade has elapsed since the United States Centers for Disease Control identified a cluster of five cases of *Pneumocystis carinii* pneumonia (PCP) [11] among young homosexual males in the Los Angeles area, two of whom soon died. To monitor this flare-up of a usually rare disease, the Centers for Disease Control (CDC) quickly established a category for people who acquired diseases that were rare except in those with profoundly depressed cellular immune function. This included people with Kaposi's

sarcoma (a rare skin cancer) [12] or any of a limited number of opportunistic infections, particularly PCP. Opportunistic implies that the infection flourishes because of defects or impaired function in an individual's immune system. With this surveillance definition, the era of AIDS was born. By 1984 the **human immunodeficiency virus (HIV)** had been isolated [13] and described, and mechanisms of transmission were being identified: intimate sexual contact; direct contamination of blood as occurs between intravenous drug abusers using contaminated equipment, or hemophiliac or transfusion recipients of contaminated blood or blood products; passage of virus from mother to a fetus, at birth or through breast milk.

Worldwide estimates place the HIV infection rate at perhaps one person in four hundred, about half of the U.S. rate. In Africa the infection rate for women is about equal to that for men, with heterosexual transmission being the principal route. By contrast, in Canada most cases are in male homosexuals, while Europe falls somewhere between the two extremes. But any statistic on HIV infection or AIDS incidence is the stark outcome of processes much more problematic and complex. No pattern of incidence should be taken as grounds for either complacence or paranoia.

HIV-1: The AIDS Virus

Most researchers accept the central importance of the human immunodeficiency virus (HIV) in the development of acquired immune deficiency syndrome (AIDS). Several features that are essential to our understanding of the transmission and replication of HIV are depicted in figure 5.24. To reproduce themselves, viruses must gain access to the genetic and metabolic machinery of a host cell. The knobs on the surface of the virus particle, called gp120 (for glycoprotein of 120,000 gram molecular weight), have affinity for a molecule called CD4, which is produced and displayed on the surface of selected cells of the body. Helper T cells (recall that they are also called T_4, because of the presence of CD4) are richly covered, as are monocyte/macrophage cells and some B cells. There is evidence that other cells in the body have gp120 receptors, for example, glial (support) cells in the brain and chromaffin (unicellular glandular) cells in the duodenum, colon, and rectum. Of all these, T_4 lymphocytes are the most numerous and widely distributed targets of HIV infection.

Entry to the host cell initially involves the binding of gp120 molecules to the outer portions of CD4 molecules. This helps bring the virus particle into close association with the T_4 cell membrane, allowing for the exposure of the gp41 molecule. Fusion of the virus and T_4 membranes follows, thus bringing the viral core and its genetic material into the cell (fig. 5.25). It is this viral core protein (usually called p24) that is involved in the tests used for detecting HIV infection.

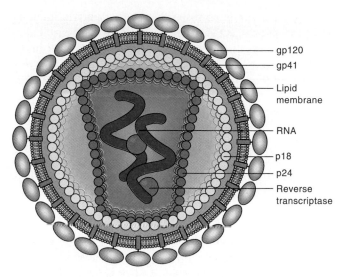

Figure 5.24   Structure of the HIV virus particle.

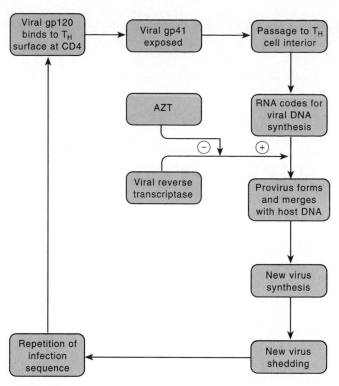

Figure 5.25   Sequence of events in HIV infection. The key function of viral reverse transcriptase is blocked by AZT to prevent synthesis of new viral particles.

You will note in figure 5.24 that the core contains two strands of RNA (rather than the DNA we usually associate with genetic information storage) and two molecules of **reverse transcriptase.** It is these features that give HIV its designation as a **retrovirus:** replication of HIV requires that RNA first be transcribed back into a DNA form (hence the reverse transcriptase enzyme). The viral DNA formed in this way is then incorporated into the host cell chromosomes and in this form is known as a **provirus.** It may remain dormant or latent here for years, or it may immediately trigger the production of viral RNA, which, using the metabolic machinery of the host cell, will trigger production and assembly of the HIV **virion** (virus particle). **Zidovudine** (also called AZT, azidothymidine, or retrovir) is an antiviral drug that delays the development of AIDS and slows its progression. It acts by interfering with the normal action of reverse transcriptase (fig. 5.25). AZT interferes by becoming incorporated into viral DNA in the place of a normal DNA building block. Other DNA constituents cannot attach to the AZT molecule, so transcription effectively terminates at that point. Zidovudine has a similar (and thereby potentially harmful) effect on host DNA replication, but only at concentrations much greater than normal therapeutic doses. In some patients, even the lower therapeutic doses produce progressive bone marrow toxicity. This usually leads to anemia, depressed neutrophil counts, and some bleeding abnormalities.

One of the elements produced by the normal transcription of HIV, gp120, is exported to the surface of the host cell. When the virion is shed from a cell, it is through a process of budding of an assembled viral core in a sheath of host cell plasma membrane studded with gp120 molecules. The virion can then go on to infect other CD4–bearing cells. As well, host cells coated with gp120 can readily stick to and fuse with other host cells that display CD4 to

form **giant cells.** These are particularly noted in brain biopsies of advanced AIDS-associated neurological disease. Their role in the pathophysiology of AIDS is not clear, but the process of giant cell formation provides a means whereby uninfected cells can incorporate HIV.

Why does full-blown AIDS occur one year after infection in one person, but not for 12 or 15 years in another? When an infected T_H cell proliferates, it duplicates its DNA, including the perhaps multiple provirus inclusions, thereby replicating the virus. The provirus also contains a segment with affinity for IL-2 that triggers viral transcription. As you will recall, activated T_H cells produce IL-2, providing another stimulus to viral replication. These mechanisms might be important for individuals with a larger exposure to pathogens, who have more T_H activation and therefore more IL-2 stimulus. This would be the case, for example, in intravenous drug users or people with weakened primary nonspecific resistance.

Before leaving the description of the AIDS virus, let us comment on the role of the monocyte/macrophage in the development of HIV infection. Recall that the monocyte is a freely traveling cell found in the bloodstream. After about three days, monocytes pass into the tissues and take on the morphology and phagocytic function of macrophages (see chapter 2). Some studies have shown these cells to have a higher rate of HIV infection than T_4 cells. However, they appear not to be involved in a major way in the immune defects of HIV infection. They may serve as a reservoir of HIV infective particles and perhaps play a role in the spread of HIV into tissues, particularly the central nervous system.

The Pathogenesis of AIDS

The current understanding is that the **latent period,** a theoretical period during which the HIV virus is present but inactive, may not really exist. That is, with more precise ways of monitoring the progression of HIV infection, it appears there is no period when viral replication does not occur. The clinical picture, on the other hand, supports and is the original source of the idea of a latent, inactive infection. Infection is followed in weeks to months by an early **acute phase** in 30–50% of people. This lasts perhaps a few weeks and resembles influenza or infectious mononucleosis. The symptoms include sore throat, muscle aches, fever, swollen glands, perhaps rash. Nervous system symptoms ranging from headache to meningitis may be present. At some point, for most people between 3 and 17 weeks after infection, **seroconversion** occurs, i.e., HIV proteins reach the blood. Blood is tested for the presence of these antigenic elements of the HIV virus with the **enzyme-linked immunosorbent assay (ELISA).** While the ELISA, if correctly done, detects 99% of individuals in whom the virus is replicating and is 99% specific to HIV, a positive ELISA is followed by a more complex and costly procedure called a **Western blot assay** 14 to confirm the presence of specific HIV proteins, e.g., p24 or gp120.

The middle or **chronic phase** of the disease can last for years. Some people are asymptomatic for much of this time, but for many others it is characterized by chronic lymphadenopathy (swollen lymph nodes). This may be the only symptom in an otherwise apparently healthy person. The swelling reflects chronic immune stimulation, particularly of B cells. These produce antibodies, but they are ineffective in neutralizing HIV. During this period HIV continues to replicate slowly, possibly being held in check by HIV-specific cytotoxic T lymphocytes. Throughout this phase there is a gradual drop in T_4 cell concentration in the blood (from the normal $800/mm^3$). As well, there is a progressive increase in the proportion of circulating T_4 cells that are infected with HIV, from perhaps 1/100,000 to 1/100 in full-blown AIDS. The rate of infection of T_4 cells in the lymph nodes is considerably higher. These changes are often clinically silent until the T_4 levels drop below $200/mm^3$.

At about this point ($T_4 < 200/mm^3$), HIV infection enters the final or **crisis phase.** The already established chronic lymphadenopathy is complicated by long-lasting fever (three months or longer), persistent night sweats, weight loss, and diarrhea. Skin tests that measure delayed hypersensitivity—that is, the individual's ability to gener-

ate a cellular immune response against specific immunogenic proteins injected under the skin—will be negative or weak. This result indicates a profound breakdown in T_H-cell-mediated immunity. T_4 counts are reduced significantly and the normal 2:1 ratio of CD4 to CD8 is reversed. This stage of the disease has been called **ARC (AIDS-related complex)** and is designated **CDC class IVa** (for the U.S. agency Centers for Disease Control). In this stage, the person probably has persistent viral or fungal infection of the skin and mucous membranes, including thrush 15 , herpes simplex (a viral infection producing painful and persistent sores in the anal, genital, and mouth areas), and infection of the vagina by *Candida albicans* (the same fungus as causes thrush). Oral hairy leukoplakia (fuzzy, adherent, white patches, usually on the tongue), may also be observed.

AIDS is diagnosed when a person positive for HIV develops any of a variety of infections or neoplasms that are highly unusual in people with normal immune function (see table 5.7). **PCP,** pneumonia 16 caused by the protozoan *Pneumocystis carinii,* is the most common life-threatening opportunistic infection contributing to the definition of AIDS. It appears in up to 50% of AIDS victims. Even with prophylactic use of inhaled pentamidine, an antiprotozoal agent, many patients develop pneumocystis pneumonia and of those, 5–30% will experience often fatal respiratory failure. The pathogenesis of AIDS is presented in figure 5.26.

Kaposi's sarcoma (KS), a skin cancer causing dark, splotchy lesions, 17 develops in 15–25% of HIV positive individuals, in whom it often follows an aggressive course. It is far more common among HIV positive homosexual men than among intravenous drug users or other risk groups and may develop while the person is otherwise relatively healthy. Kaposi's sarcoma may be more likely to develop in HIV infection because the function of antitumor natural killer (NK) cells is impaired. There is also growing evidence that factors released by a variety of cells, including activated T_H cells and the tumor cells themselves, are responsible for fostering dramatic tumor growth. The fact that KS can arise in the absence of HIV infection, among other evidence, raises the possibility that KS develops from a cancer-causing virus that infects people independently, but that its action is promoted by the development of HIV infection.

Some otherwise rare opportunistic infections associated with AIDS bear noting. The parasitic protozoan *Toxoplasmosis gondii* often infects the brain and can lead to seizures and coma. The fungus *Cryptococcus* not only can cause meningitis but may damage the liver, bone, skin, and other tissues. **Cytomegalovirus,** 18 a viral agent to which 70% of us have been exposed, can cause pneumonia, encephalitis, blindness, and inflammation of the gastrointestinal tract in AIDS.

14   451

15   21213

16   40556

17   40407

18   464

Figure 5.26   The pathogenesis of AIDS. The chronic phase follows several weeks after the initial infection and may last for months to years.

While various factors probably play a role in the development and progression of HIV infection, the current, widely accepted view is that there is an unavoidable continuum progressing from HIV infection to ARC and then to AIDS.

AZT Therapy

All therapeutic agents identified to date, including AZT (zidovudine), have potential toxic side effects and these must be balanced against anticipated benefits. Trials with zidovudine published in 1990 indicate a delay in the onset of AIDS with patients started on the drug when they experienced mild symptomatic illness and T_4 cell counts of $200–499/mm^3$. A second study began therapy in asymptomatic patients with counts below $500/mm^3$. Progression to symptomatic illness was delayed, the decline in T_4 counts slowed, and the drug was better tolerated than it was by patients with full-blown AIDS. An added benefit of early treatment may be in reducing the infectivity of the HIV positive person. Extensive use of a medication on an actively mutating microbial strain increases the likelihood of developing resistant strains and this has been observed in *in vitro* testing of zidovudine. Although our discussion has highlighted AZT because of its demonstrated efficacy, a

host of other antiviral agents and strategies are being vigorously explored, and many researchers believe that a vaccine will be available by the end of the 1990s. Much that we have written here may be outdated when you read it.

HIV and the Nervous System

Earlier, we referred to the CNS manifestations sometimes accompanying or following the period of seroconversion and acute HIV infection: headache and a condition called aseptic meningitis—"aseptic" because no microbial agent can be recovered from the cerebrospinal fluid (CSF). At the other end of the spectrum is the finding that 70–90% of those dying with AIDS or ARC show brain and spinal cord pathology at autopsy. CNS or neuromuscular abnormalities can be found in up to 80% of infected adults, so that the CDC currently recognizes dementia in HIV positive adults as an indicator of AIDS, even without the presence of other secondary infections or tumors. Other CNS disorders include primary CNS syndromes associated with HIV, opportunistic viral and nonviral CNS infections and neoplasms, and HIV-related neuromuscular diseases. Many of these conditions are described in more detail in the chapters on neuropathology. Here, we will consider only the major problems.

Table 5.8	Nervous System Disorders Associated with HIV Infection and AIDS

Central Nervous System

Disorders probably attributable to HIV infection
  Meningitis—in acute stage of HIV infection
  Spinal cord disease—principally motor disorders
  Progressive brain damage in children (2 mo–5 yr)—
  impaired growth, motor dysfunction, death
  Progressive brain damage in adults—behavioral, cognitive
  and motor impairment (AIDS dementia complex)
Opportunistic infections
  Viral—fatal demyelinating diseases and other infections
  Nonviral—fungal and/or bacterial infections causing
  meningitis and/or abscesses
Neoplasia
  Lymphomas infiltrating CNS

Peripheral Nervous System

Diseases Affecting Peripheral Nerves
  Various demyelinating diseases
  Various motor and sensory disorders

The most common primary CNS syndrome associated with HIV in adults is chronic HIV encephalopathy, widely called AIDS dementia complex. While uncommon (2–3%) in asymptomatic HIV positive people, as many as 50% of those with lymphadenopathy experience symptoms such as difficulty concentrating and slowing of verbal and motor responses. As HIV infection progresses, there is an increasing incidence of withdrawal, personality changes, clumsiness, mutism, seizures, partial paralysis, psychosis, incontinence, eventual confinement to bed, and relative unresponsiveness. The direct role of HIV is implicated by the presence of HIV in monocytes, macrophages, and multinucleated giant cells in the brains of people with AIDS dementia complex and other CNS changes. Among other explanations being explored, two bear noting. First, the dysfunction may be due to cytokines and other agents released from macrophages or astrocytes, perhaps in response to direct infection of astrocytes. Second, it is possible that gp120 alters neuronal regulation of neural function. Some other CNS complications of AIDS are presented in table 5.8.

Impact of HIV Infection on Helper T Cells

In a strict sense people do not die of HIV infection. They die of the opportunistic infections and neoplasms that thrive when normal helper T-cell function is paralyzed. What we know about HIV-associated alterations in immune function is to a large extent conjecture based on our understanding

of normal function. In many people, T_4 counts are at less than $100/mm^3$ when AIDS is diagnosed and they subsequently fall lower. This reduction in T_4 counts is central to the pathophysiology of HIV infection. Recall that a specific antigen is presented to the members of the responsive clone of T_H by APCs, which at the same time release IL-1. The T_H cell then becomes activated, produces IL-2, and subsequently proliferates. Equally important are the other cytokines released by T_H cells, those that cause activation and proliferation of B cells, stimulate lymphocyte and macrophage production, induce MHC class I and II, recruit and focus the activities of macrophages, etc. In turn, cells that respond to T_H cytokines produce cytokines of their own.

The chronic reduction of T_H cell cytokines leads to a depletion of monocyte/macrophages (reduced production of IL-1 and TNF) and neutrophils (decreased inflammatory response). With the reduction of antigen-specific antibodies, a host of secondary defects appear: decreased function of antibody-dependent cellular cytotoxicity (ADCC), decreased complement fixation to pathogens, with consequent impaired inflammatory response and decreased opsonization, and less effective phagocytosis. Also involved is a decreased expression of MHC antigens, causing impaired antigen presentation and natural killer cell (NK) function, decreased chemotaxis, activation, and phagocytic activity by macrophages and neutrophils, and failure of NK cells to proliferate and activate, causing less effective killing of tumor cells. In the face of this hypofunction how do we reconcile the lymphadenopathy and hypergammaglobulinemia (excess antibodies in circulation)? Two explanations are probable. First, opportunistic infection with certain agents such as Epstein-Barr virus (EBV) and cytomegalovirus (CMV) causes generalized direct stimulation of B cells to produce antibodies and as a consequence lymph nodes swell. Second, certain proteins or glycoproteins produced when HIV replicates may stimulate B cells. The overview in figure 5.27 provides a helpful summary.

Transmission of HIV Infection

HIV has been demonstrated in the saliva, tears, urine, CSF, serum, T_H cells, and macrophages of infected people. Semen and vaginal secretions are particularly rich in HIV and infected lymphocytes. At this point it seems likely that these T_4 cells are the principal vehicle for transmitting HIV from one person to another. The HIV virus itself is relatively fragile, so casual contact (shaking hands, eating together, living in close association) is not likely to cause infection.

What activities do carry a high risk of transmission? Any activity that can pass large numbers of infected T_4 cells directly into the bloodstream or to areas that bear receptors for HIV. Sexual activity, especially if mucous membrane damage from trauma or an infection is present,

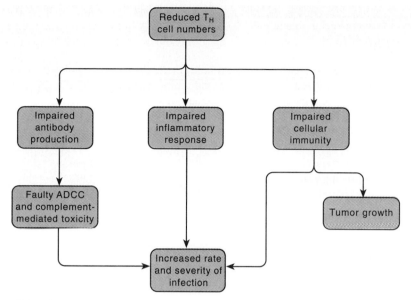

Figure 5.27 Consequences of T_H cell depletion in AIDS.

is the most common mode of transmission. Direct injection of infected lymphocytes or HIV is also a very effective means of infection, which occurs among intravenous drug users who share contaminated needles, syringes, or other drug paraphernalia. It is also the mechanism affecting recipients of transfusions of blood or blood products derived from pooled blood components from many donors. AIDS cases have been traced to a single unit of transfused blood, and, even with screening, a slight risk remains. The screening tests used have a very slight false-negative rate and, more significantly, there can be a window of infectivity (perhaps longer than four months) before an individual shows seroconversion and gives a positive test. This means that blood can test negative prior to a transfusion and still carry the virus to a transfusion recipient.

To put the problem into perspective, anyone who is infected is producing HIV particles. Infectivity probably increases with the number of HIV particles and number of infected T_4 cells produced and passed, and therefore infectivity increases as the HIV infection progresses. The wild card in this game is that apparently some individuals are inherently more infectious, perhaps because they carry a variant HIV strain that is more resilient and virulent. As we have noted, some evidence suggests that treatment with zidovudine may decrease infectivity.

The chief targets of efforts to contain the spread of HIV continue to be the established North American risk groups—homosexual and bisexual men, intravenous drug users and their sexual partners. However, spread of the virus in the heterosexual population has now become a major concern as well. AIDS is growing fastest among young, sexually active adults, and teens are at a growing risk. While condom use should be routine, this precaution merely reduces the risk of infection; some risk still remains. Of course, it makes sense to avoid sexual contact with indi-

viduals who belong to, or are in intimate contact with the members of, one of the high-risk groups. But it isn't always easy to get an accurate idea of the background of a potential sex partner. A study published in the *New England Journal of Medicine* (March 15, 1990) points out the difficulty of establishing risk if the people you ask tell lies.

Health Care Workers and the Risk of HIV Infection

Table 5.9 presents a variety of data on HIV infection among populations with which a health care worker may come in working contact. At the extreme of exposure are those nurses and doctors whose professional work is exclusively with AIDS patients. The chief source of risk for them is direct, accidental inoculation of contaminated blood or tissues by needle, wire, bone, or scalpel punctures or exposure of blood to the delicate mucous membranes of the eye. Bites by infected persons have not been shown to transmit HIV, and contact with body fluids other than blood also carries relatively low risk. Pricking with a needle is estimated to lead to HIV infection in about 0.4% of these cases (about 1/50 the risk of hepatitis B infection after a single exposure!). This may be considered low and, in fact, relatively few health care workers have contracted AIDS; however, compared with the estimated risk of a woman being infected through a single incident involving vaginal sex with an infected man (0.2%), it is significant.

Cardiac surgeons, assistants, and scrub nurses can experience a risk of HIV infection in the range of 0.5% per year or greater, depending on the nature of the surgery and the patient group. Saws and drills can produce tiny airborne fluid droplets containing infective HIV particles or lymphocytes, another source of risk for surgical or dental personnel.

Sex, Lies and HIV

A group of 665 18–25-year-old college students in southern California completed anonymous questionnaires assessing sexual behavior, HIV-related risk reduction, and their experiences with deception when dating. Of the 422 who were sexually active (196 men, 226 women) the following percentages reported dishonesty.

	Men	Women
Has told a lie in order to have sex	34%	10%*
Has been sexually involved with more than one person	32%	23%*
Has had sex with a partner who did not know HIV status	68%	59%
Has been lied to for purposes of sex	47%	60%*
Would lie about having negative HIV-antibody test	20%	4%*
Would understate number of previous partners	47%	42%
Would never disclose a single episode of sexual infidelity	43%	34%*

" The implications of our findings are clear. . . . Patients should be cautioned that safe-sex strategies are always advisable, despite arguments to the contrary from partners."

* Responses of men significantly different from responses of women.

Source: From *New England Journal of Medicine,* Vol. 322, No. 11, March 15, 1990, pp. 774–775.

Table 5.9   Prevalence or Incidence of HIV Infection in a Variety of Populations (Studies Done between 1988 and 1990)

Prevalence of HIV in Students at 19 U.S. Universities (1990)[1]

Overall	0.2% (range 0.0%–0.8%)
Men	0.5%
Women	0.02%

Seroconversion Rates—Navy and Marines (1986–1988)[2,3]

Navy	0.69/1000/year
White men	0.53
Black men	2.05 (3.9 ×)
Men	5 × rate for women
Blacks	3.5 × rate for whites

Marines 0.28/1000/year

[1]Data from Gayle et al., *NEJM,* Vol. 323, No. 22, p. 1538.
[2]Data from *JAMA,* Vol. 262, No. 22, pp. 3161–3165.
[3]Rate per 1000 people who became HIV positive per year.

HIV Prevalence for Clientele of Various Clinics

Women in an obstetrics service	2%
Women at Baltimore STD clinic	3%
Women at New York Colposcopy Clinic for evaluation of abnormal Papanicolaou smears	10.6%
All clients at inner city emergency services	20% (estimate)
All clients at New York inner city emergency service	33% (estimate)

As the number of AIDS cases increases, it becomes clear that health care workers must take routine precautions with all patients. And this, of course, is a two-way street: 1991 marked the first case in which a patient sued a health care worker (in this case an infected dentist) for liability in transmitting HIV.

AUTOIMMUNE DISEASES

Autoimmune diseases are distinguished by several criteria, which are listed in table 5.10. Applying these criteria strictly, we would arrive at a very short list but, as you may be aware, many disorders are said to be probably or possibly autoimmune. The two best candidates are strangely at

---

Table 5.10	The Criteria Applied in Determining That a Given Disease Is an Autoimmune Disorder

1. Antibody or T cells against self-antigens have been demonstrated.
2. Specific interaction between antibody or T cells and tissues involved in the disease process has been demonstrated.
3. Immune dysfunction is the primary factor in the disease.
4. Other possible nonimmune causes do not induce the immune defect.
5. Disease is transferable to others via antibody or T cells only.*
6. Autoimmune characteristics of the disease can be duplicated in experimental systems.*

Asterisks indicate more stringent criteria applied by some, but not all, investigators.

---

opposite poles of a continuum, ranging from organ-specific to systemic. They are also at the extremes of autoantibody specificity. **Hashimoto's thyroiditis,** 19 one of the first diseases to be associated with autoantibodies, affects mostly middle-aged women, causing goiter and hypothyroidism. In affected patients, the serum usually has high titers of antibodies to thyroglobulin, the protein in the thyroid follicles that binds and stores thyroid hormones, and the immune-mediated disease is restricted to the thyroid gland. Systemic lupus erythematosus (SLE), on the other hand, is a systemic disease with a bewildering assortment of autoantibodies. Arthritis, skin lesions, fever, and kidney disease are some of the disorders that recur in individuals affected by SLE.

The best-defined autoimmune diseases are also clearly influenced by genetics, as shown by familial trends toward increased autoantibodies and increased incidence of autoimmune disease. Genetics also appears to strongly influence the specific nature of the autoimmune disease; that is, there seems to be a general familial tendency toward elevations of particular autoantibodies. On the other hand, various environmental factors, including diet, drugs, chemicals, and viruses, are also implicated in the etiology of autoimmune disorders. Genetics sets a predisposition, perhaps expressed in elevated specific autoantibodies, but (in most cases) the environmental factors must also intervene to produce the immune system derangement that results in autoimmune disease. The tendency for women to be more affected than men (for example, SLE afflicts ten times as many women of childbearing age as men) presents an ongoing puzzle. Estrogen is implicated but a satisfactory explanation is lacking.

Table 5.11 lists the more commonly encountered diseases that probably have a basis in autoimmunity. We will deal with many of these in some detail in later chapters, in connection with the pathology of the system in which they primarily occur. The remainder of this chapter deals with some largely multisystem autoimmune disorders: SLE, progressive systemic sclerosis, dermatomyositis, and Sjögren's syndrome.

Systemic Lupus Erythematosus

Systemic lupus erythematosus (SLE) is an autoimmune disorder characterized by acute or insidious onset with widely variable systemic effects. Also typical are periods of remission and intense exacerbation, especially in the initial stages of the disease. However, there are so many different signs and symptoms that diagnosis is difficult. The name lupus, which means wolflike, comes from a rash over the cheeks and the bridge of the nose, which appears in some patients. SLE affects 1 in 700 women aged 20 to 64 and 1 in 245 American black women, but it can strike anyone at virtually any age.

Diagnosis has been made easier by the fact that virtually every SLE patient is positive for antinuclear antibodies (ANAs)—antibodies directed against a variety of nuclear components including DNA. With immunofluorescence tests, it is possible to identify such antibodies adhering to nuclear features. While high proportions of patients with other systemic autoimmune disorders also are positive for ANAs, this test is one of the eleven criteria proposed for the identification of SLE patients (table 5.12). A person is said to have SLE if any four or more criteria are met together or in sequence at any time.

SLE occurs when, for unknown reasons, there is a breakdown of the mechanisms that maintain self-tolerance (fig. 5.28). Genetics and environmental factors probably combine as etiological factors. Estrogens may also be involved; that would explain the greater incidence of SLE in women. Whatever the cause, the resultant production of autoantibodies to a wide variety of targets, including nuclear antigens and cytoplasmic and membrane components, leads to the formation of immune complexes that can deposit in vessel walls and vulnerable organs (glomeruli of kidneys, choroid plexus of the brain, the skin, perhaps joint connective tissue). There they activate complement, whose breakdown products mediate neutrophil attack on endothelia and basement membranes (type III hypersensitivity). Although the ANAs do not appear to have a direct role in pathology in this case by binding to nuclear proteins, other antibodies do. Those against erythrocytes, leukocytes, or platelets can produce serious blood disorders (type II hypersensitivity). IgG and IgM autoantibodies bind to the cell surface and result in cell death by any of three routes: enhanced phagocytosis through opsonization, lysis through the membrane attack complex, or antibody-dependent cellular cytotoxicity.

19 39055

Table 5.11   Selected Disorders with an Autoimmune Etiology or Pathogenesis. Also Indicated Are the Tissues Affected by Self-Antibodies or Immune Complexes.

Disorders	Target Tissues
Widely Accepted as Autoimmune	
Hashimoto's thyroiditis	Thyroid gland
Grave's disease	Thyroid, eyes, skin
Systemic lupus erythematosus	Systemic
Goodpasture's syndrome	Lung, kidney
Autoimmune thrombocytopenia	Platelets
Autoimmune atrophic gastritis of pernicious anemia	Gastric mucosa
Myasthenia gravis	Acetylcholine receptor
Insulin-dependent diabetes mellitus	Pancreatic islet cells
Rheumatoid arthritis	Systemic
Systemic sclerosis	Systemic connective tissues, especially skin
Sjögren's syndrome	Systemic
Probably Autoimmune	
Polymyositis-dermatomyositis	Muscle, skin
Chronic active hepatitis	Liver
Ulcerative colitis	Colon, small intestine
Primary biliary cirrhosis	Liver

Table 5.12   Criteria for the Diagnosis of SLE. The Disease Is Deemed To Be Present When Four of These Eleven Criteria Are Met.

Criterion	Comment
Malar rash	Erythema over the cheekbones
Discoid rash	Raised scaly patches on skin
Photosensitivity	Skin rash on exposure to sunlight
Oral ulcers	Ulcers in oropharynx and/or nasopharynx (usually painless)
Arthritis	Acute inflammation in two or more peripheral joints
Serositis	Acute inflammation in pleurae or pericardium
Renal disorder	Loss of protein in urine; blood cells or hemoglobin in tubule
Neurologic disorder	Seizures or psychoses without other identifiable cause
Blood disorder	Deficiency of platelets or white cells, anemia from red cells lysis
Immune disorder	Various antibodies identifiable
Antinuclear antibody	Antibodies to DNA in 50% of non-drug-induced SLE

Pathogenesis

The criteria for diagnosing SLE are listed in table 5.12. Chronic fever and fatigue and weight loss are experienced by the vast majority of patients. Widespread vasculitis, secondary to the immune complex deposition, affects small arteries and arterioles. Vasculitis is particularly evident in the skin and muscles and may be responsible for the muscle aching noted by one-third of patients. Immune complex disposition is probably responsible for the butterfly rash (erythema) over the cheeks and bridge of the nose, as well as for the raised, scaly, discoid rash found on the scalp and other parts of the body. Hair loss (alopecia), sometimes permanent, may accompany the disfiguring discoid lesions.

The kidney is involved, at least minimally, in almost all cases of SLE. Mild glomerular damage [20] can give rise to the passage of large molecules (proteinuria) and cells (hematuria) into the urine, where they can be identified by

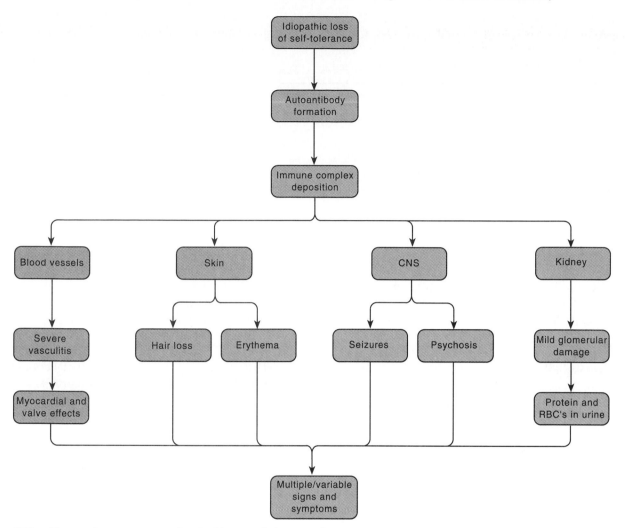

Figure 5.28   Signs and symptoms associated with systemic lupus erythematosus.

routine urinalysis. One cause of death in SLE can be renal failure. Heart problems can include pericarditis, myocarditis secondary to acute vasculitis, and the development of small (1–3 mm), warty, sterile vegetation anywhere on the valve leaflets. The basis for the disturbance of central nervous system function is not well established. Although some patients experience seizures or psychosis, many more have subtle mental and psychological disorders. Autoantibodies to neurons and to endothelial phospholipids have been demonstrated. Those to endothelia appear to initiate a thickening of the vessel intima that can limit blood flow to brain tissues and may explain some of the CNS symptoms. The arthritis, while causing pain and discomfort, doesn't damage the joint as it does in rheumatoid arthritis, and joint swelling is variable.

Treatment   As our understanding of autoimmune disorders improves, a variety of treatments, now being experimentally explored, will be used with SLE. In the meantime, two principal approaches are employed. Corticosteroids, including topical creams, are used as sparingly as possible to alleviate acute symptoms but limit the harmful side effects. In patients with serious life-threatening symptoms, cytotoxic immunosuppressants like cyclophosphamide and azathioprine can be used. These drugs can have serious side effects (e.g., increased risk of cancer for both drugs, and bladder damage for cyclophosphamide).

Drug-Induced Systemic Lupus Erythematosus

Certain drugs can induce a lupuslike syndrome in susceptible individuals. In this case, the reason is probably a genetically determined metabolic deficiency that results in the accumulation of products that adhere to nuclear and cellular molecules. The accumulation produces antigenic alterations that set off an immune-mediated, SLE-like production of autoantibodies. From that point, the two conditions are essentially indistinguishable except for one dramatic difference—drug-induced SLE completely remits when the offending drug is stopped.

Some of the many drugs implicated are procainamide (an antihypertensive), isoniazid (an antitubercular agent with liver and CNS toxicity), and D-penicillamine (a chelating agent used to treat copper, lead, or mercury poisoning and Wilson's disease, a disorder involving copper metabolism).

Progressive Systemic Sclerosis (Scleroderma)

This chronic, progressive disease of connective tissue involves the excessive deposition of collagen and affects about 3 females to 1 male. It usually emerges in early middle age and is most apparent in the skin. When well advanced, the disease results in clawlike, inflexible fingers and a face like a drawn mask. It is a systemic disorder primarily affecting the gastrointestinal tract, the heart and its vasculature, and the kidneys, **21** lungs, and musculoskeletal system. The pathology arises both from the increased activity of fibroblasts laying down collagen and from impaired local circulation. Together these lead to intense fibrosis that interferes with organ function. Formerly called **scleroderma** because of the widespread involvement of the skin, the disease is increasingly known as **progressive systemic sclerosis** (PSS).

Pathogenesis

The pathogenesis of PSS is poorly understood. There appears to be dysfunction at the level of both the fibroblasts and the microvasculature. The triggering antigen or immune defect is unknown, but apparently collagen-reactive T cells and B cells mediate the pathology. The response of autoreactive helper T cells to their encounter with collagen sets up a cycle of progression. The delayed hypersensitivity reaction (type IV) generates mediators that attract and stimulate the division of fibroblasts. These produce more collagen that is antigenic for more T cells, stimulating them to additional mediator release, and so on.

Collagen-reactive B cells could produce antibodies that form complexes and mediate vascular damage, or other autoantibodies may be involved. The vascular derangements affect small arteries and arterioles, which are subject to intimal thickening and narrowing of the lumen, both by deposition of mucinous or collagenous material and by proliferation of intimal cells. These processes set the stage for scar formation because the tissue is robbed of adequate blood supply. Platelet adherence in the injured vessels contributes to the stimulation of fibroblasts because of the factors released. As in other diseases identified as autoimmune, there are abnormalities of immune function like circulating antinuclear antibodies.

Polymyositis-Dermatomyositis

This usually chronic weakness of proximal musculature affects twice as many women as men and usually appears in middle age, although a variant affects children. Half the patients experience rashes, classically in the eyelids and the extensor surfaces of joints including the fingers, elbows, and knees. While abnormalities are found in many systems (e.g., vasculitis, lung fibrosis, transitory arthritis), it is the muscle weakness **22** that produces most difficulty. Initially, patients have difficulty raising their arms or climbing stairs. This weakness can progress to weakness of neck muscles, impaired swallowing, and difficulty breathing as intercostals and diaphragm are involved. Occasionally, a fulminant case will rapidly lead to death, perhaps due to vasculitis-induced heart failure. The presence of muscle enzymes in the plasma (e.g., creatine kinase and lactic dehydrogenase) is evidence of the muscle cell destruction that takes place.

The association of this disease with others of presumably autoimmune origin (e.g., SLE, Sjögren's syndrome, and PSS) and the presence of ANAs in many of the patients argue for this being an autoimmune disease. What elicits the autoreactive response is unknown although, as with many other of its autoimmune relatives, a virus (in this case perhaps Coxsackie virus) is suspected. There is evidence that muscle-antigen-reactive T cells may be the immune agent.

Sjögren's Syndrome

A presumed autoimmune disease with almost as wide an assortment of autoantibodies as occurs in SLE, **Sjögren's syndrome** involves destruction of the salivary and lacrimal glands and their ducts. The resultant dry eyes cause blurred vision, burning and itching, and inflammation of the conjunctiva and corneal epithelium, followed by erosion of the cornea. The dry mouth becomes cracked and fissured and ulcers develop. Food can't be tasted and swallowing of solids is difficult. In about 40% of patients this is the extent of their lesions. They are said to have primary Sjögren's syndrome or **sicca (dry) syndrome.** The other 60% have this disorder along with some other autoimmune disease, often rheumatoid arthritis. Most (90%) of the patients are middle-aged women. People with Sjögren's also have an increased risk of developing lymphoid malignancies.

Case Study

A 28-year-old black woman came to her general practitioner because she was alarmed by recent signs of blood in her urine. She explained that she had been feeling increasingly tired at her work as a nurse, and for the past five months had been troubled by periods of stiffness and swelling in her hands, mild fevers, appetite and weight loss, and a rash over her cheeks, which worsened when she was out in the sun. On examination she was otherwise normal, but reported that she was taking isoniazid, a widely used antibacterial agent that is effective against tuberculosis. Her most recent routine tuberculin test at the hospital where she was employed had been positive, and the house physician had prescribed the drug. She was also using birth control pills.

The patient was taken off isoniazid and switched to another antibacterial agent. Laboratory studies were ordered and revealed some small loss of protein and blood to the urine. They also revealed the presence of antinuclear antibodies. On the basis of these factors, a diagnosis of systemic lupus erythematosus was made.

The patient was advised to avoid stress and exertion at work and to get as much rest as possible. Prednisone, a corticosteroid anti-inflammatory agent, was prescribed for her joint pain and kidney problems. Avoidance of sun exposure was also advised, and when exposure was inevitable, the use of an effective sun-blocking agent was counselled. It was also recommended that she stop using birth control pills.

Her symptoms improved and she continued to be monitored for any side effects of her therapy.

Commentary

The signs and symptoms in this patient pointed fairly clearly to SLE and were confirmed when the tests for antinuclear antibodies were returned as positive. It was necessary to stop the use of isoniazid because in some sensitive individuals it induces anti-DNA antibodies. When the possible role of the drug was removed and the antinuclear antibodies remained, the SLE diagnosis was relatively straightforward. The suggestion to abandon the use of birth control pills was based on indications that, in many cases, estrogen use can worsen SLE symptoms.

Prednisone is likely to suppress the glomerular inflammatory damage that is disrupting renal function, but other agents with similar effects are available should side effects become a problem. If episodes of more severe signs and symptoms develop, more aggressive immunosuppressive therapy may be indicated, but the side effects of such agents would be carefully weighed against expected benefits.

Generally, prognosis in such relatively mild cases of SLE is optimistic when the diagnosis is promptly made. Unfortunately, the variation and complexity of SLE signs and symptoms often offer a confusing picture, which delays diagnosis and prompt therapeutic intervention.

Key Concepts

1. Vaccines build up immunity to a pathogen by exposing the immune system to some stably recognizable but harmless feature(s) specific to that pathogen; subsequent exposure to the pathogen results in a rapid and intense immune response (pp. 85–86).

2. Antisera can be used to neutralize pathogens at the infection site or, once the pathogens are in the bloodstream, to neutralize bacterial toxins or to avoid immune sensitization (pp. 86–89).

3. In hypersensitivity reactions, damage to tissue function and/or structure arises out of immune responses to harmless antigenic stimuli, to self-antigens, to deposited immune complexes, or to persistent foreign or modified self-antigens (pp. 89–90).

4. Allergies are an example of type I immediate hypersensitivity: the exposure of sensitized mast cells in the skin and mucosal barriers to a specific allergen elicits immediate inflammation, bronchoconstriction, and increased secretion, as well as delayed reactions (pp. 90–94).

5. Aberrant antibody production or chemical alteration of self-antigens can elicit antibody-dependent cytotoxicity (type II hypersensitivity), in which K cells, phagocytes, and complement can injure tissues (p. 92).

6. Exposure to masses of foreign antigen (e.g., pneumonoconiosis) or excessive production of antibody (autoimmune disease) can lead to the formation and deposition of small immune complexes that trigger a range of inflammatory and immune processes destructive to tissue (type III immune-complex-mediated hypersensitivity) (pp. 92–93).

7. Cell-mediated, delayed-type hypersensitivity (type IV) results when helper T cells mobilize a macrophage response to a persistent foreign antigen (e.g., tubercular bacillus or fungi) or an altered self-antigen (e.g., contact dermatitis) (pp. 93–94).

8. Each individual has a combination of cell surface proteins that is more or less unique, called human leukocyte antigens (HLA) or self-antigens. These make

possible the identification and destruction of virally infected cells but also make tissue transplantation problematic (pp. 94–95).

9. The genes producing HLA proteins (the MHC complex) are also responsible for other surface antigens and aspects of immune system function that may be the basis of autoimmune diseases. Certain specific HLA antigens are more commonly identified in individuals with particular autoimmune diseases (pp. 95–98).

10. Strategies for improving transplant graft survival include careful tissue matching, use of cytotoxic drugs to reduce the pool of sensitized T_H cells, and use of immunosuppressant drugs such as prednisone, cyclosporin A, or cyclophosphamide (p. 97).

11. Primary immune deficiencies result when one or more components of immune system function are deficient or lacking, often because of a genetic defect, with a resulting characteristic pattern of infection (pp. 100–101).

12. Secondary immune deficiencies can arise from a wide variety of infections or as a toxic effect of drugs or other medical treatments (pp. 101–104).

13. Molecular characteristics of the HIV virus particle explain its absorption, replication, and spread (p. 104).

14. HIV infection classically passes through three phases. Infection is followed in weeks to months by a brief acute phase resembling mononucleosis or flu; a prolonged chronic phase, accompanied by swollen glands and gradually dropping T_4 cell counts; and a crisis phase that includes ARC and AIDS (p. 106).

15. The AIDS phase of the disease is diagnosed when the HIV positive person develops any of a variety of opportunistic infections (particularly PCP), otherwise rare neoplasms (e.g., Kaposi's sarcoma), or dementia. Women with advanced HIV infection may show only highly resistant candidiasis and other infections (p. 106).

16. HIV infection can result if HIV particles or infected lymphocytes, which are present in large numbers in semen, vaginal secretions, and blood, and in lower numbers in other body fluids, are passed into the bloodstream or to areas that bear receptors for HIV (p. 108).

17. In autoimmune disease, a primary immune defect allows the development of self-reactive antibodies or T cells (loss of tolerance) that mediate tissue destruction (pp. 110–115).

REVIEW ACTIVITIES

1. Describe the steps involved in effective immunization, from the first step, vaccination, when antigenic features are engulfed and processed by an antigen-presenting cell, to the last step, when pathogen-specific antibodies and cytotoxic T cells mediate destruction of the naturally encountered pathogen.

2. Explain the feature that the four hypersensitivity reactions have in common. Construct a table briefly describing the principal mechanisms of injury in each case, and name a disorder in which that reaction plays a key role.

Hypersensitivity	Mechanism	Example
Type I		
Type II		
Type III		
Type IV		

3. Using figure 5.27 as a guide, explain the various ways in which depressed T_4 numbers can result in impaired immunity (both specific and nonspecific) and tumor growth.

4. What signs and symptoms would you expect to note in the case history of each of the following? (a) a child with severe combined immunodeficiency disease, (b) an adult with Sjögren's syndrome, (c) isolated IgA deficiency, (d) dermatomyositis, (e) DiGeorge syndrome.

5. You are probably familiar with the use of universal precautions when handling body fluids of someone who is HIV positive. These decrease the likelihood that the health care worker will contract the disorder. What do they do for the person with AIDS?

6. You have read that genetics may play a role in individual cases of diseases like rheumatoid arthritis or diabetes mellitus. What group of genetically programmed characteristics are thought to account for these differences? The mechanisms are not well understood. Can you suggest how these genetic patterns are expressed in intensified or inappropriately focused immune system function?

7. "Systemic lupus erythematosus is a model for the loss of self-tolerance." What is meant by this statement?

Chapter Six

Neoplasia

On some a relentless cancer has fastened its envenomed teeth.

James Hervey
Meditations and Contemplations

Neoplasia is a widespread and potentially grave growth abnormality whose more serious form is known as cancer. Neoplasia is the second ranking cause of death in North America, where approximately 25% of the population suffers from some form of the disease, and of those, 15% die as a result. It kills more people under the age of 15 than any other disease. Autopsy studies indicate that the incidence of neoplasia is so high that even those who do not die *of* the disease have a good chance of dying *with* it. For this reason, and because of pain and serious functional complications that accompany the disease, as well as the many severe side effects associated with therapy, neoplasia is widely recognized as a major threat to our health and well-being.

TISSUE GROWTH DISORDERS

Neoplasia means new tissue formation and involves the overgrowth of a tissue to form a neoplastic mass, or **neoplasm,** which is called a **tumor. [1]** (Although "tumor" was originally used to denote any abnormal swelling, the term is now restricted to use in the context of neoplasia.) To put this excessive growth into perspective, let us first review some growth changes that are beneficial. As we saw in previous chapters, alterations in cell size or number can be normal adaptive responses to changing demand.

Adaptive Growth Responses

When demand increases, but cells cannot divide, hypertrophy produces enlarged cells with increased functional capacity; skeletal muscle is one example. If demand is low, atrophy reduces cell size in response, while cell numbers are retained to provide for future demand increases. In healing, regeneration of labile and stable tissues produces new cells to replace those lost to injury.

In **hyperplasia,** mitosis produces new cells, but only in quantities needed to meet a particular demand. For example, focal hyperplasia of the epidermis is a response to increased pressure and friction at the surface of the skin. The newly formed tissue gives rise to a thicker, more protective callus, which can regress when demand is reduced. These adaptive responses are the result of closely balanced control factors that produce a growth response carefully matched to demand. The swollen lymph nodes seen in patients suffering chronic infections are the result of hyperplasia. Substances drained by the lymph flow from infected tissues presumably trigger hyperplasia in both the lymphoid tissue and the phagocytic reticuloendothelial cells of the lymph nodes.

When disease requires surgical removal of a kidney, some cells of the remaining kidney undergo hypertrophy and others become hyperplastic. Both responses compensate for the loss of one kidney by increasing the functional capacity of the remaining kidney.

Metaplasia and Dysplasia

When demand is more intense or prolonged, altered tissue growth can produce structural and functional abnormalities. These are seen most often in the epithelia, which are exposed to injurious agents at body surfaces.

Metaplasia is the conversion from one cell or tissue type to another. The respiratory epithelia most often undergo metaplasia in response to exposure to inhaled irritants, usually tobacco smoke. The process involves replacement of the normal ciliated, pseudostratified epithelium by a thicker, tougher stratified epithelium that is better able to stand up to the irritants. The new stratified tissue is well organized and its cells have a normal appearance. Metaplasia is reversible. When irritation is reduced, the normal epithelium may be restored (fig. 6.1). Note that metaplasia might, at first, be thought of as a normal adaptive response, but the loss of cilia and goblet cells means a reduced ability to clear inhaled particles and microorganisms and maintain normal mucous secretion. This change represents a significant loss of normal defense capacity, and for this reason, metaplasia should be regarded as an abnormal condition.

Dysplasia is seen when irritation is more severe and prolonged. As with metaplasia, the replacement tissue is a tougher, stratified tissue. **[2]** However, its architecture is disordered and its cells demonstrate **pleomorphism.** Pleomorphic cells are variable in their size and shape, in contrast to the regularity of cell structure seen in normal tissues. **[3]** They also have larger, more darkly stained nuclei and increased mitosis rates (see fig. 6.1). Dysplasia is also a reversible condition but is less so than metaplasia. It is associated with the chronic bronchitis commonly seen in cigarette smokers, and also in prolonged inflammations of the uterine cervix. Severely dysplastic tissues often resemble tumors (fig. 6.2), and it is generally accepted that dysplasia often precedes a tissue's becoming neoplastic. Some forms of dysplasia are known as **precancerous** lesions.

In the case of neoplasia, the formation of the tumor mass represents an irreversible alteration in a cell's growth pattern. Tissue production continues beyond the body's needs and in many cases continues until the resulting disruption of function causes the victim's death (fig. 6.3). Clearly, the growth of a tumor represents a dramatic departure from the normal pattern of tissue formation. Normal formation of new tissue represents a fine balance between growth stimulation and growth inhibition; the body produces only the tissue necessary to meet demand, and no more.

This concept of the balance of stimulus and inhibition is presented in figure 6.4. Genetic or developmental abnormalities produce the problems of **aplasia**—lack of organ development **[4]**—and **hypoplasia**—development that is inadequate, so that the resulting structure is immature and functionally deficient. Adaptive responses to changing

1   5810

2   12428

3   46363

4   46142

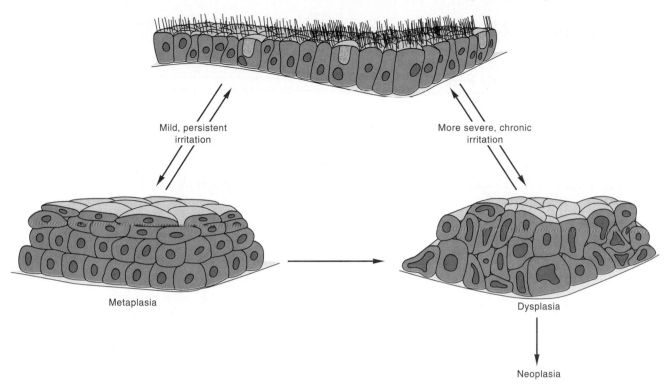

Mild, persistent irritation

More severe, chronic irritation

Metaplasia

Dysplasia

Neoplasia

Figure 6.1 Metaplasia and dysplasia: reversible changes in tissue structure induced by injury. More intense and prolonged exposure to the injurious agent can produce the irreversible transformation to neoplasia.

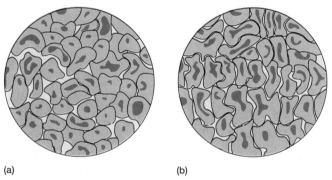

(a)   (b)

Figure 6.2 Diagrammatic comparison of (*a*) dysplasia and (*b*) neoplasia. In the representative microscope field, the dysplastic cells show varying degrees of pleomorphism, with some cells appearing to be near normal. The neoplastic (tumor) cells are all abnormal, with enlarged nuclei and more pronounced pleomorphism.

demand—atrophy, hypertrophy, hyperplasia, and regeneration—are seen to be reversible. In neoplasia, the transformation from the normal is irreversible and the newly formed tissue continues to grow without control. It is the imbalance between growth stimulus and growth inhibition that produces the inappropriate tissue overgrowth.

The principal factors that regulate tissue growth were first introduced in chapter 3. There, we considered contact inhibition, cell interactions with components of the extracellular matrix, and plasma-born regulator molecules (table 3.3) in the context of tissue regeneration following injury.

These regulatory inputs are shown in figure 6.5*A*. Generally, derangements of tissue growth could result from flawed regulatory input due to inadequate delivery of regulator molecules, from damage or loss of cell surface receptors, causing faulty growth responses, or from defective exchange of regulators between cells (fig. 6.5*B*).

TUMOR TERMINOLOGY

The study of tumors is called **oncology,** from the Greek word *oncos,* meaning tumor. In describing a tumor, two distinguishing characteristics are relevant: its pattern of growth and its tissue of origin.

In terms of its growth pattern, a tumor falls into one of two broad categories. It is said to be **benign** if its growth is relatively slow and orderly and if the tumor remains localized. A **malignant** tumor, by contrast, is characterized by more rapid, disordered growth and by aggressive invasion into adjacent normal tissues. The term **cancer,** from the Latin word for crab, refers to malignant tumors, generally. (It is unclear whether the term arose because of the claw-like growth extensions of malignancies, the crab-claw appearance of some tumor blood vessels, or the crablike tenacity with which the disease belabors its victims.) The invasiveness of a malignant tumor is usually accompanied by spread to other, distant points in the body. These differences in tumor behavior underlie the more favorable prognosis associated with benign tumors. Malignant tumors, if untreated, inevitably lead to the death of the host.

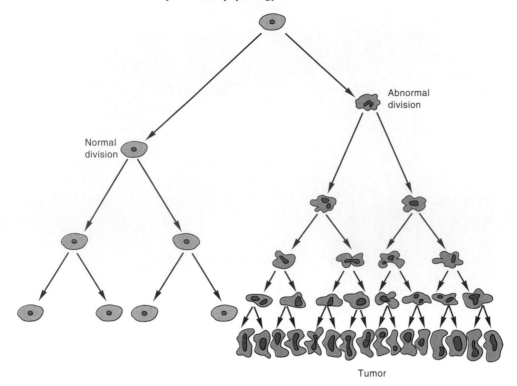

Figure 6.3   Growth of a neoplasm. Tumor growth outstrips that of normal tissue, forming a neoplastic mass.

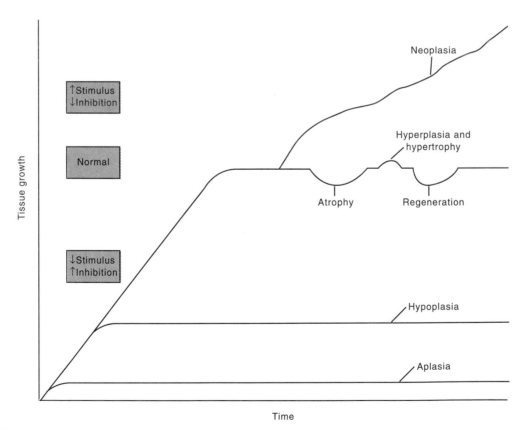

Figure 6.4   The balance between stimulus and inhibition determines the pattern of tissue growth. See text.

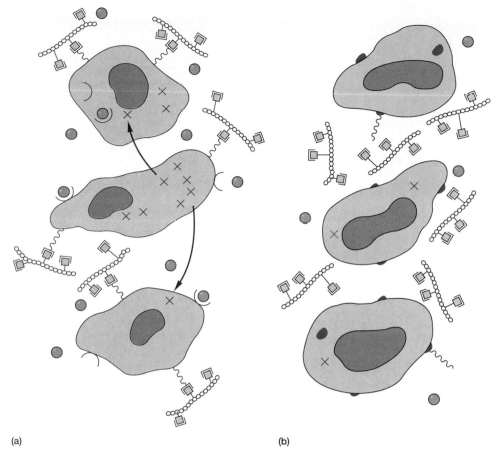

Figure 6.5   (*a*) Extracellular matrix components bind to surface receptors; plasma-borne and cellular regulators also provide appropriate growth control. (*b*) Damaged receptors and lack of adequate plasma or cellular growth factors alter growth regulation. ▲: matrix receptor ×, ●: regulator molecules.

The suffix "-oma" may be used to designate any tumor. In naming benign tumors, a root word indicating the type of tissue that has become neoplastic is used. For example, where glandular tissue is involved, the benign tumor is called an adenoma. In the case of bone, the benign tumor is called an osteoma. Other examples are given in table 6.1.

Malignant tumors are classified according to their embryonic origin. During development of an embryo, three primary tissue layers form. **Ectoderm** lines the outer surface of the body, whereas **endoderm** provides the protective lining for its internal surfaces. Malignant tumors arising in tissues derived from these primitive layers are known as **carcinomas.** Generally, carcinomas are malignant tumors of the skin and the epithelial linings of the alimentary canal and the respiratory passages. Since glandular tissue is derived from ectoderm or endoderm, malignant glandular tumors are included with the carcinomas and are called **adenocarcinomas.**

The third embryonic tissue layer is **mesoderm.** Malignancies developing in tissues that derive from meso-derm are called **sarcomas.** Specific sarcoma terminology makes reference to the particular tissue of origin; for example, tumors of cartilage and fibrous connective tissue are called chondrosarcoma and fibrosarcoma, respectively.

There are a few cases in which traditional but less precise usage persists. For example, you might think that a melanoma, lymphoma, or hepatoma is benign because of its name, but all three are actually quite malignant. The more accurate terms are malignant melanoma, lymphosarcoma, and hepatocellular carcinoma, respectively.

Table 6.1 lists only the most frequently encountered terms describing tumors. Many other terms are used to provide more specific insight into the origin and other characteristics of a given tumor. For example, in malignant tumors of stratified epithelium, usually in the skin, a tumor might involve different cells. When the cells in the deepest layer become neoplastic, the tumor is called a **basal cell carcinoma.** If cells nearer the surface are involved, the term **squamous cell carcinoma** is used. Further complexity in terminology arises when other factors are used to expand the basis of tumor classification. Most of these have clinical relevance that lies beyond the scope of this text.

Table 6.1 Tumor Terminology and Classification

Tissue of Origin	Benign	Malignant
Ectoderm/Endoderm		
Epithelium	Epithelioma (papilloma if projecting from surface)	Carcinoma
Gland	Adenoma	Adenocarcinoma
Melanocytes		Malignant melanoma
Neuroglia	Glioma	Glioma
Embryonic nervous tissue*		Neuroblastoma
Embryonic retinal cells*		Retinoblastoma
Mesoderm		
Connective tissue		
Adipose tissue	Lipoma	Liposarcoma
Cartilage	Chondroma	Chondrosarcoma
Bone	Osteoma	Osteosarcoma
Fibrous tissue	Fibroma	Fibrosarcoma
Lymphoid Tissue		Lymphosarcoma
Smooth muscle	Leioma	Leiomyosarcoma
Embryonic skeletal muscle*		Myoblastoma
Combined tissues (usually gonadal)*	Teratoma	
Leucocyte-Producing Tissues		
Red bone marrow		Myeloid leukemia
Lymphoid tissue		Lymphocytic leukemia

* Less well-differentiated cells not normally present in adults.

TUMOR STRUCTURE

Neoplastic Tissue

The major constituent of a tumor is neoplastic tissue with varying degrees of resemblance to its tissue of origin. The degree of resemblance is greater in benign tumors than in malignancies. A benign tumor contains cells of near normal size and shape, arranged in a manner that closely resembles the normal tissue architecture. Occasionally, a cell in the process of dividing can be seen in microscopic studies. A malignant tumor is usually quite different (fig. 6.6). Its cells are highly pleomorphic, with enlarged, unusually shaped nuclei and abnormalities of chromosome structure and number. The tissue configuration is disordered, and mitotic cells are seen more frequently than in benign tumors. The irregular and often bizarre configurations seen in tumor cells provide the basis for tumor diagnosis in cases where tissue samples are available. A common example of the technique occurs with the **Papanicolaou,** or **Pap, test.** In this test, named for its originator, George Papanicolaou, a microscopic study is made of epithelial cells that have been gently removed with a swab from the lining of the cervix. Cell size and shape as well as nuclear size, shape, and number are studied for indications of neoplasia. **5**

Figure 6.6 Malignant cells from a gastric carcinoma. Large pleomorphic cells have irregular and deeply staining nuclei. Normal tissue architecture is lost and the cells bear no resemblance to their normal tissue of origin.

Biochemical changes can also be detected in cancers, because the enzyme complement of a malignant cell resembles that of more primitive, undifferentiated cells. The malignant cells demonstrate a greater use of anaerobic glycolysis as an energy source, regardless of oxygen availability. Also, malignant cells typically lose some of the specialized functional capabilities characteristic of their

34787

Figure 6.7 Although tumor cells (A) are evident in this view, the dominant feature is fibrous tissue (B), which tightly binds the neoplastic cells. The fibrous tissue produces the characteristic firmness of the scirrhous tumor.
A 50-year-old assembly line worker discovered a lump in her breast during a regular breast self-examination. On the follow-up, her physician found a very firm lump of 2 cm diameter. It was joined to the skin and underlying pectoral muscle, a fact indicating that it had invaded locally. The mass was surgically removed and sectioned to reveal a significant fibrous tissue component, which accounted for the tumor's firmness. The woman suffered no further complications.

tissue of origin. The pattern of change that produces a seemingly earlier cell form is called **anaplasia.** It is often described as the reverse of normal differentiation. As tissues normally develop, differentiation yields a highly specialized cell whose reproductive capability is usually reduced in comparison with its earlier, less specialized forms. The anaplastic cell, however, seems to have regained reproductive capacity at the expense of functional specialization.

Anaplasia is not an all-or-nothing phenomenon. Rather, it is a characteristic present to different degrees in different tumors. Generally, the degree of anaplasia and the degree of malignancy are directly linked. At the extreme, highly malignant tumors may be so undifferentiated that they lack resemblance to any particular tissue, and hence cannot be classified except in their general resemblance to embryonic tissue. In such cases broadly descriptive terminology, emphasizing some obvious characteristic, is often used, for example, **giant cell carcinoma. 6**

Stroma

Another major component of a tumor is the stroma (connective tissue framework) that supports the tumor cells. It is important to note that this tissue is in itself not neoplastic. It is formed in response to the tumor's presence. Malignant tumors have been shown to secrete factors that promote vascular permeability. This supports the development of a matrix that fosters the formation of collagen and other stromal components by fibroblasts. Tumor variability in eliciting this response gives rise to a broad range of variation in the physical properties of the tumor. When there is little stroma formation, the tumor has a softer, fleshy consistency, which is typical of sarcomas. At the other extreme is a **scirrhous** (skir′us) tumor. In this case the stromal

response is exaggerated, and a densely collagenous tumor, hard to the touch, results. **7** The fibrous tissue that is newly formed may undergo contracture to add to the density of the tumor mass. Scirrhous tumors are typical of adenocarcinoma of the breast and may have as much as 90% of their volume formed of stromal elements (fig. 6.7).

Vasculature

A tumor also contains blood vessels. These, like stromal connective tissue, are nonneoplastic and are formed in response to the new tissue. Initially, a tumor can derive its nutrients from adjacent normal tissues by diffusion, but after the tumor reaches a diameter of about 1 mm, it requires additional vascular supply. Note that although this seems a minute size, over such distances diffusion is too slow to sustain tissue growth. Consider also the high metabolic demand of the one million growing cells that might be present in the tumor this size, and you can better appreciate the need for new vascular channels.

The process of new vessel formation (**angiogenesis**) in tumors seems essentially the same as in the revascularization of a healing tissue. That is, it is closely regulated by a group of tissue growth and inhibition factors. One of these is called **tumor angiogenesis factor** (TAF). Although widely distributed in normal tissues, it is also present in many tumors. It is thought that the large quantities secreted by growing tumors overcome opposing inhibitory factors so that new vascular channels are formed.

The ability to induce angiogenesis varies greatly. Generally, the newly formed vessels have a less regular pattern compared with those at healing sites. Newly formed tumor capillaries also have looser endothelial junctions and may lack basement membranes. They are more highly permeable as a result (fig. 6.8).

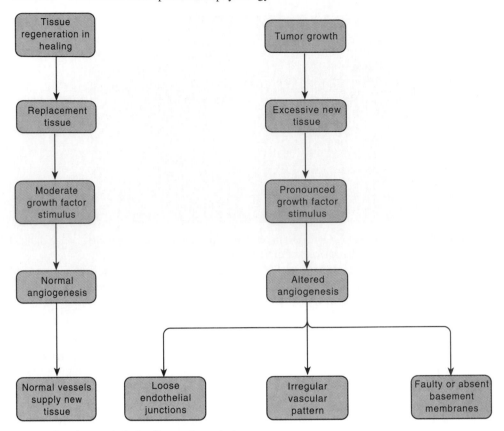

Figure 6.8   Comparison of angiogenesis in healing and neoplasia.

Tumor Products

Many cells produce some product in the course of their normal activities. Hormones and mucus are common examples, as is the keratin formed by dry-surfaced stratified epithelium. When transformed into neoplastic tissue, cells often continue such production, and the resulting tumors produce large amounts of these products. The product's properties will depend on the degree of the tumor's anaplasia. Products of a benign tumor tend to closely resemble the normal product. Those of anaplastic malignant tumors may sufficiently resemble the normal to allow some degree of normal function or physiological potency. In other cases, the products of malignant tumors may be completely nonfunctional. A squamous cell carcinoma produces excessive nonliving keratin, much of it lying below the surface of the skin, where it causes irritation that may elicit an inflammatory response. **8** Other examples of tumor products are the bony calcium deposits characteristic of osteosarcoma (fig. 6.9) and excessive erythropoietin secreted by a renal carcinoma. Tumor diagnosis may be aided by a tumor's overproduction of enzymes. As they spill into the plasma their high levels may betray the presence of a tumor that would otherwise be unnoticed.

Tumor products may also contribute to differences in the physical characteristics of a tumor. For example, tumors secreting large quantities of serous fluid (**serous tumors**)

Figure 6.9   The arrows indicate the bone matrix substance being produced by the cells of this bone tumor (osteogenic sarcoma). Note the lack of similarity to normally structured bone.

may form cysts, **9** while overproduction of mucus leads to the loose, gelatinous texture of a **mucoid tumor** such as colon carcinoma.

TUMOR BEHAVIOR: BENIGN VERSUS MALIGNANT

Benign

Benign tumors grow more rapidly than normal tissues, but more slowly than malignant tumors. In a benign tumor, the production of new tissue proceeds in an orderly pattern of

Figure 6.10 Typical tumor structure. (*a*) A benign tumor, in which near-normal cells slowly undergo expansile growth, enclosed by a connective tissue capsule. (*b*) A malignant tumor, characterized by abnormal cytology and irregular, invasive

expansile growth to form a generally regular tumor mass. Another characteristic of benign tumors is the presence of a fibrous connective tissue capsule that surrounds the tumor mass and provides a distinct line of separation between the tumor and the adjacent normal tissue in which it is growing. The capsular tissue is derived in part from newly formed connective tissues and in part from the stroma of the normal tissue that has been replaced by the tumor. Both the slower, measured, expansile growth and the surrounding capsule contribute to the more favorable prognosis typical of benign tumors. Slower growth means there is less damage to the surrounding normal cells, and the presence of the capsule makes surgical removal easier (fig. 6.10*a*).

Malignant

The behavior of a malignant tumor is a different matter. Its more rapid rate of growth can produce a larger tumor mass, but more significant is its pattern of growth, which is aggressively invasive. The tumor sends columns of cells into adjacent normal tissues, causing disruption of their structure and function (fig. 6.10*b*). **10** The occurrence of a capsule is rare. When present, it is usually incomplete and irregular. The blurred lines of demarcation between tumor and adjacent normal tissue complicate surgical removal (see fig. 6.11). **11**

An even greater factor in the poor prognosis of a malignancy is its ability to spread to distant points in the body. This type of spread is called **metastasis.** In metastasis the original tumor mass, growing at its **primary site,** is able to shed cells that become established as tumors at one or more distant **secondary sites.** There is no physical continuity between tumors at primary and secondary sites. However, the tumor growing at the secondary site is the same tissue as that growing at the primary site. That is, the normal tissue of the secondary site has not become neoplastic; rather, tumor cells have been transported to the secondary site and have resumed growth there (fig. 6.12).

Metastasis is a major problem in dealing with tumors. In a patient who has a primary malignancy, there is often doubt over whether metastasis has already occurred. On the

other hand, a secondary tumor may be the first to produce signs or symptoms, in which case the problem lies in determining the location of the primary tumor from which it arose. For example, a bone that fractures after relatively slight strain may have been weakened by tumor growth within it. **12** A biopsy might indicate a tumor whose cells are sufficiently well differentiated to be identified as glandular tissue. But there remains the problem of finding the source of the adenocarcinoma that has spread from some unknown primary site to the bone.

The ability to metastasize is the single characteristic that clearly differentiates the malignant from the benign tumor (table 6.2). Also, even though malignant growths both invade and metastasize, the two characteristics are not necessarily present to the same degree. That is, highly invasive tumors may metastasize to only a limited degree, and tumors that are minimally invasive may metastasize extensively.

Any tumor that metastasizes is, by definition, malignant. Such tumors will generally have other characteristics as indicated in table 6.2. However, in some cases the distinction between benign and malignant is not clear-cut. This is because tumor characteristics are expressed over a range, usually with an area of overlap between the extremes of benign and malignant tumor behavior. For example, some tumors that do not metastasize, and are therefore benign, might demonstrate an invasive pattern of growth. In comparison, as we have noted, a metastasizing—and therefore malignant tumor—might grow in a manner that is only mildly invasive. A similar overlap exists in tumor tissue architecture. The most precisely ordered malignant tumors may be more regularly arranged than the least orderly benign tumors (fig. 6.13). This overlap has important implications for diagnosis, because therapy and prognosis will depend on the early determination of whether a tumor is benign or malignant. Unless metastasis has clearly occurred, any tumor whose observed invasiveness or tissue architecture or other characteristics fall into the area of overlap between benign and malignant presents a problem. On the one hand, it would be regrettable to subject a person with a benign tumor to the rigorous and often unpleasant therapies intended for a malignant tumor. On the other hand, treating a malignant tumor as though it were benign could tragically shorten the patient's life. Unfortunately, in some cases it is impossible to clearly distinguish between benign and malignant tumors. Many histopathologists would agree that the process of establishing a tumor's identity is far from precise and in some ways is more of an art than a science.

Tumor Growth Rate

Tumor growth rates also overlap: the most rapidly growing benign tumors have growth rates that surpass those of the slowest growing malignancies. Although higher than normal, tumor growth rates are not extremely rapid. Normal

(a)

(b)

Figure 6.11   (*a*) Normal esophageal epithelium. (*b*) A squamous cell carcinoma of the esophagus. The solid line at upper right (arrow) indicates an area where the tumor is still confined within the tissue's basement membrane. In the central portion of the photo, the tumor is present in cords and islands of cells that have broken through to the underlying submucosa.

Table 6.2	Characteristics of Benign and Malignant Tumors	
Characteristic	**Benign**	**Malignant**
Cell structure	Near normal	Abnormal shapes, larger cell and nucleus
Tissue structure	Orderly	Disordered, irregular
Growth rate	Above normal	Rapid
Invasive growth	Uncommon	Typical
Metastasis	Never	Typical
Capsule	Typical	Rare, incomplete if present
Anaplasia	Minimal	Typical
Prognosis	Good	Poor

Figure 6.12   This section through the liver reveals numerous secondary tumor masses. They originated as multiple tumor emboli that were shed by a colon carcinoma. The site at which they lodged in the liver was determined by the flow pattern of the hepatic portal blood arriving from the colon.

The extensive secondary tumors visible in this liver section originated in the lung of an elderly man. His lung carcinoma had been assessed as inoperable when he developed signs and symptoms of liver malfunction. His damaged liver was unable to excrete bile pigments and his serum alkaline phosphatase level was elevated. He died soon after these problems developed.

Figure 6.13 Overlapping characteristics of benign and malignant tumors. B: benign; M: malignant. Note the stippled areas where the upper end of the B scale overlaps the M scale. These overlaps can complicate diagnosis.

fetal growth and regeneration in healing involve growth rates significantly higher than those found in most tumors. However, a clear understanding of tumor growth rates requires a precise distinction between two growth-related concepts. The first is **generation time**—the time between successive cell divisions. Generation time includes the time taken for mitosis itself, as well as the time when the cell rests, metabolizes, and synthesizes the molecules needed for its next mitotic division. The second concept is **doubling time**—the time required to double the number of tumor cells or the size of the tumor.

You might assume that generation time and doubling time are the same, but clinical experience indicates that doubling times for tumors are much longer than generation times. In fact, doubling times actually increase as a tumor ages. How can this be? The reason has to do with the fate of newly produced cells; not all go on to reproduce, forming new daughter cells that reproduce in turn, and so on. Some of the newly formed cells lose their mitotic ability, some enter a nondividing resting phase, while still others die. It is estimated that in tumors, as many as 90% of the newly formed cells do not immediately go on to divide. This means that several division cycles, whose generation time is unchanged, may be required to double the amount of tumor tissue. Also, as a tumor ages, reduced blood supply, nutrient depletion, and host responses can reduce the number of actively dividing cells so that doubling times increase and the rate at which new, viable tumor tissue is produced decreases. Again, note that for a given tumor, its generation time doesn't change even though its doubling time increases and its growth rate decreases (fig. 6.14).

The number of a tissue's cells that are involved in proliferation is the tissue's **growth fraction** (GF). It is usually presented as a percentage. In slowly growing tumors, studies indicate growth fractions under 10%, while the most rapidly growing malignancies have growth fractions as high as 30%. Note also that normal intestinal epithelium has a growth fraction of about 15%, producing more rapid growth than is seen in many tumors. In some tumors the generation time does increase, further extending the doubling time. This increase is due to an extended period in the mitotic stage of the cell's reproductive cycle. For human tumors studied, generation times vary from 1 to 5 days, while doubling times may be as low as 30 days or may extend to over a year. On this basis, you can appreciate that a tumor may be growing for many months, or even several years, before its presence is detected.

In normally dividing tissues, precise growth controls match cell loss to new cell production. In tumors, although all daughter cells don't survive, there is still a net increase in cell production over cell losses. From this fundamental imbalance the problem of neoplasia emerges.

Tumor Invasion

There are several essential factors involved in a tumor's invasion of the normal tissue that surrounds and contains it. One is pressure atrophy. As a tumor expands, it puts pressure on adjacent normal cells and their supporting blood supply. Tissues vary in their ability to tolerate such pressure, but ultimately they atrophy and die. The tumor can then more easily fill the newly available space. However,

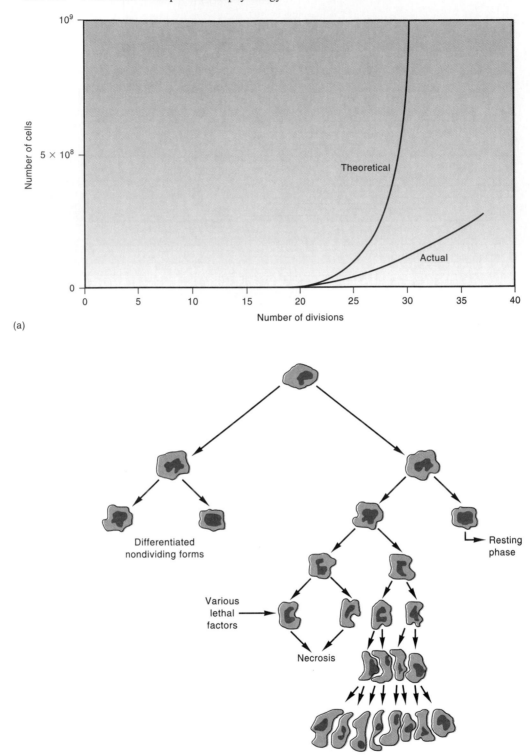

(a)

(b)

Figure 6.14   (*a*) Theoretical versus actual tumor growth. (*b*) After six divisions of a single tumor cell, the number of surviving cells is significantly lower than the 64 that is theoretically possible.

pressure atrophy is a relatively minor factor in tumor invasion, and growth rate and invasion are not necessarily related. For example, a type of benign breast tumor grows relatively rapidly, yet invades only minimally. In contrast, a malignant form of breast cancer invades extensively even though it grows more slowly than the benign tumor.

More important than pressure atrophy is tumor cell motility. Especially in malignant tumors, cells have the ability to separate from the primary tumor mass and move into surrounding tissues. Several factors contribute to this pivotal invasive capability. One is reduced adhesiveness. Unlike normal cells, which are tightly bound together,

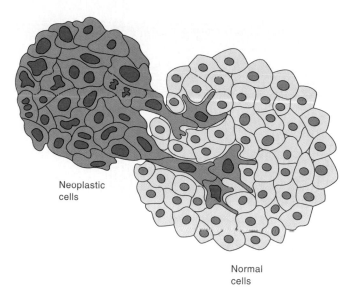

Neoplastic
cells

Normal
cells

Figure 6.15   Malignant cells grown in culture with normal cells preferentially invade the adjacent normal tissue.

tumor cells are easily released from links to their neighboring cells. Thus loosened from surrounding restraints, malignant cells are able to separate from the tumor mass and actively move into adjacent tissues. The extracellular matrix (ECM) and, in the case of epithelial tumors, the basement membrane (BM) may restrict this motility. But this restriction is met by a second adaptive capability that now comes into play.

In becoming neoplastic, cells acquire surface receptors that enable them to bind to particular elements of the extracellular matrix or basement membrane. This binding triggers the release of enzymes from the tumor cell. These degrade and loosen the ECM, or BM, to provide low-resistance invasion paths through the disrupted tissues. The result is easier penetration and infiltration by the aggressive tumor cells.

Another key aspect of tumor invasiveness is the process of chemotaxis, which draws tumor cells into the adjacent tissues. That is, the tumor cells respond to chemical stimuli from the nearby normal tissues. These chemical signals speed up and direct the tumor's invasion. When tumor cells are grown adjacent to normal cells in tissue culture, they don't spread uniformly in all directions and encounter the normal cells by chance. Instead, they grow toward the normal cells to a greater extent than they do in other directions, appearing to preferentially invade the normal tissue (fig. 6.15). Chemotaxis explains this phenomenon. Factors chemotactic for tumor cells are formed in the normal tissue, and these focus and accelerate tumor cell motility and invasion.

There are three sources of such chemotactic factors. Some products of normal cell metabolism are chemotactic for tumor cells. Some of the products of ECM and BM degradation are tumor attractants. The third source is the tumor cell itself. In becoming neoplastic, many tumors

acquire the ability to secrete substances called **autocrine motility factors** that are chemotactic to other tumor cells. The earliest invading cells secrete these, actively drawing other cells from the primary tumor mass. Figure 6.16 summarizes the mechanisms that underlie tumor invasion.

Patterns of Invasion

At the microscopic level, we have seen that the breakdown of the BM and ECM provides paths along which invading tumor cells can more easily penetrate. Similarly, at the gross level, tumors will invade along planes of low resistance. Fascia, bone, thick-walled arterioles, and the pericardial sac are examples of tissues resistant to invasion. Rather than penetrating, advancing tumors will grow around or along the low-resistance planes between an organ and its neighbors (fig. 6.17). This pattern is seen in the abdominal cavity, for example, where sheets of tumors grow along peritoneal surfaces. On the other hand, a tumor originating within an organ, and unable to break through its connective tissue capsule, might extend its growth along a low-resistance plane within the organ, just deep to the capsule.

After invading through the wall of a vein or lymphatic vessel and gaining access to the lumen, the tumor cells lie within a channel that offers a low-resistance path favoring growth along the lumen. **13** However, this pattern does not seem to occur with any significant frequency. Exceptions are renal carcinoma and the relatively rare primary hepatic tumors. These may grow along the veins that drain the organ to form elongated, cordlike tumor masses that can reach the heart via the inferior vena cava. As with other tumor characteristics, there is much difference among tumors in their invasive capability. In the case of highly invasive malignant tumors, organ capsules may only temporarily slow invasive spread before the tumor penetrates into adjacent structures.

Tumor Metastasis

Malignant tumors typically couple localized invasion with metastasis to secondary sites. This spread increases the damaging effects of the tumor, because after metastasis, destructive invasive growth can proceed at other, often widely separated locations. Although this is the usual pattern, invasion and metastasis are not necessarily linked. Some invasive malignancies metastasize only rarely, for example, basal cell carcinoma of the skin and brain glioma.

Metastasis Via Embolism

Most often, metastasizing tumor cells are carried to secondary sites as emboli in the blood or lymph. The initial event in a typical metastasis is the invasion of a vein or lymphatic vessel by a growing tumor (fig. 6.18). Once within the vessel, further growth of tumor proceeds, with cell clumps becoming separated from the intravascular mass; recall the low intercellular adhesiveness that characterizes

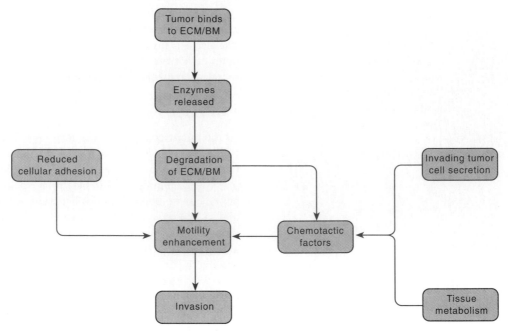

Figure 6.16   Factors underlying a tumor's invasive growth capacity.

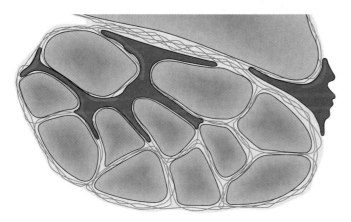

Figure 6.17   Initially impeded by the capsules of the organ, the growing tumor extends along low-resistance paths between them. Even when penetration of the capsule is achieved, growth proceeds along the internal subdivisions of the organ.

malignant tumors. Emboli formed in this way are carried along with the moving blood or lymph until they reach some part of the vascular system that prevents their passage. At such points they become trapped and resume growth. As growth proceeds, the tumor invades the vessel wall, gaining access to the tissue at the secondary site, where further invasive growth continues. After developing at secondary sites, the tumor can repeat the sequence to produce further metastatic dispersion.

Blood Vessel Metastasis The thin walls of capillaries and veins seem to allow easy penetration by aggressively invasive tumor cells. Once within a vein, a tumor embolus passes through successively larger veins, which ultimately deliver it to the left heart. The embolus then enters the pulmonary arterial system, whose branches at some point become sufficiently small to block its passage. Lodged in a small blood vessel, the tumor cells become actively invasive, secreting the enzymes and motility factors that promote passage through the vessel wall into the surrounding lung tissue. By this mechanism, the lungs trap emboli arising from many widely dispersed primary tumor sites. The lung is therefore a very common site of secondary tumor growth. **14** The major exception to this general pattern is the venous drainage of the abdominal organs. This blood passes directly to the liver in the vessels of the hepatic portal system. In the liver, vessels branch to form small-diameter sinusoids that can trap tumor emboli; for this reason, the liver is a common secondary site for primary tumors of the intestines and stomach (fig. 6.19). **15**

Arterial metastasis is much less common, probably because the thick arterial walls are harder to penetrate. Primary lung tumors provide a special case, however, in that tumor emboli arising in the pulmonary venous system are carried back to the left heart, which ejects them into the systemic arterial flow. The emboli are then widely disseminated, and extensively dispersed metastases can result. Of course, the organs that receive a larger arterial flow, the brain and kidney, **16** for example, are particularly vulnerable.

Lymphatic Vessel Metastasis Like veins, lymphatic vessels are easily invaded by malignant tumors. **17** Because lymph must pass through a succession of lymph nodes

14 ‖‖‖‖‖‖‖‖ 35232

15 ‖‖‖‖‖‖‖‖ 39549

16 ‖‖‖‖‖‖‖‖ 36908

17 ‖‖‖‖‖‖‖‖ 27065

Invasion of
vessel

Initial growth
at primary
site

Embolus in
vessel draining
primary site

Metastatic growth
established at
secondary site

Invasion of
secondary site

Small branch of
distant vessel

Figure 6.18 Metastasis by embolism. Penetration of a blood or
lymphatic vessel is followed by the formation of an embolus and
its trapping at some distant site. Invasion of the secondary tissue is
followed by growth of the secondary tumor.

before reaching the blood, you might think that lymphatic metastasis would be limited. Unfortunately, this is not the case. Lymph node involvement seems to promote metastasis by three principal mechanisms.

The first involves growth of a tumor within the lymph node. Trapped in its reticular tissues, the tumor cells grow invasively, often completely replacing normal node tissues. This growing tumor becomes the source of new emboli, which are then carried by the efferent lymph to the next lymph nodes in the chain, where the process repeats.

Second, tumor growth in the lymph nodes blocks normal lymph flow, causing lymph to be redirected through alternative channels. The result is that tumor emboli are dispersed over a wider field of secondary sites. Obstruction that produces retrograde flow can also lead to unusual and unexpected embolus dissemination, which can complicate diagnosis, therapy, and prognosis.

The third factor that favors metastasis via the lymph nodes is their vascular arrangement, which provides close intercommunication between lymph and blood vessels. This means that tumor cells arriving at the node via the lymph can gain easy access to the blood after growth is established. Once a tumor has reached a lymph node, you can assume that if blood metastasis has not yet occurred, it is soon likely (fig. 6.20).

The enlargement of regional lymph nodes is often an indication of metastatic tumor growth within the node. In some cases, however, the enlargement (**lymphadenopathy**) is due to a hyperplasia response. This proliferation of lymph node cells may be a response to substances, some antigenic, that are produced by the tumor cells and then carried to the nodes by lymph flow. Nodal hyperplasia of this sort is completely reversible and nonthreatening, but it can suggest a more extensive metastasis than has actually occurred.

Factors Affecting Secondary Tumor Growth

It is significant that not all tumor cells that gain access to the blood or lymph survive to grow at secondary sites. Only a small fraction, some evidence suggests one in a thousand, of the cells shed from a primary tumor survive transport to secondary sites. The poor survival rate of circulating tumor cells is probably due to physical disruptions arising from turbulent blood flow and to host defense mechanisms. In the blood, tumor emboli may also pick up circulating lymphocytes, platelets, and coatings of fibrin that mask their surfaces. Their presence on the embolus may be related to the observation that single cells and large emboli are less likely to establish metastases than small clumps of 5–10 cells. It may be that the intermediate-size embolus is protected by the fibrin, lymphocyte, and platelet coatings. Perhaps the single cells are destroyed by blood turbulence, while larger clumps aren't adequately screened from host attacks.

Figure 6.19   Blood-borne tumor emboli often lodge in the lungs, where they form secondary tumors. The exception to this pattern involves emboli from the GI tract, which tend to lodge in the liver.

While the distribution of secondary growth sites reflects blood and lymph flow patterns, a significant number of secondary tumors, as many as 40%, cannot be explained on this basis alone. Certain tumors seem to establish preferentially at secondary sites other than those that would be predicted by blood or lymph drainage. For example, the venous drainage of prostate, thyroid, and kidney tumors should predispose to secondary growth in the lung, but these tumors all preferentially metastasize to bone. And note, as well, that tumor emboli carried in arterial blood, and therefore widely disseminated, rarely establish secondary growth in skin or in skeletal or cardiac muscle.

Current research has established four factors that combine to determine a tumor's success in becoming established at a secondary site. The first of these involves specific binding of the tumor cells to the endothelium of the vessel in which they are lodged. Those tumors with surface receptors that match particular endothelial adhesion molecules can bind at the surface. Those lacking the receptors cannot adhere. The significance of the binding event is its triggering of a critical response in the underlying epithelial cells. When their surface adhesion molecules are bound, their edges retract to expose the underlying basement membrane. This exposure allows easier movement of tumor cells out of the vessel (**extravasation**).

The second factor is the differing complements of enzymes that tumors can produce to degrade vessel basement membranes and the extracellular matrix of the secondary site. A given tumor's enzymes will permit to gain access to certain tissue quite easily while allowing it to invade other secondary sites only with great difficulty.

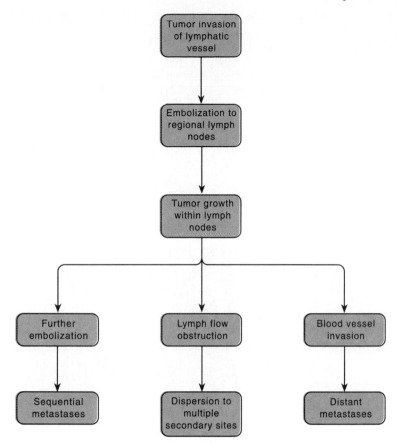

Figure 6.20   Consequences of lymphatic invasion and embolization.

Third, the metabolic activity at a secondary site will produce substances that act as attractants for certain tumor cells, while other tumor types are unresponsive to them. Thus various tissues will differ in the chemotactic coaxing they offer to cells lodged in their small vessels.

The fourth factor is the variation in the array of growth factors present in the body tissues. If a given tissue has the growth factors needed to support the particular type of tumor that has been delivered to it, then a metastatic site will be more easily established. If the necessary factors are absent, growth at the secondary site will be less likely to occur.

In summary, for secondary tumor growth to succeed, tumor emboli must be able to adhere selectively to vascular endothelium. Once they achieve adhesion, the cells must be able to release the enzymes that will allow them to escape from the vessel and infiltrate the adjacent tissue. Then, sufficient tissue chemotactic and growth factors must be present, to promote invasion and support secondary growth. Where any of these factors are lacking or deficient, secondary tumor growth is much less likely to be successful (fig. 6.21).

Metastasis Via Body Cavities

The second major mechanism of metastasis involves tumor spread by way of the body's cavities. In such cases, tumors can invade through to the exterior of the primary site organ and spread to other sites. For example, adenocarcinoma cells may be shed from the pancreas and move to the inferior extremes of the pelvic cavity, where they grow to form a shelflike mass of tumor that surrounds the rectum. In the case of a neuroblastoma whose primary site is the medulla oblongata, cells shed from the primary tumor may "seed" down the subarachnoid space to resume growth at inferior regions of the spinal canal.

Iatrogenic Metastasis

Another mechanism of metastasis is iatrogenic (due to medical intervention) and is probably very rare. In obtaining a biopsy for diagnostic purposes, or during surgical excision of a tumor, it is possible that a surgical instrument could introduce tumor tissue alt a site where it might develop into a secondary tumor. The incidence of iatrogenic metastasis is difficult to determine. However, the

The deeply pigmented masses in these various organs are the result of the widespread metastasis of a malignant melanoma. The victim was a 52-year-old man who first noticed numerous small lumps in the skin over various parts of his body. They were not painful and in some their dark coloration was visible through the skin. He also had noticed that his urine was quite dark.

One of the lesions was biopsied and was identified as metastatic melanoma. The primary site could not be identified, but the search for it revealed numerous secondary sites of tumor growth. For some reason the spleen and liver were not involved, although they normally support secondary tumor growth quite well. Large amounts of melanin were being excreted in the urine, which explained its coloration.

The patient died six months later. At autopsy, the extensive metastases shown here, as well as numerous others in the skin, lymph nodes, and lung mucosae, were found.

Certain naturally existing passages, such as intestinal, urinary, or other ducts, would seem to offer low-resistance paths that favor metastasis. This concept is especially appealing in light of the normal motion of the passage's contents, which would seem to favor the transport of tumor cells shed from a primary tumor at the point where it invades the passage. However plausible, there is little evidence to indicate such a mechanism is at all significant in tumor metastasis. Perhaps the mucous membrane or other modifications, which isolate the duct's wall from its contents' potential dangers, also minimize adherence, invasion, and growth by cells that arrive at distal parts of the passage.

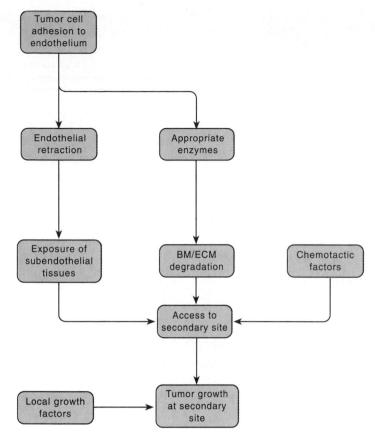

Figure 6.21   Requirements for successful metastasis of a tumor cell embolus.

Table 6.3	Typical Sites of Metastasis for Selected Primary Tumors

Primary Tumor	Typical Sites of Metastasis
Carcinoma and breast adenocarcinoma	Bone (especially vertebral column), brain, liver, adrenals, regional lymph nodes
Bronchogenic carcinoma	Brain, spinal cord, bone, skin, regional lymph nodes
Osteosarcoma	Lung, brain
Renal carcinoma	Lung, liver, bone, brain
Prostatic carcinoma	Bone (especially vertebral column)
Colon carcinoma	Liver, brain, ovary, lung, regional lymph nodes
Neuroblastoma	Bone, regional lymph nodes
Malignant melanoma	Lung, liver, spleen, regional lymph nodes

surgical team's awareness of this danger is probably sufficient to keep the incidence extremely low. Table 6.3 indicates some typical tumors and the tissues to which they characteristically metastasize.

TUMOR EFFECTS

Tissue Destruction

The presence of a tumor growing at a primary and perhaps one or more secondary sites in the body can be expected to affect normal functions. The tumor's autonomous growth produces a wide range of local and systemic effects. In the case of benign tumors, these effects may be relatively minor and slow to develop. For the malignant tumor, invasion and metastasis tend to produce an increasing burden of damage, whose effects will ultimately overwhelm the host unless vigorous therapeutic intervention can be brought to bear.

Normal tissues in the immediate vicinity of a growing tumor are directly at risk. The cells of such tissues suffer the effects of the tumor's aggressive expansion at the expense of their own structure and function. The cells that are destroyed are replaced by tumor tissue. Functional

Lung

Pleural
space

Pericardial
space

Heart

(a)

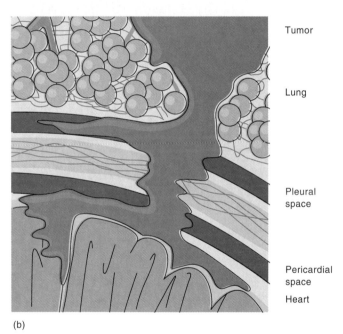

Tumor

Lung

Pleural
space

Pericardial
space

Heart

(b)

Figure 6.22   (*a*) Normal heart and lung motion is unrestricted because fluid in the pleural and pericardial space is present, reducing friction. (*b*) An invading lung tumor has penetrated to the heart, joining the two organs and restricting their normal freedom of movement.

deterioration follows as functional cells steadily decline in quantity. Cells may atrophy in response to the pressure applied by the tumor mass. Tumor growth may compress blood vessels to compromise nutrient supply and waste removal. Both mechanisms probably contribute to a tumor's local destructive effects. Release of destructive enzymes may also be a factor.

A further local complication can arise when a highly malignant tumor in one organ penetrates its capsule to invade an adjacent structure. For example, a common cause of death in cervical carcinoma is renal failure. The kidney damage is the result of tumor invasion from the cervix to the adjacent ureter and then to the kidney. Not only does such invasion from one organ to another broaden the functional deficit, but normal motion, for example, respiratory or peristaltic, may be restricted by tumor tissue that joins the two structures (fig. 6.22).

Even if no invasion occurs, a tumor's compression of an adjacent structure may be harmful. The central nervous system is especially vulnerable in having a soft consistency that is easily distorted and in being housed within the rigid walls of the skull and vertebral column. Intracranial tumors can cause damage as their expansion compresses brain tissue. **18** The spinal cord may be compressed by primary or secondary tumors of the vertebral column, and the intervertebral foramen may provide an opening through which an adjacent tumor can reach the spinal cord and compress it.

Obstruction

Depending on its location, a tumor may cause less damage through tissue destruction than it does by obstructing a duct or other passage so as to interfere with normal movement or flow. Such obstruction may arise from a tumor's growth within a duct lumen, as typically occurs in carcinomas arising in mucosal epithelia. On the other hand, a growing tumor may apply external pressure to a duct, narrowing its lumen and restricting flow (fig. 6.23). Examples of internal obstructions are tumors of the bronchi, **19** which can block air flow (fig. 6.24), and **pharyngeal or esophageal carcinoma,** which interferes with swallowing. The ureters are especially vulnerable to obstruction from the external pressures produced by ovarian, prostatic, rectal, and cervical tumors.

A small but critically situated benign tumor can be particularly dangerous in spite of its relatively low invasive capability and its inability to metastasize. For example, a benign glioma growing adjacent to the cerebral aqueduct, which connects the third and fourth ventricles of the brain, need only expand a small amount before completely stopping the flow of cerebrospinal fluid. The resulting pressure increase within the third and lateral ventricles poses a serious threat to the brain, especially since it is confined within the unyielding bone of the skull. **20** Similarly, a rather small papilloma within the bile duct system can produce significant effects by interfering with bile drainage.

Flow in the superior vena cava may be obstructed by growth of an adjoining lung tumor, or by a tumor in the lymph nodes that surround the vessel. An expanding tumor can compress the vein against the adjacent sternum and right primary bronchus. The low pressure and thin wall of

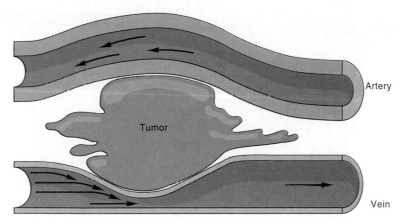

Figure 6.23   Tumor growth can compress adjacent vessels, obstructing flow. Because of their thinner walls, veins are more vulnerable than arteries.

(a)

(b)

Figure 6.24   Tumor obstruction. (*a*) Growth of a carcinoma in the trachea and primary bronchi can greatly obstruct the flow of air. (*b*) A colon carcinoma. Note the dilated proximal segment of the colon, where its contents accumulated behind the obstructing tumor. Note also the two polyps. The malignant and fatal tumor shown may well have arisen from such growths.
Acute, intense abdominal cramping and paroxysms of diarrhea were the result of the tumor shown here. It has severely restricted the lumen of this patient's colon. Lower GI scans revealed air and fluid accumulating proximal to the point of obstruction. These distressing events were superimposed on this patient's numerous other problems, stemming from a lung tumor and a damaged heart, which finally caused his death.

the vena cava make it especially vulnerable to compression, and interference with its large blood flow can have acute and serious consequences.

Infection

Infection is often associated with the presence of a tumor. This may be due, in part, to the general suppression of the immune system's anti-infection responses that is associated with some tumors, especially those of the marrow and lymphoid tissues. Also, where a tumor grows near a body surface, whether internal or external, the surface may be pene-

trated by invading tumor tissue. This disruption of the surface interferes with one of its essential functions: providing a barrier to infective organisms. When the barrier is damaged, microorganisms have easier access to the tissues and a greater chance of becoming established. Infection is often a result of tumor obstruction of the ureter, gastrointestinal tract, or respiratory passages. Patterns of motion in the intestinal tract strictly limit bacterial proliferation. The normal mucous motion produced by ciliary action in the respiratory mucosa restricts access of microorganisms to the lungs, and continuous flow of urine in the ureter prevents urethral organisms from reaching the kidney. When a tumor interferes with these normal preventive mechanisms, the risk of infection—pyelonephritis in the case of the urinary passages, bronchopneumonia in the case of the lungs—rises greatly. Infections in the small intestine or colon can erode the bowel wall to the point of perforation, posing the threat of peritoneal irritation. Peritonitis is a common complication of such tumor-related abdominal infections.

Effects on the Blood

Tumor growth can affect the blood directly, by promoting bleeding, or indirectly by its effects on red bone marrow. Blood loss may arise as tumor invasion breaks through a body surface, allowing blood to escape more rapidly from disrupted vessels. Hemorrhage at internal gastrointestinal surfaces can be particularly threatening because significant losses can occur before they are noticed.

Bone marrow abnormalities can also contribute to bleeding. When primary or secondary tumor growth replaces normal marrow, the reduced production of platelets compromises normal coagulation responses and increased bleeding is the result. The liver can exaggerate these hypocoagulation effects since it is the production site for several key blood-clotting factors. When primary, or more commonly secondary, tumor growth replaces functional liver tissue, inadequate clotting factor production can compromise coagulation and promote hemorrhage.

The marrow's production of white blood cells, especially the phagocytic neutrophils and monocytes, is also suppressed by the presence of tumor. This causes, in part, the lowered infection resistance to which we referred in the last section. More importantly, **erythropoiesis** (red cell production) is reduced, causing the systemic anemia seen in many cancer patients. Although loss of active marrow is a principal cause, other tumor-related factors often contribute to anemia. Gastrointestinal tumors that interfere with normal absorption can significantly reduce the availability of iron and Vitamin B_{12}, and thereby prevent the marrow from maintaining adequate erythrocyte production. Bleeding, another cause of iron loss, is often a major factor in anemia. Yet another contribution to reduced erythropoiesis is the lack of **purines** and **folates** that are needed by the marrow to sustain its high reproduction rates. Growing tumors, which require these substances also, are able to accumulate and store large quantities of them, thus depriving the marrow of an adequate supply.

Although primary and metastatic tumor growth within the marrow can produce the suppressive effects described earlier, other tumor-related factors often contribute to the suppression of marrow. One is the production of marrow-suppressing substances by tumors growing in other tissues. These substances enter the blood at their site of production and are then delivered to the marrow. Other factors are the infections that often accompany tumor growth and the marrow suppressant effects of many of the chemical and radiation therapies used in treating patients with malignant tumors. In the case of renal tumors, **21** an inadequate production of **erythropoietin** may suppress red cell production and give rise to anemia.

Apart from its effects on blood loss and marrow suppression, a tumor can also produce anemia by destroying circulating red blood cells. In some leukemias, lymphomas, and solid tumors, particularly in the elderly, the immune system produces antibodies directed against normal erythrocytes. The mechanism is unknown, but the resulting **hemolysis** causes red cell losses that the often suppressed marrow cannot replace. Anemia is the result.

These effects of tumor growth on the blood are summarized in figure 6.25. **Polycythemia,** where excessive production of erythrocytes occurs, is seen in renal cell carcinoma. Here, a tumor secretion is produced to excess, with harmful effect. The secretion is the hormone erythropoietin, which stimulates the marrow. As a result, the rate of erythropoiesis is increased, and excessively large numbers of red cells pour into the blood.

Pain

It is well known that pain, intermittent or constant, and often severe, is associated with tumor growth. The pain can arise in two ways. First, nerves may be directly invaded by the growing tumor. Second, as it expands, the tumor produces unusual pressure and tensions in the adjacent normal tissues; their nerve endings are affected and pain results. In the case of tumors of the spinal cord (glioma, meningioma), the rigid vertebral column or skull restricts the tumor mass, causing pain as the cord or brain is compressed.

Cachexia

The condition known as **cachexia** is seen most often in advanced malignancies. Cachexia is a syndrome involving generalized weakness, fever, wasting (weight loss), **anorexia** (loss of appetite), and pallor. This pattern of signs and symptoms is probably not the result of any single cause but rather represents the cumulative effects of the factors described above. Thus infection might contribute to weakness and fever, and hemorrhage and anemia to further weakness and pallor. Wasting would follow tumor-induced nutritional imbalance or intestinal malabsorption, in the case of small bowel tumors. Also pain, depression, and anxiety would produce anorexia and a reduced food intake. A specific growth factor, variously named **cachectin** or **tumor necrosis factor-alpha,** may play a role in cachectic wasting. The speculation is that cachectin contributes to the increased metabolic consumption of nutrients that is characteristic of cachexia. In combination with loss of appetite and reduced nutrient intake, wasting would result.

Other factors contributing to cachexia might be toxins and the necrotic debris released from damaged tissues. These substances would ordinarily be detoxified by the

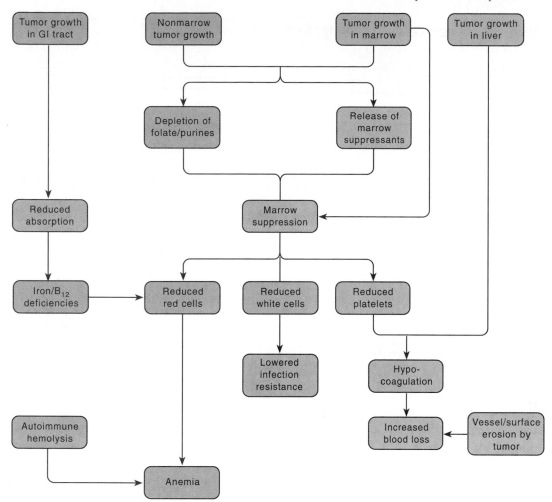

Figure 6.25   Principal effects of tumor growth on the blood.

liver, but hepatic metastases might depress such functions. As the various aspects of cachexia worsen, death may follow, with its specific cause remaining obscure. The tumor's growth, its spread, and then the multiple effects that produce cachexia increase to the point where the victim is overwhelmed.

The principal tumor effects are summarized in figure 6.26.

Hormonal Effects

Tumors of endocrine tissues produce their effects through abnormal and uncontrolled hormone secretion. Improper regulation of various body tissues follows, with potentially serious systemic consequences. In the case of benign tumors, or malignancies that are less anaplastic, functional hormone may be produced, with hypersecretion and overstimulation of target tissues the result. In the case of more anaplastic malignancies, hormones may function only partially or not at all. Hyposecretion follows, to cause a reduced input to target tissues. In either case the result can present a serious threat to the host. In pancreatic islet cell adenoma, hyperinsulinism results and can cause

hypokalemia followed by coma and death. Adenoma in the adrenal cortex can lead to systemic hypertension, the result of excessive sodium and water retention, and to hypokalemia from excessive potassium losses. Both conditions are the result of hypersecretion of aldosterone.

A phenomenon seen in the case of some tumors is **ectopic secretion.** This means that tumors of nonendocrine origin develop the ability to secrete functional hormones. For example, lung carcinomas may secrete insulin, parathormones, antidiuretic hormone, and others. (Some recent evidence indicates that the lung normally secretes certain hormones in minute amounts.) Parathormone may also be secreted by breast, ovarian, or kidney tumors. Adrenocorticotropic hormone, a normal secretion of the pituitary gland, may be secreted by tumors of the lung, parathyroids, or kidneys. Such abnormalities of secretion may be indications that the tumor cell has access to genetic information that is normally masked. On the other hand, they may be related to abnormal differentiation—the anaplasia associated with malignancy. Whether deriving from endocrine or nonendocrine tissues, a relatively small hormone-secreting tumor can cause large systemic effects.

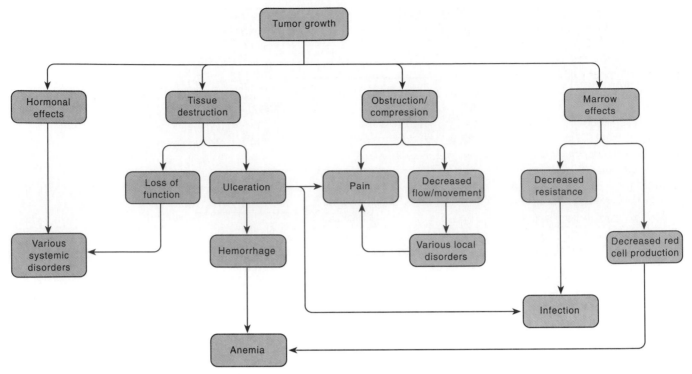

Figure 6.26   A summary of the local and systemic effects of tumor growth.

Paraneoplastic Syndromes

By **paraneoplastic syndromes** we mean the wide variety of tumor-related effects whose pathogenesis is poorly understood. The presence of the tumor and the paraneoplastic effects are easily established, but the links between them remain obscure. An example is the occurrence of leg vein thrombosis in cases of pancreatic or lung tumors. Tumor or necrotic tissue products might be implicated in damaging the endothelia of the veins that drain the region of tumor growth, but the relationship to the leg vein thrombosis is unexplained. Some lung and breast carcinomas are associated with muscle and peripheral nervous abnormalities, whereas other tumors, although not situated in the head, produce symptoms of increased intracranial pressure. Two possible explanations are circulating toxic tumor products or the deposition of tumor-derived antigen-antibody complexes in affected tissues. Further research is expected to clarify the pathogenesis of these puzzling situations.

ONCOGENESIS

As indicated earlier, tumor formation (**oncogenesis**) involves a fundamental alteration of cell reproduction and differentiation. Tumor cells seem unable to maintain a state in which they can carry out normal functions according to their particular specializations without dividing. Consider the fact that most tumors arise in tissues that have high normal rates of reproduction, namely, epithelia and marrow.

Consider also that permanent tissues that have lost their reproductive capacity almost never become neoplastic. For example, tumors of skeletal muscle and neurons are extremely rare, and may not exist at all. It is difficult, however, to be absolutely certain because tumors that are highly anaplastic may closely resemble each other, even though originating in different tissues. Also, unusual differentiation patterns, seen in some tumors, might produce characteristics similar to those of muscle or neurons. The rare primary tumors thought to derive from skeletal muscle or neurons probably originate in embryonic cells that haven't fully differentiated.

Because cell growth and differentiation are governed by information contained in the chromosomes, it is here that the fundamental neoplastic transformation must arise. Factors that alter certain critical components of a cell's genetic makeup can either stimulate the cell's growth rate or allow the cell to escape growth-limiting controls to grow autonomously. Such changes in genetic makeup raise the question of transmitting tumors to future generations: the role of heredity in oncogenesis.

Heredity

Little is known of the hereditary factors in oncogenesis because of the great difficulties associated with human genetic studies. Only a small number of tumors can be ascribed to directly transmitted genetic defects. In these cases, a family pattern of tumor incidence provides the basis for fairly accurate prediction of tumor incidence in future generations. The relatively rare **polyposis coli, xeroderma pigmentosum,** and **retinoblastoma** are examples of such directly transmitted tumors. In some tumors, such as breast cancer (when it occurs before menopause) and bronchogenic and colon carcinoma, heredity appears to be a factor, but its role is not well understood. Familial patterns of incidence seem to occur but prediction is much less precise. In such cases, it can only be said that close relatives of a cancer patient are more likely to develop the same tumor than more distant relatives, or those unrelated. Similarly, differences in tumor incidence seem related to racial background. However, since racial and ethnic differences are often accompanied by environmental or cultural differences, the hereditary effects are difficult to isolate. As with any cellular or somatic characteristic, there is an interplay between hereditary and environmental factors in oncogenesis (fig. 6.27).

Environmental Factors

A great deal is known of the role of environmental agents in oncogenesis. Experimental evidence derived from oncogenesis studies strongly supports the concept that tumor formation can result from exposure to agents in the cell's environment. These interact with and alter the DNA of the cell's chromosomes to bring about transformation from normal to neoplastic. The following are the principal environmental agents known to be capable of inducing tumor formation.

Physical Agents

Energy in the form of solar or ionizing radiation can induce tumor formation. Evidence clearly shows that increased exposure to radiation yields increased rates of **carcinogenesis,** or cancer production (the terms carcinogenesis and oncogenesis are often used interchangeably). Both solar radiation and ionizing radiation are known to damage cells and especially nucleic acids (see chapter 1). When DNA is altered in certain poorly understood ways, changes from the normal to the neoplastic come about. On the other hand, in addition to DNA damage, radiation may activate other oncogenetic factors or suppress antitumor defenses (discussed in a later section). The result in either case would be increased tumor incidence. Usually a lag period of many years is involved before radiation-induced tumors are discovered.

There are two major sources of exposure to radiation. One is the ultraviolet radiation of the sun. Those who work in the sun for long hours over many years show increased rates of skin cancer. The disease is often preceded by a dry, flaky, thickened condition of the skin called **actinic keratosis.** The second source of exposure is ionizing radiation from industrial or medical sources. Those working with

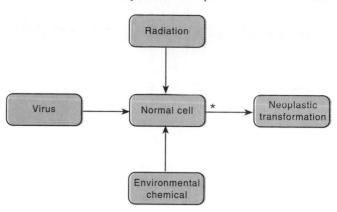

Figure 6.27   The major etiological factors in oncogenesis. Asterisk represents mediation of the process by hereditary or hormonal factors.

industrial or medical X-ray equipment or radioactive materials in mining, manufacturing, or medicine are at risk of increased tumor incidence. Any unnecessary exposure to medical or dental X-rays adds to the total burden of carcinogen exposure and should be avoided.

Viruses

Viruses are the only biological agents implicated in carcinogenesis. Because viruses are known to interact with the chromosomal DNA of the cells they infect, it seems plausible that they could introduce changes in the chromosomes that would predispose to neoplasia. Although a few human tumors strongly suggest viral involvement, the evidence is only circumstantial.

There is evidence that women who use birth control pills have a greater risk of developing cervical carcinoma, **22** as do women infected with HPV, the human papilloma virus (which causes genital warts). When epithelial cells are grown in tissue culture and then infected with HPV, no cancers arise. However, when progesterone, the hormone forming a component of many birth control pills, is added to the culture, the infected cells become neoplastic. Their growth rate increases five to six times. For various reasons, this work does not clearly show the pill to be the causative agent in cervical cancer. It does illustrate an intriguing link between a cell, an infecting virus, and their hormonal environment. The principal human tumors and their suspected viral agents are presented in table 6.4. Further research is proceeding.

Environmental Chemicals

For over 100 years it has been recognized that the transformation from normal to neoplastic can be induced by chemicals that originate in our environment. During this time many specifically carcinogenic substances have been recognized and studied. As new chemical structures are

Table 6.4	Viruses Associated with Human Tumors

Virus	Associated Tumor
Hepatitis B (HBV)	Hepatocellular carcinoma
Human papilloma virus (HPV)	Skin and cervical carcinomas
Epstein-Barr virus	Burkitt's lymphoma* and nasopharyngeal carcinoma
Human T-cell leukemia virus	Some leukemias
Cytomegalovirus	Kaposi's sarcoma*

* AIDS-related tumors

The role of these viruses in tumor etiology, if any, and their links to tumor pathogenesis are not well understood.

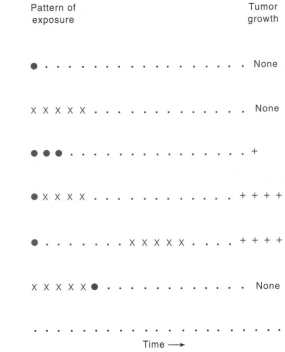

● Initiator

x Promoter

Figure 6.28   Chemical oncogenesis: the effects of various patterns of exposure to initiators and promoters on tumor development.

produced and marketed, many inevitably reach body tissues by direct or indirect routes. Those substances are either industrial by-products or consumer products specifically intended to provide some benefit. Pollutants that are inhaled or ingested (e.g., in water supplies) or substances in foods, cosmetics, clothing, or medicines may be carcinogenic. The list of chemical carcinogens has increased dramatically and will probably continue to do so. Note that exposure to a chemical carcinogen is usually prolonged before actual tumor formation occurs. In other words, a few brief encounters with a carcinogen are unlikely to produce a tumor. (In addition to the growth rates described earlier, this may be a second reason why most tumors arise in a person's later years. Over 80% of all tumors are diagnosed in those past 55 years of age.)

Mechanisms of Oncogenesis

Because oncogenesis is complex and difficult to study, details of oncogenetic mechanisms are scarce. It appears, however, that two distinct processes are involved. One is **initiation,** whereby an essential change is first introduced into the cell. This is probably an alteration of the cell's DNA that establishes the essential capacity for neoplastic change. Generally, more than one initiation event seems required for tumor production. Initiation is irreversible, but the actual development of a tumor often depends on the second process involved in oncogenesis, **promotion.** When cells are exposed to initiators, a certain, usually low, rate of tumor formation can be observed. When the same type of cell is exposed to promoters alone, no tumors develop. When both initiator and promoter are present, however, tumor formation is greatly favored. Usually, prolonged application of the promoter is required. Tumors result even when exposure to the promoter is delayed after initiation. Promotion before initiation results in no tumor formation (fig. 6.28).

The action of initiators and promoters may provide the explanation for certain long-observed characteristics of tumors in humans. For example, most tumors occur in old age. This may be the result of a long period of promotion required for tumor formation or of low rates of exposure to promoters after initiation. Many tumors are hormone-dependent. That is, their growth is greatly increased when certain hormones (usually the sex hormones) are present. These hormones may be acting as promoters in such cases. The concept of promotion may also explain why tumor incidence varies in a given family or the general population, because individuals would experience differing patterns of exposure to promoters. Numerous studies have shown that increased tumor incidence is linked to various dietary factors, e.g., increased protein, fat, and caloric intake, as well as to occupational exposure, sex, smoking, and age. Some aspect of these conditions may act as a promoting agent that enhances the development of neoplasia. Currently, only a few specific substances can be positively identified as being initiators or promoters. Until further insights are gained, we identify those agents as carcinogenic without knowing their exact role in the process.

Chemical carcinogens alter DNA, typically by binding to it. The result is a change in the cell's information pool that may give rise to the formation of the tumor. It is difficult to determine, but it may be that in some cases a particular chemical is only indirectly carcinogenic. For example,

Chemical Oncogenesis and DNA Damage

Box figure 6.2 provides some additional detail on the process of chemical oncogenesis. Note that exposure to an initiator need not produce permanent changes. The cell's enzymes, its stress protein response (see chapter 1), or other adaptive mechanisms may allow it to cope with the reactive intermediates formfed by the initiator's interaction with cell components. A cell may be exposed to the initiator but recover from its effects. If the cell is unable to clear the reactive intermediates, their binding to DNA poses a serious threat. If the cell lacks the needed DNA repair systems, the damage may destroy the cell or cause it to be permanently susceptible to neoplastic transformation by the later action of a promoter. It is thought that human tumors require a sequence of several DNA changes before full promoter susceptibility is developed; a few exposures to a carcinogen is, in most cases, unlikely to yield a tumor.

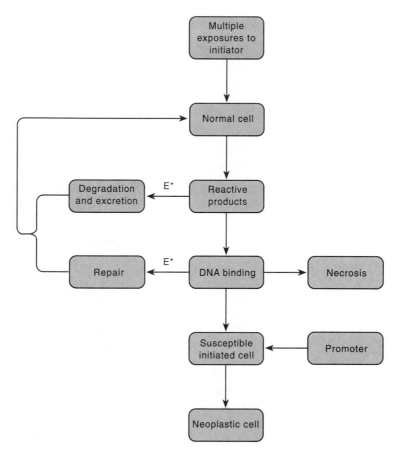

Box Figure 6.2   Initiation and promotion in oncogenesis. E* represents the role of adaptive enzyme responses in coping with the initiators' effects.

it might activate a virus already present in the cell, or by interacting with DNA or other cell constituents, it might make the cell more susceptible to initiation or promotion by other agents.

Because certain enzyme and other adaptive systems have variable occurrence within the population, some individuals have a higher risk of developing a tumor than do others. This important factor may well explain the variations in tumor incidence in groups whose individual members have similar exposure to carcinogen chemicals.

Certain classes of chemicals are known to have many carcinogenic members, although it should be noted that oncogenic potency varies within each class of carcinogenic compounds. The following are some of the major classes of chemical carcinogens.

Polycyclic Hydrocarbons

Polycyclic hydrocarbons are a class of substances derived primarily from the combustion of organic compounds. Their name is descriptive in that they consist only of hydrogen and carbon. The carbon atoms are joined to form closed rings, with three or more such rings forming the molecule. Typical exposures are the result of inhaling smoke or ingesting smoked foods (e.g., smoked fish). The potent carcinogen **benzopyrene,** for example, is a common constituent of cigarette smoke. It is thought to act as an initiator in carcinogenesis. At the same time, tobacco combustion also produces tumor promoters, so the delivery of cigarette smoke to the respiratory passages is a highly efficient carcinogenic process. It was the polycyclic hydrocarbons that were first linked to chemical carcinogenesis in chimney sweeps, who developed higher rates of scrotal tumors than those not exposed to the polycyclic hydrocarbons of chimney soot.

Aromatic Amines

These are carbon ring structures to which an amino group is linked. Many **aromatic amines** are carcinogenic. These are substances used as dyes for fabrics or as coloring agents in foodstuffs. One of this group, **methylaminobenzene,** is metabolized in the liver to produce a carcinogenic agent that causes primary hepatic tumors. Another, **II-naphthylamine,** has its carcinogenic metabolites altered in the liver to a form that can be cleared by the kidney and excreted in the urine. Unfortunately, the urinary bladder's mucosa contains an enzyme that converts the excreted form back to the carcinogenic form. The result is a high incidence of bladder carcinoma in those exposed to II-naphthylamine.

Nitrosamines

This is another class of compounds that can induce tumors. In cells, **nitrosamines** form products that interfere with DNA replication. The result is errors of DNA replication that in some way bring about the neoplastic transformation. Nitrosamines can form when nitrite ion reacts with amino acids. The process is favored by heat and acidity. Because nitrite ion is commonly used as a meat preservative, and because Western diets are rich in amino-acid-containing protein, people whose diets contain large amounts of bacon, ham, sausage, or canned meats may be at risk, especially since the high acidity of the gastric secretions would favor nitrosamine formation even if the nitrite-containing meats were not cooked. The actual risk is not known, and since nitrite is a normal constituent of saliva as well as other substances that are commonly ingested, there may be protective mechanisms operating to reduce nitrosamine formation or to minimize the effects when nitrosamines do form. It is known that ascorbic acid (vitamin C) inhibits nitrosamine formation. Perhaps the traditional vitamin C-containing orange juice before a breakfast of bacon has for many years provided unsuspected anticancer benefits.

Aflatoxin

A carcinogen of biological origin called **aflatoxin** is produced by fungi of the genus **Aspergillus.** [23] These fungi are widely distributed and grow on the surfaces of numerous vegetable products. While these products are growing or being stored before distribution for consumption, conditions of dampness and warmth favor production of the toxin. Animal experiments indicate that aflatoxin acts as a hepatocarcinogen, since liver tumors develop when it is converted to a form that binds to DNA. Improperly stored peanuts, cotton seeds, and corn are examples of farm products subject to aflatoxin contamination.

Inorganic Carcinogens

To this point the carcinogens described have all been organic chemicals, but inorganic substances are also capable of inducing tumor formation. Cadmium, cobalt, and lead are known to be carcinogenic. Workers involved with nickel are at increased risk of lung cancer, as are those exposed to asbestos, a complex inorganic molecule used in fireproofing insulation and various other applications.

Note that chronic exposure to cobalt can lead to tumor formation. Inhaled or ingested cobalt can be carcinogenic as it interacts with body tissues. This effect should not be confused with the beneficial therapeutic effects of ionizing radiation derived from a radioactive form of cobalt. The radioactive cobalt is typically housed in a system that can focus and deliver its ionizing radiation to a tumor to destroy it. (See the section on antitumor therapy, later in this chapter.)

The conclusion to be drawn from the preceding information on carcinogenesis is that many cancers are preventable. Although viruses are impossible to avoid because of their extremely wide distribution and ability to remain within cells without destroying them, their carcinogenic role is unclear. However, in the case of radiation and carcinogenic chemicals, it seems clear that minimizing their introduction to the environment will reduce tumor incidence. The reduction of exposure to those carcinogens that cannot be eliminated is, of course, also indicated. For example, lung cancer, the most common North American tumor, [24] would become a rare disease if cigarette smoking were discontinued. After only 20 years this change would result in a major reduction of all cancer-related deaths.

TUMOR IMMUNOLOGY

The fact that individual cells each carry a particular array of membrane surface antigens is well established. In recent years, evidence from animal studies has indicated that tumor cells carry a unique complement of antigens. These are known as **tumor-specific antigens** (TSAs). The implication to be drawn from their presence is the possibility that the immune system can recognize and destroy the TSA-bearing tumor cells by means similar to those used in destroying an organ transplant or invading microorganisms.

Clear evidence that TSAs are present in human tumors is lacking, but there are some indications that they are present. For example, certain tumors of the lung, breast, colon, and testes that are infiltrated by lymphocytes and

Figure 6.29 Factors that limit the ability of the immune system to suppress tumor growth.

macrophages have a better prognosis. The suggestion is that the tumor's growth and spread is impeded by immune-mediated suppression by the infiltrating cells. Another line of supporting evidence is found in the higher incidence of tumors seen in those whose immune response is suppressed or lacking. Transplant recipients who receive immune suppression therapy, AIDS sufferers whose immune response is suppressed by a virus, and people whose immune system develops inadequately all have a higher tumor incidence than those in the general population. The rare but well-documented cases of spontaneous remissions of malignant tumor could be attributable to the host's immune, anti-TSA defenses. The term **immune surveillance** refers to the theory that the immune system can recognize and eliminate tumor cells that arise and express TSA. There is a widespread research effort seeking to verify and pursue the ramifications of immune surveillance for therapy and prevention (see chapter 5).

Obviously, tumors do arise in spite of host defenses. In the case of the immune system, it may be that tumor growth outstrips the immune response or that a reduced immune capability allows the tumor to survive. An infection, some nutritional deficiency, or other factors might cause a disturbance in the normal immune response, allowing tumors to evade recognition and destruction. Furthermore, some tumors have specific immune suppression abilities that may help to increase their chance of survival. Another possibility is suggested by the fact that some highly anaplastic tumors lose their TSAs. This would enable them to escape the immune component of the host's antitumor defenses. Also, because most TSAs are only weakly antigenic, the immune system may have difficulty in mounting an adequate response. Figure 6.29 summarizes these factors.

Fetal Antigens

Another aspect of tumor immunology has been useful in the diagnosis of tumors. Some tumors carry antigens that are not normally present beyond the time of birth. These are fetal antigens that are normally suppressed after birth. Their presence on some tumors is probably a reflection of a process related to anaplasia. The emergence of the fetal antigens may be associated with the formation of a poorly differentiated tumor cell. Fetal antigens elicit only weak immune responses, but they can be detected in the plasma of tumor bearing individuals. When found, they indicate the presence of a tumor. The two fetal antigens most widely used for diagnosis are carcinoembryonic antigen (CEA) for tumors of the lung, pancreas, and gastrointestinal tract and alpha-fetoprotein (AFP) for primary hepatomas.

The immune system's role in tumor defense is greater in some tumors than in others. One of the difficulties in assessing its contribution to the overall process is the lack of information on other antitumor defenses.

ANTITUMOR THERAPY

The essential approach in antitumor therapy is the removal or destruction of the tumor. Several quite different techniques are commonly employed, but all face an essential difficulty, that of confining their effects to the tumor while sparing normal tissue. The techniques also often involve significant and unpleasant side effects. The following sections describe the major antitumor therapies currently in use.

Surgery

The surgical approach to therapy is simple and direct. It seeks to physically remove the tumor mass and thus eliminate the problem. However, the nature of tumor growth and spread presents certain, often major, difficulties. These are minimal in the case of a well-defined, encapsulated, benign tumor growing in a noncritical tissue. In such cases the tumor can easily be removed, with only minor disturbance to adjacent normal tissue. By contrast, the irregular, invasive growth of malignant tumors can present great difficulty. Because the edge of the malignant tumor is not well defined, it is not possible to excise all of it without also removing some of the adjacent normal tissue that might contain invading tumor cells. Thus, depending on the size and growth pattern of the tumor, varying amounts of normal tissue will inevitably be lost. This loss can present significant difficulties where the nervous system or a small gland is involved.

If the tumor has spread from the primary site along lymphatic channels, these channels must be removed along with any involved lymph nodes that contain tumor tissue.

Lymph node removal continues along the channels that drain the region until no further tumor is found. The lack of tumor is not necessarily a positive sign, however, since metastasis via blood embolization may have already occurred by tumor cells that have invaded blood vessels in the lymph nodes. Surgery is also complicated by the possibility that surgical manipulation of the tumor may produce large numbers of tumor emboli, which can metastasize to produce secondary growths. In cases in which the tumor is large, invasion to adjacent organs is extensive, or tumor growth involves a critical organ, the tumor may be judged to be inoperable. In such cases other therapies must be used.

Radiation Therapy

Radiation therapy seeks to deliver a destructive dose of ionizing radiation to the tumor mass. Of course, normal tissue is also susceptible to damage from ionizing radiation (see chapter 1), and this presents the major difficulty in radiation therapy. Many complex and sophisticated techniques are used to maximize the dose reaching the tumor, while minimizing destructive effects on normal tissues. Some tumors are **radiosensitive**; that is, they are much more susceptible to radiation damage than are other tumors. These are best suited to radiation therapies, because dose levels can be restricted and side effects held to a minimum (table 6.5). Because rapidly dividing cells are most sensitive to radiation damage, most radiation side effects involve the rapidly dividing epithelia of the skin, hair, and gastrointestinal tract. Another problem in radiation therapy is the heat that develops in the skin as radiation passes through it to reach an underlying tumor. Such heat may cause skin burns. Sources of ionizing radiation are radioactive isotopes such as cobalt-60 and devices that produce X-rays.

Chemotherapy

In **chemotherapy,** toxic chemical substances are used to destroy the tumor. They interfere in various ways with the cell's metabolism or division. See table 6.6 for some patterns of tumor susceptibility to chemotherapeutic agents. The essential difficulty in chemotherapy is that the therapeutic agent is not able to selectively damage only tumor cells. Normal tissues are also damaged to varying degrees, causing many and often severe side effects. These can not only injure but tend to demoralize the patient undergoing therapy (figure 6.30). Although effective in treating a few primary tumors, such as acute leukemia, most chemotherapy aims at the smaller tumor mass found at metastatic sites.

Unfortunately, chemotherapeutic agents induce a tolerance on the part of the tumor victim. That is, a slowing of tumor growth may occur initially in response to chemotherapy, but after this early period of approximately several months, the antitumor effects seem to fade and tumor growth resumes at its previous higher rate. Such

Table 6.5	Selected Tumors Grouped According to Their Relative Radiosensitivity

Radiosensitive

Neuroblastoma
Chronic leukemia
Lymphomas
Wilm's tumor (renal tumor of childhood)

Moderately Radiosensitive

Squamous cell carcinoma
Genital carcinomas
Esophageal carcinoma
Bronchogenic carcinoma

Nonradiosensitive

Fibrosarcoma
Osteogenic carcinoma
Various adenocarcinomas

Table 6.6	Tumor Susceptibility to Chemotherapeutic Agents

Highly Susceptible

Retinoblastoma
Hodgkin's disease
Wilm's tumor (renal tumor of childhood)
Testicular tumors
Acute lymphoblastic leukemia
Choriocarcinoma

Moderately Susceptible

Small cell carcinoma of lung
Various sarcomas
Lymphocytic lymphoma
Leukemia: acute myeloblastic
chronic granulocytic
Adenocarcinoma of breast and ovary

Resistant

Malignant melanoma
Carcinomas generally
Lung cancer

drug tolerance may be related to the presence in the tumor of a population of cells that are resistant to the drug's effects. On first exposure, the more numerous, drug-sensitive cells are destroyed and tumor growth is restricted. During this time, however, the resistant cells continue to divide until the tumor is large enough to again cause noticeable signs and symptoms.

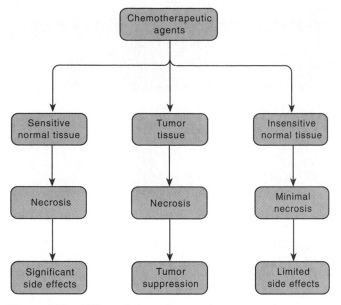

Figure 6.30   Effects of chemotherapeutic agents on the tumor-bearing host.

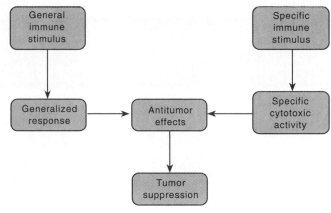

Figure 6.31   Antitumor effects of immune therapy.

Immunotherapy

Immunotherapy seeks to utilize the immune system to combat a growing tumor. Although early attempts to utilize this therapeutic approach seemed promising, its effectiveness has been disappointing. Initial attempts involved administering a substance with potent antigenic properties. The result was a strong, general stimulus to the immune system. The hope was that such a stimulus would increase the antitumor activity of host defenses along with the other parts of the immune response and thus increase tumor destruction. A common immune stimulant used in immunotherapy was the **BCG** (Bacillus-Calmette-Guerin) antigen, which is derived from mycobacteria. More recently, attempts to activate specific cytotoxic cells of the immune system using interleukin 2 (IL-2) have been pursued with some success. Figure 6.31 illustrates the immunotherapy rationale.

As in the other antitumor therapies, there are some side effects and potential problems associated with immunotherapy. Some of these are nausea, fever, liver damage, and inflammation and abscess formation at the sites of antigen injection. Also, potent stimulation of the immune system creates the risk of inducing such a strong response that autoimmune destruction of normal tissue results.

Combination Therapy

The most widely used therapeutic approach in neoplasia is **combination therapy.** This technique involves the use of two or more therapeutic modes in combination. The hope is that tumor destruction can be maximized by attacking the tumor on more than one front. At the same time, side effects are kept to a minimum, because doses of each agent,

for example, drugs or radiation, can be reduced while maintaining the same or even increased lethal effect on the tumor.

Particular therapy combinations are determined by each tumor's pattern of sensitivities to the different agents available. Typically surgery, and in some cases radiation, is first used to reduce the tumor mass, followed by chemotherapy or radiation therapy in an attempt to destroy those cells that could not be surgically removed. For example, surgical removal of a primary tumor might be followed by radiation therapy aimed at the smaller masses of tumor cells that might have spread to adjacent lymph nodes or vessels, or surgery might be followed by both radiation and chemotherapy. In any case the goal remains maximum tumor destruction with minimal discomfort to the patient.

TUMOR STAGING AND GRADING

Tumor staging and grading are means of classifying malignant tumors for the purpose of simplifying description and aiding communication between health professionals.

Tumor Staging

Tumor staging is a system of categorizing malignant tumors in terms of their potential for invasion and metastasis. Because it facilitates description and discussion, it has proved useful in assessing prognosis, selecting appropriate therapy, and carrying out **epidemiological studies,** i.e., studies that consider the relationships between tumors, their host populations, and relevant environmental factors.

Tumor staging is generally applied only to a solid tumor. In the simplest system, a tumor is said to be in stage I if its growth is restricted to its primary site, and in stage IV, if it has grown and invaded extensively and shows wide metastatic dispersal. Stages II and III describe tumors that fall between these extremes.

Various other staging systems have been developed, but because of differing clinical perspectives, degree of complexity, and areas of overlap, they have sometimes introduced confusion instead of clarifying. Here we will

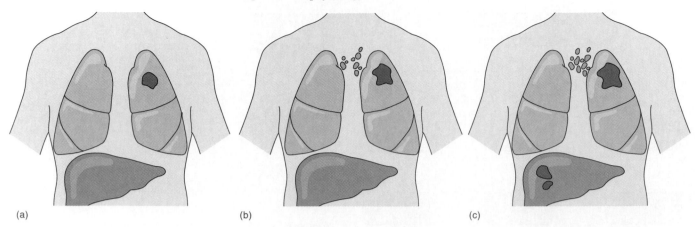

Figure 6.32 The TNM staging system in three patients with lung cancer. (*a*) $T_1N_0M_0$: This patient has a single primary tumor in the lung. It is less than 3 cm in diameter and there is no lymph node involvement or metastasis. (*b*) $T_2N_1M_0$: In this patient, the primary tumor is enlarged and adjacent lymph nodes are involved. (*c*) $T_3N_2M_1$: In the third patient, the primary tumor is large, mediastinal lymph nodes are involved, and there is metastasis to the liver.

deal only with one internationally recognized and widely used malignancy staging system, the TNM system. Again, its use is confined to discrete, solid tumors; it is less applicable to diffuse malignancies, e.g., leukemia (described in chapter 7).

In the TNM system, three tumor criteria are assigned a modifying subscript number related to size, or degree, with lower numbers indicating low values and higher numbers referring to increasing values. The T component refers to the size of the primary tumor. T_0 indicates that no tumor can be found at the primary site, while T_1, T_2, and T_3 indicate tumors of increasing size. The degree to which regional lymph nodes are involved is indicated by the N element. N_0 means there is no regional lymph node enlargement, while N_1, N_2, and N_3 reflect increasing degrees of node involvement. M refers to tumor metastasis, with M_0 meaning that no indications of metastasis are present, while M_1, M_2, and M_3 denote progressively more extensive spread. Figure 6.32 illustrates the TNM system as applied to three different lung cancer patients.

Tumor Grading

Following a biopsy, various histological characteristics of a tumor are assessed and the tumor is then assigned a descriptive designation, or grade. The degree of differentiation, the extent of pleomorphism, and the frequency of mitosis are typically studied as a means of judging the degree of malignancy that a particular tumor has achieved. A grade I tumor exhibits highly differentiated cells, is well ordered, and has few, if any, mitoses visible. At grade IV, the cells are poorly differentiated and pleomorphic, and

Table 6.7		The Relationship between Tumor Grade and Prognosis in Selected Tumors

Tumor Site	Grade	% Survival 5 Yrs After Diagnosis
Thyroid gland	I	85
	II	55
	III	11
Salivary gland	I	85
	II	80
	III	38
	IV	18
Testis	I	85
	II	55
	IV	7

mitoses are increased. Grades II and III represent intermediate degrees of malignancy between these extremes. In general, then, low grades are associated with low growth rates, invasiveness, and metastasis and with better prognosis, while the opposite situation applies at grades III and IV (table 6.7).

Grading of tumors is of limited use in dealing with any individual patient's tumor. Not only is it time-consuming, but it can be misleading, since different regions of a given tumor can exhibit different histologic characteristics. It is, however, a useful tool for studying groups of cases with regard to the effectiveness of therapy or other clinical criteria.

Case Study

The family of an 80-year-old woman noticed that, in contrast to her usual mental acuity, she had recently showed signs of being confused. The woman agreed with this assessment and stated further that she had been having difficulty in selecting appropriate words when speaking. Even more disturbing to her, were the problems she had experienced in doing her favorite crossword puzzles. She had been reluctant to see a doctor because her own physician had recently retired and she was uncertain about going to a new one. On her family's urging she did consent to be examined.

Her new general practitioner found her to have the dry, hacking cough predicted by her 60 years of moderate to heavy smoking. She also had a history of long-standing social alcohol use, but was not an alcoholic. When young she had suffered two bouts of occupational radiation exposure as a radiographic technician during World War I. On both occasions reduced platelet counts had been noted, but she had recovered fully.

Her G.P. also noted that she was taking a variety of medications (a diuretic, an anti-inflammatory, a barbiturate, and a tranquilizer) that did not seem indicated by her otherwise apparently good health. She said her previous physician had prescribed them ". . . because she was getting on . . .", but that she only used them sporadically when she ". . . was having a bad day . . ." or when she felt guilty about not following her doctor's orders.

The doctor ordered a complete blood count and plasma assessments of the BUN (blood urea nitrogen), electrolytes, and vitamin B_{12}, as well as an ECG, all of which were normal. Her liver function tests were also normal and her urine was negative.

On the basis of these findings the doctor explained that he felt she had had a mild stroke, and because routine tasks could be performed but processing new information was difficult, it might be located in the frontal lobes. Because of her previous training she asked if a chest X-ray wouldn't be a good idea. The physician agreed and it revealed the presence of a mass in the middle lobe of her right lung. A bronchoscopy, airway washings, and a transbronchial biopsy were done, but failed to confirm the nature of the mass. A follow-up CT scan of the brain indicated the presence of multiple sites of secondary tumor growth in both frontal lobes.

In the following weeks, her condition worsened, with her speech and general condition deteriorating rapidly. She died ten weeks after her initial presentation. No postmortem examination was performed, but the presumed cause of death was the effects of bronchogenic carcinoma and its brain metastases.

Commentary

Diagnosis based on an elderly patient's confusion and disrupted cognitive functioning is always difficult because of the potential overlapping effects of senility, depression, social isolation, and the multiple side effects of the numerous medications prescribed to alleviate these and other problems associated with old age. If the diet is inadequate, a deficiency of vitamin B_{12} may produce dementia to further complicate diagnosis.

This case is unusual in that a single disease process seemed solely responsible for an elderly patient's demise. More typically in the elderly, death is due to the combined effects of at least two and often several conditions such as infection, heart disease, lung disease, or arteriosclerosis, to cite a few.

The initial suspicion of a frontal lobe cerebrovascular accident (CVA, or stroke) was based on the patient's altered mental functions, which are common to such conditions. The patient had no chest-related symptoms beyond the cough, which had been present for 40 years, and it is quite unusual for a bronchogenic carcinoma not to reveal its presence in the chest in some way before age 80.

Once the tumor's presence was established, the doctor attempted to obtain a sample of the tumor tissue by biopsy or airway washings in the hope that it was an oat cell carcinoma, because they are highly sensitive to chemotherapy.

The final rate of decline was also unusual. The patient was spared the 6 to 12 months of slow deterioration that is typical in such cases.

Key Concepts

1. Because of its high incidence, the serious functional disruptions it causes, and the potentially severe side effects of therapy, neoplasia is a major threat to our health and well-being (p. 118).

2. Changing functional demands or exposure to injurious agents can induce adaptive changes in tissues, some of which involve structural and functional changes from normal (pp. 118–119).

3. The name given to a tumor usually makes reference to its benign or malignant character and to its embryonic tissue of origin (pp. 119–121).

4. A tumor consists of (1) neoplastic cells, usually exhibiting some degree of anaplasia and pleomorphism, (2) stroma and vasculature induced by the increased tissue mass, and (3) some quantity of an often dysfunctional tumor product (pp. 122–124).

5. A benign tumor usually has a better prognosis because of its slower, more regular growth, which is confined to its site of origin (pp. 124–125).

6. In comparison to benign tumors, malignant tumors grow more rapidly, invade aggressively at the primary site, and spread to distant sites to establish secondary growth (p. 125).

7. Diagnosis and therapy in neoplasia are complicated by the fact that, apart from the capacity for metastasis, the characteristics of the many different tumors are expressed over a range, with overlapping at the extremes of benign and malignant behavior (p. 125).

8. Although tumor growth rates are higher than normal cell growth rates, most tumor cells do not actively divide, so that doubling times may be as long as one year, and many years may pass before signs and symptoms appear (pp. 126–127).

9. The capacity of tumors to invade is based on their ability to detach from adjacent cells and move into normal tissues, using enzymes to disrupt basement membranes and intercellular matrix (pp. 127–129).

10. At the gross level, typical tumor invasion patterns are based on extension along paths of low resistance, i.e., along and between structures, rather than penetrating resistant surfaces such as fascia, bone, or the pericardium (p. 129).

11. Tumor metastasis arises primarily by invasion of blood or lymphatic vessels, followed by embolism and outward invasion to establish growth at the secondary site (pp. 129–130).

12. The pattern of growth in vascular metastasis is determined by the type of vessel and the tissues to which it delivers blood or lymph (pp. 130–131).

13. Various factors contribute to the successful establishment of a tumor embolus at a secondary site. Among these are plasma survival, binding to vascular endothelia, and tissue properties at the secondary site (pp. 132–133).

14. Metastasis via body cavities occurs with some frequency, but iatrogenic metastasis is assumed to be rare (pp. 133–134).

15. Tumor growth produces a broad range of physical and functional disruptions, both locally and systematically (pp. 135–140).

16. Oncogenesis is based on irreversible changes in a cell's chromosomes that enable it to escape growth controls and to grow autonomously as neoplastic tissue (pp. 140–141).

17. Direct genetic transmission of neoplasia is limited to a few rare tumors, but less precisely defined familial factors may play a part in the emergence of some other, more common tumors (p. 140).

18. Given the effects of physical, chemical, and viral agents on cellular DNA, it appears that environmental agents are the most important factor in oncogenesis (pp. 141–142).

19. In oncogenesis, an initiating agent in some way predisposes DNA to the effects of promoters, which then greatly favor tumor formation (pp. 142–143).

20. The immune system response to a tumor's characteristic surface antigens may be a significant host defense and has implications for tumor diagnosis and therapy (pp. 144–145).

21. In tumor therapy, the difficulty of removing or destroying only neoplastic tissue, while preserving normal cells, reduces success rates and introduces often unpleasant side effects (p. 145).

22. Antitumor therapy is based on surgical removal of neoplastic tissue or its destruction by chemicals, radiation, or the immune response, alone or in combination (pp. 145–147).

23. For purposes of description and ease of communication, systems of tumor staging, to assess prognosis, and tumor grading, to express the degree of malignancy, are in common use (pp. 147–148).

REVIEW ACTIVITIES

1. Examine each of the diagrams in this chapter (not flow charts or photos) and note those that clearly contain pleomorphic cells. The authors count 8; what count do you get? List the figure numbers.

2. Complete the following table:

Tumor Behavior/Tissue Descriptive Term

Malignant/lymphoid	Malignant/fibrous tissue
Benign/bone	Benign/gland
Benign/projects from surface	Benign/adipose
Malignant/red marrow	Malignant/gland

3. Using a sheet of graph paper, continue figure 6.13 by adding the characteristics prognosis, anaplasia, and metastasis. Indicate overlaps as in figure 6.13. If there is overlap in your graph for all three, see page 125.

4. On 18 small pieces of paper, copy the elements of the flow chart in figure 6.25 and sketch the connecting arrows on a blank sheet of paper. Now drop your 18 bits of paper into a container, pick them out at random, and position them to build up the flow chart. Do it, as much as possible, without referring to the figure.

5. Convince yourself that the key concept number 8 is reflected in figure 6.14. If you're not convinced, read pages 126 to 127.

Part Two

Systemic Pathophysiology

Chapter Seven

Blood Disorders

She was very anemic. Her thin lips were pale, and her skin was delicate of a faint green color, without a touch of red even in the cheeks.

W. Somerset Maugham
Of Human Bondage

The blood is a complex fluid consisting of plasma and the formed elements: erythrocytes, leukocytes, and platelets. **1** In this chapter we deal with derangements of the formed elements only, since disorders of plasma volume and concentration are better considered in chapter 16, which deals with fluid and electrolyte imbalance.

We also consider here the blood coagulation system and its abnormalities, as well as the bleeding disorders that follow from such coagulation defects. The first two sections review normal hemopoiesis and the blood's coagulation and anticoagulation systems. These sections provide the basis for the later discussion of coagulation disorders. A knowledge of coagulation and anticoagulation is also the foundation for much of the material on intravascular thrombosis, which we discuss in chapter 8.

NORMAL HEMOPOIESIS

Marrow Stem Cells and Progenitors

Hemopoiesis is the process leading to production of the blood's formed elements. It combines sequences of mitotic cell divisions and differentiation in such a way that the daughter cells produced by each cell division are slightly different from their parent cell. These changes affect the cells' structure and function, and as the process continues over several generations, daughter cells become significantly different from the ancestor cells from which they derive. Generally, the end products are cells that show greater functional specialization and the structural changes that are associated with such specialization. As well, the finally produced cells tend to have a greatly reduced, or completely lacking, reproductive capacity. They are at the end of a line of differentiation, and as their numbers are reduced in the exercise of their various functions, they must be replaced by new descendants of the same process of mitosis and differentiation.

For the most part, hemopoiesis occurs in red bone marrow. **2** The average adult's approximately two liters of red marrow is distributed within the bones of the axial skeleton and the proximal heads of the humerus and femur. It includes a supporting stroma of fibroblasts, macrophages, fat cells, and blood vessels, in particular the thin-walled and loosely joined **marrow sinusoids,** which allow mature formed elements to enter the blood by squeezing through their large endothelial gaps. On this supporting stromal network are found the parent cells and various intermediate forms (known generally as **precursors**) involved in hemopoiesis. The earlier forms of these cells are of two types. **Stem cells** are those which can differentiate into all of the mature hemopoietic cells. **3** They can also form new stem cells; that is, they have the capacity for self-renewal.

Progenitor cells derive from stem cells but lack their self-renewal capability. They have become committed to a given cell line. That is, a mature cell of a given type can be traced back to only one parental cell type: its progenitor. (Note that many stem cells, progenitors, and early cell forms can't be easily distinguished on the basis of their structure; they can only be functionally identified in complex tissue culture studies.) So, with minor exceptions, each mature formed element has a single progenitor from which it is descended. It is for this reason that abnormalities of hemopoiesis can often be identified as arising at a certain point in the hematopoietic sequence. Figure 7.1 illustrates the general scheme of hemopoiesis. The control and regulation of this process depends on a variety of circulating and locally produced factors, which will be noted in the sections that follow.

Erythropoiesis

The formation of red blood cells, **erythropoiesis,** involves several linked mitotic divisions. Beyond a certain point in the sequence the cells become smaller and smaller, and the nucleus shrinks and condenses until it is finally extruded from the cell. **4** Hemoglobin synthesis commences relatively early in the developmental sequence. During the later stages, the cell loses its organelles and retains only the metabolic capacity to maintain its membrane, hemoglobin structure, and anaerobic energy metabolism. Before it completely matures, a red cell contains a residual network of cytoplasmic RNA, which gives rise to the term **reticulocyte. 5** The network is lost after three days and the fully mature erythrocyte is the result. Because final reticulocyte maturation occurs in the bloodstream, normal blood contains about one reticulocyte for every one hundred erythrocytes. The entire red cell production sequence takes about eight days to complete.

As the erythrocyte circulates, it is subject to mechanical deformation as it is squeezed through small capillaries. It is also subject to various metabolic stresses. Together these present a challenge that the red cell, lacking a nucleus and possessing only a limited adaptive capacity, can tolerate for only four months. After about 120 days it becomes dysfunctional and is removed from the circulation by macrophages in the spleen, liver, and marrow. **6** Aging RBCs are cleared from the blood at the rate of about 1% per day. As a percentage, the loss is small, but since there are approximately 5 billion RBCs per milliliter in the adult's 5 liters of blood, the daily loss is 25 billion erythrocytes—about 173 million per minute.

The red marrow must produce a corresponding number of replacement RBCs. This enormous task requires not only a high rate of mitosis but an adequate supply of iron for

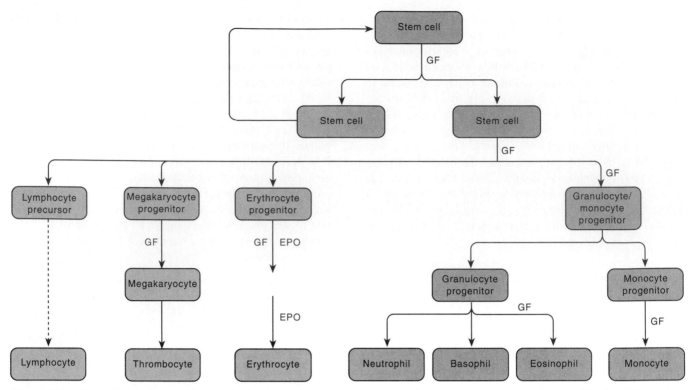

Figure 7.1   Generalized scheme of hemopoiesis. Mature formed elements derive from a single marrow stem cell, which is self-renewing. Known points at which erythropoietin (EPO) and other growth factors (GF) gave effects are also indicated. Broken line denotes lymphoid tissue.

Red Cell Units

Formed element counts have traditionally been recorded as the number of cells per cubic millimeter (mm^3) of blood. The increasingly favored SI (Système International) units use the number of cells $\times\ 10^9$ per liter for white cells and platelets, and the number of cells $\times\ 10^{12}$ per liter for red cells. A normal red cell count, therefore, might be expressed as $5,000,000/mm^3$ or 5×10^{12}/liter. 250×10^9 platelets/liter would indicate a normal thrombocyte count. Note further that because 1 mm^3 equals 1 μl or 1 millionth of a liter, a typical neutrophil count might be represented as 5000/mm^3 or 5000/μl, and in SI units as 5×10^9/liter.

hemoglobin synthesis, as well as vitamin B_{12}, needed for RBC maturation, and folic acid to promote adequate DNA synthesis in the dividing erythrocyte precursors.

The process of red cell production is controlled by the hormone **erythropoietin** (EPO) and two or more growth factors. Erythropoietin is required at several points in the red cell's maturation sequence (fig. 7.1). It is secreted by the kidney in response to changing oxygen levels detected by its oxygen-sensitive juxtaglomerular cells. Lower oxygen levels trigger increased secretion, and the resulting rise

in erythropoietin stimulates RBC production in the marrow (fig. 7.2). This mechanism provides a useful corrective response to conditions in which the blood's oxygen delivery capacity is reduced. In extreme cases, erythropoietin can generate as much as a fivefold increase in red cell production.

Apart from the hormonal control supplied by erythropoietin, growth factors are also required for erythropoiesis. They are locally derived from marrow cells. Their exact roles and significance have yet to be precisely determined.

Leukopoiesis

This discussion of leukocyte formation will be confined to granulocytes **7** and monocytes. **8** The migration of lymphocyte progenitors to widespread lymphoid tissue sites in the body and the later maturation of lymphocytes is described in chapter 5.

The approximately 7 million leukocytes present in each milliliter of blood are in transit from their production sites to the various tissues in which they will perform their essentially protective functions. At the same time, in the case of granulocytes and monocytes, an approximately equal number of cells are at work in the tissues. This means that the actual body total of these cells is roughly twice their circulating number. Their life span is considerably shorter than that of the erythrocytes, with granulocytes

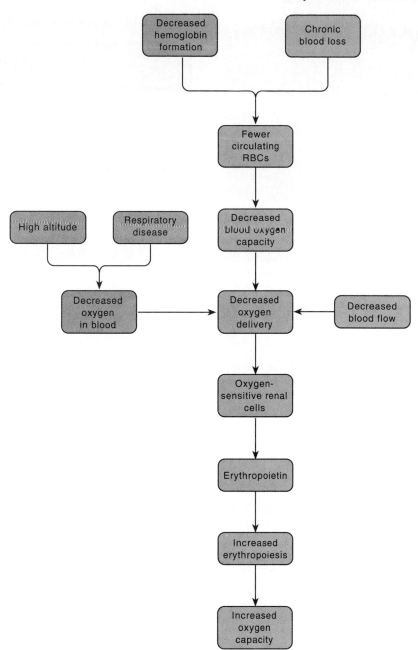

Figure 7.2   Erythropoietin and its role in erythropoiesis.

living from just hours to as long as a few days and mono-cytes perhaps as long as two to three months. Note also that the circulating granulocytes are mature and able to commence their defensive tasks upon entering the tissue spaces. By contrast, the monocyte is an immature cell and must complete its development into a macrophage in the tissues, before it can proceed with phagocytosis or immune system functions (see chapter 5).

The regulation of granulocyte and monocyte production depends on various growth factors, which interact in subtle and complex ways. As in erythropoiesis, interactions with the marrow's stroma also play an important role in the process (fig. 7.1).

Thrombopoiesis

The **thrombocyte,** or platelet, is derived from its marrow precursor, the **megakaryocyte** (fig. 7.1). Production is not by mitosis but, instead, by fragmentation. As it matures, the megakaryocyte's cytoplasm develops numerous vesicles, which give it a granular appearance. Its membranes also become discontinuous, forming gaps similar to the perforations in a sheet of stamps. The large megakaryocyte extends elongated extensions of its perforated membrane into the lumen of the marrow sinusoids, through their loose endothelial junctions. It then sheds cytoplasmic fragments

(a)

(b)

Figure 7.3   (*a*) Essential elements of a blood clot. Fibrin strands entrap red cells where a platelet plug has formed at the site of vessel wall injury. (*b*) Scanning electron micrograph of a clot fragment containing fibrin strands, red cells, and platelets.

into the blood. These assume the platelet's characteristic flattened, disklike shape. Some initially larger fragments may split off smaller portions while circulating. After losing most of its cytoplasm in this way, the megakaryocyte's nuclear remnant is cleared by marrow macrophages.

The circulating blood contains about 250 million platelets in each milliliter. Their average life span is about three days, with about one-third of the total held as a reserve in the spleen, whose specialized **red pulp** ▪9 takes up and stores platelets. They form a reservoir that can be released when demand is high.

Control of thrombopoiesis is dependent on at least two growth factors. One elicits its effects early in the maturational sequence that leads to the formation of thrombocytes, granulocytes, and monocytes. It promotes the formation of progenitors from earlier stem cells. The second substance, called **thrombopoietin** or **thrombocytosis-stimulating factor** (TSF), is probably the same as, or at least similar to, interleukin 6 (IL-6). This substance was previously mentioned in chapter 2, in the context of its role in the inflammatory response.

BLOOD COAGULATION

The importance of the blood's several functions is indicated by the elaborate mechanisms that are brought to bear when the threat of blood loss arises. The process of stopping blood loss is called **hemostasis,** and the principal hemostatic mechanism is blood coagulation. Essentially, this process involves converting the fluid blood into a nonflowing gel to prevent its escape from damaged blood vessels.

When blood coagulates, many long protein filaments form a tangled mass within the blood. ▪10 This mesh of filaments traps the blood's formed elements to form a red, gelatinous mass called a **blood clot.** The blood clot usually forms in the tissue spaces immediately adjacent to a damaged blood vessel and blocks further loss of blood from it (fig. 7.3). Note, however, that this mechanism is effective only in veins, capillaries, and small arterioles. The high blood pressure of the larger arteries interferes with clot formation. This is why it is usually necessary to apply external pressure to stop bleeding in all but the smallest arterioles.

The blood clot's filaments are composed of the protein fibrin. Fibrin is derived from a plasma protein called **fibrinogen.** When a small fragment of the fibrinogen molecule is split off, the remaining portion is called fibrin. It is able to link with other fibrin units to form long strands. (This process is called polymerization; the single fibrin unit is known as a monomer, and the long fibrin strand, formed of hundreds of linked monomers, is called a polymer.)

The enzyme **thrombin,** derived from its inactive precursor, **prothrombin,** splits fibrinogen to trigger the formation of fibrin and its polymerization. It also catalyzes the activation of factor XIII, which in turn promotes chemical cross-linking between the newly formed fibrin filaments. This process converts a loose tangle of strands into a more tightly organized and stabilized mass (fig. 7.4). Thrombin can't normally be present in the blood, but must

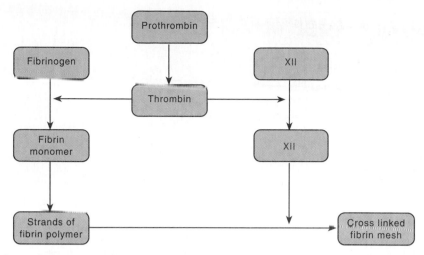

Figure 7.4   Blood coagulates when a mesh of fibrin polymer strands is formed. Thrombin and activated clotting factor XIII act as catalysts in the process. Clotting factor XII is activated also.

be activated only when there is need for blood coagulation. The activation of prothrombin is accomplished by another enzyme, which is itself activated by another enzyme, which in turn depends on yet another activation step. Thus fibrin formation depends on several linked enzyme activations. Such a sequence of reactions is called a **cascade.** The components of the coagulation cascade are called **clotting factors.**

Each of the components of the coagulation cascade has a name, but many of these are cumbersome, so a system of Roman numerals is more widely used in designating them (table 7.1). The exceptions are fibrinogen, thrombin, and prothrombin, whose names are used more frequently than their assigned numbers. Unfortunately, the various clotting factors were discovered and numbered before their positions in the cascade were fully understood. For this reason they appear in the clotting sequence in an order different from their numerical sequence.

The plasma, then, contains clotting factors normally circulating in an inactive form. When the first in the sequence is activated, it activates the next member of the cascade and so on, until the fibrin strands form a tangled mass that coagulates the blood. We need now to consider the obvious question: What initiates the activation of the coagulation cascade?

There are two triggering mechanisms involved. When tissue is damaged, a lipoprotein called **tissue thrombo-plastin,** or **tissue factor** (TF), is exposed at the surfaces of endothelium, smooth muscle, and other cells. Tissue factor can bind activated factor VII, which in turn activates factor X, giving rise to the formation of fibrin. Because the source of tissue factor is external to the blood, this cascade

Table 7.1	Clotting Factor Terminology. The Roman Numeral Designations Are More Commonly Used

Factor Name	Roman Numeral
Fibrinogen	I
Prothrombin	II
Preaccelerin	V
Proconvertin	VII
Antihemophilic factor	VIII
Christmas factor	IX
Stuart-Prower factor	X
Plasma thromboplastin antecedent	XI
Hageman factor	XII
Fibrin-stabilizing factor	XIII

initiation mechanism is called the **extrinsic pathway** (fig. 7.5). The second triggering mechanism has all its factors ipresent within the blood itself. For this reason it is called the **intrinsic pathway** (fig. 7.6). Alterations in the vessel's endothelial lining expose the blood to collagen and other subendothelial elements. This abnormal exposure activates factor XII (also known as **Hageman factor**), and another series of linked enzyme activations results in the formation of fibrin. Regardless of which pathway starts the cascade, both result in activation of factor X. Beyond this point in the cascade there is a single common pathway that leads to the formation of fibrin (fig. 7.7). Typical injuries activate both the extrinsic and intrinsic pathways. Chapter 8

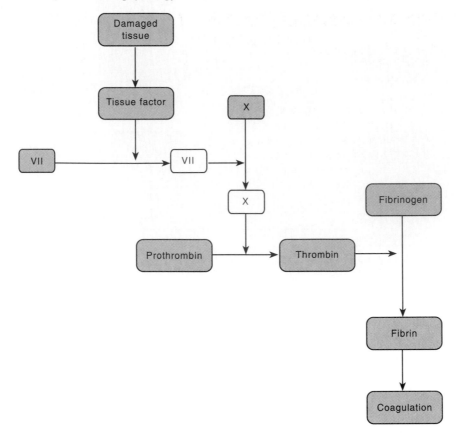

Figure 7.5   The extrinsic pathway to blood coagulation. Clotting factors in white boxes have been activated.

will describe how the intrinsic pathway can be activated, without tissue damage, to threaten potentially serious obstruction to blood flow.

Several of the cascade activations require the presence of calcium ion. Only minute amounts are required, and patients with calcium deficiencies do not suffer for lack of an adequate coagulation response. **Chelating agents** are often used to prevent the clotting of blood withdrawn for laboratory examination. They avidly take up calcium, preventing it from contributing to the coagulation cascade. Examples are oxalate and citrate ion preparations and EDTA (ethylenediaminetetraacetic acid).

Fibrinogen, prothrombin, and other clotting factors are synthesized in the liver by a process requiring vitamin K. This is a fat-soluble vitamin, and thus its availability for absorption depends on the fat-emulsifying action of bile.

The Role of the Platelet

Platelets make an important contribution to hemostasis. At the site of vessel damage, subendothelial collagen is exposed to the blood. Circulating in it is a complex of factor VIII and another substance called **von Willebrand factor** (vWF). vWF can bind to collagen and also to receptors

Figure 7.6 indicates a link between the intrinsic and extrinsic pathways. When activated, factor VII can activate factor IX just as factor XI does.

This link seems to explain the observation that people who lack factor IX suffer serious clotting deficiencies, while others who lack factor XI experience only minor clotting problems. It would appear that those with no factor IX lack the ability to activate factor X. Those whose intrinsic cascade lacks factor XI can still activate factor IX using factor VII formed via the extrinsic pathway.

on the surface of platelets. As flowing blood carries platelets to the damage site, they bind to its collagen by the vWF that is anchored there (fig. 7.8). Platelet binding is a key step in that it triggers a complex of platelet responses known collectively as **platelet activation.** These responses contribute to the massing of platelets at the site of vessel damage, to the promotion of blood coagulation, and to the control of these processes so that an excessive or inadequate response is prevented. Let us now describe in some detail the principal elements of the platelet activation response.

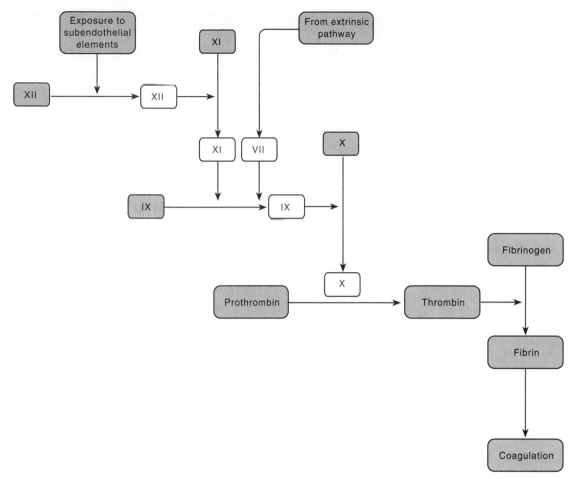

Figure 7.6   The intrinsic pathway to blood coagulation. Clotting factors in white boxes have been activated.

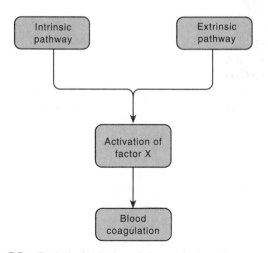

Figure 7.7   Both the intrinsic and the extrinsic pathways provide access to the activation of factor X and the coagulation of blood that follows.

Platelet Plug Formation

The platelets first arriving at the area of vessel wall damage are bound by vWF. They undergo a shape change as a result, becoming more rounded and developing membranous protrusions. As this change proceeds, surface receptors are exposed, allowing activated platelets to bind to the surfaces of other platelets brought to the scene by the flowing blood (fig. 7.8). As the new platelets stick to the surfaces of the already activated platelets, they are themselves activated. The resulting exposure of receptors binds other platelets, and the process is repeated again and again until an aggregation of platelets, bound to the damage site, is formed. The platelet mass is called a **platelet plug.** It contributes directly to hemostasis by acting as an obstruction to the flow of blood through the gap in the vessel wall (fig. 7.3).

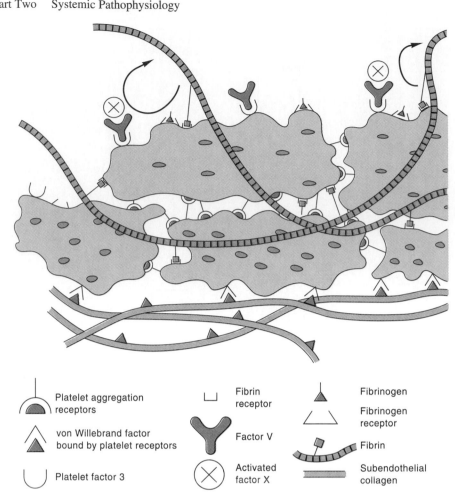

Platelet aggregation receptors		Fibrin receptor		Fibrinogen	
von Willebrand factor bound by platelet receptors		Factor V		Fibrinogen receptor	
Platelet factor 3		Activated factor X		Fibrin	
				Subendothelial collagen	

Figure 7.8   Platelets bind to von Willebrand factor (vWF) on exposed subendothelial collagen. Platelet activation follows, exposing platelet factor 3, which binds factor V, which in turn binds activated factor X. Arrows represent the sequence of steps that convert fibrinogen to fibrin. Note the receptors localizing fibrinogen and fibrin at the surface of aggregated platelets.

The Platelet Release Reaction

A second response of activated platelets is the release of several substances that regulate the overall hemostatic response. On release, these substances tend to amplify the response, promoting the rapid formation and consolidation of a mass of platelets and coagulated blood at the site of potential blood loss.

These regulatory substances are stored in membranous vesicles within the platelet's cytoplasm. The platelets employ exocytosis to release their contents into the exterior. As the process continues, the platelets' cytoplasm loses its granular appearance. For this reason, the process is often referred to as **platelet degranulation.**

One of the substances released is ADP, **adenosine diphosphate.** It has the effect of promoting platelet activation and therefore more aggregation and further degranulation with the release of additional ADP to further increase the response, and so on. Another substance released by platelets is **thromboxane A_2** (TxA$_2$). It is a derivative of arachidonic acid, which is also the precursor of the leukotrienes. These play an important role in the mediation

of the acute inflammatory response (see chapter 2). Like ADP, TxA$_2$ functions to promote further platelet activation, aggregation, and release. It also has vasoconstriction effects that promote smooth muscle contraction, to restrict the size of the gap through which blood might be lost. As ADP and TxA$_2$ are released, they also interact with thrombin, which is being simultaneously formed by the coagulation cascade. The three substances combine their effects in triggering clot retraction, which will be described shortly.

Activated platelets also release growth factors that play a role in the later stages of the process. When blood loss has been stopped, the gap in the wall must be repaired. The growth factors act to attract fibroblasts and promote healing by fibrosis. The effects of platelet activation are summarized in figure 7.9.

Exposure of Surface Receptors

Platelet membranes have receptors for elements of the hemostatic response other than those involved in platelet aggregation. When activated, the platelet membrane exposes a receptor called **platelet factor 3** (PF-3). It is

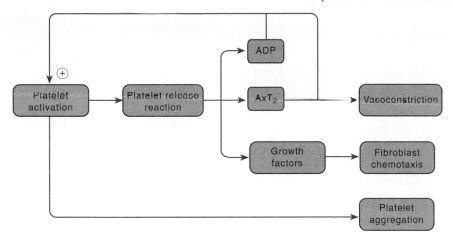

Figure 7.9   Principal effects of platelet activation and the platelet release reaction.

specific for factor VIII and factor V of the coagulation cascade. Factor VIII is needed for the activation of factor X, while factor V's role in the process is to bind activated factor X to the platelet's surface. As it catalyzes the formation of fibrin, PF-3 localizes the process at the site of the aggregated platelets. **11** It thereby confines the coagulation response to the point of damage, where it is needed.

Activated platelets also expose receptors specific to the binding of fibrinogen and fibrin. In this way, fibrinogen is positioned at the point where factor X will produce thrombin. As thrombin catalyzes fibrin formation, the resulting polymer filaments are anchored to the platelet surfaces, forming a localized mass of coagulated blood (fig. 7.8).

Clot Retraction

As platelet-mediated coagulation proceeds, fibrin forms a tangle of filaments that are anchored at the surfaces of the platelet plug. These trap red cells to form a loose, gelatinous mass at the site of the vessel wound. At this stage, platelets make another contribution. Their internal system of contractile proteins, similar to those in muscle fibers, is activated. The platelet contraction that follows pulls the fibrin strands into a more tightly packed mass. Plasma trapped in the mix of platelets, red cells, and fibrin is squeezed out and a denser, more firmly seated hemostatic gel results.

The Role of Thrombin

As established earlier, thrombin is the enzyme that converts fibrinogen into the fibrin monomer, which can link with others to form long filaments: the fibrin polymer. But this critical enzyme has other effects that promote the coagulation response. It also has effects on other clotting factors that are activated earlier in the coagulation cascade. It intensifies their activity, which in turn leads to more thrombin formation and further activity intensification of the other factors, and so on. This is a positive feedback effect, which rapidly generates a pronounced coagulation response.

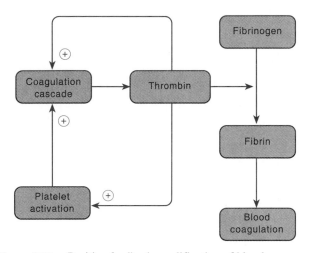

Figure 7.10   Positive feedback amplification of blood coagulation is mediated by thrombin. Note the link between platelet activation and an enhanced coagulation cascade response.

Furthermore, thrombin promotes platelet activation to enhance platelet participation in the hemostatic response. Through its effect on the coagulation cascade, platelet activation generates an increased production of thrombin to produce still further positive feedback amplification of the response. Figure 7.10 illustrates this aspect of thrombin's contribution to blood coagulation.

The Anticoagulation System

The positive feedback amplification of blood coagulation must be controlled or it could trigger widespread clotting, far beyond the amount needed to prevent blood loss. Such extensive coagulation would have serious consequences, especially for critical organs like the brain. The fact that there is enough prothrombin in a few milliliters of blood to coagulate all the blood in the body indicates the need for fine control of the coagulation response. There are three major factors that limit clotting so that only the amount needed for hemostasis is allowed to develop: hemodynamics, mediation via endothelium, and the fibrinolytic system.

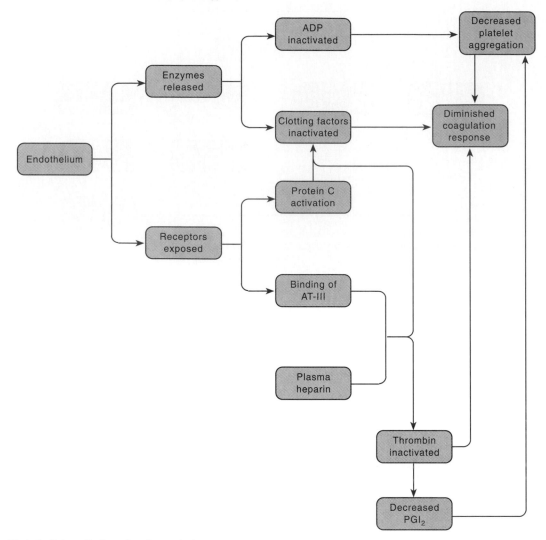

Figure 7.11   Endothelial mediation of anticoagulation.

Hemodynamics

One factor limiting coagulation is the movement of the blood itself (**hemodynamics**). As clotting factors are activated, many are carried off by the flowing blood before they can activate others or be bound to surfaces at the injury site. At the same time, newly arriving blood dilutes the region's activated factors, slowing the coagulation cascade's reactions. Activated factors removed from the area are inactivated in the liver. This prevents their returning to the scene to speed coagulation on later circulatory passes.

Endothelial Mediation

The endothelium adjacent to the site of vascular damage plays an important role in limiting clotting. As thrombin is forming, it triggers the endothelium to release a particular prostaglandin called **prostacyclin** or PGI$_2$. This substance has the effect of inhibiting platelet aggregation, preventing the spread of adhering platelets along vascular surfaces. Thus the platelets contribute to hemostasis only at the damage site; the platelet plug is confined to the injury site and can't extend to adjacent normal endothelium.

Endothelial cells also possess enzymes that degrade thrombin and the ADP released from platelets. ADP loss means less aggregation and activation of platelets, but beyond that, its breakdown products are known to specifically interfere with coagulation. Obviously, degradation of thrombin directly interferes with fibrin formation.

Vascular endothelia also limit the coagulation process by activating other enzyme systems, which degrade clotting factors. These systems are dependent on endothelial membrane receptors, which bind key elements to activate them, but also to confine them to the site where coagulation promoters are also confined.

Endothelia have receptors that bind **antithrombin III** (AT-III). When complexed with heparin, derived from the plasma, AT-III has a potent proteolytic effect on thrombin and various other clotting factors. It is intriguing to note that AT-III is effective only in degrading factors that are not bound to platelet surfaces. Those that are bound and participating in the coagulation cascade are in some way protected from AT-III's attack. A second type of endothelial receptor binds thrombin, which in turn activates another proteolytic enzyme. This one, called **protein C,** inactivates factors V and VIII to inhibit the coagulation cascade (fig. 7.11).

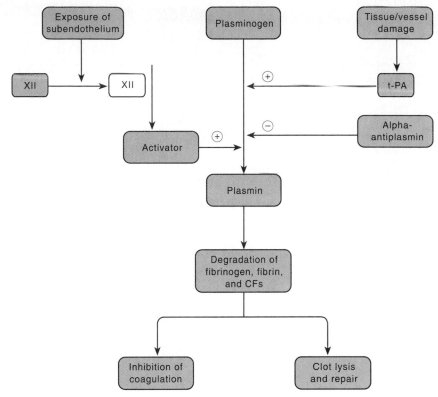

Figure 7.12   The fibrinolytic system. t-PA: tissue plasminogen activator.

The Fibrinolytic System

As hemodynamics and endothelium-dependent enzyme systems counter the factors promoting coagulation, a fine balance is struck. This allows sufficient coagulation for hemostasis while preventing a potentially troublesome overresponse. The fibrinolytic system is an important factor in providing a transition between the hemostatic response and repair of the vessel wall. It provides a means of clot breakdown, allowing phagocytosis of its remnants and clearing the area for fibroblast activity and regeneration of various vessel wall elements.

Like the coagulation reactions, the fibrinolytic system involves two cascades, which produce a final, key enzyme. In the fibrinolytic system this substance is **plasmin.** It is a proteolytic enzyme that degrades fibrinogen, fibrin, and factors V and VIII. Plasmin is derived from its inactive circulating precursor, **plasminogen.** Damaged vascular cells, especially endothelium, release the major plasminogen-activating enzyme, tissue plasminogen activator (t-PA). There is another, intrinsic, pathway that is triggered by exposure to subendothelial tissue components. This activates clotting factor XII, which in turn promotes formation of another plasminogen activator. This pathway may be more important in controlling clot formation, with the t-PA pathway primarily effecting the breakdown of clots already formed (fig. 7.12).

As fibrin is formed and localized at the injury site, circulating plasminogen binds to it. In this way, as the clot forms, the plasminogen is directly incorporated into its structure. When t-PA is released it also binds to fibrin. This means that the t-PA and plasminogen are held at the scene to facilitate the formation of plasmin, which is then in a position to directly attack the immediately adjacent fibrin. In this way the clot is lysed from within, and repair of the damaged vessel can proceed.

Of course, if the fibrinolytic process is not closely controlled, an excessive response could overwhelm the coagulation system's hemostatic effects to produce massive bleeding. Such overreaction is prevented by a circulating factor called **alpha$_2$–antiplasmin.** It has an antiplasmin action that moderates the fibrinolytic response (fig. 7.12).

Striking a Balance

We've seen how the coagulation and anticoagulation systems oppose each other, and how fine control is needed to prevent an overreaction. The goal is a coagulation response adequate to prevent blood loss, but limited so that no undesirable flow restrictions are produced.

One mechanism underlying the achievement of such fine control has been hinted at in the previous descriptions. It is the process whereby the same event triggers both coagulation and anticoagulation responses. Factor XII is one example, in that it activates both the intrinsic coagulation cascade and the formation of plasmin. Another is ADP, which is released by platelets to promote activation and coagulation while, at the same time, endothelial cells break it down to yield products with anticoagulant properties. Thrombin is a third factor that contributes to balancing the systems' responses. When formed, it activates platelets and

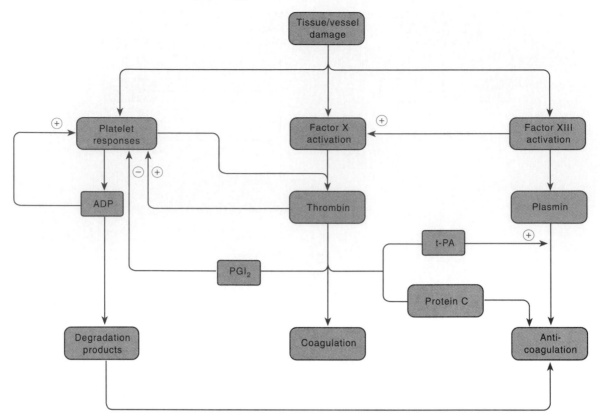

Figure 7.13   Hemostasis control. Blood coagulation is opposed by anticoagulation responses so that the degree of coagulation is not excessive. Note the role of factor XII in promoting both coagulation and anticoagulation.

catalyzes fibrin formation, but it also activates protein C and triggers endothelial cell release of t-PA. These substances then break down the same fibrin that thrombin was responsible for forming. Thrombin also promotes endothelial secretion of PGI_2, which reduces platelet aggregation and activation, lessening the coagulation response (fig. 7.13).

The complexities of the mechanisms that produce effective coagulation and finely tune the response are still being studied. The goal is to identify those points in the various systems where, by therapeutic intervention, it may be possible to restore fine control that has been lost and to correct responses that have become inadequate or excessive.

Blood Coagulation Tests

Information on the effectiveness of a patient's coagulation response can be gained from a variety of tests. These are usually aimed at measuring the time required to produce fibrin or a specific amount of an activated factor in the coagulation cascade. If the time is abnormally long, the assumption is that the inactive factor is deficient in the plasma or that the anticoagulation system is dominant. Currently used tests can pinpoint specific parts of the cascade to aid diagnosis. Some common coagulation tests are described in table 7.2.

BLEEDING DISORDERS

Loss of blood results if hemostatic mechanisms are defective. This section describes defects in both the platelet and clotting factor components of the hemostatic response. In addition, we consider bleeding that results from abnormal fragility of fine blood vessels.

Terminology

As blood escapes from the blood vessels, it is often trapped in the surrounding tissues. These accumulations may be visible at skin and mucous membrane surfaces. Pinpoints of hemorrhage seen in the skin, or in a post-mortem organ section, such as the brain, are called **petechiae** (fig. 7.14). **12** They typically follow rupture of a capillary or small arteriole. Larger and sometimes less regular areas of bleeding in the skin are called **purpura**. **13** Still larger (over 2 cm) areas of bleeding are known as **ecchymoses.** They are commonly called bruises. Their characteristic coloration, involving the progression from purple, through blue/black, to green, and finally yellow, reflects changes in the hemoglobin released from ruptured RBCs. A large volume of blood trapped in a soft tissue is a **hematoma.** **14** Hematomas present the risk of compressing an adjacent organ or duct, and can pose a serious threat by directly compressing brain tissue.

Table 7.2   Selected Laboratory Tests of Blood Coagulation

Test Name	Comments
Partial thromboplastin time (PTT)	Normal: 25–40 sec. Longer times usually indicate fault in intrinsic pathway.
Prothrombin time (PT)	Normal: 9–10 sec. Tests intrinsic system. Can indicate low levels of factors I, II, V, VII, and IX.
Thrombin time (TT)	Normal: 16 sec. Indicates time to convert fibrinogen to fibrin.
Prothrombin and preconvertin time (P and P)	Used in combination with PT to detect lack of factors II, VII, and X.
Fibrin-fibrinogen degradation products (FDP)	Also called FSP (fibrin split products). Uses immune methods to test fibrinolytic system.
Fibrinogen	Chemical analysis to indicate amount in plasma. Normal range: 200–400 mg/dl.
Bleeding time	Longer times indicate low platelet numbers, delaying coagulation. Aspirin increases bleeding time.
Platelet aggregation	Platelet aggregometer uses optical means to measure aggregation. Indicates faulty platelet function.

Figure 7.14   The tiny dark spots in this brain section are the sites of petechial hemorrhages.

Platelet Disorders

Thrombocytopenia

Inability to mount an adequate hemostatic response may be the result of **thrombocytopenia,** the condition of insufficient circulating platelets. The problem can arise because platelet production has decreased or because platelets are being cleared from the blood at higher than normal rates. In either case, hemostasis is compromised and bleeding from minor vascular pressure or trauma produces petechiae and purpura.

Impaired platelet production may result from a generalized marrow suppression, in which case reduced red and white cell numbers would also result. The marrow may be affected by antitumor radiation or chemotherapy or other therapeutic agents. Suppression may also be due to marrow replacement by tumor metastases, whose growth is well supported by marrow. Some agents are more specific in selectively inhibiting platelet formation; thiazide diuretics, gold and phenylbutazone (commonly used by arthritics), and certain antibiotics are examples. Chronic alcohol abusers may exhibit thrombocytopenia because of ethanol's marrow suppression effects. Thrombocytopenia may also result if the marrow is unable to sustain normal mitosis rates because of rare congenital defects or because of more common dietary deficiencies of folic acid and vitamin B_{12}.

Excessive clearance of platelets may result from immune-related destruction or from nonimmune mechanisms. A major nonimmune cause is **disseminated intravascular coagulation** (DIC), **15** which is described in detail in chapter 8. Essentially, widespread systemic coagulation removes large numbers of platelets from the blood, producing thrombocytopenia. A related phenomenon is seen in certain hemangiomas, benign tumors originating in the cells of blood vessels. The large masses of vessels have endothelial surfaces that bind platelets and lower circulating numbers. Some protozoan infections damage platelets, causing them to be removed from the plasma at an accelerated rate.

An interesting nonimmune mechanism causing thrombocytopenia involves the spleen. Normally, its vascular channels hold about 25% of circulating platelets. These provide a reserve that can rapidly enter the circulation, along with an erythrocyte reserve, in times of demand. When the spleen enlarges (splenomegaly), as it often does in cirrhosis and congestive heart failure, it can take up and hold additional platelets (hypersplenism). In extreme cases of splenomegaly, up to 80% of platelets may be held in the enlarged organ.

Thrombocytopenia and Blood Transfusion

A relative thrombocytopenia can result from large-scale blood transfusions. When blood is stored for prolonged periods, platelet numbers rapidly decline. Transfusion with such blood can dilute the recipient's platelets so that a relative thrombocytopenia results. Normally this is avoided by transfusing only blood and platelets that have been stored in a way that maintains their viability.

Most thrombocytopenia is caused by immune mechanisms that involve the binding of antibodies or antigen-antibody complexes to platelet surfaces. This hastens their removal from circulation and their phagocytosis by macrophages in the spleen. The causes of such an abnormal immune response are unknown. For this reason the most common disorder involving this mechanism is called **idiopathic thrombocytopenic purpura** (ITP). Its two forms are characterized by petechial and purpuric blood loss to the skin and mucous membranes. In acute ITP, children under the age of 6 are affected, but most of these cases are benign and spontaneously resolve in a period of a few weeks to six months. The bleeding disorder often arises following a viral infection, a fact suggesting that the virus might interfere with immune recognition. In chronic ITP, adults, and women in particular, are affected. No infection is associated with this condition, but in some cases it may occur in relation to other immune disorders such as lymphomas or systemic lupus erythematosus (SLE).

Certain drugs are able to induce thrombocytopenia by an immune mechanism. Thiazide diuretics, quinidine, quinine, and heparin in some way disrupt the immune response, causing antibodies to the drug to complex with it and then bind to platelet surfaces. The result is a condition that presents in much the same way as ITP.

Thrombotic thrombocytopenic purpura (TTP) may involve an antibody that damages endothelium. The resulting platelet adherence not only produces thrombocytopenia, but also induces widespread coagulation in small blood vessels. The factors that predispose to thrombocytopenia are summarized in figure 7.15.

Impaired Platelet Function

Less common than a lack of platelet numbers, platelet functional disorders usually involve altered platelet membranes that interfere with binding at damage sites or with platelet plug formation. They may be the result of genetic or acquired mechanisms. As you can appreciate, these conditions are characterized by bleeding even though platelet counts are normal.

The genetic impairment of platelet function is quite rare, with acquired conditions occurring more frequently.

Aspirin and Anticoagulation

Aspirin (ASA) is known to affect platelets by reducing their aggregation. The mechanism is different from the immune effect induced by other drugs. ASA prevents thromboxane A_2 (TxA_2) synthesis and release, which means a loss of one of the major promoters of platelet aggregation. Normal ASA doses are unlikely to produce any clinical bleeding, but in those with a preexisting bleeding disorder, aspirin therapy could exaggerate the problem. ASA may be prescribed in cases where there is a potentially dangerous increase in coagulation tendency, to counter the effect by inhibiting platelet adhesion and aggregation (see chapter 8).

In marrow tumors, abnormal megakaryocytes may produce platelets with defective membrane receptors. Also certain drugs, like penicillin in large doses, can bind to platelets and reduce their functional capacity, as can the antibodies that are present in the plasma in multiple myeloma.

Patients with uremia may also suffer from platelet function loss. The plasma in such patients is a hostile environment, as it contains toxins normally excreted by the kidneys. When renal dysfunction prevents toxin clearance, platelets can be damaged.

Clotting Factor Disorders

As established earlier, the interplay between platelets and circulating clotting factors produces an integrated hemostatic response. With adequate numbers of normally functional platelets, bleeding disorders may arise if clotting factors are deficient. For all the seeming complexity of the coagulation cascades, you might expect many opportunities for the system to malfunction. In fact these conditions are relatively rare. Clotting factor deficiencies may be of genetic origin or they may be acquired.

Genetic Clotting Factor Disorders

These disorders will arise early in life and are characterized by larger amounts of blood loss. Ecchymoses and hematomas are typical in these conditions, as opposed to the smaller petechiae and purpura seen in platelet disorders. Bleeding may arise without warning, or excessive bleeding may follow minor trauma or medical or dental surgical procedures.

Von Willebrand's Disease Genetic deficiency of von Willebrand factor (vWF) interferes with platelet binding to subendothelial surfaces at the site of blood vessel damage. This is particularly significant in vessels where blood flow rates are high. Because the defect is transmitted by autosomal dominant inheritance, an affected individual will always have an affected parent. Factor VIII is normally carried in plasma complexed with vWF, so this disease may also produce defects in the coagulation cascade.

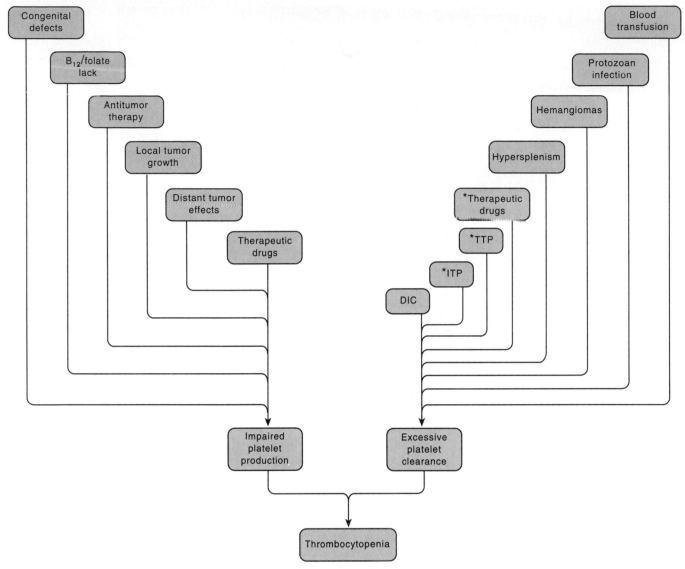

Figure 7.15   Factors predisposing to thrombocytopenia. Asterisks denote that an immune mechanism is involved.

Sufferers of von Willebrand's disease experience recurring bouts of gastric and intestinal bleeding, and women are subject to excessive menstrual hemorrhage (**menorrhagia**). Treatment of the disease is by transfusion with vWF derived from normal blood donors.

Hemophilias   Although genetic deficiencies of all of the clotting factors exist, the most common involve inherited defects of factor VIII, called **hemophilia A,** or factor IX, in which the disease is called **hemophilia B.**

Because the genes coding for factors VIII and IX are located on the X chromosome, hemophilia A and B exclusively affect males, whose parents are unaffected by a bleeding disorder. Both conditions present similar patterns of abnormal bleeding. They can be distinguished only by analyzing the plasma to identify the deficient, or absent, clotting factor. Sufferers are subject to pronounced hemorrhage after trauma, and relatively minor surgery presents a serious bleeding threat. As opposed to victims of von Willebrand's disease, hemophiliacs suffer less GI mucosal bleeding. They do, however, suffer from bleeding into the

Christmas Disease

Hemophilia B is also known as Christmas disease, since factor IX is the Christmas factor. You may, perhaps, be imagining that the name of this factor is related to a dedicated researcher's toiling late on Christmas eve to finally achieve its discovery. If so, you'll be disappointed to learn that it was named after the patient in whom its lack was first identified.

larger weight-bearing joints. Trauma in these structures is normally well tolerated, but hemophiliacs suffer repeated episodes of hemorrhage into these joints. Over time, joint deformities and fusion of the bones (**ankylosis**) are the result. Therapy typically involves transfusion with concentrates of the deficient factor from the blood of normal donors.

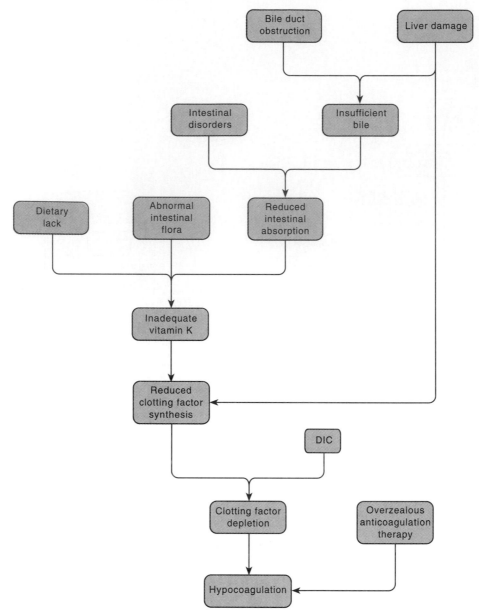

Figure 7.16   Hypocoagulation may result from acquired depletion of clotting factors or excessive anticoagulation therapy.

Acquired Clotting Factor Disorders

Given a normal genetic capacity to produce clotting factors, various acquired conditions can compromise their synthesis or function. These acquired disorders are much more likely to arise at later ages than the genetic diseases. The most common etiologies of the acquired clotting factor disorders involve impaired hepatic synthesis, disseminated intravascular coagulation, and anticoagulant therapy.

Impaired Hepatic Synthesis Since most clotting factors are produced in the liver, hepatic disease may be associated with clotting abnormalities. In practice, this problem is typically seen only when liver damage is severe, as in advanced hepatic cirrhosis. However, since the synthesis of clotting factors requires vitamin K, its lack in a normal liver can result in inadequate production. Deficiency of the vitamin might be the result of malnutrition, but since the microorganisms that normally populate the colon produce some vitamin K, dietary deficiencies must be quite severe to overcome their contribution. On the other hand, antibiotic therapy, with moxalactam in particular, can suppress these organisms and reduce the availability of vitamin K. Lack of vitamin K could also follow the various intestinal disorders in which absorption is affected. Note too that, since vitamin K is lipid-soluble, its absorption is bile-dependent. This means that obstruction of the bile ducts, or liver damage that compromises bile synthesis, can also produce a shortage of vitamin K and inadequate liver production of clotting factors (fig. 7.16).

Disseminated Intravascular Coagulation (DIC)
Disseminated intravascular coagulation can also reduce the level of available clotting factors. The same mechanism

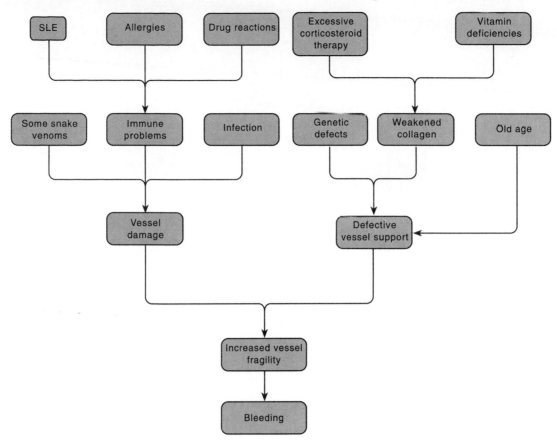

Figure 7.17   Factors contributing to the vascular fragility that causes bleeding.

that affects platelets is involved here, as well. Generalized coagulation can so dramatically deplete clotting factors that their number is inadequate to meet hemostatic demands, and excessive bleeding results.

Anticoagulant Therapy Therapy to counter excessive blood coagulation may be complicated by bleeding in up to one-third of patients. Severe hemorrhage is not usual, but bleeding into the GI lumen, as well as skin ecchymoses and hematomas, commonly occur. Patients undergoing anticoagulant therapy require continuous monitoring for signs of bleeding. Invasive procedures involving potential blood loss are deferred, if possible. Heparin and **warfarin** are commonly used anticoagulants. Information on their modes of action and some other therapeutic uses can be found in table 8.1.

Small Vessel Fragility

Bleeding from small blood vessels (the **microvasculature**) typically produces petechiae or purpura in the skin and GI mucosa. Involvement of glomerular capillaries produces petechiae in the kidney and may also result in blood loss to the urine (**hematuria**). As a group, these conditions are referred to as the **vascular purpura.** Strictly speaking, these conditions might be treated in a later chapter dealing with blood vessel abnormalities, but since bleeding is the chief problem arising from fine vessel fragility, they are

grouped with the true hemorrhagic disorders. Overall, the vascular weakness that characterizes these conditions derives from two sources: vascular damage or defective vessel support.

Vascular Damage Damage to the fine arterioles, capillaries, and venules of the microvasculature produces a vasculitis that may involve immune-mediated damage by neutrophils. Immune complex deposition in the fine vessels is associated with various immune diseases, e.g., systemic lupus erythematosus (SLE), various allergies or drug reactions, or the idiopathic Henoch-Schönlein purpura (see chapter 3 case study). Vasculitis might also be the result of direct damage to the vessels by the toxins of infectious microorganisms or the venoms of certain snakes. In either case, vessel injury results in weakness and small hemorrhage into the surrounding tissue (fig. 7.17).

Defective Vascular Support The microvasculature is braced by a supporting architecture of connective tissue. This enables its fine vessels to better withstand the pressure of the blood they carry. Deterioration of the perivascular support system can compromise this function, producing vascular rupture and microhemorrhage.

In some cases, connective tissue weakness is due to a hereditary defect, as in **hereditary hemorrhagic telangiectasis** (telangiectasis is dilation of fine vessels) or Marfan's syndrome. More commonly, acquired mechanisms underlie

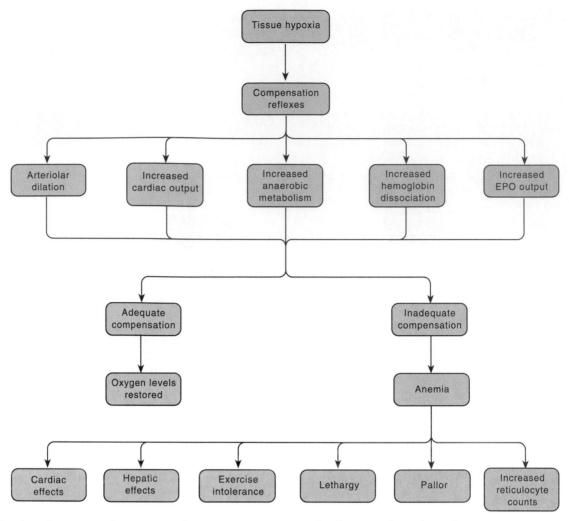

Figure 7.18   Anemia emerges when compensations cannot restore oxygen levels to meet tissue demands.

the problem. In scurvy, a dietary lack of vitamin C interferes with collagen synthesis, and in Cushing's disease, hypersecretion of corticosteroids induces the breakdown of protein, which weakens vascular supporting tissues.

Connective tissues also deteriorate with advancing age. The lessening of vascular support in the elderly causes **senile purpura.** In this condition, the vessels of the hands, wrists, upper arms, and calves are principally affected. The threat of serious blood loss in this condition is minimal.

ERYTHROCYTE DISORDERS

Problems involving erythrocytes arise if their numbers are excessive or inadequate. If numbers are excessive, the condition is known as **polycythemia.** When hemoglobin levels or erythrocyte numbers are decreased, oxygen transport is compromised and the condition of **anemia** results.

Anemia

Anemia is usually indicated by a hemoglobin level that falls below the lower limit of its normal range: 14–18 g/dl for males and 12–16 g/dl for females. The low hemoglobin levels cause a decline in the blood's oxygen transport capacity, which in turn triggers various physiologic compensations. Arteriolar dilation, accompanied by an increased cardiac output, provides for increased blood flow. A shift to anaerobic metabolism reduces oxygen consumption and indirectly promotes the dissociation of oxygen from hemoglobin. Also, increased renal secretion of erythropoietin stimulates the marrow to increase erythropoiesis and speed RBC production.

If these compensations are unable to restore oxygen delivery, and hemoglobin levels fall to 7–8 g/dl, signs and symptoms of hypoxia emerge. **Pallor** (paleness) is common, as are weakness, lethargy, and exercise intolerance. In severe cases, tissues especially sensitive to hypoxia may be affected, with abnormal cardiac rhythms and hepatic necrosis the result. Related metabolic defects may also produce fatty change in the heart and liver (fig. 7.18).

When anemia is suspected, it is usual to assess red cell numbers and size by means of red cell counts, the **hematocrit,** and tests of the **mean corpuscular volume** (MCV). The hematocrit is the volume of cells expressed as a percentage of total blood volume. Since red cells dominate in the blood, in practice its value is taken to be a measure of erythrocyte volume (normal: 45%). Information relating to the blood's oxygen transport capacity comes from testing hemoglobin levels and the **mean corpuscular hemoglobin concentration** (MCHC). The MCV and MCHC tests provide a classification based on red cell size and hemoglobin content. Erythrocytes of normal volume are said to be **normocytic,** while those with an increased and decreased volume (higher and lower MCV values) are **macrocytic** [16] and **microcytic** [17], respectively. Erythrocytes with a normal hemoglobin content are described as normochromic, those with excess hemoglobin (elevated MCHC) as **hyperchromic,** and those with a hemoglobin deficiency (low MCHC) as **hypochromic** (table 7.3).

Reticulocyte counts are also useful in the assessment of anemia. Hypoxia triggers an increased renal secretion of erythropoietin to stimulate a compensating increase in marrow activity. The marrow responds by rapidly moving immature reticulocytes into the circulation. This response provides an insight into the underlying pathophysiology of the anemia. When the anemia is caused by increased red cell destruction, a compensating rise in the reticulocyte count occurs. However, when it is caused by the marrow's inability to produce adequate red cell numbers in the first place, the increased erythropoietin will have no effect. Since the marrow can't meet normal demands for red cells, it can hardly be expected to increase its output, and so reticulocyte counts are lower than normal.

With this background, we can move to consider the etiology of anemia. As previously indicated, the condition is caused either by abnormally high red cell losses or by failure of the marrow to maintain production while normal red cell clearance continues. We will examine the latter case first.

Impaired Erythrocyte Production: Marrow Defects

Anemia is sometimes caused by abnormalities in the stem cells or progenitors of the various hemopoietic cell lines (fig. 7.1). In such conditions, the defect can be localized in the developmental sequence by analyzing the circulating formed elements. For example, if only red cells are deficient, the defect can be ascribed to one of the progenitors in the red cell line. A rare disease called pure red cell aplasia (PRCA) is caused by an abnormality of this type. By contrast, if all formed elements are deficient (**pancytopenia**),

Table 7.3	Terminology Used in Laboratory Red Cell Assessment	
	Volume	**Hemoglobin Content**
Normal	Normocytic	Normochromic
Increased	Macrocytic (higher MCV)	Hyperchromic (higher MCHC)
Decreased	Microcytic (lower MCV)	Hypochromic (lower MCHC)

the abnormality must occur earlier in the developmental sequence. In some cases it is due to specific marrow suppressants associated with infections, chemotherapy, radiation, or drug reactions, but many cases are idiopathic.

A common example of a pancytopenic disorder is **aplastic anemia.** In this condition, all the normal formed-element precursors are greatly reduced. Fat cells proliferate to replace them and dominate the marrow. Although anemia is a significant problem, bleeding due to thrombocytopenia and infections from depressed white cell numbers are important secondary features. In severe cases, mortality can be quite high; especially threatening is the aplastic anemia that can accompany viral hepatitis. Therapy may require a bone marrow transplant. An underlying autoimmune mechanism may be implicated in the large number of idiopathic cases, since immune suppression therapy has been used with some success.

Impaired Erythrocyte Production: Deficiencies

Deficiencies of substances essential to erythropoiesis may arise either from inadequate supply or from excessive losses. The red cells produced in these deficiency states demonstrate size and staining properties that are useful in diagnosis. The principal deficiencies that interfere with erythropoiesis are described in the following sections.

Iron Deficiency Iron deficiency anemia is a common condition throughout the world. [18] The essential problem is the lack of adequate iron to sustain the level of erythropoiesis needed to replace the 1% of red cells cleared from the circulation daily. As aging erythrocytes are destroyed in the spleen, marrow, and liver, the iron from their hemoglobin is efficiently recycled and used to synthesize new hemoglobin. However, small amounts, 1–2 mg daily, are lost in urine and feces, and from the skin via perspiration and sloughing of its superficial layer. These losses must be made up from dietary intake. In women, an additional average daily iron loss of 1 mg can be attributed to menstrual blood flow (fig. 7.19). Most women do not compensate by increasing their dietary intake and are in a marginal iron deficiency state. Because of this, they are more vulnerable to any additional factor that predisposes to iron deficiency.

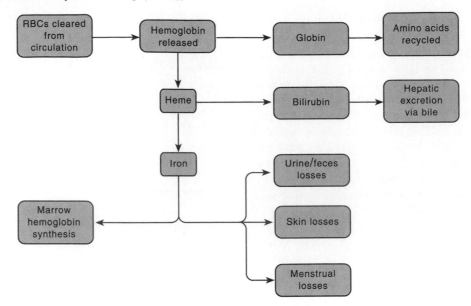

Figure 7.19   Iron recycling and the unavoidable iron loss that are related to the clearance of erythrocytes from the circulating pool.

Although iron is widely available in meat, liver, eggs, nuts, legumes, and beans, the iron in animal products is contained in heme, which is much more easily absorbed. The uptake of iron derived from plant sources depends on processing by gastric acid, which promotes the formation of soluble complexes of iron and other dietary components. These complexes remain soluble in the small intestine, favoring iron absorption. For this reason, patients who have had a total gastrectomy (stomach removal) may require iron supplementation to offset the reduced iron absorption rate that results from lack of gastric processing.

Absorbed iron is stored locally in the intestinal epithelium, in the liver, and in macrophages widely dispersed throughout the body. As iron intake is reduced or losses are increased, these stores of iron can be drawn upon to replenish supplies to the marrow. Eventually, however, the stored iron may be depleted, and if the underlying imbalance is not corrected, signs and symptoms of anemia emerge.

Iron deficiency anemia may develop as the result of an inadequate supply of iron to the marrow, which in turn may be due either to an inadequate diet or to absorption disorders (chapter 13). These causes are not common in developed countries. Far more frequently, iron deficiency anemia develops in adults as the result of blood loss, usually from gastrointestinal bleeding. Such bleeding can be sufficient to deplete iron, but not severe enough to reveal its presence by any noticeable change in stool coloration. If bleeding is prolonged, a chronic anemia may result. In cases where heavy menstrual flow is unrecognized as abnormal, increased losses can also produce a chronic iron deficiency anemia.

In iron deficiency anemia, the erythrocytes produced by the marrow are small (microcytic) and deficient in

Iron Deficiency Anemia and Pregnancy

Pregnancy can produce anemia because of the considerable transfer of iron from mother to infant during pregnancy and subsequent nursing. If pregnancies are closely spaced, the chance of developing an iron deficiency anemia increases, since there may not be enough time between them for replenishment of maternal iron stores. You might expect that the cessation of menstruation during pregnancy would compensate for losses to the infant. Unfortunately, however, blood loss associated with the delivery of the child offsets those gains.

hemoglobin (hypochromic). Once the condition is established, these defects are reflected in low MCV and MCHC values.

Vitamin B$_{12}$ Deficiency Vitamin B$_{12}$ is required for normal DNA synthesis. When it is lacking, hemopoiesis is suppressed and a pancytopenia results. There is no impairment of RNA or protein synthesis, and cell growth proceeds, but since division can't occur, marrow precursors remain enlarged. These **megaloblasts** give rise to the descriptive term **megaloblastic anemia**. Because the erythrocytes that reach the circulation are also enlarged, a macrocytic, normochromic anemia results, with an increased MCV and a normal MCHC. The anemia is compounded by the fact that the enlarged red cells are more quickly cleared from the circulation.

Vitamin B$_{12}$ is also known as **cobalamin.** It is not synthesized in our tissues, so we rely on the dietary intake of

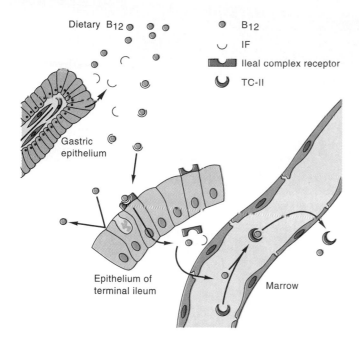

Figure 7.20   Vitamin B$_{12}$ combines with IF in the proximal small intestine. Complex receptors in the distal ileum promote absorption. Uncomplexed B$_{12}$ is not absorbed. TC-II carries the vitamin in the plasma. It is split off in the marrow, releasing B$_{12}$ for its role in hemopoiesis.

meat, liver, seafood, and dairy products to supply our needs. The small daily requirement of 1 μg is easily satisfied by most diets, and an added protection comes from body stores of 2–5 mg. This is enough to meet demand for years, should intake fall to zero. Only strictest dietary avoidance of meat and dairy products for several years could pose the threat of anemia from inadequate supplies of vitamin B$_{12}$.

Much more commonly, the lack of cobalamin is due to its inadequate absorption from the intestinal lumen. When released from food by gastric digestive processing, cobalamin is in a form that is not readily absorbed. However, a glycoprotein produced by the parietal cells of the gastric mucosa can combine with it. The glycoprotein is called **intrinsic factor** (IF). The IF-cobalamin complex passes to the intestine, where it is bound to specific IF-B$_{12}$ receptors on the epithelium of the distal portions of the ileum. Absorption can occur only after such binding. Following absorption, the cobalamin is released from IF and is taken up by a plasma transport protein called **transcobalamin II** (TC-II). The vitamin travels in the blood complexed with TC-II until it is taken up by the marrow, or by other cells with high mitotic rates that require it (fig. 7.20).

In **atrophic gastritis,** vitamin B$_{12}$ absorption is hindered by a lack of IF. According to growing evidence, the cause may be an autoimmune attack on both IF and the parietal cells that produce it. The reasons underlying the immune defect are unknown. The megaloblastic anemia associated with the IF deficiency in atrophic gastritis is known as **pernicious anemia.** Gastric resection, usually to remove a carcinoma, can also reduce or eliminate IF availability, but the term pernicious anemia is reserved for the condition where deficiency arises with the mucosa essentially intact.

Intestinal malabsorption states (chapter 13) may also affect cobalamin absorption, as can resection of the ileum. More rarely, abnormal bacterial growth in the intestine or a tapeworm (from undercooked fish) can consume vitamin B$_{12}$ to a degree that limits its availability for absorption.

Many patients who suffer a cobalamin deficiency anemia also experience some degree of neuropathy. The central or peripheral nervous systems, or both, may be affected. Symptom severity is often not linked to the degree of anemia. Loss of myelin is the underlying cause of the neuropathy, but the reasons for it are unknown.

Folic Acid Deficiency   Lack of **folic acid** (or **folate,** its salt) produces a megaloblastic anemia that is very similar to that seen in the cobalamin deficiency state. The cells of both marrow and peripheral blood are similar, so diagnosis must be made on the basis of depressed levels of folate in serum. No neuropathy is associated with folate deficiencies. The poor, elderly, and alcoholics (who have notoriously poor diets) are other groups likely to develop folate deficiency anemia.

The dietary sources of folate—meat, eggs, leafy vegetables—are readily available, so pure dietary deficiency states are rare in developed countries. Fad diets, or overcooking, which breaks down heat-sensitive folate, may produce a deficiency, but body stores provide a five-month period of tolerance for deviations from proven dietary practice.

As you might expect, intestinal resection or disease can interfere with folate absorption. In fact, in such cases deficiencies of folic acid, cobalamin, and iron can all contribute to anemia.

Folate deficiency can also be the result of high demand states. Examples of these are pregnancy, infant growth spurts, prolonged marrow overactivity to compensate for chronic blood loss, and rapid consumption by rapidly growing malignancies.

Impaired Erythrocyte Production: Chronic Disease

A variety of long-term, often systemic disease conditions can lead to mild, nonprogressive anemia. In such cases the marrow is intact and total body levels of key nutrients are normal. Infections and chronic inflammations are often involved, with anemia developing by various mechanisms. In some cases, the mechanism is a reduced red cell survival time. For some reason in chronic disease states, normal erythrocytes are prematurely removed from the blood by macrophages. In other cases, the mechanism involves erythropoietin (EPO); either marrow precursors become

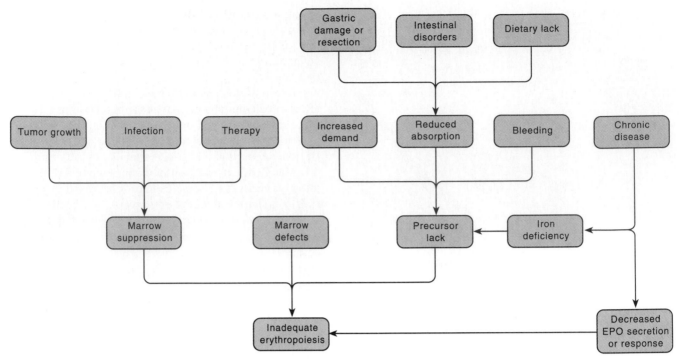

Figure 7.21 Factors that may contribute to reduced erythropoiesis.

Folic Acid Deficiency in Tumor Therapy

Some tumor therapy side effects are related to folic acid. Not only do malignant tumors consume more folic acid, but some antitumor chemotherapeutic agents work by interfering with the tumor's utilization of folate, in order to slow or stop its growth. The effect can't be limited to the tumor cells, so a critical lack of folic acid may arise in normal tissues already facing a deficiency from the tumor's high folate consumption.

less responsive to it or secretion is inadequate. Since EPO is secreted by the kidney, lack of secretion is typical in chronic and severe renal disease. Iron deficiency is another reason for anemia in chronic diseases. The problem seems to arise because, although total body iron reserves are adequate, macrophage stores can't be drawn on quickly enough to meet demand.

The marrow suppression effects of malignant tumors were described in chapter 6. We can summarize here by saying that nonmarrow malignancies seem to produce anemia by suppressing the marrow. The likely mechanism is the tumor's production of circulating marrow suppressants. The various factors that can interfere with normal erythropoiesis are summarized in figure 7.21.

Hemolytic Anemia

As we have seen, circulating erythrocyte numbers are the result of the balance between production and clearance. Having considered failure of the marrow to maintain adequate red cell output, we can now turn to the destruction of erythrocytes—**hemolysis,** in particular—and to those anemias that result from the destruction of defective red cells.

Intrinsic Hemolytic Anemia

Intrinsic hemolytic anemia derives principally from hereditary defects that promote hemolysis. These are relatively rare disorders involving flawed erythrocyte enzyme systems, defective RBC membranes, or abnormal hemoglobins. The **hemoglobinopathies** are most important, and are represented by two distinct conditions: sickle cell anemia and thalassemia.

Sickle Cell Anemia In this condition, erythrocytes contain an abnormal hemoglobin, **HbS,** as opposed to the normal **HbA.** When oxygen level is low, HbS forms aggregates by polymerizing. The result is a distortion of the cell, which assumes a less flexible crescent shape resembling a sickle (fig. 7.22). Such cells are much more likely to be cleared from the blood by marrow and spleen macrophages. **20** The typical life span of a sickled cell is 20 days, as opposed to the normal cell's 120 days. Sickled cells also tend to become trapped in the microcirculation, where they can obstruct flow and threaten the tissues that rely on it. **21**

(a)

(b)

Figure 7.22   (*a*) Normal blood, for comparison with (*b*) the abnormal cell shapes that occur in sickle cell anemia.

Either mechanism reduces cell numbers to produce the anemia. The clinical course of sickle cell anemia is quite variable. Although the disease was previously quite threatening, improved therapeutics enable many sufferers to reach maturity.

A benign condition called **sickle cell trait** is determined by the presence of one defective gene, instead of the two present in the full-blown anemia disorder. Affected individuals are asymptomatic and are threatened only if severe hypoxia develops. However, they are carriers of the defective gene and can pass it to their offspring. If both parents are carriers and contribute a defective gene to the same child, sickle cell anemia is the result.

Blacks of African origin are the population affected by sickle cell anemia. The defective allele can be detected, and screening programs have been helpful in providing information and counseling applicable to mate selection and family planning.

Thalassemia The thalassemias are a group of genetic disorders that also involve hemoglobin defects. The most common thalassemias, beta-thalassemias, arise from defective production of the beta-globin component of hemoglobin. Beta-globin normally joins to alpha-globin, but when the beta protein is lacking, alpha-globin accumulates and causes destructive membrane effects (fig. 7.23). Not only does the membrane damage cause rapid clearance of red cells from the blood, but before leaving the marrow the defective RBCs in some way suppress mitosis in stem cells so that red cell production falls.

Thalassemia major (**Cooley's anemia**) is a gravely threatening disease that requires a continuous regimen of transfusions. 22 Sufferers are homozygous for the defective gene. **Thalassemia minor** 23 is a milder form of the disease, which occurs in heterozygotes (those who have only

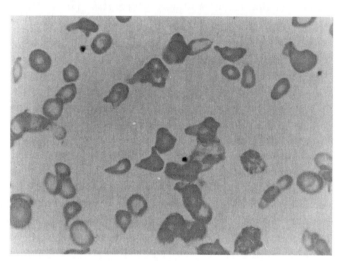

Figure 7.23   Reduced erythrocyte numbers in thalassemia. Compare with normal blood in figure 7.22.

one defective gene). It is well tolerated and essentially asymptomatic. These conditions are more prevalent in ethnic groups with origins in countries bordering the Mediterranean.

Paroxysmal Nocturnal Hemoglobinuria (PNH) This rare condition arises as a genetic defect that occurs in marrow precursors rather than in the sufferer's parents' genes. The abnormality involves a membrane defect that is passed on to daughter cells in the erythrocyte maturation sequence, but cannot be transmitted to the affected person's offspring.

The disease is characterized by a chronic anemia as well as episodes of hemolysis that occur at night. The hemoglobin that is released from the ruptured red cells is excreted by the kidneys and is detectable in the urine.

22 ‖‖‖‖‖‖‖‖‖‖‖‖‖‖
13682

23 ‖‖‖‖‖‖‖‖‖‖‖‖‖‖
16174

Table 7.4	Conditions Involving Immune-Mediated Hemolysis

Autoimmune hemolytic anemia
Warm antibody autoimmune hemolytic anemia
Cold antibody autoimmune hemolytic anemia
Drug-mediated hemolytic anemias
Paroxysmal cold hemoglobinuria
   (This rare condition is associated with syphilis and other infections. It should not be confused with paroxysmal nocturnal hemoglobinuria, a genetic condition.)

Table 7.5	Therapeutic Agents Known to Have Some Degree of Hemolytic Effect via Immune Mechanisms

Amino salicylic acid	Cephalosporine
Chlorpropamide	Cisplatin
Isoniazid	Levodopa
Mefenamic acid	Methyldopa
Penicillins	Phenacetin
Quinidine	Quinine
Rifampin	Stibophen
Sulfonamides	Sulfonylureas
Tolbutamide	

Extrinsic Hemolytic Anemias

In these conditions, hemolysis is the result of damaging influences that affect normal erythrocytes. The problem arises outside the red cell to cause surface changes that promote clearance by spleen and marrow macrophages. Alternatively, the cells might be so damaged that they rupture in the blood.

Immune Hemolysis The essential difficulty in immune hemolysis is the combining of antibodies with red cell surface antigens. This results in more rapid clearance of RBCs from the blood, on the basis of an altered cell surface, or rupture of the RBCs via complement activation (see chapter 5). In normal circumstances, antibodies against red cell surface antigens are not present, but inappropriate blood transfusions or immune incompatibilities between a mother and her fetus can introduce them. The D or Rh antigens are typically involved in maternal-fetal incompatibilities, while the ABO or other antigen systems are principally involved in transfusion-related hemolysis.

In the examples just cited, antigens from one individual interact with antibodies from another individual, but other immune hemolytic conditions involve autoimmunity. In these **autoimmune hemolytic anemias,** an individual's immune system produces antibodies against its own self-antigens. About half of such anemias arise in association with some identifiable disease, but the remainder are idiopathic. The anemias associated with various tumors, infections, and inflammatory conditions are caused by immune-related red cell destruction. Examples of these conditions are provided in table 7.4. In this table the terms **warm antibody** and **cold antibody** refer to the laboratory incubation temperatures at which the antibodies maximally combine with antigen.

Some therapeutic drugs are able to induce immune destruction of red cells. By direct or indirect means, the drug comes to be bound at the cell surface, causing lysis while in the circulating blood or more rapid clearance from it. Some agents known to elicit these effects are listed in table 7.5. Large drug doses or a pronounced patient sensitivity are usually involved.

Mechanical Hemolysis Trauma, or physical injury, can disrupt red cell membranes to induce hemolysis. As erythrocytes traverse vascular or cardiac passages, they may encounter trauma due to a variety of causes. Certain, especially older, artificial cardiac valves are known to physically damage erythrocytes, as does the jetting of blood through ventricular septal defects or abnormally rigid aortic valves. Similar traumatic damage is associated with hemodialysis devices and heart-lung machines, both of these being examples of **extracorporeal circulation.** In DIC, or more localized intravascular coagulation, adhering platelet plugs and fibrin strands present obstacles to red cells, damaging them as they are driven over obstructions in the confined spaces of the microvasculature. [24] Prolonged trauma to the soles of the feet and palms of the hands has been known to produce episodes of transient hemolysis. Running or even walking long distances with inappropriate footwear presumably causes trauma to the small vessels of the soles and damages the erythrocytes as they pass through them. As a result, fragments of erythrocytes are mechanically sheared off to yield circulating cell fragments with bizarre configurations.

Miscellaneous Hemolytic Anemias Certain drugs can damage erythrocytes by forming destructive free radicals that damage hemoglobin or the red cell membrane (table 7.6). Snake bite toxins, infectious agents, or various other substances encountered in the environment can disrupt red cells in various ways that promote their more rapid clearance from the blood.

Hypersplenism

Excessive splenic clearance of formed elements from the blood is called **hypersplenism.** It is seen in conditions of splenomegaly [25] most commonly as a result of cirrhotic congestion of the hepatic portal circulation (chapter 14). Leukopenia and thrombocytopenia may be present to varying degrees in association with the anemia produced by the spleen's exaggerated red cell clearance.

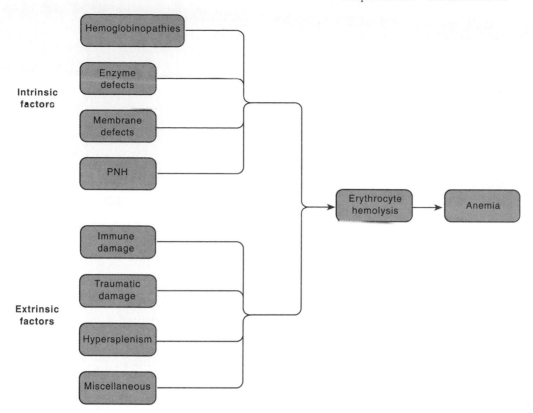

Figure 7.24   Factors in hemolytic anemia.

Table 7.6	Drugs Causing Hemolysis Through the Production of Injurious Intracellular Free Radicals (Peroxide, Superoxide)

Dapsone
Nitroglycerine
Phenacetin
Primaquine
Sodium perchlorate
Sulfasalazine
Vitamin K analogues

In some cases, therapeutic resolution of the condition producing the hypersplenism is not followed by a return to normal spleen clearance rates. To avoid chronic anemia problems, the spleen may be surgically removed without serious long-term functional deficit. The broad array of factors that can produce hemolysis is presented in figure 7.24.

Polycythemia

Polycythemia is the condition of increased red cell concentration in the blood. **26** It may be due to an increase in red cell numbers (with normal plasma volume), **absolute polycythemia,** or to normal red cell numbers suspended in a reduced plasma volume (**relative polycythemia**). The condition produces elevations of packed cell volume (PCV), the hematocrit, and the hemoglobin level.

Absolute Polycythemia

This condition involves an overproduction of erythrocytes by the marrow. If marrow activity is increased in response to elevated renal output of erythropoietin (EPO), the polycythemic condition is said to be secondary. **Secondary polycythemias** may arise as a normal physiologic response to the tissue hypoxia that is present in certain lung or heart conditions that interfere with normal blood oxygenation. High-altitude exposure has a similar effect. If there is no physiologic requirement, but EPO secretion is increased, a tumor is usually involved. Renal tumors may secrete excessive EPO, or nonrenal tumors, able to secrete EPO-like substances, may be the source of the marrow stimulus. In some cases, restricted renal blood flow will produce renal hypoxia and activate EPO secretion. An exaggerated marrow output will then cause a secondary polycythemia to develop.

Heavy smokers may also suffer a secondary polycythemia. Inhaling products of combustion delivers significant levels of carbon monoxide (CO) to the blood. CO has a tendency to bind with hemoglobin that is over 200 times that of oxygen. When CO is present in a heavy smoker's blood, oxygen delivery is compromised, and hypoxic renal sensors respond with increased EPO secretion (fig. 7.2).

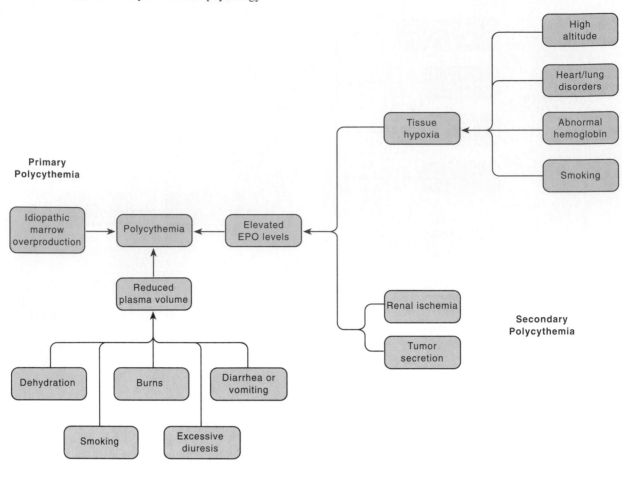

Figure 7.25   Etiological factors in primary, relative, and secondary polycythemia.

In **primary absolute polycythemia,** marrow stem cell lines proliferate without an increased EPO stimulus. This condition is, in effect, a benign tumor of the marrow, with red cell proliferation dominating over platelet or white cell production. In such cases, the normal or elevated tissue supply of oxygen suppresses EPO secretion.

Another myeloproliferative condition is referred to as **polycythemia vera** or sometimes **polycythemia rubra vera.** It is characterized by a thickened blood, which flows more sluggishly through small vessels and predisposes to coagulation within them, especially in the kidneys, spleen, and liver. Deprivation of nutrients and tissue destruction follow blockage of the vessels. Males in their 60s to 80s are most likely to be affected by this idiopathic disease.

Relative Polycythemia In these conditions, hematocrit values are increased but total red cell numbers are normal. The plasma deficiency that produces this state may be the result of generalized dehydration, extensive skin burns, or pronounced diarrhea or diuresis.

Two other conditions that involve a relative polycythemia have only poorly understood reasons for low plasma volume. One is **smoker's polycythemia,** to which heavy smoking contributes in some way, and the other is **stress polycythemia,** whose typically hard-driving, male sufferers are also at high risk of heart and brain vascular disease. A summary of etiological factors in pulmonary, secondary, and relative polycythemia is presented in figure 7.25.

LEUKOCYTE DISORDERS

As in the case of red cells, leukocyte numbers in the peripheral blood are determined by the balance between production and destruction. **Leukopenia** is the general deficiency state, while the term **leukocytosis** denotes a nonneoplastic elevation of white cell numbers. The neoplastic proliferation of leukocytes is denoted by the term **leukemia.**

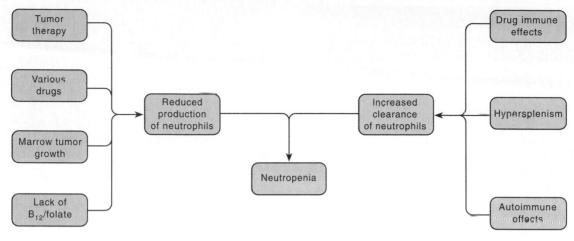

Figure 7.26   Etiology in neutropenia.

Leukopenia

Most conditions of white cell depletion involve **neutropenia,** although the other granulocytes may be affected, as well. The blood's normal range of neutrophil numbers is 1800–7200 per mm^3. Neutropenia is diagnosed on the basis of sustained counts below 1800/mm^3. When counts drop to the extremes of 200–300/mm^3, the term **agranulocytosis** is often used to describe the condition.

The usual consequence of neutropenia is an increased risk of infection as a result of a reduced phagocytosis response. Increased infection rates are significant when neutrophil counts fall to 500/mm^3 and below. The typical signs and symptoms of infection are malaise, fever, weakness, and fatigue. Infections of the oral and pharyngeal mucosa are typically seen in leukopenia. Without timely antibiotic and anti-inflammatory therapy, rapid development of massive systemic infection may occur.

Most neutropenia is the result of inadequate production by a marrow whose functions are suppressed by antitumor therapy involving drugs or radiation. Neutrophil counts decrease with increased dose level, and their lowering is taken into account in the patient's management. In many cases, however, nontumor drugs may have variable marrow suppression effects, producing neutropenia as an unexpected side effect (table 7.7). A broad variety of other causes can also produce marrow suppression and neutropenia, including marrow replacement by primary or secondary tumor growth as well as various infections, deficiencies of folic acid or vitamin B$_{12}$ (needed for DNA synthesis in neutrophil precursors), and genetic immune defects (fig. 7.26).

Excessively rapid clearance of neutrophils from the blood can also produce neutropenia. Immune destruction may be involved. Inappropriate immune responses can trigger destruction of neutrophils as part of an underlying autoimmune disorder. Some therapeutic drugs are able to bind to neutrophil membranes, acting as opsonins that promote clearance by macrophage phagocytosis. In hypersplenism, neutropenia may result when neutrophils are removed from the blood and destroyed.

Table 7.7	Selected Agents That May Suppress the Marrow to Produce Neutropenia

Alkylating Agents
  Cyclophosphamide
  Melphalan
Analgesics*
  Phenacetin
  Phenylbutazone
Antibiotics*
  Ampicillin
  Chloramphenicol
Anticonvulsants*
  Phenytoin
  Trimethadione
Antihistamines*
  Tripelennamine
Antimetabolites
  Mercaptopurine
  Methotrexate
Thyroid Antagonists*
  Methimazole
  Polypropylthiouracil
X-irradiation

*Indicates agents whose neutropenia effects are unpredictable.

Table 7.8	Specific Leukocytoses and Their Principal Associated Conditions

Polymorphonuclear leukocytosis (neutrophilia)
Acute inflammations
Basophilic leukocytosis (basophilia)
Myeloproliferative disorders
Lung malignancies
Eosinophilic leukocytosis (eosinophilia)
Allergic disorders (hay fever, asthma, drug reactions)
Parasite/fungus infection
Sarcoidosis
Skin disorders
Monocytosis
Collagen vascular disease (systemic lupus erythematosus, rheumatoid arthritis)
Chronic infections (TB, brucellosis)
Intestinal inflammations (Crohn's disease, ulcerative colitis)
Lymphocytosis
Acute viral infections
Chronic infections (TB, brucellosis)

Leukocytosis

This condition of elevated leukocyte counts is a functional response to increased demand. Specific white cells may be affected and their increased number linked to their particular defensive role (see table 7.8). Leukocytosis in the context of the inflammatory response is described in chapter 2.

Leukemia

Primary malignant tumors of leukocyte precursors in the marrow are called leukemias. They do not produce discrete tumor masses but instead are characterized by proliferation in the marrow. In most cases (65%), cells showing varying degrees of differentiation spill over into the blood to increase circulating cell numbers, and it is then that the term leukemia is used (fig. 7.27). In the cases where proliferation is confined to the marrow, the term **aleukemic leukemia** is employed.

Pathogenesis

The production of large numbers of marrow cells in the leukocyte differentiation line is not the result of a decreased generation time. The abnormality lies in later developmental stages when cells maintain the ability to divide instead of losing it as they mature and differentiate. The result is a large number of dividing cells, which expand at the expense of normal marrow. In late stages of the disease, the entire marrow volume may be replaced by tumor cells.

(a)

(b)

Figure 7.27 Blood smears from (*a*) a normal person and (*b*) a person with leukemia.

One consequence of marrow loss is severe neutropenia, or agranulocytosis, and the pronounced susceptibility to infection it produces. Another is anemia, as red cell production falls. It is compounded by the blood loss resulting from failure of normal hemostasis, which is in turn the result of the thrombocytopenia that follows the marrow's reduced platelet production. As the tumor continues to grow, it may invade to the bone that houses it, causing destruction of bone tissue and bone and joint pain. Metastasis to the spleen, liver, meninges, and lymph nodes is not uncommon and can compromise their function to yield additional systemic complications (fig. 7.28). Secondary growth may enlarge the infiltrated organ to produce hepatomegaly, splenomegaly, and enlarged lymph nodes (lymphadenopathy).

Classification

Leukemias can be classified according to their pattern of progression. They are said to be acute if the onset is abrupt, with more severe signs and symptoms and rapid progression. By contrast, chronic leukemia develops gradually and

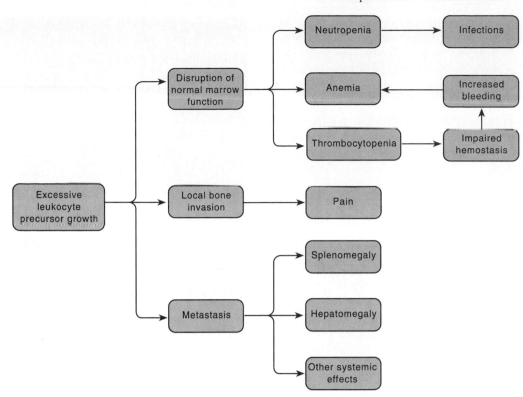

Figure 7.28   Pathogenesis of leukemia.

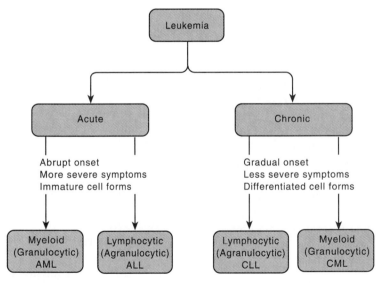

Figure 7.29   Classification terminology in leukemia.

is associated with milder, less specific early effects, e.g., fatigue or weight loss. Acute forms are also characterized by cells that are less well differentiated, while in chronic leukemia, the leukocytes are typically more mature (fig. 7.29).

Further classification is possible in that two different lines of differentiation can be the focus of the disorder. If the precursors of the granulocytes are neoplastic, the dominant marrow cell is a granular descendant. These are the **myeloblastic** or **granulocytic leukemias.** When the lymphocyte line of development is neoplastic, agranular descendants dominate and a **lymphoblastic** or **lymphocytic leukemia** is present. Rare leukemias of plasma cells and monocytes are also known.

Acute Lymphocytic Leukemia (ALL) ALL is predominantly seen in children and adolescents and is the most common malignancy affecting children. **27** Anemias due to inadequate erythropoiesis produce progressive weakness and lack of stamina. Bleeding from thrombocytopenia, susceptibility to infection, and cervical lymphadenopathy are also typical. Aggressive combination chemotherapy and the increasing mastery of bone marrow transplants have made a complete cure possible in over 50% of patients.

Acute Myeloblastic Leukemia (AML) The prognosis in AML is less optimistic. Even after intensive therapy, approximately 75% of patients will suffer recurrence of symptoms within 18 months. **28** Peak incidence is among adolescents and adults to about age 40.

ALL and AML present clinically similar pictures so that diagnostic certainty depends on analysis of a bone marrow biopsy. AML patients have characteristic chromosomal abnormalities that can be used in determining a prognosis.

Chronic Lymphocytic Leukemia (CLL) The most common of the leukemias, CLL is typically seen in later life (above 50 years of age). Its onset is gradual, and the fatigue, weight loss, and anorexia that accompany it are often accepted as being age-related. The cell most typically involved is the B lymphocyte, with extreme cases producing counts as high as 200,000/mm^3. **29** However, these cells are not functional, so a deficiency of the immune system's antibody response results in a predisposition to bacterial infection. Infiltration of lymph nodes is responsible for the lymphadenopathy that is often present in CLL. In many patients, survival is prolonged by a course of chemotherapy.

Chronic Myeloblastic Leukemia (CML) People in the age range 25–60 suffer the peak incidence of CML. In this condition, cells of the granulocyte line can reach counts as high as 100,000/mm^3. **30** Liver and spleen infiltration is marked by symptoms of abdominal heaviness or dragging due to massive splenomegaly. Most sufferers of CML experience a **blast crisis** in the disease's later stage. This is a phase that resembles acute leukemia, with large numbers of immature leukocytes rapidly entering the blood, to accelerate the patient's deterioration. The presence of a damaged chromosome (#22) is noted in over 90% of the CML patients. It is known as the **Philadelphia chromosome.**

Lymphomas

Lymphomas are the most common tumor type after carcinomas. They are solid malignant tumors arising in the cells of lymphoid tissue: lymphocytes and their precursors. Their growth produces marrow and lymphoid tissue replacement as well as local effects related to expansion of the tumor mass, e.g., invasion into adjacent tissues or compression of nearby organs. Loss of normal lymphoid tissue functions causes immune deficiencies that predispose to infection. Various mechanisms contribute to anemia, and lymphadenopathy is a typical and prominent sign.

Figure 7.30   The Reed-Sternberg cell is diagnostic for Hodgkin's disease. The arrows indicate two R-S cells in this tissue sample from a lymph node biopsy.
This axillary lymph node is typical of the many that were enlarged and heavily infiltrated in a 34-year-old male who finally succumbed to Hodgkin's disease. He had been weak and listless for some time prior to his death because of extensive metastases. This section shows complete loss of lymph node architecture and heavy cellular infiltration throughout the node. The Reed-Sternberg cell is easily distinguished by its size and the presence of several nuclei.

Hodgkin's Lymphoma This condition is also widely known as **Hodgkin's disease** (HD). Although relatively rare, it arises most often in young adults, usually in a single, painless, cervical lymph node. This is followed by spread to adjacent nodes and then more widely dispersed lymphoid organs in a consistent pattern. Splenomegaly **31** and lymphadenopathy are usually present, as are fatigue, wasting, and fever. T-cell immune functions are also usually depressed.

HD has four subtypes based on the cell types that dominate and other histological features. All HD diagnosis is substantiated on the basis of its characteristic marker, the **Reed-Sternberg (RS) cell.** **32** This is a large, multinucleate cell with other distinguishing cytologic features (fig. 7.30). Clinical staging in HD is indicated in table 7.9. Therapeutic approach and prognosis are related to the stage of the disease, with younger patients expecting a better outcome than the elderly.

Non-Hodgkin's Lymphomas (NHL) This group of tumors arises in lymphoid tissue, and its B and T lymphocyte lines in particular. Lymph nodes are the usual primary site, with spread to other nodes and lymphoid organs occurring in a less systematic pattern than is seen in HD. In some cases, following extensive metastasis, cells escape into the blood to mimic leukemia.

Table 7.9	The Ann Arbor System of Hodgkin's Disease Staging. More Hopeful Prognosis is Associated with Lower Stages.*

Stage I
Tumor present at a single lymph node region.

Stage II
Tumor present at two or more lymph node regions, all of which are on the same side of the diaphragm.

Stage III
Tumor present at two or more lymph node regions, with involvement on both sides of the diaphragm.

Stage IV
Widespread metastasis to one or more nonlymphatic organs.

*Further classification is based on the absence (A), or presence (B) of systemic symptoms (e. g., weight loss, fever). The subscript E indicates invasion to nonlymphatic organs, while the subscript S indicates invasion into the spleen. Stage IIIB would therefore indicate lymph node involvement on both sides of the diaphragm, with systemic symptoms present but no indications of splenic involvement.

Complications of Therapy for HD

Note that the radiation chemotherapy used in HD can have suppressing effects on the marrow and immune system. These can complicate the prognosis by adding to the anemia and infection burdens that the patient must bear. In a few cases, it is thought that radiation therapy for HD may actually cause a new tumor (acute leukemia) to develop.

The classification of the diverse group of lymphoid tumors is complex and has been controversial. The widely used, but not universally accepted, **Working Formulation** shown in table 7.10 combines prognosis data with cytologic features to yield a classification that distinguishes 10 NHLs (table 7.10). Generally, the prognosis in NHL is not as clearly related to its clinical stage as is the case in Hodgkin's lymphoma.

Bone Marrow Transplantation

In conditions where the marrow has been destroyed or replaced by a tumor, marrow transplantation can be effective in restoring marrow functions. In selecting marrow for transplantation, it is essential to avoid incompatibility between the donor's and recipient's human leukocyte antigens (chapter 4). Identical twins or siblings are usually selected.

The procedure begins with removal of marrow from the donor, usually from the hip bones. A volume equal to an ordinary wine bottle, 750 ml, is withdrawn and passed through a screen to free the cells from their marrow stroma

Table 7.10	Staging of the Ten Non-Hodgkins Lymphoma Subtypes

Low grade
Small lymphocytic lymphoma
Follicular lymphoma: small cleaved cell predominant
Follicular lymphoma: small and large cell types mixed

Intermediate grade
Follicular lymphoma: large cell type predominant
Diffuse, small cleaved cell lymphoma
Diffuse, mixed small and large cell lymphoma
Diffuse, large cell lymphoma

High grade
Large cell immunoblastic lymphoma
Lymphoblastic lymphoma
Small, noncleaved cell lymphoma

supports. The dispersed freed cells are then introduced into the recipient via an intravenous injection. The marrow cells circulate and selectively establish in the recipient's marrow. The mechanism involves receptor-mediated adherence to marrow stromal elements. Once in place, normal marrow differentiation can proceed.

Of course, where the human leukocyte antigens are other than identical, immune rejection may arise. To increase the likelihood that the transplant will be accepted, the recipient's immune response can be suppressed. As we have noted, this may interfere with erythropoiesis, clotting, and infection defense, so that, posttransplant red cell and platelet transfusions may be necessary. In addition, coping with the recipient's infection risk may involve elaborate isolation and special procedures for the handling of food and therapeutic agents.

Case Study

A 21-year-old university student went to his Campus Health Center. He complained of feeling weak and tired, experiencing increasing loss of appetite and periodic episodes of diarrhea and constipation. He had lost 30 pounds in the past year and was on a strictly vegetarian diet. He reported that he ate only "whole, natural foods" completely excluding animal products and taking no vitamin or mineral supplements. His goal in adopting this diet was to avoid introducing "toxins" into his body. Recent sensations of burning in his tongue and tingling in his arms had prompted him to seek medical advice.

On examination he appeared pale and emaciated with normal neurologic signs. When his blood test results were reported, they indicated a megaloblastic anemia with some distortion of red cell shapes. His hemoglobin value was 10 g/dl, the increase in MCV was pronounced, and his serum cobalamin was significantly below normal. With no history of gastric problems, the diagnosis of cobalamin deficiency anemia was made and a regimen of dietary supplementation prescribed. The patient was agreeable to the therapy and his health was soon restored.

Commentary

This classic dietary deficiency condition needs little comment, except to note that the patient's paresthesias (abnormal sensations) were an indication of a worsening condition. Had he ignored the neurological signs, the consequences might have been much more serious.

Although many who embark upon dietary regimens are not as severely affected, this individual interpreted his early signs and symptoms as being caused by the "contaminants" in his food, so he intensified his dietary vigilance, only to compound the problem. In the case of this young man, he readily accepted the recommended supplements of vitamin B_{12}, commenting that he wasn't "stupid, I just want to be healthy." In some extreme cases there may be resistance to dietary change. In these situations, the diet is seen as integral to a philosophic position or as an indication of one's discipline and worthiness. At any rate, in this case the outcome was a happy one.

Key Concepts

1. Conversion of the fluid blood to a nonflowing gel is the dominant mechanism that opposes blood loss (p. 156).

2. Blood coagulation depends on the formation of insoluble fibrin filaments via the sequential activation of a cascade of plasma enzymes called clotting factors (pp. 156–157).

3. Triggering of the coagulation cascade may be the result of damage that exposes clotting factors to tissue-derived activators or exposure to vessel wall elements when there is no threat of blood loss (pp. 157–158).

4. An anticoagulation system is balanced against the coagulation system to prevent unnecessary or too widespread coagulation that might interfere with normal blood flow (pp. 161–164).

5. An inadequate hemostatic response may be the result of decreased platelet numbers, caused by insufficient production, excessive clearance from the blood, or a functional deficit in the platelets themselves (pp. 165–168).

6. An inadequate hemostatic response may be the result of a clotting factor deficiency caused by insufficient production or by excessive clearance from the blood from widespread coagulation, which depletes their numbers (p. 168).

7. Bleeding may be caused by a weakness of small blood vessel walls resulting from damage or defective connective tissue support (pp. 169–170).

8. Anemia may result from inadequate red cell production, caused by a marrow abnormality or by a dietary deficiency that limits production by an otherwise normal marrow (pp. 170–174).

9. Red blood cell depletion sufficient to produce anemia may be caused by genetic red cell defects that favor their clearance from the blood by macrophages, by premature membrane rupture due to mechanical or immune-mediated damage, or by excessive splenic clearance (pp. 174–177).

10. Excessive RBC production may result from a benign tumor of red cell precursors or from excessive marrow stimulus by abnormally high levels of EPO or other less clearly understood control factors (pp. 176–178).

11. Neutropenia, and the increased infection risk it produces, is most often the result of therapeutic marrow suppression (p. 179).

12. Leukemia is a primary malignant tumor of leukocyte precursors in the marrow, which typically, although not in every case, spill over into the blood in large numbers (pp. 180–182).

13. Lymphomas are the solid, malignant tumors of lymphocytes and their precursors that arise in lymphoid tissue in lymph nodes and various other sites (p. 183).

14. To augment marrow function, a closely matched donor's marrow may be transplanted into a recipient whose marrow function is critically depressed by tumor growth or other suppressant factors (p. 183).

REVIEW ACTIVITIES

1. Cover the legend in figure 7.3 and identify the following features of the diagram:

RBCs and platelets in lumen	fibrin mesh
subendothelial connective tissue	platelet plug
muscle of vessel wall	RBCs in clot
vessel endothelium and BM	

2. Without reference to the text, lay out a flow chart that illustrates how thrombin contributes to three key components of the blood coagulation response. When you're done, see if your layout tells the same story as figure 7.10. Is there any positive feedback involved? Can you see why this might be usefully applied in the context of hemostasis?

3. Explain how marrow suppression might interfere with disease resistance. Mention at least three blood cell types.

4. Complete the following table.

Pattern of Bleeding	Distinguishing Characteristic
Purpura	
Ecchymosis	
Petechia	
Hematoma	

    Use an asterisk to denote the term that refers to a bruise.

5. Make up a ready reference list based on the three formed elements and the abnormal conditions involving each, in support of the concept that reduced formed element numbers may derive from inadequate production or excessive clearance from the blood.

6. Check back to figure 7.22 to verify that you can recognize the sickled cells as opposed to the normal RBCs. Note again, as well, the RBC shapes in figure 7.23.

7. Is it true that all leukemia is characterized by increased plasma leukocyte counts? Is there a descriptive term that could be included as part of your answer? If you're not clear, look late in the chapter for help.

Chapter Eight

Hemodynamic Disorders

*How should it happen that if you tie the arteries, immediately the parts
not only become torpid, and frigid, and look pale, but at length cease
even to be nourished?*

William Harvey
An Anatomical Disquisition on the Motion of the Heart and Blood in Animals

Hemodynamic disorders are those that arise from interruptions of normal blood flow. As noted in the preceding chapter, coagulation of the blood limits blood loss when vessel damage allows its escape. However, if blood coagulation is activated without the threat of blood loss, there may be undesirable consequences. These will result from the formation of a **thrombus** within a vessel by the process of **thrombosis.** Embolism and infarction are the other hemodynamic disorders that may follow thrombosis.

THROMBOSIS

A thrombus is a mass of platelets, red and white blood cells, and fibrin. **1** It is different from a clot in three ways. First, a thrombus never forms outside a blood vessel, whereas clots usually do. Second, a thrombus develops from and maintains a point of attachment to a blood vessel's wall. The third difference between a clot and a thrombus lies in the organization of their components. When a clot forms, its fibrin strands entrap formed elements to form a more or less homogeneous mass. By contrast, thrombosis yields a mass in which the blood components are highly organized. Because of these differences, the terms clot and thrombus should not be used interchangeably, although they often are.

Thrombosis starts at a point where platelets adhere to the vascular wall. As described in chapter 6, platelet adherence occurs at points where the endothelium is irregular or at points where it has been stripped away to expose subendothelial collagen. After initial contact is made, other platelets stick to those first at the scene, forming a mass of fused platelets that adheres firmly to the vessel's inner surface.

The effects of blood movement within the vessel now come into play as thrombosis proceeds. In arteries, where normal blood flow is rapid and regular, fibrin formation is limited. Because the blood carries away thrombin and other clotting factors activated by the intrinsic coagulation pathway, only small amounts of fibrin form. These strands strengthen the platelet mass at its site of attachment, but they do not accumulate. A similar process occurs in those thrombi that form on the linings of the cardiac chambers or on cardiac valve surfaces (fig. 8.1). Thus an arterial or cardiac thrombus is formed of aggregated platelets and small amounts of densely compacted fibrin. It also lacks any significant red or white cell component.

The situation is different in arteries or veins when blood flow is turbulent. In such situations, after platelet aggregation at the point of endothelial damage, fibrin builds up and traps erythrocytes and leukocytes. Turbulent blood flow forcefully washes platelets over the fibrin mass,

Figure 8.1 The damaged valve at left caused sluggish flow through this atrium, a condition favoring formation of the thrombus visible at the upper right.
This view of the floor of the left atrium was obtained from the autopsy of a man whose mitral valve was damaged as a result of an attack of rheumatic fever at the age of 9. Although he tolerated the problem fairly well, by age 39 his condition had started to deteriorate, and his heart ultimately failed when he was 46. The specimen shows the degree to which the mitral valve had been damaged so that its opening and closing were significantly affected. More details of rheumatic fever are presented in chapter 10, but of particular relevance here is the mass tucked into the auricular appendage of the atrium. This is a thrombus that is attached to the atrial endocardium. It probably formed as a result of the obstruction to atrial emptying caused by the damaged valve.

where they become activated, triggering further fibrin formation. The process continues, with the result that the thrombus is now enlarged by alternating layers of fibrin and trapped cells and layers of platelets. These alternating layers are called **lines of Zahn** (fig. 8.2) and are said to form the **mixed region** of a thrombus. **2** They usually form downstream from the attachment point.

In veins, when blood flow is very slow, activated clotting factors accumulate sufficiently to produce large quantities of fibrin. As a result, a large red cap of coagulated blood forms at the downstream end of the enlarging thrombus (fig. 8.3).

As previously indicated, the pattern of blood flow is a major determinant in the type of thrombus that will form. After somatic death, blood flow stops. This means that clotting factors activated by post-mortem tissue changes soon accumulate, causing coagulation of the blood. The

Figure 8.2   The alternating deposition of platelets and red cells trapped by fibrin produce the lines of Zahn visible in this arterial thrombus.

This is a section through the aorta of an 87-year-old man who was admitted to hospital following his arrival at the emergency room coughing blood and complaining of back pain. He died suddenly soon after admission. At autopsy he was found to have severe hardening of the arteries, but there were no signs of MI. A large aortic aneurysm (bulge) was also discovered. Its wall had weakened and bulged and a large thrombus had formed within it. The lines of Zahn can be clearly seen, as can the lining of the aorta that is badly diseased. The aorta had bulged against the adjacent lung, compressing and penetrating it to produce bleeding into the surrounding tissues and airways. The result was pain and the coughing of blood. The aorta's rupture, at a point not visible in the photograph, was the cause of death.

Figure 8.3   Arterial and venous thrombosis. (*a*) An arterial thrombus is smaller and denser than (*b*) a venous thrombus. Note the attaching mass of aggregated platelets where each thrombus originated, the mixed region of each, and the large red cap of the venous thrombus.

post-mortem clots formed in this way are large, red, gelatinous, and occlusive. They are not thrombi, as they are not joined to the vascular wall by a platelet attachment point. Sometimes a post-mortem clot will not form until the cells have begun to settle out of the blood. The result is a lighter-colored clot that lacks erythrocytes.

Factors Predisposing to Thrombosis

There are three factors that predispose to thrombus formation. These are endothelial damage, altered blood flow, and a blood hypercoagulation state.

Endothelial Damage

When a vessel's lining is damaged, endothelial cells may be stripped away or may draw away from adjacent cells to expose subendothelial collagen. This condition favors platelet adherence, activation, aggregation, and the initiation of thrombosis. A similar change can occur in the cells of the endocardial surface. The endocardium may be damaged by certain bacterial infections. It may also be affected

by damage to the myocardium, which lies immediately deep to it. In either case, platelet adherence is favored by the resulting surface changes.

In the arterial system there are two principal mechanisms that underlie most endothelial damage. The first involves the normal wear and tear to which the endothelium is subjected. This is called **hemodynamic stress,** because it is the result of the motion of blood as it is driven through the arterial tree under pressure. During each systolic contraction, the pressure developed causes the arteries to expand and elongate. They then return to their unstretched configuration because of the elastic recoil of their walls. This process is repeated an average of over 70 times per minute. It thus accounts for a major component of the wear and tear to which the endothelium is subjected. Although the endothelial cells are able to withstand the pressures to which they are exposed, elevation of systemic arterial pressures will increase the level of hemodynamic stress. Thus any factors that contribute to **hypertension** will increase endothelial damage and the thrombosis associated with it. The second major source of endothelial damage is the vascular disease called arteriosclerosis, which is described in chapter 9.

In the venous system, endothelia are less commonly damaged, but they are unable to avoid the effects of certain conditions. Some inflammations affect the venous endothelium. For example, the mesenteric veins demonstrate increased thrombosis in appendicitis, perhaps because of irritants carried by the veins from the site of tissue damage. Some tumors also seem to affect venous endothelium. Two examples are the increased thrombosis that occurs in the renal vein in cases of renal carcinoma and in the leg veins in pancreatic tumors. In the case of the kidney, venous drainage of irritating tumor products could be involved. However, the situation in the pancreatic tumor is not understood, because the region of the tumor is not drained by the leg veins.

Therapeutic intervention can cause endothelial damage in veins and thus promote **iatrogenic thrombosis.** (Recall that iatrogenic diseases are the result of medical or surgical interventions.) For example, thrombosis may follow from the effects on venous endothelium of long-term irritation from prolonged intravenous fluid administration.

Both venous and arterial endothelia are adversely affected by massive trauma. Such injury leads to increased thrombosis following auto accidents, major fractures, falls, or even surgical interventions. In particular, endothelia show an increased predisposition to platelet adherence for periods of up to two weeks after major surgery.

Flow Abnormalities

Change from the normal pattern of blood flow is the second factor that will increase platelet endothelial contact and predispose to thrombosis. The two most common hemodynamic changes are reduction in the rate of blood flow (or its complete stoppage—stasis) and turbulence in the blood.

Flow rate reduction in the arterial system causes a decrease in the axial flow of blood (see chapter 2, fig. 2.8). As a result, platelets in the central column of formed elements assume positions nearer the vessel wall. This change will increase the likelihood of contact, adherence, and thrombosis. There are two principal causes of reduced flow rates in the arterial system: cardiac damage, which reduces the heart's pumping capability, and increased blood viscosity. When blood viscosity is increased, there is more resistance to flow and hence the blood will move more slowly. (By analogy, a mechanical pump moves water more easily than pancake syrup.) Blood viscosity changes can result from increased numbers of formed elements, as in the case of increased white blood cells in leukemia. Alternatively, a dehydrated patient's blood will be more viscous because there is less plasma in which to suspend the normal number of formed elements.

In the venous system, increased blood viscosity reduces flow rates, but two other factors more often affect venous blood flow. One of these is physical inactivity.

Figure 8.4   Venous blood returning to the heart is assisted by the contraction of adjacent skeletal muscle. In conjunction with venous valves, these contractions produce forward flow and reduce retrograde flow. Inactivity, such as bed rest, compromises this action, causing slower venous flow and favoring thrombosis.

Reduction or lack of normal physical activity slows the rate of circulation because of decreased demand by the muscles and, more importantly, because of the loss of skeletal muscle pumping. Peripheral veins, and especially the leg veins, rely on the skeletal muscles to aid blood flow. As muscles contract, they shorten and thicken, compressing the veins that pass over and between the muscles. In conjunction with the veins' internal system of leaflet valves, **3** this massage of the veins makes a major contribution to venous return from the legs (fig. 8.4).

A second cause of reduced venous blood flow involves a common form of venous pathology. In **varicose veins,** blood flow rates are reduced because of deficiencies in the functioning of the leaflet valves. Venous varicosities are regions of the vein wall that become so weakened that they are unable to maintain normal muscular tone. The weakened vein walls sag away from the blood within their lumina to form irregular bulges. As a result, venous pressure drops and the rate of blood flow is reduced. Furthermore, the endothelial linings of varicose veins are less regular than those of normal veins. Both reduced rates of blood flow and the irregular endothelium will predispose to thrombosis. It is therefore not surprising that over 90% of venous thrombi are localized in the superficial veins of the legs. Venous flow rates can be reduced to the point of stasis of the blood, which further predisposes to thrombus formation by greatly favoring intravascular coagulation.

Figure 8.5   Deformation of a vessel wall by external compression (*a*) or by changes in the wall itself, such as an aneurysm (*b*), can create turbulent flow and lead to thrombosis.

Turbulent, irregular blood flow increases platelet contact with cardiac and vascular linings. Blood normally flows smoothly through open, regular channels. Turbulence results from alterations in the vascular channels that reduce the smoothness of the vessel walls or restrict the blood's passage. A common cause of such vascular changes is pressure applied externally to the vessel, by a tumor for example (fig. 8.5*a*). Weakness in vascular walls can cause bulging, which produces turbulent flow. This effect is seen not only in varicose veins **4** but in arteries, where the bulging region is called an **aneurysm** **5** (fig. 8.5*b*). Chapter 9 deals with both these conditions in more detail.

Blood Hypercoagulation

An increased tendency to blood coagulation accompanies various diseases and other conditions, such as extensive burns, some kidney diseases, heart failure, widespread metastatic tumor growth, and especially the chronic ingestion of estrogens in oral contraceptives (birth control pills). A single mechanism in these conditions has not been iden-

tified, but excessive production of procoagulants or deficiencies of endogenous anticoagulant factors are thought to be involved.

Of the many factors that predispose to thrombosis, several are often operating simultaneously in the hospitalized patient. Surgery to remove a tumor is often followed by forced inactivity. Alternatively, an elderly person might have a vascular disease, an undiagnosed tumor, and be inactive as well. In such situations the likelihood of thrombosis is greatly increased.

SEQUELAE OF THROMBOSIS

The pathological consequence of some event is the **sequela** of that event. There are several possible sequelae to thrombosis. These are resolution, organization, propagation, infarction, or embolism. The least threat is presented when a thrombus undergoes **resolution.** In resolution of a thrombus, the anticoagulation system overcomes those factors that favor thrombus formation. This means that thrombi that start to form do not all continue to develop. The anticoagulation system can cause thrombus formation to be significantly reduced. Of thrombi that do form, many are dissolved or substantially reduced in size so as to lack any significant effects. There are indications that moderate exercise increases thrombus resolution. Cardiopulmonary fitness has been shown to be associated with an increase in the activity of the fibrinolytic system.

Another sequela of thrombosis is **organization.** The process consists of phagocytic digestion of the thrombus two to three days after it forms. Platelets and fibrin are then replaced by fibrous connective tissue. Endothelium forms over the organizing tissue, with the result that the thrombus becomes incorporated into the wall. Small channels often form in a thrombus undergoing organization. The process, termed **recanalization,** allows blood to flow through the obstructing thrombus, **6** reducing ischemia downstream from the thrombus (fig. 8.6).

Propagation of the thrombus is another possible sequela (fig. 8.7). In this situation a thrombus, once formed, enlarges to extend further along the vessel, usually a vein. Propagation occurs because the surface of the initially formed thrombus serves as a site for further platelet adherence and further thrombosis. **7** It may also occur where blood flow is turbulent, such as the region around cardiac or venous valves **8** or at blood vessel branches.

Infarction

A major sequela of thrombosis is **infarction.** This is the process in which an **infarct,** a region of necrosis caused by oxygen deficiency, is formed. **9** Hypoxia typically follows

4 24526

5 38578

6 6307

7 24781

8 6286

9 6344

Figure 8.6   Recanalization of a thrombus. This diagram shows a longitudinal section through an organizing thrombus that has occluded the vessel. The newly formed channels lined by endothelium can be seen to partially restore flow.

Figure 8.7   Propagation of a venous thrombus. From an initial site of formation at A, the new deposition of platelets and fibrin from the joining vein at B has extended the process. As thrombosis proceeds, blood from the converging vessel at C continues the extension of the thrombus along the lumen.

the ischemia, which is often caused by the presence of a thrombus narrowing or completely occluding the lumen of a vessel. **10** Infarction is most common and most serious in arteries, because they directly supply oxygen and nutrients. When arterial stenosis (narrowing) occurs, it also reduces waste removal, with toxic effects adding to the tissue damage as levels of waste products rise.

Anoxia in most tissues results in the formation of a firm, relatively dry region of coagulation necrosis. After an acute inflammatory response, the necrotic tissue is broken down and replaced by scar tissue (fig. 8.8). In the brain,

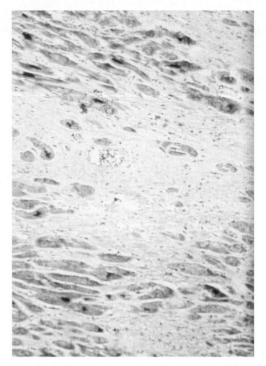

Figure 8.8   An infarct in the myocardium. The dark nuclei are present in still-living cells at the periphery of the infarct. Other nonnucleated cells are dead but still intact. The central region is scar tissue that has replaced the necrotic muscle tissue.

infarct resolution is quite different. Liquefaction necrosis causes fluid debris to accumulate at the site of infarction. When the debris is reabsorbed, a fluid-filled cavity remains. **11** Fibrosis is limited in the brain, so the cavities are not lined with scar tissue. The cavity's size is reduced somewhat by **gliosis, 12** a proliferation of the neuroglia at the margin of the cavity.

Infarction most commonly occurs as a result of arterial thrombosis. The two most seriously damaging types of infarction are cerebral infarction and myocardial infarction (MI). **13** Most infarction involving the arterial system is caused by thrombosis, but other factors can have the same result. For example, external pressure can narrow or even completely compress an artery. A tumor might affect an adjacent artery in this way. Another common cause of infarction is vascular disease, where thickening of the vessel wall reduces the size of the lumen. **14**

Venous obstruction as a cause of infarction is much less common, because of the vascular pattern of venous drainage. Several drainage vessels, called **collaterals,** usually serve the same area. If one should become occluded, blood can flow through the unobstructed collateral vessels, limiting any interference with blood drainage.

10 40417

11 17399

12 35912

13 53278

14 53262

Venous obstruction can, however, occur when a loop of intestine is twisted within the abdomen or forced out of the abdominal cavity by unusually high pressure or a weakness in the abdominal wall. The latter case is called **herniation.** In either case, the pressure at the point of twisting or herniation is great enough to compress the low-pressure veins draining that region of the intestine, but not the higher-pressure arteries. Thus blood can enter the loop of the intestine but cannot leave it. As a result, the blood hydrostatic pressure (BHP) in the vessels rises, and the pressure is backed up into the arterial system. Soon there may be so much resistance to blood flow that arterial BHP cannot overcome it, and ischemia, anoxia, and infarction follow. 15

Factors Affecting Infarction

We have seen that infarction can lead to serious and potentially fatal consequences, especially when it occurs in the brain or myocardium. However, in other tissues infarction may have little or no effect. The outcome depends, for the most part, on four factors. These are the tissue's innate vulnerability to hypoxia, the pattern of its vascular supply, the oxygen delivery capacity of the blood, and the rate of development of the occlusion.

As described in chapter 1, tissues vary in their ability to tolerate hypoxia. Nervous tissue, in particular, is very sensitive to oxygen deprivation. Even brief periods of brain hypoxia can cause a fatal infarction. In the myocardium, muscle tissue is less sensitive than nervous tissue, but it will succumb to chronic hypoxia. The fibroblasts of the myocardial stroma are much more resistant to low oxygen levels and are thus adapted for work in the repair process that may follow infarction.

The pattern of a tissue's vascular supply is another important influence on the effect of infarction. The essential element is an alternative route by which arterial blood can reach a tissue. The most important factor here is the degree of **anastomosis** the vessels demonstrate. When arteries anastomose, they branch and then rejoin. This means, in effect, that the blood can reach a given region by more than one route (fig. 8.9). A tissue with a high degree of anastomosis is more likely to resist the effects of stenosis or occlusion.

An infarct will develop more rapidly in an individual whose oxygen delivery capability is already reduced. In such cases, tissues are already partially hypoxic, and less stenosis is required to increase hypoxia sufficiently to cause infarction. Such situations exist, for example, in the anemic and in those whose weakened hearts are only marginally able to meet pumping demands.

The rate at which an artery or vein becomes occluded is another factor that affects infarction. The essential mechanism here is the time needed for new collateral vessels to form. These grow out from the existing vessels of an

(a)

(b)

Figure 8.9 Arterial anastomosis and its consequences. (*a*) Lack of anastomosis in a tissue makes it more susceptible to ischemia if a vessel is occluded. (*b*) A high degree of anastomosis greatly reduces the risk of ischemia and infarction.

ischemic tissue in a response that can reverse the tissue's oxygen deprivation. Unfortunately, the new vessels can form only slowly, so that only when stenosis and ischemia develop slowly can new collaterals be effective in limiting, or preventing, infarction.

Embolism

Another important sequela of thrombosis is **embolism.** Embolism is the sudden occlusion of a blood vessel by an **embolus,** an abnormal mass moving with the bloodstream.

Figure 8.10 Formation of thromboemboli. The gelatinous and easily fragmented red cap of a venous thrombus is a common source of emboli.

Figure 8.11 Arterial thromboembolism. The thromboembolus will lodge at some point in the artery's downstream branches to occlude the vessel.

Anything in a vessel other than the normally fluid blood constitutes an embolus. Interruption of blood flow by embolism is a common cause of infarction.

Thromboembolism

The most common type of embolus is a **thromboembolus,** formed when a thrombus or part of a thrombus breaks away from the vascular wall and is carried away in the blood. Emboli originating at arterial or cardiac surfaces consist mainly of fused platelets and fibrin, and will be smaller and more dense than those formed in the venous system. **16** As a thrombus forms in a vein, its red cap can increase greatly in size as blood coagulation continues. **17** When such a mass becomes detached, a very large embolus results. Alternatively, a large gelatinous thrombus, tailing downstream in the venous flow, might break up to release several small emboli into the bloodstream (fig. 8.10).

A thromboembolus can become detached from a vascular surface because of normal variations in blood flow. Temporary pressure changes that result from postural changes or exercise could contribute to loosening a thrombus. The resumption of normal activity, after a period of inactivity that favored formation of the thrombus, might also be a factor. Thus a patient who begins walking after prolonged bed rest runs a higher risk of thromboembolism. Surgery, physiotherapy, or other therapeutic manipulations might also contribute. Another significant factor is the fibrinolytic system, which by fibrin degradation can directly loosen the wall attachments of thrombi. Whatever the cause of thromboembolism, its effects are potentially very serious.

The principal consequence of thromboembolus formation arises when an embolus lodges in a vessel at some distance from its point of formation. Generally this results in occlusion of the vessel and possible downstream infarction. The site of occlusion and rate of infarction will vary depending on the point in the vascular system at which the thromboembolus first arises, as described in the following sections.

Arterial Thromboembolism In the arterial system, large vessels branch to form smaller vessels, which in turn branch repeatedly until capillaries with very small diameters are formed. Thus an arterial thromboembolus will be carried by the blood through successively smaller vessels until, inevitably, it becomes trapped and occlusion occurs (fig. 8.11). Such abrupt occlusion may result in an infarct, whose size depends on the size of the blocked vessel and the degree of arterial anastomosis in the tissue involved. **18** Arterial thromboemboli are most typically formed from cardiac mural thrombi, cardiac valve thrombi, or at sites of aneurysm or other points of marked endothelial irregularity. Arising from such sites, the emboli are most likely to lodge in the arteries of the kidney, spleen, brain, or lower limbs. These organs are affected more than others because of the large fraction of the cardiac output that is normally apportioned to them.

Venous Thromboembolism Throughout the venous system, vessels converge rather than branch. This means that blood flows through increasingly large vessels until it reaches the heart. Thromboemboli that are carried in the systemic venous return, therefore, have little likelihood of occluding a vessel on their way to the heart. However, from the right heart they are pumped into the pulmonary arterial system. As these vessels branch, the emboli ultimately come to an artery through which they cannot pass. Although infarction can result, the effects of the resulting occlusion will tend to be minimized by four factors. One of these is clot retraction. If retraction of thrombus fibrin occurs after it lodges in the pulmonary arterial system, it may reduce the size of the embolus. Such reduction might allow adequate blood to pass through to the dependent tissues beyond. A second factor is the double blood supply of the lung. Its tissue can extract oxygen and nutrients from the blood that comes directly from the heart as well as from the bronchial arteries, which supply the lung independently. Thus if one source of supply is cut off, the tissues are still supplied by the other. A third and quite important factor is the fibrinolytic system. In the lungs, the fibrinolytic system functions at a higher level of activation. This helps to loosen and dissolve thromboemboli that lodge in the pulmonary vessels. Fourth, the fact that many thromboemboli are small will allow occlusion of only minor pulmonary vessels, with correspondingly small effects.

Because of its position in the circulatory system, the lung will receive and trap most thromboemboli in its arteries. The factors described above, especially the dual blood supply and increased fibrinolytic activity, make the lung well suited to handle the thromboemboli that are delivered to it. The lung, in effect, acts as a filter that removes thromboemboli before they reach the systemic arteries, which might deliver them to the brain or other vital organs. [19]

However effective it is in coping with thromboemboli, when emboli are large in size or great in number, even the lung will suffer ill effects. These effects can cause partial loss of pulmonary function or even somatic death through infarction and hemorrhage. The great majority of pulmonary thromboemboli arise in the veins of the leg and contribute to a substantial number of all hospital deaths. When larger emboli occlude pulmonary vessels, upstream blood pressure is increased. This often leads to vessel damage, which causes hemorrhage into the pulmonary tissues. If sufficiently large or numerous arteries are occluded, the resulting back pressure can cause weakening and ultimate failure of the right heart. The danger posed by the massive thromboemboli that can originate in the leg veins is very great. These long, cordlike masses may lodge within the right cardiac valve orifices [20] or within the pulmonary arteries, shutting off virtually all flow to the lungs. [21] As a result, blood flow to the left heart is abruptly cut off

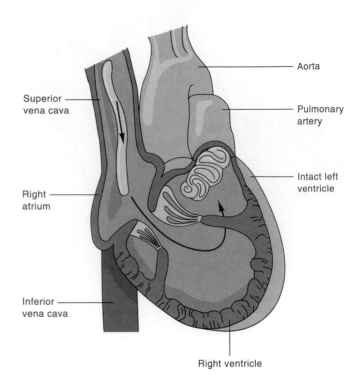

Figure 8.12   A large gelatinous thromboembolus, the red cap of a leg vein thrombus, has been carried to the right ventricle by the returning blood. It has blocked all pulmonary flow to prevent any oxygenation of the blood.

(fig. 8.12). This causes the cardiac output to fall to levels that cannot meet demand, and death follows.

Not all thromboemboli arising in veins end up in the lung. Those forming in the veins that drain the intestine, stomach, spleen, and other abdominal viscera will be carried to the liver (fig. 8.13). They travel in the hepatic portal vessels, which normally carry newly absorbed nutrients to the liver for processing. Because liver, like the lung, has a dual blood supply, infarction is not often the result of portal system embolism.

Therapy in Intravascular Thrombosis and Thromboembolism   Three categories of therapeutic agents are employed in dealing with thrombosis and thromboembolism (fig. 8.14). One consists of anticoagulants, which block or otherwise interfere with blood coagulation. The most widely used agent of this type is heparin, which is a potent blocker of thrombin and fibrin formation. Beyond its use in therapy for acute cases of pulmonary embolism and myocardial infarction, it is also commonly employed in preventing the coagulation of diagnostic blood samples, and for treating blood that must pass from its normal vascular channels through the plastic tubes or membranes of various pumps or machines used in open-heart surgery and renal dialysis.

Figure 8.13   Principal pathways of thromboemboli. Those that arise in the general systemic veins are trapped in the lungs. Those arising in vessels drained by the hepatic portal system will lodge in the liver.

Antiplatelet therapy is a second approach to limiting thrombosis. It employs agents that interfere with the platelets' role in coagulation and thrombosis by limiting their aggregation and subsequent activation. The low-cost and effective aspirin is the most widely used such agent. It has proved effective in preventive therapy for those with a predisposition to myocardial infarction.

The third therapeutic approach, rather than limiting coagulation, promotes action of the fibrinolytic system. The agents employed are enzymes that activate plasminogen to form plasmin. Increasing use is being made of preparations of tissue plasminogen activator (chapter 7), artificially produced through the application of "genetic engineering" techniques. Particular agents commonly used in these therapeutic approaches are listed in table 8.1.

Leg Vein Thrombosis

Deep vein thrombosis (DVT) of the leg is an important and often serious clinical condition. Although it can present symptoms such as tenderness, edema, and areas of focal discoloration, it often cannot be detected on clinical examination. It is thought that over 90% of pulmonary emboli arise from venous thrombi in the lower extremity. This means a high level of clinical suspicion should be maintained when the predisposing factors for thrombosis are present.

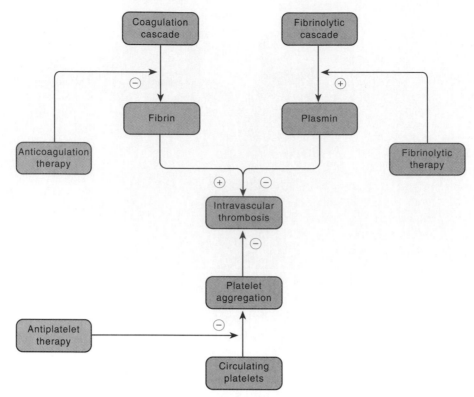

Figure 8.14   The principal therapeutic approaches to intravascular thrombosis and embolism. Anticoagulation and antiplatelet therapies limit coagulation and thrombosis. Fibrinolytic therapy promotes the formation of plasmin and its suppressing effects.

Table 8.1	Principal Pharmaceutical Agents Used in Therapy for Thrombosis and Embolism

Drug	Action	Comments
Dicumarol Phenprocoumon Warfarin	These three agents suppress the liver's synthesis of several clotting factors.	These chemically related agents are used in the prevention and therapy of chronic venous thrombosis, pulmonary embolism, coronary artery disease, and in cases of blood hypercoagulability.
Heparin	Blocking agent that interferes with the last two steps of the coagulation cascade.	Widely used to prevent coagulation of blood samples and in surgery and dialysis. Also used in acute venous thrombosis, pulmonary embolism, thrombosis in cerebral vessels, coronary artery disease, and myocardial infarction.
Aspirin (ASA)	Inhibition of platelet aggregation.	Used in cerebral embolism and acute myocardial infection. Also in the prevention of MI in high-risk individuals.
Streptokinase	Promotes fibrinolytic cascade and plasmin formation.	Extracted from bacteria. Used in acute coronary or other arterial occlusion and massive pulmonary embolism.
Urokinase	Same as for streptokinase.	Extracted from nephron tubules. Used similarly to streptokinase.
Alteplase (rt-PA, recombinant tissue plasminogen activator)	Same as for streptokinase.	Localized effects as opposed to the more systemic effects of streptokinase and urokinase.

Fat Emboli

Fat emboli are formed when fat-rich, yellow marrow gains access to the blood. They are usually small and form in large numbers. They arise most commonly as a result of long bone fractures, especially the femur and tibia, usually within 12 to 48 hours of the fracture. Because of their size, they tend to lodge only in smaller arterioles and capillaries. **22** In the lung, this can produce symptoms ranging from mild difficulty with breathing through complete respiratory failure. Because the globules that form fat emboli are compressible, and because the lung vasculature has channels that can by-pass the small capillary beds, smaller fat emboli can pass through the pulmonary microcirculation and reach the systemic arterial vessels. In this way they can reach the skin, where they often cause a diffuse rash of petechial hemorrhages. The principal threat of fat emboli is that they can't pass through small cerebral vessels. They lodge in these vessels and occlude them. The resulting pressure causes vessel damage and numerous small petechial hemorrhages as the blood is lost to the surrounding brain tissue upstream. Downstream, many small infarcts form, threatening coma and death.

Air Emboli

Gases can also enter the blood and travel as emboli. The most common such embolus is air. It can enter the blood when veins are open to the air. This is especially so when surgery, a fractured rib, or knife wounds damage the veins of the thorax, allowing air to be drawn into the blood by respiratory movements. Neck surgery, suicidal lacerations of the jugular veins, or improper administration of intravenous fluids can have the same result.

An air embolus will have significant consequences only if large. A few small bubbles introduced into the blood with an injected drug preparation are soon dispersed in the flowing blood and dissolve to pose little threat. Most diagnosed air emboli are over 100 ml in volume. Effects that are potentially fatal require an air embolus volume of about 300 ml. The principal effect of such an air embolus is on the heart. The cardiac pump is designed to handle fluids that are noncompressible. The myocardium pumps by exerting a pressure that moves the blood since it cannot be compressed. When an air embolus reaches the heart, it is drawn into a ventricle. When the ventricle contracts, pressure increases and the air yields to it, allowing itself to be compressed, but not moved out of the heart. When the pumping chamber relaxes, the air reexpands. During the next cardiac cycle, compression and expansion are repeated. Because air fills the pumping chamber, much less

blood is being pumped. Cardiac output can fall to critical levels while a strong, healthy right ventricle is filled with a bloody froth generated by the compression and expansion of the air. This churning of the blood also damages platelets and predisposes to thrombosis in the blood that does reach the pulmonary arterial system.

The situation in which a pump intended for liquids fills with air is called **air lock.** In the case of an air lock caused by an air embolus in the heart, the effect can be countered by achieving a body position in which the right heart is elevated. The air in the heart will rise, allowing blood to pass under it to reach the ventricle. As the blood continues to flow under the air embolus, small quantities will gradually be carried with the blood to be harmlessly dispersed.

In circumstances where abrupt reduction of atmospheric pressure occurs, nitrogen gas normally present in the tissues will boil out of the tissues into the blood. The presence of nitrogen gas emboli is associated with joint pain and carries the potential for brain damage. This situation is commonly called the **bends.** It occurs in accidental pressure reductions in underwater divers and in other circumstances where air pressure is artificially increased, for example, in air travelers and in tunnel workers breathing compressed air.

Amniotic Fluid Embolism

This is a rare complication of childbirth that can occur during either a spontaneous delivery or cesarean section. The term **amniotic fluid embolism** is somewhat misleading, because a fluid itself can't occlude vessels. The occluding agent is actually the infant's cells, which are shed into the amniotic fluid in which it is suspended. During the delivery, clumps of these cells enter the circulation via tears in the placental membranes or in the uterine or cervical veins. In the blood they are carried to the lungs, where they are trapped in its small vessels. Respiratory difficulty may follow, but since the amniotic fluid also contains thromboplastinlike blood coagulants, the potential for disseminated intravascular coagulation and progressive circulatory shock, with fatal consequences, is always present.

Foreign Body Embolism

Less commonly, foreign bodies may gain access to the blood and be carried by it to become emboli. An example is a bullet fragment that might enter the blood after tearing through a vessel wall. **23** As with thromboemboli, the site at which it is finally trapped depends on the point where it enters the circulation.

Case Study

While convalescing at home following a work-related foot fracture, a 57-year-old brick layer felt weak and faint, and then suffered a severe episode of labored breathing and crushing pain over his left chest. He was rushed to the hospital, where he complained of dizziness and persistence of his chest pain. On examination, he was found to be pale, with a rapid heart rate, reduced blood pressure, and distended neck veins. His electrocardiogram produced no evidence of myocardial infarction, but signs of some right ventricular strain were present. Auscultation of the left lung revealed a "friction rub" over the left lung. He was also febrile, with a temperature of 38.8° C.

He reported a history of varicose veins and a recent worsening of calf pain while recuperating from his fracture. His left calf was swollen, tender, warm, and edematous. He also stated he had no history of heart trouble and had recently had a general physical examination by his family physician, who declared him to be "in the pink," apart from minor problems like his varicose veins. His chest pain and breathing difficulties continued and intravenous heparin therapy was instituted on the basis of a presumed pulmonary embolism. Quickly obtained radiographic and radioisotope scan results confirmed a massive occlusive embolism in the left pulmonary artery, blocking all blood flow to the left lung.

In view of this confirmation of the initial tentative diagnosis, vasoconstriction therapy to support his blood pressure was started and a more aggressive anticoagulation regimen was quickly instituted. Because of the threat of further emboli forming in the leg veins, it was decided to insert a filter in the inferior vena cava, but as the patient was being prepared for the procedure he abruptly developed a sharp pain in his right chest, gasped repeatedly for breath, and died before any intervention could reverse the situation.

Autopsy findings confirmed the complete occlusion of the left pulmonary artery that presumably produced the patient's initial attack. The occluding mass was formed of a coil of gelatinous thrombus. A similar coil was found blocking the right pulmonary artery. It appeared that a long thrombus initially detached from its site of formation in the popliteal vein, reaching the right ventricle. It was then driven into the left pulmonary artery, producing the initial attack. A second, large mass of embolus, presumably from the same leg vein, was found coiled in the right pulmonary artery, where it completely blocked all lung access to the pulmonary vasculature. A small fragment of embolus, wedged within the right ventricle's floor, testified to the passage of the larger masses through the chamber en route to the lungs.

An infarcted area of the left lung was also found, verifying the lung sounds and ECG indications of pulmonary infarction. The infarct was also the likely explanation for the patient's elevated temperature. Examination of the left leg revealed pronounced varicosities in the deep calf veins and in the popliteal and great saphenous veins, with residual thrombi at several points in the vessels. In this extreme case the initial massive occlusion induced the ischemic damage, but because the lung is also supplied by the bronchial arteries, infarction in pulmonary embolism is unusual.

Commentary

The patient's rapid heart rate was compensation for the fall in cardiac output produced by the pulmonary occlusion. His chest pain was the result of right ventricular overload from the abrupt increase in resistance that the blocked pulmonary artery presented to it. Distention of the right pulmonary artery, which arose quickly as both lungs' blood supply was being forced into it, also probably contributed to the pain. Inability to cope with such high demand caused backup of blood into the large veins of the systemic circulation, producing the observed neck vein distention. The "friction rub" heard over the lung was the result of infarction damage at the lung's surface, which produced a rubbing sound as it moved against the adjacent parietal pleura.

The procedure to insert a caval filter was to have been done via the jugular vein. Such filters are able to block access of thromboemboli to the lung, at the same time offering no restriction to blood flow. They can be inserted with relative ease, avoiding full-blown surgery, and have been widely and successfully used. Had time permitted, such a filter would probably have spared this patient's life.

Subsequent discussions with the family physician of the deceased revealed that in view of the man's history of varicose veins, he had provided his patient with a series of lower leg maneuvers intended to promote venous flow and counter the tendency to sluggish venous flow in the fractured and immobilized leg. The victim's wife reported that her husband had not bothered with the exercises, nor had he reported or sought medical help for recent episodes of increased pain and swelling in the calf of his fractured limb.

Key Concepts

1. Hemodynamic factors underlie the differences between arterial versus venous thrombosis (p. 187).

2. Thrombosis is the result of blood hypercoagulation states and conditions that favor platelet adherence to endothelia: endothelial damage and irregular, turbulent blood flow (pp. 187–188).

3. Once formed, a thrombus may resolve, or it may enlarge to narrow or completely occlude a blood vessel, raising the threat of infarction (p. 190).

4. An infarct may result from thrombosis, vascular compression, or various vascular diseases that increase wall thickness at the expense of the lumen (pp. 190–191).

5. Infarction depends on a tissue's vulnerability to hypoxia, its pattern of vascular supply, the blood's oxygen delivery capacity, and the rate at which tissue deprivation develops (pp. 191–192).

6. A thromboembolus may be formed from a thrombus, producing an infarct by the mechanism of embolism (p. 193).

7. Once formed, a thromboembolus lodges in the next branching vascular bed to which the blood delivers it (p. 193).

8. In cases of thrombosis, therapeutic intervention is based on anticoagulants that inhibit thrombosis, agents that inhibit platelet aggregation, and those that promote fibrinolysis (pp. 194–195).

9. Emboli of marrow-derived adipose tissue, air, cells accumulated from amniotic fluid, or foreign bodies may be carried in the blood to disrupt blood flow at various points in the cardiovascular system (p. 197).

REVIEW ACTIVITIES

1. Use the information on pages 187–188 to make up a comparison table highlighting the difference between a clot and a thrombus.

2. A handy study aid would be a master list of all the factors that predispose to thrombosis. All the information you'd need is on pages 188–190.

3. Check all the photos and diagrams in this chapter. How many show lines of Zahn? (The authors count 6.)

4. Complete the following table.

Embolus	Origin	Likely Embolism Site
Fat	Leg fracture	
Thrombus	Renal artery	
Thrombus	Leg vein	
Air	Rib fracture	
Thrombus	Arm vein	
Amniotic cells	Placenta	
Thrombus	Mesenteric vein	
Bullet fragment	Femoral vein	

Chapter Nine

Vascular Disorders

A man is as old as his arteries.

Thomas Sydenham
Observationes Medicae

TI

IEL

TM

EEL

TA
VV

Figure 9.1 Normal arterial structure. Tunica intima (TI) consists of an endothelium, its basement membrane, and a layer of connective tissues. Tunica media (TM), consisting of muscle and elastic tissue, is bounded by the internal and external elastic laminae (IEL, EEL). The vasa vasorum (VV) supply tunica adventitia (TA) and the outer TM.

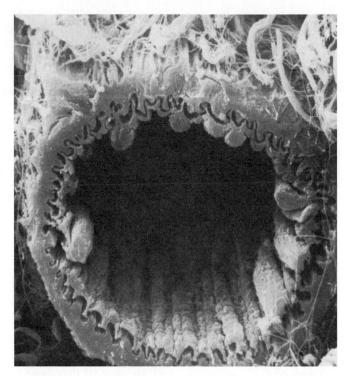

Figure 9.2 In this scanning electron micrograph the collagen fibers of tunica adventitia can be seen. Note tunica intima drawn away from the inner elastic lamina, a result of the processing needed to produce the micrograph.

D isorders of the arteries represent a major source of disease and death in North America. Vein disorders present a much smaller threat to mortality, but they are still responsible for significant clinical disease. Any consideration of these conditions must make reference to various features of arterial and venous structure. The following sections provide the essentials for those who might need a review.

VASCULAR STRUCTURE

Blood flows away from the heart in the system of branching arteries. The lumen that carries the blood is enclosed within the arterial wall, which, generally, is considered to have three layers, or coats (fig. 9.1). **1**

The innermost is called **tunica intima** (the Latin term tunica means covering, or coat). It consists of a single layer of flattened endothelial cells, which line the lumen and provide the smooth surface over which the blood flows. On the surface of the endothelium, opposite the lumen, is found a layer of glycoprotein and collagen. This layer is called the basement membrane and serves to support the endothelium. Finally, a layer of loosely organized fibrous and elastic tissues and scattered smooth muscle cells completes the internal layer of the wall. The middle layer of the arterial wall, **tunica media,** is separated from tunica intima by a thin, strong mesh of elastic connective tissue, the **internal elastic lamina.** Tunica media is the thickest part of the arterial wall. It consists of elastic connective tissue and circularly oriented smooth muscle tissue combined to form a strong yet flexible and elastic midwall region. In larger arteries, elastic tissue is the dominant component of the tunica

media, whereas smaller vessels have much more smooth muscle. **Tunica adventitia** (*adventitia* means "from afar") is the outermost of the three wall coats. It is separated from tunica media by another elastic mesh called the **external elastic lamina.** This means the media has an elastic lamina on both intimal and adventitial surfaces. Tunica adventitia is a protective layer of loosely organized fibrous connective tissue (fig. 9.2). Its outer surface is often indistinct, because it merges with surrounding connective tissues to fix the vessel securely in position.

In small arteries, cells of the wall are directly supplied with nutrients by diffusion from luminal blood into the wall. The larger arteries present something of a problem in this regard, in that their walls are too thick to be supplied by diffusion alone. In such vessels diffusion can supply only the intima and inner part of the media. The remaining part of the wall is supplied by its own system of small blood vessels, the **vasa vasorum.** These are the vessels' vessels, which deliver blood to capillary networks within the large arterial wall, supplying its external layers.

With aging, arteries undergo a characteristic and generalized pattern of change. In the intima, connective tissue and lipid content increase, as does the number of smooth muscle cells. This process can cause the intima to become as thick as the media by the sixth decade of life. These changes accompany an overall dilation and lengthening of

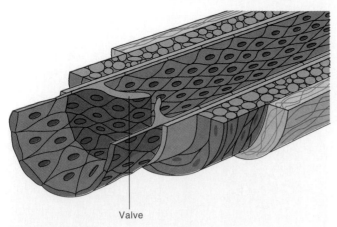

Valve

Figure 9.3 In this view into the interior of a vein, valves, formed of endothelium-lined leaflets, can be seen projecting into the lumen. This arrangement allows blood to flow toward the heart and prevents backflow.

Figure 9.4 The arteriole in this micrograph demonstrates the pronounced wall thickening characteristics of arteriolosclerosis. *This is a microscopic view of the renal cortex in malignant hypertension. The afferent arteriole in the center of the field is greatly thickened and almost completely closes the lumen. The resulting reduction of blood flow is responsible for the damage to glomeruli and tubules that is also apparent. The section is from the kidney of a 40-year-old male. From mild headaches and a somewhat elevated blood pressure of 150/100 at age 38, he progressed to severe headaches, a blood pressure of 225/150, and various CNS effects that combined with his failing kidneys to bring about his death.*

some larger arteries, which causes them to assume a more irregular, winding configuration. As time passes, the arterial wall becomes more rigid, causing more resistance to arterial pressure pulses. As well, the size of the lumen is reduced, increasing the predisposition to downstream ischemia. As collagen increases and elastic tissue and muscle are lost, the arteries' walls become more rigid. Because of the wall's rigidity, some consider these changes to be a form of arteriosclerotic disease. However, since the process is virtually universal, it seems more reasonable to consider these changes to be the result of normal aging rather than arising from some pathological process.

In contrast to the typical artery described earlier, most veins have a thinner wall and a larger lumen. Except for the largest veins, in most the elastic laminae are not present and tunica intima has a thinner connective tissue layer deep to the endothelium. Tunica media is also thinner, with its muscle and elastic tissues less uniformly distributed. Veins in the limbs are modified by the presence of leaflet valves. These are formed by foldings of the intima that project into the lumen (fig. 9.3) to prevent backflow and promote the return of blood to the heart. **2**

ARTERIOSCLEROSIS

Arteriosclerosis is a condition in which arterial walls undergo changes that reduce their normal flexibility and elasticity. This is the process of **sclerosis,** or hardening, hence the lay expression "hardening of the arteries." Given that the arterial changes noted in the previous section are a part of the normal aging process, there are three forms of arteriosclerosis. They can be distinguished on the basis of the type of artery affected and on differences in the pattern of changes in the wall that produce sclerosis. The three types of arteriosclerosis are the relatively rare **medial calcific sclerosis,** the more common **arteriolosclerosis,** and the very widespread **atherosclerosis.**

Medial Calcific Sclerosis

Medial calcific sclerosis, an uncommon and idiopathic condition, is also called **Mönckeberg's sclerosis.** It typically involves the medium-sized arteries of the limbs and genitalia in those past 50. The condition is characterized by focal calcification of tunica media at sites where its muscle tissue has degenerated. The regions of calcification may be irregular or ringlike, producing a characteristic pattern in radiographs. Calcium deposition also produces focal hardening that may be palpable in superficial vessels, but because it produces no narrowing of the lumen, it is unusual for it to produce clinical disease.

Arteriolosclerosis

In arteriolosclerosis, vessel wall changes are restricted to fine arteries and arterioles, with both intima and media usually thickened by the deposition of plasma proteins, lipids, and basement membrane. (You might check, at this point, to verify that you've noted the extra syllable in arteriolosclerosis. On hearing the term, it's easy to notice, but after having earlier read arteriosclerosis, the eye leaps ahead and can easily miss the extra "lo.") Because the microscopic appearance of the accumulating material is uniform and glasslike, **3** the descriptive term **hyaline arteriolosclerosis** is often used (fig. 9.4). As the wall thickens, downstream ischemia develops, especially since any

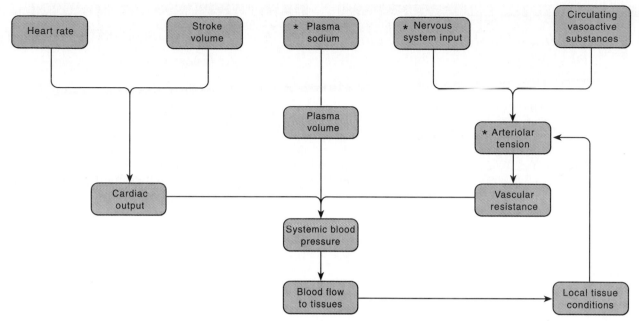

Figure 9.5 Principal determinants of systemic blood hydrostatic pressure. Asterisks indicate the points where a genetic defect might contribute to hypertension.

reflex corrective response is limited by the thickened wall's loss of dilation capacity. Although these wall changes are common in the elderly, they are also seen in diabetes mellitus, presumably as a result of that condition's fundamental metabolic derangements (chapter 17). Arteriolosclerosis is also a prominent feature of the much more common condition of **systemic hypertension,** which is described next. (If your primary interest is arterial disease, you might skip ahead to the section on atherosclerosis.)

Systemic Hypertension

This is the widespread problem of elevated blood hydrostatic pressure (BHP) in the systemic arterial system—the lay person's "high blood pressure." Use of the term systemic hypertension has value in differentiating this condition from others where abnormally high BHP is confined to the vessels of the lung (**pulmonary hypertension**) or to those of the hepatic portal system (**portal hypertension**). Once context is established, the simpler term hypertension is often used for convenience.

Currently, diagnosis of hypertension is based on a diastolic pressure in excess of 90 mmHg or a systolic pressure exceeding 140 mmHg. On this basis, 60 million people in North America are estimated to be hypertensive. Since the condition is essentially asymptomatic, as many as one-third of these are thought to be undiagnosed. Various risk factors are associated with an increased likelihood of developing systemic hypertension. Genetics, race, increased age, smoking, obesity, and stress and other ill-defined environmental factors are some of them. Although their precise roles are poorly understood, they are recognized as playing some

direct or indirect part. A genetic component is suggested, in part, by familial incidence patterns and the much higher frequency of occurrence in blacks: double the rate of whites.

Incidence Patterns and Essential Hypertension Etiology in hypertension is a problem around which much discussion and research is centered. In 90–95% of cases no specific cause can be identified. This is the condition known as **primary** or **essential hypertension.** It is widely held to be the result of some defect in the complex control mechanisms that have a bearing on systemic blood pressure maintenance. These are presented in figure 9.5, where cardiac output and peripheral resistance are indicated as the major determinants of blood pressure. Asterisks indicate those points in the system where a genetic defect may provide some degree of disruption. One of these involves a genetic defect in the kidney's sodium excretion mechanism, which in turn promotes an increase in extracellular fluid volume and cardiac output. The resulting increase in blood flow to the tissues causes local arteriolar constriction responses that increase peripheral resistance and blood pressure.

A second genetic defect may be centered in the membranes of arteriolar smooth muscle. Because the entrance of sodium ions causes the release of the calcium ions that trigger contraction, an inability to expel sodium ions at a normal rate would result in longer periods of elevated calcium levels in the cells. The consequences would be higher wall tension and an increased sensitivity to normal hormonal and neurogenic constriction inputs. These would combine to produce a generally higher level of constriction for a given level of stimulus, causing an elevation of systemic blood pressure.

Salt Intake and Cardiovascular Disease

The genetic membrane defect mentioned in the text may explain the observed link between hypertension and high salt intake. In those with the genetic inability to clear sodium from cells, hypertension would be induced by dietary salt loading. In people with normal membranes, dietary salt intake would have no effect. In fact, only about half of hypertensives respond to increased dietary salt intake with a further pressure increase. Generally, unless hypertension or heart disease is diagnosed, there is no need to restrict salt intake or to accept the layperson's idea that "salt is bad for you."

Other lines of research indicate that inadequate dietary calcium may indirectly produce hypertension, and that in salt-sensitive hypertensives chloride, as well as sodium, can contribute to the problem.

The Role of Renin in Hypertension

In approximately 35% of cases of essential hypertension, plasma renin levels are abnormal. In **high-renin hypertension** you might expect that excessive renin would promote water retention to produce hypertension. However, since drugs that block renin's effects don't reduce the blood pressure, some other underlying mechanism would seem to be operating. In **low-renin hypertension** you might think that low renin and, therefore, low angiotensin II levels would lead to water loss and a reduction of blood pressure. Since they don't, the high pressure in these cases may be produced by other, unknown adrenal cortex hormones with water retention effects, or by an excessive arteriolar sensitivity to angiotensin II. In the latter case, the sensitivity would be high enough so that even low levels of angiotensin II could produce hypertension.

The third suggested genetic defect involves an increased responsiveness on the part of the autonomic system, so that its constriction inputs to systemic arterioles are exaggerated. This mechanism may explain the link between stress and hypertension. With chronic exposure to stressful situations, sympathetic activation could result in increased vasoconstriction via direct nervous stimulation and by the effects of increased epinephrine in the blood.

Since the interactions among the various components involving blood pressure regulation are so complex, there are many possibilities for developing an imbalance that would produce systemic hypertension. Much research is attempting to sort out the precise role of each variable, but it has proved to be a difficult and often frustrating challenge.

Secondary Hypertension In 5–10% of hypertensives, hypertension is **secondary;** that is, some other specific disorder can be identified as the cause of the elevated blood pressure. In most cases the focus of the problem is the kidney or excessive levels of various hormones. In cases where disease of the renal parenchyma is established, hypertension may be the result of the kidney's failure to excrete sodium and water, to produce more of, or to activate, some unknown vasoconstrictor substance, or to secrete enough of a vasodilator. It may also be that damage to the renal tissue reduces blood flow to the nephrons and activates the **renin-angiotensin system** (RAS).

The RAS is an important mechanism in the regulation of arterial blood pressure (fig. 9.6). It involves the production of angiotensin II, a potent vasoconstrictor that also stimulates aldosterone secretion and therefore sodium and water retention. The system's activation depends on the secretion of renin by the nephron's **juxtaglomerular cells** 4 in response to blood pressure and to sodium levels in the nephron's distal

convoluted tubule. (Note: The enzyme here is renin, not rennin, a quite different gastric enzyme.) Angiotensinogen is the plasma substrate from which renin produces angiotensin I. It is activated, in turn, by a converting enzyme associated with pulmonary endothelial surfaces. If blood pressure or distal tubule sodium levels fall, increased renin secretion promotes a corrective increase in pressure.

Activation of the RAS is the principal mechanism underlying a second type of kidney-related hypertension called **renovascular hypertension.** It occurs when an intact and functional kidney is supplied by a diseased and stenotic renal artery. The reduced renal blood flow that results triggers increased renin secretion, and hypertension follows.

Excessive levels of certain hormones can also produce secondary hypertension. When the adrenal glands hypersecrete aldosterone, water retention and systemic hypertension result. In Cushing's syndrome (chapter 17), glucocorticoids are present to excess, but their precise link to hypertension is not clear. About 5% of birth control pill users experience hypertension. Probably the elevated estrogens promote the liver's synthesis of angiotensinogen, which leads to excessive plasma levels of angiotensin II. Not all users of oral contraceptives develop hypertension, however, and it may be that the presence of some additional genetic, environmental, or other factor is necessary before hypertension develops.

Whether the cause is known or unknown, most hypertension steadily progresses and is ultimately fatal unless therapy to control blood pressure intervenes. The condition characterized by a slowly progressive pressure increase is **benign hypertension.** In 1–5% of hypertensives a rapidly progressive **malignant hypertension** develops. This is a

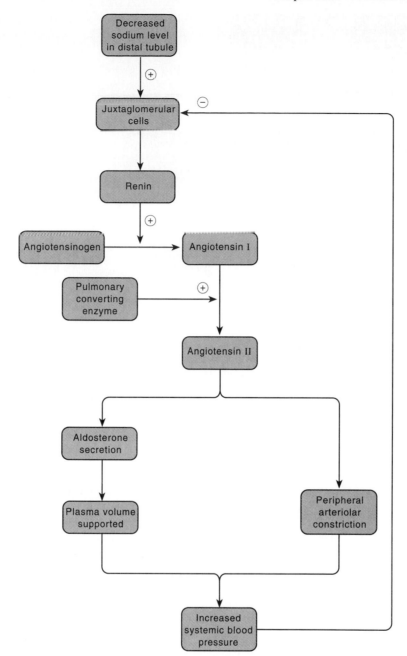

Figure 9.6   The renin-angiotensin system.

serious condition that can be triggered by renal damage from benign hypertension or other causes. The rapid pressure increases in this condition seem to promote endothelial damage in small arterioles, which in turn favors the widespread formation of microthrombi. These contribute to flow restriction and damage to red cells, causing a form of anemia called **microangiopathic hemolytic anemia** (see chapter 7). High pressure in malignant hypertension also produces a pronounced smooth muscle and endothelial proliferation response to produce **hyperplastic arteriolosclerosis** (fig. 9.4). This contrasts with the hyaline arteriolosclerosis typically present in benign hypertension.

Currently, therapy for hypertension utilizes a broad array of drugs with effects aimed at key blood pressure determinants. Their principal categories are presented in figure 9.7.

Consequences of Systemic Hypertension Broadly, there are three consequences of systemic hypertension. One is arteriolosclerosis, which, by reducing the arteriole's lumen and its ability to dilate normally, contributes to further hypertension. This mechanism can produce the positive feedback cycling that operates in some malignant hypertension. The second consequence is damage to the central nervous system, where chronic high pressure can directly and

Figure 9.7   The categories of drugs used in antihypertension therapy.

indirectly produce a variety of neurological problems. The third consequence is most significant in that systemic hypertension predisposes to earlier and more severe atherosclerosis, the last of the three types of arteriosclerosis.

Atherosclerosis (AS)

Atherosclerosis is by far the most common type of arteriosclerosis. It accounts for about half of all deaths in North America, and is the underlying disease process in most of the coronary artery disease that causes myocardial infarction and the arterial alterations that produce cerebrovascular accidents. It is the number one killer in economically developed countries worldwide.

Whereas arteriolosclerosis largely affects arterioles, it is the larger arteries that are affected by atherosclerosis. The chief vessels involved are the aorta and its principal branches, i.e., the coronary, mesenteric, renal, iliac, femoral, common, carotid, basilar and vertebral arteries (fig. 9.8). On the basis of this distribution, you can appreciate the effects the disease has on the heart, brain, kidney, intestine, and legs.

Apart from the vessels affected, AS can be differentiated from the other types of arteriosclerosis on the basis of its characteristic lesion, the **atheroma** (pl. atheromata) or **atheromatous plaque.** This is a focal thickening of the intima due to the deposition of lipid and connective tissue

and the proliferation of cells. **5** The Greek root *athero* means "gruel," and its use in describing this arterial lesion is based on the lipid-rich core of the atheroma.

Atheromata are initially distributed in a patchy, scattered pattern in the major arteries, but as the condition progresses, adjacent lesions merge to form more extensive plaques. These are initially yellow to orange in color but become increasingly pale as they develop and extend. The atheroma is formed only slowly, gradually enlarging and increasingly protruding into the lumen. Initial intimal thickening can be identified as early as ages 10–20, with subsequent progression producing symptoms as early as age 35. Beyond this age, the atheromata become further enlarged and increasingly irregular. These later changes contribute to an increasing risk of complications, which have potentially devastating effects, especially in males past the age of 40. We will consider these complications after we analyze the pathogenesis of atherosclerosis.

Pathogenesis

Early signs of intimal changes can be found in most individuals, worldwide, after the age of 1 year. These changes are seen as narrow, pale yellow streaks that run longitudinally along the intima of the aorta. Such visible lines are the result of focal proliferation of smooth muscle cells in the intima, known as **myointimal cells.** Fat is present in

Figure 9.8 Atherosclerosis distribution. Common sites of atheroma formation are indicated by heavy shading.

Figure 9.9 Fatty streaks revealed by a lipid-specific stain applied to the surface of the aorta.

these cells in the form of small cytoplasmic globules, causing minimal elevation of the endothelial surface.

The early formation of these **fatty streaks** seems to be a part of normal development. [6] They remain until about 10 years of age, by which time 10% of the aorta's surface may show streaking (fig. 9.9). At this point a critical distinction arises. In economically undeveloped areas of the world, the streaks remain static or regress, posing no further problem. Where standards of living are high, however, streaks continue to develop into potentially destructive atheromatous plaques.

Study of plaque development (**atherogenesis**) in the coronary arteries indicates that, past 10 years of age, new streaks form and are transformed into plaques by about the age of 30. The process involves the early build-up of macrophages and myointimal cells in the intima. [7] This is followed by the accumulation of fat in the cytoplasm of the cells, which gives them a bubbly appearance microscopically. For this reason they are termed **foam cells.** As the years pass, the intima becomes thicker as foam cell numbers increase. As well, proliferating smooth muscle produces fibrous connective tissue, which together with the muscle cells forms a **fibrous cap** just deep to the endothelium (fig. 9.10).

The process continues with the development of one or more of several possible complications. These **complicated lesions** (fig. 9.11) are a major factor in the wall damage

(a)

(b)

Figure 9.10 Microscopic view of a typical atheroma. (*a*) The arrow indicates the core of foam cells and lipid-rich debris. Over this central region lies the cellular fibrous cap. (*b*) A stain specific for lipid highlights its accumulation within the atheroma.
This is a section through an atheroma in the aorta of a 65-year-old male who died of pulmonary complications caused by his failing heart. The core of the atheroma contains fat and necrotic debris. The coronary arteries also exhibited extensive AS, with some lumina reduced to mere pinpoints. No large infarct was found at autopsy, but many small, diffusely scattered scars were found throughout the myocardium. These produced the myocardial weakness that caused the heart to fail.

that gives rise to the serious consequences of atherosclerosis. The complicating factors are calcification, hemorrhage, medial destruction, and ulceration. **8**

As intimal damage is prolonged over months and years, it is accompanied by the deposition of insoluble calcium salts in the intima. This process is called **dystrophic calcification.** It is not restricted to blood vessels but can

Figure 9.11 Complicated lesions of advanced atherosclerosis.

also occur elsewhere in the body, for example, in joints or cerebral infarcts. Calcification can proceed to the point where, in advanced atherosclerosis, cutting through the aorta at autopsy produces an easily audible crunching sound. As the atheroma develops, necrosis in the media elicits a normal revascularization response from the vasa vasorum. The process is typically unsuccessful, however, and hemorrhage into the atheroma often results. This causes further damage and enlargement of the lesion. The fibrous cap that forms beneath the endothelium also contributes to destruction of the media. The muscle of the media, which to this point has not been affected by the formation of the atheroma, is dependent on diffusion from the lumen for nutrient supply. When a fibrous cap is formed in the atheroma, it provides a barrier to diffusing nutrients. This reduction of oxygen and nutrient supply causes a gradual deterioration of the media. Smooth muscle atrophy and destruction of the internal elastic lamina results, and is followed by a gradual weakening of the arterial wall.

As fibrosis, calcification, hemorrhage, and enlargement of the atheroma proceed, its surface is affected (fig. 9.12). Endothelial cells lose their normally firm support as the underlying intima becomes necrotic and softened. As a

Figure 9.12 Essential features of the complicated atheroma: core of necrotic debris and free lipid, in part from rupture of foam cells. Note disruption of the internal elastic lamina and the ulcerated endothelium where a thrombus is forming. Dark masses are calcium deposits.

Figure 9.13 The arrows indicate sites of ulceration in this severely diseased aorta.

result, the endothelium becomes damaged or is stripped away, and ulceration at the surface of the atheroma follows (fig. 9.13). This exposes the interior of the atheroma to the blood, allowing either the release of necrotic debris into the blood or further disruption of the wall as blood from the lumen is forced into the lesion.

The **"response to injury" hypothesis** is the most widely accepted explanation of the process of atheroma formation. It is based on many studies carried out over many years and seeks to unify the essential components of the process as described earlier: cell proliferation, lipid deposition, and connective tissue formation. As the name implies, the "response to injury" hypothesis suggests that atheroma formation follows an initial injury to the arterial endothelium. The injury may involve only mild effects, which initially alter endothelial permeability. This change could be followed by increased lipid access to the intima. Injured endothelial cells are also known to retract their edges, drawing back from neighboring cells. The retraction exposes the subendothelial tissues, allowing platelet adherence and easier access to the intima for monocytes. These blood cells first adhere and then migrate into the intima, where they are transformed into macrophages. They then proceed to take up lipid, as do smooth muscle cells, to form the foam cells characteristic of atherosclerosis.

A key component to the continued development of the atheroma is cell proliferation. This process is driven by a variety of **growth factors** (GFs) that are released by platelets (platelet-derived growth factor, PDGF) and macrophages.

Growth factors were described in chapter 4 in the context of healing. In atherogenesis they contribute to the enlargement of the atheroma by promoting proliferation of its components. The GFs involved are chemotactic for monocytes, so more are drawn to the site. Their presence can aggravate the situation, since the adhering monocytes

can themselves secrete injurious agents (superoxides—see chapter 1) that can damage the endothelium and contribute to progression. (We will consider further implications of the effects on lipids of such oxidizing molecules later, in the section on hyperlipidemia.) GFs also promote mitosis of smooth muscle and its deposition of connective tissue within the atheroma. In particular, PDGF has these effects, but it can also promote lipid uptake by endothelium and stimulate cholesterol synthesis by smooth muscle. Figure 9.14 presents the essential elements of the pathogenesis of atherosclerosis.

Risk Factors in Atherosclerosis

Many long-term and large-scale studies of the incidence of AS have identified an association between its progression and various circumstances known as **risk factors.** Generally, the presence of a risk factor increases the likelihood of AS, and the presence of two or more significantly increases the probability of earlier and more severe complications. The AS risk factors are thought to contribute directly or indirectly to the endothelial damage or other components that play a role in the development of AS. The most important of these (table 9.1) are the following.

Hyperlipidemia The term **hyperlipidemia** is used to indicate elevated levels of fat in the blood. In the context of atherosclerosis, two particular lipids are relevant. Elevated

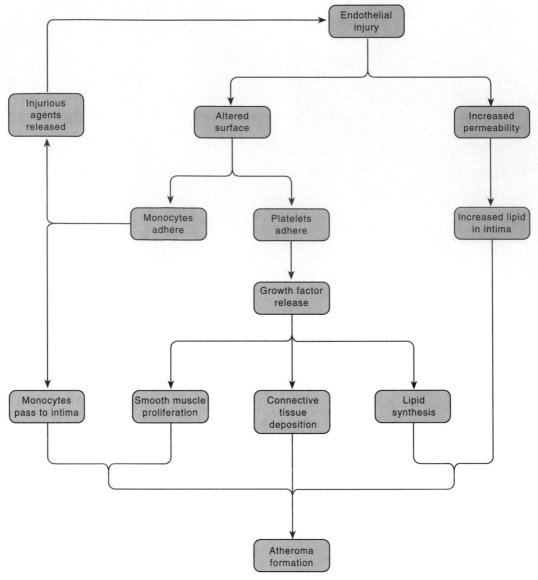

Figure 9.14   Principal factors in the "response to injury" hypothesis of atherogenesis.

Table 9.1	Risk Factors in Atherosclerosis

Major Factors	Secondary or Less Clearly Related Factors
Diabetes mellitus	Excessive (or no) alcohol use
Genetic predisposition	Obesity
Hyperlipidemia	Inadequate exercise
Male sex	Stress
Smoking	
Systemic hypertension	

plasma cholesterol **9** (**hypercholesterolemia**) and triglyceride (**hypertriglyceridemia**) are generally accepted as posing significant risk factors in atherosclerosis. Although a thorough exploration of lipid metabolism is beyond the scope of this text, an insight into the essentials is necessary to appreciate current thinking and future dietary and therapeutic implications.

Since lipids are not water-soluble, their transport in the plasma requires some specific provision for increasing their water solubility. The increase is accomplished by a specialized system of lipid and protein complexes (**lipoproteins**) that also accommodates cellular uptake of the lipids. In essence, the lipoproteins use a coating of phospholipid to

Figure 9.15   Low-density lipoprotein: an LDL and its role in cholesterol transport and cell uptake. (*a*) The cholesterol core of the LDL is enclosed by phospholipids, which shield it from plasma water. (*b*) Binding of the membrane receptor to the apoprotein of the LDL triggers endocytosis. Within the cell, cholesterol is metabolized and the receptor returns to the surface.

surround the lipid that is to be carried in the plasma. The phospholipid molecules are oriented so that their water-soluble ends interact with the plasma's water. The protein-component, called an **apoprotein,** provides for interaction at cell membrane receptors that facilitate cellular uptake of the lipid for metabolism (fig. 9.15). Refer to table 9.2 for the major plasma lipoproteins and their principal functions.

Although study of the plasma lipoproteins has produced a large body of information, much remains unclear about their precise roles in normal metabolism. The most significant information in regard to AS has to do with the plasma levels of LDLs, and HDLs. Generally these function in an **endogenous pathway** for cholesterol transport between the liver and the other tissues that metabolize cholesterol. The liver also receives newly absorbed dietary lipid via other lipoprotein complexes in the **exogenous pathway** (fig. 9.16).

In essence, the liver takes up dietary cholesterol from the plasma and uses it to synthesize bile salts. These, along with some free cholesterol, are passed to the intestinal lumen to complete the exogenous pathway. The liver's role in the endogenous pathway involves its secreting cholesterol, which is carried in VLDLs. Capillary enzymes convert these to LDLs, which can be taken up by the tissues that metabolize cholesterol: the adrenal cortex, ovary, and liver. Of the plasma's total cholesterol, 70% or more is carried in LDLs. LDLs can also be taken up by arterial endothelial cells, with their cholesterol then accumulating in the wall to be taken up by scavenging macrophages or smooth muscle cells. Any cholesterol not utilized by these tissues can be cleared from them and carried away by HDLs. These transport the cholesterol from cell membranes to the liver, where it is metabolized or lost to the intestine in bile.

Table 9.2	Principal Plasma Lipoproteins and Their Major Roles in Lipid Transport

Plasma Lipoprotein	Function
Chylomicrons	Formed in the intestinal epithelium from newly absorbed triglyceride and cholesterol; carry lipid to muscle and adipose tissue for utilization or storage.
Very-low-density lipoproteins (VLDLs)	Formed in the liver; carry triglyceride and cholesterol.
Low-density lipoproteins (LDLs)	Formed from VLDLs; carry cholesterol to various tissues for utilization, also to arteries in which lipid can accumulate.
High-density lipoproteins (HDLs)	Take up cholesterol released from tissues and carry it to the liver, which excretes it into bile.

Various studies have established that there is a direct relationship between high plasma LDL levels and myocardial infarction caused by AS in the coronary arteries. The risk declines, however, when HDL levels increase. If HDLs are clearing cholesterol from sites of accumulation in the arterial intima, this would seem to reduce the process of atheroma formation and explain the observed reduction of AS.

The role of high LDL levels is less clear. It has been suggested that simply because more cholesterol is present in the LDLs, there is greater receptor binding, uptake, and deposition in the arterial intima. It has also been suggested that high levels of LDL may affect the endothelia to promote platelet or macrophage adherence. Since cholesterol is normally present in cell membranes, it may also be that increased endothelial uptake of cholesterol, when LDLs are elevated, causes the endothelial membranes to become more susceptible to injury and AS.

Genetics Having a near relative with atherosclerosis is a significant risk factor. This predisposition is not directly transmitted by a recognizable pattern of inheritance. It may be that different individuals have a genetically determined susceptibility, such as endothelia more prone to injury, or some loss of regulatory control of the excretion of cholesterol. Of course, the link may also be the result of shared dietary, exercise, or other family practices that tend toward greater incidence of AS. Another complication is that in some cases the genetic component might be an inherited tendency toward some other risk factor, such as hypertension.

!! Diet and Plasma Cholesterol

Many studies have sought to establish that lowering dietary cholesterol intake will result in a lowering of LDL-borne cholesterol. The results of such studies are complicated by the fact that dietary cholesterol is handled by the exogenous pathway. This means that it is only indirectly related to the endogenous pathway.

Results of changing dietary cholesterol are also affected by other processes that seem to adjust cholesterol metabolism and intestinal absorption, preventing large-scale plasma LDL changes. An example is the case of a healthy, elderly man who, because of a psychological compulsion, ate a normal diet *plus* 20–30 eggs every day. He did this for over 15 years, and suffered no indications of atherosclerosis even though egg yolks are rich in cholesterol. Although his plasma cholesterol levels were elevated somewhat, his body had adapted by absorbing less cholesterol and metabolizing more to bile acids for clearance via the intestine.

Apart from these ill-defined cases, there is a group of genetically transmitted diseases that are characterized by high levels of various plasma lipoproteins. They are usually designated by use of the term familial, or they may be described with reference to a type, indicated by a Roman numeral that relates to the lipoprotein involved (table 9.3).

An example is the rare genetic disease known as **familial hypercholesterolemia,** which is characterized by defective LDL receptors. When only one defective allele is present, the lack of normal receptor numbers means that less LDL can be taken up by liver, ovary, and adrenal tissues for cholesterol metabolism. The deficiency in uptake causes high LDL levels to be sustained, which in turn causes an accelerated development of AS. In such cases, heart attacks may occur as early as age 35. In the even more rare cases (1/1,000,000) where both of an individual's alleles are defective, the absence of LDL receptor synthesis produces very high LDL levels and an even earlier onset of AS-related heart attacks, often by age 20.

In treating these familial disorders, as well as selected cases of hyperlipidemia with no genetic cause, dietary cholesterol restriction is augmented by the use of drugs that lower plasma LDL levels (table 9.4). These operate by complexing with cholesterol in the intestine to limit its absorption, or by inhibiting endogenous cholesterol synthesis, or by other less well-understood mechanisms. These types of drugs have quite unpleasant side effects, and it is often difficult to persuade patients to continue their use long enough to ensure maximum effectiveness.

Hemodynamic Stress This is the wear and tear to which the endothelia are subjected in coping with rapid arterial blood flow. One component of wear and tear is the surging of blood, which expands and stretches the arterial walls with every systolic contraction. The second is the stress

ENDOGENOUS PATHWAY   **EXOGENOUS PATHWAY**

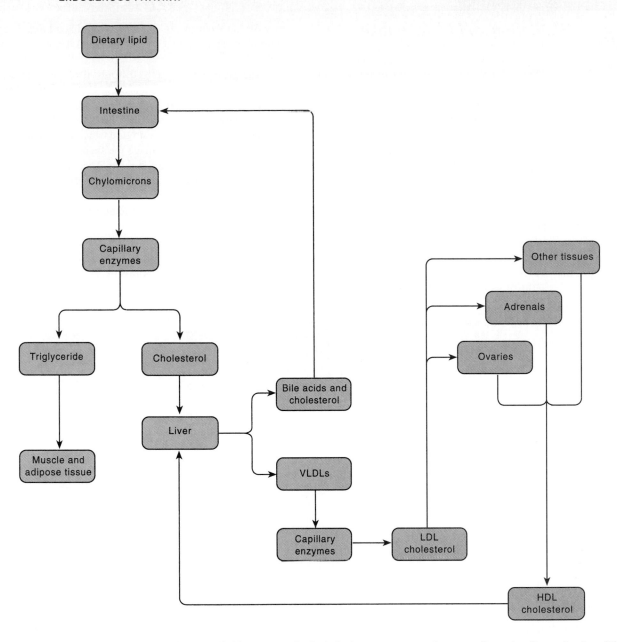

Figure 9.16   The two major pathways of plasma lipid transport. At the left, the exogenous pathway mediates the dietary intake of lipid and its return to the intestine. In the endogenous pathway, lipid carried in VLDLs and LDLs is delivered to various tissues, where it is metabolized or returned to the liver by HDLs for excretion.

caused when a rapidly moving column of blood is split at arterial branch points (fig. 9.17). The change in flow direction sets up turbulence and local pressure waves that can damage the endothelium. It is interesting to note that the high-turbulence branch points are also those sites most frequently involved in atheroma formation (see fig. 9.8).

In this context, you can appreciate the observed relation between systemic hypertension and significantly increased AS in the coronary arteries. The generally increased blood pressure increases hemodynamic stress and

favors endothelial damage. Another risk factor, inadequate exercise, may be related to hemodynamic stress. A sedentary individual has a higher resting heart rate than one who regularly engages in some activity that elevates and sustains the heart rate. Brisk walking, running, sustained swimming, squash, racquetball, and cross-country skiing are examples. Although they may promote flexibility and increase strength or coordination, golf, bowling, or weightlifting don't have the same effects in reducing the heart rate.

Oxidation and LDL Uptake

An intriguing line of research has focused on the fact that cellular uptake of lipid in the intima does not involve normal LDL receptors. The accumulating LDL-cholesterol that is taken up by macrophages and smooth muscle cells must first be modified to an oxidized form for which the scavenging cells have a receptor. Evidence indicates that the superoxide and other free radicals produced by lipid oxidation have the effect of transforming the normal LDL apoprotein into the altered form recognized by intimal macrophages. This transformation promotes rapid cellular uptake and the formation of foam cells (box fig. 9.1).

Oxidation is the critical step, but exactly what produces it is unclear. It appears that endothelia, macrophages, and smooth muscle have the enzymes that can produce oxidized free radicals, and it is possible that this pathway is activated by some early and subtle form of endothelial injury. In fact, it may be that the scavenging of these oxidized lipids is a normal defense mechanism that is overwhelmed when LDL levels are high.

The presence of oxidized lipids also fits other aspects of atherogenesis in that they are chemotactic for monocytes, which, once drawn to the intima, have their motility suppressed, preventing their passage back to the blood.

The oxidized superoxide and other free radicals are also toxic, and in time they damage the foam cells, causing them to release their cytotoxic lipid burden. There has been speculation that their release into the intima more severely damages the endothelium, allowing platelet adherence, growth factor release, and progression to the complicated atheroma. Their release would also account for the necrotic debris and free cholesterol present within the core of complicated atheromas. **10** Much study is continuing to sort out the many complexities of the AS problem, but the final resolution seems likely to involve these basics.

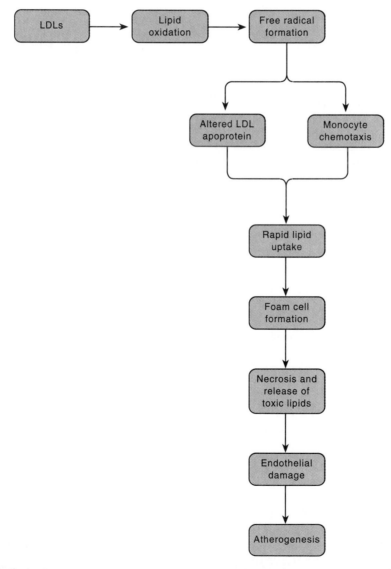

Box figure 9.1   The proposed role of lipid oxidation and free radicals in atherogenesis.

Table 9.3	Selected Genetic Hyperlipidemias and Their Major Plasma Lipid Elevations	

Disease Name	Alternative Designation	Lipoprotein Elevated
Familial hypertriglyceridemia	Type I	VLDL
Familial hypercholesterolemia	Type IIA	LDL
Familial combined hyperlipidemia	Type IIB	LDL/VLDL
Familial type 3 hyperlipoproteinemia	Type III	Chylomicron products

Table 9.4	Drugs Utilized in the Treatment of the Hyperlipoproteinemias

Drug	Action
Cholestyramine	Lowers LDLs and serum cholesterol by binding intestinal cholesterol. This promotes more cholesterol utilization, and blood levels fall.
Clofibrate	Reduces synthesis of LDL precursors and endogenous cholesterol formation.
Genfibrozil	Reduces formation of LDL precursors and promotes HDL formation.
Lovastatin	Suppresses the endogenous pathway to cholesterol synthesis.
Nicotinic acid	In large doses, lowers both cholesterol and triglycerides in plasma.
Probucol	Reduces endogenous synthesis and absorption of cholesterol and promotes LDL degradation.

Figure 9.17   Turbulent blood flow at arterial branch points increases hemodynamic stress and the potential for endothelial damage.

!! Effects of Exercise on Endothelia

A reduction in the heart rate of 10 beats per minute can be quickly achieved by a regular program of moderate exercise. This represents an annual decrease of well over 5 million heartbeats, which means over 5 million fewer systolic pressure pulses surging through the arterial tree, a substantial savings in annual wear and tear on the endothelia.

Smoking The general awareness of the hazards of smoking is usually focused on its role in the etiology of lung cancer. Too few people, however, are aware that it is a major risk factor for atherosclerosis, and coronary AS in particular. Evidence continues to accumulate that those who smoke a package of cigarettes daily have a significantly greater likelihood of coronary thrombosis and myocardial infarction. Further, when an acute MI does occur, it is more likely to be fatal in smokers than in nonsmokers. Women are also vulnerable, with as much as half their heart disease attributable to smoking. Being a nonsmoker who must spend time in the presence of smokers is also risky. Studies show an increased likelihood of death in such cases of **passive smoking.** This is particularly unfortunate in the case of infants and older children of smokers, who have little awareness of the dangers, or of the options for avoiding the hazards of their parents' ignorance or indifference. As many as one-third of the several hundred thousand annual deaths from AS in North America are due to smoking. From all causes combined, smoking-related deaths exceed 1000 per day.

Although its role as a major risk factor is clear, the specific mechanisms by which smoking contributes to AS are less so. Endothelial injury via hypoxemia may well be involved, since cigarette smoke contains carbon monoxide (CO), which replaces oxygen carried by hemoglobin. Hypoxia may also be atherogenic in that it promotes smooth muscle proliferation and LDL accumulation. The nicotine in cigarettes may contribute by its vasoconstrictive effects, producing myocardial ischemia and hypoxia, or by directly injuring the endothelium. Cigarette smoke also enhances platelet aggregation and so might promote atherogenesis by enhancing the role of platelets and the growth factors they secrete. As well, increased platelet aggregation might underlie the coronary thrombosis that is the major cause of fatal coronary infarction.

The bright spot in the smoking situation is that if smoking is stopped, its AS effects regress. After 1–5 years of nonsmoking status, a previous smoker's risk of coronary artery disease returns to normal.

Age and Sex There is firm evidence that these two factors have a strong bearing on the development of AS. Increasing age is related to increased risk of AS. As we noted earlier, intimal thickening and sclerosis are common among older people. It can be assumed that any other risk factors that predispose to AS will then operate on vessel walls already thickened and with lumina already narrowed. As well, increased age means that any such factors have had a longer time to superimpose their effects on the aging artery, so that the resulting problems are magnified.

Being male poses a serious risk to the development of AS. Males have significantly higher LDL levels and lower HDL levels than do females. Presumably, it is through this undesirable lipoprotein balance that AS is favored in males. The sex hormones of females appear not to be the reason for their more favorable high HDL and low LDL levels. Some other, more subtle factors linked to the female sex must be operating, but they remain unclear.

Diabetes Mellitus This condition, more fully considered in chapter 17, is an endocrine derangement that produces early and severe atherosclerosis in its victims. It involves widespread metabolic derangements, but in particular, it causes the plasma's glucose level to be elevated, sometimes considerably. The effect is to enhance the addition of sugar units to circulating plasma proteins, by a process called **glycation.** Glycation of LDLs has been suggested as a possible mechanism favoring AS development in diabetics. Glycated LDL might be more aggressively scavenged by intimal macrophages, or high plasma glucose levels might favor the oxidation of LDLs to promote atherogenesis by increasing their uptake by macrophages and smooth muscle or by their toxic effects on the endothelium. Study of these matters is proceeding, in part to clarify the fact that even when glucose levels are tightly controlled, presumably limiting glycation, the rates of AS among diabetics remain high. The problem is a difficult one to unravel because the metabolic effects of diabetes are so widespread.

Miscellaneous Risk Factors The previously described risk factors are those that show the strongest links to increased AS. There are other risk factors that are linked to AS, but less strongly and with less information on their underlying mechanisms.

One of these is physical activity. Sedentary individuals are more likely to develop AS than those who are more active, particularly in the kinds of activities described earlier in the context of reducing heart rate. Numerous studies have indicated various mechanisms by which exercise and fitness might have beneficial effects, but extracting clear-cut and persuasive evidence is difficult. Generally it appears that increased exercise levels are associated with reduced blood pressure, increased levels of plasma HDL, and lower plasma values of cholesterol, triglyceride, and LDL. The myocardium of strenuously training athletes shows an increased ability to extract oxygen from the blood, the implication being that it is therefore better able to resist ischemia. Other lines of research show that exercise reduces platelet aggregation, which might limit both atherogenesis and the thrombosis that often accompanies it. As well, some animal studies have suggested that exercise increases collateral circulation and stabilizes myocardial rhythmicity, both of which would allow the heart to cope better with the effects of AS.

Obesity is a risk factor for AS, but it may not operate independently. Its link to increased AS may be indirect, through its association with other risk factors such as hypertension, diabetes, hyperlipidemia, and the often sedentary activities of the obese. Note that risk factor effects have been noted only when body weights are 30%, or more, above one's "ideal" weight.

There is a widely held view, among medical personnel as well as the general public, that certain personality types are associated with a reduced ability to handle "stress" and that such individuals are at greater risk of coronary AS and MI. Despite careful analysis of the research, it is difficult to draw clear-cut conclusions to support this concept. Part of the problem may lie in the difficulty of clearly characterizing and identifying personality components or in defining "stress" and verifying its presence. It is also difficult to quantify stress levels for the type of analysis from which hard conclusions can be drawn.

Alcohol is another risk factor for AS. Evidence indicates that increased values of plasma HDL are associated with moderate alcohol consumption. Reduced HDL levels are found in those whose alcohol intake is high and, perhaps surprisingly, in those who drink no alcohol at all. No reason for these links have been widely accepted.

Risk Factors: A Summary Figure 9.18 indicates the various AS risk factors and some of the ways in which they interact. In considering risk factor interactions, note that in many individuals multiple risk factors are present. Many sedentary, obese smokers with hypertension are multiplying risks so that the question becomes less a matter of "if" and more a matter of "when" the consequences of AS will take their toll.

In assessing the best approach to one's patients and to one's own risk factor reduction program, it should be noted

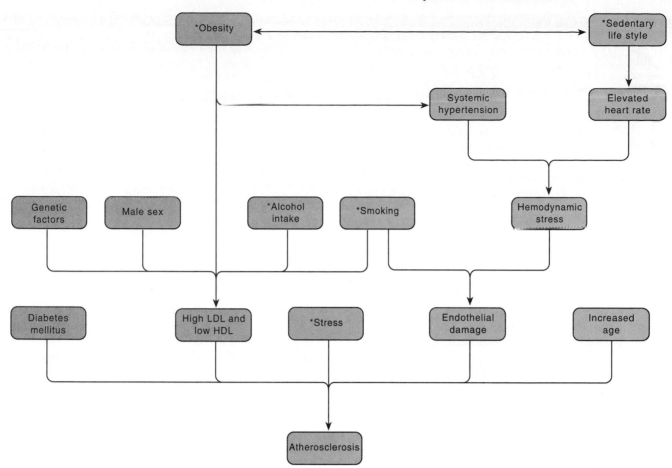

Figure 9.18   The various risk factors that directly or indirectly contribute to atherosclerosis. Note the large amount of overlap and interplay among the risk factors. Asterisks indicate the factors that are avoidable for most people.

that although age, sex, and genetic makeup can't be changed, the other risk factors can be reduced with significant benefits. Increasing exercise and fitness, therapeutic control of hypertension, elimination of smoking, reducing stress (or coping better with it), and reducing, but not completely eliminating, alcohol consumption can all be expected to reduce the predisposition to AS. Dietary changes may reduce the risk, but this topic has been the subject of many, often conflicting, claims in the medical literature as well as the popular press. Currently, there does not seem to be sufficient evidence to justify dietary extremes that seek to minimize or eliminate cholesterol intake. There is much more support for reducing caloric intake to avoid obesity and to adjust the diet so that less than one-third of its total calories derive from fat. Fat in the diet should be derived less from meats rich in saturated fat (fat which is solid, rather than liquid at room temperature) and more from fish and vegetable oils. Fat eliminated from the diet should be replaced by vegetables, and complex carbohydrates, e.g., pasta. Bon appétit!

In concluding this assessment of risk factors in AS, note that the past 20 years have seen an encouraging decline in the mortality statistics of coronary atherosclerois.

Much of this decline is due directly to the increased effectiveness of therapy for AS and indirectly to better therapeutic control of systemic hypertension. The decline in dietary fat intake and the reduction of smoking have also contributed to the decline in a significant way. Unfortunately, AS and its effects remain the major disease threat to North Americans, and further reduction of risk factors, where possible, is a continuing goal.

Sequelae of Atherosclerosis

As AS progresses, larger and more numerous plaques are present. These changes produce no signs or symptoms until well-advanced, complicated plaques develop. Then stenosis, or narrowing, of the lumen results. Other changes involve damage and deterioration of tunica media. These changes combine to produce an array of sequelae that have devastating effects.

Arterial Stenosis   Atherosclerotic stenosis of the major arteries reduces the volume of blood that can be delivered to the dependent tissues downstream. In the aorta, because of its large diameter, stenosis will have only minor impact, but atherosclerotic stenosis of the common iliac and

Links between Atherosclerosis and High Iron Levels

The difference in AS incidence between males and females may be explained by recent evidence that iron may be a factor. Some research indicates that premenopausal women who require surgical removal of the uterus, leaving ovaries in place to maintain estrogen secretion, suffer more coronary AS than other women. The suggestion is that the regular loss of menstrual blood, and the iron it contains in its hemoglobin, keeps iron in most women at a low level that protects them against AS. Also supporting this idea is the fact that meat is the source of most dietary iron, and in groups like Seventh Day Adventists, who eat no meat and have correspondingly low iron levels, coronary AS rates in males are only half those of meat eaters.

Such provocative observations have been tested in a study of coronary atherosclerosis risk factors that included iron levels in the blood. Close to 2000 men were monitored over five years and, rather than LDLs, it was iron in the blood that seemed to have the largest effect compared with any other single variable. Exactly how iron contributes to the process of atherogenesis is unclear at this early stage, but further research is under way. In the meantime it might be noted that a male donating blood three times a year achieves the same iron status as a premenopausal woman, and incidentally contributes significantly to those who need the blood.

---

femoral arteries can cause problems in the legs. For example, minor wounds may become slow to heal. As atherosclerosis develops, further stenosis may cause skin wounds of the legs to ulcerate, with increasing risk of infection and gangrene. **11** Smaller branches of the aorta may be more seriously affected. The coronary and cerebral arteries are especially significant because of the critical tissues they supply. In either brain or myocardium, the chronic ischemia caused by arterial stenosis can cause a slow, progressive deterioration of function. **12** The memory loss, confusion, and generally reduced mental functions commonly seen in the elderly are, at least in part, reflections of this reduced cerebral blood flow. AS-related stenosis of the renal artery presents a special problem. The resulting renal ischemia activates the renin-angiotensin system, which responds with fluid retention and vasoconstriction. These produce renovascular hypertension, which itself increases the progression of AS, which then aggravates the hypertension in a positive feedback cycle. In the heart, reduced blood flow will mean a steadily declining ability of the myocardium to meet its pumping demands. This decline is usually indicated by chest pain at moderate and even low levels of exertion. Chapter 11 considers the myocardial implications of **coronary artery disease** (CAD), also referred to as **ischemic heart disease** (IHD).

Thrombosis and Embolism Further complications in the coronary and cerebral vessels can result from thrombosis. As complicated plaques form, they contribute to thrombosis in two ways. First, because they protrude into the moving blood, they cause blood flow to be irregular and turbulent. This condition, as we have seen, favors the deposition of platelets in and around the plaques. Second, the complicated

lesions of advanced atherosclerosis have ulcerated, or otherwise irregular, surfaces to which platelets can readily adhere. In some cases, the loss of endothelial cells from the surfaces of advanced plaques allows platelet access to subendothelial elements that can bind them. The process of thrombosis superimposed on plaques that have already narrowed the lumen of a smaller vessel presents a serious problem. The thrombus may become organized and incorporated into the arterial wall to consolidate the stenosis and ischemia. As organization proceeds, the surface of the thrombus can provide a stimulus to further thrombosis, with still greater reduction of the vessel's lumen. As the process continues, the entire lumen may ultimately be occluded, with infarction in the brain or myocardium the result. **13** In cases of fatal myocardial infarction, it is usually thrombosis at an atheroma's surface that produces the final coronary occlusion that shuts off myocardial flow (fig. 9.19). **14**

Given that thrombosis is favored at plaque surfaces, it follows that the threat of embolism is also present. Larger complicated plaques may detach intact or may release necrotic debris into the blood. In either case, downstream occlusion of smaller vessels results. **15** This may explain some of the peripheral circulation problems commonly seen in atherosclerosis. Even though the smaller peripheral vessels are not directly affected—that is, no plaques initially form in these vessels—they may be occluded by emboli that originate in larger atheromatous vessels upstream (fig. 9.20). Emboli may also contribute to cerebral dysfunction. As thrombi form at irregular atheromatous surfaces in the carotid arteries, they may release thromboemboli that feed into the brain's vessels to occlude many small vessels.

---

11 24479

12 37622

13 6499

14 40417

15 6332

Figure 9.20   An embolus, derived from an atherosclerotic plaque, has lodged in a small artery. Note the darker masses of cellular debris, and the lighter areas, which consist of lipid. The lipid masses assume the flattened shapes because they are compressed in the lumen.

Aneurysm An **aneurysm** is a focal dilation of a blood vessel wall. Most arise in the aorta and its major branches as a result of atherosclerotic wall damage. **16** In practice, this means that males over 50 are the group at highest risk for aortic aneurysms. Some additional, much less frequent, causes of aneurysm are other diseases that involve arterial walls: **cystic medial necrosis** (CMN), **syphilis,** and **rheumatoid arthritis.** Trauma to the aorta or other vessels may also cause aneurysms. These are considered in chapter 24. When an essentially symmetrical segment of the wall is involved, the aneurysm is said to be **fusiform** (resembling a spindle), while an asymmetric bulging is described as a **saccular aneurysm** (fig. 9.21). Most commonly the aorta and cerebral vessels are affected, with aortic aneurysms able to attain a diameter of up to 20 cm. The small (maximum 1.5 cm) saccular aneurysms that affect certain cerebral vessels are called **berry aneurysms. 17** These congenital defects are considered in more detail in chapter 20.

The consequences of aneurysm are significant. One of these is thrombosis. Because the aneurysm is a dilated region of a normally symmetrical artery, blood flow is disturbed and turbulence results, predisposing to thrombosis. It is not unusual at autopsy to find the lumen of an aneurysm filled with thrombus showing a characteristic alternation of platelets and fibrin (fig. 9.21). **18** This is the result of turbulently flowing blood depositing platelets, which aggregate. Fibrin forms at the platelets' surface, and further platelet deposition and fibrin formation follow. From such a site, numerous thromboemboli can be released to occlude smaller peripheral vessels downstream. Once formed, an aneurysm may continue to expand, as it is constantly exposed to high arterial blood pressure. This is an

(a)

(b)

(c)

Figure 9.19   Coronary atherosclerosis. (*a*) Early lipid deposition yields a fatty streak: no restriction of flow results. (*b*) Progression has enlarged the lesion at the expense of the lumen. (*c*) A complicated lesion encroaches further into the lumen and has affected the media. A superimposed thrombus occludes the lumen and MI follows.

Figure 9.21   Aneurysms: (*a*) Fusiform aneurysm and
(*b*) saccular or berry aneurysm.

Figure 9.22   This aneurysm in a cerebral artery is compressing
the nearby brain tissue as arterial pressure pulses surge through it.
*This radiograph was obtained in diagnosis of a 72-year-old
woman who had been admitted to hospital complaining of a
severe headache that had suddenly developed. Soon after her
admittance she developed convulsions, lapsed into a coma, and
died. In addition to the cerebral aneurysm seen in the X-ray, a
sample of cerebrospinal fluid revealed the presence of blood. At
autopsy, the ruptured aneurysm was located, as was a large mass
of recently coagulated blood in the subarachnoid space at the
base of the brain.*

especially significant factor in those with hypertension,
where the already weakened wall must bear an even greater
burden.

A second consequence of an arterial aneurysm is the
pulsatile pressure that the expanded wall applies to adjacent
structures, e.g., the brain (fig. 9.22). **19** In the case of the
aorta, this means there is the possibility of complications
arising from compression of the esophagus, trachea, or various abdominal structures. Long-term exposure of vertebral
bodies to an aortic aneurysm can cause them to atrophy,
weaken, and distort the vertebral column.

Ultimately, the bulging wall may weaken to the point
where it cannot resist. As a result, the vessel ruptures, and high
arterial pressure drives blood into the adjacent tissues. **20** In
the aorta or its principal branches, the effect can be fatal, with
rapid blood loss quickly compromising flow to the brain
and myocardium. Since an aortic aneurysm often produces
no signs or symptoms, its often catastrophic rupture may
give no warning. In the brain, declining arterial pressure
may be less a problem than the immediate effect of rapid
hemorrhage into its delicate tissue, confined within the
skull. Chapter 23 treats this problem more fully.

The **dissecting aneurysm** is a special case, occurring
where tunica media is weakened and the intima torn. This
combination allows arterial pressure to drive blood through
the torn intima and gain access to the media. There, its
strong pulses force the separation (dissection) of the
media's layers, extending the defect around and along the
vessel (fig. 9.23). **21** Such extensions can progress along
the aorta's full length and continue into the vessels continuous with it, e.g. common carotid, renal, or coronary arteries.

There are three consequences that may follow from a
dissecting aneurysm. One is downstream ischemia as the
blood trapped in the wall forces the inner layer into the
lumen. This can produce complete occlusion of the vessel
with immediately following consequences (fig. 9.24*a*). A
second possibility is that the dissection causes the wall to
rupture, with blood rapidly lost through the defect (fig.
9.24*b*). The consequences are similarly threatening to
those following rupture of other aortic aneurysms. If the
aortic wall ruptures near its base, blood escaping the vessel
can become trapped in the pericardium. The result is called

Figure 9.23   Dissecting aneurysm. In this example, atherosclerosis has weakened the wall, allowing blood to separate (dissect) the muscle of the media. The dark coagulated blood is easily identified in the photo. The defect that allowed access to the interior of the wall is at the left.
This is the aorta of a 47-year-old male who had a history of hypertension. He died during a diagnostic procedure aimed at explaining his sudden, tearing chest pain and the loss of sensation and strength in his legs that had followed. The dark mass is coagulated blood that had been driven into the wall at a point weakened by exposure to chronically elevated blood pressure. Blood also dissected the aorta to reach the pericardial sac where it interfered with diastolic filling and reduced cardiac output (See chapter 10—cardiac tamponade). No evidence of myocardial infarction was found, but there was significant ventricular hypertrophy.

(a)   (b)

Figure 9.24   Aortic dissection may yield two serious consequences. (*a*) Blood driven into the wall has torn loose a flaplike section that acts like a valve, blocking flow. (*b*) The wall has given way and ruptured, allowing the escape of arterial blood. Note the atherosclerotic damage at the point where the dissection started.

cardiac tamponade and can be fatal (see chapter 10). The third possibility is the disruption of the aortic valve by dissection of the aortic wall adjacent to it.

Most dissecting aneurysms arise in cases of systemic hypertension, where medial damage, attributable to the idiopathic condition CMN, is also present. It is not clear whether both conditions must be present or whether the hypertension causes the medial damage. Given some medial defect, the loss of support at the site would make the intima vulnerable to tearing, especially if blood pressure is elevated. From this start, the process of dissection would then follow.

Although use of the term is well established, describing these defects as aneurysms is not accurate, in that the affected vessel doesn't have the obvious dilation seen in the saccular or fusiform types. Since dissection and bleeding into the vessel wall are the essential features in these cases, the terms **aortic dissection** and **dissecting hematoma** are increasingly encountered. A system for classifying aortic dissections is in use. It is based on the site of the dissection: type A when the ascending aorta is involved, with or without extension to the descending aorta, and type B when involvement is limited to the descending aorta.

ARTERIAL INFLAMMATIONS

Arterial inflammation, **arteritis,** is often accompanied by wall damage and some degree of stenosis. 22 It may be confined to the vessels or be one of several complications of a systemic disease. Local irritation from an infection, toxin, or some other irritant may be the cause, but an immune mechanism is usually involved. An example of vascular inflammation in a systemic disorder is **systemic lupus erythematosus** (SLE), described in chapter 5. Other conditions are **polyarteritis nodosa** (PAN) and **thromboangiitis obliterans,** which arises primarily in the veins of young male smokers.

VEIN DISORDERS

Disorders of the veins are common, but essentially only two are significant and both arise principally in the veins of the leg. These vessels are situated superficially, or travel with the deep supply arteries.

Thrombophlebitis

Thrombophlebitis is the condition of venous inflammation (**phlebitis**) that follows thrombosis. The major sites of occurrence are the deep leg veins.

Thrombophlebitis is usually the result of focal infection, disruptions of blood flow, or hypercoagulation states. Most thrombophlebitis arises in the deep leg veins and poses a significant risk of thromboembolism. The fewer cases that arise in the superficial leg veins present minimal risk of embolism, but can cause discomfort due to the congestion from reduced venous drainage, which arises when the veins communicating to the unaffected deep veins cannot handle the excess volume.

Varicose Veins

In **varicose veins,** the superficial leg veins become dilated and assume a more twisted pattern. **23** Each dilation is a **varix** and there are usually multiple such varices present (fig. 9.25). These venous deformations are thought to arise as a result of elevated venous pressure. Unable to resist, the walls stretch and dilate. Varicose veins may arise more often in the superficial vessels, probably because they lack the complete support of surrounding muscle that the deep veins enjoy. The leg veins' burden is eased by the presence of leaflet valves that prevent backflow. When the walls dilate, valve function is compromised to add to the volume and pressure load the wall must resist (fig. 9.26).

Any factors that increase venous pressure in the legs can contribute to greater loading of the veins' walls. Since an upright posture significantly increases venous pressure, those whose normal activities involve chronic and prolonged standing place increased loads on their veins. Any other condition that impedes venous drainage of the legs, such as a thrombus or compression of the communicating abdominal vessels by a tumor, abdominal fat, or a pregnant uterus, will increase venous pressure. The excessive plasma volume produced by a failing heart or kidney disease may also increase the veins' burden. Since many people who are subject to any of these predispositions do not develop varices, it may be that an inherited weakness of venous walls is an important underlying factor in their development.

The reduced rates of flow and irregular surfaces that characterize varicose veins predispose to thrombosis, which can reduce flow to aggravate the problem. However, in such cases embolism is quite rare.

Varices in the veins of the rectum and anal canal are called **hemorrhoids.** They are also caused by elevated venous pressure when abdominal factors restrict drainage, particularly in chronic constipation that involves straining

Figure 9.25   A section of leg vein, with pronounced varices. *This is a length of great saphenous vein resected from the leg of a 50-year-old male. He had had asymptomatic varicose veins since his mid-teens. Three weeks earlier, he had experienced pain and redness above his knee. On admission to hospital a large varicosity was found. It was occluded with thrombus at a point above the knee. After its removal, recovery was uneventful.*

in attempts at defecation. The abdominal pressures of pregnancy may also promote hemorrhoid formation.

Esophageal varices may arise in the veins that accompany the esophagus. These vessels carry some of the blood returning from the abdomen. They may become chronically congested in cases of liver disease, with varices forming as a result. They are considered more fully in chapter 14.

24526

(a)   (b)

Figure 9.26   Varicose veins. Compare the normal vein at left with the varicose vein on the right. The irregular bulging of the varices limits complete valve closure and allows some backflow. Note also the developing thrombi, whose formation is favored by the swirling of blood around the valve leaflets.

Case Study

While driving with his girlfriend, a 24-year-old man said that he felt "kinda funny and dizzy" and that his vision was blurred. At the woman's insistence he surrendered the wheel and she drove to a nearby hospital's emergency room.

The physician on duty examined the man and found him to be in excellent health, but with mildly elevated blood pressure. When questioned about the aroma of alcohol detected on his breath, he reported having "only a beer or two," which his girlfriend verified. He was admitted to hospital for overnight observation.

During the night he complained of feeling ill and having blurred vision, chest and abdominal pain, and tingling in the feet. His ECG showed tachycardia, and was otherwise grossly abnormal. His legs were cool and no femoral pulse could be found. A CT scan was ordered and indicated a dissecting hematoma of the aorta, distal to the ductus arteriosus. He showed signs of cardiovascular shock as he was prepared for emergency surgery.

During the procedure the presence of a 5-cm dissecting hematoma was verified. It was removed and replaced by a Dacron graft. The presence of a somewhat narrowed region of the aorta was also identified distal to the point of dissection, and this region was also removed and replaced. The postoperative period was uneventful and the patient recovered fully.

Commentary

The patient's apparent good health, and the indication that he had been drinking, might normally have resulted in his being sent home. In this case the clinician's decision, based on many years of experience, was vindicated. Had the patient not been under close medical observation, the aorta might have ruptured, threatening his survival.

Microscopic analysis of the excised segment of aorta showed evidence of medial necrosis, probably in response to the abnormally elevated pressures caused by the region of narrowing further along the vessel. It was this damage that weakened the wall, allowing the blood to gain access to it and begin its dissection.

Key Concepts

1. Aging is accompanied by a generalized change in arterial walls that involves increased wall rigidity and thickening (p. 202).

2. The rare condition of medial calcific sclerosis embodies calcification of medium-sized limb arteries, but since no loss of lumen is involved, clinical signs and symptoms seldom arise (p. 202).

3. Arteriolosclerosis involves intimal and medial thickening of arterioles, most typically in association with diabetes mellitus and systemic hypertension (pp. 202–203).

4. A broad range of risk factors predispose to systemic hypertension, but since the condition is essentially asymptomatic, it is often undiagnosed (p. 203).

5. Various genetic defects in the excretion of sodium ion by the kidney, smooth muscle's ability to expel sodium from its interior, and unbalanced autonomic input to arterioles have been suggested as contributing to essential hypertension (pp. 203–204).

6. In secondary hypertension, a specific systemic disorder can be identified as contributing to pressure elevation; usually the disorder involves an endocrine or renal problem (p. 205).

7. If untreated, systemic hypertension is associated with increasing disease occurrence, notably involving vessels or neurological problems, and may take a slowly or rapidly progressive course (pp. 205–206).

8. Atherosclerosis, the major cause of death in North America, is essentially a derangement of the aorta and its major branches and derives from internal thickening caused by its characteristic lesion, the atheroma (p. 206).

9. The atheroma develops progressively with lipid accumulation, cell and connective tissue proliferation, calcification, and surface ulceration that compromise the lumen and weaken the arterial wall (pp. 207–208).

10. The pathogenesis of AS is thought to rest on the concept of atheroma formation as a response to injury, with cell proliferation mediated by a variety of growth factors that are released by platelets and macrophages (p. 208).

11. A broad array of risk factors for AS have been identified as directly or indirectly contributing to atherogenesis by promoting endothelial damage or by other less well-defined mechanisms (pp. 209–217).

12. The sequelae of AS involve compromised blood flow via arterial stenosis, thrombosis, and embolism or by aneurysm formation, all of which present their greatest threat to the coronary and cerebral circulations (pp. 217–221).

13. A variety of factors such as toxins and infections may activate immune responses that have an irritant effect, producing a focal or systemic arteritis (p. 221).

14. Vein disorders involve inflammation or varicosities, both of which states predispose to complications of venous flow and may involve thrombosis (p. 222).

REVIEW ACTIVITIES

1. Study figure 9.12 and identify the following:

   endothelium

   basement membrane

   foam cells

   calcium deposits

   proliferated myointimal cells

   subendothelial connective tissue

   platelet plug

   internal elastic lamina

   vasa vasorum

   If you have trouble, see the relevant text sections and illustrations.

2. Complete the following table of characteristics for the indicated types of arteriosclerosis.

Vessels Affected	Wall Region Affected	Major Cause
Medial calcific sclerosis		
Arteriolosclerosis		
Atherosclerosis		

3. Compare the highlighted regions of figure 9.8 and the sites of turbulent flow in figure 9.17. Now prepare a list in point form that links events in figure 9.17 to sites of atheroma formation in figure 9.8. Be sure to include reference to the general hypothesis that governs atherogenesis.

4. In figure 9.6, use a penciled arrow to indicate an increase in renin secretion. Then follow through the system with other arrows indicating the ultimate effect on systemic blood pressure. By using light red pencil for the decreased renin condition and its consequences, you produce a quick reference diagram for renin's blood pressure effects. (As a quick verification, see figure 9.7 and note the plasma volume effects of RAS inhibitors.)

5. Draw up a list of key points to use in discouraging tobacco users from smoking. Include some MI and fatality information for pack-a-day users and five (5) mechanisms whereby smoking might contribute to AS.

Chapter Ten

Cardiac Pathophysiology

Never morning wore
To evening, but some heart did break.

Alfred, Lord Tennyson
In Memoriam

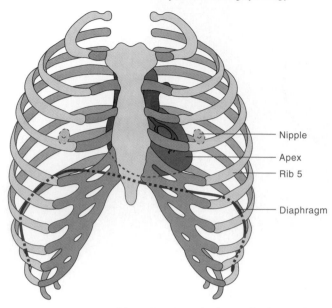

Figure 10.1   The position of the heart in the mediastinum with respect to selected skeletal reference points.

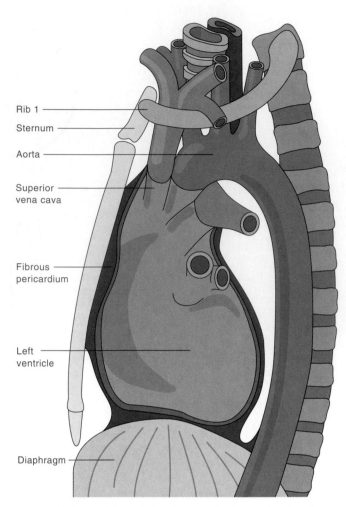

Figure 10.2   Left lateral view into mediastinum, showing the attachments of the pericardium to the diaphragm and sternum. Note also the protection provided by the sternum and vertebral column.

T he heart normally functions as a highly effective pump. In a young adult it is capable of adapting within minutes to dramatic changes in the body's requirement for oxygen, from the 5 liters pumped per minute at rest to perhaps 35 liters during continuous heavy exercise. The capacity to meet these pumping requirements depends on the coordinated action of a healthy heart muscle, valves that regulate flow direction, and vessels that facilitate distribution and return of blood. Although diseases may alter or damage different parts of this system, it is the ultimate compromise or failure of this essential pumping action that threatens health. Before turning to cardiac disease details, let us briefly review the working of the normal heart.

THE NORMAL HEART

Location of the Heart

The heart is located within the chest in the mediastinum, with much of its bulk lying posterior to the sternum. About one-third of the heart lies to the right of the midline and two-thirds to the left. **1** Typically, the apex of the heart lies between ribs 5 and 6 when one is lying down, and one space lower when one is sitting or standing. The base is directed toward the right shoulder (fig. 10.1).

The Pericardium

The pericardium consists of a substantial and tough outer layer of fibrous connective tissue, the **fibrous pericardium. 2** It anchors the heart to the great veins and arteries at its base, to the sternum anteriorly, and to the diaphragm inferiorly (fig. 10.2) It thus fixes the heart in position as it contracts and relaxes in pumping and provides the cardiac surface with a protective enclosure.

Within the fibrous pericardium is a pair of serous membranes. The one lining the inner surface of the fibrous pericardium is the **parietal pericardium** and the other, which covers the heart's surface, is the **visceral pericardium.** Both secrete a watery fluid that fills the thin

Figure 10.3   Components of the pericardium and endocardium and their relationship to the myocardium.

space between them, the **pericardial space.** The 15–50 ml of **pericardial fluid** provides lubrication to the serous membrane surfaces to reduce friction as the heart moves during its pumping cycles. The fibrous pericardium and its inner serous lining are known as the **pericardial sac,** while the visceral pericardium and the loose layer of connective tissue on the heart's surface are called the **epicardium** (fig. 10.3).

The Myocardium

The cardiac muscle tissue that forms the walls of the atria and ventricles **3** is the **myocardium.** It is anchored to an internal framework of fibrous connective tissue, sometimes known as the heart's fibrous skeleton. The tissue of the fibrous skeleton lies on a plane between the atria and ventricles, providing a framework to which myocardial muscle can attach (fig. 10.4). This arrangement provides some distinct mechanical advantages. Bands of longitudinally arranged myocardial cells circle and loop down to form the ventricular walls (fig. 10.5*a*). When these contract, they draw the walls upward in a wringing movement that reduces the ventricular lumen far more for a given shortening of fiber than would a simple parallel arrangement of

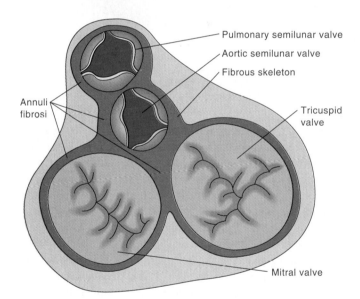

Figure 10.4   The fibrous skeleton of the heart is indicated in this diagram by stippling. Note how the annuli fibrosi form the margins of the flow tracts, providing a strong anchoring for the cardiac valves.

(a)

RV   LV

(b)

Figure 10.5 (*a*) The circular swirling of myocardial fibers. (*b*) This section shows the overlapping and continuity of the myocardial muscle sheets.

fibers. The gain in pumping efficiency can be compared to the increase in effect produced by wringing out a wet towel as opposed to just squeezing it. As well as this encircling of the ventricles, there is a continuity and integration of the fibers of the left and right myocardium. Superficial layers circle the right ventricle, wind through the interventricular septum, and then form deep muscle layers in the left ventricle. Superficial layers circling the left ventricle wind backward through the septum and form deep layers in the right ventricle (fig. 10.5*b*). Because of this arrangement, pumping between the two sides is better integrated, but pathology that affects one ventricle is also apt to eventually affect the other.

Chambers of the Heart

The heart consists of two pumps that function synchronously as an integrated unit (fig. 10.6). The right heart acts as a volume pump, propelling blood through the low-resistance vessels of the pulmonary system. The left heart

acts as a pressure pump, generating enough pressure to force the blood through the high-resistance vessels of the systemic circulation.

Each pump includes a thin-walled atrium that collects blood returning to the heart. **4** A thin interatrial septum separates the left and right atria. Both atria have small ear-like appendages (auricles) that extend anteriorly. **5** (Note that the terms atrium and auricle are not interchangeable.) Atrial contraction aids in filling the ventricles. The right atrium receives deoxygenated blood from the inferior vena cava, the superior vena cava, and the heart muscle (the myocardium) via the coronary sinus. The left atrium receives oxygenated blood from the lungs via the four pulmonary veins.

The muscular ventricles comprise more than 60% of the mass of the heart and receive most of the coronary blood flow. They are separated by the interventricular septum, which is thick and muscular except near the atrioventricular septum, where it is a thin membrane. (Failure of this membranous septum to form is the most common congenital abnormality of the heart, allowing blood to be shunted from the high-pressure left ventricle into the low-pressure right ventricle.) Blood from the right ventricle is pumped into the pulmonary artery, while blood from the left ventricle is pumped into the aorta. The left ventricular wall is three to four times thicker than the right, **6** reflecting the high workload required to overcome the resistance of the systemic vessels.

The Cardiac Valves

Blood must flow through the vascular system in one direction only. Any change from this flow pattern interferes with oxygenation of the blood and its supply to the tissues, or puts an extra load on the pump. The four cardiac valves are responsible for preventing any backflow in the system. Their structure and position allow blood to move in only the desired forward direction. Valve function in controlling flow of a liquid is illustrated in figure 10.7. This same principle is applied in the case of the cardiac valves.

The four valves are not active structures. That is, they do not contract or act by themselves to control blood flow. Their valve function instead depends on their structure and position within the heart's flow tracts and their passive responses to pressures applied to their surfaces. The delicate cardiac valve cusps or leaflets are formed of thin layers of connective tissue covered by endothelium that is continuous with the endocardium (fig. 10.8). **7** When pressure is greater on one side than the other, the valve moves passively. Depending on its location, pressure causes the valve leaflet either to move into the flow tract, where it will contact other valve leaflets and thus block flow, or to be pushed out of the way to permit forward flow.

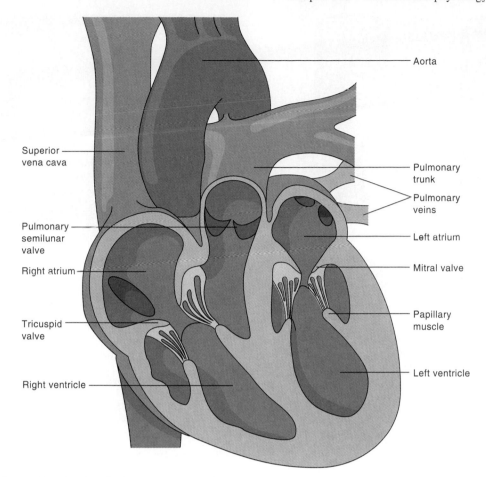

Figure 10.6   Cardiac section showing the internal structure of the heart. The aortic semilunar valve, at the base of the aorta, is hidden by the pulmonary trunk.

The valves of the heart are encircled by tough fibrous rings of the heart's fibrous skeleton to which the valve leaflets or cusps are anchored. These rings, the **annuli fibrosis,** prevent the outlets from the atria and ventricles from becoming dilated when the myocardium contracts to force blood through them. When the heart is relaxing, they form a firm margin or valve seat that makes effective valve closure possible.

There are two different types of cardiac valve. One type controls flow between an atrium and its corresponding ventricle. These are the **atrioventricular valves** (AV valves). Since the right AV valve has three cusps, it is known as the **tricuspid** valve. **8** Only two cusps form the left or **bicuspid** AV valve. The bicuspid valve is also known as the **mitral valve,** because when closed the cusp configuration resembles a miter, the ritual headdress of a bishop.

As the ventricles contract, they generate a pressure that closes the AV valves. The pressure involved is quite high, and if unaided the AV valves could not resist it. They would be abruptly pushed past their closed position (valve **eversion**), allowing blood to be regurgitated back into the atrium. This does not happen because the AV valves are tethered by the **chordae tendineae.** **9** As their name suggests, these are tendonlike cords. Each is attached, at one end, to the ventricular surface of an AV cusp. The other end is secured to a small protrusion from the ventricular myocardium called a **papillary muscle** (fig. 10.9). **10** The strong, inelastic chordae tendineae act as restraints against the ventricle's high pressure. They are long enough to allow the valve to be pushed to its full closed position, but not beyond.

Backflow of blood from the arteries into the relaxing ventricles is prevented by the **semilunar (SL) valves.** Each valve is composed of three cuplike leaflets that fold against the vessel walls as the ventricle empties. As the ventricle begins to relax, blood flow reverses, causing the cusps to fill and expand and thereby block the lumen. **11** The **pulmonary semilunar** valve separates the right ventricle from the pulmonary artery. The **aortic semilunar valve**

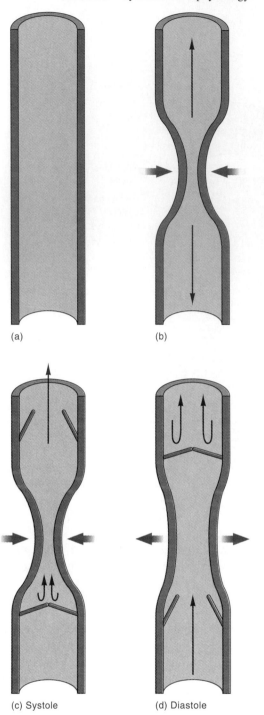

(a)   (b)

(c) Systole   (d) Diastole

Figure 10.7 Schematic representation illustrating the principles of cardiac valve function. Squeezing the fluid-filled tube (*a,b*) produces flow in both directions. With valves in place, squeezing drives blood forward (*c*). When pressure is released, backflow is prevented and more fluid moves in (*d*) to be pumped during next cycle.

Figure 10.8   The cardiac valves. See figure 10.4 for details.

separates the left ventricle from the aorta. In a semilunar valve, the smaller lumen and the support of the strong annuli fibrosi eliminate the need for the chordae tendineae associated with the AV valves.

The Cardiac Cycle

The sequence of events that comprise the repeating, pumping action of the heart is termed the **cardiac cycle.** The portion of the cycle during which the ventricles contract is termed **systole** and the remaining interval, when the ventricles are relaxing, is called **diastole.** By convention, unless specifically indicated, these terms refer to the ventricles. If the focus is on the period of atrial contraction, then atrial systole needs to be specified.

Cardiac Performance

Adequate circulation of blood through the body is achieved by maintaining an appropriate pressure gradient from the arteries through the capillaries to the veins. The arterial pressure is determined, in part, by the rate at which blood is pumped into the arteries and, in part, by the rate at which blood passes from the arterial system into the capillaries and veins. As tissue blood flow requirements change, cardiac pumping is altered to match them.

Each ventricle has a volume of up to 150 ml at the end of its filling period, the **end-diastolic volume** (EDV). During one systolic contraction, the volume of blood pumped from a ventricle is termed the **stroke volume** (SV). Not all the blood in the ventricle is pumped into the arterial system during systole. The volume remaining is termed the **end-systolic volume** (ESV). The percentage of blood pumped from the filled ventricle is the **ejection fraction,** normally about 65–70%. From these definitions it follows that taking the amount of blood in a filled ventricle (EDV)

Figure 10.9   In this sectioned heart it is easy to see the chordae tendineae joining to the margin of the cusps at one end, while their other end is firmly anchored in the myocardium at the protruding papillary muscles.

and subtracting the amount remaining after it contracts (ESV) will yield the amount pumped by the ventricle in one contraction (SV). Equation (1) presents this concept more succinctly:

$$SV = EDV - ESV \qquad \text{(Eq. 1)}$$

The ejection fraction can be expressed as in equation (2):

$$\text{Ejection fraction (\%)} = SV/EDV \times 100 \qquad \text{(Eq. 2)}$$

The volume of blood pumped from the left ventricle each minute is called the cardiac output (CO) and is dependent on both the heart rate (HR) and the stroke volume (SV). The relationship is indicated in equation (3):

$$CO \ (ml/min) = HR \ (beats/min) \times SV \ (ml/beat) \qquad \text{(Eq. 3)}$$

A typical resting heart rate is about 70 beats per minute, with a stroke volume of 80 ml. The resting cardiac output in this example is therefore about 5.6 liters per minute.

Heart Rate Control

The heart generates its own regular contraction, which is modified by both nervous and hormonal controls. This intrinsic rhythm, of about 100 beats per minute, results from the spontaneous depolarization of a tiny island of specialized myocardial tissue located in the atrium near the junction with the superior vena cava and called the **sinoa-**

trial node (SA node). This signal is passed through atrial bands of the same specialized myocardium to the **atrioventricular** (AV) node, embedded in the center of the fibrocartilagenous skeleton that forms the atrioventricular septum. Here the signal pauses very briefly, allowing the atrial contraction it has initiated to force more blood into the ventricles. Then the signal continues into the ventricles, passing along the conduction pathways (again, specialized myocardial tissue) of the bundle of His, the right and left bundle branches, and the Purkinje fibers to finally reach and activate the cells of the ventricular common myocardium. This depolarization induces ventricular contraction.

The capacity for rhythmic depolarization is found throughout the tissues of the SA and AV nodes and conduction pathways. The SA node has the fastest intrinsic rhythm and thereby sets the heart rate. For this reason it is often called the **pacemaker.** A cardiac rhythm that is dependably initiated from the SA node, whatever its rate, is termed a **sinus rhythm.** The term sinus rhythm therefore implies normally functioning signal generation and conduction. Certain disease conditions can permit other parts of the conduction system or even parts of the common myocardium to take over signal generation. These abnormally functioning bits of tissue are called **ectopic foci.** Their effect on heart function can range from minor (slightly impaired ventricular filling) to disastrous (ventricular fibrillation, a chaotically disordered ventricular contraction that can be fatal and requires immediate electrical defibrillation and restarting).

The electrochemical events that accompany signal generation and conduction in the specialized myocardium, while critical, are not normally observable on a clinical **ECG** (electrocardiogram, the tracing made of the amplified electrical events in the heart detectable at surface electrodes). However, the depolarization induced in the common myocardium of the atrium, which acts as a signal to contract, is seen as the first (or **P**) wave of the ECG. The second wave form (called the **QRS complex**) derives from ventricular depolarization while the third (**T**) wave arises during ventricular repolarizaiton (the signal to cease contracting). To produce an ECG, electrodes are applied to the wrists and ankles and also to the left chest. The presence, timing, and shapes of the P, QRS, and T waves allow the detection of any deviations from normal sinus rhythm. Tracings of the electrical activity in different combinations of electrodes essentially give different views of the contraction of the ventricles. These can also be used to detect areas of abnormal conduction and possibly areas of infarction.

The heart is continually required to adjust pump-volume to meet altered metabolic demands and pump-pressure to meet altered resistance. It has a simple repertoire of responses to meet these requirements: it can change heart rate and it can alter the force of each contraction (myocardial contractility). The commonly observed resting heart rate of 70 beats per minute is evidence that something must restrain the natural intrinsic rhythm of 100. Parasympathetic neurons reach the SA node of the heart via the vagus nerve. At rest they release small amounts of acetylcholine, which slows the rate of depolarization of the SA node to 70 bpm. Sympathetic neurons innervate the pacemaker and conduction system as well as the ventricular common myocardium. Release of norepinephrine from these neurons or release of epinephrine from the adrenal medulla speeds the rate of depolarization. It also increases the force of each contraction, an issue dealt with in the section on stroke volume control.

The sympathetic nervous system and epinephrine act as cardiac rate accelerators. For this reason they are known as **positive chronotropes.** The parasympathetic nervous system is antagonistic to them, acting as a brake on the heart rate; thus it is a **negative chronotrope.** The two systems are coordinated by the cardiac centers in the medulla oblongata of the brain stem. Pressure receptors in the right atrium and arterial system form part of a negative feedback system regulating the heart rate and blood pressure (fig. 10.10). Higher brain centers also can influence the heart rate.

Stroke Volume Control

Stroke volume is determined by three main variables: EDV, the resistance of the vascular system to emptying of the ventricle, and the contractility of the myocardium.

The EDV determines the amount of tension applied to the resting myocardium of the fully filled ventricle prior to contraction. For this reason, EDV is sometimes called the **preload.** In turn the EDV is dependent on the volume of blood available for ventricular filling (the venous return) and the resistance of the ventricle to expansion.

End-diastolic volume and stroke volume are related. The relationship was first demonstrated at the turn of the century by Frank and Starling and is known as **Starling's law of the heart.** Briefly stated, the heart adapts to different preloads by pumping the volume of blood delivered to it. This adjustment occurs automatically, without any external control by nerves or hormones, and is thus termed **autoregulation** or **intrinsic regulation** of stroke volume. The mechanism behind the Frank-Starling effect is a characteristic common to both skeletal and cardiac muscle cells: the force of contraction is greater when the muscle is stretched prior to contraction (fig. 10.11). The degree of stretch of cells in the ventricular wall is determined by the volume of blood delivered to the heart. This means that changes in venous return produce appropriate changes in contraction force that efficiently match preload to contraction force. The essential principle of Starling's law is widely accepted, but its role in normal cardiac output determination is less clear. Intrathoracic pressures vary during breathing, and this leads to unbalanced filling of left and right ventricles. Starling's law probably deals with this by automatically adjusting stroke volume to EDV. It may play a more significant role in compensating for cardiac dysfunction.

The stroke volume is also determined by the resistance of the arterial system to ventricular emptying. This resistance is called **afterload** and is determined primarily by blood viscosity and the resistance offered by the vascular system itself. Normally, vascular resistance comes principally from the arterioles and precapillary sphincters, whose tension is an important component determining the BP and which function to effectively shunt the fixed volume of blood to the most metabolically active body tissues.

The third major variable influencing stroke volume is **myocardial contractility.** It is defined as the tension that can be developed by the cardiac muscle cell independent of its starting length or tension. Contractility is dependent, in part, on the structural organization of the cell and its metabolic state. Hypoxia and certain toxins decrease myocardial contractility and are termed **negative inotropes.** Other factors, such as digitalis or its derivatives, will increase contractility and are termed **positive inotropes.** In addition, contractility can be increased by sympathetic stimulation and by the hormone epinephrine, so these are also positive inotropes.

HEART DISEASE

Death from **heart failure** is the most catastrophic outcome of the disease processes described in this chapter. For a death to be attributed to heart failure the ventricles must have failed to maintain blood circulation compatible with basic life processes despite adequate venous filling. By this definition, heart failure is a common ultimate cause of death. In practice, if the failure of the pump is indirectly caused by some other disease process, e.g., blood loss, acidosis, or widespread cancer, mortality is then attributed to that disease.

Heart failure may be intrinsic to the pump itself. For example, the myocardium may have been weakened by disease or excessive stretching. Other causes might be restrictions to cardiac blood flow that impede filling and pumping, or disturbance of the heart's intrinsic rhythm. On the other hand, the failure might be attributed to factors that place excess demands on the pump—for example, defective valves, or vessels that offer abnormal resistance to blood flow, or excessive pumping demand as in hyperthyroidism, which increases the metabolic/oxygenation demands of the body.

Heart Failure: Terms and Concepts

Acute and Chronic Heart Failure

Before we look at the various sources of heart failure, it will be useful to distinguish between acute and chronic heart failure.

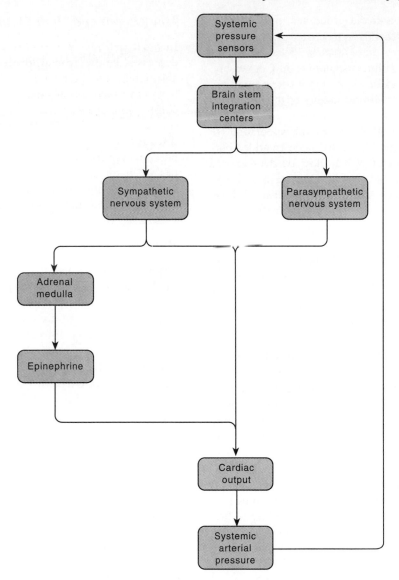

Figure 10.10   Arterial blood pressure depends, in part, on the cardiac output, which is affected by nuclei in the medulla. These monitor systemic pressure and adjust rate of stimulation in the autonomic pathways that supply the heart.

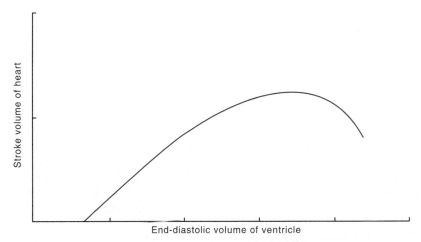

Figure 10.11   Starling's law expresses the relation between the end-diastolic volume, which stretches the myocardium, and the resulting force of contraction, which determines the stroke volume.

If the heart failure and the processes underlying it develop quickly (a few seconds to a few days), we refer to it as **acute heart failure.** Approximately 35% of individuals suffering acute heart failure succumb to it. Conversely, 65% do not; either spontaneously or with medical intervention, these people survive, with the quality of the remaining heart function dependent on the nature and extent of the cardiac damage. At the other end of the spectrum are chronic conditions that more gradually place an added burden on the individual's heart. When these burdens exceed the capacity of the heart and circulatory system to adapt, the person is said to be experiencing **chronic heart failure.** Individuals with chronic heart failure may experience a sudden deterioration of cardiac function, which threatens them with acute heart failure because of the natural progression of the disease, a failure of therapy, or sudden and excessive cardiac demand (the classic is shoveling snow). Because the heart and associated vessels are a complex anatomical and functional system, there are many routes to the end-stage of complete heart failure. Sometimes the function of the entire heart is disrupted, as for example in a sudden arrhythmia. In other cases, one ventricle alone is initially affected.

A variety of terms are used to denote either actual conditions in the heart or hypothetical mechanisms whereby the symptoms and heart failure progress. Bear in mind while you read this material that the most common underlying pathology giving rise to heart failure is ischemic heart disease. This condition will often be expressed as a weakening of the ventricular myocardium, usually that of the left ventricle. Other diseases and other sites and structures may result in chronic heart failure, but left ventricular failure secondary to ischemic heart disease is the most common starting point.

Right-Sided and Left-Sided Heart Failure

The most common pattern of heart failure is for one ventricle, usually the left, to fail first. The left is more often the first to fail because it has a much greater workload, so is thereby more stressed. The pattern of left-sided heart failure includes a number of pulmonary effects, including pulmonary congestion and edema, because the lungs empty into the left heart. As well, decreased perfusion of the kidneys and cerebral hypoxia contribute to its complications. Right-sided heart failure often follows left-sided heart failure, but it also occurs independently in primary lung diseases in which the resistance of the lung's vascular bed, and hence the pressure load on the right ventricle, increases dramatically. This situation leads to a classic pattern of signs and symptoms that we will deal with in detail in the section on congestive heart failure.

Low-Output and High-Output Heart Failure

In most patients with heart failure, cardiac output is depressed below normal levels. Because the heart is not able to meet normal resting oxygen demands, a clinical pattern of impaired peripheral circulation, due to systemic vasoconstriction, produces cold, pale, and sometimes cyanotic (bluish) extremities. On the other hand, some normal or disease states require significant increases in cardiac output to meet very high demand. In these states, the extremities are warm and flushed. If the demand for increased cardiac output outpaces the capacity of the heart to meet it, high-output heart failure will ensue.

Pericardial Disease

Percardial disease manifests itself by the accumulation of fluid in the pericardial space (**pericardial effusion**) and/or inflammation of the pericardium (**pericarditis**). Although there can be pain and discomfort associated with pericarditis, the threat to health occurs when the pumping action of the heart is impeded. The pericardial cavity can fill with up to 2 liters (normal volume 15–50 ml) of serous fluid (**hydropericardium**) or blood (**hemopericardium**) that prevents normal diastolic filling and thereby reduces cardiac output.

Acute Pericarditis

The most frequent clinical form of pericardial disease is acute pericarditis, a nonspecific inflammatory response to a variety of injuries that can be organized into three groups: intrinsic heart disease, disease in adjacent structures, and systemic disorders.

Usually the volume of intrapericardial effusion in acute pericarditis is small (not greater than 200 ml) and with varying fibrin content: **serous, serofibrinous,** or **fibrinous** (fig. 10.12). The greater the fibrin content, the greater the tendency to roughen the pericardium or form adhesions. This pattern is typical in the acute pericarditis that accompanies rheumatic fever, myocardial infarction, and immune and viral forms of pericarditis. **12** These usually resolve with no clinically significant sequelae. A **purulent suppurative effusion** is found in bacterial or fungal infections and tends to have more serious consequences. There is often fibrous obliteration of the pericardial cavity. Not only do the visceral and parietal membranes adhere, but the fibrous pericardium can adhere to adjacent structures, producing adhesive mediastinopericarditis. This condition disrupts both diastolic and systolic ventricular action, since the heart has to work against the restricting adhesions to surrounding structures.

ing the cardiac cycle.) If the volume of fluid is large or the exudate develops quickly, the filling of the ventricles may be impaired because the heart's relaxation is opposed by the high pericardial pressure (the condition called **pericardial tamponade**) and cardiac output will fall. **Pericardiocentesis**—removal of the excess fluid—relieves the pressure on the heart but may have to be repeated if the exudate continues to form. The inflammatory reaction can be therapeutically controlled with salicylate and occasionally corticosteroids, while the pain is controlled by analgesics such as codeine.

Chronic Pericarditis

Acute pericarditis typically resolves, but chronic problems can arise as a complication of healing. When fibrosis is excessive, **chronic constrictive pericarditis** may produce a diffusely and densely scarred pericardial sac. This sclerosis or hardening of the pericardium means that a nondistensible shell now encases the heart. **13** The reduced elasticity often produces stenosis at the points where veins enter the atria. The resulting restriction of venous return can increase back pressure in the systemic veins, causing enlargement of the liver (**hepatomegaly**) and spleen (**splenomegaly**). Restricted diastolic filling from the limitation of venous return can also combine to reduce cardiac output. Severe cases require surgical removal of both the visceral and parietal layers of the pericardium. This condition is most common as a complication of tuberculous pericarditis, but it is also found as a chronic development in **acute idiopathic pericarditis** (probably viral). In about 50% of cases, the heavily scarred pericardium becomes calcified and can reach a state (called **concretio cordis**) in which the heart appears to be encased in a plaster mold.

Radiation-induced pericarditis is a form of chronic pericarditis that frequently develops after prolonged radiotherapy for Hodgkin's disease, lymphoma, or breast cancer and must be anticipated in these patients. Pericardiocentesis is the common form of management. Uremic pericarditis can develop in patients with chronic renal failure who are not being dialyzed. The reason why pericarditis develops is unknown, but it promptly disappears upon initiation of dialysis.

Myocarditis

Myocarditis is a condition of inflammatory change in the myocardium. **14** Occasionally myocarditis presents as focal inflammation of the myocardium (sometimes called primary myocarditis), but usually it is one manifestation of a more general disease process (for example, rheumatic fever). Myocarditis is usually acute and mild, and followed

Figure 10.12   Acute pericarditis. In this view of the pericardial surface, a pronounced fibrinous exudate produces a shaggy appearance.
This cardiac surface is thickly coated with fibrin as the result of an acute pericarditis with a fibrinous effusion. The problem arose in a 57-year-old male who had been overwhelmed by the effects of a malignant lung tumor. He had deferred any medical assistance for his chronic productive cough, loss of voice, and progressive weakness and weight loss. Radiation therapy was unable to significantly reverse his decline, and he died one month later.

A contributing factor to his death was a weakened resistance, which had allowed the establishment of a widespread pneumococcal infection. Acute meningitis resulted, as well as the acute pericarditis that produced the shaggy pattern of fibrin deposition shown here. The surface was heavily infiltrated with polymorphonuclear cells and bacteria.

The clinical presentation of acute pericarditis is one of constant chest pain of sudden onset, which worsens on deep inspiration. Pain often lessens when the patient is sitting or leaning forward, because that posture lowers the tension on the pericardium. In 50% of patients, however, chest pain is minor or absent. On auscultation, a scratchy sound called a **friction rub** can be heard in systole and diastole as surfaces roughened by the deposition of fibrin from the exudate move over one another. If a large volume of fluid is present, heart sounds are diminished. An electrocardiogram and echocardiogram are needed for a definitive diagnosis of acute pericarditis. (In echocardiography, also called cardiac ultrasonography, ultrasound is used to image heart structure and study structure and blood flow patterns durby a complete recovery. In some cases, however, there can be scattered necrosis of myocardial cells or even heart failure due to extreme weakening of the heart muscle or faulty valve function. The causative agent may be viruses, bacteria, protozoa, parasites, hypersensitivity reactions, trauma, or that diagnostic blind alley, unknown (idiopathic myocarditis).

Viral myocarditis is the most common form, more often affecting infants and young men. Sometimes common exposure in very close living or working environments, e.g., army barracks, has been implicated. Viral forms also are more likely to be restricted to the heart. The Coxsackie B virus is most often implicated and often there is an associated pericarditis. Changes in the myocardium typically include both fluid exudate and a cellular infiltration. Among otherwise healthy adults, the viral disease is usually mild, with some pericardial pain, weakness, and fatigue. Debilitated or immune-suppressed patients can experience much more serious symptoms and even acute cardiac failure. Fetuses and newborns are also more vulnerable to the effects of viral myocarditis.

The clinical course of myocarditis can be extremely variable. Transient ECG abnormalities may be the only objective sign. Symptoms might include malaise, dyspnea (difficult breathing), low-grade fever, and tachycardia (elevated heart rate). The weakened muscle and fibrous skeleton can allow the AV valve orifices to stretch, a condition leading to mitral or tricuspid valve malfunctions. In most cases, signs and symptoms take one to two months to resolve. In some cases, the problem persists to cause chronic heart failure. Less often, acute heart failure is involved. A chronic form of myocarditis called **Chagas's disease** afflicts up to 30% of the population in certain areas of South America and South Africa.

Endocardial Disease: Infective Endocarditis

Untreated **infective endocarditis** (IE) is almost invariably fatal. Even with aggressive and appropriate antibiotic therapy, it still has a mortality range of 30–35%. Bacteria are the most usual infective agents involved in IE, so the disease is sometimes called **bacterial endocarditis.** The more inclusive term, infective endocarditis, is preferable because fungi and rickettsiae are also infective agents that are known to cause endocarditis.

There are two clinically distinct patterns of this disease, **subacute** and **acute infective endocarditis,** and one major difference between them is their response to treatment. Subacute IE has a current mortality rate of 5–10%, while that for acute IE runs in the range of 60–80%! The usual cause of death in both is acute or chronic heart failure.

In both subacute and acute IE, the basic lesion is the build-up of a large, easily fragmented infective mass called a **vegetation. 15** This is essentially a thrombus of tangled fibrin, platelets, and blood cell debris containing masses of

Figure 10.13   The vegetations on the surface of these valve cusps arose as a result of an infective endocarditis. *Exploratory abdominal surgery was performed on a 72-year-old woman who had chest pains, but no ECG confirmation of infarction. The suspicion was that chronic inflammation of the gall bladder (cholecystitis) might be involved, and the surgery indeed found an enlarged, thick-walled gall bladder, which was removed. Her postoperative course was plagued by a variety of severe complications, including dehiscence, arterial obstruction necessitating a leg amputation, and finally, by heart failure, to which she succumbed.*

At autopsy her left heart was found to have been damaged by an infective endocarditis. In the specimen small, crumbly vegetations can be seen. The valve cusps are thickened, as are the chordae tendineae. Microscopic study of the vegetations revealed them to be composed of fibrin, platelets, bacterial masses, and inflammatory cells.

bacteria or other microorganisms (fig. 10.13). Especially in acute IE, the bacteria can be effectively isolated in the core of this mass, thus being sheltered from the body's immune system or antibiotics. Vegetations can be as large as several centimeters in diameter, loosely attached, and single or multiple. They usually form at the margins of the affected valve leaflets (the mitral or aortic valve alone, in 80–90% of cases). Valvular infection, especially in acute IE, can cause erosion of the valve leaflet or associated chordae tendineae. This condition leads to impaired valve function and to the major cause of death, heart failure. Vegetations have a tendency to break up, seeding the blood with infective and potentially occlusive emboli. Embolization is more extensive in acute IE, producing petechiae, abscesses, and infarcts. The kidneys are particularly affected, but significant embolic infarction of the brain or heart can also take place.

In **acute infective endocarditis,** a classic pattern of signs and symptoms aids diagnosis. The cardinal signs are a changing heart murmur, high fever, shaking chills, splinter hemorrhages (petechiae visible beneath the fingernails), splenomegaly, anemia, and hematuria (blood in the urine). Preexisting heart disease is uncommon and the patient often has a preexisting infection. The infective agent is *Staphylococcus aureus* (a particularly virulent and antibiotic-resistant bacterium) in 50% of cases and *Streptococcus* in an additional 35%.

A bacterial infection of the valves appears to develop initially, and this is followed by thrombus formation. The course of the disease is rapid. If untreated, death can occur in two weeks, either from embolism as the loose thrombotic vegetations break up, or from heart failure secondary to mitral or aortic valve dysfunction. **16** Infection and embolic infarction of the kidney contribute to anemia by interfering with renal erythropoietin production and by allowing blood loss to the urine.

Intravenous drug use carries a risk of many infections, including acute IE. In over half of these cases the pattern of vegetation formation is quite unusual: the tricuspid valves alone are affected. Athletes who take injections of psychoactive drugs or performance-enhancing drugs comprise another growing population of people at risk of developing acute IE.

Typically, the person who develops **subacute infective endocarditis** has a preexisting heart condition (e.g., rheumatic heart disease, congenital defect, valve replacement). **17** A significant number of cases develop after cardiac surgery, particularly in valve replacements. In such cases, prophylactic antibacterial treatment can result in growth of a resistant fungus (e.g., *Candida*), which then becomes the infective agent. Apparently the blood-borne organisms colonize tiny preexisting thrombi that have developed in areas of turbulence or back eddies in the abnormal heart. Because of this vulnerability, patients with previous cardiac disease are often given prophylactic antibiotic treatment before they undergo procedures that may introduce organisms into the blood. The disease develops slowly (three to six months), often with vague symptoms: low-grade fever, anemia, debilitation, or perhaps only malaise. The spleen is often enlarged, and characteristic hemorrhages of the nailbeds may be observed.

In subacute IE, vegetations develop slowly and are not as damaging to the valves as in acute IE, although some may occur. In the 5–10% of patients who die of subacute IE, death results from chronic heart failure, unless the chordae tendineae rupture or emboli cause myocardial infarction.

Valvular Disease

Valvular diseases of the heart have many causes, but from a functional viewpoint, there are two basic types of malfunction. One is **valvular stenosis,** a narrowing of the valve so that forward flow of blood is restricted. The second is **valvular incompetence** or **insufficiency.** In this case, the valve is unable to close fully, so there is some regurgitation of blood in the backward direction.

It is not uncommon for more than one valve to be affected and for a valve to exhibit both stenosis and insufficiency at the same time. The aortic and mitral valves, subjected to much higher pressure gradients, are more frequently involved than the tricuspid and pulmonary valves.

Valvular Stenosis

When any valve fails to open effectively or is obstructed, blood accumulates in the upstream chambers and vessels. This accumulation is called **congestion** and it causes hypertension in the affected vessels. Downstream hypotension is often absent, since compensatory mechanisms maintain an adequate arterial blood pressure. Blood tends to jet through the narrow valve orifice and the resulting turbulence causes abnormal cardiac sounds called **heart murmurs.** These are often the first diagnostic clue to valve disease. Common causes of stenosis are rheumatic heart disease, infective endocarditis, congenital malformation, calcification of the valve cusps, or an extravalvular obstruction, e.g., a tumor or aneurysm.

Mitral Stenosis The most common of all valve diseases, **mitral stenosis** is frequently found in association with other valve disorders. **18** It is typically the result of rheumatic heart disease (described in the next section). Adhesion and stiffening of the valve cusps, accompanied by calcification and distortion of the scar tissue formed, all combine to impair filling of the left ventricle (fig. 10.14). The left atrium dilates and hypertrophies, and chronic heart failure may result. Cyanosis and fatigue will occur when the stenosis is severe and compensation cannot sustain downstream pressure and blood flow. (In **cyanosis,** the skin takes on a blue tinge that is due to insufficient oxygen saturation of the blood's hemoglobin.) Enlargement of the left atrium results in characteristic electrocardiogram and sometimes atrial fibrillation. Impaired swallowing (dysphagia) occurs when the enlarged atrium compresses the esophagus, which lies immediately behind it. Mitral stenosis produces a diastolic murmur, and the stiff valve opens with a snapping sound. In advanced disease, right heart failure can ensue and the cardiac output will be reduced and unable to meet varied demands. Surgical valve replacement is often necessary.

Aortic Stenosis Another common valve disorder, **aortic stenosis,** is usually due to either valve damage or obstruction caused by atherosclerosis, rheumatic scarring of the valve cusps, or calcification of a congenitally malformed valve. **19**

16 3293   **17** 3626   **18** 46251   **19** 6797

Figure 10.14   This mitral valve restricts blood flow between atrium and ventricle because the aperture is narrowed and the thickened valve cusps cannot fully open. The term "fish mouth" is often used to describe the shape of the narrowed valve opening. *This mitral valve shows severe stenosis, probably as a result of an early bout of rheumatic fever. The flow tract to the left ventricle is substantially narrowed, leaving only the small "fish mouth" opening. The restricted blood flow ultimately produced a chronic pattern of heart failure.*

The specimen was obtained after the death of a 62-year-old woman who had suffered dyspnea and a long period of declining cardiac function. Her heart was also found to be enlarged, as was her liver, from having to cope with the extra pumping demands placed on it by the stenotic mitral valve. She had previously had carcinoma of the breast and a mastectomy, but there was no indication that the tumor had contributed to her death.

The increased resistance to ventricular emptying (a greater afterload) seen in aortic stenosis results in left ventricular **dilatation** and **hypertrophy.** Since aortic stenosis is usually progressive, the left ventricle ultimately fails. The myocardial hypertrophy is necessary to overcome the resistance offered by the narrowed valve, but it makes the heart susceptible to ischemic injury and angina by increasing its workload and oxygen demand. Dizziness, **syncope** (fainting), fatigue, and skin pallor all reflect the decline in cardiac output. The pulse pressure is also reduced. Since, at least early in the disease, left ventricular hypertrophy can compensate for the stenosis, backup of blood into the lungs and pulmonary congestion are observed only when the condition is quite severe. Auscultation reveals a systolic murmur from blood jetting through the constriction as the ventricle contracts.

Tricuspid and Pulmonary Stenosis Right-sided valve disorders are uncommon, particularly alone. Tricuspid and pulmonary stenosis both produce symptoms of right heart failure, which is due to the loads imposed on it when it tries to pump through narrowed valves. The heart sounds resemble those of the corresponding valve disorder on the left side but vary in location and intensity.

Table 10.1	Conditions Causing, or Associated with, Cardiac Valvular Insufficiency (Regurgitation)

Rheumatic heart disease
Idiopathic hypertrophic subortic stenosis (see section on cardiomyopathy)
Myocardial infarction
   Postinfarction fibrosis
   With rupture of papillary muscle (cuspid valves)
Ruptured chordae tendineae
Congenital cardiac defects
Ventricular aneurysm
Pulmonary or systemic hypertension (semilunar valves)
Idiopathic calcification of mitral valve annulus
Infective endocarditis
Systemic lupus erythematosus
Rheumatoid arthritis
Ankylosing spondylitis

Valvular Insufficiency/Incompetence

In these disorders the valve fails to prevent reverse flow, and a portion of the ejected blood leaks back (regurgitates) into the upstream chamber. Typically, 40–50% of the ejected volume regurgitates, but in severe cases the proportion can reach 80–90%. Since the stroke volume of the ventricle can increase by an amount that approximates the volume regurgitated, the cardiac output is maintained. However, if the condition progresses, the heart is, at some point, overloaded by the excess volume that can't be cleared from it. The ventricle will then dilate without a significant increase in wall thickness. Ultimately, signs of dilatation and ventricular failure become evident, but the disease may go undiagnosed for many years. Some common causes of valvular insufficiency are presented in table 10.1.

Mitral Insufficiency Eversion of damaged mitral valve cusps is frequently the reason for mitral insufficiency. The eversion may be due to rupture of the papillary muscle following a left ventricular infarct, or to rupture of the chordae tendineae in rheumatic heart disease or bacterial endocarditis. **20** The eversion means that the valve cusp can fold back, allowing reverse flow into the atrium. Valve closure may also be impaired when scar tissue formation and contraction thickens, distorts, and misaligns the valve cusps or shortens the chordae tendineae. Blood flows back into the left atrium during ventricular contraction and the resulting turbulence is heard as a systolic murmur.

A surprising 5–10% of adults have an abnormality of one or both valve cusps and associated chordae tendineae that allows the mitral valve to prolapse into the atrium (floppy valve syndrome). This usually produces only interesting auscultatory sounds, but can, on occasion, give rise to serious insufficiency and other problems.

With mitral insufficiency, the atrium fills with blood normally returning from the lungs but also with blood regurgitating from the ventricle. The result is an increased pressure in the atrium, which backs up into the lungs to produce congestion, pulmonary hypertension, and an array of related lung signs. The increased atrial pressure also causes the atrium to dilate, as it is chronically stretched by the increased volumes that it can't adequately eject. The stroke volume increases so that the volume of blood ejected into the aorta is close to normal. The electrocardiogram usually indicates evidence of left ventricular hypertrophy, atrial enlargement, and arrhythmia.

Aortic Insufficiency Perforated valve cusps, which may result from infection or inflammation, and impairment of valve closure by scar tissue are two major causes of aortic insufficiency. **21** Blood regurgitates into the ventricle during diastole, sometimes causing the mitral valve or septal wall to quiver. A diastolic murmur is heard, and the rapidly falling aortic pressure is responsible for a strong, bounding pulse that reflects an increased pulse pressure. Syncope, dizziness, pounding headaches, weakness, and fatigue are common symptoms of the altered hemodynamics in aortic insufficiency, along with the typical signs and symptoms of left heart failure.

Tricuspid and Pulmonary Insufficiency Like stenosis, insufficiency of valves of the right heart is relatively infrequent, except in combination with other valve defects. **22** Isolated tricuspid or pulmonary valve disorders are usually the result of congenital malformation, although they may also be due to the infective endocarditis that occurs in intravenous drug users.

As is the situation with the corresponding left heart valves, tricuspid insufficiency and pulmonary stenosis are characterized by systolic murmurs; tricuspid stenosis and pulmonary insufficiency produce diastolic murmurs. All produce the characteristic symptoms of right heart failure. Ironically, failure of both right and left heart together diminishes the severity of pulmonary edema, since blood does not accumulate in the pulmonary vasculature.

Rheumatic Heart Disease

Rheumatic heart disease (RHD) is a potential complication of a more generalized condition called **rheumatic fever** (RF). This is an inflammatory disease that affects a variety of tissues in widespread sites in the body. Painful joints are the major complaint in probably three-quarters of the patients, but the heart, skin, serosa, blood vessels, and lungs can commonly be affected. The majority (90%) of patients have their first attack of RF when they are young (5–15 years). Boys and girls are equally affected. The great majority have suffered a streptococcal pharyngitis ("strep throat") one to four weeks before the emergence of rheumatic fever. In the heart, the focus of its effects can be the pericardial sac, the myocardium, the endocardium, the valves, or all four. Impairment of cardiac function can be acute, but the most typical pattern involves valvular damage that can ultimately lead to congestive heart failure and death.

The name rheumatic fever is derived from the joint pain that often accompanies the disease. The term **rheumatism** was formerly applied to various conditions involving painful joints, but with increased awareness of their etiology and pathogenesis, the older, more general term has been replaced by specific names that differentiate particular diseases. Degenerative joint disease and ankylosing spondylitis are examples of current terms describing conditions that might previously been known as rheumatism.

The symptoms of rheumatic fever may be sudden and intense, with fever, sore or swollen joints, and tachycardia, or they may be mild, with low-grade fever and malaise. Diagnosis can be challenging, since none of the clinical or laboratory features are specific to rheumatic fever. The diagnostic criteria for RF are presented in table 10.2.

Etiology and Pathogenesis

Although certain features of the etiology of RF are clear at this point, the underlying pathological mechanisms are still in question. Only a small proportion of those who have pharyngitis due to infection with any strain of group A beta-hemolytic streptococci will go on to develop RF. The antibodies produced to streptococcal antigens have an affinity for a wide variety of body tissues, including joint connective tissue and tissues of the heart. In certain individuals this autoimmune cross-reaction progresses dramatically. It is triggered by the streptococcal infection but then becomes self-perpetrating. At this point, the signs and symptoms of rheumatic fever emerge. Once an acute case of RF has occurred, subsequent streptococcal infections are quite likely to stimulate further bouts of RF. Treatment of the acute rheumatic fever is based on penicillin, to eliminate the infecting bacteria, and anti-inflammatory agents, principally aspirin or corticosteroids (e.g., prednisone).

The chain of events in the pathogenesis of RF probably involves binding of antibodies to body tissues, which triggers damaging responses. Damaged cells may release histamine and activate kinins, triggering an inflammatory response that promotes the arrival of more macrophages and neutrophils. These cells, and perhaps T lymphocytes, produce further damage, activate complement, and produce fever.

Rheumatic heart disease arises when the cardiac effects of RF threaten to become serious. The heart is affected in about one-third of initial attacks of RF. In younger patients, there is more likelihood of cardiac involvement. Although

Table 10.2   The Jones Criteria for Diagnosis of RF. These Criteria Are Commonly Employed in Combination, because Isolated Signs or Symptoms Might Also Arise in a Variety of Other Conditions. The Presence of Two Major Criteria, or of One Major and Two Minor Criteria, Together with Evidence of an Earlier Streptococcal Infection, Is Taken as Highly Suggestive of RF.

Major Criteria
    Carditis (as indicated by cardiac indicators, e.g., congestive heart failure, cardiomegaly, heart murmurs, pericarditis)
    Chorea (central nervous system disorder involving muscle weakness, motor and emotional disorders)
    Erythema marginatum (a characteristic skin rash)
    Polyarthritis
    Skin nodules
Minor Criteria
    Characteristic ECG changes
    Joint pain
    Previous RF or rheumatic heart disease (often indicated by *Streptococcus*-related antibodies)
    Pyrexia (fever)
    Nosebleeds

the transient symptoms associated with other sites can be troublesome, when the heart is implicated severe damage can occur, particularly to the valves.

In acute RHD, the valves become red, thickened, and swollen. On the leaflet surfaces directly exposed to forward blood flow, especially where they meet in closure, tiny (1–2 mm) wartlike vegetations form. These **verrucae** might develop through erosion of the soft, inflamed endocardial surface (fig. 10.13). The subsequent organization of the sites of inflammatory damage can produce valvular stenosis or incompetence, or both (fig. 10.14). The mitral valve is almost always involved and is the sole site of serious lesion in 50% of cases. This stenosis impedes the flow of blood from the atrium and generates a characteristic heart murmur, as well as producing congestion in the lungs and right heart that can progress to chronic heart failure. On the other hand, the valvular damage can result in incompetence, with regurgitation into the atrium. In this case, assuming mitral damage, the left ventricle hypertrophies in compensation for the lowered efficiency of pumping. As noted, the mitral valve, perhaps because of greater wear and tear, is almost always involved.

In about 50% of cases, the aortic semilunar valve is also damaged. Extensive involvement of other valves is less common. Damage to valves and the chordae tendineae, as well as thrombosis in enlarged atria, embolism, and pulmonary complications may all play a part in the emerging picture of chronic heart failure, the most usual cause of death in RHD. The pathogenesis of RHD is presented in figure 10.15.

Effective antibiotic treatment of streptococcal infections has cut the incidence of rheumatic fever and heart disease by about 70% in the last 50 years, by cutting short this

Aschoff Bodies and RHD

Microscopic examination of affected heart tissue during the active inflammatory phase of RF reveals the presence of **Aschoff bodies.** 23 These consist of a central area of fibrinous material—swollen collagen fibrils, perhaps fibrin and plasma proteins—surrounded by a rim of macrophages and large multinucleated cells called **Aschoff cells.** The presence of Aschoff bodies is diagnostic for RHD. It should be noted that these lesions are sterile; most researchers believe that the heart itself is not attacked by the streptococci.

disruption of healthy immunological response. However, in the Third World RHD is still a major health problem, accounting for 25–40% of all heart disease.

Ischemic Heart Disease

Coronary Artery Disease (CAD)

Coronary artery disease (CAD), also called **atherosclerotic heart disease** (ASHD), is the result of progressive narrowing of the coronary arteries by atherosclerosis. This is the condition, described in chapter 9, that is confined to the aorta and its major branches, including the coronary arteries. Development of atheromatous plaque in the principal coronary vessels obstructs their lumina, resulting in ischemia, chest pain, arrhythmias, and myocardial weak-

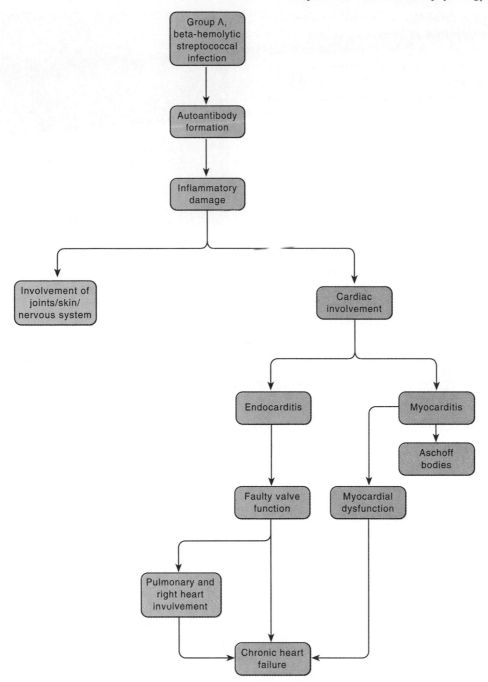

Figure 10.15   Pathogenesis of rheumatic heart disease (RHD). Initial signs and symptoms of rheumatic fever in the joints, skin, and nervous system may, over time, evolve to the more serious RHD.

ness. When the obstruction is prolonged and severe, cardiac output falls and heart failure follows. The atheroma is a common site for thrombosis, which is often responsible for sudden occlusion of the coronary vessels and acute myocardial infarction. The resulting ischemic injury affects the tissue at any sites supplied by the obstructed coronary vessels.

Current strategies for CAD treatment are designed to arrest the atherosclerotic process, reestablish myocardial flow, control symptoms, and reduce cardiac workload and oxygen requirements.

Ischemic Heart Disease

Ischemic injury of the heart is the most common cause of heart disease and the major cause of death in developed countries. Sudden or progressive loss of coronary blood flow is almost always due to atherosclerosis of the coronary arteries and its complications. Ischemia may be gradual or sudden in onset, depending on the nature of the arterial obstruction.

Acute ischemia is caused most commonly by coronary thrombosis superimposed on an atherosclerotic plaque. The vessel is rapidly occluded, and the myocardial cells supplied by it suffer hypoxic injury and undergo necrosis to produce **myocardial infarction** (MI) (fig. 10.16). **24** The severity of injury depends on the size and location of the infarct and the collateral circulation. The consequences of myocardial infarction are serious. Twenty percent of victims die before they reach hospital, and another 10% die of chronic heart failure or other complications in the following days or weeks.

Chronic ischemia occurs when atherosclerosis and perhaps small, nonocclusive thrombi cause slow but progressive narrowing of the arterial lumen. Gradual narrowing allows time for the myocardial cells to adapt partially to hypoxia and for anastomoses (alternative supply routes) to develop from vessels adjacent to the region of hypoxia. With continued occlusion, however, necrosis occurs and damaged cells are replaced by fibrous tissue, **25** making the myocardium weaker and less extensible. The consequences of chronic ischemia are angina pectoris (see the following discussion) and a gradual decline in cardiac output, which, without correction, can progress to chronic heart failure.

Elements of Ischemic Heart Disease (IHD)

There are three distinct elements of ischemic disease in the myocardium: angina pectoris, sudden cardiac death, and myocardial infarction (fig. 10.17). IHD can also present as chronic ischemic heart disease, to be considered later.

Angina Pectoris Angina pectoris is chest pain arising from transient myocardial ischemia. The pattern is similar to that experienced in myocardial infarction, although less intense. It is typically experienced as substernal or precordial pain (the **precordium** is the chest wall overlying the heart), often radiating to the left axilla, arm, shoulder, or jaw, and lasting several minutes (fig. 10.18). Radiation to the right side of the body is not unusual. There are three subsets of this general condition. **Typical angina pectoris** occurs when there is an increased demand on a poorly oxygenated myocardium, for example when stress accelerates heart rate, when increased workload is attempted, or when blood pressure rises and increases the left heart's afterload. Relaxation, rest, and vasodilation therapy relieve this form of chest pain. Often the term angina pectoris (angina is from the Greek word for choking) is shortened to angina, but it is important to establish the context before using the shortened form because there are other applications of the term. For example, sore throat may be called **acute angina,** and abdominal pain, **angina abdominis.**

Prinzmetal's variant angina is caused by coronary arterial spasm in atherosclerotic arteries and occurs without regard to the immediate workload on the myocardium. Vasodilators have no beneficial effect on these attacks,

Figure 10.16 This section through the ventricular myocardium shows the darkened region of necrosis caused by an occluded coronary artery, which has led to an acute myocardial infarction. *Two days after being driven to the emergency room by his wife, a 60-year-old male died of an acute MI. He had experienced chest pain that radiated to his left arm. He was dyspneic and anxious after being admitted. His pulse was weak and rapid and his skin was cold and "clammy."*

Autopsy findings confirmed severe coronary atherosclerosis and a massive, recent MI. In the photograph, the darkened, mottled region of the infarct shows the involvement of the left ventricle and interventricular septum. The infarction also affected the pericardium, producing an acute pericarditis.

which often occur while the person is at rest. **Unstable angina** is angina that progresses relatively rapidly. Frequency and duration of pain can both increase, and there may be direct progression to acute myocardial infarction. Like Prinzmetal's variant angina, it may occur at rest but is variable in its response to vasodilators.

Sudden Cardiac Death This condition is responsible for over half of all deaths due to IHD. Typically, the victim suffers a fatal arrhythmia produced by myocardial ischemia. The difference between this condition and myocardial infarction is that we can't assume that there has been any tissue infarction. There may well be post-mortem evidence of atherosclerosis, some degeneration of the myocardium, or some previous MI. In sudden cardiac death, the event inducing the ischemia that triggers the arrhythmia could be vasospasm, occlusion of a coronary vessel by rapid platelet aggregation and thrombosis, or increased exertion. For many, sudden cardiac death is the first indicator of IHD.

Acute Myocardial Infarction Sudden myocardial ischemia and infarction is accompanied by severe chest pain, described as an intense, crushing substernal or precordial pain, often radiating to the left shoulder, arm, or jaw, accompanied by sweating, breathlessness, and anxiety. Although similar to the pain of angina in its location, it is not relieved by rest or vasodilators.

Figure 10.17   Elements of ischemic heart disease.

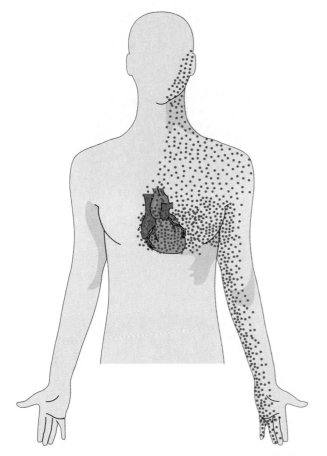

Figure 10.18   Angina pectoris. The pain is usually reported over the chest, with variable patterns of radiation to the arm, shoulder, and jaw.

Nausea and vomiting may also occur, along with characteristic indicators of a falling cardiac output. A history of angina is common. An electrocardiogram is often the first diagnostic procedure to yield results, permitting an assessment of the location and severity of the infarct and the

---

The Pain of MI

The oppressive, crushing nature of the pain associated with myocardial ischemia and infarction is a distinctive characteristic. It is often described as feeling that steel bands are tightening around the chest. The diffuse nature of the pain of angina or MI makes it easily distinguishable from the more focal pain of a pulled chest muscle, for example. A rule of thumb is that if the patient can point to the spot that hurts, it isn't angina or an MI.

---

nature of any arrhythmia that develops. After admission to hospital, continuous ECG monitoring is essential because life-threatening arrhythmias may occur at any time in the first few days after infarction. Serum enzyme assay is used to assess cellular injury. **Creatine kinase** (CK), formerly known as creatine phosphokinase (CPK), and **lactic dehydrogenase** (LDH) are both released from injured muscle. In the absence of further infarction, CK peaks in about 24 hours and LDH in 48–72 hours after injury. Neither enzyme is specific for myocardial damage, but their elevation in the presence of other cardiac signs and symptoms, without evidence of other muscle damage, can be presumed to indicate an MI. Only a more precise assessment of the plasma to determine the presence of **CK-MB** and **LDH1** can be definitive, in that these **isoenzymes** (enzyme subtypes) are specific to cardiac muscle.

Sequelae of Acute MI

If the patient survives the initial attack, damaged muscle is destroyed and replaced by scar tissue. The healing phase is fraught with hazards that can complicate recovery and threaten the patient's life.

Arrhythmias The most serious arrhythmia is **ventricular fibrillation.** It is usually fatal, since it can be eliminated only with specialized procedures and equipment. Fibrillation involves complete lack of synchronization in the contraction of the myocardial fibers. The myocardial cells are active, but they produce only quivering instead of forceful rhythmic contractions. In this situation, pumping stops and cardiac output fails. Unless a defibrillation procedure is successful within minutes, brain cells will be irreversibly damaged by anoxia. **Defibrillation** involves delivering an electric shock to the wildly contracting myocardium. The intent is to depolarize all of the myocardial cells momentarily. This change may allow a normal sinus rhythm to be reestablished and normal pumping to be restored. Ventricular fibrillation and other less severe dysrythmias are typically controlled and prevented with antiarrhythmic drugs.

Cardiogenic Shock Cardiogenic shock (see chapter 12) is the consequence of large infarcts and severe dysrhythmias that decrease cardiac output below the level required to perfuse the tissues adequately. Tissues vulnerable to hypoxia are compromised, and compensatory mechanisms may provide additional stress.

Thrombosis Thrombosis is triggered by activating factors released from injured myocardial tissues. Thrombi may form in the heart over the site of injury or where blood pools in weakly contracting chambers. **26** With cardiac output reduced by injury and the patient's immobility, venous stasis and thrombosis occur. Thrombi in the contracting heart and veins of newly ambulatory patients are prone to the production of emboli.

Rupture The necrotic myocardium of the infarct is slowly cleared by phagocytic cells prior to the formation of scar tissue. Typically, around 7–10 days after an infarct occurs, the dead muscle gradually softens (**myomalacia cordis**) and the wall is susceptible to rupture. An infarct of the ventricular wall tends to cause **ventricular aneurysm 27** (fig. 10.19), rupture of which causes blood to fill the pericardial sac. Compression caused by pressure from the distended sac (tamponade) impedes filling of the ventricle, and death ensues (fig. 10.20). Infarction of the interventricular septum may lead to rupture into the right ventricle; combined ventricular failure then rapidly develops. In the region of the papillary muscles of the left ventricle, infarction may lead to separation of the muscle from the ventricular wall. The muscle, attached by chordae tendineae to the AV valve, flails about in the left atrium and ventricle, producing sudden and severe mitral insufficiency. Left heart failure follows, and without rapid surgical intervention, the patient dies.

Figure 10.19 This section through the heart shows a prominently bulging ventricular aneurysm. Note the thinness of the myocardium, which raises the risk that the aneurysm will rupture.

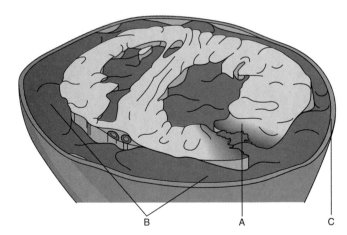

Figure 10.20 In this diagram, the pericardial space is filled with coagulated blood from a ventricular rupture. The external pressure increase compresses the heart, restricting its ability to fill adequately during diastole.

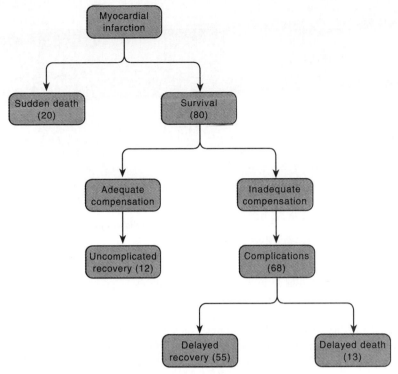

Figure 10.21   The prognosis for a representative 100 myocardial infarction patients.

Prognosis in Myocardial Infarction The serious nature of MI can be seen in the fact that only 10% of those affected experience uncomplicated recovery. The situation shows signs of improving, however, as better means of postinfarction management are developed. These are based on carefully regulated exercise programs that can increase myocardial capabilities to meet and even exceed preinfarction performance. Also, drugs can be administered immediately post-MI to limit reperfusion injury. Acute MI is suddenly fatal in over 20% of cases, usually from massive myocardial destruction or severe arrhythmia. Here too there is improvement in prognosis as cardiopulmonary resuscitation (CPR) skills are increasingly developed in medical personnel and in the general population.

Of those in whom MI is not immediately fatal, 15% will die later from related problems such as arrhythmias, myocardial rupture, or thromboembolism. Thrombosis is, of course, favored by both the reduced cardiac output of the weakened heart, which causes reduced blood flow rates, and lack of mobility in the patient recovering from the MI. In well over half of MI cases, neither fatality nor uncomplicated recovery occurs. In these cases, some factor arising out of the initial infarction event weakens the heart. It can still maintain a cardiac output adequate for survival, but undesirable chronic effects develop as well. These progress over a period of months or even years until ultimately the heart fails to maintain a minimal output. A variety of physiological compensations are brought to bear, but they may further complicate the situation rather than resolving it (fig. 10.21). This type of chronic heart failure is called congestive heart failure and is the focus of the next section.

CONGESTIVE HEART FAILURE

Ischemic heart disease is only one of many heart, respiratory, or vascular diseases that can create circulation demands that outpace the heart's ability to respond. In such circumstances, the heart and cardiovascular system can be pushed into a state of progressively decreasing capacity called **chronic heart failure.** In this slowly developing condition, cardiac output is unable to respond adequately to tissue demands.

There are four broad consequences of chronic cardiac failure. One is the backup of blood in the vessels upstream from the heart because the heart can't maintain forward blood flow. This excess of blood in the upstream vessels is called **congestion.** It in turn causes hypertension and edema in the congested tissues (fig. 10.22). Indeed, since congestion is the classic sign of the chronically failing heart, the condition is more typically known as **congestive heart failure** (CHF). The second consequence of longer-term cardiac failure is the activation of an array of circulatory compensations that normally maintain adequate blood flow to the

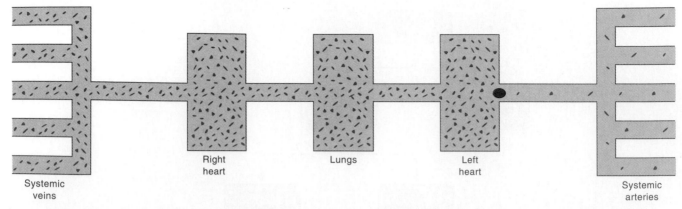

Figure 10.22   Schematic representation of the relationship between the heart's two pumps and the lungs. In this example, a damaged aortic valve (•) produces congestion upstream from its position at the entrance to the systemic circulation. Downstream flow may be reduced if compensations are inadequate.

tissues. Some of the characteristic signs and symptoms in CHF derive from these compensations, e.g., a rapid pulse rate. Third, when physiological mechanisms are unable to compensate, cardiac output declines. As a result, systemic hypoxia may produce a generalized weakness and tendency to fatigue. In severe cases, cyanosis may be present. Generally, although cardiac output may be adequate at rest, demand for increases in cardiac output cannot be fully met. A fourth consequence, reached when cardiac output is ultimately unable to supply the major organ systems adequately, is death.

Etiology of Congestive Heart Failure

The chronic inability to pump its preload may be the result of the heart's reduced pumping capability or of increased afterload. In the first case the fault may lie in the myocardium itself or in certain physical factors that interfere with pumping. These etiological factors in CHF are considered in the following sections.

Myocardial Weakness

Most commonly, the myocardium is weakened by ischemia related to atherosclerosis (AS) and its stenosis of the coronary arteries. **28** When stenosis reaches 50–70%, only resting myocardial oxygen demand can be met. As AS progresses, myocardial fibers undergo hypoxic injury and necrosis. They are replaced by fibrous connective tissue, causing a steady deterioration in myocardial pumping capacity.

Another cause of myocardial ischemia is thrombosis in the coronary arteries. The roughened endothelium lying over an atherosclerotic plaque may induce thrombus formation, further reducing blood flow and damaging the myocardium. Recent studies have also shown that subsequent to platelet adhesion at endothelial surfaces, a

sequence of chemical activations triggers constriction of the coronary vessels. This vasospasm is thought to be a factor in patients who develop MI, yet who have little atherosclerotic involvement of their coronary vessels.

In addition to weakness caused by ischemia, the myocardium may be directly affected by other factors, e.g., myocarditis or the cardiomyopathies described in a later section of this chapter.

Restrictions to Pumping

Even when the myocardium is undamaged and adequately supplied with oxygen, the heart may be unable to cope with its preload because of physical factors that restrict its pumping. Cardiac valve malfunction is one such factor. As we described earlier in this chapter, incompetent valves, which cannot tightly close, will allow backward flow in the heart or pulmonary circulation. When valves are unable to open widely, reduced blood flow through the heart may cause cardiac output to fall.

Internal obstructions may interfere with the free flow of blood through the heart. These may arise as a result of inborn malformations of the cardiac flow tracts or vessels. Such congenital malformations are described in more detail in a separate section to follow. Another internal obstruction might be a mass (e.g., a thrombus or tumor) present within a cardiac chamber. By occupying a portion of a chamber's volume, this mass reduces the chamber's blood capacity, in addition to interfering with the free flow of blood through the chamber. The most common cardiac tumor is myxoma, a connective tissue tumor usually found in the left atrium, but occurring less often in the other chambers. This may form on a slender stalk (a pedunculated myxoma), **29** allowing it to move to and fro within a chamber with changes in blood movements, often moving in and out of a valve orifice to obstruct blood flow or damage valve structures (fig. 10.23).

Figure 10.23   In this diagram, the atrial tumor is positioned to act like a ball valve. The normal movement of blood causes it to move on its stalk to block flow to the ventricle. Blockage is also favored by atrial contraction, which moves the tumor toward the ventricle.

Pumping may also be restricted by cardiac dysrhythmias. In such cases, ischemia, infarction, or other factors may initially interfere with the cardiac conduction system. Alternatively, electrolyte imbalances or chemical toxins can alter the myocardium's electrical stability. Whatever the cause, the resulting rate and/or rhythm abnormalities can seriously compromise cardiac output.

The pericardium is also a potential source of restriction to cardiac pumping. As we described earlier, changes to the pericardial surfaces involving fibrin deposition **30** or adhesions can severely limit cardiac activity. Also, the accumulation of fluid, be it a pericardial effusion, or blood, can produce significant external pressures (cardiac tamponade) that compromise cardiac filling (fig. 10.20). The factors that can restrict cardiac pumping are presented in table 10.3.

Increased Afterload

An inability to maintain cardiac output may also result from overload. When the myocardium is constantly exposed to high physical demand, the strain may ultimately overwhelm it, with the result that contractility and stroke volume steadily decline. This decline is seen most commonly when cardiac afterload is increased. The right ventricle faces such a situation in certain lung diseases where

Table 10.3	Causes of Restriction to Cardiac Pumping

Valve defects
  Stenosis
  Regurgitation
Congenital malformations
Obstructing mass
  Tumor
  Thrombus
Dysrhythmia
Pericarditis
  Chronic constrictive pericarditis
  Pericardial effusion
Cardiac tamponade

vascular damage causes pulmonary hypertension. (See the section on cor pulmonale, later in this chapter.) In systemic hypertension, chronically elevated blood pressure presents an increased resistance that the left ventricle must overcome to maintain adequate cardiac output. This is the case in essential hypertension as well as the hypertension associated with obesity. In the case of valve disease or congenital defects in the cardiac outflow tracts, valves, pulmonary trunk, or aorta, the ventricle's afterload may also be excessive.

Excessive cardiac workload may complicate preexisting CHF even when afterload is relatively low. This situation arises in high-demand states, where elevated tissue metabolism increases demand for blood flow via reflex cardiac stimulation. The resulting chronic increases in heart rate and contractility can progressively exhaust the already weakened myocardium, hastening its ultimate failure. One high-demand state that may contribute to CHF is chronic anemia, where even resting tissues are deprived of adequate oxygen delivery. Another is thyrotoxicosis, in which excessive thyroid secretion elevates systemic metabolism to levels requiring extraordinary blood supply. In such cases, cardiac output may be well above normal as the already failing heart labors to satisfy a chronic high demand for its output.

In summary, a variety of etiologies can produce a chronic and progressive decline in the heart's pumping capability. They affect the heart by weakening the myocardium either directly, as in the case of ischemia or infection, or indirectly by increasing afterload. On the other hand, internal obstructions or factors external to the heart may interfere with its contraction or rhythm. In either case, in the absence of intervention, the ability of the heart to respond to demands progressively declines until failure of the pump is complete (fig. 10.24).

Figure 10.24   Etiological factors in congestive heart failure.

Pathogenesis of Congestive Heart Failure

CHF presents an excellent demonstration of the relationship between a functional abnormality and its related pattern of signs and symptoms. In considering the pathogenesis of CHF, two factors are significant. One is the essential problem of the heart's inability to clear itself of the blood delivered to it. The second is the comparatively long time over which signs and symptoms develop. In the following analysis, mitral stenosis is used as an example of a condition that produces the characteristic signs and symptoms of CHF. These are weakness and fatigue, pulmonary congestion and edema, dyspnea, cardiomegaly, systemic congestion and edema, hepatomegaly, and splenomegaly.

Stenosis of the mitral valve is often the result of fibrosis and calcification. The hardened, thicker valve cusps can't fully open, and the flow tract between left atrium and left ventricle is reduced in size. Stenosis interferes with ventricular filling and causes a decline in stroke volume and cardiac output. As the stenosis increases, cardiac output may even fail to meet demand at rest. Weakness, quickness to fatigue, and fainting may result.

Upstream from the narrowed mitral valve, the effects are more extensively felt. Blood that can't easily clear the atrioventricular flow tract backs up into the right atrium and then into the lungs (fig. 10.22). This **pulmonary congestion** produces pulmonary hypertension, with pressures sometimes rising to three to five times normal. The high pressures cause an accumulation of fluid in the lung interstitium: **pulmonary edema** (fig. 10.25). **31** Edema causes

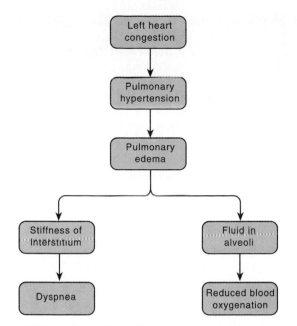

```
Left heart
congestion
    ↓
Pulmonary
hypertension
    ↓
Pulmonary
edema
   ↙     ↘
Stiffness of      Fluid in
interstitium      alveoli
    ↓              ↓
Dyspnea       Reduced blood
              oxygenation
```

Figure 10.25 The problem of pulmonary edema is an important aspect of chronic left heart failure.

(a)

(b)

Figure 10.26 Pulmonary congestion in CHF. (*a*) Normal alveoli. (*b*) Lung in CHF with fluid filling the alveoli. Numerous phagocytic cells are also present.

a stiffening of the lungs; they become firm and less elastic. As the condition progresses, higher pressures force fluid from the pulmonary tissues into alveolar air spaces (fig. 10.26). This process reduces the surface available for diffusion and leads to airway obstruction as fluid accumulates in the alveoli and bronchioles.

Both airway obstruction and the loss of normal lung elasticity contribute to another problem, difficulty of breathing, or **dyspnea.** Dyspnea in heart failure may be intensified when lying down. This condition is called **orthopnea,** and seems to result from an increased loading of the failing heart as the reclining position favors movement of blood from the legs and abdomen to the heart. The additional burden causes more pulmonary congestion, edema, and increased respiratory difficulty. Orthopnea is quickly relieved by elevating the head and shoulders. Severe bouts of dyspnea also often occur at night in CHF patients. However, this condition of **paroxysmal nocturnal dyspnea** is not quickly relieved by assuming an upright posture; as much as thirty minutes in an upright position may be required for breathing to become easier. Although the underlying mechanism is not well understood, it appears that partial depression of the brain's respiration and cardiac centers during sleep contributes to the problem.

In addition to breathing difficulties, pulmonary hypertension can cause aneurysms in small pulmonary vessels. These may rupture to yield small areas of hemorrhage in the lungs. Pulmonary hypertension and congestion predispose to secondary infection; bronchopneumonia is a common complication of CHF.

Further progression of CHF involves the backup of blood into the right heart (fig. 10.22). This means an increase in the right heart's preload—another burden that is added to the increased afterload presented by the elevated pressures in the pulmonary vessels. The right atrium responds, as does the similarly congested left atrium, with a hypertrophy response that increases their strength and enables them to compensate with an increased stroke volume. The result is an enlarged heart, the **cardiomegaly** that characterizes the chronically failing heart. **32** We will deal with another aspect of cardiomegaly, cardiac dilatation, in the section on myocardial compensations later in this chapter.

As right heart congestion develops, blood returning to it from systemic veins confronts a high resistance, and systemic venous congestion results. This is evident in

(a)   (b)

Figure 10.27   (*a*) The characteristic microscopic pattern of liver damage caused by hepatic congestion. It resembles a slice through a whole nutmeg (*b*), hence the descriptive term nutmeg liver. In (*a*), the dark regions represent islands of surviving cells at a distance from the congested vessels. The cells near the vessels are damaged and appear pale.

the swelling of the major superficial veins, especially the internal jugulars, that is often observed in CHF patients. Elevated systemic venous pressure is also reflected in increased capillary pressures, which causes systemic edema. As tissue fluid accumulates, it tends to percolate through the tissue spaces following the pull of gravity. It collects at low points, such as the ankles, when the person is sitting or standing, producing the condition of **dependent edema.**

Beyond widespread systemic edema, venous congestion has significant effects in the liver and, in some cases, the spleen, which drains into it. Hepatic congestion arises when the hepatic vein is unable to empty into the congested inferior vena cava. The resulting blood accumulation in the liver causes it to enlarge, the condition of **hepatomegaly.** In the hepatic sinusoids, hepatic congestion produces high pressures that can damage hepatocytes or cause hemorrhage as the vessels rupture. Pressure damages those cells that are adjacent to the congested vessels, while tissues further removed from the vessels are unaffected. These retain their normal dark color. Damaged tissue is lighter in color, providing a contrasting pattern that resembles the coloration of a nutmeg, hence the descriptive term **nutmeg liver** 33 (fig. 10.27).

Hepatic portal system hypertension may cause back pressure, which leads to congestion in the spleen. The resulting **splenomegaly** is associated with severe and advanced CHF. In such cases, the effects of congestion may also be seen in a reduced intestinal absorption as drainage from the congested mesenteric veins is impeded by hepatic congestion. The major elements of pathogenesis in CHF are presented in figure 10.28.

In summary, the dominant clinical pattern in CHF can be seen to arise from the pulmonary and systemic congestion that follows the heart's failure to deal effectively with

Heart Failure in Infants

Newborns and young infants with heart failure present a special diagnostic challenge, since many of the characteristic signs and symptoms are different from those seen in adults or may be confused with those of lung disease.

Common features of heart failure in infants include:

*   repeated pulmonary infections
*   excessive sweating
*   feeding difficulties
*   failure to grow and gain weight
*   rapid breathing
*   facial edema (versus peripheral edema)

Respiratory distress, experienced as in the adult, may be expressed as flaring of the nostrils, grunting, and retraction of the ribs (i.e., depression of the rib cage). These children will tend to become cyanotic when crying because of the added demands this action places on their compromised heart function. The infant whose primary problem is compromised lung function, on the other hand, will tend to become pinker while crying because of improved ventilation of the lungs.

its preload. Most often, right heart failure follows left heart failure, as in the preceding example. A similar pathogenesis may result from heart failure that originates in the right heart.

Cor Pulmonale   Numerous diseases of the lung produce alterations of the lung tissue and vasculature that directly or indirectly cause pulmonary hypertension. The resulting increase in the right heart's afterload causes hypertrophy and dilatation in the right atrium and ventricle. Right heart enlargement that arises as a result of primary lung disease is called **cor pulmonale.** Its effects typically produce CHF without left heart involvement. Chronic bronchitis and emphysema most often cause cor pulmonale, but a large number of other lung diseases may also give rise to this condition, which is responsible for 10–30% of North American hospital admissions for CHF (table 10.4).

There are two essential mechanisms underlying the pulmonary hypertension that causes cor pulmonale. The first is damage or reduction in the number of pulmonary vessels, which, because it forces blood through fewer vessels, causes congestion and hypertension. The second is a reflex vasoconstriction of pulmonary arterioles in response to the hypoxia, hypercapnia (excessive carbon dioxide), and acidosis that often accompany lung disease. These conditions are discussed more fully in chapter 12.

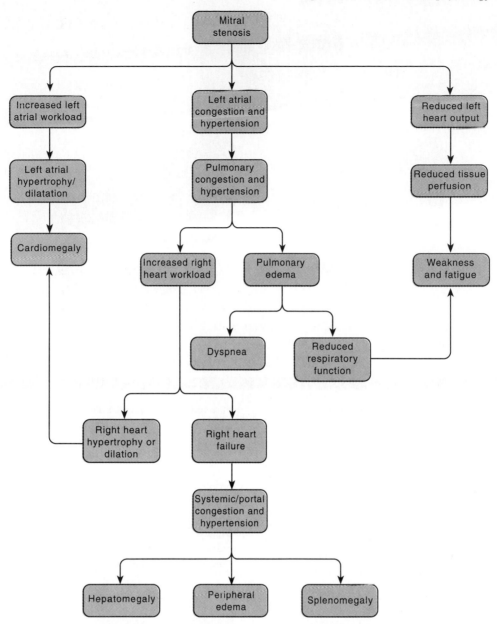

Figure 10.28 Pathogenesis of congestive heart failure (CHF). In this example, a narrowed left atrioventricular valve (mitral stenosis) produces a chronic condition that compromises downstream blood supply and generates upstream congestion, which in turn gives rise to an often seen pattern of cardiac, pulmonary, and systemic complications.

Table 10.4	Pulmonary Conditions Causing Cor Pulmonale

Pulmonary embolism
Pulmonary fibrosis
Chronic bronchitis*
Emphysema*
Idiopathic pulmonary hypertension[+]
Disorders involving reduced air flow (for example, distortions of the vertebral column, obesity or muscle weakness)

*These may be present to varying degrees in the clinical syndrome known as chronic obstructive lung disease (COLD).

[+]This condition is rare.

Physiological Compensations in Congestive Heart Failure

Myocardial Compensations

The failing myocardium has two responses that enable it to better cope with its pumping task. One is triggered by the increased EDV that occurs when the heart fails to maintain an adequate ejection fraction. The larger EDV stretches the myocardium to induce a more forceful contraction, an application of Starling's law. This response provides increases in stroke volume that support cardiac output and reduce congestion. However, as the myocardium must

Figure 10.29   The distinction between dilatation and hypertrophy can be easily seen in these cardiac sections. The middle section is through normal ventricles; hypertrophy is on the left, dilatation on the right.

Normal versus Abnormal Compensation

It is important to recognize that hypertrophy also occurs in a normal heart that is regularly subjected to high demand, as in laborers or those who regularly pursue some form of athletics or fitness training. In such cases the heart's weight can double. With such a strengthened myocardium, stroke volume increases to the degree that resting cardiac output can be maintained at lower heart rates. The savings in hemodynamic stress may reduce the risk of atherosclerosis and ischemic heart disease. In CHF, cardiac weight can triple. Also note that CHF may involve both increased EDV and increased afterload. In such cases, both hypertrophy and dilatation can contribute to cardiac enlargement. For example, the increased afterload problem of the hypertensive may induce an adaptive hypertrophy response. As well, the elevated blood pressures may damage the coronary endothelium, predisposing to coronary atherosclerosis and a weakened myocardium. This in turn leads to a reduction of the ejection fraction, increases in EDV, and, in time, cardiac dilatation.

chronically cope with excessive volume, the increased stretching involved becomes disruptive to its tissues. The myocardium becomes thinner and less elastic, and normal tone is reduced. This is called **myocardial dilatation.** [34] It contributes to the cardiomegaly seen in CHF. Thus the cost of maintaining an adequate stroke volume is contraction under conditions of increasing myocardial distortion, causing dilatation. As dilatation increases, the myocardium's ability to develop adequate contraction force is reduced. This is the state of decompensation indicated by the downward sloping portion to the right in the Starling curve (fig. 10.11).

The second myocardial compensation is hypertrophy. In confronting a greater afterload, myocardial cells quickly respond by enlarging. [35] They synthesize new contractile proteins and thus increase overall myocardial thickness and strength. Formation of additional supporting connective tissue accompanies this enlargement of the myocardium. Hypertrophy, like dilatation, can contribute to cardiomegaly (fig. 10.29).

Nervous System Compensations

Several compensations involving sympathetic nervous system reflexes are activated by declining cardiac output and systemic blood pressure. In response, autonomic input to the SA node causes elevation of the heart rate. At the same time, sympathetic stimulation to the myocardium promotes a positive inotropic response, increasing stroke volume. Both responses increase cardiac output and hence blood pressure. Sympathetic stimulation also causes vasoconstriction in systemic arterioles, which supports systemic blood

Digitalis Toxicity

When cardiac glycosides are used, drug dosage must be calculated carefully, because they have an extremely narrow margin of safety. There is very little difference between a therapeutic and a toxic dose. Studies indicate that as many as 20% of patients taking digitalis show some form of toxic response.

Prominent among the effects of digitalis overdose are cardiac arrhythmias. Spontaneous depolarization (automaticity) is increased, leading to ectopic beats, tachycardia, and fibrillation. The conduction rate of the muscle action potential may decrease, particularly at the AV node, and varying degrees of heart block may result. There are characteristic ECG changes that aid in the diagnosis of digitalis toxicity. The ECG of the digitalized patient on a cardiac monitor should be examined frequently and carefully, since potentially fatal arrhythmias may be the first signs of digitalis toxicity.

Nausea, vomiting, and diarrhea are the gastrointestinal manifestations of glycoside toxicity. Neurologic symptoms include headache, anorexia, dizziness, and visual disturbances, particularly in color perception.

Although simple overdose is the most common cause of digitalis toxicity, several factors increase the sensitivity of the heart to digitalis doses that would otherwise be acceptable. A low plasma and intracellular potassium concentration (hypokalemia) markedly increases the risk of toxicity. Since the glycosides may be prescribed in combination with diuretics, which promote renal potassium loss, great care must be taken to maintain a proper potassium balance. Acidosis also provokes intracellular potassium depletion (see chapter 16). Hypokalemia and acidosis are both caused or aggravated by diarrhea.

---

pressure. The vasoconstriction reflex reduces blood flow to the skin's surface. This means that less heat reaches the skin and so the evaporation of perspiration fluid is reduced. The result is the cold, "clammy" skin of the CHF patient in compensation.

Renal Compensation

Recall from chapter 9 our discussion of the renin-angiotensin system (RAS). When cardiac output falls in CHF, renal blood flow is reduced. In response, the kidney increases its secretion of the enzyme **renin.** This favors formation of a plasma protein called **angiotensin I,** which is converted to its active form, **angiotensin II,** as it passes through the lungs. When activated, angiotensin II stimulates secretion of aldosterone, the principal mineral corticoid of the adrenal cortex. Aldosterone stimulates renal retention of sodium ion, and water is increasingly retained by the kidney. This effect in turn causes an increase in plasma volume, which contributes to increasing blood pressure in compensation for a reduced cardiac output. However, this compensation attempt also complicates the situation, since the extra plasma volume also contributes to congestion, already a major problem in CHF. In this case the compensation attempt hinders more than it helps.

Another renal compensation response is based on **atriopeptin** or **atrial natriuretic factor** (ANF). It is released from the atrial myocardium in response to atrial tachycardia or distention. As its name implies, it induces sodium loss via the kidney. This loss results in diuresis that reduces fluid volume and, therefore, cardiac workload. Renin secretion and release of ADH (antidiuretic hormone) are both suppressed by ANF, a factor that further contributes to renal water loss. Another benefit derives from ANF's

vasodilation effects, which reduce cardiac workload. Why this potent substance is unable to counter the antagonistic effects of enhanced renin secretion in CHF is unclear. Its effects are being analyzed for potential therapeutic application. Physiological compensations in CHF are summarized in figure 10.30.

Ultimately, the chronic progression of CHF overcomes available compensations, with total heart failure the result. This outcome can be delayed by therapeutic intervention.

Therapy in Congestive Heart Failure

In CHF it is sometimes possible to eliminate the cause of the heart's reduced pumping ability. Surgical replacement of defective valves or correction of certain arrhythmias with electronic pacemakers are two, often successful, examples. Recently, much has also been achieved in **coronary by-pass surgery.** In such procedures, part of a coronary vessel narrowed by atherosclerosis is by-passed by an additional vessel that is surgically implanted, and full blood supply to the myocardium is restored. **Angioplasty,** in which stenosed coronary arteries are mechanically stretched and widened by an arterial catheter, is less intrusive and apparently as effective. Often, however, it is not possible to eliminate the cause of CHF, and therapy must be directed toward increasing the heart's ability to maintain its output.

A major thrust of therapy in CHF is aimed at strengthening the myocardium while reducing afterload. This is achieved by various pharmaceutical agents with enhanced myocardial inotropic effects. Various of these agents as well as those that promote diuresis are described in the following section.

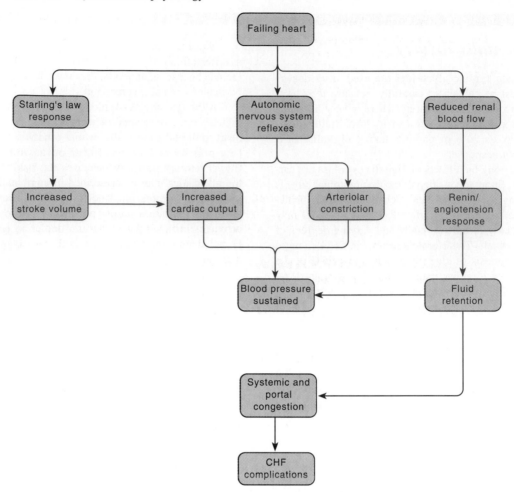

Figure 10.30   Physiologic compensations for a failing heart may be able to maintain adequate blood pressure to meet a reduced level of demand, but complications may be introduced by the fluid retention responses.

Principles of Cardiac Pharmacology

A wide variety of drugs influence the performance of the heart. They do so by modulating the electrical and mechanical events of the cardiac cycle or the regulatory systems that influence cardiac output. Cardiac drugs can be classified in various ways, but clinically, only five types are typically encountered: drugs with chronotropic, inotropic, diuretic, antiarrhythmic, or vasodilation effects.

Chronotropic drugs alter the heart rate. Positive chronotropic agents increase heart rate, while negative chronotropic agents decrease it. **Inotropic drugs** alter myocardial contractility and therefore stroke volume. Positive inotropic drugs increase contractility, negative inotropic drugs decrease it. **Digitalis** and its derivatives **digoxin** and **digitoxin** are widely used positive inotropic agents. **Diuretics** indirectly affect the heart by promoting urinary fluid loss. This limits volume overload and reduces edema. **Antiarrhythmics** alter the electrical properties of the myocardial cells to restore normal rate and rhythm, and **vasodilators** relax smooth muscle in arterioles. Some agents have most effect in the coronary vessels, increasing myocardial blood flow. Others dilate systemic arterioles to decrease afterload. This effect eases myocardial workload and reduces angina.

Because the effects of these clinically important groups overlap, they are organized in a different order in the following section.

Cardiac Glycosides Digitalis and its derivatives form a group of drugs, termed **cardiac glycosides,** that are widely used in the treatment of the failing heart. Although they affect the heart and vasculature in several different ways, their principal action is to augment the inotropic response of the myocardium by raising stroke volume and cardiac output. When the inotropic effect is enhanced, an increased contraction force is obtained at lower degrees of myocardial distention. This means less myocardial strain and an improved ability to meet increased demand (fig. 10.31).

The cardiac glycosides increase contractility by raising the intracellular concentration of calcium ions. In fact, it seems that all drugs with a positive inotropic effect function in this way. At the same time, they act as positive chronotropes. This tendency to increase heart rate, which

Figure 10.31   The inotropic effect of digitalis provides more cardiac output for smaller degrees of myocardial stretch. This alteration provides some additional capacity to cope in higher-demand conditions. See figure 10.11.

would increase the oxygen demand of an already compromised myocardium, is offset by other effects. The increase in cardiac output achieved by effective use of digitalis raises the arterial blood pressure, tissue perfusion, and venous return. There is thus a reflex decline in sympathetic nervous system output, causing arteriolar and venous vasodilation and a decline in heart rate, in spite of the direct increase in automaticity that digitalis produces. This is a good example of a normal homeostatic regulatory response.

Diuretics   In response to declining cardiac output and arterial blood pressure in congestive heart failure, the renin-angiotensin-aldosterone pathway induces fluid retention. This is of value to the degree that it raises blood volume, venous return, and stroke volume. However, excess fluid retention causes edema and injurious overdilation of the ventricles, which in turn reduces the ejection fraction and stroke volume. Salt restriction in the diet can reduce sodium levels and promote water loss. Diuretic agents can be used to further stimulate urinary water loss in an effort to ease the heart's fluid volume burden.

The multitude of diuretics can be divided into four major groups as shown in table 10.5. Most operate on the renal tubules by interfering with the reabsorption of sodium, chloride, and various other ions. This in turn reduces the osmotic reabsorption of water, and urinary water loss is increased. The major problem encountered with diuretic use is electrolyte imbalance, particularly hypokalemia. This is usually handled by using a diuretic that causes potassium loss in combination with one that counters this effect by retaining potassium, such as aldactone. These problems are explored in more detail in chapter 16.

Antiarrhythmic Drugs   An arrhythmia is an abnormality in the cardiac rate or rhythm caused by an abnormal origin of cardiac impulses, or a defect in cardiac conduction.

These abnormalities are the consequence of altered myocardial depolarization (automaticity), faulty conduction pathways, or a combination of both. Normally the specialized conducting cells of the heart exhibit spontaneous activity, generating the myogenic rhythm. The rate of firing of these cells is dependent on three factors: the inflow of sodium and/or calcium or the outflow of potassium, the resting potential, and the threshold potential. Lowering the threshold, raising the resting potential, and increasing sodium or calcium influx, for example, all cause the myocardium to reach threshold sooner and accelerate the myogenic rhythm.

Figure 10.32 illustrates these effects. In the figure, the solid curve provides a reference. The broken-line curves show the effects and changes caused by more rapid sodium inflow (curve A), raised resting potential (curve B), and a lowered threshold potential (curve C). These effects are primarily elicited by digitalis and the catecholamines (norepinephrine and epinephrine). Atropine achieves its accelerating effects by blocking the inhibiting effects of parasympathetic stimulation on the heart rate.

In contrast, various antiarrhythmic drugs slow the myogenic rhythm. Some interfere with sodium availability, while others block calcium flow through calcium channels in the cell membranes. Various antiarrhythmic agents are listed in table 10.6.

Drugs Used for Treatment of Angina Pectoris   As we have noted, angina is the characteristic crushing chest pain associated with myocardial hypoxia. The pain can occur at rest but is usually triggered by exercise, emotion, or physiological stress. It represents an imbalance between oxygen demand and supply to local areas of the myocardium. The underlying cause in the vast majority of cases is ischemia from coronary atherosclerosis. Oxygen demand is proportional to cardiac workload; thus the approach to therapy is two-pronged: to increase the blood supply and to decrease myocardial workload and the heart's oxygen demand.

Since coronary blood flow is almost entirely regulated by local control mechanisms that in the poorly perfused myocardium are working at maximum, vasodilators have very little direct effect on the coronary vessels in relieving angina. A reduction of cardiac workload is the only alternative, and it is achieved by the use of three types of drugs: beta blockers, peripheral-vasodilating nitrates, and calcium-channel blockers. These drugs are often used in combination.

Propranolol and nadolol are both drugs that block the beta receptors that mediate the effects of the sympathetic nervous system on the heart. Thus the heart rate and contractility of the myocardium are reduced and the blood pressure falls. Since beta blockers also induce bronchospasm, they are not appropriate for patients with asthma and should be used cautiously for patients with any respiratory disease.

Table 10.5	Major Classes of Diuretics and Some Specific Agents That Might Be Encountered Clinically. (Other types of diuretic antagonize the action of aldosterone and so promotes diuresis. These agents also reduce the secretion of fluid into the eye, and so are more often used to reduce the increased pressure in glaucoma.)

Osmotic Diuretics

These indirectly promote sodium loss and diuresis by increasing filtrate concentration.

Mannitol	Urea
Isosorbide	Glycerine

Loop Diuretics

These reduce sodium, chloride, and other electrolyte reabsorption, which decreases water reabsorption to induce diuresis.

Bumetanide	Ethacrynate sodium
Ethacrynic acid	Furosemide

Thiazide Diuretics

These increase the loss of sodium and chloride, which promotes water loss.

Bendroflumethiazide	Benthiazide
Chlorothiazide	Cyclothiazide
Hydrochlorothiazide	Hydroflumethiazide
Methyclothiazide	Polythiazide
Trichloromethiazide	

Carbonic Anhydrase Inhibitors

Inhibition of this key enzyme indirectly induces water loss by limiting bicarbonate reabsorption and hydrogen ion secretion.

Acetazolamide	Acetazolamide sodium
Dichlorphenamide	Methazolamide

Figure 10.32 Possible mechanisms underlying the acceleration of the myogenic rhythm employed by various positive chronotropic agents. Solid curves represent a slower reference rhythm. In curve A, inflow of positive ions is increased. The distance from rest to threshold is decreased in curve B by raising resting potential and in curve C by lowering the threshold. Most antiarrhythmics have the opposite effect (slowing myogenic rhythm) by the reversal of any combination of these mechanisms.

Table 10.6	Drugs That Influence the Myogenic Rhythm

Drugs That Increase the Heart Rate	Drugs That Decrease the Heart Rate
Digitalis	Quinidine
Epinephrine	Procainamide
Norepinephrine	Lidocaine
Atropine	Propranolol
	Disopyramide

Nitrates and other vasodilators indirectly relieve angina by slowing peripheral flow. By causing blood to pool in capillaries and veins, they reduce venous return, stroke volume, and cardiac output, and thereby the workload and oxygen demand of the heart. **Nitroglycerine** and related compounds cause some coronary vasodilation, as well, which adds to their effectiveness.

Calcium antagonists such as **verapamil, nifedipine,** and **diltiazen** are examples of calcium-channel blockers that inhibit calcium influx into myocardial and vascular smooth muscle cells. This means they have the dual effect of reducing contractility and promoting coronary artery vasodilation; that is, they simultaneously reduce cardiac

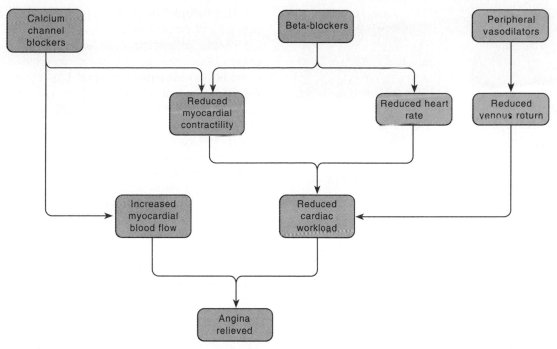

Figure 10.33   Relief of angina pectoris is achieved by the use of agents that either reduce cardiac workload or increase myocardial blood flow. With a better balance between work demand and blood supply, angina is alleviated.

Breaking Therapy

An often unexpected, yet common, cause of heart failure is the inappropriate withdrawal of therapy. This often occurs when digitalis, or another agent, is effective in alleviating symptoms. Too often patients will, without informing their physicians, reduce the prescribed dosage. Alternatively, frustration with sodium or other dietary restrictions may induce binges of excess intake, often on vacations or special occasions. Either can trigger a severe and potentially fatal episode of cardiac decompensation.

workload and increase blood flow to the myocardium. The actions of some common agents used in treating angina pectoris are summarized in figure 10.33.

CARDIOMYOPATHIES

The **cardiomyopathies** are those noninflammatory conditions that cause impaired myocardial function and that are unrelated to the more common causes of heart failure: coronary artery disease, valve dysfunction, hypertension, or congenital defects. Because the cardiomyopathies are diverse, their classification takes two approaches.

Etiology is the basis for one approach, with two categories identified. In **primary cardiomyopathy,** two criteria are applied. First, the myocardium, rather than valves or the pericardium, is the focus of damage, and second, etiology is

unknown or unrelated to some other systemic disease. In **secondary cardiomyopathy,** the direct cause of damage can be identified or at least seen to be the result of some systemic disorder, e.g., uremia or Cushing's syndrome. The secondary cardiomyopathies may be further categorized on the basis of etiology, with infiltrative, toxic, and other categories recognized. However, since over half of cardiomyopathies are idiopathic, the etiological approach to classification is less useful than one based on functional abnormalities.

From a functional viewpoint, the cardiomyopathies are divided into three groups. **Dilated (congestive) cardiomyopathy** is characterized by pronounced dilation and failure of the ventricle. In **hypertrophic cardiomyopathy,** the major feature is ventricular hypertrophy, which is so pronounced that it reduces ventricular volume and obstructs outflow from the heart. The third type, **restrictive cardiomyopathy,** has the key feature of a stiffened ventricular wall, which is only poorly distensible.

Although we will describe these groups separately, note that some degree of overlap exists between them.

Dilated Cardiomyopathy

Diffuse myocardial injury that impairs contractility is the underlying abnormality in this condition. As a result of the impairment, the ejection fraction typically falls to 40% or less (55–78% is normal), while end-systolic volume and end-diastolic volume increase, producing a chronic stretching of the myocardium. This causes damage, scarring, thinning, and dilation of the ventricles. **36** Some hypertrophy

(a)   (b)

Figure 10.34 (*a*) The characteristic pattern of myocardial tissue is clearly evident in this micrograph of hypertrophic cardiomyopathy. (*b*) Normal tissue for comparison.

is often present as well, accounting for observed increases in the heart's weight, which in extremes can double to reach 700 gm.

With diminished contractility, signs and symptoms of heart failure appear, but since the right ventricle is also failing, the pulmonary vessels are partially protected from hypertension and edema. Onset of symptoms is usually gradual, but an inexorably downhill course is typical as the ejection fraction and cardiac output continue to fall, in spite of cardiac compensations. Prognosis is quite variable, with many patients surviving for years, while others with acute and severe (fulminant) attacks may die within weeks of diagnosis.

Since etiology in dilated cardiomyopathy is usually unknown, therapy cannot be directed at a specific cause. Instead, a general treatment for patients with heart failure is instituted. The usual regimen seeks to maintain stroke volume by means of cardiac glycosides and to limit fluid accumulation and edema by means of salt restriction and diuretics. Anticoagulant therapy is also frequently employed, since a reduced ejection fraction predisposes to intravascular and intraventricular thrombosis. Vasodilators may also be used to lower peripheral resistance and reduce cardiac workload.

Alcohol is the major cause of nonischemic dilated cardiomyopathy. It is seen primarily in males aged 30–55, where consumption of alcoholic beverages is heavy for 10 years or longer.

Hypertrophic Cardiomyopathy

Etiology in this condition is usually poorly identified, but most cases have a genetic component. The dominant feature is focal, asymmetric hypertrophy of the myocardium. Microscopically, the myocardial tissue can be seen to be disorganized, with shortened, nonparallel cell arrangements and fibrosis. **37** Intracellular organization of myofibrils is also distorted (fig. 10.34).

Hypertrophy is often asymmetric, with the septum enlarging disproportionately, sometimes enough to impede left ventricular emptying and aortic valve function. When either of these features dominates, descriptive terminology is employed: **asymmetric septal hypertrophy** (ASH) in the first case and **idiopathic hypertrophic subaortic stenosis** (IHSS) in the second. If outflow obstruction dominates the functional disruption, the term **hypertrophic obstructive cardiomyopathy** (HOCM) is employed.

The congestive heart failure that develops in these patients generally arises from three problems: obstruction of ventricular outflow, mitral insufficiency, or **reduced ventricular compliance** (the ventricle stiffens). The ejection fraction is often elevated, although in severe disease the end-diastolic volume is reduced by the enlarged and encroaching myocardium. Although surgery may be used to repair valve dysfunction, pharmacotherapy is more commonly employed.

Restrictive Cardiomyopathy

The least common type of cardiomyopathy is characterized by the deposition of amyloid, glycogen, or mucopolysaccharide in the myocardium. Such infiltration is typically accompanied by fibrosis and is the result of an inherited metabolic disease. The rare primary tumors of the heart and more common metastatic tumors may also be responsible for the infiltration.

Typically, heart failure in restrictive cardiomyopathy occurs because of loss of resilience and contractility in the myocardium. Falling values of EDV, SV, and cardiac output are typically present. Pharmacological therapy is usually unable to restore cardiac output, and death ultimately occurs from arrhythmia or congestive heart failure.

CONGENITAL HEART DEFECTS

Congenital heart disease develops as a result of malformations in the heart and includes, by convention, defects in the great vessels. Congenital cardiac defects are present in under 1% of live births, with a greater proportion found in stillborn infants; cardiac defects presumably contribute to the increased prenatal mortality. Generally, the mechanisms underlying these abnormalities are the persistence of normal fetal blood channels into extrauterine life and faulty embryologic development during the third through eighth weeks of gestation.

Complex interactions between genetic and environmental factors appear to be responsible for most congenital cardiac defects. Those in which hereditary factors predominate will often be found in association with other genetic conditions such as DiGeorge's syndrome, osteogenesis imperfecta, trisomy 21 (Down's syndrome), trisomy 13, trisomy 18, and Turner's syndrome. Environmental factors

Table 10.7	Incidence of Congenital Cardiac Defects as a Percentage of All Such Abnormalities. Various Studies of the Incidence of These Conditions Yield Values that Fall Within the Indicated Range. The Incidence of Congenital Cardiac Defects Is Estimated at Less than 1% of all Live Births.

Ventricular septal defect (VSD)	20±5%
Atrial septal defect (ASD)	12±2%
Patent ductus arteriosus (PDA)	15±5%
Tetralogy of Fallot	10±5%
Aortic coarctation	6±1%

known to be involved during pregnancy are maternal rubella (German measles), or other infections, certain drugs, e.g., lithium, and maternal alcohol abuse. However, with that said, it should be noted that currently over 90% of congenital cardiac disease is idiopathic. Severe, complex cardiac abnormalities are a significant cause of neonatal death or require surgery in infancy. If untreated, survivors typically face a declining course of congestive heart failure.

The structural abnormalities present in these conditions divert blood through the heart and pulmonary circulation to other than normal passages. For example, blood flow may be diverted from the pulmonary circulation to the systemic circulation to produce a **right-to-left shunt.** In such cases, blood is poorly oxygenated, often to the degree that cyanosis results. Cyanosis starts to develop when hemoglobin saturation falls below 65%, and may be accompanied by polycythemia. This excess of red blood cells results from the response to systemic hypoxia. A hematocrit of 60% is typical in polycythemia (45% is normal). In a **left-to-right shunt,** blood flow is diverted from the systemic circulation to the lungs, producing congestion in the pulmonary vessels.

Abnormal flow of blood through malformed cardiac or great vessel passages often produces unusual sounds called heart murmurs. These are often early signs of the presence of congenital cardiac defects.

The incidence of congenital defects in the heart is indicated in table 10.7. Those with most clinical significance are the following.

Ventricular Septal Defects (VSD)

Although they are the most common cardiac malformation of infancy, **ventricular septal defects** are rare in adults because they either close spontaneously or result in a high rate of infant mortality. **38** Only small defects (less than 1 cm in diameter) are compatible with survival beyond childhood. These are usually the result of a failure to close the membranous portion of the interventricular septum,

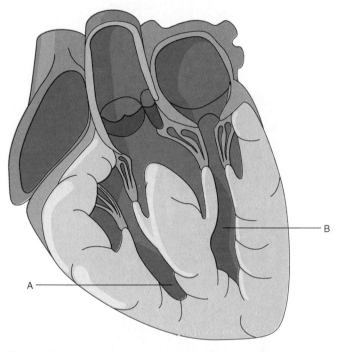

Figure 10.35   In this typical case, the thin membranous portion of the interventricular septum has failed to close the opening between the ventricles.

which lies adjacent to the floor of the atria (fig. 10.35). The pathogenesis is predictable. Blood is driven from the higher-pressure left ventricle to the lower-pressure right ventricle, producing a loud murmur during systole. The resulting right heart overload increases pulmonary congestion, causing hypertension, dyspnea, fatigue, and a susceptibility to pulmonary infections. If the condition is prolonged for months and years, hypertension in the pulmonary vascular bed can lead to sclerosis, raised pulmonary resistance, and shunt reversal in late stages (fig. 10.36). Right-sided congestive heart failure is the usual end-stage of the unrepaired defect.

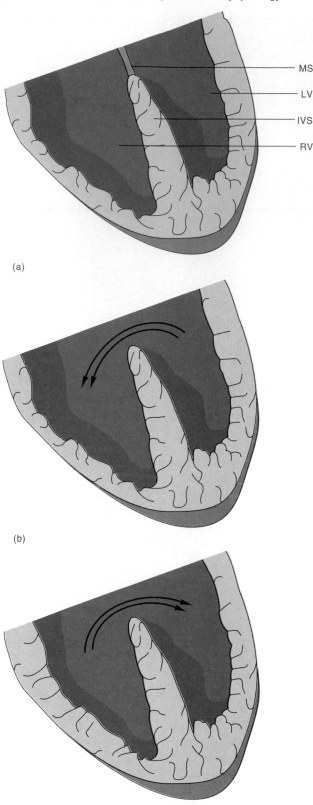

(a)

(b)

(c)

Figure 10.36 (*a*) The normal isolation of the right ventricle (RV) from the left ventricle (LV). The interventricular septum (IVS) is muscular except for the membranous system (MS). (*b*) In cases where lack of closure allows communication between ventricles, left-to-right shunting results. (*c*) Later, with lung damage, the shunt reverses.

Figure 10.37 During embryonic development, if the normally present foramen ovale does not close, an atrial septal defect is the result.

This is the heart of a 72-year-old woman, showing a large defect in the atrial septum due to the failure of closure of the foramen ovale. The woman's history included long-standing hypertension and several bouts of heart failure, which she had survived until her last hospital admittance. At that time, a chest X-ray indicated a possible aneurysm in the pulmonary artery, but no definitive clinical diagnosis was made. She soon died of a suspected acute MI.

At autopsy the atrial septal defect, which had previously escaped detection and which caused the overloading of the right heart and pulmonary trunk, was discovered. This condition explained the X-ray findings and revealed that it was cor pulmonale, rather than a MI, to which the unfortunate woman ultimately succumbed.

Atrial Septal Defects (ASD)

Atrial septal defects often arise as the result of an abnormal fusing of the interatrial septum during embryonic development. They may also arise when the **foramen ovale** (fig. 10.37) fails to close. During fetal life, the foramen ovale provides a direct route to the left heart atrium, bypassing the nonfunctioning lungs. Normally this passage closes during the early postnatal period.

Atrial septal defects are often not diagnosed or treated in childhood and therefore represent a significant group among adults with congenital heart disease. The opening in the septum allows blood to be shunted from the left atrium to the right atrium. **39** Increased right heart volume increases flow through the pulmonary valve, causing a systolic murmur. Another finding on auscultation is a characteristic alteration of the second heart sound.

Fatigue, pulmonary congestion, dyspnea, and frequent upper respiratory tract infections are common findings in severe left-to-right shunting, although many young victims are asymptomatic. With increasing age, the chronic overcirculation of blood through the lungs causes pulmonary

(a)

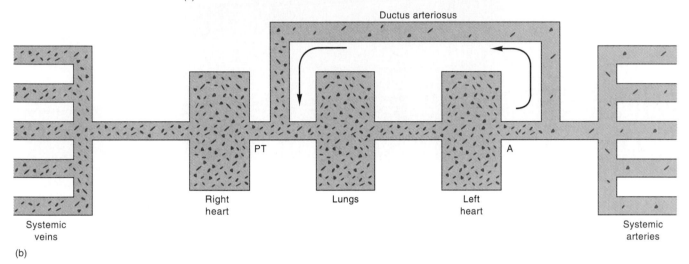

(b)

Figure 10.38 Patent ductus arteriosus. (*a*) The arrow shows the connecting link between the aorta (A) and the pulmonary trunk (PT) that failed to close off after birth. (*b*) Schematic representation of the relation between the aorta and pulmonary trunk, and of the cardiac and pulmonary overloading that results when the fetal vessel is retained.

The history behind this photo is sadly brief. This is the heart of a family's fourth child. He had developed normally for two months, but then had become listless and irritable, demonstrating bouts of cyanosis and crying. During one such episode he suddenly went limp and died. In the photo, the explanation can be easily seen: a patent ductus arteriosus. It is large and afforded too little flow to accommodate the circulatory demands of the infant's normal development.

sclerosis. Later in the course, pulmonary arterial pressure increases and the left-to-right shunt declines, becomes variable, and finally reverses (fig. 10.36). This puts a great burden on the right heart, and right heart failure is a likely outcome. As pulmonary blood flow diminishes and blood by-passes the lungs, cyanosis, fatigue, and fainting spells develop. Surgical repair is a safe and effective procedure, but is usually not done if shunt reversal has occurred.

Patent Ductus Arteriosus (PDA)

During fetal life the ductus arteriosus joins the aorta and pulmonary artery, shunting blood from the pulmonary circulation into the systemic vessels to by-pass the nonfunctioning lungs. Following birth the lungs inflate, pulmonary

resistance declines, and blood flow through the duct is reversed. Within hours of birth, the high concentration of dissolved oxygen in the systemic arterial blood and the reversal of flow through ductus arteriosus cause the duct to become stenotic and finally close.

Persistence of the ductus arteriosus **40** causes chronic shunting of blood from the high-pressure aorta into the low-pressure pulmonary artery (fig. 10.38). This is sustained throughout the cardiac cycle so that a continuous (systolic and diastolic) murmur is evident. The severity of the disorder is proportional to the degree of patency, most children being asymptomatic. Volume overload of the left ventricle, with pulmonary congestion and hypertension, occurs in severe cases. When present over many years, pulmonary sclerosis develops raising pulmonary arterial

(a)

(b)   (c)

Figure 10.39 Patterns of blood flow in preductal (*b*) and postductal (*a, c*) coarctation of the aorta. Broken lines indicate site of ductus arteriosus. Note how the position of the point of coarctation has implications for the cranial circulation. [In (*a*), the left ventricle is being viewed from the right side.]

In this photo, a coarctation at the base of the aortic arch can be seen. It was responsible for the early death of an infant, caused by the inability of the heart to drive blood past the coarctation. As the photo shows, the lumen of the aorta was extremely narrow, offering high resistance that even the markedly hypertrophied ventricle could not overcome.

Additional evidence of high ventricular pressure can be seen in the thickness of the endocardium, which had adapted to the abnormal pressures to which it was subjected. Also note an additional congenital defect: a bicuspid aortic valve.

pressure and reversing flow. Pressure overload on the right heart eventually causes right-sided congestive heart failure. When the condition is diagnosed before shunt reversal has occurred, surgical correction is the treatment of choice.

Coarctation of the Aorta

Coarctation of the aorta is a congenital narrowing (fig. 10.39*a*) that primarily occurs in males and exists in two quite distinct forms, based on the position of the coarctation

with respect to the ductus arteriosus. In both types, there is a large pressure gradient across the coarctation, producing downstream hypotension and upstream hypertension.

Preductal or **infantile coarctation** occurs at a point proximal to the ductus arteriosus, which remains open following birth since pressure in the distal aorta is insufficient to reverse flow and initiate duct closure (fig. 10.39). Left ventricular failure follows, as a result of the increased resistance to flow offered by the narrowed aorta. This produces symptoms of left heart failure. Also, volume overload of the right ventricle develops, since part of the ejected blood is shunted into the aorta. Cyanosis, dyspnea, and heart failure are all observed. Death may follow unless surgical intervention is prompt.

Postductal coarctation usually arises distal to the left subclavian artery and is compatible with survival to maturity, hence the designation **adult-type coarctation.** The characteristic high pressure in the aortic arch leads to the normal post-partum flow reversal in the ductus arteriosus, which closes in the usual way. Some relief of the distal hypotension and ischemia is achieved by way of a multitude of collateral vessels that develop to by-pass the point of coarctation, particularly branches of the subclavian and intercostal arteries. This adaptation permits survival to middle age. There is hypertension in the head and upper limbs, hypotension in the lower limbs and abdomen. Left ventricular hypertrophy is evident, and left heart failure may ultimately occur if surgical repair is not performed. The young individual may suffer aneurysm, thrombosis, or rupture of cerebral vessels, or aortic aneurysm.

Tetralogy of Fallot

In this condition, four structural abnormalities are present. They include a ventricular septal defect, pulmonary stenosis, and an aorta that is shifted to the right (dextroposed aorta) to lie over the right as well as the left ventricle. The fourth component, right ventricular hypertrophy, is not a malformation but rather the adaptation of the right ventricle to the high afterload presented by a narrowed pulmonary outflow tract. The four elements of this condition were first described by a French physician, E. A. Fallot. Of those affected, 40% have one or more additional cardiac defects. In over 20% of cases, abnormalities in other organs are also present.

Right-to-left shunting occurs in this complex malformation as the narrowed entrance to the pulmonary trunk diverts blood through the septal defect into the left ventricle. When a lesser degree of stenosis is present, pulmonary blood flow may be sufficient to prevent cyanosis, but more typically, cyanosis is present at birth or develops within the first year of life.

A temporary by-pass vessel between a systemic artery and the pulmonary artery may be surgically introduced in the infant's first year. This allows sufficient oxygenation to sustain growth and development to later childhood, when a complete surgical correction of the defect is better tolerated. Without surgical intervention, the outlook is bleak, with death occurring in infancy or early childhood. Various

complications beyond systemic hypoxia contribute to the decline: cardia arrhythmias, infective endocarditis, coagulation disorders, and cerebral abscess or infarction, among others.

CARDIAC DISEASE: IMPACT ON MORTALITY

We have chosen to organize our discussion of heart disease to parallel our treatment of basic cardiac anatomy. This ordering, however, does not reflect the relative incidence with which you will encounter specific heart diseases. The incidence in clinical populations will, of course, vary immensely: in infant cardiac wards you may see a much higher proportion of congenital heart disease, for example, while in respiratory wards you will more commonly encounter cor pulmonale associated with chronic lung disease. Mortality statistics give us a more balanced way of ranking the significance of competing pathologies. On this basis, cardiac disease is the major killer in industrialized societies, responsible for perhaps 35% of all deaths. Of those deaths, the vast majority (about 85%) are attributable to atherosclerosis and ischemic heart disease.

Although the coronary atherosclerosis progresses slowly, processes superimposed upon it make its expression in ischemic heart disease quite variable. Resultant conditions include angina pectoris, sudden cardiac death, myocardial infarction, and chronic ischemic heart disease. The incidence of, and recovery from, IHD have been improving over the past two decades, a function of decreases in coronary atherosclerosis. This in turn is possibly due to improved medical intervention, diet, exercise, and life style. Certainly, an increasing amount of attention is being directed to these factors in efforts to lessen the life-shortening effects of epidemic atherosclerotic disease. A large proportion of the 6–7% of deaths due to cerebrovascular disease are atherosclerotic in origin, as are all of the additional 1% of deaths directly attributable to atherosclerotic degeneration of the aorta, renal, or other systemic, noncerebral arteries.

Of fatal cardiac disease, 85% is caused by IHD. What of the remaining 15%? Five specific diseases account for almost half of this number. Hypertensive heart disease gives rise to about 2%, while rheumatic heart disease, congenital heart disease, infective endocarditis, and cor pulmonale account for about 1% each. The remainder, a wide variety of specific diseases, can be grouped effectively into pericardial, myocardial, or endocardial valvular diseases.

Case Study I: Acute Heart Failure

A 63-year-old male was admitted to the emergency room (ER) at 2130 hrs after suddenly collapsing while reading a newspaper at his home. An emergency inhalator crew found him unconscious and gasping for breath. He was resuscitated with some difficulty and rushed to hospital.

On arrival at the ER he was found to be in ventricular fibrillation. He was successfully defibrillated, and an airway was established by intubation. Oxygen, anticoagulant, and digoxin therapies were promptly instituted. After he was stabilized, he was transferred to the intensive care unit (ICU), where a second defibrillation was required.

He regained consciousness the next morning and could speak, describing a 10-year history of angina and nitroglycerine therapy. His skin was pale and cool, consistent with compensatory peripheral vasoconstriction. He was sweating, was restless, and his urinary output was low. BP was 80/60 mmHg. Blood chemistry studies showed an SGOT level of 300 IU (normal: 6–22) and an LDH level of 900 IU (normal: 90–210). His condition deteriorated and he succumbed at 1230 hrs the same day.

At autopsy six rib fractures were noted, the result of the inhalator crew's resuscitation attempts. The right coronary artery was occluded by a large, gelatinous thrombus. The left anterior descending and circumflex arteries showed signs of severe atherosclerosis and were narrowed to only pinpoint lumina. Extensive recent infarction was noted in the left ventricle, as were areas of old, healed, subendocardial infarction in both ventricles and the septal myocardium.

Commentary

This history is, unfortunately, not unusual. About 20% of acute MI patients die of the initial attack, while others may ultimately succumb to its complications or to subsequent infarction. Serious arrhythmias are common, resulting from direct damage to the conduction system or from more generalized ischemic damage to the myocardium.

Following admission, findings were consistent with acute MI, the low BP and high serum enzymes indicating significant myocardial injury. Low urinary output follows widespread vasoconstriction and fluid retention. Physiological compensations and therapeutic intervention were unable to protect against the devastating loss of functional myocardium.

Case Study II: Congestive Heart Failure

A mentally confused 37-year-old male was admitted to a large hospital's intensive care unit (ICU). He was pale, sweating, and suffered severe dyspnea. He was diagnosed as suffering from right heart failure due to mitral insufficiency, with associated pulmonary and right ventricular congestion and hypertension. His blood pressure measured 110/90 mmHg and his heart rate was 120 beats per minute. He had dependent edema and pronounced jugular venous distention, and was mildly jaundiced.

Although he was too ill to provide any history, according to previous records that were obtained he had suffered nine years previously from rheumatic fever complicated by bacterial endocarditis. The resulting damage had necessitated surgical replacement of the mitral valve.

During open-heart surgery the patient was supported by cardiopulmonary by-pass. It was found that some of the sutures of the old mitral prosthesis had pulled away from their anchorage, producing an orifice that allowed regurgitation into the left atrium. A new valve was secured in position, and the patient was removed from cardiopulmonary by-pass. A very low cardiac output was in evidence, and BP could not be sustained without cardiopulmonary support, which was therefore resumed. Adrenalin, isoproterenol, and calcium were administered to support myocardial function, but all attempts failed and the patient was finally pronounced dead after two hours on the by-pass apparatus.

At autopsy the heart was found to be markedly enlarged, particularly the left ventricle. Cardiac weight was 950 g (normal: 375 g). The pericardium showed evidence of previous rheumatic fever damage; it was completely adherent with no detectable pericardial fluid. The myocardium was seen to be seriously weakened by extensive areas of fibrosis and calcification. The coronary vessels were widely patent, with only minor focal indications of early atherosclerotic involvement.

The liver weighed 1550 g (normal: 1350 g) and was cirrhotic, with prominent nutmeg patterning. Both spleen and kidneys showed signs of minor infarctions, possibly from thromboemboli. Examination of the brain revealed indications of previous surgery to relieve pressure at the site of an earlier cerebral hemorrhage. Various small infarcts were also observed.

Commentary

This interesting case demonstrates the risks associated with rheumatic heart disease and with valve replacement. Left-sided valve damage is a common result of rheumatic heart disease; pericarditis and myocardial involvement are found less frequently. Following surgery, the patient's condition had improved, but he later suffered a cerebral hemorrhage, presumably related to his anticoagulant therapy which was instituted to prevent thrombosis and embolism from the surfaces of his mechanical valve prosthesis. He had undergone surgery to relieve the pressure that developed as a sequela of the cerebral hemorrhage. His records indicated that he had also suffered transient attacks of ischemia involving the cerebral vasculature, probably from small thromboemboli. His mental condition had progressively deteriorated following these small embolisms. For the preceding two years he had had a steadily declining course of fatigue, exercise intolerance, and exertional dyspnea, characteristic of chronic cardiac decompensation.

Previous cardiac diagnostic procedures, carried out in the referring hospital, had revealed significant mitral regurgitation and a left ventricular end-diastolic pressure of 30 mmHg (normal: 9–12 mmHg). This finding indicated a weakened ventricular myocardium, unable to eject its preload, and stretched at the end of diastole into the decompensating portion of the Starling curve. Pulmonary hypertension was severe, with pulmonary arterial pressure of 100/50 mmHg (normal: 22/8 mmHg).

Further ECG, radiographic, and laboratory analyses indicated CHF with cardiomegaly, pulmonary hypertension, hepatomegaly, and serious liver dysfunction. Echocardiography indicated left atrial and left ventricular dilatation, and color flow Doppler studies revealed a regurgitant jet around the valve prosthesis. Although he was a poor candidate, it was determined that surgery offered the only possibility of saving this unfortunate patient.

Thrombosis and embolism are persistent problems with valve prostheses, but, as this case illustrates, preventive anticoagulant therapy also has its hazards. The failing heart produced the classic features of left-sided CHF, with blood backing up through the lungs and liver. The prosthetic valve failure and volume overload of the left ventricle was complicated by the rheumatic myocardial injury, which could not be relieved by surgery.

Key Concepts

1. Heart failure implies that the heart is not pumping sufficient blood to meet normal demands, acute heart failure develops quickly, while the conditions that underlie chronic heart failure progress more slowly (p. 232).

2. The most common underlying pathology giving rise to either acute or chronic heart failure is ischemic heart disease affecting the left ventricle (p. 234).

3. Anything that interferes with the pumping capacity of the heart can lead to acute or chronic heart failure. This includes conditions that restrict its filling, impair valve efficiency, weaken the muscle, disturb its coordinated rhythm, or present abnormal resistance to the blood pumped (p. 234).

4. A less common cause of heart failure is any condition, such as extreme anemia, that places excessive pumping demands on the heart (p. 234).

5. Pericarditis can present problems in two ways: the accumulated fluid can restrict the heart and impair filling, or alternatively it can produce adhesions that restrain heart movement (p. 234).

6. Inflammatory disease of the heart muscle (myocarditis) is usually acute and mild, although chronic conditions can be very debilitating and rare acute cases can weaken the heart sufficiently to produce acute heart failure (p. 235).

7. Acute infective endocarditis, which can cause valvular degeneration and throw off infective emboli that damage kidney, brain, or heart, is lethal in a significant proportion of cases (p. 236).

8. Stenosis of heart valves (commonly the mitral and aortic) increases the resistance to blood movement and leads to compensatory hypertrophy and potential chronic heart failure (p. 237).

9. An improperly closing valve (valvular insufficiency or incompetence) allows the partial return of already pumped blood, adding to the volume the heart must pump to maintain adequate perfusion (p. 238).

10. Rheumatic heart disease results when a cross-reacting antibody binds to valve leaflets and initiates inflammatory degradation that may produce both stenosis and insufficiency (pp. 239–240).

11. Atherosclerosis of the coronary arteries and superimposed thrombosis causes ischemia, which may produce pain, focal or diffuse infarction, or a life-threatening arrhythmia (p. 240).

12. Suddenly impaired local circulation or increased cardiac demand can precipitate acute myocardial infarction, which may cause death, predispose to many short-term complications, or set the stage for chronic heart failure (pp. 242–245).

13. A wide variety of cardiac, vascular, hematological, and respiratory conditions can create excessive demands on the heart or impair its function and push it into a state of progressively decreasing capacity called chronic or congestive heart failure (CHF) (p. 245).

14. A decrease in the pumping capacity of the heart, so that it fails to clear the blood delivered to it, leads to congestion of upstream vessels and tissues and elicits a variety of compensatory mechanisms, the normal function of which is to sustain perfusion (pp. 245–253).

15. Normal adaptations to increased cardiac demand (e.g., dilatation, hypertrophy, increased heart rate and force of contraction, retention of plasma fluid volume) extract relatively increased performance from the failing heart but also contribute to the pathophysiology of CHF (pp. 248–253).

16. Pharmacological agents can improve the performance of the failing heart by increasing its force of contraction, relieving the volume overload, stabilizing its rhythm, or reducing the resistance to pumped blood (pp. 254–257).

17. The term cardiomyopathy applies to a diverse collection of noninflammatory disorders of the myocardium that impair pumping by weakening the muscle or interfering with filling or outflow (pp. 257–258).

18. Congenital heart defects result from malformations or the persistence of normal fetal blood channels and impair the pumping of blood or its appropriate routing (pp. 258–263).

REVIEW ACTIVITIES

1. Lay out a flow chart that indicates the cause-effect relationships that develop in the pathogenesis of congestive heart failure. Start on the premise that an area of atherosclerotic artery has developed a thrombus that caused infarction of a substantial area of the left ventricular wall.

2. Assume that a clinical instructor has asked how a patient's body was compensating for congestive heart failure, and prepare a response.

3. Explain the use of diuretics and salt restriction for the patient in activity 2.

4. List the possible outcomes of myocardial infarction. When are the crisis points in the recovery from a myocardial infarction, and to what are they related?

5. Explain how left heart failure might become combined heart failure.

6. Differentiate the various types of angina.

7. Using figure 10.15 as your guide, describe and explain the development of rheumatic heart disease.

8. Cover all of figure 10.33 except for the top line and then construct your own flow chart to explain the actions of these agents (i.e. calcium-channel blockers, beta blockers, etc.).

9. Figure 10.24 summarizes the etiologic factors in congestive heart failure. Cover the column on the left-hand side and generate it on your own with appropriate explanations.

Chapter Eleven

Circulatory Shock

Yet who would have thought the old man to have had so much blood in him?

William Shakespeare
Macbeth

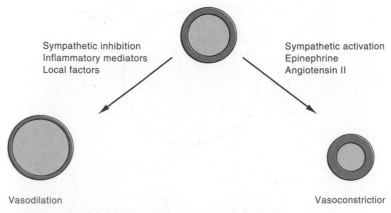

Sympathetic inhibition
Inflammatory mediators
Local factors

Sympathetic activation
Epinephrine
Angiotensin II

Vasodilation

Vasoconstriction

Figure 11.1   Factors that play a role in determining the wall tension of systemic arterioles.

The condition of **circulatory shock** is an acute and serious one. It is a state in which there is an imbalance between the supply of blood to the tissues and the amount of blood they need to meet their metabolic demands. An abnormally elevated metabolic rate may cause tissue demands to be excessive, or an overwhelming infection may lead to cell damage and the inability of cells to utilize the available blood supply. More usually, the situation involves failure of the cardiovascular system to provide adequate blood flow to meet normal metabolic demand.

To understand the pathogenesis of shock, it will be helpful to review the essential factors that determine blood flow in the cardiovascular system.

NORMAL BLOOD FLOW

To maintain normal homeostatic balance, tissues depend on an adequate blood flow reaching the **microcirculation.** This term describes the extensive networks of capillaries that pass among the cells of almost all tissues, including the arterioles that supply them and the venules that drain them. **1** It is only in the capillaries that vascular walls are adapted to accommodate the passage of fluid, nutrient, and waste molecules between the blood and tissue spaces. When blood adequately perfuses the microcirculation, nutrient supply and waste removal are consistent with normal function. When perfusion declines, the tissue's life is threatened.

Adequate blood flow in the microcirculation depends on arterial blood hydrostatic pressure (BHP). This is the driving force that moves blood through the body's vessels. Those factors that affect BHP, then, are the factors that might cause it to fall to the point at which it could no longer drive sufficient blood into the microcirculation. One such factor is the cardiac output. This is the blood forced by the left heart into the systemic arteries. As cardiac output changes, changes in systemic BHP follow.

Another factor that contributes to BHP is the tension in the walls of the arterioles, which is maintained by smooth muscle. Arteriolar tension can be varied to meet the needs of normal blood distribution throughout the body. Vasoconstriction is caused by input from the sympathetic branch of the autonomic nervous system and by the effects of several circulating vasoconstrictor substances. Two of these are epinephrine and angiotensin II (fig. 11.1).

MECHANISMS OF CIRCULATORY SHOCK

It is the relationship between the arterial system and the amount of blood it contains that determines the systemic BHP. In circulatory shock, this normally balanced relationship is abruptly thrown out of equilibrium. Although many etiologies are involved, only three basic patterns of pathogenesis contribute to the development of shock. One of these is cardiac malfunction, which causes cardiac output to decline. With less blood entering the vascular system, pumping pressure drops, and the result is **cardiogenic shock.** Even with normal heart and vessel functions, a loss of blood from the circulatory system can cause a rapid fall in BHP. Shock due to such lack of circulating blood volume is **hypovolemic shock.** The third type of shock is caused by changes in the vascular system. **Vascular shock** results from widespread dilation of the systemic arterioles. In dilating, their walls, in effect, draw away from the blood within them. This change causes pressure to fall, since the blood now occupies a larger volume. Such a response can abruptly reduce BHP (fig. 11.2). The vessels of the abdominal viscera, the **splanchnic circulation,** are especially significant in vascular shock. Because they are so numerous and their capacity is so large, their dilation can cause significant drops in pressure.

Primary Shock

Any given case of circulatory shock will usually be the result of one of these three basic mechanisms. But often two or even three may contribute to the overall loss of circulatory function. A good example is **primary shock,** which is also known as **neurogenic shock.** This condition

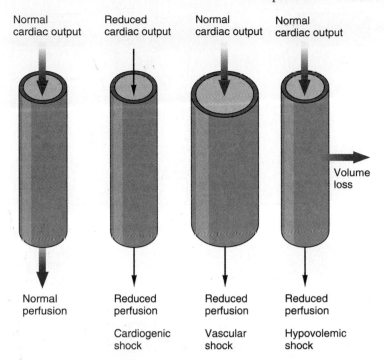

Figure 11.2   The three essential patterns of circulatory shock. In each case, one specific mechanism is responsible for reduced tissue perfusion.

usually passes quickly and is followed by rapid recovery. In primary shock, rapidly falling blood pressure sharply reduces cerebral blood flow, causing loss of consciousness. This is fainting, or **syncope.** Emotional trauma, intense pain, or other threateningly vivid experience (for some, merely the sight of blood) can result in altered nervous system output to the vessels and heart. (The term neurogenic shock makes reference to this nervous system involvement.) The response is vasodilation, causing a fall in BHP and a decline in the heart rate, which reduces cardiac output and then BHP. It is also significant that when blood enters dilated arteriolar networks, especially the extensive splanchnic circulation, venous blood flow is sharply reduced. The blood, in filling these enlarged spaces, moves less quickly to the veins on its return to the heart. The sequestering of blood in peripheral vessels is called **peripheral pooling.** It reduces the systemic venous return, which can in turn cause further reduction of cardiac output.

In primary shock, then, we have cardiogenic and vascular components both contributing to an abrupt fall in BHP. Insufficient cerebral flow follows, and the affected individual experiences a feeling of light-headedness and then loses consciousness. It is this loss of consciousness that interrupts the emotional stimulus to the autonomic centers that control heart and vessel activity. As a result, normal cardiac output and vasoconstriction are restored.

Neurogenic shock can be more serious when other than emotional factors are involved. In the case of brain damage or central nervous system (CNS) depression from drugs such as barbiturates or anesthetics, neural output to the heart and vessels may be inadequate to maintain BHP. If the spinal cord is injured, or in cases of excessive spinal anesthesia, normal CNS output may be blocked and prevented from reaching the heart and vessels. In either case, the abnormal output to arterioles results in widespread vasodilation and peripheral pooling (fig. 11.3).

In primary shock the onset of signs and symptoms is immediate. Most shock, however, is characterized by signs and symptoms that are slower to develop. This more common type is called **secondary shock.** It can develop from a wide variety of etiological factors, but all involve the three essential patterns of pathogenesis already described. These can now be considered in greater detail.

Cardiogenic Shock

Cardiac malfunction leading to a decline of cardiac output is the basis of cardiogenic shock. Its most common cause is failure of the left ventricle due to myocardial infarction. In many cases of MI, loss of myocardial function is limited, so that cardiac output is adequate to meet resting tissue demands. In over 10% of all MI cases, however, loss of myocardium is substantial, and these needs cannot be met. When 40% or more of the myocardium is lost, cardiogenic shock will result. **2** In over 80% of such cases, death will follow in spite of therapeutic intervention.

Although MI is the most common cause of cardiogenic shock, several other etiologies that produce a relatively rapid failure of the myocardium may be involved. These were treated in chapter 10 as factors contributing to acute heart failure. The relatively rare cardiomyopathies **3** or bacterial toxins (e.g., diphtheria toxin) can weaken the

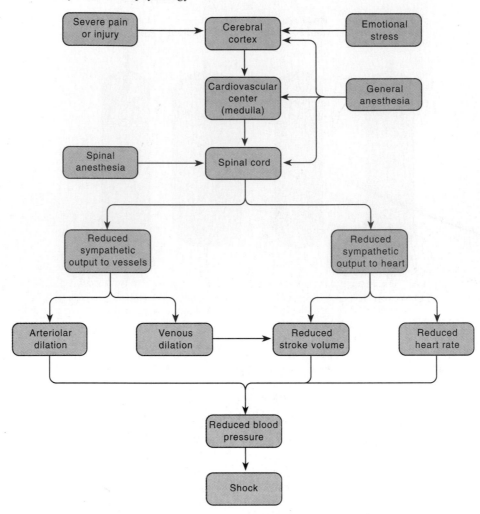

Figure 11.3. Neurogenic shock. Note that both cardiac and vascular mechanisms play a contributing role.

myocardium. Other circulating substances, such as narcotic drugs or excessively high levels of potassium ion, can also depress myocardial function.

Cardiac output may also fall rapidly as a result of factors that restrict normal pumping. Mural thrombi can block blood flow through the heart, **4** as can cardiac tamponade, which produces external pressures that interfere with normal filling. Inadequate venous return may also result in a reduced cardiac output. Venous return can be reduced by compression of the venae cavae as in cardiac tamponade **5** or **tension pneumothorax.** In the latter condition, air gains access to the pleural cavity and causes the lung to collapse. If air continues to enter more rapidly than it can escape, the increasing pressure that results is applied to the venae cavae, causing their compression and a drop in venous return. Another way that blood flow to the heart can be restricted involves the pulmonary circulation. Extensive pulmonary embolism can interfere with flow through the lungs so that blood reaching the left heart will be greatly

reduced in volume. **6** A rapid fall in cardiac output results. Various patterns of cardiac arrhythmia can also cause significant reduction in cardiac output so that shock develops. Whatever the etiology, a sharply reduced cardiac output is the significant event of cardiogenic shock. Figure 11.4 summarizes the etiology of cardiogenic shock.

Hypovolemic Shock

Hypovolemic shock is the condition arising from inadequate circulating blood volume. Most hypovolemic shock is **hemorrhagic shock.** That is, it is usually the result of severe bleeding following massive trauma. Blood escaping the body's vascular channels is usually easily seen, and quick intervention can often prevent shock from developing. However, intervention may be delayed, or bleeding may occur without visible blood loss, as in the cases of hemorrhage into body cavities, muscle groups, or the GI tract. **7** For example, blood lost into the abdominal

Figure 11.4   Principal causes of cardiogenic shock.

cavity following rupture of the aorta or into the muscle mass surrounding a fractured femur can result in serious drops in blood pressure. In some cases, hypovolemic shock may arise without the loss of whole blood from the vessels. Examples are fluid losses due to vascular changes that can accompany severe inflammation, to skin burns, or to dehydration from inadequate fluid intake, pronounced perspiration, or prolonged vomiting and diarrhea.

When excess fluid is lost to the tissues across intact capillary walls, shock may result. Such fluid losses may be the result of an abrupt obstruction in the venous system—from thromboembolism, for example. The obstruction prevents normal drainage of the microcirculation, and congestion and higher BHP result. The elevated BHP can rapidly drive substantial volumes of fluid into the tissue spaces. The result is **hypovolemia,** a reduction of circulating blood volume. A similar result follows damage to capillaries, usually from anoxia or immune causes. When a capillary wall is damaged, its permeability increases, allowing the escape of fluid to the tissues. In either case, although total body fluid volume is not reduced, the volume of blood circulating in the vessels is. Shock follows, as venous return falls to levels that cannot sustain the output. Such increased capillary permeability can complicate hemorrhagic shock, since both often accompany massive trauma.

Shock may also be caused by extensive skin burns, where fluid loss can be substantial. The greatest losses occur in **third-degree burns,** in which both epidermis and dermis are lost. (**First-degree burns** are mild and involve only the epidermis, which can quickly regenerate; **second-degree burns** are more severe because they involve both epidermal loss as well as some dermal damage.) Two factors contribute to fluid loss at burned surfaces. One is a pronounced inflammatory response in the severely damaged tissue. Massive exudate formation follows when large volumes of fluid rapidly leave the vascular spaces. Also, because blood vessels damaged by burns tend to lose protein, tissue osmotic pressure increases, drawing further fluid from the vessels by osmosis. The second fluid loss factor in burns is the loss of the body's protective surface lining. The skin normally prevents loss of tissue fluid by evaporation to the surrounding dry air. When the skin is

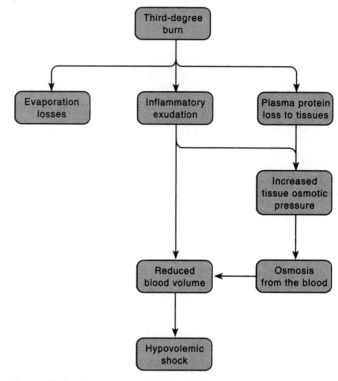

Figure 11.5   Burns and shock. Severe burns present the risk of fluid loss and hypovolemic shock.

lost, evaporation to the surrounding air can be considerable (fig. 11.5). So great is this loss in third-degree burns, that when over 15% of the body's surface is involved, therapy must first be directed to preventing shock. Only then can attention be directed to the burned tissues.

In dehydration, substantial water is lost from the body. The result is a drop in plasma volume followed by a fall in BHP. When the dehydration is severe, hypovolemic shock can result. Sustained vomiting or diarrhea can lead to large losses of body water. Children are especially susceptible to this type of dehydration. Dehydration can also result from kidney disease. For example, in one type of kidney disease, large amounts of protein are lost into the urine. This in turn causes large urinary water losses, plasma volume reduction, and the potential for shock. In another type of disease, the

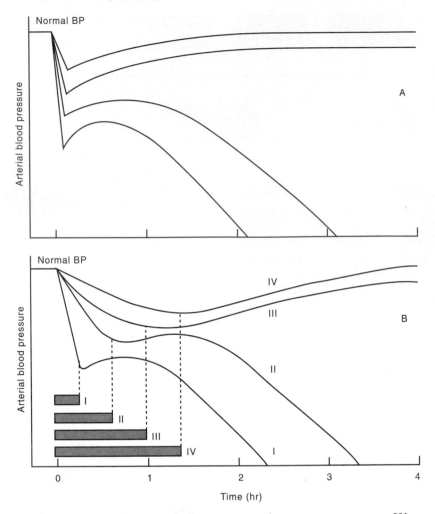

Figure 11.6   (*a*) In the face of small volume and pressure declines, compensations can restore pressure. If losses are large, no recovery may be possible. (*b*) Outcomes of the same fluid volume lost over different time periods. Slow losses (III, IV) allow compensations to take effect and restore BHP. Rapid loss (I, II) of the same volume is fatal.

Source: Modified from A.C. Guyton, *Textbook of Medical Physiology,* 5th edition, 1971, W.B. Saunders, Philadelphia.

kidney may be unable to regulate electrolyte levels properly. The resulting electrolyte imbalance can also cause large water losses (see chapter 16). Even prolonged and intense exertion in warm temperatures can lead to such large perspiration losses that shock from dehydration is a threat.

Hypovolemic shock develops on the basis of a reduction in circulating blood volume. However, any such losses will have much more severe effects if they occur over a short time span. Although much information on the effects of hemorrhage has been derived from studies using dogs or other animals, similar patterns are assumed to apply to the human. At one extreme, 10% of the body's approximately 5-liter blood volume can be lost, even abruptly, with minimal effect. At the other extreme, rapid loss of 50% of the blood is almost invariably fatal. Between these, the time factor becomes more significant. The rapid loss of only 20% of blood volume will pose a greater threat than the

gradual loss of 35% or even more (fig. 11.6). The reason for these different effects has to do with physiological compensations that are activated by a falling BHP. These are explained in detail following a description of vascular shock.

Vascular Shock

In vascular shock, rapid and widespread vasodilation expands vascular capacity. For a given volume of blood within the vascular system, the result is reduced BHP. This means that even though no blood is lost, the relationship between the normal blood volume and the vascular capacity has been thrown out of balance. In this situation of **relative hypovolemia,** the existing blood volume is unable to fill the enlarged vascular space adequately. The result is a fall in BHP and a decline in venous return to the heart. As the heart receives less blood to pump, cardiac output may fall to reduce the BHP further.

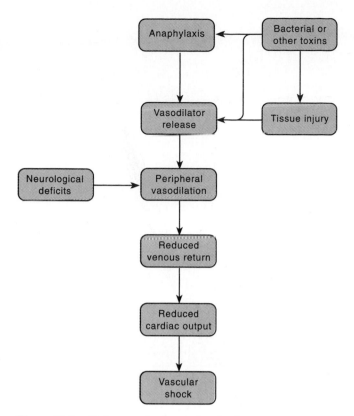

Figure 11.7   Pathogenesis of vascular shock.

Distributive Shock

You may encounter use of the term **distributive shock** in some clinical settings. It is essentially the same as vascular shock, but with a different focus. Rather than the essential vascular mechanism that produces the problem, its use emphasizes the inappropriate distribution of blood in peripheral tissues, which reduces venous return and compromises cardiac output. You are likely to meet the term in cases of anaphylactic, septic, and neurogenic shock, the most frequently encountered types of vascular shock.

The significant vasodilation component of primary shock has already been described. The pathogenesis of vascular shock is summarized in figure 11.7.

COMPENSATION IN SHOCK

In response to falling BHP, several reflex compensations are triggered. These reflexes are part of the cardiovascular regulation mechanism, which is based on the principles of negative feedback control (chapter 3). They include baroreceptor reflexes, which support cardiac function and vasoconstriction, and renal fluid retention.

The cardiovascular system has pressure-sensitive receptors (**baroreceptors**) distributed throughout the body. Some are located in the arch of the aorta. A second concentration of baroreceptors is found near the division of the common carotid artery. This region is called the **carotid sinus.** From these sites, the baroreceptors send BHP-related information to the medulla oblongata, where integration for blood pressure regulation occurs. These medullary integration centers can be collectively described as the **cardiovascular center.** Output from the medulla elicits a response from effectors that appropriately adjusts BHP. The control system's effectors are the heart and blood vessels. By controlling cardiac output and constriction in arterioles and veins, BHP can be maintained at set point.

In the heart, output is altered by changing both heart rate and myocardial contractility. When autonomic input to the sinoatrial node is dominated by the sympathetic branch, heart rate increases. The opposite response results when the parasympathetic system is dominant. Myocardial contractility depends in part on sympathetic stimulation. When stimulation is increased, contractility is greater, and vice versa. (The myocardium is only minimally affected by the parasympathetic system. As contractility is increased, greater stroke volume and cardiac output result.)

Similarly, only the sympathetic system is required to produce changes in the constriction state of arterioles and venules. When sympathetic stimulation is increased above normal levels, the result is arteriolar constriction. In veins,

The most common type of vascular shock is **septic shock,** in which falling BHP is the result of peripheral vasodilation caused by circulating vasodilator substances. In some cases, these are bacterial endotoxins that reach the blood when infection is uncontrolled. Most often, Gram-negative organisms from urinary or gastrointestinal tract infections are involved. In other cases, the bacterial toxins cause tissue damage, which liberates histamine, kinins, or other vasodilators. A complicating factor in septic shock is that cellular damage caused by bacterial toxins also renders the cells less able to utilize the nutrients supplied by the already diminished blood supply. This handicap contributes to the overall reduction of metabolic activity in the affected tissues.

Next to cardiogenic shock, septic shock is the most common cause of fatality from circulatory shock. Risk is especially great in peritonitis. When circulating vasodilators are toxins of nonbacterial origin, the term **toxic shock** is used. Such toxins may be released from damaged tissues or they may achieve high levels when liver damage causes a depression of normal hepatic detoxification functions.

Another type of vascular shock is **anaphylactic shock.** It involves an immune response following a second exposure to a foreign antigen. The antigens react with sensitized cells, causing the massive release of histamine and other vasodilators. Insect bites, blood transfusions, and some therapeutic or diagnostic agents can trigger the response. Anaphylactic shock presents significant risks, because it can develop with dramatic speed and intensity.

Figure 11.8   Baroreceptor-mediated compensations in shock.

with a much less well-developed tunica media, more sympathetic stimulation causes a greater wall tension. In this way, the venous wall better resists stretching in response to the pressure of blood in its lumen. Although not actually constricting, this greater wall tension, or **tone,** will maintain higher venous pressure. This in turn promotes venous blood flow and increases venous return to the heart (fig. 11.8). Most compensating vasoconstriction occurs in dermal and splanchnic arterioles. As a result, not only is BHP increased, but more blood volume can be diverted from the skin and abdominal viscera to structures critical to the circulation, such as the brain and the heart.

The cardiovascular reflexes function to adjust BHP during normal activities, for example, during exercise or when changing from a reclining to an upright posture. They are also available when circulatory shock develops, and can greatly reduce its threat. It has been estimated that

these reflexes approximately double the volume of blood loss that can be tolerated before hypovolemic shock develops (fig. 11.6b).

In cases of extreme BHP reduction, to about half of normal levels, the cardiovascular center's neurons are directly affected by ischemia. In response to the resulting hypoxia, the cardiovascular center produces an intense outpouring of sympathetic stimulation in an emergency attempt to raise BHP and avoid serious anoxic damage. This is known as the **central nervous system ischemic response.**

There are other compensations that can counter the effects of shock. As BHP declines, the pressure balance across capillary walls between the blood and tissues is disturbed. Since BHP is the major factor in moving fluid into the tissue spaces, when it is reduced, less tissue fluid is formed. With less fluid leaving the vessels, BHP falls less

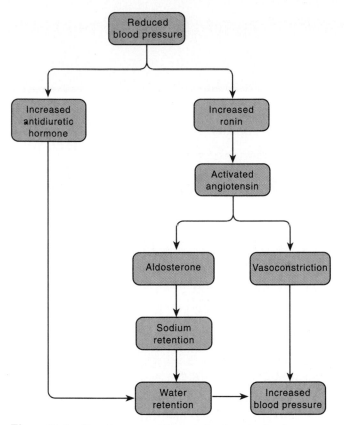

Figure 11.9   Renal compensation mechanisms in shock.

rapidly. A lower BHP also promotes the drawing of more tissue fluid into the blood from the tissue spaces. The additional fluid raises plasma volume and supports BHP.

The kidney is also involved in shock compensation. Because of falling BHP and the compensating vasoconstriction that follows, blood flow to the kidney is reduced in shock. In response, the kidney's water retention mechanisms are activated. Total plasma volume, and hence BHP, are maintained in this way. Another reflex mechanism involves the renin-angiotensin system. When it is activated, blood levels of angiotensin II are increased. This most potent of the endogenous vasoconstrictors supports the CNS reflexes that maintain BHP by vasoconstriction. In addition, angiotensin II stimulates aldosterone secretion by the adrenal cortex. This steroid hormone promotes renal sodium retention, which in turn results in more water retention by the kidney. Retention of water maintains plasma volume, with favorable effects on BHP (fig. 11.9).

THERAPY IN CIRCULATORY SHOCK

Therapeutic intervention in shock must first restore adequate levels of blood flow to dependent tissues. Then, attempts to eliminate the cause of shock and to cope with its secondary effects can be made. In hypovolemic shock, the lost blood volume must be replaced to restore pressure

and blood flow. Whole blood, plasma, or plasma substitutes may be used in such cases.

Various drug therapies are also useful in shock. They are especially beneficial in correcting unfavorable vascular dilation states. For example, in neurogenic or vascular shock, where vasodilation is a major problem, a vasoconstrictor such as norepinephrine might be used. On the other hand, in cardiogenic shock, vasoconstriction reflexes may place an increased burden of afterload on a heart that is already experiencing difficulty in maintaining cardiac output. In such cases, administration of isoproterenol is of benefit because it increases heart rate and myocardial contractility while at the same time reducing afterload by inducing vasodilation. The increases in cardiac output produced by the drug cause an elevation of BHP that outweighs any BHP reduction resulting from vasodilation. Alternatively, vasoconstrictors may be used to augment BHP if further flow reduction in dermal and splanchnic capillaries will not result in tissue damage. There are many drugs available and most have multiple sites of action; therefore, great care must be taken in selecting and administering an appropriate vasoactive agent to avoid aggravating the situation instead of helping it. For the same reason, it is important to establish the cause of shock before a therapeutic course is selected.

Elimination of the cause of shock may be difficult in cardiogenic shock, because infarction often involves a large volume of myocardium and because of the acute onset of the attack. In the case of tamponade, some surgical correction is possible. Antibiotic therapy can sometimes eliminate the bacteria responsible for septic shock, but the time required for achieving adequate control is often too long to save the situation. In general, hypovolemic shock has a better prognosis than does cardiogenic or septic shock, because of the speed and relative ease with which fluid replacement therapy can be instituted.

Secondary effects in shock are also usually corrected when an adequate blood flow is restored. This is the case with the muscular weakness, restlessness, and confusion often seen in shock. Body temperature is also restored as renewed oxygen and glucose supplies return aerobic metabolism to the normal levels that contribute to body temperature maintenance. Antibiotic therapy favors resolution of the secondary pulmonary infections that often accompany cardiogenic shock. Infections readily develop in **shock lung,** which is characterized by pulmonary congestion, edema, and thrombosis.

The kidney is nearly always affected in shock, as reflex vasoconstriction restricts its blood flow. The result is a decreased filtration rate and hence a substantial reduction in urinary output. This condition is called **oliguria** and is a hallmark characteristic of shock. When vasoconstriction is prolonged, renal ischemia can cause necrosis from anoxia, because renal oxygen requirements are high. A critical

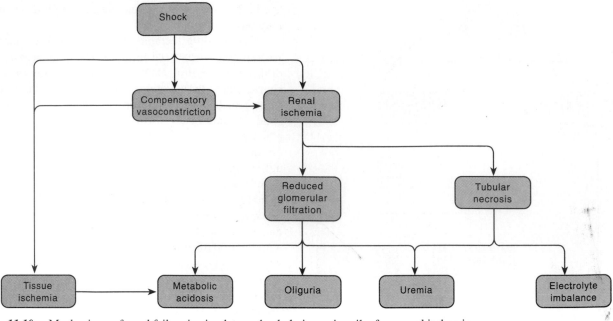

Figure 11.10   Mechanisms of renal failure in circulatory shock derive, primarily, from renal ischemia.

reduction in renal function may result, leading to a build-up in the blood of the toxic substances normally excreted by the kidney. Electrolyte imbalances will also often result from such renal damage. These problems can contribute to tissue damage and further complicate an already serious shock situation. In many cases death from shock is caused by renal failure (fig. 11.10).

Another problem in shock therapy involves coping with pH imbalance. Lactic acid production by the anaerobic metabolism of hypoxic tissues may produce a **metabolic acidosis.** This can be further complicated by **respiratory acidosis** because fluid retention reflexes may produce congestion in the lungs, impairing ventilation and the clearance of carbon dioxide. Alkaline sodium bicarbonate is usually injected to counter the acidosis and restore normal plasma pH values. (Details of these pH imbalance conditions are available in chapter 16.)

PROGRESSION IN CIRCULATORY SHOCK

Circulatory shock is a dynamic state that, if uncorrected, can lead to death. It has the potential for progressing through a sequence of three stages. The first is **nonprogressive shock,** in which a combination of physiological compensations and therapy may overcome the process and lead to recovery. The second stage is **progressive shock,** which is characterized by tissue hypoperfusion and organ damage. In the third stage, **irreversible shock,** organ and tissue damage is so severe that death is inevitable, even though aggressive therapy restores BHP.

These stages of circulatory shock lie on a continuum and do not represent isolated clinical states, but it is useful to examine each one to gain an insight into their specific mechanisms.

Nonprogressive Shock

In nonprogressive shock, reflex compensatory mechanisms are activated and BHP and microcirculation flow are restored. Tissues return to their normal functional status. In those tissues damaged by hypoxia, adequate flow is available to meet the demands of regeneration and repair. Secondary problems of metabolic acidosis, shock lung, and renal disturbances are relieved by the restoration of blood flow and corrective therapy.

Progressive Shock

The situation in progressive shock is potentially much more serious. In this situation, BHP and microcirculation flow progressively decline because of the severity of blood loss or the lack or failure of therapeutic intervention. The result is hypoxic cell injury to the vital organs. This leads to the initiation of positive feedback cycling, which increases the damage and decreases the likelihood of effective compensation.

Depression of cardiac function is an important feature of progressive shock and is due to a number of factors. First, with falling blood pressure, the coronary circulation may be compromised, with the myocardium becoming ischemic, damaged, and weakened. This condition leads to a reduction of cardiac output, further declines in BHP, and further declines in myocardial perfusion, etc. A second factor involves the cardiovascular center in the medulla. With hypoperfusion of the hypoxia-sensitive brain, its function may be depressed, with less autonomic output to the heart and systemic arterioles producing a lower BHP, further brain perfusion decline, and continued positive feedback cycling. A third factor in progressive shock is the release of **myocardial depressant factor** (MDF) by the ischemic

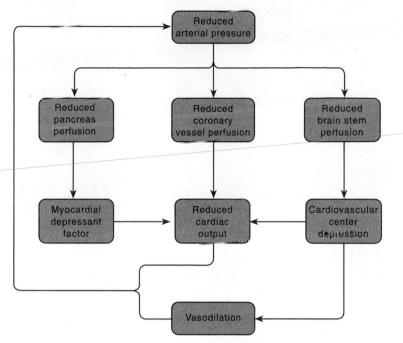

Figure 11.11   Positive feedback cycling in progressive shock. The essential factor in progression is the declining functional capacity of the heart and vessels.

pancreas. This substance has the effect of compromising myocardial contractility. Thus, whether the heart is directly or indirectly involved, an initial drop in BHP and blood flow affects the brain and heart, resulting in further declines in pressure and flow. Continuation of the positive feedback cycling causes rapid deterioration of an already serious situation (fig. 11.11).

Another major problem in progressive shock is peripheral pooling, which reduces venous return to the heart. There are a number of causes of this accumulation of blood in the peripheral veins. With a persistent cellular oxygen deficit, a shift to anaerobic metabolism produces a lactic acidosis, which affects arterioles. The chronic acidity interferes with their normal vasoconstriction responses and they dilate, allowing blood to accumulate in the veins. Peripheral pooling is also favored by the reduced sympathetic nervous system output from the hypoxic cardiovascular center. Such input is a major factor in sustaining the vasoconstriction that normally promotes rapid blood flow.

Vasodilation and pooling may also result from functional deterioration of the vessels themselves. Compensatory constriction demands greatly exaggerate the vessels' workload at a time when their own nutritional needs are compromised by reduced blood flow. Fatigue may then cause failure of the vessels, with consequent vasodilation and pooling. As previously discussed, there are other factors that may contribute to vasodilation, e.g., bacterial toxins in septic shock.

The combination of cardiac suppression and peripheral pooling produces a deteriorating pattern of diminished car-

diac output, which is driven by the positive feedback cycling characteristic of progressive shock. The various contributing factors are summarized in figure 11.12.

Progressive shock may also develop from other causes, either cardiac or vascular. When blood flow rates decline, for whatever reason, risk of intravascular thrombosis is increased. Some bacterial endotoxins also stimulate thrombosis. In shock, DIC (disseminated intravascular coagulation) may develop, causing further reduction in blood flow or even complete stasis. **8** In addition, toxins released from necrotic tissues can damage capillaries, greatly increasing their fluid permeability. Massive losses of fluid to the tissue spaces result, followed by great reductions in circulating plasma volume, venous return, cardiac output, and further downward spiraling of circulatory function.

Irreversible Shock

When shock is acute and severe, or when prolonged without therapeutic support, such positive feedback cycles may be impossible to interrupt. Unless therapeutic intervention is quickly and aggressively applied, the prognosis is poor. In fact, beyond a certain level of anoxic and toxic damage, even restoration of normal BHP by fluid replacement or other therapy will not prevent the patient's death. This is the situation of irreversible shock. That a given shock victim is at the point of irreversible damage is impossible to determine. Therefore, therapy is always vigorously maintained until either shock progression is arrested or the patient dies (fig. 11.13).

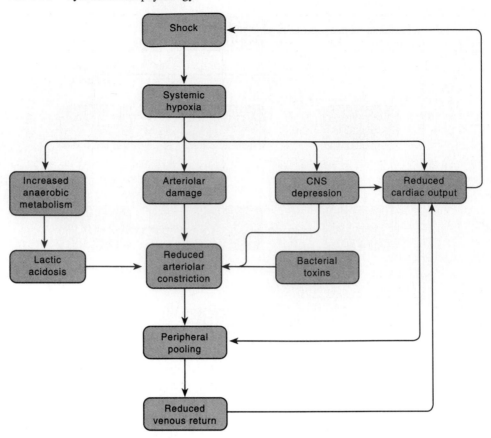

Figure 11.12   Summary of the essential features of progressive shock. Note the characteristic positive feedback component.

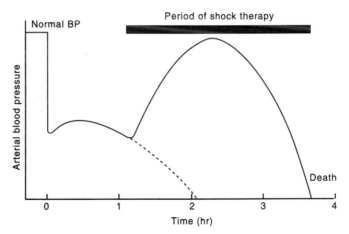

Figure 11.13   Irreversible shock. The loss of arterial pressure causes damage from which recovery is ultimately impossible, even though therapy may temporarily restore BHP.

Case Study

A 66-year-old male arrived by ambulance at a hospital's emergency room on IV fluids and oxygen. He had collapsed at work after complaining of heartburn over a 30-minute period. His wife had accompanied the ambulance and was able to provide some medical history to the effect that although the man had been in generally good health, he had been experiencing heartburn and dull pains in his chest and left shoulder over the past few weeks.

On examination, the ER physicians found him to be confused and lethargic, with pale, cool, "clammy" skin. His pulse was "thready," i.e., rapid and weak, and his respiration rate was elevated. The ambulance crew's blood pressure report of "70/unrecordable" was verified in the ER. A tentative diagnosis of MI and cardiogenic shock was made.

IV lines and ECG monitoring were quickly established, after which the patient almost immediately lost consciousness, with the ECG indicating ventricular fibrillation.

Cardiac stimulant drugs and defibrillation were unable to reverse the arrythmia, and the patient died.

Commentary

In this all too typical case, cardiogenic shock due to MI quickly overwhelmed the victim before supportive therapy could reverse the process. The low arterial pressure noted in the ambulance had compromised cerebral flow to induce the patient's loss of consciousness and lethargy. The pulse, respiration, and skin signs all testified to a marshalling of the sympathetic nervous system's reflexes in the face of rapidly declining arterial pressure.

At autopsy a massive left ventricular infarct was found, as were coronary arteries showing evidence of severe atherosclerosis. Fibrillation in such cases is common, as the widespread destruction of cardiac tissue so disrupts conduction that maintaining myocardial contraction coordination becomes impossible.

Key Concepts

1. Circulatory shock is the result of the cardiovascular system's inability to maintain blood flow adequate to meet tissue requirements (p. 268).

2. Although specific etiologies are numerous, only three essential mechanisms of shock are involved: cardiac malfunction, which causes cardiogenic shock; inadequate blood volume, which causes hypovolemic shock; and widespread vasodilation, which causes vascular shock (p. 268).

3. In primary shock, a neurogenic mechanism produces both cardiac and vascular alterations that combine to produce a critical fall in BHP (p. 268).

4. Primary shock may arise as a result of emotional trauma or some compromise of CNS function that interferes with normal output to the heart and arterioles (p. 268).

5. Although myocardial infarction is the most common cause of cardiac shock, many other factors may contribute to the heart's inability to maintain adequate output (p. 269).

6. Hypovolemic shock is produced by the direct and rapid loss of fluid from blood vessels, or by various indirect means such as burns or kidney malfunction (p. 270).

7. The widespread vasodilation that characterizes vascular shock may be triggered by bacterial endotoxins, by other chemical vasodilators, or by immune or neurogenic mechanisms (p. 272).

8. Various physiological compensations are activated in the face of falling BHP (p. 273).

9. Therapy in shock first addresses the problem of restoring adequate blood flow, then seeks to eliminate the cause of shock and deal with its secondary effects (p. 275).

10. Progression in shock may be prevented by physiological compensations and therapy, but if cardiovascular structures malfunction because of ischemia, shock may progress to cause severe organ damage that may be fatal (p. 276).

REVIEW ACTIVITIES

1. Using CS (cardiogenic shock), HS (hypovolemic shock), or VS (vascular shock), categorize each of the following specific shock types. Note that some types might fall into two categories.

   Septic shock   Toxic shock   Neurogenic shock
   Primary shock   Hemorrhagic   Distributive shock
                      shock
   Anaphylactic   Burn shock
   shock

2. Complete the following table by using ST (short term) or LT (long term) to indicate the time over which each of the cardiovascular compensations is likely to have an effect when BHP declines.

   Increased heart rate
   Increased myocardial
       contraction strength
   Arteriolar constriction
   CNS ischemic response
   RAS-mediated water retention
   Increased venous tone

3. Cover the legend in figure 11.11. Pick any starting point and from it, follow the process through successive steps. Once you start the sequence can you stop? What kind of feedback is involved? Is it the same type that operates in the body's temperature regulation system, described in chapter 3? Is this relevant to progression in shock? Why?

4. In the case study, explain why the patient's heart rate was elevated. Assess this case of shock in terms of progression: was it progressive or nonprogressive, reversible or irreversible?

Chapter Twelve

Respiratory Pathophysiology

Oft fetchying of the winde, declares a sicknesse of the lungus.

Thomas Wilson
Logike

Figure 12.1   Essential features of lung and airway structure. Note that the right lung has three lobes, while the left lung has two.

Disordered respiratory function can have serious and even lethal consequences. It also accounts for the usually less serious, but widespread, misery associated with the common cold and the numerous influenza infections that plague us. Before we consider respiratory pathophysiology, it will be helpful to review the normal structure and function of the respiratory system.

ANATOMY AND PHYSIOLOGY

The Lungs

The paired lungs occupy the pleural cavities, which lie within the larger thoracic cavity. **1** **2** Each lung has a superior extreme, the **apex,** which lies opposite its **base.** The base is concave to accommodate the superior thrust of the diaphragm on which it rests. The region of the lung's medial surface where blood vessels and bronchi enter the lung is called the **hilum** (or hilus). The cluster of blood vessels, lymphatic vessels, and bronchi entering at the hilum is the **root** of the lung. Each lung is separated into subdivisions, called **lobes,** by fissures that penetrate deep into the pulmonary mass. A single fissure in the left lung yields a superior and inferior lobe, while two fissures in the right lung give rise to superior, middle, and inferior lobes (fig. 12.1).

Associated with the lungs is a system of membranes called the pleural membranes, or **pleurae.** The pleurae are sheets of squamous epithelial cells that rest on a supporting bed of collagenous and elastic connective tissue. These are serous membranes, which secrete a watery fluid that coats their surfaces. They are arranged so that one part of the pleural membrane, the **visceral pleura,** covers the lungs'

surface, while the other part, the **parietal pleura,** folds back to line the inner surfaces of the thoracic cavity. The **pleural fluid** is found in the **pleural space** between the two pleurae (fig. 12.2a). In this way, during respiration, the lung surface glides over a film of fluid as it moves against the thoracic wall.

Because pressure in the pleural space is always lower than that of atmospheric air, air in the pulmonary airways is always at greater pressure. The pressure difference between the two regions is normally large enough to overcome the lung tissue's elasticity, causing the lung to be pushed firmly against the thoracic wall. This elastic property derives from the abundant elastic connective tissue present in the pulmonary tissues between the lung's airways and its vasculature. The lung's elastic tissue is organized in a way that tends to draw the lung into a smaller, less expanded configuration. A second factor contributes to the effect, namely, the surface tension present at the inner alveolar surfaces. This is the result of the thin fluid layer that coats their surfaces. Alveolar surface tension is normally quite low because of the presence of **pulmonary surfactant.** This phospholipid is secreted by the specialized type II alveolar cells (see fig. 12.6). Both surface tension and the lungs' elasticity must be overcome to keep the lungs fully expanded against the thoracic wall. The same forces must be overcome to produce an inhalation.

Respiratory Airways

Air is delivered to the alveoli of each lung by the upper and lower respiratory passages, or airways. These communicate directly with the atmospheric air. Inhaled air first enters the upper respiratory passages: the nasal **fossae** and then the **pharynx.** **3** Communicating with the nasal fossae are

(a)   (b)

Figure 12.2   (*a*) The pleurae. The visceral pleura is adherent to the surface of the lung, while the parietal pleura is attached to the thoracic wall. The thin pleural space between them contains the pleural fluid. (*b*) Pressure in the pleural space is lower than atmospheric pressure, and the differential causes the lung to expand against the chest wall. Broken arrow represents opposing lung elasticity and surface tension forces.

the **paranasal sinuses.** These are air spaces that protrude from each nasal fossa into the adjacent facial and cranial bones. They take their names from the bones in which they lie: the maxillary sphenoidal, ethmoidal, and frontal sinuses (fig. 12.3). The pharynx is the muscular tube that is continuous with the nasal fossae, the mouth, and the lower respiratory passages, which consist of the larynx, the trachea, and the bronchi.

The **larynx** lies at the base of the pharynx. It is structured of several cartilage pieces that provide sufficient strength and rigidity to prevent its collapse. **4** Positioned in the throat, the larynx is subjected to the twisting and folding that accompanies head movement. Without a rigid wall, such movement could interfere with air flow through the larynx. The vocal cords are situated within the larynx. **5** Their vibration produces the basic sound that is modified by the tongue, lips, and sinuses in voice production (fig. 12.4).

The **trachea** emerges at the inferior end of the larynx. **6** It is a hollow tube formed of incomplete cartilage ring segments, some of which branch. These are stacked and held in place by fibrous and elastic connective tissues to yield a tubular structure with a characteristic segmented appearance (fig. 12.5). At about the midpoint of the mediastinum, the trachea divides to form the two **primary bronchi.** Each primary bronchus conducts air to a complex of smaller bronchi, which repeatedly branch within the lung to form the **bronchial tree.**

Like the trachea, the bronchi have walls containing cartilage segments that allow them to resist collapse. As their branching continues, many small **bronchioles** are formed, **7** the largest of which have a diameter of about 1 mm. Bronchioles have no cartilage in their walls, but smooth muscle tissue is present. The elasticity of the adja-

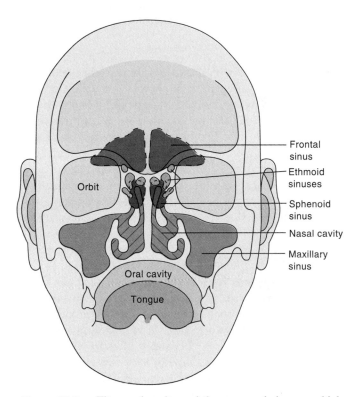

Figure 12.3   The nasal cavity and the paranasal sinuses, which communicate with it. The ethmoid sinuses consist of several small, interconnected air spaces that lie anterior to the sphenoid sinuses.

cent lung tissues exerts a tension on their external surfaces that prevents their collapse.

The smallest bronchioles are called terminal bronchioles. They branch to form still finer ducts, which have periodic bulges where the wall becomes very thin. Pulmonary

4 ‖‖‖‖ 53346

5 ‖‖‖‖ 53365

6 ‖‖‖‖ 53347

7 ‖‖‖‖ 44372

Figure 12.4 The nasal cavity and pharynx. Mucus and trapped particles are swept from the airways by cilia to the oropharynx for swallowing. Solid arrow shows the path of swallowed food.

capillaries associate with these, and some exchange of carbon dioxide and oxygen occurs across the wall. For this reason, these airways are called **respiratory bronchioles.** From their smallest branches, air passes into **alveolar ducts, 8** which have a succession of thin-walled, alveoluslike bulges forming their walls. Each alveolar duct delivers air to a small number of **alveolar sacs.** These dead-end pouches form the termination of the respiratory passages. They are formed of many **alveoli** (singular: alveolus), **9 10** which present the large surface across which the blood gases diffuse (fig. 12.6). The lungs have an average of about 400 million alveoli, with a total surface area of about 75 m^2.

The term **acinus** is used to describe the functional unit of the lung. It consists of the airways and alveoli supplied by each terminal bronchiole: the respiratory bronchioles, alveolar ducts, and alveolar sacs. In normal lungs, three to five acini are supported by thin sheets of connective tissue. Each of these is known as a **lobule.**

Both the upper and lower respiratory passages are lined by mucous membrane. It consists of an epithelium supported by a layer of connective tissue, which in turn is limited by a thin layer of smooth muscle, the **muscularis mucosa.** In the bronchioles, this muscle layer can alter the airway's diameter by changing tension. The mucosal epithelium, with only few exceptions, is a protective pseudostratified type. It has cilia that project into the mucous layer present at its luminal surface. **11** Mucus is secreted by the specialized goblet cells of the epithelium and by glands in the submucosa. These glands also secrete a serous fluid and so are called **seromucous glands.**

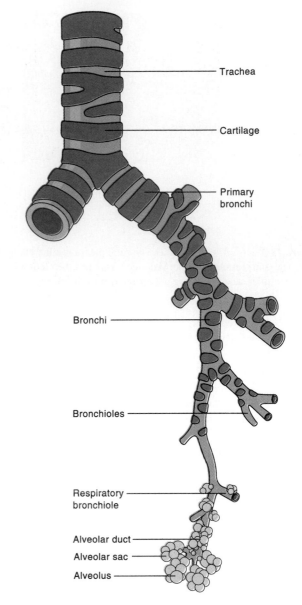

Figure 12.5 The bronchial tree and the pattern of its branching to form the distal airways, where respiratory gas exchange occurs.

Respiratory Movements

At rest, air is moved into the lungs and then expelled. The approximately 500 ml of air moved in this way is called the **tidal volume.** Inhalation is achieved by contracting the inspiratory muscles—mainly the **diaphragm,** with a small contribution from the **internal intercostal muscles.** Their contraction produces a taller and wider thoracic cavity by lowering its floor (the diaphragm) and elevating the ribs. As the walls of the cavity expand to these positions, the adhesion of the pleurae causes the lungs to be drawn into an expanded configuration. Because pulmonary tissue is attached to the walls of the lung's airways, expansion of the

8 44375

9 44378

10 27226

11 46201

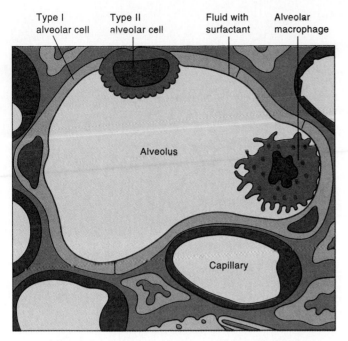

Type I alveolar cell   Type II alveolar cell   Fluid with surfactant   Alveolar macrophage

Alveolus

Capillary

Figure 12.6 Structural elements of the respiratory membrane. The endothelium and basement membrane of the capillary lie adjacent to the epithelium of the alveolus, with only a thin layer of elastic lung tissue between them. Most alveolar cells are type I pneumocytes. The type II cell is the source of pulmonary surfactant. An alveolar macrophage is also shown.

lung causes the airways to expand as well. The result is an increase in the total volume of the pulmonary airways. This in turn causes a drop in pressure within them. As pressure falls below atmospheric levels, air is pushed into the lungs. Relaxation of the inspiratory muscles and the recoil of the lung's elastic tissues return thoracic dimensions to normal. This reduction of volume raises air pressure within the pulmonary airways, and air is forced from the lungs. Note that, at rest, exhalation is passive; that is, it requires no muscle contractions.

The usual rate of respiration is in the range of 10–18 breaths per minute. When increased **ventilation** (the total volume of air moving in and out of the lungs) is required, both rate and depth of respiration are usually increased. These changes are the result of output from centers in the pons and medulla oblongata. In response, the respiratory muscles contract more often and more forcefully, producing a greater volume of air flow. To expel such increased volumes, active expiration is required, and the abdominal muscles are called upon. In tensing, they increase abdominal pressure, which causes the abdominal viscera to push the diaphragm past its rest position. The external intercostal muscles are also employed. As they contract, the ribs are depressed beyond their rest position. Both these movements further decrease thoracic volume to increase exhalation pressure. When lung disease makes breathing especially difficult, even the sternomastoids and those muscles that

straighten the vertebral column are brought into use to increase the force of inspiration. To meet the high ventilation demand of vigorous exercise, energy expenditure to contract the respiratory muscles can approach 3% of the body's total output.

Oxygen and Carbon Dioxide Exchange

The respiratory system's principal contribution to overall somatic function is the exchange of carbon dioxide (CO_2) and oxygen (O_2) between the blood and atmospheric air. This exchange is accomplished in the lungs, where pulmonary capillaries are in intimate contact with the linings of the lung's terminal air spaces, the alveoli. Each alveolus has a wall, or septum, formed by a thin epithelial cell and its basement membrane (BM). The pulmonary capillary walls are formed of a thin endothelium, also with a BM on its tissue surface. Where the alveolar wall and capillary wall are in contact, their BMs merge to form a single layer. This arrangement provides only a thin (0.5 μm) layer of cytoplasm and BM between capillary blood and alveolar air. **12** This layer is the **respiratory membrane,** across which exchange of oxygen and carbon dioxide occurs (fig. 12.6).

After returning to the right heart from the systemic circulation, blood is delivered to the pulmonary capillaries. They provide a large surface area that matches the large surface presented by the alveoli. Blood in the pulmonary vessels carries carbon dioxide produced by systemic cells as a by-product of their energy metabolism. It contains about 100 times the carbon dioxide of arterial blood.

In the blood, carbon dioxide is transported in three forms. About 25% is combined with hemoglobin (Hb) in erythrocytes, not with the heme group where oxygen binds, but with the protein portion of the molecule: globin. This means that carbon dioxide and oxygen do not compete for the same bond sites on the hemoglobin molecule; both carbon dioxide and oxygen are simultaneously carried on the hemoglobin molecule. About 65% of carbon dioxide is present in the form of bicarbonate ion (HCO_3^-) derived from carbonic acid (H_2CO_3). Carbonic acid is formed from water and carbon dioxide, which combine within the erythrocyte in a reaction catalyzed by the enzyme **carbonic anhydrase.** As the carbonic acid is formed, it dissociates to yield bicarbonate ion and hydrogen ion by the formula

$$CO_2 + H_2O \leftrightarrow H_2CO_3 \leftrightarrow H^+ + HCO_3^-$$

This is the carbonic acid equilibrium. As carbon dioxide enters red blood cells from the systemic tissue spaces, the equilibrium shifts to the right to produce bicarbonate ion (fig. 12.7). As this ion accumulates, a concentration gradient is established between the red cell and the plasma. This gradient favors the diffusion of the bicarbonate ion into the plasma, where it remains until it reaches the pulmonary capillaries.

Figure 12.7   The uptake of CO_2 from the tissues and the delivery of oxygen to the tissues depend on their interaction with hemoglobin (Hb) within the erythrocyte.

A small amount (about 10%) of the blood's carbon dioxide is carried as a gas, directly dissolved in the plasma's water. As a dissolved gas, it contributes to the total pressure exerted by all of the gas molecules dissolved in the plasma (others are nitrogen and oxygen). The portion of the total pressure contributed by the carbon dioxide is called the **partial pressure** of carbon dioxide. This is usually written PCO_2.

As carbon dioxide enters the blood in systemic capillaries, oxygen diffuses from the blood to the tissue spaces. Some of this oxygen was carried in the blood as a dissolved gas, producing a certain partial pressure of oxygen (PO_2). Only a small amount (1–2%) of all the blood's oxygen travels in this way, however. Most is carried in the erythrocyte, bound to the iron atom found in each of the four heme groups of hemoglobin. This combined form is **oxyhemoglobin** (HbO_2). The oxygen-hemoglobin equilibrium can be expressed as follows:

$$O_2 + Hb \leftrightarrow HbO_2$$

(It should be understood that Hb is an abbreviation and not a chemical symbol.) In the tissues, cells consume oxygen and a lowered tissue PO_2 results. This change favors the diffusion of oxygen from the plasma and red blood cells into the tissues. As a result, red blood cell PO_2 falls, causing the hemoglobin equilibrium to shift to the left. This shift releases oxygen, making it available for diffusion to the tissues (fig. 12.7). From the tissues, blood is delivered by way of the right heart to the pulmonary capillaries, where it is separated from the alveolar air by the thin respiratory membrane.

The relative partial pressures of carbon dioxide and oxygen between blood and air favor diffusion of oxygen into the blood and of carbon dioxide into the alveolar air. As a result, plasma PCO_2 falls, favoring the release of hemoglobin's carbon dioxide. Shifting of the carbonic acid equilibrium to the left is also favored by a lower PCO_2, so that additional CO_2 is formed, followed by its diffusion into the adjacent alveolus. Similarly, the arrival in the blood of newly diffused oxygen elevates the red blood cell's PO_2. This increase in PO_2 drives the hemoglobin equilibrium to the right, and oxyhemoglobin is formed. In this way, the blood is continually cleared of its carbon dioxide burden at the same time that it takes up needed oxygen (fig. 12.8).

Respiratory Defense Mechanisms

High pulmonary air flow moving over the extensive pulmonary surfaces presents a situation with great potential for airway irritation and damage. Microorganisms and irritants in the air are drawn into the airways with each inhalation, but an array of defense mechanisms is normally able to resist their damaging effects. These mechanisms also provide for adjusting the temperature and humidity of the air that will be exposed to the delicate alveolar endothelium.

The mucous membrane of the respiratory airways has a well-developed blood supply. **13** This means that air, which is normally cooler than the lungs, and whose humidity may be quite low, is warmed and moisturized as the blood warmth and moisture pass to it from mucosal surfaces. The nasal septum and conchae, or turbinates, increase the surface of the nasal fossae to enhance this effect.

The mucous coating of the respiratory passages plays an important role in preventing particles from reaching the distal airways. Inhaled particles pass over the mucous-covered surface and stick to it. The cilia of the psuedostratified epithelium beat rhythmically to move the particle-laden **mucus blanket** down toward the oropharynx from the upper passages, and up toward the oropharynx from the lower passages. At the pharynx the mucus and particles are swallowed and broken down by gastric acid.

Figure 12.8   The delivery of CO_2 to the lung for excretion and the uptake of oxygen from the alveolus.

Mucosal Damage in Tracheostomy

The value of the warming and moisturizing of inhaled air can be appreciated in patients who have had a **tracheostomy.** **14** In this procedure, an opening into the trachea is made to allow air to by-pass an obstruction that lies in the pharynx or larynx, above the site of the tracheostomy (box fig. 12.1). The procedure permits air to be drawn directly into the lower airways without the benefit of exposure to the moisturizing and warming mucosae of the upper respiratory passages. As a result, long-term tracheostomy patients have a much greater risk of damage to their bronchial mucosal surfaces and of subsequently developing chronic bronchitis (described later in this chapter).

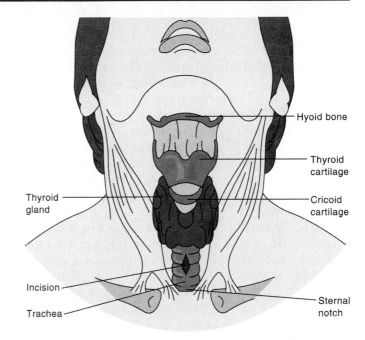

Box Figure 12.1
A tracheostomy involves an incision in the trachea that provides an alternative airway when an obstruction arises in the pharynx or larynx.

The branching pattern of the bronchial tree contributes to the process of particle clearing as each branch point diverts the air flow and increases its exposure to the mucus-covered surfaces. It has been estimated that inhaled air passes an average of 16 branchings of the airways before reaching the respiratory bronchioles.

Larger particles are initially trapped by the nasal hairs and upper respiratory surfaces, while medium-sized particles deposit on bronchial surfaces. These are cleared by the action of the epithelium's cilia. The fine particles that reach the alveoli are cleared by macrophages that are present within the alveoli. **15** If the inhaled particles are bacteria,

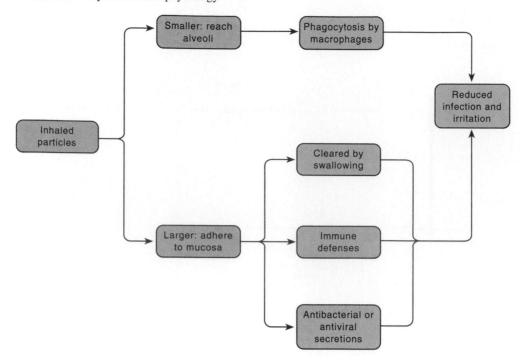

Figure 12.9   Airway defenses that are arrayed against inhaled particles.

they will be killed. If nonliving particles, they may be broken down or remain intact within the macrophage. Following phagocytosis of alveolar particles, the macrophages and the particles they carry may be picked up by the moving mucus blanket, or they may enter the lymph to be carried to the region's lymph nodes.

Macrophages, surfactant, and free particles are known to move from alveoli to the edges of the moving mucus blanket for clearance. The mechanisms underlying these movements are ill understood, but surface tension and pressure gradients may be involved. Whatever the precise mechanisms, they are adversely affected by hypoventilation. It is important to note that factors that reduce a patient's respiratory air flow may compromise clearance and predispose to infection. In many of the hospitalized, restricted lung movement and ventilation may arise due to positioning, constricting bandages, central nervous system depression, or coma. The high rate of pneumonia in hospitalized patients is due, in large part, to impaired ventilation that leads to reducing of clearance.

In addition to its function in particle clearance, the mucus blanket of the respiratory passages contains various secretions that have antibacterial (lysosome and lactoferrin) and antiviral functions (interferon). Complement is also present to augment anti-infection inflammatory responses. It may be that pulmonary surfactant also has a defensive role in promoting phagocytosis. The immune system is active in the lung, with pulmonary secretions containing specific antibodies against bacteria and viruses (fig. 12.9).

Summary

In normal respiratory function, central nervous system output provides the appropriate degree of thoracic cavity expansion and contraction. In response, pulmonary tissues expand sufficiently to move air through unobstructed airways to reach the alveoli. Exchange of carbon dioxide and oxygen follows, provided that blood flow matches air flow and that the respiratory membrane is not altered. Defense mechanisms directed against inhaled microorganisms and nonliving particles are present. Changes in one or more of these requirements interfere with respiratory function to produce lung disease.

RESPIRATORY DISEASE

In considering the function of the respiratory system as providing for the exchange of carbon dioxide and oxygen between blood and air, it should be clear that abnormal oxygenation and carbon dioxide clearance will result from any interference with this process. Therefore, respiratory insufficiency can arise from an inadequate blood volume perfusing the pulmonary capillaries (**hypoperfusion**) or an inadequate air flow reaching the alveoli (**hypoventilation**).

The following sections consider how pulmonary embolism or heart failure can contribute to hypoperfusion of the lungs. Also discussed are the airway obstruction and the pulmonary or other disorders that limit normal lung expansion, in the context of their ability to compromise ventilation (fig. 12.10).

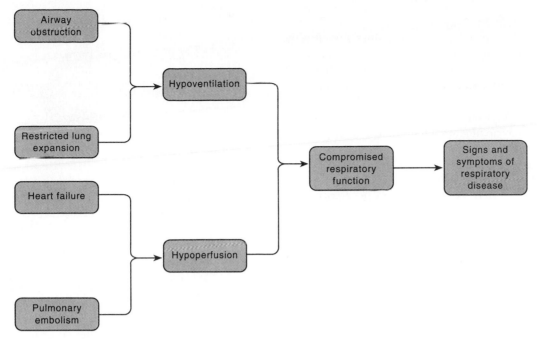

Figure 12.10   The overall pattern of respiratory disease.

Before turning to these major patterns of respiratory pathophysiology, it will be useful to consider the principal signs and symptoms associated with respiratory disease and various pulmonary function tests.

Signs and Symptoms

Cough

Cough is a common sign associated with respiratory disorders. This is a reflex response that attempts to clear the lower respiratory passages by the abrupt and forceful expulsion of air. It is effective when particulate matter, such as food, accidentally enters the respiratory airways. It is most commonly found in lung disease when mucus or other fluids accumulate in the lower airways. Such accumulations may result from inflammation of the lung parenchyma or from increased secretion in response to mucosal irritation. Irritation might arise from the inhalation of irritants or from intrinsic sources of mucosal disruptions, for example, a tumor that invades a bronchial wall. Fluid may also accumulate as a result of excessive blood hydrostatic pressure in the pulmonary capillaries. This causes pulmonary edema, with excess tissue fluid passing into the adjacent airways.

When cough is successful in raising fluid to the pharynx, from where it can be cleared by swallowing or **expectoration** (spitting), it is described as **productive cough.** The fluid so produced is called **sputum.** Production of a bloody sputum is called **hemoptysis.** It usually involves only small amounts of blood loss, so the risk of serious pulmonary blood loss in this way is small. Although the loss of blood is not in itself serious, its presence may indicate serious pulmonary disease. If sputum is purulent, an infection in the lung or airways is usually indicated. Cough that is not productive of sputum is called dry, **nonproductive,** or **hacking,** cough.

Dyspnea

A second common symptom of lung disease is **dyspnea.** This is the shortness of breath reported by patients who experience the need for greater respiratory effort at a given level of physical activity. It ranges from mild discomfort during exertion to extreme difficulty in breathing even at rest. In such cases, all the respiratory muscles may be required to exchange only the small tidal volume.

Dyspnea may result from airway obstruction. In such cases, greater force is necessary to produce adequate ventilation. The wheezing sound associated with many obstructive conditions is the result of greater pressures pushing air through airways narrowed by fluid accumulation. Another common cause of dyspnea is the stiffness of pulmonary tissues present in many lung diseases. Such stiffness means that the lung's **compliance** is reduced. Compliance of the lung refers to the amount the lung tissues will expand in response to a given inspiratory pressure. If, because of changes in the lung tissue, a normal inspiratory pressure produces a reduced lung expansion, then the lung is said to have decreased compliance.

Cyanosis

Cyanosis is a third sign of respiratory malfunction. It is the condition in which the blood contains large quantities of reduced (unoxygenated) hemoglobin. As a result, the blood has a dark red-blue color, which produces a characteristic bluish appearance in the skin. (The effect is masked in those with heavier skin pigmentation, but it may be visible in the sclerae or mucous membranes, which are not pigmented.)

Most cyanosis arises because of peripheral vasoconstriction. The result is reduced flow, which allows hemoglobin to yield up more of its oxygen to the tissues, thus producing venous blood with a high level of reduced hemoglobin. This is called **peripheral cyanosis.**

Central cyanosis involves inadequate blood oxygenation, which can arise because of an abnormality of the respiratory membrane or from a mismatch between air flow and blood flow. This mismatch is described in terms of a change in the ventilation (V) to perfusion (Q) ratio. A larger V/Q ratio is produced, for example, in the case of pulmonary thromboembolism, where blood flow through a region of the lung is reduced. Various causes of hypoventilation, such as airway obstruction, will cause the V/Q ratio to decrease with the same result: inadequate blood oxygenation and clinically detectable central cyanosis when reduced hemoglobin levels reach 5 gm/dl (fig. 12.11).

Pulmonary Function Tests

A variety of laboratory studies of pulmonary function are useful in diagnosing respiratory disorders, determining their severity, and monitoring the disease's response to therapy. The most commonly used pulmonary function test employs **spirometry** to assess air flow versus time in a forced exhalation from maximally inflated lungs. This is a convenient method of assessing airway obstruction, indicated by a reduction in the volume of air exhaled during the first second of the test: **one-second forced expiratory volume** (FEV_1). The maximum exhaled volume is the **vital capacity** (VC). A low VC indicates airway obstruction or restricted lung expansion.

Tests of **diffusing capacity** use uptake of carbon monoxide to indicate the status of the respiratory membrane. In combination with other pulmonary function tests, diffusing capacity is applied to the diagnosis of interstitial fibrosis and in differentiating emphysema from chronic bronchitis and asthma.

Arterial blood gas studies provide information on blood levels of oxygenated carbon dioxide and of arterial blood pH. In particular, alterations in the V/Q will produce lower values of PO_2, while elevated arterial PCO_2 indicates reduced alveolar ventilation.

Less commonly employed are tests for **lung elasticity** (compliance) in assessing the lungs' ability to expand and recoil normally. **Lung volume** tests provide information on the ability of the respiratory system to ventilate the pul-

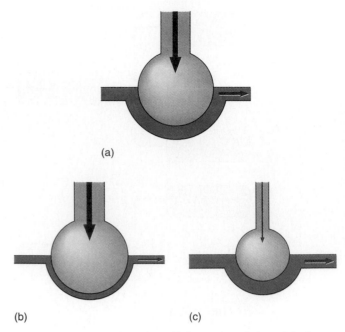

Figure 12.11   (*a*) Normal ventilation and perfusion of the lungs permits adequate gaseous exchange. Hypoxia is threatened if perfusion is impaired (*b*) or if ventilation is impaired (*c*).

monary airways normally. In particular, alterations in the **residual volume** (RV) and **total lung capacity** (TLC) are useful in the diagnosis of hypoventilation problems (fig. 12.12). The major pulmonary function tests are listed in table 12.1.

HYPOPERFUSION

The major factor that limits perfusion of pulmonary capillary beds is pulmonary hypertension, which can result from left heart failure, thromboembolism, or hypoventilation. These were described in earlier chapters, but will be briefly treated here in the context of their impact upon the V/Q and respiratory function.

Heart Failure

When the acutely or chronically failing left heart is unable to cope adequately with its preload, pulmonary congestion and hypertension arise. The result can be a limiting of pulmonary blood flow as the higher pressure in the lung's vessels offers increasing resistance to the right heart's pumping efforts. If pulmonary hypertension is chronic, pulmonary arteriosclerosis may develop, with progressive thickening of the media and intima, causing stenosis and reduced vascular elasticity. The increased mitosis caused by tissue growth factors released from pressure-damaged endothelia or activated platelets is thought to play a role in the medial hyperplasia that characterizes this condition. Of course, vascular stenosis increases pulmonary blood pressure to aggravate the existing hypertension, and a progressive deterioration that can lead to cor pulmonale may

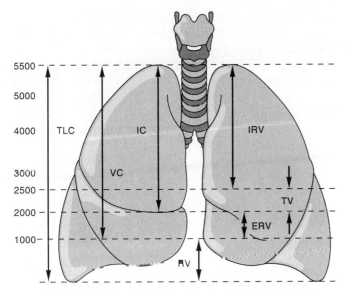

Figure 12.12 Lung volumes in milliliters. TV: Tidal volume; exchanged during resting breathing. ERV: Expiratory reserve volume; exhaled below TV. RV: Residual volume; cannot be voluntarily exhaled. IRV: Inspiratory reserve volume; maximum inhalation above TV. IC: Inspiratory capacity after tidal volume exhalation. VC: Ventilatory capacity, the total volume voluntarily exchanged. TLC: Total lung capacity.

Table 12.1	Selected Pulmonary Function Tests and Their Application in the Assessment of Respiratory Function
Test	**Variables Measured**
Spirometry	One-second forced expiratory volume (FEV_1) Vital capacity
Diffusing capacity	CO_2 uptake as an indication of respiratory membrane functioning
Arterial blood gases	Arterial PO_2, PCO_2, pH as indications of respiratory function
Lung elasticity (compliance)	Lung's elastic properties, relevant in emphysema and restrictive disease
Lung volumes	Residual volume (RV) and total lung capacity (TLC) used as indicators of obstructive or restrictive disease

develop (chapter 10). In severe cases, vascular wall necrosis and pulmonary hemorrhage are present. Rather than a mild infarct weakening the ventricle, cardiac obstructions, e.g., mitral stenosis, are more likely to produce severe pulmonary hypertension. Of course, in the case of right heart failure, hypoperfusion is due to the inability of the pump to maintain an adequate output.

Thromboembolism

Most thromboemboli arise in the deep veins of the calf or thigh. As they lodge in the pulmonary vessels, flow is blocked to a degree determined by their size and number. Pulmonary thromboembolism is typically accompanied by some degree of pulmonary hypertension. Two mechanisms are usually involved. One is the blocking of a vessel by the embolus, which causes higher pressures upstream from the occlusion. The second involves the release of vasoconstrictors from platelets that are activated when they contact and adhere to the surface of the embolus (fig. 12.13). Depending on the degree to which blood flow is reduced in pulmonary thromboembolism, an increased V/Q, as well as varying degrees of dyspnea, **tachypnea** (elevated respiratory rate), and PO_2 reduction may follow.

Infarction following pulmonary embolism is uncommon because of the presence of links between the pulmonary circulation's vessels and the bronchial arteries that supply the bronchial tree. Following pulmonary embolism, flow from the bronchial arteries to an area of ischemia is usually adequate to prevent infarction, although V/Q

increases may still arise. Of course, when a thromboembolism is massive and occludes the pulmonary trunk, the abrupt fall in blood flow to the lungs deprives dependent brain tissue of oxygen, and death follows. **16**

Reduced Ventilation

In hypoventilation states, there is a reflex vasoconstriction response by the pulmonary arterioles. This is a useful response in normal circumstances, where regions of transient hypoventilation can be matched with regions of reduced flow to maintain a balanced V/Q. However, when ventilation is chronically reduced, the resulting vasoconstriction reflex produces pulmonary hypertension, which offers an increased load to the right heart and produces pulmonary hypoperfusion to complicate the existing hypoventilation problem. The principal conditions that can give rise to reduced ventilation are the focus of the following sections.

HYPOVENTILATION

In addition to hypoperfusion, the second principal mechanism that commonly contributes to respiratory insufficiency is reduced air flow: hypoventilation. In this condition, a normal pulmonary blood flow is delivered to underventilated alveoli so that carbon dioxide can't be adequately cleared from the blood and not enough oxygen can enter the blood. This effect of a larger V/Q ratio is called **shunting,** because it produces the same effect that would result if blood were by-passing, or shunting, the lungs. As figure 12.10 indicates,

Figure 12.13 Pulmonary embolism can produce vasoconstriction as well as obstructing a blood vessel. Activated platelets at the surface of the embolus release constrictors that affect vessel B. Airways associated with vessels A and B constrict in response to low blood flow. Airways associated with vessel C are dilated but cannot compensate fully, and shunting effects emerge.

pulmonary air flow may be reduced by factors that restrict normal lung expansion and by those that obstruct the airways.

Obstructive Lung Disease

Upper respiratory inflammation produces increased mucus and serous fluid secretion by the mucous membranes that line the nasal fossae and pharynx. **17** Usually this is in response to viral infection, but inhaled irritants are often involved as well. Although annoying, the excessive fluid at mucosal surfaces presents no threat. A more serious situation arises, however, when the virus or irritant gains access to the lower respiratory passages. In the larynx, trachea, and bronchial tree, excessive mucus and fluid can obstruct air flow. Acute inflammations of these respiratory passages (e.g., laryngitis and bronchitis) will usually resolve without significant functional loss. **18** A productive cough will

tend to clear excess secretions, and body defenses will usually cope with the damaging agent. Cough is especially important in unblocking these passages, because the infectious agent or irritant may interfere with the action of cilia and alveolar macrophages. The loss of clearing function may also allow bacteria to become established. It is the usual case that bacterial infections develop secondary to viral infections in the lower respiratory passages. In addition to viral and bacterial infections, acute bronchitis may result from exposure to irritant fumes from solvents, acids, ammonia, or industrial pollutants.

Lung airway obstruction typically produces hypoventilation, essentially due to reduced expiration, which is indicated by smaller FEV_1 values. Outflow is restricted by reduced airway size, the presence of excessive secretions, or by a reduction of the lung's elastic recoil that reduces expiration pressure. The principal pulmonary obstructive conditions are asthma, emphysema, and chronic bronchitis.

Chronic Bronchitis

This is the most common chronic obstructive disease in the Western world, with peak incidence in males over the age of 45. To distinguish this condition from a recurrent acute inflammation, it is usually diagnosed on the basis of two consecutive years in which a productive cough is present for three months of each year. The cough is an attempt to clear excessive secretions formed in response to chronic irritation of the respiratory mucous membranes.

The principal etiologic factor in chronic bronchitis is long-term inhalation of irritants: cigarette smoke in the large majority of cases, with contributions from other air pollutants becoming an increasing problem. Sulphur dioxide and nitrogen dioxide are two particularly damaging industrial air pollutants. After ten or more years of heavy smoking, the pattern of productive cough, dyspnea, and increased respiratory infections that characterizes chronic bronchitis becomes established.

Pathogenesis in chronic bronchitis reflects the mucous membranes' response to long-term irritant exposure (fig. 12.14). Inflammatory hyperemia and exudate cause thickening of the mucosa, **19** as does hypertrophy and hyperplasia of its mucus-secreting glands **20** (fig. 12.15). Chronic cough to clear the excessive mucus is typical of the heavy smoker.

Metaplasia of the bronchial epithelium also develops, causing loss of cilia and their contribution to movement of mucus from the lower airways to the oropharynx. This factor, coupled with heavier mucus secretion that can plug smaller airways to isolate inhaled microorganisms, contributes to reduced infection resistance. The increased susceptibility to respiratory infection in turn complicates the existing mucosal disruption.

17 24759

18 6254

19 29135

20 29137

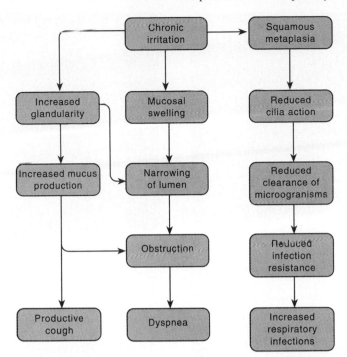

Figure 12.14 Effects of chronic irritation on the bronchial mucous membrane in chronic bronchitis.

Figure 12.15 (*a*) The mucous membrane in chronic bronchitis. Note the increased number of glands in the submucosa, and the inflammatory swelling and excessive mucus. A residual region of normal epithelium is present to the right of the field, but squamous metaplasia of the epithelium predominates. (*b*) Normal respiratory mucus.

In advanced chronic bronchitis, hypoventilation produces hypoxemia and **hypercapnia** (CO_2 excess). These in turn trigger a pulmonary vasoconstriction reflex (described earlier, in the thromboembolism section) that elevates pulmonary pressure to increase the right heart's workload. Chronic hypoxemia also increases renal secretion of erythropoietin (EPO), but the increased blood viscosity that results from EPO's stimulus to marrow red cell output can present an additional load to the heart. The elevated hematocrit, which is characteristic of advanced chronic bronchitis, is the result of this hypoxemia response.

(a)   (b)

Figure 12.16 (*a*) Normal lung alveoli. (*b*) Loss of respiratory surface area in emphysema. The alveolar sacs are greatly enlarged and many septa have been lost.

(a)   (b)

Figure 12.17 Emphysema. (*a*) A normal lung in section. (*b*) A similar section through an emphysematous lung. Note the numerous bullae.
The marked emphysema apparent in this lung was the reason that a 59-year-old man led the life of a "respiratory cripple" in his last years. A chronic productive cough and a gradually emerging dyspnea were early indications of the problem. At autopsy, an enlarged right heart and hepatic congestion were noted. These were probably the result of the high resistance to blood flow presented to the heart by the compromised vasculature of the lungs.

Pulmonary Emphysema

This lung disease is characterized by abnormal enlargement of the lung's airways, beyond the level of the terminal bronchioles. Enlargement is accompanied by the destruction of alveolar septa. **21** **22** As septal damage progresses, adjacent, already distended airways merge to form even more extensively enlarged sacs, which contrast markedly with the precisely ordered structure of normal lung parenchyma **23** (fig. 12.16). The term **bulla** **24** is applied to air spaces that enlarge to diameters above 1 cm (fig. 12.17).

The classification of emphysema uses terminology that refers to the lung's acini or its lobules. When only the proximal respiratory bronchioles are involved, the terms **centriacinar** or **centrilobular** are used. When enlargement and septal loss are primarily seen at the more distal alveolar sacs, the condition is known as **paraseptal emphysema.** Reference here is to the connective tissue septa that lie adjacent to the distal alveolar sacs of a lung lobule. When the emphysematous changes are distributed over both proximal and distal airways, the terms **panacinar** or **panlobular** are used (fig. 12.18). Note that these designations can be made only on the basis of surgically removed lung tissue, often

(a)

(b) Centrilobular emphysema   (c) Panlobular emphysema

Figure 12.18   Schematic illustration of the effects of emphysema. (*a*) Distal airways in normal lung. (*b*) The more proximal, central airways are affected in centrilobular emphysema, while in panlobular emphysema (*c*), the more distal airways are primarily involved.

related to lung cancer, or at autopsy. Although the terms are commonly encountered, the different emphysema types cannot be distinguished clinically.

The obstructive effects of emphysema follow from the loss of alveolar septa. The lung tissue's architecture uses the air-filled alveoli to apply tension to the walls of the smaller airways. This outward pull keeps the airways open during an exhalation to allow for adequate outflow of air. With the destruction of the alveolar walls, small airway support is lost and they tend to collapse during exhalation, obstructing outflow (fig. 12.19). At the same time, decreased lung elasticity provides less expiratory drive and air is exhaled only with additional expiratory effort.

Pathogenesis in emphysema is clearly linked to the inhalation of tobacco smoke. Normal aging is accompanied by emphysematous changes in the lungs. From early to middle adulthood, alveolar septa are lost at a low but steady rate, decreasing alveolar surface area as much as 0.5% per year. Only minimal functional losses result from this apparently normal aging process. Most smokers exhibit no acceleration of the process, but there is a subset of this group in which signs of declining FEV_1 values appear after 10 or 20

years of smoking. These individuals are especially sensitive to the destructive process, which may well progress to emphysema and its serious consequences.

The most widely accepted explanation of tobacco smoke's role in emphysema is related to the lung's normal response to injury from infections and the sporadic inhalation of irritants. In coping with the debris and the cellular infiltrates associated with pulmonary damage, macrophages and neutrophils release a specific enzyme, **serine elastase,** that degrades elastic tissue. The process is controlled by a plasma antagonist called **alpha₁-antitrypsin,** which antagonizes elastase action. In normal nonsmokers, the balance between the promotion and limitation of elastic connective tissue degradation is maintained, and new synthesis of elastic fibers follows. In a proportion of smokers this balance is upset; septal walls are lost, and emphysema develops.

Specifically, smoke particles cause macrophages to release substances chemotactic for neutrophils. These cells have high elastase levels, which enhance the breakdown of septal walls. At the same time, some cigarette smoke components, together with macrophage peroxides, significantly inhibit alpha₁-antitrypsin's activity. There is

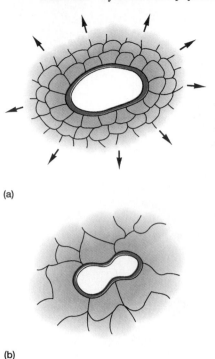

(a)

(b)

Figure 12.19 (*a*) The normal arrangement of lung septa produces tension (arrows) that supports the airways, aiding in maintaining their dilation, particularly during exhalation. (*b*) The loss of septal support in emphysema allows the airways to collapse. See figure 12.16*b*.

also evidence that cigarette smoke interferes with the synthesis of new elastic fibers. This delays repair and also contributes to the loss of elastic tissue and the progressive decline in pulmonary elastic recoil that characterize emphysema (fig. 12.20).

Small Airway Disease

It has recently become apparent that nonrespiratory bronchioles with diameters less than 2 mm are damaged by tobacco smoke. They initially exhibit mild inflammatory changes that may induce some degree of fibrosis in the airway wall. Progression intensifies the changes, with obstruction of air flow developing from lumen reduction by fibrosis in the airway walls. Bronchiolar constriction responses to inflammatory mediators might also play a role, as might the dilution of surfactant by inflammatory exudate. Although this condition is actually **bronchiolitis,** the term **small airway disease** has found wide acceptance. In the case of many smokers, it is felt that the early effects of small airway disease are present, but that since the small airways are so numerous, any early narrowing has little impact on FEV_1 values. Since at this early stage no other symptoms are present, smoking and its irritant effects may well continue. By the time full-blown chronic bronchitis and/or emphysema develops, falling FEV_1 values are attributed to then widely recognized bronchitic obstruction

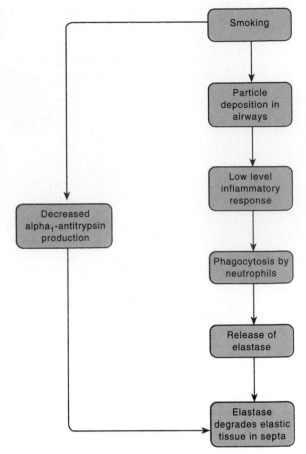

Figure 12.20 Pathogenesis of emphysema. Although there are some cases caused by hereditary alpha₁-antitrypsin deficiency, most emphysema can be linked to the effects of smoking. Note that smoking not only activates the inflammatory response, which destroys the septa, but inhibits the response that protects them.

mechanisms. It seems likely that the late obstruction effects of advanced small airway disease make an important contribution to reduced expiratory capacity.

The impact of smoking on nonsmokers is increasingly demonstrated by specialized pulmonary function tests that can provide evidence of small airway disease. Indications of small airway involvement are present in nonsmokers who breath air containing tobacco smoke. There may be small consolation in being a nonsmoker if it is necessary to spend much time with smoking companions in smoke-filled environments. Consider, in particular, the risks to the children who are subjected to breathing the products of their parents' addiction.

Chronic Airway Obstruction

In many cases, the clinical picture of pulmonary obstruction presented by many patients does not allow a definitive diagnosis. Often elements of chronic bronchitis and emphysema are both present, and although difficult to accurately assess, it can be assumed that some degree of small airway involvement is also present. It is likely that a subsequent

Table 12.2   Comparison of Some Key Features in Chronic Bronchitis and Emphysema

	Chronic Bronchitis	Emphysema
Signs and symptoms	Productive cough	Dyspnea
	Increased respiratory infections	Lung hyperinflation
	Right heart failure	Exercise intolerance
	Episodic hemoptysis	Expiratory wheezing
Laboratory studies	Shunting: Higher PCO_2 lower PO_2	Variable blood gas analyses
	Higher hematocrit	Higher TLC
	Pulmonary hypertension common	Some pulmonary hypertension
	Higher airway resistance	Higher airway resistance
	Higher residual volume	Higher residual volume
		Lower compliance

autopsy will confirm the degree to which each of these commonly overlapping conditions may have contributed to the patient's respiratory difficulties. To deal with this situation, several terms have been proposed that deemphasize diagnosis in favor of clinical descriptive value. Two of these are **chronic obstructive lung disease** (COLD) and **chronic obstructive pulmonary disease** (COPD). Recently the term **chronic airway obstruction** (CAO) has become widely used, with a variation also proposed: **chronic airway limitation** (CAL). It may be some time before the clear favorite emerges, so you should recognize that, essentially, they all describe the same condition.

A typical CAO patient initially presents with a degree of dyspnea and exercise intolerance that has finally prompted the seeking of medical attention. A history of long-term cough and sputum production is usually reported. The slowly progressing exertional dyspnea is usually attributed to increasing age or lack of physical fitness to explain not seeking medical assistance. By the time that severe dyspnea develops, irreversible lung damage is likely to produce progressive bouts of respiratory insufficiency and its complications.

The degree to which chronic bronchitis or emphysema is present in a given individual determines the emergence of signs and symptoms, so a wide range of clinical variability is characteristic of CAO. Table 12.2 indicates the principal features of advanced CAO when chronic bronchitis or emphysema is clearly dominant.

The incidence of CAO is high, accounting annually for over 1,500,000 cases in North America. Its contribution to loss of working days is second only to that of heart disease. CAO also has an important effect on its sufferer's ability to cope with many everyday demands. Their lack of tolerance for exertion is often so pronounced that they can justifiably be described as respiratory cripples.

Therapy In CAO   With irreversible destructive effects on lung tissues, therapy in CAO can only seek to avoid further damage and to cope with the respiratory consequences of the particular combination of chronic bronchitis and emphysema found in a given patient. Cessation of smoking is paramount and can prevent further pulmonary damage and reduce cough and sputum production. Greatest benefits are seen in earlier, less advanced cases. Beyond this, a regimen of therapy will typically involve oxygen therapy to cope with hypoxemia, and various combinations of agents that reflect a given patient's condition. Many benefits are derived from bronchodilator therapy, corticosteroids, antibiotics, and, when right heart failure develops, diuretics and vasodilators.

Bronchial Asthma

Asthmatics suffer from acute episodes of bronchial obstruction. For this reason, bronchial asthma may represent a component of a given patient's overall CAO problems. Although it is far less frequently involved than chronic bronchitis or emphysema, its potential contribution to CAO should not be overlooked. Also note that many asthmatics can be shown to have some degree of chronic bronchial obstruction on which acute attacks are superimposed. The significant feature of asthma that sets it apart from chronic bronchitis and emphysema is its reversibility. Following an attack of dyspnea, extended periods of essentially normal respiratory function are typical.

The major airway events in an acute asthma attack are bronchiolar constriction, mucus hypersecretion, and inflammatory swelling (fig. 12.21). These obstruct air flow, principally during expiration, to produce dyspnea, bouts of often severe cough, and a wheezing exhalation, which results from the forcing of air through constricted, edematous, and mucus-filled airways. **25** Attacks are usually of one to two hours' duration, but they may be more severe and continue for days and even weeks.

On the basis of their different underlying mechanisms, two forms of bronchial asthma are widely recognized. Where both types are involved in a given individual, the condition is described as **mixed asthma.**

(a)   (b)

Figure 12.21   (*a*) In this micrograph of a section through the airway of an asthmatic, the lower region is thick mucus containing epithelial debris and inflammatory cells. Note how the mucus blocks the lumen. Inflammatory cells can be seen crowding into the subepithelial regions of the bronchial wall in the top part of the micrograph. Also note the wall's dilated blood vessels. (*b*) Normal wall for comparison.

Extrinsic Asthma This condition arises principally in childhood and accounts for less than 10% of all bronchial asthma. Its underlying mechanism involves an immune hypersensitivity response mediated by antibodies (IgE) that form in response to air-borne allergens (see chapter 5). Usually pollen, animal danders, household dusts, or insect excretions are involved. Upon formation, the antibodies bind to airway mucosal surfaces, mast cells, and basophils. Subsequent exposure to the allergen produces a dramatic mast cell response (fig. 12.22). They degranulate explosively, releasing an array of chemical mediators that induce bronchospasm, pronounced mucus secretion, and increased capillary permeability. Table 12.3 lists various mediators known to be involved in extrinsic asthma. Their precise contributions have yet to be definitely determined.

Extrinsic asthma has a definite, yet ill-defined, genetic component. Those with family histories of asthma and allergy are more likely to develop an extrinsic asthma.

Intrinsic Asthma In many cases, asthma affects adults with no history of allergy problems. In these individuals, autonomic nervous system stimulus of the airways is the principal factor in producing smooth muscle constriction, mucus hypersecretion, and increased vessel permeability. Intrinsic asthma involves an increased parasympathetic input to airway gland and muscle in response to the activation of irritant receptors in the airway's epithelium. The activating agents are any of a variety of irritants that contact the mucosal surface (fig. 12.22). For example, asthma attacks may be induced by air pollutants, a broad range of work-related particles, such as industrial chemicals or various dusts, infections, therapeutic drugs (aspirin in particular), or physical exertion. The high ventilation rates associated with exercise seem to affect the airway receptors by excessively cooling the surface.

Eosinophils in Asthma

In asthma, the role of the eosinophil, drawn to the site of mast cell degranulation by chemotactic agents, is beginning to be better understood. The eosinophil releases substances that promote further mast cell degranulation in a positive feedback loop, and this may explain, in part, the rapidity with which the immune-mediated asthmatic attack develops. Eosinophils also release substances that are toxic to epithelium. These toxins may damage the respiratory epithelium, allowing inhaled allergens to trigger mast cell degranulation more easily.

Mixed Asthma Intrinsic and extrinsic asthma represent two conditions at opposite ends of a spectrum. The majority of asthmatics lie somewhere between these "pure" conditions and suffer airway narrowing due to an overlap of both allergic and autonomic mechanisms. The narrowing may be caused, in part, by the ability of some mast cell products to stimulate the epithelium's irritant receptors. Or inhaled irritants might damage the endothelium to produce an asthmatic attack, while at the same time allowing allergens to gain access to the mucosa. The allergens induce IgE formation, setting the stage for future immune reactions.

It is not difficult to appreciate how a given individual might confront more than one factor capable of inducing an attack of asthma. A worker doing heavy labor in an environment of industrial fumes and a cigarette smoking co-worker might need to open containers of some allergenic substance to which the workers had been previously exposed and sensitized. An emotional component might be

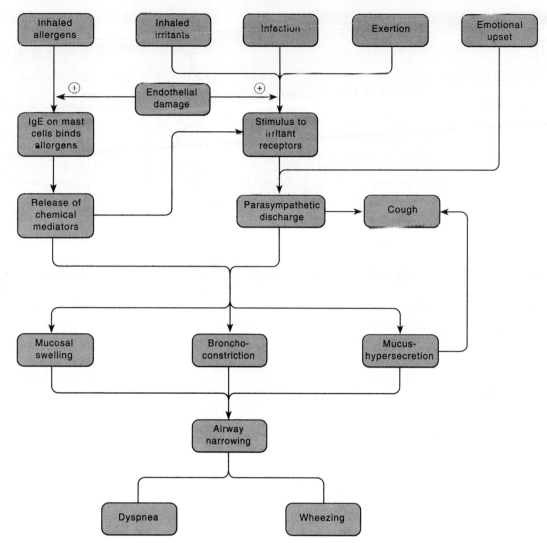

Figure 12.22 Pathogenesis of extrinsic and intrinsic asthma. Note the enhancing effect of endothelial damage, which increases access to both irritant receptors and IgE.

Table 12.3	Mediators of the Extrinsic Asthma Response. As Their Precise Roles Are Determined, Therapeutic Antagonism of These Agents May Prove Beneficial

Bradykinin
Eosinophil chemotactic factor of anaphylaxis (ECFa)
Histamine
Leukotrienes
Neutrophil chemotactic factor (NCF)
Platelet-activating factor
Prostaglandins
Slow-reacting substance of anaphylaxis
Thromboxane (TxA_2)

superimposed if one of the workers had just received a lay-off notice. Furthermore, once an attack was under way, the stress of not being able to ventilate adequately can aggravate the situation and introduce a vicious circle of positive feedback cycling.

Therapy for Asthma Therapy seeks to eliminate exposure to the allergen or other inhaled stimulant to interrupt induction of the response. Attempts to counter airway narrowing are based on bronchodilators and agents that oppose autonomic vasoconstriction. When infection is involved, or a threatened complication, appropriate antibiotics are used. A potential complication can arise in the prolonged inhalation of bronchodilators. These may have irritant effects on the airways that can aggravate the problem. Where emotional upset is a factor, sedatives may be indicated. The patient's confidence in the attending medical personnel is also an important factor in reducing anxiety.

Asthma Terminology

As in CAO, descriptive terminology in asthma reflects increasing awareness of underlying mechanisms. It has been proposed that the extrinsic/intrinsic/mixed asthma designations be dropped. The rationale is based on the idea that airway hyperactivity is the essential problem, and that a given individual's asthma derives from excessive chemical stimulus or some ill-defined combination of excessive or inadequate autonomic responses. Until these factors become better sorted out, you can expect to encounter the traditional terminology.

Some Cautions for Bronchodilator Use

Recent approaches to therapy have focused on the inflammatory component of asthma. The vascular leakiness that contributes to mucosal swelling and airway lumen reduction plays an important role in the asthmatic's reduced ventilation capacity. Bronchodilators and constriction antagonists bring relatively rapid results and so have been accepted widely, but there are some problems with their long-term use. Moreover, in spite of their extensive use, chronic asthma incidence and severity seem to be increasing.

It has been suggested that bronchoconstriction reflexes are a normal means of restricting irritant and antigen access to the lower airways. Therefore, long-term bronchodilator therapy may actually expose the lower airways to a greater irritant burden and more pronounced and chronic symptoms. By contrast, longer-term benefits have been identified in therapy based on inhalation of anti-inflammatory agents, especially cortico-steroids and cromolyn sodium. By reducing mucosal edema, over the long term, these agents seem to promote a mucosal state better able to tolerate an acute asthma attack. On the basis of preliminary studies, side effects at therapeutic doses appear not to be significant.

Status Asthmaticus This is the condition that results when a prolonged and severe asthmatic attack does not respond to therapy. It may continue over days and even weeks, compromising ventilation to produce pronounced cyanosis. It is a life-threatening condition that often follows hospital emergency room attempts to subdue a severe asthmatic attack. Patients suffer extreme dyspnea and most resort to recruiting the sternocleidomastoid muscles to assist in breathing. Aggressive therapy often reverses the airway blockage, but several days may be required to fully restore ventilation.

The Role of Ion Transport in CF

It appears that abnormal membrane transport of sodium and calcium ions produces a critical reduction of mucus water content, causing its high viscosity. Recently, the CF gene, which codes for a particular protein involved in ion transport, has been identified. This discovery opens the door to earlier, more reliable diagnosis, better insight into the underlying pathogenesis of CF, improved therapy, and a potential cure.

An example of therapy following from newly gained research information is the inhalation of **amiloride.** This drug is normally used as a diuretic because it blocks sodium absorption. When inhaled and delivered to bronchial mucosal surfaces, it prevents sodium uptake into the epithelium, which in turn reduces water absorption from the mucus. The result is a more normal viscosity that promotes mucus clearance.

In fatal asthma attacks, typical post-mortem findings are hyperinflated lungs containing air trapped behind mucus-plugged airways that are narrowed by edema. **26** The mucus is usually thick and often contains remnants of epithelium and inflammatory cells. **27** Increased numbers of goblet cells in the epithelium and bronchial muscle hyperplasia are also characteristic and point to the persistence and severity of the condition.

Cystic Fibrosis (CF)

This disease is a systemic condition that involves defective exocrine secretions. Electrolyte abnormalities produce increased viscosity of the secretions of the pancreas, salivary glands, liver, intestine, and lungs. The involvement of the different organs is variable, but the lungs are affected in almost every case, with a particularly viscous mucus obstructing the airways. This viscous property of secretions in CF is the basis for its alternative, but much less frequently used, name, **mucoviscidosis.**

CF is a genetic (autosomal recessive) disease most commonly arising in Caucasian children of normal parents. Sufferers experience an inability to clear the respiratory passages of accumulations of thickened mucus. Airway obstruction reduces ventilation and inadequate mucus clearance gives rise to a pattern of recurrent respiratory infections that begin in childhood and continue throughout the victims' shortened lives. Repeated bouts of bronchitis and bronchopneumonia cause damage that is followed by fibrosis, causing further loss of respiratory function, pulmonary hypertension, and ultimately cor pulmonale. Although there is no cure for this disease, therapeutic advances have reduced the respiratory disability of CF sufferers and extended their life span. However, survival beyond age 30 is unusual. Most death is the result of respiratory failure.

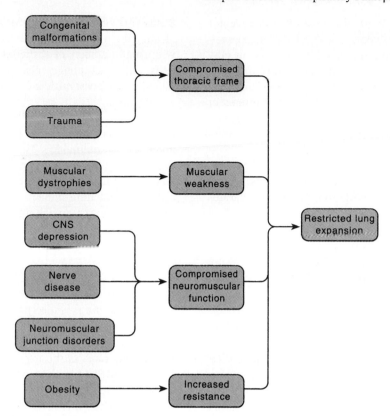

Figure 12.23   Etiology in extrinsic restrictive lung disease.

Restrictive Lung Disease

In this major category of pulmonary dysfunction, the essential problem is restricted expansion of the lungs (fig. 12.10). Reduced lung expansion may be the result of changes in the **pulmonary interstitium,** i.e., the lung tissue itself, as opposed to its airways. This condition can be described as **intrinsic restriction.** The other factors that limit lung expansion produce **extrinsic restriction.** These involve abnormalities in the system that generates the respiratory movements. In either case, sufferers exhibit a decreased total lung capacity as a result of their inability to expand the lungs normally.

Extrinsic Restriction

Normal ventilation not only requires unobstructed airways, but also depends on a normally structured and intact thoracic framework that is expanded by sufficiently strong muscular contractions triggered by an appropriate neural input from the brain stem. Derangements in any of these components can compromise ventilation (fig. 12.23).

Defective Thoracic Framework Congenital malformations, skeletal disease, or trauma can alter the thoracic skeleton and interfere with normal lung expansion. Deformities of the spinal column are **kyphosis,** an anterior displacement of the thoracic vertebrae causing "rounding" of the shoulders, and **scoliosis,** a pronounced lateral curvature of the spine. Both may be present when the column is rotated and bent laterally: **kyphoscoliosis.** [28] Most often, these conditions are idiopathic and produce a diminished vital capacity, reduced total lung capacity, and impaired ventilation. They are described more fully in chapter 18.

Trauma can damage the thoracic cage to compromise ventilation. Pain associated with bone fractures can significantly inhibit inspiration. In auto accidents, when an unrestrained driver is thrown against the steering wheel, rib fractures on both sides of the sternum may result. As a consequence, the anterior segment of the thoracic wall is detached from its supports and floats freely on the chest's surface. On inspiration, the floating segment is drawn inward, and on expiration, it is pushed outward. (These movements are described as paradoxical respiration. See flail chest in chapter 24.) The result is diminished chest expansion and reduced ventilation.

Respiratory Muscle Weakness This term covers several relatively rare conditions that have a genetic cause or are idiopathic. They are usually referred to as one or another type of muscular dystrophy. The weakened respiratory muscles are unable to generate sufficient chest expansion and diaphragm depression to sustain adequate ventilation. It is not unusual to have respiratory difficulties as first indications of such an abnormality.

Neural and Neuromuscular Defects These problems can be considered in terms of faulty output from the brain stem's respiratory control centers or as defects in the neural pathways from brain stem to respiratory muscles. At the neuromuscular junction, the neurotransmitter or receptor may be the focus of the problem.

Damage to the brain stem or CNS depression may result in an inadequate stimulus to the respiratory musculature. Direct brain stem injury or compression from increased intracranial pressure following cranial trauma or surgery may be involved. CNS depression may be caused by accidental or suicidal drug overdoses, excessive anesthesia, and, rarely, epileptic seizures.

Neural pathways from the brain stem travel the spinal cord, and injury in the high cervical region where they leave the cord can depress ventilation. Otherwise, various nerve disorders (neuropathies) may produce sufficient interference with conduction to compromise ventilation. In **poliomyelitis,** viral damage to the motor neurons that supply the respiratory muscles can be life-threatening. Motor neurons are also involved in **amyotrophic lateral sclerosis** (ALS), also known as **Lou Gehrig's disease** after the famous baseball player who died from its effects. In this fatal disease, respiratory failure often develops in its later stages. In the **Guillain-Barré syndrome,** acute respiratory failure is a common result of faulty stimulus to the respiratory muscles. Demyelination of the motor neurons causes faulty nerve conduction in this rare disease.

The neuromuscular junction, between the respiratory motor neurons and the respiratory muscles it supplies, is another potential site for the development of hypoventilation problems. In **botulism,** caused by the extremely potent toxin of a bacterium (*Clostridium botulinum*), respiratory failure from paralysis of the respiratory muscles is a common cause of death. The toxin blocks the release of acetylcholine (ACh) from motor nerve endings. Without the stimulation of ACh, respiratory muscles can't contract. The other side of the junction is involved in **myasthenia gravis.** In this disease, the ACh receptors are damaged by an autoimmune mechanism. A completely normal brain stem, conduction paths, and strong, intact muscles are present, but loss of the minute ACh receptors can sufficiently compromise ventilation to produce respiratory failure.

Increased Resistance to Expansion This problem may arise in extreme obesity. Excessive accumulations of thoracic wall fat, particularly in females with large breast fat deposits, can restrict thoracic expansion. Increased abdominal pressure from large masses of stored fat or accumulations of fluid (see ascites in chapter 14) may also offer resistance to depression of the diaphragm. If pronounced and prolonged, these resistance factors can exceed the ability of skeletal muscles to adapt by hypertrophy, and hypoventilation results.

Intrinsic Restriction

Various lung disorders produce alterations whose dominant effects are seen in the pulmonary interstitium. These disorders are grouped under the title **interstitial lung disease** (ILD). They involve the supporting connective tissue framework of the lung. This tissue consists of collagen and elastic fibers imbedded in extracellular ground substance, with small numbers of scattered fibroblasts, smooth muscle cells, and macrophages also present. The elasticity of the interstitium is a significant factor in the lung's recoil after an inhalation.

In intrinsic restrictive lung disease, diffuse changes in the pulmonary interstitium produce stiffening of the lung and reduced compliance. This means that the lung's normal expansibility [29] is compromised and it becomes more difficult to inhale. [30] Low compliance is the cause of the reduced total lung capacity (TLC) that is characteristic of intrinsic restrictive lung disease. Low compliance is also associated with increased recoil of the lung's interstitium. Greater recoil contributes to the expiratory drive in exhalation.

Dyspnea and a reduced tidal volume typically accompany intrinsic restrictive disease. Tachypnea (rapid and shallow breathing) is also present, indicating compensation to maintain ventilation. The rapid breathing is especially pronounced during exertion, producing hyperventilation that exaggerates carbon dioxide clearance and produces low arterial PCO_2 values while providing arterial oxygen levels that are relatively high.

Hyperventilation is also promoted by the lung's increased recoil, which drives exhalation and supports airways to keep them dilated. This helps to offset the higher energy expenditures required to overcome the lung's resistance to expansion during inhalation.

Cough is common in ILD and may be present without other signs of respiratory disease. It is typically nonproductive and may be the result of interstitial changes affecting airway irritant receptors. Productive cough is associated with more acute damage to the interstitium, where accumulating exudate and mucus may require clearance to avoid airway obstruction.

Restrictive lung disease typically arises in one of two forms. One is usually acute or subacute, and can quickly produce respiratory failure and death. It is characterized by pulmonary edema, which produces a pattern of signs and symptoms called **adult respiratory distress syndrome** (ARDS). The second form of restrictive disease in the lung involves long-term changes in the pulmonary interstitium. This condition is called **chronic intrinsic restrictive lung disease** (CIRLD).

ARDS: Pulmonary Edema Edema of the pulmonary interstitium is the most common restrictive lung disorder because it arises secondary to the most common disease in the Western world: heart disease. Failure of the left heart causes congestion in the pulmonary vasculature, which produces pulmonary hypertension. This in turn forces more fluid from the pulmonary capillaries. The increased fluid, under pressure, thickens and stiffens the pulmonary interstitium, decreasing compliance and restricting lung expansion. [31] This condition is described as **cardiogenic pulmonary edema.**

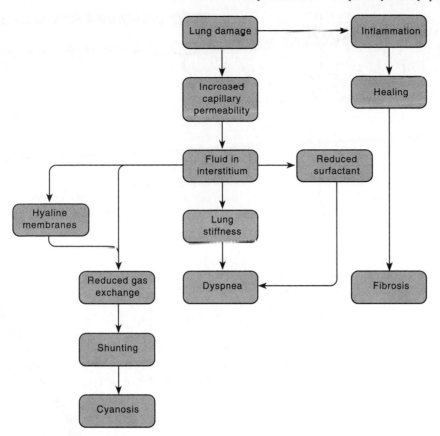

Figure 12.24   Pathogenesis of ARDS.

Another important mechanism underlying pulmonary edema involves damage to pulmonary capillaries that causes them to become highly permeable. As a result, water, electrolytes, and protein pass from the blood to the pulmonary tissues. When the pulmonary capillaries are severely damaged, even erythrocytes may escape. As this protein-rich exudate forms, compliance is reduced. With increasing interstitial pressures, the exudate is forced into the alveoli to further compromise respiratory function. The resulting pattern of signs and symptoms is known as ARDS: adult respiratory distress syndrome. (The designation "adult" distinguishes this condition from the surfactant deficiency state that may arise in the newborn. See the section on RDN, later in this chapter.) Onset of ARDS typically follows some injurious event, usually after a period varying from a few hours to two days in which no respiratory disorder is apparent. In some cases, early respiratory difficulties may be masked by other, nonrespiratory effects of the injury. Tachypnea, dyspnea, and cyanosis then emerge, with the threat of rapid progression to complete respiratory failure. ARDS is fatal in over 50% of cases.

Pathogenesis in ARDS involves intrinsic restriction from the presence of nondistensible fluid filling the interstitial spaces. The loss of compliance is complicated by the dilution or washing away of pulmonary surfactant by exudate passing to alveolar surfaces. The reduction in surfactant increases surface tension, which means that increased effort is required to achieve inspiration. Fluid in the interstitium also presents an obstacle to diffusion, so that oxygenation of the blood is also reduced. Carbon dioxide levels are less affected, since the higher water solubility of carbon dioxide means that more of it can be carried to the alveoli for exhalation, even though less oxygen is entering the blood.

The presence of fluid in the alveoli also leads to loss of respiratory surface and reduced airway volume. The result is a lowered V/Q ratio, causing shunting, which contributes to the cyanosis associated with ARDS. The situation is aggravated by the protein component of the exudate. On exposure to alveolar air, the protein denatures and forms a layer of hyaline membrane that can line the respiratory surfaces extending as far as the respiratory bronchioles. **32** In addition to plasma proteins, hyaline membranes contain cellular and basement membrane debris.

If a severe ARDS attack is not fatal, it is often followed by fibrosis in the interstitium, which can lead to chronic loss of compliance (fig. 12.24).

ARDS can result from a broad array of injuries, all affecting the integrity of the pulmonary capillaries. In many cases, the cause of damage to capillary endothelia is unknown. Trauma, biological toxins from infectious agents, or inhaled irritants may be involved either directly or indirectly, alone or in combination. A most common cause of ARDS is circulatory shock (see chapter 11). The

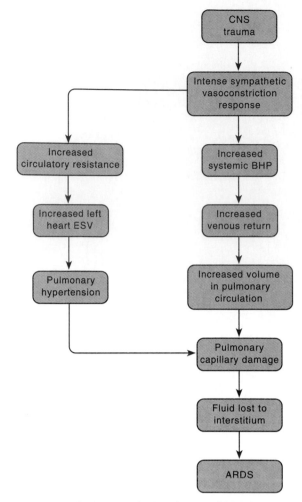

Figure 12.25   CNS trauma in the etiology of ARDS.

Although drowning fatalities are usually due to water in the lungs, 10–30% of drowning victims have a laryngospasm reflex that blocks water aspiration. In such cases, death is caused by asphyxiation. In near-drowning, aspiration of seawater (hypertonic to plasma) causes osmotic water flow from the plasma to the alveoli. The rapid loss of blood volume that follows poses the threat of hypovolemic shock. If fresh water (hypotonic to plasma) is aspirated, it moves by osmosis into the plasma and then into RBCs. The large water inflow can quickly produce widespread rupture of cells, releasing sufficient K^+ to cause cardiac arrhythmias.

characteristic pulmonary changes associated with ARDS in circulatory shock are collectively called **shock lung.** Trauma is also capable of producing ARDS, either directly, by effects at the thoracic wall that can bruise the underlying lung, or indirectly via the central nervous system. In severe CNS injury, a pronounced vasoconstriction response greatly increases pulmonary blood pressures. This forces fluid into the pulmonary interstitium, causes capillary endothelial damage, and increases capillary permeability [33] (fig. 12.25).

Infection may produce ARDS when severe. **Pneumonia** is a common example. This condition is an acute inflammation of the lung parenchyma that is normally reversible. Viral pneumonia is most common and most likely to produce ARDS. Bacterial pneumonia may follow an initial viral attack. Most bacterial pneumonia is caused by organisms of the genus *Pneumococcus,* although pneumonia resulting from many other bacteria is also common.

(The rare but notorious **legionnaire's disease** involves ARDS that follows bacterial infection.) Pneumonia may also develop without infection. When gastric contents are inhaled, their acidity induces a pronounced inflammatory response that can produce ARDS. Usually such **aspiration pneumonia** is associated with the aspiration of vomitus while unconscious. For example, aspiration pneumonia may follow general anesthesia or an alcoholic stupor. Mortality associated with aspiration pneumonia is high.

In disseminated intravascular coagulation (DIC—see chapter 7), multiple sites of microcirculation coagulation damage endothelia and increase permeability. At the same time, thrombi obstructing the capillaries produce increased BHP. [34] This additional pressure adds to fluid losses through the more permeable capillaries to favor the development of ARDS. Near-drowning can also produce ARDS. In such cases, the exposure of the lungs to seawater or fresh water presumably causes damage via pronounced osmotic water movement.

Pulmonary capillary endothelium is also subject to damage from toxins or irritants that are inhaled or blood-borne. Inhalation of smoke, from fires as opposed to tobacco, or toxic fumes can induce ARDS, as can prolonged inhalation of therapeutically enriched oxygen mixtures. Oxygen toxicity is related to the production of oxygen-derived free radicals, which damage endothelia.

Blood-borne irritants may arrive at the lungs from an inflamed pancreas that is releasing its digestive enzymes. In fat embolism, pulmonary enzymes produce injurious degradation products from the breakdown of the emboli. Since fat emboli are usually multiple, lung capillary damage can be extensive. The blood may also bring additional fluid to the lung to produce pulmonary hypertension, apart from the problem of a failing left heart. If IV fluid administration leads to overloading of the pulmonary vasculature, damage

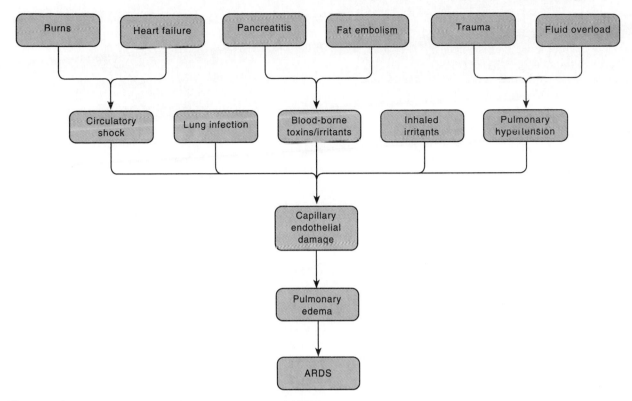

Figure 12.26   Etiological factors in the development of ARDS.

Oxygen Therapy and ARDS

Oxygen therapy for correction of hypoxia and cyanosis is indicated in ARDS. However, since extended inhalation therapy can damage the respiratory membrane, careful monitoring of patient responses is necessary. Prolonged inhalation of air with a 40% oxygen content is usually not harmful, but in ARDS, higher oxygen levels may be necessary to reestablish adequate arterial PO_2 values. The danger is a vicious circle of oxygen therapy to cope with lung damage, which causes further damage, necessitating more oxygen therapy.

from congestion and hypertension can occur. This is particularly dangerous in patients with renal damage and a reduced capacity for urinary water loss (diuresis). The etiology of ARDS is summarized in figure 12.26.

Whatever the cause, treatment of ARDS requires immediate relief of hypoxemia, usually with oxygen inhalation therapy. Ventilation assistance is often provided by a mechanical ventilator that uses positive pressure to increase air flow. Attempts to reduce lung fluid loading by the use of diuretics may be effective, but only in the absence of

heart failure that might compromise arterial BHP. Even with prompt and aggressive intervention, high mortality can be anticipated.

Chronic Intrinsic Restrictive Lung Disease (CIRLD)

This is the restrictive lung condition that involves long-term changes in the pulmonary interstitium, as opposed to the acutely developing problems of ARDS. In this condition, lung stiffness develops over a long period following initial damage. Because of the resulting infiltration of inflammatory and immune system cells, destruction of the interstitial tissues continues. Also released are chemical mediators that promote a fibrogenic response. Over time, collagen deposition by fibroblasts proceeds at the expense of the normal elastic tissues, causing a progressive loss of compliance.

A broad array of damaging agents are able to induce chronic restrictive changes in the lung. In most cases, they involve low-level occupational exposure to the irritant over a long period of time. The irritants may be dust particles, industrial gases or air-borne liquid droplets, drugs, or infectious agents. The usual occupational exposure involves irritant levels that are low enough to be tolerated so that work

Table 12.4	Selected Intrinsic Restrictive Diseases and the Inhaled Agents That Are Implicated in Their Etiology
Disease	**Agent**
Asbestosis	Asbestos
Aspergillosis	Fungal spores of *Aspergillus* species
Berylliosis	Beryllium
Bird-breeder's lung	Ill-defined bird antigens
Coalworker's lung	Carbon dust
Farmer's lung	Molds in hay or grain
Silicosis	Silicon
Welder's lung	Iron oxide

Figure 12.27   In this microscopic field, two distinctively shaped asbestos bodies are represented by the club-shaped dark masses. The pale surrounding structures are phagocytes attempting to engulf and degrade the asbestos bodies. Such efforts inevitably fail.

and inhalation continue. If levels are too high, acute effects become intolerable, thus preventing further exposure and long-term damage. Typically, low-level exposures of several months to two years, or more, are required before progressive cell infiltration and fibrosis produce clinical signs of impaired respiratory function. Because sufferers often adapt to the slow deterioration, clinical presentation may well be deferred until significant damage has occurred.

Overall, infection and dust inhalation are the two principal categories in the etiology of CIRLD. A third, miscellaneous category serves as a catchall for the large number of its diverse and less common causes.

Pneumoconioses These are conditions of chronic restrictive lung disease caused by inhalation of irritant dusts or droplets. Most involve prolonged occupational dust inhalation in mining or secondary industrial processing. [35] Levels of dust inhalation gradually overwhelm the airways' particle clearance defenses, resulting in particle accumulation in the alveoli and interstitium. The pattern of damage and fibrosis that follows particle deposition varies with the physical, chemical, and antigenic properties of the particular dust, but all are characterized by inflammatory and/or immune cell infiltration, fibroblast proliferation, and fibrosis. Specific terminology is applied to describe a particular pneumoconiosis when the damaging dust component is known. For example, **asbestosis** is used when asbestos crystals are involved, and **silicosis** when the retained dust is silica. [36] Where the inhaled irritant is unknown, reference is typically made to the occupation in which exposure occurs (table 12.4). The most common pneumoconioses follow prolonged inhalation of coal dust, dusts containing silica or silicates, and dust that contains asbestos. Although specific differences in pathogenesis exist, there are broad similarities between advanced coalworker's pneumoconiosis, silicosis, and asbestosis.

Typically, early fibrosis develops at foci of particle deposition to form nodules of fibrous tissue. A more diffuse fibrosis, lacking nodules, is characteristic of asbestosis, as is the presence of **asbestos bodies.** [37] These are crystals coated with protein and iron, often club-shaped (fig. 12.27). As fibrosis continues, nodules may enlarge to reach several centimeters in diameter. This condition is called **progressive massive fibrosis.** [38] It is a complication seen most often in silicosis and severe coalworker's pneumonoconiosis. Other, less common pneumoconioses may involve granulomatous inflammation in the lung. An example is **berylliosis,** [39] which involves granuloma formation in response to retention of dust containing particles of the metal beryllium.

Pneumoconiosis is often asymptomatic for many years. With increased particle retention and fibrosis, dyspnea may develop progressively as lung compliance is reduced. Cough is also characteristic and may be productive or not, depending on the particle involved. Those suffering from pneumoconiosis are also at increased risk of respiratory infection because of the enormous demand placed on airway clearance mechanisms. Susceptibility to the effects of dust inhalation is widely variable, so that workers exposed to an identical particle burden may suffer significant debility on the one hand and be asymptomatic on the other. The differences may be explained, in part, on the basis of individual variations in the immune system's response to a particular retained particle. Smoking is a common additional risk factor.

Infection CIRLD may follow infection, with fibrosis the response to the presence of the infectious agent, its products, or the products of tissue damage. Bacteria, viruses, and fungi [40] have all been implicated in the etiology of CIRLD. Even the common and usually benign influenza virus may be a causative factor when it is followed by

| 35 | 27459 | 36 | 27463 | 37 | 24668 |
| 38 | 32147 | 39 | 27503 | 40 | 39672 |

pneumonia. The organisms induce a chronic inflammatory response that may involve a diffuse or granulomatous pattern of cell infiltration and fibrosis. (See the section on lung infection, later in this chapter.)

Miscellaneous Etiologies Some infectious agents, their spores, and a wide variety of inhaled organic dusts induce an allergic response in the lung. The result is a widespread cellular infiltration, with granuloma formation throughout followed by diffuse fibrosis. Such a condition is described as **hypersensitivity pneumonitis** or **extrinsic allergic alveolitis.** Many animal and plant antigens are known to induce this response. Exposure often occurs as the result of long-term low-level inhalation of the antigen while doing farm work.

Therapeutic agents may induce chronic fibrosis and lung restriction. Radiation and various antitumor drugs may damage normal lung tissues and trigger the progression to interstitial infiltration and fibrosis. Various other drugs are known to have similar capabilities in susceptible individuals.

Idiopathic Pulmonary Fibrosis (IPF) This is a condition involving immune complex deposition, but the initiating antigens have not been identified. Males from 30 to 50 years of age are predominantly affected by slow progression and loss of interstitium, **41** with steadily worsening dyspnea and hypoxemia (fig. 12.28). Another idiopathic condition, **sarcoidosis,** involves widespread granuloma formation, usually favoring the lungs. Interstitial fibrosis typically follows long-term granulomatous damage, complicated by lymphocyte and macrophage mediated interstitial damage.

In **Goodpasture's syndrome,** an autoimmune defect causes antibody formation against lung and kidney basement membranes. The result is a linking of a type of glomerulonephritis (chapter 15) and a pattern of pulmonary damage causing interstitial hemorrhage and varying degrees of fibrosis. Although a serious complication, pulmonary dysfunction is usually overshadowed by more rapidly developing kidney failure. Goodpasture's syndrome predominates in young males and is a particular example of a more general category of disorder known as **diffuse pulmonary hemorrhage.** CIRLD etiologies are summarized in table 12.5.

Therapy in CIRLD Therapeutic options are relatively limited in ILD because of the essentially nonreversible nature of its interstitial damage. If an irritant is known to be inhaled or a therapeutic agent is suspected, stopping exposure is the first step. This is not possible where the agent is unknown, so treatment of such conditions as IPF or sarcoidosis is much more difficult. In some cases steroidal anti-inflammatory agents, such as prednisone, can limit the

Figure 12.28 The lung in idiopathic pulmonary fibrosis. Compare with the normal surface in figure 12.17a.
This is the lung of a heroin addict who died of respiratory failure at 34. Pronounced pulmonary fibrosis can be seen throughout the specimen. Severe dyspnea and a productive cough had confined her to her home for the previous year. On admission to hospital she looked old and emaciated, had markedly reduced ventilation and a left pneumothorax. At autopsy, evidence of her addiction history was apparent in fibrotic arm veins damaged by excessive injection injury, suicidal scars at the wrists, and numerous foreign body granulomas and fibrosis, which were induced by the deposition of talc used by her heroin suppliers to dilute the drug.

Table 12.5	Principal Types of CIRLD, Based on Etiology

Drug-induced CIRLD
Hypersensitivity pneumonitis
Infectious and postinfectious CIRLD
Inhalation of irritant gases
Pneumoconiosis
Radiation pneumonia
Sarcoidosis*
Collagen vascular diseases*
Eosinophilic granulomas*

Asterisks indicate systemic disorders that may be associated with CIRLD.

damage caused by inflammatory cells. However, this treatment does not eliminate the underlying cause of the inflammation, and the ultimate interstitial losses are only delayed. Overall, there is much disagreement on the modes and actions of anti-inflammatory drugs for ILD.

LUNG INFECTION

Lung infections are a major cause of death in North America. The lung's exposure to large volumes of inhaled air makes them vulnerable to potent infectious agents that can overwhelm or elude defenses. This is particularly true in the elderly, whose defenses are less vigorous, and in those whose immune systems are suppressed. The latter case is often related to immune suppression therapy in transplant recipients and, indirectly, as a side effect, to anti-tumor therapy. In the case of AIDS, one infecting organism suppresses the immune system to allow other organisms to establish a secondary infection.

Bacterial infections, now much less common because of their susceptibility to antibiotics, typically cause an acute inflammatory response that is characterized by exudate formation centered in the alveoli. Subsequent infiltration by inflammatory cells produces a solidification of the affected area called **consolidation.** **42** By contrast, viral damage focuses inflammatory cells in the interstitium. In both cases the pattern of acute inflammation is termed pneumonia, although **pneumonitis** is increasingly employed to describe the viral disease.

Two particular forms of pneumonia are worth noting. One is a type of bronchopneumonia caused by an obscure organism first studied as a result of an outbreak of severe respiratory symptoms at an American Legion convention in a major U.S. city. Some fatalities due to ARDS occurred. The organism has since been named *Legionella pneumophilia.* It seems to propagate in warm, standing water in air conditioning or heating systems, from which it periodically escapes to produce scattered outbreaks. Hospitals and nursing homes are particularly dangerous locations, as many occupants have compromised infection resistance.

The second pneumonia is caused by the protozoan *Pneumocystis carinii.* Usually this organism can't overcome a normal infection resistance. However, if the immune system is suppressed, the organism can become established in the lungs, with lethal consequences. **43** Those most at risk are AIDS sufferers and transplant recipients whose immune system is suppressed to reduce rejection of an implanted donor's organ. Various other agents may infect the lung. The most important of these are listed in table 12.6.

The terms **lobar pneumonia** and **bronchopneumonia** attempt to describe bacterial infections that are limited to a

Table 12.6   Selected Organisms Implicated in Pneumonia

Bacteria
Escherichia coli
Group A beta-hemolytic streptococci
Hemophilus influenzae
Klebsiella pneumoniae
Pseudomonas species
Staphylococcus aureus
Streptococcus pneumoniae (pneumococcus)
Viruses
Adenovirus
Influenza virus
Measles virus
Varicella
Rickettsiae
Coxiella burneti
Mycobacteria
Mycobacteria tuberculosis
Chlamydia
Chlamydiae psittaci

lung lobe or that originate in the bronchioles. Because there often is overlap and lack of a clear distinction, the terms have limited clinical relevance.

RESPIRATORY FAILURE

Given the lung's primary task of oxygenating the blood and clearing it of carbon dioxide, inability to perform these tasks constitutes respiratory failure. Whether it arises by an acute mechanism, as in pulmonary embolism or ARDS, or as the result of a long period of progressive hypoventilation from airway obstruction or restrictive disease, the inability to maintain adequate pulmonary function presents a serious threat. Dyspnea is virtually always present, but it may be difficult to identify the slight increases in breathing effort that indicate respiratory failure, since they are often superimposed on the chronic dyspnea that is present in various respiratory disorders. Since nervous tissue is highly oxygen-dependent, CNS signs and symptoms will also emerge in respiratory failure. Memory loss, visual impairment, and drowsiness are typical. Headache may be present as a result of the increased intracranial pressure that follows cerebral vasodilation in response to hypoxemia.

Two principal patterns are recognized, one in which arterial hypoxemia is the dominant feature and one in which arterial hypoxemia is accompanied by hypercapnia (elevated carbon dioxide).

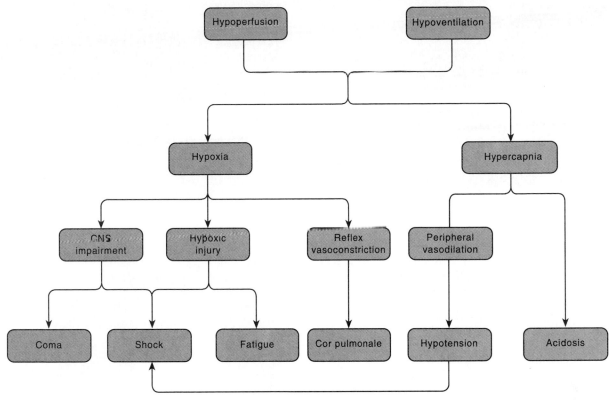

Figure 12.29   Respiratory failure and its systemic consequences.

Hypoxic Respiratory Failure

This condition is present when PO_2 falls to, or below, 60 mmHg. It is typically seen in chronic bronchitis and emphysema, in lung consolidation due to bacterial infection, in lung collapse (see the discussion of atelectasis, later in this chapter), or in pulmonary hypertension. High V/Q values due to intracardiac right-to-left shunting or pulmonary embolism are also able to lower PO_2 critically. This is also the typical result of ARDS.

Initially, hypoxemia produces headache and nervous agitation, which is soon followed by a decline in mental activity and by confusion. With progressive lowering of PO_2 values, more widespread tissue damage and loss of consciousness can be expected. In the event of brain stem hypoxia, CNS output to the heart and systemic arterioles can produce circulatory shock. Hypoxic renal damage, and the loss of homeostatic balance and waste accumulation that follow, complicate the problem.

Hypoxic-Hypercapnic Respiratory Failure

When arterial PCO_2, normally at 40 mmHg, exceeds 45 mmHg, hypercapnia is present. Most often, obstructive conditions produce this form of respiratory failure, as may

hypoventilation from CNS, thoracic cage, or neuromuscular abnormalities. Attempts to compensate include an increased heart rate and vasodilation, which produce a warm, moist skin. CNS effects produce muscular tremors, drowsiness, and, at extremes, coma. Hypercapnia also produces an acidosis in the body fluids via the plasma bicarbonate equilibrium.

The pathogenesis of respiratory failure is presented in figure 12.29. The acid-base imbalances related to respiratory failure are considered in chapter 16.

MISCELLANEOUS PULMONARY CONDITIONS

Atelectasis

Atelectasis is the collapse of a portion of the lung. **44** **45** It is usually associated with bronchial obstruction. Following airway blockage, over a period of several hours, the air in alveolar sacs is absorbed into the blood. If the obstructed airway prevents new air from replacing the absorbed air, the affected region collapses (fig. 12.30). If the degree of

(a)

(b)

Figure 12.30   Atelectasis. In this case an object has obstructed an airway. Air trapped beyond the blockage has been absorbed by the blood, causing the isolated region to collapse.

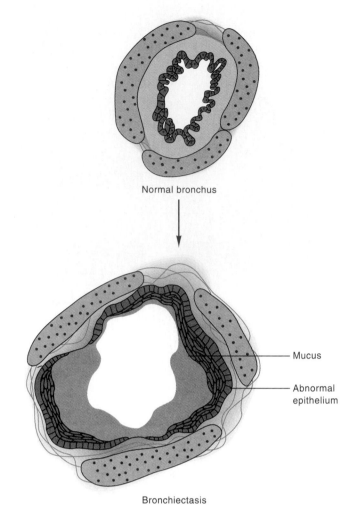

Normal bronchus

Mucus

Abnormal epithelium

Bronchiectasis

Figure 12.31   Bronchiectasis. Abnormal dilation of small airways is accompanied by replacement of normal epithelium by a stratified squamous epithelium. Excessive secretions, which cannot be cleared by compromised clearance mechanisms, accumulate to cause airway obstruction.

collapse is small, the collapse will probably be asymptomatic, but if large, the perfusing blood neither receives oxygen nor loses carbon dioxide. The various obstructive diseases of the lung may all produce atelectasis, as may aspiration of a foreign body that lodges in a bronchus.

Obstruction may also stem from a tumor's growth within an airway, or by a tumor or other factors compressing the airway from without. The latter condition is called **compression atelectasis. Postsurgical atelectasis** is the most common type. It seems to result from anesthesia effects, which cause obstruction by increasing mucus secretion. Atelectasis is also often associated with ARDS. It is assumed that whatever factor produces the altered capillary permeability also, in some way, depresses surfactant production or release. The resulting increase of surface tension causes collapse of the small terminal airways.

Bronchiectasis

In **bronchiectasis,** the medium- to small-sized bronchi are abnormally dilated because of muscle and connective tissue damage in their walls (fig. 12.31). In some cases, the cause

is congenital, but in most cases, damage is secondary to necrosis associated with recurrent infection, in particular, bronchial inflammations and pneumonia. After damage, the respiratory epithelium is lost or replaced by a stratified squamous epithelium. **46** The dilated bronchi are unable to clear secretions, so obstruction and cough result. The inability to clear secretions also predisposes to further infection, purulent sputum, and further bronchial damage. Hemoptysis is a common sign in bronchiectasis. It is probably the result of damage associated with the severe paroxysms of coughing that may accompany this disorder.

Pneumothorax

In **pneumothorax,** collapse of the lung follows the entrance of atmospheric air into the pleural space. The air removes the normal pressure gradient that provides for the

Figure 12.32 Pneumothorax. The lung collapses as air enters the pleural cavity. The combination of lung elasticity and surface tension causes the collapse when pleural and airway pressures equalize. The arrows indicate two access routes to the pleural space, from within the lung and through the thoracic wall.

expansion of the lungs against the thoracic wall. As a result, the elastic recoil of the lung draws it into a collapsed configuration. **47**

Pneumothorax may result from trauma, as when a fractured rib, knife blade, or bullet lacerates the parietal pleura, or it may occur secondary to thoracic surgery (fig. 12.32). Most commonly, it occurs accidentally, as a result of a medical procedure such as aspiration (suction) of fluid from the pleural space (see pleural effusion in the following section) or a lung biopsy. Pneumothorax is also associated with emphysema when enlarging bullae form near the surface of the lung. With destruction of lung surface tissue, the visceral pleura may be the only barrier separating the pleural space and the atmospheric air in the airways. Such an air space at the lung's surface is called a **bleb.** With rupture of the visceral pleura, air enters the pleural space and lung collapse follows. Pneumothorax is also common in ILD. Tumor invasion might penetrate the visceral pleura to produce pneumothorax. In some cases, especially in males 20–40 years of age, pneumothorax occurs without a known predisposing condition. This is **spontaneous pneumothorax.** It may result from the rupture of an apical bleb that is present at the lung's surface because of undiscovered lung disease, or because of some partial airway obstruction that produces terminal airway hyperinflation.

In pneumothorax, the defect that allows air to enter the pleural space usually closes as the lung collapses. With subsequent healing of the defect, the lung expands. In some cases, however, the atmospheric air in the pleural space does not rapidly reabsorb air. The sustained higher pressure on one side of the mediastinum can displace its contents, causing them to shift to the lower-pressure side. This condition is called **tension pneumothorax.** It is a serious condition requiring prompt intervention, since the lung compression that is caused by the shifted mediastinal structures can compromise the only remaining source of respiratory function.

Pleurisy

Pleurisy is the same as **pleuritis,** that is, inflammation of the pleurae. **48** The condition is not a disease in itself but is the result of some other abnormality. Usually this is an infection in the adjacent lung parenchyma, but thoracic trauma or an invading tumor might also be at fault. In some cases, inflammatory exudate is minimal, so the description **dry pleurisy** is used. More typically, significant exudate accumulates between the pleurae. This is termed **pleural effusion.** **49** **50**

The presence of a substantial effusion may produce sufficient pressure on the adjacent lung tissue to cause compression atelectasis. It may also restrict lung movements in respiration, causing dyspnea and outright pain, especially on coughing. The accumulated fluid may be reabsorbed as the underlying cause subsides, as in the case of infection. In other cases, as in tumor invasion of the pleurae, excess fluid may be drawn off therapeutically by aspiration. If the pleural effusion contains pus, the condition is **pleural empyema;** the presence of blood in the pleural space is called **hemothorax.**

Respiratory Disease of the Newborn

Respiratory distress syndrome (RDS), also known as **respiratory disease of the newborn** (RDN), is seen in a significant number of infants who are premature, whether by spontaneous delivery or by cesarean section. Also, full-term infants of diabetic mothers are at greater risk of RDN. Affected infants suffer from extreme dyspnea that develops with first breathing, or normal respiration may occur for several hours before the onset of the dyspnea. Breathing difficulty is the result of a lack of pulmonary surfactant. It appears that a critical mark of the lung's maturity is its production of pulmonary surfactant. If delivery occurs before this maturity is achieved, alveolar surface tension becomes a significant force that interferes with respiration in two ways. First, high surface tension means that a greater effort is required to achieve inspiration. This produces dyspnea and chronic fatigue, as a larger portion of total energy output is required just to breathe. The second problem arises during expiration. When increased surface tension combines with the normal forces that reduce alveolar volume,

47 20165

48 39847

49 41342

50 41343

the result is collapse of the terminal airways when alveolar air pressure is exceeded. Because of this, during each inspiration, collapsed airways must be reinflated. Atelectasis occurs when inspiratory effort can't reinflate them.

In RDN the alveolar surfaces are lined by a characteristic coating. It consists of a protein-rich fluid that is drawn out of the lung's interstitium by the increased surface tension, and necrotic debris, present as a result of hypoxic tissue damage. This lining of the alveolar surface is called a hyaline membrane. For this reason, RDN is often described as **hyaline membrane disease.** Because hyaline membranes greatly slow diffusion, and because increasingly widespread atelectasis reduces the surface available to diffusion, hypoxemia and hypercapnia result. Formerly, death often followed in a matter of hours or days because of acute respiratory failure, with mortality rates in the range of 20–30%. Recently, improvements in oxygen administration and ventilation techniques have improved the prognosis in RDS. In particular, the more effective use of pulmonary surfactant therapy has brought a significant reduction in mortality for RDS infants.

LUNG TUMORS

Primary malignant lung tumors are the most common of all tumors and are highly lethal. They are responsible for more deaths than any other tumor. Highest incidence is found in males between 50 and 60 years of age. This is about four times the rate in women, but the incidence in females is steadily rising. It is widely accepted that the single most significant etiological factor in pulmonary malignancies is cigarette smoking. The rising incidence of primary lung cancer in women is probably a reflection of their increased use of tobacco. Those chronically exposed to airborne industrial contaminants show a higher incidence of primary lung cancer, and those who also smoke have a higher incidence still. It may be that air pollutants are promoters that increase the carcinogenic effects of initiators in tobacco smoke (see chapter 5). The effect is also seen in asbestosis. Nonsmokers with asbestosis have a low incidence of lung cancer. Smokers with asbestosis have incidence rates higher than smokers who have no asbestosis involvement.

Over 90% of primary lung cancer develops in the mucous membranes of the larger bronchi. It is therefore called **bronchogenic carcinoma.** **51** The most common form is **squamous cell carcinoma,** which produces characteristic whorled masses of keratin. Another form consists of

Figure 12.33 Bronchogenic carcinoma. The white tumor tissue can easily be identified in contrast to the darker lung tissue. Note that the tumor originated in the bronchial epithelium and invaded the wall, gaining access to the lung parenchyma. Segments of bronchial cartilage can still be identified, delineating the boundaries of the airway.
X-rays had revealed a lesion in the right upper lobe of a 60-year-old male. He had refused therapy and was readmitted some time later with severe dyspnea and marked jugular distention. He died soon thereafter. Autopsy revealed a tumor in the right lung that had invaded extensively. It had spread from its site of origin in the bronchus and penetrated into the lung and beyond to the pericardium. Metastasis was widespread, involving the liver, adrenals, stomach, bone and brain.

small, highly anaplastic cells that resemble oat grains. This tumor is called a **small cell** or **oat cell carcinoma.** **52** It metastasizes early, and by the time of diagnosis is likely to have spread to multiple secondary sites. **53** Small cell carcinoma and the squamous cell type are the tumors most strongly associated with smoking. They are also the most lethal forms. An adenocarcinoma may also arise in the mucus glands of the bronchial mucous membrane. This is the form most common in women.

The impact of cigarette smoking on the bronchi and lungs is reflected in a continuum of effect that can be seen in young smokers. Bronchial irritation results in mucosal inflammatory changes accompanied by hyperplasia in the epithelium. Inflammatory exudate produces pulmonary edema accompanied by fibrosis, particularly in the small

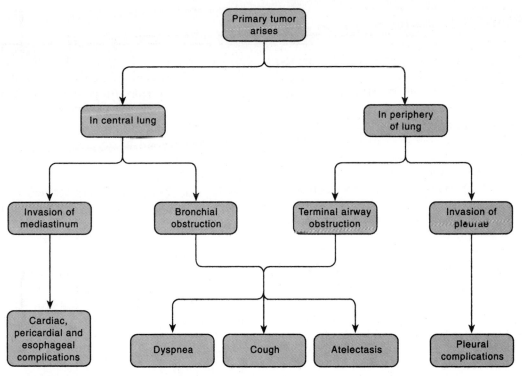

Figure 12.34   The effects of primary lung tumors may vary with the location of the tumor.

airways. Epithelial changes also involve loss of cilia. These early airway changes cause productive cough and an increase in respiratory infections in the smoker. As time passes and cigarette smoking increases (the usual pattern), bronchial damage increases, with chronic bronchitis and emphysema much more likely to develop. Mucosal epithelia thicken as chronic irritation produces early hypertrophy and later hyperplasia, metaplasia, and all too frequently, neoplasia.

As the tumor enlarges, a typical early sign is cough. This is unremarkable, however, because cough is a way of life among heavy smokers, those most at risk of lung cancer. Hemoptysis is often the first indication that the situation is serious. The tumor mass usually invades the bronchial wall. As it grows around the airway's circumference, greater and greater obstruction to air flow occurs (see fig. 12.33). With complete obstruction, atelectasis distal to the blockage is common. Another result of infiltration of the bronchial wall is bronchiectasis from damage that causes airway dilatation. There is also an increased likelihood of lung abcess formation as infection resistance is further eroded.

Bronchogenic carcinoma tends to spread as a large, irregularly expanding mass rather than by narrow invasions into the lungs' parenchyma. **54** Such spread may produce focal compression and atelectasis in the adjacent parenchyma. Collapse occurs when external pressure from the tumor exceeds the pressure of air within the terminal airways. About half of all lung tumors originate at the lung's root and, therefore, often invade the mediastinum, where the pericardium or heart may become involved, introducing the possibility of pericarditis and cardiac arrhythmias. More peripheral tumors may invade to the thoracic cavity's wall. Pain is experienced in such cases, because the parietal pleura is much more sensitive to painful stimuli than are the visceral pleura and lung parenchyma. Irritation of the pleurae by an invading tumor often produces substantial pleural effusion. The effects of primary lung tumors are summarized in figure 12.34.

Prognosis in primary lung cancer is poor. Metastasis is frequent and widespread, typically involving the brain, lymph nodes, bone, and liver.

Case Study

A general practitioner was seen by a 50-year-old male who was worried by a shortness of breath that had developed over the previous month. He indicated that he had had a recent "cold" and cough, which had since improved. On questioning by the doctor, he indicated that he smoked two packs of cigarettes each day and had developed a "smoker's cough" in the last five years. He replied to further inquiries that for the past two years he had experienced some difficulty breathing while climbing stairs and in similar demand situations. When pressed, he further revealed that his "smoker's cough" was sometimes productive of a thick and occasionally colored sputum, and that every winter he tended to develop what his previous doctors had called bronchitis. He was quick to point out that the prescribed antibiotics were able to deal with the problem quite effectively.

On examination, he appeared normal with no apparent cyanosis. Lung auscultation revealed slight wheezing on expiration. Spirometry revealed a depressed FEV_1, while a chest X-ray and complete blood count proved normal.

On the basis of these findings, a diagnosis of early COPD was made. Antibiotic therapy was started to control any residual infection, along with a bronchodilator to ease the patient's breathing. The patient was also urged to stop smoking and to return for periodic reassessment. He failed to return and no follow-up was possible.

Commentary

This patient is all too typical of the long-term, heavy smoker. Note that he had to be persistently questioned to obtain the full story of his condition. The history and FEV_1 results were strongly indicative of his problem, the blood counts established no anemia, and the radiograph was useful in establishing that no significant infection was present.

The fact that bronchodilation was able to improve, if only somewhat, the patient's FEV_1 values indicates some degree of reversibility. With appropriate monitoring, therapy for recurring infections, and support for the patient's efforts to stop smoking, the progression can be slowed, but not avoided.

The patient's failure to return was not unusual in that many require a great deal of time to come to grips with the need to break their addiction. Of course, while the resolve is being mustered, the disease is progressing.

Key Concepts

1. Cough, dyspnea, and cyanosis are the typical signs and symptoms that accompany various respiratory disorders (pp. 289–290).

2. Various studies of pulmonary function are employed in the diagnosis of respiratory disorders, the determination of their severity, and the monitoring of the disease's response to therapy (p. 290).

3. Compromised respiratory function may be the result of hypoperfusion of the pulmonary vasculature due to heart failure, thromboembolism, or the reflex vasoconstriction triggered by hypoventilation (pp. 290–291).

4. Pulmonary shunting is the result of a decreased V/Q ratio caused by hypoventilation, which is in turn caused by airway obstruction or restriction of lung expansion (p. 291).

5. Airway obstruction is characterized by reduced ventilation caused by smaller airway size, accumulated secretions, or loss of pulmonary elastic recoil (p. 292).

6. The long-term inhalation of irritants, most commonly cigarette smoke, is the stimulus to hypersecretion and mucus gland hyperplasia typical of chronic bronchitis (pp. 292–293).

7. The distinguishing features of pulmonary emphysema are bronchiolar stenosis, alveolar enlargement, and septal loss, which reduce respiratory surface and pulmonary perfusion (pp. 293–295).

8. An essential component of the pathogenesis of emphysema is the role of cigarette smoke in inhibiting the action of alpha$_1$-antitrypsin (p. 295).

9. The term chronic airway obstruction (CAO) has clinical descriptive value for those obstructive conditions in which elements of chronic bronchitis, emphysema, or bronchial asthma combine to an extent that may be difficult to determine for a given patient (pp. 296–297).

10. The essential elements of a bronchial asthma attack—bronchiolar constriction, mucus hypersecretion, and inflammation—may be the result of an allergic response, inappropriate autonomic stimulation, or a combination of both (pp. 297–301).

11. Hypoventilation may be caused by extrinsic factors that restrict lung expansion: a defective thoracic framework, insufficient respiratory muscle strength, or faulty neural input from the brain stem (pp. 301–303).

12. Intrinsic restriction of the lung involves diffuse changes in the pulmonary interstitium that produce stiffness and reduced compliance, which may emerge in an acute form, ARDS, or a chronic form, CIRLD (p. 303).

13. The principal feature of ARDS is acute pulmonary edema from capillary damage, which might arise from a broad array of etiologies (pp. 303–306).

14. Most CIRLD is due to long-term, low-level occupational exposure to inhaled irritants, producing inflammatory and immune-mediated damage that is superimposed on the effects of particle accumulation (pp. 306–308).

15. In respiratory failure, the clinical picture may be dominated by either hypoxia or hypoxia and hypercapnia (p. 309).

16. Absorption of air by a portion of a lung isolated by airway blockage can lower pressure sufficiently to allow the lung portion to collapse, producing atelectasis (pp. 309–310).

17. Collapse of an entire lung (pneumothorax) results when atmospheric air gains access to the pleural space, eliminating the pressure gradient that provides for the lung's expansion against the thoracic wall (pp. 310–311).

18. A premature infant's lack of pulmonary surfactant can produce a life-threatening combination of dyspnea, atelectasis, and hyaline membrane formation called respiratory disease of the newborn (pp. 311–312).

19. Bronchogenic carcinoma is the principal primary malignant lung tumor, whose poor prognosis is due to its frequent and extensive metastasis to vital tissues (pp. 312–313).

REVIEW ACTIVITIES

1. In figure 12.5, use a pencil to encircle the area that contains an acinus. (The acinus is not completely shown in the diagram.) The key can be found on p. 284.

2. Rough out a flow chart that indicates the difference in the fate of inhaled particles, based on their size. Indicate the specific fates and, when you're through, compare with figure 12.9 to see how well you did.

3. State how the V/Q ratios in figure 12.11b,c would compare with normal. See page 290 if you have any uncertainty in answering. Now get more practice by similarly assessing figure 12.13, points A, B, and C. The legend may offer help if you need it.

4. Cover the legend in figure 12.15. Of a and b, which is normal? Can you identify each factor that differs between a and b and relate it to the etiology and pathogenesis of chronic bronchitis? If you can't, refer to pages 292–293.

5. List the respiratory disorders mentioned in this chapter that are identified as being caused or complicated by smoking. For each, indicate the essential mechanism involved.

6. Complete the following table.

Key Characteristic	Respiratory Condition
Airway dilation	
Lung portion collapses	
Airway clearance reflex (sign)	
High blood level of reduced hemoglobin	
Inadequate pulmonary surfactant	
Entire lung collapses	
Allergy triggers	
Pleural effusion	
Difficulty breathing (sign)	

7. Jot down the principal differences in the effects a primary malignant lung tumor produces when it originates in a primary bronchus as opposed to a peripheral airway. Don't overlook pain as one effect. Include any effects that might arise regardless of the site of the tumor's origin. A certain flow chart will be useful if you aren't certain your jottings are complete and accurate.

Chapter Thirteen

Gastrointestinal Pathophysiology

A mannerly belly is a great part of a man's liberty.

Michel de Montaigne
Essays

D igestion and the absorption of nutrients that follows it occur in the **alimentary canal,** which extends from the mouth to the anus. This chapter will not deal with diseases of the mouth, and will follow the common usage of the term gastrointestinal (GI). That is, although the usage is not strictly accurate, gastrointestinal will be taken to include the esophagus along with the stomach and intestines.

ANATOMY AND PHYSIOLOGY

The fundamental task we face in obtaining nutrients is their passage from the body's exterior to its internal compartments. Nutrients present in the lumen of the GI tract are considered external to these compartments, since the alimentary canal is open to the exterior at both ends. This concept may not be obvious because of the manner in which the rest of the body is ingeniously folded around the GI lumen, but it is an important one (fig. 13.1). It means that digestion occurs outside the body, and that the crucial event that provides access to the nutrients is absorption. Absorption involves the passage of nutrients from the lumen through the membranes of the epithelial cells that line it, and then to the blood and lymph for distribution to appropriate sites of utilization or storage.

Most absorption occurs in the small intestine. It is particularly well adapted for this purpose, as it presents to the lumen the enormous surface area required for efficient absorption. Two major factors that contribute to the small intestine's large surface area are its length and the configuration of its internal lining. The small intestine (or small bowel—the terms are used interchangeably) is quite long. It can be drawn out to a length of over 20 feet and so is repeatedly folded back on itself to fit within the shorter abdominal cavity. Its proximal portion, the **duodenum,** receives the stomach's contents and passes them to its midportion, the **jejunum.** The **ileum** is the distal segment of the small bowel. It joins to the **cecum,** the inferior portion of the large bowel, or **colon.**

The small intestine, in fact the entire alimentary canal, has its internal surface lined by a **mucous membrane** or **mucosa.** This consists of an epithelium resting on a cushion of loosely organized fibrous connective tissue, under which lies a thin layer of smooth muscle. For most of its length the epithelium is only one cell layer thick, to accommodate nutrient absorption. In the mouth and esophagus, a thicker and stratified epithelium that is better adapted to protection is present. Specialized cells of the epithelium, and glands beneath it in the **submucosa** (the layer of fibrous connective tissues that supports the mucosa), secrete mucus onto the epithelial surface. **1** This viscous, protein-containing fluid acts as a protective covering and lubricant that promotes easy passage of **chyme** from one part of the canal to the next. (Chyme is the preferred term for the contents of the stomach and small intestine. With the addition of

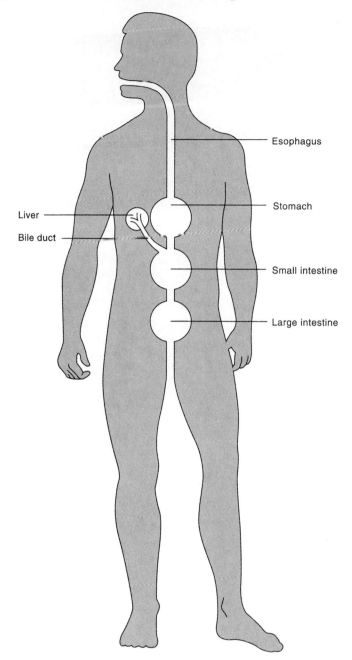

Figure 13.1   The lumen of the alimentary canal (GI tract) is an external space. In the schematic diagram the tract has been simplified to illustrate this important concept.

various secreted substances and the start of digestion, the contents of the stomach and small bowel are quite different from the food that entered the mouth.)

In the small intestine, three structural modifications are present that provide increased surface area for absorption. In the first, the mucous membrane is thrown into a pattern of circular folds. In effect, the internal mucous membrane is longer than the wall of the small bowel and must be collapsed into a folded configuration in order to fit the intestine's shorter length. A second modification of the mucosa

Figure 13.2 Microvilli at the luminal surface of the intestinal epithelium greatly increase the surface area available for absorption.

involves the **villi.** Thousands of these mucosal projections protrude into the lumen to greatly increase absorptive surface. **2** A third and very large increase in surface area derives from the **microvilli,** which cover the luminal surface of each epithelial cell in the villus. These are extremely fine, hairlike projections of the cell's membrane across which nutrients are absorbed (fig. 13.2). The small intestine's length and its mucosal configuration combine to provide an absorptive surface estimated to be in excess of 3000 square feet.

Digestion is the processing of food that converts it into forms that are capable of being absorbed. Most food is in the form of macromolecules, which cannot cross the mucosal epithelium. Digestion reduces these macromolecules to their simpler, absorbable subunits. The process depends on enzymes that catalyze a series of several chemical changes in small steps. The products of these reactions are the simpler units, which can then be readily absorbed. The necessary digestive fluids are produced by the mucosal epithelium and by glands whose secretions are poured into the alimentary canal's lumen. Such secretions contain not only enzymes but also other substances that contribute to digestion. Since the salivary glands, liver, and pancreas are situated apart from the canal, long ducts are needed to deliver their secretions to the lumen.

A significant amount of digestive activity is devoted to reducing the physical size of food particles, because chemical digestion is more efficient if food particle size is small. This physical digestion of food has three components: mastication, secretion, and alimentary wall motility. In chewing or **mastication,** the tongue and cheeks position food so the teeth can tear and crush it. Secretion involves the movement of digestive fluids into the lumen to promote physical breakdown of the food. For example, water is secreted into the mouth, stomach, and small intestine to loosen, soften, and dissolve food components. Acid is secreted into the stomach to disrupt the connective tissues binding the cells of the plant and animal tissues in food. The acid also kills bacteria, activates gastric enzymes, and prepares protein for chemical digestion. Bile, which is secreted by the liver, travels to the duodenum by way of a duct system. The bile salts it contains act to convert large fat globules to large numbers of tiny globules. This process, called **emulsification,** is a physical change that greatly increases the surface area available to fat-splitting enzymes. The third component of physical digestion involves the activity of the GI wall. In it are two layers of smooth muscle, one longitudinally and one circumferentially arranged. Unlike the rest of the alimentary canal, the stomach has a third, partial layer, which contributes to the vigorous contractions that churn and mix food with the water, acid, and enzyme secretions of the stomach. Mastication, secretion, and gastric churning combine to yield the small particle size required for efficient enzyme functioning.

The process of digestion requires that food in the alimentary canal be moved through its lumen at an appropriate rate. The canal wall's smooth muscle layers provide this motion by producing a series of coordinated, rhythmic contractions called **peristalsis.** This pattern of contractions provides the required direction and rate of motion along the length of the alimentary canal. Generally, the direction of peristalsis is from the esophagus toward the anus, but in the small intestine small retrograde movements ensure adequate mixing of chyme with digestive fluids, as well as increasing the time available for digestion.

Throughout the alimentary canal the process of digestion is regulated to provide close coordination between secretory and muscular activity. Nervous reflexes are involved, some confined to the canal and others involving the central nervous system. At times of stress or emotional disturbances, input from the central nervous system (CNS) can adversely affect the functioning of the system. The endocrine system is also involved in the regulation of digestion. Hormones secreted by glands in the stomach and

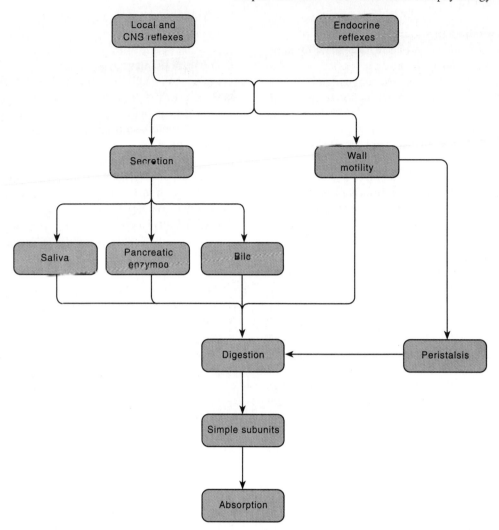

Figure 13.3 Summary of the essential elements of digestion. Control of secretion and muscle contraction is mediated by nervous and endocrine reflexes.

small bowel contribute to the responses needed to meet changing digestive requirements. These essentials are summarized in figure 13.3.

GI PATHOPHYSIOLOGY

Much of North American hospitalization involves the digestive system: the alimentary canal and its associated glands. In this chapter we consider those disorders that principally involve the GI tract. Although there is a fairly large number of these disorders, their effects produce only a relative small number of GI manifestations. Each of these will be considered in the sections which follow.

Expulsion from the GI Tract

Expulsion of the GI contents, by vomiting or diarrhea, is a common indicator of tract irritation or malfunction. Although the episodes are typically of short duration, producing minimal disturbance and resolving promptly, severe or prolonged bouts can have serious systemic consequences.

Vomiting

In expelling the gastric contents, close coordination of several interrelated processes is required. Pallor and increased salivary output precede vomiting as a result of altered CNS output. Peristaltic contractions in the stomach and small intestine stop, and the pyloric sphincter, between the stomach and duodenum, closes. Access to adjacent airways is cut off as the glottis, the larynx's opening to the lower respiratory passages, is closed and the soft palate moves back to tightly seal off the posterior openings into the nasal passages. In this way only a single path for expulsion is provided.

Following these preparations, an abrupt increase of abdominal pressure develops as the diaphragm, the intercostal muscles, and the muscles of the abdominal wall contract. (The fairly common experience of soreness in the abdominal muscles following a vigorous bout of vomiting testifies to their forceful contribution to the process.) The mounting pressure is applied to the stomach and adds to that produced by its own contractions. The result is a high pressure that is applied to the closed gastroesophageal sphincter, causing it to open and allowing gastric contents to be forced into the esophagus, past the opened hypopharyngeal sphincter at the top of the esophagus, and into the mouth. This process clears the vomited material, the **vomitus,** from the tract. The occasional presence of bile in vomitus is evidence of the small intestine's participation in vigorous vomiting episodes. Contraction of its proximal portion can generate sufficient pressure to drive bile through the pyloric sphincter to the stomach.

The sequence of responses just described is the result of nervous output from an integrating center for the vomiting reflex, located in the medulla oblongata. This **vomiting center** initiates the vomiting reflexes as it receives input from sensitive receptor cells in the walls of the GI tract, abdominal viscera, or other parts of the nervous system. Irritating substances from chemical or biological sources, inflammatory changes in the mucosa, or distortion of the canal—usually small bowel distention—typically induce the vomiting reflex. **Nausea,** the awareness of the tendency or need to vomit, occurs because activity in the vomiting center is being signaled to the cerebral cortex.

The vomiting center also receives input from another part of the brain nearby called the **chemoreceptor trigger zone** (CTZ). This area has a rich blood supply and is highly sensitive to certain circulating chemicals that stimulate the CTZ and, in turn, the vomiting center. Some of these are substances released from tissues damaged by bacterial infection or ionizing radiation. CTZ activity may also result from exposure to circulating therapeutic drugs administered for problems unrelated to GI problems. This is the reason for the nausea and vomiting side effects associated with the use of certain drugs. Various neurological disturbances are also associated with vomiting, as they directly or indirectly affect the vomiting center or the CTZ. Such conditions as meningitis, cerebral ischemia, and increased intracranial pressure are examples. The CTZ also receives input from the inner ear structures involved with the maintenance of somatic equilibrium. In sensitive individuals, visual and other activities associated with the motions of air, sea, or land travel can cause these inner ear structures to activate the CTZ, with the nausea and vomiting of motion sickness the result.

In certain individuals, merely the aroma or sight of vomitus or the sensations evoked by the memory of a previous episode of vomiting may induce the response. A case in point is the author, who has been aware of a distinct abdominal queasiness while researching and writing this material. Psychological disturbances can also produce chronic vomiting, for example, where there is some compulsive fear of poisoning, or where the mere thought of eating can induce nausea. The latter case is typical of **anorexia nervosa,** a potentially grave condition deriving from an obsession with weight loss. Figure 13.4 summarizes the steps in the vomiting response.

Most vomiting is a direct approach to clearing the upper GI tract of irritants. Usually, as the offending material is expelled, normal functions are quickly restored. Complications may arise, however, in the case of chronic vomiting, especially in children. Loss of fluid in such cases may lead to dehydration, and loss of needed electrolytes may lead to potentially severe fluid and electrolyte imbalances. Chronic vomiting may also lead to deficiencies of essential nutrients, especially vitamins. Another source of complications is frequent or particularly vigorous vomiting. In such cases, the mucosa may tear, with subsequent bleeding into the lumen and the vomitus. The **Mallory-Weiss syndrome** involves such gastric and esophageal bleeding. It results from lacerations of the mucosa caused by paroxysms of retching, typically seen in chronic alcohol abuse.

In the unconscious, CNS reflex coordination may be sufficiently depressed to produce faulty vomiting responses. If the stomach's contents are expelled to the oropharynx while the glottis remains open, aspiration of vomitus may result. The potential consequences are pulmonary damage or complete blockage of the respiratory passages. Those in an alcoholic stupor or those recovering from surgical anesthesia are particularly at risk.

Diarrhea

The large bowel functions to complete the absorption process by removing up to 900 ml of water and various salts from the colon's lumen daily. This process prepares the contents of the colon (the **feces**) for expulsion from the alimentary canal. The colon's smooth muscle undergoes two to three periods of vigorous peristalsis per day. One of these may fill the rectum, stimulating receptors there. In response, the spinal cord activates the defecation reflex, and fecal matter is expelled. There is wide variation in the frequency of defecation among normal individuals, from as few as two per week to as many as three per day.

Diarrhea is usually defined in terms of increased fecal fluidity, but increased volume of feces or frequency of defecation in a given individual may also indicate an abnormality. The essential cause of diarrhea is increased colonic fluid volume, which, by producing distention, activates the defecation reflex. Greater colonic distention will also lead to increased frequency of the response.

The fluid accumulates in the intestinal lumen by three distinct mechanisms. One is an active secretion process, while the second involves passive water movement, by osmosis. The third mechanism is based on faulty intestinal or colonic water absorption.

Secretion The secretion of water into the intestinal lumen is a common response to irritation. In some cases, bacterial toxins, in particular from *Vibrio cholera* and *Escherichia coli,* and irritation from laxatives or unabsorbed fatty acids are known to produce an intestinal secretion response. The movement of fluid to the lumen promotes distention, and the resulting defecation would seem a beneficial response

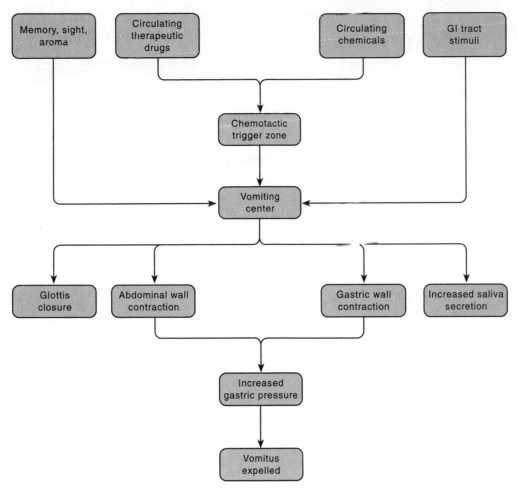

Figure 13.4   Mechanisms underlying the vomiting reflexes. Local GI stimuli, circulating therapeutic drugs or other chemicals, as well as sensory and memory inputs, can all induce the response.

in that tract irritants are initially diluted and then evacuated from the tract. In other cases, patients who undergo removal of all, or part, of the ileum are unable to reabsorb bile salts, since the ileum is the principal site for their uptake for recycling via the liver. As a result, abnormally large amounts of these irritant salts are present to elicit a secretion response. Also, certain GI tumors stimulate intestinal secretion by direct or indirect means that are not well understood. In these cases, the related bouts of diarrhea can be quite intense.

Osmosis Osmotic flow of water to the lumen depends on high luminal osmotic pressures. These are the result of increased particle concentrations, which are usually caused by faulty digestion, impaired particle absorption, or an increased intake of indigestible or unabsorbable molecules. Digestive problems may arise from a lack of bile or the enzymes needed to degrade food macromolecules to their absorbable subunits. As a consequence, the particles remain in the lumen and raise its osmotic pressure.

The slowing of intestinal motility favors bacterial growth, which is normally inhibited. As they proliferate, the bacteria metabolize luminal nutrients to produce greater numbers of product molecules. These increase osmotic pressure and thus lead to diarrhea, even though no toxic or infectious damage is involved. Impaired absorption of digestion products has the same effect: an increased luminal osmotic pressure, which draws water from the intestinal wall.

Increased dietary or therapeutic intake can also raise lumen osmotic pressure. Diets rich in legumes and carbohydrates have a high content of indigestible elements and can produce diarrhea. Also, patients undergoing antacid therapy to reduce gastric hyperacidity may ingest preparations with high concentrations of poorly absorbed ions, such as magnesium. Therapy based on these preparations often produces an osmosis-mediated diarrhea as a side effect.

Impaired Water Absorption Certain diseases of the intestine and colon reduce the mucosa's permeability to water and therefore impede water absorption. This effect is significant in light of the 2 liters of dietary fluid ingested daily and the addition of 7 liters of digestive fluids secreted into the lumen each day. Since normal daily fecal loss is only about 400 ml, the small intestine and colon must absorb 8600 ml daily. Thus a reduction of water absorption can

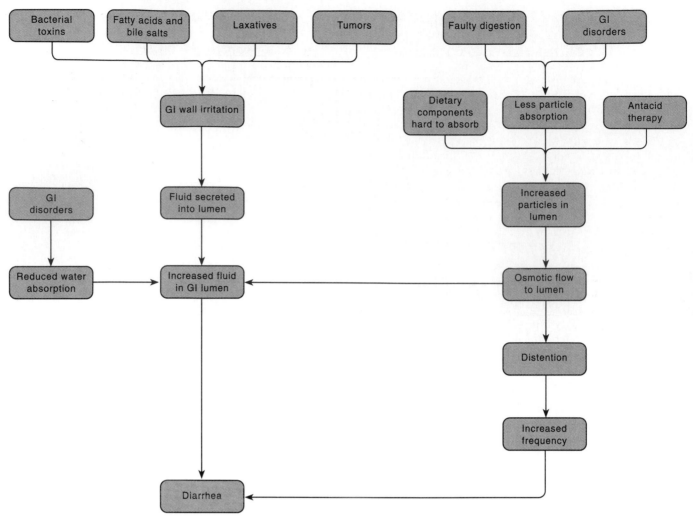

Figure 13.5   Factors contributing to diarrhea.

readily generate significant intestinal fluid volume and diarrhea. Various malabsorption syndromes are described in a later section.

Alcohol and certain classes of therapeutic agents can produce diarrhea as a side effect. Antibiotics and antitumor agents are the principal drugs involved. They may act either to irritate the intestine, promoting fluid secretion, or to interfere with water absorption. The various factors predisposing to diarrhea are summarized in figure 13.5.

Of course, **laxatives**—agents that promote defecation—might also cause diarrhea. These are normally administered to counter **constipation** (difficulty in defecation), which may be due to altered intestinal motility (see irritable bowel syndrome, in a later section) or to faulty rectal reflexes. Whatever the cause of the constipation, excessive laxative use can produce diarrhea in those particularly sensitive to their effects.

The principal consequences of diarrhea are water loss, leading to dehydration, and acidosis, due to the loss of alkaline bicarbonate ions. These are particularly threatening in the very young, the elderly, and those already weakened by disease or other debilitating factors.

Dehydration and acidosis are less likely to occur in acute diarrhea, which typically resolves without intervention. They are more likely to arise in cases of liver or pancreatic dysfunction, intestinal resection, or severe mucosal damage where diarrhea becomes chronic. If diarrhea is severe or chronic, therapy may attempt to inhibit motility in the intestines to reduce frequency and promote fluid absorption. Typical antidiarrheal agents are preparations of loperamide and paregoric.

Irritable Bowel Syndrome This condition, also known as **spastic colon** or **mucous colitis,** is involved in as many as half of the GI problems for which people seek medical consultation. It is characterized by a varying symptom mix that may include abdominal discomfort or pronounced cramping, fatigue, episodes of tachycardia, constipation, pain radiating down the left arm, and diarrhea. The diarrhea typically involves increased frequency and urgency of defecation, even though stool volume is low. A higher than normal mucus content is also characteristic of the stool in the irritable bowel syndrome.

Diarrhea in this condition appears to be the result of increased intestinal motility, which reduces the time avail-

Mechanisms of Laxative Action

Insights into the mechanisms that increase intestinal fluid volume to cause diarrhea can be applied to promoting bowel evacuation in cases of constipation. Four laxative mechanisms are currently employed by various agents. Some add water-binding materials to the GI tract to prevent water absorption. The objective is to maintain sufficient colonic water volume to increase distention and thus stimulate the defecation reflex. An example of such a **bulk-forming agent** is methylcellulose. Other laxatives rely on an **osmotic** or **saline** mechanism to draw water from the mucosa by using high ion concentrations to produce high luminal osmotic pressure. Because of its low absorption by intestinal epithelium, osmotic laxatives often utilize magnesium ion as their principal active agent. A third laxative category contains **irritant** or **stimulant** agents. These irritate the intestinal mucosa to promote secretion and enhance distention. Where longer periods of constipation have allowed for increased colonic water absorption, a hardened and difficult-to-evacuate fecal mass may result. In such cases a member of the fourth laxative category, a **stool-softening** agent, such as **docusate potassium,** may be used. It acts as an emulsifying agent to promote the mixture of water and fecal fat. This action softens the stool and provides for easier evacuation.

able for adequate fluid absorption. The associated abdominal pain is thought to be linked to bouts of intense and prolonged intestinal spasm.

The mechanism underlying the irritable bowel syndrome is not clearly understood. It may involve a neurogenic component that produces an exaggerated motility response to the presence of chyme. The high incidence in those with personalities that seem driven to high achievement suggests a psychological component as well.

Gastrointestinal Inflammation

Acute inflammation in the GI tract is quite common. Most of it is an acute response to local injury or irritation. It produces the expected inflammatory symptoms and signs: congestion and exudate formation in the mucosa, along with pain and redness. As healing follows, there is usually little problem with epithelial regeneration, but fibrosis in the submucosa may arise, followed by contracture to produce strictures in the GI tract that narrow the lumen, impede normal motility, and obstruct passage along its length.

Esophagitis

Most inflammation in the alimentary canal occurs in the stomach and intestines. The esophagus is less commonly involved, but irritation typically stems from the reflux of gastric contents into it. The intense acidity of gastric juice

Laxative Abuse

In some cases of chronic diarrhea for which no cause can be found, laxative abuse may be a hidden factor. Excessive and concealed laxative use has been identified in those, usually young women, who have eating disorders and who try to reduce their weight by inducing diarrhea. Another group of abusers, for less clear but presumably psychogenic reasons, includes people who work in medically related jobs. Women also predominate in this group, whose members' ages range from young to middle years.

Diagnosis of laxative overuse can be made on the basis of stool ion concentrations, which are altered by the laxative. This analysis can be particularly important in undiagnosed chronic diarrhea in children, where an abusive parent is forcing the child to ingest a laxative when one is not needed.

is the major factor in such irritation, because the esophageal mucosa lacks the gastric adaptations that provide acid tolerance. The resulting **reflux esophagitis** is associated with epigastric pain, usually described as a dull or burning ache that may radiate to the neck. **3** This sensation is commonly known as **heartburn.** A wide variety of commonly encountered agents can induce a lowering of tension in the region of the gastroesophageal junction known as the **lower esophageal sphincter** (LES). This change allows gastric pressures to drive acidic chyme into the esophagus. CNS depressants such as valium or morphine can reduce normal input to the LES, and certain foods, e.g., chocolate or fats, and alcohol and smoking are also known to elicit this response.

Reflux esophagitis is also associated with pregnancy and obesity. In both situations, increased abdominal pressures can combine with gastric pressures to overcome resistance of the LES. Reflux of gastric contents is also associated with **hiatal hernia** of the stomach. In this condition, a segment of the stomach herniates (projects from its normal cavity) into the thoracic cavity through an enlarged or loosened **esophageal hiatus**—the opening in the diaphragm by which the esophagus gains entry to the abdominal cavity. This idiopathic condition may take two forms: **sliding hiatal hernia** or **paraesophageal hiatal hernia** (fig. 13.6). Most cases of either type are essentially asymptomatic, but some sliding herniation is associated with reflux esophagitis.

Acute esophagitis may also be the result of damage that follows esophageal infection, e.g., by herpes simplex virus, or irradiation for thoracic tumors. Less common, but much more severe, is the esophagitis that follows accidental or suicidal ingestion of corrosive liquids such as strong acids or lye. In such cases the potential for scarring and stricture is high.

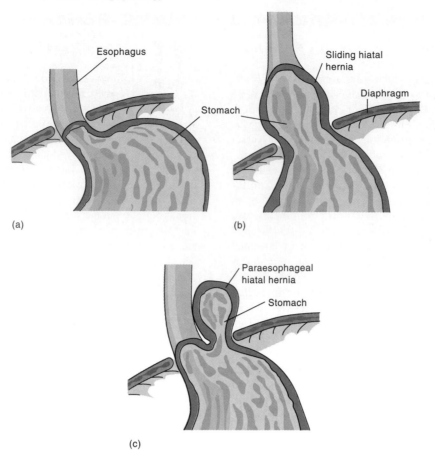

Esophagus

Stomach

(a)

Sliding hiatal
hernia

Diaphragm

(b)

Paraesophageal
hiatal hernia

Stomach

(c)

Figure 13.6   Hiatal hernia. This condition involves herniation of the stomach into the thoracic cavity by way of the esophageal hiatus. (*a*) Normal. (*b*) Sliding hernia. (*c*) Paraesophageal hernia. This type may progressively enlarge.

Inflammations of the Stomach and Intestines

In the stomach and intestines, various irritants can provoke fairly mild inflammations of short duration. Many are idiopathic. These conditions are termed gastritis, enteritis, gastroenteritis, enterocolitis, or colitis, depending on the organs involved. Most such inflammations are the result of ingested irritants of biological or chemical origin, which often trigger vomiting and diarrhea. Damage is usually minimal, with rapid healing of mucosal damage.

The gastric mucosa is especially sensitive to alcohol, aspirin (ASA), and other nonsteroidal anti-inflammatory drugs (NSAIDs). Chronic ingesters of such substances may suffer from acute gastritis combined with bleeding erosions of the mucosa, **4** a condition called **acute erosive gastritis.** The loss of mucosal surface in these cases is superficial. More severe erosions of the GI mucosa are considered in the section on ulceration, later in this chapter.

Sufferers of chronic pain or non-GI inflammatory conditions, rheumatoid arthritics for example, may become dependent on ASA or NSAID use and suffer significant gastric mucosal disruption, which raises the threat of chronic bleeding. (Note that although ASA has anti-inflammatory effects, and therefore can be grouped with the NSAIDs, e.g., ibuprofen or indomethacin, it is separately identified here because much of its use is based primarily on its analgesic properties.) Individuals who suffer **dyspepsia** (generalized gastrointestinal upset involving pain, gas, poor appetite, nausea, and vomiting) as a result of alcohol abuse often seek to correct the discomfort with aspirin. Of course, this only compounds the problem by adding to the mucosal damage already caused by previous alcohol ingestion.

Appendicitis

The vermiform appendix is a potential site of inflammation. This 8–10 cm long structure is a slender extension of the cecum containing nodules of lymphoid tissue in its submucosa **5** (fig. 13.7*a*). These nodules enlarge during adolescence and may play some special role in the development of a fully competent immune system, but their exact contribution is not known. Acute inflammation of the appendix **6** can occur at any age, but the highest incidence is in the range 10–30. Incidence favors males within the range, but when appendicitis occurs in those younger or older, the sexes are equally affected. It is the most common cause of abdominal surgery in children.

(a)   (b)   (c)

Figure 13.7 (*a*) Cross section through normal appendix, showing lumen and lymphatic nodules. (*b*) Acute appendicitis, showing swelling and bacterial proliferation. Ischemic injury may follow. (*c*) Necrosis from hypoxia or bacteria toxins may result in perforation of the wall, allowing bacteria and debris to spill into the abdominal cavity.

The pathogenesis of acute appendicitis involves obstruction of its narrow lumen, which appears to establish conditions favoring resident bacterial growth. The obstruction is often a hardened mass of fecal material called a **fecalith.** [7] External compression by a tumor or other mass may also provide luminal blockage, but in many cases no obstruction seems to exist. Once bacterial growth is established, the resulting mucosal irritation induces an inflammatory response (fig. 13.7*b*). Acute pain in the lower right quadrant accompanies these changes, as do anorexia (loss of appetite) and vomiting.

With progression, swelling of the appendix can compress its veins to produce ischemia and hypoxia. These conditions favor the growth of anaerobic organisms, whose digestion of necrotic tissue produces gas and other noxious products. This condition is called **gangrene.** A major risk in appendicitis is that the damaged appendix wall will weaken and perforate, allowing the lumen's bacteria-laden contents to spill into the abdominal cavity [8] (fig. 13.6*c*). The pathogenesis of acute appendicitis is summarized in figure 13.8.

Peritonitis

The **peritoneum** is an extensive serous membrane system in the abdominal cavity. Its parietal layer lines the inner walls of the cavity, whereas its visceral layer is adherent to the surfaces of most abdominal organs. The smooth peritoneal surfaces are coated with a thin film of protective lubricating fluid. Its presence greatly reduces friction between the viscera, and between them and the cavity's wall, during peristaltic and other normal movements. In addition, the peritoneum supports the viscera and aids in maintaining their relative positions within the abdomen. The sheets of peritoneum also carry blood, lymphatic vessels, and nerves to and from the intestines.

Peritonitis [9] is caused most commonly by perforation of an inflamed abdominal organ, often the appendix, but it may also result from abdominal wounds, surgical or other trauma, bleeding from the GI tract, or perforation of the colon's wall by an invading tumor.

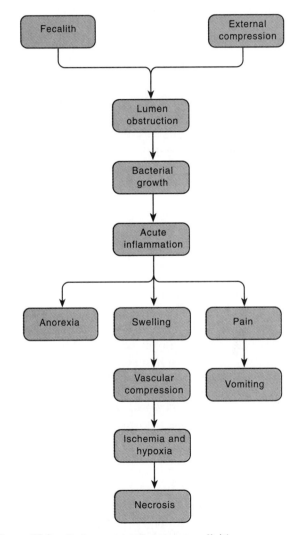

Figure 13.8 Pathogenesis of acute appendicitis.

Peritonitis often produces the syndrome of acute pain onset, fever, and vomiting that is called the **acute abdomen.** It is typical in cases of acute appendicitis, cholecystitis (gall bladder inflammation), GI wall perforation, and various other abdominal disorders.

[7] 20088   [8] 18701   [9] 39645

Pathogenesis of peritonitis involves peritoneal inflammation at the point where it overlays an inflamed abdominal organ. At the affected peritoneal surface a fibrinous exudate forms. A fibrin mesh, which is continuous between peritoneum and the adjacent organ, walls off the inflamed area, isolating the irritants from the rest of the abdominal organs.

In some cases, an abscess will form at the site if exudate and pus clearance is delayed. In others, postinflammatory scarring can produce adhesions and compromise normal intestinal motility. If stricture results, obstruction of normal movement within the lumen is likely. In the case of peritonitis resulting from colon perforation, the inflammation following fecal contamination may be complicated by abscess formation and perforation of the wall of an adjacent pelvic structure. This complication may result in fibrosis that joins the two adjacent organs in such a way that a passage forms between their normally separate lumina. Such a passage is called a **fistula.** The same term applies when the perforated organ's lumen communicates with another surface or cavity instead of another organ's lumen (fig. 13.9).

When fistulae form, problems arise because substances normally confined to one site may well produce irritation or infection when abnormally exposed to surfaces or mucosae that are not able to resist their effects. Bile is particularly irritating to tissues other than the gall bladder or bile duct linings, and it is not difficult to appreciate the irritation and infection threat when colon contents pass through a fistula connecting with the urinary bladder, small intestine, or vagina.

Following perforation of a GI organ, irritation of the peritoneum may not remain localized. More widespread involvement is called **generalized peritonitis** and presents the potential for more serious consequences. Since the peritoneal membranes are continuous throughout the abdominopelvic cavity, irritants and infectious agents have access to an extensive array of potential damage sites. The large surface also accommodates absorption of toxins spilled from the perforated organ. These can produce various systemic complications such as fever, septicemia, and vascular shock. Mortality in generalized peritonitis is high if the leaking perforation can't be closed. The elderly and debilitated are particularly at risk.

Diverticulitis

Diverticula are thought to be present in as much as 10% of the population of economically well-developed nations, usually in people over 50. Each **diverticulum** is a pouchlike sac of intestinal mucous membrane that protrudes through the wall of the large intestine (fig. 13.10). The presence of diverticula is described by the term **diverticulosis. 10** Most diverticula form in the colon, and most of these (95%) occur in the sigmoid colon. In many cases they are asymp-

Figure 13.9 A fistula (arrow) between the colon and the vagina.

tomatic, but in some they may produce cramping pain, less intense abdominal discomfort, and constipation. A few cases involve mild to severe bleeding into the colon's lumen.

It is widely held that diverticula are formed by high intraluminal pressures, which force the mucosal pouches to project through the colon wall at the weakened points where nutrient arteries pass through it. The high pressures are believed to be the result of the more intense peristaltic contractions needed to evacuate low-volume stools from the alimentary canal. A diet rich in indigestible residues, collectively referred to as fiber, provides a large fecal volume that readily triggers defecation. The shorter time spent in the colon (the **transit time**) also means that less water is absorbed. The result is a moister, more easily evacuated stool. A low-residue diet stimulates less colonic peristalsis and thus promotes water absorption. The smaller, dryer stool may then require more forceful colonic contractions, which raise pressures and promote formation of diverticula.

Although there is no hard evidence of the relationship between intraluminal pressure and diverticulosis, the problem is nonexistent in countries where high-fiber diets, based on cereal grains and vegetables, are the norm, in striking contrast to the incidence in countries where refined carbohydrate and meat form a high proportion of the diet. Vegetarians have a much lower incidence of diverticulosis, and in animals that eat only vegetable matter, the problem is unknown, even though they have points of weakness in their colon walls similar to those in humans.

A few scattered diverticula may be present in diverticulosis, or there may be over a hundred. In about 15% of affected individuals, fecal matter becomes impacted in the diverticula to form fecaliths. Irritation and bacterial damage to the wall may follow to produce **diverticulitis.** In these cases, lower left quadrant abdominal pain, fever, and episodes of diarrhea or constipation, or both, are characteristic.

(a)   (b)

Figure 13.10   (*a*) Diverticula are flask-shaped sacs of mucosa that project through the muscular layers of the intestine, usually the colon. (*b*) Numerous colon diverticula can be seen as the rounded masses projecting from this sectioned length of colon. The arrows indicate the openings of the diverticula, which communicate to the bowel lumen.
This colon segment was removed from the abdomen of a 58-year-old man who had suffered years of intermittent bouts of pain, fever, and vomiting. On one such occasion, swelling in the lower left abdominal quadrant was pronounced, and a radiographic study revealed extensive diverticular disease in the sigmoid colon. The patient elected to have the affected segment of bowel removed, and he was no longer troubled. The specimen shown here has been cut on its long axis to reveal the openings into several diverticula. The resection was done during a period of remission so no signs of inflammation are apparent.

‼ A Caution about High-Fiber Diets

Of course, it doesn't necessarily follow that if a little is good, more must be better. In those seeking a high degree of immediate protection against diverticulosis, a sudden change to a high-fiber diet can induce rectal gas accumulation and frequent, forceful, even explosive episodes of diarrhea. As in most things, a gradual change in fiber intake, with monitoring of any ill effects, is the wise course.

The principal threat of diverticulitis is necrosis of the wall of the diverticulum, followed by its perforation. The resulting spill of colon contents onto adjacent organ surfaces presents the risk of peritonitis and formation of fistulae to adjacent organs. Furthermore, fibrosis following successive bouts of diverticulitis may cause stenosis of the colon, obstructing free passage through it.

The presence of diverticulosis is often unnoticed, and because, after an episode of diverticulitis, the condition may again become asymptomatic, it is often difficult to determine the status of the situation in a given patient. For

this reason, the term **diverticular disease** is increasingly used. It implies the condition of diverticulosis and the possibility of periods of diverticular inflammation, without the need to select a term whose clinical precision may vary in each case.

Inflammatory Bowel Disease

The designation **inflammatory bowel disease** (IBD) includes two conditions that have certain underlying features in common. Both **Crohn's disease** and **ulcerative colitis** are inflammatory diseases with no known cause and a well-established pattern of familial incidence. Both conditions often have an insidious onset of abdominal cramping, diarrhea and fever. The two bowel disorders also occur in similar populations: whites, especially Jews of European extraction, in the 20–40-year age range. Many investigations have pursued the cause of Crohn's disease and ulcerative colitis, but without definitive results. Presumably a genetic predisposition to attack by some infectious agent is involved, but beyond that, little can be said with certainty. Apart from these broad similarities, the following specific differences in pathogenesis and clinical course are known.

Crohn's Disease In this condition, granuloma formation and sometimes more diffuse cellular infiltrations produce mucosal swelling and erosion of the mucosal surface, **11** often producing a linear pattern of ulceration. Fibrosis in the submucosa and hypertrophy of muscle layers often contribute to intestinal stenosis. **12** **13** As these changes affect a given section of the colon or small intestine, adjacent areas may remain uninvolved, hence the designation **regional enteritis.** Symptoms are quite variable among those affected, with intervals of pain and discomfort separated by asymptomatic periods of remission, which usually last weeks to months, and in some cases years. A pattern of chronic recurrence, producing progressive weight loss and anemia from inadequate absorption of iron or vitamin B_{12}, is common in Crohn's disease. Reduced red cell production may also be caused by a folate lack, secondary to food intake reduction caused by an accompanying anorexia.

Ulcerative Colitis (UC) In this condition, blood in the stool often accompanies diarrhea and abdominal pain. **14** As in Crohn's disease, bouts of remission separate the attacks, but onset is usually more abrupt. Among sufferers, 90% have mild or moderate symptoms, but 10% have a much more threatening **fulminant** or **severe ulcerative colitis.** Fluid and electrolyte losses can be serious in this condition, as can hemorrhage, which poses the threat of hypovolemic shock. The mortality rate in this condition is 15%.

Ulcerative colitis is limited to the colon and is characterized by a diffuse involvement confined to the mucosa. Inflammatory swelling, redness, and cellular infiltration are typical, but the mucosal surface also displays a progressive loss of epithelium (fig. 13.11). This surface erosion, or ulceration, begins in deep epithelial folds where foci of purulent necrosis arise. These abscesses enlarge and merge with adjacent abscesses to produce extensive mucosal ulceration. Over the course of the disease, inflammation in the mucosa takes on a more cellular characteristic typical of a chronic inflammatory response. A comparison of relevant aspects of Crohn's disease and ulcerative colitis is presented in table 13.1.

Complications and Therapy The two conditions that contribute to IBD have similar complications, which are related to weakening and perforation of the wall of the bowel. The potential consequences are peritonitis and fistula formation. Scarring during periods of remission may produce intestinal stricture, more so with Crohn's disease than ulcerative colitis. Systemic effects include eye and joint inflammation, liver damage, and cancer. The increased cancer rate is more significant in cases of ulcerative colitis that are of prolonged duration and generalized colon involvement. The cancer risk in Crohn's disease is above normal, but smaller than in ulcerative colitis (table 13.1).

Figure 13.11 Ulcerative colitis. These colon segments show a thickened wall with longitudinal ridges in the mucosae. Between the ridges are depressions of ulcerated mucosa.
A 13-year-old girl suffered from ulcerative colitis and had a long history of diarrhea, bleeding, and pain. Therapy had been ineffective, and because she was having trouble avoiding malnutrition, the affected segments of her colon and rectum were surgically removed. Her condition improved and she gained weight, although the postsurgical period was complicated by various intestinal disturbances. The colon segments shown here have elongated ridges of thickened wall separated by linear troughs of ulcerated mucosa. Various regions of fibrosis are also present, with some sites of acute inflammation. No indications of malignancy were found.

Therapy in IBD involves easing symptoms with antidiarrheal drugs and attempts to limit the disease with anti-inflammatory agents. Since there is no known way to suppress the unknown causative mechanism, surgical resection of an affected bowel segment or the entire colon may be necessary in severe cases or if cancer indications arise. Removal of a segment of bowel is often followed by recurrence and exacerbation of symptoms in the remaining sections.

Previously, it was thought that psychological or emotional stress contributed to IBD. In such cases, psychotherapy was often instituted to alleviate any psychogenic component of the process. However, various recent studies have shown no evidence of psychogenic stress exaggerating symptoms in IBD.

Table 13.1   Comparison of Selected Characteristics of Ulcerative Colitis versus Crohn's Disease

Characteristic	Ulcerative Colitis	Crohn's Disease
Inflammation type	Acute/chronic mix; no granulomas	Chronic; granulomas present
Site of lesion	Confined to mucosa	Mucosa with wall penetration
Affected bowel	Colon only	Small intestine or colon; both in 50% of cases
Pattern of onset	Gradual or acute	Insidious, low level, slow to develop
Ulceration pattern	Irregular and superficial	Linear and penetrating
Stool	Watery; blood and mucus typical	Blood is uncommon
Complications are similar except:	More anemia and hemorrhage	More malabsorption and stricture
Lesion distribution	Diffuse; more uniform mucosal involvement	Unaffected segments between areas of involvement
Association with cancer	Approx. 8% when disease active more than 8 years	Approx. 1%

Ulceration

As indicated at the beginning of this chapter, the process of digestion, which produces the nutrient forms that we can absorb, occurs outside the body in the external space that is the GI lumen (fig. 13.1). One benefit that derives from this arrangement is the opportunity to use harsh acid and potent enzymes to degrade food molecules. Isolating these substances to the external lumen of the tract means that the body fluids and tissues are not subject to disruption by the extreme conditions tolerated by the GI mucosa's epithelial lining. For example, at its most acid, the H^+ concentration of gastric juice is about 3 million times that of plasma.

To tolerate such conditions, the stomach and small intestine have a complex array of protective mechanisms. One is the mucus blanket that coats its epithelial surfaces. Protein and bicarbonate components of this lining are able to reduce acidity so that the immediate epithelial cell environment is much less acid. Secondly, adjacent epithelial cells are joined by specialized membrane structures called **tight junctions.** These effectively block the diffusion of hydrogen ions back into the submucosa. This is particularly important, given the enormous concentration gradient favoring diffusion of H^+ from the lumen across the mucosa's epithelium. Another factor is the continual sloughing of epithelial cells into the lumen. Any damage the cells do sustain presents little problem, as the injured cells are soon lost and replaced with new, resistant cells.

Taken together, these defenses allow the GI's lining epithelium to stand up to the acid and enzyme challenge it normally confronts. If they are weakened or if the challenge is intensified, the surface epithelium may be overwhelmed. Undefended subepithelial tissues then become exposed to the acid and enzymes, which can digest them as they normally do food . The result is an ulcer (fig. 13.12). **15**

Figure 13.12   Peptic ulceration of the duodenum. Two ulcers are visible in this specimen. The smaller appears to have been healing, but the larger one had eroded an artery, causing massive blood loss.

This segment of duodenum shows the large peptic ulcer that was responsible for the death of an 11-year-old boy. The ulcer had eroded an artery in its base, causing massive bleeding and hypovolemic shock, which proved fatal. At autopsy, the stomach was found to contain 1.5 liters of blood. The child had an unfortunate history of a lymphoid tumor, which had been effectively treated, as well as liver cirrhosis, which developed from a case of hepatitis B that he had contracted while living in the Orient. These conditions were apparently unrelated to the development of the peptic ulcer.

Peptic Ulcers

Since the protein-digesting enzyme pepsin is involved in its production, the term **peptic ulcer** is applied to distinguish this common ulcer from the other, much less common GI ulcers. For example, the mucosal ulceration that occurs in ulcerative colitis and Crohn's disease derives from a disease process within the mucosa, as opposed to the peptic ulcer, in which erosion proceeds from the surface.

Peptic ulcers may arise throughout the esophagus, stomach, and small intestine, i.e., those sites subjected to the action of the acid and pepsin of the gastric juice. In the esophagus, they are uncommon, but may occur in patients with chronic reflux of gastric juice. They are also much less likely to occur in the jejunum or ileum, most (98%) arising in the stomach and duodenum. They typically arise singly; only 20% of cases involve multiple sites. The size of a peptic ulcer ranges between 1 and 3 cm. Its margin is usually smooth, **16** as opposed to the more irregular pattern seen in ulcers caused by surface disruption from tumors.

The relatively high incidence of peptic ulceration has prompted much examination of its etiology and pathogenesis. Although new insights continue, there still is no definitive description of the process that accounts for all the elements known to play some direct or indirect part in it. The most widely held view of ulcerogenesis proposed that the less common gastric ulcers were the result of some compromise in mucosal defense mechanisms. Duodenal ulceration was thought to arise because a normal mucosa was exposed to excess gastric juice as a result of gastric hypersecretion and/or too-rapid gastric emptying. In light of continuing analysis, it is more probable that hypersecretion alone is unlikely to produce peptic ulceration, and that impaired defenses permit erosion from exposure to excessive, normal, and even lower than normal amounts of gastric acid.

Gastric Hypersecretion In many patients who suffer from duodenal ulcers, hyperplasia of acid-producing **parietal cells** and pepsin-secreting **chief cells** is typical. In addition, the same patients often demonstrate an exaggerated secretion response to normal levels of stimulus. The excessive gastric wall motility also seen in many such cases increases duodenal exposure to gastric juice. Cigarette smoking is known to be strongly associated with peptic ulcers, and its role in promoting secretion has been suggested, but not proved. The idea that gastric hypersecretion due to psychologic stress causes peptic ulcers is solidly entrenched in the folk wisdom. However, evidence to substantiate it is lacking and its contribution is increasingly discounted.

Impaired Defenses The number of factors known to compromise mucosal defenses against acid and pepsin is growing. Increasingly accepted is the role of the bacterium *Helicobacter pylori*. This organism is thought to predispose the gastric mucosa to ulceration by inducing a gastritis which weakens its defenses. The relation between gastric and duodenal ulcers and gastritis induced by *Helicobacter*

Spicy Food and Gastric Irritation

Direct viewing of the interior of the digestive tract can be achieved with an **endoscope,** a tubular instrument that is passed through the mouth and esophagus to reach the stomach or duodenum. In experiments to assess the gastric and duodenal effects of various foods and aspirin, subjects were given bland and spicy meals, and a meal with aspirin. The effects on the mucosa were then viewed with an endoscope. The results showed that 11 of 12 subjects suffered no irritation when they ate either bland or spicy (jalapeño peppers, pepperoni) foods. Even when ground jalapeño peppers were inserted into the stomach and placed directly on its lining, no irritation resulted. However, in 11 of the 12 subjects, a bland meal (steak and potatoes) containing aspirin produced pronounced irritation and multiple erosions in the stomach's mucosa.

---

pylori is quite strong, but in many cases the organism is present in those without ulcers. This finding suggests that other factors may contribute to the breakdown of mucosal defenses and that *Helicobacter pylori* infection may enhance their effects.

A second important factor that predisposes to mucosal disruption is the effect of NSAIDs such as aspirin, indomethacin, and phenylbutazone. These widely used preparations are known to cause damage and bleeding in the gastric and duodenal mucosae. Superficial erosion of these surfaces exposes deeper layers to acid and pepsin to promote peptic ulceration. NSAIDs also have relevant systemic effects in inhibiting prostaglandin synthesis, because certain prostaglandins contribute to mucosal defenses by promoting secretion of mucus and acid-neutralizing bicarbonate and by maintaining local blood flow.

Since there is a familial tendency to peptic ulceration, genetics may play an important role. The parietal and chief cell hyperplasia that promotes secretion is probably genetically determined, and a genetically determined reduction of defenses may also be involved. Similarly, smoking may have an impact in compromising mucosal defenses, as it is known to reduce blood flow and prostaglandin synthesis. There is little experimental support for other factors commonly associated with mucosal damage and ulcer formation, such as alcohol, spicy foods, or stress.

In summary, the pathogenesis of peptic ulcers involves various factors that combine to compromise gastroduodenal defenses. The effects of acid and pepsin can then produce the ulcer, even at normal or low levels (fig. 13.13).

Incidence and Complications Adult males in the industrialized Western nations who have other family members with peptic ulcers represent the high-risk population. Middle age and beyond are the years of greatest risk, and the male-to-female preponderance is 2 or 3 to 1. There is

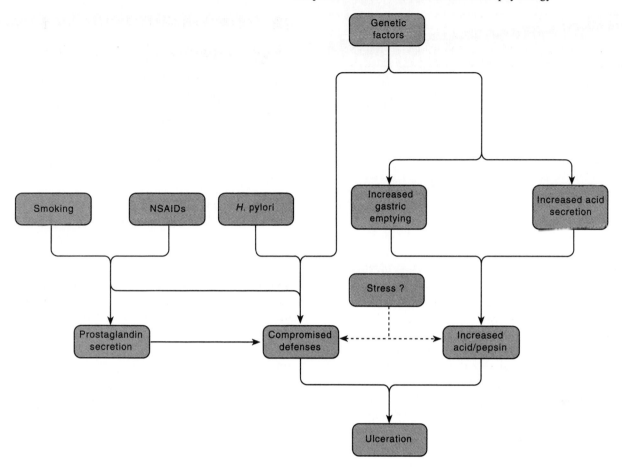

Figure 13.13   Pathogenesis of peptic ulcer formation. It should be emphasized that the various contributing factors are more likely to operate in combination than in isolation.

also some evidence suggesting more peptic ulcers in those with hepatic cirrhosis, obstructive lung disorders, and rheumatoid arthritis.

Ulcer sufferers complain of 15–60-minute periods of gnawing or burning pain over the **epigastrium,** the central and superior surface of the abdomen. Food intake has varying effects on ulcer pain, which are often dependent on the ulcer's location. Sufferers of duodenal ulceration often report pain onset 30–45 minutes after a meal, with later food intake offering relief. Presumably the initial ingestion of food triggers a secretion response that brings on the pain, then subsequent food intake absorbs the gastric juice to minimize irritation. Many who suffer from gastric ulcers report anorexia and vomiting and often experience weight loss as a result. Food often increases bouts of epigastric pain in these individuals. Aspirin has the effect of intensifying the epigastric ache.

In uncomplicated peptic ulcer disease, patients are otherwise normal. The condition is chronic, and episodes of recurrence are separated by varying time intervals. Most peptic ulcers are resolved by healing that involves epithelial, but not glandular, regeneration and scarring in the submucosa and deeper layers. Healing is typically slower in the stomach because of its high acid levels.

Complications are uncommon, but 20% of patients suffer hemorrhage from the ulcer. Normally only small blood loss occurs, but if the ulceration penetrates deeply enough to erode an artery in the wall, severe bleeding and cardiovascular shock may result. Seriously bleeding peptic ulcers have a mortality of about 10% and are not to be taken lightly.

Perforation of the stomach or duodenal wall **17** may also occur to present the threat of peritonitis. Involvement of the adjacent pancreas can also induce acute pancreatitis (chapter 14). Mortality is high if perforation occurs, particularly with involvement of the gastric wall.

Gastric obstruction may also complicate peptic ulcer disease. The obstruction typically involves the gastric outlet at the pylorus, where ulcers may induce muscle spasm or hypertrophy. Healing may also contribute to obstruction if stricture follows scarring.

Therapy in Peptic Ulcer Disease The most effective therapeutic approach to peptic ulcers involves the diet and control of acid secretion. The assumption is that if acidity is reduced and irritants are avoided, healing will follow. Previously, ulcer patients were advised to eat bland diets and consume milk or cream regularly. In fact, this regimen is unnecessary (indeed, milk products may stimulate acid

Table 13.2	Some Side Effects Associated with the Use of Selected H$_2$ Blocking Agents

Agent	Side Effects
Cimetidine	Mental confusion, diarrhea, hepatitis, pancreatitis, impotence
Famotidine	Headache, insomnia, diarrhea, constipation, anorexia, impotence
Ranitidine	Headache, dizziness, cardiac arrhythmias, diarrhea, constipation, hepatitis

secretion), and any diet that does not aggravate ulcer pain is acceptable. Usually, patients soon recognize the irritation and pain associated with caffeine, any acid stimulus, or casual NSAID use, and restrict their intake.

In reducing acid levels to limit ulceration and promote healing, two approaches are taken. In one, antacids are used to neutralize existing acid. Many low-cost and effective agents are available, hence this is the most widely used therapy. An increasingly popular second approach suppresses acid secretion by interfering with a normal histamine stimulus to the parietal cells. Antihistamine drugs that belong to a class called **H$_2$ blockers** are employed in this task. The more common antihistamines affect H$_1$ receptors that histamine activates to promote vascular and bronchial constriction, but histamine also can activate H$_2$ receptors to promote gastric acid secretion. H$_2$ blockers selectively inhibit this response to reduce gastric acidity, thus allowing more rapid ulcer healing (table 13.2).

In severe cases of chronic ulceration that resists therapy, surgery may be indicated. Surgery may involve sectioning the vagus nerve by which the CNS stimulus to acid secretion reaches the stomach. This procedure is now used less frequently, since H$_2$ blocker therapy can achieve smaller benefits with less risk and cost. In extreme cases, surgical removal of the affected portion of the stomach may be required.

Stress Ulcers

The term for these primarily gastric ulcers relates to their occurrence in response to a wide variety of acute systemic stresses. They are usually multiple and smaller than peptic ulcers. They arise following severe trauma, e.g., automobile accidents, falls or crushing injuries, CNS damage, or extensive skin burns. Serious illness, generally, can also induce stress ulcers, as can bacterial infections that spread through the blood. Cardiovascular shock, in relation to the above conditions or due to other causes, also promote the development of stress ulcers.

Meckel's Diverticulum

Meckel's diverticulum is a congenital malformation of the ileum consisting of an elongated (up to 6 cm) pouch. **18** It occurs in only about 1% of the population and is clinically insignificant except for the few cases in which it undergoes peptic ulceration and perforates.

The mechanisms involved are thought to be gastric juice hypersecretion, especially in CNS injury that is associated with a pronounced secretion stimulus to the stomach. Other mechanisms are based on mucosal ischemia that develops secondary to a widespread vasoconstriction response or to hypotension related to cardiovascular shock. The reduced mucosal blood flow weakens defenses or damages the mucosa, and gastric acid is able to produce widespread surface erosions.

Typically, stress ulcers are asymptomatic and present minimal difficulties, especially in the context of the generally severe systemic conditions with which they are associated. Mild bleeding may occur, but only rarely is hemorrhage a problem. Perforation of the wall is also rare, but when it does occur, the duodenum is the usual site.

Gastrointestinal Bleeding

Blood loss into the GI lumen may be indicated by the presence of blood in vomitus or feces. The vomiting of blood (**hematemesis**) is typically associated with gastric or esophageal bleeding. **19** Gastric ulceration, peptic or otherwise, may be the source of the blood. It might also originate at a laceration of the gastroesophageal junction, as in the Mallory-Weiss syndrome described earlier, in the section on vomiting.

When blood spends some time in the stomach before being vomited, gastric acid and enzymes alter it, producing a dark, granular material resembling coffee grounds. Blood lost directly into the small intestine, or reaching it from a gastric lesion, is similarly darkened. It affects the stool, producing a darker, tarlike coloration. This condition is called **melena**. Bleeding peptic ulcers are the most common cause of such blood loss into the stomach and small intestine.

Bleeding from the colon's wall usually appears bright red in the stool, since the blood is not exposed to acid or enzymes to any significant degree. Diverticulitis is the common cause of colonic hemorrhage. Of course, at all levels of the GI tract, surface erosion by a benign or malignant tumor can produce bleeding. Table 13.3 indicates the relative frequency of the principal sources of upper and lower GI blood loss.

Table 13.3	Major Causes of Upper and Lower Gastrointestinal Bleeding	

	Cause	Incidence
Upper GI bleeding	Erosive gastritis/duodenitis	$9x$
	Duodenal peptic ulcer	$7x$
	Esophageal varices	$5x$
	Peptic/gastric ulcer	$4x$
	Mallory-Weiss laceration	$2x$
	Carcinoma	x
Lower GI bleeding	Colon cancer	$8x$
	Benign polyps	$4x$
	Diverticulitis	$2x$
	Inflammatory bowel disease	x

Relative incidence is expressed in terms of a base unit, x, which has an approximate value of 3%.

The level of the duodenum is the commonly used line of demarcation between the upper and lower regions of the GI tract.

In cases of GI bleeding, the source is often difficult to determine. Assessment of the patient's stool or vomitus may provide information based on coloration and the obvious presence of blood, but these can be confusing. For example, when blood is lost rapidly from an upper GI site it may be darkened only slightly, so that when seen in the stool it suggests colonic bleeding.

Long-term bleeding of smaller quantities of blood may not be detected in the stool on casual inspection by the affected person. The presence of a low-grade anemia may be evidence of the slow bleeding, and confirmation can be had by laboratory analysis of a stool sample to detect **occult** (hidden) **blood.** At the other extreme, acute hemorrhage may be so severe that it is immediately life-threatening, [20] requiring emergency treatment to avoid cardiovascular shock.

Therapy for episodes of acute GI bleeding is not usually necessary, since it tends to be self-limiting. If the bleeding is acute and severe, fluid replacement therapy to restore and stabilize blood volume and to counter hypovolemic shock may be necessary. Beyond such an immediate threat, therapy specific to the underlying disorder must be instituted.

Obstruction

Restriction or blockage of the movement of chyme along the GI tract is referred to as **ileus.** If a physical blockage is responsible, the condition is usually described as a mechanical obstruction, or mechanical ileus. If peristalsis stops, it is described as adynamic ileus.

Mechanical Obstruction

Mechanical blockage of the GI tract may result from an internally obstructing mass, e.g., a swallowed foreign object or colon tumor, from compression or distortion of the bowel, usually the small intestine, or from a congenital malformation. [21] Although uncommon, a congenitally narrowed or closed esophagus can present an obstruction to the swallowing of food, and **congenital pyloric stenosis** (narrowing of the opening to the duodenum) may limit gastric emptying. Surgery in early childhood is usually necessary to cope with such inborn obstructive malformations.

A malignant tumor [22] or benign polyp [23] may physically block the GI lumen. Most such growths occur in the colon as adenomas or carcinomas of the sigmoid colon and rectum. Tumors that metastasize to the colon may also mechanically obstruct its lumen. Swallowed foreign objects that can act as obstructions are highly varied. Virtually any object that fits into the mouth and resists breakdown by gastric acid has the potential for obstructing the tract. Children are particularly at risk. Tangles of roundworms or other parasites, though not swallowed, can also be considered as obstructing foreign objects. The obstruction of the esophagus by dilated veins is described in relation to cirrhosis of the liver in chapter 14.

Various abnormalities can produce obstructive distortion or compression of the GI tract, with the small intestine often involved. The most common is herniation of a loop of small intestine through the abdominal wall. This condition is usually seen at points where the scrotum is continuous with the abdominal cavity (the inguinal canal), at the

Figure 13.14 Herniation of a loop of small intestine through a weak spot in the abdominal wall. In such cases, if strangulation occurs, the complications of ischemic injury may be added to those of obstruction.

umbilicus, or at weakened surgical scars. In uncomplicated herniation, the loop of bowel may be easily drawn back into the abdominal cavity, but compression of the loop of intestine at the point of herniation can obstruct the passage of chyme (fig. 13.14). (Note that hiatal hernia, described earlier, does not usually produce obstruction effects.) However, if the compression is severe enough to collapse the vessels that supply and drain the herniated loop, **strangulation** of the bowel results. In such cases, the resulting ischemic injury can produce necrosis and gangrene, **24** adding the risk of perforation and peritonitis to the problems associated with bowel obstruction.

Healing complications following bouts of peritonitis or abdominal surgery can also produce bowel obstruction. Most often involved are adhesions that form at the healing serous membrane surfaces of abdominal organs **25** and the abdominal wall. If a loop of bowel is joined to the wall by an adhesion, it may kink to form a narrowed point (fig. 13.15*a*). Adhesions can also contribute to obstruction by abnormally isolating regions in which an adjacent bowel loop may then become trapped (fig. 13.15*b*). Another complication of healing ulcers, or of intestinal surgery, is contracture of fibrous tissue at the site of healing, which can produce a stricture that obstructs the bowel (fig. 13.16).

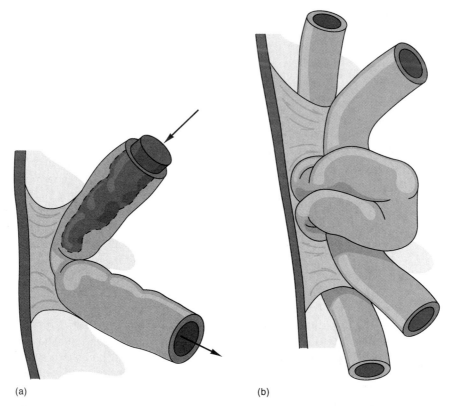

(a)   (b)

Figure 13.15 Intestinal obstruction as a complication of adhesion formation. (*a*) An adhesion causes a kink that narrows the lumen. (*b*) Adhesions between a bowel loop and the abdominal wall form an opening in which another loop can become trapped and compressed.

Figure 13.16   Stricture of the intestine caused by contracture of scar tissue at the site of a healing peptic ulcer. Inflammation, trauma, or tumors may all produce stricture.

Figure 13.17   Volvulus. A loop of intestine and its mesentery have undergone a twisting, which has caused an obstruction. The segment isolated by the twist is distended and darkened in comparison to the lighter sections adjacent to the twist.
An elderly male came to a hospital emergency room complaining that he had awakened at night with intense abdominal cramping pain. There were no signs of an acute abdomen, but he vomited once following his admission. Blood studies revealed no indication of infection; however, an enema showed the presence of blood in the stool. His symptoms intensified and an exploratory abdominal operation (laparotomy) was performed. It revealed the 12-in. loop of bowel shown here. The segment had become twisted, and was swollen, thick-walled, and hemorrhagic, with the outer surface covered in a fibrinous exudate. Bowel segments adjacent to the volvulus had a normal appearance. With resection of the damaged section, recovery was uneventful.

In North America, most GI tract obstructions are caused by herniation, adhesions, or primary tumors. Much less frequently a **volvulus** is involved. **26** In this condition, a loop of intestine rotates around its supporting mesentery, forming a point where it twists around itself (fig. 13.17). The point of twisting presents an obstruction, but more importantly, it compresses the arteries and veins in the mesentery. Strangulation and the risk of necrosis and perforation are typical consequences.

An even less common bowel obstruction problem is **intussusception. 27** The problem here is the telescoping of a segment of small intestine into the immediately distal portion of the bowel. This condition may arise as a mucosal polyp in the proximal segment is drawn, by peristalsis, into the distal portion, or the proximal portion may constrict to form a small, dense region on which peristaltic waves can act. Whatever the mechanism, the result is a compressed bowel segment that obstructs normal transit along its lumen (fig. 13.18).

Adynamic Ileus

This is a GI tract functional disorder that involves a loss of motility in the intestines. Two types are usually identified: **paralytic ileus** and **vascular ileus.**

Paralytic ileus involves a neurogenic reflex that halts normal intestinal motility. It is triggered by various abdominal stimuli such as pain, peritonitis, appendicitis, trauma, or acute distention of an abdominal organ. Paralytic ileus also frequently accompanies certain systemic conditions such as infections or renal disease, and those involving electrolyte imbalances, especially potassium deficiencies.

In vascular ileus, the failure to sustain normal motility is due to a compromised blood supply. **28** Thrombosis, atherosclerosis, or compression of the mesenteric vessels that

Figure 13.18 Intussusception. A section through the point where a segment of small intestine has been drawn, by peristalsis, into the immediately adjacent proximal segment. Note the proximal distention caused by chyme unable to pass the obstructions.

An abrupt episode of abdominal distention, severe cramping pain, and vomiting was diagnosed as intestinal obstruction and an emergency laparotomy was performed. The section of small intestine shown here was found. The intussusception had compressed the veins of the bowel, causing congestion, hemorrhage, and the risk of gangrene. The situation could not be corrected by pulling the affected region to straighten it, and it had to be removed.

supply the intestines is usually the underlying cause. Beyond the immediate problem of focal loss of motility, this condition carries the risk of infection, necrosis, and gangrene.

Sequelae of Obstruction

GI obstruction is associated with four clinical features that may vary with the degree of obstruction and its location: vomiting, abdominal distention, pain, and **obstipation** (lack of fecal or gas evacuation, due to obstruction).

Vomiting is the response to obstruction in the upper GI tract, especially from stricture at sites of gastric or duodenal peptic ulcer healing. The vomiting reflex is triggered by distention as food accumulates proximal to the point of obstruction. Vomiting in such cases is often persistent, with large volumes of undigested food expelled from the tract. When the blockage is in the proximal small intestine, its contents may reflux back to the stomach, with bile appearing in the vomitus. The consequences of persistent vomiting are as would be expected: fluid loss leading to dehydration, electrolyte imbalance, as needed ions are lost in the vomitus, and the loss of nutrients.

When obstruction occurs in the lower GI tract, vomiting is less able to clear backed-up lumen contents. The consequence is intestinal distention, as parts of the GI tract proximal to the obstruction dilate to accommodate the increased volume. **29** Obvious abdominal bloating results, as does cramping pain from the pronounced peristaltic waves that drive the lumen's contents to the point of blockage. The pain can be quite intense, with crescendos associated with peaking peristaltic intensity.

Paralytic Ileus and Bowel Sounds

The intestinal response to the trauma of abdominal surgery, or to associated general anesthesia, is paralytic ileus. It usually lasts for two to three days, and then normal bowel motility patterns are spontaneously restored. The restoration of bowel activity is accompanied by characteristic bubbling and gurgling sounds that can be easily detected with a stethoscope. A delay in the return of normal bowel sounds may indicate a complication. In cases of mechanical bowel obstruction, bowel sounds are typically intensified as chyme is forced past the narrowed point by strong peristaltic waves.

GI tract distention is also associated with mucosal ion and fluid secretion into the lumen. The increase in luminal distention can promote compression of mesenteric vessels, increasing the risk of ischemic necrosis. The holding of fluid in the GI lumen can also pose the threat of hypovolemic shock. As well, more intense vomiting bouts may result as distention increases, even when the obstruction is situated in the distal small bowel or colon. In these cases, backup of lumen contents prevents small intestine and gastric emptying, and the severity of the resultant vomiting may yield fecal material in the vomitus.

In cases of colon obstruction, stasis favors bacterial proliferation and thereby increases the possibility of bowel necrosis, perforation peritonitis, and more widespread infection. The sequelae of GI obstruction are presented in figure 13.19.

Malabsorption

The problem of inadequate absorption of nutrients, **malabsorption,** may be generalized, affecting most nutrients, or it may be specific to a particular nutrient, e.g., vitamin B_{12}. Malabsorption conditions may be mild and of short duration, or more severe and chronic. They are the result of three essential defects: of digestion, of absorption, and of transit from the intestinal mucosa.

Defective Digestion

Since absorption requires that the digestion process convert nutrients to forms that are absorbable, it is clear that interference with digestion will lead to malabsorption. Most commonly, defective digestion is due to lack of pancreatic enzymes or bile, in severe pancreas or liver failure, respectively. Obstruction of the bile or pancreatic ducts produces similar effects. Bile insufficiency may also arise following surgical resection of the ileum, the site of bile salt absorption and recycling via the liver, or in conditions involving bacterial overgrowth in the small intestine. Factors that

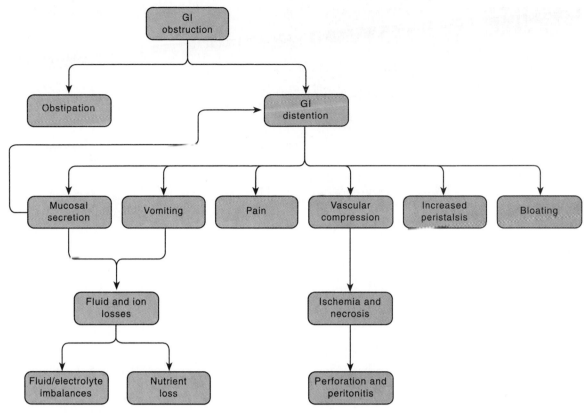

Figure 13.19   The potential derangements that can arise as a consequence of GI obstruction.

impede normal intestinal motion, such as an obstruction or paralytic ileus, can have this effect. Bacterial metabolism alters bile salts and makes them much less likely to be recycled, thus producing a bile deficiency. They can also enhance osmotic water movement to the intestinal lumen to produce diarrhea.

Defective digestion might also be due to a resection of part of the stomach and/or small intestine and the surgical rejoining of the remaining structures. The resulting problems are caused by inadequate digestive processing by the resected regions and by the loss of their normal contribution to the feedback control mechanisms that regulate digestion.

Defective Absorption

The small intestine's major adaptations to absorption are its very large surface area and its epithelial transport and enzyme systems. Interference with these compromises the absorptive capabilities of the small bowel, and malabsorption results.

Loss of surface area may be due to resection of an intestinal tumor or to extensive intestinal trauma. Specific disease states may also reduce surface area by damaging or infiltrating the mucosa. Relatively mild and transient malabsorption may accompany enteritis **30** from whatever cause. The following are conditions in which the results of malabsorption are clinically prominent.

Celiac sprue or **nontropical sprue** involves a genetic sensitivity to gluten, a protein component of wheat, barley and rye. The result is a flattening of the intestinal villi that greatly reduces absorptive area. This is a rare condition, but **tropical sprue,** thought to be caused by an infection, is more common, especially in the tropics, and produces similar effects. Mucosal surface loss due to inflammatory cell infiltration is responsible for the malabsorption associated with Crohn's disease, described earlier, and **Whipple's disease,** a systemic infectious condition characterized by mucosal infiltration by bacteria-filled macrophages. A rare tumor of the intestine, **primary intestinal lymphoma,** is characterized by extensive tumor spread through the mucosa that causes a flattening of the villi. In this respect, the condition resembles celiac sprue. Malabsorption may also be caused by absent or defective membrane enzyme systems, which compromise digestion (usually genetic defects involving the intestinal disaccharidases lactase, sucrase, or maltase.) These are relatively rare conditions, as are the genetic defects that produce malabsorption as a result of loss of membrane transport systems specific to carbohydrate or amino acid absorption.

Transit Defects

Even if digestion and absorption occur, transport of absorbed nutrients via lymph and blood to systemic utilization sites is still required. Any conditions that compromise this transit will cause a deficiency, as if absorption had not

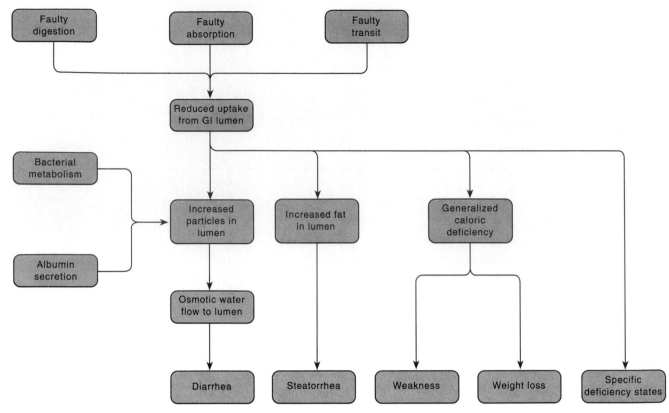

Figure 13.20   Pathogenesis of GI malabsorption.

occurred. For this reason, such conditions are regarded as malabsorption syndromes. Two examples of diseases that compromise lymph flow, and therefore transit of lipids, are Whipple's disease and **lymphangiectasia.** In Whipple's disease, the pronounced infiltration of the mucosa compresses its lacteals and other small lymphatics to obstruct lymph flow. In lymphangiectasia, lymph obstruction is due to lymph channels that are narrowed or closed. This rare condition is idiopathic.

Another genetic defect reduces lipid transit from the intestinal epithelium because of the lack of beta lipoproteins. Without these, chylomicrons cannot be formed and absorbed fat is confined to the epithelial cells, which become engorged. This rare condition is called **abetalipoproteinemia.**

Sequelae of Malabsorption

The signs and symptoms associated with malabsorption states reflect the deficiencies that such states produce and the intestinal disturbances that are often present. In generalized malabsorption states, an overall caloric deficiency will typically produce weakness, weight loss, fatigue, and variable anorexia. Particular deficiencies may give rise to specific systemic problems, such as coagulation disorders resulting from a lack of vitamin K, anemia resulting from a vitamin B_{12} deficiency, or abnormal muscle function resulting from a lack of calcium.

Steatorrhea, excessive fat in the stool, is often seen in malabsorption states. The excess of fat is due, in part, to its lack of uptake from the intestinal lumen, but to another reason if digestion is defective. In such cases, lack of adequate caloric intake triggers an increased appetite, which brings more fat-containing food into the lumen, and it passes to the colon undigested and unabsorbed. If malabsorption is due to an intestinal defect, anorexia is more often present, and steatorrhea may be characterized by large volumes of foul-smelling feces. More often, stool changes are less pronounced and may only involve the stool's floating as a result of its increased content of low-density fat. A patient's first indication of a problem may be difficulty in flushing bulky, floating stools from the toilet.

Diarrhea is often present in malabsorption states. It may be the direct result of inadequate water absorption or the indirect result of the underlying malabsorption. When lumen solute concentration is high, osmotic water movement into the lumen follows. Such concentration increases may be due to the accumulation of nutrient molecules that can't be absorbed, or to products of bacterial action, if stasis fosters their proliferation. During digestion, much albumin, a small and plentiful plasma protein, is secreted into the intestinal lumen, but if it can't be digested and reabsorbed, it contributes to the lumen's osmotic pressure and aggravates the predisposition to diarrhea. These factors are summarized in figure 13.20.

Gastrointestinal Tumors

The most common tumors of the GI tract are carcinomas, arising, in order of frequency, in the colon, stomach, esophagus, and small intestine. Their typical effects are pain, obstruction, and bleeding, where tumor growth breaks through the mucosal surface. Metastasis by blood and lymph is common, but may be delayed, so that early detection is important.

Benign adenomas are also common in the GI tract, principally in the stomach and colon. Such growths may be broad-based or may project into the lumen, supported by a stalk **31**—a **pedunculated polyp** (fig. 13.21). Although benign, pedunculated tumors have a predisposition to bleeding. In the colon, an adenoma may have fingerlike extensions that resemble intestinal villi. This is a **villous adenoma. 32**

In some adenomatous polyps of the colon, malignant cells may arise. Their more rapid growth dominates to produce an invasive adenocarcinoma. It is thought that most colon cancers arise in this way. Currently, improved technique and instrumentation provides for easy and safe polyp removal in a **colonoscopy.** No surgical access through the abdominal wall is required for this procedure, which is routinely used to remove colon polyps. The term **hyperplastic polyp** refers to the benign colon polyp that does not become malignant.

A rare genetic defect of the colon involves multiple adenomatous polyps associated with a high risk of colon carcinoma. This condition is known as **familial polyposis**

Figure 13.21   A pedunculated adenoma of the colon. *This polyp was found at the autopsy of an elderly man who had died of the cumulative effects of a colon carcinoma that had metastasized extensively, especially affecting the lungs and liver. The pedunculated adenoma shown here was found in the colon. Although, the adenoma was benign, it may well be that the fatal carcinoma developed from such a small, innocent-appearing mass.*

coli (FPC). **33** The problem of multiple polyp growth in the colon may not emerge until as late as age 30, with an average of 1000 polyps present in those affected. The risk of cancer is sufficiently strong that resection of the colon may be necessary in FPC. Drug therapy to reduce polyp formation is being investigated.

Case Study

A hospital emergency room received a 23-year-old male with complaints of severe diarrhea, abdominal cramping, nausea, and "just not feeling too good." He reported that similar symptoms had been present for the past 10 days, but the intensity of the current bout of symptoms had frightened him and he felt the ER was a better choice than his regular doctor.

His history revealed no significant previous illness except for a similar, milder GI attack six months prior, as well as periodic episodes of mild diarrhea, which he diagnosed as "allergies to all the stuff they put in food these days," but for which he'd sought no medical help. His temperature was mildly elevated (37.9), he had a slight tachycardia, and his blood pressure was normal. His right lower quadrant was tender on palpation, and rebound tenderness was present. Bowel sounds were normal. Blood tests indicated a reduced hemoglobin of 11 g/dl and an increased WBC count.

The young man was admitted with a possible diagnosis of acute appendicitis. A general surgeon agreed with the diagnosis and the patient was scheduled for surgery.

During the operation the appendix appeared only mildly hyperemic and no other abnormalities were noted, except for some mild swelling in a few mesenteric lymph nodes. A routine appendectomy was performed, and the patient's recovery was uneventful. Subsequent microscopic study revealed the appendix to have been normal. The patient was discharged after three days.

After six weeks he reported to his GP that his symptoms had returned after going back to his normal solid food diet. He also complained of feeling fatigued and reported weight loss since the operation. He was examined and found to be tender in the lower right quadrant as before. A rectal examination revealed additional sensitivity, and blood was noted in the stool.

Blood tests showed WBC counts increased and Hb decreased (9 g/dl) with respect to their previous levels. Urinalysis and blood tests were normal, and blood and urine cultures for bacteria and parasites were negative. A lower GI radiographic study revealed a normal ileal lumen except for a 6-cm segment that demonstrated pronounced stenosis.

On the basis of these observations, a tentative diagnosis of Crohn's disease was made, and the patient was referred to a gastroenterologist. Following an endoscopic study of the ileum, she confirmed the diagnosis and prescribed prednisone in a tapering dose for six weeks. This regimen proved successful in alleviating the acute symptoms.

Over the next two years the patient experienced several repetitions of the same signs and symptoms, with periodic hospitalizations during which total parenteral nutrition (TPN) was employed to rest the bowel. Increasingly frustrated with this situation, the patient opted for surgical resection of the affected ileal segment. He was advised of the likelihood of recurrence, but accepted the risk and proceeded with the surgery.

At operation the affected bowel segment was resected and the adjacent edges of the normal ileum were joined (an end-to-end anastomosis). Postoperative recovery was uneventful, and the patient was discharged. Follow-ups at three, six, nine, and twelve months found him well and without symptoms.

Commentary

This is an example of the difficulties present in the assessment of abdominal signs and symptoms. Had the patient noticed his rectal bleeding, the appendectomy might have been avoided, but the small quantity of blood involved was easily missed. The dangers associated with perforation in acute appendicitis justify appendectomy on what may seem inadequate evidence, but the general opinion among surgeons is that if a high percentage of removed appendices aren't later found to be normal, surgery is being delayed too long.

Initial diagnostic testing in acute abdominal attacks seeks to establish the absence of infection before other diagnoses are considered, hence the blood and urine studies and stool cultures. The episodes of exacerbation and remission illustrated in this case are unfortunately typical of Crohn's disease. The sufferer must avoid any irritation to the intestine that might trigger further episodes, but often there is no apparent reason for a renewed attack.

Key Concepts

1. Vomiting and diarrhea expel excessive or irritating GI contents and are usually minimally disruptive, unless prolonged or severe, in which case serious systemic consequences may result (p. 319).

2. Various factors other than GI wall irritation can induce vomiting by means of the effects that circulating substances have on the chemoreceptor trigger zone (p. 320).

3. Acute inflammation of the GI mucosa is common, usually only moderately disruptive, and readily healed, although serious postinflammation complications may arise in some cases (p. 323).

4. The pathogenesis of acute appendicitis often involves a fecalith, which promotes bacterial growth and the threat of gangrene and wall rupture (pp. 324–325).

5. Rupture of an abdominal organ is a common cause of peritonitis, which can in turn give rise to abscess formation, perforation, fistulae, or generalized peritonitis, with its threat of widespread and serious damage (pp. 325–326).

6. Diverticulosis is relatively common and may be asymptomatic, but some cases involve pain, bleeding, or constipation, and if the walls of the diverticula are irritated, inflammation and rupture may give rise to peritonitis (pp. 327–328).

7. Although of essentially different pathogenesis, Crohn's disease and ulcerative colitis are both characterized by abdominal cramping, diarrhea, and fever, causing them to be included together under the clinical designation inflammatory bowel disease (IBD) (p. 328).

8. The GI wall's defenses against its lumen's acid and enzymes may be weakened to allow formation of a peptic ulcer, usually in the stomach or duodenum (pp. 329–330).

9. The bacterium *Helicobacter pylori* is increasingly accepted as directly or indirectly contributing to the weakening of GI mucosal defenses and peptic ulcer formation (p. 330).

10. Bleeding into the GI lumen is often revealed in vomitus or feces, but the precise site of the wall damage may be difficult to determine without special diagnostic procedures, such as endoscopy (p. 332).

11. Interference with peristalsis may be the result of mechanical blockage of the GI tract by an internally obstructing mass, external compression, or a congenital malformation (pp. 333–334).

12. Consequences similar to those produced by mechanical obstruction may be the result of a cessation of tract motility that is due to neurogenic disturbances or compromised blood supply (p. 335).

13. GI obstruction is associated with four clinical features determined by the location and degree of obstruction: vomiting, abdominal distention, pain, and obstipation (pp. 335–336).

14. Malabsorption arises principally from defects of digestion, absorption, or nutrient transit from the intestinal mucosa, and may be generalized or specific to a particular nutrient (pp. 336–338).

15. GI tumors may produce pain, obstruction, or bleeding, and, if malignant, may metastasize by both blood and lymph (pp. 338–339).

REVIEW ACTIVITIES

1. Explain why, in eliciting the vomiting reflex, the CTZ's blood supply is more important than its nervous input, and why the opposite case is true for the medulla's vomiting center.

2. Construct a flow chart that ends with the words "Bowel Evacuation." Have it begin with four types of laxative, and include the essential features of the action of each.

3. Refer to pages 323–327 to compile a list of irritants known to cause GI inflammation.

4. Having been told that IBD is involved, and given a single clinical feature to go on, as listed below, determine in each case whether the disease is more likely to be ulcerative colitis or Crohn's disease.

CLINICAL FEATURE	UC/CROHN'S?
Superficial mucosal ulceration	_____
Only colon involved	_____
Acute onset	_____
Affected and normal regions in same bowel segment	_____
No blood in stool	_____
Granulomas present	_____

5. Test your knowledge of GI ulceration by listing the key points of its pathogenesis. (Don't forget to mention *H. pylori*.) Check figure 13.13 to be sure you've left nothing important off your list.

6. Your aunt Harriet phones to say that she lost the dietary suggestions her doctor gave her after her peptic ulcer was diagnosed. She wants to know if a soothing glass of milk before bed would be a good idea. She also wonders about the H_2 blocker that was prescribed for her. Decide what you should tell her on each count.

7. Make up a ready reference chart showing specific causes of malabsorption and its specific sequelae.

Chapter Fourteen

Hepatobiliary and Pancreatic Pathophysiology

All seems infected that the infected spy,
As all looks yellow to the jaundiced eye.

Alexander Pope
An Essay on Criticism

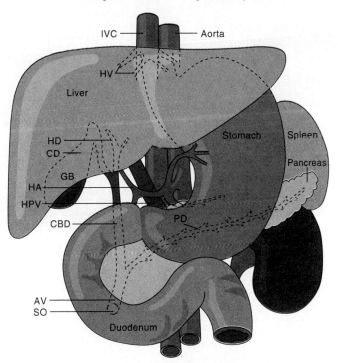

Figure 14.1   The hepatobiliary system. The liver receives blood via the hepatic artery (HA) and the hepatic portal vein (HPV), which drains the GI tract. Blood leaves the liver via the hepatic veins (HV) to reach the inferior vena cava (IVC). The hepatic duct (HD) and cystic duct (CD) form the common bile duct (CBD), which carries bile from the liver and gall.

The liver and pancreas are the principal accessory organs of the digestive system. For this reason, and because pancreatic disorders can cause hepatic disturbances, and vice versa, the two organs are considered together in this chapter, beginning with the liver. **1** **2**

The hepatocyte's remarkable metabolic capabilities make a vital contribution to several of the body's critical functions. Damage to the liver or its associated bile system causes a wide variety of physiological disturbances. These may be short-lived and relatively benign, or so serious as to be life-threatening. In either case, such large numbers of people suffer from the effects of some form of liver failure that it constitutes a major medical threat. Before discussing the pathogenesis of the different forms of liver failure let us describe normal liver structure and function.

STRUCTURE OF THE LIVER AND BILE SYSTEM

The liver is situated in the superior extreme of the right abdominal quadrant. It is the largest of the body's internal organs, contributing about 2% of body weight. It consists of two principal lobes: a large right lobe and a much smaller left lobe, which extends somewhat beyond the midline. Liver cells utilize their elaborate metabolic capabilities to chemically alter various of the substances they take up from the blood. Large metabolic capacity is therefore consistent with the enormous volume of blood that flows through the liver: 1.5 liters per minute, the equivalent of about 2000 liters per day. This blood volume arrives via the liver's dual blood supply, which involves both the arterial and the venous systems. The hepatic artery (fig. 14.1) provides about one-third of the total hepatic flow. (The hepatic artery is a branch of the celiac artery, which in turn arises from the aorta.) The remaining two-thirds of its blood flow comes to the liver by way of the hepatic portal vein, a large vein that receives blood from the veins that drain the spleen, pancreas, stomach, and intestines. This arrangement provides for the direct delivery to the liver of newly absorbed nutrients instead of their being dispersed in the general circulation. The liver cells thus have quick access to substances absorbed from the intestine, in order to provide for their prompt and efficient metabolism. The portal blood also provides over 50% of the liver's oxygen supply. After passing through the liver, blood is returned to the inferior vena cava (IVC) by the hepatic veins. These usually consist of two or three larger and several smaller vessels.

Within the liver, blood passes from the portal vein to a complex of fine blood channels called **sinusoids.** These are thin-walled vessels like capillaries, but they are somewhat larger and more permeable. The hepatic artery's branches also supply arterial blood to the sinusoids, where it mixes with portal venous blood. The sinusoids converge to form

Central vein

Hepatocytes

Bile canaliculi

Hepatic portal vein

Sinusoid

Bile duct

Hepatic artery

Figure 14.2   Liver histology. Plates of hepatocytes lie parallel to the hepatic sinusoids. These fine vessels carry a mixture of blood from the hepatic portal vein and the hepatic artery. The circle indicates the point where the two blood sources join to supply the sinusoid.

the central veins, which deliver blood to the hepatic veins and then to the systemic venous return (fig. 14.2). Adjacent to the sinusoids are rows of hepatocytes, each having one surface directly abutting the thin space that surrounds the sinusoid walls **3** (fig. 14.3). Their ready access to the sinusoids allows the hepatocytes to absorb from, or secrete into, the sinusoidal blood directly. In this way, substances arriving via the portal vein can pass from the sinusoids to the liver cells, where their metabolism proceeds. Products of metabolism can then be secreted into the sinusoids for distribution with the blood that reaches the IVC via the central and hepatic veins.

The liver's major secretion, bile, is drained from it in a separate system of ducts so that it does not enter the blood. Instead, hepatocytes secrete bile into **bile canaliculi.** These fine ducts originate between adjacent liver cells and converge to form larger ducts, which ultimately deliver bile to the small intestine.

The converging system of bile ducts drains the right and left lobes of the liver into the **hepatic duct.** A short distance below the liver the hepatic duct is intersected by the **cystic duct,** which communicates with the **gall bladder. 4** (The term gall refers to bile and is no longer in common usage.) The cystic duct and hepatic duct in this way join to form the **common bile duct** (CBD), which proceeds to the duodenum and then passes through the duodenal wall to open into the intestinal lumen. The **pancreatic duct,** draining the digestive secretions of the pancreas, also joins the duodenum in this region, the **hepatopancreatic ampulla (ampulla of Vater)** designated AV in figure 14.1. The passage of bile into the duodenum is controlled by the **sphincter of Oddi,** located at the distal end of the ampulla of Vater (as in fig. 14.1).

When the sphincter is closed, bile secreted by the liver backs up into the duct system and then into the gall bladder. The gall bladder can store about 50 ml of bile until such time as it is required in the small intestine. When fat arrives at the duodenum from the stomach, it indirectly stimulates the gall bladder to contract and the sphincter of Oddi to relax. Normal duodenal peristalsis will also draw small

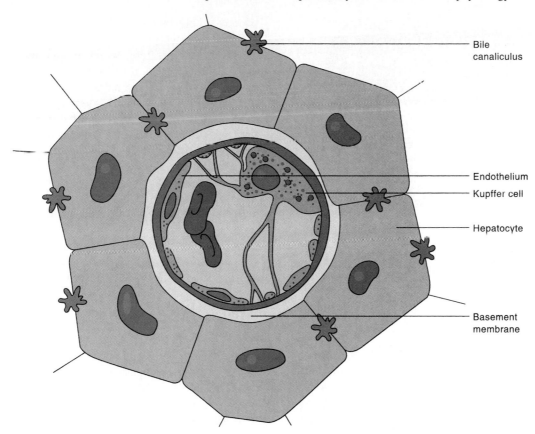

Figure 14.3   Cross-sectional view of a hepatic sinusoid, showing a Kupffer cell whose cytoplasmic extensions span the lumen of the sinusoid. This increases exposure to the blood to enhance the cell's phagocytic activity. The endothelium of the sinusoid is fenestrated (perforated) to permit rapid exchange between hepatocytes and the blood. The bile canaliculi between adjacent hepatocytes receive bile and carry it to the hepatic duct.

amounts of bile into the duodenum. The gall bladder empties in this way in about 1 hour. The gall bladder is also able to concentrate bile by removing nonessential electrolytes and water. This process allows for the storage of increased quantities of the active ingredients of bile, the bile salts.

FUNCTIONS OF THE LIVER AND BILE SYSTEM

Bile Secretion

The secretion of bile is a major hepatic function. From 800 to 1000 ml of bile are secreted daily to supply the bile salts needed for fat digestion and absorption. The liver synthesizes two major bile acids, **cholic** and **chenodeoxycholic acids,** and secretes their sodium and potassium salts into the bile ducts. In the intestine, the bile salts perform two essential functions in the digestion of fat. First, they emulsify it. This means they work to prevent the small fat globules, formed by mechanical digestion, from coalescing to form larger globules. Small fat globules would tend to merge to form larger globules in the watery chyme in the same way

that the oil and vinegar in a salad dressing separate after standing. Emulsification keeps the globules small, thus maintaining the large surface area that favors the efficient action of digestive lipases.

The second function of bile has to do with the absorption of the products of fat digestion: fatty acids, monoglycerides, and fat-soluble vitamins. Bile salts combine with them in a way that makes them water-soluble. They remain in this soluble form until they contact the small intestine's epithelium. There the bile salts release their lipids to dissolve in the membrane, which allows their absorption. The bile salts are now free and available to form complexes with other lipids to repeat the process. This sequence continues until the bile salts are themselves reabsorbed at the distal ileum. In this way, most (about 90%) of the bile salts are available for resecretion into the bile. The circulation of the bile salts from the intestine to the liver and back to the intestine is called the **enterohepatic** circulation. Bile salts may be cycled through it from five to ten times per day. This efficient use of the bile salts means that the liver must newly synthesize only the amount needed to replace the small quantity lost in the feces (fig. 14.4)

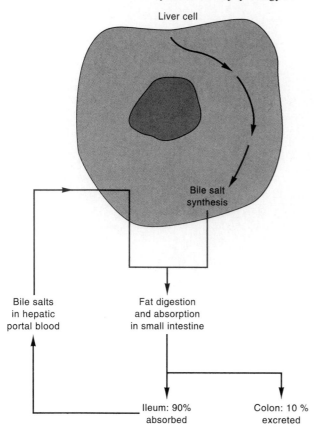

Liver cell

Bile salt
synthesis

Bile salts
in hepatic
portal blood

Fat digestion
and absorption
in small intestine

Ileum: 90%
absorbed

Colon: 10 %
excreted

Figure 14.4 The enterohepatic circulation of bile salts between the small intestine and the liver: an efficient recycling mechanism.

Bile is also important as the vehicle of **bilirubin** excretion. Bilirubin is a product of hemoglobin degradation and is toxic if allowed to accumulate. It is formed primarily in the spleen, where most aging erythrocytes are removed from the circulation. There hemoglobin is degraded to form **biliverdin** and the protein globin. The globin is then metabolized to release its amino acids and the biliverdin is converted into the yellow-brown pigment bilirubin. Lesser amounts of bilirubin are also formed in the marrow and liver. From the spleen and marrow, bilirubin is carried by the blood, combined with the plasma protein albumin, to the liver. There it is picked up by hepatocytes and chemically modified by the addition of two molecules of glucuronic acid. This process is called **conjugation.** Its product is bilirubin diglucuronide or, more simply, conjugated bilirubin (CB).

There are two significant consequences of the bilirubin conjugation. One is that CB is much less toxic than unconjugated bilirubin (UCB). The other is that CB is water-soluble and UCB is not. (This is why UCB transport in the plasma is facilitated by albumin.) By converting bilirubin to a water-soluble form, the liver facilitates its incorporation into bile for the purpose of excretion. Some bilirubin is converted to a sulfate, which is also water-soluble. The excretion of bilirubin in bile is one of the few cases in which the alimentary canal is used for excretion. Because the intestine's lumen is an external space, and because the bile duct system directly communicates with it, at the moment when bile enters a bile canaliculus it is technically outside the body and has been excreted (fig. 14.1). In this way bilirubin is cleared from the blood and prevented from accumulating in the body tissues. On reaching the colon, bilirubin is converted by bacterial action to **urobilinogen** and then the darkly colored **urobilin** pigments that are responsible for the color of feces. Bilinogens are also absorbed from the colon and carried to the liver, where they are again secreted into bile. Small amounts are also excreted by the kidney into the urine (fig. 14.5).

Metabolic Functions

The liver makes major contributions to the metabolism of carbohydrate, lipid, and protein. Its cells contain the array of specialized enzymes needed to accomplish these complex metabolic tasks. In lipid metabolism, the liver takes up fatty acids from fat stores around the body. About one-half are converted to lipoprotein and returned to the blood for transport back to adipose tissue. The remaining half are used in a variety of metabolic pathways, for example, the synthesis of **cholesterol.** This steroid lipid serves as a precursor of the steroid hormones and the bile salts. It is also found in cell membranes. Cholesterol made in the liver is also present in bile. It is normally kept in water solution by the action of the bile salts, aided by a phospholipid, **lecithin,** that is also synthesized by the liver from triglyceride. The liver can also synthesize fat from carbohydrate and protein when these are present in oversupply. The resulting fat is then stored against future demand (fig. 14.6).

In the metabolism of carbohydrate, the role of the liver is vital because the simple sugar glucose is the principal fuel of energy metabolism. As newly absorbed glucose enters the blood after a meal, the liver converts much of it to a stored form, **glycogen.** This process is called **glycogenesis.** Later, as glucose is utilized, the liver can degrade glycogen in a process called **glycogenolysis,** which provides the glucose needed to maintain its level in the blood. When necessary, the liver can synthesize glucose from amino acid precursors by a process termed **gluconeogenesis.**

Protein metabolism in the liver includes the **deamination** of amino acids. In this process the amino group is removed from an amino acid, leaving a carbon-containing

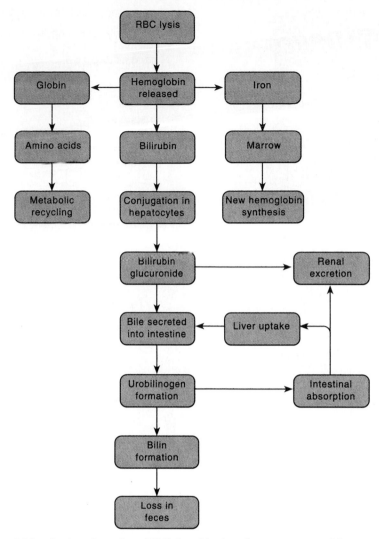

Figure 14.5   The fate of hemoglobin after its release from RBCs lysed in the spleen, marrow, and liver.

molecule that can be used in various synthetic pathways, for example, in glucose synthesis or energy metabolism. The amino groups produced by deamination are used by the liver to make **urea,** which is then excreted by the kidney. The liver also uses ammonia absorbed from the colon, where it is formed by bacteria, to synthesize urea. In addition, hepatocytes synthesize most of the plasma proteins and the protein clotting factors of the blood's coagulation system. Also produced in the liver are some components of the fibrinolytic system. The liver's major metabolic functions are presented in table 14.1.

Detoxification

The liver cells' smooth endoplasmic reticulum contains an array of enzymes that chemically alter certain substances so that they can be cleared from the blood, especially hormones and exogenous substances. In the case of circulating hormones, the benefit of their inactivation by liver enzymes is that new secretion is required to replace them. This requirement allows for the closely regulated secretion that provides fine hormonal control of various body functions. The hormones of the pancreas, adrenal cortex, and thyroid gland are inactivated by enzymatic degradation in the liver.

The process of enzymatic degradation (or **catabolism**) is called **detoxification** when exogenous substances are involved. Drugs, harmful chemicals, and biological toxins can be cleared from the blood by the liver in this way, providing an early defense against potentially threatening substances. The process is similar to that seen in preparing bilirubin for excretion. The drug or chemical is metabolically altered and the product converted to conjugated forms that are water-soluble. This makes them suitable for renal

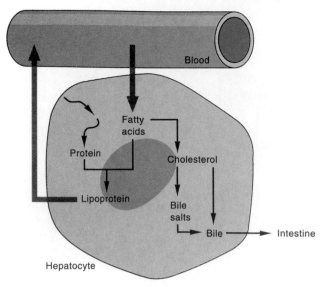

Figure 14.6 Some important hepatic lipid metabolism pathways. Fatty acids from the blood are metabolized in the production of bile salts or in other pathways not shown. Combination of lipid and protein synthesized within the cell (curved arrows) forms lipoprotein. Only in this form can unmetabolized fat be cleared from the cell.

excretion (fig. 14.7). The liver's blood supply arrangement has significance for detoxification in that toxins or chemicals absorbed from the GI tract are carried directly to the liver. The liver clears the blood of a certain fraction of the toxic chemical during each passage through its sinusoids. This arrangement greatly reduces the amount to which the systemic tissues are exposed.

The liver's detoxification enzymes may not be present at all times. However, the presence of the substrate (the molecule on which the enzyme has its effect) induces the liver cell to produce the enzyme and so eliminate the substrate. This process is called **enzyme induction** and is nonspecific; that is, a single substrate can induce the production of many different enzymes. A related function is performed by specialized phagocytes called **Kupffer cells** (fig. 14.3), which are found in the liver's sinusoids. These cells can expand to bulge into or cross the sinusoids' lumen. In this way they increase their contact with the blood and with any potentially threatening substance being carried by it. The Kupffer cells make an important protective contribution in removing antigen-antibody complexes, colonic bacteria, or tissue debris that finds its way into the portal blood.

Vitamin and Nutrient Storage

Hepatocytes also contribute to metabolism by storing several needed nutrient substances. These can't be synthesized, and hence the diet must supply them. When amounts greater than immediately required are available, the liver

Table 14.1	Principal Liver Functions
Detoxification of toxins/drugs	Synthesis of plasma proteins
Vitamin storage	Hormone inactivation
Clotting factor synthesis	Protein/lipid metabolism
Glycogen formation/storage	Urea production
Phagocytosis	Bile production

Liver damage may affect any of these to a greater or lesser degree, depending on the severity of the injury, the nature of the injury, and other variables.

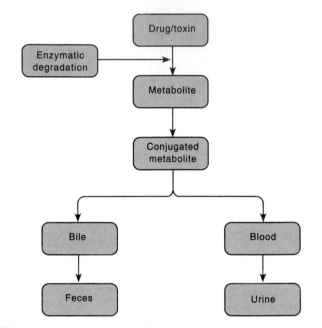

Figure 14.7 Hepatic detoxification of drugs and toxins.

stores them. If supplies should decline at some later time, the liver releases its stored nutrients for use. The quantities stored are usually adequate to meet the body's needs for periods of weeks to months. The important vitamins stored by the liver's cells are vitamins A, B_{12}, D, and K. Other nutrients stored are glycogen, triglycerides, riboflavin, nicotinamide, copper, and iron.

LIVER FAILURE

Because it receives the direct venous drainage of the stomach and the intestines, the liver is subject to substantial threat. This threat takes the form of absorbed microorganisms, their products, and any toxic chemicals or drugs in the intestinal drainage. To cope with this situation the liver brings two powerful defenses to bear. One is its enormous reserve capacity: the liver is estimated to use only 10% of its cells in meeting normal day-to-day requirements. The other defense is the liver's highly developed regenerative capacity, which can produce large amounts of functional cells to replace those lost to injury. However, any advantages gained by these hepatic capabilities may be offset by the fact that a disease process may be well advanced before sufficient liver tissue is destroyed to produce significant signs and symptoms. This means that, aside from some acute infections or focal trauma, much liver disease involves diffuse damage that affects large amounts of the liver's parenchyma before a person recognizes a problem. The result is often chronic and severe disease, because a long period of tissue destruction may overwhelm the liver's reserve and regeneration capacities. The major sequelae of liver disease that are commonly seen, regardless of etiology, are considered in the following sections.

Jaundice

Hyperbilirubinemia is the condition in which bilirubin levels in the blood are elevated above the normal range of 0.3–1 mg/dl. In **jaundice,** a yellow-brown color becomes visible in the skin and the sclera of the eye when the bilirubin level in the blood reaches three to four times the normal value. In liver failure, jaundice is almost always present and serves as an easily observed sign of some disturbance in the liver or bile system. (**Icterus** is an older, less commonly used term meaning jaundice.) Jaundice may be the result of one or more of three problems that can arise in the liver and bile (hepatobiliary) system. One is excessive lysis of red blood cells, which are normally the source of most bilirubin. (Some bilirubin, about 20% of the total, is produced from other heme-containing proteins, for example myoglobin and heme-containing enzymes.) Another is a breakdown in the liver's ability to conjugate or excrete bilirubin, while the third is obstruction of the bile duct system.

Hemolytic Jaundice

Jaundice resulting from excessive erythrocyte lysis is called **hemolytic jaundice.** Hemolysis is red blood cell rupture followed by hemoglobin release. It is seen most frequently in cases of red blood cell membrane damage by immune mechanisms. These cases may arise from incompatibility of blood types between a transfusion recipient's blood and that of the donor. Another such immune incompatibility may develop between a mother and the child she carries in her uterus. These usually involve the Rh antigen (see chapter 7).

Whatever etiology produces the hemolysis, the result is an increase in the bilirubin conjugation and excretion load that the liver must bear. Initially, the liver can cope because of its large reserve. During this early stage the urine will be darker because increased hepatic bilirubin excretion produces larger quantities of bilinogens in the intestine.

Increased amounts then enter the enterohepatic circulation, and as a result more are excreted via the kidney. When the liver reaches the point at which its excretory capacity is overwhelmed, bilirubin levels in the blood and tissues rise. Because liver conjugation and excretion are operating at maximum, the bilirubin that appears in the blood and tissues will be toxic UCB. This can pose a special threat to newborns since their blood-brain barrier is unable to prevent higher levels of UCB from gaining access to the brain and threatening serious damage. This condition is called **kernicterus.** **5** Renal excretion of bilirubin can't increase to reduce high UCB levels because the kidney can excrete only the conjugated diglucuronide form of bilirubin, and only when it is present in high plasma concentrations.

Hepatocellular Jaundice

A second type of jaundice results from a failure of the liver cell to take up, conjugate, or excrete bilirubin. This type is called **hepatocellular jaundice.** It is the most common type of jaundice seen clinically, usually in association with viral hepatitis (see the discussion of hepatitis in a later section). Faulty hepatic uptake of bilirubin is sometimes at fault, but failure to conjugate and secrete bilirubin is a more common problem. It may result from damage to liver cells caused by infection, tumors, therapeutic drugs (e.g., steroids), or toxic chemicals. In some cases, a genetic lack of the conjugating enzymes is the underlying problem. A mild and transient form of hepatocellular jaundice is often seen in the newborn. Because the liver conjugation enzymes may not be functional for the first 7–14 postnatal days, even normal hemolysis releases more bilirubin than can be excreted by the immature liver cells. A mild jaundice results, but it soon passes as the liver enzymes develop. This condition is quite common and is known as **neonatal jaundice.**

Obstructive Jaundice

Obstruction of the bile duct system is the third mechanism causing jaundice. In **obstructive jaundice,** the normal draining of bile into the duodenum is substantially reduced or completely stopped (**cholestasis**). As a result, bilirubin and bile salts accumulate, first in the liver and then in the blood. The bilirubin initially entering the blood is CB, but later UCB uptake by hepatocytes is reduced as well, causing a hyperbilirubinemia characterized by both CB and UCB. As bile salts are carried in the blood to peripheral tissues, they can produce an intense itching sensation in the skin called **pruritus.** Complete obstruction of the hepatic duct or common bile duct results in gray-colored feces, since urobilins are absent from the colon. In such cases, urinary urobilinogens are also lacking. Microscopic studies of liver affected by obstructive jaundice may show dilated bile canaliculi with leakage of bile into the surrounding tissues. These bile accumulations are known as **bile lakes.** **6**

Obstruction of the bile ducts may be caused by abnormalities inside or outside the liver. **Intrahepatic obstruction** occurs when viral or other infections, or drugs, damage the liver. Swelling of the liver follows injury, as in the case of fatty liver, or because of infiltration by inflammatory cells. As a result, the fine intrahepatic bile canaliculi may be compressed, reducing or stopping bile flow. In **extrahepatic obstruction,** mechanical blockage of the bile ducts is involved, e.g., a carcinoma of the bile duct epithelium or another externally compressing tumor. Inflammation or neoplasia of the adjacent pancreas might also be involved, since swelling might compress the hepatopancreatic ampulla to block flow. A common cause of extrahepatic obstructive jaundice is inflammation of the bile ducts, **cholangitis.** Other causes are accumulating pus from a bacterial infection and bile duct stricture associated with postinfection repair of the ducts. Obstructive jaundice is also commonly caused by gallstones, which can lodge in the ducts. Details of their formation are discussed in the cholelithiasis section, later in this chapter.

In **biliary atresia,** obstruction is the result of congenitally deficient bile ducts that are inadequate to drain bile from the liver. The atresia, or absence, of ducts may be intrahepatic or extrahepatic and presents serious risks of progressive irritation and necrosis from accumulating bile salts. The consequences are fibrosis and cirrhosis (discussed in a later section), and the affected child is unlikely to survive. Although quite rare, the cases often gain attention via the news media, where pleas for a liver donor are often made. Transplantation offers the only hope of a cure.

The various causes of jaundice are summarized in figure. 14.8.

Malabsorption

Because of its role in digestion and absorption, liver damage may be associated with malabsorption. Following obstruction of the bile duct system, malabsorption of fat often occurs. With the loss of bile salts, fat emulsification and absorption are diminished, falling to about half of normal levels. This is one factor in the weight loss and steatorrhea characteristics of chronic liver failure.

Another problem indirectly related to malabsorption is abnormal blood coagulation. Vitamin K is required for normal hepatic synthesis of various plasma clotting factors. Because vitamin K is fat-soluble, it is dependent on bile salts for its absorption. When liver damage interferes with bile secretion, or when obstruction prevents its reaching the duodenum, vitamin K levels may be depressed.

Disordered Hepatic Metabolism

When hepatocytes are damaged, their numerous metabolic functions may become disrupted. A few cells, or many, may be affected to differing degree, with systemic effects producing a variety of signs and symptoms. For example,

the overall effects of chronically depressed hepatic metabolism are generalized weakness and weight loss. On the other hand, more specific effects are seen when a particular hepatic function is affected. For example, the blood coagulation abnormalities that result from malabsorption of vitamin K are enhanced by defects in hepatic protein synthesis. The result is a deficiency of prothrombin and other clotting factors. With protein synthesis depressed, a deficiency of plasma proteins follows and produces hypoalbuminemia. Lack of albumin reduces blood osmotic pressure, with peripheral edema the result. As fluid accumulates in the tissue spaces, a finger's pressure on the skin produces a pit that only slowly returns to normal. For this reason, the condition is called **pitting edema.** The pit results because the excess tissue fluids can move only slowly through the tissue spaces to refill the depression produced by the finger's pressure.

Another sequela of hepatic injury is called **hepatic encephalopathy.** It is characterized by a series of neurological abnormalities thought to be related to the failing liver's altered protein metabolism. Although amino groups continue to be split off amino acids, the damaged liver can't synthesize enough urea to clear them. They accumulate as ammonia, which has toxic CNS effects that cause the encephalopathy. Other toxic substances that can't be inactivated by the damaged liver have been implicated in hepatic encephalopathy, but their precise roles and interrelations are not clearly understood. Mild forms may produce only a passing sluggishness or lethargy. More severe expressions involve disorientation and coma. In severe hepatic failure, hepatic encephalopathy produces a characteristic flapping tremor of the hand when the arm is extended, called **asterixis.** Usually the prognosis is less favorable if hepatic encephalopathy develops in acute liver damage rather than in chronic cases.

Injury that prevents hepatic lipoprotein synthesis leads to altered lipid metabolism. As discussed in chapter 1, such injury disrupts the normal exchange of fat and lipoprotein between the liver and adipose tissue stores around the body, and fat accumulates in the liver cells. This fatty liver condition is reversible, but if damage is severe or chronic, the cells may not survive. **7** **8**

Other effects are often seen as a result of altered hepatic metabolism. With depression of the liver's chemical and drug detoxification function, the effects of a given toxin may be exaggerated as its removal from the blood proceeds more slowly. Similarly, therapeutic drug doses may require adjustment; because less will be inactivated by a damaged liver, greater effects will be produced by a smaller than normal dosage.

Another type of metabolic effect involves hormone inactivation. As this hepatic function diminishes, higher levels of circulating hormones may result if feedback controls can't compensate. For example, in male alcoholics, liver damage appears to interfere with inactivation of the small amounts of estrogens produced by the adrenal cortex.

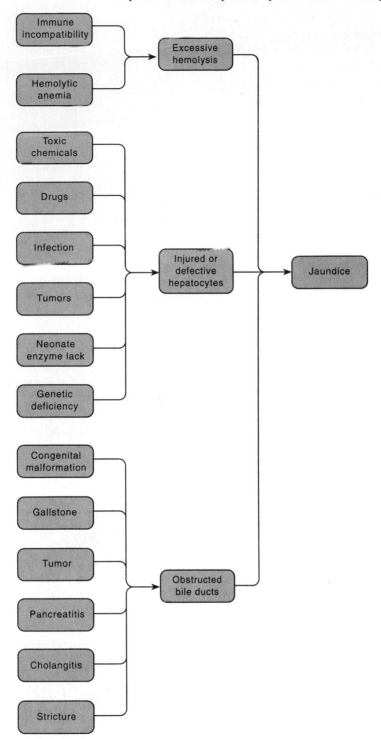

Figure 14.8   Principal etiologies in hemolytic, hepatocellular, and obstructive jaundice.

The result is the exposure of the tissues to estrogen levels that produce **feminization**: **gynecomastia** (breast enlargement) and a female pattern of pubic hair distribution. The increased incidence of peptic ulcer in association with liver damage may similarly be the result of reduced hepatic inactivation of the hormone gastrin. Higher levels of gastrin in the blood lead to excessive stimulation of the stomach's parietal cells, and therefore to oversecretion of acid and a tendency to ulceration.

Renal failure may follow liver failure. This condition, known as the **hepatorenal syndrome,** usually arises late in the course of severe liver disease and indicates a poor prognosis. Although its pathogenesis is not well understood, it is possible that elevated levels of circulating vasoconstrictors, normally destroyed in the liver, damage the kidney by interfering with its blood flow. Although the kidney is functionally impaired, a renal biopsy reveals no structural changes; indeed, such kidneys have been successfully donated in transplant procedures. Normal function follows restoration of an adequate blood supply.

With this survey of the typical sequelae of liver damage as a foundation, we can now consider the principal patterns of pathogenesis that produce them.

HEPATITIS

Viral infections and toxic drug reactions commonly cause hepatic damage sufficient to produce at least some disruption of liver function. The result is an inflammatory response in the liver, called **hepatitis.** Two forms of hepatitis, acute and chronic, are commonly recognized. Although the "-itis" suffix implies certain inflammatory changes in the liver, they are not typical of the usual acute inflammatory response. For example, in the acute liver condition there is little fluid exudate, and lymphocytes are characteristically present, dominating over macrophages and neutrophils.

Acute hepatitis is often caused by viruses, but chemical toxin damage frequently produces the same pattern of hepatic change. The result is moderate injury with scattered areas of necrosis and regenerating hepatic parenchyma. The liver is swollen and may be discolored by bile that damaged cells can't pass to the bile canaliculi, or that can't clear canaliculi that are compressed by the swollen hepatic parenchyma. The victim feels weak and fatigued and typically experiences nausea, anorexia, fever, and jaundice. Various hepatic functions will be sufficiently depressed to produce abnormal diagnostic test results. The typical course of the disease involves a 4–6 week period of symptoms, followed by restoration of normal functions and complete recovery.

In a small percentage of acute hepatitis cases, hepatic damage is extreme and death may follow the initial attack in a matter of days or weeks. This pattern of hepatic damage is called **massive liver necrosis** or **fulminant hepatitis.** It is seen in a type of viral hepatitis, but toxic damage from various drugs or chemicals may also produce the same extensive damage. When acute hepatitis produces massive liver necrosis, most hepatic functioning is disrupted, and prognosis is poor, with mortality rates exceeding 70%. Hepatic encephalopathy is a common complication of massive liver necrosis.

Viral Hepatitis

Most viral hepatitis is produced by a group of viruses that specifically attack the liver. These are grouped in a separate category from the various other viruses that can incidentally affect the liver as part of a systemic infection; Epstein-Barr virus, herpes virus, adenovirus, enterovirus, and cytomegalovirus are examples. Essentials of the principal hepatitis viruses and their related conditions follow.

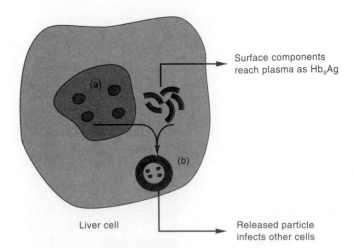

Figure 14.9 The nucleic acid core of the hepatitis B virus in the nucleus of an infected cell (A). In passing through the cytoplasm it acquires its protein coat (B). Some of this coating spills over into the plasma, where it can be identified as HB_sAg.

Hepatitis A Virus (HAV)

This virus is the cause of hepatitis A, **9** an acute and usually mild condition that resolves with minimal therapeutic intervention. It has a relatively short (3–6 weeks) **incubation period,** that is, the time during which the infection is proceeding without producing signs or symptoms. As the viruses become established in the liver, they pass to the intestine, where they contaminate the feces. As a result, the organisms typically are spread by contact where hygiene is faulty or when a water supply suffers fecal contamination. Shellfish, such as clams and oysters, may be contaminated by sewage to become a source of infection in human populations. Hepatitis A is often involved in epidemic outbreaks that are confined to a closed population, such as on naval vessels or at boarding schools. Although the term hepatitis A is now widely accepted as standard, you may still encounter the previous term for this condition, **infectious hepatitis.** Hepatitis A is also referred to as **short-incubation hepatitis.**

Hepatitis B Virus (HBV)

The hepatitis B virus **10** is the causative agent of hepatitis B, a potentially more serious condition than hepatitis A. Since HBV can be transmitted by infected blood or blood products, hepatitis B was previously known as **serum hepatitis. Long-incubation hepatitis** is another, seldom-used term for hepatitis B, derived from its usual 6–24-week incubation period.

HBV, sometimes known as the **Dane particle, 11** has an antigenic surface coat that surrounds its infective core (fig. 14.9). The core contains the DNA strand and an accompanying enzyme that allows the virus to infect hepatocytes and proliferate inside them. Infected cells produce the viral surface coat to great excess and it spills over into

Table 14.2	A Comparison of Some Key Characteristics of Hepatitis A, Hepatitis B, and Hepatitis C (NANB)		
Characteristic	**Hepatitis A**	**Hepatitis B**	**Hepatitis C (NANB)**
Mode of transmission	Fecal-oral	Skin* or venereal	Skin*
Time to postinfection symptoms	3–6 weeks	6–24 weeks	7–8 weeks
Carrier state	No	Yes	Yes
Chronic hepatitis	No	Up to 10% of cases	Up to 50% of cases
Association with hepatocarcinoma	No	Yes	Unknown
Mortality	Negligible	Up to 1.5%	Unknown

*Most often via contaminated intravenous needles.

HAV in Day Care Centers

The risk that children may develop hepatitis A from contact at day care centers seems to be increasing. The increase is due, in part, to the more widespread use of day care centers at the same time that there is increasing use of cloth diapers, based on environmental concerns. A recent study showed that cloth diapers, even when doubled, were more likely to allow fecal leakage, significantly increasing contamination of the hands of the children who wear them. Increased infections in the day care population were found, as communal toys and other surfaces were soon contaminated. The study showed that disposable paper diapers were better able to reduce contamination and the incidence of infection.

the blood, where it can be detected on the basis of its antigenic properties. It bears the designation **HB$_s$Ag** but may also be referred to as the **Australia antigen** because it was first isolated from an Australian aborigine.

Detection of HB$_s$Ag can be used to verify HBV infection and is the basis for screening donors of blood to be used in transfusions. Although the viral coat is not itself infective, finding HB$_s$Ag is presumed to indicate the presence of the more difficult-to-detect infective core. Such screening has greatly reduced transfusion transmission, but higher risks remain for medical personnel who can't avoid blood contact and for illicit drug injectors who use contaminated needles. It is also known that HBV is present in saliva and semen, which is why, today, venereal transmission accounts for most of the incidence of hepatitis B.

Hepatitis C Virus (HCV)

The hepatitis C virus is one of a group known as the **non-A, non-B** (NANB) **viruses**. The term was developed to describe the hepatitis conditions that differed from hepatitis A and B, but for which no infective virus could be identified. Continuing research has revealed several distinct viruses in the NANB group, and as these are better studied the NANB term will no longer be required.

HCV was the first of the NANB group to be identified. It is known to be the agent responsible for over 95% of posttransfusion hepatitis. Further study may also support the speculation that HCV is responsible for some localized outbreaks of hepatitis that did not involve transfusion.

Selected features of hepatitis A, hepatitis B, and hepatitis C are presented in table 14.2.

Other NANB Viruses

Two other viruses previously included in the NANB group may be encountered by health care professionals. One is the **hepatitis D virus** (or **delta agent**), an apparently incomplete agent that can't infect alone, but only in concert with HBV. It is usually not detected, but may combine its effects with those of an existing hepatitis B to produce a more severe attack. **Hepatitis E virus** is not usually encountered in North America. It may be implicated in some acute hepatitis in developing countries, in which outbreaks seem based on water-borne and therefore possibly fecal contamination.

The Carrier State

A subset of hepatitis B sufferers are unable to completely eliminate HBV particles, for reasons that are obscure. It may be they have some degree of immune incompetence or that they are genetically predisposed to susceptibility. In these individuals, the infection persists, in some cases with minimal signs of liver derangement and in other cases with no indication of abnormality. Such **carriers** present a constant hazard in that they remain capable of spreading the disease, sometimes for many years, and may not realize it. The problem of identifying carriers is difficult because in many cases, the initial acute attack of hepatitis may be mild enough to be overlooked or passed off as a brief period of "feeling under the weather."

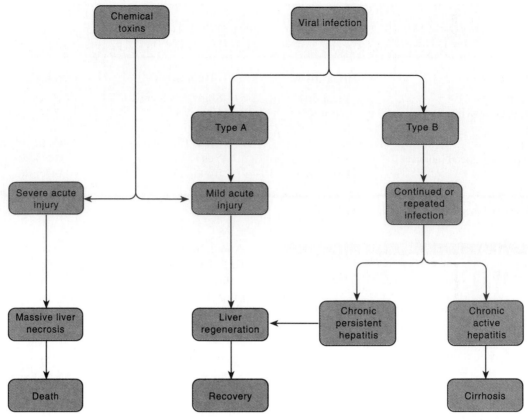

Figure 14.10   Pathogenesis of acute and chronic hepatitis.

Although the carrier state does not exist for HAV, it is well established not only for HBV, but for HCV and HEV as well. Data on HCV and HEV carriers is limited, but estimates put the number of HBV carriers in North America in excess of 1 million. This represents a large pool of infection, especially with an increasing population mobility producing greater numbers of contacts and, therefore, higher infection risk. Carrier incidence is high among homosexuals and intravenous drug users.

Chronic Hepatitis

A large majority of acute hepatitis cases resolve without complication. However, in up to 10% of cases the disease persists beyond six months and enters a chronic phase that may last for many months or years. Viruses or drugs may be responsible for the initial acute attack, but 80–90% of chronic hepatitis cases are idiopathic. Where the causative agent of chronic hepatitis is identified, it is usually HBV.

In chronic hepatitis, two forms are traditionally recognized. **Chronic persistent hepatitis** (CPH) is characterized by years to decades of limited hepatic necrosis and only minor symptoms such as mild fatigue, or in some cases no symptoms at all. Hepatic regeneration can replace lost parenchyma so that functional losses do not occur. Therapy is usually not indicated, but information on infection risks to others should be provided to the patient.

Chronic active hepatitis (CAH) is a more threatening progressive condition that may emerge from acute HBV or HCV attacks. Some cases of CAH may be the result of HDV infection superimposed on cases of CPH. The signs and symptoms of CAH are quite variable and may be so mild that the condition may be confused with CPH. On the other hand, intermittent bouts of abdominal pain, jaundice, anorexia, splenomegaly, or encephalopathy may be quite severe. Various extrahepatic derangements of the GI tract, pericardium and heart, pleurae and kidneys may also accompany CAH. In this condition the mortality rate can be as high as 50% five years after diagnosis, as parenchymal regeneration is unable to keep pace with necrosis. Scarring and the development of liver cirrhosis follows.

The pathogenesis of acute and chronic hepatitis is summarized in figure 14.10.

Drug and Chemical Hepatitis

A large variety of chemicals, some of which are used therapeutically, are known to have hepatotoxic effects. **12** These effects may be acute or chronic and will vary in intensity from mild injury to massive liver necrosis.

Many chemical agents known to be directly hepatotoxic are not available to the general public, or access to them is strictly controlled. Of course, in the case of a therapeutic drug, unequivocal hepatotoxicity would prevent its

(a)   (b)

Figure 14.11   Micrographs of (a) normal and (b) cirrhotic liver. Note the bands of fibrous tissue and regenerating parenchyma that are characteristic of cirrhosis.

being approved for use. More problematic are agents that produce **idiosyncratic** reactions, that is, reactions that are unpredictable because individuals vary in their susceptibility to damaging effects. Table 14.3 lists various hepatotoxic agents.

Drug hepatitis has no distinguishing characteristics that allow it to be differentiated from viral hepatitis. The patient's history may provide a clue, and rapid recovery when use of a suspected chemical or drug is stopped is usually taken as confirmation of its role in causation.

CIRRHOSIS OF THE LIVER

Long-term necrosis caused by infection, by drug or chemical damage, from alcohol in particular, or by extrahepatic bile obstruction can eventually overwhelm the liver's regeneration capacity. In response to such chronic destruction of parenchyma, scarring becomes increasingly prominent until sheets of fibrous repair tissue form throughout the liver **13** (fig. 14.11). These are diffusely distributed, isolating areas of hepatocytes that retain their regenerative capacity. Such foci of regeneration are called nodules, and are readily apparent at the affected liver's surface **14** (fig. 14.12). This condition of nodularity and fibrosis is called **cirrhosis.** Since differing patterns of parenchymal loss and scarring can produce smaller nodules (<3 mm) or larger ones (up to several centimeters), you may encounter references to

Table 14.3		Selected Drugs and Chemicals Known to Have Hepatotoxic Effects
	Category	**Examples**
Directly toxic	Industrial chemicals	Carbon tetrachloride, vinyl chloride, benzene, and related compounds
	Plant toxins	Mushroom toxins (*Amanita*)
Unpredictable toxicity	Anesthetics	Halothane, methoxyflurane
	Antibiotics	Isoniazid, rifampin, sulfonamides
	Anticonvulsants	Diphenylhydantoin
	NSAIDs	Phenylbutazone
	Oral contraceptives	All, as a class
	Tranquilizers	Phenothiazines

Figure 14.12   Cirrhosis of the liver. The large rounded masses are foci of regeneration. Contracture in the scar tissue that separates them has drawn in the fibrous bands to produce pronounced irregularity at the hepatic surface.

micronodular or **macronodular** cirrhosis; **15** however, the size of the nodules has no bearing on the clinical presentation of the disease or its course.

Cirrhosis is a nonspecific end-stage toward which various pathogenic sequences converge. Its signs and symptoms are variable, reflecting differing degrees of functional loss and typically involving jaundice, wasting, blood coagulation disorders, and plasma protein deficiencies, hypoalbuminemia in particular. As well, various indications of a deranged intrahepatic vasculature may be present. In some cases, however, parenchymal regeneration may be just able to compensate for necrosis, so that only minimal symptoms, or even none, are present. The consequence is a slowly progressing destruction of liver cells that goes unnoticed until it reaches the point at which adequate function can't be sustained. Continued necrosis then depletes functional reserves so rapidly that complete liver failure can't be avoided. In some cases, death from other causes comes before the liver is overwhelmed, and "silent" cirrhosis is discovered as an incidental finding at autopsy.

Portal Hypertension

The **hepatic portal vein** drains the intestines, stomach, pancreas, and spleen and carries their blood to the liver. Increased blood pressures in this system, **portal hypertension,** are the result of restricted flow of blood through the liver to the inferior vena cava (IVC) and beyond. Although portal hypertension may be caused by thrombosis or by compression of the inferior vena cava, hepatic, or portal veins, in most cases it is a consequence of liver cirrhosis.

Two factors seem principally responsible for the liver changes that induce elevated portal system pressures: vascular compression and increased arterial loading. In cirrhosis,

both regenerating nodules and scar tissue deposition occur at the expense of the fine sinusoids and intrahepatic venules, compressing them and thus increasing their resistance to flow. The resulting portal congestion elevates portal pressures. Arterial loading is the result of an increased flow through the hepatic artery that accompanies cirrhosis for unknown reasons. This flow increases the volume with which the sinusoids and venules must cope and adds to an already increased vascular congestion. The principal consequences of portal hypertension derive from the diversion or shunting of blood past the liver and as direct consequences of elevated blood hydrostatic pressures in the liver and splanchnic (intestinal) veins.

Hepatic Shunting

Cirrhosis leads to a decrease in the liver's functional capacity, not only through destruction of its parenchyma, but because portal hypertension causes portal system blood to by-pass the congested liver vessels, returning to the IVC via alternative routes. The remaining functional hepatocytes are therefore exposed to less blood flow. The result is an overall reduction in oxygen and nutrient delivery to the liver, as well as a further general reduction of liver function for lack of adequate access to the blood. In this way, already existing coagulation defects, hypoalbuminemia, or other signs of compromised liver function may be exaggerated. Of particular significance is the ammonia produced from the breakdown of amino acids. Its normal incorporation into urea in the liver is reduced in cases of portal hypertension. Instead of being excreted as urea, the ammonia remains in the blood, causing an increased risk of hepatic encephalopathy. Less blood flow to the liver also means hepatocytes have less exposure to the circulating substances that require detoxification. As a result, they will also be more highly concentrated in the blood and therefore more likely to produce damaging effects.

When hepatic blood pressure is increased, blood bypasses the liver by way of collateral vessels that connect the portal veins to other venous channels. The collateral vessels normally carry limited amounts of blood, but when portal pressures rise, they can deliver additional blood to the superior and inferior venae cavae. Of particular significance are the collaterals that accompany the esophagus, because they are thin-walled and have little surrounding connective tissue support. As they receive increasing portal flow and their pressure rises, focal dilatations called **esophageal varices** may form. **16** (These are analogous to the varices or varicosities seen in superficial leg veins.)

Because they cause the esophageal mucosa to protrude into the lumen (fig. 14.13) esophageal varices are subject to trauma as food is swallowed, and they may be exposed to the reflux of gastric juice. The precise mechanism is not understood, but trauma, gastric juice, and the high pressure

Figure 14.13   In this view of the esophageal mucosa (right), the enlarged and tortuous varices of the esophageal veins can be clearly seen.

This specimen is from the liver and esophagus of a male alcoholic cirrhosis victim. It shows the nodular character of the hepatic surface and the internal disorganization of the liver tissue architecture. On the right can be seen the esophageal varices that had ruptured to cause the man's death. He had been a very heavy drinker for 20 of his middle years and had been hospitalized for the last three years of his life. He suffered severe lower limb edema and pronounced ascites. Repeated abdominal taps were necessary to reduce his abdominal distention, often yielding as much as 4 liters of fluid.

Figure 14.14   This drawing shows the degree of abdominal distention often seen in ascites.

within the varices probably combine to produce the erosions, rupture, and bleeding that make esophageal varices a serious complication of cirrhosis.

Usually without symptoms until they rupture, esophageal varices can produce sudden, large-scale blood loss that may be difficult to identify as originating in the esophagus. Hematemesis is a common accompanying sign, and bleeding may be complicated because the damaged liver can't maintain an adequate coagulation response. Bleeding of esophageal varices is a serious condition, with mortality approaching 40% in those whose initial indication of damage is an episode of hemorrhage. Subsequent bleeds and continuing liver failure contribute to the poor prognosis.

Therapy for bleeding esophageal varices may rely on compression of the bleeding veins from inside the esophagus by a balloon device inserted into its lumen. Alternatively, an agent that promotes a pronounced fibrosis response (a **sclerosing agent**) may be directly injected, via an endoscope, at the point of bleeding. In extreme cases, pressure in the esophageal veins may be relieved surgically by the introduction of a by-pass that carries blood to a point in the systemic venous return. This approach is usually undertaken when other attempts to stop the bleeding have failed.

Portal hypertension produces two other major complications of cirrhosis: ascites and splenomegaly. **Ascites** is the condition of fluid accumulation in the peritoneal cavity. It can be quite pronounced, leading to significant abdominal distention, **17** which in turn can compromise breathing and compress the abdominal viscera (fig. 14.14). The ascitic fluid derives from the plasma and "sweats" off hepatic and intestinal surfaces because of the increased BHP in the sinusoids and capillary beds of the hepatic and splanchnic tissues. Also contributing is reduced hepatic albumin production, which lowers BOP and reduces the

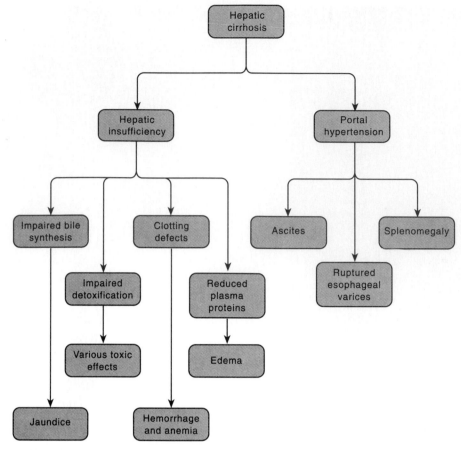

Figure 14.15   Sequelae of hepatic cirrhosis.

return of fluid to the blood. A third factor is the backup of blood in the splanchnic vessels, which diminishes venous return to the heart. This in turn can trigger sodium and water retention reflexes that add to the already exaggerated fluid burden.

An uncommon, but serious, complication of ascites is **spontaneous bacterial peritonitis.** By mechanisms unknown, but presumably related to high vascular pressures, intestinal organisms gain access to the peritoneal cavity. In it they find a medium that readily supports their growth and rapid proliferation, and peritonitis follows. This complication of cirrhosis can be fatal.

Splenomegaly is the result of congestion and hypertension in the spleen, **18** which arise as its veins, working against high portal system pressures, are unable to drain it adequately. The enlargement may produce spleen weights of up to 1000 g, over seven times normal. Splenomegaly is often accompanied by hypersplenism. In this condition, formed elements are increasingly taken up and held by the enlarged spleen. Hypersplenism can produce thrombocytopenia exaggerating any preexisting cirrhotic coagulation defects. Anemia may also develop as erythrocytes held in

the spleen add to circulatory red cell losses caused by bleeding from esophageal varices or other sites. The sequelae of liver cirrhosis are presented in figure 14.15.

Alcoholic Cirrhosis

About half of all cirrhosis involves an alcohol abuse etiology, with 15% of alcoholics becoming cirrhotic after ten years of high alcohol intake, at least one pint of spirits per day. Alcoholism is the single most common cause of hospitalization for liver derangements in North America.

The mechanism of alcohol toxicity involves the production of high levels of metabolites that have damaging effects. Also, the chronic need to detoxify large amounts of alcohol depletes detoxification enzymes so that toxins continue their effects for a longer period.

Other metabolic disturbances contribute to the fibrosis that characterizes cirrhosis. These metabolic derangements also produce the asymptomatic fatty degeneration that often precedes irreversible alcoholic liver damage (fig. 14.16). Such fatty degeneration **19** can produce liver enlargements as much as two to three times normal. As alcohol abuse

Figure 14.16   Fatty change in the liver. Note the swollen appearance of this section through a liver severely damaged by chronic alcohol abuse. Only traces of the normal dark liver coloration remain because fat, much of it extracellular at this late stage, has largely replaced functional parenchyma.

In sectioning this liver, it was noted to be heavy, and was greasy to the touch from the additional pound of accumulated fat it contained (weight 1980 gm, normal 1550 gm). The autopsy revealed no evidence of cirrhosis or esophageal varices. Although this degree of fatty change is extreme, the immediate cause of death of this 45-year-old male alcoholic was pneumonia. He had a history of many years of alcohol abuse and was generally debilitated.

persists, chronic damage is followed by cirrhotic scarring. [20] [21] In the alcoholic, steadily declining liver function is typically exaggerated by binges of alcohol intake, which can produce acute alcoholic hepatitis. This insult may overwhelm the already damaged liver and cause complete hepatic failure and death. Once cirrhosis is established and alcohol intake is not reduced, there is greater than an 80% likelihood of death within five years from liver failure or ruptured esophageal varices. Most alcoholic cirrhosis is seen between the ages of 40 and 65 in the male, whereas in the female the highest incidence occurs between 30 and 45 years of age. The pathogenesis of alcoholic liver damage is presented in figure 14.17.

Other Cirrhoses

After alcoholic cirrhosis, the second most common type is known as **postnecrotic cirrhosis.** [22] It is the most common type of cirrhosis worldwide, but the high consumption of alcohol in North America distorts the overall incidence figures. The term postnecrotic is misleading, but has unfortunately been retained in describing this condition. As must by now be apparent, all cirrhosis follows chronic hepatic necrosis, so the term offers no descriptive advantage. However, common usage reserves the term for the cirrhosis that follows chronic toxic or viral damage, most often the result of chronic hepatitis B. Indeed, postnecrotic cirrhosis is the end-stage condition toward which CAH progresses.

In another type, biliary cirrhosis, two forms are recognized, primary and secondary. **Primary biliary cirrhosis** arises most often in middle-aged females. It appears to involve chronic autoimmune destruction of the intrahepatic bile ducts, progressing to cirrhosis. There is no way to reverse the process, and liver transplantation may offer the only therapeutic option. **Secondary biliary cirrhosis** is the result of a chronic extrahepatic obstruction that allows bile to accumulate within the liver. The result is inflammation, necrosis, and fibrosis.

HEPATIC TUMORS

The liver greatly favors metastatic growth, and the vast majority of hepatic tumors are secondary growths, usually originating in the colon, breast, or lung. [23] Multiple tumor emboli typically establish several metastatic foci in the liver, with distribution reflecting their path through the hepatic vasculature. In advanced stages they may produce pronounced liver enlargement. Approximately one-third of all patients with malignant tumors have secondary hepatic involvement (fig. 6.12).

By comparison, primary hepatic tumors are rare. If benign, such as the **liver cell adenoma** or **bile duct adenoma,** they are well tolerated and seldom produce liver enlargement. The incidence of liver cell adenoma is low but seems linked to the use of birth control pills. The hormones they contain seem, in some way, to favor the development or growth of liver cell adenomas. Because their capsules are thin, when these tumors are present at the liver's surface they may rupture the surface and produce serious hemorrhage. Rupture occurs more often during pregnancy, perhaps because of the higher abdominal pressures caused by the enlarging uterus.

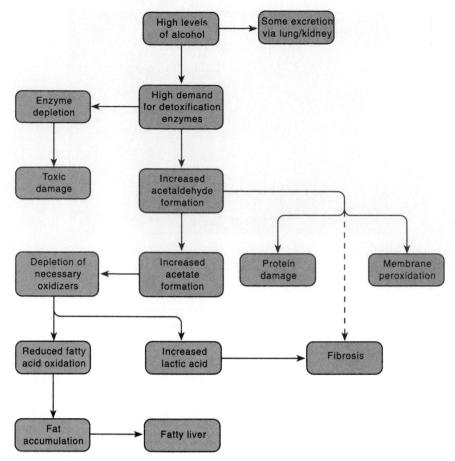

Figure 14.17   The pathogenesis of alcohol damage to the liver. The broken line denotes a less certain casual link.

Malignant tumors arise from two different hepatic cell types. The most common (80%) is the **hepatocellular carcinoma,** or **hepatoma, [24]** which derives from the hepatocyte (fig. 14.18). These are rare in North America but much more frequently encountered in parts of Africa, Japan, and Southeast Asia. These regions have high HBV infection rates and large numbers of HBV carriers. It is thought that since the virus is known to associate with the hepatocyte's DNA, it may also be able to induce the neoplastic transformation that yields the malignancy. The long-term effects of a chronic hepatitis B infection may indirectly contribute to the process by in some way producing conditions within the infected cell that facilitate the transformation. Of primary hepatic malignancies, 20% originate in bile duct epithelium, forming a scirrhous tumor termed **cholangiocarcinoma. [25]**

There is a strong association between primary liver malignancies and cirrhosis: about 70% arise in cirrhotic livers. In most cases, an HBV infection is the cause of the cirrhosis, but the precise links between the virus and the tumor are not understood.

CHOLELITHIASIS

Hospitalization in North America is often the result of complications arising from the presence of a stone in the bile ducts. Such stones usually form in the gall bladder from bile. For this reason they are called **gallstones. [26]** Gallstone formation is a common occurrence, with autopsy studies indicating their presence in approximately 15% of adults. Increasing age is correlated with an increasing incidence of their formation, with peak occurrence seen in obese females who are past the age of 40. Increased gallstone formation is also linked to high calorie diets and to genetic factors. The process of gallstone formation is called **cholelithiasis.**

The major constituents of normal bile are water, various inorganic ions, bile salts, cholesterol, lecithin, and conjugated bilirubin. Since cholesterol is a lipid, it has low water solubility. However, bile salts and lecithin combine with cholesterol to form large water-soluble complexes. When a change in bile permits low-solubility bile components to come out of the solution, they are said to **precipitate** out of the bile. As they do, they form small crystals on

Figure 14.18 Hepatocellular carcinoma. The large tumor mass is easily distinguished from the normal liver visible at the lower right of the photo. Note the large area of necrosis.
This portion of liver contains a very large hepatocellular tumor. The mass was soft and fragile compared with normal liver. Its cells retained the ability to form bile, which imparted a greenish tinge to the tumor. The mass was removed from a 15-year-old girl who died of a hemorrhage into her peritoneal cavity after the tumor broke through the liver's surface. The child had refused food and run a fever three months preceding this terminal event. Lung metastases were found at autopsy.

Figure 14.19 Gallstones. This gall bladder is filled with gallstones, whose principal constituent is cholesterol.
This is the gall bladder of a 56-year-old woman. It was removed after a severe attack of right upper quadrant abdominal pain. She reported that prior to the attack she had experienced six years of indigestion and flatulence, particularly after eating fatty foods. The gall bladder was nonfunctional, with its mucosa atrophied and its wall thickened and scarred from working against its stony contents. The pearly stones that fill the lumen are composed largely of cholesterol.

the gall bladder's mucosal surface. **27** Over time, these enlarge to produce grossly visible stones, some in excess of 1 cm in diameter. Several or many stones commonly form instead of only one or two (fig. 14.19). Three substances usually precipitate to form gallstones. One is cholesterol, another is the calcium salt of bilirubin (calcium bilirubinate), and the third is calcium carbonate ($CaCO_3$). These may be present alone in some stones, but most stones are formed of two or more of these, **28** with cholesterol being dominant in 80–90% of all gallstones. Where calcium bilirubinate dominates, the stones are called **pigment stones.**

Although the condition is idiopathic, the pathogenesis of cholelithiasis seems to follow from an imbalance in the composition of bile. For example, factors that increase the amount of cholesterol in bile may overwhelm the bile salts' ability to dissolve it. This may be a factor in the obese, who have elevated cholesterol levels and at the same time exhibit an increased tendency to cholelithiasis. If, on the other hand, bile acid production is depressed, or if intestinal absorption of bile acids is impaired, they may not be able to dissolve cholesterol adequately. In particular, ileal resection and Crohn's disease seem to lower bile salt absorption, reducing the amounts available for dissolving bile cholesterol.

Although excess cholesterol and/or insufficient bile salts may cause gallstone formation, other functional derangements may be involved. Beyond the excess or deficiency of bile components, there exists a further requirement for a site at which precipitation can be initiated. Here the gall bladder mucosa contributes. In gallstone patients, a component of the gall bladder's mucous membrane is altered, causing the surface to act as a site for tiny points of precipitation. Such a focus is called a **nidus;** once it is formed, precipitating crystals provide a surface that favors further precipitation, and a grossly visible stone develops.

The most common condition associated with cholelithiasis is inflammation of the gall bladder (**chole-cystitis**). It most often arises secondary to irritation of the mucosa by an obstructing gallstone at the outlet of the gall bladder. Following inflammation and repair, bile-concentrating ability is reduced or may be lost altogether. In chronic cholecystitis, long-term exposure to stone irritation and repeated acute attacks may make surgical removal of the gall bladder necessary. This treatment often resolves the typical pattern of upper right quadrant pain that often accompanies chronic cholecystitis.

In many cases, the presence of stones in the gall bladder produces no symptoms; in fact, many are first discovered in X-rays of the abdomen taken for reasons unrelated to their presence. The major complications of cholelithiasis

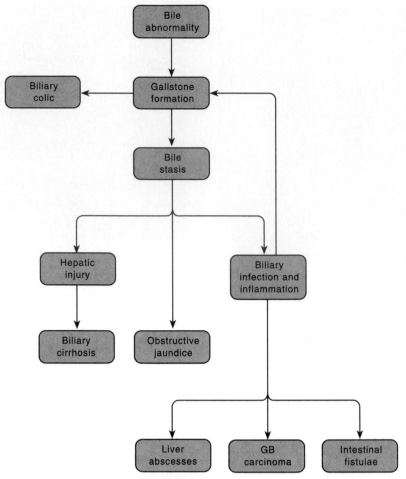

Figure 14.20   Pathogenesis of cholelithiasis. Infection and inflammation in the gall bladder may result from stone formation or these conditions may arise first and then cause stone formation.

follow from the movement of a stone into the duct system, where it obstructs bile flow. **29** The immediate effect is an intensely sharp upper abdominal pain that strikes abruptly and then gradually fades. This pain is known as **biliary colic.** If the blockage is not corrected, obstructive jaundice may also develop as a consequence of bile flow obstruction. Lack of normal bile flow can also favor ascent of bacteria from the intestine to the biliary system. Inflammation in the ducts and gall bladder then follows from bacterial activity, as well as from irritation by the obstructing stone. Bacterial damage and compression of gall bladder vessels may contribute to necrosis of its wall and raise the threat of rupture and peritonitis (fig. 14.20).

The usual therapy for gallstones that obstruct the duct system is surgical removal. However, surgical risk may be high because of the patient's advanced age (a common problem) or because of a reduced clotting response that is caused by depressed hepatic synthesis of clotting factors. In such cases, an alternative treatment is the long-term administration of bile acids to dissolve existing cholesterol

!! *Gallstones as a Side Effect*

Because of the link between high serum lipid levels and coronary atherosclerosis (see chapter 9), drug therapy to lower those levels has become more common. As a rule, pharmaceuticals are employed only when dietary control of hyperlipidemia is unsuccessful or when lipid levels are extremely high. The agents involved are generally directed at cholesterol and the serum lipoproteins that carry it. Two such drugs, clofibrate and gemfibrozil, have cholelithiasis as a potential side effect, particularly after long-term use. Although the exact mechanism of action is not fully understood, their use in some way disrupts the balance of bile constituents, or the gall bladder mucosa, to increase stone formation.

stones and prevent the formation of others. Another alternative is to fragment the stones with ultrasound energy, because the small pieces that result are more easily passed to the intestine for evacuation.

Table 14.4   Common Liver Function Tests Used to Assess Liver Damage

Test	Comments
Blood	
Serum bilirubin	Both CB and UCB are elevated in hepatitis. In obstructive jaundice, CB is higher than UCB; in hemolytic jaundice, UCB is higher.
Serum albumin	Depressed in chronic hepatitis and cirrhosis.
Bromsulphthalein (BSP)	A damaged liver cannot clear BSP injected into the blood.
Plasma alkaline phosphatase and glutamine pyruvate transaminase	These enzymes are released from a damaged liver. They are assessed in diagnosis of hepatitis and obstructive jaundice.
Urine	
Bilirubin	CB present in hepatitis and obstructive jaundice.
Urobilinogen	Excreted in urine when liver damage reduces uptake from blood. Elevated in hepatitis.

DIAGNOSTIC TESTS FOR LIVER FAILURE

Blood and Urine Tests

The usual approach to the diagnosis of liver disease is an evaluation of the blood and urine. Abnormally high or low levels of substances derived from normal hepatic functions are taken as an indication of liver damage. The level of serum bilirubin is a commonly used diagnostic indicator. Because it is possible not only to determine the total bilirubin but also to distinguish between CB and UCB, serum bilirubin analysis yields some information as to the specific nature of the malfunction. For example, in hepatitis, plasma levels of both CB and UCB are elevated, whereas in obstructive jaundice, CB is dominant. If the excess of bilirubin derives from increased hemolysis, the UCB level will be elevated above that of the conjugated form. Urinalysis for the presence of CB is also of diagnostic value, because the kidney will excrete CB only when its plasma level is abnormally high. This is the case in hepatitis and obstructive jaundice. Also, urinary urobilinogen will be increased in hepatitis, since the damaged liver can't take it up from the blood. The result is an increase in its renal excretion.

The liver's protein metabolism functions can also be assessed to gain insight into the functional status of the liver. Such assessment is most significant in chronic hepatic parenchymal disease, for example, cirrhosis or chronic hepatitis. The most common indicator in such cases is hypoalbuminemia due to impaired hepatic albumin synthesis.

If liver disease is suspected, but no jaundice is evident, the liver's functional ability can be challenged by presenting a specific task and then evaluating hepatic performance. One such evaluation involves the substance bromsulphthalein (BSP), which is excreted exclusively by the liver. Forty-five minutes after injecting the dye, the level of BSP in serum is measured. An elevated level indicates the liver is unable to remove BSP from the blood and is therefore malfunctioning.

Like other necrotic tissues, necrotic hepatic tissue releases certain characteristic enzymes whose presence in plasma can be taken as an indication of liver damage. For example, increased plasma values of alkaline phosphatase and glutamic-pyruvic transaminase (GPT) are useful in diagnosing acute and chronic hepatitis and obstructive jaundice. Some basic liver function tests are summarized in table 14.4.

Imaging

Radiation imaging plays a role in diagnosing liver damage. Scanning the liver to assess its uptake of radioisotopes is useful in localizing hepatic tumors. The focus of increased uptake indicates a primary tumor. An area of decreased uptake indicates a secondary growth, since it lacks the phagocytic cells needed for uptake of the isotope. Because only about 25% of gallstones contain calcium, most of them can't be visualized in X-ray studies. For this reason, ultrasound or computerized tomography (CT) scans are much more accurate in assessing their presence and location.

Biopsy

Sometimes it is helpful to obtain a sample of liver tissue for microscopic study. The procedure used is a **needle biopsy,** in which a hollow needle is passed through the abdominal wall into the liver and then withdrawn. The tissue in the needle is then removed for examination. Although the procedure is not safe if a bleeding tendency is established, it is useful in diagnosis of hepatomegaly and jaundice, and in monitoring liver transplants for rejection. It is also an important means of assessing the status of a hepatic tumor. The serious complications associated with the procedure are peritonitis, from bile leakage, and hemorrhage.

LIVER TRANSPLANTATION

This procedure is becoming increasingly successful as suitable recipients are better defined and more carefully selected, and as rejection suppression techniques are refined. In the latter case, the immunosuppressive agent cyclosporine has been an important factor. Candidates for a liver transplant are those who suffer massive liver damage or whose bile duct system is malformed from birth (biliary atresia).

The transplantation procedure involves surgical removal of the diseased organ. This may prove more difficult if the organ is badly scarred or if blood coagulation is compromised by the damaged liver's inability to sustain normal production of clotting factors. Donor livers are removed from individuals who are gravely ill and without hope of recovery. The liver's arteries, veins, and bile duct are severed and the donor's blood thoroughly flushed from it as it is quickly cooled. Liver tissue can successfully tolerate anoxia and nutrient deprivation for up to eight hours, if its metabolic demands are depressed by cooling. Without cooling, the entire procedure would have to be completed within about one hour.

During transplantation, the recipient's blood supply is connected to the donor liver and the bile duct is joined to the duodenum. A bile drain to the abdominal surface may be used to reduce bile irritation during healing at the duct sutures. The entire procedure is usually completed in under ten hours.

The "new" liver starts metabolic activity as its temperature and blood flow are restored. Improvement in the patient's condition soon follows, as previously deficient liver functions are reestablished. Monitoring of progress is based on blood tests and needle biopsies to detect any sign of rejection. Should rejection occur, another transplant procedure is required. In such cases, only minimal time, two or three days, may be available for locating another donor.

PANCREATIC PATHOPHYSIOLOGY

Apart from some quite rare developmental abnormalities, the pancreas is affected by only two disease processes, inflammation and neoplasia. Although these disorders are uncommon, when they do arise they can have severe consequences. This chapter will consider only derangements of the exocrine component of the pancreas. Its endocrine disorders are described in chapter 17. Before we consider pancreatic pathophysiology, a review of the normal pancreas may be useful.

Figure 14.21   A typical section of normal pancreas, showing the darkly stained exocrine cells with lighter islets of Langerhans (arrows) interspersed among them. A duct can be seen at the upper left, supported by the gland's connective tissue.

Anatomy and Physiology of the Pancreas

The pancreas is positioned with its **head** lying in the curve of the duodenum and its tapered **tail** lying against the hilus of the spleen (fig. 14.1). The intervening central portion is the **body.** Its parenchyma **30** is dominated by exocrine tissue, which secretes a collection of approximately 20 digestive enzymes (fig. 14.21). These enzymes are delivered to the small intestine by a duct system that terminates at the hepatopancreatic ampulla, alongside the common bile duct. The pancreatic duct cells secrete an alkaline secretion of concentrated bicarbonate, which neutralizes acid arriving in the duodenum from the stomach. Nervous and hormonal mechanisms control the daily secretion of 1500 to 3000 ml of pancreatic juice. Also present in the pancreas are islands of endocrine tissue known as the islets of Langerhans. Their pathophysiology is described in chapter 17.

Pancreatitis

An inflammatory response to damage of the exocrine tissue of the pancreas takes two forms, an acute pancreatitis, which can be life-threatening, and a chronic form involving recurring acute episodes.

Acute Pancreatitis

This condition typically presents with midepigastric pain. Nausea and vomiting may accompany the pain, and although fever is sometimes present, an underlying infection is rarely involved. Many attacks are relatively mild, involve no pancreatic necrosis, and resolve without intervention. More severe attacks are characterized by a more intense,

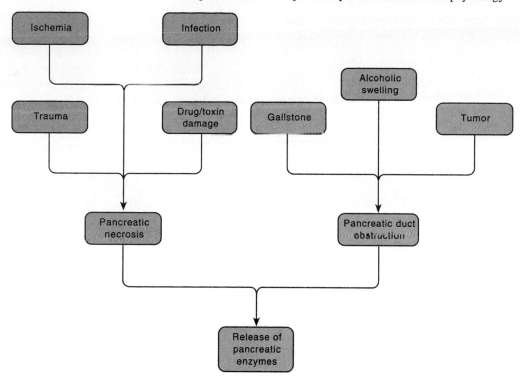

Figure 14.22   Principal factors that cause the release of pancreatic enzymes to produce acute pancreatitis.

radiating pain, pancreatic necrosis, **31** and extensive local hemorrhage. Vascular shock, renal failure, and ARDS may also arise to profoundly threaten the victim. Survivors may develop cysts filled with necrotic debris, blood degradation products, and pancreatic enzymes. These can enlarge to compress the adjacent duodenum and, in particular, the hepatopancreatic ampulla.

Etiology in acute pancreatitis has been much studied, but exact mechanisms have yet to be determined. In considering the problem, there are three key factors. First, the potent proteolytic and lipolytic enzymes of the pancreas are normally prevented from access to pancreatic tissue. They are held in inactive forms within the cytoplasm, in the cisternae of the ER and Golgi complex, until secretion. They are activated only when they enter the fine pancreatic ductules. Second, the digestion of pancreatic tissue and blood vessels by the gland's own enzymes is the underlying cause of the necrosis and hemorrhage that characterize severe attacks. Third, most acute pancreatitis is seen in alcohol abusers and in association with cholelithiasis.

On the basis of these three factors, anything that limits normal drainage of the ducts would seem to favor access of the enzymes to the normally protected pancreatic tissue (fig. 14.22). Sources of obstruction, or at least limitation, of flow might be gallstones or an adjacent tumor, or they might be alcohol-related. Bouts of alcohol intake are known to have an irritant effect on the duodenal mucosa and can produce inflammatory swelling at the sphincter of Oddi, limiting drainage of pancreatic juice from the ducts.

At the same time, alcohol has an indirect stimulating effect on pancreatic secretion. As a result, additional enzymes enter the ducts at a time when drainage is limited, and thus there is a greater likelihood that enzymes will escape to the adjacent glandular parenchyma. In cases linked to cholelithiasis, an obstructing stone may favor the retrograde movement of bile into the pancreas. Its irritant effect on the duct lining may then promote the loss of actuated enzymes to the tissues.

In the rare cases of acute pancreatitis not linked to alcohol or cholelithiasis, damage to the pancreas by various means may involve release and activation of its digestive enzymes and the destruction of pancreatic tissue (fig. 14.23). For example, tissue destruction from trauma, ischemia, an infection, or some chemical agent may induce an attack of acute pancreatitis. Some therapeutic agents are also known to be potentially damaging to the pancreas, e.g., corticosteroids, thiazides and furosemide.

Pathogenesis of acute pancreatitis is based upon the effects of enzyme release and tissue and vessel destruction. Pancreatic lipases digest fat stored within the pancreas and fat adjacent to it. The enzymes produce fatty acids from triglycerides, which then react with plasma ions to form pale masses of necrotic fat. The calcium and magnesium salts of fatty acids have a soapy consistency (fig. 14.24). In extreme cases, the uptake of calcium ions by fatty acids can deplete plasma calcium levels and produce peripheral muscle hyperactivity.

Figure 14.23   Acute pancreatitis; compare with normal pancreas in figure 14.21. Organization has been enormously disrupted. Two pale circular islets (arrows) can still be faintly seen, as can a few ducts (D). The acinar cells have been greatly damaged; their debris and large numbers of inflammatory cells dominate the site.

Figure 14.24   Acute pancreatitis. Pale areas of soapy necrosis are visible at the surface of the swollen gland.

A 60-year-old male developed a severe infection as he was convalescing from surgery for a cardiac valve replacement. He then experienced bouts of increasingly severe abdominal pain and died during attempts to diagnose and treat these complications. The pancreas shown here was found to be severely necrotic and heavily damaged by the infecting organisms and polymorphonuclear cells. Although most acute pancreatitis is related to alcohol abuse, there was none in this patient's history.

!! *A Short Historical Note*

You may recall stories of early settlers making soap from animal fat and lye. The animal fat was a source of triglyceride, while the lye, which is concentrated sodium hydroxide, was a source of sodium ions. When combined, the two ingredients formed sodium salts of the fatty acids: soap.

In an attack of acute pancreatitis, the combined effect of extensive inflammatory exudate formation and hemorrhage can lead to hypovolemic shock. Renal ischemia and renal failure may follow in extreme cases. In cases where ARDS develops, it seems to be because pancreatic enzymes are carried by the blood to the lungs, where they damage susceptible pulmonary capillaries. Digestive disruptions and malabsorption may also arise because of the lack of adequate pancreatic secretions (fig. 14.25).

Chronic pancreatitis is a condition that seems to involve repeated moderate attacks of acute pancreatitis. Successive episodes produce a progressive loss of functional parenchyma, which is replaced by scar tissue. The situation is complicated by calcified masses forming in the pancreatic ducts. **32** With progression and islet cell loss, diabetes mellitus may develop. The high-risk population is composed of males who suffer an initial alcohol-related attack and who continue to indulge, i.e., chronic alcoholics, and of those with persistent and severe cholelithiasis.

Pancreatic Tumors

The benign pancreatic **cystadenoma** is a rare condition that arises principally in women in their middle to later years. The tumors may derive from ductal elements and typically take the form of multiple small masses.

By contrast, the malignant carcinoma of the pancreas is a much more common and threatening disease, which is increasing in frequency in North America. Some correlation with smoking and high caloric intake has been identified. Most of such tumors arise from pancreatic duct cells, and although most appear late in life, emergence in the 20s is not unusual.

Prognosis in this condition is very poor, with approximately 90% of victims dying within the first year after diagnosis. Pancreatic carcinoma has its devastating effects because of early and widespread metastasis. This seems based, in part, on its location, which has elaborate venous and lymphatic drainage and therefore readily accessible metastasis routes.

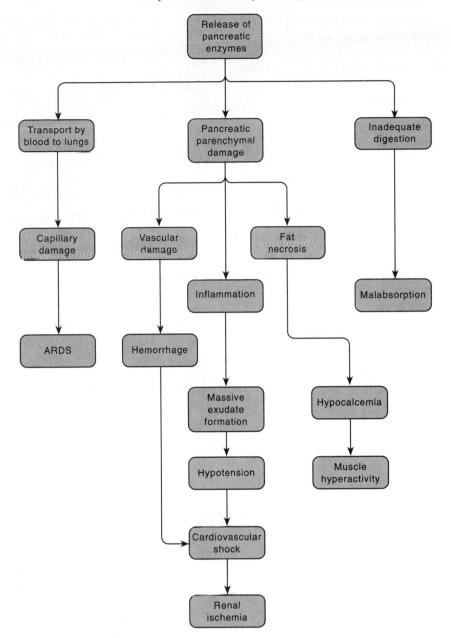

Figure 14.25   Pathogenesis of acute pancreatitis.

Case Study

At a general physical examination for his insurance company, a 55-year-old businessman mentioned that over the past year he had lost about six pounds, experienced some loss of appetite, and had some vague bowel and bladder problems. These had not particularly alarmed him, since they didn't suggest any heart disease, and he had attributed them to his age. He reported that he was a nonsmoker, exercised little, used no drugs, and was a "social" drinker.

On examination he appeared generally well, but with a slight pallor. Some borderline palmar erythema (redness) was noted, and there were several spider angiomata (singular: angioma) on his chest and abdomen (see commentary). There was a slight abdominal fullness and the just palpable margin of the liver was smooth and nontender. Asterixis was not present, and other neurological findings were normal.

The palmar erythema, spider angiomata, and slightly enlarged liver suggested liver damage, so the physician questioned the man further on his drinking habits. He again reiterated that he was "just a social drinker," but when pressed to be more specific, his typical drinking pattern proved to be one or two cocktails at lunch, three or four drinks with office associates after work, and a drink or two before dinner. He admitted that at dinner, since his "wife didn't much like wine" he drank most of a bottle of dinner wine. He also was in the habit of having "a little brandy at night" before retiring. His weekend "social" drinking was increased even above this weekday intake, but he insisted that he was never drunk, never craved alcohol, and was not an alcoholic.

Blood tests revealed a hemoglobin level of 10 g/dl, with normal values for BUN and creatinine. Liver function tests were generally abnormal, and his prothrombin time (PTT) was delayed. Serum levels of gamma-glutamyl transpeptidase (GGT) and alkaline phosphatase were both elevated.

On the basis of these findings the patient was referred to a gastroenterologist, who agreed with the probable diagnosis of liver cirrhosis. A liver biopsy was performed and confirmed the cirrhotic damage to the liver.

The patient was advised that there was no treatment for this condition, but a regimen of abstention from alcohol and a balanced and nutritious diet, supplemented by vitamins and iron, might help prevent further decline in his liver's functional capacity. He was also given information on contacting Alcoholics Anonymous and asked to come back for a follow-up, but he never returned.

Commentary

Although sometimes present, jaundice more often appears later in the course of cirrhosis. Spider angiomata are isolated arterioles that dilate and appear as focal red points with tiny radiations. They are often present in women, especially during pregnancy, but they are abnormal in men. Both these and the vasodilation that produces reddening of the palms are linked to liver damage in men by mechanisms that are obscure, but that may involve a damaged liver's reduced inactivation of adrenocortical estrogen. These signs, coupled with the indications of liver enlargement, were sufficient to establish some doubt about the patient's claims to only moderate drinking.

The elevation of both GGT and alkaline phosphatase, while not specific for liver disease, are strongly indicative when there is no evidence of a cardiac, renal, or pulmonary disorder. An increased PTT is attributed to the liver's inadequate synthesis of clotting factors and the low hemoglobin level to reduced absorption of the vitamin K needed for normal erythropoiesis.

Although there was no further contact with this patient, and no evidence that he didn't adhere to the prescribed regimen, his failure to return for any follow-up was not surprising. Many who abuse alcohol have great difficulty in coping with their addiction, and the likelihood that cirrhotic complications will progress to liver failure is unfortunately high.

Key Concepts

1. The liver's immediate exposure to potential damage from newly absorbed microorganisms or toxins is countered by a large functional reserve and a highly developed capacity to regenerate damaged cells (pp. 348–349).

2. Jaundice, the accumulation of bile salts, may be caused by excessive red cell lysis, injury to liver cells, or obstructions that reduce clearance of bile from the liver (pp. 349–350).

3. Liver damage produces a variety of systemic signs and symptoms reflecting the disruption of one or more of the liver's numerous metabolic functions (pp. 350–352).

4. Acute hepatitis is the liver's response to moderate injury from viruses or toxins, which produces a characteristic pattern of nausea, anorexia, fever, and jaundice (p. 352).

5. While HAV typically produces a relatively mild and self-limiting acute hepatitis, HBV infection is more serious in its potential for spread through sexual contact and exposure to blood or saliva (pp. 352–353).

6. HCV is the major cause of posttransfusion hepatitis (p. 353).

7. HBV and some members of the NANB group are associated with an often undiagnosed carrier state, which presents a constant threat of transmission to the noninfected population (pp. 353–354).

8. Some acute hepatitis sufferers progress to chronic hepatitis, with the disease taking either a relatively mild course or a form that can be life-threatening (p. 354).

9. Chronic or severe injury that overwhelms the liver's regenerative capacity causes cirrhosis, which is characterized by scattered areas of focal regeneration separated by sheets of scar tissue (pp. 355–356).

10. Cirrhotic changes in the liver's architecture cause congestion and hypertension in the hepatic portal vessels, producing a variety of complications, some of which may be life-threatening (pp. 356–358).

11. Alcohol abuse is the single most important factor contributing to hepatic cirrhosis in North America (p. 358).

12. Primary liver tumors are rare, but tissue-specific factors and its large blood flow make the liver a site that greatly favors secondary tumor growth (p. 360).

13. Alterations in bile composition can trigger the formation of insoluble gallstones, which are typically composed of cholesterol and other bile constituents (p. 360).

14. Most cholelithiasis is idiopathic, but in some cases an imbalance of plasma or bile constituents can be identified as leading to gallstone formation (p. 361).

15. The major threat of cholelithiasis is obstruction of the bile ducts, which may lead to jaundice, and irritation of the duct or gall bladder walls, presenting the threat of rupture and peritonitis (p. 362).

16. Various liver diagnostic tests are based on analysis of the plasma or urine for evidence of disrupted hepatic function, on imaging techniques that can localize tumors or gallstones, or on needle biopsy for the direct visualization of hepatic tissue (p. 363).

17. Liver transplants to save those with severely damaged tissue are increasingly successful, provided that immune rejection of the implant can be avoided (p. 364).

18. Obstruction of pancreatic flow caused by alcohol-related inflammation, gallstones, or tumors can produce attacks of acute pancreatitis from the destructive affects of pancreatic enzymes on the tissue of the pancreas (pp. 364–366).

REVIEW ACTIVITIES

1. For each of the following conditions, indicate the liver-related problem that contributes to it

   Jaundice

   Hepatic encephalopathy

   Hypoalbuminemia

   Pruritus

   Hypocoagulation

   Steatorrhea

   Kernicterus

   Gynecomastia

2. Explain why the terms infectious hepatitis and serum hepatitis are potentially misleading. With that as a warm-up, explain how hepatitis A and hepatitis B differ (at least three ways). Then point out the meaning of CAH and CPH and the essential differences between them.

3. Examine figure 14.11. Is the section shown in (b) normal? Why are the cells in (b) swollen with lipids? What term describes this condition? What are the dark bands that pass through (b)? Why are they there? What consequences outside the liver often result from this condition?

4. Make a photocopy of figure 14.15. Cut out the boxes and drop them into a container. Then pick out the boxes at random and arrange them to reflect in logical fashion the sequelae of hepatic cirrhosis. Tape them down when you're sure, and draw the appropriate connecting arrows. Now check against the original to verify.

5. Cover the comments column of table 14.4. Now, for each blood or urine test, quickly jot down whether the analyzed substance will be increased or decreased, and why. Uncover the comments column. How did you do? Try this again tomorrow.

6. Look at figure 14.3. Note the position of the bile canaliculi. How do you think they'd be affected by damage to hepatocytes that might cause them to swell? What is the name of the condition in which these bile channels do not develop normally? What can be done for infants born with such a liver defect?

7. Without first checking figures 14.22, or 14.25, list the principal causes of acute pancreatitis. Then name four body organs likely to be affected by the release of pancreatic enzymes from a damaged pancreas.

8. Referring to figure 14.1, speculate on how two conditions described in this chapter might arise from a tumor growing in the vicinity of the ampulla of Vater.

Chapter Fifteen

Renal Pathophysiology

What is man, when you come to think about him, but a minutely set, ingenious machine for turning with infinite artfulness, the red wine of Shiraz into urine?

Isak Dinesen
Seven Gothic Tales

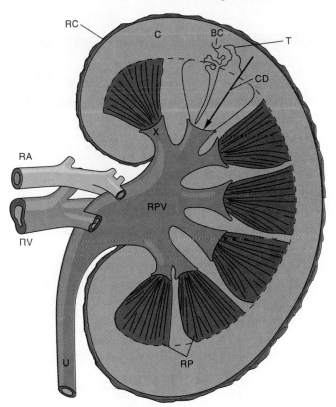

Figure 15.1   Normal renal anatomy. Indicated structures are the renal capsule (RC), the cortex (C), renal pyramids (RP), the renal artery (RA), and renal vein (RV). The renal medulla contains the renal pyramids and lies deep to the broken line. Also indicated are the ureter (U), the renal pelvis (RPV), and a calyx (X). An enlarged nephron tubule (T) with Bowman's capsule (BC) is shown in relation to the cortex and a renal pyramid. The tubule is joined to a collecting duct (CD).

THE NORMAL KIDNEY

A principal function of the kidney is excretion. This process involves the removal of certain substances from the blood and their passage to the body's exterior. Such substances are either toxic or potentially so; hence the kidney's ability to reduce their levels in the blood is an important one. Because of their toxicity, the nitrogen-containing products of protein metabolism—urea, creatinine, and uric acid—are especially significant in renal excretion. Hydrogen ion and several other potentially troublesome substances are also excreted.

A second function of the kidney lies in its ability to directly influence the composition of the body fluids. This renal function is therefore homeostatic, in that it maintains the levels of the particular substances required for optimum cellular functioning. In addition, the kidney is indirectly able to provide homeostatic regulation by means of its secretion of renin and erythropoietin. Release of renin into the blood causes a series of responses that affect the systemic blood pressure both directly by the formation of a vasoactive substance, angiotensin II, and indirectly by renin's effects on sodium ion. The hormone erythropoietin is also secreted by the kidney and serves as a means of regulating normal blood cell production in red bone marrow.

The essential structural features of the kidney are indicated in figure 15.1. These are often used in referring to renal disease, which may be centered in a particular section of the kidney. Note the position of the nephron tubule with respect to the renal cortex and medulla.

The Nephron: Structure

Renal functions derive from the functional unit of the kidney, the **nephron.** Approximately 1 million of these are present in each kidney. The nephron has two distinct components: a tubule and its associated vasculature.

The nephron tubule is an elongated, hollow duct whose walls are one cell thick. **1** One end is modified to form a cup-shaped enlargement, **Bowman's capsule,** whose hollow interior communicates directly with the lumen of the rest of the tubule. Two parts of the tubule are thrown into twists and folds, and between them a characteristic loop is formed as a straight-running portion of the tubule folds back on itself. These are the proximal and distal convoluted tubules and the loop of Henle, respectively (fig. 15.2).

The nephron's vasculature consists of two capillary beds and their associated arterioles and venules. The first capillary bed is the glomerulus. It rests in the cup-shaped hollow of Bowman's capsule with its capillaries' walls in

Distal convoluted tubule

Proximal convoluted tubule

Bowman's capsule

Bowman's space

Glomerulus

Afferent arteriole

Efferent arteriole

From renal artery

To renal artery

Collecting duct

Peritubular capillaries

Loop of Henle

Figure 15.2   The structure of the nephron.

intimate contact with the epithelial cells of the capsule. These cells, called **podocytes,** have an unusual configuration of footlike extensions that provide points of attachment and support for the glomerular vessels **2** (fig. 15.3). Blood flows to the kidney via the renal artery, which ultimately branches to deliver blood to the glomerulus by means of the **afferent arteriole.** Blood then drains from the glomerulus, not by the expected venule, but instead by another arteriole called the **efferent arteriole.** This vessel carried blood from the glomerulus to a second,

larger capillary network. These capillaries, which surround the nephron tubule, are called the **peritubular capillaries.** From these vessels, blood moves into the venous system for removal from the nephron and ultimately from the kidney by the renal vein (fig. 15.4).

The Nephron: Function

The essential task of the nephron is modifying the blood delivered to it so that the blood will have a lesser quantity of toxic products and a composition otherwise adjusted to

Podocyte

Basement membrane

Fenestrated endothelium

Pedicel

Bowman's space

Figure 15.3   The microstructure of the filtration membrane. Fluid from the lumen of the glomerular capillary passes through the perforations (fenestrations) in the endothelium, the basement membrane, and the narrow slits formed by the podocyte's pedicels to arrive in Bowman's space.

meet the demands of homeostasis. How does this modification of the blood occur?

The ability of the nephron to alter the blood's composition is based on three processes. In combination they allow for both the removal of waste products and necessary homeostatic regulation. The first of these processes is **filtration.** The filtration of the blood involves no removal of waste or toxic products, but is instead the physical separation of the blood's formed elements and most of its plasma proteins from the fluid component of the blood. This separation occurs in the glomerulus as a result of blood pressure applied to the **filtration membrane.** The filtration membrane is a filter consisting of the glomerular endothelial cells, **3** their basement membranes (BMs) and the specially modified podocytes of the epithelium of Bowman's capsule. **4** This arrangement allows water and the small molecules dissolved in it to move from the glomerular capillary into the lumen of Bowman's capsule (**Bowman's space**) **5** (fig. 15.3). There, this fluid product of the filtration process is called **glomerular filtrate.** The rate of filtration over 24 hours is the **glomerular filtration rate** (GFR). It has a normal value of about 180 liters per day.

Following the nephron's formation of a filtrate, some further action is required, because if left to itself, filtrate will pass along the tubule to the kidney's collecting system, the urinary bladder, and finally to the body's exterior. This means that anything in the glomerular blood is inside the body and anything in the tubule is outside; there is no middle ground. As a result of filtration our body fluids are being lost.

To cope with this situation, the nephron employs the second principal mechanism of renal function: **selective reabsorption.** By this process, substances in the filtrate pass from the nephron's lumen back into the blood of the peritubular capillaries, and their loss is prevented. They have been reabsorbed and hence retained for the body's use (fig. 15.5). Note, however, that not all of the constituents of filtrate are reabsorbed. Some are allowed to remain in the

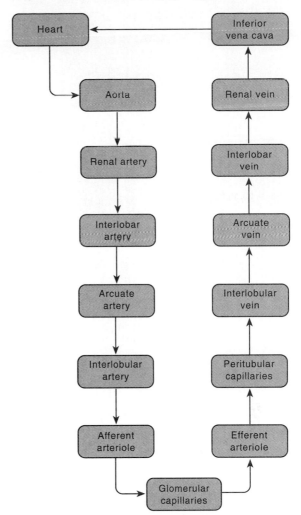

Figure 15.4   The sequence of blood flow through the renal vasculature. In essence, blood entering the kidney is directed to a nephron. After processing by the nephron, blood is returned to the systemic veins.

lumen and will be excreted. Thus there is a selection process involved in reabsorption. It is based, essentially, on the relative permeability of the tubule wall to the various filtrate constituents. Some substances may pass to the peritubular spaces by simple diffusion through the tubule wall, whereas others are carried by specific membrane transport systems.

With certain substances, the nephron employs a third mechanism to bring about adjustments in the makeup of the contents of the nephron tubule. It is called **tubular secretion,** and involves the movement of substances from the blood of the peritubular capillaries into the tubule lumen (fig. 15.5). Tubular secretion in this way adds to the substances to be excreted in the urine. (The term tubular secretion is defined in the context of excretion into the lumen and should not be confused with the more general concept of secretion, where the substance that passes from a cell serves some useful purpose.) As in the case of selective reabsorption, a system of simple diffusion and specific

Blood

Glomerular filtration

Tubular reabsorption

Tubular secretion

Urine

Figure 15.5   Essential mechanisms of nephron blood processing and urine production.

Table 15.1	Comparative Composition of Renal Fluids	
Blood	**Filtrate**	**Urine**
Formed elements	Trace	Trace
H_2O	H_2O	
H_2O_E	H_2O_E	H_2O_E
Plasma proteins	Trace	Trace
Na^+	Na^+	
Na^+_E	Na^+_E	Na^+_E
K^+	K^+	
K^+_E	K^+_E	K^+_E
HCO_3^-	HCO_3^-	
$HCO_3^-{}_E$	$HCO_3^-{}_E$	$HCO_3^-{}_E$
Glucose	Glucose	
Amino acids	Amino acids	
H^+		
H^+_E	H^+_E	H^+_E
Urea	Urea	Urea
Creatinine	Creatinine	Creatinine
Uric acid	Uric acid	Uric acid
Cl^-	Cl^-	
Cl^-_E	Cl^-_E	Cl^-_E
Mg^{++}	Mg^{++}	
Mg^{++}_E	Mg^{++}_E	Mg^{++}_E
NH_3	NH_3	
NH_{3E}	$NH_4^+{}_E$	$NH_4^+{}_E$

The subscript E indicates a quantity in excess of the homeostatic optimum. These are excreted in the urine with metabolic wastes such as urea, uric acid, and creatinine, as well as others not indicated in the table. Essential filtrate components are retained by reabsorption from filtrate. (NH_3 is converted to NH_4^+ in the nephron tubule.) The essential similarity of plasma and filtrate reflects the nonspecific nature of the filtration process. Urine composition is determined by the tubule cells as they process filtrate by means of selective reabsorption and tubular secretion.

membrane transport mechanisms is involved, the latter in particular. Filtration, reabsorption, and tubular secretion rates are subject to variation based on the body's overall need to excrete or retain various substances. In this way, these nephron processes form the basis of renal homeostatic functions.

Urine Production

It should be apparent from the preceding discussion that the excretion of a particular constituent of the blood plasma is determined by its ability to be filtered, the degree to which it is reabsorbed, and the amount of it, if any, that is added to the nephron lumen by tubular secretion mechanisms. All such excreted substances are passed to the urinary bladder for elimination in the form of urine. Urine is therefore derived from the blood plasma and contains anything that has been filtered and/or secreted but not reabsorbed. Some of these urine constituents are toxic if allowed to reach high levels in the tissues. Others are present in the urine because their levels exceed homeostatic requirements. For example, water, sodium ion, and bicarbonate ion are not in themselves toxic. However, if their respective levels are not precisely maintained, serious problems can arise. Normally, any such substances present in urine represent amounts in excess of those required for homeostatic balance. Table 15.1 compares the composition of the blood, nephron filtrate, and urine. It shows that blood and filtrate composition differ only in the filtrate's almost complete lack of formed elements and plasma proteins. In comparing the filtrate and urine, it can be seen that all substances not toxic or present to excess in filtrate remain in the tubule to form urine.

ALTERED RENAL FUNCTION

Since renal disease involves inadequate renal function, it typically involves some degree of waste retention or of fluid water and electrolyte imbalance. Several etiologies and patterns of pathogenesis are recognized as contributing to loss of nephron function. In many cases, this loss is reversible, but nephrons may be permanently lost. The large number of nephrons in the kidney seems to allow for a wide safety margin, and as more and more losses occur, existing nephrons can increase in size, enabling them to process more filtrate. This hypertrophy response can't com-

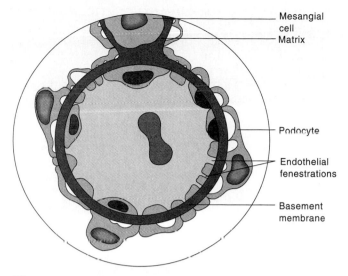

Figure 15.6 Cross section through a glomerular capillary, showing its fenestrated endothelium, podocytes, and their pedicels. Note that mesangial cells are present in a matrix that is continuous with the basement membrane of the capillary.

pensate completely, however, and functional deterioration continues, with lost nephrons being replaced by scar tissue. Initially, malfunction may derive from a problem in the nephron itself or from infections that arise in the urinary tract or collecting system and then spread to the tissues of the renal medulla. Either situation may quickly resolve, but if the problem persists, it can involve the permanent loss of entire nephrons.

Glomerular Disorders

The filtration process provides the fluid that tubule cells modify to produce urine. It follows, then, that any change in the glomerular components that make up the filtration membrane will have an effect on the filtration process. Unwanted substances may be retained, or needed substances may be lost.

Impaired filtration is the common element in a broad range of kidney disorders. Before we turn to the details of these conditions, it will be useful to analyze figure 15.6, which presents a simplified section through a single glomerular capillary loop lying near the epithelium of Bowman's capsule. Note the supporting mesangial cells and their intercellular matrix, which is continuous with the capillary basement membrane. These mesangial elements are not included in figure 15.3.

In normal filtration, fluid passes from the glomerular capillary lumen to Bowman's space through the endothelial fenestrations, the basement membrane, and the slits formed by the pedicels. Therefore, any disease process that alters or distorts any of these components will have an effect on filtration. The conditions that will be described shortly are examples involving loss of pedicels, and immune-mediated

BM damage that affects glomerular function. Proliferation of endothelial, mesangial, or Bowman's capsule cells may also occur to obstruct blood flow, filtrate flow, or both.

Terminology

A complex terminology has arisen around the various glomerular disorders, reflecting the focus of the clinician, histologist, and pathologist. Glomerular disorders are usually grouped under the term **glomerulonephritis** (GN), even though some glomerular disease lacks a clearly inflammatory component. More precise usage is emerging, but traditional usage is difficult to change.

From the clinician's perspective, GN is described as acute, rapidly progressive, or chronic. **Acute GN** is typically benign and relatively quick to resolve, whereas **rapidly progressive GN** **6** is a swiftly advancing disorder that can lead to death in a matter of a few months. **Chronic GN** is long-term disease that may take from years to decades to run its course.

From the pathologist's point of view, the distribution of the glomerular lesions throughout the cortical tissue might well be significant, and the terminology will reflect this fact. **Diffuse GN** involves most or all glomeruli, whereas in **focal GN,** only some of the glomeruli are abnormal. The term **segmental GN** indicates that some capillary loops in a given glomerulus are involved while others are unaffected.

Study of the histology of glomerular disease gives rise to still other terms differentiating three types of glomerular change. In **minimal change** disease, **7** little histological alteration is seen except for changes in the processes of the podocytes. Although the abnormality may be histologically minimal, the defect can certainly give rise to clinical disease. This is one of the conditions often grouped with GN, even though it lacks an inflammatory component. The classification of a GN as **proliferative** indicates an increase in some cellular component of the glomerulus or the tissues associated with it. Thus the capsular cells, glomerular endothelium, or supporting mesangium might proliferate and cause interference with the filtration process (fig. 15.7a). Another histological change involves the complexing of antibody with antigens of the basement membrane of the glomerular capillaries. When antibody deposition forms a uniform layer, the result is a smooth, unbroken, membranelike appearance, and the condition is designated **membranous GN** (fig. 15.8).

A complication in describing a particular pattern of GN arises from histological complexity. For example, both cellular proliferation and basement membrane thickening may be present. In such cases, the term **membranoproliferative GN** is appropriate, if cumbersome. Terminology can be further complicated by adding information regarding the distribution of the lesions, as in **diffuse proliferative GN.**

Figure 15.7   (*a*) Normal renal cortex with glomeruli and various tubule sections. (*b*) In proliferative glomerulonephritis, the increased number and size of the glomerular components give rise to the appearance of congestion in this photomicrograph (1). Note the tubular atrophy (2). (*c*) Chronic pyelonephritis. Some glomeruli are normal (2), while others have been replaced by scar tissue (1). Tubular necrosis is extensive and numerous inflammatory cells have infiltrated (3). (*d*) Chronic glomerulonephritis. Glomeruli are enlarged and exhibit some hyalinization (1). Proliferation of glomerular and capsular cells has almost obliterated Bowman's space (2). Tubules are atrophied and there is extensive scarring (3).

However you may encounter these terms, if you recognize their patterns of use, and also the user's frame of reference, you will get insight into the essential nature of the glomerular abnormality.

Pathogenesis of GN

From research into the pathogenesis of GN, the animal and human evidence indicates that the dominant factor in the destruction of the glomerulus is the immune system. Its activation gives rise to a sequence of events that damages or occludes the glomerular capillaries. This destructive process is initiated by the presence of immune complexes in the glomerulus. These may form in two ways. Antibody against the glomerular basement membrane may reach the glomerulus and bind to capillary basement membranes. Alternatively, antibody against a circulating antigen may combine with it in the plasma to form a complex that is sub-

sequently trapped at the filtration membrane. In either case, complement activation and/or inflammatory changes follow, producing cell damage, scarring, and glomerular loss.

Immune complexes produce the great majority of acute GN. As they become trapped in the BM, they activate complement, producing chemotactic proteins that promote infiltration of the glomerulus by macrophages and polymorphonuclear leukocytes. These cells engulf the immune complexes, releasing enzymes and toxins that disrupt the capillary walls by destroying their endothelial lining cells and BM. The exposed BM promotes platelet aggregation, which is followed by fibrin formation and deposition in the glomerulus (fig. 15.9). Fibrin thus formed will subsequently be organized and replaced by scar tissue, with resulting permanent loss of the glomerulus.

In chronic GN, the prolonged course of the disease seems related to the enormous reserve capacity of the kidneys. Glomerular malfunction and destruction may go unnoticed as immune or other damage proceeds, since the

Figure 15.8   Interaction of circulating antibody and glomerular basement membrane antigen produces a pattern of deposition that appears linear in microscope preparations. Compare with figure 15.6.

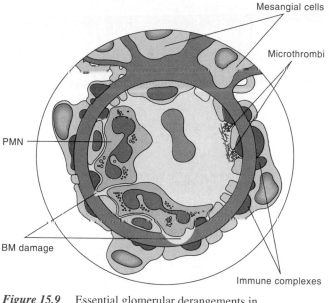

Figure 15.9   Essential glomerular derangements in glomerulonephritis. Dark antigen/antibody complexes are deposited in the basement membrane, producing a granular appearance in microscopic studies. PMNs are disrupting the glomerulus and fibrin deposition is also under way. Proliferation of mesangial cells, their supporting matrix, and the basement membrane are also present.

Histological Staining and GN Diagnosis

Special histological staining techniques can demonstrate the difference between the deposition of immune complexes that are preformed in the plasma and anti-BM antibody that reacts with the BM. When the uncomplexed antibody is exposed to the BM, it can bind to it all along its surface to produce a uniform, linear staining pattern. The preformed complexes, by contrast, produce a granular appearance as they are trapped at their points of filtration, forming nonuniform clumps. This difference can be useful in diagnosis when tissue from a renal biopsy is specially stained, and you may encounter reference to the staining pattern in lab reports.

undamaged nephrons in reserve are able to provide essentially normal function. Unfortunately, the emergence of signs and symptoms is an indication that the reserve nephrons have been destroyed with no possibility of regeneration. Another element is the defensive clearing of complexes after their deposition. Migrating macrophages and the phagocytic mesangial cells can perform this job to a degree, delaying complex deposition. However, continued deposition can overwhelm them and give rise to glomerular destruction (fig. 15.7*d*).

In proliferative GN, **8** the specific mechanisms that bring about the increased production of endothelial, epithelial, or mesangial components of the glomerulus and Bowman's capsule are not clearly understood. They appear to be responses to damage or inflammatory changes. The pathogenesis of GN is summarized in figure 15.10.

Having noted the destructive effects of the immune response in the pathogenesis of GN, let us consider the source of immune complexes or anti-BM antibody. In the case of anti-BM antibody, the problem is one of autoimmunity. The mechanisms whereby antibodies against one's self-antigens are formed were considered in chapter 5. In the context of GN, there is little precise information, but some cases are linked to viral (hepatitis B) or bacterial (streptococcal) infections. The presumption is that these have antigenic components that elicit antibody formation. Complexes then form in the plasma, and BM deposition follows as the blood carries them to the glomeruli. **9** In most cases, however, the initiating antigen is unknown. Minimal change disease is interesting in this regard, in that not only does it involve no inflammatory damage, but no immune complexes are deposited in glomeruli.

In addition to the glomerular disorders described here, various systemic diseases produce secondary glomerular disease. These are discussed in detail in their appropriate chapters. Some important examples are diabetes mellitus, systemic lupus erythematosus, Goodpasture's syndrome, and bacterial endocarditis.

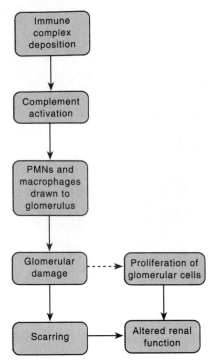

Figure 15.10   Pathogenesis of glomerulonephritis. The broken line indicates uncertainty as to the cause of proliferation of glomerular elements.

Mechanisms Underlying the Nephrotic and Nephritic Syndromes

You may be wondering how, in the nephritic syndrome, red cells can escape a damaged glomerulus while much smaller proteins like albumin are retained in the blood. The explanation has to do with a specialized property of the glomerular BM. Its components carry negative charges, which repel the negative charges on plasma proteins. In the nephrotic syndrome, BM damage disrupts these charges. No longer repelled, protein can more easily escape. Over the extensive glomerular BM surface, protein loss by this mechanism can be significant.

In the nephritic syndrome, capillary endothelial damage is associated with cellular proliferation. These changes may generate pressures that can expel erythrocytes at points where the endothelium gives way. This would occur only at certain points, allowing red cell loss but minimizing protein escape because the BM and its negative repulsive charges remain largely intact.

Sequelae of Glomerular Change

Regardless of the specific sequence of pathogenesis, damage to the glomerulus yields a predictable pattern of nephron malfunction. Essentially, the altered glomerulus will retain substances normally lost and allow the escape of plasma constituents that are normally retained. Of the many different glomerular disorders, all converge to form two clinical patterns: the **nephrotic syndrome** and the **nephritic syndrome.**

Nephrotic Syndrome This is the clinical condition in which the dominant feature is a pronounced proteinuria caused by the inability of the glomeruli to retain protein. Because they are small, the albumins are the first to pass a defective filtration membrane and, once they are in the tubule, their reabsorption is limited. They are also the most numerous of plasma proteins, so their loss can quickly produce systemic effects. The most important of these is systemic edema, arising because hypoalbuminemia reduces blood osmotic pressure so that fluid cannot readily return to the blood from the tissue spaces. As glomerular damage reduces overall filtration, a falling GFR activates reflexes that promote aldosterone secretion. This hormone in turn promotes salt and water retention, which often complicates the edema problem. Figure 15.11 summarizes the essential elements of pathogenesis in the nephrotic syndrome.

Minimal change glomerular disease and membranous GN most usually produce the nephrotic syndrome. Proliferative GN is another condition that can be expected to produce proteinuria. **Focal nephrosclerosis** is a noninflammatory glomerular disease characterized by segments of the glomerulus that are lost to scarring. **10** **11** It may accompany other glomerular diseases or arise in conjunction with nonrenal disorders such as AIDS. Damage in focal nephrosclerosis tends to produce the nephrotic syndrome.

Nephritic Syndrome In this condition, the clinical picture is dominated by the results of glomerular damage that restricts filtration and allows erythrocytes to escape the blood to reach the urine (hematuria). A reduced GFR gives rise to reduced urinary output (**oliguria**), water retention, and the accumulation of nitrogenous wastes in the blood (**azotemia**). Glomerular damage may also allow protein loss, but this is a variable occurrence and the amounts are less than in the nephrotic syndrome (fig. 15.12).

The nephritic syndrome typically follows proliferative changes in the glomerulus. For example, **postinfection GN** produces mild symptoms in children, usually after streptococcal or other bacterial infections. It usually resolves with minimal intervention. On the other hand, membranoproliferative GN may produce a nephritic syndrome that slowly progresses to the point of renal failure. Following proliferative changes, the increasing mass of glomerular, capsular, or basement membrane material impedes normal blood flow, thus reducing filtration. The decreasing demand on tubule cells results in their atrophy in response. Ultimately, lost nephrons are replaced by scarring. In rare cases, rapidly progressive GN produces an acute and severe

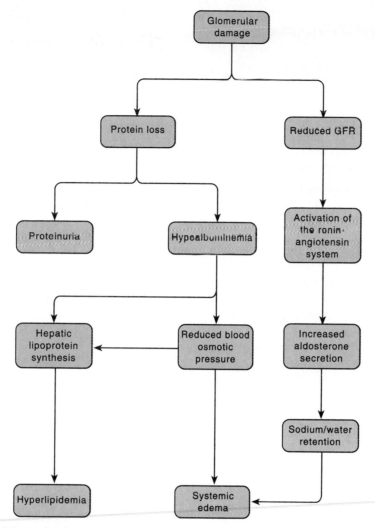

Figure 15.11   Pathogenesis of the nephrotic syndrome.

Figure 15.12   Pathogenesis of the nephritic syndrome. Although fluid retention and some protein loss occur in the nephritic syndrome, edema does not usually develop.

nephritic syndrome that does not respond to therapy. Complete renal failure is the result. Much rapidly progressive GN is idiopathic, but may follow infection (table 15.2).

Tubulointerstitial Disorders

The renal medulla contains the straight-running arms of Henle's loop and the collecting ducts that receive processed filtrate from the nephrons. The remaining medullary tissues, consisting of a supporting intercellular matrix and the peritubular capillaries, are referred to as the renal interstitium. Problems arising in one area have immediate impact on the other and so may be difficult to separate in diagnosis. Just as glomerular disease produces clinical consequences based on defective filtration, tubulointerstitial disorders are based on altered tubular processing. Generally, the consequences are water and sodium loss and the retention of acid. There are two principal forms of tubulointerstitial disease, **pyelonephritis** and **interstitial nephritis.**

Table 15.2	The Glomerular Disorders Most Commonly Associated with the Nephrotic and Nephritic Syndromes

Nephrotic Syndrome	Nephritic Syndrome
Minimal change disease	Membranoproliferative GN
Membranous GN	Acute, diffuse, proliferative GN
Membranoproliferative GN	Postinfection GN
Focal glomerulosclerosis	Rapidly progressive GN

Pyelonephritis

Pyelonephritis (PN) is an inflammatory condition of the renal interstitium that also affects the calyces and pelvis of the collecting system. **12** Glomeruli are not normally affected, or are only minimally so, unless the condition is prolonged. Bacterial infections are the usual cause of such inflammation, although viral or other agents may be involved. Pyelonephritis is the most common renal disease, the kidneys' involvement deriving from the frequent occurrence of urinary tract infections in the adult. Chronic PN is the second most common source of renal failure, next to chronic glomerulonephritis.

PN may be **hematogenous,** with blood-borne bacteria from an infected site being carried to the kidney. In such cases, the typical result is abscess formation and necrosis in the renal cortex. Subsequent spread to lower parts of the urinary tract distinguishes descending PN from the much more common cases (over 90%) of ascending PN, in which bacteria reach the kidney from lower parts of the urinary tract. These are often of fecal origin (e.g., *Escherichia coli, Proteus,* and *Enterococcus* species), but vaginal and exogenous organisms are also commonly involved (fig. 15.13). It would seem that the observed higher incidence of ascending PN in the female is related to the shorter length of the urethra in that sex. A longer urethra and antibacterial properties of the prostate gland secretions favor a lower incidence in the male.

Pathogenesis

Normally the urine and the urinary tract are sterile, excepting the distal urethra. With normal flushing of the urinary tract by the usual pattern of urine flow, bacteria cannot proliferate. If bladder emptying is incomplete, the remaining urine may serve as a growth medium for urethral bacteria. Bladder abnormalities that involve inadequate urine expulsion pressures or blockage of urine outflow are the main sources of incomplete bladder emptying. Factors contributing to obstruction of the urinary tract are urinary calculi, or kidney stones (see the section on urinary calculi), prostatic hypertrophy in the male, pregnancy

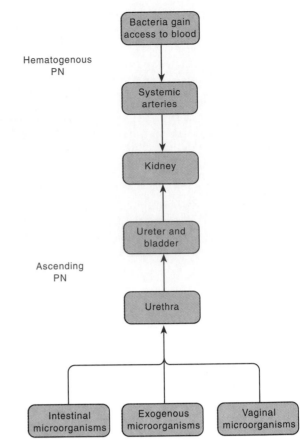

Figure 15.13   Etiology of pyelonephritis.

(involving increased pelvic pressure), pelvic inflammations related to disease or trauma, and tumors.

Once bacterial growth is established, ascent to the ureters, collecting system, and kidney may follow. The driving force for ascent up the urinary tract seems to depend on a structural defect in the joining of the ureter to the bladder. Normally the joining provides for closure of the ureter during bladder contraction, preventing backflow. In a subset of the population, this mechanism is deficient and bladder contraction develops pressures that can force urine and bacteria up the urinary tract. Those who lack the normal protection against this backflow have a greater predisposition to developing PN.

Two types of PN, acute and chronic, can be distinguished on the basis of the duration and severity of their signs and symptoms.

Acute Pyelonephritis Acute PN is a common, comparatively mild condition of primarily bacterial etiology, ranking as the second most common infectious disease, after those of the respiratory system. It involves inflammation of renal tissues, which can lead to suppuration and necrosis **13** as well as bleeding in the mucous membrane of the adjacent collecting system (fig. 15.14). Acute PN may involve one or both kidneys and is characterized by sudden onset accompanied by pain, chills, and fever, **pyuria** (pus

Figure 15.14 Abscesses are easily seen in this view of the kidney in PN, as pale areas in the medulla (1). The surfaces of the renal pelvis and calyces are inflamed (2) and the entire kidney is swollen.
This is the kidney of an elderly man who was admitted to hospital with seizures. He was unable to convey any elements of his medical history that might aid in diagnosis, and he was admitted in the hope that antiseizure medication would stabilize him. His urinary incontinence was assumed to be related to his seizures, and when a urinary catheter was inserted, his prostate was found to be enlarged. Although his seizure activity subsided somewhat, he soon became feverish and his urine became cloudy and odorous. Culture revealed E. coli *to be the contaminant. In spite of antibiotic therapy, the infection quickly became systemic and he died. Autopsy revealed acute bilateral pyelonephritis, probably from an ascending infection that had become established as a result of urinary obstruction. The swollen kidney shown here has inflamed calyces, and pale abscesses can be seen in the medulla.*

in the urine), and bacteriuria, although the latter is not always observed. This acute form of the disease is typically mild and self-limiting, but overwhelming infections can lead to necrosis of the renal medulla, which is followed by renal failure. **14** Although treatment with antibiotics is normally successful, recurrent infection is not uncommon.

Chronic Pyelonephritis The devastating pattern of development in chronic PN consists of a slow, long-term deterioration of renal function that is often asymptomatic until substantial renal damage has occurred. As in the case of GN, this leads to loss of functional parenchyma, which is replaced by scar tissue (fig. 15.7c). Because of the slow onset of the disease, the patient is normally not moved to seek help until end-stage renal failure develops. This is usually indicated by the kidneys' inability to prevent water loss, regulate pH, or retain sodium. Grossly, the surface of the kidney shows evidence of substantial scarring where infection has destroyed the tubulointerstitium and, often, the adjacent cortex (fig. 4.15). Where urinary obstruction is involved, long-term back pressure produces dilation of the collecting system and proximal ureter. In a significant number of cases, chronic PN results in renal failure, necessitating dialysis or kidney transplantation.

Interstitial Nephritis

This term denotes the tubulointerstitial disorders that have an etiology other than infection. The principal damaging agents are therapeutic drugs, other exogenous toxins, or endogenous substances that are toxic to the interstitium. One aspect of this problem is large blood flow. Although they represent less than 1% of the body's weight, the kidneys receive 20–25% of the resting cardiac output. As a result, the entire plasma volume circulates through the kidneys about 60 times a day. Any circulatory substance with toxic effects will have numerous opportunities to exert them on renal tissues.

A number of antibiotic and analgesic preparations, as well as lithium salts and the increasingly used immunosuppressant cyclosporine, are implicated in interstitial nephritis. **15** Note, in particular, that chronic pain sufferers such as rheumatoid arthritics or those with low back pain have a significant risk of nephrotoxic damage from their long-term analgesic ingestion. As well, derangements that increase plasma levels of calcium and uric acid, e.g., gout and polycythemia, or that decrease potassium levels have roles in its etiology. Lead, mercury, and cadmium poisoning can produce interstitial nephritis, but these occur less commonly.

Selected nephrotoxins are presented in table 15.3. Signs and symptoms of interstitial nephritis reflect evidence of varying degrees of tubular malfunction. Additional effects based on hypersensitivity reaction to the drug may also develop: fever, skin rashes, hematuria.

Renal Vascular Disorders

Many vascular disorders have prominent renal effects even though, for the most part, the renal vessels are themselves not abnormal. For example, atherosclerotic narrowing of the aorta and renal artery can produce renal ischemia that will affect kidney function. Emboli from an atherosclerotic aorta may cause diffuse cortical damage. Similar damage is also seen in circulatory shock, where falling BHP is the cause of ischemia.

Other systemic disorders have effects on the renal vasculature. In diabetes mellitus, the glomerular capillaries are affected (see chapter 17). In systemic hypertension, the renal arterioles undergo thickening, the condition referred to in chapter 9 as arteriolosclerosis. In the context of the kidney, this arteriolar thickening is known as **nephrosclerosis.** It typically results in renal ischemia and scattered areas of atrophy and necrosis.

The two types of systemic hypertension produce different patterns of nephrosclerosis. In **benign nephrosclerosis,** the damage is usually mild, with minimal polyuria or filtration abnormalities and little risk of renal failure. As we indicated in chapter 9, the biggest risk in benign hypertension is its related cardiac and cerebrovascular morbidity.

The renal vascular problems associated with malignant hypertension, **malignant nephrosclerosis,** are much more likely to lead to serious complications and renal failure.

Table 15.3	Selected Nephrotoxins

Metals

Mercury compounds	Cadmium
Arsenic	Copper
Uranium	

Organic Solvents

Carbon tetrachloride	Tetrachloroethylene
Methanol	Ethylene glycol (automobile antifreeze)

Therapeutic Agents

Antibiotics

Ampicillin	Penicillin
Methicillin	Sulfonamides
Tetracycline	Streptomycin

Analgesics

Aspirin (ASA)	Acetaminophen

Various Diuretics and Nsaids

Insecticides

Chlorinated hydrocarbons	Biphenyl compounds

Miscellaneous

Carbon monoxide	Cresol
Mushroom poisons	Mannitol

Figure 15.15 Staghorn calculus. This large kidney stone is, essentially, a cast of the renal pelvis and calyces. It resembles a deer's antler.
This staghorn calculus was an incidental autopsy finding in a middle-aged male who died of an acute MI. In this view the loss of renal cortex and medulla is apparent. The pelvis is filled with the stone, which sends rough projections into the calyces. In addition to the nephrolithiasis, microscopic studies confirmed the presence of tubular atrophy and scarring consistent with chronic pyelonephritis.

A key feature in this condition is the escape of fibrinogen to the vessel walls, whose permeability has been altered, probably because of the pronounced pressure increases to which the walls have been subjected. Diffuse coagulation follows, **16** blocking blood flow and producing severe renal ischemia. In response, the renin-angiotensin system is activated, triggering reflexes that increase the already elevated BHP. Cycles of further ischemia and pressure rises continue to exaggerate the problem. Another consequence of diffuse coagulation within the narrowed arterioles is trauma to red blood cells. As they are driven over fibrin deposits, their membranes are damaged. The damaged erythrocytes are cleared from the circulation faster than they can be replaced, and a **microangiopathic hemolytic anemia** develops.

With the increased kidney damage associated with malignant nephrosclerosis, renal dysfunction gives rise to hematuria, proteinuria, and decreased acid and waste excretion. If untreated, it will steadily progress to complete renal failure, often within one year. Therapeutic intervention to lower blood pressure can greatly reduce mortality.

URINARY CALCULI

The process of **nephrolithiasis,** or **urolithiasis,** involves the formation of insoluble stones, or **calculi,** in the urinary tract. A calculus usually forms in a single kidney. Once formed, it may remain in the kidney's collecting system or be passed through the ureter and then to the urinary bladder. Often it will lodge at some point of the tract to obstruct urine flow. **17**

Most urolithiasis presents only minor problems, because small stones that remain in the kidney are well tolerated, and others may be unknowingly passed in the urine. Thus, although the incidence of calculi seen at autopsy is relatively high (1 in 100), the incidence of hospitalization for urolithiasis is quite low (1 in 1000). The disorder is three times more likely to occur in males than in females, with peak incidence at 30–50 years of age.

Calculi vary in size and number. One or several stones may form, ranging in size from the microscopic to those with diameters of several centimeters. They may have smoothly rounded or polygonal shapes, or their surfaces may be jagged and rough. **18** When a large calculus forms in the renal pelvis with extension into the calyces, the resulting shape resembles a deer antler and is referred to as a staghorn calculus **19** (fig. 15.15). Most calculi are composed of crystals of inorganic ions imbedded in a matrix of protein. Many different ions have been found in calculi, with composition generally reflecting pathogenesis. Most commonly involved are calcium, oxalate, phosphate, and urate ions.

Stone formation is usually associated with an increased urine concentration of the ions found in the stone. The change in concentration most often derives from increased renal excretion, but might also involve a diminished urine volume, as in dehydration states. Even when urine concentration is normal, changes in urinary acidity can lead to stone formation. For example, a lowered urine pH favors precipitation of uric acid, while a more alkaline urine predisposes to phosphate stone formation.

Etiology in urolithiasis is complex and usually reflects disturbances in the metabolism of the ions involved. Most cases involve **hypercalciuria** (high levels of calcium in the urine), which may be the result of an idiopathic increase in intestinal calcium absorption, with an attendant increase in the need for calcium excretion. Alternatively, excessive calcium absorption, and thus an increase in the kidneys' calcium excretion burden, may be due to increased dietary levels of vitamin D. In the parathyroid glands, an elevated secretion of parahormone causes plasma calcium levels to increase. Again, the excess calcium ion must be excreted by the kidney, and the resulting hypercalciuria may then contribute to stone formation. Not only calcium but other substances, such as oxalate ion, may become incorporated into calculi as a result of the increased urinary excretion that follows increased dietary intake. Urinary tract infections and chronic pyelonephritis also predispose to urolithiasis.

After obstruction of the urinary tract by a stone, urinary stasis and increased back pressure may result. This can lead to destruction of renal parenchyma, a predisposition to secondary infection, and further renal damage.

The presence of a renal stone may often be asymptomatic, but if a large stone enters the ureter, **renal colic** follows. This is pain of an exquisite and excruciating character, originating at the ureter and often radiating to the upper leg. It derives from the periodic waves of ureteral peristalsis that press upon the stone. Chills and fever are often associated with the ureteral passage of a stone, and hematuria often follows, the result of ureteral damage from abrasion of the mucosa.

In cases of unacceptable pain, infection, or bleeding, obstructing calculi that are not passed from the urinary tract may be removed surgically or with instruments introduced into the urinary tract via the urethra. Alternatively, cystoscopes introduced into the ureter or collecting system can be used to break stones mechanically or by ultrasound energy, so that they can be passed in the urine. Once the stones are removed, prognosis is excellent.

If there is no pressing need for surgery, therapy may simply be directed toward reducing the stones to a size easily passed to the bladder for evacuation. Some drugs can

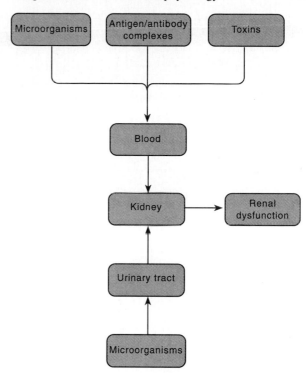

Figure 15.16   Pathways to renal damage and dysfunction.

cause existing stones to dissolve or can prevent their enlargement. Other drugs can help by reducing excessive excretion or by changing urine pH, which aids in dissolving the stone.

A condition related to urolithiasis, but only about one-tenth as common, is **nephrocalcinosis.** This involves the formation of minute, insoluble calcium deposits in the nephron tubules and collecting ducts. Fine crystals also form at the papillae. Nephrocalcinosis may occur alone or in association with nephrolithiasis.

OVERVIEW OF ETIOLOGY IN RENAL DYSFUNCTION

Clinicians often use a system that distinguishes different patterns of etiology in renal disorders. It is based on the position of the kidney with respect to its blood supply and the urinary tract that drains it. These components are, of course, essential to normal renal functioning, but each can also be a source of potentially damaging agents. Microorganisms can be blood-borne, or they can reach the kidney via the urinary tract. The blood may also deliver antibodies or immune complexes (earlier implicated in glomerular damage) or any number of toxins also previously considered. The situation is further complicated by the high volumes of blood that perfuse the renal vessels, providing high exposure to any damaging agents that might be present. On the other hand, the dependence of renal function on high blood flow rates can be a source of disruption should blood flow be reduced. Figure 15.16 summarizes the essentials.

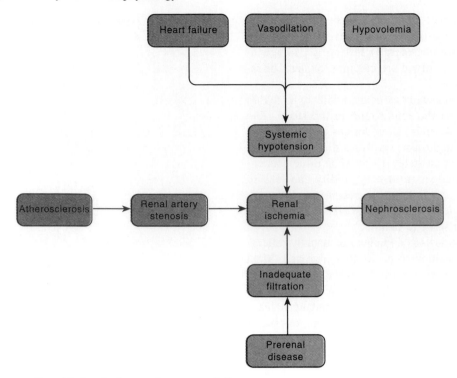

Figure 15.17   The causes of renal ischemia that produce prerenal disease.

Given the situation of the kidney with respect to its blood supply and the urinary tract, it can be useful to classify renal disease as **prerenal, renal** (sometimes **intrarenal**), or **postrenal.** In essence, this system describes renal problems whose root cause lies in the renal blood supply, the kidney itself, or in the urinary tract, respectively.

Prerenal Disease

The essential problem in prerenal disease is renal ischemia. However it may come about, any reduction of renal blood flow produces a state of inadequate glomerular filtration, with a consequent decline in the kidney's ability to meet the need for homeostatic regulation and excretion. Clinically this produces a characteristic oliguria and loss of excretory function.

Figure 15.17 indicates the essential ways in which renal ischemia might arise to produce the signs and symptoms of prerenal disease. They should look familiar because they were mentioned earlier, in the section on renal vascular disorders. An important one of these is renal artery stenosis. Atherosclerosis, and the thrombosis often associated with it, is the usual cause of the vessel's narrowing.

A second cause of renal ischemia is low systemic blood pressure, which leads to reduced perfusion of the renal vessels. With normal fluctuations in systemic arterial pressure, the kidney arterioles respond to provide a constant glomerular filtration pressure. This process is known as **renal autoregulation.** However, in circulatory shock

states, arterial pressure falls below the kidney's compensation capacity, and filtration is compromised. The specific mechanisms underlying the development of circulatory shock were treated in some detail in chapter 11, so you will quickly recognize the obvious carcinogenic, vascular, and hypovolemic mechanisms as being relevant. In cases of severe renal ischemia, perfusion may be inadequate to maintain renal tissues, and kidney necrosis results. This condition of reduced filtration and renal necrosis is called **shock kidney.**

A third major source of renal ischemia is the nephrosclerosis associated with systemic hypertension (as opposed to hypotension). Various other conditions are also known to reduce renal blood flow, the hepatorenal syndrome mentioned in the last chapter, for example. Most of these are relatively uncommon.

Postrenal Disease

The essential problem in **postrenal** disease is urinary obstruction. With blockage of flow through the urinary tract, often exaggerated by a faulty joining of the ureter and bladder, back pressure causes urine to accumulate in the kidney. This can compromise excretory function and directly damage renal tissues. [20]

There are two principal sources of urinary tract obstruction. One is the lodging of a kidney stone (or stones) within the ureter or renal pelvis. A second is blockage or compression of the tract by swollen or neoplastic tissues. In males, obstruction arises in the relatively common problem of prostatic hyperplasia, where prostate enlargement directly compresses the urethra. [21]

Before we proceed to the third renal etiology classification, note that in both prerenal and postrenal disease, the kidney is initially able to function normally. That is, a problem first arises outside the kidney, and altered renal function then follows. Without renal ischemia or urinary tract obstruction, the kidney continues to function normally.

Renal Disease

Renal, or intrarenal, disease is different from prerenal or postrenal disease in that the problem stems from changes within the kidney itself. One example is the glomerular changes in GN that lead to development of the nephritic and nephrotic syndromes. The other major intrarenal diseases arise in the tubulointerstitium. Remember that although bacterial infections are the most common causes of these infections, drug and toxic damage can also be significant.

RENAL FAILURE

Renal damage, from whatever source, sooner or later produces signs of renal failure, which may be either acute or chronic. Since both conditions are associated with some degree of uremia, we will consider this topic first.

Uremia

In renal failure, progressive loss of renal function results in the accumulation of waste products, particularly those deriving from the metabolism of protein. Carbohydrate and lipid are metabolized to carbon dioxide and water, which are easily excreted, but protein metabolites are more difficult to excrete. The best known of these are urea, the guanilidines (creatine, creatinine, guanidine), and uric acid. Of these, urea is the most toxic. Together, their presence in the blood produces a clinical syndrome called **uremia.** A group of somewhat larger nitrogenous molecules also seems to be involved in uremia, but their precise roles are unclear. At the cellular level, uremia toxins seem to exert an inhibitory effect on membrane ion transport mechanisms, which apparently underlies the variable and wide-ranging systemic effects associated with uremia.

Fluid and electrolyte imbalances are prominent in uremia and involve water retention and acid-base disturbances. Excessive potassium retention and calcium loss can produce cardiac arrhythmias and cardiac and skeletal muscle weakness. Loss of body weight is common and is related to the anorexia, vomiting, and diarrhea that the uremia toxins induce. They also affect the nervous system, producing a pattern of confusion, apathy, convulsions, and coma called **uremic encephalopathy.** Pericarditis often develops in uremia, but it is unusual for it to interfere with cardiac

function. More serious are the blood coagulation problems that result from inhibition of platelet factor 3 (PF-3). They include bleeding at mucosal surfaces or into the pericardial sac or meninges.

The list continues, but suffice it to say that since the accumulating uremia toxins affect cells at a fundamental functional level, almost all organ systems will suffer some degree of derangement in uremia. Usually, by the time uremia develops, the underlying renal disease has progressed too far to be responsive to treatment.

Acute Renal Failure

Rapid, usually reversible decline of renal function is known as **acute renal failure** (ARF). When kidney function is depressed, urinary output falls to about 400 ml per day, or 25% of its normal value (oliguria). Many factors can produce rapidly developing oliguria, but they may be grouped into three categories: acute pyelonephritis, toxic nephropathy, and renal ischemia.

Bilateral renal ischemia occurs whenever there is a pronounced drop in the systemic blood pressure. Such cardiovascular shock can take many forms, the most common of which are the result of surgical or other trauma, hemorrhage, burns, infection, or cardiac damage. The toxic agents listed in table 15.3 may be involved in ARF.

The most common cause of ARF is the result of ischemia or of nephrotoxic injury called **acute tubular necrosis**(ATN). This condition involves damage to nephron tubules varying over a wide range of severity [22] (fig. 15.18). Regeneration of tubule epithelium, and hence restoration of function, depends on the degree of damage to the tubule's basement membrane. Nephrotoxins usually damage the basement membrane much less then renal ischemia, hence the poorer prognosis when renal blood flow is reduced.

In acute renal failure, oliguria may continue for several weeks, depending on the severity of damage and on tubular regeneration capacity. As restoration of function proceeds, a period of diuresis is usual, as previously retained water is lost to restore fluid balance. The regeneration of tubular epithelium, and the restoration of function that follows, occurs gradually over several weeks. Where damage is severe, or infection or other complications are present, acute renal failure may prove to be fatal.

Chronic Renal Failure

As renal parenchymal damage increases, the declining number of functional nephrons leads inevitably to increased excretory loading on the remaining nephrons and a progressive reduction of function. This is the case following chronic GN or severe PN. In chronic renal failure, effects are irreversible and derangements of homeostatic regulation and excretion will be in evidence, but only after nephron losses exceed 50–70% of the total. At this point

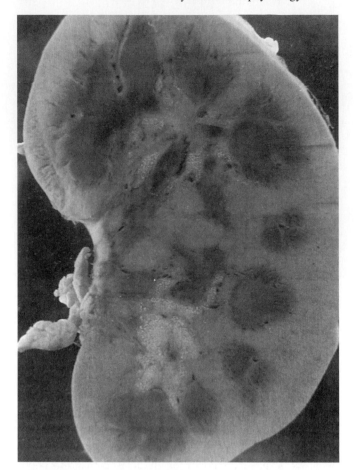

Figure 15.18 Severe tubular necrosis in acute renal failure. The tubules of the cortex were heavily damaged by exposure to a nephrotoxin, as evidenced by the pale, swollen cortex.
Large-scale kidney and liver damage were responsible for the death of a woman who broke a large bottle of carbon tetrachloride she had been using as a cleaning solvent. She had been cautioned about its hazards, but stubbornly maintained that her mother and grandmother had used it in preference to "modern" cleaners, and furthermore, she was always careful. In cleaning up the spill, she could not avoid heavy fume inhalation and exposure to the skin of her hands and ankles. In bed at night she developed a headache and became drowsy. The next morning she was admitted to the emergency room in a coma and severely oliguric. She died soon after admission. Kidney damage from the solvent produced the swelling, the cortical pallor, and the hyperemia in the medulla seen here. Most damage involved the proximal portions of the tubules, since these are the tubule segments first exposed to the solvent after it is filtered at the glomerulus. These proximal segments lie in the cortex.

the consequences of renal insufficiency emerge, and **chronic renal failure** develops. It is characterized by the combination of derangements associated with uremia, which progress toward the condition known as the **end-stage kidney.** 23 24 Chronic GN or PN is usually the cause, with damage from malignant nephrosclerosis also common. This last condition is typically superimposed on a long-standing benign nephrosclerosis.

Another condition, called **polycystic kidney disease** (PKD), 25 accounts for up to 10% of chronic renal failure even though its incidence is quite low: only 1 in 1000. It is a genetic disorder in which the kidneys are filled with multiple fluid-filled cysts, causing them to become hugely distended.

Excessive water loss dominates during early end-stage disease because the loss of reabsorptive capacity by the tubules is greater than the reduction in filtration at the glomeruli. For example, if the glomerular filtration rate falls 90%, to 18 liters a day, but the tubules can reabsorb only 50% as opposed to their normal 99%, the result is a daily loss of 9 liters, a significant increase over the normal liter and a half. Later, as glomerular function is even further reduced, oliguria or even anuria can result. Urine that is produced is characteristically dilute, usually with a fixed specific gravity, the result of failing tubular concentration mechanisms.

When chronic renal failure gives rise to irreversible and progressive uremia, only aggressive therapeutic intervention can cope with the situation. The two possibilities are dialysis and transplantation.

RENAL DIALYSIS

In **renal dialysis,** wastes and uremia toxins are cleared from the blood and electrolyte balances are restored. Two methods are commonly used, both based on establishing favorable concentration gradients between the patient's blood and an appropriately constituted dialysis fluid, the **dialysate.**

Hemodialysis

Hemodialysis involves moving the patient's blood to a device called a **hemodialyzer,** where it flows through a series of chambers bounded by a semipermeable membrane. Because the hemodialyzer lies outside the body, this procedure is also called **extracorporeal dialysis.** Surrounding the dialyzer's membrane chambers is the dialysate. Its composition favors the diffusion of waste products, toxins, and unwanted electrolytes out of the blood and the diffusion of needed substances into the blood. The dialysis membrane characteristics and the dialysate composition are both critical to successful hemodialysis.

The dialysis membrane must have permeability properties that will allow water, electrolytes, and small toxin and waste molecules to pass through it. At the same time, its pores must not allow the loss of formed elements, plasma proteins, or other larger molecules from the blood, nor the movement of bacteria or viruses into the blood.

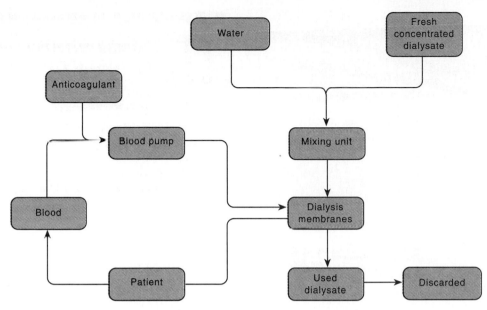

Figure 15.19   The essential elements of extracorporeal dialysis.

The dialysate's composition can be varied to meet individual requirements, but its basic composition is such that electrolytes are present in concentrations near to those of normal plasma. As a result, if any plasma ions are present to excess because of faulty renal excretions, the concentration gradients are selected to favor diffusion of those ions out of the blood and into the dialysate. Conversely, if there are electrolytes that the failing kidney can't retain, the gradients will favor their diffusion from the dialysate into the plasma. Typically, the failing kidney retains sodium and potassium ions while losing calcium ion. Dialysate composition will also adjust chlorine and magnesium ion concentrations.

To maximize removal of waste products, no urea, creatinine, or uric acid is present in dialysate. Thus there is a maximum concentration gradient across the dialysis membrane, which ensures maximum diffusion of these unwanted substances out of the blood. Other uremic toxins, whose exact identities are unknown, are also removed by diffusion, since they are not present in the dialysate solution.

Dialysis also attempts to compensate for the kidney's inability to excrete water adequately. It does so by using a pump to raise the pressure under which blood is driven through the dialysis chamber. This elevated pressure directly forces more water out of the blood by filtration. The same effect is achieved in some systems by lowering the pressure in the dialysate through the application of suction.

Since the tubing and dialyzer membranes activate the coagulation system, heparin or other anticoagulant is used to inhibit clotting. Various therapeutic manipulations, beyond the scope of this text, are employed to deal with the problem of patients who are at risk of bleeding and need all the coagulation they can muster, but who also require dialysis. This situation is not uncommon because, as you may recall, the uremia that necessitates dialysis also interferes with coagulation. Postoperative patients are similarly at risk. The essential elements of extracorporeal dialysis are shown in figure 15.19.

In typical cases, hemodialysis will be repeated several times. To avoid vessel damage from repeated venipuncture, there must be a special means of gaining access to the patient's blood for efficient delivery to and return from the hemodialyzer. The most widely used approach is based on the direct surgical joining of an artery of the forearm or leg with its parallel vein, thus creating an **arteriovenous fistula.** This exposes the vein to arterial pressure, and over a period of time it enlarges in response, forming a larger vessel that more easily accommodates venipuncture (fig. 15.20).

Another technique, the **external arteriovenous shunt** or by-pass, involves exposing an artery and vein in the forearm or leg. Into these parallel vessels are placed rigid cannula (thin metal tubes), which are then passed through the skin, where they are secured with sutures and tape. The arterial cannula is then connected to the venous cannula by a length of flexible tubing (fig. 15.20). Prior to dialysis, the flexible tubing is removed to provide access to arterial blood for the dialyzer, as well as access to a vein for return of the blood after dialysis. The shunt apparatus provides ready access to the blood but is often complicated by infection, clotting, or bleeding as a result of becoming dislodged. For this reason, the external shunt is used only for short-term dialysis.

(a)

(b)

Figure 15.20 Two methods of gaining access to the blood in hemodialysis. (*a*) Arteriovenous fistula. (*b*) External arteriovenous shunt.

Peritoneal Dialysis

Compared with hemodialysis, **peritoneal dialysis** is a simpler and easier approach. It uses the peritoneal cavity as a dialysis chamber and the peritoneal membranes as the dialysis membranes. These membranes provide over two square meters of surface across which diffusion can occur. A cannula passes the dialysate into the peritoneal cavity by gravity. The dialysate is allowed to remain for a period during which diffusion and osmosis provide exchange between blood and the dialysate. The cavity is then cleared of dialysate by means of gravity drainage, and the process is repeated until the desired blood chemistry restoration is achieved.

KIDNEY TRANSPLANTATION

As the function of any organ progressively deteriorates, it becomes apparent that available therapies can only extend the time until its failure is complete. In the case of renal failure, we are fortunate in possessing sophisticated dialysis technology. However, although there is increasing use of CAPD (see box), hemodialysis is still the most widely used dialysis technique. Overall, given the cost, inconvenience, and patient morale problems associated with hemodialysis, transplanting a functional replacement kidney into the ailing recipient is obviously appealing. The advantages of replacing a diseased kidney with a normally functioning

‼ *Continuous Ambulatory Peritoneal Dialysis*

Recently, **continuous ambulatory peritoneal dialysis** (CAPD) has become a popular alternative to hemodialysis. This procedure is based on the surgical placement of an indwelling catheter through which dialysate can be passed to the peritoneal cavity. Patients can perform the procedure at home with convenient plastic bags of dialysate. They can then continue their near-normal daily activities with less reliance on the medical delivery system. This approach fosters a generally improved morale, avoids coagulation complications, and minimizes the use of expensive equipment. Also, because it is slower than extracorporeal hemodialysis, blood chemistry changes develop gradually. CAPD thus eliminates the more rapid swings associated with hemodialysis, which many uremic and generally debilitated patients have difficulty tolerating.

organ have long been recognized, but only in the last 20 years has kidney transplantation become a widely available therapeutic option demonstrated in the human. As the technique has become more widespread, its rate of success has steadily improved.

In transplantation of the kidney there are two obstacles that must be overcome. One is that of obtaining a replacement kidney. The other is the need to work very quickly, to avoid ischemic damage to the organ.

Two sources of kidneys are currently relied upon. The most desirable source is a living donor (LD) closely related to the recipient. A living unrelated donor or a cadaver donor (CD) may also be used. Because related donors are not always available or able to donate, and living unrelated donors are in short supply, cadaver donors are a valuable source of kidneys for transplantation.

The kidney can tolerate anoxia for up to one hour at body temperature (its **warm ischemic time**). If the organ is quickly cooled to 4°C, the tissue's metabolic demands decrease and its viability can be maintained for up to ten hours (its **cold ischemic time**). Cooling thus allows for more leeway between the time when the organ becomes available and the time required for preparation of the recipient.

Implantation

The currently favored site for implantation is perhaps different from what one might expect. Instead of being positioned in the space previously occupied by the diseased kidney, the implant is placed in the right iliac fossa. This site is well protected by the innominate bone and the abdominal musculature, but more importantly, it is nearer

Figure 15.21   Typical implantation of a renal transplant.

to the urinary bladder than is the usual kidney location. This is significant because of the ureter's blood supply. Branches of the renal artery supply the proximal parts of the ureter, and these vessels can be retained during the donor's nephrectomy (kidney removal). The distal ureter relies more on vessels that can't be retained during nephrectomy, so it is difficult to support in the recipient. Implantation in the iliac fossa allows the shorter proximal ureter, with its better blood supply, to reach the nearby urinary bladder.

The implantation procedure starts with an oblique incision into the right abdominal wall. The iliac arteries and veins are located, and the donor's renal arteries and veins are joined to them to establish a renal blood supply. After the blood flow to the implant is restored, urine formation follows, usually within a few minutes in the case of a related LD. Next, the urinary bladder is opened and a small incision is made in its base to accommodate the attachment of the ureter. The urinary bladder is then closed, and closure of the abdomen completes the procedure (fig. 15.21). The recipient's diseased kidneys are not usually removed after a donor's kidney is implanted.

Care of the recipient after the implantation is similar to that of most postoperative patients. Recipients are able to leave bed on the first postoperative day and to remain up for increasing periods thereafter. Urinary output is closely monitored, because falling urinary output is indicative of

the major complication of an implantation, namely, immune rejection of the donor kidney. Cellular and humoral mechanisms may combine to effect rejection, either immediately, where the antigenic match is not sufficiently close, or over a prolonged period.

Immune Rejection

Immune rejection may take one of three forms. In **hyperacute rejection,** urinary output may decline by 90% within minutes to hours after implantation. **26** After several weeks the cortex undergoes necrosis and the kidney is lost. This sequence of events is due to the presence of antikidney antibodies circulating in the blood of the recipient. These may have arisen from previous exposure to antigens by way of blood transfusion, a previous transplantation, a pregnancy in which fetal antigens gained access to the maternal circulation, or exposure to bacterial antigens that cross-react with kidney antigens. However the antibodies arose, their presence in the recipient allows them to bind to the endothelial linings of the renal vasculature. As a result, complement is activated, and in response PMNs are attracted to the site, where they strip away the endothelium. This exposes the subendothelial tissues, allowing platelets to adhere. Thrombosis and vascular occlusion follow, causing ischemia and necrosis.

The second pattern of rejection is based on both cellular and humoral immune attack and is called **acute rejection.** It occurs between the 1st and the 16th postoperative week in the case of an LD. The potential threat extends to two years when a CD is used (fig. 15.22).

Chronic rejection may take two years to develop. In this case, antibody against the graft binds to the implant's vascular endothelium. In response the endothelia proliferate, producing stenosis and ultimately occlusion of the vessel. In glomeruli, anti-BM antibody attacks and disrupts the basement membrane, leading to protein loss and the nephrotic syndrome. By whatever mechanism the rejection occurs, the end result is the same: loss of renal function.

Immune Suppression

In view of the devastating potential of immune rejection mechanisms, increased success in transplantation depends on therapeutic suppression of the response. This is achieved by the use of chemical immunosuppressant agents, often in combination. Cyclosporine is the basis of most such therapy, especially in combination with drugs with additional immunosuppressive and anti-inflammatory effects, such as prednisone and azathioprine. The goal is the inactivation of those cells of the immune system that mount the immune attack. This approach yields consistently good results, but it carries with it certain hazards, which in some cases are potentially as grave as the renal loss that the immune suppression seeks to prevent.

46309

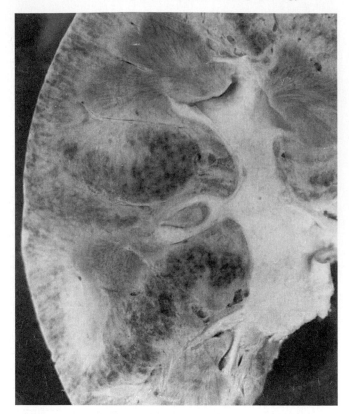

Figure 15.22 Transplant rejection. In this portion of a sectioned renal implant, the organ is generally swollen and edematous. Congestion and small hemorrhages are responsible for the dark mottling of the cortex and medulla.

This is a cadaver donor kidney that was rejected 16 months after implantation. Evidence of immune-mediated vascular damage can be seen in the swollen, edematous organ and in the fine hemorrhages scattered throughout both cortex and medulla. Microscopic study showed degenerated glomeruli and numerous casts in the tubules as evidence of faulty filtration in the glomeruli. The recipient was a 50-year-old man who had polycystic kidneys. After 11 years of hypertension, proteinuria, and hematuria, one kidney was removed. Eighteen months later a suitable cadaver donor kidney became available, allowing the removal of the other abnormal kidney and a kidney transplant. The failure of the implant developed rapidly, and uremia and kidney failure could not be prevented.

Apart from the side effects of individual suppressant drugs, nephrotoxicity in the case of the commonly used cyclosporine, and a cost of several thousands of dollars annually, the major problem associated with immune suppression is infection. This is because the immune system that rejects the implanted kidney is also the principal means of defense against invading microorganisms. When its defensive ability is therapeutically suppressed, the danger of infection increases. It is ironic that the most common cause of death associated with transplantation of the kidney or other organs is not rejection of the transplant but rather infection following immune suppression. A secondary complication of immune suppression involves tumors. It is possible that a renal tumor may be implanted with the donor kidney, but this is less likely than is the development of a primary tumor. Immune-suppressed patients are more likely than the normal population to develop leukemia, for example. Of course, the fact that the development of the tumor might take many years before presenting a significant threat must be balanced against the immediate requirement for a new kidney.

Results

The success rate of renal transplantation has steadily increased with improvements in the ability to match donor and recipient antigens and to control the complications of the procedure. Currently, the recipient of a related LD's kidney has a high likelihood of indefinite survival. The advent of cyclosporine therapy has also increased the success rate of CD implants, so that they currently compare favorably with those of an unrelated LD.

URINARY TRACT TUMORS

Benign renal tumors are fairly common but produce no signs or symptoms and may come to attention only as an incidental post-mortem finding. Two malignancies of the kidney are important. **Renal cell carcinoma or adenocarcinoma of the kidneys** [27] is the dominant malignant renal tumor in adults. It makes up over 90% of all adult kidney cancers. It metastasizes extensively, especially to lung and bone, before clinical indications warn of its presence. Prognosis is poor unless therapy can be instituted before metastasis occurs. An enlarging renal cell carcinoma is the most frequent cause of inferior vena cava compression by a tumor.

Wilms' tumor, also known as **nephroblastoma,** [28] is a common tumor of childhood. It often reaches large size before its presence is detected in investigating abdominal distention in children 2–4 years of age. Results of combined surgical, radiation, and chemotherapy are favorable, and the prognosis is generally good.

The urinary tract is the site of few benign tumors, but carcinomas do arise in the epithelium of the collecting system and urinary bladder. Obstruction and the risk of PN are superimposed on the local damage caused by invasion. Metastasis via the lymphatic system is typical.

ASSESSMENT OF RENAL FUNCTION

A wide range of diagnostic techniques is applied to the assessment of renal functional capacity. Various tests focus on excretion, because the kidney removes unwanted substances from the blood to form urine. High levels of such substances in the blood or low levels in the urine suggest certain diagnostic conclusions. The tests described in this section are used primarily to assess nephron function. Normal values for these tests are indicated in table 15.4.

Table 15.4	Reference Values for Some Commonly Performed Tests of Renal Function

Test	Reference Value
Blood	
Plasma creatinine	0.7–1.5 mg/dl
Blood urea nitrogen (BUN)	10–20 mg/dl
Urine	
Specific gravity	1.025–1.032
Protein	<150 mg/day
Blood cells	0–5/high-power field
Casts	Occasional, hyaline
Bacteria	Urethral organisms only
Clearance Tests	
Creatinine clearance	91–130 ml/min
Urea clearance	60–100 ml/min
Inulin clearance	105–150 ml/min

Blood Tests

Blood is routinely studied to determine its content of toxic substances. Most typically these are the nitrogen-containing products of protein metabolism. If their level in the blood is elevated, renal excretion is probably impaired.

Plasma Creatinine Level

Creatinine is a normal plasma constituent and is derived from the creatine normally found in muscle tissue. Creatinine is toxic and is excreted primarily by the kidney. Under normal circumstances, its level in the blood is quite stable.

Blood Urea Nitrogen Level (BUN)

Urea is synthesized in the liver from nitrogen derived from the metabolism of amino acids. It is excreted only by the kidney. Its level in the blood is expressed in terms of the nitrogen it contains. Values can vary depending on changes in dietary protein or protein metabolism. The blood urea nitrogen (BUN) determination is widely used to screen for renal malfunction.

Elevation of the plasma creatinine or BUN is interpreted as a nonspecific indication of impaired renal function. Because of its stability, the plasma creatinine is regarded as being a somewhat more reliable indicator. Neither test can warn of early pathological changes in the kidneys, since creatinine and urea levels are not elevated until damage is severe enough to reduce the kidney's substantial reserve capacity.

Urinalysis

The constituents and characteristics of normal urine are well known. Changes in the makeup of the urine can provide an indication of altered renal function, often with some specificity as to the part of the nephron involved.

Physical Examination of the Urine: Urine Volume and Specific Gravity

Because urine production derives from renal function, an altered urine volume can be taken to reflect altered renal function, assuming normal fluid intake. Urine production normally varies throughout the day, so urinary output is typically monitored over a 24-hour period. An increased urine volume (**polyuria**) is an indication of the tubules' inability to reabsorb water. This might result from damage to the tubules or from an excessive demand for solute reabsorption. As solutes are left in the tubule, reabsorption is reduced and water loss is increased. Decreased urine volume (oliguria) is associated with nephron damage, as seen, for example, in certain types of GN and PN. A complete lack of urinary output (anuria) might result from substantially reduced renal blood flow, urinary tract obstruction, or severe renal damage, especially toxic damage.

In measuring **specific gravity,** a solution's weight is compared with that of pure water. Because it is a ratio, the result has no units of measure. In all body fluids, water is the solvent, so in comparing solutions the weight of the solute particles is the major cause of difference. As particle number increases, so does the specific gravity. Specific gravity is thus related to concentration, and because it can be measured more easily, specific gravity is more commonly used in urinalysis than are direct concentration measurements. Specific gravity is used as an indicator of the kidney's ability to excrete a concentrated urine. Loss of tubular concentrating function will produce urine with a specific gravity equal to that of plasma, which is 1.001.

Chemical Examination of the Urine: Protein Levels

Of the small amount of protein filtered, most is reabsorbed. This means that normal levels of urinary protein are quite low. The presence of larger quantities of protein in the urine (proteinuria) is an indication of faulty filtration, since the filtration membrane must be passing protein that it would normally withhold. Albumin, the smallest and most prevalent plasma protein, is found most commonly in the urine, so much so that **albuminuria** is often used synonymously with proteinuria. The appearance of more and larger proteins in urine indicates more extensive damage of the filtration membrane. Proteinuria is typically seen in GN and in cases of glomerular damage secondary to PN. In the later stages of chronic GN or PN, proteinuria diminishes because scarring reduces nephron numbers so that filtration generally is reduced.

Microscopic Examination of the Urine: Particulate Matter

Information on the number and type of any particles in the urine can provide important insights into the nature of a renal malfunction.

Urine will normally contain very small numbers of both red and white blood cells, as well as some epithelial cells from nephron tubules, the bladder, or the urethra. Erythrocytes gain increased access to the urine when glomerular damage allows the escape of erythrocytes into the nephron tubule. In acute GN, this loss of erythrocytes to the urine is so pronounced that the disease is often called **hemorrhagic GN.** Disruption of other parts of the nephron vasculature or damage to the urinary tract can also allow blood to appear in the urine.

Elevated counts of white blood cells are indicative of an inflammatory process in the kidney or urinary tract. Laboratory reports of urine cell counts will seem to be quite small, but because only a minute volume of urine is examined, even small numbers in a microscope field can represent a large loss of cells in each day of urinary output. For example, the normal urine erythrocyte count of one to two cells per field represents a daily loss of over 100,000 cells.

Casts are particles in the urine that originate when tubule material first gels and then dislodges to pass to the urine. Casts form when the tubule secretes a protein into its lumen. This protein may be the only constituent of the cast (the so-called **hyaline cast**), **29** or cells reaching the tubule may imbed in the protein, forming more complex casts. Because red and/or white blood cells and/or tubule cells may imbed in the protein matrix of the cast, **30** analysis of the cast components may provide indications of diagnostic value. For example, red blood cells in casts are most commonly associated with the glomerular damage of GN. A predominance of white blood cells in casts is seen in PN as well as GN, whereas tubule cells in casts might result from PN, advanced GN, or toxic damage such as from heavy metals. In the nephrotic syndrome, in which protein loss is pronounced, damaged tubule cells become engorged with fat. As these cells are sloughed from the tubule they may lodge in its lumen to form fatty casts. Whatever the composition of a particular cast, its principal diagnostic significance lies in localizing the problem in the kidney as opposed to other parts of the urinary tract.

Bacteriological Examination of the Urine

Urine is tested for bacteria to establish bacterial involvement in cases of inflammation. As previously stated, urine produced by the kidney is sterile, as is the normal urinary tract with the exception of the distal urethra. For this reason, normally voided urine is contaminated only by small quantities of urethral bacteria so elevated bacterial counts indicate infection. The therapy chosen depends, in part, on bacteriological testing to determine the nature of the infecting organism(s). These may travel to the kidney via the blood, but they more commonly enter the urinary bladder, which allows them access to the ureters and kidney.

Clearance Tests

Clearance tests are a valuable means of assessing renal function. Essentially they attempt to assess how the nephron processes the blood delivered to it. Each clearance test focuses on a specific substance in the plasma, one that may be normally present, or one that has been injected into the blood for the purpose of the test. The test involves a comparison of the amount of the substance in the blood with the amount found in the urine. The result provides a measure of the kidney's ability to remove, or clear, the substance from the blood, and hence of renal functional capacity. Since the nephron applies different combinations of filtration, reabsorption, and tubular secretion in processing plasma, the different clearance tests can provide information about a specific nephron process that might be abnormal.

Clearance test values are obtained by a calculation that takes into account the concentration of a particular substance in plasma and urine, urine output, and a correction factor for body surface area, since this is related to clearance. Results may be reported in terms of the amount of substance cleared per volume of blood (e.g., milligrams per hundred milliliters) or as a volume of blood cleared of the substance per unit of time (e.g., milliliters per minute).

Creatinine Clearance

Because creatinine is freely filtered at the glomerulus and none is reabsorbed, the amount present in urine reflects the glomerular filtration rate (GFR). There is, however, some tubular secretion of creatinine, so that test results may tend to indicate a somewhat elevated GFR. Test results are regarded as a useful approximation of renal filtration.

Urea Clearance

Renal clearance of urea is also used as an indication of the GFR. Since some urea is reabsorbed from the nephron tubule lumen, the reported value of urea clearance will be approximately 60% of the actual GFR. The normal value of urea clearance is about 60–100 ml/min. Test results are often reported as a percentage of this reference value.

Inulin Clearance

The carbohydrate inulin is not normally present in the blood. After injection it is freely filtered at the glomerulus. Because none is subsequently secreted into the tubule, nor is any reabsorbed, inulin clearance accurately reflects glomerular filtration. The test unfortunately requires rather elaborate and costly procedures, so it is not commonly performed.

Renal Biopsy

Obtaining a sample of kidney tissue for microscopic study is not routinely done. It may, however, prove valuable in cases where an accurate diagnosis of renal malfunction is needed for selection of an appropriate course of therapy. In a renal biopsy, the kidney is localized via X-ray technique in order to identify a point on the skin that overlies the lateral margin of the kidney's inferior pole. Next, under local anesthesia, a long needle guide is passed through skin and muscle to reach the kidney. The guide is then removed and the hollow biopsy needle quickly introduced into the track established by the guide. Finally, the tissue obtained is prepared for microscopic study.

Case Study

A 9-year-old native Indian boy, living in an isolated village, experienced significant weight gain and some abdominal distention in a period of only two weeks. Also noting his general malaise, his complaints of abdominal discomfort, and traces of blood in his urine, his parents took him to the nearest medical facility, a small cottage hospital.

They reported that he had recently had a bad cold with sore throat, but since it seemed to get better, no medical treatment had been thought necessary. On physical examination, a generalized massive edema was apparent, the abdomen, including the genitalia, being particularly swollen.

Blood tests were done, and blood cell counts, the BUN and plasma electrolyte and creatinine levels were all essentially normal, with the exception of a positive test for serum antistreptolysin "O" antibodies and a significant degree of hypoalbuminemia.

Urinalysis revealed severe proteinuria (2.5 g/day) and traces of blood in the urine. Microscopic study indicated the presence of red cell and hemoglobin casts.

A nephrologist at the nearest referral center, who was consulted by phone, said that in view of the child's age, a biopsy need not be done, and that local treatment should be adequate. The boy was hospitalized and prednisone therapy started, with the dose tapering down after two weeks. A supportive low-protein, high-carbohydrate diet was also started, and fluids were restricted.

After ten days the boy experienced a pronounced diuresis and his weight returned to normal. He was released two weeks later with normal blood and urine values, and has since been well.

Commentary

In this case, it seems likely that the boy's previous streptococcal infection was the initiating factor in an acute glomerulonephritis of autoimmune pathogenesis. The resulting glomerular dysfunction produced the classic complex of proteinuria, hypoalbuminemia, and widespread edema. The anti-inflammatory action of prednisone was able to suppress the process of glomerular damage and prevent any progression.

A more severe attack might have required a renal biopsy to obtain a more precise diagnosis on which to base therapy. In this case, because of the child's age and the relative mildness of his condition, a biopsy proved to be unnecessary.

This case also illustrates the lack of a clear line of distinction between the nephrotic and nephritic syndromes. A daily urinary loss of 3.5 g of protein is the amount usually taken as defining the nephrotic syndrome. Although the level here was significantly lower, it induced a massive edema. On the other hand, the nephritic syndrome usually involves more prominent hematuria than was detected in this case.

It is also interesting to note that the incidence of severe streptococcal infections is on the rise in North America. This increase appears not to be the result of the past years of antibiotic therapy, which might have allowed only resistant strains to survive. Instead, there is evidence that spontaneous genetic mutations in the organisms have produced streptococcal strains of greater virulence.

Key Concepts

1. Any disease process that compromises glomerular filtration produces signs and symptoms related to renal retention of potentially toxic substances or the loss of needed substances to the urine (p. 374).

2. Immune destruction of glomerular elements is the dominant feature of glomerulonephritis and may involve antibody directed against the glomerular basement membrane or damage caused by the trapping of immune complexes in the glomerulus (p. 375)

3. Immune complexes in the glomerulus induce PMN and macrophage responses that produce glomerular damage via complement activation, the release of enzymes and toxins, fibrin deposition, and scarring (p. 376).

4. In some GN, the pattern of glomerular damage allows the loss of albumins from plasma, producing a syndrome of hypoalbuminemia, proteinuria, and systemic edema known as the nephrotic syndrome (pp. 378–379).

5. Glomerular damage that results in the retention of wastes and water, with some loss of blood to the urine, produces the clinical syndrome of oliguria, azotemia, and hematuria known as the nephritic syndrome (p. 379).

6. Tubulointerstitial disorders are characterized by altered tubule processing, typically producing loss of water and sodium and the retention of acid (p. 379).

7. The most common tubulointerstitial disorder is pyelonephritis, in which infectious agents reach the renal medulla either by ascent from the urinary tract or by transport in the blood from an infection site (p. 380).

8. Acute PN is usually of bacterial origin and readily resolves after a relatively mild illness in which pyuria may be present, while chronic PN is potentially much more threatening, since signs and symptoms may not arise until substantial nephron loss has occurred (pp. 380–381).

9. Interstitial nephritis is the tubulointerstitial disease that is caused by damage from toxins, among which are therapeutic agents such as some antibiotics and analgesics (p. 381).

10. Various diseases, such as hypertension, diabetes mellitus, and atherosclerosis, may affect the kidney's functions by their effects on renal vasculature, which lead to renal ischemia (pp. 381–382).

11. Insoluble calculi may form in the kidney, producing pain and urinary obstruction and increasing the risk of infection and renal parenchymal damage (pp. 382–383).

12. A widely used clinical approach to etiology in kidney disorders employs the categories of: renal disease, where the fault lies with the kidney, prerenal disease, in which an initially normal kidney is compromised by ischemia, and postrenal disease, where the normal kidney is affected by urinary obstruction (pp. 383–385).

13. The widespread functional derangements associated with failing kidneys are the result of waste retention and fluid and electrolyte imbalance, which are clinically designated as uremia (p. 385).

14. PN, toxic nephritis, and renal ischemia produce the rapidly progressing decline of renal function called acute renal failure (p. 385).

15. More severe and irreversible nephron loss produces chronic renal failure, which is characterized by more pronounced functional derangements, progressing to uremia (pp. 385–386).

16. Given evidence of renal failure, therapeutic intervention to clear toxins and provide homeostatic adjustments may employ hemodialysis, where an external hemodialyzer is used, or peritoneal dialysis, where dialysate is infused into the peritoneal cavity (pp. 386–388).

17. When a suitable donor kidney is available and immune rejection responses can be suppressed, renal transplantation is the optimal therapeutic choice in cases of irreversible renal failure (pp. 388–390).

18. Assessment of renal function is accomplished by examining the blood and urine for indications of retained wastes, excretion of needed plasma constituents, or homeostatic imbalance (pp. 390–393).

REVIEW ACTIVITIES

1. The longest term in this chapter is membrano/proliferative glomerulo/nephr/itis. For each of the indicated word elements, write out its meaning and briefly relate it to altered kidney function. Consult your medical dictionary if you must.

2. With respect to figure 15.9, answer the following: How did the immune complexes shown trapped in the BM form? Why are PMNs present? How are the PMNs linked to glomerular damage? Check your answers by consulting pages 375–378.

3. Both the nephrotic and the nephritic syndromes may involve oliguria, but it is produced by different mechanisms in each case. If you think about it, you may be able to work out what they are. If not, see figures 15.11 and 15.12.

4. From the information presented on pages 382–383, lay out a handy reference flow chart showing the pathogenesis of urolithiasis. Add the principal sequelae of urolithiasis. Check back to the diagram at least twice before your next exam.

5. With a pad of sticky notes, make ten labels, one each for the elements that contribute to the development of prerenal disease. Stick them to a large sheet of paper and draw connecting arrows. You could put the notes down randomly, but if their positions and the arrows reflect the actual sequence (figure 15.17), the exercise will be more worthwhile.

6. On a blank sheet of paper, draw a vertical line and label it "Dialysis Membrane." Label the space to its left "Blood" and the space to the right "Dialysate." Add large and small symbols on either side to indicate high and low concentrations of metabolic wastes (MW), Na^+, K^+, and Ca^{++}. Now add arrows to indicate the direction of net diffusion of each. Will your arrow directions produce a blood lower in waste Na^+ and K^+ and higher in Ca^{++}? Is this the condition needed for blood returning to the patient in figure 15.19? If yes, good! If no, see page 387.

7. Before checking pages 374–379 and the case study commentary, recall the situation in the case study. The young boy's urinalysis indicated a pronounced proteinuria. Of the plasma proteins in the urine, which one would have been most prevalent? Why? The case study also notes that the nephrotic and nephritic syndromes were not clearly separated. Which aspect of the boy's urinalysis pointed toward the nephrotic syndrome and which toward the nephritic syndrome?

Chapter Sixteen

Fluid and Electrolyte Imbalances

*There is in man the bitter and the salt, the sweet and the acid, the sour and the
insipid. . . . These, when all mixed and mingled up in one another, are not
apparent, neither do they hurt a man; but when any of them is separate, and
stands by itself, then it becomes perceptible and hurts a man.*

Hippocrates
On Ancient Medicine

FLUID AND ELECTROLYTE BASICS

Overall somatic functions are a product of the smoothly coordinated activities of the body's various organ systems. These depend on the functioning of the vast numbers of cells that form the tissues of the different organs. Cellular functioning in turn depends on numerous chemical reactions that occur in an environment dominated by water. Water is not only the cells' principal internal constituent, it also bathes their external surfaces and fills the spaces between them. It is not difficult to appreciate, then, an essential requirement of cellular homeostasis: that the quantity and composition of body water, both inside and outside cells, be carefully controlled. Only when such body fluid homeostasis is achieved can normal functioning occur. When there are imbalances in the body fluids, disease and even death can result.

Body Fluid Compartments

Water contributes about 55% of a typical female's body weight and about 65% of a male's. The rest of the body weight is derived from fat and fat-free solids. All water in the body (**total body water, TBW**) is distributed among four separate fluid compartments (fig. 16.1). One compartment contains the **intracellular fluid** (ICF). The ICF consists of all water present within the body's cells. The remaining body water, that found outside the cells, is the **extracellular fluid** (ECF). Of the total body water, 65% is found in cells and 35% in the ECF. Within the ECF are three subcompartments. About 25% of TBW is found between cells, forming the **intercellular fluid,** also referred to as the interstitial fluid. About 8% of TBW is found in the **plasma.** A small compartment is also recognized as part of the ECF. This contains the **transcellular fluid,** constituting only about 2% of TBW. It consists of the fluids in the GI tract, glandular secretions, eyes, urinary tract, and airways. Its volume is sufficiently small to leave little impact on overall water distribution, so it is usually excluded from therapeutic calculations in fluid imbalance cases.

From this description, it should be clear that the boundary between the extracellular fluid and the intracellular fluid is the cell membrane, and that the plasma and interstitial fluid are separated by the blood capillary wall. Both these dividing membranes are freely permeable to water, so that it normally moves easily between plasma, the interstitial spaces, and the cells. Much of the water movement that occurs is the normal exchange of fluid between the plasma and interstitium; blood hydrostatic pressure drives water from the blood into the intercellular spaces, and blood osmotic pressure draws it back from the intercellular spaces into the blood. This movement is an example of the **bulk flow** of water. That is, water and any dissolved substances move together from one compartment to another. Bulk flow also occurs as interstitial water moves into lymphatic ves-

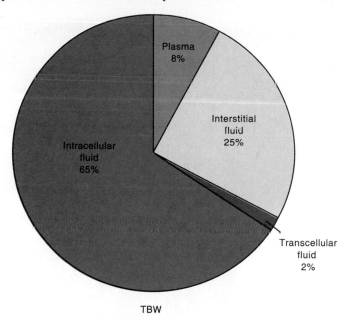

Figure 16.1 Relative size of the body fluid compartments expressed as a percentage of total body water (TBW).

sels, which return it to the plasma. In terms of body water compartments, the lymphatic vessels can be thought of as an extension of the blood vessels, because lymphatics empty lymph directly into the blood. The body's water, therefore, is continually exchanged between plasma, interstitium, cells, and lymph (fig. 16.2). Let us now consider these fluid movements in the context of the balance between overall input and output of fluid and electrolytes.

The Balance Concept

Fluid and electrolyte homeostasis can be viewed in terms of a balance between inputs and outputs. These will change in the course of normal activities, but the optimum amounts of water and electrolytes must still be maintained. This means that if input is increased, a corresponding increase in output is required to balance it. When input matches output in this way, a state of **neutral balance** is said to exist, or a patient is said to be **in balance.** If input exceeds output for a particular substance, it accumulates and the patient is said to be in **positive balance.** If output exceeds input, a deficit develops, and the patient is said to be in **negative balance.**

Water Balance

Normal physiology involves a continual loss of body water. This water must be replaced, and when water input matches water loss, water balance is achieved. The typical daily balance of water input versus output, averaged over a range of normal variation, is approximately 2500 ml. The input total is based on drinking 1300 ml as pure water or in various beverages, with about 900 ml contained in solid food. After

Figure 16.2   Fluid moves freely between the plasma, interstitial spaces, lymph, and cells.

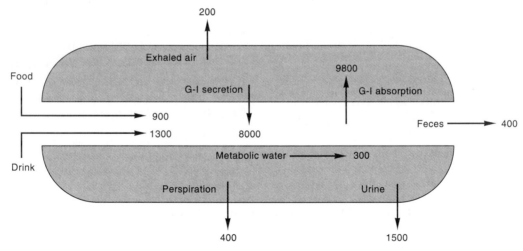

Figure 16.3   Principal inputs and outputs that determine normal body water balance. All volumes are in milliliter units.

ingestion, water is absorbed and enters the ECF. The remaining 300 ml of input is formed as a product of cellular energy metabolism.

Body water is lost primarily in the urine, which accounts for a daily output of about 1500 ml. Another 400 ml is lost in feces, and a similar volume leaves the body via the skin. This skin loss occurs as perspiration fluid is moved to the skin's surface by sweat gland ducts, and as tissue fluid slowly percolates to the skin's surface by way of the spaces between its cells. The remaining 200 ml escapes from the large alveolar surface and is lost in expired air. In addition, approximately 8000 ml of fluids,

containing mostly water, is secreted into the gastrointestinal lumen every day. This, however, is not an output from the body, because almost all is reabsorbed in the small and large intestine (fig. 16.3).

Electrolyte Concentration

The body's water molecules have numerous molecular-sized particles mixed among them. These are called **solute** particles. They are described as being **dissolved** in the water, which is called the **solvent.** The resulting mixture is a **solution.** Most solutes have a positive or negative charge associated with them. Such solutes are called ions. Their presence in a water solution enables it to conduct an electrical current, which would not flow through pure water. For this reason, such charged particles are called **electrolytes.** Those with a positive charge are called **cations,** while those with a negative charge are called **anions.**

Although many different solutes are present in the body fluids, relatively few are responsible for most conditions that produce potentially serious disease. Of the cations, sodium (Na^+), potassium (K^+), calcium (Ca^{++}), and hydrogen (H^+) ions are most important. The more significant anions are chloride (Cl^-), bicarbonate (HCO_3^-), and phosphate ($PO_4^=$). Because protein has a negative charge associated with its constituent amino acids, it also makes a significant contribution to the total anion complement of the body fluids. In this context it is referred to as **proteinate.**

The **concentration** of a solution is based on the ratio between the amount of solute and the amount of solvent. The total of all solutes present can be used to express the overall concentration of the solution. For example, a solution that contains little solute is said to be **dilute** compared with the same volume of a **concentrated** solution, which contains a large amount of solute. Concentration may also apply to a single solute; a solution may have a certain concentration of Na^+ and a different concentration of K^+. Brackets are used to denote the concentration of a solute. The expression [Na^+], for example, is read "the concentration of sodium ion".

The terms concentrated and dilute provide only a rough approximation of the solute/solvent ratio. In dealing with fluid and electrolyte balance, it is often necessary to express the specific quantity of solute present in a specific volume of solution. In solution chemistry, the ratio is expressed as the weight of solute present in a liter of solvent. The solute weight is often expressed in terms of **gram molecular weight.** This is the molecular weight of a substance expressed in grams. The term is often shortened to **mole (M).** A liter of solution containing 1 M of a solute is said to be a 1 molar (1M) solution; if the liter of solution contains 2 M of solute it is a 2 molar (2M) solution. Specifically, since sodium chloride (NaCl) has a molecular weight of 58 atomic mass units, a gram molecular weight of NaCl weighs 58 g. A 1.5M solution of NaCl would therefore contain 1.5 × 58 or 87 g of the salt in each liter of solution.

Expressing solution concentration in this way has many advantages, but physiologically it is often less appropriate. Another system of expressing concentration is therefore quite common. It is based on the number of **equivalents (Eq)** present in a liter of solution (Eq/L). An equivalent is the weight of a substance that will interact with one equivalent of another substance when the interaction is based on charge. Thus the number of equivalents is determined by the charge (or valence number). A liter of solution containing 1 Eq of solute is described as a

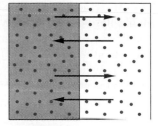

Diffusion down the concentration gradient

Equilibrium

Figure 16.4 Simple diffusion of particles through a permeable membrane. At equilibrium, diffusion continues but rates in both directions are equal, so no net displacement of particles occurs.

1 normal (1N) solution. If there were 0.3 Eq present, the concentration would be 0.3N. For example, 1 M of Na^+ in a liter of solution is the same as 1 Eq, since there is a single positive charge on the sodium ion. The same holds for the hydroxide ion (OH^-), with its single negative charge. By contrast, 1 M of Ca^{++} contains 2 Eq, since the calcium ion has a charge of 2. This means that 1 M of Ca^{++} has the potential to react with 2 M of OH^-. By the same logic, 0.5 M of Ca^{++} has the same number of equivalents as 1 mole of OH^-, and they would completely interact on that basis. To summarize, using normality to express concentration puts emphasis on the number of ions that react, rather than on the weight of the solute.

Because the mole and equivalent are inconveniently large for dealing with physiological concentrations, the **milliequivalent** (mEQ, 1/1000 of an equivalent) and the **millimole** (mM, 1/1000 of a mole) are commonly used.

Diffusion

The concentration of ECF electrolytes is the same in the plasma and interstitial fluid compartments, because of the ease of fluid motion between the blood and tissue spaces. The only significant exception is proteinate. Because the large plasma proteins can't pass through the capillary walls as easily as water, the interstitial concentration of protein is only about 1/15 that of plasma. For most electrolytes, any change of concentration in either division of the ECF is quickly followed by a compensating shift of electrolytes between the divisions until their concentrations are again equal.

Molecular or ionic movement of this sort in solutions occurs by **diffusion** (fig. 16.4). The frequent and random collision of solute and solvent particles produces a net particle motion down a concentration gradient, that is, from a region of high solute concentration to a region of lower solute concentration, until an equilibrium is established, meaning that the concentrations of the two regions are equal. At equilibrium, even though there is much diffusion, there is no net change of concentration between the two areas because there is no concentration gradient.

Movement through cell membranes occurs when small molecules and ions diffuse through membrane pores, when molecules dissolve in membrane lipid, or when a specialized **membrane transport system** (MTS) assists the passage of a specific ion or molecule. Such systems transport molecules whose size or other properties prevent their diffusion through the cell membrane (fig. 16.5). Some MTSs can move a specific ion or molecule from a region where it is in low concentration to one in which its concentration is higher. In other words, the ion or molecule is moved against its concentration gradient. To do this a cell must expend energy. For this reason such systems are often called **pumps.** They are said to work by **active transport,** as opposed to passive diffusion, which requires no expenditure of cellular energy.

By contrast to the situation that exists between the plasma and the interstitial fluid, electrolyte concentrations between the intracellular and extracellular compartments are substantially different for some ions (table 16.1). Such differences are the result of two factors. One is the permeability characteristics of the cell membrane, which limit the passage of certain electrolytes. The other is the action of ion pumps in the cell membrane. These produce and maintain an intracellular fluid that has, for example, a much higher concentration of K^+ and a much lower concentration of Na^+ than the ECF.

Osmosis

Not only electrolytes pass through cell membranes. Water freely passes through them by the process of **osmosis.** Osmosis is based on the same molecular collisions that produce diffusion, but the term osmosis is reserved for use specifically with reference to the motion of water molecules.

Osmosis is significant when water can move more easily than solute particles through a membrane that separates solutions with different concentrations. The solution's concentrations are determined by calculating the ratio between the total of all solute particles and the volume of water in which they are dissolved. The particle concentration is expressed in terms of **osmolality,** which describes a solution in terms of the total number of its solute particles per unit volume of water. The unit of osmolality is the **osmole.** It is the concentration of particles produced when 1 M of a solute that does not dissociate in water is added to 1 kg of water. In the case of glucose, therefore, the gram molecular weight dissolved in 1 kg of water produces a solution of 1 osmole. For sodium chloride (NaCl), 2 osmoles are present in 1 kg of water, because NaCl dissociates to yield two particles: a sodium ion and a chloride ion. For potassium phosphate (K_2PO_4), 3 osmoles would be produced, since this molecule splits into two potassium ions and one phosphate ion. Because an osmole is too large a unit for practical use in describing body fluid concentrations, the **milliosmole** (1/1000 osmole) is generally used.

The significance of osmolality as an expression of a solution's concentration lies in its emphasis on particle

(a)

(b)

(c)

Figure 16.5   (*a*) Some ions and larger molecules cannot pass through cell membranes. (*b*) Membrane transport systems (dark boxes) assist in moving such particles through the membrane. (*c*) Active transport, in which the transport system moves particles against the concentration gradient.

Table 16.1	Ion Concentration of the Intracellular (ICF) and Extracellular (ECF) Fluid Compartments	
	Concentration	
Ion	**ICF**	**ECF**
Sodium	10	147
Potassium	140	4
Chloride	4	114
Bicarbonate	10	30
Biphosphate	100	2

Values are in milliequivalents per liter of water.

number. Osmolality is dependent only on the number of particles and not on the particle size. This means that from 1 g of a high-molecular-weight protein that contains few particles, there is a much smaller osmotic effect than from 1 g of a low-molecular-weight material that contains many particles. In osmosis, water moves from an area of lower osmolality (lower total solute particle concentration or higher water concentration) to one of higher osmolality (higher total solute particle concentration or lower water concentration).

Under normal circumstances, the intracellular and extracellular compartments have the same osmolality, even though the concentrations of particular ions may vary greatly on either side of the cell's membrane. In this case, the two solutions are said to be **isotonic.** When the ECF has

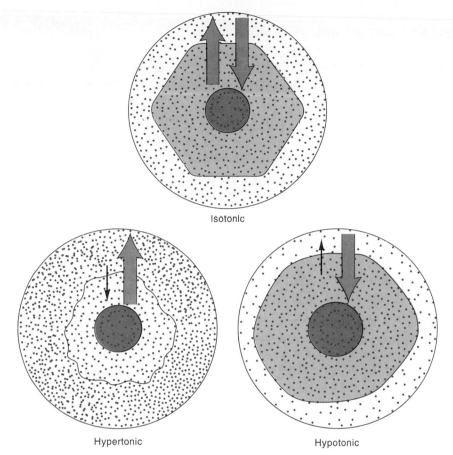

Isotonic

Hypertonic

Hypotonic

Figure 16.6   Osmosis. When the extracellular fluid (ECF) is isotonic to a cell, no net water displacement occurs even though osmotic exchange proceeds. If the ECF is hypertonic to the cell, then net osmotic loss from the cell causes cell shrinking. When the ECF is hypotonic to the cell, osmotic inflow exceeds outflow and the cell swells.

a greater osmolality than that within cells, the ECF is said to be **hypertonic** to the intracellular fluid. When ECF osmolality is less than that of intracellular fluid, the ECF is described as **hypotonic** compared to the intracellular fluid. Note that the concept of osmolality allows expression of overall solute concentration in precise units, whereas the terms hypertonic and hypotonic provide only comparative information. Cells exposed to hypotonic solutions accumulate water by osmosis and swell. The intracellular pressure may rise to the point where the cells rupture. Cells exposed to hypertonic solutions lose water by osmosis and shrink (fig. 16.6).

Electrolyte Balance

The level of electrolytes in the body fluids is determined by the balance between their input and their loss. All normal electrolyte input is derived from the diet. The plant and animal tissues, and their derivatives, that make up most well-balanced diets contain all the electrolytes needed to maintain normal homeostasis. Losses occur mainly in three ways. First, as perspiration fluid passes to the body surface, it carries with it various electrolytes, which are then lost. Second, substantial quantities of electrolytes are present in

the secretions passed into the alimentary canal daily. Most of these are absorbed along the GI tract, but small amounts are not, and these are lost in feces. The third and most important route of electrolyte loss is the urine. Under normal circumstances, urinary losses of electrolytes far exceed losses from the skin and feces. The kidney receives a very large plasma flow from which it can remove and excrete water and various ions to achieve fluid and electrolyte balance.

Renal Regulation of Fluid and Electrolytes

The role of the kidney in fluid and electrolyte balance is vital. On the one hand, the kidney functions to excrete any fluid and/or electrolytes present in excess of homeostatic set points. On the other hand, it can retain fluid and/or electrolytes when they fall below the required level. Note here the importance of dietary input. When an electrolyte deficiency occurs, the kidney can only reduce loss of that electrolyte via the urine. It thus supports the existing level and reduces further losses, but this is still not the same as providing an additional input. In the case of water deficiency, when the body fluids are hypertonic, the thirst drive is activated to stimulate new water input. In the case of electrolytes, however, the situation is different. There is no potassium drive or calcium hunger to induce a new electrolyte input; people don't develop a craving for chloride. So when an electrolyte deficiency does exist, if the diet does not make enough of these ions available for uptake from the GI tract, renal retention mechanisms can only delay a worsening of the deficiency state.

The essential nephron mechanisms of filtration, selective reabsorption, and tubular secretion were described in chapter 15. These mechanisms are applied to water and the various body electrolytes to achieve the appropriate balance of loss and retention needed to maintain homeostasis. The ability of the nephron to regulate a particular ion depends on its diffusion properties and the membrane transport systems of the nephron's tubular cells, which determine the rates of reabsorption or tubular secretion of that ion. These processes are important to fluid and electrolyte balance because they selectively transport specific ions out of the tubule lumen to achieve retention, or into it for excretion. By comparison, filtration is nonspecific. It affects water and all its solutes, excepting the large plasma proteins. The rate of activity of nephron membrane transport systems is regulated to achieve varying degrees of retention or excretion. One such regulating factor is the tubule cells' response to changes in the ion's concentration in the fluids that bathe its surface. Other controlling inputs are hormones, whose level in the blood determines the transport rate. However regulated, nephron excretion of the major electrolytes—Na^+, K^+, and Cl^-—has a major impact on water balance.

The high concentration of Na^+ in the ECF (140 mEq/L) means that a large amount will enter the nephron tubule lumen after filtration at the glomerulus. The proximal convoluted tubule reabsorbs about 90% of the filtered Na^+, which accumulates in the peritubular tissue spaces. Cl^- and HCO_3^- passively accompany Na^+ ion, maintaining a balance of positive and negative charges. K^+ is almost completely reabsorbed, but its low concentration in filtrate produces a smaller effect than that of Na^+, Cl^-, and HCO_3^-. As these ions enter the peritubular spaces they increase osmotic pressure, and the resulting osmosis causes large volumes of water to be reabsorbed from the tubule. By this mechanism, over 80% of filtrate is returned to the blood that circulates through the peritubular capillaries (fig. 16.7). This process provides retention of the greatest portion of Na^+, Cl^-, and water.

Most homeostatic regulation is accomplished in the distal convoluted tubule, even though the bulk of the filtrate is reabsorbed in the proximal tubule. The composition of blood is adjusted by secretion into, and reabsorption from, the fluid in the distal tubules under the influence of several controlling inputs. The adrenocortical hormone **aldosterone** regulates uptake of Na^+ from the tubule lumen. For each Na^+ reabsorbed, one K^+ is secreted into the lumen. Na^+ excretion is also regulated by one or more natriuretic factors, so named because they promote urinary sodium

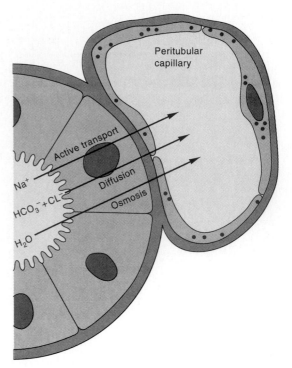

Figure 16.7   Reabsorption through the nephron tubule. Sodium is actively transported from filtrate to the blood. Chloride and bicarbonate ions follow the positively charged sodium, maintaining the charge equilibrium. The resulting concentration gradient is responsible for the osmosis of water that follows.

loss, **natriuresis.** The best-known of these is **atrial natriuretic factor** (ANF). It is secreted by the atria in response to their distention by increased plasma volume. The increase in ANF increases filtration and blocks sodium reabsorption, producing sodium loss, water loss, and a reduction of circulating plasma volume.

Urinary water loss is regulated by **antidiuretic hormone** (ADH), also known as **arginine vasopressin,** which is released from the posterior pituitary gland. ADH increases the water permeability of collecting duct cells and to a lesser extent those of the distal convoluted tubule. Because the collecting duct is relatively impermeable to ions, water is drawn by osmosis into the hypertonic interstitial fluid of the renal medulla. ADH is therefore an important component of the system regulating the osmotic pressure of the extracellular fluid (fig. 16.8). ADH is released into the blood in response to input from pressure receptors, principally those in the heart, and osmoreceptors in the brain. Decreased BHP, cardiac pressure, and increased osmolality stimulate ADH secretion. Water retention tends to expand plasma volume and reduce osmolality. Receptor input to the thirst center, in the hypothalamus, also activates the thirst drive, causing additional water intake.

Aldosterone secretion depends on the concentration of K^+ in plasma and on the renin-angiotensin system, which is

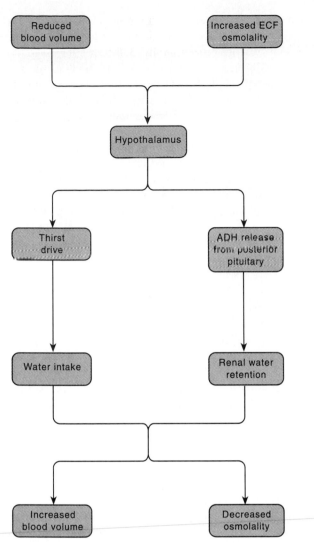

Figure 16.8   ADH-mediated compensation can reduce losses when the body fluid osmolality or volume is increased. The thirst drive provides new input to aid the corrective response.

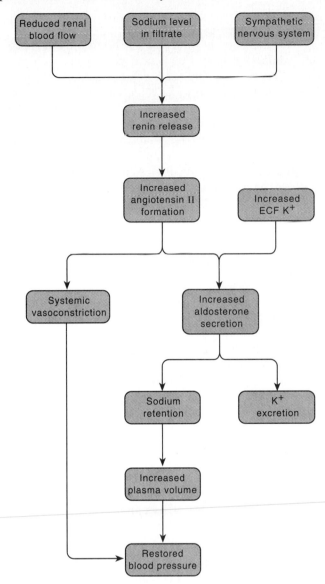

Figure 16.9   Compensations that restore falling blood pressure are mediated, in part, by the renin-angiotensin system.

sensitive to the Na$^+$ level in filtrate, to renal blood flow, and to sympathetic input from the CNS (fig. 16.9). Changes in BHP are related to plasma volume, which in turn is dependent on the overall volume of ECF. Should normal ECF volume or osmolality change, appropriate alterations in aldosterone and ADH secretion produce corrective responses in the nephron that restore fluid volume and osmolality.

BODY FLUID IMBALANCE

The preceding discussion of water and Na$^+$ regulation illustrates two essential factors that have a bearing on fluid imbalances. The first is the close linking of Na$^+$ and water. Since Na$^+$ is the dominant single electrolyte in the ECF—indeed, contributing about half its osmolality—a change in Na$^+$ level has significant effects on water balance. Simi-

larly, any gain or loss of pure water will soon have an effect on Na$^+$ concentration. The second factor worthy of note is that, apart from changes in Na$^+$ or water intake, fluid imbalance problems are often based on defects in the mechanisms that maintain body fluid concentration and volume homeostasis.

In the following sections, and in clinical situations, it is important to use appropriate terminology to describe fluid imbalance. The term **volume** implies that both water and Na$^+$ are involved. For example, you may encounter a patient who is threatened with hypovolemic shock due to **volume depletion.** On the other hand, if water loss or gain dominates the clinical picture, and Na$^+$ gain or loss is minimal, then **dehydration** and **water intoxication** are the correct descriptive terms. Let us consider these two conditions before we deal with volume derangements.

Dehydration

This is the condition in which there is decreased total body water, while total body Na^+ is near normal. It may come about as the result of reduced water intake or excessive losses. Lack of access to water is unusual, but may arise in those dependent on others to supply it. Children, the elderly, the bedridden or crippled, or those with some compromised mental capacity are particularly at risk. If there is no water replacement, skin, respiratory, and GI losses continue and dehydration results. Abnormally high water losses may be present in certain disease conditions. In diabetes insipidus, a condition described in chapter 17, ADH secretion is suppressed and the resulting inhibition of renal water reabsorption promotes heavy water loss. In untreated diabetes mellitus, high blood glucose increases the osmotic pressure of nephron filtrate, and thereby also inhibits water reabsorption.

Under the threat of developing dehydration, both increased ECF osmolality and BHP decreases can activate the thirst drive. This drive is usually able to restore normal ECF concentration even when losses are quite high, as in cases of heavy perspiration and diabetes. However, in members of the dependent groups indicated earlier, or in those with a defective thirst mechanism, correction of water depletion may not occur, and if losses are heavy, severe dehydration may develop quite rapidly.

In dehydration, Na^+ levels are near normal, but since there is a decreased water volume, the body fluids become hypertonic. Considered in terms of Na^+, the dominant ECF ion, the situation is one of **hypernatremia** (*natrium* is the Latin word for sodium). This condition is sometimes described as **relative hypernatremia** to imply that water loss, rather than Na^+ gain, is at the heart of the matter.

Water Intoxication

An increase in total body water, with no changes in the body's total Na^+ level, dilutes the ECF and produces the condition of water intoxication. Increased water intake is normally not able to dilute the body fluids significantly because the renal diuresis responses are so efficient. With normally functioning kidneys, even an intake of over 15 liters per day can be cleared by a correspondingly large urinary output. Even if there is an extreme **polydipsia** (excessive water drinking), as might be found in some mental aberrations, water intoxication will rarely develop. Much more frequently, it arises from an impaired water excretion capacity based on excessive ADH secretion. When it occurs, nephron tubule water permeability is increased to produce excessive water retention at normal renal osmolality gradients.

Excessive ADH secretion produces the **syndrome of inappropriate ADH secretion** (SIADH). It arises because of excessive ADH release by the posterior pituitary when there is no physiological requirement for it. Various CNS disturbances, such as infection, trauma (including surgery), cerebral hemorrhage, pain, or anesthesia may be involved, as may various psychogenic disorders. The underlying mechanism seems to involve disturbances in the control system that regulates ADH secretion. These disturbances produce a lower set point for body fluid osmolality, and the posterior pituitary responds with increased ADH output.

Although ADH is normally secreted by the posterior pituitary, some nonendocrine tumors can also secrete ADH or functionally similar substances. The tumors involved include oat cell carcinoma of the lung and certain tumors of the pancreas, intestine, or brain. Lung secretion of ADH is associated with some nontumor conditions, COPD, tuberculosis, and asthma, but the mechanisms are unclear. Certain drugs can produce SIADH, either by stimulating ADH secretion or by increasing renal tubule sensitivity to it. Chlorpropamide (used by diabetics), carbamazepine (an antiepileptic), cyclophosphamide (a cancer chemotherapy agent), and clofibrate (an antihyperlipidemic) are the drugs most often involved.

Like dehydration, water intoxication may be considered in terms of Na^+. In that context, we refer to the situation as one of **relative hyponatremia:** normal total Na^+ in an increased volume of solvent. In many clinical settings, the terms dehydration and water intoxication are not even used. Instead, attention is centered on Na^+, and only the relevant "natremia" terms are employed.

Gains or Losses of Water and Sodium

Pure water loss or gain is much less common than conditions in which both water and Na^+ are involved. Usually the fluid volume change is due to an initial Na^+ change, with water effects following. Note that Na^+ and water levels may not always be altered to the same degree. In some cases, Na^+ loss may exceed water loss, producing a hypotonic ECF. In other cases, where water loss exceeds Na^+ loss, the ECF becomes hypertonic. Of course, if water and Na^+ changes are matched, then the ECF remains isotonic even though the volume may be increased (expanded) or decreased (depleted). Table 16.2 presents the possible water and volume changes using this terminology.

Volume Depletion

When water and electrolytes are lost from the ECF, volume depletion is the result. Losses may arise through heavy perspiration, vomiting or diarrhea, or intestinal resection or GI fistulas that reduce absorption. Renal losses may also be involved when kidney disease impairs Na^+ reabsorption or in cases of adrenal cortex insufficiency, which reduces aldosterone output. Of course, diuretic therapy can also produce exaggerated volume losses via the kidney, if dosage is imprecise or if the drug is misused by the patient. Skin burns may also result in volume depletion as the skin's barrier function is lost and evaporative losses are

Table 16.2   Changes Associated with Volume Depletion and Expansion

Precipitating Condition	Descriptive Terminology	Volume Change ECF	ICF	Sodium Change
Chronic diarrhea	Isotonic depletion	D	—	—
Intense perspiration	Hypertonic depletion	D	D	I
Renal Na$^+$ loss	Hypotonic depletion	D	I	D
Normal saline infusion	Isotonic expansion	I	—	—
Hypertonic saline infusion	Hypertonic expansion	I	D	I
Water intoxication	Hypotonic expansion	I	I	D

D = decrease, I = increase, — = unchanged.

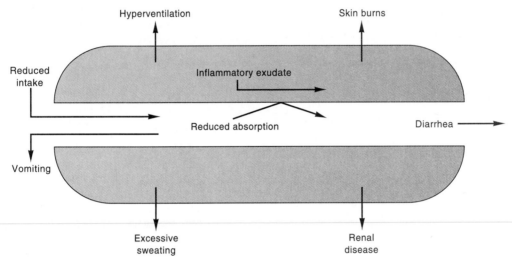

Figure 16.10   Factors contributing to volume depletion.

exaggerated. A water-dominated organism in a dry environment relies heavily on the skin to prevent fluid loss, and burns are a serious threat if they are extensive. Whereas GI, kidney, and skin losses are true losses from the body fluids, various **sequestration states** (states in which inflammatory exudate or blood is rapidly lost from the vessels) can produce volume depletion effects. Acute peritonitis, pancreatitis, and hemorrhage in trauma are examples (fig. 16.10). Note that in edema and ascites, which are slow to develop, volume compensation reflexes are usually able to prevent volume depletion. Specifics of the balance between Na$^+$ and water loss are presented in table 16.2.

Volume Excess

This condition is largely the result of renal Na$^+$ and water retention, which may be due to kidney disease or to cardiac or liver conditions that promote water and sodium retention. In renal failure, the kidneys lose the ability to excrete Na$^+$, usually as a result of declining filtration. Water

retention follows, and the ECF volume increases. In congestive heart failure, as well as in liver cirrhosis, edema and ascites are often present. In these conditions, the loss of fluid from the plasma activates reflexes that seek to restore volume by retaining Na$^+$. As they expand plasma volume, additional fluid is lost from the plasma and the cycle repeats. This can lead to serious consequences, as described in the earlier chapters dealing with CHF and cirrhosis. Urinary protein losses associated with the nephrotic syndrome can also produce edema as a result of the attendant decrease in plasma osmotic pressure. Cycling of volume expansion reflexes follows as in CHF and cirrhosis.

Fluid retention can also arise in cases of aldosterone hypersecretion. The cause may be adrenal cortex hyperplasia or a benign tumor. In other cases, excessive renin secretion may be responsible, often as a response to renal ischemia. Overall, these conditions contribute to fluid volume excess much less than do CHF, cirrhosis, and renal failure.

Figure 16.11   Principal effects of fluid imbalance.

Consequences of Fluid Imbalance

Volume expansion or contraction primarily produces circulatory and osmotic effects. Circulatory effects are the result of changes in plasma volume and therefore BHP. At modest volume changes, pressure-regulating reflexes may be able to maintain normal BHP. If larger volume decreases develop, some pressure drop may result, or if increased plasma volume raises pressure beyond correctable levels, BHP increases and systemic edema will follow. Of course, if fluid losses are large and rapid, for example at a badly burned surface or from hemorrhage in massive trauma, then hypovolemic shock may arise.

In volume depletion states where the plasma remains isotonic, water retention reflexes will produce thirsty patients with dry oral mucous membranes, reduced perspiration, and lower urinary output. As well, there is usually a reduction in skin **turgor.** This is the firmness and fullness of the skin that results from a normal interstitial fluid pressure. If plasma volume is depleted, interstitial fluid moves from the tissue spaces to compensate, and reduced turgor is the result. In the elderly, however, skin aging changes may make the assessment of turgor difficult. Reduced plasma volume is also reflected in an increased hematocrit.

In many fluid imbalance cases, where plasma osmolarity is changed, signs and symptoms arise from the shrinking or swelling of CNS cells and the resulting disruption of their normal sodium concentration. When dehydration produces a hypertonic plasma (relative hypernatremia), the higher plasma osmolality draws water from the intracellular compartment (fig. 16.11). If volume depletion is due to Na^+ loss exceeding water loss, the plasma becomes hypotonic and water enters the cells, causing them to swell.

In volume excess states, similar osmotic swelling or shrinkage occurs. In water intoxication, the plasma becomes hypotonic, favoring osmotic flow into the cellular compartment (fig. 16.11). When Na^+ retention arises as a result of renal malfunction or aldosterone hypersecretion, water retention tends to exceed Na^+ retention, so the plasma is also hypotonic in such cases.

When CNS cells undergo mild osmotic shrinkage, the patient exhibits weakness, lassitude, and irritability. With progression to more profound levels of derangement, seizures, coma, and death may occur. If brain shrinkage develops rapidly, hemorrhage from torn cerebral veins may result to compound the problem.

In fluid excess states, the ECF volume is increased and is usually hypotonic. (Recall that when both are retained, water retention exceeds Na^+ retention to produce a relative hyponatremia.) The result is an osmotic shift to the cellular compartment and the swelling of the CNS. This condition is sometimes referred to as cerebral edema. Swelling in the brain produces headache, nausea, and vomiting. The relative intracellular hyponatremia also produces malaise and lethargy at low levels, with seizures and coma more prevalent if swelling is increased (fig. 16.12).

Therapy in Fluid Imbalance

Volume depletion due to hemorrhage can be restored with carefully matched whole blood or an appropriate blood fraction. **Normal saline** (isotonic) solutions can readily restore volume and plasma concentration. If the kidneys are functioning, they will soon correct Na^+ and water imbalance as long as they have an adequate volume of infused saline on which to work. If fluid is present to excess,

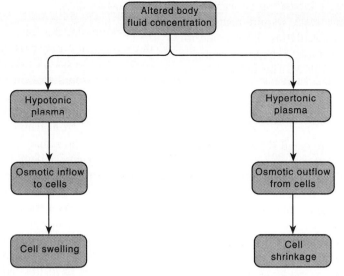

Figure 16.12   Cellular consequences of undesirable osmotic shifts when body fluid concentration is disrupted.

Iatrogenic Fluid Imbalance

!!

If therapy is imprecise or overzealous, fluid imbalance may be worsened. An example of such an iatrogenic complication is fluid excess caused by excessive saline infusion during volume depletion therapy. Another example is a too-vigorous application of diuretics, intended to promote diuresis but unintentionally producing a depletion state.

diuretic therapy can restore volume if the kidneys are unable to compensate after the underlying problem has been addressed.

ELECTROLYTE IMBALANCE

For the sake of clarity, the major electrolytes are considered separately in the following sections. However, in clinical situations, excess or deficiency of one ion often produces imbalance in other ions. These effects, and those of the water imbalance that often accompanies them, combine to produce the pattern of signs and symptoms seen in a given patient.

Sodium Imbalance

The intimate relation between Na^+ imbalance and body water alterations has already been described in the context of fluid imbalance. The key points of Na^+ level alterations are considered in the following sections.

Hyponatremia

Na^+ deficiencies are almost always the result of body fluid loss rather than inadequate Na^+ intake. Na^+ is plentiful in even minimal diets, so meeting normal requirements is rarely a problem. Note also that much hyponatremia is relative, that is, the result of excessive body water rather than a true Na^+ depletion. Where renal defects prevent adequate Na^+ retention, or when aldosterone levels are depressed, Na^+ losses occur, but they are soon matched by water losses that produce an isotonic ECF. Thus, even though Na^+ has been lost, its concentration is normal.

Hypernatremia

The Na^+ excess state most often arises when water losses exceed Na^+ losses, producing a relative hypernatremia. True hypernatremia is rare, but may arise where therapeutic administration of NaCl infusions is excessive. If Na^+ is excessively retained, corresponding water retention produces systemic edema.

Potassium Imbalance

Potassium (K^+) is the dominant cation of the intracellular fluid compartment, which contains about 98% of the body's total K^+. Its concentration in the ICF is about 40 times that of the ECF and thus it represents the principal osmotic determinant of cellular volume. K^+ also plays an important role in neuromuscular activity, through its contribution to the membrane potentials on which neuron and muscle function depend.

Perspiration and fecal losses of K^+ are normally low. Most dietary K^+ is excreted in the urine by two mechanisms. In one, tubule cells directly respond to K^+ concentration in the renal interstitium, appropriately increasing or decreasing tubular secretion to match homeostatic requirements. The second mechanism depends on circulating aldosterone to regulate K^+ reabsorption via tubule transport systems. Increased aldosterone levels are followed by reduced reabsorption and increased renal K^+ excretion.

Hypokalemia

Hypokalemia is the condition of lowered K^+ concentration (*kalium* is Latin for potassium). It may be due to a total body K^+ deficit or to shifts of K^+ from the ECF into the cellular compartment. Such shifts may arise as cellular K^+ uptake is stimulated, for example by insulin, glucose, or drugs that mimic certain sympathetic nervous system effects. K^+ also shifts into cells in the acid imbalance condition called alkalosis, described in a later section.

K^+ deficiency may result from inadequate dietary K^+ intake. This is unlikely, but there is increased risk when appetite is depressed, as it commonly is in the elderly, those with CNS or GI disturbances that cause chronic nausea, and those with a psychogenic aversion to eating. Hypokalemia is more likely to be caused by excessive loss of K^+ in ways similar to those in which Na^+ is lost: in vomiting, heavy perspiration, and, particularly in cases of chronic diarrhea, as liquid stool content. Laxative abusers are also therefore at risk of K^+ depletion. Absorption difficulties can lower K^+ intake, especially where a GI fistula allows by-passing of absorptive intestinal surface or in cases of intestinal resection.

Kidney tubule reabsorption defects or aldosterone hypersecretion states may also increase K^+ losses. Drugs can play a role as well, particularly diuretics such as furosemide, ethacrynic acid, acetazolamide, and thiazides. As in the case of most electrolytes, there is the potential for an imbalance following inappropriate administration of intravenous fluid, in this case a solution deficient in K^+ (fig. 16.13).

In hypokalemia, the dominant signs and symptoms are a reflection of disordered neuromuscular function. Weakness, muscle twitching, and depressed neuromuscular reflex responses are typical. Skeletal muscles may lose their normal firmness, i.e., they demonstrate a loss of neuromuscular tone. A characteristic electrocardiographic change is seen in hypokalemia. It involves depression of the S-T segment, flattening of the T wave, and a prominent U wave (fig. 16.14). The U wave is a minor deflection of the ECG that follows the T wave. Its underlying cause is unknown, as is the reason for its prominence in hypokalemia. Intestinal smooth muscle may be affected, causing paralytic ileus and vomiting.

Hypokalemia also has an impact on the kidney. Low K^+ levels seems to promote prostaglandin synthesis. They reduce the tubule's sensitivity to ADH, and diuresis and polyuria result.

Hyperkalemia

Hyperkalemia, the state of K^+ excess, is potentially life-threatening and may arise in aldosterone deficiency states in which depression of renal excretion causes K^+ retention. Of course, renal failure or excessive intravenous fluid administration can also cause hyperkalemia. In cases of extensive trauma, especially crushing injuries, massive release of K^+ from damaged cells may produce a K^+ load that exceeds the kidneys' excretion capacity. In conditions involving extensive hemolysis, large amounts of K^+ may be released from damaged red cells. In blood stored for transfusion, erythrocytes are unable to maintain intracellular K^+ concentration. As a result, K^+ leaks into the plasma and can cause hyperkalemia in the recipient following transfusion. The effect is most pronounced when a large amount of blood is used after prolonged storage.

K^+ shifts from the cellular compartment can increase ICF K^+ levels. This occurs most often in acid-base imbalances and is described later in this chapter. Just as insulin and certain drugs promote K^+ uptake and hypokalemia, beta blockers and insulin deficiency have the opposite effect, limiting K^+ uptake from the ECF.

Prolonged and severe hyperkalemia is potentially grave. Its major effect is on the myocardium, causing arrhythmias. Characteristic ECG changes are also present in hyperkalemia. Initially, the S-T segment is depressed, whereas T waves are increased with progression of K^+ build-up. The P wave is lost, the QRS complex broadens, and the T waves become especially prominent (fig. 16.15).

Chloride Imbalance

Chloride (Cl^-) is another of the principal anions in the ECF. It passively follows Na^+, both when it is absorbed from the GI lumen and when it is reabsorbed in the nephron. For this reason **hypochloremia,** the condition of Cl^- deficiency, is typically associated with Na^+ deficiency. Thus, increased loss of GI fluids, perspiration, or renal failure can produce hypochloremia. In hypokalemia, K^+ retention mechanisms may produce a corresponding loss of Na^+. When loss of Cl^- follows that of Na^+, hypochloremia may result. In **hyperchloremia,** excessive Cl^- is usually present from increased intake. This might be the result of dietary excess or excessive intravenous infusion of NaCl in Na^+ depletion therapy. The influx of Na^+ adequate to correct hyponatremia can easily produce hyperchloremia, because the Na^+ and Cl^- in the intravenous infusion are present in equal concentrations. The exceptions to the similarity in conditions that give rise to Na^+ and Cl^- imbalances are acid-base changes, which can affect Cl^- but not Na^+. These are described in the acid-base section, later in the chapter.

Signs and symptoms of Cl^- imbalance are similar to those seen in Na^+ imbalance, that is, those reflecting fluid imbalance: edema and acute weight gain in hyperchloremia and dehydration effects in hypochloremia.

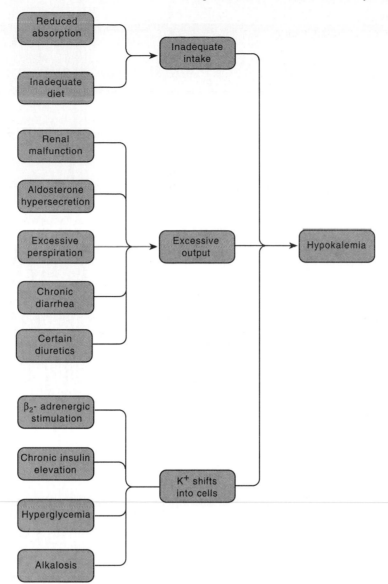

Figure 16.13   Principal factors in the pathogenesis of hypokalemia.

Calcium Imbalance

Calcium ion (Ca^{++}) is present in both the ECF and the ICF. The ECF concentration is twice that of the ICF. Ca^{++} is present in two forms, which exist in equilibrium. One form is ionized calcium, and the other is calcium bound to citrate ion or protein. If more of the ionized form is present, the equilibrium shifts to restore balance by binding more of the ionized form to protein or citrate. A deficiency of ionized calcium causes an opposite shift of the equilibrium as calcium is split from its binding molecule.

Ca^{++} homeostasis is principally mediated by **parathyroid hormone** (PTH). Parathyroid cells modify their secretion of this hormone when ECF Ca^{++} deviates from its normal range. PTH increases GI absorption and renal retention of Ca^{++} and it also mobilizes Ca^{++} from bone. Vitamin D functions similarly in supporting ECF Ca^{++} concentration.

The thyroid hormone **calcitonin** also affects ECF Ca^{++} by promoting excretion when Ca^{++} is present to excess.

The state of Ca^{++} excess is called **hypercalcemia.** It may result from hyperparathyroidism or hypothyroid states, both of which favor Ca^{++} retention. Similarly, in renal disease, the major excretory pathway of Ca^{++} may be suppressed, causing Ca^{++} retention. Because vitamin D is required for Ca^{++} absorption, hypercalcemia may be caused by excessive therapeutic intake of the vitamin. Increased ICF Ca^{++} is also associated with the presence of various malignant tumors, as a result of their secretion of substances with PTH-like effects. Renal Ca^{++} retention is linked to the excretion of phosphate ion, $PO_4^{=}$. As a result, hypercalcemia stemming from renal Ca^{++} retention is often accompanied by phosphate deficiency, or **hypophosphatemia.**

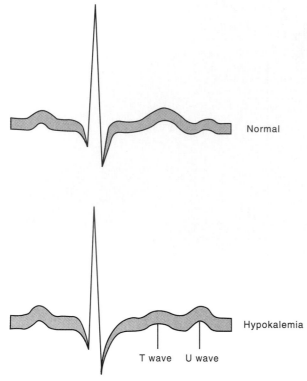

Figure 16.14   The ECG in hypokalemia. The T wave is depressed and the U wave is elevated.

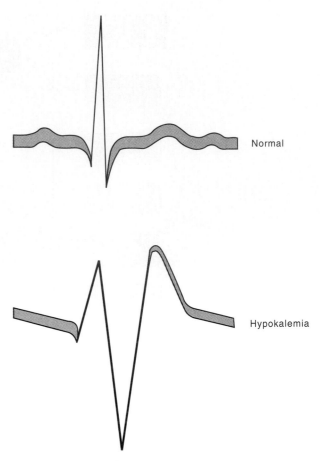

Figure 16.15   The ECG in hyperkalemia. All elements are abnormal.

Hypercalcemia is typically associated with nephrolithiasis, muscle cramps, and pain. Some GI hyperactivity is also common, producing nausea, abdominal cramps, and diarrhea. The widespread tissue deposition of calcium seen in chronic hypercalcemia is termed **metastatic calcification** and should not be confused with dystrophic calcification, the Ca^{++} deposition at sites of necrosis, described in chapter 1.

Although abdominal cramps are also seen in **hypocalcemia,** hyperactive neuromuscular reflexes and **tetany** differentiate it from Ca^{++} excess states. Tetany is a pattern of excessive muscle irritability involving intense, paroxysmal muscle spasms in the extremities. A deficiency of Ca^{++} may result from a dietary lack of vitamin D, suppression of parathyroid function, or hypersecretion of calcitonin. Sprue or other malabsorption states can also produce hypocalcemia. Because the absorption of Ca^{++} depends on normal intestinal acidity, antacid therapy for peptic ulcers or gastric resection may so reduce intestinal acidity that absorption of Ca^{++} is depressed. Widespread infection and pancreatic or peritoneal inflammation may also produce hypocalcemia because they promote the binding of Ca^{++} so that its ionized form is less available to the ECF (fig. 16.16). Ca^{++} also has effects on acid-base balance, which are described shortly.

THERAPY IN FLUID AND ELECTROLYTE IMBALANCE

As in any therapy, in cases of fluid and electrolyte imbalance, an attempt is made to correct the initial cause of the imbalance. Then interventions promoting loss in excess states, or increased input in deficiency states, can proceed. In deficiency states, intravenous administration of the appropriate fluid and electrolytes can restore balance. Water movement from the plasma to the tissue spaces or to the ICF and vice versa can be accomplished by intravenous infusion to produce an appropriate change in plasma osmolality.

When total body fluid is excessive, diuretics are used to stimulate renal water loss. Most depress nephron Na^+ reabsorption, so that water is lost and fluid volume is reduced. Note, here, the potential for excessive diuretic therapy that could produce hyponatremia and hyperkalemia. Other diuretics function by interfering with passive reabsorption of Cl^- in the nephron. This reduces the osmolality gradient between the nephron and the peritubular tissues and therefore limits osmotic water reabsorption. Another approach involves diuretics that reduce the response of the nephron tubule to ADH. The reduction of

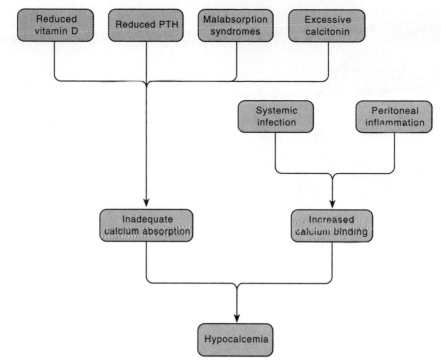

Figure 16.16   Major factors that may contribute to hypocalcemia.

water permeability that results produces the desired water loss while at the same time retaining electrolytes.

ACID-BASE IMBALANCE

The acidity of the body fluids is a critical variable in normal metabolism. Even small changes in acidity can produce major disturbances of function, because many physiological chemical reactions are strongly influenced by pH. In particular, most cellular enzymes function only within a narrow range of pH change, beyond which reaction rates fall sharply. Changes in acid-base balance also affect several electrolytes, Na^+, K^+ and Cl^-, in particular, which can further disrupt homeostasis. The normal range of pH is between 7.35 and 7.45, with an average value of 7.40. When pH falls below 7.35, a condition of **acidosis** is said to exist, whereas above 7.45 the term **alkalosis** is used. The critical nature of pH is indicated by the fact that it need vary only slightly to produce disease. Symptoms develop when pH falls below 6.85 or rises above 7.65. Below pH 6.8 and above pH 8.0, death occurs.

The hydrogen ion (H^+) of the body fluids is produced directly or indirectly as a result of cellular metabolism. Protein and fat metabolism produces organic or inorganic acids, but these amounts are small. Aerobic energy metabolism contributes over 100 times more by constantly producing carbon dioxide, which affects pH via the carbonic acid equilibrium:

$$CO_2 + H_2O \;\rightleftarrows\; H_2CO_3 \;\rightleftarrows\; H^+ + HCO_3^-$$

The essential requirement in maintaining correct pH is that H^+ be excreted at a rate that matches its production. The lungs are crucial to this process, in that by exhaling CO_2, they can bring about a shift in the carbonic acid equilibrium that reduces H^+ levels. Because CO_2 gas is linked to acid via carbonic acid, it is sometimes referred to as **volatile acid.** Acids produced in protein and lipid metabolism are excreted in the kidney. These are known as **fixed acids.**

Although fixed and volatile acids can be efficiently excreted, a potential problem arises in the cells where H^+ is initially produced. Because only slight increases in [H^+] can disrupt cellular function, it is necessary to cope with this newly produced acid until it can be excreted. This task is accomplished by a **buffer system,** which functions to resist changes in pH by taking up or releasing H^+ when its concentration changes. Only free, unassociated H^+ contributes to acidity. When taken up by another molecule, the hydrogen is no longer free and no longer acts as an acid. This is the essence of a buffer's function.

Immediately on its formation in cells, H^+ is taken up by a phosphate buffer system. It is then passed to the major ECF buffer system, which is based on the carbonic acid equilibrium. In cells and in both ECF compartments, proteins, including plasma proteins and the hemoglobin in red cells, also function as buffers in that they can take up H^+ when it is in high concentration and release it should pH rise (fig. 16.17). It is the buffers of the ICF and ECF that take up and hold H^+ until it can be excreted.

Figure 16.17   Principal buffer systems that take up H^+ in cells are cell proteins (P^-) and a phosphate system. Bicarbonate buffering occurs in the interstitium and plasma. Plasma proteins (PP) and hemoglobin (Hb) are other important buffers.

Hydrogen Ion Excretion

Most H^+ excretion occurs by the exhalation of volatile acid in the lungs. This system has the ability to adjust its excretion by changes in ventilation. A system of systemic chemoreceptors sensitive to acid have input to the brain stem, where respiratory control centers are housed. When ECF H^+ level is increased, an increased ventilation response drives off CO_2 to lower the H^+ concentration. This system can effectively cope with the CO_2 generated by aerobic energy metabolism, but additional regulation capacity is needed for three reasons. One is to provide a backup system for acid excretion in situations where respiratory insufficiency compromises CO_2 clearance. The second is the need to excrete the fixed acid produced by protein and lipid metabolism, which the lungs can't excrete. The third reason is the need to insure the reabsorption of filtered bicarbonate and to generate additional HCO_3^- to replace the amount expended in buffering activities. Renal processes provide these needed regulatory capabilities.

Immediate local production of H^+ for excretion occurs in the nephron tubule, using CO_2 from the plasma and its own metabolism. Carbonic anhydrase catalyzes the reaction between CO_2 and water to form H_2CO_3, which then dissociates to yield H^+. It is secreted into the lumen as Na^+ is reabsorbed. This insures that there is no positive charge excess in the lumen. The HCO_3^- produced by the dissociation of H_2CO_3 leaves the tubule cell to enter the blood and

(a)

(b)

Figure 16.18   Excretion of H^+ in the nephron tubule. C. A. is the enzyme carbonic anhydrase, which catalyzes the reversible carbonic acid equilibrium. (*a*) Filtered bicarbonate combines with H^+ formed in tubule. H_E^+ is excess for which no HCO_3^- is available so it is lost in urine. (*b*) In this case, since body fluids are too alkaline, less H^+ is available to combine with HCO_3^-, which is lost to make the body fluids more acid.

is now available for buffering action in the ECF. This regeneration of buffering capacity is an important aspect of renal acid-base regulation and is quite efficient in that the excretion of acid is directly linked to retention of base.

As H^+ secretion occurs, filtration at the glomerulus is proceeding. The filtrate contains a good deal of HCO_3^- which combines with excreted H^+ to form H_2CO_3. Carbonic anhydrase at the luminal epithelial membrane surface promptly breaks the H_2CO_3 into CO_2 and H_2O, and the CO_2 returns to the peritubular blood (fig. 16.18*a*). In

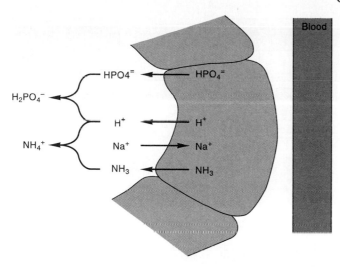

Figure 16.19 H^+ tends to diffuse back into the tubule and blood unless combined to form the low-permeability ammonium and dihydrogen phosphate ions. The exchange of sodium for H^+ is also indicated.

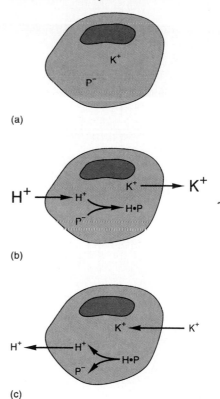

Figure 16.20 (a) Normal homeostatic balance with proteinate (P^-) and K^+ within a cell. (b) Acidosis produces a secondary hyperkalemia. (c) Alkalosis favors outward diffusion of H^+, which is replaced by K^+ to cause a secondary hypokalemia in the ECF.

normal circumstances, the amount of fixed acid slightly exceeds the amount of HCO_3^- available for combination. When acid production is above normal, the tubule cells respond with more H^+ secretion. This means a greater than usual number of hydrogen ions will have no HCO_3^- with which to combine, so more will remain in the urine. If acid production is lower than usual, or if HCO_3^- levels are increased, H^+ will be insufficient to combine with all the filtered HCO_3^- and more HCO_3^- will be lost (fig. 16.18b). In this way, renal compensation for excessive acid or base can restore homeostasis.

Buffers, in cells and the ECF, can respond in a matter of seconds to shifts in pH, while respiratory responses take a bit longer: a few minutes. By contrast, renal excretion may take hours to respond, but it can continue compensation for an extended period, with the added benefit that its action restores buffering capacity. This renal response, once fully activated, can excrete up to 500 mM of excess H^+ or HCO_3^- daily. This is roughly ten times normal daily production. If acid or base is produced above this level, excretion capacity is exceeded and a net accumulation results in a pronounced acidosis or alkalosis.

Following its excretion into the tubule lumen, there is a tendency for the excess H^+ to diffuse back into the peritubular tissues. This is prevented by the tubule cells' secretion of ammonia (NH_3) into the lumen. There the NH_3 and H^+ combine to form the ammonium ion (NH_4^+). Ammonium has a low permeability and can't readily diffuse back into the peritubular spaces. This renal process effectively confines excreted H^+, in the form of NH_4^+, to the lumen and ultimately the urine. The formation of dihydrogen phosphate ($HPO_4^=$) in the lumen has a similar effect (fig. 16.19).

Related Ion Effects

Altered pH in the ECF can produce secondary changes in the level of other ions. When acidosis is present, high ECF concentrations of H^+ cause it to diffuse into cells where H^+ concentration is lower. As a result of the accumulating positive charge inside the cell, positive ions move out of the cell, and since K^+ is the dominant intracellular ion, its passage to the ECF will be most significant. Hyperkalemia is the result. Similarly, in alkalosis, ECF H^+ concentration is reduced, favoring its diffusion from cells to the ECF. K^+ diffuses in to compensate for lost intracellular cations, the ECF K^+ level falls, and hypokalemia results (fig. 16.20).

In the preceding examples, the acid-base shift arises initially, with K^+ effects then developing in response. When K^+ imbalances are first present, secondary acid-base derangements may arise. Consider the situation in the nephron tubule cells generally. In hypokalemia, a reduced K^+ level in the ECF causes K^+ to diffuse out of the cell. The cation loss is answered by the diffusion of H^+ into the cell. The resulting increase in intracellular acid triggers its excretion, and as the process continues, the ECF acid-base status shifts toward alkalosis. The opposite effect is seen in hyperkalemia, where the tendency is to acidosis (fig. 16.21).

The relation between H^+ and ECF volume regulation is based largely on renal reabsorption of Na^+ ion. As Na^+ is

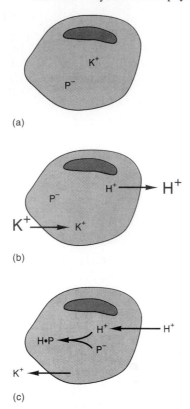

(a)

(b)

(c)

Figure 16.21   (*a*) Normal homeostatic balance with proteinate and K$^+$ in a cell. (*b*) Hyperkalemia favors K$^+$ diffusion into the cell and H$^+$ diffuses out to compensate for positive charge build-up. A secondary acidosis results. (*c*) Hypokalemia favors loss of K$^+$ from the cell, and compensating H$^+$ diffusion produces a secondary alkalosis in the ECF.

exchanged for H$^+$ in the nephron, pH shifts may occur. If ECF volume is excessive, Na$^+$ reabsorption falls and reduced H$^+$ exchange occurs, meaning that retention is increased and a shift toward acidosis develops. Similarly, when ECF volume is low, increased Na$^+$ reabsorption occurs while H$^+$ is passed to the lumen, and a tendency to alkalosis emerges.

You may recall, from the earlier discussion of calcium imbalance, that Ca^{++} is present in the body fluids as a free ion or bound to protein or citrate. This binding is acid-dependent, so that in acidosis more Ca^{++} is taken up by protein and citrate, and hypocalcemia may develop. In alkalosis, hypercalcemia is also often present, as a result of the opposite effect of increased pH.

Increased aldosterone secretion may come about as part of the response to diuretic therapy. As diuresis proceeds, fluid loss activates the renin-angiotensin system, which increases aldosterone secretion and H$^+$ loss to produce alkalosis. When aldosterone secretion is below normal levels, its stimulus to K$^+$ and H$^+$ excretion is reduced. The result is retention of both ions and concurrent acidosis and hyperkalemia. Figure 16.22 presents the links between acid-base shifts and other electrolytes.

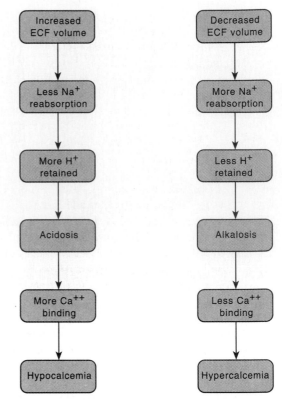

Figure 16.22   Links between fluid imbalance and acid-base and calcium derangements.

Diuretic Use and Acid-Base Imbalance

H$^+$ shifts may be caused by diuretic therapy where the diuretic acts by suppressing Na$^+$ or HCO$_3^-$ absorption to promote water loss. The ion involved and the segment of the tubule where the diuretic acts determine the direction of the pH shift.

The popular **loop diuretics,** such as furosemide or ethacrynic acid, exert their effect by blocking Na$^+$ absorption from Henle's loop. This leaves unusually large volumes of sodium-rich filtrate, which pass to the distal tubule. There Na$^+$ absorption proceeds at a high rate, linked to H$^+$ loss. The potential side effect is a shift toward alkalosis. By contrast, the **thiazide diuretics** work by blocking Na$^+$ absorption in the distal tubule segments. This means less H$^+$ secretion and a lowered risk of alkalosis.

The class of diuretics called **carbonic anhydrase inhibitors** functions by interfering with carbonic anhydrase activity at the nephron tubule's luminal surface. This reduces the formation of H$_2$CO$_3$ in the lumen, leaving HCO$_3^-$ to exert an osmotic diuresis effect. With increased bicarbonate losses, acidosis may develop.

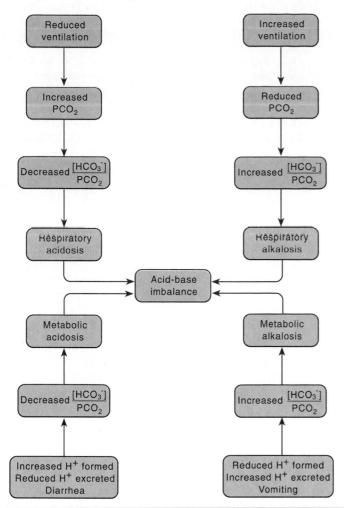

Figure 16.23   Pathogenesis in the major patterns of acid-base imbalance.

Patterns of Acid-Base Imbalance

Intracellular buffers are responsible for most buffering, but the carbonic acid system is especially significant in determining the acid-base status of the plasma. Because the plasma is easily analyzed, the state of its carbonic acid buffer system is often used as an indicator of pH in the ECF generally, as well as in the intracellular compartment. A useful expression of pH is the **Henderson-Hasselbalch equation,** which expresses pH in terms of the components of the carbonic acid buffer system:

$$pH = K + \log \frac{[HCO_3^-]}{[H_2CO_3]} \qquad \text{(Eq. 1)}$$

The value of the constant K is 6.1, and under normal circumstances the ratio of $[HCO_3^-]$ to $[H_2CO_3]$ is 20:1. The log of 20 is 1.3. Substituting this value, the value of K, into equation (1) yields the normal pH value:

$$pH = 6.1 + 1.3 = 7.4$$

Because the value of K does not change, any difference in pH is the result of a change in the ratio of the concentrations of HCO_3^- and H_2CO_3. Furthermore, because $[H_2CO_3]$ is related to the partial pressure of CO_2, equation (1) can take the form

$$pH = K' + \log \frac{[HCO_3^-]}{PCO_2} \qquad \text{(Eq. 2)}$$

The new constant, K', adjusts for the relationship between PCO_2 and H_2CO_3. Equation (2) is significant because it expresses pH in terms of PCO_2, which is altered by changes in ventilation, and in terms of plasma $[HCO_3^-]$, which is modified as a result of renal hydrogen ion excretion.

Acid-base imbalances are classified on the basis of equation (2). Those pH imbalances caused by changes in the elimination of CO_2 by the lungs are classified as respiratory imbalances. For example, as PCO_2 increases because of inadequate ventilation, the denominator of equation (2) increases. This produces a smaller value for the ratio $[HCO_3^-]: PCO_2$, and therefore a lower pH. This condition is termed **respiratory acidosis.** On the other hand, if PCO_2 is diminished, the ratio increases and so does the value of pH, to produce **respiratory alkalosis.** Alternatively, when pH imbalance is caused by changes in acid production, renal excretion, or digestive losses, the imbalance is said to be of metabolic origin. In such cases, the ratio $[HCO_3^-]: PCO_2$ will shift because of changes in $[HCO_3^-]$ indirectly linked to changes in H^+ ion production or loss. So, in **metabolic acidosis,** increased H^+ ion shifts the carbonic acid equilibrium to the left. This decreases the $[HCO_3^-]$, the ratio decreases, and therefore the pH decreases as well. In **metabolic alkalosis,** reduced $[H^+]$ forces a shift to the right in the carbonic acid equilibrium. The result is an increase in the $[HCO_3^-]$, an increased ratio of $[HCO_3^-]$ to PCO_2, and therefore a larger, more alkaline pH (fig. 16.23).

It is important to recognize that changes in pH are the result of a shift in the ratio of these two key variables. If, for example, $[HCO_3^-]$ is decreased as a result of excessive acid production, compensation can be achieved by suitably reducing PCO_2. This can be accomplished by hyperventilation until the desired ratio and therefore pH is achieved. Alternatively, if lung disease causes a decrease in the $[HCO_3^-]: PCO_2$ ratio because of the accumulation of CO_2, then renal excretion of H^+ ion increases to elevate the $[HCO_3^-]$ until the $[HCO_3^-]: PCO_2$ ratio approaches the desired value. If the respiratory system causes pH to change, then renal hydrogen ion excretion and its indirect $[HCO_3^-]$ effects will compensate. When acid production changes, compensation is achieved by ventilation changes that alter PCO_2. This means that following compensation, both $[HCO_3^-]$ and PCO_2 will have values higher or lower than normal, but still within normal limits (fig. 16.24).

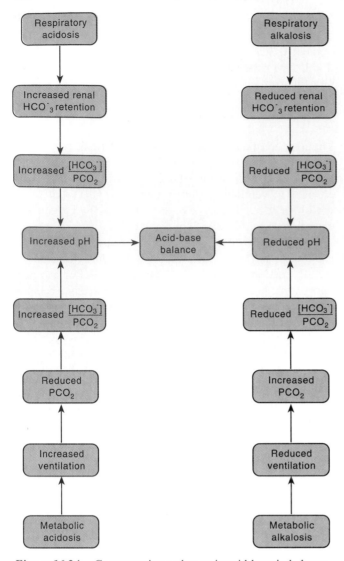

Figure 16.24   Compensation pathways in acid-base imbalance.

Respiratory Acidosis

In respiratory acidosis, a decrease in pulmonary function causes a build-up of CO_2 in plasma, which lowers pH. Asthma, emphysema, and chronic bronchitis are common causes. Respiratory insufficiency may also follow trauma or other damage to the brain stem, where the respiratory control centers are located. Similar effects are also produced by inappropriate dosage of drugs that depress CNS function. Renal compensation is slow and may require several days to restore a normal pH. Renal disease compromises compensation and greatly increases the threat of acidosis. A general weakness is characteristic of acidosis, with deranged CNS function the greatest threat. Confusion and disorientation may be followed by coma and finally death.

Respiratory Alkalosis

Respiratory alkalosis is the result of excessive pulmonary CO_2 clearance. It is much less common than respiratory acidosis. It may arise as the result of hyperventilation that attempts to compensate for hypoxemia or for inhaling air with a reduced PO_2, such as at high altitude. Disorders of the pulmonary interstitium can also produce hyperventilation. Excessive anxiety or other psychogenic disorders may induce hyperventilation, as well. Patients may complain of numbness, a generally increased sensitivity (paresthesia), lightheadedness, and even tetany in extreme cases.

Metabolic Acidosis

In this condition, declining pH is the result of a fall in $[HCO_3^-]$ or a rise in $[H^+]$. Most often this is the result of increased production of acid metabolic products, as in prolonged hypoxia, where the shift to glycolysis produces lactic acid. **Lactic acidosis** is also associated with certain tumors, drug or toxin ingestion, and respiratory failure. In those suffering from diabetes mellitus, altered metabolism produces keto acids (see chapter 17). Alcoholics may also produce excess ketoacids. In renal failure, a decline in H^+ excretion capability often follows the loss of nephrons in glomerulonephritis, or the reduced H^+ secretion typical of pyelonephritis. In either case, normal H^+ production exceeds available excretory capability, and pH falls. Thiazide diuretics are another source of excess acid. Direct loss of HCO_3^- can also produce acidosis, usually in chronic diarrhea, but also in cases of intestinal fistulae, where intestinal absorption is substantially reduced.

In metabolic acidosis, respiratory compensation produces a rapid and deep pattern of breathing. As in respiratory acidosis, the symptoms include generalized weakness, fatigue, and CNS depression.

Metabolic Alkalosis

In this condition, acid is lost from the GI tract by vomiting or diarrhea. Renal mechanisms are most often related to the use of loop diuretics. In response to an initial H^+ loss, HCO_3^- losses can rapidly provide compensation. For this reason, metabolic alkalosis is unlikely to develop without some factor that compromises renal HCO_3^- compensation. Volume depletion states, for example, involve pronounced Na^+ reabsorption, and HCO_3^- is retained to balance charge. In adrenal cortex tumors that hypersecrete aldosterone, H^+ is excessively secreted. In either case, alkalosis is sustained. Often, too-vigorous antacid therapy for gastric hypersecretion will produce a metabolic acidosis.

Signs and symptoms are nonspecific: anorexia, nausea, lethargy, loss of mental acuity, and, at extremes, loss of consciousness. These may derive more from the related K^+ deficits that follow alkalosis than as a result of the pH change.

Table 16.3 Typical Urine and Blood Changes in Acute (Uncompensated) and Partially Compensated Acid-Base Imbalances

Condition	Blood pH	Blood PCO_2	Blood HCO_3^-	Urine pH
Acute respiratory acidosis	SD	SE	E	D
Compensated respiratory acidosis	D	SE	SE	D
Acute respiratory alkalosis	SE	SD	D	E
Compensated respiratory alkalosis	E	SD	SD	E
Acute metabolic acidosis	SD	N	SD	D
Compensated metabolic acidosis	D	D	SD	D
Acute metabolic alkalosis	SE	N	SE	E
Compensated metabolic alkalosis	E	E	SE	E

E = elevated, SE = significantly elevated, D = depressed, SD = significantly depressed

Compensation in Acid-Base Imbalance

The two mechanisms that have an impact on ECF pH—ventilation and renal H^+ and HCO_3^- excretion—are available to compensate for acid-base imbalances (fig. 16.24). Although compensatory acid-base shifts are important in minimizing the adverse effects of an elevated or depressed pH, they can complicate diagnosis, with a compensation effect being confused with the original cause. For example, an acute metabolic acidosis that develops because of renal failure activates a hyperventilation response. This may reduce the acidosis, but since shifting the carbonic equilibrium has reduced $[HCO_3^-]$, this effect may be taken as the original cause of the problem (table 16.3). Generally, the term **uncompensated** is applied to acidosis or alkalosis in which no compensation response is activated. In **partially compensated** imbalances, pH is abnormal, but it is closer to normal than if compensation had not occurred. **Fully compensated** (or chronic) acidosis or alkalosis involves restoration of a normal pH although other ion imbalances may be present.

Therapy in Acid-Base Imbalance

Generally, respiratory compensation in metabolic acidosis or alkalosis is less capable of restoring a normal pH than is the kidney in correcting for respiratory acidosis or alkalosis. Therapy attempts to correct the cause of the initial imbalance, but often this is not possible. Efforts are therefore made to adjust the pH of the ECF via oral or intravenous administration of appropriate agents. These may have a direct effect, as in the oral administration of sodium bicarbonate ($NaHCO_3$) to correct acidosis. Alternatively, a substance may be used that is in itself not directly corrective, but that is metabolized to form products that produce the desired pH shift. In acidosis, for example, solutions containing sodium gluconate or sodium lactate ions are used, because their metabolism produces Na^+ to hold HCO_3^- in the ECF. In alkalosis, ammonium chloride (NH_4Cl) is used, because the metabolism of the ammonium ion produces acid products that offset the excessive alkalinity.

Case Study

A 1-year-old child worried his parents when he ran a fever and refused any food or drink for 24 hours. The following day the child developed diarrhea and vomited periodically. The parents phoned their general practitioner, who advised them to give the child clear fluids only for a day and then to gradually reintroduce solid foods.

The child took the clear fluids offered, but vomited them soon after they were given. He also continued with intermittent diarrhea for the remainder of the day. On the next day the parents' concerns were worsened when the pattern continued and the child became listless and refused

even liquids. With no improvement by evening, and six consecutive hours of dry diapers, the parents took the child to the hospital emergency room.

The attending ER physician's examination determined the child to be generally normal and well developed. The exceptions were dryness of the mouth, sunken eyes, a rapid pulse, and a generally diminished skin turgor. On the basis of these findings, a diagnosis of gastroenteritis with dehydration due to diarrhea and vomiting emerged. A viral etiology was suspected.

The child was admitted to hospital, and IV fluids were administered to rehydrate him. Nothing was given by mouth until the vomiting subsided, about 14 hours later. A series of blood analyses proved normal, and the child was released to his parents with instructions to continue with fluids and then slowly add increasingly solid food as improvement continued. They were also advised to monitor closely for any interruption of the recovery. The child's progress was rapid and no further complications developed.

Commentary
The night admission via the ER is not uncommon since, to concerned parents, all signs and symptoms in their children seem worse at night. In this case, all indications were consistent with a dehydration state. The suspicion of a viral eti-

ology, without direct evidence, was based on the high incidence of transient and benign gastroenteritis among children. It was further supported by the lack of any travel or day care contacts where exposure to other infection sources was possible.

The blood studies were done primarily to assess whether metabolic acidosis or hypokalemia had resulted from the bouts of diarrhea and vomiting. Since most such viral gastroenteritis is self-limiting, more extensive stool studies for parasites or other agents would have been undertaken only if the signs and symptoms had persisted. Admission to hospital was prudent in view of children's susceptibility to rapidly developing, more severe complications of fluid and acid loss without prompt intervention.

Key Concepts

1. If the quantity and composition of the body fluids is not maintained within homeostatic limits, serious functional disturbances and even death may result (p. 403).

2. Water and sodium are closely interrelated, and any deficiency or excess in one may well produce an effect in the other (p. 403).

3. Dehydration typically results from excessive water loss and rarely from inadequate intake (p. 404).

4. Water intoxication is typically produced by a defective water excretion mechanism and only rarely as a result of excessive intake (p. 404).

5. Most water intoxication is due to an excessive secretion of ADH, arising from faulty neurologic control, from the effect of certain therapeutic drugs, or from the hypersecretion of ADH, or functionally similar substances, by tumors (p. 404).

6. Volume depletion may result from body fluid losses via the GI tract, kidneys, skin, or develop in various sequestration states in which fluid is lost from the vessels but retained in the extracellular compartment (pp. 404–405).

7. Fluid volume excess is usually mediated via the kidneys when they are diseased, or through inappropriate fluid retention reflexes related to heart failure or cirrhosis (p. 405).

8. Fluid volume expansion or depletion induces effects through changes in plasma volume, and therefore arterial BHP, or through osmolarity and osmosis effects to which cells of the CNS are particularly vulnerable (p. 406).

9. Therapy in fluid imbalance typically involves the infusion of blood vessels with fluids whose composition restores normal volume and osmolarity (p. 406).

10. A given patient's pattern of fluid and electrolyte balance is the result of complex interrelations among the various electrolytes dissolved in the body water, with deficiency or excess in one often producing imbalances among the others (p. 407).

11. Excesses or deficiencies of sodium are usually relative changes produced by excessive loss or retention of body water (p. 407).

12. Most hypokalemia is due to excessive loss of potassium via the GI tract, skin, or kidneys, while the potassium excess state may arise from aldosterone hyposecretion, renal failure, or widespread cell damage associated with extensive trauma (pp. 407–408).

13. Since the chloride ion passively follows the sodium ion, most chloride imbalance is a secondary effect linked to sodium deficiency or excess (p. 408).

14. Hypercalcemia, caused by excessive retention or impaired excretion, may produce nephrolithiasis, muscle cramps, and pain, while hypocalcemia, caused by a dietary deficiency, inadequate absorption, or excessive renal excretion, is typically accompanied by muscle hyperactivity and tetany (p. 409).

15. Therapy in electrolyte imbalance is directed at correcting the initial cause and at restoring balance by the intravenous administration of an appropriately balanced solution (p. 410).

16. Acidosis and alkalosis may produce secondary imbalances in both potassium and calcium (pp. 413–414).

17. Reduced pulmonary excretion of carbon dioxide produces respiratory acidosis, while excessive carbon dioxide excretion via the lungs increases the ratio, causing respiratory alkalosis (p. 416).

18. Increased metabolic acid production, or loss of bicarbonate, produces the condition of metabolic acidosis, while in metabolic alkalosis, acid is lost via the GI tract or the kidneys (p. 417).

19. Reference to a given patient's degree of pulmonary or renal compensation for an acid-base imbalance is indicated by the terms uncompensated, in which pH imbalance is not reduced, partially compensated, where the degree of imbalance is reduced, and fully compensated, in which pH is restored to normal (p. 417).

REVIEW ACTIVITIES

1. From left to right across the bottom of a piece of paper, write the following five items: systemic edema, increased hematocrit, shock, fluid retention reflexes, cerebral swelling or shrinking. Above the first four, add the plasma volume changes that would cause them. Above cerebral swelling or shrinking, add their cause. Does your page look like the bottom part of figure 16.11?

2. Look at the lower two cells in figure 16.6. If these were cells in the brain, what kind of problems might develop in each case illustrated?

3. Complete the following quick reference table, which will give you a quick check on some important links between the major electrolytes. All you need to do is to replace the question mark with an appropriate arrow in the right column. Pages 404–414 have all the information you'll need.

If	Then
↑ H_2O	? Na^+
↓ H_2O	? Na^+
↑ Na^+	? Cl^-
↓ Na^+	? Cl^-
↑ K^+	? H^+
↓ K^+	? H^+
↑ H^+	? K^+
↓ H^+	? K^+
↑ Ca^{++}	? $PO_4^=$
↓ Ca^{++}	? $PO_4^=$
↑ H^+	? Ca^{++}
↓ H^+	? Ca^{++}

4. Complete the following table by indicating the electrolyte change that each therapeutic agent might produce. The agents indicated by an asterisk often have effects on two ions. You needn't start looking in the text before page 404.

Therapeutic Agent	Possible Electrolyte Effect
Thiazides*	
Sodium bicarbonate	
Ammonium chloride	
Ethacrynic acid*	
Furosemide*	
Vitamin D supplementation	
Carbonic anhydrase inhibitors	
Sodium gluconate	
Antacids	
Acetazolamide	

5. Think back to the case study. If lab tests on the plasma had indicated that acidosis was present, would it have been respiratory or metabolic acidosis, and how would the ratio of bicarbonate to the partial pressure of carbon dioxide have changed to produce it?

Chapter Seventeen

Endocrine Pathophysiology

Tie off pancreas ducts of dogs. Wait six or eight weeks. Remove and extract.

Sir Frederick Banting, codiscoverer of insulin
from his experimental notebook

T he excessive or inadequate secretion of the body's many hormones produces a broad array of endocrine disorders. As background for a description of the major endocrine diseases, this chapter starts with a review of the endocrine system and the general principles that govern its function.

ESSENTIALS OF ENDOCRINOLOGY

The endocrine system is traditionally described as consisting of ductless glands whose secretions are carried away and delivered by the blood. This is in contrast to the exocrine system, whose secretions are delivered to their sites of action by ducts (fig. 17.1). The endocrine system employs its secretions, called **hormones** (from the Greek word meaning "to set in motion" or "to excite") to provide controlling input to cells. Hormonal control of cellular activities serves the overall somatic requirement for homeostasis and is the principal function of the endocrine system.

There are some variations on this essential endocrine mechanism. For example, **paracrine** cells secrete hormones that diffuse to adjacent cells and regulate their actions, and **autocrine** cells secrete substances that control their own function. Note that in these cases, the hormones never reach the general circulation in appreciable quantities.

The presence of many small deposits of endocrine tissue, in widespread parts of the body, supports the concept of a dispersed regulatory system. In this broad sense, a dispersed regulatory system would include the nervous system because of its release of chemical substances (at synapses and junctions) that elicit responses from adjacent cells (paracrine function). The nervous system also exerts broad regulatory and control functions, some directly, and others indirectly by its links to the endocrine system. Such **neuroendocrine** activity can be seen in the release of the posterior pituitary gland's hormones in response to nervous stimulus from the hypothalamus. **1** The anterior pituitary gland is also largely dependent on the hypothalamus for its control, but in this case control is mediated by **releasing hormones,** rather than by action potentials. The hypothalamus secretes the releasing hormones, which travel directly to the adjacent pituitary to govern release of its hormones. When an endocrine gland's hormone controls the secretion of a second endocrine gland, the hormone is said to be a **tropic hormone.** In these ways the endocrine and nervous systems are closely linked in providing the body's requirements for precise regulation of its many functions (fig. 17.2).

Consider the example of sex cell production in either sex. It depends on the sex hormones secreted by the ovary and testis (endocrine glands in their own right, in addition to being sites of gametogenesis). Sex hormone production is dependent on anterior pituitary tropic hormones, which in turn rely on hypothalamic releasing hormones for their

(a)

(b)

Figure 17.1   (*a*) In exocrine secretion, ducts carry the gland's product to its site of action. (*b*) Endocrine glands secrete directly into the blood, which widely disperses their hormones.

secretion. Here is a case of the nervous system influencing the release of three levels of control chemicals, which ultimately determine a single response: spermatozoan and oocyte production. In cases of infertility, the underlying defect might lie in the sex gland itself, its endocrine cells, the anterior pituitary, the hypothalamus, or other brain areas.

Despite the existence of paracrine and autocrine functions, most hormones depend on the blood for delivery. Many hormones are water-soluble and travel freely

1 ‖‖‖‖ ‖‖‖‖‖‖‖‖ ‖ ‖‖ ‖‖‖‖
28279

Figure 17.2 Nervous and endocrine roles often combine to determine the regulatory input to a given target tissue.

Figure 17.3 Receptor binding by a hormone at its target tissue. Fat-soluble hormones interact with intracellular receptors, since the hormone can readily pass into the cell. Protein hormones are unable to enter the cell easily. Instead they bind to surface receptors. In either case, hormone binding triggers the cell's metabolic responses.

dispersed in the plasma, but the steroid and thyroid hormones have low water solubility and are carried in plasma complexed with albumin or specific carrier proteins. Protein-bound hormones exist in equilibrium with small amounts of unbound hormone. The protein-bound hormone seems to provide a reservoir of hormone that is available should secretion be reduced. In normal circumstances, it is the tiny amount of free hormone that is responsible for eliciting tissue effects.

Endocrine Specificity

Since hormones are carried throughout the body by the blood, they reach all tissues. However, not all tissues respond to them. Only certain tissues, and in some cases only one tissue, alter their activity in response to a particu-

lar hormone. These responding tissues are the hormone's **target tissues.** As we noted earlier, if a hormone has another endocrine gland as its target tissue, it is known as a tropic hormone. A given hormone's target, then, responds to that hormone whereas all other tissues do not. This is an example of endocrine system specificity. It is based on the binding of hormones at specific cellular receptors. The receptor has a particular shape that is matched by only one of the many circulating hormones, and this match allows the two to fit closely enough for binding to occur.

There are two broad classes of target tissue receptor, which correspond to the two chemical categories of hormones. The **intracellular receptors** are present in the cytoplasm or at the surface of the nuclear membrane. These can bind to steroid hormones because steroids are lipid-soluble and can readily pass through the cell membrane to reach receptors in the cell's interior. For protein, peptide, and single amino acid hormones, the situation is different. Having low lipid solubility, they can't easily enter the cell. Instead, they interact with the second type of receptor at the cell's surface. Binding at these **membrane receptors** or at intracellular receptors has the same effect: an alteration of the target cell's level of activity (fig. 17.3).

The key to endocrine specificity lies in the differing patterns of receptor distribution in the many body tissues. A given cell has a particular array of receptors specific for many hormones. Other cells may have some receptors in common with it, but will also have some receptors that it lacks. The differences explain the differing tissue responses to the particular hormones in the blood at a given time (fig. 17.4).

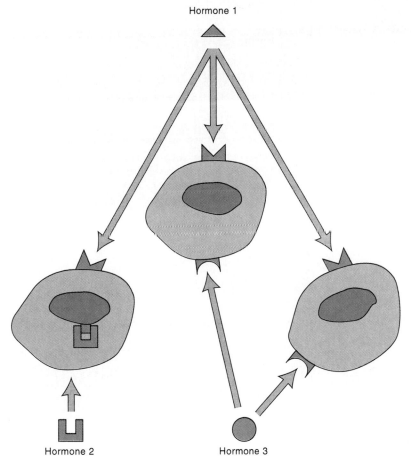

Figure 17.4   The tissue specificity of hormone responses is determined by the presence or absence of tissue receptors. Those with receptors (target tissues) are responsive to the hormone, those without them are not. Hormone 1 elicits responses from several tissues, while hormone 2 is highly specific, with one target tissue only.

Mechanisms of Target Tissue Response

The frequency at which target tissue receptors bind hormone is linked to the tissue's activity: increased binding rates induce an increased response. The response is, in some cases, greater cellular activity and, in other cases, inhibition of cellular processes, but basically, more hormone binding means more target tissue response, and vice versa. How, then, does hormone binding alter cellular functioning?

Two fundamental processes are involved. In the case of the steroid and thyroid hormones, their binding to intracellular receptors forms complexes that enter the nucleus. There they interact with regulatory elements of the chromosome's DNA. The result is an increase in the production of enzymes that will enhance a metabolic pathway's activity, thus producing an appropriate alteration of the target tissue's function (fig. 17.5a).

In the case of those target tissues that respond to binding of their surface receptors, membrane transport systems may be involved. These increase or decrease activity in response to receptor binding, altering cytoplasmic concentrations of various molecules or ions on which cell processes depend. In most cases, membrane receptor binding is followed by the triggering of a sequence of activation steps that ultimately affect the cell's functions. The largest number of hormones activate one of two receptor systems that are designated as **G proteins** or **protein kinases.** These systems in turn activate various intermediate processes catalyzed by specific enzymes (fig. 17.5b). Much research is devoted to clarifying these intermediate steps, in an effort to increase our ability to therapeutically manipulate cellular responses.

The Determinants of Plasma Hormone Level

From the preceding, you can see that the determining factor in an effector's response is the frequency of receptor binding. With greater binding frequency there is increased cellular response, and vice versa. The frequency of receptor binding is in turn dependent on the amount of hormone delivered by the blood at any given time. This amount is

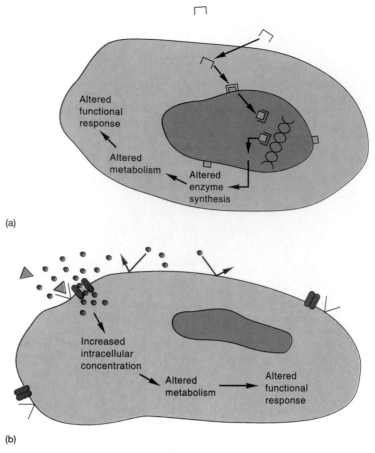

Figure 17.5   (*a*) Receptor binding linked to the synthesis of enzymes that regulate cell functions. (*b*) Surface receptors bind hormone and alter membrane transport of ions or molecules linked to key cellular responses.

determined by the balance between the rate at which hormone enters the blood and the rate at which it is cleared from the blood by inactivation or excretion. Inactivation of hormones usually occurs at two sites. One is the target tissue, where enzymes degrade hormones and convert them to nonfunctional forms. The other inactivation site is the liver. Hormones reaching the liver are chemically converted to inactive forms by hepatic enzyme systems, a process related to the liver's detoxification functions. Hormones are also cleared from the body by the kidney. They are excreted in the urine, often entering the nephron tubule by tubular secretion mechanisms. The products of target tissue and hepatic hormone inactivation may also be excreted in the urine (fig. 17.6).

Hormone inactivation by liver and target tissues or hormone excretion normally occurs at steady rates. This means that the blood's level of a given hormone is primarily determined by changes in its rate of secretion. For increased target tissue response, more secretion increases the level of circulating hormone, whereas reduced secretion causes it to decline as inactivation and excretion continue.

Hormone secretion has two components. One is the rate of hormone synthesis from dietary or endogenous precursors. Controlling stimuli to the gland directly or indirectly affects its synthesis of hormone, speeding or slowing the process. Increased or decreased secretion is the result. The second factor that determines secretion is the rate at which hormone is released from the endocrine cell. In some cases, hormone is stored within the gland, with release determined by nervous, hormonal, or other stimuli (fig. 17.7).

Secretion control is typically based on the principle of negative feedback. For example, the level of circulating hormone is inversely related to its own secretion rate. That is, when hormone level is excessive, secretion is inhibited; an inadequate hormone level acts as a stimulus to secretion. The thyroid and sex hormones are controlled in this way. Another regulatory input is the level of some variable that is controlled by a hormone. Calcium concentration in the plasma is an example. This variable is principally regulated by parathyroid hormone (PTH). As calcium levels change, parathyroid cells appropriately modify PTH secretion.

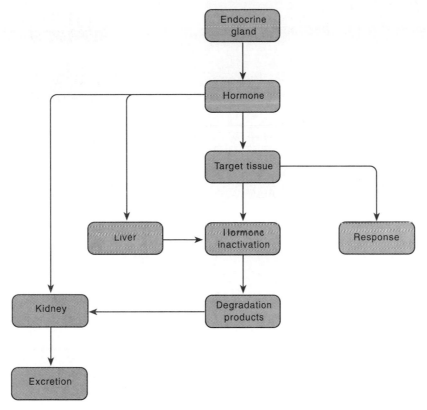

Figure 17.6   Hormone clearance from the blood.

Another example is insulin, which is regulated by the blood glucose level that it controls. The nervous system may also control hormone secretion directly, as in its interaction with the posterior pituitary adrenal medulla, or indirectly by way of anterior pituitary tropic hormones. Figure 17.7 summarizes these secretion control inputs.

ENDOCRINE DYSFUNCTION

Essentially, disordered endocrine function produces only two types of defect: excessive target tissue responses, caused by endocrine hypersecretion, or inadequate tissue responses, usually due to endocrine hyposecretion. Broadly, an inappropriate target tissue response can be assessed in terms of the source of the inputs that control it, that is, the endocrine gland and its hormone output. The endocrine gland may be damaged and unable to maintain hormone output, or excessively stimulated to hypersecrete. In some cases, there may be a flaw in the controlling inputs that leads to inappropriate stimulation of a normally functioning gland. Much endocrine pathophysiology rests on these basic concepts, and they should be the first factors to consider in clinical situations involving endocrine disorders. They are reflected in the descriptive terminology encountered clinically, e.g., hyperpituitarism or the hypothyroid state.

The following section deals with the principles of endocrine dysfunction generally, while the rest of the chapter is devoted to particular endocrine glands and their specific disorders.

Endocrine Hypofunction

In endocrine hypofunction states, target tissue responses are inadequate. The cause may be hyposecretion or it may be a loss of target tissue sensitivity to its controlling hormone.

Hyposecretion

In rare cases, inadequate secretion is due to **agenesis,** or lack of gland development. This is a clear-cut example of hyposecretion, as no hormone source is present. In other cases, a genetic defect may produce a metabolic abnormality that prevents synthesis of normal hormone. Of course, hyposecretion may be due to a dietary deficiency that causes a lack of hormone precursors, but more commonly, it arises because a normally developed gland is damaged and is unable to maintain normal secretion. Infection, infarction, or autoimmune mechanisms are most often involved, with chronic inflammation less often responsible for the damage.

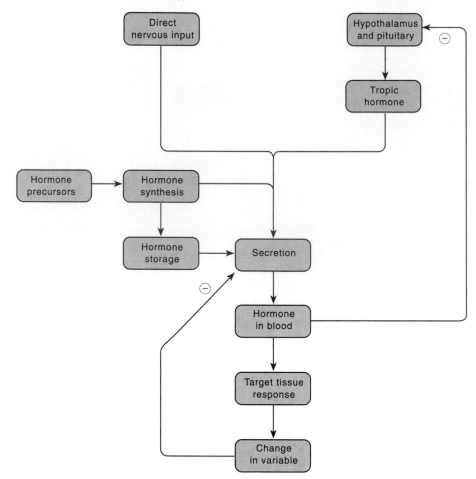

Figure 17.7 Endocrine secretion control. Once synthesized, hormone may be stored prior to secretion. The nervous system may control secretion directly or via the hypothalamus-pituitary link, which leads to tropic hormone secretion. The change in the variable may be monitored to control secretion, or the hormone level in the blood may be fed back to regulate tropic hormone secretion.

Another cause of hyposecretion is atrophy of an endocrine gland. This is most often due to a lack of tropic hormone input, which reduces demand for hormone secretion. Autoimmune destruction of tropic hormone receptors may also be followed by atrophy. In such cases, normal or even elevated tropic hormone levels are ineffective, since they are deprived of access to the cell's mechanism of response.

Tumor growth can be the cause of endocrine hyposecretion when primary or secondary malignant growth replaces functional endocrine tissue. Secretion is reduced if the tumor cells are sufficiently anaplastic to produce no hormone, or if they secrete altered hormone forms that are nonfunctional or of reduced potency.

A special case of endocrine hypofunction is based on therapy for hypersecretion. Surgery to remove part of an excessively active gland may resect too much tissue, inadvertently producing a hyposecretion state. The essential factors in endocrine hypofunction are summarized in figure 17.8.

Hyposecretion states are often accompanied by elevated levels of control hormones. These result from the negative feedback stimulus presented by subnormal hor-

mone levels (fig. 17.7). Tropic hormones of the anterior pituitary or hypothalamic releasing hormones are typically involved. Recovery or therapeutic restoration of normal hormone levels suppresses secretion of pituitary and hypothalamic control hormones, restoring their normal values.

Hormone Resistance

Resistance is the term often used to describe insensitivity of a target tissue to its hormone. This phenomenon, which is increasingly recognized, often involves a hereditary defect that compromises the target tissue's ability to synthesize hormone receptors. Other genetic defects may be present in the intracellular systems activated by normal hormone binding. The consequence is a depressed target tissue response even though hormone levels are normal, or even elevated. Higher than normal hormone levels may be a reflection of the negative feedback response to reduced target tissue activity (fig. 17.8).

The immune system is often a factor in hormone resistance. In such cases, an autoimmune mechanism produces an antibody against hormone receptors that is similar to the

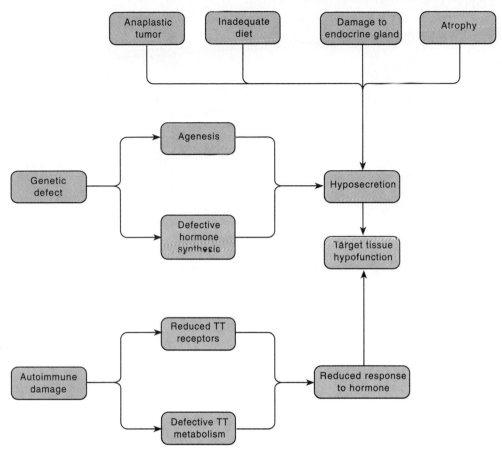

Figure 17.8   Factors in endocrine hypofunction. Inadequate secretion of hormone or a reduced target tissue (TT) response when hormone secretion is normal can both produce target tissue hypofunction.

normal hormone. Its shape allows the antibody to fit the receptor, but not closely enough to elicit the usual cell response. The result is reduced target tissue activity. Furthermore, since the antibody cannot be rapidly degraded by the target tissue's hormone inactivation systems, it remains bound to the receptor for a longer period, blocking normal hormone access to the receptor and further reducing secretion.

Endocrine Hyperfunction

In hyperfunction states, exaggerated target tissue responses are present. The usual cause is hormone hypersecretion.

Hypersecretion

The second major pattern of endocrine dysfunction is hypersecretion, in which circulating hormone is present at levels that are inappropriately high. Excessive hormone secretion may arise when an endocrine gland is exposed to unusually high levels of its tropic hormone. Its response is an increased synthesis and release of hormone. In such cases, hypertrophy or hyperplasia can cause gland enlargement in response to the increased stimulus. Defective feed-

back control may be a factor in endocrine hypersecretion, but details of such mechanisms are scarce because of the difficulties of studying the disease in nonhuman systems.

Tumors of endocrine glands may produce hyperfunction states if the neoplastic tissue retains the ability to secrete functional hormone. Even if only partially functional, the tumor's growth rate and uncontrolled secretion can produce exaggerated target tissue responses. The production of hormones or hormonelike substances by nonendocrine tumors was described in chapter 6. Such cases can confuse diagnosis. For example, when a small and difficult-to-locate tumor secretes excessive hormone, endocrine hyperfunction effects may be present without any other sign of endocrine gland abnormality.

Because most hormones produce effects by speeding or retarding widespread metabolic reactions, it is not surprising that the signs and symptoms of endocrine disease often present a puzzling picture of altered function simultaneously involving many of the body's organ systems. Excessive or inadequate secretion of only one hormone can produce extensive effects, as metabolism is altered by the synergistic and antagonistic interplay of hormonal stimuli. The remainder of this chapter deals with the major

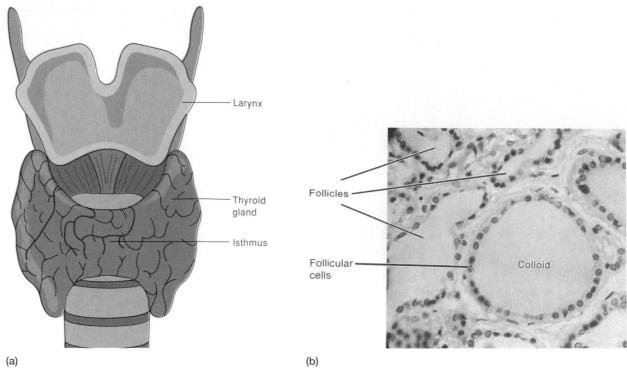

(a)   (b)

Figure 17.9   (*a*) The normal thyroid gland. Note the isthmus crossing the center line to connect the gland's lateral masses. (*b*) Thyroid histology, showing characteristic follicles and hormone-containing colloid.

endocrine glands and their most common disorders. The testis and ovary will be considered in chapter 20, in the context of reproductive disorders.

THE THYROID GLAND

The thyroid is involved in some of the most commonly encountered endocrine diseases. The associated functional disruptions may be quite extensive because of the broad effects of the thyroid hormones. Before considering thyroid abnormalities, let us review the gland's normal structure and function.

Normal Anatomy and Physiology

The thyroid gland is positioned in the region of the throat. It consists of two lateral masses on either side of the trachea, joined by a connecting **isthmus** that crosses the midline, **2** just inferior to the larynx (fig. 17.9).

The cells of the thyroid gland are cuboidal cells arranged in a single layer to form the wall of a hollow sphere. These are the **thyroid follicles,** which make up thyroid tissue. **3** Secretion of the thyroid hormones involves synthesis by the follicle cells, storage within the follicle, and then release into the blood (fig. 17.10*a*).

The two thyroid hormones are unique among the body's chemical regulators in that they contain iodine. Derived from dietary sources, especially seafoods, the iodide ion is taken up from the body by the thyroid's folli-

cle cells after its absorption from the intestine. This is an active transport process that concentrates iodide within the follicular cells. The process is called **iodide trapping.** Normally, the thyroid achieves an iodide concentration up to 50 times greater than that of plasma. In hyperactive states, the cellular concentration of iodide produced by iodide trapping may exceed 300 times the plasma levels. Because of iodide trapping, over half the total body's iodide is found in the thyroid (fig. 17.11*a*).

Once inside the cell, iodide is oxidized to iodine and released into the fluid of the follicle, which is called **colloid.** A major constituent of colloid is the protein **thyroglobulin.** It contains the amino acid tyrosine, with which iodide combines to form both monoiodotyrosine (MIT) and diiodotyrosine (DIT). These are then converted to the two active thyroid hormones, **triiodothyronine** (T_3) and **thyroxine** (T_4) (fig. 17.11*b*). The hormones remain a part of the thyroglobulin structure and are stored in the follicle in this form until needed for secretion. There is sufficient T_3 and T_4 stored in the thyroid's follicles to provide normal secretion for about three months, should all synthesis stop.

Prior to secretion, small quantities of colloid are moved back into the follicle cells by pinocytosis. There the pinocytotic vesicles merge with lysosomes whose enzymes split T_3 and T_4 from thyroglobulin. Once freed, the hormones diffuse into the plasma for distribution throughout the body. Some thyroglobulin is also secreted. In the blood, most T_3 and T_4 is transported bound to alpha globulins and albumin. The principal protein involved is known

(a)

(h)

(c)

(d)

Figure 17.10   Thyroid follicles. (*a*) Note the uniform colloid texture within each of these normal follicles. (*b*) In Hashimoto's thyroiditis, colloid deficiency and inflammatory cell infiltration are apparent. (*c*) Graves' disease. Note the hyperplasia of the follicle's epithelium, which produces the irregular folding. (*d*) Benign follicular adenoma.

as **thyroxine-binding globulin** (TBG). This binding means that the thyroid hormones responsible for stimulating target tissues are the very small unbound quantities that circulate in the plasma.

Control of Thyroid Secretion The control of thyroid secretion depends on the anterior pituitary and hypothalamus. **Thyroid-stimulating hormone** (TSH), also known as **thyrotropin,** is the immediate stimulus to the thyroid cells. It is secreted by the anterior pituitary gland and binds to follicle cells, triggering their release of stored hormones. It also increases both iodine uptake and hormone synthesis. TSH secretion is in turn dependent on **thyrotropin-releasing hormone** (TRH), which is produced in the hypothalamus. TRH reaches the pituitary directly via the portal circulation, which joins it to the hypothalamus. High levels of the thyroid hormones cause an inhibition of TRH and thyrotropin and therefore of T_3 and T_4 secretion. They also antagonize TRH by in some way decreasing TRH receptor numbers on TSH-secreting cells in the anterior pituitary. Very high plasma iodide concentrations (on the order of about 100 times normal) also suppress thyroid function.

Prolonged exposure to cold also increases thyroid secretion, which in turn stimulates metabolism and generates body heat. Emotional states can affect thyroid secretion as well, with varying conditions stimulating or suppressing the gland's activity. These thyroid-controlling inputs are summarized in figure 17.12.

Thyroid Hormone Effects On reaching the tissues, especially the liver and kidney, target cells convert most T_4 to T_3. T_3 binds much more readily than T_4 to nuclear thyroid receptors in target cells. About 90% of thyroid hormone effects are the result of T_3 binding, with the remaining 10% due to T_4. After binding, target tissue enzymes degrade T_3/T_4, removing its iodine, which is then recirculated. Most is taken up by the thyroid gland for reuse, and a small amount is excreted in the urine. Other degradation products are lost in the urine and bile.

Thyroid hormones have a very wide range of target tissues, virtually all cells of the body. Their major effect is metabolic, generally promoting protein, carbohydrate, and lipid utilization. Aerobic energy metabolism is also affected, with changes in T_3/T_4 levels reducing it by half or

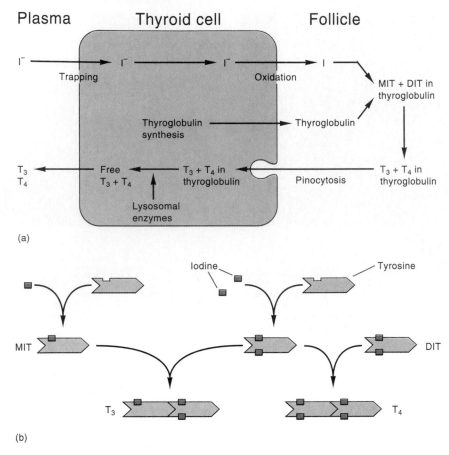

Figure 17.11   (*a*) Iodide trapping, thyroglobulin formation, and T_3T_4 secretion by the thyroid gland. (*b*) In the colloid within the follicle, iodine combines with the tyrosine of thyroglobulin to form MIT and DIT. These then combine to form T_3 and T_4.

increasing it to as much as twice the normal rate. Normal growth and development is also regulated by T_3/T_4. The nervous system is particularly dependent, so that infants exposed to deficiencies of the hormones in the first six months of life suffer irreversible mental retardation. Because of their widespread metabolic effects, thyroid hormones are important to many organ system functions. The most significant are listed in table 17.1.

Thyroid Pathophysiology

Broadly speaking, thyroid disorders produce excessive levels of T_3/T_4 and exaggerated target tissue effects, or depressed levels and reduced activity. The gland itself may be the source of the malfunction, or some defects in the hypothalamus-anterior pituitary control system may be at fault. Whatever the underlying etiology, the thyroid gland is a good example of endocrine dysfunction because the signs and symptoms of altered secretion are closely related to the effects of T_3/T_4 on target tissues.

Thyroid Hypofunction

The hypothyroid state is one in which thyroid hormone secretion is inadequate to maintain normal levels of target tissue stimulation. The result is a generalized fall in the metabolic rate. Less metabolic heat is generated, body temperature drops, and the skin cools as body heat retention reflexes are activated. The decline in metabolism also produces weaker, more sluggish muscular contractions throughout the body. In the gastrointestinal tract the result is a slowing of motility, which can produce constipation, while in the myocardium, contractility is reduced and hence cardiac output may decline. In the hypothyroid state, an increase of body weight is typical, because dietary habits provide normal input to a system whose caloric expenditures are reduced. The excess is stored as fat. The lack of T_3 and T_4 also causes a rise in the blood cholesterol level, which, if maintained for prolonged periods, may contribute to the development of atherosclerosis. Hypothyroidism may also produce a decreased sex drive in both sexes and cause irregularities in the pattern and intensity of the menstrual flow.

Lack of thyroid hormone stimulation to the CNS produces a depression of overall mental functioning. Instead of responses that are quick and alert, in the hypothyroid state mental processes are slower and dulled. An affected individual also requires a great deal of sleep. CNS suppression also contributes to a decline in the heart rate and hence the cardiac output, although some of this effect follows the lowering of tissue demands for oxygen and waste removal by a depressed metabolism.

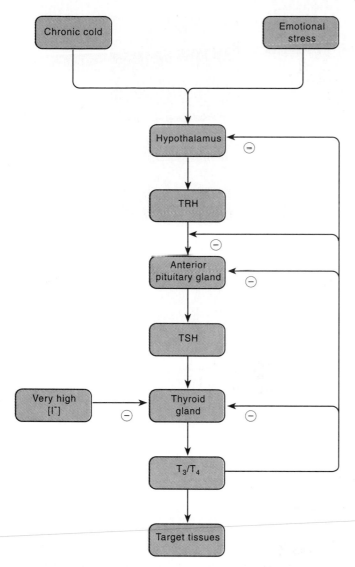

Figure 17.12   Normal controlling inputs and other factors that regulate thyroid secretion. T_3 and T_4 levels in the blood inhibit thyroid secretion and TRH and TSH release, as well as antagonizing the effects of TRH on the pituitary.

Table 17.1   Principal Effects of the Thyroid Hormones

Primary Effects
  Aerobic energy metabolism
  Glucose metabolism
  Protein metabolism
  Lipid metabolism
  Ion transport
Secondary Effects
  Growth/development
  Cardiac output
  Ventilation
  CNS activity
  Thermoregulation
  Muscle function
  GI activity
  Reproductive functions

In myxedema the usual signs and symptoms of hypothyroidism are exaggerated, with a greater decline in overall metabolism producing increased physical weakness. At the same time, mental functions become increasingly slow and confused. Because heat retention compensations are needed at even normal temperatures, the ability to adjust to cold environmental temperature is compromised in myxedema. In severe, untreated myxedema, the sufferer may lapse into a coma characterized by low body temperature. The elderly are particularly at risk of **myxedema coma,** which may be fatal. Table 17.2 lists the predominant clinical effects of adult hypothyroidism.

Cretinism   When thyroid hypofunction occurs in the newborn infant, normal growth and tissue differentiation are impaired. If the condition is untreated, physical and mental retardation result. The affected individual is called a **cretin,** and the condition characterized by the abnormality is known as **cretinism.** Physically, a cretin is short because of greatly reduced growth. Somatic proportions are altered because skeletal development is retarded more than that of soft tissues (fig. 17.13). A stocky, thick body with infantile proportions is the result.

Obesity is typical, but some of the appearance of obesity is due to the presence of near-normal abdominal viscera in a smaller than normal body frame. Thickening of the tongue, which is also symptomatic of cretinism, may interfere with swallowing and presents the risk of choking, especially in infants. Tooth and hair development is faulty as well, and the cretin's skin has a characteristic coarseness and scaliness. A yellow tinge to the skin may be present from accumulating carotene pigments, which are normally metabolized under the influence of thyroid hormones. Sexual development is also retarded.

Myxedema   When, in the adult, secretion of thyroid hormones is chronically reduced, the resulting condition is called **myxedema.** It is so named because of a characteristic edematous swelling around the eyes and lips **4** and at the fingers. A metabolic derangement, assumed to be the result of thyroid hormone lack, causes **glycoprotein** to be deposited in the dermis. (Glycoprotein is protein with some carbohydrate incorporated into its structure.) The term myxedema refers to the presence of this glycoprotein, which binds water to form a gel in the dermis and thus produces the facial puffiness associated with severe and prolonged hypothyroid states. Because the water is chemically bound, it cannot move freely through the tissues, so no pitting edema is usually seen, nor does the tissue fluid settle to dependent regions of the body as in congestive heart failure. Edema of the fingers causes them to thicken, while edema of the vocal cords produces a lowering of the voice.

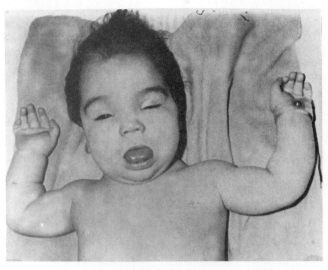

Figure 17.13   Characteristic facial features associated with cretinism.

Figure 17.14   Iodine deficiency goiter.

Table 17.2	Clinical Effects of Adult Hypothyroidism

Decreased energy production
  Weakness
  Fatigue
  Cold intolerance
  Lassitude
  Weight gain
  Decreased ventilation (decreased oxygen requirement)
  Constipation
  Bradycardia (slow heart rate)
  Hypotension
Decreased protein synthesis
  Anemia
  Dry sparse hair
  Dry scaly skin
Decreased CNS activity
  Memory loss
  Drowsiness
  Apathy
Mucoprotein synthesis
  Water retention
  Nonpitting edema (myxedema)
  Edema of vocal cords—husky voice
Decreased liver function
  Elevated plasma lipids
  Elevated plasma cholesterol   } Atherosclerosis
  Decreased vitamin A synthesis

Table 17.3	Clinical Effects of Juvenile Hypothyroidism

Myxedema
Mental retardation
Sexual immaturity
Delayed skeletal maturation
Short stature
Increased subcutaneous tissue
Protrusion of a thickened tongue
Dry, scaly skin
Slow growth and weight gain
Goiter

The CNS requirement for thyroid hormones is unsatisfied in cretinism. Brain development suffers and mental retardation is the result. Emotional derangements often accompany defective mental functions (table 17.3). In cretinism, maternal hormones can satisfy the newborn's earliest demands, but within a few weeks slowed mental response and lethargic behavior are noticeable.

Goiter Goiter is the condition of thyroid gland enlargement. Swelling may be minimal and difficult to recognize, or the gland may enlarge to over ten times its normal 30-g size **5** (fig. 17.14). Goiter is typical of thyroid hyposecretion states since, as thyroid hormone levels fall, the inhibition of TSH is removed and its secretion is increased. In response to continued exposure to high TSH levels, follicular hyperplasia develops, with follicle cells secreting abundant additional thyroglobulin. The result is a generalized enlargement of the thyroid called **diffuse colloid goiter.** The colloid reference is to the presence of the excess thyroglobulin.

Some goiter is characterized by the presence of irregular nodules within the thyroid tissue. **6** This condition is called **nodular goiter.** The nodules form when regions of follicular atrophy and fibrosis are present among normal or hyperplastic follicles. Nodular goiter has greater incidence in females past the age of 30. In unusual cases, a nodular goiter will hypersecrete. This phenomenon complicates diagnosis because it suggests a thyroid tumor. In such cases, the condition is called **toxic goiter** because hyperthyroid effects develop (see the discussion later in this chapter). The threat imposed by the more common hyposecreting goiter, or **nontoxic goiter,** is secondary to its enlargement: compression of adjacent throat structures, with the esophagus, jugular veins, and larynx being at greatest risk.

Etiology of Thyroid Hypofunction Most adult thyroid hyposecretion is the result of surgical resection or radiation therapy for thyroid hypersecretion states, usually Graves' disease (to be discussed later). In cretinism the problem derives from either a congenital lack of thyroid tissue or a rare genetic defect that prevents hormone synthesis. With these exceptions, hypothyroid states develop secondary to thyroid trauma and thyroiditis. This is most clearly seen in penetrating wounds of the neck that produce acute inflammation. However, bacterial or viral infections, especially in the mouth and throat regions, may produce subacute or chronic changes that are minor or even pass unnoticed. The most common thyroid hyposecretion state associated with goiter is a chronic granulomatous disease called **Hashimoto's thyroiditis** (fig. 17.10*b*). In this condition, fibrosis and infiltration of thyroid tissue by inflammatory cells occur at the expense of functional gland tissue. Hyposecretion is the result, with glandular hyperplasia and goiter following as falling thyroid hormone levels stimulate TSH release. Even though hyperplasia occurs, tissue damage dominates to yield a net loss of functioning follicles.

In Hashimoto's thyroiditis, other thyroid inflammations, and primary (idiopathic) myxedema, most patients have humoral and cellular immune responses directed against their own thyroid tissues. Antibodies against both follicle cells and thyroglobulin have been identified in patients with Hashimoto's thyroiditis. The condition is usually mild, with symptoms of myxedema occurring if prolonged. In severe cases, pericardial and pleural effusion and myocardial dilatation may complicate the course of the disease.

Some goiter is caused by a deficiency of dietary iodine. In such cases, although the gland is unable to maintain its normal output of hormone, thyroid secretion is usually sufficient to avoid or at least minimize symptoms. Iodine deficiency goiter has become uncommon since the practice of adding potassium iodide (KI) to table salt has been widely adopted.

In about 5% of hypothyroidism, disturbances of the hypothalamus or anterior pituitary produce insufficient stimulus to the thyroid, and hyposecretion follows. Some therapeutic drugs have thyroid-blocking side effects and may produce symptoms of hyposecretion. Examples are lithium preparations, phenylbutazone, and para-aminosalicylic acid.

Transient conditions of relative thyroid hyposecretion also occur. Periods such as pregnancy and puberty generate a high demand for thyroid hormones because of the rapid growth and development rates prevalent in those conditions. At such times, normal hormone levels are initially inadequate, and a condition of relative hyposecretion exists. Mild, temporary thyroid hyperplasia usually provides the needed additional hormone to correct the deficiency. The etiological factors in hypothyroidism are summarized in figure 17.15.

Therapy in Thyroid Hypofunction Therapy for thyroid deficiency is straightforward. It is a matter of providing thyroid hormone, which is readily available in oral preparations. Once the appropriate dose level has been determined, a reversal of symptoms usually follows. Thyroid hormone preparations offer the further benefits of being inexpensive and having no significant toxic or other side effects. Many people have successfully maintained thyroid hormone therapy for decades without symptoms or side effects. In the case of congenital thyroid hormone deficiencies arising at birth, therapy must be started promptly to avoid irreversible physical and mental retardation.

Thyroid Hyperfunction

When thyroid hormones are present to excess, exaggerated target tissue responses result. This condition is called **thyrotoxicosis.** With hypersecretion, several characteristic signs and symptoms develop. One is an increase in metabolic heat production. In response, heat loss reflexes produce a flushed skin and a high rate of perspiration. Many individuals suffering from thyroid hypersecretion are almost constantly perspiring. Excessive production of metabolic heat also limits the ability to tolerate high environmental temperature, because heat loss compensations are already activated.

Another characteristic of the hyperthyroid state is nervous excitability. The affected person is highly active physically and mentally. In contrast to the victim of hyposecretion, who is lethargic, in hypersecretion states **insomnia** (the inability to sleep) is the problem. Such individuals may be highly irritable, emotionally unstable, and subject to attacks of anxiety and paranoia. Another characteristic neurological sign is a slow tremor of the hand.

Cardiovascular effects are also seen in thyrotoxicosis. The heart rate is increased, in response both to the increased metabolic demands for oxygen supply and waste removal and to the direct cardiac stimulation effects of thyroid hormones. Blood hydrostatic pressure remains at near-normal values as increased cardiac output is countered by the systemic vasodilation needed to meet high tissue demands for blood flow.

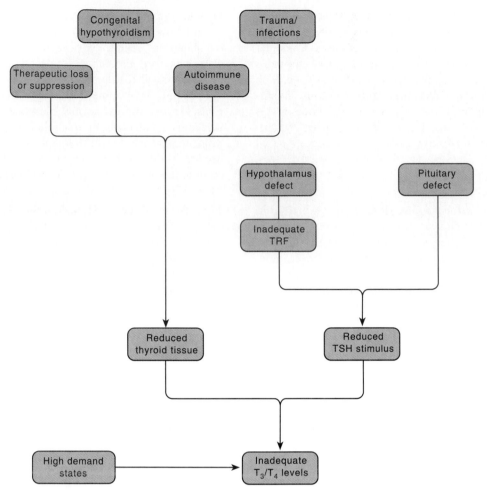

Figure 17.15   The principal factors that may induce thyroid hyposecretion. Note that in high-demand states the deficiency of hormone is relative.

Excessive energy demands produce metabolic shifts in hyperthyroid states. Plasma lipid levels fall as fat in the adipose tissue stores is consumed, and substantial weight loss often follows even though appetite and food intake increase. Thyroid hormone excess also stimulates breakdown of muscle protein for use as an energy source. This protein loss can affect muscle contractility in both skeletal muscle and the myocardium. The greatest threat in such cases is that of heart failure, because the myocardium is weakened at the same time that the demand for cardiac output is high. However, failure of the myocardium is a risk only when thyrotoxicosis is severe.

A distinctive sign in thyrotoxicosis is **exophthalmos** (fig. 17.16). In this condition, the eyes appear to protrude from their orbits. The principal cause is an exaggerated sympathetic nervous system output, which produces pronounced retraction of the eyelids and hence a wide-eyed appearance. When lid retraction is extreme, it may interfere with closing the eye, so that drying, infection, and ulceration are more likely to damage the cornea.

Other typical signs and symptoms of thyrotoxicosis are a tendency to hyperventilate, as a means of clearing the additional carbon dioxide produced by the elevated meta-bolic rate, and hyperactivity in the GI tract, which often results in attacks of diarrhea. An increased metabolic rate may produce vitamin deficiencies when demand outstrips dietary supplies. In males, impotence may develop, whereas in females, menstruation may decrease or stop entirely (**amenorrhea**). These effects are summarized in table 17.4.

Etiology of Thyroid Hypersecretion The most common thyroid hypersecretion syndrome usually affects young females. It is called **Graves' disease.** This is an autoimmune condition, as are the major hyposecretion diseases. In Graves' disease, the thyroid gland exhibits a diffuse hyperplasia, with its size increasing to two to three times normal **10** (fig. 17.10c). The result is a toxic goiter condition in spite of normal or very low TSH levels. Onset of symptoms is slow and progression is gradual. Weight loss, hyperactivity, and the other components of the thyrotoxicosis syndrome are usually seen, with exophthalmos typically present to varying degrees.

As noted earlier, an autoimmune etiology is involved in Graves' disease, causing the destruction of thyroid tissue. **11** And yet, this condition involves thyroid hypersecretion. What is the explanation for this seeming contradiction? The

Figure 17.16 Exophthalmos: eyelid retraction suggesting eye protrusion in hyperthyroidism.

Table 17.4	Clinical Effects Seen in Hyperthyroidism

Increased metabolic rate
  Muscle wasting
  Increased activity
  Heat intolerance—sweating and skin flushing
  Weight loss
  Insomnia
  Hyperventilation
  Diarrhea, nausea, and vomiting
  Tachycardia and congestive heart failure
  Hypertension
Increased CNS activity
  Rapid speech
  Emotional instability
  Nervousness and irritability
  Tremor of the limbs
Other findings
  Exophthalmos (protrusion of the eyeball)
  Goiter (enlargement of the thyroid gland)

Terminology Variations in Graves' Disease

The reason that the autoimmune response develops in Graves' disease is unknown. It has been suggested that a genetic defect is involved or possibly an unusual release of thyroid antigens that act as a stimulus to the system.

As with many diseases, as more information accumulates, new terminology emerges. In Graves' disease, use of the term TSAb is relatively new. Earlier, the term **long-acting thyroid stimulator** (LATS) was used, and it is still frequently encountered. In some cases, the term TSAb will be used as it is in our description of the mechanism underlying Graves' disease. You may also find the term **TRAb** employed in this context. It refers to **TSH receptor antibody,** which appears to be an antibody subtype specific for the TSH receptor, which can be distinguished from another TSAb that promotes growth and secretion, but apparently not via the TSH receptor. Another variant that is also in use is **TSI,** a general term referring to **thyroid-stimulating immunoglobulins.** More precision in terminology will emerge as our understanding is increased, but until then you can expect to find all of these various forms in clinical and laboratory settings.

answer is that the autoimmune response is not directed against the thyroid cells or thyroglobulin. Instead, antibodies against the TSH receptor are present. They are known as **thyroid-stimulating antibodies** (TSAb), and since they closely resemble TSH, they can bind to TSH receptors and stimulate thyroid secretion. They are also sufficiently different from TSH to resist enzymic degradation, and therefore to be active ten times as long as TSH. As well, the high plasma levels of thyroid hormones suppress TSH secretion (fig. 17.12), reducing competition for TSH receptors and allowing TSAb to dominate.

Other, less commonly encountered thyrotoxicosis conditions are known that do not involve autoimmunity. One condition is toxic goiter, in which a simple goiter develops

regions of tissue that hypersecrete and do not respond to lowered TSH levels. For this reason, they are said to be secreting autonomously. The hypersecreting foci may enlarge to form one or more large nodules in the thyroid gland. Hemorrhage and fibrosis are also present and contribute to the nodularity. If hypersecreting, this condition is described as **toxic multinodular goiter.** Another, rare hyperthyroid condition is the result of idiopathic TSH hypersecretion, which leads to thyroid enlargement and toxic goiter. The excess TSH may be secreted because of exaggerated anterior pituitary activity (of unknown origin) or because of hypersecretion of TRH by the hypothalamus. Incorrect dosage in hypothyroid therapy can also produce the hyperthyroid state.

A major threat in thyrotoxicosis is **thyroid storm** or **crisis,** in which high levels of thyroid hormones exacerbate the symptoms of an already hyperthyroid state. Rather than a burst of secretion, a large release of hormone from TBG is thought to be responsible. The precise trigger for this release is unknown, but it is often associated with the postoperative state and systemic infections.

Thyroid crisis involves a dramatic further increase in metabolism, which abruptly drives up body temperature, producing **hyperpyrexia.** This can have adverse CNS effects, including delirium and convulsions. Loss of fluid from extreme perspiration and from the diarrhea and vomiting caused by pronounced GI hyperactivity can combine to produce electrolyte imbalance and hypovolemia. High

Lowering Surgical Risk in Thyrotoxicosis

Prior to thyroid surgery to deal with thyrotoxicosis, a regimen of iodide (I^-) therapy is instituted for a period of about ten days. The high concentration used has the effect of suppressing gland function (fig. 17.12). The gland atrophies in response, forming a smaller mass with a reduced blood supply. A much lower surgical complication rate is the result.

thyroid hormone levels can also induce cardiac arrhythmias, which, with hypovolemia, can contribute to cardiovascular shock and death.

Therapy in Thyroid Hypersecretion Unfortunately, most therapy to counter hyperthyroidism cannot eliminate its primary cause. The alternative approach is to remove the source of thyroid hormones by surgical removal of part or most of the gland. Although several drugs are known to suppress T_3 and T_4 synthesis, such as methimazole and propylthiouracil, the problems and cost of a lifetime of drug therapy side effects seem an unwarranted burden on the patient. Destruction of the thyroid's hypersecreting tissue is sometimes achieved by the use of ionizing radiation. Dose determination is difficult, however, and if excessive can so depress secretion that myxedema results. Surgical removal of some hyperactive tissue is effective. Although it may also lead to a hyposecretion state as time passes, the problem is easily corrected because thyroid extract therapy is inexpensive and problem-free.

Tumors of the Thyroid Gland Most tumors of the thyroid are benign adenomas (fig. 17.10*d*) that grow only gradually. **12** The gland's normal tissue usually maintains adequate secretion, and hypothyroid conditions are uncommon. Some thyroid tumors, however, have well-developed follicles. These retain the ability to secrete functional hormone and can produce thyrotoxicosis. Malignancies are rare and have the highest incidence in females past the age of 40. Invasion to adjacent throat structures and lymphatic metastases are typical. Although an unusual primary carcinoma site, the thyroid gland is often the site of secondary growth from breast and lung metastases.

As with most tumors, identifying a specific etiology is difficult. However, early exposure of the thyroid to irradiation, as in nonthyroid tumor therapy, and prolonged exposure to high levels of TSH are known to be associated with increased rates of malignant tumor incidence.

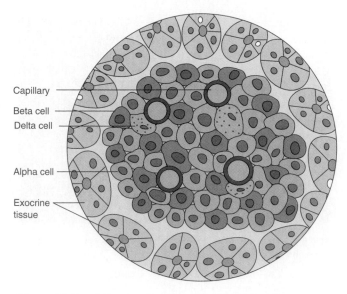

Figure 17.17 Microscopic view of a typical islet of Langerhans.

PANCREATIC ISLET CELLS

Blood glucose is a variable that requires close regulation because it is the dominant fuel of cellular energy metabolism. The brain, with its numerous functions critical to survival, and a few other tissues are absolutely dependent on glucose as an energy source. Most other tissues have alternative energy metabolism pathways that they can use when glucose is in short supply. However, the brain lacks this ability, and close regulation of the blood's glucose is essential to prevent its fall below the critical value needed for brain function. Also, blood glucose regulation must prevent glucose excess, which increases ECF osmolality and thus causes water to be drawn from the ICF by osmosis. The resulting increase in ECF volume can lead to diuresis and dehydration.

Normal Histology and Physiology

The cells of the **islets of Langerhans** are the primary regulators of blood glucose. The islets are microscopic masses of endocrine tissue scattered among the exocrine cells of the pancreas. **13** Each islet contains three principal cell types. One is the **alpha cell,** which secretes the hormone **glucagon.** These cells make up about 25% of the islet's total. The most common cell type is the **beta cell,** which is the source of the hormone **insulin.** This cell type makes up about 70% of islet cell numbers. The beta cells normally have an abundance of characteristic cytoplasmic granules. These are insulin-filled Golgi vesicles (described in chapter 1), which release their contents into the islet's blood capillaries. The remaining 5% of islet cells are **delta cells,** which secrete the hormone **somatostatin.** This hormone suppresses secretion of insulin and glucagon (fig. 17.17). Together, glucagon, insulin, and somatostatin closely regulate blood glucose. A fourth hormone, **pancreatic polypeptide,** is also secreted by the islets, but its regulatory functions are not well understood.

Functions of Insulin and Glucagon

Insulin is a polypeptide that is increasingly secreted into the blood when glucose is available for cell use. The beta cells are sensitive to glucose level and alter their secretion in direct response to its presence. They may also respond to hormones that are secreted by the intestine when glucose is digested. This response allows some initial insulin secretion in anticipation of glucose absorption. Beta cells increase secretion of insulin in response to elevated blood glucose levels, and glucagon is secreted by alpha cells when blood glucose levels are depressed. The effects of glucagon are opposite to those of insulin. This functional antagonism allows for closer control of this important plasma variable. In the following discussion of insulin's functions, keep in mind that for each one, the effect of glucagon will be its opposite.

Glucose is the primary energy source in cell metabolism. Following its absorption from the intestine, the blood level of glucose rises. The result is an increase in insulin secretion, which stimulates cell uptake, utilization, and storage of glucose. At the same time, insulin suppresses the use of fat as an energy source. When glucose levels fall, reduced insulin secretion favors the release of glucose from storage and the use of lipid-based energy sources.

One of the major effects of insulin is on cellular glucose uptake. Because it has low solubility in cell membrane lipid, glucose uptake depends on a specific membrane transport system (MTS). This system operates in the tissues that make up two-thirds of the body's weight: skeletal muscle, adipose tissue, and connective tissue fibroblasts. The major exceptions are brain, liver, and red blood cells, whose glucose uptake is not insulin-dependent. The rate of MTS activity is insulin-dependent and normally accounts for 75% of a cell's glucose uptake.

In the liver, insulin has an important effect on **glycogenesis.** When ample glucose is available, higher insulin levels promote the formation of glycogen as a means of storing glucose for later use. Numerous glucose units are polymerized to form the glycogen macromolecule. At the same time, insulin activates the hepatic synthesis of free fatty acids (FFAs) from glucose. These are then combined with

Table 17.5   The Antagonistic Metabolic Effects of Insulin and Glucagon

Cellular Activity	Insulin	Glucagon
Glycogenesis	↑	↓
Glycogenolysis	↓	↑
Gluconeogenesis	↓	↑
Ketogenesis	↓	↑
Lipolysis	↓	↑
Lipogenesis	↑	↓

protein and enter the blood, which carries them to adipose tissue for storage. Insulin also inhibits the normal release of FFAs from adipose tissue. These are normally metabolized in the liver, but because the liver has sufficient glucose to make its own FFAs, those in adipose tissue are not required.

When glucose levels fall, insulin secretion declines, causing a reversal of the effects just described. That is, cell uptake and utilization of glucose in muscle and adipose tissue are reduced. The result is a tendency to maintain the plasma glucose level, making more available to the brain and other tissues that depend on it. In the liver, glycogen synthesis is suppressed, and the low level of insulin activates two other metabolic pathways. One is **glycogenolysis,** in which glucose is produced from the breakdown of glycogen. The other is **gluconeogenesis,** in which new glucose is synthesized. Both these reaction pathways provide glucose to maintain an adequate plasma level. Also in the liver, lowered insulin levels activate lipolytic metabolism. In **lipolysis,** FFAs are converted to keto acids. These reach the systemic tissues, where they may be utilized as an energy source.

Glucose scarcity, with the drop in insulin that follows, stimulates the secretion of glucagon and other hormones. Their combined metabolic effects generally compensate for the lack of glucose. The hormones involved are glucagon from the islet alpha cells, growth hormone from the anterior pituitary, epinephrine from the adrenal medulla, and glucocorticoids from the adrenal cortex. Together, these stimulate protein breakdown to provide molecules needed for gluconeogenesis. They also increase the amount of lipid available for energy metabolism, indirectly producing an elevated plasma lipid level. The focus here is on the islet hormones, whose antagonistic effects are summarized in table 17.5.

Diabetes Mellitus

Diabetes mellitus (DM) is the major disease involving the islet cell hormones. It is, in fact, the single most common endocrine disorder. Estimates of the incidence of DM range from 1% to 2% of the North American population. Of these, many are undiagnosed and receive no treatment until the disease is well advanced. Although DM is recognized to have a genetic component, its precise pattern of transmission is not known.

DM is a metabolic disorder with wide-ranging and serious effects, many of which are life-threatening. It may occur in either of two forms, which differ in pathogenesis but produce essentially similar metabolic derangements. The more severe of the two forms, which typically affects the young, is the less common. It develops following failure of the beta cells and requires insulin therapy. This type of DM has been variously described as **juvenile onset DM, type 1 DM,** or, because insulin therapy is always required, **insulin-dependent DM** (IDDM). The last term is probably the best, because it makes reference to an unambiguous characteristic of the disease. The term type 1 DM is arbitrary and lacks descriptive value. The term juvenile onset DM is somewhat misleading, because some IDDM occurs as late as age 25. Of the two types of DM, IDDM makes up about 10% of the total.

The second type of DM has a slow, gradual development of symptoms, so that often years pass without the victim being aware of any change. Insulin therapy is required much less often in this type, so the term **non-insulin-dependent DM** (NIDDM) is descriptive. It is also called **type 2 DM** or **maturity onset DM,** because most cases are diagnosed past the age of 40. In NIDDM, beta cells are capable of producing insulin, but target tissues show reduced sensitivity to it.

Etiology of IDDM

The essential component of IDDM's etiology is autoimmune destruction of beta cells in the islets of Langerhans. **14** As is so often the case in autoimmune disease, the precise reason why normal self-antigens in a particular tissue become altered and vulnerable to immune attack is unclear. Familial patterns of IDDM incidence suggest a genetic predisposition, but some environmental agent is thought to be required to take advantage of it. Several lines of evidence indicate that a beta cell viral infection is a factor, although environmental chemicals may also be involved. The infected, or otherwise damaged, beta cells elicit an inflammatory response that brings lymphocytes to the scene. These in some way alter the beta cells' antigens, which are then recognized as nonself. A humoral cellular immune attack follows, with signs and symptoms of diabetes mellitus emerging as insulin secretion declines to critically low levels, when 90% of beta cells are destroyed (fig. 17.18).

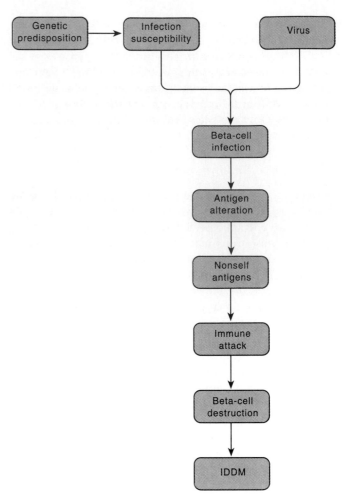

Figure 17.18   Etiology of insulin-dependent diabetes mellitus.

This may occur over a period of years without symptoms because of the beta cells' reserve secretion capacity.

Pathogenesis of IDDM

The chief signs and symptoms in IDDM can be directly traced to lack of insulin secretion. The immediate result is an increase in blood glucose (**hyperglycemia),** because without insulin, cellular uptake and utilization of glucose is limited. In the fasting state, blood glucose varies in the range of 70–100 mg/dl. In IDDM this value is increased to exceed 180 mg/dl, and at extremes may reach 1200 mg/dl. One effect of hyperglycemia is the urinary loss of glucose (**glucosuria**). When glucose levels are elevated, filtration at the glomerulus produces a filtrate with an abnormally high glucose content. Such high levels exceed the capacity of the tubule cells to reabsorb glucose, so that any glucose in filtrate that exceeds the maximum reabsorption limit is lost in the urine. Normally, only minute amounts of glucose reach the urine. Glucosuria, therefore, is a principal diagnostic indicator of IDDM.

The loss of glucose in the urine has further consequences. High levels of glucose in nephron filtrate increase the nephron tubules' osmotic hold on water, preventing its normal reabsorption and causing an **osmotic diuresis.** Polyuria and a compensating increase in thirst and water intake (polydipsia) are typical of untreated IDDM.

In IDDM, reduced insulin secretion stimulates hepatic glycogenolysis and gluconeogenesis, both of which produce glucose, which is released into the blood. The result is to increase hyperglycemia and the amount of glucose lost in the urine. Another complication follows chronically increased gluconeogenesis. This is the depletion of body proteins that are broken down to supply the subunits from which glucose is synthesized in gluconeogenesis. Essentially, this means that protein (from muscle, for example) is converted to glucose and then lost in the urine. The result is weakness, fatigue, and weight loss.

Lipid metabolism is also stimulated by low insulin levels, causing hyperlipidemia and the excessive production of **ketone bodies.** These products of lipid metabolism are **acetone** and the keto acids **aceto-acetic acid** and **hydroxybutyric acid.** As they accumulate, they produce a metabolic acidosis called **ketoacidosis,** which is often seen in the diabetic. They can produce nausea and vomiting and are toxic to brain tissue. Ketone bodies are volatile and have a characteristic odor that is often detected on the breath of the diabetic. In IDDM, there is a constant risk of **acidotic coma,** a result of the combined effects of ketoacidosis, dehydration, and the toxic effects of ketone bodies on the brain. The major signs in IDDM are presented in table 17.6.

Hypoglycemic coma is the result of brain glucose deprivation. It may be caused by inadequate dietary intake, high glucose utilization, as in exercise, or from an accidentally excessive insulin dose. In the last case, high insulin levels promote widespread glucose uptake, which can reduce the amount available to the brain. Deprived of its major energy source, it can't maintain normal levels of activity, and loss of consciousness results.

Pathogenesis of NIDDM

The pathogenesis of NIDDM is not well understood. Like IDDM, it has a genetic component, and some evidence suggests a more direct autosomal dominant pattern of transmission. In NIDDM, beta cells are essentially undamaged, although some fibrosis and amyloid deposition is present in the islets. Insulin levels are normal or elevated, but secretion in response to stimulation by glucose may be delayed. One of the key defects in NIDDM is a loss of target tissue insulin receptors and a flawed intracellular response to binding of the receptors that are present. This target tissue insensitivity produces hyperglycemia even though insulin levels are normal or above normal. Figure 17.19 illustrates the contrasting defects that underlie IDDM and NIDDM.

Table 17.6	Major Signs and Symptoms of IDDM
Signs and Symptoms	**Comments**
Hyperglycemia	High blood glucose from reduced cell uptake and increased release from liver
Glucosuria	From high blood levels of glucose
Polyuria	Hyperglycemia reduces renal water reabsorption
Weakness/fatigue/ weight loss	Caused by disordered protein and carbohydrate metabolism
Ketoacidosis	The result of excessive lipid energy metabolism and other metabolic derangements

The fact that NIDDM is usually found in the obese and in those past 40 has suggested a reason for insulin insensitivity. The high caloric loads that produced the obesity may cause cells to respond by reducing their insulin receptor numbers and their intracellular responses to receptor binding. Such a response is known to occur in other systems, e.g., lipid uptake, and would seem to be a reasonable adaptation to excessive intracellular glucose associated with caloric overload. A relatively slow adaptation rate would mean delay of hyperglycemia signs and symptoms until later years.

In some cases of uncompensated NIDDM, a nonacidotic coma may arise. The coma is caused by cerebral dehydration, which results from water movement to the extracellular compartment in compensation for pronounced urinary water loss. The diuresis is in turn the result of an exaggerated hyperglycemia, which may reach glucose levels in excess of 2000 mg/dl. Because of the hyperosmolarity and the lack of ketoacidosis (for reasons unknown), this condition is known as **hyperglycemic, hyperosmolar, nonketotic coma** (HHNC). It is most likely to occur in the elderly who can't adequately replace lost fluids, with the result that dehydration can build rapidly. Some significant points of comparison between IDDM and NIDDM are presented in table 17.7.

Chronic Effects in Diabetes Mellitus

In both IDDM and NIDDM there is a widespread pattern of long-term vascular and neurological change, which stems from basic derangements of metabolism. Two fundamental mechanisms underlying these changes are being studied. In one, products of abnormal glucose metabolism, which can

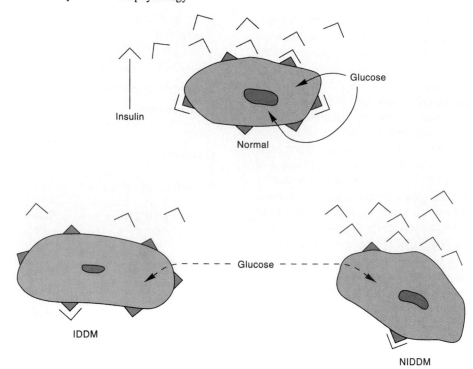

Figure 17.19　Mechanisms in DM. Glucose uptake in a normal cell depends on insulin binding at the cell surface. In IDDM, insulin is deficient, and glucose uptake and metabolism are compromised. NIDDM arises when receptor numbers are inadequate and insulin level is normal, or even increased.

Table 17.7	A Comparison of Some Selected Features of IDDM and NIDDM	
	IDDM	**NIDDM**
Frequency among diabetics	10%	90%
Family history of DM	Less than 1/5	Over 1/2
Age of onset	Under 40, most under 20	Over 40, most over 30
Clinical course	Acute onset, rapid progress	Delayed recognition, gradual progress
Physique	Normal or wasted	Usually obese
Plasma insulin	Low or absent	Normal or elevated
Sulfonyl urea stimulus	No insulin response	Insulin response
Acute threat	Ketoacidosis	HHNC
Therapy	Insulin, diet	Diet, exercise, some drug/insulin

be directly or indirectly damaging, are formed. The second mechanism involves **glycated proteins** (sometimes known as **glycosylated proteins**). These are proteins to which glucose has been added. Glycated proteins are often incapable of functioning normally, and the hyperglycemia of DM favors their formation. Hemoglobin, albumin, lipoprotein, eye lens protein, and collagen are known to be affected by glycation. Both these mechanisms are implicated in the vascular and neurologic complications of DM described in this section.

Emergence of complications is variable, based on the severity of the diabetes and the time in which its metabolic derangements have been present. In some cases systemic problems arise early, in others, not at all, but an average period of onset is 15 years or so after hyperglycemia develops.

Microangiopathy In small vessels, altered carbohydrate metabolism causes faulty deposition of basement membrane material. This weakens the vessels and interferes with normal capillary permeability. The role of glycosylated proteins in the BM may involve inducing endothelial changes and platelet aggregation that reduce blood flow. This is often superimposed on an already compromised blood flow from the arteriolosclerosis present in many diabetics, thought to be secondary to the systemic hypertension present in 50% of adult diabetics. By whatever mech-anisms, the reduced blood flow produces a compromised healing response, especially in the lower legs, where vascular involvement is pronounced. Minor wounds, which normally should heal quickly, can pose a serious threat in DM. Because of reduced blood flow and oxygen delivery, the growth of anaerobic bacteria is also favored. These organisms can produce gangrene, which can be severe enough to warrant amputation of a limb with extensively compromised circulation.

Fine retinal blood vessels are also affected in DM. Because hypertension often accompanies NIDDM, especially in the obese, the weakened vessels of the diabetic are also often subjected to an elevated BHP. **15** As a result, small aneurysms readily form and may then rupture within the retina. Such retinal damage produces a progressive loss of vision, which can become total. Some degree of blindness is 25 times more likely to occur in the diabetic as compared with the nondiabetic. **Cataracts** (clouding of the cornea caused by altered proteins) **16** and **glaucoma** (increased pressure within the eye) **17** also have increased incidence in the diabetic.

The glomerular vessels are also subject to BM damage. With the passage of time, nephron function is progressively lost. The immediate cause is the faulty BM of the glomerular capillaries, which produces abnormal filtration. Initially, filtration is increased, then a period of increasing proteinuria follows, and in later stages filtration progressively declines. Ultimately, renal failure is the result. It is the leading cause of death in DM. In extreme cases, an acute necrosis of the renal papillae causes them to be sloughed, causing a rapid loss of renal function. This condition is **necrotizing papillitis.** **18**

Atherosclerosis The second most common cause of death in DM is atherosclerosis, leading to myocardial infarction and cerebrovascular accident (CVA). The chronic hyperlipidemia of DM seems to promote atheroma formation. The process starts early in the course of DM and rapidly progresses. The hypertension often found in the diabetic also favors the development of atherosclerosis (see chapter 7). As well, atherosclerosis in the large cerebral supply vessels adds to the brain ischemia that may be present as a result of the small vessel damage associated with DM. The result is an increased likelihood of CVA. Many of the heart attacks and strokes attributed to vascular disease in mortality statistics are, in fact, complications of DM.

The glycation of proteins may also contribute to the more extensive and rapid atherosclerotic involvement of the large vessels seen in diabetes. It is suspected that glycated LDLs may not be recognized by normal cell membrane receptors, thus elevating their levels in plasma. At the same time, there is evidence that glycosylated collagen binds LDLs at high rates. This might give rise to their increased deposition in the intima to escalate the rate of atherogenesis. Glycated collagen may also enhance platelet binding and aggregation to promote thrombosis and infarction.

Table 17.8	Vascular and Neurologic Conditions Associated with Long-Term Diabetes Mellitus

Small vessel damage
   Depressed peripheral healing response; gangrene risk
   Impaired vision from retinal damage, cataracts, glaucoma
   Depressed renal function; long-term renal failure
Large vessel damage
   Early and severe atherosclerosis; higher incidence of MI and CVA
Peripheral neurologic abnormalities
   Pain, bladder and bowel dysfunction

Peripheral Neuropathy Widespread effects in the peripheral nerves often accompany DM. They may affect neuron processes directly, or their supporting myelin sheaths, or both. Whatever the mechanism, the result is a variety of neurological disturbances, which may not be life-threatening but which are a great source of distress to the sufferer of DM.

Sensory loss is often present, with skeletal motor dysfunction found less frequently. In either case, abnormal reflexes are common. Numbness, tingling sensations, or heightened sensitivity may be experienced, or sensory defects may produce deep and intense pain. When autonomic pathways are affected, a broad range of malfunctions may arise, including disturbances of GI motility, bladder dysfunction, impotence in males, and fainting from neurogenic vascular shock.

DM is known to affect the brain, but disturbances there are thought to derive primarily from small vessel changes that compromise circulation. For this reason, peripheral neuropathy is the term most commonly used in relation to the nervous system abnormalities associated with DM (table 17.8).

Diagnosis of Diabetes Mellitus

Diagnosis in DM is based on the presence of hyperglycemia, glucosuria, and polyuria resulting from lack of insulin secretion. This is a relatively straightforward matter in IDDM. In NIDDM the situation is less clear, and in these cases the glucose tolerance test (GTT) is used. This test assesses the ability of an individual's cells to take up and metabolize glucose. After an oral dose of glucose is given, its level in the blood and urine is monitored. If blood glucose goes up and remains elevated, it is a sign that insulin secretion is inadequate to cope with the absorbed glucose (fig. 17.20).

15 46515

16 27191

17 22486

18 38888

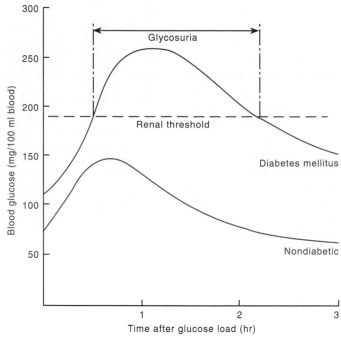

Figure 17.20 The glucose tolerance test. The two curves indicate blood glucose level in the diabetic and the nondiabetic following oral administration of 100 g of glucose (glucose load). Note that when blood glucose level exceeds 190 mg/100 ml, renal reabsorption capacity is exceeded and glucose appears in the urine.

In some individuals, GTT results are above normal but below the level of clear-cut DM. Such individuals are said to have **impaired glucose tolerance.** They will only infrequently progress to diabetes, but they have a greater likelihood of developing coronary atherosclerosis. High stress states, which place an increased demand on the blood glucose control systems, may also produce transient glucose intolerance. Conditions such as trauma or infections are examples. Previously these cases were described by the terms **chemical, latent,** or **subclinical DM,** but the implication that DM was present, yet undiscovered, has led to the decline in the use of these terms. Again, in these cases there is little expectation that diabetes will develop.

Treatment of Diabetes Mellitus

Treatment of IDDM is predominantly by subcutaneous insulin injection. The aim is restoration of glucose metabolism, so that its dietary intake must be closely regulated and matched to insulin dose. This usually means that meals must be taken at regularly timed intervals, with frequent snacks between meals. Caloric levels are closely monitored for all food intake. Foods rich in sugars are strictly limited because they release glucose from the G-I lumen into the blood more rapidly than insulin can cope with it.

Recently, battery-powered insulin infusion pumps have been increasingly used. These provide a continuous insulin supply through a subcutaneous needle or intravenously. They have their own set of complications, e.g., battery failure or hypoglycemia from overdose, and are not indicated for all IDDM patients.

DM in Pregnancy

In **gestational diabetes,** DM emerges in 1–2% of pregnant women with no previous indication of the disease. This idiopathic condition gives rise to delivery complications that are due to the large size of the infants born to diabetic mothers.

The derangements of maternal metabolism also produce congenital malformations in as many as 10% of newborns. Cardiovascular and neurological defects are most often involved. These may cause spontaneous abortion or death in the early post-partum period. In the majority of cases, the DM does not persist beyond pregnancy.

In NIDDM, insulin is required much less often. In many cases the loss of excess weight provides a substantial correction of the problem. Moderate exercise also promotes carbohydrate metabolism and can contribute to normalization without drug therapy. If needed, one of several **sulfonyl urea** preparations may be used to stimulate insulin release from beta cells. Other drugs, which mimic the action of insulin, are finding increasing use in NIDDM therapy.

Secondary DM

When insulin hyposecretion is due to other than beta cell destruction or hormone resistance, the condition is described as **secondary DM.** In these conditions, a variety

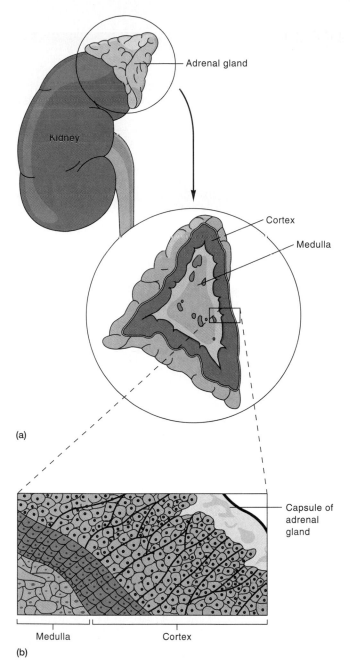

(a)

(b)

Figure 17.21   The adrenal gland. Its cortex and medulla can easily be distinguished in these (*a*) gross and (*b*) microscopic sections.

Table 17.9	Principal Adrenal Cortex Hormones

Mineralocorticoids
   Aldosterone
   Deoxycorticosterone
Glucocorticoids
   Cortisol
   Corticosterone
Gonadocorticoids
   Dehydroepiandrosterone (metabolized to sex hormones in tissues)

Note that mineralocorticoids have some glucocorticoid effects and that glucocorticoids have some mineralocorticoid effect.

THE ADRENAL GLANDS

Broadly speaking, the adrenal glands produce hormones that enable us to better cope with a changing environment. Important homeostatic adaptations mediated by the adrenal hormones include the maintenance of body fluid balance and blood glucose level, as well as various cardiovascular responses.

Normal Anatomy and Physiology

The adrenal or **suprarenal glands** are a pair of small (about 5 g each), approximately pyramidal masses **19** that rest on the superior pole of each kidney (fig. 17.21*a*). Each gland is, in fact, two separate glands of quite different embryologic origins. The larger (85%) adrenal cortex is true glandular tissue, while the internal medulla is derived from embryonic nervous tissue (fig. 17.21*b*). The glands' blood supply derives from the adrenal arteries and other branches of the abdominal aorta. A single vein drains each gland, the right adrenal vein joining the inferior vena cava and the left emptying into the left renal vein.

The hormones of the adrenal cortex are a closely related group of steroid hormones, known collectively as **corticosteroids.** Some of these, because they affect sodium and potassium levels, are called **mineralocorticoids,** while others, which regulate carbohydrate metabolism, are classed as **glucocorticoids** (table 17.9). Of the mineralocorticoids, the most important is aldosterone. It has high potency and is responsible for over 90% of mineralocorticoid stimulus to target tissues. The dominant glucocorticoid is **cortisol,** providing over 95% of glucocorticoid response. Note that cortisol also has some slight mineralocorticoid effect (table 17.9). The adrenal cortex also secretes small quantities of the male and female sex hormone precursor (**gonadocorticoid**) that is converted to testosterone or estrogen in systemic tissues. The components of this

of conditions may contribute to the loss of pancreatic tissue and produce diabetes as a result of insulin hyposecretion.

Factors that are known to produce secondary DM are pancreatic inflammations or trauma, pancreatic surgery, or drug or chemical suppression of the insulin secretion. Various endocrinopathies may also affect insulin secretion, directly or indirectly. Examples are acromegaly, Cushing's syndrome, and pheochromocytoma, three conditions that will be described later in this chapter. Adrenocorticosteroid therapy may also induce secondary DM.

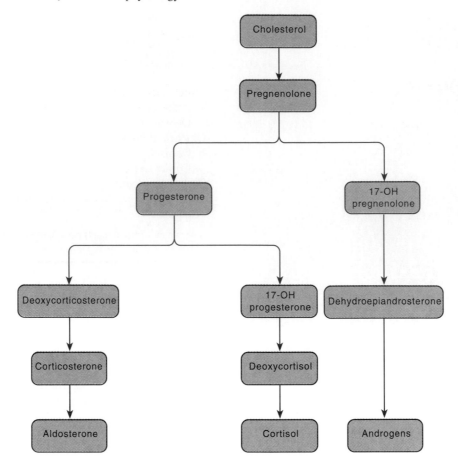

Figure 17.22   Synthetic pathways of the adrenal corticosteroids. Final androgen formation occurs in peripheral tissues.

pathway are referred to as **androgenic.** Normally, only insignificant amounts are secreted, but they may be important in disease states.

Adrenal synthesis of the corticosteroids starts with the uptake of LDL by membrane LDL receptors. The cholesterol carried in large quantities by LDL is released to enter the cell's synthetic pathways. These are catalyzed by mitochondrial and ER enzyme systems and produce the three major steroid hormone types (fig. 17.22).

Control of adrenal secretion is achieved by two major controlling inputs. **ACTH (adrenocorticotropic hormone)** from the anterior pituitary regulates glucocorticoid and gonadocorticoid synthesis, while angiotensin II regulates the mineralocorticoid pathway. The factors determining the feedback control of aldosterone were described in chapter 16. ACTH is under the control of **corticotropin-releasing hormone** (CRH), produced in the hypothalamus and delivered to the pituitary by its connecting portal circulation. Cortisol is the key to regulation. Its blood level exerts a negative feedback effect at the pituitary and hypothalamus to control both glucocorticoid and gonadocorticoid levels (fig. 17.23).

Once in the blood, cortisol travels bound to a specific transport protein called **cortisol-binding globulin** (CBG), and to a lesser degree to albumin. Only small amounts of

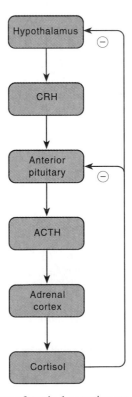

Figure 17.23   Pathway of cortisol secretion control.

Figure 17.24   Catecholamine synthesis pathways in the adrenal medulla.

Table 17.10	Stressors Capable of Inducing the GAS

Trauma (including surgery)	Pain
Intense/prolonged exercise	Emotional distress
Severe disease/infection	(anxiety/depression)
Systemic hypoxia	Severe hemorrhage
Temperature extremes	

Side Effects of Corticosteroid Therapy

The therapeutic use of synthetic cortisol preparations to suppress inflammation is widespread. These anti-inflammatory effects emerge only at pharmacologic doses that are much higher than the physiological levels measured during the GAS. At physiological concentrations the cortisol may exert some role in inflammation regulation, but the degree to which this occurs is unclear.

Also, note that the prolonged therapeutic use of corticosteroids can promote the suppression or loss of normal cortical function. The high therapeutic doses have a suppressive effect on the hypothalamus and pituitary (fig. 17.23). A long-term decrease in ACTH stimulus can cause the cortex to lose sensitivity to ACTH. After a prolonged regimen of corticosteroid therapy, the cortex may require weeks or even months to recover from its highly suppressed state. Patients may be more vulnerable to stressors during this period.

unbound hormone are present in the plasma. Those corticosteroids not inactivated by target tissues are excreted in bile and urine.

In the small, internal core of the adrenal glands, the catecholamines norepinephrine and epinephrine are produced. The amino acid phenylalanine is the initial point in the synthetic pathway (fig. 17.24). The levels of norepinephrine and epinephrine exert feedback control at a key point in the metabolic sequence. Norepinephrine and epinephrine are stored in cytoplasmic granules, from which they are released by exocytosis in response to input from the sympathetic nervous system. Of the adrenal medulla's secretion, 80% is epinephrine, and the remaining 20% is norepinephrine.

General Adaptation Syndrome The adrenal cortex and the adrenal medulla have complementary roles in promoting a widespread adaptation to stress. Broadly, stress consists of either a deviation from some variable's homeostatic optimum or a more acute and immediate threat to physical or emotional well-being. Whenever stresses arise, a coordinated adaptive response follows, mediated by the adrenal cortex's increased secretion of cortisol and the adrenal medulla's enhanced release of catecholamines. This combined response has been termed the **general adaptation syndrome** (GAS). The surge in cortisol is so characteristic that those who study the response define a **stressor** as anything that triggers increased cortisol secretion.

Stressors vary greatly (table 17.10), but the GAS that follows produces a stereotyped response regardless of the stressor. On activation, the hypothalamus, the CRF-ACTH-cortisol pathway, and the sympathetic adrenal medulla responses combine to provide an integrated and widespread ability to meet the stressor's challenge (fig. 17.25).

The effect of these responses is to supply cells with increased cellular fuels (glucose, lipid), increased protein synthesis components (amino acids), and increased oxygen as a result of higher respiration rates, and to increase blood flow to deliver them more efficiently. The benefits of the GAS in coping with physiological disruption seem clear enough, but their adaptive aid in psychological or emotional stress is less clear. Indeed, as noted in earlier chapters, such long-term stress may contribute to atherosclerosis and systemic hypertension.

The GAS has been described as having three stages. The **alarm phase** is the initial response, which principally activates the adrenal medulla and promotes rapid release of catecholamines. It is followed by the **resistance phase,** in which corticosteroids provide a longer-term response that

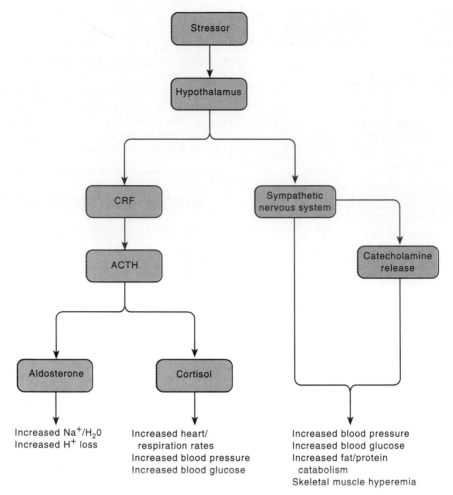

Figure 17.25   The GAS responses as mediated by the adrenals and the sympathetic nervous system.

stabilizes to produce steady-state compensation for the high demands generated by the initial emergency. In the **exhaustion phase,** adaptive capacity has been overwhelmed, and unless therapy can intervene, the result may be rapid decline and death. This phase is characterized by loss of potassium as a result of its exchange for sodium in the nephron tubule, in attempts to sustain blood volume and blood pressure. It may prove useful to identify the GAS phase in which you find your patients. Often, your contribution to diagnosis and therapy allows them to prolong their resistant phase or to avoid the exhaustion phase.

Adrenal Pathophysiology

Most adrenal disorders involve the cortex. Only two, relatively uncommon, tumors produce hyperfunction of the adrenal medulla. We will consider these briefly after describing the more common cortical disorders.

Adrenocortical Hypersecretion

Since there are three classes of hormone produced by the adrenal cortex, there are three principal disorders related to their excessive secretion.

Cushing's Syndrome   The term applied to the glucocorticoid hypersecretion state is **Cushing's syndrome**. The signs and symptoms are predictable on the basis of the glucocorticoid effects already described. Victims of Cushing's syndrome are often obese, with a typical pattern of fat deposition in the face, at the base of the neck, and in the abdomen. A rounded "moon face" is characteristic of the Cushing's syndrome sufferer [20] (fig. 17.26). Lipids made available by the action of cortisol are preferentially deposited in these areas, if they are not metabolized. Chronic protein catabolism produces muscle weakness, bone loss, as its protein matrix components are degraded, and bruising and striae (stretch marks) [21] in the skin. High levels of cortisol also have mineralocorticoid effects, so sodium and water retention typically give rise to systemic hypertension and to hypokalemia. Prolonged hyperglycemia, induced by high levels of cortisol, can also produce insulin insensitivity and impair glucose tolerance. Increased androgenic secretion may also be present in Cushing's syndrome, with women experiencing menstrual dysfunctions and some male-pattern hair growth and acne as a result. Mild to severe emotional or psychological disturbances may also be present to varying degrees (table 17.11).

Figure 17.26   The rounded, puffy facial features seen in this photograph are characteristic of Cushing's disease.

Table 17.11	Principal Signs and Symptoms in Cushing's Syndrome
Obesity	Altered GTT
Characteristic face appearance	Menstrual disorders
Weakness	Psychological
Systemic hypertension	disturbances
Hypokalemia	Tendency to bruising
	Striae

The high levels of glucocorticoids in Cushing's syndrome arise most often as a side effect of prolonged ACTH or glucocorticoid therapy for other conditions. Other causes of hypersecretion are adrenal tumors. Benign adenomas and malignant carcinomas may produce a similar Cushing's pattern of signs and symptoms, but the carcinoma metastasizes extensively and so has a very poor prognosis. Note, however, that about half of cortical carcinomas are so anaplastic that no functional hormones are produced. In these cases, no Cushing's syndrome signs or symptoms are present, and the effects of local invasion and metastasis dominate the clinical picture. Note also that in cortical tumors and therapeutically induced Cushing's syndrome, high glucocorticoid levels suppress ACTH production. In such cases, its low level can be useful in drawing diagnostic conclusions as to etiology.

By contrast, the two remaining causes of Cushing's syndrome are characterized by elevated plasma ACTH values. These may arise as a result of the ectopic secretion of ACTH by a nonendocrine tumor, usually bronchogenic carcinoma. Another, less common source might be the excessive ACTH output of a pituitary adenoma or a hypothalamic tumor that releases excessive CRF to stimulate ACTH secretion. In either case, the pronounced ACTH stimulus to the adrenal cortex induces high cortical output, and Cushing's syndrome results.

Hyperaldosteronism In hyperaldosteronism the problem is hypersecretion by the aldosterone-secreting cells of the adrenal cortex. This condition usually affects those 30–50 years of age, with men affected twice as often as women. It usually arises as the result of a cortical adenoma, sometimes referred to as **Conn's syndrome,** and rarely from a carcinoma's hypersecretion. In other cases, a nonneoplastic and idiopathic cortical hyperplasia is the cause. Excessive renal secretion of renin may also cause excessive aldosterone output. In such cases, a renal tumor or chronic volume depletion is the underlying cause.

The major effect of hyperaldosteronism is systemic hypertension due to sodium and water retention by the kidney. Hypokalemia and alkalosis secondary to sodium reten-tion may also be present. About one in a hundred cases of systemic hypertension result from this condition.

Adrenal Virilism The result of androgen hypersecretion in females is **adrenal virilism.** Normally androgenic effects are masked by high androgen levels in males, but in females they induce various masculine traits such as beard growth, acne, voice deepening, and hair loss. Taken together, these changes are known as **virilization.** Menstrual abnormalities are also common. If androgen hypersecretion occurs in a young male, it leads to **sexual precocity.** In this condition, sexual development is rapid and premature. In such cases, the male sex organs and sexual drive of an adult may be present in a quite young individual. Etiology of the hypersecretion state is based either on hyperplasia or neoplasia of the androgen-secreting region of the cortex or a congenital enzyme derangement that promotes excessive androgen synthesis.

Adrenocortical Hyposecretion

Failure to secrete adequate amounts of corticosteroids gives rise to **hypoadrenalism** or **Addison's disease.** In this uncommon condition, corticosteroid deficiency may be due to destruction of the adrenal cortex or to suppression of ACTH by high therapeutic doses of glucocorticoids. In rare instances, a congenital enzyme deficiency is the cause. In most cases, destruction of the gland occurs by an ill-understood autoimmune mechanism, but infection, tumor invasion, or infarction may be also involved.

The clinical pattern in Addison's disease is one of slowly developing weakness and fatigue, appetite and weight loss, and a characteristic pigmentation excess. The pigmentation increase is sometimes blotchy and is due to the pigment-stimulating effects of high ACTH levels caused by the feedback effects of low cortisol secretion (fig. 17.23). Because Addison's patients have little ability to secrete cortisol and mount an adequate GAS, they are highly vulnerable to stress. If they are challenged by some stressor, an acute condition called an **Addisonian crisis** may emerge. It typically involves fever, nausea, vomiting, hyponatremia, and hyperkalemia, as well as hypotension and dehydration, which pose the threat of circulatory shock.

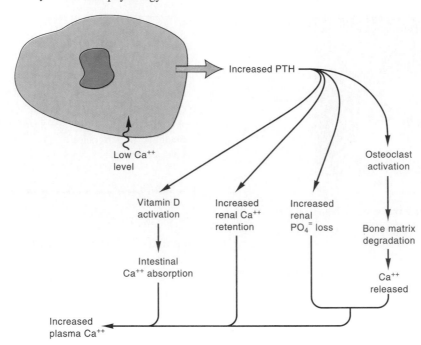

Figure 17.27 PTH regulates four responses that contribute to CA⁺⁺ homeostasis.

Adrenal Medulla Pathophysiology

The derangements that arise in the adrenal medulla are rare tumors. One, **pheochromocytoma, 22** is usually benign, and the other, **neuroblastoma,** is malignant.

Pheochromocytoma This tumor arises in the catecholamine-secreting **chromaffin cells** of the medulla. Although most pheochromocytomas are benign, 10% are malignant. Sufferers typically develop systemic hypertension, with superimposed bouts of headache, heavy perspiration, tachycardia, and anxiety due to unregulated surges in catecholamine output from the tumor. Surgical resection has a high probability of success.

Neuroblastoma This highly malignant tumor occurs most frequently in children under the age of 15. Its effects are similar to the pheochromocytoma in deriving from excessive catecholamine secretion, but its rapid and extensive metastasis is its most serious threat. If it is identified and surgically removed prior to an infant's first year, prognosis is quite good. After the first year, widespread metastasis makes the prognosis grim.

THE PARATHYROID GLANDS

The parathyroid glands are important regulators of calcium and other minerals, and as a result, have significant impact on bone and indirectly on muscle function.

Normal Anatomy and Physiology

The parathyroid glands are small nodules of endocrine tissue held to the posterior surface of the thyroid gland by its capsule. **23** Their number varies from two to twelve, but four is typical. Their hormone is **parathyroid hormone** (PTH), also known as **parathormone.**

PTH is a peptide hormone synthesized in the **chief cells** of the parathyroids. Little is stored in the gland, and secretion is closely linked to synthesis. In the plasma, PTH travels as a free molecule, rather than bound to a carrier protein. Secretion of PTH is controlled by Ca^{++} concentration in the extracellular fluid compartment (ECF). When Ca^{++} concentration is low, PTH secretion is increased, and when high, it is suppressed (fig. 17.27). Magnesium ion (Mg^{++}) concentrations also affect PTH secretion similarly, but their input to the regulatory system seems less important than that of calcium. PTH acts directly or indirectly on various effector tissues to regulate plasma Ca^{++} levels. It also affects Mg^{++}, $PO_4^=$, and HCO_3^-. Its regulatory role is based on its effects on bone, nephron tubules, and vitamin D.

In response to a prolonged lowering of plasma Ca^{++} levels, increased PTH secretion will promote Ca^{++} and Mg^{++} reabsorption by the nephron. This directly cuts Ca^{++} losses to support the level of plasma Ca^{++}. PTH also activates osteoclasts in bone, stimulating their breakdown of bone matrix to make more Ca^{++} available. This effect is enhanced by another PTH-mediated action, renal $PO_4^=$ excretion. Since $PO_4^=$ and Ca^{++} concentrations are inversely related, lowering $PO_4^=$ levels promotes the movement of Ca^{++} from bone into the plasma. In addition, PTH activates vitamin D, which stimulates additional Ca^{++}

Anatomical Variability and the Hypoparathyroid State

Not only the number of parathyroid glands is subject to variation; their location also differs from one individual to the next. Some of these small nodules may not be associated with the thyroid gland at all. Instead they may be dispersed to various locations in the region of the neck. As well, some may be present in the superior mediastinum, so that surgery or trauma there may give rise to an unanticipated hypoparathyroid state.

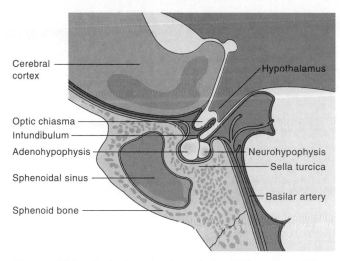

Figure 17.28 Sagittal section through the pituitary gland. The adenohypophysis is distinct from the neurologically derived neurohypophysis.

absorption from the small intestine. These last two mechanisms are a new input of Ca^{++} into the plasma from body stores and the diet (fig. 17.27).

Hyperparathyroidism

Hyperparathyroidism is usually the result of a benign or malignant tumor or of parathyroid hyperplasia. These conditions arise more often in females than males and primarily produce loss of bone tissue from excessive osteoclast stimulus. The resulting bone weakness predisposes to bone pain, deformity, and fracture.

The result of chronic PTH hypersecretion is hypercalcemia, which may reach twice the normal Ca^{++} concentration of 8.5–10.5 mg/dl. It produces a range of muscular and neurologic defects (see the section on hypercalcemia in chapter 17) as well as predisposing to kidney stone formation. In extreme cases, widespread deposition of insoluble calcium phosphate in soft tissues may occur. This is known as **metastatic calcification.**

In renal disease, if $PO_4^=$ is retained, then Ca^{++} levels are depressed by the mechanism of their inverse relationship, as previously described and as indicated in figure 17.27. In such cases, PTH secretion is increased and bone degradation follows. When excessive secretion of PTH is caused by such a derangement, the condition is known as **secondary hyperparathyroidism.** If it is prolonged, parathyroid hyperplasia results. GI malabsorption or vitamin D deficiencies may also play a role in the etiology of secondary hyperparathyroidism, where inadequate Ca^{++} levels act as stimuli that induce PTH hypersecretion.

Hypoparathyroidism

Hypoparathyroidism is less frequently encountered than the hypersecretion state. Previously, the most common cause of hypoparathyroidism was the inadvertent removal of parathyroid glands during thyroid or other neck surgery.

More recently, awareness of the need to maintain parathyroid tissue, and the increasing application of nonsur-

gical therapies for hyperthyroidism, has reduced the incidence of hypoparathyroidism. Hereditary gland deficiency and gland destruction from various causes are now more significant factors in this condition. When target tissue insensitivity to PTH yields signs and symptoms, the condition is described as **pseudohypoparathyroidism** (PHP).

The principal result of diminished PTH secretion, or target tissue insensitivity to it, is hypocalcemia due to inadequate renal Ca^{++} retention or $PO_4^=$ excretion. Impaired GI absorption and reduced Ca^{++} release from bone are also involved. Weakness, altered mental processes, and faulty muscular functions are the result (see the section on hypocalcemia in chapter 16).

THE PITUITARY GLAND

The pituitary derives its name from the Latin for phlegm, since it was originally thought to be the source of the mucus that coats the nasal mucous membranes. This important regulatory gland has intimate structural and functional links to the hypothalamus, and we will therefore consider both in this section.

Normal Anatomy and Physiology

The position of the pituitary gland, under the base of the brain, gives rise to its alternative name, **hypophysis,** which means "growing under" (fig. 17.28). The pituitary stalk emerges from the hypothalamus to support the small (1 cm diam) glandular mass, **24** which projects into and is surrounded by a depression in the skull's sphenoid bone called the **sella turcica.** This elaborate protection gives testimony to the functional importance of the pituitary.

The gland consists of two regions, the **adenohypophysis** (anterior pituitary), composed of true glandular tissue,

Table 17.12   The Principal Anterior Pituitary Hormones and Their Major Functions

Hormone/Abbreviation	Major Function
Human growth hormone (GH)	Stimulation of overall body growth and development
Thyroid-stimulating hormone (TSH)	Regulation of thyroid secretion
Follicle-stimulating hormone (FSH)	Stimulation of male and female gamete production
Luteinizing hormone (LH)	Stimulation of testosterone secretion; triggers ovulation and corpus luteum secretion
Prolactin (PRL)	Stimulation of mammary gland milk production
Adrenocorticotropic hormone (ACTH)	Regulation of adrenal cortical secretion
Melanocyte-stimulating hormone (MSH)	Stimulation of pigment production in skin melanocytes

and the **neurohypophysis** (posterior pituitary), which derives from embryonic nervous tissue and which is continuous with the hypothalamus. The posterior pituitary, rather than synthesizing and secreting hormone, acts as a storage site for hormones produced in the hypothalamus. The hormones migrate to the neurohypophysis along neurons that reach it via the pituitary stalk. From these the hormones are released in response to action potentials from the hypothalamus. The two neurohypophyseal hormones are **vasopressin,** also called **antidiuretic hormone** (ADH), and **oxytocin** (table 17.12).

The adenohypophysis synthesizes and secretes six major hormones from cells specialized for each hormone type. All but two of the anterior pituitary hormones are tropic hormones, that is, they control another endocrine gland's secretion. The exceptions are **prolactin** and **somatotropin,** or **growth hormone** (GH), which elicits its target tissue effects by activating the liver to release substances called **somatomedins.** These exert a potent growth stimulus to most body tissues.

Table 17.12 lists the pituitary's hormones and their principal functions.

Adenohypophyseal Hypersecretion

Hypersecretion of the anterior pituitary may be caused by a tropic-hormone-secreting adenoma. Malignancies or hypothalamic disorders are much less frequently involved. The adenomas are often tiny and cause no local invasive or compressive effects. However, because of the bony surrounding walls of the sella turcica, any that do enlarge significantly can compress the adjacent **optic chiasma.** This structure is formed by the merging of the two optic nerves prior to their entering the brain. The visual defects that accompany pituitary tumors are usually due to its compression or invasion.

The signs and symptoms in a given condition usually reflect hyperactivity in the pituitary's target gland. Cushing's syndrome is most often caused by ACTH hypersecretion and a thyroid hyperfunction state that resembles Graves' disease, but without its autoimmune component.

Hypersecretion of the two nontropic anterior pituitary hormones may also occur. When prolactin is present at high plasma levels, males experience impotence as a sole disturbance. In females, irregularities of menstruation are typical, often accompanied by varying degrees of breast milk production without pregnancy **(galactorrhea).**

Growth Hormone Hypersecretion

The effects of this condition depend on the age at which the hypersecretion state arises. If it is during childhood, prior to closure of the epiphyseal plates, rapid overall body growth is promoted by somatotropin's exaggerated stimulus to growth. The afflicted individual may reach a height of 8–9 feet with a proportionately large body. This is the condition known as **giantism** or **gigantism.** If the pituitary tumor that causes this condition is not surgically removed or otherwise suppressed, it may completely destroy the pituitary by compressing it against the walls of the sella turcica. Death at an early adult age is the usual result without intervention.

When somatotropic hormone hypersecretion occurs after adolescence, **acromegaly** develops. In this condition, although long bone length is fixed, bones enlarge by thickening. This change is accompanied by excessive growth of soft tissue, which produces a characteristic enlarging and coarsening of the features (fig. 17.29). Internal organs, such as the liver and kidney, are also affected. These changes occur quite gradually and may go unnoticed for some time.

Adenohypophyseal Hyposecretion

Hyposecretion may be the result of infection, primary or metastatic tumor damage, infarction, or various other injuries. The result is the suppression of all or most hor-

A Diagnostic Note from the Ancient Greeks

Both diabetes mellitus and diabetes insipidus are characterized by diuresis. In DM the cause is the osmotic effect of high glucose levels in nephron tubule filtrate, whereas in diabetes insipidus it is the lack of ADH. Even in ancient times, a patient complaining of large urinary water losses might be asked to produce a urine specimen. Lacking modern laboratory analytical machinery, and indeed, anything to plug them into, the canny physician would taste the specimen. The Greek word for honey is *meli,* so sweet-tasting urine would yield the diagnosis diabetes mellitus (the passing of sweet urine). On the other hand, insipid or flat-tasting urine would indicate a different condition, and hence the distinguishing term diabetes insipidus would be applied.

Note that it was not necessary to ingest large quantities of urine to arrive at the diagnosis; a small taste was enough. Of course, urine is normally sterile, so no infection was likely to follow from such tasting. Although their knowledge was primitive in many ways, early physicians weren't fools, and we can be sure they would avoid tasting any urine that was cloudy, blood-tinged, or otherwise abnormal.

(a)

(b)

(c)

(d)

Figure 17.29   The progressive coarsening of facial features in acromegaly is seen in this sequence of photographs taken at age 9 (*a*), 16 (*b*), 33 (*c*), and 52 (*d*).

mone secretion, the condition of **panhypopituitarism.** The resulting signs and symptoms are highly variable and generally reflect hypoactivity in target tissues. In the case of tumors, various consequences of brain compression or invasion of the brain may be superimposed on endocrine hypofunction, e.g., headache or visual disturbances.

Congenital or hereditary defects may produce hyposecretion of only a single anterior pituitary hormone. As you would expect, deficiency of a tropic hormone reveals itself as hypoactivity in its endocrine target gland. Hyposecretion of growth hormone is rare, but a prolactin hyposecretion state may arise as a result of hypotension related to perinatal hemorrhage. Because the adenohypophysis enlarges during pregnancy, it may compress the vessels that supply its blood. These vessels are arranged in a pattern that supplies the prolactin-secreting cells last, so they are at greatest risk of becoming ischemic as pregnancy proceeds. If at the time of delivery there is excessive blood loss, the fall in BHP can cause infarction of the prolactin-secreting cells. Of course, failure to lactate is the result, and at the very time when lactation is most needed. Abnormal menstruation is another consequence of inadequate prolactin secretion. This condition of perinatal pituitary infarction is known as **Sheehan's syndrome.**

Neurohypophyseal Dysfunction

Neurohypophyseal dysfunction, which is relatively rare, affects the secretion of ADH. Abnormalities of oxytocin secretion are unknown.

Diabetes Insipidus

This is a vasopressin hyposecretion state that may be caused by tumors, infection, trauma, or inadvertent damage from radiation therapy. The result is a significant diuresis due to a reduction of the nephron tubule's water permeability, which ADH controls. Thirst and polydipsia are the expected responses, which can at least partially compensate for the sometimes enormous water losses (as much as 20 liters daily) that characterize this condition.

Syndrome of Inappropriate ADH Secretion

This condition was discussed in chapter 16 in the context of the excessive extracellular fluid volume that it produces. Most SIADH is due to production of ADH-like substances by nonendocrine tumors, usually of the lung, lymphoid tissue, or thymus. Other conditions that less frequently cause SIADH are disturbances of the hypothalamus, meningitis, infections, cerebral trauma, and infarction.

Case Study

A 23-year-old female university student saw her general practitioner and complained of severe constipation, headaches, fatigue, and menstrual periods characterized by prolonged and excessive flow (**menorrhagia**). She had been experiencing fatigue and some degree of bowel irregularity for the past two years. These initially mild symptoms, combined with a slight swelling in her throat, had prompted a previous physician to measure her thyroxine levels, which were found to be normal. The diffuse nature of her complaints, combined with the emotional upset, at the time, of poor grades and a broken wedding engagement, prompted her previous doctor to suspect that her problems were stress-related.

She now reported that in addition to the general worsening of her symptoms, her throat was much more swollen and she was experiencing difficulty in coping with cold temperatures, saying she "had a hard time keeping warm." In view of these more recent developments, a blood test was done. It revealed that her thyroxine levels were abnormally low, and she was referred to an endocrinologist.

On physical examination the patient appeared generally well, with a normal body weight that had not recently changed. Her thyroid gland was diffusely enlarged, to approximately twice normal size, with no nodularity detectable on palpation. Her reflexes were normal, except for some delay in the relaxation phase of her biceps muscle. Other physical findings were normal. A blood test confirmed the depressed thyroxine levels: 2.3 µgm% (normal: 4–10 µgm%). A technetium radioisotope scan showed normal uptake in both thyroid lobes, with no obvious abnormal areas.

On the basis of these findings, a diagnosis of idiopathic primary hypothyroidism was made. Thyroxine replacement therapy was prescribed on a continuing, life-long basis. The patient's signs and symptoms subsided and she suffers no side effects.

Commentary

The slow onset and progression of the initial thyroid changes produced no drop in plasma thyroxine levels, and the diffuse nature of the early complaints were easily confused with psychological illness or stress-related disorders. Weight loss (in hyperthyroid states) or gain (in hypothyroid conditions) is common, but not always present, and any coincidental change in activity levels and appetite can affect body weight to further confuse the picture.

Menstrual irregularities are also typical findings in thyroid disorders: amenorrhea with thyroid excess and menorrhagia in deficiency states. But since such irregularities also accompany a wide variety of other conditions, they may not provide much diagnostic help. In this patient, once the thyroid's hyperplasia response proved inadequate to maintain adequate thyroxine in the blood, the emerging cold intolerance, constipation, and slowed muscle reflexes soon clarified the diagnostic picture.

Key Concepts

1. Endocrine disease is most often the result of excessive or inadequate hormone secretion, due to an imbalance in the gland's controlling inputs or to damage to the gland itself (p. 425).

2. Endocrine hyposecretion may be the result of a metabolic defect, gland agenesis, atrophy of a developed gland, or damage to an otherwise normal gland by infection, infarction, autoimmune mechanisms, or tumor growth (pp. 425–429).

3. In response to endocrine hyposecretion, negative feedback reflexes produce increased levels of tropic hormones or hypothalamic releasing hormones, whose suppression may be monitored to confirm restoration of normal function (p. 426).

4. Hormone resistance is often the result of autoimmune hormone receptor destruction, which produces target tissue insensitivity and hyposecretion effects (p. 426).

5. Endocrine hypersecretion is the result of excessive secretion of tropic hormones, defective feedback control mechanisms, or endocrine gland tumors (p. 427).

6. Thyroid hypofunction produces a systemic decline in the metabolic rate, causing cold intolerance, weight gain, and sluggish muscular and neurologic activity (pp. 430–431).

7. Chronically low plasma levels of thyroxine promote increased secretion of TSH, which induces the condition of thyroid hyperplasia known as goiter (p. 431).

8. Thyroid hyperfunction produces a systemic elevation of the metabolic rate, causing heat intolerance, neurologic excitability, insomnia, weight loss, cardiac effects, and exophthalmos (pp. 433–435).

9. Diabetes mellitus exists in two forms, IDDM, the true islet hypofunction disease, and NIDDM, which is a hormone resistance state based on insulin insensitivity (pp. 434–435).

10. A variety of chronic effects in DM involve small and large blood vessels and the nervous system, producing numerous and serious long-term consequences for the diabetic (pp. 439–441).

11. A range of adaptive responses to stress are mediated by the adrenal cortex and medulla, grouped under the title general adaptation syndrome (GAS) (p. 446).

12. Adrenocorticotropic hypersecretion may involve glucocorticoids, producing Cushing's syndrome, aldosterone, to yield hyperaldosteronism, or androgens in women, causing adrenal virilism (pp. 447–449).

13. The principal adrenocortical hyposecretion state involves a deficit of the corticosteroids, producing Addison's disease, which may compromise the GAS response (p. 448).

14. Hyperparathyroidism, which is usually caused by a parathyroid tumor, produces high levels of bone resorption, to the degree of compromising skeletal integrity (pp. 448–449).

15. The numerous hormones of the adenohypophysis may be individually hypersecreted by an adenoma of a specific pituitary cell type, limiting effects to the target tissue regulated by each hormone (p. 450).

16. Hypersecretion of growth hormone prior to closure of the epiphyseal plates can so stimulate growth that body height might attain 8 or 9 feet, while hypersecretion after closure results in the enlargement and thickening of various tissues without any increase in height (p. 450).

17. Hyposecretion of adenohypophyseal hormones is usually due to tissue damage that affects all cell types to produce more widespread and variable systemic hypofunction effects (p. 450).

18. In the neurohypophysis, disturbances of oxytocin secretion are unknown, but ADH secretion may be excessive, causing SIADH, or inadequate, causing diabetes insipidus (p. 451).

REVIEW ACTIVITIES

1. For each of the following situations, use upward or downward pointing arrows to show how each situation would cause plasma hormone levels to change.

   Tropic hormone hypersecretion
   Liver failure
   Target tissue hormone receptor damage
   Reduced target tissue hormone inactivation
   Kidney failure
   Anaplastic endocrine tumor

2. See figure 17.12. Why are the feedback effects of T_3/T_4 represented by minus signs? What would happen if they were plus signs?

3. The patient in this chapter's case study asks you to explain why she can't seem to keep warm. For help in answering her, see page 430.

4. Use pages 438–439 to assist in laying out a flow chart illustrating the pathogenesis of IDDM. Start with "Decreased Insulin Output" at the top, and end with "Hypoglycemic Coma" on the bottom.

5. In figure 17.8, identify the section showing the steps that are thought to produce NIDDM. What is the name of this hypofunction mechanism? Page 426 may provide a clue. Which part of figure 17.19 would be useful to help make the point?

6. Write out a list of known or at least plausible links between each GAS response component in figure 17.25 and a physiological benefit that might contribute to coping with a stressor.

7. Prepare a giant quick reference list. For each major endocrine gland, indicate its principal hypo/hypersecretion states and the general pattern of target tissue problems that result.

Chapter Eighteen

Skeletal and Muscular Pathophysiology

He knew the anguish of the marrow,
The ague of the skeleton;
No contact possible to flesh
Allayed the fever of the bone

T. S. Elliot
Whispers of Immortality

The osseous tissue that forms the skeleton and the muscle tissue of skeletal muscles are substantially different, but the organs they form have a close functional relationship. For this reason it is useful to consider their pathophysiology in a single chapter. This chapter also includes treatment of joint diseases, since most skeletal muscle action produces bone motion at joints. Bone fractures, however, are described separately in chapter 24, where you will also find the definitions of particular types of fractures (e.g., compression fracture, pathological fracture) to which passing reference may be made here.

NORMAL BONE PHYSIOLOGY

Bone formation, or **ossification,** involves the deposition of inorganic crystals in the organic matrix of a preformed cartilage bone model or **template.** The crystals are composed of calcium, phosphate, and hydroxide, and form the water-insoluble salt called **hydroxyapatite.** Various other ions, e.g., sodium, carbonate, and magnesium, may join to the hydroxyapatite plates that are bound to the template's collagen. The imbedding of compression-resistant hydroxyapatite plates in a matrix of high-tensile-strength collagen yields a greater combined strength. The principle is the same as the one applied in so much industrial technology: materials with differing properties can be combined to form a new material with enhanced performance. Examples are fiberglass, which combines glass fibers in a resin matrix, and reinforced concrete, in which steel rods are imbedded in a concrete matrix. Binding between the dissimilar components is based on interactions at the molecular level that yield pronounced increases in the material's strength, resilience, or other properties.

The process of bone formation starts prior to birth and continues throughout the period of growth and development. Elongation of the body's long bones continues during this period because new cartilage forms at a rate that outpaces ossification. This process occurs at the **epiphyseal plate** or **growth plate** (fig. 18.1a). As full skeletal growth is achieved, ossification overtakes cartilage formation and the epiphyseal plate disappears. At this point, the length of the bone is permanently fixed (fig. 18.1b).

The skeletal structures formed during early development are crude approximations of their final, mature form. Following the initial formation of a bone, its structure is continually modified to better respond to functional demands. These are the result of altered patterns of weight-bearing and other stresses that increase and change with normal development. For example, the transition from a child's crawling, through brief periods of standing upright, to unassisted toddling, and then to running over a playing field, places increased demand on the skeleton for the development of overall strength and weight-bearing capacity. As well, the tensions generated by increasingly strong muscles require modifications of the bone to form stronger muscle attachment points.

(a)

(b)

Figure 18.1   (a) The epiphyseal plates (P) that can be seen in this radiograph indicate that ossification has not yet been completed. (b) This radiograph shows an adult's hand, with no epiphyseal plate visible.

To accommodate these demands, a process of **bone remodeling** continues throughout life. In response to demand, bone remodeling involves a constantly shifting of the balance between bone deposition by **osteo-blasts** and its breakdown (resorption) by **osteoclasts.** **1** The result is a continually active bone, which, once formed and

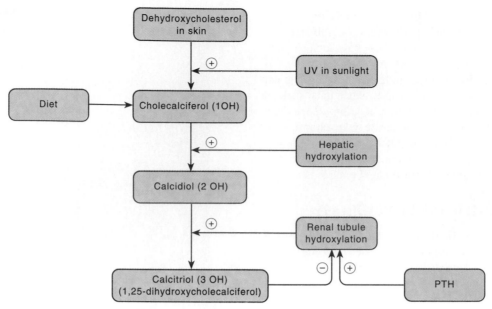

Figure 18.2   Vitamin D production and related regulatory factors. Hypoparathyroidism and renal or liver failure may produce calcitriol deficiencies, necessitating therapeutic supplementation to counter calcium imbalances.

remodeled to its mature configuration, remains sensitive to any changes in demand that may arise. Vigorous body activity is matched by a stronger skeleton, while the skeleton that experiences lower activity levels, or is bedridden for a prolonged period, loses bone tissue and weakens in response. Even in an adult with an unchanging level of activity, remodeling continues in a steady state in which deposition is exactly matched by resorption. It is thought that this process continually renews bone structure to offset the aging of osteocytes, the cells resident in mature bone, and to replace or restore damaged **trabeculae.** These critical stress-bearing plates in the interior of bone may suffer microfractures in the course of normal loading that can be repaired by bone remodeling.

Bone Metabolism and Its Regulation

Beyond its direct structural role in the skeleton, bone acts as a reservoir that can take up or supply calcium if its plasma level alters from the optimum. Accordingly, about 1% of bone's calcium is available to meet an immediate calcium demand. This **exchangeable calcium** is only loosely bound in the form of calcium phosphate and can be quickly released in response to short-term increases in PTH (parathyroid hormone) levels. When plasma PTH remains elevated over a longer period, it activates osteoclasts, and their resorption of bone makes further calcium available to the extracellular fluid. PTH also promotes the renal retention of calcium in support of falling plasma calcium levels and promotes intestinal calcium absorption through its indirect effects on vitamin D.

Vitamin D, **cholecalciferol,** was originally studied in the context of its natural occurrence in butter, eggs, and fish and was initially thought to be a vitamin, that is, an essen-

Dietary Supplementation of Vitamin D

During the winter in northern latitudes, the sun's angle may reduce skin activation of vitamin D to negligible levels for months. During this time dietary sources can meet most needs, provided that intake is adequate and well balanced. Across North America, cholecalciferol is widely added to milk, cereals, and various processed foods to insure adequate dietary intake, particularly in children, whose growing skeletons have a high calcium demand. This practice has been effective in preventing deficiencies in children of low-income parents, especially those living in northern urban centers.

tial nutrient obtainable only in the diet. Now, it is known to be produced endogenously, so it can more accurately be regarded as a hormone. However, its status as a vitamin is so well established that the name persists. Circulating cholecalciferol may have its origin in dietary sources or it may have been produced internally.

Most cholecalciferol is produced in the skin, where exposure to the sun's ultraviolet (UV) light activates dehydroxycholesterol to form cholecalciferol, which contains one OH (hydroxyl) group. As the blood transports it through the liver, cholecalciferol is modified by the addition of an OH group and given the name **calcidiol.** The kidney's nephron tubules complete formation of the active hormone with addition of another OH group to yield **calcitriol,** or 1,2,5-dihydroxycholecalciferol, the term that may appear on laboratory blood chemistry reports.

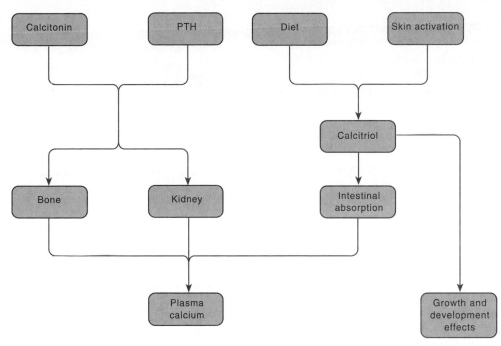

Figure 18.3   Factors determining plasma calcium levels. Note that calcitriol has some additional systemic effects and that the role of calcitonin is minor.

Calcitriol is 100 times more potent than calcidiol and 1000 times more potent than cholecalciferol. The last activation step is controlled by PTH, so that increases in plasma calcitriol follow increases in PTH secretion. Once activated, calcitriol is principally taken up by the intestinal epithelium, where it indirectly promotes the active absorption of calcium from the lumen. Note also the feedback regulation that calcitriol exerts: a direct effect on the kidney and an indirect input to the kidney via the suppression of PTH secretion. Because of these regulatory links, calcitriol may be administered therapeutically in cases of hypoparathyroidism or chronic renal failure to counter calcium imbalances (fig. 18.2).

At normal physiological levels, calcitriol promotes bone deposition, a logical link in the context of ossification. However, at high levels it works with PTH to activate bone resorption and calcium release. In addition to its impact on mineral metabolism, calcitriol has a broad array of recently recognized effects in other areas. It appears to function in regulating the growth and development of several important tissues, e.g., skin, red marrow blood cell precursors, and the insulin-secreting cells of the pancreas. Some tumor growth suppression has also been reported, and research into further therapeutic use of calcitriol is under way.

Calcitonin, from the thyroid gland, also has an effect on plasma calcium levels, one that is opposite to that of PTH. Increased calcitonin triggers renal calcium excretion and suppresses osteoclast activity to lower calcium in the extracellular fluid. Beyond this, calcitonin's links to the other calcium-regulating mechanisms are unknown. Its role may be only a subsidiary one, in that no calcium derangements are caused by its excessive or inadequate secretion. Calcium homeostasis is summarized in figure 18.3.

Because it suppresses osteoclast activity, calcitonin has increasingly been used as a therapeutic agent to counter bone loss in osteoporosis and Paget's disease, both of which are described in the following section.

BONE PATHOPHYSIOLOGY

Bone disorders are essentially derived from infection, tumor growth, abnormal ossification, or an imbalance in bone remodeling. In metabolic bone disease, a net loss of bone (**osteopenia**) is the usual result, but conditions involving excessive (**hyperostosis**), irregular, or otherwise inappropriate bone formation also occur. Deficiency of an essential ossification factor or some derangement of its regulatory system may be involved, but some bone diseases remain in the idiopathic category. Bone disorders are described here on the basis of whether they are inherited or acquired.

Genetic Bone Disorders

These rare conditions are transmitted by varying patterns of inheritance. They usually produce defects in a single factor essential to normal bone metabolism, which then gives rise to various skeletal abnormalities.

Osteopetrosis

This condition is also known as **Albers-Schönberg disease** or **marble bone disease.** It is transmitted by a recessive pattern of inheritance and can therefore arise in the child of parents who have no skeletal disorder. The essential defect in osteopetrosis involves the osteoclasts. They are either functionally deficient or completely absent, because of some abnormality of differentiation in the cell line from which they arise. In either case, the result is defective ossification, which produces excessive deposition of a bone tissue that is flawed in being brittle and easily fractured.

In mild cases, the typical signs are short stature and a tendency to easy fracturing of the bones. Such cases may go unnoticed until adulthood, when a radiograph reveals an unusually dense bone structure. Severe cases arise early and the victims have little chance of survival. Excessive bone formation typically encroaches on bone marrow cavities to produce a progressively debilitating anemia. Bone deformities in the floor of the brain case can cause increased intracranial pressure and can compress and damage cranial nerves, causing blindness, deafness, paralysis of the facial muscles, and various other cranial nerve disorders.

One therapeutic approach that has been tried is the use of marrow transplants to provide a source of osteoclast precursors. Although this has met with some success, the problems of suitable donor availability and the procedure's risks to anemic and otherwise weakened children are often difficult to overcome. Another approach takes advantage of the bone degradation effects of high levels of calcitriol. Administration of this substance has been beneficial in some cases.

Osteogenesis Imperfecta

The term **osteogenesis imperfecta** (OI) includes a number of related conditions that have in common an inherited defect in collagen synthesis. Specifically involved is the collagen that dominates bone matrix and on which mineral deposition occurs. **2** The result is a faulty ossification, which produces osteopenia and brittle bones. Defective tooth formation, a blue discoloration of the sclerae, and faulty hearing are also often present in OI.

Inheritance is by both recessive and dominant mechanisms, but scattered mutations also arise so that either, both, or neither of a victim's parents may exhibit signs of the disease. Several degrees of severity are recognized, from quite mild to an extremely severe form that is fatal in the perinatal period. In mild cases, skeletal abnormalities may be noticed only as minor defects in radiographs. In severe cases, pronounced stunting of growth, incomplete ossification, and various other skeletal defects may be present, e.g., long bone shafts of variable thickness or length **3** **4** and **scoliosis** (lateral deformation of the vertebral column that can cause hypoventilation and a tendency to lung infections). **5** **6**

Achondroplastic Dwarfism

As its name indicates, this condition involves a defect in normal cartilage development. The problem is a lack of cartilage formation at the epiphyseal plates of long bones, which causes ossification to seal the plates early, preventing their further elongation. Normal ossification of other parts of the skeleton proceeds, but the abnormally short limbs and normal-sized spinal column and skull produce the characteristic skeletal disproportion that characterizes the dwarf. **7** To exaggerate the effect, some bones may grow by thickening, even though they can't elongate.

The dominant inheritance of this condition means that an affected individual will probably have an affected parent. Development of other organ systems proceeds normally, and a short but otherwise normal adult may achieve a full life span. In some cases, however, **lordosis** (anterior convexity) of the spinal column may arise, causing spinal cord and spinal nerve compression. **8** In the very rare case where each parent contributes a defective gene, the condition is quite severe and the victim rarely survives much past birth.

Acquired Bone Disorders

We will consider bone infection and tumors of bone after describing the major metabolic bone disorders. In this group, osteopenia is typical, and only one disorder—Paget's disease—is characterized by significant bone deposition to compensate for increased bone resorption.

Paget's Disease (Osteitis Deformans)

In this condition, focal derangements of bone resorption and deposition occur over the course of the disease. In the initial stages, bone resorption dominates (the **osteolytic phase**). Later, in the **mixed phase,** bone deposition rates approximate resorption rates, but the newly formed bone is abnormal. It is coarsely structured and crudely organized, often forming dense, focal masses. This characteristic tissue is known as **pagetic bone 9** (fig. 18.4). In the late, or **osteosclerotic phase,** resorption declines and harder, more dense bone tissue is formed, again in a focal pattern.

2 46393

3 45502

4 45510

5 25609

6 45063

7 25610

8 30253

9 38210

Figure 18.4   Histologic examination of pagetic bone reveals a characteristic pattern of irregular and crudely structured bone. The dark spots aligned at the trabecular surfaces are the nuclei of osteoblasts (B), while the larger, multinucleated cells are osteoclasts (C).

Classification Terminology in OI

You may encounter a classification system that groups the various OI conditions according to when signs of bone weakness emerge. One category includes conditions marked by the occurrence of bone fractures at birth, which are classified as **OI congenita.** Any condition with later emergence of fractures is classified as **OI tarda.** This system is being replaced by a more sophisticated one, which designates the mildest form of OI as **type I** and the early, fatal form as **type II.** As opposed to a tumor grading system, where the highest number has the worst prognosis, in this system there is potential for confusion, in that types III and IV indicate severity intermediate between types I and II. This means that, in order of increasing disease severity, the sequence is I, III, IV, II.

To compound the problem, type II is in some systems subdivided into groups that also have Roman numeral designations. Of these, group I conditions show severe radiographic abnormalities and group V only minor abnormalities. Needless to say, it is important to recognize and use the correct designation in clinical settings.

Many individuals with Paget's disease are asymptomatic, but incidental radiographic studies may reveal the sites of pagetic bone deposition, as may elevations of serum alkaline phosphase levels that result from the high bone turnover rates in Paget's disease. In later stages, patients may become aware of focal limb deformities or of skull thickening **10** on the basis of a hat size change.

Bones of the skull, vertebral column, and proximal portions of the major long bones are most typically involved (fig. 18.5). Skull weight can be significantly increased, so much so that patients carry the head in a characteristic

Figure 18.5   Paget's disease. Note the excessive deposition of coarsely structured bone in this section of the tibia. The curvature is also abnormal.

This is the tibia of an 83-year-old man who died of respiratory complications of Paget's disease. Following diagnosis, the disease slowly progressed, causing various skull and long bone deformities, as well as a degree of vertebral collapse. In the sectioned and dried tibia shown here, elongation and anterior bowing can be seen, as well as significant thickening of cortical bone and coarsely structured cancellous bone at the epiphysis (top).

45072

bowed posture. In extreme cases, the heavy skull can cause compression fractures of the superior vertebrae. Hearing disorders are often present as well, and may derive from thickening of the ossicles or from compression of the vestibulocochlear (eighth cranial) nerve. Compression of adjacent tissues may be a cause of the pain experienced in Paget's disease. Also, it has been suggested that the high rate of turnover at affected bone surfaces may itself cause bone pain.

Bone fractures may occur at sites of bone resorption in the initial osteolytic phase. Because the bone is weakened, normally trivial stresses may cause the break. Although painful and delayed, healing does occur. In rare cases, the abnormal blood vessel configuration of pagetic bone allows blood to by-pass normal capillary channels. The by-passed tissues become ischemic and, in response, local vasodilation triggers compensation reflexes that increase cardiac output. Where skeletal involvement is extensive, this extra cardiac demand can lead to high-output heart failure if the heart is already compromised by some other myocardial or valvular defect.

Another serious threat confronts about 1 in 100 Paget's sufferers. In these, osteogenic or other sarcomas arise in affected bones, often at multiple sites. These tumors seem more resistant to therapy than the sarcomas that arise apart from Paget's disease. As a result, prognosis is poor.

Because it is asymptomatic, much Paget's disease is undiagnosed. Estimates of incidence vary from 1% to 3% of adults, with significant worldwide variations. Most of those affected are over 60, and incidence increases with age, reaching as high as 10% of those age 80. Etiology is not definitively established, but a viral cause is increasingly implicated. Various lines of evidence suggest a specific viral attack on osteoclasts. This may be the factor that increases early bone destruction and causes the imbalance between bone resorption and deposition that is characteristic of this disease.

Osteoporosis

Osteoporosis is the most common North American disorder of bone metabolism. Its predominant feature is fracture as a result of bone weakness, which is due to an imbalance in the remodeling process that favors bone resorption. **11** The vertebral bodies, **12** distal radius, and proximal femur are the sites where the process is most pronounced. Fractures may follow trauma, but compression fractures of the vertebral bodies usually occur spontaneously. The condition typically produces no symptoms, and its diagnosis is complicated by the difficulty of accurately assessing the status of bone. As a result, a fracture is the usual indicator of the underlying disease.

Bone metabolism, like many physiological processes, is affected by advancing age. The tendency is for bone resorption to exceed bone deposition so that a net loss of bone mass occurs with increased age (fig. 18.6). The process is generally more rapid in women and is exaggerated in a

(a)

(b)

(c)

Figure 18.6   Osteoporosis. (*a*) Note the loss of bone density (1) in this radiograph of the skull. Instead of a normally dense, white appearance (2), the area of bone loss appears mottled and less dense. (*b*) Scanning electron micrograph of normal bone trabeculae compared to those in osteoporosis (*c*).

11   46508   12   46507

Other "Paget's" Conditions

The term **Paget's disease** is also applied to a rare group of epithelial tumors that primarily affect the nipple, breast glands, vulva, penis, and scrotum. This section describes Paget's disease **of bone.** Once a bone context is clearly established, the term Paget's disease is descriptive and widely used. In other contexts, it is important to specify, say, Paget's disease **of the nipple** (a type of breast cancer) or **of the scrotum,** to avoid confusion with the bone disorder.

---

subset of females at the time of the menopause. In these women, the disease is focused in the internal trabecular bone of the vertebral bodies and in the distal radii. This condition is designated **type I osteoporosis** or sometimes **postmenopausal osteoporosis.** In this type, fractures arise about ten years after the menopause. **Type II osteoporosis** affects both sexes who are over 70, with the neck of the proximal femur, humerus, tibia, and hip most often involved. Both the internal trabeculae and the external bone cortex are affected in this condition, which is sometimes called **senile osteoporosis.** With an increasingly elderly North American population, the early 21st century may very well see a major public health problem associated with epidemic levels of osteoporosis-linked bone fracture. Currently, 50% of 80-year-olds suffer vertebral compression fractures, and over 90% of all hip fractures occur in those past 70.

Etiology The etiology of osteoporosis is unknown, although there is evidence that in some women a hereditary factor determines a skeleton with lower bone mass. With less bone to begin with, later resorption more quickly reduces bone mass to the point where fractures occur. This is thought to be the reason for the greater incidence of osteoporosis in Caucasians, since their peak skeletal mass is less than that of other races.

Abnormalities of calcitonin, PTH, or vitamin D have not been implicated in osteoporosis. Research has therefore shifted its focus to the various local factors that regulate bone remodeling. Various growth factors and mediators have been considered, and evidence indicates that the prostaglandins and interleukins may be involved. One of the confounding factors in such research is the complexity of the growth factors' interactions and the difficulty of studying bone metabolism in tissue culture. The estrogen decline in postmenopausal women is associated with increased osteoporosis risk, because of estrogen's inhibitory effect on bone resorption. The inhibition is probably not directed at osteoclasts, but may be elicited indirectly by effects on one or more of the local factors that regulate bone metabolism.

The link between female hormones and osteoporosis is revealed in young female athletes, whose training and competition stresses produce lowered estrogen levels and menstrual irregularities; either a reduction in menstruation or its complete cessation. Note that the women affected are serious athletes who train vigorously and often, for example those who train six days a week for over two hours per day, often running over thirty miles a week. In such athletes, menstrual irregularities have been linked to losses of vertebral bone mass that were not fully restored after normal menstrual patterns resumed. A high incidence of fractures in young female athletes has been recognized for some time, and this link to estrogen and menstrual irregularities may be the explanation.

Prevention and Therapy There is currently no known therapy that can reverse the progression of osteoporosis. In some cases, estrogen or calcitonin is employed to suppress bone resorption, and this is effective in reducing bone loss. Exceptions are the many elderly in whom bone metabolism is greatly slowed or even stopped altogether. For these, even estrogen or calcitonin is ineffective. Although bone loss rates can be slowed in some, there is unfortunately no known way to promote the build-up of bone to replace lost tissue and restore skeletal strength. Recall that fractures most often occur before the diagnosis of osteoporosis is made. This means that by the time the disease is recognized, loss of bone is already at the level where functional demand can't be met, and no new bone formation can be induced. Some studies have shown that fluoride therapy can promote new bone formation, but the new bone is irregular and weak, and no reduction of fracture rate has been achieved with this approach. Calcium and vitamin D supplementation has similarly been shown to be ineffective in promoting replacement of lost bone.

Indications are that, as with many conditions, prevention is the best means of coping with osteoporosis. The key, essentially, is developing the maximal skeletal mass that one's genetic makeup allows. This means insuring that during the period of growth and development, there is an adequate dietary intake of calcium and vitamin D, as well as all the other nutrients. Once the skeleton is fully developed, by about age 28 in most cases, its strength must be maintained through a lifelong pattern of physical activity that provides adequate skeletal loading, and by sufficient nutrient support for the remodeling process. In an age in which modern therapeutics offer quick solutions to many medical problems, this recommendation may not seem like much, but an optimally developed and functioning skeleton provides an excellent first line of defense against osteoporosis.

In the elderly, whose bone mass is already reduced, preventive measures that reduce the likelihood of a fall and fracture are important. Such measures must take into account the reduced vision, confusion, and altered balance and gait that are common among the elderly. Relevant side effects of medications must also not be overlooked.

Table 18.1	Conditions in Which Osteoporosis Is Identified as a Secondary Feature			

Endocrine Conditions	Nutritional Deficiencies	Genetic Conditions	Miscellaneous
Diabetes mellitus	Malabsorption syndromes	Osteogenesis imperfecta	Prolonged immobilization
Adrenocortical hypersecretion	Scurvy	Marfan's syndrome	Various metabolic bone diseases
Thyroid hypersecretion	Hypocalcemia		Rheumatoid arthritis*
Ovarian/testicular hyposecretion			Alcoholism*
Chronic steroid therapy			Chronic obstructive pulmonary disease*
			Epilepsy*

*Pathogenesis unclear.

Secondary Osteoporosis A loss of bone mass due to an excess of resorption over deposition may also arise as the result of some other derangement. This condition is known as **secondary osteoporosis.** The primary cause may be a nutritional deficiency, a genetic or endocrine abnormality, therapeutic drugs, certain tumors, or some other disease states. Various of these conditions are listed in table 18.1.

Rickets and Osteomalacia

In these conditions, the defect in bone metabolism involves inadequate mineral deposition in an essentially normal organic matrix. The result is a softened bone that is subject to malformation or distortion, which causes pain. A broad range of etiologies reflect the various nutritional requirements, regulatory functions, and tissues involved in calcium and bone metabolism.

Rickets The condition of **rickets** is due to inadequate mineralization of the developing skeleton. It is primarily a condition of dietary vitamin D deficiency in infants and children and is rarely seen in the industrialized Western world, except for isolated pockets of poverty and ignorance of nutritional requirements. Softened bones in the developing skeleton are subject to deformity as soft tissue mass and skeletal loading progress. Shortened, deformed limbs are the result, bowed legs for example **13** (fig. 18.7). As well, other characteristic deformities of the skull, chest, and teeth are typical, as is an increased tendency to bone fractures. Therapy to supply adequate vitamin D and calcium is usually successful in correcting the condition.

Osteomalacia The term **osteomalacia** is applied to the condition of inadequate bone mineralization that occurs in the adult. Because initial skeletal development is normal, the later inability to maintain bone deposition during remodeling usually produces no bone deformities or other gross indications of the problem. A common symptom in later stages is bone pain, which may be accompanied by generalized muscle weakness and an increased predisposition to fractures. **14**

Figure 18.7 Rickets. The lack of normal bone strength causes the legs to bow under the weight of the upper body.

In the general population, dietary vitamin D deficiencies are seldom the cause of osteomalacia, except for isolated cases where the elderly or institutionalized receive improper care. More often, osteomalacia is due to a GI malabsorption problem, to a renal defect of phosphate retention that results in hypophosphatemia and defective

Figure 18.8   (*a*) Normally ossified trabeculae are interconnected to isolate regions of yellow marrow, which contain deposits of adipose tissue. (*b*) Osteoporosis is characterized by loss of bone mass and thinning of trabeculae. (*c*) Osteomalaria. The darkened regions represent the surfaces at which abnormal remodeling has produced inadequately mineralized matrix.

Figure 18.9   Osteomyelitis. Note the areas of necrosis (1) and reactive bone (2) in this radiograph.

A 12-year-old girl deeply lacerated her arm in the region of the elbow in a fall from a tree. The underlying bone subsequently became infected, producing the bone necrosis evident in this X-ray. Antibiotic therapy was able to arrest the process after surgery to clear necrotic bone and establish drainage of the infection site. Some permanent damage to the adjacent joint was unavoidable, however, and the patient was left with some restriction of movement.

bone mineralization, or to faulty activation of cholecalciferol in chronic liver or kidney diseases. The elderly are a population subgroup more often affected as a result of inadequate diet or, more commonly, a lack of outdoor activity, which reduces the sun's activation of vitamin D in the skin. Osteomalacia may accompany and complicate osteoporosis. Both conditions can be asymptomatic for years, but the bone aches and pains associated with osteomalacia may draw attention to the problem, which might otherwise be unnoticed until a fracture occurs. Figure 18.8 illustrates the essential changes from normal in osteomalacia and osteoporosis.

Osteomyelitis

This is the condition of bone inflammation, usually in response to its infection by a pyogenic (pus-producing) bacterium. Usually a staphylococcal or streptococcal organism is involved, but various other organisms are also known to infect bone. The source of such bacteria may be the blood, which delivers organisms from some already infected distant site, but the widespread use of antibiotics to control infections has greatly reduced this cause. More often the organisms are introduced as a result of bone trauma involving a fracture, penetrating wound, or surgery. The long bones of children are most often involved, but the spinal column may also be the focus of infection, this site more so in adults.

In acute osteomyelitis, proliferation of the bacteria is followed by the formation of a pus-filled abscess. As it enlarges, it disrupts ossification and interferes with blood supply to the site, causing ischemia and bone necrosis. **15** If there is no therapeutic intervention, the abscess may penetrate to an adjacent surface. Occasionally a nearby joint is involved, with bacteria, pus, and necrotic debris entering the joint space. In response, new **reactive bone** is formed and has the effect of isolating the infection site. Coupled with the already established local ischemia, such isolation may also reduce the ability of antibiotics to reach the scene of infection. In this way, some organisms can avoid destruction and may then periodically proliferate, so that episodes of recurrence become chronic (fig. 18.9).

Clinically, osteomyelitis is characterized by pain and swelling at the infection site. Chills and fever are also typical, with lab reports confirming the presence of the infecting agent in only 50% of cases. Therapy usually requires surgical clearing of necrotic bone and the draining of abscesses in addition to the administration of antibiotics. If

Table 18.2   Selected Features of Principal Bone Tumors

Tumor	Status	Site	Affected Sex	Affected Age	Comment
Osteoid osteoma	B	Long bone diaphyses	Male	Under 25	Pain is significant
Osteochondroma	B	Metaphyses	=	Under 20	Common bone tumor
Chondroblastoma	B	Epiphyses	Male	Under 25	Rare, significant pain
Osteogenic sarcoma	M	Long bones, knee	Male	10–20	Most common bone tumor, lung metastases
Chondrosarcoma	M	Pelvis, ribs, proximal femur, and humerus	Male	20–30	Second most common bone tumor
Ewing's tumor (sarcoma)	M	Distal femur and radius, proximal tibia	=	20–40	Hemopoietic cell tumor, limited metastasis
Giant cell tumor	B/M	Epiphyses, pelvis/sacrum	Female	20–30	Benign form may damage locally

B: benign; M: malignant; =: equal incidence among males and females

therapy is unavailable or unduly delayed, complications can include rapid progression throughout the infected bone, joint damage, and pathological fracture. There is also a risk that organisms may be carried to other parts of the body to produce more extensive infection.

Bone Tumors

Bone provides a supportive environment for metastases and so is a very common site of secondary tumor growth. A carcinoma is the usual primary tumor, most often arising in the prostate, breast, thyroid, bladder, lung, or kidney. Access to bone is by way of the blood, rather than lymph, and the sites most often involved are the bones of the axial skeleton (except the skull) and the proximal femur and humerus. Once established, a secondary tumor may grow and invade locally, disrupting the organization of the osseous tissue by inducing bone breakdown (**osteolysis**) or new bone formation. These effects are due to the release by the metastatic cells of substances that activate local osteoclasts, osteoblasts, or both. The result is a mix of growing tumor, resorbing bone, and new bone formation at the secondary site. Carcinomas, and some sarcomas, differ in their abilities to stimulate resident bone cells, so each produces its characteristic pattern of secondary growth, involving greater, lesser, or no effects on osteoclasts or osteoblasts.

Primary Bone Tumors These are much less common than secondary tumors, but can have devastating effects in that they arise most often in the young. Actively growing bone is much more likely to undergo a neoplastic transformation, and pain is an early indication of the tumor's expansion within the densely organized bone tissue. Like secondary tumors, primary bone tumors induce osteolysis, so that weakening of the bone, which produces a tendency to pathological fracture, is a common feature. In addition, normal bone adjacent to the tumor may respond to tumor pressure by altering its pattern of remodeling. This response produces the altered and expanded contours of the bone's surface that are seen in the area of tumor growth. The danger in malignancies is, of course, metastasis, and in bone tumors, it typically involves the lung. In many tragic cases, amputation is necessary to cope with the primary tumor when other therapy is too little or too late. For unknown reasons, most bone tumors arise more frequently in males than females with one exception, the giant cell tumor (see table 18.2).

About one-third of primary bone tumors are benign. They arise from bone or cartilage cells and can be either of minimal significance or quite painful and predisposing to fracture. They can be surgically removed, and a bone graft used to restore the damaged site. Prosthetic devices are employed where a limb resection is unavoidable. Examples of benign bone tumors are the rare **osteoma,** which typically affects the skull, and the **osteoid osteoma,** [16] usually seen in long bone diaphyses. Osteoid osteoma occurs more frequently in males and, although the tumor mass is small, it is usually quite painful. **Osteoblastoma** usually involves a larger tumor mass and primarily arises in vertebrae and long bones. [17] A rare benign bone tumor arising from bone cartilage is the **chondroblastoma.** It usually develops in the epiphyses of the arm and leg bones.

Osteogenic sarcoma (osteosarcoma) is the most common malignant tumor of bone. [18] It usually arises in the age range 10–20 and has a great predisposition to

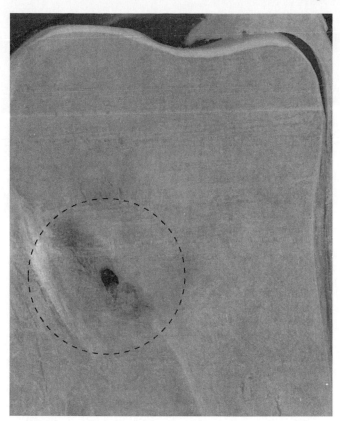

Figure 18.10   Osteogenic sarcoma. The tumor and its necrotic core can be seen in the epiphysis of this long bone.

This osteogenic sarcoma of the tibia caused amputation of the leg of a 19-year-old woman. She had experienced some knee pain for two to three months before seeing her physician, who attributed the pain to a basketball injury. The pain persisted for six months, and when it increased to the point where she couldn't sleep, she saw another physician. She was five months pregnant by this time. No swelling or other surface abnormality could be identified, but X-ray studies and a biopsy confirmed the presence of the tumor. To spare her developing infant from exposure to chemotherapeutic agents, the woman opted for amputation of her leg above the knee. The infant was successfully brought to term, but the mother died of lung and liver metastases 18 months later. Figure 6.9 shows a microscope field from the biopsy specimen.

blood-borne metastasis to the lung. The region of the knee is most often involved, but the other long bones may be affected (fig. 18.10). The previously very poor prognosis for this tumor has improved with recent chemotherapy advances. By the time the diagnosis is made, metastasis has already occurred. However, chemotherapeutic agents are quite effective in destroying secondary growth, and up to 80% of patients remain disease-free after five years. Even when limb amputation is necessary, currently available artificial limbs offer far better possibilities for more normal mobility.

Chondrosarcoma, [19] the second most common bone malignancy, is atypical in that it arises later than most bone tumors: ages 30–50. Many of these slow-growing malignancies are thought to arise in benign cartilage tumors in bone, some of whose cells become malignant. The tumor typically arises and grows in the interior of the pelvis, ribs, and proximal femur and humerus. It slowly expands, inducing osteolysis and sometimes breaking through the bone's surface. The cartilaginous tumor mass may contain variable regions of ossification. Although it is slow-growing, metastasis to the lung is not uncommon.

Ewing's tumor (Ewing's sarcoma) is a rare and highly malignant tumor of uncertain cellular origin. It arises principally in the limbs of young males. [20] Extensive and early metastasis, as well as rapid local bone invasion, contribute to the destructive effects of this condition. Although it is a threatening malignancy, progress in chemotherapy has significantly improved prognosis in Ewing's tumor.

Giant cell tumor is also known as **osteoclastoma.** The tumor's dominant cell type derives from precursors that resemble fibroblasts. Also present, and perhaps induced to form by the dominant tumor cells, are giant multinucleated cells that resemble osteoclasts. This tumor typically grows only locally, resorbing bone as it expands. It produces early local pain and swelling, often eliciting early surgical treatment that can completely remove the tumor. In such cases, prognosis is excellent, but if all tumor elements are not excised, recurrence at the original site is common. [21] Some giant cell tumors metastasize early to cloud the prognosis. This is the only major bone tumor that occurs more frequently in females than it does in males.

Table 18.2 summarizes some of the features of the principal bone tumors.

JOINT DISORDERS

Bones meet to form joints, or articulations. Most of these are freely movable joints known as **synovial** or **diarthrodial joints.** The less numerous **synarthrotic joints** are essentially incapable of movement, but provide strong binding of the joint elements. Pain and loss of mobility from joint disorders are very common around the world. The two most frequently encountered disorders are osteoarthritis and rheumatoid arthritis. This section will describe these and some less common conditions. First, however, a brief review of normal joint anatomy and physiology is in order.

Normal Diarthrodial Joints

The diarthrodial joint (fig. 18.11), which is most often involved in joint disease, is characterized by the presence of a **synovial cavity** containing a lubricant, the **synovial**

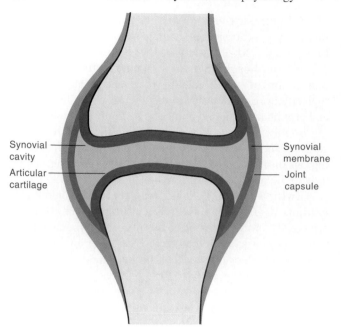

Synovial cavity

Articular cartilage

Synovial membrane

Joint capsule

Figure 18.11   The essential structure of a typical diarthrodial joint, seen in section.

fluid. This fluid is also the nutrient medium that supplies the cells of the **articular cartilages,** which line the articular surfaces of the bones that form the joint. Synovial fluid is produced by the **synovial membrane** or **synovium,** which lines the **fibrous capsule,** the tough, protective sleeve of fibrous tissue that seals and protects diarthrodial joints. The synovial membrane or synovium lines all internal joint surfaces except those of the articular cartilages. Its villi and microvilli provide a very large surface area that favors the formation of synovial fluid. The free motion of diarthrodial joints is principally due to the smooth surface of the highly polished articular cartilages and the lubricating film of synovial fluid.

Providing for freedom of motion is one major joint function. The second is that of weight-bearing and weight transfer from one bone to another. The chief factors that make this possible are the related muscle masses, which absorb much of the energy being transferred across the joint, and the internal cancellous (spongy) bone architecture of the epiphysis. Its resilience combines with the effect of the joint's muscles to relieve most joint stress. This means that loading of the articular cartilages is normally kept to low levels, well tolerated by these thin (maximum 6 mm) layers of hyaline cartilage.

A Terminology Clarification

Note that free, unrestricted joint motion is not the same as a joint's **mobility,** or **range of motion.** The shoulder joints and those between the articular processes of adjacent vertebrae are both diarthrodial joints. The range of motion is great in the shoulder and quite small between the vertebrae, but in both cases, what movement does occur is free and unimpeded.

Osteoarthritis

Osteoarthritis (OA) is the most commonly encountered joint disease in North America. Despite its name, this disease has only a minimal inflammatory component, and it is increasingly designated by the more descriptive term **degenerative joint disease** (DJD). It is DJD that is responsible for the pain and loss of mobility associated with the aging process. Its incidence is low in the young, but increasing age finds more and more cases of DJD emerging, so that by age 60 the majority are affected, and past age 75, 85% have DJD.

The underlying process begins in the articular cartilage with the death of chondrocytes and the thinning and degeneration of the intercellular matrix that surrounds them. Cracks or fissures then develop in the articular cartilage, and with progression they fill with synovial fluid and penetrate to the underlying bone. **22** Such fissures may extend through the thin surface of articular bone to form fluid-filled cysts, around which reactive bone may form. Microfractures in the subchondral bone may also arise. The response to these changes is mitosis of chondrocytes and a new vascular supply to the damaged region, which leads to the formation of fibrocartilage repair plugs. As a result of the joint loading associated with normal activities, these plugs may be loosened and stripped away, exposing the bone's surface. Continued loading and function of these surfaces causes them to become burnished; that is, they develop a smooth, hardened, ivorylike texture.

The synovial membrane is indirectly affected by these changes. Fragments of fibrocartilage, dislodged from their site of formation, can react at the synovial membrane's surface and induce an inflammatory response. This may be a factor in the pain of DJD. Subsequent fibrous repair in the adjacent joint capsule may also restrict joint motion. To further complicate the problem, cells from the synovial membrane adjacent to the articular cartilage can develop

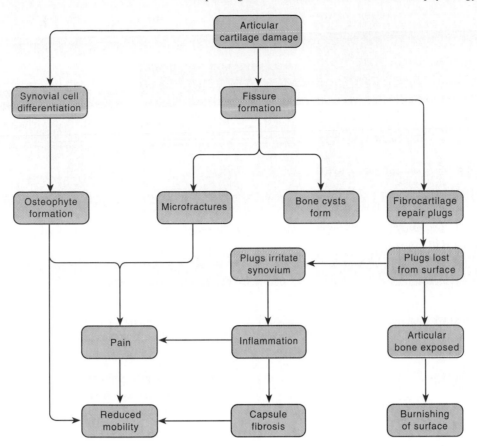

Figure 18.12   Pathogenesis of degenerative joint disease.

into osteoblasts as a response to the damage. The result is the formation of bony outcroppings, called **osteophytes** or **bone spurs,** at the periphery of the joint. **23** These are thought to be a significant factor in the pain and limitation of joint mobility that are characteristic of DJD (fig. 18.12).

The degenerative process primarily affects one or more of the larger weight-bearing joints, although finger joints are sometimes involved (fig. 18.13). Often, a link to long-term occupational or athletic joint stress is an underlying factor. For this reason DJD is considered to be the result of wear and tear on the articular cartilages. In some cases, a malformed joint, or obesity, or some postural defect may be the cause of excessive joint loading. There is also some evidence for a genetic component to this disease, but its exact nature is difficult to determine because patterns of activity in a family can influence joint use and wear. When a contributing factor to joint stress can be identified, the term **secondary OA** is used. Such cases may involve young people who have suffered joint injury in athletics or automobile or other accidents, and who face the difficult prospect of many years of joint pain. Where no particular etiology is detectable, the condition is called **primary OA.**

Typically, joint aches and stiffness arise gradually in middle age, signaling that the process of degeneration has begun. These symptoms increase with activity and diminish with rest, and there is usually no pronounced inflammatory swelling or redness in the adjacent tissues. DJD effects are confined to the joint and produce no systemic signs or symptoms. Increasing age finds the condition progressing, with pain and stiffness intensifying and becoming persistent. Most of the serious loss of mobility results from hip or knee involvement. When present in the distal interphalangeal joints, osteophytes are known as **Heberden's nodes.** At the proximal interphalangeals they are termed **Bouchard's nodes.**

Since there is no known way to prevent or arrest the degenerative process in OA, therapy is quite limited. For most sufferers analgesics are helpful, as are activities that minimize joint strain. Of course, reducing any obvious aggravating factor, such as occupational joint stresses or obesity, will be beneficial. In severe cases, surgical removal of bone spurs or replacement of joints may be indicated.

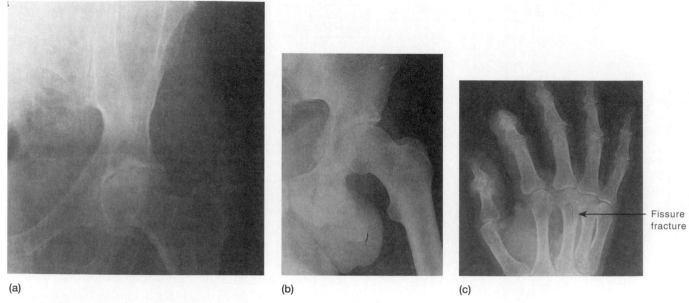

(a)   (b)   (c)

Fissure
fracture

Figure 18.13   Degenerative joint disease. Compare the articular surfaces of (*a*) a femur and hip damaged by DJD with (*b*) the normal hip joint. (*c*) Finger involvement in DJD. Note the fissure fracture that extends from the distal articular surface of one of the right metacarpals.

Rheumatoid Arthritis

In contrast to DJD, **rheumatoid arthritis** (RA) originates in the synovium, with later effects in articular cartilage and bone. It is an inflammatory condition that primarily affects the joints of the hands, wrists, ankles, and feet, but that may also produce systemic effects involving the heart, lungs, skin, and other organs. It is variable in its severity, from so mild that it is almost unnoticed, to a severe condition that destroys the joints and grossly distorts them. Also characteristic is its variable clinical pattern of remission and exacerbation. About 1% of the adult population is affected, with incidence among women about three times that among men. Age of onset is usually in the 20s or 30s, but RA has been known to arise as early as infancy or as late as the 90s.

Etiology

Rheumatoid arthritis is an essentially idiopathic disease that is characterized by immune-mediated destruction of joints. It appears that a genetic predisposition is in some way involved. In affected individuals, synovial macrophage receptors bind antigens, which in turn triggers the sequence of events that destroy the joint. The nature of the antigens that can induce this response in sensitive individuals is the subject of much research.

Some evidence suggests that the antigens are introduced by an infection, with suspicion falling on the Epstein-Barr virus, paroviruses, and mycobacteria. Other evidence suggests that RA may be an autoimmune disorder. In this proposed scheme, anticollagen antibodies are involved, but rather than causing the initial damage in RA, they may play more of a role in its progression. An autoim-

mune role is also indicated by the presence of **rheumatoid factor** (RF) in most cases of RA. RF is an antibody against immunoglobulin G (IgG), which plays a role in the pathogenesis of RA.

Pathogenesis of RA

Analysis of the joint changes associated with RA reveals a pattern of chronic inflammation that dominates in the synovium, with acute inflammation seen in the synovial fluid of the joint space. In the synovium, early changes involve cellular proliferation and damage to its microcirculation, perhaps due to an immune mechanism. Thrombosis and new vessel formation are also associated with the early joint changes in RA.

Synovial cells, T and B lymphocytes, and fibroblasts contribute to the increased cellularity in the synovium. The immune cells are activated, a fact suggesting that an immune stimulus is present, but its source is unclear. The thickening synovium becomes irregular, with its surface thrown into fingerlike projections that extend into the joint space. Its extension and covering of adjacent joint surfaces resembles a cloth, so the term **pannus,** from the Latin for cloth, is used to describe it. **24** Swelling accompanies these changes, as does stiffness and pain.

The acute inflammatory component in these early stages of RA is seen in the excessive production of synovial fluid and the presence in it of large numbers of PMNs. Immune complexes, histamine, and other mediators are thought to induce the increased blood flow, neutrophil emigration, and fluid exudate formation. Pain, swelling, and joint stiffness are also produced by the acute inflammation effects.

Heat Shock Proteins in RA

Recent research is focusing on the role of a particular heat shock protein (hsp, see chapter 1) in RA. The hsp in question, designated p65, has a shape that is very similar to that of a protein component of mycobacteria. It has been suggested that a minor early mycobacteria infection could sensitize the immune system to this protein. When some later joint stress causes hsp's to be released, macrophages with receptors to the protein could bind p65 because of the similarity in shape. This would trigger a T-cell response involving cytokine release, further damage, and more hsp release, and so on in a continuing positive feedback cycle that leads to progressive joint destruction. If this analysis is correct, then therapeutic suppression of hsp release, or neutralizing of its autoimmune stimulus, may be able to prevent or greatly limit its destructive effects in RA.

If therapy is instituted at this early stage of the disease, inflammation can be limited and progression prevented, or at least delayed and reduced in severity. This stage is critical, in that beyond it, irreversible articular cartilage and bone destruction occur. This is the result of an immune-mediated process involving T lymphocytes, macrophages, and neutrophils in the synovial fluid. These cells release cytokines that trigger the release of enzymes and destructive oxidants from cells of the pannus and the release of collagenase and other enzymes from articular cartilage cells. Their combined effect is the erosion of articular cartilage and destruction of the bone that lies deep to it. **25** Prostaglandin E_2 (PGE_2), from macrophages and pannus cells, also promotes the breakdown of bone by osteoclasts to add to the destructive process. The cytokine mediators also prolong the acute inflammatory component of the disease mechanism.

B lymphocytes are also involved and form antibodies. Initially, RF is produced, but it is thought that the degradation of joint macromolecules may alter their antigenic configurations so that antibodies against them are also formed. In either case, phagocytosis of the immune complexes in joint cartilage and in synovial fluid triggers the further release of destructive enzymes and oxidants by the phagocytes and further joint erosion follows. Immune complex formation also activates the complement cascade, producing intermediates that are chemotactic for neutrophils. Their increased numbers at the scene continue the process as they engulf immune complexes and release the erosive contents of their cytoplasmic granules.

Cytokines in the pannus and joint space not only cause damage, they also cause the release of cytokine inhibitors that antagonize their effects. This role may explain the different degrees of severity and rates of progression seen in RA. Mild or slowly progressive cases may be the result of higher levels of cytokine inhibitors than are present in the more severe and rapidly progressive conditions. Their periodically increased production could also explain the episodes of remission that characterize RA.

With continued hyperplasia and hypertrophy of the pannus, it encroaches further into the joint space. As it extends over joint surfaces, cartilage and bone erosion continue. Ultimately, the pannus may enlarge to fill the joint space completely. By this stage, the articular cartilages on both sides of the joint, and much of their underlying bone, will have been lost. In late stages, **ankylosis,** or fixing of the joint, may develop **26** as fibrous tissue or bone replaces the pannus. Figure 18.14 summarizes the principal elements of the pathogenesis of RA.

Joint distortion is a characteristic change in later stages of RA. It arises as ligaments and tendons adjacent to the affected joint are damaged. **27** Joint pain often means reduced joint use, so muscle atrophy may also contribute to the loss of soft tissue support of the joint. With reduced support the bones can move from their normal positions, and the result is often severe joint distortion (fig. 18.15).

Systemic Effects

A variety of systemic effects of RA are known, but their incidence is quite variable from one case to another. Most sufferers experience a generalized weakness and malaise, particularly in the early stages of the disease. Up to 35% develop characteristic granulomas called **rheumatoid nodules.** These are regions of focal subcutaneous swelling **28** found most often in the region of the elbow, heel, and the dorsal surface of the head. Other superficial sites are affected, especially those subjected to pressure, but internal nodules may also arise, for example, in the heart, pleural membranes, intestine, or meninges. Rheumatoid nodules consist of large concentrations of macrophages, lymphocytes, collagen, and granulation tissue that surround a central zone of necrosis and cellular debris. They may attain a diameter of 2 cm, but are typically painless and cause little functional disturbance. They are associated with high levels of circulating RF.

A systemic inflammation of the blood vessels, **rheumatoid vasculitis,** is also a common feature of RA, especially when RF levels are high. It may be related to nodule formation, but the precise link is unclear. Serous membranes may also be affected, producing effects in the heart (pericarditis) or lungs (pleural effusion). Eye involvement may occur but

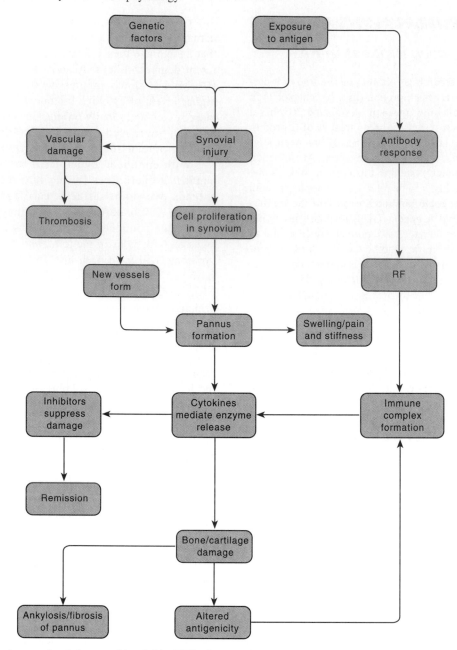

Figure 18.14 The pathogenesis of rheumatoid arthritis. RF is rheumatoid factor.

is rare. Most of these nonarticular conditions are thought to be related to immune complex deposition, but definitive evidence is lacking.

Therapy in RA

There is no cure for RA; the underlying cause can't be eliminated, and the destruction of joint structures can't be reversed. This means that therapy can only seek to relieve pain and reduce swelling, to allow the retention of as much joint function as possible. Generally, the treatment consists

of anti-inflammation therapy, coupled with a regimen that reduces stress to affected joints. This may involve simply resting the joint, but in some cases binding or splinting to reduce movement may be indicated. Strengthening of associated muscles can be effective in maintaining joint mobility.

Drug therapy is based on NSAIDs, whose analgesic and anti-inflammation effects can be quite beneficial. Table 18.3 lists the NSAIDs that are commonly used in treating RA. Other agents seem able to alter the course of the disease, producing beneficial clinical results by other than an anti-inflammation effect. In 50–70% of patients, it

(a)

(b)

Figure 18.15   Rheumatoid arthritis. The pronounced distortion of the finger joints is easily seen in both views.

Table 18.3	NSAIDs Employed in Therapy for RA

Aspirin	Naproxen
Diflunisal	Oxyphenbutazone
Fenoprophen	Phenylbutazone
Ibuprofen	Piroxicam
Indomethacin	Salsalate
Ketoprofen	Sulindac
Meclofenamate	Tolmetin

is possible to reduce symptoms for prolonged periods by supporting NSAID therapy with gold salts, antimalarials, hydroxychloroquinone, penicillamine, or sulfasalazine. When NSAIDs and disease-altering agents are unable to produce relief, immunosuppression therapy may be successful, but as always, its application is associated with significant side effects. When joint damage is pronounced, surgery may be necessary to restore deformed joints and improve function. In severe cases, replacement with an artificial joint may be necessary.

Other Joint Disorders

In osteoarthritis and rheumatoid arthritis, the principal focus of the disease is the synovial joint. In OA, the process starts in the joint cartilage and later affects the synovial membrane, while in RA, the initial damage arises in the synovium and only later affects the articular cartilage. By contrast with OA and RA, the less common conditions described next are ones that have an initial derangement in some other part of the body, which produces secondary effects in the joints.

Gout

This disease is characterized by high levels of urate ions in the plasma. Uric acid is produced as a normal product of nucleic acid metabolism and is normally excreted in the urine and feces. If production is excessive, or excretion inadequate, urate ions accumulate and spill over into the urine to produce a characteristic **hyperuricemia.**

A genetic factor seems to operate in gout, but some cases arise with no family history of the disorder. This genetic factor may be a susceptibility to the effects of urate ion, since only a small percentage of those with hyperuricemia develop gout.

The problems of gout arise from the deposition of urate crystals in joint structures. **29** These induce initial attacks of exquisitely painful arthritis in the foot, usually at a single metatarsophalangeal joint. **30** In some cases, several joints may be involved. The initial episode is typically followed by an interval without symptoms, which may last from one to ten years. If no treatment intervenes to reduce uric acid levels, urate crystals deposition may become more extensive, affecting soft tissues, tendons, and synovial membranes. This deposition elicits a local inflammatory response that produces subcutaneous swellings in the forearm, elbow, heal, ear, and other sites. These resemble the rheumatoid nodules of RA and each is designated a **tophus** (pl. tophi). **31** Therapy directed against hyperuricemia can usually prevent tophus formation. If therapy is delayed, a chronic arthritis from urate deposition can become more widespread and severe. Renal dysfunction is a common correlate of gout, often involving nephrolithiasis.

The incidence of gout is highest in adult males; only 5% of sufferers are female. Most initial attacks arise in the 40s. As indicated, timely therapeutic intervention can control progression and formation of tophi.

Ankylosing Spondylitis

In this condition, adolescent or young adult males experience fusion of the vertebral column. The process usually starts at the sacroiliac joints **32** and proceeds slowly up the spinal column, initially affecting the synovial joints

29 38228

30 45634

31 38246

32 45662

(a)

(b)

Figure 18.16   Ankylosing spondylitis. Compare the clearly separate joint surfaces between adjacent vertebrae in the normal column (*a*) with those in the ankylosing spondylosis patient (*b*). The arrow in (*b*) indicates a clearly visible point of vertebral ankylosis.

Are Gout Sufferers Overindulgent?

Because an initial episode of gout can be precipitated by episodes of excessive food or alcohol intake, the folk wisdom has it that gout is a disease of the overindulgent. In fact, various other factors not related to dietary or alcohol excess can trigger attacks. Examples are emotional stress, trauma (including surgery), drugs, various illnesses, or, surprisingly, periods of fasting.

between articular processes of adjacent vertebrae. As joint structures are destroyed and replaced by fibrocartilage and bone, the spinal column becomes fused and the increased weight-bearing of the dorsally fused processes induces bone resorption in the vertebral bodies, in response to the corresponding reduction in their weight-bearing load (fig. 18.16). The resorption produces an osteoporosislike thinning and yields a characteristic radiographic appearance that resembles a length of bamboo, hence the term **bamboo spine.** Peripheral joints and some nonjoint structures may also be involved in ankylosing spondylitis, most often an eye inflammation.

An immune pathogenesis is implicated in ankylosing spondylitis and many regard it as a form of RA. However, no RF or rheumatoid nodules are associated with cases of ankylosing spondylitis. As with RA, therapy can only alleviate symptoms and seek to slow the progress of the disease. The early onset of the disease seems to provide more time for serious consequences to develop, and the prognosis is therefore less optimistic. A major problem in severe ankylosing spondylitis is spinal fracture, but most sufferers are able to maintain adequate mobility.

Systemic Lupus Erythematosus (SLE)

This is an autoimmune condition more fully described in chapter 5. It is characterized by the widespread deposition of immune complexes in various tissues, especially joints. Over 90% of cases involve joint pain and swelling related to the synovitis that develops in response to the immune complexes. The joints most often affected are those of the fingers, wrists, and knees. Deformation and destruction of joint structures is unusual.

As in all autoimmune diseases, females are predominantly affected, in particular those between puberty and age 40. A genetic predisposition is suspected to be a significant factor in this disorder.

DISORDERS OF SKELETAL MUSCLE

With its nerve and blood supply intact, skeletal muscle is remarkably resistant to disturbances that might compromise its function. Fluctuations in demand are met with hypertrophy or atrophy to provide a muscle mass adapted to changing circumstances.

In response to inadequate contraction stimulus, skeletal muscle atrophies and weakens. In most cases, the cause is a neurological defect involving CNS motor centers, PNS motor neurons (polio), or the neuromuscular junction (myasthenia gravis), all of which are treated in chapter 21.

In **myositis,** inflammation may arise in response to systemic infections in which viruses, bacteria, fungi, or parasites gain access to skeletal muscle. Less commonly encountered inflammatory conditions involve a predominantly cellular infiltration in response to a suspected autoimmune defect. The term **polymyositis** describes the condition in which most signs and symptoms derive from muscle damage. In about 30% of cases, an accompanying skin rash is present, presumably due to dermal immune complex deposition. In these cases the disease is termed **dermatomyositis.** 33 Because of their supposed, but not proven, autoimmune etiology, both these disorders are considered in more detail in chapter 5.

Muscular Dystrophy

The term **muscular dystrophy** is used to denote a group of rare diseases characterized by a genetic etiology and the progressive degeneration of skeletal muscle. Differences in the degree of progression, pattern of inheritance, and age of onset are the basis for distinguishing among them.

Duchenne Muscular Dystrophy

This X-linked recessive defect is the most common of the muscular dystrophies. It arises in about 20 of every 100,000 live births (0.0002%) and, because of its pattern of inheritance, affects males almost without exception. Most cases arise in families with a history of the disorder, but there is

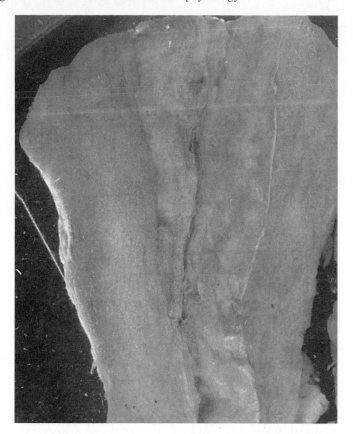

Figure 18.17   Muscular dystrophy. The quadriceps specimen shown here is pale because fat has replaced its muscle fibers.

Portion of the quadriceps muscle from a victim of muscular dystrophy who had been essentially bedridden since his early years. He died at age 19. The specimen contains only faintly visible streaks of muscle tissue, the atrophied fibers having been replaced by fat.

no way to determine accurately whether a woman who is herself normal might be a carrier of the defective gene. To complicate matters, the gene involved has a high rate of spontaneous mutation. This means that up to 30% of cases arise as the result of a new mutation, so there is no family history on the basis of which parents might anticipate the disease.

If suspected, the disease can be diagnosed immediately at birth on the basis of high serum levels of **creatine kinase** (CK). This enzyme is released from damaged muscle fibers at multiple sites. In affected children, it is possible by close observation to detect muscle weakness and delayed motor development quite early. Obvious loss of strength and motor skills emerges by age 5. From this point, the disease progresses to induce increasing muscle degeneration, 34 35 in particular in the larger proximal muscle masses of the legs (fig. 18.17). By age 10 most victims require leg bracing to walk. Confinement to a wheelchair follows by age 12, and beyond age 15 most are completely bedridden. Fibrosis, to repair degenerating or otherwise damaged muscle, is pronounced and is often followed by contracture,

Figure 18.18 In this section through a skeletal muscle, the individual muscle fibers are seen as rounded masses. The pale areas within each cell are the sites of degeneration.

which produces distorting forces on the developing skeleton. **36** Lordosis (anterior curvature) and scoliosis (lateral curvature) can result, leading to compromised respiration because the skeletal deformities prevent normal chest expansion. With muscle weakness also contributing, respiratory insufficiency is a major problem in the later stages of muscular dystrophy, with a superimposed respiratory infection often precipitating complete respiratory failure and early death. Survival to age 30 is unusual in those afflicted by this tragic disease. Cardiac muscle tissue is also involved in the degenerative process, although clinically significant heart problems are uncommon. Mental retardation typically accompanies Duchenne muscular dystrophy, and is presumably linked to the mechanism responsible for the loss of muscle tissue.

Recent genetic studies have revealed that the underlying defect in this condition is based on the deficiency of a muscle membrane protein called **dystrophin.** The precise pathogenesis is unknown, but the membrane abnormality appears to be linked to widely distributed sites of muscle damage and CK loss. After macrophages clear the debris, the damaged portion of the muscle fiber regenerates. But the essential membrane defect causes renewed damage, and ultimately degeneration overwhelms the cell's regenerative capacity. Fibrous connective tissue and fatty deposits then replace functional muscle fibers (fig. 18.18). There is no known means of replacing the deficient dystrophin in this disease. Therapy can only intervene to sustain mobility and respiratory function for as long as possible.

A milder condition called **Becker's muscular dystrophy** is also due to abnormal dystrophin. It is essentially similar to Duchenne muscular dystrophy but has a later onset and is more slowly progressive, allowing survival to as late as age 40.

Myotonic Dystrophy

This is the second most common of these rare muscular dystrophies. Its transmission is by autosomal dominant inheritance. This means that it can more readily be traced through a family's history, since no carrier state is possible. In other words, if the defective gene is present, the disease is present, and affected individuals are easily identified. **37**

Myotonic dystrophy has a variable pattern of onset. Symptoms may arise in the teens and 20s, after which they follow a slowly progressive course. The muscles of the face, neck, and distal limbs are the focus of the degenerative process. **38** The delayed relaxation of muscle after contraction (**myotonia**) associated with this condition sets it apart from the other muscular dystrophies. In addition to skeletal muscle weakness, the disease may also produce myocardial degeneration, cataracts, atrophy of the testicles, and impaired mental functioning.

In the heart, defects in the conduction system pose the threat of serious dysrhythmias, while weakness in the respiratory muscles can compromise ventilation. In most sufferers, muscle defects are mild, producing only minimal interference with normal activity. In severe cases, severe disability may emerge as early as age 20–30.

Facioscapulohumeral Muscular Dystrophy

This genetic condition is transmitted by autosomal dominant inheritance, so males and females are affected equally. As its name indicates, the affected muscles are those of the face, shoulder, and upper arm, **39** but the lower leg and foot muscles may also be involved. Their degeneration and weakness usually emerge between adolescence and age 40, with rates of progression slower than those seen in the Duchenne form.

No cardiac or other tissues are involved in facioscapulohumeral dystrophy, and mental development is normal. Although an early onset seems to allow time for more severe muscle involvement, the slow progression of the disease may make a near-normal life span possible.

Limb-Girdle Dystrophy

Transmission of this disease is by autosomal recessive inheritance. This means that parents will usually have no sign of the disease but, being carriers, can each contribute a defective gene to produce the disease in their unfortunate offspring.

Onset of symptoms may be early or delayed to as late as age 30, with degeneration of the shoulder and pelvic girdles usually progressing only slowly. Relatively normal walking may be possible for many years after onset of the disease. Mental functions are not compromised, but a cardiomyopathy may give rise to arrhythmias or congestive heart failure. Respiratory failure is typical late in the course of the disease.

Case Study

Because of intermittent low back pain, a 22-year-old male student saw his physician. He explained that he had been troubled by low back stiffness when he got up in the morning, and that with his normal routine of activities the stiffness eased and he felt better. He had had no injuries, and he was rather sedentary, so it seemed unlikely that exercise strain could account for the problem. He described the pain as a "dull stiffness" with no radiation down the leg. When questioned, he recalled that his father, a construction worker, had suffered from back pain that was attributed to the rigors of his work, but he couldn't remember much since his father had died relatively young in a work-related accident.

On examination the patient was apparently healthy, with no grossly observable back defects, and had a full range of flexion, extension, and rotation at the waist. Palpation over the sacroiliac joints, however, revealed some tenderness.

X-rays of the chest and low back indicated no chest abnormalities, but did reveal some blurring of the SA joints and some degree of bilateral erosion of their bony margins. The erythrocyte sedimentation rate (ESR) was elevated. These findings were suggestive of ankylosing spondylitis. A blood test was returned as positive for HLA-B27 antigen and negative for rheumatoid factor, verifying the diagnosis.

In addition to counseling as to the possibility of progression of the disease, the patient was given various exercises to build strength and support his posture. He was also advised to use a small pillow when sleeping and to follow a course of NSAID therapy. He was asked to return for annual assessment.

Commentary

The age and sex of this patient are typical. The common finding of a hereditary component is also suggested in the father's back problems, with his untimely death probably preventing development of spinal deformity at a time when the disease and its treatment were less well understood.

The chest X-ray was requested because, although the patient had not complained of chest pain, early changes at the manubriosternal joint are common in this condition. The elevated ESR is a nonspecific indication that an inflammatory process may be active. It involves increased time for RBCs to settle from plasma, presumably because in inflammatory conditions, its greater content of immune globulins and fibrinogen makes the plasma more viscous. The HLA-B27 antigen is present in 90% of ankylosing spondylitis sufferers and confirmed the diagnosis in the context of the history and other findings.

The physician's pillow recommendation was aimed at reducing neck flexion to relieve strain on the lower back, while the exercise regimen was designed not only to build strength, but also to reduce the degree of deformation that might develop. NSAIDs have proven quite successful in limiting pain, but there is little more that can be done for ankylosing spondylitis patients. When the initial symptoms are as mild as these, they may well remain so for 10–20 years, offering only minor interference with work. With maintenance of an appropriate exercise program, much deformity can be avoided.

Key Concepts

1. Apart from infections and tumors, bone disease derives from abnormalities of bone formation or later imbalances in the bone remodeling process (p. 457).

2. Apart from infections and tumors, most of the more common bone disorders produce osteopenia, with the exception of Paget's disease, which involves both osteopenia and hyperostosis (pp. 457–458).

3. Genetic bone diseases are rare and involve various patterns of inheritance of traits that produce defects in the cartilage template on which ossification depends, or in the activities of osteoblasts or osteoclasts (p. 457).

4. Pain, skeletal malformations, and pathological fractures are the principal derangements produced by acquired bone disorders (p. 458).

5. The most important factor in preventing the osteopenia that characterizes osteoporosis is the early

development and maintenance of the maximum skeletal mass provided by one's genetic makeup, to counter the inevitable loss of bone in later life (p. 461).

6. Osteomyelitis is usually caused by a pyogenic exogenous bacterial infection that arises secondary to bone trauma, but organisms from previously established infection sites may reach bone via the blood (p. 463).

7. Most bone tumors are secondary carcinomas from various body sites; of primary bone tumors, two-thirds are malignant and one-third benign (p. 464).

8. Degenerative joint disease, the most common North American joint disease, involves the degradation of articular cartilage in response to long-term overloading of the larger weight-bearing joints (pp. 466–467).

9. Rheumatoid arthritis typically involves the joints of the wrists, hands, ankles, and feet and derives from inflammatory damage to the synovium, with later effects in articular cartilage and adjacent bone (p. 468).

10. RA is caused by the immune destruction of joint structures, which may depend on a genetic predisposition (pp. 468–469).

11. Superimposed on its alternating pattern of exacerbation and remission in affected joints, RA exhibits a range of variably occurring systemic effects (p. 469).

12. Although essentially a systemic autoimmune disorder, 90% of SLE is accompanied by joint pain and swelling due to synovitis induced by immune complex deposition (p. 471).

13. With nerve and blood supply intact, skeletal muscle is remarkably resistant to disease, but with inadequate neurological stimulus, its cells atrophy and weaken (p. 473).

14. Duchenne muscular dystrophy is the most common of a group of rare genetic diseases characterized by progressive degeneration of muscle tissue (pp. 473–474).

REVIEW ACTIVITIES

1. Write out the reasons that vitamin D can be considered a hormone as well as a vitamin. Refer to pages 456–457 for help.

2. List all the factors that have a bearing on the etiology and pathogenesis of osteoporosis. There's no section labeled "Pathogenesis," so you'll have to dig around in the material on pages 460–462.

3. Complete the following table.

Essential Bone Derangement	Etiological Factor	Pathogenesis Factor	Disease
Focal loss and deposition	Possibly viral	Rare tumor incidence	
Osteopenia	Deficiency state	Adults affected	
Excessive deposition	Genetic	Little chance of survival if severe	
Shortness of stature	Genetic	Defective cartilage matrix	
Osteopenia	Vitamin D deficiency	Children affected	
Infection	Bacteria	Trauma	
Osteopenia	Low skeletal mass	Fractures in later years	

4. Since you're likely to encounter so much DJD, it's a good idea to be conversant with its pathogenesis. To see if you are, check figure 18.12 and verify that you know the following:

(a) the link between fissure formation and bone cyst formation,

(b) what osteophytes are and why they might affect joint mobility and cause pain,

(c) what burnishing means,

(d) the essential difference between DJD and RA (this emerges pretty clearly in figures 18.12 and 18.14 when the words "injury" or "damage" are used at the top of each).

Pages 466–471 are the source for this material.

5. Given the information on pages 473–474, construct a flow chart that explains the current thinking on the pathogenesis of Duchenne muscular dystrophy. Lay it out top-to-bottom, starting with "Genetic Defect" at the top and "Muscular Weakness" at the bottom. Include the term "CK."

Chapter Nineteen

Reproductive Pathophysiology

*—I would very much rather stand
Three times in the front of a battle than bear one child.*

Euripedes
Medea

The reproductive system is distinctive in that its continued functioning is not as critical as that of other organ systems. In kidney, liver, or heart failure, for example, loss of essential functions is incompatible with life. Even when modern therapeutic resources sustain life, they bring their own burdens and demands to the survivor. In the reproductive system, by contrast, the failure of essential function usually produces only sterility or the inability to sustain normal prenatal development of offspring. However disappointing this may be, the physiological consequences are usually not serious. Furthermore, because a reproductive disorder may arise after one or more children are born, the inability to produce additional offspring has less impact. On the other hand, some disorders of the reproductive system do pose significant threats. For example, serious problems of bleeding and miscarriage can arise in pregnancy, and tumors of the reproductive organs, like most tumors, can have serious effects both locally and at sites of distant metastatic growth.

This chapter will consider only those reproductive disorders that arise in the testis, ovary and uterus, and their associated ducts and glands. Disorders that arise in the hypothalamus and anterior pituitary, affecting the neuroendocrine controlling neuroendocrine inputs to the reproductive system, were considered in chapter 17. Many psychological factors influence reproductive activities, but these are beyond the scope of this book, as are the rare genetic disorders that may produce sterility.

DISORDERS OF THE MALE REPRODUCTIVE SYSTEM

Of the male reproductive structures (fig. 19.1), disorders of the penis/urethra, bulbourethral glands, seminal vesicles, and vas deferens (ductus deferens) are rare. For example, the congenital abnormality called **epispadias,** in which the urethral orifice opens at the upper surface of the penis, occurs only once in 50,000 live births. **Venereal infections,** those transmitted by sexual intercourse, may provide a threat to reproductive structures **1** or distant organs, e.g., the brain in syphilis. These conditions, however, are usually readily controlled by antibiotics, which limit serious consequences. Most male reproductive disorders other than infection arise in the testis and prostate gland.

Testicular Disorders

The paired testes (sing. testis) are housed in the scrotum, outside the pelvic cavity. Although this location may expose the testes to a greater risk of damage from trauma, it appears to allow for closer temperature regulation of the process of **spermatogenesis**—the production of male sex cells, called **spermatozoa.** Scrotal temperature is about 2° C lower than that of the pelvic cavity, and this difference seems to be critical, for as testis temperature increases, spermatozoa production decreases. Spermatogenesis occurs within the testes, in the seminiferous tubules. **2** These tiny, tightly coiled ducts have a total length of about 250 m and produce over 200 million spermatozoa daily (fig. 19.2).

Broadly, disorders of the testes are congenital or involve acquired abnormalities arising from infection, compromised circulation, or neoplasia.

Congenital Abnormalities of the Testes

Development of the testes normally proceeds within the pelvic cavity. Prior to birth, a passage, the **inguinal canal,** forms between the pelvic cavity and scrotum. The testes enter the canal and descend along it, through the abdominal wall, to take up their normal location in the scrotum (fig. 19.3). The **spermatic cord** remains as a link to the abdominal cavity and contains the testes' blood and nerve supply as well as the **cremaster muscle.** This muscle alters its tension to draw the testes nearer to the warmth of the abdominal cavity in cold conditions, and to allow descent from it when temperatures are increased. In this way it helps to maintain optimal temperatures for spermatogenesis.

The most common congenital defect involving the testes is their failure to descend to the scrotum, a condition called **cryptorchidism.** In this term, Greek word elements refer to the testis (*orchido*) being hidden (*crypto*) within the pelvic cavity. The condition usually involves only one testis, which remains inside the pelvic cavity or within the pelvic canal. The reasons why this might occur are difficult to establish, since the mechanisms underlying normal testicular descent are poorly understood.

An undescended testis seems able to maintain testosterone secretion, but spermatogenesis is suppressed by the warmer pelvic cavity temperatures to which it is exposed. As a result, the seminiferous tubules and the entire gland

Sacrum

Seminal vesicle

Rectum

Prostate

Bulbourethral gland

Ductus deferens

Bladder

Symphysis pubis

Penis

Urethra

Epididymis

Testis

Scrotum

Urethral orifice

Figure 19.1   The male reproductive structures. Note the anatomic relation that facilitates palpation of the prostate gland via the rectum.

(a)   (b)

Figure 19.2   Seminiferous tubules in cross section. (*a*) The numerous tails of developing spermatozoa produce the fibrous appearance of the lumen of the tubule at left. (*b*) The essential tubule elements.

Testis

Abdominal wall

Lower abdominal cavity

Symphysis pubis

Developing penis

(a)

Peritoneum

Testis

Rectum

(b)

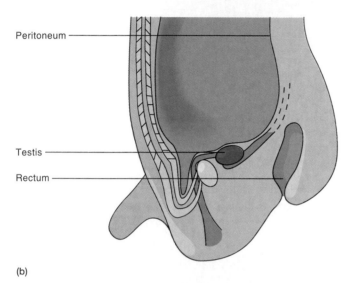

Inguinal canal

Vas deferens

Spermatic cord

Testis

Scrotum

(c)

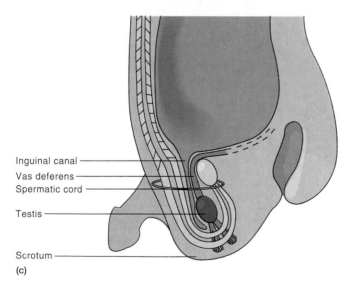

Figure 19.3   The sequence of testicular descent from the abdomen to the scrotum: (*a*) Predescent position. (*b*) The descent under way. (*c*) Arrival at the developing scrotum. Note the components of the spermatic cord.

atrophy (fig. 19.4). Loss of fertility usually accompanies cryptorchidism. Without intervention to move an undescended testis to the scrotum (the procedure is called **orchiopexy**), a much greater danger emerges. Presumably because of the elevated temperatures to which it is subjected, an undescended testis is at an increased risk of developing tumors. After five years without descent, the cancer risk increases to thirty times normal.

Testicular Tumors

Although the **interstitial cells** (**cells of Leydig**), which secrete testosterone, **3** and the **Sertoli cells,** which support developing spermatozoa, are present in the seminiferous tubules, 95% of testicular tumors arise in the precursor cells that ultimately give rise to mature spermatozoa. For this reason they are known as **germ cell tumors.** The cells involved are largely undifferentiated, and when they become neoplastic, the tumor may develop along various paths of differentiation to produce differing cell types. In most cases a single cell type is present, but in 40% of cases, two or more types can be identified. The major types are listed in table 19.1.

Germ cell tumors present the risk of local invasion to the epididymis and pelvic cavity. Metastasis via the lymph involves the chains of lymph nodes that lie alongside the aorta, while blood-borne metastases typically involve the lung, liver, brain, and bone. Initially, the only sign of a tumor may be testicular swelling that is due to the increasing tumor mass. Pain incidence is variable, at least in the early stages, before swelling generates pressure against the testicles' essentially inelastic protective coat, **tunica albuginea** (fig. 19.5). Later invasion may produce urinary obstruction, and metastases often produce back and abdominal pain due to growth in secondary lymph nodes. Dyspnea from the effects of pulmonary metastases, weight loss, and gynecomastia (breast enlargement) may also be present to varying degrees.

About 70% of germ cell tumors secrete chorionic gonadotropin (hCG), α-fetoprotein, or both. Their detection in the plasma can be a useful diagnostic aid.

The average incidence of germ cell tumors is 2–3 per 100,000 males, but peaks of higher incidence occur in the young, mostly related to cryptorchidism, and at age 20–35, perhaps because of the higher testosterone levels associated with sexual activity during these years. As with so many tumors, etiology in germ cell tumors is unclear. Different racial incidence, significantly higher in whites than blacks, suggests that a genetic factor is involved, and varying geographic distribution of the victims points to some role for environmental agents. It is interesting to note that in cases associated with cryptorchidism, the incidence of germ cell tumors is the same in descended and undescended testes.

(a)

(b)

Figure 19.5   Sections through the testis. Tightly coiled seminiferous tubules are isolated by septa of the tough tunica albuginea that protects the testis.

Figure 19.4   Atrophy of seminiferous tubules: normal tubules (*a*) for comparison with atrophied tubules (*b*).

Table 19.1	Principal Types of Testicular Tumors

Germ Cell Tumors	**Stromal Tumors**
One cell type present:	Leydig (interstitial) cell
Seminoma	Sertoli cell
Embryonal carcinoma	Granulosa cell
Choriocarcinoma	Undifferentiated
Teratoma	
More than one cell type present:	
Combinations of two or more of the above	

This finding seems to counter the idea that higher abdominal temperature plays an important role in the neoplastic conversion and suggests, instead, that a single underlying cause may be responsible for both the failure of descent and induction of the tumor.

Therapy in germ cell tumors consists of first removing the primary tumor via surgery and then following with a regimen of radiation therapy, chemotherapy, or both. The goal is to prevent metastasis, since tumor growth at

!! *hCG in Pregnancy Testing*

hCG (the "h" denotes "human" to distinguish it from therapeutic preparations derived from animal sources) is the normal product of trophoblasts present in a newly formed embryo. Its presence in a female's plasma or urine is therefore a sign of pregnancy. Since hCG is often produced by nonendocrine germ cell tumors, affected males could test positive for pregnancy.

secondary sites is the cause of most deaths. Cure rates are quite high when therapy can be initiated prior to metastasis. Unfortunately, a quarter of all cases are diagnosed only after metastases have already become established.

Compromise of Testicular Circulation

Reduced blood flow to the testis is most often the result of twisting or **torsion** of the spermatic cord, which carries its vascular supply. Often, particularly vigorous exercise or physical trauma produces the torsion, but if the scrotum is more loosely suspended, even moderately vigorous activity may allow the spermatic cord to twist.

If torsion only partially compresses the testicular veins, varying degrees of congestion and swelling occur as a result of restricted venous drainage. Pain arises and is due both to the initial torsion and to the congestion and swelling that follow. If the torsion can't be resolved by manipulation or surgery, or if compression blocks all blood flow, necrosis, hemorrhage, and infarction follow. **4**

Disorders of the Prostate Gland

The most common prostatic disorder is **prostatic hyperplasia.** It may be referred to as **benign prostatic hypertrophy** (BPH), but this term is inaccurate in that the essential problem is not enlargement of existing cells (hypertrophy), but the production of new tissue (hyperplasia). Since the same initials can also refer to **benign prostatic hyperplasia,** they are widely used.

Normally, at birth the prostate is a small mass weighing a few grams, which grows to a weight of approximately 20 g by age 20. This size is sustained until about the age of 45, when a second period of slow growth begins. By age 70, over 90% of males show some degree of prostatic hyperplasia. Symptoms indicating some degree of urinary obstruction by the prostate (fig. 19.6) emerge at an average age of 65. **5** Such obstruction increases the risk of bladder infections and pyelonephritis, since longer urine retention favors bacterial growth.

If obstruction is pronounced, the excess prostatic tissue can be surgically removed to restore normal voiding. In the absence of surgical correction, the back pressure of urine can produce dilatation of the ureters and can involve the kidney's calyces and pelvis. This is the condition of **hydronephrosis. 6** Not only does continued renal filtration add pressure to the system, which can distort the tissues involved, but the back pressures can compromise renal blood flow and precipitate renal failure.

Prostatic Carcinoma

In males, prostate cancer is the second most common malignancy (lung cancer is first) and the third highest cause of death from tumors (lung and colon tumors are first and second). Tumors of the prostate most often produce symp-

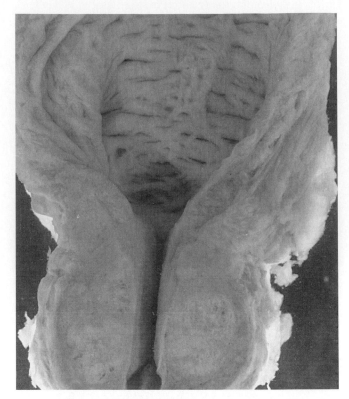

Figure 19.6   Prostatic hyperplasia. The enlarged prostatic masses can easily be seen in this section. Cutting through the enlarged gland relieves its compression of the urethra, so its narrowing is not apparent in this photo.

toms after the age of 50, with peak incidence emerging in the 70s. Although malignant, these tumors are usually smaller than the size reached in prostatic hyperplasia. Also, because many arise near the periphery of the gland, they cause little urinary obstruction and may remain undiscovered until local invasion produces pain. Initially, metastasis involves the regional lymph nodes, then later, the lungs and other distant sites. A widely used staging system for prostatic carcinoma is based on the size and spread of the tumor. In stages A and B, growth is confined to the prostate, and in stages C and D, spread beyond the gland is involved (table 19.2).

Like that of testicular germ cell tumors, the etiology of prostatic carcinoma seems to involve a genetic component, since incidence in blacks is greater than in whites. Environmental factors may also play a role, as indicated by a varying geographic distribution of age-adjusted death rates; Japan has a very low rate, Sweden's is very high, and the rate for North American males is between those extremes. There is no evidence that prostatic hyperplasia predisposes to germ cell tumors.

Prostatic carcinoma growth is supported by testosterone. Therefore, after surgical resection of the tumor, treatment includes radiation and alteration of the tumor's endocrine support, which are often effective in limiting

39994

38932

40263

Table 19.2		Staging of Prostatic Carcinoma
Stage	**Substage**	**Clinical Criteria**
A		No tumor symptoms reported. Tumor discovered in biopsy of BPH.
	A1	Low number of well-differentiated tumor cells.
	A2	Larger number of poorly differentiated cells.
B		Tumor palpable in prostate via rectal examination. Mass confined within gland's capsule.
	B1	Single mass palpable.
	B2	More extensive gland involvement.
C		Invasion beyond capsule, based on evidence of local signs and symptoms and CT scan.
	C1	No invasion of seminal vesicles.
	C2	Invasion of seminal vesicles.
D		Indications of metastasis.
	D1	Secondary growth confined to pelvic lymph nodes.
	D2	Distant metastases: lung, bone.

further growth. One way to counter testosterone secretion is to administer estrogens, which antagonize testosterone's effects. In some cases, surgical removal of the testes, **orchiectomy,** is performed to abolish the source of the growth-supporting testosterone.

The prognosis is better when therapy is instituted at stage A or B, with ten-year survival rates as high as 80% in some studies. Over half of prostatic tumors are diagnosed at these earlier stages. If diagnosis and therapy are delayed until stage C or D, the prognosis is much poorer, with ten-year survival rates ranging from 10% to less than 50%.

DISORDERS OF THE FEMALE REPRODUCTIVE SYSTEM

The emphasis in this discussion will be on the ovary and uterus (fig. 19.7), which account for the most serious reproductive system diseases suffered by women. **7** Let us start, however, by describing the condition of ascending infection called pelvic inflammatory disease (PID). Since it can damage the reproductive structures, it often leads to sterility.

Pelvic Inflammatory Disease

Pelvic inflammatory disease (PID) is due to infection that usually originates in the vagina, ascends through the uterus and Fallopian tubes, and then spreads to the ovaries, **8**

broad ligaments, peritoneal surfaces, and various other abdominal organs, in some cases as far removed as the liver. The associated inflammatory response usually involves a purulent exudate, which may be discharged via the vagina or which may be sequestered in tubal or ovarian abscesses. Postinflammatory scarring makes infertility a common sequela of PID.

Most PID arises as a result of sexually transmitted organisms, most often *Neisseria gonorrhoeae* or *Chlamydia trachomatis.* These organisms are quite virulent, and exposure to them is associated with a high rate of infection. Various other vaginal and cervical organisms may also be involved when the initial venereal infection disrupts the balance of host factors that normally limit their growth (table 19.3). Less commonly, PID may originate with various medical procedures, such as insertion or manipulation of an IUD, **cesarean section** (surgical delivery of an infant through the uterine and abdominal walls when a normal delivery is not possible), or **dilatation** and **curettage** (D and C: dilating the cervix to allow introduction of an instrument or suction device to strip away the endometrium, for the purpose of abortion or the removal of polyps or unexpelled placental remnants following an infant's delivery). From these facts you can see that PID is a disease that is limited, almost without exception, to sexually active women. Younger women are more vulnerable than mature women, perhaps because of the thinner epithelium and less acid epithelial secretions that are typical of younger women. Women who have never borne a child (nulliparous) are also at greater risk of developing PID. In rare instances the precipitating infection may spread from an initially infected adjacent organ, e.g., the appendix or colon, or from a distant focus of infection via the blood.

The pathogenesis of PID is based on an inflammatory response elicited by the infecting organisms at the mucosal surfaces of the vagina and uterus, which produces an exudate that contains mucus and pus and so is described as **mucopurulent.** The organisms' access and spread through the reproductive passages may be facilitated by their ability to attach to spermatozoa. Tissue culture studies suggest that, on reaching the Fallopian tube mucosa, gonococcal or chlamydial organisms are taken into its columnar cells where they produce damage, either by inducing the sloughing of ciliated cells or by eliciting an infiltration by PMNs, lymphocytes, and other host cells. Involvement beyond the tubes is common, with ovarian and peritoneal surfaces serving as sites from which the infection may spread to various adjacent and distant organs. Inflammations of the peritoneal surfaces of these various organs are denoted by specific terminology, e.g., **periappendicitis, perigastritis, perihepatitis.**

The inflammatory response in the Fallopian tubes (**salpingitis**) poses particular problems in that swelling can seal its ends, trapping the progressively increasing volumes of exudate. **9** This causes the tubes to swell, distorting their shape and predisposing to abscess formation. The

15779

39832

40120

(a)

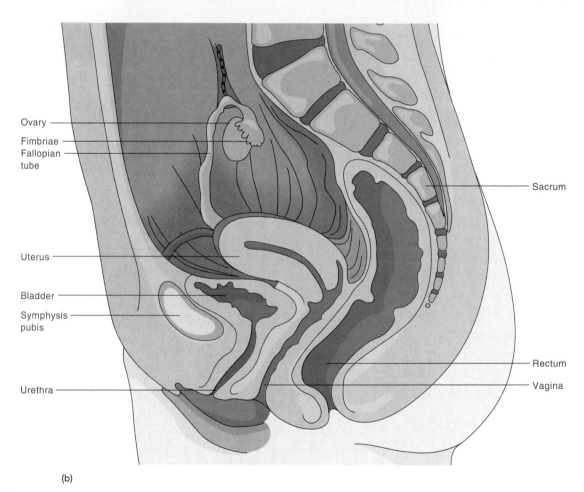

Ovary
Fimbriae
Fallopian
tube

Uterus

Bladder

Symphysis
pubis

Urethra

Sacrum

Rectum

Vagina

(b)

Figure 19.7   *(a)* Female reproductive structures. Note the normal forward bending (anteflexion) of the uterus in the diagram *(b)*.

Table 19.3	Organisms Typically Involved in PID
Neisseria gonorrhoeae	Clostridium perfringens
Chlamydia trachomatis	Coliform bacteria
Streptococci	Actinomyces
Staphylococci	Mycoplasma

Vaginal Douching As a Risk Factor in PID

Many women routinely practice vaginal douching in regular hygiene or following menstruation or sexual intercourse. Unfortunately, this practice is associated with an increased risk of PID. Perhaps the process is irritating and provides sites of erosion where organisms can establish an infection. Alternatively, it may cause organisms from proximal sites to be flushed to deeper regions within the uterus.

ovaries are also subject to abscess formation as a result of their close proximity to the Fallopian tubes. Such abscesses are known as **tubo-ovarian abscesses.** Abscesses may also arise at various other pelvic or abdominal sites, including the liver and inferior surface of the diaphragm. In such abscesses various organisms, other than those of the initial infection, may proliferate and contribute to the destructive process.

Signs and symptoms in PID are related to the inflammatory process. Vaginal discharge of blood and mucopurulent exudate from vaginal and uterine surfaces is common. Pain associated with infection of the rectum and urethra may be present, and urethritis and bladder involvement may produce frequent urination and dysuria (painful urination). With extension to the Fallopian tubes and beyond, abdominal pain may arise, initially dull or aching, and later more severe and localized, depending on the infecting organisms and the organs involved.

The bleeding and abdominal pain of PID may cause the condition to be confused with various other disorders, e.g., acute appendicitis, ectopic pregnancy, endometriosis, or an ovarian tumor (these last three are described in later sections). For this reason, it may be necessary to perform a **laparoscopy** (endoscopic viewing of the abdomen's contents) to arrive at a definitive diagnosis. Once the diagnosis of PID is established, treatment consists of various antibiotic regimens to suppress the infection. Usually, more than

one antibiotic is required because two or more bacteria may be involved. In some cases, the treatment may require surgical intervention to drain abscesses.

Long-term consequences of PID derive from postinflammatory scarring and the formation of adhesions between the tubes, ovaries, and adjacent organ surfaces. Stricture of the Fallopian tubes is also common. These changes can lead to infertility because they block the passage of spermatozoa to the distal Fallopian tubes, the usual site of fertilization. When fertilization does occur, passage of the embryo to the uterus is also blocked, and implantation into the tube's mucosa (ectopic pregnancy) may occur. In the abdomen, adhesions can interfere with normal intestinal motility or cause pain when they restrain organs from shifting in response to body movements. In some cases, chronic abdominal pain and recurring bouts of salpingitis follow the initial acute attack and may continue for years.

Disorders of the Uterus

The normal uterus consists of the muscular myometrium and an internal lining, the endometrium (figs. 19.7 and 19.8). Broadly, the problems arising in these tissues relate to tumors of the myometrium and cervical epithelium and to various disorders of the endometrium, which are often characterized by uterine bleeding. Let us consider endometrial disorders first.

Dysfunctional Uterine Bleeding

Uterine bleeding disorders are the most common problem affecting women of childbearing age. They may be related to various diseases, but when none can be identified, the condition is described as **dysfunctional uterine bleeding.** Abnormalities of bleeding that may occur during the menstrual period include prolonged, excessive, or meager flow. Another abnormality is bleeding between menstrual periods, which is usually not associated with abdominal discomfort.

The cause of most dysfunctional uterine bleeding is failure to ovulate, as a result of some disturbance in the endocrine control of the ovarian cycle. Cycles that pass without ovulation are described as **anovulatory cycles.** They are thought to arise when the corpus luteum of one cycle continues to secrete beyond its normal ten-day life span into what would be the next cycle. High levels of hormones are thus prolonged enough to suppress normal follicle development in the ovary before the corpus luteum finally loses secretory ability. In consequence, no ovulation occurs, no new corpus luteum forms, and the resulting lack of estrogen and progesterone secretion produces bleeding abnormalities.

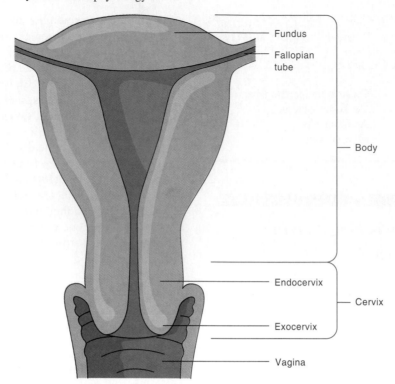

Fundus

Fallopian tube

Body

Endocervix

Cervix

Exocervix

Vagina

Figure 19.8   Section through the uterus and proximal vagina. The transition zone between exocervix and endocervix is the site at which carcinoma is most likely to emerge.

Dysfunctional Uterine Bleeding and Intense Athletic Training

Women engaged in vigorous and prolonged physical activity are subject to dysfunctional uterine bleeding and in many cases to cessation of all menstruation, **amenor-rhea.** If a normal menarche is followed at some later time by cessation of menstruation cycling, the condition is called **secondary amenorrhea.** If the menarche does not occur, the condition is called **primary amenorrhea.** Intense physical training is associated with stress and with nutritional and metabolic alterations, which appear to contribute to the endocrine changes that interfere with ovulation. When exercise patterns are restored to more typical levels, apparently normal menstrual cycles return.

Anovulatory cycles are more common around the time of the **menarche** (onset of menstruation) and the **menopause** (cessation of menstruation), probably because of delay in the acquisition of fine endocrine control as cycle patterns are established and because of its loss as cycles are ending. Between these times, anovulatory cycles may be caused by various metabolic disturbances, such as systemic disease, obesity, psychological stress, or some abnormality in the endocrine links between hypothalamus-anterior pituitary and ovary.

Endometriosis

In this condition, deposits of endometrial tissue are present at various sites external to the uterus. They are thought to arise from endometrial fragments that are expelled through the infundibulum of the Fallopian tube to reach the pelvic cavity, where they become established. Alternatively, and less commonly, endometrial cells may gain access to lymphatics or veins that transport them to regional lymph nodes or more distant sites, e.g., lung or bone. Since they contain endometrial cells, which retain mitotic capacity, these deposits of endometrial tissue are able to proliferate at their ectopic sites. **10**

Because they are essentially normal endometrial tissue, these deposits are subject to changes induced by normal endocrine cycles. This means that they not only proliferate under the influence of rising estrogen and progesterone levels, but that they become necrotic and bleed when levels decline. This bleeding at pelvic sites typically causes peritoneal irritation and pain at the time of menstruation (dysmenorrhea). After bleeding, organization of the coagulated pelvic blood may produce adhesions between affected organ surfaces and pelvic walls. These can cause pain because they restrict normal visceral movements during exercise, defecation, urination, or sexual intercourse.

Infertility is a common consequence of endometriosis and results from disruption of the ovarian surface and blockage of the Fallopian tubes. In some cases, cysts filled with coagulated blood (**chocolate cysts**) are formed on the ovaries. These can reach diameters of 10–15 cm.

10

39843

Figure 19.9   Epithelium of the cervical transition zone. (*a*) Normal immature epithelium. (*b*) Squamous metaplasia adapts to the changed conditions of maturity. (*c*) Dysplasia, with deeper cells exhibiting pleomorphism. (*d*) Carcinoma-in-situ with all cells abnormal.

Menstrual Pain and Premenstrual Syndrome

The term **dysmenorrhea** describes the abdominal cramping that accompanies ovulation cycles in many women. In most cases it is trivial or mildly uncomfortable, but in some individuals the pain is severe and interferes with, or prevents, normal activity. Dysmenorrhea is due to uterine cramping in response to myometrial ischemia. The underlying mechanism appears to depend on the action of high levels of prostaglandins that are present during the second half of the cycle, when high progesterone levels exaggerate their effect on myometrial arterioles. The result is pronounced vaso-constriction, ischemia, and pain.

The term **premenstrual syndrome** (PMS) refers to the array of signs and symptoms experienced by some women during the 7–10-day period that precedes the onset of menstrual bleeding. Those most commonly reported include edema, abdominal discomfort, breast fullness, and headache. A psychological component, involving varying degrees of irritability, anxiety or depression, aggressiveness, and alterations in libido, is often superimposed on the physical changes. The subsiding of PMS symptoms after the start of menstrual bleeding suggests an underlying hormonal mechanism that directly or indirectly produces them.

Hormonal effects on neurotransmitters, various metabolic pathways, salt and water retention, and other factors have been proposed as being involved in causing PMS, but there is no clear evidence for any of these. With no known etiology, therapy is usually directed at alleviating the particular combination of signs and symptoms present in each patient. Diuretics for systemic edema, NSAIDs for abdominal pain or headache, and various agents to reduce breast discomfort are typically employed.

Cervical Carcinoma

The cervix (neck) forms the lower third of the uterus. **11** The portion of the cervix that projects into the superior vagina is the **exocervix,** while the remainder, leading to the body of the uterus, is called the **endocervix** (fig. 19.8). The exocervix is protected by a stratified squamous epithelium, while the endocervix is lined by a simple columnar epithelium. In the transition zone between these two tissues, the epithelium is thrown into a complex pattern of folding. In the young adult, the folds are lined by an epithelium of columnar cells resting on a bed of reserve cells, which are the source of new cells needed to replace those normally sloughed from the surface. With maturity, the folded epithelium of the transition zone is exposed to various vaginal irritants, as well as pH and estrogen changes, and to the trauma of coitus and childbirth. These induce an adaptive thickening and strengthening of the epithelium, termed **squamous metaplasia** (fig. 19.9). Such adaptations produce the essentially normal adult epithelium of the endocervix, which is the site where the transformation to carcinoma usually occurs.

The development of an invasive carcinoma from the metaplastic cells of the cervix occurs over a period of years and involves a predictable sequence of changes. (Before proceeding, you may find it useful to refer to chapter 6 for a brief review of terminology related to tissue growth abnormalities.) The early change from normal sees the epithelial cells exhibiting mild degrees of dysplasia. These initial changes are seen in the deepest layers, with the more superficial regions exhibiting pleomorphism in later stages. **12** Surface cells retain their normal appearance until the last, but ultimately dysplasia is in evidence in all

Table 19.4	Grading of Cervical Intraepithelial Neoplasia (CIN)
Grade	**Criteria**
CIN I	Mild dysplasia
CIN II	Moderate dysplasia, less than two-thirds of epithelium's cells are dysplastic
CIN III	Carcinoma-in-situ; severe dysplasia in more than two-thirds of epithelium's cells

Table 19.5	Staging of Cervical Carcinoma
Stage	**Criteria**
0	Carcinoma-in-situ.
I	Tumor confined to region of cervix.
II	Invasion to adjacent structures, but excluding lower one-third of vagina and wall of pelvis.
III	Invasion to lower one-third of vagina or wall of pelvis.
IV	Extension to bladder or rectum or structures beyond pelvis.

epithelial layers. The next stage involves the critical transformation from dysplasia to neoplasia, with increasing anaplasia and more extreme pleomorphism characteristic of a full-blown carcinoma seen in all layers. Because the tumor is, at this point, confined to the epithelium, it is described as **carcinoma-in-situ** (CIS). Since the development of CIS is thought always to follow this sequence, all of these development stages are grouped under the title of **cervical intraepithelial neoplasia** (CIN), with an accompanying grading system that is widely used (table 19.4).

Unless there is intervention to interrupt the progression, tumor cells break through the basement membrane to invade locally. **13** With more extensive invasion, adjacent organs are affected and access to lymphatics is achieved, followed by metastasis to regional lymph nodes, ultimately involving the lungs and liver. Blood-borne metastasis is a less common route for the spread of cervical carcinoma.

Previously more common, cervical carcinoma has been declining because of the ease with which a sample of cervical epithelium can be obtained via a Pap smear. **14** Assessment of cervical cells can reveal the status of the epithelium in the context of the progressive changes that precede CIS and invasion. On findings of abnormal cytology, there is ample time to confirm the diagnosis and consider various interventions, given the long times involved in progression through the stages of CIN. Studies indicate that of all cases of mild dysplasia (CIN I), 40–50% will develop into CIS (CIN III) over a period of 5–20 years. Incidence of CIS has a peak at about age 30, while invasive carcinoma peaks in the early 40s. Most specialists insist on annual Pap smears starting at age 18 or at the onset of sexual activity.

Because CIN is confined to the cervical epithelium, it produces no symptoms. The tumor betrays its presence only when invasion has occurred, at which point there may be abnormal bleeding, vaginal discharge (**leukorrhea**), and pain from the irritation or compression of adjacent pelvic structures. Compression of the ureter, a common occurrence, may cause hydronephrosis, which can ultimately lead to renal failure and death. Invasion through the walls

of the nearby rectum and bladder can lead to fistula formation between their lumina and the uterus. Although metastasis does occur, most of the serious consequences of cervical carcinoma derive from its invasion of pelvic structures.

Early detection is strongly related to therapeutic success in carcinoma of the cervix. When diagnosis is made at Stage 0 (see table 19.5), it is relatively simple to remove or destroy the lesion, and survival rates approach 100%. At later stages the treatment may include **hysterectomy** (surgical removal of the uterus), excision of invading tumor, and radiation therapy. As is to be expected, survival rates are higher in the earlier stages. The staging system for cervical carcinoma is indicated in table 19.5. Five years after diagnosis, survival rates are: Stage I—up to 95%, Stage II—up to 75%, Stage III—35%, and Stage IV—10%.

Studies of etiology in cervical carcinoma indicate that sexual transmission of a viral agent plays a key role. Incidence of the tumor is high when sexual activity starts early and involves multiple partners. A woman faces a particularly high risk when her partner has had previous sexual relations with a woman who had developed cervical carcinoma, the implication being that either he transmitted the oncogenic agent to the original partner or he picked it up from her and can now transmit it to others. The situation can be summed up in the stark contrast between the virtual nonexistence of cervical carcinoma in virgins and its very high incidence in prostitutes.

The principal viral agent implicated in cervical carcinoma is the human papilloma virus (HPV), although its exact role is unclear. Also suspected of contributing are the herpes type II virus, other microbial agents, and various environmental factors such as smoking and even passive inhalation of cigarette smoke. Again, the precise role these play in the processes of initiation and promotion is not yet known, but some interplay between them presumably generates the progressive epithelial changes characteristic of CIN.

13 46557

14 9755

Figure 19.10   In this sectioned uterus a smaller, rounded leiomyoma can be seen at the right, contained within the uterine wall. The larger mass is another leiomyoma projecting from the surface into the uterine cavity.

This uterus has been sectioned to reveal a leiomyoma, the size of a hen's egg, occupying the uterine cavity. Its presence was not betrayed by any signs or symptoms; at least none were reported. The mass was discovered incidentally, in examining a 50-year-old woman who had suffered a massive myocardial infarct from which she did not recover.

Myometrial Tumors

These tumors are principally of two types: a rare malignant form, **leiomyosarcoma,** and a common benign form, **leiomyoma.** The benign form is also known as a **fibroid** and occurs in one out of four women over 30. The fact that many fibroids regress after menopause, whereas their growth is increased during pregnancy, suggests that estrogen is important to their development.

Leiomyomas vary greatly in size, from tiny growths to large, spherical, unencapsulated masses of over 25 cm diameter (fig. 19.10). In some cases, they take the form of a polyp projecting into the uterine cavity. **15** Depending on their size and location, they may be asymptomatic or produce varying patterns of excessive menstrual bleeding and discomfort or pain, which is due to their compression and impingement upon other pelvic structures.

The leiomyosarcoma **16** presents a much more serious prognosis, with survival rates of only 20–40% five years

after diagnosis. Extensive metastasis contributes to the high lethality of these tumors. Incidence is highest at about the age of 50.

Disorders of the Ovary

Previous sections of this chapter have described secondary involvement of the ovary in PID and endometriosis. Apart from genetic defects in its ova, there are only two primary ovarian abnormalities of any significance: cysts and tumors.

Ovarian Cysts

The most common ovarian cysts form from Graafian follicles that do not degenerate normally, or that ovulate and then become sealed, forming an enlarged corpus luteum cyst. These fluid-filled **follicle** or **luteal** cysts are usually 1–2 cm in diameter, but at extremes may exceed 8 cm. Smaller cysts may present no signs or symptoms, but increasing size may be associated with abdominal discomfort. **17** Since they continue to secrete estrogens or both estrogens and progesterone, anovulatory cycles and irregularities of menstrual bleeding often accompany ovarian cysts. Although they may resolve spontaneously, they present the risk of rupture, at which point their released fluid contents and blood can cause acute irritation and abdominal pain.

A less common cystic condition of the ovaries is **polycystic ovarian (PCO) disease,** also known as the **Stein-Leventhal syndrome.** It is usually seen in young women and involves the presence of multiple cysts in both ovaries **18** (fig. 19.11). Its essential characteristics are secondary amenorrhea, increased body and facial hair (**hirsutism**), enlarged ovaries, and variable obesity.

The root of the problem in PCO disease appears to be an exaggerated secretion of androgens near the time of the menarche. It is not clear whether an anterior pituitary or hypothalamic disorder is involved, but whatever the source of the androgens, they are converted to estrogens in the liver and adipose tissue. The high estrogen levels that result have a stimulatory effect on the hypothalamus, which then begins steady secretion of an increased level of **gonadotropin-releasing hormone** (GnRH), which then stimulates secretion of **luteinizing hormone** (LH) by the anterior pituitary. The excessive LH induces an increased output of hormones from the ovaries, including androgen, which are in turn converted to more estrogen, and a positive feedback cycle is established that perpetuates the problem. The androgens are also responsible for inducing the growth of body hair.

Note that the normal interaction between elevated estrogen and the hypothalamus produces a short surge of

15 39739
16 39662
17 40759
18 105

Figure 19.11   Ovarian cysts. This section through an enlarged ovary reveals that its interior is dominated by numerous fluid-filled cysts.

A 15-year-old girl experienced three months of dysmenorrhea followed by a week of abdominal swelling. When fever developed, and persisted for 36 hours, she was examined and a large mass was found adjacent to her umbilicus. Exploratory surgery revealed a 6-kg (13-lb) growth, which had replaced her left ovary. It contained numerous cysts that were filled with a milky looking, mucinous fluid. The tumor was removed and postsurgical progress was satisfactory.

LH output that triggers ovulation, which then subsides, but in PCO disease the high LH output is sustained. The exaggerated estrogen levels also exert the usual inhibitory effects on the anterior pituitary, suppressing its release of **follicle-stimulating hormone** (FSH). This means that no normal ovarian follicle development occurs, and amenorrhea and anovulatory cycles result. The common association of obesity and PCO disease is thought to lie in the capacity of adipose tissue to convert androgen to estrogen. Obesity alone is not likely to produce high enough estrogen levels to initiate the cycling, but once excess androgen is present, obesity can add to the estrogen excess problem and exaggerate its effects (fig. 19.12).

PCO disease is a common cause of infertility and is treated by reducing obesity or by various regimens of hormone therapy, which seek to restore a more normal balance and to interrupt the cycle of positive feedback that drives this derangement.

Ovarian Tumors

Ovarian tumors have a relatively low incidence ($\approx$1/100 females), but they rank fourth in the list of tumor fatalities in females. The danger arises from the lack of signs and symptoms in the early growth stages of ovarian malignancies. By the time indications of abnormality emerge, the tumor's growth, invasion, and metastasis have developed to the point where aggressive combination therapy is required. In spite of improved therapy, prognosis in advanced cases remains poor, and as with so many tumors, the importance of early detection can hardly be overemphasized.

Most ovarian tumors arise in the age range 50–70, but no age is without risk. Various studies implicate ill-defined environmental factors in their etiology, but specifics are few. Because they occur less often in multiparous women, their etiology may have a hormonal component, but studies of birth control pill use and ovarian tumor incidence have been inconclusive.

Ovarian enlargement due to tumor growth may be substantial, [19] involving one or both ovaries and producing significant and even enormous pelvic and abdominal bulk before signs and symptoms arise (fig. 19.13). The tumor's presence may first be detected in an incidental pelvic or abdominal examination, or it may reveal itself through various indications of abdominopelvic disturbance, such as pain or disruptions of normal intestinal or urinary function. In some cases, the bulk caused by a large tumor mass may be mistaken for simple obesity, while in other cases, preexisting obesity may mask the tumor's growth. A common feature of ovarian tumors is abdominopelvic distention, usually associated with the production of large volumes of fluid resembling serous fluid or mucous. These secretions are usually confined to large cysts within the bulky ovarian mass, but in some cases a mucin-secreting tumor releases its gelatinous fluid into the peritoneal cavity. These products may also accumulate at metastatic sites, extensively coating abdominal surfaces. Another factor producing abdominal distention is ascites, which develops as a result of the tumor's compression of lymphatic vessels. This condition prevents adequate lymph drainage and leads to the accumulation of fluid in the peritoneal cavity.

The most beneficial tumor product is produced by tumors that are sufficiently well differentiated to retain estrogen or progesterone secretion capacity. These can produce early systemic effects that call attention to the tumor's presence before it can spread, thus allowing early therapeutic intervention.

Metastasis of ovarian tumors is by direct seeding onto adjacent pelvic surfaces [20] and by way of the lymphatics. These routes can give rise to widespread growth at secondary sites, [21] some as far removed as the diaphragm. Metastasis by the blood to more distant sites, outside the abdominopelvic cavity, is less common. A widely used staging system for ovarian tumors is presented in table 19.6.

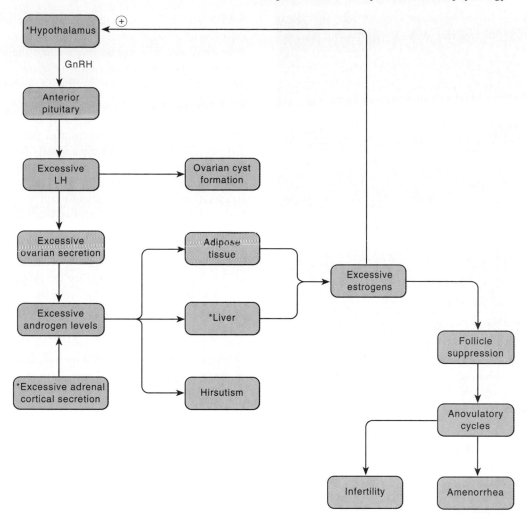

Figure 19.12 Pathogenesis of polycystic ovarian disease. It is unclear which of several initiating events (indicated by asterisks) may produce excessive LH, but once it is produced they trigger positive feedback cycling (+). In obesity, high levels of adipose tissue can contribute to, but probably not initiate, PCO disease.

An Extreme Case of Ovarian Cyst

Recently, a woman diagnosed as having an ovarian cyst refused to allow its surgical removal because she was concerned she would die during the operation. It grew for ten years and reached a size that caused the woman to be bedridden for two years before finally agreeing to consent to its removal.

After the resection, the cyst was found to have a diameter of 1 meter and to weigh over 300 pounds (137 kg). The mass consisted of 50 separate benign ovarian cysts filled with mucous, serous, or fatty liquid contents. The 5-foot 10-inch woman weighed 200 pounds after the procedure and suffered no ill effects.

Table 19.6	Staging of Ovarian Cancers. Substages (not shown) Carry A/B/C Designations and Indicate Increasing Tissue Involvement and Severity Within a Given Stage.

Stage	Criteria
I	Tumor confined to ovaries.
II	Extension of tumor growth to adjacent pelvic structures, one or both ovaries involved.
III	Extension beyond pelvis to peritoneal surfaces, bowel, or liver.
IV	Distant metastases.

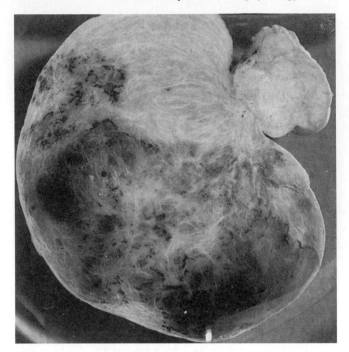

Figure 19.13   An ovarian tumor. This benign mass derives from the ovarian stroma (thecoma). It is about the size of a grapefruit. Compare with the ovary, which is about the size of an unshelled almond.

This grapefruit-sized mass was discovered arising from the ovary of a 57-year-old woman. She had complained of no symptoms that could be attributed to the tumor. After removal, the specimen could be seen to have a thin capsule enclosing its firm mass. Note the lighter-colored stromal bands interlacing the neoplastic tissue. Evidence of scarring at the sites of previous hemorrhage are also present.

There is great diversity in the types of benign and malignant ovarian tumors (table 19.7). Each possesses its own specific diagnostic and therapeutic characteristics, but these are beyond the scope of this text. The following sections briefly describe the major features of the three principal categories of ovarian tumors.

Tumors of the Ovarian Epithelium Tumors originating in the ovarian epithelium constitute over 70% of ovarian tumors. For this reason, they are known as the ovary's **common epithelial tumors.** Differing lines of tumor cell development produce different types of epithelial cell tumors, which resemble various epithelia of the female urogenital passages. The **endometrioid adenocarcinoma,** for example, resembles endometrium, and Brenner's tumor resembles urinary tract epithelium. Among the epithelial

tumors are the serous and mucin-producing tumors mentioned earlier. Epithelial cell tumors most often produce late signs and symptoms. Even when these emerge, they may be ignored or denied, allowing more extensive growth and spread and reducing the likelihood of successful therapy.

Ovarian Germ Cell Tumors These are mostly benign and rare following menopause, but malignant forms can arise in children. Because they originate in the precursors of the female sex cells, they have the capacity for widely differing lines of differentiation. As a consequence, the tumors of this group are quite diverse and will vary in their sensitivity to radiation or chemotherapeutic agents. Some tumors of this group produce hCG and α-fetoprotein, but not in detectable amounts until the later stages of their development. This means they are of little help in making an early diagnosis; but once the diagnosis is established, their levels in plasma can be used to monitor the progress of therapy.

About one-quarter of all ovarian tumors are benign germ cell tumors, which have peak incidence at ages 20–30. They are called **mature cystic teratomas** or **dermoid cysts,** 22 and derive from a defect in meiosis that produces a diploid cell, which then proceeds to differentiate to form a cyst containing any number of mature tissue types. Most often the tissues are epithelial derivatives, with skin lining the cyst's interior. From this lining, hair and sebaceous glands may develop, and the cyst's interior may be filled with a sebumlike fluid or keratinlike material. Other tissues and organ elements may be found, including tooth, bronchus, smooth muscle, nervous tissue, and various glands. Upon discovery, these cysts can be surgically removed to effect a cure.

Tumors of the Ovarian Stroma These are the least common of the ovarian tumors. Microscopically, the stroma of the ovary has a fibrous appearance that is due to the presence of numerous spindle-shaped cells, resembling smooth muscle cells, and fibroblasts, which have some capacity for contraction and for collagen synthesis. Other cells of the stroma are more specialized in being able to secrete estrogen, progesterone, and in some cases, androgens. These, you will recall, can be critical as early indications of the tumor's presence. Stromal cell tumors constitute approximately 10% of all ovarian tumors and only 2% of the malignancies.

Pregnancy-Related Disorders

The following sections deal with the major conditions that are related to pregnancy and that present a threat to its successful outcome.

Table 19.7   Principal Types of Ovarian Tumors

Epithelial Tumors (70%)	Stromal Tumors (10%)	Germ Cell Tumors (20%)
Serous tumors	Granulosa cell tumor	Teratoma
Mucinous tumors	Thecoma	Dysgerminoma
Endometrioid tumors	Fibroma	Choriocarcinoma
Clear cell tumor	Sertoli-Leydig tumor	Endodermal sinus tumor
Brenner's tumor		Embryonal carcinoma

Ectopic Pregnancy

As the term ectopic implies, this is a pregnancy in which the fertilized ovum is implanted at a site other than the endometrium (fig. 19.14). Usually the cause is some defect or blockage along the uterine tube, leading to implantation in its wall. [23] Most ectopic pregnancies, 90% or more, occur in this way, and in many cases obstructions related to PID or endometriosis are responsible. However, in about half of ectopic pregnancies, the Fallopian tubes appear to be normal, so more subtle defects in the transport mechanism, or some exaggerated capacity for adherence on the part of the developing embryo, may be involved. In rare cases, instead of entering the infundibulum, a fertilized ovum may fall to a lower peritoneal surface, where it implants, or fertilization may occur at the ovarian surface and confine the embryo to the ovary.

Implantation in the oviduct raises the threat of rupture of its wall, followed by pelvic bleeding. This crisis usually induces pronounced abdominal pain and often leads to cardiovascular shock. Initially, there may be no sign of anything unusual, because relatively normal development proceeds in the tubal mucosa. But the thin Fallopian tube wall can't sustain the embryo's presence, and rupture usually occurs 2–12 weeks after fertilization. The variations of timing and degree of blood loss in ectopic pregnancies are due to differences in wall thickness and blood supply along its length.

In some cases, there is a seemingly spontaneous interruption of the ectopic development, followed by degeneration and absorption of the failed embryo. This occurrence may be related, not to the ectopic implantation, but to the fact that approximately 40% of all pregnancies abort spontaneously, presumably as a result of genetic defects or congenital factors such as infection or endocrine disorders.

Figure 19.14   Ectopic pregnancy. The fully formed fetus lies in the lumen of the uterine tube. Note the placental vessels below the feet.

The fetus in this photograph developed for three months in the left Fallopian tube of a 23-year-old woman. At that time the invading placenta broke through the tube's wall, causing intense lower left quadrant abdominal pain. The hemorrhage that followed produced an acute drop in blood pressure, causing the woman to collapse. Pelvic examination revealed an orange-sized mass, lateral to the uterus, which was surgically removed. In the specimen, note the stretching of the tube in response to the expansion of the developing fetus, amniotic sac, and placenta. The woman's recovery from shock and surgery was uneventful.

Gestational Tumors

Three major tumors, which derive from the developing placenta and which involve excessive hCG production by its trophoblasts, are grouped under the term **gestational trophoblast disease** (GTD). One of these is a benign tumor composed of large masses of grapelike swellings of the placenta's chorionic villi. It is known as an **hydatidiform mole** (HM). **24** With early detection by ultrasound imaging, the mole can be removed by suction curettage. Most are readily dealt with in this way.

A second type of GTD is the **invasive mole,** which does not metastasize but which can invade from the endometrium into the myometrium. Extension of tumor to adjacent structures may also occur, but the greatest risk is perforation of the uterine wall and hemorrhage.

The third type of GTD is **choriocarcinoma,** a rare but highly malignant tumor that may develop in association with HM, spontaneous abortion, or even a normal pregnancy. The tumor mass is typically soft and bulky, with prominent areas of hemorrhage and necrosis. It metastasizes early and widely via the blood to the lung, vagina, brain, and liver. Both choriocarcinoma and invasive mole are quite susceptible to chemotherapy.

HM and choriocarcinoma are very rare in the Western world, but have higher incidence in Asia and Africa. Most cases occur in women younger than 15 and older than 40. Following curettage of an HM, 10% of GTD cases are found to be invasive moles, while 2–3% emerge as choriocarcinoma.

Abnormalities of Placental Attachment

Following fertilization, three or four days are required for transport of the developing embryo to the uterus. On arrival, it spends an additional three days or so at the endometrial surface, where it develops to the stage of a hollow cell mass called the **blastocyst.** It is this embryonic form that initiates implantation into the endometrium, which has undergone various changes to accommodate its further development.

Implantation normally occurs in the upper portion of the uterus. While embryonic development proceeds, the endometrium underlying the blastocyst undergoes modification to become the **decidua basalis.** One aspect of this process involves formation of the early placental blood channels. The **placenta** provides for the passage of nutrients, blood gases, and fetal metabolic wastes between the maternal and fetal circulations. **25** The exchange occurs via a particular arrangement of embryonic capillaries that occupy projections of the embryonic membranes called **chorionic villi** (fig. 19.15). These extend into pools of maternal blood present in the placenta. After the infant is delivered, the placenta separates from the supporting

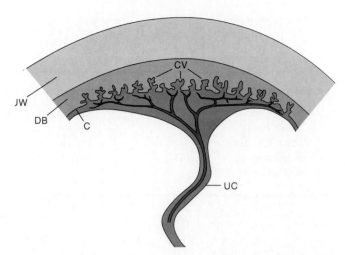

Figure 19.15   Essential components of the placenta. Projections of the embryonic chorion (C), the chorionic villi (CV), carry fetal capillaries that project into the region of the decidua basalis (DB), which contains pools of maternal blood. After exchange between the two circulations, the umbilical cord (UC) returns blood to the fetus. UW: uterine wall.

decidua basalis and is expelled by uterine contraction. (The lay term for the expelled placenta and its associated membranes is **afterbirth.**)

An abnormal implantation in the lower portion of the uterus positions the developing fetus, and sometimes the placenta, over the opening to the cervix. This condition, called **placenta previa,** presents the risk of serious hemorrhage because the elongation and thinning of the cervix that occurs in the later stages of pregnancy is exaggerated during the delivery. As the cervix elongates, the decidua moves from under the placenta, tearing out the placental vessels and causing blood loss. The result is a reduction, or complete loss, of blood supply to the infant and the threat of hypovolemic shock to the mother. A cesarean section is often necessary in placenta previa.

When an endometrial abnormality at the site of implantation provides no decidua basalis to anchor the placenta, the embryo's chorionic villi invade the myometrium. This is the condition of **placenta accreta.** **26** The lack of normal decidua formation may be due to endometrial abnormalities at sites of previous uterine disruption—for example, scarring caused by infection, previous curettage procedures, healing at the site of a previous cesarean section, or an underlying tumor. Placenta accreta may take the form **placenta increta,** where invasion is superficial and limited, or **placenta pancreta,** where there is penetration of the complete myometrial thickness. In the latter case, hemorrhage associated with rupture of the uterus is usually serious, occurring before or during the delivery. In all cases of placenta accreta, the delivery poses a serious risk of blood loss, since, in the absence of the decidua basalis, there is no provision for the orderly separation of placenta from uterus. When bleeding is severe, surgical removal of the uterus (hysterectomy) may be necessary.

The condition of **abruptio placentae** 27 is one that arises in the later stages of pregnancy, but prior to the actual delivery. In this disorder, a portion of the placenta may separate from its underlying decidua. The resulting disruption of the placental vessels produces bleeding, which forms a hematoma within the placenta, thereby compressing it and restricting fetal blood flow. As the blood coagulates, it rapidly consumes clotting factors, limiting the blood coagulation response at other sites where it may be needed. This interference with the coagulation response is especially threatening when delivery and the associated bleeding follow soon after abruptio placentae develops.

When blood is also lost to the pelvic cavity following a premature separation of the placenta, shock may present a serious threat to both mother and infant. Another danger, although rare, is pulmonary embolism by masses of fetal cells in the amniotic fluid that bathes the fetus. As these gain access to the disrupted maternal vessels, they can be carried to the right heart and then the lungs' vessels, where they become trapped. The amniotic cells also release thromboplastins, which can initiate disseminated intravascular coagulation (DIC) because the cells are widely distributed in the circulation.

Toxemia of Pregnancy

This is another condition whose descriptive terminology is in a state of transition. Although in widespread use, the term toxemia is inappropriate since no toxins are known to be involved in its etiology. More currently, emphasis on the most common abnormality of the condition has generated the term **pregnancy-induced hypertension.** In addition to hypertension, albuminuria and edema are often present, together forming the syndrome called **preeclampsia.** The term refers to the late occurrence of convulsions and coma, whose emergence in this context is described as **eclampsia.**

The hypertension, albuminuria, and edema of preeclampsia, usually arise after 32 weeks of pregnancy, and are often accompanied by headache, abdominal pain, vomiting, and disruptions of vision. Early increases in blood pressure are often successfully countered with bedrest and restriction of salt intake. However, in more severe cases, a therapeutic dilemma may emerge because more aggressive intervention may put the infant at risk. For example, antihypertensive agents may reduce pressure so that placental perfusion is compromised, or pronounced restriction of salt intake and beta blocker use may directly damage the fetus.

The etiology of pregnancy-induced hypertension is not well established, but the underlying pathogenesis seems based on restricted blood flow to the placenta. Most cases occur in a woman's first pregnancy, and various immune, genetic, or other factors have been proposed to explain the development of the placental ischemia, but none have been widely accepted. Beyond directly threatening the developing fetus, the altered placental flow is associated with an increased incidence of abruptio placentae.

The pathogenesis of preeclampsia follows from the response of the placenta to ischemia; it releases vasoconstrictors that induce the widespread constriction response leading to systemic hypertension. The constriction of renal vessels produces renal effects that are responsible for two major elements of the toxemia of pregnancy syndrome. These are glomerular damage, which allows the loss of protein to the urine, and salt and fluid retention responses, which contribute to the systemic edema and which can exacerbate preexisting hypertension.

Placental ischemia also results in the release of coagulation promoters, which induce DIC, which can in turn cause widespread systemic ischemia and thromboembolism (fig. 19.16). If progression is limited, vascular tension returns to normal on delivery of the infant and expulsion of the placenta, and signs and symptoms subside.

Breast Disorders

The significant breast lesions include lumps that may be either cysts or tumors, and which range from small, asymptomatic, and trivial, to life-threatening in their impact.

Fibrocystic Disease

In breast fibrocystic disease (FCD), rounded masses consisting of hyperplastic gland epithelium, fibrous stromal tissue, a combination of the two, or fluid-filled cysts arise in the breasts. 28 The cysts are usually palpable as lumps and may be quite small or may exceed 5 cm in diameter. 29 They may occur singly or in greater numbers, to occupy a significant proportion of the breast's volume. The incidence of FCD is low in young women, increases through adolescence, peaks between 20 and 40, and then subsides to be rare after menopause. Although they may be tender following ovulation, most of the cysts are essentially nonthreatening and are easily removed. Sometimes FCD is characterized by a predominance of fibrosis and proliferation of fine gland ducts, in this case it is called **sclerosing adenosis.** In those FCD lumps that contain hyperplastic glandular epithelium, the risk of breast cancer is increased.

FCD is an idiopathic condition, but there are various indications that it arises from an endocrine imbalance involving the estrogens. They may be present at excessive levels, or breast tissues may become unduly sensitive to normal estrogen levels.

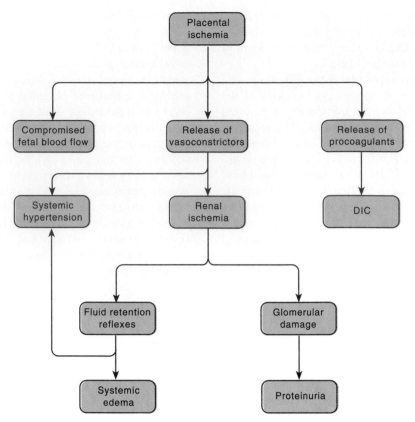

Figure 19.16   The pathogenesis of pregnancy-induced hypertension.

Role of the Immune System in Pregnancy-Induced Hypertension

Recent research has focused on the role of the immune system in pregnancy-induced hypertension. This research is based on the fact that although the placenta has different tissue antigens than the endometrium that supports it, a maternal response in some way masks the "foreign" placental antigens so that the placenta is not rejected. However, if the masking mechanism is disrupted, placental antigens are exposed to the maternal immune system's responses at the point where invading placental arterioles and anchoring cells are most intimately associated with the maternal tissues. The result is immune attack, with immune complex deposition, vasculitis, and necrosis of the vessels causing ischemic damage to the decidua. In response, tissue thromboplastins are released, followed by thrombosis and thromboembolism. Also released are prostaglandins and thromboxane A_2 (TxA_2), a vasoconstrictor that may trigger the characteristic systemic hypertension seen in this condition. One of the prostaglandins released may mediate ischemia by promoting platelet aggregation, while another may contribute to the uterine contractions also often seen in toxemia of pregnancy. Immune damage to the decidual anchoring cells would also explain the increased rate of abruptio placentae seen in preeclampsia.

Certain patterns of incidence of pregnancy-induced hypertension lend support to the idea of an immune system etiology. Those whose immune system is deficient are at higher risk, and a second pregnancy is less likely to involve a preeclampsia problem. Perhaps the masking factors that were induced by the first pregnancy, though inadequate at that time, proliferate to provide adequate masking in later pregnancies.

The use of barrier methods of birth control appears to double the risk of pregnancy-induced hypertension. The explanation for this observation is that a component of semen provides an antigenic stimulus that functions to help activate the female's antigen-masking system. Apparently, blocking access of the seminal antigenic stimulus, e.g., by condoms, diaphragms, or foams, means that less masking potential is available and preeclampsia is more likely to occur. This conclusion is consistent with the observation that more toxemia of pregnancy occurs in the first pregnancies of women with minimal previous sexual intercourse. Presumably, although no barrier contraceptives are involved, minimal prepregnancy exposure to semen (or perhaps a particularly large and invasive placenta) results in a mismatch between the masking response and exposure to foreign antigens.

Fibroadenoma

This benign tumor is the most commonly encountered form of breast neoplasia. The tumor mass is encapsulated and consists of varying combinations of fibrous tissue and glandular cells. Most fibroadenomas have diameters less than 4 cm, but some may achieve 10 cm size. They typically arise in the reproductive years and, if not removed, they usually regress after the menopause. This pattern is due to the sensitivity of their glandular tissue to estrogen levels, which are low after the cessation of menstrual cycling.

Breast Cancer

Currently about one in ten North American women can be expected to develop some form of carcinoma of the breast. **30** Most cases are diagnosed in menopausal and postmenopausal women with much lower incidence prior to the mid 20s. Factors that predispose to greater risk are an early menarche and late menopause, presumably because the breast glands have a longer period of mitotic activity, during which the tissues are more sensitive to oncogenic initiating and promoting agents. Other predisposing factors are nulliparous states or a late (>30–35) first pregnancy, radiation exposure, especially to the chest, and breast gland hyperplasia. The most significant predisposing factor is a family history of breast cancer, particularly in the immediate relatives, i.e., mother, sister, or daughter.

Genetic studies indicate that the majority of breast cancers are linked to a mutation on chromosome number 17. Possibly this mutation makes the individual vulnerable to an environmental factor such as radiation. Although obesity and even moderate alcohol consumption have also been linked with a higher risk of breast cancer, some doubt still exists as to the strength of the association. Prolonged or high exposure to estrogens appears to promote the mitosis and gene activation involved in the appearance of the tumor. This effect may be due to the presence of estrogen receptors on breast glandular epithelium. The link between obesity and breast cancer may also be related to high levels of estrogens, which are formed from adrenal cortical androstenedione in the excess adipose tissue of the obese (see PCO disease, earlier). Ultimately, breast carcinoma appears to result from a complex interplay between genetic predisposition and environmental agents interacting in a supportive hormonal milieu.

Almost all cancers of the breast arise in its glands and are therefore adenocarcinomas. The various specific subtypes that are recognized are listed in table 19.8. Broadly, there are two classes of breast cancer, one in which growth is confined within the basement membrane of the duct or gland in which it arises, called carcinoma-in-situ (CIS), and invasive carcinoma, where tumor cells infiltrate adjacent

Breast Cancer Etiology

There is no evidence that breast cancer has a viral etiology in humans. Speculation about a viral role is based on the finding that in certain strains of mice, females develop breast carcinoma if exposed to a specific virus while they are nursing their young. However, no such link to a virus in humans has been found. Also, contrary to some suggestions, it seems unlikely that silicone breast implants play any causative role in breast cancer.

Table 19.8	Classification of Breast Cancer

Noninvasive	Invasive
Intraductal carcinoma	Invasive ductal carcinoma
Intraductal papillary carcinoma	Invasive lobular carcinoma
	Medullary carcinoma
Lobular CIS	Tubular carcinoma
	Mucinous carcinoma
	Adenoid cystic carcinoma
	Paget's disease
	Invasive papillary carcinoma
	Apocrine carcinoma

tissues, gain access to lymphatics, and metastasize. Most noninvasive breast carcinoma arises in the ducts and grows without inducing changes that betray its presence; in particular, it induces no fibrous response in the stroma, since the tumor is isolated from the stroma by a basement membrane. Without fibrosis the tumor is difficult to detect as a lump. In about one-third of cases, a noninvasive tumor acquires invasion capability and a stromal fibrous response follows, but by the time the resulting fibrous proliferation produces a palpable mass, some degree of metastasis may have already occurred.

Invasive tumors may produce various changes at the breast's surface due to contraction of the tumor's fibrous stroma. Surface dimples may result or the nipple may be drawn inward. When the invading tumor cells reach the overlying dermis, they may infiltrate and obstruct its lymphatics. The result is a local reddening and hardening of the skin that is termed **peau d'orange,** since it has some resemblance to an orange peel.

Tumor (T)

T_0—No evidence of tumor
T_1—Tumor diameter less than 2 cm
T_2—Tumor diameter 2–5 cm
T_3—Tumor diameter greater than 5 cm
T_4—Tumor of any size extending
       to chest wall or skin

Nodes (N)

N_0—No lymph node involvement
N_1—Involvement of axillary lymph
       nodes that remain movable
N_2—Involvement of axillary lymph
       nodes that are fixed to each other
       or adjacent structures
N_3—Involvement of internal mammary
       nodes

Metastasis (M)

M_0—No distant metastases
M_1—Distant metastases

Figure 19.17   The TNM system of breast cancer staging. ▲:
tumor growth.

Metastasis of most breast cancers is via lymphatic drainage **31** to the regional nodes of the axilla, but blood-borne spread also occurs. The tumor emboli disseminate widely to grow at multiple sites, most often the lung, liver, adrenal glands, brain, and the skin, and bone, e.g., vertebral bodies.

The TNM system (see chapter 6) is commonly used in breast cancer staging (fig. 19.17). As you may recognize by now, intervention in early stages is related to better prognosis. In most centers, when a tumor is diagnosed as malignant on the basis of a biopsy study, therapy currently involves removal of the tumor mass or the entire breast (**mastectomy**). Affected lymph nodes are also removed, and postmastectomy radiation or chemotherapy is typical.

Treatment in some cases involves a regimen of chemotherapy, using cytotoxic agents and usually not lasting beyond six months. This approach is effective in destroying the small groups of cells, at both primary and secondary sites, that surgery or radiation can't readily eliminate. Because many breast cancers retain their cell-surface estrogen receptors, a chemotherapeutic agent that binds to estrogen receptors, **tamoxifen,** is widely used. By acting as a blocking agent, it deprives the tumor of the estrogen stimulus that sustains it, and its growth is suppressed. As an added benefit, tamoxifen has few serious side effects and so is well tolerated by its users. There is also some evidence that it can prevent the initial development of breast cancer, and may therefore be suitable for prophylactic use in selected high-risk patients.

It is widely accepted that by the time of diagnosis 50% of breast cancers have already metastasized. This means that, once the primary tumor or mass has been removed, long-term survival is determined by growth at secondary sites. These secondary sites therefore are an important focus of therapy.

Case Study

A 29-year-old woman reported to her general practitioner that for the past two months she had been experiencing lower abdominal pain, urinary frequency, and some nausea. She had stopped taking oral contraceptive pills four months ago, had a menstrual period immediately following, but had had no menstrual periods since. Her weight had been stable for the past two years.

On physical examination she looked generally healthy, but her abdomen was tender on the left side, exhibiting a slight fullness. She showed no obvious signs of vaginitis

and her cervix appeared normal. Blood tests proved normal, as did urinalysis, including a determination of chorionic gonadotropin (hCG).

The patient was referred to a radiologist for a pelvic ultrasound examination. It revealed the presence of a 5-cm ovarian mass. The radiologist recommended that she return in one month for reexamination. She returned as advised and reported that she had had an apparently normal menstrual period two weeks previously. The follow-up ultrasound scan showed that the mass had increased in size, and she was referred to a gynecologist.

On the gynecologist's recommendation, she was admitted to hospital, and during an exploratory laparoscopy procedure the cyst was located and removed. Postoperative examination of the excised ovarian mass revealed that it contained endometrial tissue into which bleeding had occurred, forming a chocolate cyst.

The patient was given the option of resuming oral contraceptive therapy to suppress the hormonal swings that could exacerbate the endometriosis. She had earlier stated her intention of becoming pregnant at some future time and was advised that endometrial deposits in the uterine tubes might affect the passage of ova or spermatozoa, reducing the chance of a successful pregnancy.

Commentary

In view of the patient's complaints, blood and urine tests were required to rule out urinary infections, while testing for hCG levels would reveal a normal or ectopic pregnancy.

Since oral contraceptives supply a small additional amount of hormones, sufficient to suppress follicle development and therefore endogenous estrogen secretion, this woman's use of the pill may have suppressed bleeding from the deposit of endometrial tissue that had reached her ovary.

The radiologist's recommendation to defer any action for a month was based on the fact that, given the patient's age, an ovarian tumor was unlikely to be present, and a delay might allow the resumption of normal hormonal and ovarian cycling. If the enlargement was a follicular cyst, it might well have regressed when estrogen and progesterone levels declined during a normal cycle. If that had occurred, the patient would probably have been spared surgery. Since menstruation resumed and the mass had not regressed (had in fact increased), surgery was necessary to ascertain its nature.

Key Concepts

1. Disorders of the penis/urethra, bulbourethral glands, seminal vesicles, and vas deferens are rare, with most male reproductive disease arising in the testis and prostate gland (p. 478).

2. The most common congenital defect of the male reproductive system is cryptorchidism, in which there is a failure of the testes to descend to the scrotum from the abdomen, where they initially form (p. 478).

3. The great majority of testicular tumors are malignant and are called germ cell tumors because they arise from spermatozoan precursors in the seminiferous tubules (pp. 478–482).

4. Torsion of the spermatic cord's vessels can compromise testicular venous drainage to produce congestion and swelling, or if extreme, infarction (p. 482).

5. Hyperplasia of the prostate, beyond the limited amount present in most males after age 45, can produce urinary obstruction and predispose to bladder infection, pyelonephritis, and hydronephrosis (p. 482).

6. Carcinoma of the prostate is unrelated to benign prostatic hyperplasia and typically produces symptoms after age 50, with detection often delayed until local invasion causes pain (pp. 482–483).

7. Pelvic inflammatory disease usually involves an initial vaginal infection with subsequent ascent to involve the uterus, uterine tubes, ovaries, and other abdominal structures, often producing infertility due to postinflammatory scarring and adhesions (pp. 483–485).

8. Anovulatory cycles and their associated hormone imbalances are the principal cause of dysfunctional uterine bleeding (pp. 485–486).

9. The expulsion of endometrial tissue into the pelvic cavity can produce endometriosis, the condition in which the endometrial tissue becomes established and subject to proliferation and bleeding in synchrony with the uterine cycle, causing irritation, pain, adhesions, and the risk of infertility (p. 486).

10. High levels of prostaglandins seem to trigger myometrial ischemia, which causes the uterine cramping associated with menstruation (p. 487).

11. An ill-defined hormonal imbalance is thought to underlie the array of signs and symptoms and psychological swings known as PMS, which accompanies the menstrual cycle in some women (p. 487).

12. Cervical carcinoma usually originates in the epithelium's transitional zone after a slowly developing sequence of changes starting with mild dysplasia through carcinoma-in-situ (p. 487).

13. The ability to monitor changes in the cervical epithelium is largely responsible for the decline in the incidence of cervical carcinoma (pp. 487–488).

14. Various nonbiological environmental agents and microorganisms are suspected of contributing to the etiology of cervical carcinoma, as indicated by incidence and transmission patterns (p. 488).

15. Graafian follicles are the most common source of ovarian cysts, which are associated with anovulatory cycles, irregular menstrual bleeding, and the risk of ovarian rupture (p. 489).

16. Polycystic ovarian disease, characterized by amenorrhea, hirsutism, enlarged ovaries, and obesity, derives from some imbalance in the complex interplay

between estrogens, the hypothalamus, and the anterior pituitary, triggered by excessive androgen secretion from the anterior pituitary or the adrenals (pp. 489–490).

17. Ovarian tumors produce high mortality because of the lack of signs or symptoms prior to the point at which invasion and metastasis have clouded the prognosis (p. 490).

18. There are many types of benign and malignant ovarian tumors, which exhibit a broad array of characteristics (p. 490).

19. Ectopic pregnancy usually arises from an obstruction that promotes implantation in the uterine tube, posing the threat of its rupture and the possibility of hypovolemic shock (p. 493).

20. Hydatidiform mole, invasive mole, and choriocarcinoma are three tumors of the placenta that secret high levels of hCG and that are grouped together as gestational trophoblastic disease (GTD) (p. 493).

21. Various abnormalities of placental attachment can cause bleeding sufficiently serious to produce hypovolemic shock in the mother and the infant who depends on the placenta for blood supply (p. 493).

22. Pregnancy-induced hypertension presents a picture of hypertension, albuminemia, and edema in response to placental ischemia, perhaps induced by a failure of the system that masks self-antigens to produce immune-mediated damage to placental vessels (p. 495).

23. A fundamental estrogen-mediated mechanism is thought to underlie the nonthreatening single or multiple masses formed of epithelium, fibrous connective tissue, or cysts that characterize breast fibrocystic disease (p. 495).

24. Breast carcinoma appears to be the result of the interplay between a genetic predisposition and various suspected environmental agents in a supportive hormonal environment (p. 497).

25. Most breast cancer arises in the glands and ducts of the breast, rather than in its fibrous or adipose tissues, and is dangerous because metastases may occur prior to the development of the signs and symptoms that betray its presence (pp. 497–499).

REVIEW ACTIVITIES

1. Supply short written answers to the following: In endometriosis, how is endometrial tissue thought to reach the pelvic cavity? How might it reach the lungs? What is the consequence of the presence of ectopic endometrial tissue? Check your answers against the information on page 488.

2. Carefully review the material on cervical cancer on pages 487–488. Make a ready reference list of relevant breast cancer and Pap smear information. In chatting with anyone you know who isn't getting regular Pap smears, use the list to be informative and supportive, but in particular, persuasive.

3. Write a list of the toxins known to be involved in toxemia of pregnancy. Now suggest a better name for this condition and identify why it is better. Reflect upon two ways that vasoconstrictors are implicated in the pathogenesis of preeclampsia.

4. List the essential differences between placenta previa, placenta accreta, placenta increta, and abruptio placentae. Check pages 494–495 if you have to.

5. Trace the outlines of one of the diagrams in figure 19.17. Add sites of tumor involvement for a patient whose TNM staging is $T_2N_1M_1$.

6. Complete the following table. If you use initials, be certain you know what they stand for.

Essential Problem	Name of Disease/Condition
Failure to ovulate	
Inadequate placental anchoring	
Myometrial ischemia	
Failure of testes' descent	
Grapelike placental tumor	
Pregnancy-related convulsions/coma	
Scarring and infertility	
Compromised testicular blood flow	
Embryonic implantation outside uterus	
Multiple, bilateral ovarian cysts	
Prostatic urinary obstruction	
Placenta obstructs cervix	
Albuminemia, edema, hypertension	
Nonneoplastic breast masses	
Ectopic menstrual responses	

Chapter Twenty

Disorders of Central Nervous System Development, Vascular Support, and Protection

*The brain is the highest of the organs, and it is protected
by the vault of the head; it has no flesh, or blood
or refuse. It is the citadel of sense-perception.*

Pliny the Elder
(AD 25–79)

CENTRAL NERVOUS SYSTEM PROTECTION

Protection of the delicate tissues of the brain and spinal cord is normally insured by the scalp, bony structures, and meningeal layers enclosing the cerebrospinal fluid. Trauma to or disease in these structures may compromise this protection.

Surface Landmarks

Surface structures are routinely used to localize brain and spinal cord features. The **nasion,** illustrated in figure 20.1, is the depression at the root of the nose where it joins the bones of the cranial vault. The **inion** is the point on the scalp that overlies the midpoint of the external occipital protuberance, which is a bony projection at the lower center of the skull, above the attachment of the posterior neck muscles. This point corresponds to the junction, on the inside of the skull, of the major venous sinuses draining blood from the brain. The inion also marks the most posterior extent of the loose connective tissue that allows the scalp to move freely and is part of the attachment of the broad, thin sheet of muscle called the **occipitalis** portion of the **epicranius** muscle. Some people can voluntarily contract this muscle and shrug their scalp backwards. The anterior portion of the epicranius, called the **frontalis,** is the muscle that enables a person to wrinkle the forehead or raise the eyebrows.

The **external auditory** (or acoustic) **meatus** (the ear canal) is easy to locate. Above it and just posterior to the area normally called the temple is the **pterion.** This is the area at the irregular, H-shaped meeting of the sutures of four bones: the frontal, sphenoid, parietal, and temporal (fig. 20.1). In this region (called the **temporal fossa**), the bones of the skull tend to be thin and blows are likely to produce fractures, especially at the pterion. The anterior branch of the middle meningeal artery (one of the arteries that supply the skull bones with blood) underlies the skull at the pterion. Skull fractures in the region of the pterion may cause this artery and/or its accompanying veins to be torn, with resulting intracranial hemorrhage. Figure 20.2 illustrates the location of significant brain structures relative to the pterion.

The **vertebral column** or spine functions in three ways: it supports the head, trunk, and limbs, it allows movement of the head and trunk, and it protects the spinal cord. Certain landmarks are essential reference points (fig. 20.3).

If you move your fingers down a person's neck with the neck flexed forward, you will feel a prominent bump in the spine at the base of the neck. This bump marks the **vertebra prominens,** which is formed by the spinous process of the seventh—the lowest—cervical vertebra (C7). (The number of cervical vertebrae in humans is always seven.) A second prominent bump, which may be larger or smaller than the vertebra prominens, marks the first thoracic vertebra (T1). Starting from this point and palpating firmly at the center of the spine, you can count the spinous processes of the thoracic (usually 12) and lumbar (usually 5) vertebrae. The lowest of the lumbar vertebrae (L5) articulates with the top of the five fused vertebrae that form the sacrum. The delicate spinal cord extends down the meninges-lined vertebral canal from C1 to about the disk between L1 and L2. It is protected dorsally by vertebral arches, ligamentous structures, and muscle.

During embryonic and first-year postnatal development, growth of the vertebral column outpaces the lengthening of the cord. Because of this disparity, the cord and its spinal nerve extensions appear to be "drawn up" the vertebral canal so that lower nerves must travel several segments before they pierce the dura (protective coverings of the cord) and exit through the intervertebral foramen. Below L2, therefore, there is a mass of spinal nerves, which arises at cord levels L2 and lower and ends at coccygeal 1, that together is called the **cauda equina** (horse's tail). These nerves are contained in an extension of the dural sac that ends about the middle of the sacrum. As illustrated in figure 20.4, a bevelled, large-bore needle can be pushed into this space, usually at L3–L4 or L4–L5, to sample an individual's cerebrospinal fluid (CSF) or introduce anesthetic drugs. (The procedure is called a **lumbar puncture** or **spinal tap.**) There is little danger of damaging these nerves. Contact with the needle creates distinct motor or sensory effects (e.g., muscle twitch or shooting pain), upon which the needle is withdrawn slightly, turned so the bevel is at a different angle, and reinserted.

Locating L3–L4 by counting down from the vertebra prominens is a laborious process, and the result may be inaccurate because of variations in the number of thoracic and lumbar vertebrae. Two other approaches are commonly used. L4 can be located directly because it lies at about the same level as the top of the iliac bones in a standing person. Alternatively, since the top of the median crest (formed by the fused spinous process of the sacrum) is S2, L4 can be located by counting up from S2 (see fig. 20.3).

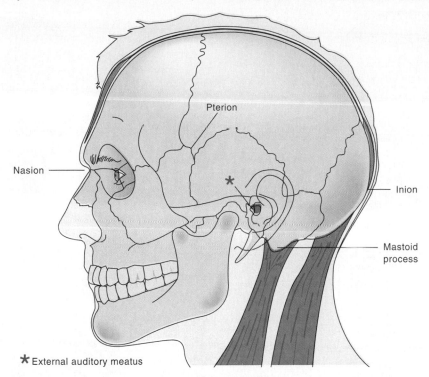

Figure 20.1   The relationship of key surface features on the head to underlying bony structures. The nasion, inion, pterion, external auditory meatus, and mastoid process are shown.

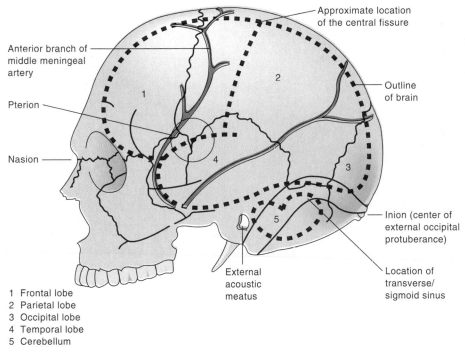

Figure 20.2   Relationship of skull landmarks to important vascular and brain structures.

Posterior   **Anterior**

Figure 20.3   Features of vertebral column in lateral and anterior views.

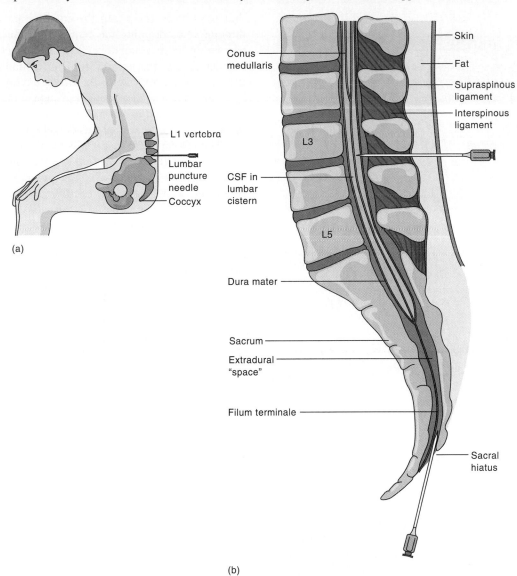

Conus
medullaris

L1 vertebra

Lumbar
puncture
needle

Coccyx

(a)

Skin

Fat

Supraspinous
ligament

Interspinous
ligament

L3

CSF in
lumbar
cistern

L5

Dura mater

Sacrum

Extradural
"space"

Filum terminale

Sacral
hiatus

(b)

Figure 20.4   (*a*) The technique of lumbar puncture (spinal tap). Note that the person's back is flexed; this is done to open the spaces between the spinous processes and laminae of the vertebrae. (*b*) Median section of the inferior end of the vertebral column, showing the spinal cord and its membranes. A lumbar puncture needle has been inserted at L3/L4 for withdrawal of CSF. A needle is also shown in the sacral hiatus, the site sometimes used for extradural (epidural) anesthesia.

Protection of the Brain: The Scalp

The scalp has five layers (fig. 20.5), of which the first three (skin, connective tissue, galea aponeurotica) form the scalp proper. This part can be quite easily separated from the head in a car crash. The dermal layer (connective tissue) is richly vascularized and the arteries anastomose freely. Because this connective tissue is attached to the flat, fibrous sheet of connective tissue called the galea aponeu-rotica (galea is Greek for helmet), the arteries can't retract as they would in soft tissue. Thus bleeding from superficial scalp wounds will tend to be profuse and prolonged. The galea is attached anteriorly at the frontalis muscle and pos-teriorly at the occipitalis. Deep wounds that split or cut the

galea will gape widely because of the divergent pull of the frontal and occipital parts of the epicranius muscle and, unlike superficial scalp wounds, will require deep sutures even though they may not bleed as profusely.

The **loose connective tissue** forms a subaponeurotic space or layer that is somewhat like a collapsed sponge. It allows free movement of the scalp proper. This layer can be easily torn in deep scalp lacerations and is capable of becoming distended with fluid if blood vessels are damaged or infection causes an accumulation of exudate. Figure 20.6 illustrates the attachments of the galea aponeurotica that limit fluid spread. Infection can be transmitted to veins and venous sinuses of the cranial cavity through emissary veins

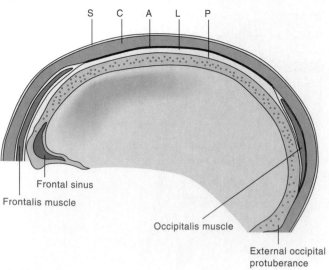

Frontal sinus

Frontalis muscle

Occipitalis muscle

External occipital protuberance

S— Skin
C— Connective tissue (dense subcutaneous)
A— Aponeurosis epicranalis (usually called the galea aponeurotica)
L— Loose (areolar) connective tissue
P— Pericranium (periosteum)

Figure 20.5   Section through the scalp and calvaria, with a key to remembering the five layers of the scalp.

that pass from the scalp through the cranial bones or through veins draining the central face. Such an infection can set up an inflammatory process, with resultant thrombophlebitis and the possibility of infarction of portions of the cerebral cortex due to blocked venous drainage. Infection may also pass from the venous system to the cerebrospinal fluid or the neural tissue itself. Any of the foregoing are potentially very serious conditions.

The last layer of the scalp is the periosteum of the cranium, the **pericranium.** In contrast to the periosteum in other regions of the body, the pericranium has poor osteogenic or bone repair properties. Hence large traumatic insults to the cranial bones don't usually fill in and must be replaced with plastic (formerly metal) plates inserted to protect the brain. Burr holes drilled through the skull to monitor intracranial pressure or reduce a hematoma may be filled with cold-cure epoxy.

Nerves and vessels supplying the scalp enter from the neck, temporal area, and forehead, i.e., from below, and ascend through either of the two connective tissue layers. When a surgeon needs to expose the skull, surgical **pedicle flaps** are made. That is, a detached mass of tissue is cut

Line of attachment of the galea

Figure 20.6   Attachments of the galea aponeurotica.

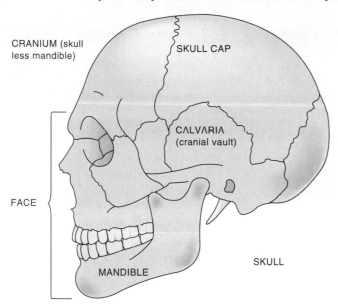

Figure 20.7   Terminology applied to the skull.

Figure 20.8   Section through skull bone.

away from underlying parts but is left attached at the lower edge. The numerous arterial anastomoses insure that adequate blood supplies will continue to reach the detached scalp. The cranial bones are supplied from arteries within the cranium.

Protection of the Brain: The Skull

The **skull** is the most complex bony structure of the body and performs many functions. It encloses and protects the brain, which is the central concern here. But as well, the organs of special sense (seeing, hearing, smelling, tasting, static and dynamic balance) are housed and strategically positioned within it. It also encloses the openings into the digestive and respiratory tracts.

The skull is composed of two parts. The first is the **calvaria** (not calvarium), which encloses the brain and is sometimes called the cranial vault or brain case. The second part is the **face,** which is attached to the anteroinferior part of the calvaria. While skull refers to the entire skeletal structure of the head, **cranium** implies the skeleton of the head excluding the lower jaw or **mandible.** The roof of the calvaria is sometimes referred to as the **skull cap** (fig. 20.7).

In cross section (fig. 20.8) the cranial bones have an outer and an inner table of compact bone, with an intervening layer of cancellous or spongy bone (the diploë). This structuring gives great strength to cranial bones while keeping weight to a minimum. It also raises the possibility, particularly with the younger patient, that the outer table of the skull may remain intact, rebounding after a blow, even

though the inner table and diploë have been broken into bits (comminuted) and forced into the meningeal and even brain tissues (depressed). So manual inspection for suspected fractures is not sufficient and X-ray is routine.

Note the terms (fig. 20.9*b*) applied to the subdivisions of the floor of the cranial vault **1** (anterior, middle, and posterior fossae). In Latin, **fossa** means "ditch" or "depression." The **crista galli** **2** is in the middle of the anterior fossa. This is a spur of bone that extends from the relatively tiny ethmoid bone up about 1 cm into the brain case. It is the anterior point of attachment of a tough membrane (**falx cerebri**) that separates the two hemispheres of the brain. Rotational trauma may rip this membrane loose, and the spur of bone can do serious damage to the frontal lobes of the brain. The **cribriform plate** of the ethmoid bone is perforated. Filaments of the olfactory nerve pierce the protective membranes of the brain (the meninges) and pass through the cribriform plate into the upper portions of the nasal cavity, providing a sense of smell. A blunt blow to the skull, such as might happen when the head is driven into the windshield in a car accident, can cause the base of the skull to fracture (basal skull fracture). Such a linear fracture can cut through the cribriform meninges, allowing cerebrospinal fluid to leak into the nasal cavity, a condition called **rhinorrhea.** As will shortly be detailed, cerebrospinal fluid (CSF) contains glucose. Testing a posttraumatic nasal discharge with a ketostick (normally used to detect sugar in a diabetic's urine) will allow one to discriminate between CSF, indicating a probable basal skull fracture with rupture of the meninges, and nasal mucous discharge, which contains no glucose. A basal skull fracture may also sever elements of the olfactory nerve, thereby leading to a loss of smell in one or both nasal cavities.

The bony recess of the **sella turcica** **3** **4** houses the pituitary gland, which is richly supplied with blood vessels to carry the trophic hormones released by this "master gland" to their target organs in all parts of the body. The sella can be used as a reference point in viewing MRI or CT scans. Enlargement of the pituitary fossa and erosion of

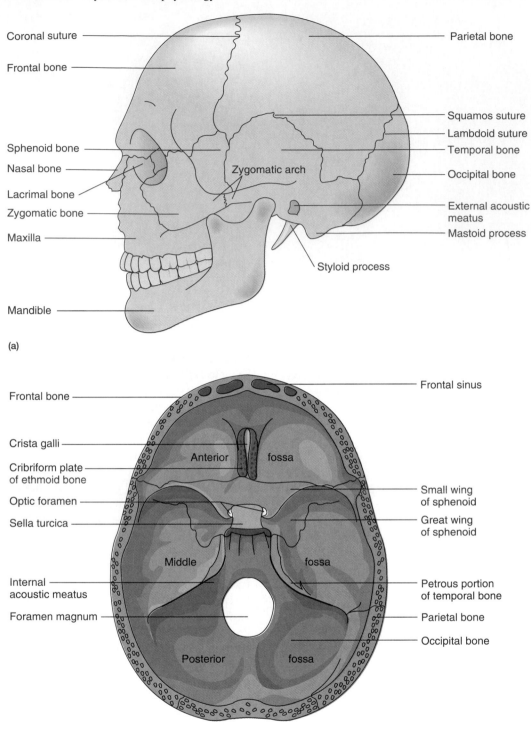

(a)

(b)

Figure 20.9 Review of skull anatomy: (*a*) Lateral view of the skull, showing principal bones and sutures. (*b*) View of the base of the skull from above, showing the internal surfaces and some of the cranial bones.

Figure 20.10   Production, circulation, and reabsorption of cerebrospinal fluid.

A Hight lateral ventricle
B Foramen of Monro
C Third ventricle
D Cerebral aqueduct
E Fourth ventricle
F Foramen of Magendie
G Foramina of Luschka

Choroid plexus
CSF flow
Venous flow

the sella turcica will accompany the expansion of a pituitary tumor and was diagnostic before assays of specific pituitary hormones became common.

The **sphenoid** (wedge-shaped) **bone,** which creates most of the sella turcica, is a major bone in the floor of the skull. The temporal lobes nestle into the middle fossa and are subject to trauma when accelerated against the ridge between the small and great wings of the sphenoid bone. The floor of the middle fossa is largely formed by the **temporal bone,** the petrous (rocklike) portion of which is often a site of linear fracture in basal skull fractures. It houses the elaborate structure of the semicircular canals and inner ear. Fracture through these structures can provide a potentially serious port of entry for infection of the central nervous system, as well as allowing CSF to leak into the middle ear or, with perforation of the eardrum, into the auditory canal. This condition is called **otorrhea.**

The spinal cord communicates with the brain stem through the foramen magnum (great opening), as do the arteries that travel up the spine and supply the posterior aspects of the brain. The dotted line on the right side of the occipital bone (fig. 20.9*b*) indicates the groove that houses the major venous sinus (a specialized blood vessel) that drains the right side of the brain.

Meningeal Protection

If the brain were housed directly in the skull, brain on bone, any jolt or jar would be conducted immediately to the brain tissue. As well, the 1500-g weight of the average brain would present a considerable mass, which, once moving, would tend to persist in its movement. This tendency could be disastrous if the skull suddenly stopped its linear or rotational movement, since it could lead to compressing or shearing of delicate nervous tissue. Further, the central nervous system has no lymphatic vessels. In the rest of the body, lymphatics carry any excess of extracellular fluid (that has passed out of the capillaries) back into the general circulation. What provisions exist in the central nervous system (CNS) to deal with these circumstances?

The brain floats in a thin pool of cerebrospinal fluid. This layer poses a significant cushion and, more importantly, reduces the effective weight of the brain to about 50 g. Much of the CSF is produced in specialized vascular tissue called **choroid plexus.** Concentrations of choroid plexus are found lining cavities deep within the brain. In its very early embryological development, the CNS is a hollow, tubelike structure. As the forebrain grows and elaborates, this central cavity, through which important blood vessels course, maintains its integrity and becomes quite complex in shape forming four ventricles. The mature brain has two paired **lateral ventricles,** which are located in a continuous chamber from the frontal, through the parietal, occipital, and finally temporal lobes of the brain. They communicate with one another, and the **third ventricle,** **5** at the approximate center of the brain (fig. 20.10), through the interventricular **foramen of Monro.** CSF is produced in the choroid plexus in both lateral ventricles and passes into the third (through the foramen of Monro), where additional CSF is added from further choroidal tissue. From the third ventricle, CSF passes down the narrow **aqueduct of Sylvius** (also called the **cerebral aqueduct**) into the **fourth ventricle.** **6** More CSF is added and the entire production is pushed through three further foramina, then passes into

Superior sagittal sinus
Subarachnoid space
Jugular vein

Dura mater:
Periosteal layer
Meningeal layer

Bone of skull
Periosteum
Dura
Arachnoid membrane
Pia mater
Superior sagittal sinus
Arachnoid villi
Subarachnoid space
Falx cerebri

Cerebral hemisphere   Cerebral hemisphere

Inferior sagittal sinus
Corpus callosum

(a)

Epidural fat
Dura mater
Spinal cord
Subarachnoid space
Pia mater
Bone of vertebra

(b)

Figure 20.11   Three meningeal layers and their relation to bone and brain and to the vertebral column and spinal cord.

the thin space that surrounds the entire brain and spinal cord. The circulation of CSF continues around the brain and cord structures to its eventual destination at the top of the cranial vault. Here specialized structures called arachnoid villi **7** pass the CSF into the venous blood. These are also called arachnoid granulations, as they have a granular appearance to the naked eye. The fluid is replaced three to five times per day.

Under normal conditions, CSF has the following stable characteristics that differentiate it from blood plasma or mucous secretions. It has approximately 60% of the glucose of plasma (mucous secretions have no glucose). It has almost no protein (20 mg/100 ml, versus 6000 mg/100 ml for plasma) and about half as much potassium ion as plasma. The white blood cell count in CSF is below $5/mm^3$ and the fluid is clear and essentially colorless. In the context

of diagnosis, note that bacterial infections of the protective membranes of the brain and spinal cord (meningitis) will deplete the glucose, increase the protein content, drive the white blood cell count up to perhaps $5000/mm^3$, and cause the CSF to become cloudy. Recent hemorrhage will turn it bloody, older hemorrhage a shade of yellow (xanthochromia).

There are three distinct layers between the brain tissue and the bony calvaria (fig. 20.11). A delicate epithelium intimately covers the entire CNS, following all the convolutions of the brain and lining the passageways of the major vessels within the brain tissue. This is the **pia mater** (Latin for gentle or delicate mother). (The ventricles just described are lined with a different, single-cell-thick membrane called the **ependyma.**) The cushioning, supportive pool of CSF is found in the narrow space between the pia and the tough outer membrane that actually makes contact with the bone, the **dura mater** (strong mother). **8** This intervening membrane that actually allows for the circulation of CSF is called the **arachnoid mater,** or **arachnoid membrane. 9** If we strip off the outer dura, the arachnoid will appear as a delicate membrane, dark and irregular (arachnoid refers to its resemblance to tangled cobwebs). If we look at it in cross section, we will find that although it is a continuous membrane where it contacts the dura, most of its thickness is a tracery of short fibers that bridge the space between the outer membrane of the arachnoid and the pia mater. It is in this **subarachnoid space** that the CSF travels. As well, this space contains both veins and arteries that are supplying the brain and the meninges themselves.

The dura mater makes direct contact with the inner periosteum of the calvaria. Normally this contact allows only for a potential space; in other words, there is nothing between the layers except perhaps for extracellular fluid. However, if a blood vessel traveling in the dura or passing through the skull were to rupture, particularly an artery, the pressure of the blood could separate the layers and a bubble or pool of blood would form (a hematoma). Because of its location, this would be called an **extradural** or **epidural** hematoma. As a person ages, these two connective tissue layers become less separable and the likelihood of this form of hematoma therefore decreases. Hemorrhage could also occur in the potential space between the dura and the arachnoid mater (**subdural hematoma**) or into the subarachnoid space itself (**subarachnoid hemorrhage**). The characteristics and effects of each will be discussed at a later point.

The CSF layer does a lot to protect the CNS (estimates have been made that the brain would be seven times more vulnerable to trauma without it). The structure of the meninges increases this protection by subdividing the cranial vault (and thereby the brain tissue) into smaller compartments. These partitions minimize the movement of neural tissue in response to lateral or rotational acceleration. One major reflection or fold of the dura (the falx cerebri) passes backward in the longitudinal fissure between the two hemispheres. The falx fuses with a second transverse fold, called the **tentorium cerebelli, 10** that cradles the occipital lobes. Both folds of dura carry large venous sinuses, vessels that are formed in the dura and are usually triangular in cross section. These large-diameter sinuses offer very little resistance to the passage of venous blood and thereby enhance cerebral circulation. A third, less significant reflection of the dura (**falx cerebelli**) separates the cerebellar hemispheres. These dural structures also can serve as referents; for example, a lesion is located **supratentorially** (above the tentorium) or **infratentorially** or **subtentorially** (below the tentorium).

A special feature of the tentorium should be noted (fig. 20.12). The **tentorial notch** provides an opening for the brain stem, as well as certain nerves and vessels. At the

(a)

(b)

Figure 20.12   Reflections of the cranial dura mater. The tentorium arches over the cerebellum and cradles the occipital and the posterior temporal lobes. The falx divides the cerebrum and extends between the inferior and superior sagittal sinuses.

same time, it is tightly stretched in place. An expanding tumor, for example, could shift the brain stem to one side, pressing it against the side of the tentorial notch. Sensory and motor fibers generally cross over (**decussate**) below the level of the tentorium, so that left brain lesions cause right body symptoms. This normal expectation, that symptoms will appear contralateral to the lesion, reverses in the situation just described. That is, a mass on the right would push the left side of the midbrain against the tentorium, entrapping the fibers from the left hemisphere. Since the result would be right-sided symptoms, on the same side as the lesion, such findings are called **paradoxical.**

Like other connective tissue, the dura carries blood vessels and nerves. Many headaches are actually caused and felt in the dura. To illustrate, a spinal tap will temporarily reduce the volume of CSF. If a person stands up too soon after the spinal tap, the sagging that occurs as the brain is displaced slightly downward, in its only partially filled pool, can put tension on the dura. This tension may be felt as a splitting headache. A fuller treatment of the role of the dura in headaches is given in chapter 23.

Protection of the Spinal Cord: The Vertebral Column

The vertebral column **11** protects the spinal cord. It has a host of other roles: articulation with the head, ribs, pectoral and pelvic girdles; a hemopoietic and immune system role, particularly in childhood; points of attachment for trunk and limb musculature; an avenue for the vertebral arteries, which provide 30% of the brain's blood supply. Some of these tasks are made more precarious by the adaptation of the vertebral column to our upright posture. At the most obvious level, the lower vertebrae must bear more weight than those located higher in the vertebral column. This difference is dealt with by the increasing size of the vertebrae's bodies, but it still subjects lower intervertebral disks to large loads with attendant stresses. Second, the thoracic and abdominal cavities are obviously anterior to the vertebral column, so that the load on the spine is not symmetrically distributed. Partial compensation for this load displacement is supplied by the abdominal musculature, which can make the trunk behave like a column that rests on the pelvic girdle rather than a mass suspended from the spine. The weakness in this design appears when the abdominal muscles themselves weaken. The back musculature must then take on an excessive load, which results in the **lordosis** identified in figure 20.13d.

The natural curvatures (fig. 20.13a), which develop to a certain extent to balance the loads on the spine, can become exaggerated as a result of excessive loads, muscular weakness, or degeneration of vertebral bodies. One of the effects of increased curvature is to place unusual loads and compression on the posterior side of the lumbar intervertebral disks, the consequences of which will be discussed shortly. Moreover, because the loads on the vertebrae are to some extent stacked, a load distribution problem in one part of the vertebral column may well be expressed throughout the spine. In **scoliosis**, **12** a lateral displacement of the vertebral column in the thoracic area, which may have originated from unbalanced muscular strength, leads to extensive rotation of the thoracic and lumbar spine (fig. 20.13b). Major deviation from normal alignment can irritate and entrap spinal nerves and associated plexi and even impair the cord. Surgical correction of orthopedic defects also carries a risk of cord or nerve dysfunction.

Figure 20.14 highlights relevant features of the vertebrae. The second cervical vertebra (the **axis**) possesses an anterior vertical structure, the **dens** or **odontoid process,** around which the first cervical vertebra (the **atlas**)

articulates. Severe hyperextension of the neck can fracture the dens and drive it into the cord. Such a lesion would prove fatal if immediate ventilation were not provided, because the phrenic nerve supplying the diaphragm originates below this (at levels C3–C5) and would be isolated from its source of stimulation. The vertebral arch is formed by two pedicles, from which the transverse processes project, and two laminae, which produce the spinous process. A **laminectomy** involves the surgical resection of a part or all of the lamina and may include part of the pedicle. This is done to gain access to the vertebral canal or to relieve pressure on nerve roots or the cord itself. Spinal fusion involves removal of damaged intervertebral disks and fusion of adjacent vertebral bodies, with provision for enlargement of the consequently narrowed intervertebral foramenae. Experimentation with the insertion of artificial disk material has not proven effective. Sometimes bone grafted from the person's pelvis has been used to replace the lost disk material.

The **intervertebral disks** are specialized points of articulation that allow limited flexibility between adjacent vertebrae while sustaining the weight of the body above them and incorporating substantial shock absorption and tensile strength. The intriguing design that meets these diverse challenges is also the origin of the most common pathologies affecting the vertebral column. The core of the disk (the **nucleus pulposus**) is relatively soft. It is cradled in a tough, fibrous capsule (the **annulus fibrosus**) that restricts the movement of the core. The collagen and elastin fibers that form the annulus extend out of the vertebrae themselves, thereby anchoring the disks and uniting adjacent vertebrae. During flexion the core acts like a pivot point in the center of the disk. This allows more movement, without unduly restricting the foramina between the vertebrae (through which the spinal nerves pass), than would be possible if it were achieved by simply compressing the edge of the disk. Also, sudden compressive forces, such as would be generated upon landing from a jump, can be absorbed. The core squashes by distending the annulus fibrosus, which then recoils, returning the core to its original shape.

As a person ages, the substance of the nucleus pulposus changes, reducing its capacity to bind water but increasing its strength. Between the ages of about 35 and 50 these trends (decreasing water and therefore size and resilience, but increasing strength) cause the intervertebral spaces to narrow, making nerve entrapment and resultant pain and hypofunction a possibility. Nerve root irritation can lead to inappropriate firing of motor neurons and muscle spasm. Altered relationships between articular surfaces (e.g., the inferior and superior articular facets) may be a source of pain. As well, one-time or cumulative injuries to the annulus fibrosus may cause it to rupture, allowing the still-soft

Cervical

Thoracic

Lumbar

Sacral

(a)   (b)   (c)   (d)

Figure 20.13   (*a*) The four natural curvatures of the vertebral column are achieved by the time the child has acquired mature walking and running gait (about age 3). (*b*) In scoliosis (Greek for crookedness), the curve is convex to the side (lateral curvature). There may be a single curve or complex curves, including kyphosis, as the vertebral column rotates to redistribute the altered load. This is a relatively common condition, particularly in adolescent girls, and often requires bracing or even surgical correction. (*c*) In kyphosis (Greek for humpbacked), there is abnormal dorsal curvature, usually in the thoracic region, which results in increased flexion in the upper back. This abnormality has been called "widow's hump" and is often associated with degeneration of vertebral bodies associated with osteoporosis. (*d*) In lordosis (Greek for backward bending), the curve is convex anteriorly, often in the lumbar region. The condition (called swayback) may be congenital or due to the weak abdominal musculature and excess abdominal fat.

nucleus to protrude or herniate. The layman's term for this condition, "slipped disk," is misleading, because the disk itself does not shift out of position. The anterior longitudinal ligament reinforces the anterior extent of the disk, while the narrower posterior longitudinal ligament limits disk protrusion directly onto the cord. These constraints favor herniation in a lateral/posterior direction. Limited herniation may press on the ventral (motor) roots of the cord, while more extensive herniation may affect dorsal (sensory)

roots and the cord itself. These potential problems often lessen with advancing age, as the disk becomes thinner but tougher.

In another type of disk herniation, compressive trauma can cause the nucleus to herniate into the body of the adjacent vertebra. This is a relatively common condition with the uncommon name of **Schmorl's lesion.** It may go undetected unless the shift of nucleus pulposus and the resultant narrowing of intervertebral space causes nerve

Figure 20.14   Details of the vertebral column bony, disk, and ligamentous structures.

entrapment or pain. The latter may also arise from altered articulation of the facets on the transverse processes or the rib articulations on thoracic vertebrae. An X-ray would reveal an abnormal narrowing of the affected intervertebral space. **13**

The normal treatment for disk herniation is bed rest with the knees over a support (most herniations occur in the lumbar region, and this position produces a sort of traction). Sometimes a proteolytic enzyme (e.g., chymopapain) is injected into the core of the ruptured nucleus pulposus to hasten retraction and reconstitution of disk structure.

CENTRAL NERVOUS SYSTEM STRUCTURE AND FUNCTION

Metabolic Support: Cerebral Vasculature

Metabolism

The proper functioning of the central nervous system depends on appropriate blood supply and drainage. Three factors make the brain's continuous dependence on adequate blood supply more critical than that of any other organ. First, under normal dietary circumstances, the only fuel the brain is able to utilize for ATP production is glucose. (In a fast that lasts longer than three days, the brain will improve its ability to use fatty acids, products of fat breakdown, as an alternative fuel.) Second, there are no energy reserves in the brain analogous to the fat reserves in the body or the glycogen stores in the liver or skeletal muscle. This point leads directly to the third factor. The anaerobic capacity of neural tissue is very limited: the brain requires a constant supply of oxygenated blood. At the same time, the energy demands in the brain are extreme. It is a very metabolically active tissue.

What is this energy used for? Almost half goes to maintain the plasma membrane electrochemical gradients that are the basis of signal transfer. Another significant amount supports neurotransmitter manufacture and movement and the active transport of metabolites across the blood-brain barrier. These take place at comparable rates whether the brain is sleeping or alert and active. Because of these factors, the blood requirements of the brain are for a constant perfusion of 750–1000 ml per minute (about 15% of the resting cardiac output) for a tissue mass (1500 g) that is about 2% of the body's weight. As well, at rest almost 70% of the blood glucose and 25% of the oxygen carried are consumed by the brain. The only other organ that maintains such a steady metabolic rate is the heart, and, fortunately for the brain's glucose supply, the heart uses principally lipids during periods of low to moderate activity.

Cerebral Blood Flow

Cerebral blood flow (CBF), as we have noted, remains relatively constant. Factors both outside and inside the skull interact to maintain or challenge that constant blood flow. The overriding extracranial factor is the systemic blood pressure, monitored in the carotid baroreceptors at the vessels carrying the largest amount of blood to the brain. As well, there are vasomotor neurons in the medulla that fire in response to ischemia and massively increase sympathetic discharge. This is a backup system to ensure maintenance of cerebral blood flow. A second extracranial factor, cardiovascular function, is an issue when the cardiovascular system fails, as happens during ventricular fibrillation. The resultant brain ischemia can give rise to edema that can kill a person hours after heart function has been effectively restored.

Of intracranial factors affecting cerebral blood flow, the most important is **autoregulation.** This is an intrinsic capacity of healthy brain arterioles to regulate local blood flow, a capacity that they share, in degree, with arterioles in much of the rest of the body. There are two facets to autoregulation. First, cerebral blood vessels reflexively constrict when systemic blood pressure rises, thereby damping the potential increase in cerebral blood flow. Conversely, if blood pressure suddenly drops, as when a person quickly stands up, the vessels reflexively dilate, thereby compensating for the potential decrease in CBF. Second, when focused activity in one region of the brain increases its metabolic rate, and therefore its circulatory requirements, that region simultaneously increases its production of carbon dioxide, the single most potent dilator of cerebral blood vessels. The vessels in the area respond with vasodilation, increasing local perfusion and balancing glucose and oxygen requirements while clearing waste products. Decreasing pH and oxygen tension also cause vasodilation and local increases in CBF. Autoregulation can maintain a constant cerebral blood flow even though diastolic systemic pressure may go as low as 60 mmHg or as high as 140 mmHg. This capacity for autoregulation is lost in severely hypoxic tissue and can worsen the degree and effects of ischemia.

The second major intracranial factor affecting cerebral blood flow is the intracranial pressure itself. This pressure might rise because of an expanding tumor, edema, or perhaps a hemorrhage. As the pressure within the cranial vault approaches the diastolic pressure of the arterial blood, CBF will be progressively compromised. The difference between the systemic arterial pressure (SAP) and the intracranial pressure is the **cerebral perfusion pressure** (CPP): CPP = Mean SAP − ICP, where Mean SAP = 1/3 (Systolic − Diastolic) + Diastolic. The normal range of CPP is approximately 80–100 mmHg. If the CPP drops below 60 mmHg, ischemia will develop. The effects of the resulting hypoxia are most severe in the boundary zones between the major arterial fields, areas known as the watersheds. There are also specific anatomical sites whose neurons are particularly sensitive to hypoxia, for example the hippocampus (part of the limbic system and involved in memory and attention), the outer layers of the cortex, the sulci (grooves in the brain's surface), and certain critical cells in the cerebellum. A CPP of less than 30 mmHg is incompatible with life.

Cerebral Vasculature

As shown in figure 20.15a, the brain is supplied by two pairs of arteries. The internal carotid arteries (which together carry over 70% of the cerebral blood) branch from the common carotids, which in turn arise from the aortic arch (left common carotid) or the brachiocephalic artery (right common carotid). As the internal carotid arteries enter through special foramina into the cranial vault, they take an S-shaped detour through a blood-filled venous sinus called the cavernous sinus. This site is significant because a variety of cranial nerves course through the sinus. They are vulnerable to pressure from an aneurysm in the carotid artery or infection of the cavernous sinus. As the internal carotids finally pierce the dura and enter the area at the base of the brain, each branches to form the middle cerebral artery, **14** the anterior cerebral artery, **15** and the anastomotic posterior communicating artery.

The second pair of supply arteries are the vertebrals. These arise from the subclavian arteries, then pass up the transverse foramina in the cervical vertebrae and enter

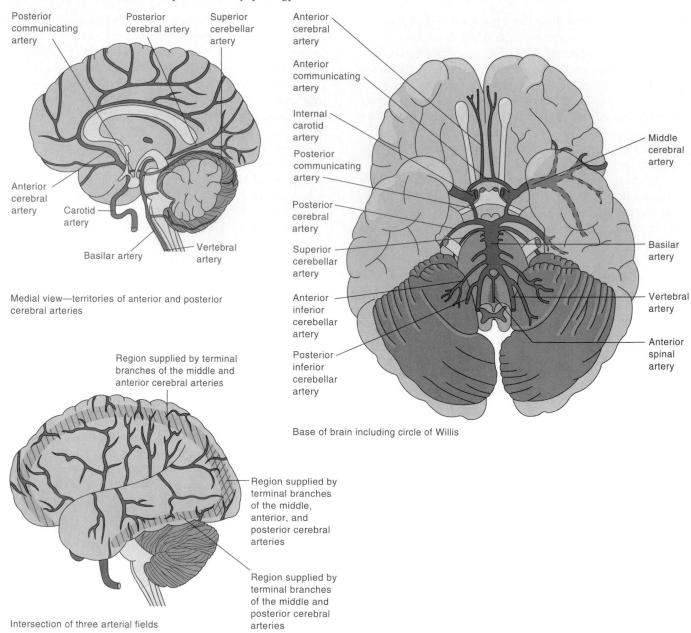

Medial view—territories of anterior and posterior cerebral arteries

Base of brain including circle of Willis

Region supplied by terminal branches of the middle and anterior cerebral arteries

Region supplied by terminal branches of the middle, anterior, and posterior cerebral arteries

Region supplied by terminal branches of the middle and posterior cerebral arteries

Intersection of three arterial fields

(a)

Figure 20.15(a)   Cerebral vasculature. (*a*) Arterial supply of the brain. In the intersection of three arterial fields, the area with cross-hatching is the watershed area.

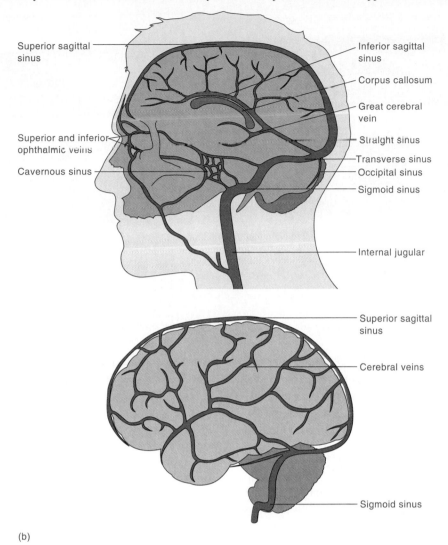

Superior sagittal sinus

Inferior sagittal sinus

Corpus callosum

Great cerebral vein

Superior and inferior ophthalmic veins

Straight sinus

Transverse sinus

Cavernous sinus

Occipital sinus

Sigmoid sinus

Internal jugular

Superior sagittal sinus

Cerebral veins

Sigmoid sinus

(b)

Figure 20.15(b)   Cerebral vasculature. (*b*) Venous drainage of the brain.

through the foramen magnum. They join to form the basilar artery, which throws off a variety of smaller arteries to supply the cerebellum and brain stem and finally branches into the two posterior cerebral arteries, which supply the posterior temporal lobe, the occipital cortex, and the posterior longitudinal fissure. The branches of the internal carotids and two posterior cerebral arteries contribute to a unique vascular structure, the cerebral arterial circle of Willis (**circle of Willis**). This interconnecting system probably serves no anastomotic role in the normal functioning of the cerebral vasculature (i.e., it doesn't shift blood back and forth to meet demands). However, in the event of obstruction of

a major cerebral artery, the alternative pathways it provides can make the difference between minimal functional loss and massive impairment. The details of the tissues supplied by specific arteries will be provided when we discuss cerebrovascular accidents.

The venous drainage of the brain is unique in that the veins have no valves and do not retrace the course of the corresponding arteries. Figure 20.15*b* shows the major venous sinuses that drain the bulk of the cerebral tissue. The superior sagittal sinus **16** is the site of uptake of the CSF in the arachnoid granulations. Many of the veins coming from deep in the tissue of the cerebral hemispheres

Figure 20.16   The blood-brain barrier compared with endothelial junctions in systemic capillaries.

course through the subarachnoid space to empty into this sinus. The blood passes posteriorly to the junction of the falx cerebri and the tentorium, where its flow is added to by blood passing from the inferior sagittal sinus through the straight sinus. The sinus then splits into a left and right transverse sinus, **17** **18** each of which takes an S-shaped course (now called the sigmoid sinus) **19** until it passes out of the floor of the cranial vault through the jugular foramen to become the left or right internal jugular vein. Other veins drain central structures of the cerebrum. Much of this blood passes backward into the great vein of Galen to join the blood from the inferior sagittal sinus in the straight sinus.

The Blood-Brain Barrier

The structure of capillaries in the CNS is quite distinct from that of capillaries in the rest of the body. The junctions between capillary endothelial cells in the brain are tight, unlike systemic capillaries; brain capillaries are surrounded by and encased in the foot processes of glial cells called astrocytes; mitochondria are more numerous in the endothelial cells of brain capillaries. These mechanisms all contribute to an effective **blood-brain barrier.** The tight junctions limit movement of solute and water, as these must pass through the endothelial cells, not through the junctions as can happen in other organs. The astrocytes form a transport system, picking up glucose, oxygen, and other metabolites and delivering waste products back to the capillary circulation. They also serve a structural support function (fig. 20.16). The endothelial mitochondria generate the ATP necessary to drive active transport. There is an analogous blood-CSF barrier that actively secretes the cerebrospinal fluid, which accounts for the fact that CSF normally has only 0.5% as much albumin as blood plasma.

The blood-brain barrier functions to exclude substances that are of low solubility in lipid (e.g., organic acids), highly ionized polar compounds, large molecules, and substances that are not transported by specific carrier-mediated transport systems. These would include albumin and substances bound to albumin (e.g., bilirubin, many hormones and drugs), many organic and inorganic toxins, and many drugs. Sugars, other metabolic substrates, and some amino acids have specific carriers within the endothelial cells. An example of a substrate normally excluded from the brain is penicillin. It is an organic acid that travels bound to albumin (a large molecule), and there is no transport carrier to move it into the brain. These factors limit its usefulness in treating CNS infection. Erythromycin, on the other hand, will easily pass through the capillaries. Dopamine, a neurotransmitter that is deficient in people with Parkinson's disease, will not pass, while L-DOPA, its precursor, will. In summary, these barriers provide a system that preserves homeostasis in the nervous system by facilitating access of necessary metabolites while, at the same time, blocking entry or promoting the removal of unnecessary metabolites or toxic substances.

Structure and Localized Function of the Brain

The Cerebral Cortex

Gray matter, whether of the superficial cortex or deep nuclei and central spinal cord, is the origin or destination and site of integration of all signals in the nervous system: it is the site of processing (fig. 20.17). White matter constitutes the pathways of intercommunication: it functions in relay. A lesion of gray matter obliterates the signal or its capacity to generate further signals; white matter lesions have the same effect by interrupting signal transfer.

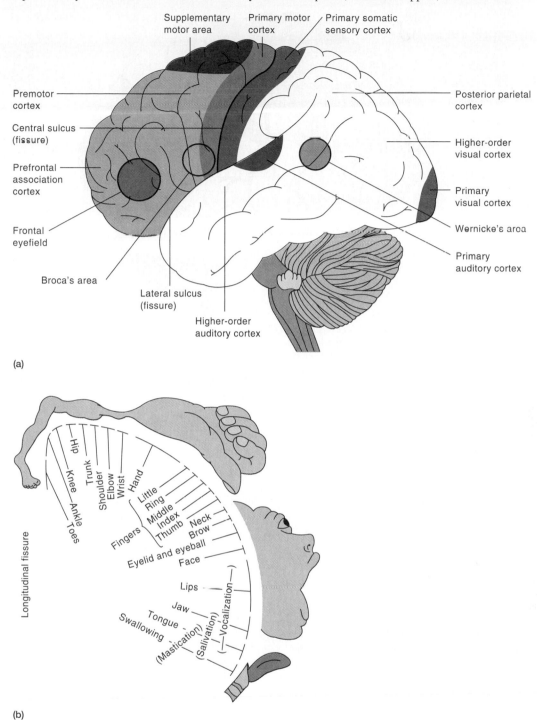

Figure 20.17   Cortical localization of function. (*a*) Lateral surface of cortex. (*b*) Motor "homunculus" (little man), picturing the relative size of areas of cortex dedicated to specific function.

The cerebral cortex **20** can be considered in terms of the territory supplied by a given major artery. The **middle cerebral artery** supplies the lion's share of the lateral cortex (fig. 20.18). Functions that are mediated here include skin sensations, voluntary movement and awareness of movement, particularly above the waist, hearing and the interpretation of sound, awareness of taste, the production and reception of spoken speech (usually concentrated on the left hemisphere), the interpretation and labeling of visual perceptions, aspects of the control of eye movements, and some of our capacity for planning and foresight. Except for language, which is localized in the left hemisphere (and perhaps specialized capacities for music, mathematics, and creative thought, which are understood to be

Figure 20.18 Territories supplied by the major cerebral arteries.

right hemispheric), these functional areas are on both lateral surfaces and act contralaterally (left hemisphere integrated with the right side of the body).

The territory of the **anterior cerebral artery** is largely the anterior two-thirds of the medial cortex. Functions here include voluntary movement, skin sensations and awareness of movement in the lower limbs, and an area with bilateral representation that is involved in the initiation of movements called the supplementary motor area. This artery carries perhaps 10% of the blood feeding the hemisphere and is proportionately as likely to be the site of pathology.

The **posterior cerebral artery** is part of an independent supply to the brain, the **vertebrobasilar system.** This feeds the primary visual cortex on the posterior medial surface and the posterior part of the corpus callosum (the splenium), which provides a pathway for the integration of images from both sides of the visual field (fig. 20.17). The vertebrobasilar system also supplies the cerebellum, the inferior temporal lobes, and the brain stem, sustaining the crucial functions of attention, arousal, and consciousness, as well as swallowing, breathing, adaptation of heart function, and less conscious aspects of movement. Gagging, vomiting, eye movement defects, dizziness, and altered patterns of breathing may all indicate a lesion that affects the brain stem, as may altered consciousness (see chapter 22).

At the margins of these adjacent vascular fields there is a C-shaped area termed the **watershed zone.** Because this area is at the furthest extent of the vascular tree, it is more susceptible to factors that interfere with oxygenation, particularly impaired cardiac function, where both blood

pressure and cardiac output are a concern. The classic problem here is the watershed zone infarct secondary to heart fibrillation, but infarcts may also be seen with carbon monoxide poisoning, near-suffocation, drowning, and severe anemia. Such infarcts **21** may be quite limited and confined to the watershed zone and certain other susceptible brain structures. Figure 20.19 shows atrophy secondary to a bilateral watershed zone infarct. As you can see by inspection of figures 20.17 and 20.18, the damage would have little effect on critical motor or sensory function. Dysfunction would be more subtle in these cases. However, sometimes a fairly dramatic disorder called **unilateral neglect** arises. This results from a white matter lesion in the watershed zone that interrupts the integration of visual and physical-sensory information in one hemisphere (in the parieto occipital area). **22** Affected individuals behave as though the opposite side of their body doesn't belong to them: the hair isn't combed and clothing is disheveled, even though motor control and sensation are intact. Other impairments of integrated function, like dressing or manipulating objects, can result from watershed zone and other scattered lesions. This is an example of a group of disorders often called **disconnection syndromes.**

Deep Nuclei and White Matter

Figure 20.20 shows some of the deep nuclei and white matter structures of the brain. The nuclei surrounding the third ventricle are vulnerable to hemorrhagic damage, particularly while the brain is developing (fig. 20.21). But while more prone to hemorrhage, the fetal brain is less susceptible

Figure 20.19   Watershed infarcts. This coronal section of the brain shows atrophy secondary to resolution of old watershed infarcts (arrows).

The darkened and collapsed regions in this photo are watershed infarcts, which were caused by a rapidly progressive cardiovascular shock that could not be corrected before becoming irreversible. The hypotension-sustained blood deprivation also caused focal infarction in the kidneys. The shock was the result of an explosion in a small gas stove that a 60-year-old man was refilling with fuel. He was severely burned and survived only three weeks.

to its consequences or can at least survive a hemorrhage that would prove fatal in an adult. This difference is due partly to the relatively low fetal blood pressure and the expandable nature of the fetal cranial vault, and partly to the plasticity of the developing nervous system. That is, if fetal brain tissues suffer hemorrhagic damage, their functions can apparently be assumed by healthy surviving tissue. In the adult, the blood from hemorrhage into brain tissue can travel to the third ventricle, where it meets only the resistance of the CSF pressure. Because of the rapid movement of blood at arterial pressure, the blood dilates the ventricles and transfers pressure to the brain tissue itself, producing a massive back pressure against normal perfusion. This and the attendant movement of brain tissue are enough to cause rapid death in any but the most minor of hemorrhages.

The internal capsule (fig. 20.20*b*) provides a massive conduit for information flow in the brain. Descending signals that produce movement and modify incoming information and ascending signals that carry sensation, arousal, and information about the effects of movement all travel in the internal capsule. A hemorrhage in the internal capsule is prone to dissect along the lines of these sensory and motor fibers and extend to greater distances than might be expected. As well, a relatively small lesion that blocks the path of the internal capsule can have effects on movement and/or sensation out of all proportion to its size.

Some conditions, for example hypertensive microaneurysms or leukemia, can cause widespread tiny hemorrhages into white matter which isolate scattered areas of gray matter. Each area is a lacuna, hence the descriptive name **lacunar syndrome.** Its symptoms are highly varied and often very challenging to identify.

GENERAL CNS PATHOLOGY

Edema in the CNS

Edema is an increase in tissue mass that results from the excess movement of body fluid from the vascular compartment or its abnormal retention in the tissue. Although the basic mechanisms creating CNS edema **23** are not unique to the CNS, certain conditions require that it be treated as a special case. For one, an increase in mass in the CNS, whatever its source, competes for the limited space within the meningeal and bony protection. The result may be destructive compression or movement of tissue or increased intracranial pressure (the next topic). For another, the CNS has no system for draining extracellular fluid that is analogous to the systemic lymphatics as already detailed. Most of the fluid that passes out of the capillaries to support neural function returns to the circulation via the capillaries and postcapillary venules. This dependence on adequate venous drainage is made more significant in the CNS by a relative absence of alternative anastomotic venous drainage. Blockage of veins or venous sinuses, such as may occur in thrombophlebitis, compression, or kinking due to shifts in tissue may rapidly induce edema, which can interfere with function and further complicate the picture.

These differences give rise to distinctions in patterns of edema that aren't made outside the CNS. **Vasogenic edema** is closest to the pattern of edema typical of inflammation in the rest of the body. It is largely confined to the white matter of the brain and spinal cord. In this case, something perturbs the usually intact blood-brain barrier. The agent might be inflammation associated with infection, a toxic agent that damages capillary endothelial cells, or the abnormally permeable capillaries that are stimulated by and supply a malignant neoplasm. (The latter is the most common cause of vasogenic edema.) These situations favor the outflow of small plasma proteins that would normally be confined to the vascular compartment. With the resultant change in osmotic gradients, there is a net flow of fluid into the intercellular space, which causes swelling. As well, the plasma filtrate accumulates in the extracellular spaces, where the altered ionic balance impairs function.

Cytotoxic edema is, by contrast, an intracellular phenomenon. The typical agent is hypoxia. This may be secondary to ischemia that results from a cardiac arrest. Near-drowning and strangulation are other causes of generalized hypoxia. Focal edema will result from partial occlusion of an end artery; again ischemia/hypoxia is the agent. Less common causes are toxic substances that directly impair the functioning of the sodium-potassium-ATPase pump or the metabolic processes that produce ATP. Since the neurons are the most active cells in the brain, cytotoxic edema tends

37799

1 Rostrum ⎤ of
2 Genu   ⎬ corpus
3 Body   ⎦ callosum
4 Cingulate gyrus
5 Precentral gyrus
6 Central sulcus
7 Postcentral gyrus
8 Calcarine sulcus
9 Cerebellum
10 Medulla oblongata
11 Median aperture
   of fourth ventricle
12 Fourth ventricle
13 Pons
14 Arbor vitae
15 Aqueduct ⎤
16 Inferior   ⎬ of
   colliculus ⎬ midbrain
17 Superior   ⎦
   colliculus
18 Splenium of
   corpus callosum
19 Fornix
20 Body of lateral ventricle
21 Thalamus
22 Hypothalamus
23 Pituitary gland
24 Optic chiasma

(a)

1 Insula
2 Putamen
3 Globus pallidus
4 Internal capsule
5 Caudate nucleus
6 Corpus callosum
7 Lateral ventricle
8 Septum pellucidum
9 Fornix
10 Interventricular foramen
11 Choroid plexus
12 Thalamus
13 Third ventricle
14 Inferior horn of lateral ventricle
15 Hippocampus
16 Pons
17 Pyramid
18 Substantia nigra
19 Red nucleus

(b)

Figure 20.20 (*a*) Sagittal and (*b*) coronal sections through the brain, showing relevant structures. The coronal section is through the interventricular foramen, midbrain, and pons.

Figure 20.21   Fetal brain showing hemorrhage in the area of the germinal eminence.
This brain came, not from a fetus, but from an infant born at 32 weeks. The difficulty in distinguishing between white and gray matter arises because the structures are not yet complete at this early point of development. Also typical of premature infants are the periventricular hemorrhages that are clearly visible. These, and a variety of kidney and heart problems, combined to overwhelm the infant, who was able to survive only nine days.

to be focused here. The swelling therefore is largely cellular. It should be noted that some authors differentiate cytotoxic from hypoxic edema. Although the agent (toxin versus hypoxia) is different, the cellular mechanism is the same, so they are grouped together here.

In practice, edema is often a result of both vasogenic and cytotoxic processes. For instance, temporary ventricular fibrillation that results in grossly impaired cerebral perfusion will probably induce both neural swelling and a transitory breakdown in the blood-brain barrier. Where this distinction may be particularly important is in the treatment of cerebral edema. When the edema is principally cytotoxic, that is, due to cellular swelling, passing a bolus of hypertonic solution, for example mannitol, through the cerebral vasculature will draw fluid out of the extracellular space. By reducing extracellular volume, this procedure will make more room for the swollen cells. As well, it will increase the osmotic concentration of the extracellular fluid, thereby arresting or reversing the movement of water into the cells. However, if the blood-brain barrier were defective, as for example in the swollen tissue of a neoplastic growth, this strategy could instead add to the problem. Mannitol would move into the extracellular space and, since it would act as an additional osmotic attractant, it would add to the swelling.

Increased Intracranial Pressure

The intact cranium and associated dural sheath are essentially inexpandable. The spinal dural sac in its protective vertebral cage is capable of a small amount of distention.

These boundaries contain three incompressible elements: CNS tissue, cerebrospinal fluid, and blood. Expansion of any one of these elements must be balanced by proportional constriction of either or both of the other two, or there will be an increase in intracranial pressure. This relationship is known as the **Monro-Kellie hypothesis.**

The normal intracranial pressure is between 5 and 15 mmHg. (For reference, this is slightly higher than venous pressure, but considerably lower than mean systemic arterial pressure of about 95 mmHg.) Minor natural fluctuations occur that are linked to the respiratory cycle and the 24-hour cycle of rest and wakefulness. These largely reflect changes in intrathoracic venous pressure and resultant changes in CSF reabsorption. During exhalation there is a temporary increase in intrathoracic pressure. Reclining facilitates venous return from the extremities, which leads to a slight pooling of blood and an increased central venous pressure. Both of these impair cerebral venous drainage and thereby the reabsorption of CSF.

An increase in CSF, according to the Monro-Kellie hypothesis, will lead to an increase in intracranial pressure (ICP) unless blood is expelled or brain tissue shrinks. Slightly increased ICP is what is observed. The same mechanism is responsible for the brief increase in ICP that is observed during the Valsalva maneuver (attempting to exhale against a closed glottis), coughing, sneezing, or straining at stool. Some of the potential increase is absorbed by the temporary distention of the spinal dural sac. These situations also generate brief increases in blood pressure and volume that are conducted to large and mid-sized cerebral arteries. For this reason they are to be avoided by people at risk of cerebral hemorrhage as well as those with increased ICP. (For example, stool softeners are prescribed for constipation.)

Chronically increased systemic arterial pressure has little impact on CSF volume and ICP because of the reflex constriction of precapillary arterioles that results in constant cerebral perfusion. However, supplying air enriched in carbon dioxide, such as used to be done for a patient with a recent cerebrovascular accident in an effort to improve perfusion of surviving tissue, can raise ICP. The carbon dioxide powerfully dilates arterioles, including those of the chorionic villi, which increases CSF production. By contrast, hyperventilation reduces PCO_2 and increases pH, which leads to arteriolar constriction and reduced CSF production. Decreasing blood and CSF volumes can bring down ICP, and mechanically-assisted hyperventilation is commonly used to control increased ICP.

Increased ICP is a potential complication of a variety of pathological conditions. CNS edema and tumor masses are increases in CNS tissue volume that must be compensated for by expansion of the spinal dural sac and decreases in CSF and blood volume, or they will raise ICP. A slowly growing mass can also be accommodated by reabsorption of adjacent cranial bone. Such bone erosion is detectable in X-rays or CT scans and is suggestive of a tumor. Blocked venous return can increase ICP by impeding CSF reabsorption or generating edema, as can heart failure. Hemorrhage into tissue, or the subarachnoid space, or a subdural or extradural hematoma creates a trapped mass of blood that can increase pressure. If the source is arterial, this rise can be dramatic. Finally, increased CSF and hydrocephalus (see later discussion) can be responsible for raising ICP.

The mechanisms that can dangerously raise ICP—edema, tumor, hematoma, hydrocephalus, venous obstruction, and increased CSF volume—often produce their effects in a gradual, linearly increasing fashion. Rising ICP can be countered by specific compensations: expansion of the spinal dural sac, decreased CSF and blood volume, bone erosion, and atrophy of neural tissue. These compensations are capable of accommodating quite large increases in brain mass with little increase in ICP. This phase of the potential danger is sometimes referred to as stage 1.

As the mass continues to increase, a point is reached when compensatory capacity is exceeded. The result is a gradually rising ICP, characteristic of stage 2. As ICP rises, effective cerebral perfusion pressure drops. The resulting decrease in oxygenation stimulates the vasomotor centers in the medulla to induce peripheral vasoconstriction and to temporarily increase cardiac output through increased sympathetic discharge. The result is increased mean systemic arterial pressure and net cerebral perfusion pressure (treated in detail earlier in this chapter). If the source of pressure is a tumor, brain oxygenation will improve on a transitory basis. If it is a hemorrhage, however, the increased blood pressure will exaggerate the problem. It is likely that a patient will have lowered consciousness by stage 2.

Stage 3 establishes the conditions for a very rapid increase in ICP. This is sometimes called the point or stage of **decompensation.** Autoregulation is lost, so increased arterial pressure is expressed in an increased blood volume in the brain. Hypoxia, which has worsened with the rise in ICP and the drop in cerebral perfusion pressure, leads to generalized cytotoxic edema and further increases in ICP. Coma deepens. Respiratory drive depends increasingly on arterial carbon dioxide levels, a system that normally acts as an "emergency backup." A pattern called **Cheyne-Stokes respiration** results: a period of apnea (15–60 seconds) is followed by deep, labored breathing that gradually becomes shallow and then apneic again. During the apnea, carbon dioxide accumulates until it triggers another breathing cycle, which clears the carbon dioxide and removes the drive to breathe. The raised arterial pressure that was caused by brain stem hypoxia and peripheral vasoconstriction stretches the pressure receptors in the carotid arteries. They signal the cardiac centers in the medulla, which in turn induces bradycardia.

Stage 4 is reached when the cerebral perfusion pressure falls below 30 mmHg, and widespread necrosis begins.

Compression of brain stem respiratory centers will then lead to respiratory arrest and death.

A quick assessment of ICP can be made by viewing the optic disk of the retina. In the past, ICP was directly assessed by performing a lumbar puncture. This procedure, however, creates the risk of making a zone of lower pressure below the foramen magnum, into which delicate brain and brain stem tissues may be driven by the higher pressure in the cranium. Now ICP is measured by drilling a small burr hole through the skull and introducing a pressure transducer, often into the space between the skull and the dura mater. Alternatively, it may be placed under the dura, or a large-bore needle may be introduced into a ventricle.

Where it is not possible to remove the cause of increased ICP, treatment consists of taking comfort measures while it runs its inevitable course. With treatable or reversible conditions a variety of strategies are employed. It may be necessary to supply mechanical hyperventilation to a medicated and comatose patient. Blood pressure is reduced by the use of diuretics, to slow CSF production and reduce brain-blood volume. Drugs, usually barbiturates, are administered to slow brain metabolism so that hypoxia has a less destructive effect. An emergency craniotomy may be done to relieve pressure. The availability of ongoing monitoring and these other procedures may be critical to survival in cases where severely increased ICP may be a complication, as in near-drowning, carbon monoxide poisoning, prolonged cardiac arrest, and bacterial meningitis.

Herniation Syndromes

The correspondence between physical features of the brain and their adjacent bony and meningeal structures can produce a potential for lesion. Recall, for example, the situation of the brain stem in the tentorial notch. In general, any focal, expanding mass, whether edema, a tumor, or an area of hemorrhage, generates pressure on adjacent tissue. This sort of **compression syndrome** can result in localized impairment of function. It can also displace tissue, in which case it is referred to as a **herniation syndrome.**

If the increase in mass is in the frontal lobe, it can push the lower gyrus of the medial cortex, the cingulate gyrus, under the barrier of the falx cerebri (fig. 20.22). Such a **cingulate herniation** 24 occurs deep in the longitudinal fissure and produces ambiguous symptoms until it is well advanced: clouded consciousness, perhaps partial complex seizures (see chapter 22). In another kind of herniation, a mass above the tentorium may push the medial temporal lobe down over the edge of the tentorium. A small hillock of tissue, the uncus, normally projects over the free edge of the tentorium. Since the uncus leads the advance of herniating tissue, this pattern is called **uncal herniation.** 25 If swelling is either massive or generalized, the compression

Flattened gyri and decreased subarachnoid CSF

Cingulate herniation

Midline shift and distortion of ventricles

Uncal herniation (transtentoral)

Midbrain pushed against tentorium compressing cerebral peduncles; tension on cranial nerves

Foramen magnum

Skull

Dura

Falx

Expanding extradural hemorrhage

Tentorium cerebelli

Central (tonsilar) herniation

(a)

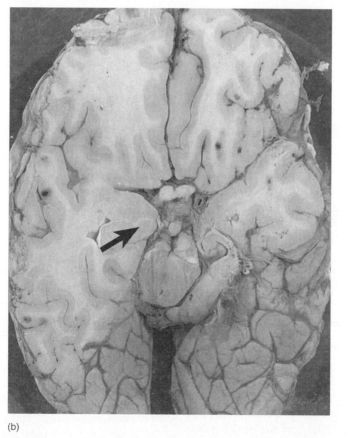

(b)

Figure 20.22 (*a*) The herniation pattern that might accompany the evolution of a massive extradural hematoma. A generalized swelling, on the other hand, may not produce a midline shift but would compress the ventricles and cause uncal and tonsillar herniation. (*b*) Photo of a transverse section of a brain with fatally increased intracranial pressure. Uncal herniation is apparent at the arrow.

The enlarging mass of a glioblastoma, combined with cerebral edema that developed in response to it, led to the brain herniation pictured here. Midline distortions are the result of displacement by the enlarging tumor, which cannot be seen in this section. These distortions of the brain contributed to the death of a 76-year-old woman who developed left-sided paralysis and hemianesthesia prior to her death.

and herniation can be focused on the only sizable exit from the cranial vault, the foramen magnum. This condition may be referred to as **central herniation.** Because the midline cerebellar tissue, descriptively called the cerebellar tonsils, leads the advance and directly compresses the brain stem, it is also called **tonsillar herniation.** **26**

In the context of central herniation, you may encounter the term **coning,** as in cerebellar coning. This outmoded usage implies that the concave cranial vault focuses the tissue displacement into a "pressure cone" that is some distance from the expanding lesion, much as rays of light are focused by a magnifying glass. In reality, pressure is conducted through the relatively soft brain tissue in the same way that it is conducted through fluid. As noted, the spinal dural sac is subject to slight expansion. What might be abnormally elevated but otherwise evenly distributed intracranial pressure is thereby focused at the foramen magnum as brain stem and cerebellar tissue move downward.

If the agent causing the increased pressure is generalized, e.g., edema due to hypoxia, brain displacement may be very even. Gyri may be flattened and sulci difficult to discriminate. The ventricles will be smaller as CSF is reduced to accommodate increased brain mass. If the pressure source is focal, chances are it will produce midline deviation. This may be detectable as off-center ventricles on a CT scan or a ventricle with an obvious protrusion into it. If the herniation causes kinking of the veins draining the central parts of the brain (where the great vein of Galen joins the straight sinus in the tentorium, fig. 20.15*b*), edema can rapidly add to the expanding mass. Kinking or compression of the cerebral aqueduct will impede CSF outflow and lead to a rapid increase in ICP.

Hydrocephalus

The term **hydrocephalus** indicates an increase in the volume of the cerebral ventricles. **27** **28** It is used whenever in the life span this condition might occur. A CT scan or MRI would reveal enlarged ventricles, their shape and evenness dependent on the cause of the hydrocephalus. There are three possible mechanisms: oversecretion of CSF, impaired absorption of CSF, and obstruction of CSF pathways.

Oversecretion, perhaps due to a tumor of the choroid plexus, is rarely encountered. Absorption of CSF can be impaired in many ways. Anything that raises venous pressure (e.g., venous or venous sinus thrombosis or severe congestive heart failure) will interfere with CSF reabsorption at the arachnoid granulations. These can be plugged or impeded by the protein and cellular and molecular debris that are produced in meningitis or subarachnoid hemorrhage, or by the high-protein CSF that may be produced from a spinal cord tumor or in Guillain-Barré syndrome. In

obstruction, the pathways for the circulation of CSF can be blocked or narrowed sufficiently to produce back pressure in the CSF and distend the ventricles. The obstruction might result from a tumor or from fibrosis associated with inflammation and infection, or it might be the result of congenital malformation. If the ventricular enlargement is due to a loss of cerebral mass, such as might be the case in advanced Alzheimer's disease or adjacent to an old infarct, the condition is not accepted as hydrocephalus proper. Instead, it is sometimes called **hydrocephalus ex vacuo.**

Hydrocephalus can have the same clinical presentation while having varied causes. One example is a child who displays the **congenital** or **infantile** pattern of hydrocephalus. This child may be born with or develop an enlarged head (giving rise to the term overt hydrocephalus) with thinned skin over the cranium. The ventricles can be massively enlarged, with a corresponding thinning of the white matter. Since the fetal skull is normally deformable because of the cartilaginous fontanelles, **29** distention of the ventricles can occur with little corresponding increase in intracranial pressure. Hence there are few of the complications you might expect. As well, because of the plasticity in localization of function that appears to characterize the developing nervous system, normal function is possible as long as correction of the hydrocephalus is achieved before irreversible damage has occurred. Infantile hydrocephalus may result from impaired CSF reabsorption, which is perhaps due, in turn, to fetal or neonatal meningitis or hemorrhage. Alternatively, it may result from a congenital malformation that obstructs CSF circulation. An example is failure of development (atresia) of the foramina that allow CSF to exit from the fourth ventricle to the subarachnoid space. Two conditions to be discussed later—Dandy-Walker syndrome and Arnold-Chiari **30** **31** malformation (fig. 20.23)—may compress these foramina or the aqueduct of Sylvius, producing the same effect.

Children and adults are also subject to a number of nondevelopmental disorders that can produce hydrocephalus, by one or another of the three mechanisms that have been described. When the condition develops acutely, it is the resultant increase in ICP that creates a clinical emergency. Such a condition is referred to as **tension hydrocephalus.** Overproduction of CSF is very rarely the mechanism, while obstruction of CSF pathways is most common. The blockage is often at the cerebral aqueduct, and is often caused by a tumor mass or focal edema, but it may also be at the third ventricle, in the subarachnoid space, or in the arachnoid granulations. The inaccurate term "noncommunicating" hydrocephalus is sometimes applied to those cases in which the obstruction is more extensive. Complete obstruction (true "noncommunication") will cause fatally raised ICP in a matter of hours. Almost all hydrocephalus is in fact "communicating."

26 18291   **27** 17815   **28** 34688

29 44583   **30** 30273   **31** 5227

(a)

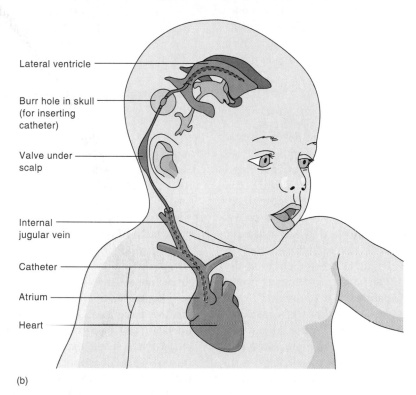

Lateral ventricle

Burr hole in skull
(for inserting
catheter)

Valve under
scalp

Internal
jugular vein

Catheter

Atrium

Heart

(b)

Figure 20.23   Hydrocephalus. (*a*) Enormous expansion of the lateral ventricle due to obstruction associated with Arnold-Chiari malformation. Vessels lie in the medial wall of the ventricle. (*b*) Placement of a ventriculo-atrial shunt.

A child born with Arnold-Chiari syndrome had at birth an unusually large head, which continued to expand, reaching enormous size. He had only a small degree of motor activity, and even this declined. Only brain-stem level functions were sustained for six months until his death. The photo shows the left half of the brain, with cerebellum and pons visible in the lower section. Above is the enormously distended space formed by the lateral and third ventricles. The cerebral tissue is present only as a thin shell a few millimeters thick. The clearly defined blood vessels lie in the medial wall of the ventricle.

528   Part Two   Systemic Pathophysiology

Some adults have enlarged ventricles without an increased ICP. They also may be confused or demented, walk with difficulty, and have lost bladder control. Such **normal-pressure** or **normotensive** hydrocephalus is now thought to have resulted from a temporarily raised intraventricular pressure that stabilized and dropped. The response to shunting is excellent.

Shunting is the provision of an artificial passage for CSF flow to detour an obstruction. This is the treatment of choice for infantile hydrocephalus. As just noted, it is effective in reversing the symptoms of normal-pressure hydrocephalus. With cases of simple obstruction, e.g., aqueductal atresia, the shunt may consist of a short by-pass. With more complex obstruction or where CSF reabsorption is impaired, a sterile tube is laid from the lateral or third ventricle to the right atrium (ventriculoatrial shunt) or abdominal cavity (ventriculoperitoneal shunt), where a one-way valve permits CSF outflow. An alternative is to place the shunt from the lumbar cistern, the same region from which a lumbar puncture is taken, to the abdominal cavity (lumboperitoneal shunt).

Coma

Normal and altered consciousness, and the description of the neurological structures that mediate consciousness, are covered in chapter 22. There the principal focus is the level of consciousness before, during, and after a seizure. But consciousness is affected by a wide variety of other medical conditions. The mechanisms responsible and the parts of the nervous system affected will vary with the disease. Remember that consciousness is a state of functioning of the nervous system, and that it can therefore be profoundly disrupted by a fully reversible and even very limited lesion.

It is not unusual for a patient to be delivered to the emergency ward in a coma, the lowest level of consciousness, without benefit of a witness who knows the circumstances surrounding the coma. This situation presents a critical diagnostic puzzle. The possible causes range from alcohol or barbiturate overdose through craniocerebral trauma, stroke, epilepsy, or bacterial meningitis, to diabetes, kidney failure or heart disease. A sophisticated knowledge of the patterns of coma characteristic of each of these disorders guides the emergency room staff in arriving at an appropriate diagnosis and treatment plan. In general, the basic emergency interventions and the assessment of level of consciousness are similar from case to case. A patent airway is assured; cardiorespiratory status is assessed (Is the patient in shock? Is breathing adequate?); if bleeding has occurred, steps are taken to prevent further blood loss; and blood chemistry is assessed (e.g., blood glucose).

Table 20.1	Terminology Commonly Employed in Differentiating Levels of Consciousness
Term	**Comments**
Normal consciousness	Patient fully responsive, with same awareness of self and surroundings as examiner.
Inattention	Patient has difficulty identifying and attending to relevant stimuli.
Confusion	Thinking is slower and less clear, patient is easily distracted.
Clouding of consciousness (obtundation)	Inattention and confusion are more profound; rousing patient is more difficult.
Stupor	Physical and mental activity at a minimum, persistent and vigorous stimulation needed for arousal, patient orients to examiner but responds minimally.
Coma	Patient can't be aroused, but may produce patterned behavior if stimulus is intense.

The description of level of consciousness requires some precision, as it indicates the status of the patient's medical condition and reflects the response to treatment (table 20.1). The most critical concern is with the patient who is in the deepest levels of stupor or coma itself. A widely used and effective scheme for standardizing the description of level of consciousness is the Glasgow Coma Scale, presented in table 20.2. It can be used with little instruction to give a regular (perhaps hourly) score that will reflect the progress of the condition or treatment.

The depth of coma is variable and is reflected in the level of integration of the response to stimulation. In the lightest levels of coma, the response may be integrated and purposive, e.g., the examiner's hand may be pushed away. In somewhat deeper coma, withdrawal of a stimulated limb will be observed. The movement is largely reflex in nature. At deeper levels, only reflex behavior can be elicited, although a patient may still moan or stir in response to painful stimulation or a distended bladder. As coma becomes more profound, normal neuromuscular reflexes may be replaced by more primitive ones. For example, the response to firmly drawing a sharp object up the lateral surface of the sole of the foot changes from plantar flexion (normal plantar reflex) to a fleeting dorsiflexion (extension) of the great toe with fanning of the other toes. This is called the **Babinski sign** or a positive Babinski and would be the normal reflex elicited in an infant below 18 months. In the

Table 20.2	The Glasgow Coma Scale

The patient is rated on all three scales and scores summed. The total (3 = deep coma, 15 = normal consciousness) is recorded.

Eyes Open

Never	1
To pain	2
To verbal stimuli	3
Spontaneously	4

Best Verbal Response

No response	1
Incomprehensible sounds	2
Inappropriate words	3
Disoriented and converses	4
Oriented and converses	5

Best Motor Response

No response	1
Extension (decerebrate rigidity)*	2
Flexion abnormal (decorticate rigidity)*	3
Flexion withdrawal*	4
Localizes pain	5
Obeys	6
Total	3–15

* These terms are explained in table 20.3.

deepest levels of coma, no reflex response is elicited even with intense painful stimulation, generated by pressing a pencil against the base of the fingernails (nailbed stimulation), pressing the thumbs into the orbits, or squeezing the testicles of a male.

For intense stimulation to elicit a reflex neuromuscular response, the reflex arc must be intact. That is, sense organs that pick up the stimulus must be functioning, and likewise the pathway that carries this signal, the center that mediates the reflex, the pathway that carries the signal out, and the structures that express the reflex. When using reflex responses, the examiner must be confident that the absence of a response is due to a lesion in the CNS where the reflex is mediated, rather than in reception or expression. Table 20.3 describes a variety of automatic or reflex behaviors that are commonly used to assess consciousness or localize the site or spread of a lesion in the CNS, particularly in the brain stem.

DEVELOPMENTAL ANOMALIES: NEURAL TUBE DEFECTS

The central nervous system is one of the first structures observable in the developing embryo. By day 18 of gestation, the pancake of cells that will produce the body's organ systems, the embryonic disk, has begun developing a longitudinal **neural plate.** Ridges form along the margins of the length of this plate and thus produce a central **neural groove.** This deepens while the ridges grow to meet in the center, creating a **neural tube** that will subsequently elaborate to form the primary structures of the CNS. Associated islands of tissue running parallel and lateral to the neural tube contribute other central and peripheral nervous system structures, the muscles that some of them supply, and the vertebral column and bones of the skull.

The formation of the neural tube begins at the level of what will become the brain stem and then proceeds both rostrally and caudally. The rostral or cranial extent of the tube, which is completed and closes about day 26, produces the brain, while the central lumen and lining give rise to the system of ventricles. The caudal extension of the tube forms the spinal cord with its small central canal and is complete about day 30 (fig. 20.24).

The development of the neural tube can be interrupted at any point, producing a defect, whereafter the tube may form normally. Moreover, the disruption may range from very limited, perhaps a defect in skull closure or formation of a single vertebral arch, to extensive, for example, failure of brain development. Neural tube defects are responsible for the majority of fetal deaths and are an important source of congenital malformations and perinatal illness and death. They appear in a total of about 2 per 1000 live births in the United States and Canada.

For the most part, conditions arising from neural tube defects are named descriptively, and the more limited the defect, the less serious and disabling the resultant condition. A general term referring to problems in the caudal neural tube is **spina bifida,** so named because the vertebral arch, which fails to close completely, may produce two palpable bases instead of the single, central spinous process. **Spina bifida occulta** is the least serious of these conditions. It is often asymptomatic, perhaps noted incidentally in an X-ray or at physical exam. In many cases, a mole with a tuft of coarse or silky hair or a small birth mark is evident over the vertebral column. Sometimes chronic back pain, enuresis (urinary incontinence), cold feet, or lateness in learning to walk is traced to this minor vertebral arch defect.

Table 20.3	Functions or Reflexes Commonly Used to Assess Consciousness or Localize the Site or Spread of a Lesion to the CNS

Breathing Patterns

Normal breathing depends on a complex of stimuli in which both P_{CO_2} and P_{O_2} are important. Rhythms are generated in the respiratory center in the medulla, and respiratory rate and depth are modified by the apneustic center in the pons.

•Slow breathing	May indicate opiate or barbiturate intoxication.
•Rapid breathing	May be due to metabolic or respiratory acidosis or a lesion that isolates the apneustic center.
•Cheyne-Stokes respirations (CSR)	Slow increase in rate and depth of respiration, which peaks and wanes, and is followed by 10–60 seconds of apnea. Due to bilateral cerebral lesion or metabolic disturbance. Respiration driven by P_{CO_2}, which increases in apnea and begins respiratory drive. May be accompanied by snoring, so-called "death rattle."
•Central neurogenic hyperventilation (CNH)	Also called Kussmaul respiration. Regular, increased rate and depth of respiration without pause. Due to lesion in lower midbrain or upper pons (respiratory center in medulla released from control of apneustic center).
•Biot breathing	Sometimes called ataxic breathing. Chaotic breathing rhythm, each breath varies in rate and depth. Lesion in the medulla. (Sometimes CSR changes to CNH and then to Biot as thelesion extends from upper to lower brain stem.)
•Apneustic breathing	Pause of 2–3 seconds after full inspiration. Lesion in lower pons (apneustic center does not function to limit inspiration).

Visual System—Eye Movements

•Corneal reflex	Stimulus: stroke conjunctiva with a wisp of cotton. Normal response: reflex eyeblink. Sensation travels via facial (fifth) cranial nerve, reflex is effected via oculomotor (third) cranial nerve. Lesion of either nerve or nucleus abolishes reflex.
•Pupillary response	Stimulus: shine bright light into one retina. Normal response: stimulated pupil constricts (direct reflex) and unexposed pupil constricts to same degree (consensual reflex).
•Doll's eyes	Stimulus: tilt the cradled head of patient. Normal response: compensatory eye movements (eyes will continue to look up despite position of head). Underlying mechanism maintains an image in the center of the retina (fovea) by moving eyes in the direction opposite and to the degree the head moves. Signal from semicircular canals is processed in the vestibular nuclei (dorsal-lateral junction of pons and medulla). Lesion abolishes doll's eyes.
•Caloric test	Stimulus: irrigate ear canal of reclining patient with cold water. Normal response: nystagmus—fast flicking (beating) of the eyes— away from the stimulated side. Warm water produces nystagmus toward stimulation. Same mechanism as doll's eyes. Temperature change in semicircular canal mimics fluid movement during head movement; lesion at pons-medulla junction abolishes response.

Neuromuscular Reflexes

•Babinski sign	Stimulation of lateral surface of sole of foot elicits plantar flexion in normal or light coma, fleeting extension of great toe and fanning of toes in deeper coma.
•Flexor withdrawal	Painful stimulation of limb evokes withdrawal in lighter coma.
•Decorticate rigidity	May occur spontaneously or in response to painful stimuli or passive movement; may be unilateral or bilateral. Posturing involves arm adduction, flexion at elbows, wrists, and hands; may include extension of lower limbs, plantar flexion of feet. Lesion has functionally isolated the cerebrum from the brain stem above the midbrain. Deepening coma progresses to decerebrate rigidity.
•Decerebrate rigidity	Stimuli same as decorticate rigidity. Posturing includes opisthotonus (rigidity and hyperextension of vertebral column), extension of arms with flexed, inturned wrists/hands, lower limbs extended, feet plantar flexed, toes inturned. Unilateral or bilateral. As in decorticate, may be sustained or fleeting response to stimulus or spontaneous. Isolation of higher function is between pons and midbrain.
•Primitive reflexes	These can emerge in lighter coma and in conditions with severe cortical impairment, e.g., late Alzheimer's disease. Characteristic of newborns, later inhibited. Rooting—turning mouth towards stimulated cheek; grasp (Darwinian) reflex—hand will close when palm stroked; sucking elicited by stroking cheek or object in mouth; Moro (startle) reflex—sudden change of posture, loud noise, or vibration elicits violent extension and then flexion of all limbs.

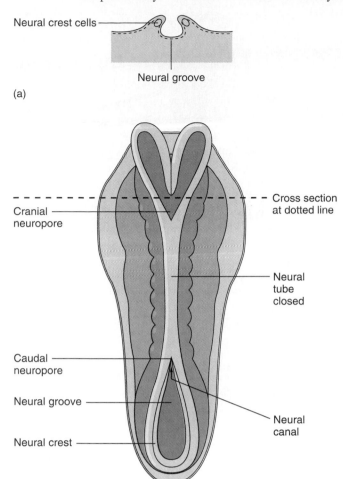

Neural crest cells

Neural groove

(a)

Cross section
at dotted line

Cranial
neuropore

Neural
tube
closed

Caudal
neuropore

Neural groove

Neural crest

Neural
canal

(b) 22-day-old embryo

Figure 20.24 (*a*) Cross section of the closing neural tube at the same level as (dotted line in *b*), showing neural groove and neural crest cells. (*b*) Embryo at 22 days. Much of the neural tube has closed. The cranial and caudal neuropore are in the process of closing.

More extensive arch, meningeal, and cord malformations exist. One of these, **meningocele,** occurs with equal incidence at cervical, thoracic, or lumbar regions of the spine. A sac containing CSF, lined with meninges and usually covered with intact skin, protrudes from the vertebral column defect. There may be no neurological deficit, and surgical correction is often very successful. Such intervention is advisable because any breach in the skin may provide a portal for infection. The resulting spinal meningitis could readily spread to the cranial meninges, and secondary encephalomyelitis (infection of the brain and cord tissue) is a distinct risk. The protruding meningocele is also vulnerable to trauma, another argument for surgical correction. Figure 20.25 provides a diagrammatic overview of neural tube defects expressed in the spinal cord, and figure 20.26 shows an infant with meningocele.

In **meningomyelocele,** [32] there is a similar protrusion, but it contains spinal nerves and part of the cord (or the cauda equina in the lumbar area) as well as the

meninges and CSF. The condition may also be called myelomeningocele or spina bifida cystica. In this situation, fully normal neurological function is rare, and there is an increased tendency for loss of CSF and risk of infection. The majority of cases are in the lumbar and lumbosacral regions, and in about half of these there is an associated brain stem defect called **Arnold-Chiari malformation.** Arnold-Chiari (II) is the specific form encountered. It is characterized by a lengthening and downward displacement of the vermis and tonsils of the cerebellum. These midline and medial structures are not accommodated in the abnormally small and shallow posterior fossa and pass through the enlarged foramen magnum to form a mass at the foramen magnum and over the upper cervical cord. An abnormal kink at the junction of the medulla and cord often combines with the foregoing herniation to produce hydrocephalus. As previously noted, hydrocephalus refers to any abnormal increase in the brain's cerebrospinal fluid volume. In this case, normal circulation is impeded by compression of the cerebral aqueduct. CSF then backs up and dilates the ventricles. Surgical introduction of a shunt may be required to manage the hydrocephalus. Besides Arnold-Chiari malformation, some meningomyelocele is complicated with encephalocele, yet to be described.

Neurological function below the meningomyelocele is usually altered. Partial or total paralysis (paraplegia) is common, as is partial or complete sensory loss. Voluntary control of bowel and bladder is often impaired. Sometimes there is an obliteration of bowel and bladder reflexes if the areas of the cord mediating these are involved. The impaired emptying that results may lead to bladder and bowel complications, for example, chronic bladder and kidney infections. The cord and nerve root lesions that are responsible may have been caused by a combination of impaired development, physical trauma due to displacement into the sac or consequent tension and abrasion, impaired perfusion, and/or fibrosis secondary to infection.

Another term you will sometimes see is **syringomyelocele.** In this condition, the central canal of the spinal cord is massively dilated, with parts of the dorsal cord protruding into the CSF-filled sac.

While meningomyelocele is found in a relatively high proportion of live births (about 0.3 per 1000), **anencephaly** (at between 0.5 and 2 per 1000) is the most common neural tube defect. It is also the most profound compatible with survival to term. This is one of a group of neural tube defects that arise with a failure of the development of the cranial neural tube. In anencephaly, the roof of the cranium is missing, and there is only a small, undeveloped vascular mass lying in the base of the skull. Brain stem development may be normal and functional, so that while many victims are stillborn, some are capable of breathing and reflex swallowing. Although controversy exists around the care of these newborns, the common resolution is to maintain hydration and a humane level of physical care. Survival is usually only for a few hours or days. The rate of

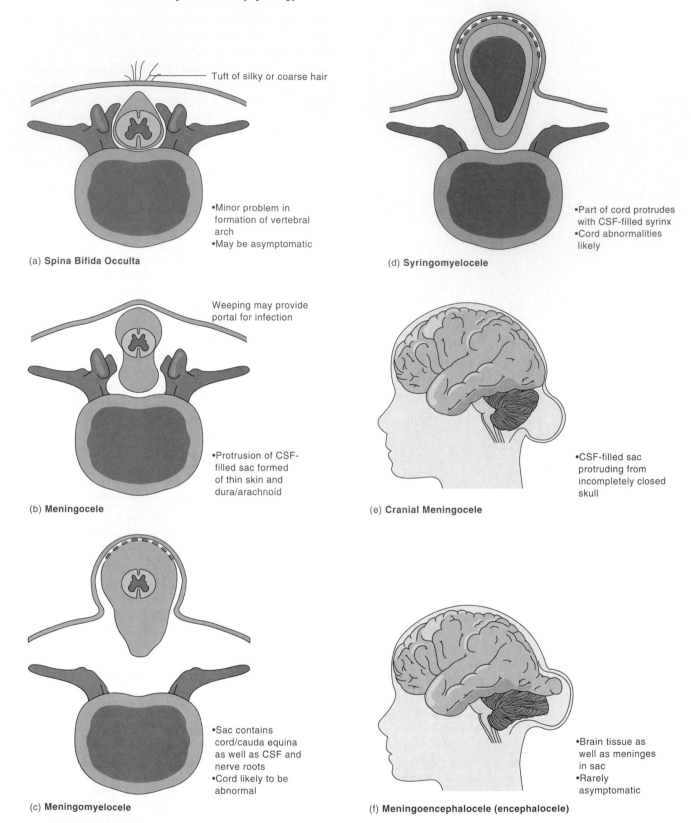

Tuft of silky or coarse hair

•Minor problem in formation of vertebral arch
•May be asymptomatic

(a) **Spina Bifida Occulta**

Weeping may provide portal for infection

•Protrusion of CSF-filled sac formed of thin skin and dura/arachnoid

(b) **Meningocele**

•Sac contains cord/cauda equina as well as CSF and nerve roots
•Cord likely to be abnormal

(c) **Meningomyelocele**

•Part of cord protrudes with CSF-filled syrinx
•Cord abnormalities likely

(d) **Syringomyelocele**

•CSF-filled sac protruding from incompletely closed skull

(e) **Cranial Meningocele**

•Brain tissue as well as meninges in sac
•Rarely asymptomatic

(f) **Meningoencephalocele (encephalocele)**

Figure 20.25   Neural tube defects. Spina bifida refers to problems in the formation and closure of the caudal neural tube and neuropore. Cranial meningocele and encephalocele result from problems in rostral neural tube/neural pore.

Figure 20.26   Meningocele.

anencephaly varies rather dramatically, with Wales and Ireland showing peaks of up to 7 per 1000 live births. This variation raises the possibility that the condition is a response to some factor in the environment. On the other hand, the 3–7-fold preponderance among female fetuses provides some balance of evidence for a genetically mediated basis. As with many developmental anomalies, solid explanations for an individual case are often elusive.

Cranial meningocele describes a meningocele in the cranial region. About 60% of those who are born with this condition and undergo surgical correction develop normal neurological and intellectual function. **Meningoencephalocele,** less accurately but more commonly called **encephalocele,** is a rarer condition (1 in 6500 live births). For the three-quarters of cases in which the defect is located in the occipital region, **33** it is also more disabling, with only 10% developing normally after surgical correction. Those with the encephalocele into the nasal cavity or through the frontal or parietal bones have a somewhat better prognosis.

Dandy-Walker syndrome may be rarely found in association with any of the above or on its own. This is an impairment in the development of the midline cerebellar structures. **34** Instead there may be a cystlike structure in the center of the posterior cranial fossa. Hydrocephalus is found. Although impairment of function is variable, gait and eye movement disorders are common, as these are mediated by the midline cerebellum. Children born with this syndrome are also susceptible to seizure disorders.

Most neural tube defects can be detected prenatally by assaying maternal blood for α-fetoprotein. This substance is elevated in a normal pregnancy at weeks 16 to 18. It is produced by the fetus during neural tube and nervous system development and crosses the placental barrier into the mother's circulation. It is released in larger amounts when

there are neural tube defects. Amniocentesis gives more accurate estimates of α-fetoprotein, and ultrasound can be used to detect major defects in the fetus.

The Arnold-Chiari and Dandy-Walker syndromes are often presented as posterior midline defects rather than neural tube defects proper. In specialized settings, it is common to encounter numerous other abnormalities of skull and brain development, but they are outside the scope of this text.

CEREBROVASCULAR DISORDERS

This section will focus on a range of disorders that can bring people into cerebrovascular care or complicate their treatment for other conditions. You will be provided with a fairly brief treatment of topics including cerebral aneurysm, vasospasm, arteriovenous malformation, and thrombophlebitis. Then you will find a more extensive discussion of transient ischemic attacks and cerebrovascular accidents.

Cerebral Aneurysm

A **cerebral aneurysm** is a distention of a cerebral arterial wall that develops at a point of weakness. **Berry aneurysms, 35 36** which tend to develop at points of bifurcation, initially appear as small balloons (berries). **Saccular** or **fusiform aneurysms,** as the name suggests, are elongated dilatations developing along an artery and may be 3 cm or more in diameter. **Microaneurysms** may be found diffusely in the brain. The weakness that sets the stage for the development of berry aneurysms is usually thought to be a developmental defect in the muscle layer of the arterial wall, in which case the aneurysm may be present from a young age. Or the weakness may be due to wear and tear associated with hypertension (saccular and microaneurysms) or possibly head injury. Most berry aneurysms, about 90%, develop in or near the circle of Willis (fig. 20.27). Most other aneurysms (except microaneurysms) are located within the subarachnoid space. Berry and microaneurysms are often completely asymptomatic, breaking their silence only if they happen to hemorrhage.

Large aneurysms behave like space-occupying lesions, which means that they can displace and compress nerves, nervous tissue, or other blood vessels. The signs and symptoms will depend on the size and location of the aneurysm: possibly cranial nerve dysfunction, headaches, lethargy, neck pain, perhaps a **bruit,** that is, a noise detectable over the site of the aneurysm, due to turbulence of the blood passing through. Although they may cause problems at any age, middle age is the most common time for aneurysms to enlarge or, more seriously, to rupture. Hemorrhage **37** of preexisting aneurysms is the usual cause of bleeding

(a)   (b)

Figure 20.27   (*a*) Diagram of common sites for the development of Berry aneurysms. The size of the aneurysm reflects its relative frequency. (*b*) Berry aneurysm of the basilar artery, filled with coagulated blood.
This photo shows a ruptured berry aneurysm, filled with thrombus, which caused the death of a 53-year-old woman. It projected upward to block the outflow of CSF from the lateral ventricles, causing hydrocephalus to develop. Two years later, confusion and drowsiness prompted a scan of the ventricles. This revealed the hydrocephalus and a smooth round mass thought to be an inoperable tumor. The obstructed CSF was by-passed to the subarachnoid space and she recovered. Soon after, however, symptoms recurred, the aneurysm ruptured, and she died. The error of diagnosing the aneurysm as a tumor might well have been avoided with more sophisticated imaging, but it was not available.

into the subarachnoid space. Such bleeding is accompanied by violent (explosive) headaches, and by symptoms of nerve root irritation due to the blood in the CSF. These include stiff neck, Kernig's sign, and Brudzinski's sign, which will be described in the section on CNS infection. Mortality is in the range of 20–40%. If the hemorrhage occurs into the brain tissue, there is a rapid development of symptoms: explosive headaches again, and decreased level of consciousness as the intracerebral hematoma enlarges, leading to a mortality in the vicinity of 70%. This pattern is an example of a hemorrhagic cerebrovascular accident and will be discussed in more detail later.

Hemorrhage, as described, is a serious potential complication with cerebral aneurysms. Although a person may survive or recover from such a bleed, the risk of a serious, perhaps fatal rebleed is high. Increased intracranial pressure, either with larger aneurysms or a hematoma, can be another serious complication. As well, cerebral aneurysms make an individual vulnerable to chronic or transitory cerebral hypertension. For this reason, control of essential hypertension is crucial. The person should also avoid any condition that raises intrathoracic pressure, for example straining at stool or exerting force with a closed glottis (Valsalva), as well as circumstances that tend to temporarily raise systemic blood pressure, for example stress, emotional shock, etc.

Subarachnoid Vasospasm

Subarachnoid vasospasm is a transitory constriction or narrowing of an artery or branch of an artery. It may be localized or affect a large section of the artery. Of patients with subarachnoid hemorrhage, 30–50% will experience subsequent vasospasm, frequently in the vicinity of the ruptured aneurysm. It is a common potential complication (65%) of surgery done to evacuate a hematoma or correct an aneurysm. An initially localized constriction can spread to become a diffuse vasospasm that can lead to significant ischemia. The signs and symptoms will depend on the territory subjected to hypoxia and the duration of the vasospasm, with death being a possible outcome. A common occurrence with people surviving an intracerebral hemorrhage (with possible associated vasospasm) is that about ten days later there is a serious rebleed. At this point, vasospasm can again be a significant complication.

The pathogenesis has the following course. Although the initiation of subarachnoid vasospasm can apparently be spontaneous, most often it is in response to the irritation of blood breakdown products in the subarachnoid space. The vasospasm produces a decrease in cerebral blood flow that can complicate existing cytotoxic edema in damaged tissue. The subsequent swelling adds to the mass of the original bleed and further increases the intracranial pressure. In turn, a generalized drop in cerebral perfusion pressure will occur, with possible effects on cerebral blood flow.

Figure 20.28   Section of cerebrum with a moderate-sized arteriovenous malformation (arrow). Death was due to massive hemorrhage from this AVM.
Two seemingly unrelated cerebrovascular accidents, separated by 41 years, are involved in this case. At 25 this man suffered a cerebral hemorrhage from an arteriovenous malformation in his right parietal lobe. He recovered but suffered from residual partial paralysis and periodic seizures. At age 66 a berry aneurysm ruptured, causing the escape of blood into the ventricle pictured here. To the left is the cyst formed at the site of the earlier AVM bleed.

Vasospasm can put an additional stress on vasculature so that local autoregulation is lost as well. Through this chain of events it is possible that a relatively small, asymptomatic subarachnoid bleed could lead to subarachnoid vasospasm, thence to cerebral ischemia and a much broader pattern of symptoms.

Arteriovenous Malformations

An **arteriovenous malformation** (AVM) is a tangled mass of dilated blood vessels that pass from large or medium-sized arteries directly into a vein or venous sinus, by-passing the normal capillary bed (fig. 20.28). They range from small local lesions to networks that may cover an entire hemisphere. They are varied in shape and location as well. They may be restricted to the subarachnoid space or dura, or they may form a cone-shaped tangle that extends from the surface of the cortex deep into the cerebrum. **38 39 40** Dural AVM may have several arterial feeders. The veins or venous sinuses draining an AVM may be dilated or even form aneurysms because of the abnormally high pressure in the venous system.

Arteriovenous malformations are a congenital anomaly. As such, they grow in step with the developing nervous system, and even very large ones can be accommodated without disrupting normal neural function. The structure of the vessel walls is also often abnormal, particularly with advancing age, being more permeable and more subject to hemorrhage.

AVM can cause problems in a number of ways. The blood shunted through the AVM is by-passing the tissue surrounding or underlying it. Especially if the AVM becomes progressively dilated, the result can be ischemia in that tissue. Second, the AVM itself and the dilated vein or venous sinus can compress adjacent tissue. Hemorrhage is the major potential complication. Depending on location and severity of the bleed, it could result in vasospasm (irritation), dissection and destruction of brain tissue, or the formation of an expanding hematoma. Particularly if an AVM aneurysm or expanding AVM mass deep in brain tissue is located above or surrounding the brain stem, compression of the cerebral aqueduct can lead to hydrocephalus and increased intracranial pressure.

Parallel to the varied routes of pathological impact, there can be widely varied signs and symptoms. Ischemia can lead to symptoms similar to those found in occlusive cerebrovascular accident (more later in this section). Local compression can give rise to a host of problems. Seizure activity due to local changes in brain tissue (e.g., gliosis, proliferation of glial cells) is one of the most common symptoms found with AVM. Headaches may be experienced. A bruit may be heard over the AVM. If there is a bleed from the AVM into the subarachnoid space, xanthochromia (yellow coloration of the CSF) will be detectable.

Figure 20.29   Principal venous structures involved in thrombophlebitis of the cavernous sinus.

With regard to complications of AVM, there is a steadily increasing potential for (further) hemorrhage. As well, the continued expansion of the AVM, dural sinus, vein, or venous aneurysm has attendant effects on local compression of vessels, nerves, or brain tissue, and, as an expanding lesion, can increase intracranial pressure. Treatment of these congenital abnormalities may involve the introduction of small Silastic beads that occlude the AVM, use of proton beam radiation, or surgical excision.

Intracranial Thrombophlebitis

Intracranial thrombophlebitis is a condition marked by inflammation and clot formation in the dural venous sinuses, and perhaps invading the cerebral veins. It most often arises as a result of infections of the middle ear, the mastoid air cells within the temporal bone, the paranasal sinuses, the scalp, or the skin around the upper lip, nose, and eyes. Such an infection can enter the lymphatic vessels in the veins draining these structures and generate an inflammatory response in the walls of the veins, producing conditions that favor thrombosis. The thrombophlebitis may then extend along the emissary veins linking these areas with the dural sinuses. For example, an infection in the upper lip may cause thrombophlebitis in the facial vein, which then extends along the ophthalmic vein into the cavernous sinus (fig. 20.29). Left and right cavernous sinuses communicate via the intercavernous sinuses, through which thrombophlebitis then commonly spreads. The infection that causes the thrombophlebitis may alternatively have been introduced during a basal skull fracture or a skull fracture, tearing the dural venous sinuses themselves.

Streptococci and staphylococci are the bacteria most often responsible. Figure 20.29 shows the principal venous structures that may be implicated.

Signs and symptoms will depend to a certain extent on the site of the thrombophlebitis. A history of infected middle ear, mastoid bone, nose, face, or scalp is common, as is generalized headache. Also, **papilledema**—a swelling of the region of the retina where the nerves and vessels enter the eye (due to impaired venous drainage into a thrombosed cavernous sinus)—as well as eye movement abnormalities and pain (due to pressure on the third, fourth, sixth, and ophthalmic division of the fifth cranial nerves) and edema in the eyelids may be present. If the thrombophlebitis is interfering with venous drainage of cortical tissue, the resulting back pressure will in turn impede arterial supply. Other effects may include focal abnormalities (due to local cortical hypoxia) and seizures.

In some cases, thrombophlebitis spreads to adjacent sinuses, thereby increasing obstruction to venous flow. Cortical infarction can result if drainage of cortical tissue is seriously compromised by the involvement of cerebral veins. The introduction of infectious agents frequently complicates these cases with other forms of intracranial infection (e.g., meningitis and brain abscess).

Cerebrovascular Accidents

Cerebrovascular accidents (CVAs) afflict approximately half a million North Americans a year. Although more a disease of aging people, no age group is spared. About one-third of those suffering a CVA (or "stroke") will die from it. Many of those who survive will be physically and socially disabled. On the positive side, there has been a significant decline in the incidence of CVA over the last 30 years, which is possibly due to more effective antihypertensive therapy. As well, with appropriate nursing and medical care, potential secondary complications of CVA can be limited and the post-CVA recovery enhanced.

What differentiates CVA from the other vascular disorders just reviewed is that the sudden onset of symptoms and neurological impairment associated with CVA are due directly or indirectly to a deficiency in blood supply. The "deficiency" can range from a transitory interruption that temporarily affects function to a permanent disruption that leads to necrosis of cerebral tissue and even death. Two mechanisms can alter blood flow: occlusion and hemorrhage.

Occlusive strokes can develop because an embolism lodges in a narrowing arterial vessel, obstructing downstream blood flow. More commonly the obstruction has evolved at the site as a thrombus has formed about an atheromatous plaque. Hence we have two forms of occlusive CVA: embolic and thrombotic. "Little" strokes that affect only function and last from a few minutes to less than a day are called transient ischemic attacks (TIAs). They are usually seen as symptoms associated with developing thrombosis and are therefore often classified as minor thrombotic CVA. Hemorrhagic CVAs can range from petechial to massive, with parallel damage to the CNS. They can result from hypertensive intracerebral hemorrhage (most commonly) or from a ruptured cerebral aneurysm or arteriovenous malformation.

Occlusive CVA: Transient Ischemic Attacks

Cerebral **transient ischemic attacks** (TIAs) are episodes of neurological dysfunction that develop suddenly, last from five minutes to usually less than one hour (never more than 24 hours), and clear completely. Certain risk factors for TIAs are common to *all* CVAs, presumably because they are related to the development of cerebral vascular disease: hypertension, heart disease, elevated plasma cholesterol, diabetes mellitus, atherosclerosis, increasing age, oral contraceptives, and smoking (particularly in combination with oral contraception use in women over 35).

In 80% of people suffering a thrombotic CVA, there has been a history of one or more TIAs. This connection is rare (some say nonexistent) in other forms of CVA. The relationship of TIA to the developing thrombosis is, however, not entirely clear. It may be that bits of the thrombus (aggregated platelets, fibrin, and entrapped red blood cells) break off and are carried downstream to some point in the vascular bed (thromboemboli). These microemboli rapidly fragment and are then transported through the capillary bed and into the venous circulation. The usually suspected site of the primary thrombus is at the bifurcation of the common carotid artery (just below the rear angle of the jaw). Other sources of emboli are the left atrium (emboli thrown off during atrial fibrillation), thrombotic plaques formed on and then thrown off the mitral valves, and thrombi forming in the left ventricle as a result of endocarditis or myocardial infarction.

This account doesn't explain the common finding that successive TIAs often present with the same symptoms. How does a thromboembolism randomly end up plugging the same field in the arteriolar bed? An explanation consistent with this recurrence is that cerebral blood vessels are diseased and irritated beyond the site of the thrombosis. These areas induce an intermittent vasospasm, which, by reducing blood flow, leads to ischemia. Whether the immediate cause is embolism or vasospasm, the subsequent ischemia and hypoxia lead to the appearance of symptoms that are reversible when blood flow returns to normal.

The symptoms associated with TIA depend on the arteries involved. If the ophthalmic branch of the internal carotid artery is involved in embolism, the person might experience **amaurosis fugax** (literally, fleeting blindness). It will appear to the person as though a shade is being pulled down or up over one eye. When the microembolism clears the retinal capillary bed, vision will return to normal. Symptoms of cerebral ischemia in part of the field of the anterior or middle cerebral arteries may include contralateral monoparesis (weakness or paralysis of one limb) affecting the lower limbs (with anterior cerebral artery occlusion) or hemiparesis affecting both limbs (with middle cerebral artery occlusion), localized tingling numbness, loss of vision in the left or right visual field, or aphasia (impaired language capacity). TIA of the vertebrobasilar arterial system may include drop attacks (the person suddenly loses postural tone in the legs), bilateral visual disturbance (dim, gray, or blurry vision or even total blindness), diplopia (double vision), vertigo, nausea, or dysarthria (difficulty forming or enunciating words).

By definition, there are no neurological impairments left when the TIA resolves. Nevertheless, a recent onset of TIAs is grounds for great concern. Since most TIAs are apparently related to evolving thrombotic lesions, there is always the danger of continued development of the thrombus, which may lead to permanent cerebral infarction. Note, however, that people do experience TIA without going on to develop full-blown thrombotic CVA.

Occlusive CVA: Thrombotic CVA

A **thrombotic CVA** involves permanent damage to part of the brain, caused by ischemia that has resulted from the thrombotic occlusion of an artery. This is the most common form of CVA and is related to the risk factors cited earlier. The thrombosis is usually due to atherosclerosis, very often associated with hypertension, diabetes mellitus, and coronary or peripheral vascular disease. Alternatively, trauma to the head or neck may cause thrombosis of major arteries and subsequent CVA.

Area supplied by middle cerebral artery

End arteries to basal ganglia and internal capsule

Middle cerebral artery

Cortex partially protected

Area of infarct

Occlusion of artery

Figure 20.30   Internal structures supplied by end arterial branches tend to be more vulnerable to local arterial occlusion, while the cortex often has protective anastomoses. Arrows indicate this collateral perfusion. The occlusion pictured is of a major branch of a middle cerebral artery.

A thrombus (often at the bifurcation of the internal carotid or middle cerebral artery) usually takes a long time to develop, perhaps many years, and is usually asymptomatic until there is major stenosis of the arterial lumen. At this point the symptoms of extreme ischemia will evolve over minutes or hours. Occasionally the stroke progresses stepwise for a period of days or weeks (this condition is often called stroke-in-evolution). Anything that lowers systemic blood pressure will exacerbate the symptoms of ischemia (e.g., acute myocardial infarction, heart block, shock, surgical anesthesia, too vigorous treatment of chronic hypertension). The slight hypotension that prevails in sleep accounts for the fact that about 60% of thrombotic CVAs occur during sleep.

The area affected by the CVA will depend on the distribution of the artery occluded and the degree of anastomosis by other cerebral arteries. Internal structures supplied by end arterial branches are particularly vulnerable because there is little anastomotic supply from other arteries. Some of the cortex supplied by the occluded artery is protected from ischemic infarction by anastomoses of other cerebral arteries (fig. 20.30).

The functional areas that immediately succumb to the CVA are typically much larger than the actual brain tissue that is infarcted. The edema responsible for much of this disruption results from two mechanisms. In the center, hypoxia compromises ATP production so that cytotoxic edema occurs (the neuronal and glial cells allow the influx of sodium and associated chloride and water, and thereby swell). This process is compounded by the loss of autoregulation. The same tissue vasculature loses its normal response to lowered oxygen, increased carbon dioxide, and increased lactic acid. So there is no compensatory dilation of arterioles and consequently no increase in blood flow. Formerly, carbon dioxide was administered to thrombotic CVA patients with the idea that this would increase focal

vasodilation in the infarcted area. In fact, the reverse occurs: normal tissue is better perfused and the blood is diverted away from the infarcted area. At the margins of the infarcted zone, maximum vasodilation results from lactic acid formed during anaerobic glycolysis. This marginal region is then the site of vasogenic edema (arterioles dilate, tight junctions between capillary endothelial cells loosen). Besides broadening the area of functional impairment, this edema can contribute to increased intracranial pressure and consequent decreased cerebral perfusion pressure. This can, in turn, exaggerate the focal ischemia, or even precipitate further sites of thrombotic CVA.

Further serious complications may evolve in cases of extensive cerebral edema: displacement of brain tissue, herniation syndromes, possible brain stem herniation and death. Cerebral edema reaches its peak at 72 hours and resolves in approximately two weeks (fig. 20.31). Only then can the extent of infarction be known. Some people who experience profound temporary disablement, e.g., complete right hemiplegia and loss of speech, may recover with barely detectable sequelae. Once having had and survived a thrombotic CVA, however, a patient is at risk of suffering another.

The symptoms associated with thrombotic CVA will, to a large extent, depend on the specific area infarcted, although clinical syndromes will often overlap to some degree. Table 20.4 lists the symptoms that correlate with specific arterial occlusions. This information is of direct relevance to embolic and hemorrhagic CVA as well. Some of the terms will look unfamiliar, but do not be concerned at this point. The details of motor and sensory abnormalities are described in chapters 21 and 23, respectively.

Cerebral tissue that becomes infarcted undergoes a pattern of necrosis and resolution that is unique to the central nervous system: **liquefaction necrosis.** The support structure of organs outside the CNS is largely composed of a variety of connective tissue elements, both cells and extra-

(a)

(b)

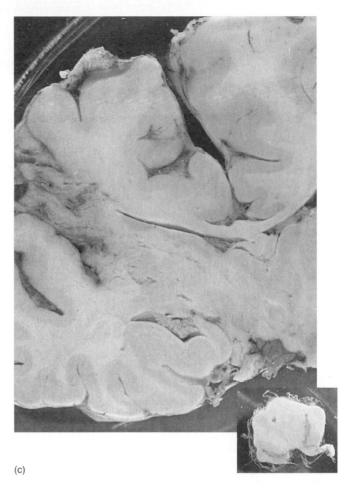

(c)

Figure 20.31   Progression of a thrombotic CVA in the region supplied by the middle cerebral artery. (*a*) Edema and functional loss decline, but some loss remains after resolution. (*b*) Recent infarct in right cerebral hemisphere (left center). (*c*) Infarct after resolution (left center). Inset shows degeneration and atrophy in the corresponding cerebral peduncle.

Thinning of the cortex and discoloration of the white matter deep to it can be seen in this eight-day-old infarct of the right cerebral hemisphere. The brain section is from a 71-year-old woman who was severely injured when she fell down stairs. She soon lost movement of her left arm, and after eight days, surgery was necessary to resect a segment of bowel infarcted by an embolus from her heart, which had formed as a consequence of cardiac trauma caused by the fall. She died in hospital as a result of bronchopneumonia. The infarct was yet a another sequela of the fall.

cellular matrix, and injury/necrosis results in an increase in these, through scarring. Except for the meninges and blood vessels, the CNS contains no connective tissue. The bulk of the brain and cord is made up of cells, particularly astrocytes and oligodendrocytes. Necrosis in the neurons and these glial support cells leads to their enzymatic and phagocytic destruction. Rather than being replaced by connective tissue as would happen elsewhere, they are replaced by a fluid-filled cyst. The area of necrosis may initially be pale to dark red (hemorrhagic infarct). **41** The process of degradation takes some weeks, leaving a brownish soup that is eventually replaced by a clear, straw-colored fluid. In the surviving tissue adjacent to an area of injury or necrosis, there will be proliferation of astrocytes, a process called astrocytosis or gliosis.

Occlusive CVA: Embolic CVA

An **embolic stroke** results when an embolus, usually a fragment of a thrombus located in the heart, lodges in a brain artery and creates ischemia that leads to an infarct. The second most common form of CVA, it is often associated with atrial fibrillation, a condition favorable to both the formation of thrombi in the atrium and their fragmentation. Another source of emboli is a mural thrombus associated with either myocardial infarction or endocarditis. Less commonly, bone fracture may allow marrow fat cells to enter the sinusoids in the medullary cavity and thereby the venous circulation. Fat emboli tend to lodge in the lung but are deformable and can pass through the lung vessels to reach the brain. Other emboli are tumor cells and septic

Table 20.4	Clinical Syndromes Produced by Occlusion of the Cerebral Arteries

Artery	Region Supplied	Symptoms Produced
Internal carotid artery (supplies both the anterior and middle cerebral arteries)	Frontal, parietal, and temporal areas; basal ganglia; internal capsule; optic nerve and retina.	**Acute:** coma, aphasia (if dominant hemisphere), contralateral hemiplegia, hemianesthesia, and homonymous hemianopsia, ipsilateral blindness. **Chronic:** transient attacks of hemiparesis, hemianesthesia, etc., and monocular visual disturbances (amaurosis fugax).
Anterior cerebral artery	Anterior part of internal capsule, tip of frontal lobe, anterior two-thirds of medial surface of cerebral hemisphere.	Dementia, confusion, or coma; contralateral hemiplegia and sensory loss affecting primarily the leg; urinary incontinence.
Middle cerebral artery	Lateral cortex and much of white matter of frontal, parietal, occipital, and tip of temporal lobes. Perforating branches supply internal capsule, basal ganglia, and anterior thalamus.	Syndrome similar to internal carotid occlusion or stenosis except for absence of visual disturbances. **Total occlusion:** coma, contralateral facial weakness, hemiplegia, hemianesthesia, and homonymous hemianopsia with aphasia (if dominant hemisphere). **Occlusion of part of the territory:** partial contralateral involvement; sensory loss and weakness affecting arm more than leg.
Posterior cerebral artery (supplied by the basilar artery, which is supplied by the vertebral arteries)	Midbrain, posterior part of thalamus, posterior part of internal capsule, base and posterior two-thirds of temporal lobe, medial surface of occipital lobe (visual cortex).	**Infarction of thalamus:** contralateral hemianopsia and hemianesthesia. **Occlusion of branch to midbrain:** ipsilateral eye movement defects and contralateral hemiplegia with or without contralateral tremor.
Basilar artery (vertebrobasilar system)	Structures of the posterior fossa (pons, medulla, cerebellum); inner ear.	Clinical criteria of disease in basilar system: (1) signs of abnormality involving 3rd–12th cranial nerves in any combination, 3rd, 6th, 7th most commonly, (2) cerebellar dysfunction, and (3) various signs of upper motor neuron lesion. Some examples of symptoms associated with interruption of circulation: stupor or coma, eye movement defects, ipsilateral Horner's syndrome,* drop attacks, ataxia, complex sensory defects, dysphagia, dysarthria.

* Horner's syndrome—eye affected has a narrowed pupil (miosis), the conjunctiva is reddened, the eyelid may droop (ptosis), the same side of the face is noticeably dry. This is due to an interruption of sympathetic supply to that side of the face.

emboli (particularly the vegetations associated with infectious endocarditis—composed of infectious bacteria, fibrin, platelets, and red blood cells). Some emboli will arise intracerebrally from a developing thrombus or from a thrombus at the carotid bifurcation.

The mechanisms of pathological impact on brain structure and function are identical with those in thrombotic CVA once occlusion has been achieved: ischemia, broad functional loss, edema and infarction, resolution of edema, and then permanent functional loss. The feature that differentiates embolic CVA is the rapid development of symptoms (within seconds to one minute) and the absence of immediate warning signs (although embolic TIAs are sometimes seen, and one embolic CVA will often be followed by others). Emboli arising in the heart or passing the lung most often enter the brain via the internal carotid artery and tend to pass directly into the middle cerebral artery, as this is the most direct path of blood flow with the largest volume. Emboli entering through the vertebral arteries tend to lodge in the vascular bed of the posterior cerebral arteries for the same reasons. For symptoms consult table 20.4.

Hemorrhagic CVA

Hemorrhagic CVA causes infarction by interrupting blood flow to a region of the brain downstream from the hemorrhage. Further damage is done if the hemorrhage creates an expanding hematoma, creating local shifts in tissue and perhaps elevating intracranial pressure. As well, the high-pressure pool of arterial blood can dissect delicate cerebral tissue, causing widespread damage (fig. 20.32). Intracerebral hemorrhages, often associated with hypertension, result from the rupture of a small penetrating arteriole, often in the putamen **42** (one of the basal ganglia) or the thalamus. In the posterior fossa, the pons and cerebellum are preferred sites. The onset of symptoms is rapid, but less abrupt than with embolic CVA, often evolving over an hour or two. Elevated blood pressure is evident in most cases and BP may continue to rise as the stroke develops. About half of the individuals will report severe headache. The symptoms associated with hemorrhage into specific sites are presented in table 20.5 (again, explanations of some terms are postponed).

The intracerebral bleeding often enters the ventricles. **43** There, as well as coloring the CSF (xanthochromia), it often causes rapid escalation of intracranial pressure. In about 70% of cases of intracerebral hemorrhage, the hematoma continues to expand and thus leads to destruction of vital brain centers and/or to large shifts of brain tissue, brain stem herniation, stupor, coma, decerebrate rigidity, and death.

CNS INFECTION

Any interruption of the vascular, meningeal, and bony protection of the CNS can expose the brain and its meningeal tissues to infectious agents. Compared with the incidence of infection in the rest of the body, CNS infection is relatively rare. When it occurs, however, the effects can range from unpleasant but fully reversible, as is the case with some viral infections, to catastrophic. The protection that serves so well in isolating the CNS from infection has the downside of isolating an established infection from normal access and attack by the immune system. As well, it sometimes frustrates the pharmacological support that would effectively assist in the elimination of a systemic infection. Because there are growing numbers of people with chronically suppressed immune function (e.g., transplant recipients, people with AIDS), the management of nervous system infections is an expanding problem.

With any such infection, rapid identification of the infecting agent is a crucial first step. As described at the beginning of this chapter, usually a lumbar puncture is performed to determine the specific agent. The CSF findings associated with bacterial meningitis were noted earlier, in the discussion of meningeal protection. Viral meningitis produces a lymphocyte-rich exudate. Assuming that the agent is one for which effective therapy exists, treatment according to the sensitivities of the organism cultured must begin without delay.

Infections of the central nervous system may be limited to the subarachnoid space (**meningitis**), may affect the meninges and adjacent brain tissue (**meningoencephalitis**), may be focused in the brain tissue (**encephalitis**) or cord (**myelitis**), or may be focal (**abscesses**). The infective organisms, the mechanisms establishing infection and producing pathology, and the pathologic outcomes can be quite distinct.

Acute Bacterial Meningitis

Acute bacterial meningitis **44** (also called **pyogenic meningitis**) presents a true medical emergency. If it is untreated, 50–60% of cases are fatal, and even with aggressive medical care 5–6% succumb. The subarachnoid space, which is the focus of this infection, is continuous around the brain, spinal cord, and optic nerves. The CSF there contains very few lymphocytes and very little complement or antibody to attack microorganisms, but it does have glucose and electrolytes that can act as a medium. Any microorganism gaining entry can multiply and spread through the CNS with little host defense. Once established, an infection will induce an inflammatory response, producing the cellular and then fibrinous exudate that give the

Table 20.5	Symptoms Associated with Hemorrhage into Specific Sites in the Brain and Brain Stem

Site	Symptoms
Putamen or internal capsule	Flaccid hemiplegia, hemianopsia, tonic deviation of eyes to injured side, speech is slurred, Babinski sign.
Thalamus	Eyes may be deviated downward, hemorrhage may compress internal capsule causing hemiplegia and hemianesthesia.
Pons	Paralysis of conjugate gaze, pupillary miosis (constriction), flaccid quadriplegia, absence or weakness in response to caloric testing, absence of doll's eye responses, often coma.
Cerebellum	Headache, vomiting, inability to walk or unsteadiness of gait, collapse.

Figure 20.32   Coronal section through the ventricles of a brain after a fatal hemorrhage. The approximate course of the expanding/dissecting intracerebral hemorrhage from the putamen through the internal capsule into the left ventricle is indicated by the dotted line.

This large hemorrhage in the left cerebral hemisphere has ruptured into ..the lateral ventricle. The victim was a 79-year-old male who was driving home from a wedding when his wife noticed him acting strangely. He was unable to find his way home without her direction. On finally arriving, he went to bed, but next morning was deeply comatose; his pupils were fixed and neither plantar nor brain stem reflexes could be elicited. His left side was found to be flaccid when he was admitted to the hospital, and he died a few hours later.

condition its name (fig. 20.33). As well, veins and arteries traveling in the subarachnoid space become inflamed (vasculitis). **45** The cellular debris and fibrin can block CSF outflow, which may rapidly raise intracranial pressure. Vasculitis may induce necrosis of vessel walls and thrombosis, which can lead to brain infarction.

The prognosis depends on whether rapid and effective antibiotic treatment can arrest the disease before any permanent damage has occurred. In such cases, full recovery is possible. Persistent meningitis can lead to cranial nerve damage, abscess, tissue infarction, or extension into the subdural space (empyema formation, explained later). Acute death results from blockage of CSF outflow and edema, which cause increased intracranial pressure. Pneumonia or circulatory failure may be secondary causes of death.

The microorganisms responsible for bacterial meningitis vary with the age of the patient and the mechanism of infection. Epidemics among adults living in close quarters are often due to the meningococcal bacterium *Nisseria meningitides.* Pneumococcus (*Streptococcus pneumoniae*) and *Hemophilus influenzae* are common agents in both children and adults. They are frequently found among the normal bacterial flora of the nasopharynx. Immunization against *Hemophilus* is recommended for young children, especially those in close contact with many other children, as in day care. Newborns can develop a very resistant

meningitis that is due to Gram-negative bacteria (especially *E. coli* and group B streptococci). Most cases of meningitis result from hematogenous spread from an upper respiratory tract infection, otitis media, or pneumonia. Direct spread from an established infection or neurosurgical procedure is also possible.

Other Meningeal Inflammations

Viral (or lymphocytic) **meningitis,** while unpleasant (severe headaches, light sensitivity, malaise), is generally self-limiting. Treatment is symptomatic and almost all patients recover without problems. Individuals with a primary tuberculosis infection may develop tuberculous infection of the meninges and adjacent brain tissue (meningoencephalitis). Those with fungal and syphilitic infections may also develop meningoencephalitis.

Figure 20.33 Bacterial meningitis. The production of exudate has yielded the thickening and clouding of the meninges seen in this view of the superior surface of the brain.

Meningeal Signs

Some of the signs of meningeal inflammation are the light sensitivity, severe headache, and general malaise that were just mentioned. In acute meningitis, fever, vomiting, drowsiness, stiff neck, muscle aches, and backache are common. Rapid development of infection may lead to confusion, deepening obtundation, and coma. **Brudzinki's sign** is seen when abrupt flexion of the neck of a supine patient results in involuntary flexion of the knees. **Kernig's sign** is seen when an attempt to extend the knee while holding the thigh in a flexed position results in reflex resistance and pain in the hamstring group. Both of these responses probably result from irritation of motor and sensory nerve roots passing through the inflamed meninges. Brudzinki's sign is a hyperactive hip flexion reflex in response to neck flexion (this would be evident in a normal infant). Kernig's sign is simply a hyperactive deep tendon hamstring reflex. Both may be exaggerated by the position assumed, which

Creutzfeldt-Jacob Disease

While not a viral infection, Creutzfeldt-Jacob disease (CJD) merits mention here. This progressive and fatally destructive brain disease is apparently caused by an abnormal form of a normal brain protein. The agent is called a prion (for proteinaceous infective particle). Although it appears to have no genetic material itself, prion protein can apparently induce brain cells to produce it in quantities sufficient to disrupt brain structure and function. After a very long incubation period, this leads to a rapidly (often less than 12 months) progressive dementia. Prions are remarkably resistant to conventional destructive techniques (autoclave, formalin, caustic soda, chlorine bleach). A number of cases have been traced to infected depth electrodes in EEG or corneal transplant. The usual means of infection is not established.

may increase pressure within the spinal dural sac. In infants and old people, meningeal signs may not be distinct or clearly evident, and examination of CSF may be necessary to establish a diagnosis.

Viral Infections of the CNS

Viral infections of the CNS tend to be either acute, in which case the immune system usually mounts defense (poliomyelitis and smallpox are examples), or latent, chronic, and so-called slow virus infections. The latter can be very destructive. In this group, herpes simplex and varicella zoster can occur acutely, then appear to become latent.

Herpes can recur as a potentially fatal encephalitis in infants. Varicella zoster produces chickenpox **46** in its acute form and later can cause inflammation of cranial and spinal nerve roots and ganglia and the painful skin lesions characteristic of **shingles. 47** Rubella and cytomegalovirus can do extensive brain damage as congenital infections. Measles virus can also infect the nervous system. Because the nervous system produces only very small amounts of a protein (M protein) required by the virus for the formation of part of its viral coat, viral replication is exceedingly slow. However, eventually in two to three years this slow virus appears to produce a fatal chronic disease in infants and children called **subacute sclerosing panencephalitis** (SSPE).

Another relentlessly progressive (six months to one year) and fatal encephalitis, which is focused on the myelinating oligodendrocytes, is **progressive multifocal leukoencephalopathy** (PML). It is usually found only in debilitated patients with some form of immune suppression.

Reye's Syndrome

This potentially fatal postviral condition has recently received wide public attention because of the suspected role of aspirin in its pathogenesis. A minority of children in the age range 6 months to 15 years who have had a viral infection (usually influenza A or B or varicella), go on after three to five days to develop **Reye's syndrome.** They have a (perhaps renewed) period of vomiting and lethargy. In about three-quarters of them, the CNS effects might deepen to clouded consciousness or hyperexcitability, but then the condition resolves to full recovery. One-quarter of the victims, unfortunately, experience degenerating consciousness due to progressive brain edema. This condition leads to deepening coma and death in 10% or more of Reye's syndrome cases. Aggressive intensive care, aimed at controlling the increased intracranial pressure secondary to edema, has resulted in this improved prognosis. Formerly death rates were as high as 40%.

In a few cases, the cause of death is liver failure. This fact draws our attention to the underlying pathophysiology, which is still not understood. Early in its course, blood tests will show hypoglycemia, acidosis due to lactic acid accumulation, and increased free fatty acids. Within a week, signs of liver disfunction appear: elevated ammonia, bilirubin, liver enzymes. Biopsy will show widespread (brain, liver, other tissues) mitochondrial injury and accumulation of fats in tiny intracellular vesicles, **48** art, and kidneys. Although the cause is not clear, brain edema is the root of the CNS symptoms.

A variety of factors may contribute to the conversion of a viral infection to Reye's syndrome. Vomiting and resultant fasting lead to exhaustion of glycogen (glucose) stores and hence the mobilization of fatty acids. These may interfere with mitochondrial function and thereby cause hyperammonia. Genetic predisposition may play a role, as may endotoxins or lymphokines released in the immune response. Salicylates (e.g., aspirin) may simply tip the balance of an already disordered metabolism. With the exception of mitochondrial injury, the pattern in salicylate toxicity is similar to that in Reye's syndrome. However, children with Reye's, while often having been given aspirin to control fever and aches associated with flu, don't show toxic salicylate levels. Whatever the connection may be, the decline in use of aspirin to control fever in children has been accompanied by a lower incidence of Reye's syndrome.

Brain Abscesses

A **brain abscess** **49** is a localized, fairly circumscribed area of necrosis and pyogenic (pus forming) bacterial infection principally found in the white matter (fig. 20.34). The presence of both necrosis and infection distinguishes this condition from encephalitis and tells us something about how abscess formation takes place. The infection is introduced at the same time as an area of infarct is produced. This usually takes place in either of two ways.

In the first mechanism, a septic embolus may pass into the cerebral vasculature, perhaps by breaking off from an established set of valve vegetations that have developed in bacterial endocarditis. Infection in the lung is another common source. A distant infection (e.g., in burns, pelvic infection, or bones) is also possible. The embolus is composed of fibrin, trapped blood cells, and the sequestered infective organisms. It lodges in the narrowing artery or arteriole and produces a small ischemic infarct. In this region the infective agent (*Staphylococcus aureus* is common, although a variety of bacteria, yeast, fungi, etc., may be involved) can get established in relative isolation from immune system interference. As the infection expands, the infected tissue will undergo liquefaction necrosis, and an extensive capsule of astrocytic gliosis may evolve. Inflammation and edema will surround this cystic space.

The other major mechanism for producing simultaneous infarction and infection is by spread from an established chronic infection. This will be in an area contiguous to the brain, for example middle ear infection, mastoiditis, paranasal sinusitis, oral or dental infections, face or scalp infections. Spread is probably through thrombosed veins or their lymphatic drainage. The occlusion of veins impairs drainage and leads to infarction of cerebral tissue. Rarely, infection and infarction may be established by brain surgery or a penetrating head wound.

A person with an abscess may experience no distinct symptoms, in which case the condition may be identified as an incidental finding in a CT scan done for some other reason. Despite the primary infection and spread to the brain, about half of those affected experience no fevers. If the abscess expands or if there are multiple abscesses, as may be the case with hematogenous spread, symptoms related to the expansion of a mass lesion are likely to appear. Clouded consciousness, headaches, and more focal symptoms like seizures or neurological deficits may occur. There may be high fever and the possibility of very rapid progression, some people succumbing in 5–15 days. Symptoms may resemble those of CVA in nature and evolution. An abscess can break through to the surface of the cortex or the ventricular system and produce meningitis.

Treatment includes antibiotics, to eliminate both the primary and the abscess infection, and surgical excision or drainage. Seizures are a relatively common long-term result

Figure 20.34   Brain abscess. The circular mass at the left is a pus-filled abscess that has extended to the adjacent ventricle.
This is the brain of a middle-aged man who died of meningitis. He had suffered for several years from a chronic middle ear infection that had drained pus intermittently. Then he developed signs and symptoms of meningitis: headache, drowsiness, and vomiting. A lumbar puncture revealed that his CSF was clouded with pus, and it was cultured to determine the antibiotic sensitivity of the causative organism. Exploratory surgery to locate a suspected brain tumor was undertaken, but none was found. In spite of large doses of an appropriate antibiotic, death followed five weeks after the onset of meningitis. The specimen reveals the large cerebral abscess that had formed by extension from the infected middle ear. It was filled with a creamy pus, which had ruptured into the lateral ventricle.

associated with the surrounding gliosis, and patients may require prolonged anticonvulsant therapy. Depending on the location and extent of the abscess, focal neurological deficits may remain after treatment.

Subdural Empyema

Subdural empyema is the collection of pus between the dura and the arachnoid membrane. The suppurative infection gets established here by spread from a contiguous infection as with abscess. It can expand, producing symptoms associated with a mass lesion, and can in turn induce thrombophlebitis in cerebral veins and infarction in their territory. As well, infection can spread to the brain or subarachnoid space (meningitis). Treatment consists of surgical drainage and antibiotic therapy. As with abscess, long-term disablement is variable.

CNS TUMORS

Tumors of the central nervous system constitute about 2% (20,000) of the over one million cases of cancer diagnosed in adults every year in North America. In children, cancer is much less common (perhaps 8500 new cases per year), but by contrast, 20% of the cancers identified are in the eye, brain, or spinal cord (2000 plus cases). A further distinction is that in adults, 70% of tumors are found above the tentorium (within the cerebral hemispheres, the thalamus, etc.), while in children, 70% are subtentorial (brain stem, cerebellum, fourth ventricle).

Since tumors can arise only in tissues capable of mitosis, tumors in adults largely exclude those arising from neurons or primitive precursor cells. Mitotically active cells, therefore those capable of tumorigenesis, include **astrocytes,** which contribute to the blood-brain barrier and provide metabolic and structural support and stabilize the environment for neurons; **oligodendrocytes,** which provide the myelin sheaths in the CNS that ensure rapid, effective signal conduction; **ependymal cells,** which line the ventricles and central canal of the spinal cord; certain cells of the arachnoid membrane (giving rise to the meningioma); **Schwann cells,** which provide myelination in the peripheral nervous system; and connective tissue cells forming the endoneureal matrix surrounding peripheral nerve processes (giving rise to the neurofibroma). Cells producing blood vessels can also give rise to tumors (e.g., arteriovenous malformations). Infants and children are subject to neural and precursor cell tumors as well (e.g., neuroblastoma and medulloblastoma, respectively).

Outside the brain the danger posed by a neoplastic growth is largely a function of its malignancy (see chapter 6). In the cranial vault, malignancy is only one factor that may affect morbidity and mortality. If it is located in or near strategic sites, e.g., adjacent to the cerebral aqueduct or in the brain stem, even a small, slowly growing benign tumor can have devastating effects. Tumor excision is usually the treatment of choice in the CNS, as it is elsewhere in the body. However, CNS tumors may be physically inaccessible, may have infiltrated diffusely and require the resection of too much tissue, or may be small but located in vital brain centers. The blood-brain barrier makes chemotherapy ineffective for most tumors, and this fact, combined with the foregoing, often makes radiation the chief acceptable therapy. The limited capacity of the cranial vault is an additional variable that blurs the distinction between malignant and benign. Even though the malignant neoplasm will probably increase in mass faster, the ultimate impact of compression, herniation, and increased intracranial pressure from a benign but inoperable tumor will probably be the same.

Table 20.6 summarizes the relative incidence of CNS tumors. The bulk of tumors of the spinal cord arise from cells of the arachnoid membrane (meningioma) or the Schwann cells that myelinate spinal nerves (Schwannoma). They are slow growing and create symptoms by compressing nerve roots or the cord. Surgical resection, with its attendant risks of cord and nerve damage, and radiation to kill actively dividing cells are alternative treatments.

Table 20.6	Approximate Relative Incidence of CNS Tumors

Adults

Spinal Cord—20%

•Majority are benign meningiomas and Schwannomas, with about 20% ependymomas and some gliomas

Brain—80%

Secondary (metastatic)—30%

•Malignant melanomas (from primary skin or other secondary), renal cell and intestinal carcinomas also a source

Primary (originating in brain)—70%

•Gliomas—48%
(includes astrocytoma, glioblastoma, oligodendroglioma, and ependymoma)
•Meningioma—13%
•Neurilemmoma (Schwannoma) and neurofibroma—9%
(mostly acoustic nerve tumors)

Children

Medulloblastoma—30%
Astrocytoma I and II—30%
Ependymoma—12%
Other—28%

Figure 20.35 Secondary brain tumor. Malignant melanoma has metastasized from the stem to the brain.
In this photo, hemorrhage can be seen surrounding a tumor that had metastasized to the brain. It, and numerous other widely disseminated secondary tumors, caused the death of a 72-year-old woman who had initially noticed a lump on her back and then others on the abdomen and arm. Six months later, scans revealed the presence of a tumor in her lung and a biopsy of one of the skin nodules revealed it to be a malignant melanoma.

Most secondary brain tumors metastasize through the blood to the brain, where multiple, randomly distributed tumors may became established. The most common sources, in order of incidence, are carcinomas of the lung, **50** breast, skin (malignant melanoma), **51** kidney (renal cell carcinoma), and intestine. The incidence and distribution reflect both hemodynamics and tumor affinity for cerebral capillaries (see chapter 6). Usually the tumors are sharply demarcated from the surrounding brain tissue. Figure 20.35 shows a single malignant melanoma located near the falx. Occasionally, metastasis is to the subarachnoid space, where the tumor nodules can cover brain and cord surfaces (**carcinomatous meningitis**). **52** Most metastasis is of highly malignant tumor types, so treatment is usually oriented to comfort and reduction of pain.

Of primary brain tumors, gliomas account for about 70%. Most of these arise from **astrocytomas.** Relatively benign astrocytomas (called I and II) are slow-growing and often broadly infiltrative. If solid and circumscribed, they may be surgically removed. While often resistant to radiotherapy, their growth may be slowed, giving five-year survival rates of about 50%. Astrocytomas III and IV are fast-growing and highly invasive. They are called **glioblastoma multiforme** because the appearance of the tumor is vari-

50 39091   **51** 18280   **52** 34637

Figure 20.36   Glioblastomae multiforme. The large tumor mass occupies the left temporal lobe (lower right). Note the distortion of the brain and ventricle that has resulted.
A 63-year-old cab driver was forced to give up his work because of progressive difficulty in speaking, reading, and making change. A CT scan found the lesion pictured here in his left parietal and temporal lobes. A needle biopsy revealed the mass to be a glioblastoma. No treatment was given and death followed four months after the diagnosis.

able, with areas of necrosis, hemorrhage, and cyst formation dispersed through the white substance of the astrocytoma **53** (fig. 20.36). These are usually inoperable because of their size and infiltration, and are highly resistant to radiotherapy. The tumor may spread across the corpus callosum into the other hemisphere. Survival beyond 12 months of the point when the tumor is recognized is unusual. Both astrocytomas I and II and glioblastoma multiforme are usually located in the cerebral hemisphere and may be diagnosed after they precipitate either a simple or complex partial seizure.

The **meningioma** is a benign, slow-growing tumor that arises from cells in the arachnoid membrane and accounts for about 20% of primary intracranial tumors. The one in figure 20.37 is flat and spreading, but focal, spherical growths are more common. **54** They are highly vascular, so they show up well when CT scans are done with a contrast medium that passes the relatively permeable capillaries supplying the tumor and concentrates in the extracellular space. When focal, the pressure on adjacent bone can stimulate osteoclastic activity, and the resultant remodeling and thinning of bone may be evident on routine X-ray. Meningiomas tend to occur singly in the front half of the skull, in the superficial meninges or the falx or along the ridge of the sphenoid bone or groove of the olfactory nerve. Symptoms can occur over years and depend on the location of the tumor. They can include any of the following: paraparesis (weakness or paralysis of the legs), bitemporal hemianopsia if located near the optic chiasm (see chapter 21), or blindness in one eye. Surgical resection is usually effective, but its feasibility is, again, dependent on the location of the tumor.

The **acoustic neuroma** **55** (also called **acoustic Schwannoma**) accounts for most of the peripheral nerve tumors that intrude into the cranial vault. It tends to develop in the foramen of the eighth cranial nerve, where pressure produces tinnitus (ringing) and progressive hearing loss. Protrusion into the cranial vault at the base of the brain, at the juncture of the medulla and pons, can stretch a variety of cranial nerves and press on motor tracts in the

Figure 20.37 Meningioma. Although most are spherical, this meningioma is flattened and is spreading over the surface of the brain.

The tumor shown here was an incidental autopsy finding. A 73-year-old woman with a history of chronic alcohol abuse underwent rapid physical and mental deterioration. She developed pneumonia but was unresponsive to antibiotic therapy because of her state of debilitation. Death followed some weeks later. The flattened meningioma covers the vertex of the brain and extends into the longitudinal fissure. This difference from the usual spherical shape accounts for the lack of focal symptoms that a round and compressing mass would have produced. The widening of sulci and dilation of the ventricles result from generalized brain atrophy, probably due to aging and alcohol abuse.

brain stem, producing unilateral sensory/motor deficits. Because it tends to grow off to the side of the vestibulo-cochlear nerve, resection with preservation of hearing and balance is possible. Bilateral tumor development is usually attributable to a **neurofibroma.** This mass grows more intimately into the nerve, so complete resection without nerve damage is unlikely.

Tumors of developmentally primitive cells or mitotically active neural cells produce about 40% of CNS neoplasia in children. The **medulloblastoma** 56 is a highly malignant tumor arising in the cerebellum and spreading over its surface, often invading the fourth ventricle. Metastasis through the CSF is common. Symptoms result from destruction of functional cerebellum (see chapter 21) and restriction of CSF outflow (hydrocephalus). 57 A combination of partial resection and radiotherapy currently yields a 50% ten-year survival rate.

Many of the mechanisms whereby tumors produce symptoms have been covered earlier in this chapter. Figure 20.38 provides an overview. It should be noted that massive infiltration of functional brain tissue can occur (for example, by an astrocytoma) with few clinical signs. This means that tumor progression can take place without the patient's perception, a characteristic of tumors outside the CNS. Also, symptoms usually develop slowly, then dramatically accelerate to a crisis that may send the patient for diagnosis or be part of the final evolution of an untreatable condition.

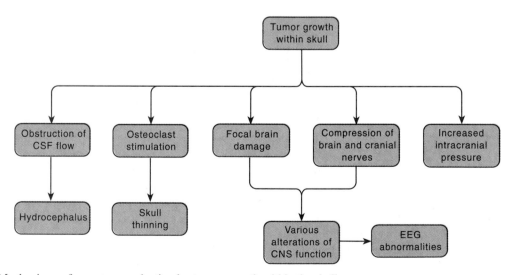

Figure 20.38 Mechanisms of symptom production by tumor growth within the skull.

Case Study

A frantic mother brought her 12-year-old daughter to a hospital's emergency room at 2300 hours. The child was rigid and in a stupor. Although the mother's English was quite poor and there was no one available to translate, it was determined that the attack was of sudden onset 30 minutes earlier. The child had experienced a mild upper respiratory infection and an earache in the last 24 hours. When her temperature started to rise, her mother gave her an aspirin and put her to bed. On later checking on the child's condition, she noticed that the fever had risen significantly and she was unable to arouse the child.

In the ER the patient's temperature was 39.5° C and she was unresponsive, showing increased muscle tone and unconscious irritability during her examination, which also uncovered evidence of otitis media. Her lungs were clear and her heart rate elevated. A well-healed scar over the upper left abdominal quadrant was present, and upon questioning the mother it was determined that the child had had her spleen removed following its rupture in a motor vehicle accident three years previously.

Blood and urine samples were obtained for testing and a chest X-ray was taken. A lumbar puncture was also done and indicated a cloudy CSF under increased pressure. An IV line was established, and a broad spectrum antibiotic was administered, pending results of blood and urine tests.

When test results were obtained, the urine and chest X-ray were normal, while white cell counts were elevated. In the CSF, the glucose level was depressed, protein and WBC counts were elevated, and there was Gram-positive diplococci present. The diplococci were identified and a diagnosis of pneumococcal meningitis was made. Tests showed the organisms to be penicillin-sensitive, and this antibiotic was substituted for the broad spectrum antibiotic.

Within 24 hours of the start of penicillin therapy, which was administered with another agent to increase the permeability of the blood-brain barrier to penicillin, the child's condition improved. After 48 hours had passed, she was sitting up in bed and communicating. In ten days she had fully recovered and was discharged from the hospital.

Commentary

Elevation of intracranial pressure is a hallmark of bacterial meningitis, which in this case can be assumed to have originated in the child's middle ear infection. The cloudiness of the CSF was due both to its elevated protein level and the presence of pus. The chest X-ray was important in establishing that there was no pneumonia or endocardial involvement, two common accompaniments of bacterial meningitis. Before the infecting organism is identified, ampicillin offers a broad effectiveness, but penicillin is more effective against most pneumococcal strains.

Although various bacterial species such as *Neisseria, Hemophilus,* or *Staphylococcus* may cause meningitis, in those who lack a spleen (and in those with sickle cell disease) it is particularly likely to be *Streptococcus pneumoniae.* The reasons for this are unclear, but the link is so well established that immediately following splenectomy, anti-pneumococcus vaccine is typically administered. The vaccine protects against the pneumococci responsible for about 90% of infections, but in the case of this child, the infecting strain was apparently one against which there was no protection. Her mother's quick response, in spite of a language deficit that might have deterred less assertive parents, was important, since pneumococcal meningeal infections are fatal in about 15% of cases.

Key Concepts

1. The scalp effectively protects the skull but can allow infection to enter the cranial vault through veins draining the face or loose connective tissue beneath the galea (pp. 505–507).

2. The skull may be subject to direct trauma, perhaps producing a hematoma or basal skull fracture that may expose the brain to infective agents (pp. 507–509).

3. Cerebrospinal fluid confers significant protection but is subject to infection, and the meningeal layers can be the site of hemorrhage and hematoma formation (pp. 509–512).

4. The vertebral column can be subject to dislocation, fracture, or disk protrusion, any of which can affect cord or nerve root function (pp. 512–514).

5. Infarcts may occur at the margins of adjacent vascular fields supplying the cortex (watershed zone) secondary to conditions that impair perfusion (e.g., fibrillation) or oxygenation (e.g., carbon monoxide poisoning, near-drowning) (p. 520).

6. Brain tissue can swell if capillaries become permeable and allow an extracellular accumulation of fluid in the white matter (vasogenic edema) or if cortical cells are injured and swell (cytotoxic edema) (pp. 521–523).

7. Any uncompensated expansion of brain, CSF, or blood within the relatively fixed cranial vault can lead to an increase in intracranial pressure, which can impair cerebral perfusion and compress, shift, or tear neural tissue (p. 523).

8. Oversecretion, impaired absorption, or obstructed circulation of cerebrospinal fluid can lead to an expansion of the CSF compartment, particularly the cerebral ventricles, that is termed hydrocephalus (p. 524).

9. Assessment and description of level of consciousness provides a significant approximate gauge of generalized neural function and the progression of pathology and treatment (p. 528).

10. A variety of reflex and automatic functions can aid in the localization of CNS lesions and in monitoring their progression or resolution (pp. 528–529).

11. Problems in the closure and development of the neural tube can lead to defects in bony or meningeal protection or abnormal development of neural tissue. Defects of the caudal neural tube are termed spina bifida, while rostral defects range from minor to failure of brain development (anencephaly) (pp. 529–534).

12. An aneurysm is a dilatation of a section of an artery that occurs at an injury or a site of congenital weakness of the arterial wall, in the case of berry or fusiform aneurysms, or secondary to hypertension in the case of microaneurysms (p. 534).

13. Transitory constriction of subarachnoid arteries (subarachnoid vasospasm) can result spontaneously or secondary to subarachnoid hemorrhage, perhaps from an aneurysm, or surgery (pp. 534–535).

14. Tangled masses of blood vessels that shunt blood directly from arteries to the venous drainage, called arteriovenous malformations, develop congenitally and are increasingly susceptible to hemorrhage (p. 535).

15. Infection or inflammation in adjacent tissues can induce clot formation in cerebral veins or venous sinuses, thereby impairing venous drainage and cerebral perfusion and perhaps spreading infection (p. 536).

16. Cerebrovascular accident (CVA) is the term applied to a group of conditions in which localized cerebral blood flow is impaired by either occlusion or hemorrhage (p. 537).

17. In a transient ischemic attack, a brief vasospasm of diseased artery downstream from a developing plaque impairs perfusion of localized tissue, producing fully reversible hypofunction (pp. 537–538).

18. A thrombotic CVA evolves when the thrombus on a chronic plaque stenoses or occludes an arterial lumen, leading to downstream ischemia and necrosis (pp. 538–540).

19. Transitory edema usually produces broader impairment in a CVA than that eventually attributable to the necrosis of specific functional cortex or white matter tracts (p. 539).

20. Occlusive CVAs are usually attributable to intra- or extracranial thrombotic emboli and produce symptoms similar to thrombotic CVA, but evolve more rapidly (p. 540).

21. Hemorrhage interferes with downstream perfusion but also may produce a hematoma mass, dissect delicate neural tissues, or enter the ventricles or subarachnoid space (p. 540).

22. Bacterial infection of the subarachnoid space (pyogenic meningitis) is a medical emergency producing classic signs like stiff neck, fever, vomiting, and Brudzinski's and Kernig's signs (pp. 542–543).

23. Viral infections of the CNS vary from usually benign viral meningitis to fatal encephalitis (pp. 543–544).

24. The relative incidence, type, and location of CNS tumors vary between children and adults (p. 545).

25. CNS tumors vary in cell type of origin, pattern and speed of development, and prognosis (pp. 545–548).

REVIEW ACTIVITIES

1. Without reference to your text figures, lay out a flow chart that terminates at a box labeled "Increased Intracranial Pressure" and that starts with boxes labeled "Abscess," "Intracranial Bleeding," "Tumor," "Blocked Arachnoid Villi," "Blocked Cerebral Aqueduct," "Trauma," "Hypoxia." Be sure to include a box labeled "Cerebral Edema" somewhere in your chart. Then insert additional boxes so that the chart accurately reflects the pathogenesis of increased intracranial pressure.

2. Do another flow chart, this time starting with "Increased Intracranial Pressure" and ending with all of the logically expected outcomes.

3. Without reference to the figures in your text, explain the processes of symptom production that are associated with the development of an intracranial tumor.

4. Construct a table that presents the progression of increased intracranial pressure to a fatal outcome.

5. Prepare a brief table summarizing the categories of neural tube defects.

6. Describe development of one of the CVA syndromes in specific terms such that it could be used in the exam question "Identify the following clinically observed CVA and defend your answer."

7. Many problems in the CNS develop as the downside of an otherwise effective design. Identify the problem(s) associated with each of the following: (a) the protection of the sturdy, solid cranial vault, (b) the lightness and strength of the thin, sandwiched skull bone, (c) the stabilizing compartmentalization of the cranial vault by the falx and tentorium, (d) the proliferative capacity of astrocytes, oligodendrocytes, and meningeal cells that allow for CNS repair, (e) the elaborate system for production, circulation, and absorption of the CSF that floats and cushions the CNS, and (f) the protective blood-brain barrier.

8. How would you differentiate clinically between a bacterial and a viral meningitis? What is the difference in the pathogenesis of a cyst that follows an embolic infarct and abscess formation?

9. How could you explain the use of stool softeners to a patient who was at risk of hemorrhagic CVA?

10. Many of the topics dealt with in this chapter can have rather bleak prognoses. To end on a lighter note, describe the most positive clinical picture or outcome for each of the following: neural tube defects, CVA, CNS infection, CNS neoplasia, aneurysm, AVM.

Chapter Twenty-One

Disorders of Movement, Sensation, and Mental Function

Man is the shuttle, to whose winding quest
And passage through these looms
God order'd motion, but ordain'd no rest.

Henry Vaughan
(1622–1695)

This chapter deals with disorders arising either centrally or peripherally that might disrupt normal movement or sensation, autonomic function, or higher mental processes. We begin with the background necessary to understand these.

CONTEXT FOR THE ASSESSMENT OF DYSFUNCTION

The Autonomic Nervous System

The **autonomic nervous system** is active in regulating a host of very important homeostatic, reactive, and sensory functions. Control of cardiac output, blood pressure, digestive processes and salivation, bladder contraction and micturition (urination), visual responses to changing light conditions or distance, temperature regulation: all are effected through the autonomic nervous system (ANS). So are the physical and physiological aspects of emotion, arousal, and stress response.

Somewhat arbitrarily, anatomists have defined the autonomic nervous system to be purely efferent; they include in this system only the nerves that travel out from the CNS to smooth muscle (in blood vessels, the lungs, digestive and urinary tract, etc.), cardiac muscle, and glandular/secretory structures. There is elaborate sensory input on this system. Information about blood pressure, filling of the stomach, intestine, or bladder, skin temperature, the availability of food, the presence of danger or sexual opportunity—all of this is constantly being relayed to the brain. Central processing occurs, and at least some of the response to these challenges to homeostasis flows out through the nuclei and fibers of the ANS.

There are two clear divisions to the ANS, parasympathetic and sympathetic, which are distinguished by anatomical, functional, and neurotransmitter differences (fig. 21.1). The fibers of the **parasympathetic** branch begin in nuclei found in the brain stem and sacral portion of the spinal cord (craniosacral division). As is the case for all autonomic innervation except that to the adrenal medulla, there is a two-neuron chain between the nucleus and the effector organ. The first fiber, the **preganglionic fiber,** communicates with the second by means of the neurotransmitter acetylcholine. This is the case in both the sympathetic and parasympathetic branches. In the parasympathetic division, acetylcholine is also the neurotransmitter released from the second neuron (the **postganglionic fiber**) to affect the activity of the effector organ (smooth muscle, gland, etc.). Nuclei of the **sympathetic** division are found in the midlateral gray matter of the spinal cord between segments T1 (first thoracic) and L2 (second lumbar). In this case, most postganglionic fibers release norepinephrine (exceptions will be noted later).

Certain terms relating to these neurotransmitters require explanation. Fibers releasing acetylcholine from their end terminals are called **cholinergic.** Even though acetylcholine (ACh) is the same substance wherever it is released in the nervous system, the receptors for it (on muscle, postganglionic fibers, autonomic effectors, CNS neurons) can differ slightly. These differences make it possible to use a drug that is active in one set of receptors, but has virtually no activity at the rest. Atropine will be described as an example later.

Terminology associated with norepinephrine has its own peculiarities. Norepinephrine and epinephrine are closely related agents, examples of biological substances called **catecholamines.** Both are released from the adrenal medulla when it is subjected to sympathetic stimulation and are important agents in the very generalized "fight or flight" response to arousal. An older name for the substance now usually called epinephrine is **adrenalin,** hence the term **adrenergic** when referring to its effects. For example, an **adrenergic agonist** is a substance, often a drug, that has the same effect on the body as do epinephrine and norepinephrine. Conversely, an **adrenergic antagonist** counteracts the activity of these two substances.

The autonomic nuclei just described, which are the avenues of activation of the ANS, must, of course, be acted upon themselves. Some impulses, for example from the cardiovascular centers in the medulla, synapse directly with the appropriate sympathetic or parasympathetic nuclei. Most impulses originate in the hypothalamus. This complex structure integrates autonomic and endocrine control systems for maintaining homeostasis and responding to environmental demands.

Parasympathetic and sympathetic divisions of the ANS are often presented as having antagonistic functions—conserving versus activating responses, respectively. A more informative view is to recognize the range of autonomic innervation and function. Some structures have only parasympathetic innervation (e.g., bronchial glands) and some have only sympathetic innervation (e.g., the spleen, the adrenal medulla, sweat glands, and most blood vessels). Most structures are dually innervated. Some of these demonstrate complementary interaction of both divisions (e.g., parasympathetic stimulation is responsible for erection, while ejaculation depends on sympathetic activity). Other dually innervated organs do demonstrate antagonist action, but with many of these the interaction of opposite effects has a synergistic effect. For example, sympathetic stimulation increases heart rate and contractility, while parasympathetic stimulation decreases both; however, in a situation demanding increased cardiac output, not only does sympathetic outflow increase but also vagal outflow is inhibited. (The vagus nerve carries parasympathetic impulses to the viscera.) This interaction greatly increases the effect of sympathetic stimulation beyond its isolated impact.

Autonomic responses are capable of being focused by the selective activation of fibers to one organ or system (e.g., sympathetic stimulation of the heart). But also, even the diffuse arousal implicit in the release into the general

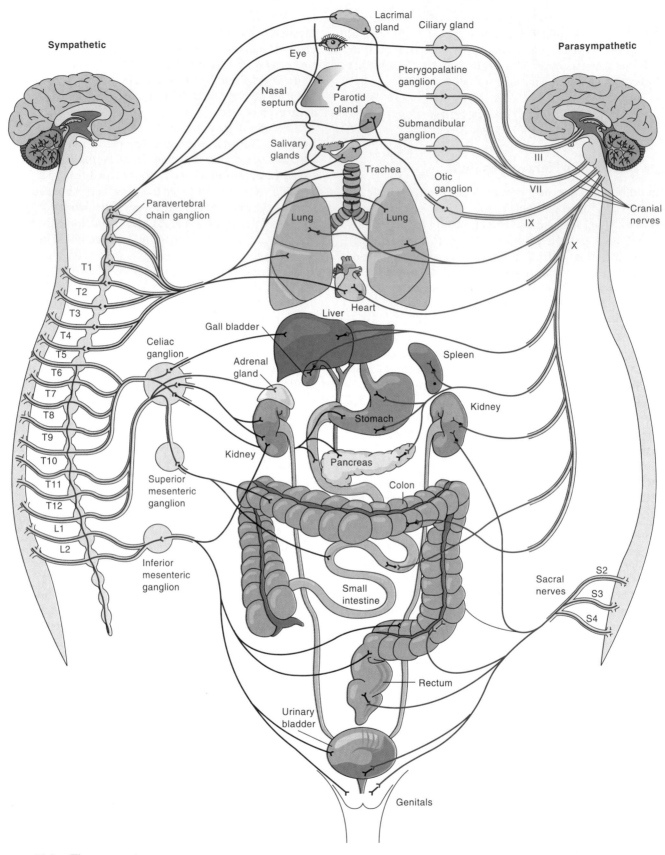

Figure 21.1 The autonomic nervous system.

Table 21.1   Major Responses of Selected Effector Organs to Autonomic Nerve Impulses

Effector Organs	Sympathetic Activation (Mostly Adrenergic Impulses)		Parasympathetic Activation (Cholinergic Impulses)
	Receptor Type	*Responses*	*Responses*
Eye			
Radial muscle, iris	α	Dilation (mydriasis)$^+$	—
Sphincter muscle, iris		—	Constriction (miosis)$^{++}$
Heart			
SA node	β_1	Increase in heart rate$^+$	Decrease in heart rate; vagal arrest^{+++}
AV node	β_1	Increase in automaticity and conduction velocity$^+$	Decrease in conduction velocity; AV block^{++}
Ventricles	β_1	Increase in contractility, conduction velocity, automaticity, and rate of idioventricular pacemaker^{++}	—
Arterioles			
Skin and mucosa	α	Constriction^{++}	—
Pulmonary	α, β_2	Dilation predominates$^+$	—
Abdominal viscera, renal	α, β_2	Constriction predominates$^+$	—
Skeletal muscle	α, β_2	Dilation predominates$^+$	—
Lung			
Bronchial muscle	β_2	Relaxation$^+$	Contraction^{++}
Spleen capsule	α, β_2	Contraction^{++}	—
Skin, sweat glands	ACh*	Generalized secretions$^+$	—
Adrenal medulla	ACh**	Secretion of epinephrine and norepinephrine^{++}	—

$^+$ Minor activation $^{++}$ Moderate activation $^{+++}$ Intensive activation

*Most sympathetic nerves ending on sweat glands release acetylcholine as a neurotransmitter.

**Sympathetic preganglionic fibers terminate directly on the adrenal medulla; all preganglionic neurons release acetylcholine.

circulation of catecholamines (epinephrine and norepinephrine) from the adrenal medulla has a different effect on different organs. This is because, like the cholinergic receptors, different receptors for the catecholamines have specific, different effects on their respective organs. Four different catecholamine receptors have been identified. Three of these have particular relevance. β_1 (beta one) receptors are found almost exclusively in the heart. When epinephrine or norepinephrine fills these receptors (having been released either from sympathetic fibers or from the adrenal medulla via the general circulation), the effect is excitatory. β_2 receptors, found on smooth muscle and gland cells, are inhibitory on the activity of these cells. α_1 (alpha one) receptors, found on smooth muscle and gland cells, have an excitatory effect. In this case, epinephrine would cause the smooth muscle cells to contract and, in arterioles, would thereby cause vasoconstriction. Table 21.1 presents a relevant selection of organs affected by autonomic activity.

Pharmacological Agents Acting through Autonomic Receptors

Agents Blocking the Effect of Parasympathetic Stimulation Atropine and atropinelike drugs have a strong affinity for the acetylcholine receptors on parasympathetic effectors, which they occupy without activating. They thereby block parasympathetic action. Atropine can be used to paralyze the sphincter muscle in the iris, thus allowing the unopposed action of the sympathetically innervated radial muscle of the iris to dilate the pupil (mydriasis) for fuller examination of the fundus (the area of the retina including the fovea, optic disk, and retinal blood vessels). It may be used preoperatively as a bronchodilator (blocks bronchial smooth muscle contraction) and to dry mucous membranes. It has a limited use in early myocardial infarction to relieve severe bradycardia (slow heart rate) or AV block.

Cholinergic blockers that have affinity for the whole range of acetylcholine receptors can be used to control the potentially fatal cholinergic crisis induced by certain insecticides that contain anticholinesterase agents. Without treatment, these substances allow acetylcholine to accumulate in autonomic pre- and postganglionic, neuromuscular, and central nervous system synaptic clefts, a condition that can lead to motor paralysis, lung congestion, convulsions, and death. Atropine, although not removing the anticholinesterase agent, blocks the action of the excess acetylcholine. Cholinesterase inhibitors are used to diagnose (Tensilon) or treat (neostigmine) myasthenia gravis (see later section). Atropinelike agents must be available to reverse the cholinergic crisis that could result from the excess action of these drugs on the myasthenic patient.

Agents Acting Via Sympathetic Receptors to Increase Sympathetic Activity Epinephrine tends to act broadly on all sympathetic effector organs if used systemically, so it tends to be used locally, for example to control superficial hemorrhage by constricting arterioles and precapillary sphincters. **Isoproterenol** attaches to all β receptors but has almost no affinity to α receptors, and therefore has a bronchodilator effect of value in respiratory disorders and a cardiac stimulant effect of value in heart block, cardiogenic shock, and after myocardial infarction. **Dopamine,** an agonist (stimulating agent) at mainly β_1 receptors, produces increased contractility in the myocardium while maintaining blood flow through renal and intestinal vascular beds. These qualities make it useful in treating certain forms of shock. **Dobutamine,** a closely related β_1 adrenergic agonist, increases contractility and cardiac output while producing little change in total peripheral resistance. This makes it a useful drug in treating congestive heart failure.

Agents Blocking the Effect of α-receptor Sympathetic Stimulation One approach to reducing chronic essential hypertension is to inhibit sympathetic vasoconstrictor tone, thereby reducing peripheral resistance and, consequently, systemic blood pressure. **Prazosin** acts as an α_1 blocking agent, selectively reducing vascular resistance without the inotropic (increased force of contraction) or chronotropic (increased heart rate) effects of a β agonist.

Agents Blocking the Effect of β-receptor Sympathetic Stimulation A drug that blocks the cardiovascular effects of β sympathetic activity could reduce heart rate and contractility (β_1), thus reducing the work load on the heart, and still compensate for reduced cardiac output by increasing resistance of vessels in lungs and skeletal muscles (β_2), leaving sympathetic vasoconstriction of skin and mucosa (α) intact. **Propranolol** is such a nonselective β-blocking agent. These effects are desirable in treatment of hypertension, prevention of angina pectoris, and the control of cardiac arrhythmias. **Metoprolol,** a selective β_1 blocker, is also effective in treating hypertension.

Cranial Nerve Function and Assessment

Cranial nerves (CN) are so named because they arise from the brain or brain stem. **1** **2** CN I (the olfactory nerve) and CN II (the optic nerve) are actually extensions of the brain, being myelinated by oligodendrocytes and possessing complex sensory end organs. In the case of the optic nerve, meningeal protection, typical of the brain, including dural sheath and CSF-filled subarachnoid space, extends to the eyeball.

The neurons that interact with the millions of photoreceptors in the retina are gathered together and leave the retina at the optic disk to pass along the optic nerve. Retinal blood vessels enter and leave at the optic disk and travel in the center of the optic nerve. The whole of the disk lacks photoreceptors, and their absence creates a blind spot in the lower temporal portion of each visual field that can become significantly enlarged in conditions like glaucoma (increased intraocular pressure). The normal disk is pinkish and round or oval, with sharply defined margins and a slightly cupped center. Increased intracranial pressure is conducted along the optic nerve in the CSF that surrounds it and can cause the disk to protrude. The margin of the disk will be swollen and less distinct, and the entire disk will have a reddish hue, presumably because the abnormal pressure interferes with venous drainage. This condition is called **papilledema** (choked disk). On the other hand, increased intraocular pressure may enlarge the depression in the center of the disk, a phenomenon called cupping.

Testing of cranial nerve function is a routine part of a neurological examination (the brief details are found in table 21.2). By combining the pattern and extent of deficits with a detailed knowledge of brain stem anatomy and the particular course of each cranial nerve (fig. 21.2), the clinician can localize a lesion and make educated guesses as to its nature.

Rinne's test can be used as an example. The subject has suffered hearing loss. The examiner strikes a special tuning fork and holds it next to the subject's ear. When the subject can no longer hear it, the stem of the fork is pressed against the mastoid process. If this allows the sound to be heard again, the deafness must be due to a problem in picking up vibrations at the eardrum or conducting them to the inner ear (conduction deafness). If there is no increased sensitivity, then deafness must be attributable to the inner ear (so-called "nerve deafness").

Visual Pathways

A variety of distinct problems can interfere with the processing of visual information: demyelination, tumors, emboli, edema, thrombosis, hemorrhage, contusion, for a not exhaustive list. Despite this variability in cause, the net effect will depend almost solely on the site at which the lesion interrupts the pathways of vision.

Table 21.2   Cranial Nerve Function and Assessment

Cranial Nerve	Function	Testing and Deficit
I. Olfactory	Sensory—sense of smell	Each nostril tested separately with aromatic substance. Basal skull fracture a common trauma.
II. Optic	Sensory—vision	Visual acuity tested with eye chart; to estimate extent of visual field, patient reports on object moved into field from periphery.
III. Oculomotor	Motor—eye movements other than those attributed for CN IV and CN VI; raises eyelids, constricts pupil, focuses lens Sensory—state of contraction/tension in innervated external eye muscles	Ability to follow object, raise eyelids against pressure, constrict pupils to light.
IV. Trochlear	Motor—superior oblique external eye muscle Sensory—state of contraction/tension	Difficulty shifting gaze in and down, a deficit noticeable when walking downstairs.
V. Trigeminal		
Ophthalmic branch	Sensory—surface of eyes, scalp, forehead, upper eyelid (motor to tear glands)	Whisp of cotton touched to surface of eyeball.
Maxillary branch	Sensory—upper teeth, gum and lip, palate, face	Pinprick to face.
Mandibular branch	Sensory—skin of jaw, lower teeth, gum and lip Motor—muscles for chewing and in floor of mouth	Pinprick to jaw, gum, lip; make chewing movements.
VI. Abducens	Motor—lateral rectus external eye muscle Sensory—state of contraction/tension	Impaired lateral gaze in left eye when looking left, etc.
VII. Facial	Sensory—taste anterior tongue Motor—muscles of facial expression, tear gland, salivary glands	Taste tested (sweet, sour, salt); grimace, smile, purse lips; tearing in response to ammonia.
VIII. Vestibulocochlear (auditory)	Sensory—hearing, balance and movement	Rinne's test.
X. Glossopharyngeal	Sensory—pharynx, tonsils, posterior tongue (taste), baroreceptors at bifurcation of carotids Motor—pharyngeal muscles used in swallowing, salivary glands	Gag reflex and swallowing tested; speech; taste for bitter.
X. Vagus	Sensory—pharynx, larynx, esophagus, visceral organs of thorax and abdomen Motor—parasympathetic innervation of viscera including heart; swallowing and speech	Swallowing and speech.
XI. Accessory	Motor—muscles of soft palate, pharynx, larynx; muscles of neck and back	Speech, shrug shoulders, push forehead forward against resistance, turn head.
XII. Hypoglossal	Motor and sensory for tongue movements	Tongue protruded and moved.

A quick review of visual processing from the retina to the visual association cortex is in order. First, what is the **visual field?** When our eyes are fixed on an object, everything to the left of the point of fixation is in the left visual field, and vice versa for everything to the right. **Macular (or foveal) vision** is very acute because the image is focused on the center of the retina (the **fovea**), where there is a particularly dense array of the photoreceptors responsible for the perception of color and detail. The image is inverted and turned left for right as it passes through the lens. Because of this, information in the upper portion of the right half of the visual field is cast upon the lower-left

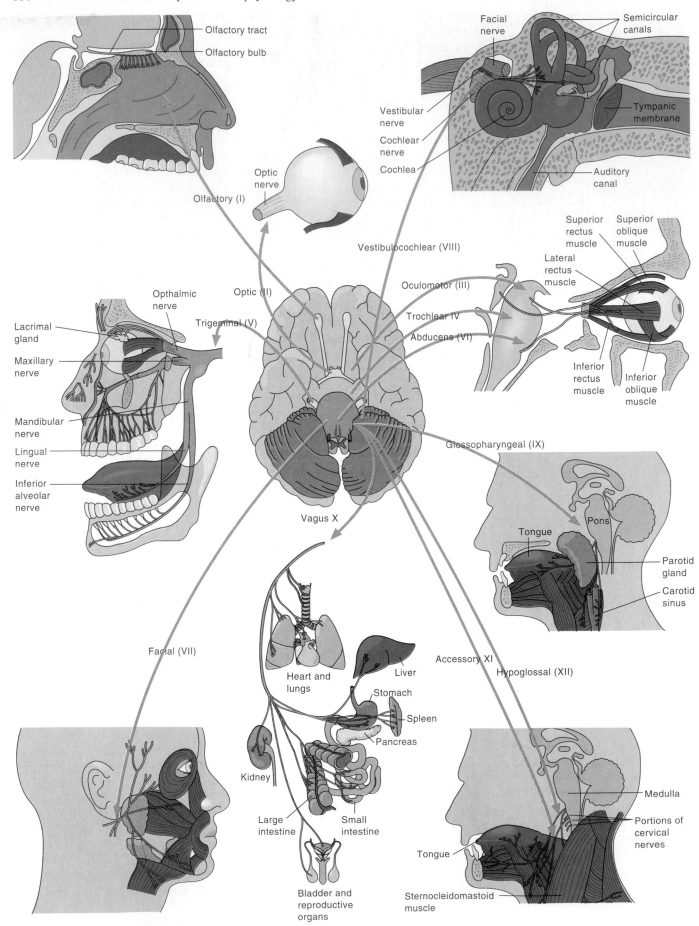

Figure 21.2 Cranial nerve pathways and innervation.

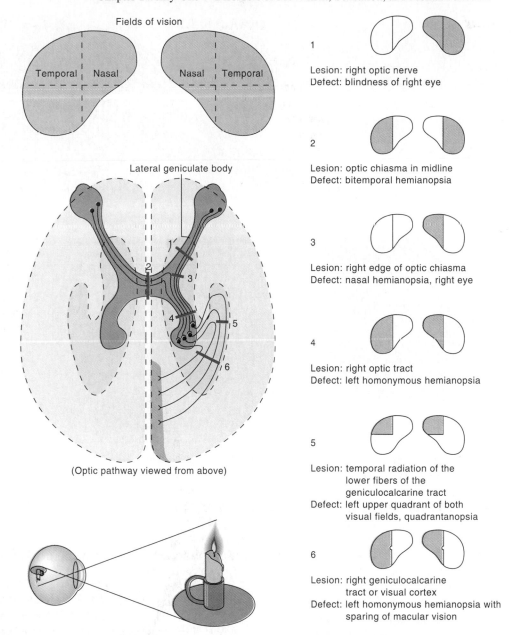

Figure 21.3   Visual field defects caused by lesions of the visual pathways. The inserted figure of the candle illustrates the 180-degree rotation of the visual image that occurs through the lens.

quadrant of each retina. That information is ultimately received and processed in the lower half of the left visual area in the occipital cortex. So, as a general rule, the neural pathways through which information from the visual fields is processed will be located top-for-bottom and left-for-right. Conversely, blindness in the left visual field will indicate disruption of the right visual pathways.

Axons from the retina come together at the optic disk and pass into the optic nerve, which proceeds posteriorly through a fissure at the back of the orbit. At the base of the brain, just anterior to the stalk that connects the hypothalamus to the pituitary, the axons from the medial half of each retina cross over at the optic chiasm. For this reason, the information from the right half of each retina, i.e., the left

visual field from both eyes, is now gathered together on the right side. This pathway is called the **right optic tract.** To restate this, axons from the left nasal retina are combined with axons from the right temporal retina to form the right optic tract (fig. 21.3). A lesion at the optic chiasm will most likely interrupt those crossing-over nasal retinal fibers. It will therefore affect vision in the outside or temporal fields, leaving nasal fields intact and producing a sort of tunnel vision. The condition is called **bitemporal hemianopsia.**

Left and right optic tracts pass on to their respective thalamic nuclei (the left and right lateral geniculate bodies) for processing and routing to the primary visual cortex. (As well, they pass off collaterals that go to areas at the back of the midbrain called the superior colliculi, where this visual

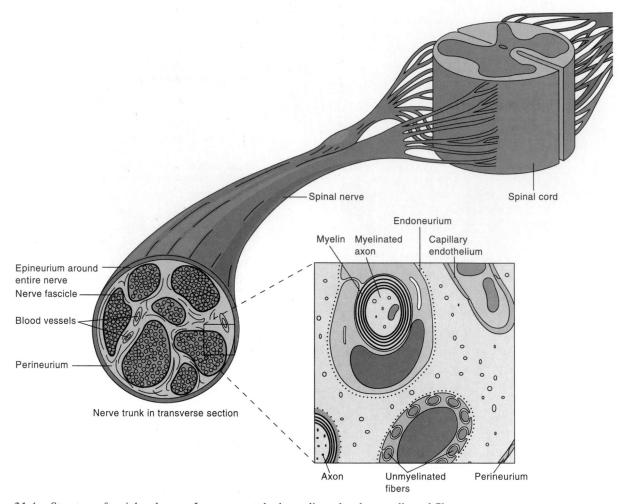

Epineurium around entire nerve

Nerve fascicle

Blood vessels

Perineurium

Nerve trunk in transverse section

Spinal nerve

Spinal cord

Myelin   Myelinated axon

Endoneurium

Capillary endothelium

Axon   Unmyelinated fibers   Perineurium

Figure 21.4   Structure of peripheral nerve. Inset presents both myelinated and unmyelinated fibers.

information makes possible certain visual reflexes and coordinated head and eye movements.) A lesion of the tract between the optic chiasm and the thalamus will wipe out sensitivity to an entire visual field for both eyes, a condition called **complete homonymous hemianopsia.** On their way from the lateral geniculate nucleus of the thalamus to the visual cortex, the fibers from the lower half of each right retina take an excursion around the lateral ventricle in the right temporal lobe (the temporal radiation of the optic tract). Here they may be subjected to lesion that would have no effect on the upper fibers that take a more direct route. This lesion would affect the upper *left* visual field (can you explain why?) and is called **upper left quadrantanopsia.** If the lesion occurs where the fibers have been reunited or at the visual cortex, we will have a condition called **incomplete homonymous hemianopsia.** In this case, there is apparent sparing of macular (central foveal) vision. This sparing is probably a result of incomplete clinical lesions rather than some bilateral representation of foveal information. For clinical purposes, the field defects that you should have at your fingertips are: single-eye blindness, bitemporal hemianopsia, and homonymous hemianopsia.

Peripheral Nerve Damage and Repair

A peripheral nerve is typically composed of the neuronal processes or **axons** 3 from a variety of motor, sensory, and autonomic neurons. The larger, rapidly conducting axons are wrapped in multiple layers of myelin. This is produced by individual **Schwann cells,** 4 which are interrupted at regular intervals by **nodes of Ranvier.** These exposed nodes are richly invested with sodium channels. It is this feature that produces the rapid, **saltatory** (jumping) signal transmission characteristic of myelinated axons. Motor neurons and the fibers carrying information about tendon and muscle tension, limb position, joint pressure, and the precisely discriminated skin sensations of light touch, vibration, and movement are examples of such well-myelinated axons.

Unmyelinated or lightly myelinated fibers carry the sensations of slow and fast pain and temperature and autonomic signals to the sweat glands and blood vessels of the skin. These axons are all imbedded in a fibrous connective tissue matrix that is named according to its location (epineurium, 5 endoneurium) (fig. 21.4). This connective tissue carries the blood vessels that maintain the axons and

3   694

4   698

5   00696

Schwann cells. The endoneurium conforms to the outer margin of the Schwann cell membrane and as such forms an **endoneurial tube,** which would remain patent if the axon and associated myelin sheath were removed.

Damage to a peripheral nerve can range from a temporary interruption of function, in which the axon and Schwann cell constituents are intact (neurapraxia), through interruption of the axon only, to severing of the entire peripheral nerve. To illustrate axon degeneration and repair, we will be using an example that is midway in this continuum—a crush injury that breaks the axons but leaves the endoneurial tubes intact. An even more desirable condition is set if the nerve is cleanly cut and then exactly repositioned, a distinct possibility with modern microsurgery.

Axon reaction is the term applied to changes that are seen in the neuron cell body (soma) within three days of the injury. The normal grainy appearance of the cytoplasm decreases (chromatolysis). This change is due to the dispersion and increased synthetic activity of protein-producing ribosomes preparatory to the repair process. As well, the nucleus swells and shifts out of its central position, and synaptic contacts from other neurons are withdrawn. The axon and its associated myelin sheath, for the whole length distal to the injury, begin simultaneous degeneration after about three days. This **Wallerian degeneration** results in ellipsoids of myelin and axonal fragments that undergo rapid autolysis (self-digestion) and phagocytosis by macrophages normally resident in the endoneurium. At the same time, the myelin-free Schwann cells, which have contributed lysosomal enzymes to the breakdown process, multiply and fill the emptying endoneurial tube. After two weeks the process is complete and macrophages have withdrawn, leaving a Schwann-cell-filled endoneurial tube.

As soon as a day after severing, the end of the proximal section of axon, which has remained intact, begins sprouting. Effective regrowth occurs only in the environment of the Schwann cells, so the dominant sprout is drawn down the intact endoneurial tube to eventually reinnervate the appropriate end organ. Consult figure 21.5 for an overview of nerve degeneration and repair. The rate of regrowth varies with the nature of the injury and size of axon, but an average regeneration rate of about 1.5 mm per day is reasonable to expect.

In the adult central nervous system, the prospects of repair after a serious injury to neurons in the brain and spinal cord are very poor. Not only do the axons degenerate and not regrow distal to the point of injury, but most of their associated cell bodies will degenerate as well. Indeed, the preceding or subsequent neurons in a multineuron chain may also die back (processes called **retrograde** and **orthograde transneuronal degeneration,** 6 respectively). Apparently neurons require functional interaction in the way of stimulation and the interchange of trophic (sustaining) factors to survive, in the same way that isolated muscle cells, having no workload, may atrophy and be replaced by fibrous connective tissue. The brain and spinal

Crocodile Tears

Crush injuries result in slower sprouting but more effective reinnervation of end organs. If sensory axons sprout down a motor neuron tube, no reinnervation of the motor unit muscle fibers by the sensory axon will occur, although the abandoned fibers may be reinnervated by processes from an adjacent motor neuron. One patient who in a fight had suffered traumatic separation of the facial nerve in its course through the cheek developed a reversal of the expected pattern of innervation. When he was hungry and smelled food, his eyes teared up; when he was very sad, he salivated. This case of "crocodile tears" resulted from the growth of fibers normally associated with stimulation of the salivary glands into the lacrimal gland and vice versa.

Repair in the CNS

The failure of regrowth of axons in the CNS is a result of the unfavorable interaction between mature neurons and their microenvironment, formed principally by astrocytes. Axonal growth proceeds as the molecules in the region of growth interact with molecules of the extracellular matrix in the presence of trophic factors like neuron growth factor. Peripheral nerves that have been separated from their proximal axons create an environment favorable to axonal regrowth. This is partly due to the maintenance of a patent tube to guide the developing axon, but it appears to be mostly a result of trophic factors released by proliferating Schwann cells that fill the endoneurium. If a section of peripheral nerve is inserted into the spinal cord distal to severed motor neuron axons, axonal regrowth down this nerve will be rapid and effective. However, it will arrest as the normal cord environment is encountered. Active research proceeds into the trophic and extracellular matrix factors that might support CNS regrowth.

The growth inhibition of the microenvironment appears to affect only mature neurons. Fetal neural tissue has been implanted into adult brains with apparently successful and appropriate axonal growth and synapse formation. Some patients with extreme parkinsonism (impoverished voluntary movement accompanied by resting tremor) have had extensive functional recovery after the midbrain implantation of fetal midbrain tissue. Scientific and ethical controversy surrounds these experiments. The use of autografts of tissue from the patient's own adrenal gland avoids these issues, as well as the prospect of tissue rejection.

At Injury

Synaptic inputs

Muscle cell

Motor endplate

Macrophage

Contractile elements

Three Days Later

Ellipsoids

One Week Later

Two Weeks Later

Reinnervation and Remyelination

Figure 21.5   Wallerian degeneration and peripheral nerve regeneration.

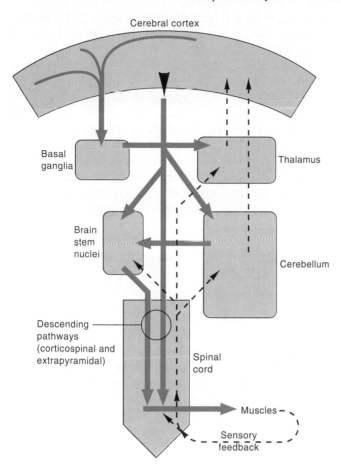

Cerebral cortex

Basal ganglia

Thalamus

Brain stem nuclei

Cerebellum

Descending pathways (corticospinal and extrapyramidal)

Spinal cord

Muscles

Sensory feedback

Figure 21.6   Overview of integrated motor function. All elements are involved in any voluntary movement.

cord tracts (pathways) that are supplied by the degenerating neurons likewise atrophy, so the lesion may be apparent at some distance from its original source. A specimen of the spinal cord would have demonstrated atrophy in the opposite dorsolateral white matter, due to degeneration of the continuing fibers in the lateral corticospinal tract.

Motor System Overview

The way a person moves voluntarily or in response to direct stimulation gives us a window into the integrity and state of functioning of that person's motor system and the sensory input necessary for its normal operation. When we tap the patellar tendon and elicit a knee jerk, we observe a fragment of an integrated motor system. The reaction we get (exaggerated, brisk, slow, reduced, absent), when put together with other relevant data, can tell us a lot about general state of health, as well as the presence, location, and perhaps the nature of the lesion. By repeating our observations, we will have evidence as to whether the effects of the lesion are spreading. But, unlike the bits we regard as motor tests or signs, any adaptive movement involves the cooperative activation of diverse elements in

the nervous system. Figure 21.6 presents a diagrammatic overview of the elements involved in movement. These motor subsystems and a few of the important integrative pathways that connect them, including signs associated with their dysfunction, are the topic of this section.

Lower Motor Neurons

The cells that are attached to and activate skeletal muscles have their cell bodies in the anterior horn of gray matter in the spinal cord. They are variously called **anterior horn cells, 7 motor neurons, alpha motor neurons,** or **lower motor neurons** to distinguish them from the fibers that connect them to the brain and brain stem. Their axons pass through the ventral root and out along the peripheral nerves, then branch and innervate the muscle cells with which they are associated. A motor neuron and the group of muscle cells it innervates is called a **motor unit.** It is these motor neuron cell bodies that are susceptible to attack by polio viruses.

The following clinical features are observed when lower motor neurons are injured. Muscle tone is reduced or absent and the muscle is paralyzed **(flaccid paralysis).** The absence or scarcity of motor neurons disrupts both voluntary movement and the expression of normal reflexes. For this reason, tendon jerks are weak or absent. Muscles supplied by the lesioned motor nerves atrophy rapidly **(neurogenic atrophy)** because they are deprived of stimulation and normal trophic factors. Tiny spontaneous electrical discharges called **fibrillation potentials** will be noted within days of the denervation, using special electrodiagnostic techniques. Later, visible uncoordinated twitching and wriggling may be noticed in the denervated muscle. These are called **fasciculations.**

Healthy lower motor neurons in the vicinity of the denervated muscle cells may gradually reinnervate the denervated cells. These enlarged motor units are not capable of producing the finely graduated force generation characteristic of the original motor unit pool. As well, expansion of the motor unit taxes the motor neuron, making it susceptible to fatigue. In the case of polio, the phenomena of postpolio syndrome may be observed (see boxed material).

Spinal Mechanisms

A great deal of important motor behavior is mediated in the spinal cord itself. Reflexive withdrawal from pain stimuli (heat, prick, etc.) can involve one or many integrated segments of the cord. The withdrawal is initiated before a person is consciously aware of the pain. Tendon reflexes (myotatic stretch reflexes) result when the action potentials generated in stretch sensors within the muscle pass into the cord, where they synapse with the large motor neurons in the anterior horn. These in turn will depolarize and pass an impulse to the stretched muscle, causing it to contract

!! *Polio victims facing a whole new battle*

News Clipping—Thousands of polio victims around the world who survived pre-vaccine epidemics of the crippling disease are battling a cruel second coming of problems.

Experts studying the syndrome agree it is not a recurrence of the actual polio virus. The syndrome is characterized by an onset of fatigue, pain and muscle weakness caused by failing nerve cells which have been working overtime for 30 years or more to compensate for the damage done by the original disease.

In Canada and the U.S. as many as a third of the polio victims who survived post-Second World War epidemics of the disease are believed at risk for developing post-polio syndrome.

There are 55 clinics and 200 support groups in the U.S. devoted to the problem, in addition to another 50 support groups in Canada, Europe, Australia and New Zealand and parts of Asia, says the International Polio Network in St. Louis.

"Fatigue seems to be one thing a lot of people are concerned about. People talk about the 'polio wall'—they hit it at maybe 3 in the afternoon and it's not just being tired. It's definite fatigue."

The syndrome is not life-threatening but it can be incapacitating.

---

reflexively. The functional significance of these stretch reflexes is that they are in place to maintain adaptive muscle tone (tension). Upright posture is maintained, to an extent, by the unconscious action of these reflexes. They are also involved in complex ways with activities like walking, swimming, and so forth.

The functioning of the stretch reflexes can be isolated for diagnostic purposes. Tapping the tendon of a muscle rapidly stretches the muscle and initiates the events just described. The reflex reaction is reflected in joint movement or tensing of the muscle. **Hyporeflexia** indicates a weaker response than normal. This may be due to muscle weakness, damage to the stretch sensors, some impairment at the cord, or lesion of the motor neurons themselves. If the hyporeflexia is exhibited bilaterally, we might suspect generalized depression of nerve function, perhaps due to electrolyte imbalance.

Hyperreflexia is an exaggeration of reflex response. This is seen transitorily in a very nervous individual as a normal facet of generalized nervous system activation. It emerges gradually as a pathological condition in individuals with significant damage to the motor neurons from the

brain and brain stem to the anterior horn cells, for instance in people with spinal cord injury. The intensification of reflex response can be extreme.

Areflexia is the absence of reflex action. This is seen in the posttrauma period for people with acute, complete spinal cord lesion. It appears to be due to the loss of the facilitating influence of upper motor neurons upon segmental reflex mechanisms. It is gradually replaced with normal reflexes if the lesion resolves or with hyperreflexia if it does not. It should be stressed that these spinal reflexes operate at the level of the cord under the facilitating or inhibiting influence of (particularly) descending motor impulses. Even if the cord above the specific segment has been completely destroyed, the basic neural machinery necessary to generate reflex actions can remain fully intact and functioning.

Cord Pathways (Upper Motor Neurons)

You may note, in figure 21.6, that there are two descending (upper motor neuron) pathways. The one that starts at the cerebral cortex (at the precentral gyrus) is called the **corticospinal tract** (origin—cortex, destination—anterior horn cells in the spinal cord). It is also called the **pyramidal tract** because most of its fibers cross over below two pyramid-shaped areas at the front of the medulla. Fibers course from the primary motor area, through the internal capsule (an extensive band of projection fibers communicating between the cerebral hemispheres and lower brain centers), through the midbrain and pons. Most decussate **8** (cross over) below the medullary pyramids and then continue down the dorsolateral white matter in the cord (corticospinal tract) to finally enter the cord gray matter and synapse in the anterior horn. This tract is responsible for finely controlled movements, particularly of the hands and feet.

The other pathway (actually several distinct pathways) is called the **extrapyramidal** or **multineuronal tract.** These cord fibers originate in certain brain stem nuclei that are the target of motor impulses that arise in the cortex, particularly from the area anterior to the primary motor cortex. The cortical inputs activate or inhibit these brain stem nuclei, which in turn influence the alpha motor neurons. The extrapyramidal fibers are responsible for maintaining balance, adjusting to changes in position, and orienting to visual and auditory stimuli. As well, they mediate repetitive rhythmic movements (walking, bicycling, etc.) and maintain posture. They are particularly focused on proximal and axial musculature. In a sense they provide the background activity that makes possible the effective execution of the fine motor activities that are the domain of the corticospinal pathways. Figure 21.7 shows the origin, course, and destination of the pyramidal and extrapyramidal tracts.

Lesions of the upper motor neurons will give rise to the following clinical features. Voluntary movements of the affected muscles are absent or weak, while the tone of the

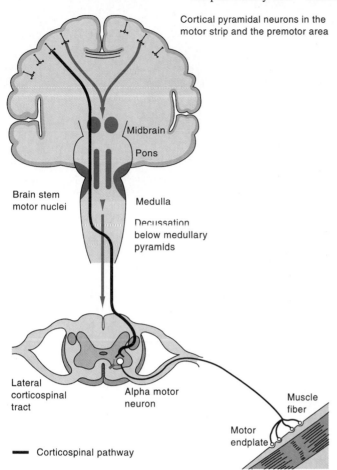

Cortical pyramidal neurons in the motor strip and the premotor area

Midbrain

Pons

Brain stem motor nuclei

Medulla

Decussation below medullary pyramids

Lateral corticospinal tract

Alpha motor neuron

Muscle fiber

Motor endplate

— Corticospinal pathway

Figure 21.7 Anatomical pathways involved in the corticospinal and extrapyramidal motor systems.

muscles is increased. This is known as **spastic paralysis.** Normal stretch reflex arcs are intact and may become stronger, perhaps because of the formation of additional synapses. Tendon reflexes are increased (the **hyperreflexia** already noted). When the examiner attempts to passively extend a flexed joint, the limb at first resists extension and then suddenly relaxes **(clasp-knife rigidity).** Muscle atrophy is slow and not complete **(disuse atrophy)** as a result of the continued release of trophic factors and reflex stimulation of muscles. Abnormal plantar reflex **(Babinski sign)** is observed. The Babinski sign in a person with cerebral trauma indicates that the upper motor neuron pathways are functionally (and perhaps structurally) disrupted.

Brain Stem Nuclei

Four distinct pairs of nuclei in the brain stem mediate motor behavior via the extrapyramidal system (as just described). The precise location of a lesion within this relatively small area (about 1½ inches long) will have a profound effect on motor behavior. If it occurs very high, where the upper motor neurons traveling in the internal

capsule enter the midbrain, the person, who is probably in a state of coma, will react to intense stimulation with decorticate rigidity, described in more detail in the section on coma (chapter 20). A lesion ½ inch lower, which will isolate the top pair of nuclei plus the cortex, will produce decerebrate rigidity (table 20.3).

Cerebellum

The cerebellum mediates the coordinated contractions of agonist and antagonist muscles to produce a smooth, well-controlled movement **(synergy).** As well, it is significant in maintaining appropriate **muscle tone,** the slight constant tension of healthy muscles such that they offer modest resistance to movement when moved passively. In brief, the cerebellum performs these roles in the following way. When a motor activity is "decided upon" by the cortex, a copy of the motor plan is sent to the cerebellum, while the various brain stem nuclei and the alpha motor neurons receive the original. The motor units react by executing the directions from the corticospinal and extrapyramidal tracts. Information about how much movement of muscles and joints actually took place is fed back from the stretch, tendon, and joint capsule receptors to the sensory cortex (awareness of movement) and unconsciously to the cerebellum (via the ascending pathways in figure 21.6). The cerebellum is essentially a very elaborate on-line computer (it has as many nerve cells as the much larger cerebrum) and it does a comparison between what was expected and what was delivered. If there was either too much or too little movement, the cerebellum discharges to the appropriate cortical or brain stem areas to correct the error. This is very rapid and continually ongoing. Figure 21.8 summarizes cerebellar function as well as illustrating anatomy.

The cerebellum mediates the smooth acceleration and then rapid deceleration characteristic of natural movements, whether of the limbs, voice, or eyes. Because it is particularly active in acceleration, deceleration, and arrest, functional deficits show up most dramatically in these phases of movement. Lesions to the cerebellum may produce any of the clinical signs or symptoms indicated in table 21.3.

Basal Ganglia

The **basal ganglia** are nuclei of gray matter deep within the cerebrum. The term basal ganglia is actually a misnomer. A more accurate term might be basal nuclei or cerebral nuclei. Unfortunately, the older term has predominance.

Basal ganglia **9** (fig. 21.9) lesions produce a very different pattern of clinical signs from those associated with cerebellar injury. A major disabling condition is **bradykinesia.** This is a general impoverishment of movement, in which the person finds it very difficult to initiate movement. **Tardive dyskinesia** is, however, the most prevalent disorder due to lesion of the basal ganglia. The lesions

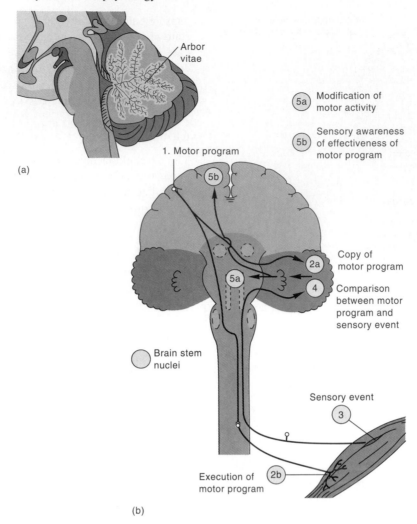

Figure 21.8   (*a*) Anatomy of the cerebellum. (*b*) Order of events in the execution of voluntary movement.

causing tardive dyskinesia usually arise from excess pro-longed use of medications like tricyclic antidepressants. The person makes involuntary writhing movements of the face, tongue, head, and neck and may pull up the knees while sitting. It is often associated with **dystonia,** frozen movement. **Resting tremor,** a steady rapid (8 per second) involuntary tremor, is a common symptom. What differentiates this from the intention or terminal tremor of a cerebellar lesion is that it is repressed during voluntary movements. Many individuals develop strategies to make this resting tremor less noticeable.

Chorea (rapid, flicklike movements of the wrists and hands and face) and **athetosis** (slow, writhing movements of fingers and hands and sometimes the toes, feet, and proximal parts of the limbs, and even the face) are also found in people affected by diseases of the basal ganglia. As well, there may be a distinctive form of rigidity (**lead-pipe rigidity**) that presents a steady exaggerated resistance to passive movement. Another possible effect is **cogwheel**

rigidity, in which the flexed limb provides a rhythmically interrupted, ratchetlike resistance to extension.

A dramatic form of explosive involuntary movement may be observed in people who suffer a lesion, usually vascular, to the region of the small subthalamic nucleus. The limbs may be intermittently and violently flung outward without warning. These movements are called **ballisms** and the most usual pattern is for one of the two nuclei to be affected, producing hemiballismus. The condition is usually transitory.

The basal ganglia probably function as programmers of motor behavior. Diffuse areas of the cortex (particularly the frontal lobes) cooperate in the formation of the intent to perform a complex movement. The cortex communicates this general "intent" to the basal ganglia, which do the hard work of creating the complex pattern of programs that can release those behaviors from the spinal mechanisms. These programs are fed back to the cortex, which reviews and edits them and then sends one copy to the cerebellum and a

Table 21.3	Terminology Describing Signs and Symptoms Associated with Cerebellar Injury

Past-pointing: When rapidly reaching out to touch an object, the person overshoots the mark. The test for this may be to get the person to touch, in rapid alteration, her nose and your fingertip held 18 inches away.

Intention tremor: This tremor emerges during the execution of movement. As the limb reaches the end of its planned movement (say, to pick up a cup of tea), the tremor, which was present during movement, worsens, giving rise to the term **terminal tremor.**

Hypotonia: Muscle tone is abnormally weak.

Dysdiadochokinesia: Rapidly alternating movements (like patting the thighs with palms up and then palms down) are difficult or impossible.

Ataxia: Gait is characterized by a wide stance and unsteady walking ("drunken sailor's" gait).

Dysarthria: Difficulty in speaking. With cerebellar lesions the result is sometimes called "scanning speech" because it resembles the struggles of someone who is having trouble reading out loud and develops a sing-song, emotionless sort of rhythm.

(a)

(b)

second copy to the motor and premotor cortex, to turn on the cells that will activate the corticospinal and extrapyramidal tracts. The behavior of **frozen addicts,** i.e., people who took street drugs contaminated with the chemical MPTP that damaged their basal ganglia, illustrates how crucial these centers are to the initiation and execution of movement. Some of these people are totally incapable of voluntary movement, but if stood up and walked seem able to passively respond, all without any gross impairment of consciousness.

Thalamus

This 10 is the part of the CNS through which all sensation except smell and all information about the form or results of movement are channeled. Small lesions here can produce many of the signs associated with cerebellar or basal ganglia dysfunction by interrupting the relay of signals from these systems. However, this sort of tiny focal lesion is very unusual.

Internal Capsule

As noted, this is the major pathway for motor information flowing out of the cerebrum and for sensory and sensory-motor information flowing in. The effect of lesions here

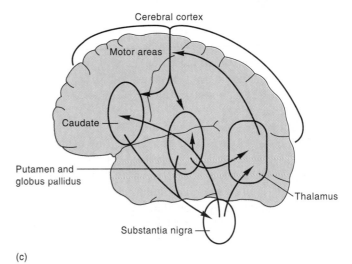

(c)

Figure 21.9   Basal ganglia structures (*a* and *b*) and functional interrelationships (*c*).

depends on the position and extent of the lesion. **Locked-in syndrome** involves the functional or structural interruption of just the motor pathways and renders a person totally paralyzed except for the respiratory muscles, which are innervated further down the brain stem. This person will have intact sensation and normal consciousness but complete paralysis of voluntary movement.

Cerebral Cortex

The functions of the primary motor cortex and the premotor cortex have already been described. Lesions restricted to the motor cortex are rare. Usually a broader territory 11 is involved, perhaps including some basal ganglia and part of the internal capsule or the underlying white matter. Given this background, we can describe some classic syndromes that include the motor cortex. **Hemiplegia** is paralysis restricted to the half of the body contralateral (on the opposite side) to the site of the lesion. The paralysis, since it is arising from an upper motor neuron lesion, will be spastic (rigid or hyperreflexive). As well, because brain stem nuclei are isolated from cortical modulation, the person will assume a classic hemiplegic stance: the hand, wrist, and elbow are flexed and the toe is extended. This is reminiscent of a unilateral decorticate rigidity (see chapter 20) and may be based on the same neural mechanisms. Hemiplegia would result if all the motor fibers in one internal capsule were disrupted. As well, a person would be functionally hemiplegic if the lateral precentral gyrus were lesioned, say by occlusion of the middle cerebral artery.

If the ischemia was on the language dominant hemisphere (the left for most people), the person would most likely have a deficit in the ability to form and enunciate words—**productive aphasia,** specifically Broca's aphasia. There may also be a difficulty in finding the words to express the ideas in the first place—another form of productive and often receptive aphasia called **Wernicke's aphasia. (Receptive aphasia** implies a difficulty in comprehending written or spoken language.) Broca's area and Wernicke's area are noted in figures 20.17 and 20.18 in the previous chapter.

Monoplegia (paralysis of only one extremity) could result from a very small lesion in the lateral precentral gyrus, in which case it could paralyze the arm and perhaps half the face (contralateral to the lesion). More probably the monoplegia is due to an interruption to the territory of the anterior cerebral artery deep in the longitudinal fissure, in which case the contralateral leg will be the area most affected by the paralysis. Bladder and bowel control would also be reduced.

Extensive diffuse injury of the cerebral cortex, as may occur in diffuse arteriosclerosis or Alzheimer's disease, can give rise to a strange form of rigidity called **gegenhalten** (German for go-stop). In this case, when a limb is passively moved it gives an apparently willed resistance or opposition quite different from lead pipe or clasp-knife rigidity. What appears to be happening is that the person, because of extensive cortical damage, can't cooperatively relax the limb.

Diagnosis in Movement Disorders

Something should be said about the diagnostic techniques commonly used to differentiate between the disorders that can affect movement. Degeneration of numbers of muscle fibers will release abnormal amounts of intracellular enzymes into the plasma, and these can be detected. For example, elevated creatine kinase is found in Duchenne-type muscular dystrophy. Electrical properties, assessed by inserting needle electrodes into muscle, give a variety of suggestive if nonspecific clues to the status of the muscle tissue and the health of its nervous supply. **Electromyography** (EMG) focuses on the muscle's response to needle insertion or movement (electrical activity should be crisp and brief), ongoing spontaneous activity (should be essentially electrically silent), the summed activity of a motor neuron and the hundreds of muscle fibers it supplies (the motor unit potential), and the massed activity that a person is able to induce voluntarily with varying effort (recruitment pattern). Muscle biopsies, which extract a tiny core of tissue, are done to examine the tissue microscopically. Studies of nerve conduction velocities can localize slowing or loss of signal strength in a peripheral nerve. And sensory-evoked potentials can follow a peripherally generated signal to its destination in the primary somatosensory cortex of the contralateral hemisphere.

IMPAIRED MOVEMENT THAT RESULTS FROM DISORDERS OF MUSCLE, NEUROMUSCULAR JUNCTION, NERVE, OR SPINAL CORD

The following disorders produce muscular weakness as their primary disability. If this occurs during musculoskeletal development, extreme joint deformities may develop along with the major disturbances of movement, including gait or grasp. In the adult frame, generalized or focal weakness can lead to less severe but recognizable limb or joint distortions. If a sensory deficit accompanies or causes the motor disability, neurogenic joint degeneration (called **Charcot's joint**) may occur. This is partly because the joint isn't held in the physiological orientation for which it was designed. It is also probably due to increased wear and tear that ensues when normal sensation, including pain, is lost. The sensory phenomena that may accompany these disorders will be variable. In some, Duchenne-type muscular dystrophy for example, ongoing pain is not characteristic; on the other hand, in polymyositis about half those afflicted experience significant pain. Motor deficits with a sensory component may produce a variety of sensory abnormalities, as detailed in the section on neurogenic pain in chapter 23.

Primary Myopathies

Diseases intrinsic to the muscle fiber (**primary myopathies**) derive principally from either heritable or autoimmune disorders. The precise pathogenetic mechanisms and focus are subjects of active research and are largely beyond our scope. A traditional categorization produces dystrophies, myotonias, and polymyositis/dermatomyositis. Table 21.4 presents the relevant information.

Table 21.4   Disorders of Muscle Tissue (Primary Myopathies)

Dystrophies

DUCHENNE'S DYSTROPHY—Transmission: X-linked recessive, almost all affected are males. Disease apparent by 2–5 years, begins with hip girdle weakness **12** (waddling gait), weakness and wasting, rapidly progressive, death usual before 25 years. Cardiomyopathy often present. Elevated CK in patients; as many as 90% of adolescent female carriers have elevated CK. Also called pseudohypertrophic dystrophy because 80% show enlargement particularly of calf **13** due to fibrosis and fat. Membrane and intracellular calcium storage defect responsible. **14**

FACIOSCAPULOHUMERAL DYSTROPHY **15** —Transmission: autosomal dominant, both sexes equally affected. Onset in adolescence, mild and slowly progressive, course variable. Wasting of facial, pectoral, and shoulder girdle muscles. CK seldom elevated, heart uninvolved. Normal longevity possible.

LIMB-GIRDLE DYSTROPHY—Actually a group of disorders. Transmission: usually autosomal recessive, both sexes affected equally. Onset adolescence or adulthood. Affects either shoulder or hip girdle, usually mild progression.

Myotonias

MYOTONIA CONGENITA (THOMSEN'S DISEASE)—Transmission: usually autosomal dominant. Myotonia *without* weakness. Stimulated muscle maintains prolonged contraction. Early onset, compatible with normal longevity, affects all skeletal muscles. Muscle hypertrophy common. Exercise relieves symptoms. Decreased chloride channel density in muscle membranes slows repolarization.

MYOTONIC MUSCULAR DYSTROPHY (STEINERT DISEASE)—Transmission: autosomal dominant. Myotonia *with* weakness. Onset in adulthood. Affects principally cranial and shoulder girdle muscles. Multisystem disease: baldness and testicular atrophy in males, cataracts in all patients.

Myositis

POLYMYOSITIS/DERMATOMYOSITIS **16** — Multisystem immune-mediated disease with muscle weakness major symptom. Half of patients experience rashes (dermatomyositis) on eyelids, extensor surfaces of joints. Begins with limb girdle weakness, can progress to neck weakness, impaired swallowing and breathing. Eyelid strength maintained (vs. myasthenia gravis). Elevated serum CK.

Disorders of Neuromuscular Junction

Myasthenia gravis (severe weakness and malaise) is an autoimmune disorder in which antibodies are produced to acetylcholine receptors. These neurotransmitter receptors are produced on the folded surface of a skeletal muscle membrane where it is in intimate association with the end processes of a motor neuron axon (the motor endplate **17** region). In normal function, the arrival at the end of processes of a nerve signal causes the release of perhaps 200,000 molecules of acetylcholine (ACh), which diffuse across the synaptic space or cleft, bind to ACh receptors, and open membrane channels. These allow the movement of sodium ions into the muscle cell and induce a second signal, this time in the muscle membrane, which triggers the contractile process in the muscle cell. After the signal is begun, the channels lose their affinity for ACh. It diffuses back into the synaptic cleft, is broken down by an enzyme called acetylcholinesterase that resides there, and the breakdown products are taken back up into the end processes for reuse. This chain of events allows for the rapid, controlled turning on of muscle tension and its equally important turning off. Binding of anti-ACh-receptor antibodies has no stimulatory effect, but neither is the antibody easily released. Two pathologic processes are instigated. Bound antibody stimulates neutrophil phagocytosis of the endplate muscle membrane. It also serves as a signal to the muscle cell and induces uptake and degradation of these receptor channels. The combined rate of degradation/phagocytosis exceeds the production capacity, and a net impoverishment of receptor channels occurs. Gradually the muscle response to nerve stimulation is impaired and weakness increases.

12 ||||||||||||||||| 14443

13 ||||||||||||||||| 14443

14 ||||||||||||||||| 14385

15 ||||||||||||||||| 14515

16 ||||||||||||||||| 5846

17 ||||||||||||||||| 1601

Typical of many autoimmune disorders, the pattern is one of flare-up and remission. The classic form of MG (myasthenia gravis) affects the muscles of the face, neck, and limb girdles. It gets worse during the day and with fatigue. The eyelids droop (ptosis), the face becomes inexpressive, the head tips forward, and the sternocleidomastoids become weak, the nasal voice becomes slurred, it is difficult to raise the arms or climb stairs. As the usually chronic, progressive syndrome persists, it worsens and muscle wasting may occur. The course is highly variable. Some people develop only the eyelid and ocular muscle weakness (ocular myasthenia). Those with more generalized MG can respond well to therapy. Some have a very fulminant, progressive form with muscle wasting and poor response to therapy. These people can die within five years, usually of pneumonia secondary to immobility.

Chemicals that block the action of acetylcholinesterase allow ACh to accumulate in the cleft. This can compensate for the impoverishment of receptors and allow somewhat normal neuromuscular transmission. **Tensilon** (edrophonium) is a potent antiacetylcholinesterase drug. It is only used diagnostically. The patient suspected of having MG is given an injection of Tensilon. Within 10–30 seconds, life comes back to the face, the eyelids rise, and neck strength and shoulder girdle strength return, confirming a diagnosis of MG. Within ten minutes the effects are reversed. Physostigmine and neostigmine are related drugs that can be used therapeutically. This chemical management has its downsides. ACh in relatively normal neuromuscular junctions is allowed to accumulate to excess amounts, producing muscle tetany. It can also produce abnormal patterns of autonomic discharge.

In this context, the emergency treatment of a person with a suspected **myasthenic crisis** is illustrative. This person would have an inability to swallow, clear secretions, or breathe adequately because of a sudden flare-up of myasthenic weakness. This condition must be discriminated from a similar-appearing **cholinergic crisis,** which is probably due to excessive plasma levels of antiacetylcholinesterase drug. These people would have excess bronchial secretions, excessive sweating, and impaired swallowing and breathing due to muscle paralysis. Life support must be available because the administration of Tensilon will deepen a cholinergic crisis, which can be reversed with the administration of an anticholinergic drug like atropine.

Other therapies focus on quenching the intensity of the immune response. Thymectomy used to be done fairly often and with varying results. (Thymic hyperplasia is a common finding.) More currently, management focuses on immunosuppressants and steroidal anti-inflammatories. Plasmapheresis, in which blood is circulated extracorporeally past a membrane that absorbs antibodies (gamma globulins) and then returned to the patient, is used to reverse a serious exacerbation. Because none of these techniques are selective for the anti-ACh antibodies, they render the person susceptible to infection, particularly bacterial.

Eton-Lambert syndrome produces many of the same symptoms as MG but results from an impaired release of ACh. This generalized weakness may be seen as a paraneoplastic phenomenon in the late stages of cancer. ACh release is better after a few contractions and this, and other findings, differentiate it from MG.

Peripheral Nerve Disorders

Diffuse Polyneuropathies

A variety of metabolic, toxic, and nutritional conditions can cause scattered peripheral nerve lesions, so-called **diffuse polyneuropathies.** These are usually chronic problems that may have a variety of mechanisms of injury. Vascular pathology in large and small arteries develops in diabetes, which may affect oxygenation of peripheral nerves. Substances accumulate in toxic levels in diabetes, in liver and kidney failure, in alcohol abuse, and in the chronic use of some drugs (e.g., isoniazid and hydralazine). Vitamin and substrate deficiencies can be associated with nutritional deficiencies or inflammatory conditions of the stomach or intestine.

The pattern of motor and sensory loss is varied. **Glove-and-stocking anesthesia** can develop through the selective lesioning of pain receptors and lightly myelinated fibers in the distal extremities (fig. 21.10). Loss of larger fibers leads to impaired proprioception—that is, sensation of movement and limb position—and loss of function that depends on incoming, well-discriminated sensation. As a result stretch reflexes will be diminished, vibratory sense in the periphery is decreased, and walking is impaired. The person may show foot drop due to impaired sensory input or muscle weakness that may develop peripherally. Paresthesias like numbness, tingling or "pins and needles" (see chapter 23) are common.

Many of these conditions are irreversible at the late stage at which they are often detected, but progression may be halted if correction of the underlying pathology is possible. Electromyography and nerve conduction velocity tests are invaluable diagnostic aids.

Guillain-Barré Syndrome

This peripheral neuropathy results from an immune-mediated attack on the sheaths of well-myelinated fibers. Therefore, in Guillain-Barré syndrome, both movement and well-discriminated sensation are affected. The typical course follows about a week after a flu or upper respiratory tract viral

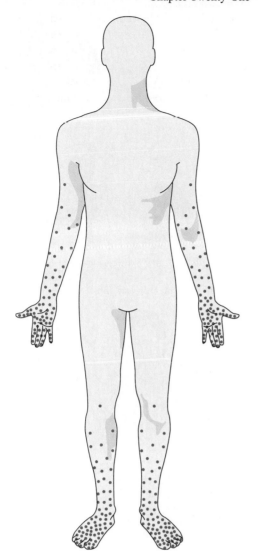

Figure 21.10   Glove-and-stocking anesthesia associated with diffuse peripheral neuropathy.

infection. In the United States a rash of cases was noted after widespread vaccination in the swine-flu epidemic of the early 1980s. In its most extreme form, paresthesias, for example, tingling of the hands and feet, are followed by progressive weakness, areflexia, and distal sensory loss. Paralysis including respiratory arrest can occur, requiring mechanical ventilation. Survival of this crisis leads to a positive prognosis: 85% make a complete recovery in 4–6 months. Immunosuppressants and steroids or ACTH have varied efficacy.

The pathology results from infiltration of the endoneurial tube by lymphocytes and, later, macrophages. Demyelination is a direct result of the binding of antibodies to a variety of Schwann cell myelin proteins. The pattern of demyelination may be very focal. There may also be wide-spread axonal degeneration, which explains the slow recovery of function. Because the endoneureal tube remains intact for the most part, regrowth and reinnervation is usually effective. But the recovery of function may be incomplete, with enduring or permanent focal sensory or motor loss. Figure 21.11 provides a summary. Again, EMG and nerve conduction studies are a valuable diagnostic and prognostic aid.

Entrapment Syndromes

The general category **entrapment syndromes** groups together peripheral nerve lesions that are clearly due to local compression and trauma (e.g., Saturday night palsy or tardy ulnar palsy) with those that are related to overuse or repetitive motion injury (e.g., pronator terres syndrome) and with those that are probably a combination of overuse and genetic predisposition (e.g., carpal tunnel syndrome). The common problem in all these conditions is a focal slowing and loss of intensity of motor and sensory signals. Prolonged signal impairment will result in muscle wasting and eventually irreversible fibrosis, so prompt diagnosis and correction, if effective, is critical. More conservative approaches, including rest, physiotherapy, and learning ways of moving that don't irritate or compress the nerve, are usually considered before surgery. Surgery releases surrounding muscle tissue, removes connective tissue to facilitate vascular perfusion and reduce pressure, and repositions nerves that have been traumatized in their course. Particularly with carpal tunnel syndrome, the response to surgery is variable, independent of the chronicity of the condition.

Any peripheral nerve can be subject to compression or trauma. The common conditions of the upper limb are presented here. Table 21.5 summarizes these.

Charcot-Marie-Tooth Disease

This heritable atrophy of peripheral motor and sensory neurons is usually passed by autosomal dominant transmission (see Huntington's disease later for an explanation). Degeneration of dorsal and ventral cord roots, the dorsal root ganglion, and alpha motor neurons is also observed. Both the axons and myelin sheaths are affected by this unexplained pathology. It begins with weakness and atrophy in the distal muscles of the lower limb, giving it the less complicated name **peroneal muscular atrophy.** Later the hands and arms are involved as the condition progresses proximally. Onset is usually in late childhood or adolescence but can be postponed until middle age in mild cases. The extent of progression is variable and usually arrests at the lower thigh and proximal forearm. A variety of limb deformities result from the muscle wasting. These require periodic orthotic correction.

(a) Upper respiratory tract viral infection.

(b) Tingling and numbness in scattered areas, particularly the periphery.

(c) Scattered weakness, decreased stretch reflexes (e.g., ↓ knee jerk).

(d) On ventilator, complete paralysis.

(e) Gradual recovery; walking with assistance (walker).

(f) Complete recovery.

Figure 21.11   Stages in the progression of Guillain-Barré syndrome.

Table 21.5	Summary of Major Peripheral Nerve Entrapment Syndromes Affecting the Upper Limbs, Presented in Order of the Site of Lesion (Distal to Proximal)

Radial Nerve

(normally responsible for extension of elbow, wrist, and fingers, forearm supination, and sensation in the back of the hand, including proximal surface of thumb and first two fingers)

Posterior Interosseus Syndrome

Lesion in upper dorsal forearm (perhaps due to overuse of the supinator muscle in actions like that used in driving in a screw). Weakness in extension of wrist and fingers, supination strength intact, no noticeable sensory loss.

Saturday Night Palsy

Temporary (6–8 weeks) neuropathy due to compression in the posterior upper arm, named for common occurrence in people who have passed out and subjected nerve to prolonged compression. Triceps unaffected (normal extension at elbow) but extension of wrist and fingers impaired, as is forearm supination. Sensory loss restricted to back of hand, thumb, and first and second fingers.

Compression can also occur at the axilla, often from improperly used crutch, same symptoms as Saturday night palsy but includes impaired extension at elbow.

Median Nerve

(normally responsible for forearm pronation; contributes to wrist flexion, finger flexion, and a complex variety of finger movements, sensation in palm and palmar surface of thumb, first two fingers and radial half of third)

Carpal Tunnel Syndrome

Lesion is in the ventral wrist where tendons, blood vessels, and median nerve enter the hand (carpal tunnel). Best-known and most common entrapment neuropathy. Incidence highest in fifth and sixth decades and in women. Frequently bilateral but dominant hand more affected; a majority of patients do considerable work with their hands. Painful paresthesias, which can awaken the patient, are often referred to elbow or shoulder; sensory loss in territory described above. Symptoms worsen after passive flexion or hyperextension of wrist of affected hand. Atrophy of thumb muscles causes flattening of palm called "ape hand."

Anterior Interosseus Syndrome

This nerve branches about halfway between elbow and wrist. Lesion causes pain in the forearm and elbow and impairs intrinsic hand muscles such that when patient is asked to form an "OK" sign, thumb and forefinger will make a "pinch sign" instead of an "O."

Ulnar Nerve

(normally contributes to wrist flexion, innervation of a variety of muscles intrinsic to the hand, sensation of palm, little finger, and medial half of third finger)

Tardy Ulnar Palsy

Collective name for ulnar nerve lesions between shoulder and wrist. Two most common are cubital tunnel syndrome, where the nerve passes medially around the elbow (at the "funny bone") and lesion is due to repeated minor trauma (e.g., those who work long hours with elbows on a table) or immobilization following fracture, and a second in which the lesion is about four inches distal to the cubital tunnel where the ulnar nerve passes through the medial muscle contributing to wrist flexion (flexor carpi ulnaris), in which case overuse or congenital predisposition are explanations. Impaired sensation in territory described; weakness in a variety of abduction and adduction movements of fingers and thumb, and thumb flexion; wasting of hand intrinsics, when advanced called "claw hand."

General Comments on Treatment

If overuse is the cause, a change in activity or technique can reverse symptoms. Response to anti-inflammatory agents is variable. Response to surgical decompression and sometimes movement of nerve continues to improve with advances in surgical technique; in some conditions success is excellent while in others it is variable.

Disorders of the Spinal Cord

Cord Structure and Function

The primary structural distinction in the cord (white matter pathways consisting of variably myelinated axons, surrounding gray matter consisting of cell bodies and their synaptic interconnections) is straightforward. The central butterfly of gray matter can be further subdivided into collections of motor neurons with related function in the anterior horns and sensory relay neurons in the posterior horns. The gray matter interconnections allow for the subtle modulation of both ascending sensory and descending motor information. Many distinct and consistent pathways have been identified in the white matter of the cord, each carrying its own information destined to initiate or modify nervous system outflow or inputs.

Outflow includes all movement excluding those of speech and facial expression, whose outflow signals leave the CNS along the cranial nerves before the cord starts. It also includes the modification of autonomic functions like digestion, cardiac function, vascular tone, sweating, etc. Except for the small sacral parasympathetic portion, most cord autonomic discharge is sympathetic, a fact that can have profound consequences for a person with extensive spinal cord damage.

Input includes sensation arising in the skin below the head, as well as the joints, muscles, and tendons. All sensation from the organs of special sense (eyes, ears, nose, mouth) passes to the CNS along cranial nerves. Input also includes the sensory feedback upon which autonomic nervous system function relies. The presence in a cord isolated by spinal cord lesion of both feedback to the autonomic nervous system and unmediated sympathetic outflow sets the stage for a condition called **autonomic dysreflexia.** This is seen as a chronic problem in individuals with complete high cord lesions (quadriplegia). The smallest stimulus (cold, pressure from a blanket, bladder pressure) may elicit a **mass reflex.** There is massive sympathetic discharge, which causes sweating, flushing, dangerously increased blood pressure, intense headache, and bradycardia. The latter requires explanation. The initial cardiovascular response to sympathetic discharge is vasoconstriction in arterioles (increased peripheral resistance and increased blood pressure) and increased rate and force of cardiac contraction. The increased blood pressure induces distention in the carotid baroreceptors, which are still normally functioning. Resultant increases in parasympathetic discharge from the cardiac center in the medulla are carried along the intact vagus nerve (CN X), which slows the heart rate. Uncontrolled sympathetic discharge is such that vasoconstriction maintains the elevated blood pressure. The violent headaches produced are an indicator of the extreme elevation of cerebral blood pressure. This condition must be medically controlled or risk cerebral hemorrhage.

!! Brown-Séquard Syndrome

The different pathways of the spinal cord tracts are illustrated by observations of the nineteenth century French physician Henri Brown-Séquard. He attended a young man who had been stabbed in the back in a barroom brawl. The lesion severed the right half of the cord in the midthoracic region (right hemisection of the cord). Most of the clinical findings were consistent with Brown-Séquard's commonsense expectations: the man couldn't move his right foot, he had no awareness of light touch or whether the doctor had moved his right great toe up or down, stroking his right sole elicited a Babinski, and in time the right limb became hyperreflexive. The left leg, on the other hand, was normal. Well, not completely normal. He had lost his sensitivity to both pain and temperature in that leg. And even more curious, these sensations were intact in the right leg. What Brown-Séquard had stumbled on was the decussation of pain and temperature at the level of the cord at which it enters.

Table 21.6 and figure 21.12 present the clinically relevant cord tracts.

Spinal Cord Injury: Chronic Adaptation

The long-term response to cord injury will depend on both the level and the extent of the injury. Incomplete lesions will leave unaffected any sensation or movement for which open pathways remain. Conversely, if an area of gray matter is destroyed, so is any reflex activity it mediated. Individual assessment of all movement, sensation, and reflex activity is necessary to assess these issues. Complete lesions are simpler to assess in terms of the lowest level of intact sensation and motor control. But again, the possibility of cord damage below the point must be carefully assessed to predict the integrity of perhaps useful reflex function. An example is reflex emptying of bladder or bowel. If the centers mediating these are intact, then filling of the bladder beyond about 650 ml or distention of the rectum following an automatic mass peristaltic movement in the colon will elicit reflex relaxation of the internal sphincters and contraction of smooth muscle in the wall of the bladder or rectum, causing voiding. This tends to insure, at least with the bladder, that emptying is more complete and the attendant risk of infection less. It also opens the possibility of "tricking" intact sensory and motor capacity to improve the quality of independent living. Manual pressure on the lower abdomenopelvic area can stretch the bladder and bowel and induce reflex emptying. Intact reflex innervation of the bladder is not an unmixed blessing. Excessive bladder tone (neurogenic bladder) can restrict bladder filling and lead to constant overflow.

Table 21.6   Summary of Ascending and Descending Cord Tracts

Ascending (Sensory) Pathways

Anterolateral spinothalamic tract

carries information from pain, temperature, and crude touch* receptors to the thalamus (a relay station in the brain). It is then relayed to the cerebral cortex and conscious awareness. 1st neuron passes from receptor to synapse in the dorsal horn (cell body in the dorsal root ganglion). 2nd neuron crosses the cord in the region ventral to the central canal and travels in this spinothalamic tract to the thalamus. 3rd neuron passes from the thalamus to the cerebral cortex. This is a crossed pathway, i.e., damage to left pathway gives symptoms on the right side of the body; for example, a lesion to the left side of the cord in the spinothalamic tract will impair any temperature sensation from the *right* side of the body below the lesion.

Dorsal columns—medial lemniscal pathway

carries information from receptors in the skin (light touch, vibration, capacity to discriminate between adjacent stimuli, pressure), particularly from the lower and upper limbs; also carries information from shoulder, arm, and finger on position and tension in muscles and tendons, movements, etc. 1st neuron passes from receptor to the cord (cell body in the dorsal root ganglion) and then passes up the dorsal column of white matter (the fibers from the legs travel in the fasciculus gracilis and from the arms in the fasciculus cuneatus) to a nucleus in the medulla. The 2nd neuron passes from this nucleus across the brain stem to the thalamus. The 3rd neuron then passes from the thalamus to the cortex for conscious perception. This is an uncrossed pathway: damage to the left side of the cord results in sensory deficits in the left side of the body. This pathway also supplies the cerebellum with movement information from the upper limbs.

Descending (Motor) Pathways

Lateral corticospinal tract

carries movement signals from the cerebral cortex to the motor neurons in the spinal cord. A single neuron passes from the cerebral cortex, crosses over in the medulla, and travels down the cord in a lateral position. At the level of the motor neuron, the fiber passes into the gray matter of the cord to synapse with the motor neuron. This pathway is particularly significant in skilled hand and foot movements. Damage to the left side of the cord results in motor deficits on the left side. (Also called the "pyramidal tract.")

Extrapyramidal pathways

These are pathways that provide for the support of movements of the lateral corticospinal tract. This includes movements of the trunk and proximal limb muscles, balance, posture, orienting to sight or sound and more. While working in coordination with the corticospinal tract, these tracts are distinct from it, hence the name extrapyramidal. Because activation of these tracts requires the successive involvement of more than one neuron (vs. the corticospinal) they are sometimes called the multineuronal pathways.

*This is mechanical stimulation that is intense enough to begin to cause tissue damage.

Complete lesion has a predictable pattern of functional loss depending on the level of damage. Table 21.7 provides an overview.

Sexual function and sensation is a major concern for the victim of a spinal cord lesion. Partial lesion may leave sensation intact, and as long as the level of the cord mediating sexual responses (parasympathetic—erection, at sacral 2–4; sympathetic—ejaculation, at thoracic 10–12) is unharmed, normal sexual function is a possibility even with motor impairment. Complete lesions prevent sensory awareness of genital stimulation, but intact reflex erection and ejaculation may be a significant component of a paralyzed person's sexual repertoire.

Hyperreflexia, like the autonomic dysreflexia already described, may create a significant management problem, since it disrupts weak voluntary movement or interferes with the passive movement of limbs that is necessary when the person is dressed or positioned. It can be treated medically, or, if necessary, by surgical interruption of spinal nerve roots.

Syringomyelia

This condition, which produces a cavity in the central cord, arises in principally two circumstances. In **idiopathic syringomyelia,** a person with no other neurological history

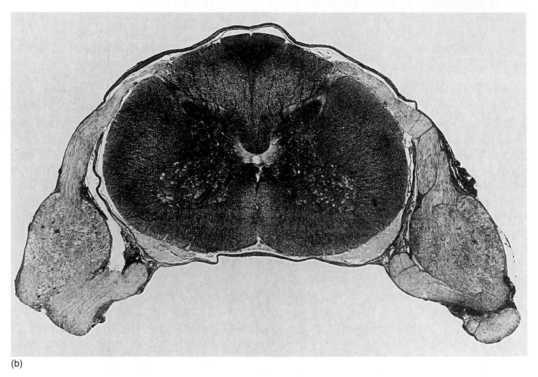

Figure 21.12   (*a*) Principal cord tracts and regions of gray matter. (*b*) Photomicrograph of spinal cord.

will gradually develop an unexplained dilatation of the central canal of the spinal cord, usually in the cervical region. **18** As this **syrinx** expands, it first compresses the decussating fibers carrying pain and temperature information across the cord. This interrupts the function of these fibers and produces a classic pattern of pain and temperature insensitivity in the arms and upper trunk, called, because of its distribution, **shawl anesthesia** (fig. 21.13). Fibers that have decussated below the lesion continue uninterrupted in the anterolateral-spinothalamic tract, so pain and temperature sensation in the lower trunk and limbs is normal. If the cavity continues to expand, compression of

motor and sensory neurons in the gray matter will depress motor behavior in the arms. Eventually obliteration of transmission in the outer white tracts will cause quadriplegia. Usually a person will go for care well before this point. Unexplained insensitivity to burns and cuts is the usual complaint. By-passing accumulated CSF (shunting) will usually arrest the progression of the dilatation, although there is likelihood of permanent sensory deficits.

The other situation in which syringomyelia occurs is secondary to spinal cord trauma. Many people who have survived the original injury and are well on their way to adapting to whatever functional loss they have experienced

Table 21.7   Functional Capacity Associated with Complete Cord Transection at a Variety of Cervical and Lumbosacral Levels

Cervical Injuries

If these muscles are normal and	these muscles are weak and	these muscles are nonfunctioning then	the level of the lesion is below
		Diaphragm	C1 or C2
	Diaphragm	Elbow flexors	C3 or C4
Diaphragm	Elbow flexors	Wrist extensors	C5
Elbow flexors	Wrist extensors	Elbow extensor	C6
Wrist extensors	Elbow extensor	Hand intrinsics	C7
Elbow extensor	Hand intrinsics		C8
Hand intrinsics			T1 or below

Dorsolumbar Injuries

If these muscles are normal and	these muscles are weak and	these muscles are nonfunctioning then	the level of the lesion is below
		Hip adductors	L1 or above
	Hip adductors	Knee extensors	L2
Hip adductors	Knee extensors	Ankle dorsiflexors	L3
Knee extensors	Ankle dorsiflexors	Great toe extensor	L4
Ankle dorsiflexors	Great toe extensor	Ankle plantarflexors	L5
Great toe extensor	Ankle plantarflexors	Anal sphincter	S1
Ankle plantarflexors	Anal sphincter		S2

From Frank Netter, *Clinical Symposia*, vol. 30, no. 2. Reprinted by permission.

are hit with a second wave of cord destruction. Again, no effective explanation exists. The cavity is more likely to be in the gray matter of the cord, and shunting is the usual treatment.

Subacute Combined Degeneration of the Cord

This generalized lesion of the posterior half of the spinal cord is often associated with a constellation of disorders that are related to its most common though not invariable cause: chronic alcohol abuse. The lesion gradually obliterates the function of the lateral corticospinal tract, the dorsal columns, and the pathways carrying proprioceptive information from the legs. This results in impaired (particularly finely controlled distal) movement, ataxic (drunken sailor) gait, toe drop, impaired skin and proprioceptive sensation, and hyporeflexia. The pathogenetic mechanism is related to inflammation of the gastric mucosa, which impairs the secretion of the intrinsic factor that is essential for the absorption of vitamin B_{12}. This B_{12} deficiency gives rise to a severe form of anemia called **pernicious anemia,** which appears to be a mechanism of cord lesion. The pattern of cord lesion may result from an interaction between the anemia (hypoxia) and the vascular supply to the cord. The dorsal white matter is supplied by two small posterior spinal

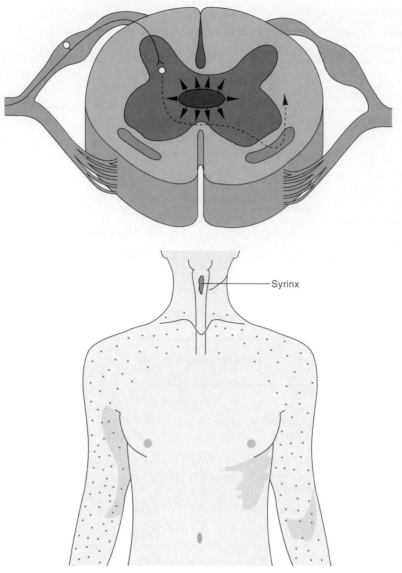

Syrinx

Figure 21.13   Syringomyelia produced a CSF-filled cyst in the spinal cord that compresses crossing spinothalamic axons. This gives rise to pain and temperature insensitivity in the area innervated, in this case a shawl anesthesia due to a cervical syrinx.

arteries, while the anterior cord and gray matter are supplied by the larger anterior spinal artery.

People who smoke and drink to excess are considerably more likely to develop this form of gastritis, although those who abstain can as well. The other disorders that are found in chronic alcoholics include cerebellar degeneration, lesions to the hypothalamus and hippocampal outflow paths that impair new memory formation, and a broad dementia called **Korsakoff's psychosis.** The latter may be more directly related to deficiencies in other vitamins, including thiamine, and direct alcohol toxicity. Subacute combined degeneration is reversible in its very early stages by administration of B_{12}. This must be injected, as oral doses would not be absorbed.

In **tabes dorsalis** (dorsal wasting) a similar pattern is observed, with involvement of the dorsal root ganglia as

well. Syphilis spirochetes are the agent in this case. They enter and damage the small dorsal arteries and produce deficits similar to those in subacute combined degeneration.

Amyotrophic Lateral Sclerosis

Variously called Lou Gehrig's disease and motor neuron disease, **amyotrophic lateral sclerosis** (ALS) is named because of the combination of loss of trophic factors to the muscles (lower motor neuron lesion) and the gross appearance of the cord at autopsy (lateral scarring because of lesions to the lateral corticospinal tract, upper motor neuron lesion). This ultimately fatal disorder is purely motor in nature. About 80% of people with ALS die within three years of diagnosis. For the other 20%, the disease follows a slow course, taking ten or more years to progress. The initial loss is particularly of corticospinal neurons, which produces clumsy and weakened hand movements and the signs one expects with a principally upper motor neuron lesion. Gradually more alpha motor neurons are involved, as are upper motor neurons innervating proximal and axial muscles. Muscle wasting, due to both disuse and denervation, becomes profound. EMG shows extensive pathology. Fasciculations may be observed. Breathing and swallowing are difficult. Death usually comes from intercurrent infection, choking, or aspiration in a severely debilitated person with fully normal cognitive capacities.

ALS is now seen as related to a variety of degenerative CNS conditions like Parkinson's disease. Mechanisms that are being explored as possible causes include environmental toxins, slow viruses, and excitotoxicity, the potentially destructive response of neurons to excessive and abnormal stimulation. No treatments are effective at present.

There are other patterns of motor neuron disease, the causes of which are equally mysterious. **Progressive muscular atrophy** affects lower motor neurons in an uneven pattern, with varied degrees of progression. **Bulbar palsy** affects mostly the motor neurons in the brain stem (ALS usually spares these until late in its course). It has a variable course but is, as well, ultimately fatal.

Spinal Muscular Atrophies of Infancy and Childhood

This group includes a variety of rare heritable motor disorders that leave sensory capacities intact. They vary in age of onset, severity, and course and pattern of transmission. The pattern of lesion is similar to ALS. **Werdnig-Hoffmann disease** is the general name applied to those with onset in infancy. The most common form has early onset and sometimes rapid progression. The child is weak and limp from birth (called **floppy baby syndrome**). **19** The classic presentation is an infant whose arms fall to the sides (jug handles) and whose legs relax in weak flexion (frog legs). Others show apparently normal development for several months, with subsequent motor degeneration. The baby has normal intelligence, and brain stem motor control is usually intact. The bright, responsive face is in contrast to the immobile body. **20** All these early onset forms are ultimately fatal. Transmission is by the autosomal recessive pattern.

Wohlfart-Kugelberg-Welander 21 disease is a milder form of heritable motor neuron disease with two distinct patterns, onset before 2 years or in the range of 5–18 years. Males are more often affected, and the usual pattern of transmission is autosomal recessive. Proximal muscles are denervated, while bulbar and corticospinal tracts are spared. The earlier the onset, the more severe the progression, but the worst affected child is able to walk for at least ten years. Gradually, distal musculature is involved.

Friedrich Ataxia

A fatal motor-sensory disorder with an average course of 15 to 20 years, **Friedrich ataxia** appears in two different patterns of inheritance and course. With autosomal recessive inheritance, the symptoms emerge at 12 years of age and death occurs at about 21. With autosomal dominant inheritance, onset is at age 20 and death occurs at an average age of 40. In both the pathology is the same. The cord is small. The posterior columns and corticospinal and spinocerebellar tracts are depleted of fibers. Bulbar motor neurons are largely spared. Cerebellar lesions are also noted. Gait ataxia is the initial symptom for most. There is difficulty standing steadily and running. A variety of joint deformities result from the sensory and motor impairments. Since the unconscious proprioceptive information doesn't ascend from the feet and legs, closing the eyes causes the person to sway and fall. Tremoring and choreiform movements are often seen. Intelligence is unimpaired. About half of those with this ataxia develop cardiomyopathies. Many die as a result of cardiac arrhythmias.

DISORDERS ARISING IN THE BASAL GANGLIA

Parkinson's Disease

Over 180 years have elapsed since James Parkinson described the syndrome that now bears his name. The odd combination of slowed, reduced movement and restless tremoring suggested the name paralysis agitans. **Parkinson's disease** (also called Parkinsonism) is a slowly degenerative CNS disorder affecting perhaps 80,000 middle-aged and older adults in North America. The disease has a course of 10–20 years, and twice as many men are affected as women.

The principal lesion in Parkinson's disease is in the substantia nigra, normally two darkly pigmented, dopamine-producing nuclei that are located in the midbrain. Their normal role is to provide an outflow pathway from the basal ganglia to the cortex via the thalamus and a feedback loop to the caudate and putamen. This loop appears to even out the discharge from these higher nuclei in the basal ganglia. Damage to the substantia nigra **22** impairs the flow of motor programs from the basal ganglia, which is expressed as difficulty initiating movement and a general impoverishment and slowing of movement (bradykinesia). Loss of the feedback loop impairs the steady flow of programs and expresses itself as resting tremor.

In many cases, Parkinson's disease is idiopathic; there is simply a gradual and unexplained loss of these dopamine-producing cells (fig. 21.14). In some cases, it can

19 ‖‖‖‖‖‖‖‖‖‖‖‖‖‖‖‖
15370

20 ‖‖‖‖‖‖‖‖‖‖‖‖‖‖‖‖
14351

21 ‖‖‖‖‖‖‖‖‖‖‖‖‖‖‖‖
14377

22 ‖‖‖‖‖‖‖‖‖‖‖‖‖‖‖‖
25625

(a)

(b)

Figure 21.14   Parkinson's disease. Sections through the midbrain showing normal substantia nigra pigmentation (lower section) and the loss of pigmented neurons in Parkinsonism (upper section).

The top section through the pons is from a 50-year-old man who died in a nursing home. He had developed severe and progressive Parkinson's disease in his thirties. Thalamic surgery to limit his dysfunction was unsuccessful, and he deteriorated until his death of a cerebral hemorrhage. The lower, normally pigmented specimen is provided for comparison with the victim's substantia nigra, whose neurons are almost completely lacking in pigment.

result from lesion by toxins like the MPTP that contaminated certain street drugs and produced the frozen addict syndrome described earlier. Although rare now, viral encephalopathy associated with the great influenza epidemic of 1914–18 produced hundreds of cases of postencephalitic Parkinsonism. Lesions to other areas of the basal ganglia can also produce Parkinsonism or a variety of other movement disorders.

The most disabling symptoms in Parkinson's disease are muscle rigidity, which can be lead pipe or oscillating cogwheel rigidity, and bradykinesia. The patient—typically an elderly male—experiences tiredness and weakness, but muscle strength is more or less normal. He has a slow (4–5 per second) resting tremor, sometimes with an alternating flexion-extension of the fingers called pill-rolling tremor. The tremor is typically suppressed during movement and exaggerated when the limb is held in extension. The person

has poor balance and maintains a stooped posture with the neck flexed. He shuffles and may adopt a gait in which he chases his pitched-forward center of gravity (festinating gait). Arm swing is absent, and he turns the body as a unit (en bloc). Rolling over or getting up out of a crouching position or out of a chair is difficult. Fine movements like buttoning become laborious. Handwriting becomes small and speech quiet. The face becomes immobile and inexpressive ("masklike"), the skin becomes oily, and inflamed seborrhea is found at the hairline and crevices of the face. Autonomic function is altered as well: the patient experiences orthostatic hypotension (blood pressure drops when they stand), excess sweating, constipation, and other autonomic disorders. Some patients suffer dementia similar to that found in Alzheimer's disease (see later section). While not fatal, Parkinson's disease shortens life expectancy significantly.

A variety of medical approaches are used to alleviate the symptoms as the disease progresses. Active exercise is encouraged, walking with swinging the arms, swimming, etc. As well, the person is taught strategies to overcome the bradykinesia: "throwing" himself up to get out of a chair, lifting the toes when "glued to the floor," practicing rapid "explosive" activities. When symptoms have progressed to a point of severe disability, drug therapy with levodopa is begun. This is a dopamine precursor that will cross the blood-brain barrier, where it is converted to dopamine to augment the diminished production from the substantia nigra. It is administered with a substance (carbidopa) that blocks the enzymatic degradation of levodopa in peripheral tissue so lower, better controlled dosages can be given. Use of levodopa is postponed because of the risk of its common side and toxic effects: cardiac arrhythmias, gastrointestinal hemorrhage, the psychiatric problems experienced by about 30% of patients, and—the most serious and ironic problem—unpredictable involuntary movement disorders. Implantation of foreign or autograft tissue has been tested, but such procedures remain experimental.

Huntington's Disease

Huntington's disease affects about 1 person in 10,000 and produces characteristic rapid, writhing flicklike contortions of the hands, arms, and face, truncal writhing, and a profound dementia. The dementia tends to consist of progressive loss of cognitive function. The movements, which have been characterized as dancelike, give this disorder its alternative name, **Huntington's chorea,** which has gone out of usage because it doesn't describe the rigidity and tremor seen in younger patients or the bradykinesia that replaces choreiform movements with age.

The disease is due to a dominant genetic defect on chromosome 4. Heritable autosomal dominant conditions must be either relatively compatible with normal life if manifested early or delayed in expression if more severe; otherwise they would interfere with reproduction and

Figure 21.15   Section through the brain of a person who died with Huntington's disease. The basal ganglia, particularly the putamen, have atrophied and the cortex and underlying white matter have thinned. These conditions led to hydrocephalus ex vacuo.

Between ages 32 and 42, a woman progressed from neck pains, weakness, and tremor to confusion and significant intellectual deterioration. Although she was initially diagnosed as having MS, by age 42 choreiform movements indicated Huntington's disease. She survived only a further ten years. No family history of the disease could be ascertained. This coronal section through the brain shows marked atrophy of the caudate nucleus, which allowed expansion of the ventricles.

consequently remove themselves from the gene pool. Huntington's is an example of the latter case. Obvious clinical onset is usually at 35–45 years of age (range 20–50), and those who inherit from their father show the disease earlier than those who inherit it from their mother (cytoplasmic constituents like maternal mitochondria appear to play a role). While the precise gene has not been localized, prenatal or postnatal predictive testing is accurate in almost 100% of cases. The uncertainty that used to hang over the heads of children of an affected adult can now be replaced with accurate information. In half of those tested, the news will be painful.

The pathology focuses on massive cellular loss from the caudate and putamen, with secondary loss of cells in particularly the frontal cortex. The ventricles are dilated **23** (hydrocephalus ex vacuo), as indicated in figure 21.15. Current investigation of the pathophysiology concentrates on the role of excessive stimulation (excitotoxicity). The drug Lamontrigene, which has been used to control progressive epilepsies in England, is now being used experimentally in attempts to slow or arrest the progression of Huntington's disease. Other medications are used to control chorea and tremoring, and antipsychotics are used to subdue the emotional outbursts that accompany the dementia. The average course of the disease to complete incapacitation and death is about 15 years.

COMPLEX DISORDERS

Cerebral Palsy

The term **cerebral palsy** (CP) is applied to a disparate collection of disabilities that derive from perinatal brain injury. Movement problems are prominent and readily observable, but sensory and cognitive deficits are also common. The mechanism, extent, and location of the injury will vary, but the child has survived and the injury is nonprogressive. The presence or severity of CP may not be evident in the young infant. But as deficits in voluntary movement and abnormally strong reflex patterns emerge, the original injury will become apparent. Also, in the absence of adequate supportive physiotherapy and training, the range of motor behavior may be restricted and musculoskeletal deformities may progress, but this does not indicate a worsening of brain function.

Because the term cerebral palsy has little descriptive or prognostic value and may carry a burden of erroneous meaning, many authorities would prefer more precise and specific terminology. Nevertheless, the term endures. Since its meaning can be so variable, however, neither the public nor the health care professional should be satisfied with less than a clear description of the extent of a given person's disability and a program of how best to work with it. Court cases over possible negligence or malpractice by those attending a birth have forced medical personnel to be much more precise in describing the timing and mechanism of the injuries that give rise to these disorders.

To understand the symptom complex possible in cerebral palsy, it is necessary to recognize that the injuries that cause it usually affect a relatively mature fetal or neonatal nervous system. The varied brain lesions generally act to separate well-developed and functioning components of the motor system (see the motor systems overview provided in figure 21.6). In this context, remember that the cord and brain stem, which are largely unaffected, house a host of motor reflexes that either are present at birth or emerge with the maturation of the infant and are overridden by voluntary motor behavior. Table 21.8 focuses on these normal reflex patterns that can become problematic in CP.

Infection, toxins, or anoxia can also damage highly cellular structures (areas of the cortex or hippocampus, the basal ganglia, the cerebellum, other smaller nuclei). This combination of disconnection and injury can result in impaired voluntary movement, exaggeration of reflex activity, and the development of abnormal movements. Interruption of pathways from the cortex to brain stem nuclei and the spinal cord similarly results in impaired voluntary movement. It also releases the reflex activity of the cord (hyperreflexia) and allows the unmediated activity of brain stem nuclei (e.g., increased flexor or extensor tone, reflex extension of the arms if the head is tipped back in dressing—symmetrical tonic neck reflex).

Table 21.8	Normal Reflexes in Infancy

Primitive Reflexes

These are present at birth or in the early months. Loss of certain of these (by CNS override or suppression) is necessary for development of other reflexes or conscious motor control.

Stepping reflex: baby held under arms, held over a table with soles of feet pressed against it, produces stepping movement.

Placing reflex: when dorsal aspect of foot is stimulated, leg is raised.

(These can be seen as preparatory to walking. They are replaced by "leg straightening" and "standing balance" reflexes as noted.)

Moro response (startle response): arms and legs thrust out, then arms drawn in, crying. Stimulus is a sudden position change or thump on bed; fades by 5 months.

Palmar grasp (Darwinian reflex): clasping response to insertion of object into palm. Fades at 3 months as grasp is more consciously controlled.

Asymmetrical tonic neck reflex: baby supine; when head turned to one side, arm and leg on that side extend, opposite side flexes. May prevent rolling; fades by 6 months. Also called the "fencing reflex."

Symmetrical tonic neck reflex: on all fours; extension of neck causes extension of arms and flexion of legs; flexion of neck elicits the reverse. Appears briefly at 6 months before infant learns to crawl; must be lost to crawl effectively.

Landau manoeuver: suspend infant horizontally in prone position; by 6 months most will extend neck and trunk. Flexion of neck will elicit flexion of hips, knees, and elbows.

Crossed extension reflex: when the sole of the held foot of a supine baby is stroked, the opposite leg is flexed, abducted, and then extended.

Reflexes that Develop Postnatally and Persist

Leg straightening: pressure to soles of feet elicits straightening of leg. Appears at 6–8 months.

Balance reaction: sitting (appears at 6 months).   } (These emerge when a seated or standing infant is thrown off balance;
Balance reaction: standing (appears at 6 months).   } the arms go out in the direction of the fall.)

Parachute reaction: on sudden lowering of infant, arms extend over head and legs extend. Appears at 8 months.

(These reflexes are generally adaptive but must be suppressed in sports like tumbling and judo.)

Permanent Reflexes

Babinski: before 2 years, extension of big toe and fanning of other toes. After 2 years, plantar flexion.

Tendon jerks: can be elicited in any large muscle with narrow tendinous insertion; also called myotatic stretch reflexes or deep tendon reflexes.

Note: Abnormalities of reflex patterns (e.g., exaggerated, diminished, asymmetrical responses or delay in age of onset or disappearance) suggest cerebral damage or abnormalities of brain development.

The person's limited voluntary movement may itself excite these reflex behaviors. To these may be added impaired or abnormal movements symptomatic of either basal ganglia or cerebellar lesion (see table 21.9).

These motor disabilities are the most obvious signs of cerebral palsy. However, the precipitating lesions are undiscriminating. It is reasonable to expect deficits in sensation from congenitally paralyzed or partially paralyzed limbs, although these will be difficult to assess and not, of course, apparent to the individual affected by CP, because he has only his own sensory experience to compare it to. Impairment of special sensation (vision, hearing, taste and smell) will be variable, depending on the nature and location of the causative lesion. The mechanisms of injury are such that much cortical function can remain intact.

Therefore, normal or superior intelligence is certainly possible, even in people with profound motor impairments. However, lesions sufficient to cause CP are also likely to impair general intelligence. With exceptions, there is a rough correlation between the degree of motor and mental impairment. Even those with normal intelligence may be hyperkinetic or distractable, have a short attention span, be subject to preseveration (getting stuck on one activity or stimulus), or have apraxias (inability to organize movements consistently in appropriate sequence).

It is common to classify CP on the basis of the area of the body most affected. Thus you may encounter terms like quadriplegic CP (all four limbs affected more or less equally), diplegic CP (lower limbs more affected than upper), and monoplegic CP (only one limb affected).

Table 21.9   Possible Symptom Complex in Cerebral Palsy Associated with Lesions to
Motor Tracts, the Cerebellum, and the Basal Ganglia. For Explanation, See
Section on Motor System Function.

Motor Tracts	Cerebellum	Basal Ganglia
Impaired voluntary movement (both fine and gross)	Hypotonia or atonia	Bradykinesia
Spasticity	Ataxia	Choreiform movements
Limb deformities due to unbalanced muscle tone (flexion at wrists, elbows, knees, hips, plantar-flexion of feet)	Intention/terminal tremor	Athetosis
	Nystagmus	Ballism
Contractures	Dysdiadochokinesia	Rigidity
Hyperreflexia (stretch, crossed extension, symmetrical and asymmetrical neck, Moro)	Dysarthria	Dystonia (athetoid movements frozen, usually, in extreme extension).

Alternatively, classification may focus on the predominant motor impairment, e.g., spastic CP or athetoid CP.

The disconnections are largely due to a variety of vascular lesions in white matter. The relatively low blood pressure and expandable nature of the fetal skull allow fetuses and newborns to survive lesions that would threaten an adult. Perhaps 50% of preterm infants are subject to hemorrhage into the delicate germinal eminence **24** (also called the subependymal plate), embryonic tissue that remains on the surface of the wall of the lateral ventricles until about 32–33 weeks into gestation. This hemorrhage may be confined to the immediate tissue and be asymptomatic. Rupture into the ventricles has more devastating and widespread consequences, **25** compressing tissues including the internal capsule and basal ganglia. Cerebellar hemorrhage can occur in premature and full-term infants, causing damage to the cerebellar hemisphere. The white matter surrounding the ventricles is subject to both hemorrhage and ischemic infarct, which can damage the internal capsule or association fibers. Gray matter can suffer ischemic/hypoxic, toxic, or infective injury.

Although some CP can be attributed to birth trauma, these cases are in the minority. Many lesions arise well before or after delivery. The best preventive care is that oriented to the prevention of prematurity or other complications of pregnancy, with emphasis on good maternal nutrition, postponing pregnancy until full adulthood, and healthy maternal life style.

Multiple Sclerosis

It is helpful to consider **multiple sclerosis** (MS) in the context of cerebral palsy. Unlike CP, MS arises through a single mechanism of lesion: focal, chronic, progressive, usually exacerbating and remitting demyelination of CNS tracts. As in CP, however, the lesions can occur in a wide variety of locations and hence give rise to complex symptom patterns. The areas of demyelination are called **plaques** and, while confined to white matter, can occur at any site where oligodendrocytes produce the myelin sheaths that facilitate the conduction of signals. This includes the cerebrum **26** (where plaques tend to occur around the ventricles), the brain stem, the cerebellum, and the spinal cord. **27** Involvement of the optic nerve produces monocular visual disturbance, which is the first reported symptom in about one-quarter of patients. While the plaques remain and mature, the specific symptoms usually worsen and then improve or resolve. The apparent movement of symptoms that is related to the development of new active plaques, and their emergence over time, gave rise to the older name for this disorder, disseminated sclerosis.

The clinical presentation depends on the location, extent, and pattern of development of the active plaques. This is a disease of young people (20–40 years), rarely having onset before 15 or after 50. As noted, many people experience a transitory, usually unilateral visual impairment or blindness. About half of those who present with this **optic neuritis** go on to be diagnosed with MS. Double vision, caused by demyelination of the brain stem tract that coordinates the actions of the three nuclei responsible for eye movements (**internuclear ophthalmoplegia),** is common while not specific to MS. **Lhermitte's sign** (tingling in the back and anterior thigh upon neck flexion) is frequently seen but again, not specific. A patient who becomes heated—either passively (from hot weather or from sitting in a hot tub) or actively (from exercise)—often experiences worsening of symptoms. This effect of heat is called **Uthoff's phenomenon.**

Laboratory investigation of suspected MS often starts with a lumbar puncture. A slight increase in proteins may be noted, with a pattern of electrophoretic migration called **oligoclonal banding.** [28] This finding, which is fairly specific to MS, is due to the presence of antibodies within the CSF, suggestive of an immune mediation of the disease. Changes in the conduction velocities along visual or auditory pathways in the CNS are detected by testing responses to visual and auditory stimuli. MRI is proving invaluable at imaging active and burned-out or silent plaques. Because the diagnosis of MS is problematic and has obvious import to the patient, the detection of a second plaque by means of electrodiagnostic tests, CT, or MRI is actively pursued.

The predominant pattern in MS is chronic exacerbation and remission (chronic MS). Symptoms become worse for two or three weeks, then partially resolve for perhaps one to five years, only to become worse again. The second occurrence can bring about a worsening of existing symptoms or the onset of entirely new ones. The third may be sooner and more extensive again. Various stresses can apparently trigger an exacerbation (infection, medication, stress, fatigue). The course of MS is unstable and unpredictable. About 10% of cases undergo a severe, rapid, progressive deterioration (acute progressive MS). Some individuals have died within seven months of first symptoms because of a combination of acute brain inflammation associated with the plaques and intercurrent infection. On the other hand, a significant number of people are never severely incapacitated, and some apparently experience a single episode that arrests and resolves (acute MS). Death, when it occurs, is usually attributable to the complications of MS (respiratory infection because of impaired ventilation, bladder and then kidney infection secondary to ineffective emptying, etc.).

The symptom complex includes most of those on the list for cerebral palsy (table 21.9). Hyperreflexia is certainly detectable, but the exaggerated movements associated with basal ganglia involvement are not a problem (choreiform movements, athetosis, dystonia, ballism). The person may experience increased urinary frequency and urgency, and difficulty in urinating, as well as difficulty in swallowing, dysarthria, and extreme intolerance of heat. Large lesions in the frontal or temporal lobes may lead to emotional outbursts (swearing, weeping, laughing) that are unrelated to the situation or the person's apparent feeling state. Depression or euphoria can be a problem. This may have both a neurological and psychological basis. The unpredictable progression and attendant disability can overtax an individual's capacity to cope. Occasionally an MS plaque and associated edema can block transmission in the cord **(transverse myelitis),** causing paraplegia or quadriplegia.

Of the many drug therapies attempted, only corticosteroids and ACTH (adrenocorticotropic hormone) appear to have any effect. They can reduce the duration of an exacerbation but have no impact on the long-term outcome of the disease. Recent experimental work with interferon β (IFN_β) has shown some promising results in arresting the progression of MS. However, maintaining a healthy outlook and life style, while easy to prescribe and difficult to carry out, will benefit a patient more than any approaches at a cure that are currently available.

Study of the underlying pathophysiology is continuing. From such research it appears that the active plaque [29] is a region of ongoing demyelination, in which myelin sheaths undergo breakdown and phagocytic destruction. The presence of antibodies against certain myelin proteins may play a role in this attack. The decreased signal conduction through a plaque is attributable to a combination of edema, disturbing the extracellular environment, and demyelination, exposing normally hidden potassium channels on the axons that short-circuit the signal. Resolution of edema and partial remyelination subsequently restore at least partial function. Eventually an active plaque is converted to a silent (burned-out) plaque in which widespread demyelination is again the rule, with extensive astrocytosis. Further exacerbation, however, produces new plaques. MRI has revealed that gradually plaques coalesce, expanding the area of impaired conduction and producing permanent dysfunction.

The epidemiology of MS hints at an interaction between a viral illness in the teen years and a genetic predisposition. People who grow up in northern temperate climates have increased risk, which they carry with them if they move after adolescence. Likewise, people from tropical regions are protected unless they move to a temperate clime as a child. Another finding in support of a genetic predisposition is the greater susceptibility of non-Orientals, wherever they live.

Alzheimer's Disease

Dementia, the loss of ordered neural function, is a major symptom in a number of unrelated disorders. Dementia is, in practice, a broad term that may denote disorder in many independent capacities: discrimination of and attending to stimuli, storing new memories and retrieving old ones, planning and the delay of gratification, abstraction and problem solving, judgment and reasoning, orientation in time and space, language processing, the appropriate use of objects, the planning and execution of voluntary movement. In **Alzheimer's disease** there is a slow (usually five years or more) but inexorable progression of dementia in which mental function is surrendered more or less in the order just stated.

The memory loss initially affects only short-term storage and retrieval, but gradually extends to well-consolidated memories as well. Many people experience restlessness, sometimes almost a compulsion to walk. Combined with failing memory, this wandering can be a major problem for both the patient and others responsible. Many patients retain insight, at least in the early stages of the disease, which is another source of anxiety and depression. Ultimately the person is left mute and paralyzed. Death comes from infection of a weakened, dehydrated patient. In parallel, the personality—the combined qualities of cognition and temperament that are unique to a person—also suffers fragmentation. It is often this loss, perhaps years before the physical death of the person, that is most difficult for friends and family.

Senility, that is, age-related dementia, used to be evoked as a catch-all explanation for any disturbances of mental functioning that might appear in old age. The implication was that these were part and parcel of growing old, and could not be helped. But many such conditions are reversible, such as altered mental function due to depression, impaired heart function, or anemia. The bottom line is that no dementia should be seen as a normal concomitant of aging. The pathological basis should be vigorously explored and treated where possible. Of dementias that result from degenerative brain disorders (old term: organic brain syndrome, OBS), two have pathology concentrated in the cerebral cortex: Pick's disease and Alzheimer's disease. Pick's is rarer and symptomatically indistinguishable from Alzheimer's. It tends to focus on the frontal and temporal lobes and leads to marked atrophy of the gyri, called walnut brain at autopsy. This difference from the more generalized pattern of atrophy in Alzheimer's may be detectable in CT or MRI scans. The distinction may be academic, as the course is very similar.

Alzheimer's may appear in patients as young as 50, in which case it used to be called presenile dementia. With advancing age the incidence of Alzheimer's increases. About 6% of the population of older adults (post-65) are afflicted. Pathology is restricted to the cerebral cortex, the hippocampus, **30** a nearby nucleus called the amygdala, and another called the basal nucleus of Meynert. Cells in the latter normally produce the neurotransmitter acetylcholine, which travels along widely branching axons to synapses in the cerebral cortex. Loss of cells in this nucleus results in widespread cortical depletion of acetylcholine and related chemicals, and presumably results in impaired neural function. A generalized loss of mainly pyramidal cells (see chapter 22) occurs in the areas named. As pyramidal cells die, so do their associated axons, which leads to loss of white matter. Gyri shrink **31** **32** and the ventricles expand **33** (hypocephalus ex vacuo), reflecting the atrophy.

Three microscopic findings correlate with the severity and progression of the disease. **Neurofibrillary tangles** **34** **35** are cytoplasmic bundles of filaments that encircle or displace the nucleus of the pyramidal cells. They are apparent with silver staining methods and are thought to be helically coiled microtubules. They can be seen as "ghost tangles" long after the neuron has died. **Neuritic (senile) plaques** **36** consist of a cluster of neural processes filled with filaments, such as are found in tangles, surrounding a poorly staining core. This core is composed of a variant of proteins that are collectively called **amyloid** (starchlike) because they appear like clear starch. Neither the tangles nor the plaques are specific to Alzheimer's but are found in smaller numbers in normal aging brains and in other pathological conditions. **Amyloid angiopathy** is found only in cortical and small subarachnoid arteries. The amyloid is the same as that in the plaque cores and will be found as a clear zone in the muscle layer of these vessels.

About 10% of cases are familial, more commonly with early onset. The gene responsible is located on chromosome 21, as is the gene that produces the amyloid protein. Much research is investigating this and its connection to Down's syndrome (trisomy 21). Interestingly, almost all people with Down's syndrome who live beyond 45 develop Alzheimer's disease.

This disease has thus far proved resistant to medical treatment. Potentially, knowledge of the formation, processing, and perhaps degradation of amyloid protein may provide methods of treatment. In addition, the raised levels of aluminum found in the brains of Alzheimer's patients have been an active research focus. It is not clear whether aluminum levels are raised secondarily by release from dying neurons or play a direct or cofactor role, in combination with other toxins or a genetic predisposition. Chelating agents that bind and remove aluminum have shown some promise, temporarily arresting or reversing some symptoms. THA (tetrahydroaminoacridine) has been used experimentally, particularly in the early stages, to enhance memory function. Despite major risks of liver toxicity, careful steps are being taken to make THA available on a limited basis because of its apparent effectiveness.

30 ‖‖‖‖‖‖‖‖‖‖‖‖‖‖
34445

31 ‖‖‖‖‖‖‖‖‖‖‖‖‖‖
34478

32 ‖‖‖‖‖‖‖‖‖‖‖‖‖‖
34481

33 ‖‖‖‖‖‖‖‖‖‖‖‖‖‖
40143

34 ‖‖‖‖‖‖‖‖‖‖‖‖‖‖
34454

35 ‖‖‖‖‖‖‖‖‖‖‖‖‖‖
34457

36 ‖‖‖‖‖‖‖‖‖‖‖‖‖‖
37652

In the meantime, the predominant therapy continues to center on minimizing the problems and frustration created by failing cognitive skills and on encouraging the exercise of remaining skills. A great deal can be done by simplifying the environment while maintaining elements that are familiar and personal. Remaining capacity can be exercised through intensely focused rehearsal and stimulation and the use of redundant cues (color coding plus labeling plus symbols, etc.). There is an emphasis on diet and exercise. Keeping the family involved by giving them the support and encouragement they require anchors this approach.

Figure 21.16 provides an overview of the various derangements that can affect motor functions.

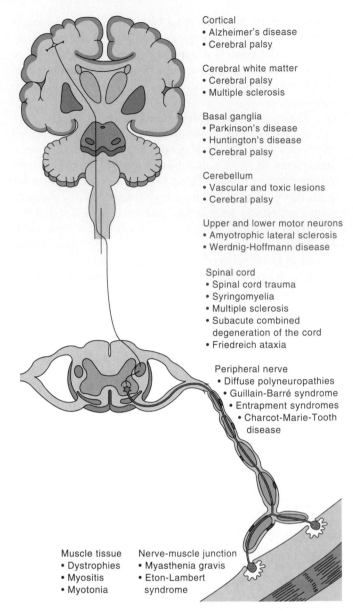

Cortical
• Alzheimer's disease
• Cerebral palsy

Cerebral white matter
• Cerebral palsy
• Multiple sclerosis

Basal ganglia
• Parkinson's disease
• Huntington's disease
• Cerebral palsy

Cerebellum
• Vascular and toxic lesions
• Cerebral palsy

Upper and lower motor neurons
• Amyotrophic lateral sclerosis
• Werdnig-Hoffmann disease

Spinal cord
• Spinal cord trauma
• Syringomyelia
• Multiple sclerosis
• Subacute combined degeneration of the cord
• Friedreich ataxia

Peripheral nerve
• Diffuse polyneuropathies
• Guillain-Barré syndrome
• Entrapment syndromes
• Charcot-Marie-Tooth disease

Muscle tissue
• Dystrophies
• Myositis
• Myotonia

Nerve-muscle junction
• Myasthenia gravis
• Eton-Lambert syndrome

Figure 21.16   Overview of pathologies that affect movement.

Case Study

This case involves a 21-year-old cocktail server. She had been well previously and had no history of any serious illness. According to her statement, she "was into alternative holistic life style remedies" and had pursued various fad diets.

On her 21st birthday she celebrated by eating half of a box of chocolates, and a few hours later experienced a loss of vision in her left eye. She attributed this effect to the "heavy sugar rush" from the chocolates she had ingested, and so she initially sought no medical attention. She finally did see her doctor because, over the next four days, her eye became quite painful and her vision remained poor. She appeared generally healthy, and because no obvious abnormalities were detected by an eye examination, her general practitioner referred her to an ophthalmologist.

His diagnosis was optic neuritis, which, in the young and otherwise healthy, is strongly associated with multiple sclerosis. No treatment was given because the patient refused prednisone to alleviate her eye symptoms. She was referred to an MS clinic, where the diagnosis was verified on the basis of her history and the ophthalmologist's work-up, but the patient refused any further tests. No treatment was prescribed, although annual follow-up examinations were recommended. She was then lost to the clinic's and her GP's office follow-up procedures.

Six months later she was admitted to the psychiatric ward of a major hospital for aggression and psychosis. She was brought to the hospital by a neighbor, who reported that for the past three or four days she had been complaining of being unable to sleep and was combative, delusional, and paranoid, expressing bizarre and grandiose ideas. The neighbor didn't know the name of her GP (or even if she had one), so her medical records or history could not be obtained. She was diagnosed as manic-depressive, and lithium carbonate therapy was initiated.

Six months after this episode, she returned to her GP for treatment of a minor injury sustained in an aerobics workout. In the course of their discussions she reported her experience of being committed to a psychiatric ward and stated that she had discontinued her medication because "it wouldn't let me get tuned into my cocktail lounge customers and my tips were bottoming out." She refused her doctor's recommendation of further testing, left, and was again lost to further follow-up.

Eight months later she was again admitted to a psychiatric ward, and a diagnosis of manic/depressive illness was made. After reinstatement of lithium carbonate therapy, she improved and was released. She had no known medical contacts subsequently, and three months later committed suicide.

Commentary

The altered mental states experienced by this unfortunate woman are a common feature of MS, e.g., emotional instability, depression, or euphoria. It was these that the lithium carbonate therapy sought to counter. Severe changes such as mania may also occur, but these are more often seen late in the course. The alternating pattern of remission and relapse seen in this patient is also typical.

Unfortunately, MS presents many diagnostic difficulties, and this patient was not unusual in rejecting further investigations for fear that a relatively minor problem might reveal some serious illness. In this case, the patient insisted that MS was an unlikely diagnosis on the basis of, in her words "the sorry evidence of a few little eye problems."

Key Concepts

1. Drugs that affect autonomic function can produce broad or focused effects by taking advantage of variability in naturally occurring receptors (pp. 555–556).

2. While peripheral injuries can undergo repair, this is generally not the case with central neuron lesions (pp. 560–562).

3. The symptoms associated with lesions of the peripheral nerves or alpha motor neurons in the cord (lower motor neurons) are decreased muscle tone, weakness or paralysis of voluntary movement, decreased or absent reflexes, rapid muscle atrophy, and electromuscular signs of denervation (pp. 563–564).

4. The symptoms associated with lesion to the upper motor neuron (all motor pathways above the alpha motor neuron) are increased muscle tone, weakness or paralysis of voluntary movement, increased reflexes, slow (disuse) atrophy, and abnormal plantar reflex (pp. 564–565).

5. Lesions affecting the cerebellum may produce any of a constellation of symptoms including imprecision and tremor in directing movements and difficulty in walking, speaking, or performing rapidly alternating movements or eye movements (p. 565).

6. Lesions affecting the basal ganglia may produce difficulty in initiating movement, as well as tremoring, writhing or flicking movements at rest, and rigidity (pp. 565–567).

7. Diseases affecting muscle, which usually derive from genetic or autoimmune disorders and result from a variety of mechanisms, tend to produce muscle weakness (p. 568).

8. The principal disorder of the neuromuscular junction, myasthenia gravis, results from an autoimmune-mediated loss of neurotransmitter receptors (pp. 569–570).

9. A variety of agents can cause scattered lesions to the peripheral nerves, giving rise to a variety of symptoms of sensory and/or motor impairment (pp. 570–571).

10. Entrapment syndromes produce focal lesions in peripheral nerves, impairing signal transmission and leading to muscle weakness and wasting and impaired sensation, accompanied by characteristic paresthesias (p. 571).

11. While injury to the spinal cord may interrupt sensory or motor pathways and destroy reflex or integration centers, the long-term adaptation involves increased reflex activity below the site of motor lesion and a variety of other problems (p. 574).

12. The syndrome of symptoms accompanying a specific spinal lesion depends on the site and extent of the lesion (p. 574).

13. Cerebral palsy results when an ante- or perinatal lesion to a normal nervous system impairs voluntary control while producing hyperreflexia and perhaps symptoms characteristic of lesions to either the basal ganglia or cerebellum (pp. 581–583).

14. Multiple sclerosis produces episodically progressive sensory, motor, and psychic abnormalities through an unexplained, immune-mediated attack on central myelin (pp. 583–584).

15. Alzheimer's disease results in progressive loss of functional cortical neurons and is the dominant degenerative dementia, ultimately affecting all mental function (pp. 584–586).

REVIEW ACTIVITIES

1. Describe as completely as you can the difference between (a) the sympathetic and parasympathetic nervous systems, (b) acetylcholine and norepinephrine, (c) alpha and beta adrenergic receptors, (d) $beta_1$ and $beta_2$ blockers, (e) agonist and blocker.

2. Explain the difference between MS and Guillain-Barré syndrome.

3. Prepare a table that highlights the similarities and differences between (a) Huntington's disease and Parkinson's disease, (b) Cerebral palsy and MS, (c) ALS and Werdnig-Hoffmann disease, (d) Alzheimer's disease and Huntington's disease.

4. You are playing charades with your three best friends, who are all neurologists. You decide to act out a lower motor lesion. What would you actually *do?*

5. List the symptoms that lesions to either the cerebellum or basal ganglia have in common. Now list the symptoms that are different.

6. Differentiate between the weakness associated with polymyositis and that of myasthenia gravis.

Chapter Twenty-Two

Seizures and Epilepsy

And when the fit was upon him, I did mark how he did shake . . .

William Shakespeare
Julius Caesar

In North America seizures are a relatively common occurrence, with approximately 1,800,000 people subject to active epilepsy. That is, they have a continuing susceptibility to seizures that is not attributable to some other medical condition. Among acute neurological disorders, only stroke is more common. Epileptic seizures occur over a wide range of intensities from the trivial, e.g., a spontaneous perception of odor, to the life-threatening.

In addition to epilepsy, a large number of people experience convulsive states arising from another illness, for example acute renal failure or cardiac arrest. This chapter is intended to provide information about both sorts of seizure activity and to establish the basis for understanding seizure development and progression.

SOME BACKGROUND CONCEPTS AND TERMINOLOGY

In discussing seizures and epilepsy, some familiarity with a core of basic terms and concepts is essential. The following sections deal with those most frequently encountered by health care professionals.

General Concepts

When dealing with seizures, a patient's level of consciousness can be of central importance, and any departure from full consciousness should be noted. Such **impaired consciousness** in a patient might be noted as "It was difficult to catch her attention" or "He appeared awake but didn't respond to questions."

A **convulsion** is an episode of widespread and intense motor activity. These may occur in isolation or in a series and may often, but not always, be associated with a loss of consciousness. By contrast, a **seizure** is a rapidly evolving disturbance of brain function that produces impaired consciousness, abnormalities of sensation or mental functioning, or convulsive movements. Because these may arise in combination, particular descriptive terms are used, such as **convulsive seizure** or **sensory seizure,** depending on which derangements are most prominent.

Epilepsy

This is the condition characterized by a relatively long-term disturbance of brain structure and/or function that produces an increased susceptibility to seizures. The strict diagnosis of epilepsy requires a history of at least two seizures that can't reasonably be attributed to some other disease. In epilepsy, the underlying abnormality is centered within the brain itself. If seizure activity can be eliminated by correction of some metabolic disorder or by removal of a brain tumor, the diagnosis of epilepsy can't be made.

Seizure Terminology

The word element -ictal refers to activity during a seizure (*ictus* is Latin for a blow). **Interictal** is used in reference to the situation between periods of seizure activity. Another term encountered in the context of seizures is **photic stimulation.** It refers to the use of an intense flashing light to elicit an abnormal electroencephalogram (EEG) or an actual seizure, which is related to some underlying epilepsy-related abnormality. Photic stimulation, in combination with an EEG, can localize the focus of abnormal brain activity and may be encountered in the diagnosis of both epileptic and nonepileptic seizures.

A **partial seizure** is seizure activity that is caused by an abnormal discharge from a relatively restricted set of brain structures. For this reason it may also be known as a **focal** or **local** seizure. Partial seizures are characterized by only limited behavioral, mental, sensory, or motor expression. In contrast, a **generalized seizure** involves more widespread derangements arising from abnormal brain activity occurring over large areas of the cerebral cortex of both hemispheres at once. Such seizures may be varied, involving major convulsive activity or perhaps impaired consciousness accompanied by lip smacking or eye blinking. Generalized seizures affect both sides of the body, or at least produce bilateral abnormalities of brain wave activity.

A **tonic-clonic seizure** is a generalized convulsive seizure involving loss of consciousness. It starts with a stiffening of the muscles (tonic) and progresses to alternating spasms of contraction and relaxation (clonic). The term **myoclonic seizure** refers to muscle twitching and/or limb jerking movements due to abnormal cortical activity. Its actions are more localized than the coordinated whole body spasms seen in a clonic seizure, but note the special case of the **myoclonic jerk,** in which the entire body is thrown into one or two pronounced twitches. When serious progressive brain pathology induces myoclonic seizures, the condition is designated **myoclonus epilepsy.**

Hyperactivity of the stretch reflexes is known as **clonus.** It derives principally from defective functioning at the level of the spinal cord, although higher central nervous system pathology may also be the cause.

NONEPILEPTIC SEIZURES

Many seizures encountered in a health care setting will be **nonepileptic.** They will typically arise as a result of an extreme metabolic disruption associated with systemic disease, specific toxins, a deficiency state, or the local effects of a brain tumor. The following conditions produce most nonepileptic seizures.

Alcohol Withdrawal and Seizures

Recent work has shown that chronic alcohol abuse induces the production and release of GABA, an inhibitory neurotransmitter. In time the brain adapts to this inhibition by increasing its level of excitation. Withdrawal from alcohol removes GABA's inhibitory effects, leaving the brain at a level of excitation that can produce seizures over the short-term. Drugs like phenobarbital and diazepam (Valium), which appear to have their anticonvulsant effect by raising GABA levels, are used temporarily to treat such seizures and then are slowly tapered off.

Withdrawal from Sedative/Hypnotic Drugs

Generalized tonic-clonic seizures are a potential hazard complicating withdrawal from barbiturates and other sedative/hypnotic drugs, alcohol, and, interestingly, anticonvulsants (drugs used to suppress seizures or convulsions). The seizures may come in clusters, and victims are prone to convulsive **status epilepticus,** a life-threatening chaining of seizure activity that will be discussed later. If acute withdrawal is the precipitating factor in the seizures, other symptoms should be evident, at least with alcohol and barbiturates: trembling, disturbed sleep, disorientation, illusions or hallucinations. (Also common is a high sensitivity to photic stimulation.) Gradual withdrawal, which is appropriate when removing a habituated patient from a prescribed barbiturate or other sedative drug, minimizes most of these symptoms and risks.

Bacterial Meningitis

Seizures often accompany bacterial meningitis, particularly with children. Meningeal signs (see chapter 20) and a lumbar puncture would have already established the diagnosis in most cases, but for some it is the myoclonic jerks or full tonic-clonic seizure that brings them to the emergency ward.

Renal Failure

The crisis stage of renal failure follows about two or three days after the kidneys cease urine production (anuria). The resultant uremia and associated electrolyte changes can cause a dramatic convulsive display that includes twitching and trembling, myoclonic jerks, generalized convulsions, and possible tetany. These symptoms arise from complex metabolic derangements that include hyperkalemia, hypocalcemia, and elevated blood levels of urea and creatinine. Dialysis is used to control these conditions while the underlying renal failure either resolves (perhaps with transplant) or progresses to the end-stage, coma and death.

Hypoxic Encephalopathy

Individuals who have experienced cerebral hypoxia (resulting from cardiac arrest, carbon monoxide poisoning, near-drowning, suffocation, respiratory failure, etc.) often experience seizures when oxygen supply to the brain is restored. Myoclonic jerks affecting any part of the body or full-blown tonic-clonic seizures may result. Susceptibility usually lasts for a few days in association with stupor and confusion. Some people will have a persistent **intention myoclonus** in which voluntary movements may elicit myoclonic jerks. They may also show sensory and motor deficits attributable to watershed infarcts (see chapter 20) and extensive memory and mental processing deficits.

Febrile Convulsions

The developing nervous system is somewhat more susceptible to seizures, including those induced by fever. Perhaps 5% of children 3 months to 5 years of age will experience seizures with fever (febrile convulsions or seizures), and in about one-third of that number they will recur. Febrile seizures usually take the form of a brief, generalized motor convulsion. They occur in the absence of any brain infection or other CNS abnormality and are not usually classified as epileptic. Essentially three very different situations can give rise to seizures during fever: a normal brain may be destabilized by fever, fever may trigger an epileptic brain's first seizure, or a brain with other serious progressive pathology can first generate a seizure during fever.

Historically physicians have tended to suspect that febrile seizures, particularly recurrent ones, might lead to a permanent alteration of brain function and epilepsy and so have aggressively administered anticonvulsants (especially phenobarbital). However, only a small minority (perhaps 3%) of children who experience febrile seizures subsequently develop epilepsy, and the connection between epilepsy and *recurrent* febrile seizures is only slightly stronger. Currently, therefore, the therapeutic approach is more conservative. Only those with abnormal neurological or other development, a family history of epilepsy, or unusually prolonged or focal febrile seizures are subjected to preventative anticonvulsant therapy. For the vast majority, standard care for the control of fevers appears to be appropriate.

Brain Tumor

A nonepileptic seizure may result from the effects of a brain tumor. Presumably, the relatively intact tissues at a tumor's edges are affected in a way that produces seizure-inducing activity. In fact, it is not unusual for a tumor's presence to be initially revealed by an abnormal EEG or a seizure. Where the tumor can be removed or otherwise suppressed, the seizure activity subsides.

Cerebrovascular Accident

Seizures will infrequently accompany an embolic, thrombotic, or hemorrhagic CVA. A more common occurrence is for the cortical region adjacent to an area infarcted by a CVA to become a focus of seizure activity. As many as one-quarter of those who survive a CVA will have some continuing, usually focal, seizure activity. Note that in these cases the individuals have become epileptic.

EPILEPTIC SEIZURES

While nonepileptic seizures present certain medical care challenges, they are usually not the primary concern. Treat the primary disease, and the seizure activity will cease (except perhaps as noted in the case of CVA). We now consider epilepsy, in which the seizure itself is the primary derangement.

The term epilepsy is derived from the Greek, meaning "to seize upon" or "a taking hold of," an apt description of the seizures that occur with epilepsy. The storm of abnormal brain activity giving rise to a seizure may be experienced as a hallucination, an unprovoked set of sensations, limited involuntary movements, or twitching. In some seizures the person may lose consciousness and have a major motor convulsion. Our understanding of epilepsy in some ways hasn't progressed significantly since John Hughlings Jackson proposed, a century ago, that seizures were caused by "occasional, sudden, excessive, rapid and local discharges of gray matter" and that a generalized convulsion resulted "when normal brain tissue was invaded by the seizure activity initiated in the abnormal focus."

Epilepsy: The Underlying Mechanism

Modern studies have confirmed Jackson's intuition that gray matter is the origin of seizure activity. More specifically, it is the cortical tissue that forms the outer layer of the entire cerebrum, forming its bumps (gyri) and its grooves (sulci and fissures) and also contributing a major part of the hippocampal formation. **1** The hippocampal formation is crucial to memory processing and is one of the cortical regions that is inherently more prone to seizure generation. It is considered to be part of the limbic system and in common with certain other limbic components has a C-shape when viewed from the side (fig. 22.1). In contrast

Elements of hippocampal formation

Figure 22.1   Location of the hippocampal formation. Dotted line indicates the hippocampal formation and its major extension into the hypothalamus.

to the superficial cerebral cortex, the hippocampus (the principal cortical portion of the hippocampal formation) develops deep on the wall of the lateral ventricles, like the basal ganglia. The bottom of the C begins on the medial wall of the temporal horn of the lateral ventricle and extends around as far as the parietal lobe. Because of its deep location, seizures originating in the hippocampus are difficult to localize with the usual scalp electrodes used in a routine electroencephalogram (EEG).

The Epileptogenic Focus

Although some truly generalized seizures can begin with a sudden shift in the activity of millions of widely distributed cortical neurons, most seizures begin at an **epileptogenic focus.** This is a group of abnormal neurons that spontaneously repolarize, firing thousands of action potentials without an identifiable cause. In theory, any collection of neurons could become epileptogenic, but in practice, the focus usually develops in either the cerebral cortex or the hippocampus. If these cells are able to activate the relatively normal neurons with which they are associated, a seizure results. This recruitment of additional neurons can be quite limited, restricted perhaps to those cortical neurons immediately surrounding the focus, in which case the result is a partial seizure. If the recruitment is on a broader scale, causing a larger disruption of neural function,

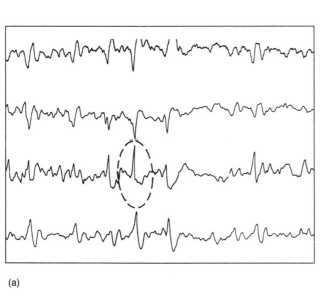

(a)   (b)

Figure 22.2   Typical EEG traces of a spike (*a*) and a spike-and-wave (*b*). The spike-and-wave has been affected by the setting of the EEG in that the top of the wave is leveled off in several traces.

a more generalized seizure results. A seizure that begins focally, however, can spread in seconds or minutes to become **secondarily generalized.**

While the significance of the distinction between focal and generalized seizures should be obvious, at least in terms of the impact on the person experiencing them, the therapeutic implications may not be so clear. Most seizures fall between the two extremes: a strictly limited focal (partial) seizure with no secondary spread or generalization on one hand, and an apparently instantaneously generalized bilateral seizure on the other. Pure focal seizures have a discrete and limited focus. In theory, generalized seizures have no focus but develop from a more or less simultaneous disruption of normal cortical function. In practice, it appears that the vast majority of what seem from the outset to be true generalized seizures also originate from discrete foci, but in this case there may be multiple foci that show an extreme tendency to generalize secondarily. Many seizures that appear to be generalized, on the basis of behavioral and EEG criteria, are actually secondarily generalized from one or more foci.

An epileptogenic focus can be examined in detail by applying multiple closely spaced electrodes on the surgically exposed surface of a section of cortex (electrocorticography). This technique reveals a relatively large area (10 cm^2 or more) in which innumerable random action potentials can be observed. On a routine EEG, such **spike foci** are too small to be individually recorded through the layers of meninges, bone, and scalp. Only when many

Considerations in Seizure Surgery

In a therapeutic context, the distinction between focal and generalized seizures is far from academic. The issue becomes more concrete when it is reduced to the questions, "Are all these seizures triggered from one focus?" and "If this focus were resected, is there a secondary focus capable of generating seizures?" Such questions are raised when considering surgery for disabling seizures that won't respond effectively to more conservative medical management. For surgery to be considered, the disruption of function that results from the removal of the affected cortex must not be worse than that created by the uncontrolled seizure activity.

small spike foci fire synchronously is their action observable at the scalp as a **spike-and-wave,** the electrical sign of an epileptogenic focus (fig. 22.2). The absence of identifiable spike-and-wave phenomena in a routine EEG is therefore not evidence of the absence of an epileptogenic focus; that is, a negative EEG does not exclude epilepsy. The tendency for nerve cells in a focus to fire synchronously is related to their capacity to recruit other cortical tissue and produce a seizure. Individuals with frequent seizures are much more likely to have a focus that can be identified during a routine EEG. Beyond the spike-and-wave, there is an

Nonspecific stimulation of
branches of apical dendrite

Dendrite booster zone—small
number of stimuli can initiate
an action potential in the apical
dendrite

Dendrite spines

**Apical Dendrite
(mainly excitatory synapses)**

Direction of
action potential

Soma (cell body)

Basal Dendrites
(mainly inhibitory
synapses)

Axon carrying
stimulation
specific to
this PC
column

Initial segment
of PC axon
(action potential
generated here
if action potential
in apical dendrite
passes the soma)

Action
potentials

Recurrent collateral
(informs cortex of
PC action potential)

Figure 22.3   Diagram of the principal features of a cortical pyramidal cell (PC). The presence of "booster zones" that can readily initiate an action potential and the dependence on ongoing inhibition of the cell body and basal dendrites to limit discharge predispose the pyramidal cell to the "spontaneous" generation of action potentials that could cause a seizure.

array of well-recognized abnormal EEG patterns that can be directly related to impaired consciousness and the behavior observed during a seizure. These details are beyond the scope of this text.

Epileptogenesis at the Cellular Level

The physical and physiological characteristics of the normal cortical **pyramidal cell** 2 (the neuron in the cortex that produces its final excitatory outflow) give rise to the EEG and set the basis for the disordered function that produces a seizure focus. Figure 22.3 presents the principal features of the pyramidal cell, a neuron that is densely distributed in the lower levels of the cortex. Many neurons in the central nervous system respond to stimulation in an essentially additive way: if significantly more excitation than inhibition occurs, the cell produces a transmittable signal, an action potential. Signal generation in the pyramidal cell (PC) is a more complex and interesting phenomenon. Excitation typically occurs on the apical dendrite and its branches. Because of the presence of dendritic booster zones, 3 a relatively small input stimulus can produce an action potential in the apical dendrite that travels towards the soma (cell body). 4 This activity is a major component of a normal EEG.

Most action potentials are arrested because of the high level of inhibition that is normally focused on the soma and

2 611

3 613

4 35825

Columns: The Functional Units of Cortical Organization

Each pyramidal cell is an element in the basic unit of cortical function, called a **column.** It consists of several hundred pyramidal and various associated cells organized around a single cortical input. This column has a unified function, for example, in the perception of a specific visual stimulus or tonal pattern, or perhaps the activation of a muscle group. Discharge of action potentials that affect the perception or movement is accompanied by a variety of other signals from the column that supply information to other areas of the cortex or promote coordination of contractions. Output from the column indirectly inhibits the surrounding cortical tissue. This limiting of cortical activity to the appropriate column is called **surround inhibition.** Box figure 22.1 presents the relationship between the principal cells contributing to the activity of a column.

If a number of cells in a column become abnormally excitable or are released from normal inhibition, they may serve as an epileptogenic focus, spontaneously and unpredictably emitting a burst of action potentials. This burst is immediately followed by surround inhibition. In theory, such a sequence accounts for the spike (action potentials) and wave (surround inhibition) characteristic of a focus. It may also provide the basis for the rhythmic alternation of massive excitation and subsequent inhibition that characterizes the convulsive tonic-clonic seizure. In this view the synchronous firing of millions of pyramidal cells is followed by their reflex inhibition, which in turn passes, leaving them vulnerable to the next wave of excitation. These volleys may continue to the point of exhaustion of the majority of cortical pyramidal cells or of those pyramidal cells in the focus that are driving the seizure.

PC - Pyramidal cell
EC - Excitatory cell
IC - Inhibitory cell
RC - Recurrent collateral

Surface of cortex

Boundary of white matter

Stimulatory input to the column

Outflow from pyramidal cells that belong to the same column

Box Figure 22.1   Diagram of the relationship between the principal cells involved in the organization of cortical function. Activation of a column of pyramidal cells (only two are indicated) through either stimulatory input or removal of inhibition (or both) induces action potentials in associated axons and inhibition of the cells surrounding the column (shaded area) through the activation by recurrent collaterals (RC) of inhibitory cells (IC).

basal dendrites. If excitation is intense enough, or if inhibition is removed, an action potential (AP) will be generated in the PC axon and a signal will leave the cortex. This interplay of excitation and inhibition allows for very subtle modulation of cortical activity; a very weak stimulatory signal can be "heard" while a very intense signal may be "ignored." In the context of epilepsy, a seizure might develop because of excess excitation or insufficient inhibition. The intense firing of an abnormally active pyramidal cell can readily recruit additional normal PCs. Conversely, if the normal inhibitory inputs to pyramidal cells are reduced in any way, these cells can become epileptogenic, i.e., fire spontaneously.

Hippocampal PCs have an added characteristic that increases their epileptogenic potential. Rather than firing a single AP and then remaining in a resistant state as do most neurons, hippocampal PCs fire bursts of action potentials and then remain susceptible to subsequent activation for a brief period. Anything that destabilizes these cells or interferes with their physiological inhibition can, for this reason, be potentially epileptogenic.

Patterns of Seizure Activity

Because of the link between cortical activity and various observable seizure phenomena (behavioral, sensory, mental, EEG patterns), it is important to make careful clinical observations of a given seizure's components. These can be useful both in diagnosis and in assessing a patient's response to therapy.

Typically, an epileptic's recurrent seizures have a relatively predictable pattern. The individual may experience a **prodrome**—that is, a set of symptoms that warns of a seizure's approach—minutes, hours, or even days before it occurs. As the seizure begins, an **aura** (from the Greek term meaning "breeze"), may be experienced. Auras include mental, sensory, or motor phenomena that the person later remembers as signaling the onset of the seizure. The seizure itself consists of a set of sensory, mental, and/or motor activities that is fairly consistent for a given individual. These persist for a usually consistent period of time and then resolve. They are followed by a postseizure state that differs for each person and seizure type. The aura that the patient notes and the characteristics of the first observable seizure are very useful in pinpointing the area(s) of the brain in which the seizure activity is initiated. Such localization is particularly important if the seizure is not medically correctable and surgery is contemplated.

Although the preceding generalization holds, variations in seizure patterns do occur. The most common variation, particularly if the person is on anticonvulsants, is a lesser version of the person's full-blown seizure pattern, often involving the aura or the aura and the first parts of the complete seizure pattern. As well, many people experience tonic-clonic seizures as a complication of their fundamental seizure type. Less commonly, individuals may exhibit two or more distinctly different types of seizures, in succession or simultaneously.

Seizure Classification

The material in this section is organized around the classification of epileptic seizures proposed by the Commission on Classification and Terminology of the International League Against Epilepsy (1981), with certain clarifying modifications. Although there is considerable complexity in the various categories of seizure, only the essential types are considered here.

Partial Seizures

Partial seizures typically begin at a discrete and relatively limited focus. The specific seizure pattern depends on the function of the area of the brain that is involved. For example, **focal motor without march** denotes a seizure that arises in neurons in a specific part of the motor cortex and may involve twitching that is restricted to one hand or one side of the face, but does not spread. If there is limited spread (march), the seizure pattern will become more extensive, as in a **focal motor with march** seizure, in which case the twitching in the hand spreads to the forearm, then the upper arm, shoulder, and even one side of the face. This "Jacksonian motor seizure" beautifully illustrates the progressive involvement of contiguous areas of the motor cortex. It is, however, a very rarely observed phenomenon.

Simple Partial Seizures If the spread is very limited, the seizure will remain **simple,** with **elementary symptomatology.** These terms indicate that the seizure is relatively uncomplicated, affecting only one aspect of neural function. Postural abnormalities or various sensory deficits are examples. In simple partial seizures, consciousness is relatively undisturbed.

Complex Partial Seizures In complex partial seizures (CPS), an alteration of consciousness follows the initial simple seizure. Although the victims may appear relatively alert and aware of their surroundings, their consciousness is definitely impaired. They typically appear confused or totally preoccupied and may exhibit various **automatisms.** These are purposeless and automatic behaviors undertaken without intent or awareness. Typical automatisms include lip smacking, sucking, chewing or swallowing movements, perhaps undressing or incoherent talking or the uninterrupted continuation of habitual acts like driving or turning the page of a book. It is estimated that 70% of complex partial seizures arise from a focus in the temporal lobe.

How Safe Are You?

Understandably, health care workers may be concerned for their safety when they see the restless, fearful behavior that a person in a complex partial seizure can display. By way of reassurance, you should be aware that unprovoked violence is very rare as an accompaniment of epileptic seizures. Of course, it is sensible to exercise caution when working closely with someone who could, in a confused state, lash out or defensively ward off a person who is trying to help. A directed attack, however, is so uncommon (19 cases out of 100,000 in one study of a group of the most difficult and potentially violent patients) that it is not a realistic concern.

There are some other conditions that might readily be confused with a CPS. For example, a panic attack (phobic-anxiety syndrome) may produce psychic symptoms suggestive of the auras associated with CPS, such as a sense that everything has happened before (déjà vu), a sense of detachment (depersonalization), and various illusions or distortions of perception. When these are epileptic phenomena, they tend to be more stereotyped and vivid and of relatively rapid onset and brief duration (seconds to minutes). The evolution of a transient ischemic attack (TIA) may also produce symptoms that resemble a CPS or its aura, especially if the TIA alters the person's level of consciousness. Such a case may be a real diagnostic puzzle because the person may have developed an epileptogenic focus associated with an old embolic infarct and also be experiencing TIA. EEG recording during the experience usually settles the issue.

Simple partial and complex partial seizures may be observed in an acute care hospital setting, but rarely are they the reason for admission. Partial seizures that spread (secondarily generalize) into tonic-clonic convulsions are much more likely to be a reason for admission. Either the initial, less serious seizure pattern has begun to generalize or control of seizure spread may have broken down. For example, another illness or condition may make the person more susceptible to generalization, or the effectiveness of drug therapy may decline, either because the person has stopped taking the medication or because illness or another drug is interfering with its absorption. Many of the epileptic seizures encountered clinically arise for reasons such as these.

As was noted earlier, careful observation of the prodrome, aura, and details of the seizure is very helpful in establishing accurate diagnosis and effective treatment. Among seizures classified as generalized tonic-clonic, most are in fact secondarily generalized partial seizures. Often the generalization is so rapid that the true nature of the seizure can be confirmed only by very careful observations of behavior and correlation of these with EEG traces.

Partial Seizure Progression A simple partial seizure may exist on its own with no alteration of consciousness, and a complex partial seizure (consciousness altered from the onset) may be experienced without complication. Apart from these cases, there are a limited number of ways in which seizure patterns can progress. A simple partial might progress to a complex partial seizure (at which point consciousness becomes altered) or to a generalized tonic-clonic seizure (fig. 22.4) with loss of consciousness. In similar fashion, a complex partial seizure might progress to a generalized tonic-clonic seizure. The most complex sequence would be found in an episode that begins with a simple partial seizure and progresses to a complex partial seizure (alteration of consciousness), which in turn progresses to a generalized tonic-clonic seizure (loss of consciousness).

Generalized Seizures

Generalized seizures are by definition incapable of being linked to a specific focus. That is, routine EEG tracings, observed behaviors, and patient recollections do not give any clues as to localization. The category commonly includes seizures that vary immensely in terms of their severity and the amount of brain tissue that is recruited into the abnormal paroxysmal discharge.

Absence Seizures Absence seizures ("absence" is usually pronounced as in French, so that "en" sounds like "on") may also be called **petit mal seizures** (again with a French pronunciation, similar to "petty mal"). They have a typical brain wave pattern and usually involve only minor impairment of consciousness arising from changes in relatively small areas of the brain (fig. 22.5). A blank stare **5** or other facial signs indicate the impaired consciousness (the person becomes "absent"). After two to ten seconds the patient suddenly resumes all preseizure activity, perhaps having lost only the thread of conversation. These typical absence seizures often include lip smacking, pouting, and eye blinking. They may also include clonic twitching of the fingers or both arms, postural tone may decrease or increase, and there may be autonomic components. The longer the absence continues, the more likely it is to include these behaviors, which indicate a progressively deeper seizure state. Because absence seizures may occur hundreds of times in a day, they can seriously interfere with learning or work performance.

Simple absence is typically an epilepsy of childhood or adolescence. Absence episodes begin in childhood (peaking at ages 6–7) or adolescence and produce a classic EEG display. The childhood form of the disease, which can produce frequent absence, often spontaneously remits as

Simple partial seizure

Complex partial seizure

Generalized tonic-clonic seizure

Figure 22.4   Pathways whereby a simple partial seizure could theoretically spread to become complex and/or a secondarily generalized tonic-clonic seizure. (*a*) Epileptogenic focus recruits associated cortical tissue, producing a simple partial seizure. (*b*) Focal seizure projects to an association area connected to the hippocampal formation on the right side, which projects, in turn, to the left hippocampal formation. This results in a complex partial seizure. (*c*) Extensive spread leads to a secondarily generalized tonic-clonic seizure.

the nervous system matures. If it doesn't do so, generalized tonic-clonic seizures (GTCS) often develop in adolescence, but response to therapy is generally very good. The adolescent form (juvenile absence epilepsy) has a lower seizure frequency (less than daily), is also complicated with GTCS, and responds well to therapy. Above-average intelligence, normal background EEG, the absence of GTCS, and a negative family history of seizures are excellent positive prognostic factors.

Atypical absence or **absence variant,** although behaviorally indistinguishable from simple absence except perhaps for a slower resolution, has quite a different clinical course. It is associated with a clinical syndrome called Lennox-Gastaut that usually afflicts children of ages 1 year

and older. These children **6** exhibit a wide range of seizures (myoclonic, astatic, absence, tonic-clonic), are usually mentally retarded, and are typically difficult to treat effectively. The absence is accompanied by an EEG trace that is much more irregular and chaotic than that of simple absence. The course and outcome of this syndrome are variable, and some children perish from an underlying progressive encephalopathy.

Tonic-Clonic Seizures Tonic-clonic **(grand mal)** seizures are a fairly common type, representing a maximal seizure response of the brain in which all brain systems can be recruited into the paroxysmal discharge. The seizure is classified as "generalized" if it commences simultaneously in both hemispheres. This is the only feature that

Figure 22.5   Bilateral and synchronous 3-per-second spike-and-wave display associated with simple absence seizures. Note the sudden fully generalized onset and the similar, instantaneous resolution. This was a very brief seizure (approximately 1½ sec).

discriminates it from the secondarily generalized tonic-clonic seizure (see earlier). Tonic-clonic seizures are the most serious seizures you will encounter in a health care setting.

The pattern of seizure is quite stereotyped (fig. 22.6), whether it is truly generalized from the start, secondarily generalized from another seizure form, or precipitated by alcohol or barbiturate withdrawal. Some patients have a prodrome, which is some change that signals the subsequent GTCS. This may occur days in advance. The prodrome might include depression, irritability, apathy or malaise or, rarely, euphoria (the Russian novelist Dostoyevsky experienced such ecstasy that he considered his seizures a blessing!). The person may have one or more myoclonic jerks upon awakening, the day of the seizure. About half of those whose principal seizure is the GTCS have a distinct aura a few seconds before the onslaught of

the GTCS. This is evidence of the simple partial onset of their seizure and may be helpful in localization of the focus. Typically, the seizure itself goes through three phases: an initial **tonic phase** lasting 10–20 seconds, a ½–2-minute **clonic phase,** and then a **terminal phase** lasting about 5 minutes.

The tonic phase starts with a brief period of muscle flexing, which is accompanied by raising of the arms and opening of the eyes and mouth. Next there is a 10–15-second interval of pronounced extension, characterized by generally high muscle tension. During this period, the jaws close sharply and air is rapidly expelled to produce a characteristic **epileptic cry.** The arms and legs are extended, respiration stops with air fully expired, bladder tension may evacuate the bladder, and the pupils become unresponsive to light. The end of the tonic phase is indicated by a short period of muscle tremor.

Figure 22.6   A generalized tonic-clonic (grand mal) seizure as it appears in a typical EEG. This trace shows generalization from a simple focus (→) as is typical of most tonic-clonic seizures. The generalization, however, is very rapid.

The onset of the clonic phase is indicated by an initial muscle relaxation, which is then followed by violent spasms of contraction and relaxation. In these, the strongest muscle groups dominate to produce a characteristic pattern of elbow flexion, leg extension, and torso hyperextension. These muscle spasms can be so intense that they result in torn muscles or bone fractures. During the clonic phase, respiration resumes but is ineffective, and cyanosis may develop. The autonomic system is also active, inducing pronounced perspiration, alternating constriction and dilation of the pupils, and heavy salivary secretion. The saliva may combine with blood from a tongue bitten during the tonic phase to produce a froth of blood in the mouth.

In the longer terminal phase that follows, the victim becomes limp and quiet, with normal breathing restored. This comalike state is characterized by a period of minutes during which the EEG is "flat." It may be followed by up to a hour of deep sleep, or the patient may become conscious with no recollection of the events of the seizure. Normal autonomic function is also restored during the terminal phase. Figure 22.7 presents an analysis of the various features of a typical GTCS.

Tonic-clonic seizures usually occur singly but may come in a cluster of two or three. A small proportion of patients (estimated at 5–8%) are at risk of lapsing into series of GTCS without fully regaining consciousness. This condition, termed **status epilepticus,** is a severe medical emergency and is treated in a later section.

Other Generalized Seizures Two seizures can best be seen as subvariants of the complete tonic-clonic seizure. Both are more commonly found in children. The **clonic seizure** is like a tonic-clonic without the tonic phase. It is a generalized seizure characterized by rhythmic contractions of all muscles, loss of consciousness, and marked autonomic manifestations. **Tonic seizures** involve brief generalized tonic extension of all four limbs and head extension with marked autonomic manifestations. These two are rare in adults. The sort of tonic-clonic variant likely to be encountered clinically involves a few massive myoclonic jerks that leave the person dazed or unconscious.

Atonic seizures are characterized by a sudden loss of muscle tone. The result will vary from head or body sagging, with full consciousness, to loss of consciousness, falling, and a complete loss of muscle tone. The term **akinetic**

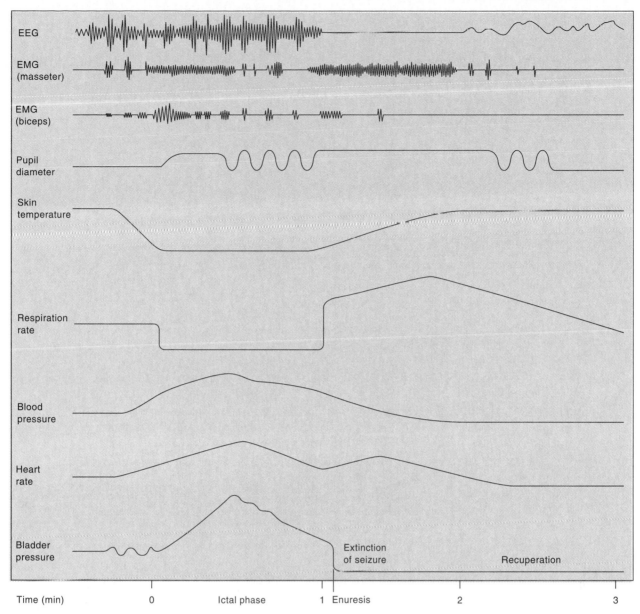

EEG

EMG
(masseter)

EMG
(biceps)

Pupil
diameter

Skin
temperature

Respiration
rate

Blood
pressure

Heart
rate

Bladder
pressure

Extinction
of seizure

Recuperation

Time (min)   0   Ictal phase   1 Enuresis   2   3

Figure 22.7   Analysis of relevant variables in a generalized tonic-clonic seizure (GTCS).

usually denotes a transient arrest of all motor activity, while the term **astatic** has been used to label drop attacks, sudden spells during which the person, usually a child, falls without warning. In current usage, the term atonic covers all of these variants.

Other patterns of seizure are usually seen only in infants or children and are often symptomatic of a broader clinical syndrome. The seizures expressed in very young babies may go unnoticed or at least unrecognized: horizontal eye movements, eyelid blinking or fluttering, sucking, smacking, swimming or pedaling movements, perhaps spells of apnea. Slightly older children may show a variety of myoclonic jerks. These have been aptly called lightning

spasms. The term infantile spasms refers to a varied expression of flexor, extensor, or lightning spasms or neck flexion (nods) that are associated with a condition called **West's syndrome** and affect infants over 8 months of age. While children who have no other evidence of neurological abnormality have been known to recover fully, many children with this syndrome suffer severe neurological impairment or progressive encephalopathy. Lennox-Gastaut, another childhood syndrome that affects slightly older infants (1 year plus), was described earlier.

An overview of the current system for classifying seizures is presented in table 22.1.

Table 22.1	Classification of Epileptic Seizures

I. *PARTIAL SEIZURES* (begin locally, also called focal or local)

    A. *PARTIAL SEIZURES WITH SIMPLE OR ELEMENTARY SYMPTOMATOLOGY* (consciousness is usually not impaired)

        1. WITH MOTOR SIGNS:

            a. Focal motor without march

            b. Focal motor with march (Jacksonian)

            c. Versive (also called adversive)

            d. Postural

            e. Phonatory (vocalization or arrest of speech)

        2. With SOMATOSENSORY or SPECIAL SENSORY SYMPTOMS (simple hallucinations, e.g., tingling, light flashes, buzzing)

            a. Somatosensory (superficial cutaneous, muscle, joint and visceral)

            b. Visual

            c. Auditory

            d. Olfactory (smells)

            e. Gustatory (tastes)

            f. Vertiginous (sudden dizziness or vertigo)

        3. With AUTONOMIC SYMPTOMS OR SIGNS (including epigastric sensation, pallor, sweating, flushing, piloerection and pupillary dilation)

        4. With PSYCHIC SYMPTOMS (disturbances of higher cerebral function—these **rarely** occur without impairment of consciousness and are therefore more commonly experienced as (part of) complex partial seizures. Examples are déjà vu, dreamy states, distortions of time sense, fear, anger and more elaborate hallucinations.

    B. *COMPLEX PARTIAL SEIZURES* (with impairment of consciousness; may sometimes begin with simple symptomatology)

        1. SIMPLE PARTIAL ONSET, FOLLOWED BY IMPAIRMENT OF CONSCIOUSNESS—may begin with simple partial features (A1–A4 above) followed by impaired consciousness or may include automatism (non-purposive 'automatic' behaviors, e.g., fumbling).

        2. With IMPAIRMENT OF CONSCIOUSNESS AT ONSET—may only involve impairment of consciousness or may also include automatisms.

    C. *PARTIAL SEIZURES EVOLVING TO SECONDARY GENERALIZED SEIZURES* (tonic-clonic, tonic or clonic)

        1. Simple partial seizures evolving to generalized seizures.

        2. Complex partial seizures evolving to generalized seizures.

        3. Simple partial seizures evolving to complex partial seizures evolving to generalized seizures.

II. *GENERALIZED SEIZURES* (seizure activity begins bilaterally, may be convulsive, e.g., B, C, D and E or non-convulsive, e.g., absence and atonic seizures)

    A. ABSENCE SEIZURES

    B. MYOCLONIC SEIZURES (myoclonic jerks, single or multiple)

    C. CLONIC SEIZURES

    D. TONIC SEIZURES

    E. TONIC-CLONIC SEIZURES

    F. ATONIC SEIZURES (Astatic, Akinetic)

    (Combinations may occur of B through F, e.g., B & F, B & D)

Source: Abstracted from Gastaut (1970) with revisions proposed by the Commission on Classification and Terminology of the International League Against Epilepsy (1981). Only seizure patterns commonly found in adults have been included.

Cortex

RAS (reticular
activating system)

Hippocampal
formation

Sensory
stimuli

Sensory stimuli
(tactile, kinesthetic,
visual, auditory, etc.)

(a)   (b)

Figure 22.8   Components of consciousness. (*a*) Lateral view illustrates four components described in text. Outflow from RAS passes to the thalamus and is then directed diffusely to the cortex to mediate level of consciousness. The relative location of the hippocampus is identified in heavy dots. (*b*) As well as tracing RAS outflow (right side of diagram) an attempt is made to suggest the inputs/outputs for the hippocampal formation (left side). Arrowheads at either end of lines suggest the reciprocal communications between cortical areas, where information arises and is eventually consolidated and stored, and the hippocampal formation. Pathways that unite the hippocampal formation with the autonomic nervous system and the pituitary have been omitted for simplicity. Dashed line in (*a*) indicates approximate section shown in (*b*).

SEIZURES AND THE ALTERATION OF CONSCIOUSNESS

A major factor in monitoring a seizure in progress is the continual assessment of the patient's state of consciousness. This is an interactive process because, in this context, consciousness is equated with the capacity to respond. Appropriate responses depend, of course, on an intact capacity to orient, attend, receive, and process prior to producing a response. Additionally, normal consciousness implies memory, the ongoing running of a "backup tape" that may or may not be consolidated into lasting memory traces.

Components of Consciousness

A full discussion of consciousness is beyond our current focus. Suffice it to say that normal consciousness depends on the integrated function of at least these major components (fig. 22.8): appropriate sensory stimulation and their normal nervous system processing, appropriate output from the reticular activating system (RAS), a functional cerebral

cortex, and access to a functional hippocampal formation. To understand the ways in which consciousness can be altered in a seizure, a brief review of these is necessary.

Sensory Input and Processing

The effects of massive sensory deprivation have been investigated by suspending subjects in silent darkness in body-temperature tanks, with their limbs padded. These people have trouble concentrating within a few hours, and most experience the chaotic thought processes associated with outright psychosis within 12–18 hours. Such results illustrate our need for at least minimal sensory stimulation to maintain normal consciousness.

Reticular Activating System (RAS)

This is a network of brain stem neurons **7** with extensive projections to almost every part of the central nervous system. In the RAS, sensory and cortical inputs are integrated with daily sleep and waking rhythms to produce patterns of output that maintain our level of consciousness. Any altered RAS function produces changes in level of consciousness. These might range from hyperactivity to profound coma, including every intervening degree: aroused, normal, dull, stuporous, responsive only to painful stimuli, or unresponsive with exaggerated reflexes.

Physiological Cortical Functioning

The cerebral cortex is seen as the seat of consciousness, since this is where we presume it is experienced. Limited focal cortical damage appears to leave consciousness intact, although it may severely impair some other specific capacity. On the other hand, a massive diffuse derangement (as in Alzheimer's disease) or a severe systemic disorder (as in extreme liver failure) may completely abolish consciousness.

Hippocampal Formation

Each temporal lobe houses a hippocampal formation (fig. 22.1). This elongated structure, which includes the hippocampus, is in communication with widely distributed brain structures, including large areas of the cerebral cortex. It is directly responsible for the ongoing consolidation of memory and for the attentional behavior that makes specific memories possible. If both hippocampal formations are disrupted simultaneously, attention and short-term memory deficits result.

Seizure Type and Impaired Consciousness

The different patterns of seizure activity produce various impairments of consciousness. These result from the effects of abnormal electrical discharge on the CNS components that contribute to normal consciousness. The following sections explore some of the basics.

Impaired Consciousness in Partial Seizures

Simple partial seizures, because of their limited nature, do not impair consciousness directly, although they can produce mental states that so distract or disturb that much more effort is required to get and hold the patient's attention.

The impaired consciousness that characterizes the complex partial seizure derives from disruption of both hippocampal formations and perhaps other of the CNS centers noted earlier. Although varying depths of altered consciousness are recognized, *any* interference with a person's capacity to respond, if it can't be voluntarily overcome, leads to a diagnosis of complex partial seizure. For example, when asked a simple question, the patient may respond with a puzzled, uncomprehending, or blank stare. Depending on the extent of cortical spread in CPS, the alteration of consciousness may be profound, resembling

the "away" of absence seizures, or it may be barely noticeable to a casual observer. In subtle cases, extensive questioning may be required to confirm the alteration of consciousness.

Impaired Consciousness in Generalized Seizures

Absence seizures are principally cortical in nature. By superimposing a widespread seizure-generated pattern of cortical excitation and inhibition, absence disrupts the normal rhythms that constitute normal consciousness. Because this disruption can be confined to the cortex, there may be no other evidence of neurological impairment. There is an "away" or "absence" (preseizure behavior ceases), but functions dependent on lower centers (maintenance of posture and muscle tone, autonomic function, routine behaviors like walking or cycling) can continue undisturbed. Because cortical memory functions are disrupted, no memory of the seizure is retained.

In tonic-clonic or grand mal seizures, the alteration of consciousness is by far the most profound. The massive volleys of seizure-generated excitation and inhibition dominate the entire central nervous system, seriously disrupting the normal function of all the centers to which we have attributed consciousness: the hippocampal formation, the cortex, and the reticular activating system. With these centers suppressed, attentional behavior, memory, thought, and consciousness itself are lost, with the victim temporarily lapsing into a coma.

Postseizure States of Consciousness

Particular attention must also be paid to the state of consciousness immediately after the seizure. After a grand mal seizure the patient may not be rousable for five minutes and then awakes looking confused and groggy. There is no memory of events during this immediate postseizure period, but with time, memory processes gradually resume normal function. In a CPS, the immediate postseizure state of consciousness allows an observer to differentiate between a CPS that arises in the temporal lobe (gradual return to normal consciousness) and one that arises in the frontal lobe (almost instantaneous restitution of waking consciousness). Similarly, restoration of normal consciousness can be helpful in discriminating simple absence (instantaneous) from absence variant (slower recovery).

GRAND MAL STATUS EPILEPTICUS

A relatively rare but critical occurrence in those with ongoing epilepsy, or those with seizures precipitated by drug or alcohol withdrawal or illness, is the prolonged continuation of their seizure state. A tonic-clonic seizure may recur with incomplete recovery between seizures, or the patient may experience continuous seizure activity. If the activity goes on for more than 30 minutes, major physiological changes occur. These are marked acidosis, significantly elevated PCO_2, hypoglycemia, and a fall in blood pressure that can compromise glucose and oxygen supply to the brain tissue. If untreated, status epilepticus can lead to severe brain damage or death. The mortality in *treated* cases is 10–37%.

A variety of factors can precipitate a status attack (table 22.2). Once established, the massive, abnormal neural activity can itself cause brain damage by depleting oxygen and building up excess harmful metabolic by-products, as well as locally lowering the pH. As the systemic PO_2, PCO_2, and pH change beyond tolerable limits, the cardiovascular centers in the medulla are compromised and the threat of progressive circulatory shock arises. In such cases, quick, aggressive therapeutic intervention is imperative.

Other types of seizure can also assume a status pattern. A person who is having 200–300 absence seizures in 24 hours is considered to be in **absence status epilepticus.** Although not life-threatening in the manner of status tonic-clonic, this is an entirely disabling condition and is aggressively treated in much the same way. When a focal (partial) seizure is maintained continuously (usually with no loss of consciousness), it is called **epilepsia partialis continua.** It also tends to be treated aggressively because of the risk of engendering further brain damage or generalizing into tonic-clonic seizures. **Electrical status** exists when, despite little or no clinical evidence of seizure activity, the EEG shows continuous abnormal spike discharges. Electrical status is rarely encountered in a typical clinical setting, but it may be seen in the emergency room, where it may be confused with a street drug problem.

DIAGNOSTIC EVALUATION

The electroencephalograph **8** was first used for diagnostic exploration of seizure disorders in the early 1940s and it is still the chief evaluative tool. About 30–50% of patients with suspected epilepsy will have characteristic abnormalities on their first standard EEG, and follow-up studies increase that proportion to 60–90%. For the purposes of diagnosis, hyperventilation, which reduces cerebral perfusion, and photic stimulation are effective in inducing some seizures or interictal abnormalities. The more frequent the seizures, the more likely it is that the patient will show abnormalities on routine EEG. These are strong confirmations of epilepsy, since few normal individuals produce EEG patterns with epilepsy-related components.

Procedures that include placement of electrodes in the nasopharynx and sphenoid bone, as well as the use of depth electrodes that are surgically introduced into the cranial vault, increase the probability of detection and allow precise localization of seizure foci. Ideally the EEG should be observed during the development and expression of a

Table 22.2   Factors That Can Precipitate Status Epilepticus

Infections, of the CNS or others, e.g., flu that impair absorption of antiepileptic agents
Alcohol deprivation in chronic alcoholism
Withdrawal of antiepileptic therapy
Electroconvulsive shock therapy
Brain tumors
Acute withdrawal from sedative or depressant drugs
Various metabolic disorders, e.g., uremia, hypoglycemia, hyponatremia

seizure. Most large metropolitan centers have seizure monitoring units **9 10 11** that make round-the-clock EEG and simultaneous videotaping possible. These are very helpful in the diagnosis of difficult cases and the precise localization required for surgical intervention. EEG monitoring of the target cortex during surgery (electrocorticography) is routine, since it allows resection of only that cortical tissue that is generating abnormal discharges.

A variety of other diagnostic techniques may also be employed. Although CT scans are often done, **magnetic resonance imaging** (MRI) has proved more effective at identifying structural abnormalities in the cortex (tumors, arteriovenous malformations, healed infarcts) or other lesions that may correlate with EEG abnormalities and an epileptogenic focus. Techniques that allow the imaging of neural function, for example glucose metabolism, can be helpful in identifying areas of altered brain metabolism or perfusion during a seizure or during an interictal period. Such sites correlate well with areas that generate EEG abnormalities and with areas of structural change that are common at an epileptogenic focus. **Positron-emission tomography** (PET) and **single-photon-emission CT** (SPECT) are used in some centers for this purpose.

THE MEDICAL MANAGEMENT OF EPILEPSY

Accurate diagnosis of the seizure pattern or epileptic syndrome goes hand-in-hand with the effective management of epilepsy. For most individuals, management means the routine use of antiepileptic medication. The choice of drug depends on the individual's particular seizure type (table 22.3), because medications that are effective with one may be quite ineffective with another. The initial effort is to control the seizure with a single drug. This goal is achievable in more than 80% of the seizures that can be controlled with drugs. The major benefit of using a single drug is that there are fewer and less confusing side effects. Only after

8 53716 **9** 53728 **10** 53729 **11** 53730

Table 22.3	Drugs of Choice for the Pharmacological Control of Typical Seizure Patterns. The Order Reflects the Ranking of Preference Common Among Physicians, Although Many Factors Will Influence the Choice for a Given Patient.

Type of Seizure	Antiepileptic Drug
Simple partial and secondarily generalized tonic-clonic seizures	Carbamazepine, phenytoin, both, either, and primidone
Partial complex	Carbamazepine or phenytoin, primidone, valproic acid,* methsuximide
Simple absence	Ethosuximide, valproic acid
Primary generalized tonic-clonic	Valproic acid, ethosuximide, carbamazepine, or phenytoin
Myoclonic	Valproic acid, clonazepam, or nitrazepam (if available)
Seizures associated with West's or Lennox-Gastaut syndrome	Clonazepam or nitrazepam (if available), ACTH, valproic acid, ketogenic diet†

*Valproic acid or valproate or sodium valproate

†These seizures are particularly difficult to control. ACTH stimulates endogenous release of hydrocortisone (an anti-inflammatory agent). A high-fat diet (ketogenic) induces moderate acidosis and is effective in some cases.

several single drugs have failed will combinations be tried, usually in cases of epilepsy that involve several seizure types.

Currently, pharmaceutical agents provide excellent or at least quite acceptable levels of control in epilepsy. In the relatively small proportion of cases where they don't, surgical intervention may be indicated. In such procedures, the epileptogenic focus is first identified and then surgically removed. Of course, various factors can complicate the issue. For example, a focus may be identified but it may be in a location to which surgical access is limited. Another problem is posed by multiple or diffuse foci, whose removal would produce unacceptable functional losses.

As noted earlier, electrocorticography is used to monitor cortical activity during surgery to resect an epileptogenic focus. The goal is to limit the loss of cortical tissue to the volume responsible for the seizures, and no more. During the procedure the patient remains conscious so that testing can monitor relevant neurological functioning. The aim, as always, is to balance any functional deficits against resolution of the seizure disorder.

Other, nonpharmacological approaches to seizure control are largely supportive. Patients need to learn to cope effectively with stress, eat well, and get sufficient rest. Avoidance of eliciting stimuli is effective in controlling some forms of what are called **reflex epilepsies.** Examples of these are the rare seizures brought on by gazing through the fingers while the hand is rapidly moved, hearing certain musical passages, reading, or tooth brushing.

Case Study

The patient in this case was a 40-year-old male who had had seizures since he was 15, with their frequency recently increasing. Although his measured IQ was within normal range, he appeared slow, had poor general knowledge, and had short-term memory processing deficits. These, combined with seizures occurring up to six times daily, had made regular employment impossible, and he had been receiving a handicap pension for the past two years. He was referred for seizure investigation with the ultimate possibility of surgical intervention.

The patient was the fourth of ten children. There was no family history of seizure disorders except that his father had appeared to have a seizure secondary to a stroke that he suffered at 73. The only event in the patient's childhood that might be significant was a fall off a cliff, at age 8 or 9.

He received a laceration but did not lose consciousness. A slight skull deformity in the left parietal region might be related to this accident. He had been quite slow in school even before his seizures began, at which point his performance worsened, and he left school after grade 10. He had attempted a variety of jobs since then, but frequent seizures interfered with success. He lived with a woman for seven or eight years in a common-law relationship and was married for two or three years, beginning at age 27 or 28, but eventually separated. He had one daughter who was medically fine. Short-term memory had become worse lately, and social and sexual relationships were becoming more difficult. Medication (including phenytoin, methsuximide, and the antidepressant amytriptyline) was being taken regularly.

The seizure investigation covered almost five years, some of that time absorbed in waiting for specialist interviews and access to the seizure investigation unit. Observations by that unit showed that he appeared to experience two distinct patterns of seizure onset. With the first, he had a distinct aura that consisted of an undescribable cephalic sensation with a strong déjà-vu feeling. This was followed by visual searching, perhaps spontaneous vocalizations ("I, ah . . . ," "Oh," "Humh"), and fumbling with glasses or other objects. When questioned, he might be appropriately responsive, identifying objects and answering simple questions. He usually passed urine in the latter part of the seizure. He might change his underwear or bedding while still appearing to be in the state of altered conscious ness. These seizures with a simple partial onset were usually mild, seldom generalized, and didn't leave him confused. He might remember some of the events of the seizure, but this was highly variable. His other seizures were without aura; they were clinically quite similar in their complex phase (i.e., during the fumbling, etc.) but left him feeling much more confused for longer periods of time (10–15 minutes). His responses to questioning were less integrated, and often he was nonresponsive. The seizures themselves were longer (2–3 minutes), and were much more likely to generalize. When this happened, the convulsion consisted of jerky movements of the head and eyes to one side, with raising and abduction of the ipsilateral arm.

His CT was normal, but MRI indicated an abnormality in the right medial inferior temporal lobe. Testing of speech lateralization and memory showed that his speech and language were localized to the right hemisphere (he was left-handed). Short-term memory was better in the right hemisphere than in the left. The findings from EEG monitoring during seizures were difficult to interpret, as there were widespread abnormalities in the traces. There was no clearly identifiable focus, although episodic sharp/slow wave activity in the anterior right temporal region was associated with drowsiness.

The patient was recommended for surgical investigation with the use of electrocorticography. This showed a fairly circumscribed focus, localized in the region identified by MRI (inferior, medial temporal lobe). While simultaneous memory and language testing and electrocorticography were done, tiny portions of abnormal cortex were removed. Most of the area identified on MRI was ablated, with no impact on language or language function. Drug therapy was continued after surgery, and a significant reduction in seizure frequency was noted (less than one per week). With this improvement, he was encouraged to attempt a preemployment program at a local college, and is currently enrolled in that program.

Commentary

This case is an example of a complex partial seizure with a poor response to usual medical management. For such patients, surgery is a possible and sometimes very effective alternative.

Key Concepts

1. Nonepileptic seizures are secondary to some other potentially reversible or transitory conditions such as alcohol withdrawal, bacterial meningitis, or liver or kidney failure (pp. 590–592).

2. Epileptic seizures result when a relatively permanent change in the environment, inputs, or nature of cortical pyramidal cells allows a portion of them (the focus) to discharge spontaneously and to recruit the involvement of larger portions of the cortex (pp. 592–594).

3. Physical and physiological characteristics of pyramidal cells predispose them to becoming seizure generators (pp. 594–596).

4. The majority of seizures begin focally, producing, at least temporarily, some evidence of limited recruitment, e.g., an aura, localized EEG activity, focal abnormal movements or sensation, altered consciousness or psychic function (p. 596).

5. A simple partial seizure may spread to become a complex or a generalized seizure (called a secondarily generalized tonic-clonic seizure) (pp. 596–597).

6. Generalized seizures (i.e., seizures that are generalized from the start, like absence, some tonic-clonic, and other rare seizures) arise more or less instantly with no evidence of focal origin (pp. 597–603).

7. Normal consciousness depends on appropriate sensory stimulation and processing and the integrated function of the reticular activating system, the cerebral cortex, and the hippocampal formation (pp. 603–604).

8. Consciousness is unimpaired in simple partial seizures and impaired in different and characteristic ways in partial complex seizures and specific generalized seizures (p. 604).

9. Grand mal status epilepticus (tonic-clonic status) is a medical emergency (pp. 604–605).

10. Evaluation of a tendency to have seizures involves minimally a routine EEG (a negative EEG does not rule out epilepsy) and perhaps further diagnostics including seizure monitoring, CT, or MRI (p. 605).

11. Drug therapy with a single anticonvulsant medication is the usual choice for medical management of epileptic conditions (p. 605).

REVIEW ACTIVITIES

1. Explain what the following have in common and in what ways they are different.

   Simple absence seizures and atypical absence seizures

   Tonic-clonic seizures and simple absence seizures

   Simple partial seizures with psychic symptoms and complex partial seizures

   West's syndrome and Lennox-Gastaut syndrome

   Ethosuximide and carbamazepine

2. Describe what you would see if you observed the evolution of a seizure from a simple partial with motor signs to a complex partial to a full tonic-clonic seizure.

3. Imagine a worst-case scenario in which a person has the seizure pattern described in activity 2, and it is resistant to normal medical management. Describe the diagnostic procedures and choices that would probably be explored, from most conservative to most radical.

4. From memory, sketch a typical pyramidal cell and label the features that are of relevance to its role as a seizure-generating cell. What are its normal inputs and where do its outputs flow?

Chapter Twenty-Three

Pain and Pain Management

*"We must all die. But that I can save (a person) from days of torture,
that is what I feel as my great and ever new privilege. Pain is a more
terrible lord of mankind than even death himself."*

Albert Schweitzer

Pain is a significant, often central factor for many patients. In confronting pain, their experience will be highly variable. Procedures that induce agony in some will appear to be only mildly uncomfortable to others. Some will describe their pain in clear, precise terms, while others will have difficulty pinpointing the problem. Patients may regard their pain as a challenge, but too many are seriously debilitated, depressed, and almost broken by their experience.

PAIN: ACUTE AND CHRONIC

To begin our discussion, let us first note the distinction between acute pain and chronic pain. Although the term acute is often used in clinical settings to imply sudden and severe, in the context of pain, it refers instead to the transitory nature of the pain experience. Acute pain may range from mild to severe, but its overall duration is relatively short, because the pain is usually related to the progression of disease and subsequent healing. An example is the pain associated with a fracture that heals satisfactorily or with a kidney stone successfully removed from its point of lodgement in a ureter. By contrast, chronic pain may also vary in severity but is of long duration (the usual rule of thumb is six months or more). It is often subclassified on the basis of its underlying cause. Where the pathogenesis of a well-characterized disease underlies the experience—for example, a poorly controlled cancer or a degenerative joint disease—the pain is termed **chronic malignant** or **symptomatic pain.** Where no such disease or degeneration can be identified, it is called **chronic benign** or **chronic nonmalignant pain.** Despite the use of the word benign, this type of pain can be a very disabling condition in its own right. Table 23.1 presents a pain classification scheme. Here the focus shifts from the objective nature of the pain experience (acute versus chronic) to a combination of pain and supposed cause that occurs in individuals.

At least two important principles emerge from the acute/chronic categorization. The first is that in the neurophysiology of pain, significant differences exist in the neurological processing, perception, and impact of acute pain compared with that of the chronic pain. The second principle is that different approaches to pain management are effective with different sorts of pain. This has a bearing on the selection of an appropriate therapeutic regimen to cope with it.

The Acute Pain Model and Pain Relief

In its most straightforward form, the experience of pain is based on the chain of events depicted in figure 23.1. Pain stimuli may directly affect a tissue's nerve endings or indirectly cause tissue damage, releasing substances which then depolarize the nerve endings. These fine nerve endings are called **nociceptors** (*noci* is from the Latin to hurt). The activation of the pain fibers associated with nociceptors is called **nociception.** Pain is the central sensory experience

Table 23.1	Classification of Patients According To Their Pain Experience and Underlying Pathology

Acute Pain

Underlying cause transitory.
Treatment of pain symptomatic.
Resolution based on resolution of underlying cause.
Physiological: part of a natural or therapeutic process, vaccinations, injections, some activity related pain, childbirth.
Posttraumatic or Postsurgery: e.g., immediate response to whiplash, recovery from shoulder surgery.
Secondary to Acute Illness: e.g., biliary colic associated with cholelithiasis.

Chronic Pain

Underlying cause protracted or ongoing, perhaps untreatable or not identifiable.
Long (six months?) duration.
Pain is a (perhaps "the") major focus of care.

Chronic Malignant/Symptomatic Pain
(underlying pathology causes pain)

Recurrent Acute: unresolved cause, pain-free periods, only symptomatic care available, e.g., migraine headaches.
Ongoing, Acute: pain a significant component of chronic disease, e.g., joint pain in rheumatoid arthritis.
Ongoing, Time Limited: e.g., cancer pain ends with death or control of disease.

Chronic Nonmalignant Pain
(pain itself and disablement that results are the major problem, response to drugs often poor) e.g., lower back pain.

Chronic Intractable Nonmalignant Pain Syndrome: same as above except patient is largely disabled by pain.

Source: Adapted fron N.T. Meinhart and M. McCaffery, *Pain: A Nursing Approach to Assessment and Analysis.* Copyright © 1983 Appleton & Lange.

of nociceptive input. It has two quite separate components. Pain perception, like vision or audition, gives information about the nature, location, intensity, and duration of the nociception. Suffering, on the other hand, involves the reactions to pain, including varying combinations of autonomic, emotional, or behavioral responses.

Autonomic responses to intense pain typically consist of increased heart rate and blood pressure, increased secretion of epinephrine, raised blood glucose, decreased gastric secretions and motility, decreased blood flow to the viscera and skin, dilated pupils, and sweating. The emotional responses may involve fear, anger, anxiety, panic, depression, even passive resignation. The simplest behavioral

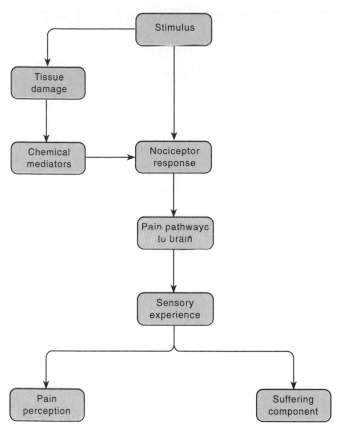

Figure 23.1   The essential aspects of acute pain processing and experience.

responses are spinal cord reflexes, but behaviors may range from lowered mobility to complex coping and avoidance behaviors. Behavioral responses may even include maladaptive patterns of adjustment that can complicate or even interfere with a person's recovery.

The model described in figure 23.1 best addresses the experience of acute pain that is based on trauma or disease, which is called **somatic** pain. In this case, pain is beneficial in that it informs us of danger and then mobilizes a drive state that attempts to remove the stimulus, correct the damage, or at least reduce the intensity of the pain or suffering. Treatment that is based on this model depends on a continued monitoring of signs and symptoms so that changes in a patient's status may be noted, providing the basis for a more refined or altered diagnosis. Any clinical consideration of pain and pain relief must assume that the underlying disease is accurately diagnosed and effectively treated.

This acute pain model is important to keep in mind because many currently used approaches to pain management may focus less on the causes of pain (since they may not be therapeutically accessible) and more on the patient's response to it. Reducing the patient's level of anxiety or tension and relieving depression or anger are a few examples. These are sometimes called **palliative pain relief methods** and are designed to alleviate pain, even if the underlying cause is not reversible. They exert their effects

primarily by modifying reactions to the sensory experience (autonomic, emotional, or behavioral responses) or modulating the sensory experience itself in indirect ways.

THE PHYSIOLOGICAL BASIS OF PAIN PERCEPTION

With an understanding of the essentials of acute and chronic pain, and a basic model for acute pain, we can now turn to the structure and function of the specific neurological components of pain perception.

Nociception

Nociceptors, the finely branched nerve endings whose stimulation gives rise to pain, all appear the same when viewed with an electron microscope. In practice, however, some respond only to strong, mechanical stimulation, especially by sharp objects, or to temperatures above 45° C. These endings converge on small, fine myelinated fibers that conduct their action potentials relatively quickly (5 to 30 m/sec). Fibers of this type are called Aδ (**A delta**) **fibers.** They are distributed only to the skin, mucous membranes, and selected serous membranes (e.g., the parietal peritoneum). They tend to fire immediately upon (intense) stimulation and cease firing when the stimulus is removed, producing the sensation of **sharp pain.** As well, they rapidly adapt to a stimulus. That is, you feel the needle pierce your skin but soon the sense of sharp pain goes away, even though the needle (stimulus) remains. You may experience some sharp pain again as the needle is withdrawn. Essentially, these fibers carry information about sharp, pricking, acute pain that is relatively well localized and discriminated (you know where it is and what's causing it!).

A second population of pain fibers, smaller in diameter and unmyelinated, are called **C fibers.** They are distributed to the same areas as the Aδ fibers, but with much greater density. In addition, they are very widely distributed in deep tissue: in muscle and tendon, visceral peritoneum, and the visceral organs themselves (e.g., the myocardium, the stomach and intestines). Action potentials in these fibers tend to be generated by substances that are associated with tissue damage or insult. These impulses travel in a continuous fashion and are therefore much slower (0.5–2 m/sec) than those conducted over the Aδ fibers. As well, the initiation of firing is not as closely related to the onset or withdrawal of the stimulus. Firing is slow to develop, so pain may emerge some time after stimulus application, perhaps because of the slow release or formation of the triggering substance. Once initiated, action potential firing can persist long after the original stimulus has been removed. C fibers carry information related to long-lasting, burning, often called **dull pain,** which is poorly localized and more diffusely distressing. Dull pain is the sort of pain that typically brings people to seek medical attention for relief.

The Experience of Fast and Slow Pain

A simple illustration may demonstrate this division of peripheral nociception into Aδ and C fibers. Using the nails of your thumb and index finger of one hand, pinch the web of skin between the base of two fingers on the other hand and note the sensations. First, and within a fraction of a second, you should have felt a sharp pain emanating precisely from the pinched area. Then, perhaps two seconds later, a duller, less clearly localized aching or burning sensation should have developed. These sensations were mediated first by Aδ fibers and then by C fibers, hence the commonly used terms **fast** and **slow pain.**

Pain Fiber Connections in the Spinal Cord

Like those of other sensory fibers, the cell bodies of the Aδ and C fibers are found in the dorsal root ganglia. Their axons continue from the dorsal root ganglion into the spinal cord, where they synapse with the next neuron in the chain, called a **second-order neuron.** As Aδ and C fibers enter the cord, some send branches (collaterals) up or down the cord for short distances. They then travel deeper to their points of synapse (fig. 23.2a). This provides for the involvement of several cord segments in the mediation of complex pain reflexes (e.g., crossed extension, table 21.8).

Most of the second-order neurons pass across the cord and then proceed toward the brain in the anterolateral-spinothalamic tract (fig. 23.2b). The term spinothalamic tract is somewhat misleading here, because the vast majority of second-order pain fibers traveling in the anterolateral-spinothalamic tract do not end up in the thalamus at all. Instead they terminate in the reticular formation of the brain stem (fig. 23.2c). Here, through the reticular activating system, they mediate an increase in general consciousness, alertness, and attention. These are important orienting and defense reactions to pain. They occur whatever the specific nature of the pain stimulus and explain some of the jumpiness, irritability, and perhaps obsessiveness of pain sufferers.

A large number of the fibers in the anterolateral system enter an area of cells surrounding the cerebral aqueduct in the midbrain (called, therefore, the **mesencephalic periaqueductal gray matter**). From here, action potentials can be relayed to the hypothalamus and thence to the limbic system and cerebral cortex (fig. 23.2d). This is part of the neurological basis for the endocrine, autonomic, and emotional components of the reaction to pain. The pain pathway, thought to be the evolutionarily most primitive, is one that activates cells in the region of the dorsal midbrain (fig. 23.2e). (This area is called the **tectum** of the midbrain and is associated with orienting responses to visual and auditory stimuli.) In response, these cells appear to promote

Flexor-Withdrawal Reflex Physiology

The neural explanation of the flexor-withdrawal reflex involves action potentials generated in Aδ fibers by cutaneous receptors. The action potentials pass into the dorsal horn, where they synapse with excitatory second-order neurons, which in turn synapse with Alpha motor neurons in the ipsilateral ventral horn. These motor neurons then stimulate the contraction of flexor muscles that draw the stimulated area away from the source of the painful stimulus. These same Aδ fibers simultaneously synapse with inhibitory interneurons (box fig. 23.1) that produce relaxation of the related extensor muscle group to facilitate the flexion of the limb.

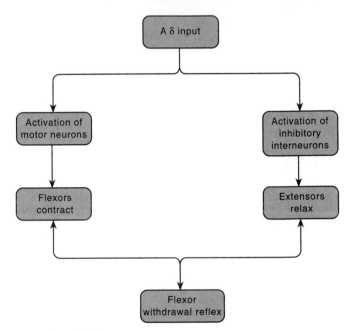

Box Figure 23.1
The flexor-withdrawal reflex depends on activation of flexors at the same time that extensors are inhibited.

spinal cord motor mechanisms, thereby enhancing spinal reflexes and facilitating behavioral responses.

Neospinothalamic Pain Pathways

Many Aδ fibers synapse immediately upon entering lamina I, the first of five layers or laminae of the cord's dorsal horn. Axons from the cell bodies in this layer cross the cord and travel the anterolateral-spinothalamic system to their destinations (fig. 23.3). About one-third of Aδ fibers terminate in the **posterior nuclear group** in the thalamus. These fibers have been called the **neospinothalamic pain system** to denote that this is an evolutionarily advanced and sophisticated pain discrimination pathway. The effectiveness and

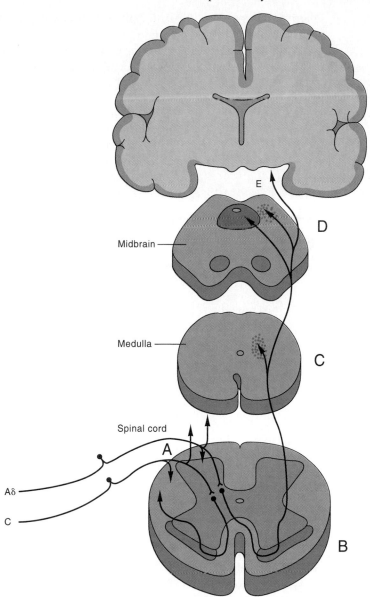

Figure 23.2   An overview of the essential neuronal interrelations for dull and sharp pain perception. Letters *a* through *e* are keyed to the text. The shaded areas of the spinal cord represent the anterolateral-spinothalamic tracts.

specificity of neospinothalamic pain discrimination is due to the convergence on these same thalamic nuclei of the medial lemniscal fibers that carry highly differentiated sensory information for light touch, two-point discrimination, stretch, etc. Pain discrimination is enhanced through the addition of these sensations to the relatively well-discriminated Aδ impulses. Because the posterior nuclear group of thalamic nuclei provide direct access to the primary and secondary somatosensory cortex, conscious appreciation of sharp, well-discriminated, and localized pain is realized.

Activity in Aδ fibers is the principal factor in eliciting pain-induced spinal reflexes. In the simplest of these, the **flexor-withdrawal** reflex, touching something sharp or hot causes rapid withdrawal of the stimulated limb. The withdrawal occurs so rapidly that it is accomplished even before we become conscious of the sensation of pain. This reflex

minimizes exposure to the potentially harmful stimulus. In the **crossed-extension reflex,** reflex extension of the opposite limb is added to the flexor-withdrawal reflex. For example, if you step on a tack, you will simultaneously lift the pricked foot and extend the other leg so that your weight is borne on the unstimulated foot.

Paleospinothalamic Pain Pathways

The C fibers have a slightly more complex fate in the cord: they synapse in either lamina II or V. But they form a major input to a much more complicated local processing system that feeds into a separate pain pathway that originates in lamina V. Fibers from cell bodies in lamina V pass into the ascending reticular system, the mesencephalic periaqueductal gray matter, and the midbrain tectum, as do the

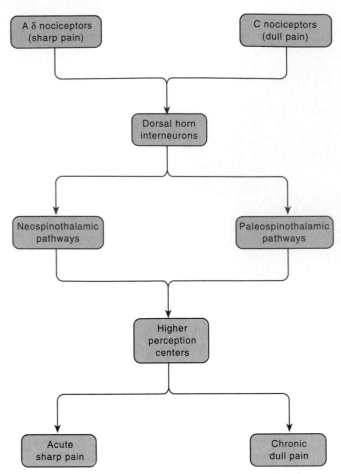

Figure 23.3   The general scheme for underlying perception of the two types of pain.

fibers from lamina I. But, as well, some continue to the thalamus, particularly its **intralaminar nuclei,** from which they diffusely project to various parts of the cortex. The number of fibers arriving at the thalamus is small compared with the vast number of original C fibers, and there is also little overlap or convergence with fibers arising from Aδ. For these reasons, discrimination and localization of pain in this system is quite imprecise. The pathways involved are called the **paleospinothalamic pathways.**

The spinal cord processing of information that feeds into the paleospinothalamic pathway is shown in figure 23.4. It shows the array of interconnections in the laminae of the dorsal horn that make possible the varieties of pain fiber activity. Incoming Aδ fibers synapse in lamina I, then cross the cord to ascend in the contralateral spinothalamic tract. C fibers end in either lamina II or lamina V. Another element is the lamina V neuron itself. It receives inputs from C and second-order Aδ fibers. A portion of these lamina V neurons contribute to the paleospinothalamic pathway.

Summary of Ascending Pain Processing

Much of the neural activity generated by pain stimuli feeds into the ascending reticular system to increase alertness, attentiveness, and readiness to identify and respond to stimuli (**spinoreticular component**). A portion of the input ends up in the periaqueductal gray region of the midbrain, gaining access to the hypothalamus and therefore both the limbic and endocrine systems. Some excitation arrives at the tectum of the midbrain and thereby increases the motor responsiveness of spinal cord mechanisms that enhance reflex activity (**spinotectal component**). The strictly "spinothalamic" component is divided into two elements: a highly discriminated neospinothalamic pathway that provides direct access to the specialized sensory cortex, and a less well-discriminated paleospinothalamic pathway that appears to play an important role in the mediation of chronic pain. Figure 23.5 presents these principles in schematic form.

Endorphins and Descending Systems of Pain Inhibition

We have already noted the role of pain in alerting us to danger and activating some coping responses. Once this role has been served, however, it is desirable to limit the pain and much therapeutic effort is devoted to this goal. One long-standing approach has been the use of narcotic agents, e.g., morphine, to dull the pain. Most narcotics are derived from plants and produce their effects by binding to specific receptors in the brain stem. Once the presence of such receptors was discovered, an intriguing speculation arose. Presumably they would have developed in a system that used some internally produced substance that would bind to them; it was just a coincidence that plant-derived narcotics were sufficiently similar to bind to the same receptors (fig. 23.6). This speculation has proved to be correct, and the presence of endogenous morphinelike substances is now well established. Certain of them, known as **endorphins,** are the subject of much study in their role as pain inhibitors.

The actual inhibitory effects of the endorphins are achieved indirectly. Endorphin receptors are richly distributed in the brain stem. When activated by endorphins, they promote the flow of action potentials down the cord, to lamina II of the dorsal horn. The arrival of these action potentials triggers the release of another member of the endorphin group called **leucine enkephalin.** This is a key step, in that leucine enkephalin exerts an inhibitory effect at the synapses between Aδ and C inputs to their second-order neurons. In this way, the descending pathways are able to limit pain inputs to the higher perception centers (fig. 23.7). The principal inhibitory effect of this descending system is on the paleospinothalamic pathways and their contribution to dull, aching pain. Since this is the case, we might predict that exogenous substances that can bind to endorphin receptors would be most effective against this type of pain, and this is, indeed, the case.

Another approach to analgesia uses harmless electrical stimulation of the skin that overlies the painful area, the peripheral nerve that serves the area, or the dorsal horn

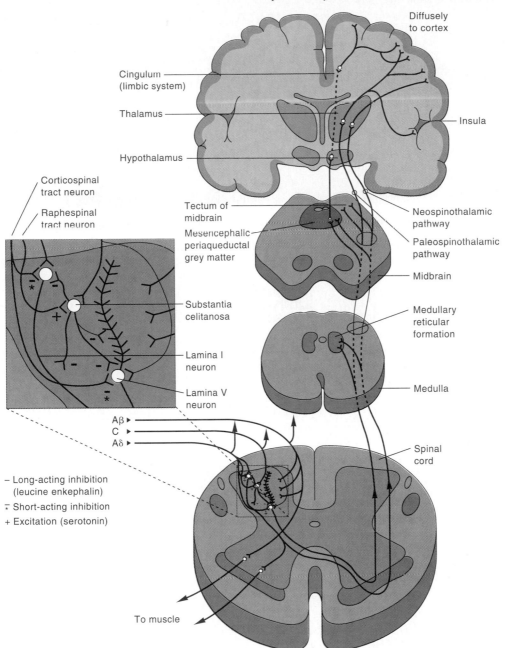

Diffusely
to cortex

Cingulum
(limbic system)

Thalamus

Insula

Hypothalamus

Corticospinal
tract neuron

Raphespinal
tract neuron

Tectum of
midbrain

Neospinothalamic
pathway

Mesencephalic
periaqueductal
grey matter

Paleospinothalamic
pathway

Midbrain

Substantia
celitanosa

Medullary
reticular
formation

Lamina I
neuron

Medulla

Lamina V
neuron

Aβ ▶
C ▶
Aδ ▶

Spinal
cord

– Long-acting inhibition
   (leucine enkephalin)
☆ Short-acting inhibition
+ Excitation (serotonin)

To muscle

Figure 23.4   Scheme of Aδ and C nociceptor synapses in the dorsal horn of the spinal cord. Shading highlights the horn's laminae, designated by Roman numerals. Most output from lamina V passes to higher perception centers via contralateral spinothalamic tracts. Ipsilateral tracts omitted for clarity.

into which its input is relayed. This method is known as **transcutaneous electric nerve stimulation** (TENS). Its analgesic effects are thought to derive from the direct or indirect stimulation of the endorphin system. Yet another technique, used when pain is severe and unresponsive to other analgesics, is **stimulus-produced analgesia.** It involves the placement of electrodes directly within the brain stem, from where their stimulus directly activates the descending pathways that induce pain inhibition.

Referred Pain

As a later section will show, adequate observation of a patient's pain experience requires a precise description of the pain and its localization. This can be quite straightforward, e.g., a burning sensation at the incision site. But it can also be puzzling, e.g., the radiating pains in the left axilla and arm that are associated with a heart attack. In such cases, it is important to recognize that all pain is really "felt" in the brain. The mind projects that perception of

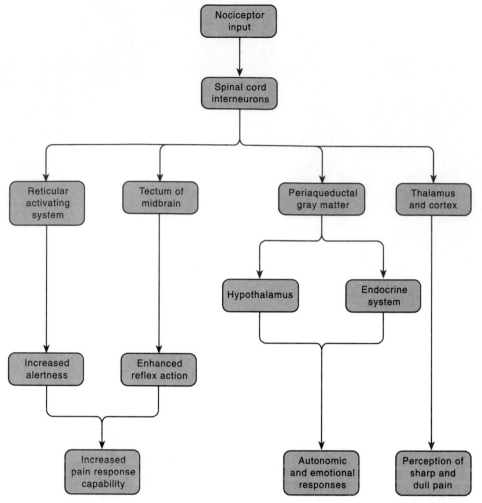

Figure 23.5 Summary of the components of the system for processing nociceptor input to the central nervous system.

pain to an area of the body that is in many cases, but not always, the same as the spot whose stimulation gave rise to the sensation in the first place. Sensations arising at the skin or in the mucous membranes and in some of the parietal serous membranes are quite accurately projected. When a mosquito bites you in the back of the leg you know exactly where to swat, without even looking. On the other hand, pain arising from internal organs, **visceral pain,** is not nearly this accurately projected. It may be perceived as arising on the skin surface or in muscles quite remote from the site of nociception. In this case the sensation is called **referred pain.**

The most widely accepted explanation for referred pain is based on the concept of **dermatomes.** Each of these is the area of skin supplied by a single spinal nerve. This means that cutaneous stimuli from a given dermatome produce action potentials that are always delivered to the corresponding spinal cord segment. The relationship is very straightforward during early embryonic development (fig. 23.8a), when each of the dermatomes lies directly over its corresponding cord segment. However, as development

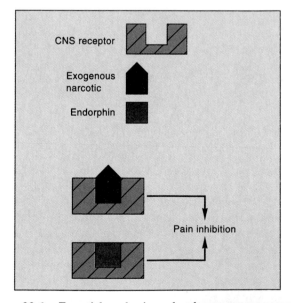

Figure 23.6 Essential mechanism whereby exogenous narcotics work via the endogenous analgesia receptors of the central nervous system.

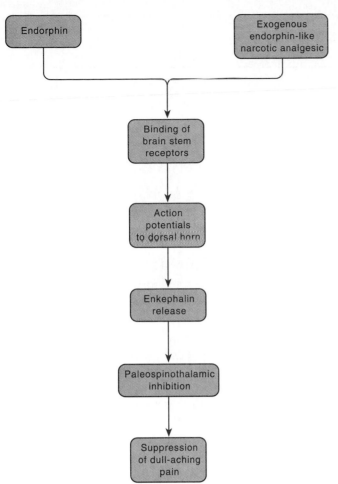

Figure 23.7   Essential elements of the descending analgesic system used by narcotics.

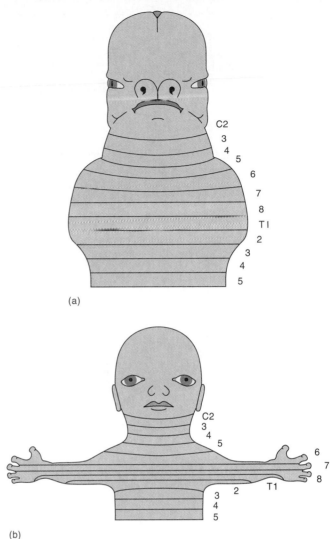

Figure 23.8   Dermatome migration during embryologic development. (*a*) At about 4 weeks, the dermatomes are quite uniform and correspond closely to cord segments. Note early limb buds. (*b*) By week 16, dermatomes C6–T1 have migrated with the developing arms.

proceeds and limb buds emerge and differentiate, the spatial relationship between dermatome and cord becomes distorted (fig. 23.8*b*). Even though some parts of the dermatomes are stretched some distance from their cord segment, the connecting nerves elongate to maintain the links previously established. As you might expect, the situation is actually somewhat more complex, because there is some overlap in the actual distribution of dermatomes. The treatment here is simplified only to make the point.

The connection between this developmental pattern and referred pain is that the sensory nerves from various body organs enter the cord at points that coincide with those of a given dermatome. Early sensory input from a given dermatome seems to become a reference that higher processing centers rely upon. Since most pain-related input is from the skin, interpretation centers seem to "assume" that all input is from the skin. When an organ is damaged, its pain afferents are interpreted as originating in the skin of the reference dermatome. For example, impulses entering the cord at levels T1 to T4 or T5 from pain receptors stimulated by myocardial ischemia are interpreted as impulses from dermatomes associated with T1–T4. Hence the

referred pain that is characteristic of cardiac ischemia: chest pains on the left side (including the shoulder and axilla), which radiate down the left arm and perhaps from the base of the neck into the jaw. The general, but not invariable, left localization is presumably due to the entry of the majority of the fibers carrying pain information from the heart into the left side of the spinal cord. (Some people with myocardial ischemia will report bilateral pain, and—rarely—a person may report principally right-sided pain. Some typical patterns of pain referral are presented in table 23.2.)

Phantom Pain

In connection with the physiological basis of pain, we should touch on the puzzling pain experience called **phantom pain. Phantoms** are tactile and movement perceptions that

Table 23.2   Typical Surfaces to Which Selected Organs Refer Pain

Organ	Site of Referred Pain
Heart	Usually left shoulder and axilla, with radiation down inside of left arm; also radiation from neck to jaw
Esophagus	Pharynx, lower neck and arm, substernum near heart
Stomach	Epigastric region, usually between umbilicus and xiphoid process
Bile duct/Gall bladder	Midepigastric region, radiating to tip of right scapula
Pancreas	Midback, sometimes low epigastric region
Large bowel	Hypogastric region, lower abdomen, and periumbilical area
Kidney/Ureter	Edge of rectus abdominis muscle below level of umbilicus, radiation to flank and groin
Bladder/Testis	Suprapubic region
Uterus	Low abdomen or low back and side
Appendix	Initially near umbilicus, then shifting to lower right as parietal peritoneum becomes involved

remain after a part of the body has been amputated. There can be a very real sense that the leg, for example, is still there, has bulk and weight, can be moved at will, gets itchy, or, to the great distress of the amputee, is a source of extreme pain. Phantoms can exist for any lost body part (e.g., breasts, hands, legs), but the greater the extent of cortical representation, the more likely it is that there will be a phantom.

Phantoms are more common in adults than children, and are thought to be quite unusual in young children. They may also occur when an area has been denervated, for example in a spinal cord injury that severs all cord pathways at T12. Some people with spinal cord lesions experience such realistic phantoms, capable of "movement" and apparent sensation, that the phenomena can be quite disturbing.

There is great variability in the persistence of phantoms. Some are only briefly apparent after an amputation, some fade or shrink gradually, some persist or reoccur for years. In emergency situations, a long-dormant but realistic phantom may arise with unfortunate consequences. For example, a person may reach out with a nonexistent arm to fend off a flying object.

Sensory reeducation can help a great deal in coping with phantoms connected to nerve damage. Where repeated opportunities for reeducation of the cortex exist, for example in the paraplegic who repeatedly has his legs stimulated with clearly no corresponding sensation, the phantom tends to fade. Such reeducation may not be possible if the limb is missing, and the phantom may then persist, but the proximal portions (which are more poorly represented on the cortex than the distal portions) may fade, with a subsequent shrinking of the phantom.

Pain is not associated with all phantoms but when it does occur it can be a very troubling problem. Many amputees have transient phantom pain, and about 5–10% of

this special population have serious, persistent phantom pain. The circumstances that bring on the phantom pain will vary. For some it comes without warning, or it may be associated with fatigue, pressure sores, or a poorly fitting prosthesis. In other cases, stimulation or irritation of certain consistent trigger points will be the cause.

The approaches that have been used to treat phantom pain present a catalogue of modern pain treatment, ranging from physical and electrical stimulation (including acupuncture), through peripheral and spinal nerve sections and blocks, psychosurgery, psychotropic drugs, and megavitamin therapy, to a host of psychologically based approaches. The results vary from approach to approach, and even more from patient to patient. Individuals experiencing such pain will possibly require extensive and highly specialized referral, assessment, and care.

Cancer Pain

Part of the problem with cancer is that many forms can be well advanced before they produce definitive symptoms, including pain, and some people never experience pain generated by their cancer. The pain, when produced, can be extremely variable, depending on its specific source. Tumor masses impinging on neural structures can cause pain ranging from sharp and stabbing neuralgias (table 23.4) to diffuse paresthesias. Invasion and displacement of functional tissue (bone, muscle, skin) can result in dull aching pain that becomes more severe with tumor progression. Compression of or growth into a tubular structure can cause pain in a variety of ways. Backing up of glandular secretions can cause distention and pain before the organ slows or shuts down its secretion. If the tube is a ureter, pain may be the only sign before the kidney is irreparably damaged. Masses in or near the esophagus can render swallowing painful, and stenosis of the gut can lead to distention and diffuse

Impediments to Accurate and Complete Pain Reporting

Effective communication about pain requires a positive desire and capacity on the patient's part to send accurate information and an equivalent capacity and desire in the health care team to receive it. The following points are worth considering if pain assessment or management is not going well.

The first step is to look more closely at the person who is in pain. Some individuals may be playing the good patient role, not wishing to trouble you, or, at a simpler level, they may simply be misinformed about the sort of pain to expect and what input from them is required. On the other hand, the patient who has learned to cope with the chronic pain associated with arthritis or chronic pelvic inflammatory disease may well have a fear of wearing out the listener. This person is probably at least as common as the person who likes to complain. And some unfortunate people will have lapsed into a learned helplessness, defeated by their pain and without the optimism that an attempt at communication requires.

Other patients may have specific reasons for concealing pain. Perhaps they are anxious to protect their family from the severity of their pain or the progression of disease they think it represents. Perhaps they fear that a report of intense pain will cause postponement of long-awaited surgery, in the same way a systemic infection might. Some people harbor common misconceptions about narcotic analgesics: that they will become addicted; that taking narcotics for pain when it is less severe will build up a tolerance so that the drug will not be effective later when they really need it; that the withdrawal from the narcotic will be worse than the pain. Or they may associate narcotics with addicts and degeneracy. Whatever the underlying concern, by sensitive and supportive questioning you may be able to help the patient to identify it so that you can address it.

A more subtle problem arises when dealing with people of different cultures and social backgrounds, whose behavior may be affected by deeply ingrained differences in the ways they understand, relate to, and express themselves about pain. If people produce pain behaviors that are recognizable and familiar to us, we are more likely to believe the expression as genuine and act to alleviate it. It is important, therefore, to make allowances for social and cultural differences when interpreting pain reports.

---

pain. Arterial occlusion may result in ischemic pain, the nature of which will depend on the structure or organ occluded (if visceral, then referred pain, etc.). Venous or lymphatic blockage can lead to diffuse dull aching. A lung tumor growing into a bronchus can lead to infection in the unventilated region. This can produce dull chest pain or extend to the pleural membranes, producing the sharp pain of pleurisy. Advanced cancer, especially that accompanied by extensive necrosis as tumors outgrow their blood supplies, can produce excruciating pain. Potent central analgesics like morphine, given in appropriate doses and intervals, are necessary to help the patient cope. These efforts may be supplemented with therapeutic blocking of peripheral nerves where appropriate. In some cases even these measures are inadequate.

DESCRIPTION OF PAIN PHENOMENA

Compared with sights or sounds, the perception, expression, and effect of pain sensations are subject to great variability both between individuals and within a given person. But this complexity shouldn't be allowed to interfere with effective clinical observation. Pain associated with disease processes or trauma can provide important clues to suggest or confirm diagnoses. And here, every detail can be meaningful: What is it like? Does it change or move? Is the pain clearly localized? To what events or circumstances is it related? What makes it better or worse? All of this data has to be evaluated in the context of the medical, personal, and social history within which it occurs. When evaluating what the patient says, it is helpful to bear in mind that "real pain" can't be distinguished from "imaginary pain," since the only true pain to the patient is what is felt.

The Patient's Description of Pain

The patient's verbal description of pain can present problems, either because the pain itself is difficult to describe (diffuse, wandering, etc.) or because of imprecision or variation in the patient's use of words. Some commonly used words that seem to denote clearly different subjective pain qualities are presented in table 23.3. The clusters of adjectives denote particular qualities of pain perception (e.g., intensity, timing, or location, etc.) and, where appropriate, the specific words have been scaled. With regard to one quality, changes in the intensity may be quite clear to the patient, especially when they are rapid, but this aspect of pain perception is greatly affected by fatigue, stress, lack of effective support, or inadequate management. The sensation of pain may be constant, while the perception of its intensity increases as the person becomes worn out.

In clinical settings where pain diagnosis and management is a central task, protocols incorporating such verbal and other pain assessment scales and questions are often used to standardize the documentation of the patient's pain experience. These ensure consistency and thoroughness and,

Table 23.3   Adjectives Used to Describe Pain. The Clusters Suggest Differing Intensities of a Variety of Independent Qualities of Pain

Onset or Specific Nature of Pain?

1) numb	2a) penetrating	2b) tearing
dull	boring	rasping
tingling	piercing	gnawing
pricking	stabbing	lacerating
sharp	(referred to as	
cutting	"lancinating")	

Intensity?

"The pain is"	"The painful area is"
mild	tender
bothersome	sore
discomforting	hurting
moderate	smarting
intense	aching
horrible	splitting
excruciating	blinding
unbearable	

Time Component?

1) constant	3) steady
periodic	flickering
intermittent	pulsing
	throbbing
2) brief	pounding
enduring	

Spatial Quality?

1a) generalized	1b) deep	2) fixed
diffuse	superficial	spreading
focal		radiating
		jumping
		shooting

Tension or Pressure?

1) tugging	3) tight
pulling	pinching
taut	pressing
	heavy
2) cramping	squeezing
wrenching	crushing
	suffocating

Temperature?

1) hot	2) cool
burning	cold
scalding	freezing
searing	
(referred to as	
"causalgia")	

Emotional/Visceral Aspects?

1) haunting	3) sickening
fearful	nauseating
frightful	
terrifying	4) miserable
	punishing
2) distressing	wretched
agonizing	cruel
killing	vicious

Impact of Pain?

annoying
troublesome
nagging
tiring
grueling
exhausting
debilitating

Source: Adapted and modified from R. Melzack, *The McGill Pain Questionnaire,* McGill University, Montreal, 1975.

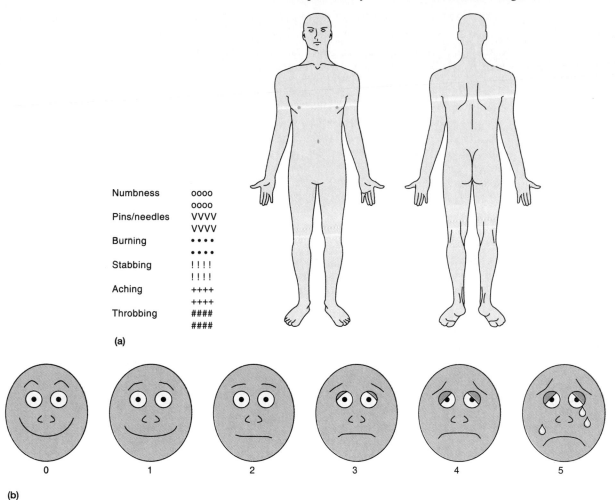

Numbness   oooo
                oooo
Pins/needles   VVVV
                VVVV
Burning   • • • •
                • • • •
Stabbing   ! ! ! !
                ! ! ! !
Aching   ++++
                ++++
Throbbing   ####
                ####

(a)

(b)

Figure 23.9   Examples of graphic representations useful in helping a patient describe their pain. (*a*) A system for adults, which localizes and indicates intensity. (*b*) A method designed for children.

with the inclusion of pain pictures like the one in figure 23.9*a*, give the patient an easier vehicle for self-expression than simple self-report. With children the use of a pain intensity rating scale like the faces in figure 23.9*b* ensures a consistency and accuracy well beyond that from verbal reports.

Clinical Terminology

The need for precision in describing the varieties of pain experience has given rise to an elaborate terminology (table 23.4). For a phenomenon as complex as pain, a variety of medical terms have evolved. We can relate to many of these terms because we have experienced the acute pain with which they are associated.

The term **somatic pain** describes a potentially tissue-damaging stimulus that leads to the activation of nociceptors, the transmission of this information to the brain, and its interpretation there. This transmission and interpretation

can be straightforward, as it is with stepping on a tack, or more complex, as with the referred pain of myocardial infarction. In every such case, there is a significant stimulus (e.g., myocardial ischemia) and a fairly predictable response (e.g., perception of pain in the left axilla and superficial chest, etc.). In chronic pain, the satisfactory explanations for an individual's pain experience are most often made in terms of a complex interaction between altered neural input and/or processing and social/psychological and behavioral factors. The special case of pain that is due to altered neural input or processing, is sometimes called **neuropathic pain** (i.e., pain associated with neuropathy). Table 23.5 contrasts the characteristics of somatic and neuropathic pain.

Although acute pain and somatic pain are often associated (as are chronic pain and neuropathic pain), we must be clear that the terms are not synonyms. Acute and chronic strictly denote patterns of onset and duration, while somatic and neuropathic propose different physiological mechanisms for the production of pain.

Table 23.4   Definitions for Medical Terms Applying to Selected Peripheral and Central Neuropathics and Altered Perception of Sensation Sometimes Associated

Symptoms	Definitions
Paresthesias	General term referring to any of a variety of spontaneous abnormal sensations and sensitivities including (but not restricted to) burning, numbness, pricking, tingling, increased sensitivity to somatic sensation.
Dysesthesia	Ongoing background aching or burning sensation in the absence of apparent stimulus.
Hyperpathia	General term applied to increased and sometimes abnormal sensitivity to stimuli (includes hyperesthesia, hyperalgesia, and allodynia).
Hyperesthesia	Extreme sensitivity to touch.
Hyperalgesia	Exaggerated sensitivity to painful stimuli.
Allodynia	Condition in which a variety of stimuli (e.g., light touch, breeze on the skin) are perceived as intensely painful.
Formication	A spontaneous sensation like insects (ants) crawling on the skin.
Causalgia	Continuous burning, searing sensation in which a variety of stimuli can cause pain (allodynia) often initially accompanied by flushing of the skin; most common following peripheral nerve injury. Chronic causalgia is associated with vasoconstriction.
Hemianesthesia	Loss of sensation from one side of the body, usually from a CVA.

Peripheral Nerve Syndromes

Focal peripheral neuropathy	Peripheral nerve damage due to trauma, vascular compromise, compression, etc; will affect sensory and motor function; not necessarily painful.
Neuralgia	Pain in the distribution of a single peripheral nerve; usually combines ongoing aching and burning with intermittent sharp pain.
Trigeminal Neuralgia (Tic douloureux)	A neuralgia in the distribution of the fifth (trigeminal) cranial nerve; principal symptom is intermittent intense, paroxysmal, lancinating pain; triggered by eating, cold air current, talking, or spontaneous.
Root avulsion	Severe trauma to spinal roots at the level of the cord caused by wrenching trauma to a limb; chronic pain common.
Generalized peripheral neuropathy	Damage to peripheral nerves, may be principally sensory or sensorimotor, symmetric or asymmetric, diffuse or focal; classically a diffuse peripheral neuropathy is symmetric and distal with a "glove-and-stocking" anesthesia (i.e., loss of sensitivity to pain first in the feet then the hands) accompanied by a variety of paresthesias.
Postherpetic pain	Following or during active herpes zoster infection; sudden lancinating pain, perhaps background of causalgia; can be elicited by light touch, cold, sometimes spontaneous.
Myofascial pain	Following injury or disease in a joint and/or associated muscles some patients develop "fibromyositis" with pain elicited by muscle contraction. This myofascial pain may be a factor in lower back and neck pain, and temporomandibular joint disorders.

Syndromes Attributable to Central Lesions

Multiple sclerosis	Often associated with a variety of paresthesias.
Tabetic pain	Associated with lesions to posterior roots and dorsal columns caused by syphilis (tabes dorsalis); skin and joint sensation impaired, paresthesias and dysesthesias.
Acute spinal cord trauma	A variety of paresthesias and dysesthesias as well as autonomic dysfunctions occur.
Thalamic pain syndrome	Damage to the thalamic nucleus involved in the referral of discriminative sensation (ventroposteriolateral nucleus) causes intense, paroxysmal pain, often causalgia, in the limbs opposite the lesion.

Table 23.5	Comparison of the Principal Differences between Somatic Pain (Arising from Tissue Damage) and Neuropathic Pain (Arising as a Result of Faulty Neural Input and/or Processing)

Somatic Pain

1. Pain stimulus usually identified easily.
2. Surface pain well localized; if visceral, felt in predictable referral areas.
3. Pain characteristics match previous pain experience.
4. Analgesics usually effective.

Neuropathic Pain

1. Pain stimulus difficult to identify.
2. Pain often difficult to localize, felt in unusual referral sites.
3. Pain qualities unusual in patient's experience.
4. Poor response to analgesics.

PHARMACOLOGICAL MANAGEMENT OF PAIN

Pharmaceutical agents that limit pain, **analgesics,** are the mainstay of pain management in most medical and nonmedical settings. Broadly speaking, analgesics act peripherally, attenuating or blocking the generation of pain signals in the tissues, or they act centrally, raising thresholds for pain transmission at a variety of sites in the central nervous system.

Peripheral versus Central Analgesics

Peripheral analgesics act by blocking the production of prostaglandins, particularly prostaglandin E_2 (PGE_2). PGE_2 appears to mediate nociception by sensitizing pain receptors to the stimulating effect of bradykinin. Blocking PGE_2 formation therefore leads to reduced peripheral pain stimulation for a given level of pain-producing bradykinin. You may recall from chapter 2 that both PGE_2 and bradykinin are produced in an inflammatory response. Along with other substances, they are responsible for the delayed but prolonged vasodilation and increased vascular permeability that promote the delivery of cells and plasma products to the site of injury. Bradykinin is generated from a plasma precursor. Prostaglandins, on the other hand, are generated from cell-membrane-derived arachidonic acid. Cyclooxygenase, the enzyme responsible for prostaglandin production from arachidonic acid, is inactivated by aspirin, acetaminophen, and nonsteroidal anti-inflammatory drugs. These drugs will produce analgesia (by raising the threshold for bradykinin stimulation of nociceptors) at levels lower than those required to reduce the inflammation (fig. 23.10).

Central analgesics, by contrast, are narcotic drugs. As noted earlier, narcotics bind to a variety of receptors in the cord, brain stem, and cerebrum that are the normal receptors for certain endogenously produced morphinelike neurotransmitters, including the endorphins. These receptors are thought to be involved in mediating pain and some aspects of pleasure or reward. A variety of natural and synthetic narcotics are used, alone or in combination with substances intended to focus their action more effectively, to impede or block pain signals once they have entered the central nervous system.

Nonnarcotic Analgesics

Although usage does vary, it is typical to refer to aspirin, acetaminophen, and nonsteroidal anti-inflammatory drugs (NSAIDs)—in other words, to the peripheral analgesics—as nonnarcotic analgesics. Aspirin (acetylsalicylic acid—ASA) is one of a group of salicylates that are potent peripheral analgesics. Unfortunately, it tends to irritate the gastric mucosa more than other salicylates (enteric-coated preparations avoid some of this); it can also depress platelet numbers and function, and is associated with Reye's syndrome in children. Acetaminophen doesn't have these risks, but on the other hand, it is not a very effective anti-inflammatory agent.

Nonsteroidal anti-inflammatory drugs (NSAIDs) are generally equal or superior to ASA in analgesia. They act by interfering with prostaglandin production in the same

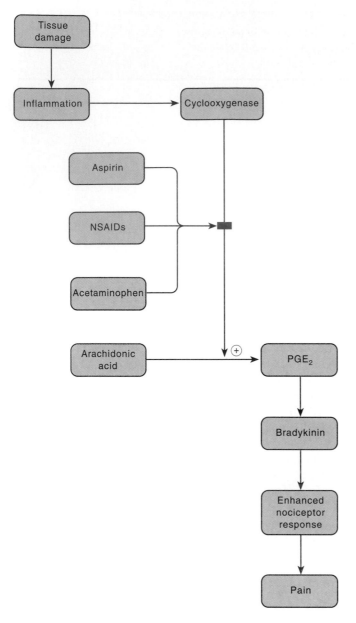

Figure 23.10   Mechanism underlying the analgesics that act peripherally to limit nociception. The three most commonly used analgesics block the formation of PGE$_2$ (■) to limit nociceptor responses and reduce pain.

Table 23.6	Selected Analgesic Agents Commonly Encountered in Clinical Settings

Nonnarcotic Analgesics

Acetylsalicylic acid (ASA, aspirin)
Magnesium trisalicylate
Acetaminophen
Nonsteroidal anti-inflammatory drugs (NSAIDs):
    Ibuprofen
    Naproxen
    Indomethacin

Narcotic Analgesics

Mild to moderate pain:
    Codeine
    Oxycodone
    Propoxyphene
Moderate to severe pain:
    Meperidine
    Pentazocine
    Morphine
    Hydromorphone
    Methadone
    Levorphanol
    Nalbuphine

peripheral component. Incidentally, as far as we know, headaches are generated in tissue external to the brain's neural tissue, i.e., vessels, the dura, muscles, etc. In this sense headache is "peripheral" and therefore often responds to nonnarcotic analgesics. A more detailed discussion of headache appears at the end of this chapter.

Narcotic Analgesics

By binding to the central nervous system endorphin receptors, narcotics activate the descending analgesia pathways, which work at the level of nociceptor input to second-order neurons in the pain pathways. There are different endorphin receptors distributed throughout the CNS. Each narcotic (see list in table 23.6) will have a different pattern of affinities with these receptors and thereby a different set of actions mediated by the receptors.

There is no significant foundation to the fear of developing addiction from the use of narcotic analgesics. Appropriate dose levels, to meet the need for analgesia, can be closely monitored and any dependence that does emerge can be readily dealt with by gradual withdrawal. Prolonged administration of narcotics does, however, lead to **tolerance,** the decreased effect of a given dose over time. When it occurs, as in cancer patients, it can be overcome by adjusting dosage and frequency of administration while monitoring for any CNS effects, such as respiratory depression.

way as ASA. Their antiplatelet effect is rapidly reversible, unlike that of ASA, and some are less irritating to the gastric mucosa. They are used with low back pain, migraine, postoperative pain, cancer pain, and dysmenorrhea.

Table 23.6 lists some common nonnarcotic analgesics. There is a limitation to the analgesia provided by these drugs, so they are best used to control mild to moderate pain. Also, unlike narcotics, many are effective antipyretics (i.e., they can control fever). They do not cause sedation, nor do they lead to tolerance or dependence. For these reasons, it is usually recommended that maximum use be made of nonnarcotic analgesics for any pain that has a

Although widely used, the synthetic narcotic meperidine (Demerol) has significant hazards. Normeperidine is produced as a metabolite of the breakdown of meperidine. It is much more slowly cleared from the tissues than meperidine and therefore accumulates in the plasma. It can produce tremors, anxiety, myoclonus (exaggerated tendon reflexes), and generalized seizures, particularly in patients with compromised kidney function, who can't excrete it. Codeine and oxycodone are morphinelike substances suitable for treating moderate pain. They are often used effectively in combination with nonnarcotic analgesics.

Potentiators

Potentiators are medications administered with an analgesic, to enhance the effect of a given dose. The theory is that, in this way, greater analgesia can be achieved without increasing side effects or risk of toxicity. In fact, these drugs may act in different ways. Some are actually additive drugs, i.e., medications that have an analgesic effect on their own that is added to that of the primary analgesic. Hydroxyzine (Atarax, Vistaril), an antihistamine, is probably an example. Other drugs, e.g., cimetidine (Tagamet), appear to potentiate by interfering with the normal metabolic breakdown of analgesics in the liver. The result is slower clearance and higher plasma drug levels. The same effect can be achieved with more control by simply increasing the dose of analgesic or its frequency of administration, or both.

Other potentiators, e.g., phenothiazines, have varied effects on pain. The phenothiazine chlorpromazine (Thorazine), a drug whose primary use is as an antipsychotic, has some analgesic effect. However, the most popular phenothiazine (Phenergan), an antihistamine, is ineffective or even an antianalgesic. There probably are no dependable pure potentiators for narcotics, with the possible exception of aspirin and acetaminophen, which appear to potentiate codeine. On the other hand, adding 100–200 mg of caffeine (a strong cup of coffee contains about 150 mg) to either acetaminophen or ASA (650 mg) will significantly improve analgesia.

Anticonvulsants and Tricyclic Antidepressants

Neuropathic pain presents real challenges to pharmacological management because it seldom responds to either narcotic or nonnarcotic analgesics. The sharp, stabbing pain of trigeminal neuralgia and some other focal neuralgias is often controlled by anticonvulsants (carbamazepine, phenytoin, or clonazepam), while tricyclic antidepressants can be effective in controlling the pain arising in postherpetic neuralgia and peripheral nerve injury. Recall that one of the descending pain limitation systems causes the release of

leucine enkephalin in the dorsal horn of the cord. Some tricyclic antidepressants enhance this effect. Whatever their route of action, these substances appear to be analgesic, whether or not the person is depressed.

HEADACHE

Headache is a relatively common form of pain experience. Although it may be temporarily completely disabling, the vast majority of headaches are benign, nonprogressive disorders. Headaches associated with excess alcohol use, smoking, stress, or fatigue are best treated by taking two aspirin and, rather than calling the physician in the morning, avoiding the cause in the future. Headache is the unfortunate accompaniment of a variety of medical disorders: fever of any cause, food poisoning, carbon monoxide poisoning, diseases producing hypercapnia (e.g., chronic lung disease), hypothyroidism, and others. In some syndromes, headache is the central complaint. These are various forms of migraine, cluster headaches, and tension headaches. Finally, in some cases headache is symptomatic of some serious underlying pathology.

Pain-Sensitive Structures

A knowledge of the structures of the head that are capable of generating pain is helpful in understanding the pathophysiology of headache. The bone of the skull and much of the dura, arachnoid, and pia are insensitive, as is all the brain itself. By contrast, the venous sinuses and tributary veins, the dura at the base of the brain, and the arteries within the meninges and the subarachnoid space are highly sensitive to any stimulation that can produce the sensation of pain. Similarly, certain nerves (e.g., trigeminal, vagus, upper cervical) generate pain when inflamed, compressed, or under tension. Superficial tissues are also capable of generating pain that is experienced as headache: skin, connective tissues, muscles, arteries, and periosteum of the skull. Other sensitive structures are the eye, the ear, and the nasal and sinus cavities.

Headaches can thus be produced by mechanical stimulation (traction, dilatation, distention) of intracranial or extracranial arteries, large intracranial veins, venous sinuses or associated dura, the nasal cavity, and the paranasal sinuses. Inflammation or irritation of the meninges and raised intracranial pressure, as well as spasm, injury, or inflammation of extracranial muscles, can also result in headache. For an intracranial mass to generate pain, it usually has to stretch or displace vessels, nerves, or dura at the base of the brain. This can occur well in advance of any change in intracranial pressure (that is, while the tumor may still be quite small).

Symptomatic Headaches

Brain tumor produces headaches in about two-thirds of all patients. Sometimes the pain is triggered by activity or postural changes (e.g., stooping), but there may be no provoking factor. Typically, headaches due to tumors are deep seated, variably throbbing, perhaps "aching" or "bursting," and occur with increasing frequency and severity. They may last minutes to an hour or more and occur once to many times per day, in some cases accompanied by forceful (projectile) vomiting. Rest will sometimes diminish the pain.

Headaches that are precipitated by cough or exertion are usually benign, although they raise the question of some intracranial mass (e.g., a tumor, an arteriovenous malformation—AVM) or developmental abnormality. The mechanism is presumably the increase in intrathoracic pressure during cough or exertion, which both raises the intrathoracic blood pressure and impedes venous drainage.

With arteriovenous malformation or aneurysm, there is little correlation between the size and the progression of the pathology and the nature of the symptomatic headache. Hemorrhage of an AVM or aneurysm, however, produces a highly symptomatic headache: rapidly developing, extremely severe, lasting many days, and localizing in the occiput and neck. Blood turbulence detected by auscultation and blood in the CSF are diagnostic. Those that survive the hemorrhage are candidates for surgical correction of the defective vasculature before a more serious rebleed occurs.

Headache that follows trauma, for example concussion or whiplash injury, is varied. It can be severe and chronic, with either continuous or intermittent pain. There is often also giddiness, vertigo, or tinnitus (ringing or whistling in the ears), and sometimes there is **posttraumatic nervous instability,** a condition of agitated restlessness and hypersensitivity not directly associated with headache. Headache immediately following trauma may signal the development of a subdural hematoma. In such cases, the headache is supplanted by drowsiness, confusion, stupor, and then coma.

Headache that is due to inflammation and blockage of the paranasal sinuses can result from the pressure of accumulated fluid; alternatively, as fluid is reabsorbed, the exit may remain blocked from tension on the mucous membranes, a condition leading to the so-called vacuum sinus headache. Headache of ocular origin (perhaps due to eyestrain) tends to be steady and aching and located in the orbit, forehead, and temple. It often occurs after sustained use of the eyes in close focusing and resolves with appropriate corrective lenses.

The headache of meningeal irritation, whether caused by inflammation from infection or by irritation from the breakdown of blood from a subarachnoid bleed or other cause, has an acute onset and becomes severe and generalized (or bioccipital or bifrontal). As with other meningeal signs, it worsens if the head is bent forward and is often accompanied by a stiff neck. Lumbar puncture produces an immediate headache upon arising from the procedure; in this case the pain is attributable to the loss of fluid and consequent tension placed on dural, venous, and arterial structures at the base of the brain as it sags within the cranial space.

Headache Syndromes and Their Treatment

There are several headache syndromes which, while nonprogressive and for the most part benign, can be cruelly disabling. They require diagnosis and appropriate symptomatic care.

Tension Headaches

This is one of the most common of headache syndromes. It is also one of the most poorly understood, and is often ineffectively treated. The sufferer experiences a bilateral, generalized sense of nonthrobbing pressure, fullness, or tightness that is characteristic. Onset is gradual and the headache can persist in continuous or variable intensity day and night for days, weeks, even years. At one time the pain was thought to develop from muscle tension associated with stress, but careful studies using electromyography have failed to support that theory. In some cases, however, relaxation training using muscle tension biofeedback has apparently been effective in treating these hard-to-manage headaches. Since fatigue, nervous strain, and worry tend to provoke episodes of tension headache, strategies that reduce stress, improve coping, or restrain reactions, as with antidepressant or antianxiety drugs, will tend to reduce their incidence or severity. Nonnarcotic analgesics (e.g., aspirin or acetaminophen) may lessen the intensity of the pain but rarely get rid of it, and sufferers often take 6–8 pills a day with little effect.

Migraine Headaches

These headaches, with throbbing-to-dull pain often accompanied by nausea and vomiting, are frequently localized to one side of the head perhaps behind one eye or ear, and hence the French term *migraine,* derived from the Latin *hemicrania*—half the skull. Perhaps 20–30% of the population have some degree of migraine, with females being three times as susceptible. About 60% of migraine sufferers have a relative in the immediate family that has shared the complaint. Onset is often in childhood and adolescence or young adulthood, and most people experience extensive relief with middle age. Women are more likely to have the migraine begin during the premenstrual part of their cycle. During pregnancy the headaches typically lessen. Although the pathophysiology has yet to be fully defined, all the variants of migraine appear to result from arteriolar constriction and decreased cerebral blood flow. These variants include classic migraine, common migraine, and complicated migraine.

Classic migraine follows a typical course. The person may have premonitory symptoms hours before the attack: a sense of elation or energy or foreboding, cravings, drowsiness, or depression. Visual disturbances like scintillations, light sensitivity, bright zigzag lines or scotomas (blind spots) affecting one or both visual fields and even extending to blindness, or dizziness and tinnitus signal the start of the attack. These symptoms, sometimes called the prodrome, develop slowly, at least over minutes, and may spread or change. As with other symptoms of migraine, the gradual time course of development allows us to distinguish these symptoms of onset from epileptic phenomena. The pain and photophobia that follow the prodome are often so extreme that the person must withdraw to a darkened room to wait it out or sleep it off. The throbbing pain behind one eye or ear becomes a dull generalized ache, and the scalp may be sensitive. The duration is hours to one or two days, and bouts may recur at irregular intervals of weeks or months.

In **common migraine** the headache is not preceded by the visual or other symptoms but otherwise follows the same course. An additional feature may be frequent nausea and occasional vomiting, which give rise to the name sick headache.

Complicated migraine, also sometimes called neurological migraine, is distinguished by the presence of neurological symptoms other than (and perhaps in addition to) the visual symptoms of classic migraine. These may include unilateral numbness and tingling of the lips, face, hand, or leg, which may deepen to weakness or paralysis imitating a stroke. The person also may have difficulty speaking or understanding speech. Such symptoms may occur before or during the aching phase of the headache and may spread slowly over a period of minutes; they usually resolve in minutes or hours.

The condition is termed "complicated" for another reason. Some people experience long-term, even permanent neurological deficits: hemianopsia, hemiplegia or hemianesthesia, or eye movement defects. Furthermore, some people experience the neurological symptoms without headache. Children may have nausea, abdominal pain, and vomiting without headache or may have intense spells of vertigo. Adults may have these symptoms or localized pain, bouts of fever, or mood disturbances. Migraine must be considered when other explanations for these symptoms have been ruled out. Diagnosis is made even more difficult because some older adults, with no earlier history of migraine, will develop migrainous neurological symptoms that resemble those of transient ischemic attacks.

The pathophysiological basis to migraine has not been established. The older theory was that the pain is caused by the vasodilation and vascular distention that follows a prodromal episode of vascular spasm and ischemia, but this theory has been shown to be incorrect. During the evolution of an attack, studies of cerebral blood flow show a slow drop in cerebral perfusion, usually beginning in the occipital region. Throughout the attack there are areas of hypoperfusion, and there is no evidence of localized or generalized dilation or hyperperfusion. Current explanations of migraine center on a defect in the neural regulation of vascular tone that in some way involves serotonin released locally from platelets. Antiserotonin drugs like methysergide are effective in arresting attacks, while drugs that trigger serotonin release, like reserpine, precipitate attacks. Many other neurotransmitters that affect vascular tone are being considered for their contribution to migraine.

Conventional medical control of migraines depends on treating the acute attack at its first sign, using ergot preparations (ergot is derived from a mold affecting rye grain). Once the pain becomes intense, codeine sulfate may control it, but aspirin and acetaminophen are ineffective. The new antiserotonin drug sumatriptan, unlike other migraine medications available by prescription, can often arrest a migraine even after it has started to evolve. While expensive and not universally effective, for some it offers control that was formerly accessible only through the emergency ward.

Cluster Headaches

These headaches are so named because they tend to occur nightly for weeks to a few months (in a cluster). Although the underlying mechanisms may be quite different from those causing migraine, cluster headaches are usually described as a migraine variant. Men are four times as likely as women to have them, in contrast to the pattern with migraines. Two or three hours after falling asleep the person awakens with steady, intense pain in one orbit and flowing tears. The nostril on the same side is plugged and later begins to run. The affected pupil may be constricted, the eyelid drooped, and the cheek flushed and edematous. The attack may last from ten minutes to two hours. The majority of people with cluster headaches show no history of migraine.

Cluster headaches are very difficult to treat effectively. If stress or fatigue is implicated, efforts are made to reduce it. Some people can interrupt an excruciating attack by administering oxygen or using an inhaled ergot preparation. Prophylactic administration of the tricyclic antidepressant amitriptyline is the method of choice, while methysergide, corticosteroids like prednisone, and the antidepressant lithium are used with very resistant cases.

Case Study

A 35-year-old male carpenter suffered an injury at work while lifting a heavy object. He stopped work and saw a physician, who identified muscle spasm and a reduced range of spinal mobility. Based on her diagnosis of low back strain, she prescribed a benzodiazepam drug as a muscle relaxant and a codeine/acetaminophen agent for pain, and recommended rest and a return for evaluation in two weeks. At that time improvement was minimal and a regimen of physiotherapy was implemented, along with continuation of the drug regimen, which the patient requested for his pain. Improvement failed to materialize over the next several weeks, and an orthopedic specialist was called in for an assessment. X-rays and a CT scan indicated some evidence of low lumbar degeneration. The specialist recommended that the man not return to his occupation and that he approach the worker's compensation agency, which provides benefits in cases of work-related disability, for retraining in some less strenuous work.

The carpenter's approach to the compensation agency led to an assessment by an agency physician some 16 weeks after the initial injury. He found the patient to have been continuing with his medications and to have developed a marked degree of hostility and depression. He further found significant disagreement between the patient's complaints of pain and loss of movement and any objective findings. The patient was also quite deconditioned from the lack of normal activity during the past weeks. On some probing interrogation and reference to the agency's files, the physician discovered that the patient had a history of a broken home, work injury claims, and alcohol and drug abuse. Because he couldn't work his wife had been forced to work in a disagreeable, low-paying job, and their family was rapidly becoming dysfunctional.

Rather than defer to the man's demands for further medical consultations and surgery to prevent his becoming a cripple, the doctor prescribed a low-dose antidepressant and withdrawal of the narcotic medication, suspecting it had been enhancing the patient's pain by endorphin depletion. He also arranged for a program of physiotherapy aimed at restoring conditioning and persuaded the man to accept some family counseling. As a result of this regimen, the patient reported loss of half his pain two weeks after withdrawal of the narcotics, and significant overall improvement after six weeks of gradually increased physical activity. Between family counseling and the employer's willingness to accommodate a gradual return to work, he achieved full resumption of work and a greatly improved home situation 25 weeks postinjury.

Commentary

Had this patient had a family physician aware of his history, recovery might have occurred much sooner. The pattern of an insecure upbringing, substance abuse, and depression are indicators of an increased likelihood of developing the pattern of chronic pain and disability behavior seen in this case. The depletion of endorphins and a resulting increase in passive pain should have been recognized earlier as being related to the extended use of narcotics and benzodiazepine agents. Endorphin replenishment following withdrawal of these agents was speeded by the antidepressant agent prescribed. It was also sound practice not to assume too quickly that the patient was motivated solely by a desire for a large insurance compensation award, and to attempt some degree of rehabilitation and renewal of self-esteem. Unfortunately, not all such cases resolve as successfully.

Key Concepts

1. Acute and chronic pain differ in their neurological processing, impact, and treatment (pp. 610–611).

2. Pain stimuli can produce physiological and psychic arousal, a variety of orienting responses, precise localization (via the neospinothalamic pathway), or chronic pain responses (via the paleospinothalamic pathway) (pp. 612–613).

3. Narcotics produce their analgesic effects by binding to endorphin receptors in the brain stem, thereby stimulating fibers that release a neurotransmitter that inhibits pain signals as they enter the cord. TENS and stimulus-produced analgesia probably induce the same neurotransmitter release (pp. 614–615).

4. Referred pain is of great clinical diagnostic utility (pp. 615–617).

5. Phantom pain illustrates the role of central processing in pain perception and is a significant clinical problem (pp. 617–618).

6. The pain that may accompany cancer is highly variable in both nature and pathological basis (pp. 618–619).

7. The complexity and variability of the experience and causation of pain have given rise to a precise and detailed vocabulary (pp. 619–622).

8. Peripheral analgesics inhibit the production of prostaglandins, thereby raising the pain threshold (p. 623).

9. Narcotics act centrally and, depending on their binding characteristics, can produce respiratory depression, euphoria, and other effects (pp. 623–625).

10. A minority of headaches are symptomatic of serious underlying pathology, and in some conditions the pattern and localization of pain is quite characteristic (pp. 625–626).

11. A variety of headache syndromes, while nonprogressive and not life-threatening, can produce significant disability (pp. 626–627).

REVIEW ACTIVITIES

1. Recall your last significant experience with pain. Go through each cluster in table 23.3 and choose the appropriate terms to describe your experience.

2. Make a copy of table 23.4. Cut up the paper in such a way as to separate all the symptoms from their definitions, and keep them in one pile. Do the same with the peripheral and central syndromes, only mix them up. Now attempt to unite symptoms and definitions, separate peripheral from central syndromes, and unite each syndrome with its definition.

3. The point was made that acute pain is processed preponderantly by the neospinothalamic pathway, while chronic pain is processed via the paleospinothalamic pathway. In table form, list the features common to both pathways. Then list the ways in which they differ.

4. Find a few people who experience migraine or tension or cluster headaches (if you're unfortunate, one of them may be you!). Question them about their pain experience and try to classify their headaches.

Chapter Twenty-Four

Trauma

For he breaketh me with a tempest, and multiplieth
my wounds without cause.

The Book of Job

Chapter 1 defined trauma as physical injury and considered the mechanisms and tissue effects by which various physical agents (heat, radiation, mechanical force, etc.) produce injury. There, emphasis was on the production of cellular change that could lead to disease. In this chapter, emphasis is on mechanical trauma and burn trauma, and the damage they produce at the organ and somatic levels of organization. These types of trauma are the most common type encountered in emergency services.

OVERVIEW OF TRAUMATIC INJURY

Automobile accidents, fires, falls, explosions, criminal assaults, and athletics are frequent sources of often severe physical injury. They typically involve an interruption of a tissue or an organ's surface to produce a **wound.** We begin the chapter by describing the essentials of wound production and the various wound types.

FACTORS AFFECTING WOUND PRODUCTION

Wound production is most often the result of the transfer of **kinetic energy,** energy of motion, from one object to another. Four factors contribute to wound production by mechanical trauma: the amount of energy involved, the duration of the impact that causes energy transfer to body tissues, the surface area over which the transfer occurs, and the physical characteristics of the tissue that receives the energy.

Amount of Energy

The kinetic energy of a moving object is expressed by the equation

$$E = \frac{1}{2}\frac{MV^2}{g}$$

where E = energy, M = mass (or, for our purpose, weight), V = velocity, and g = force of gravity. Since the force of gravity is essentially constant, the variables that determine the kinetic energy are mass and velocity. For the case of simple forward motion, figure 24.1 illustrates the impact between the human body and an object. From the kinetic energy equation you can see that a heavier moving object possesses more kinetic energy, i.e., doubling the weight produces twice the energy. Note, however, that because the velocity's value is squared, a doubling of velocity produces four times the energy. Applying this principle to baseball, you can see that a batter develops more energy by increasing the bat's speed than he does by using a heavier bat.

Duration of Impact

This is the time over which energy is transferred to body structures. For a given amount of energy, if the duration of energy input is longer, there is more time for an organ to

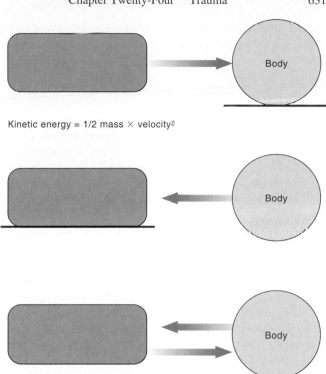

Kinetic energy = 1/2 mass × velocity²

Figure 24.1   Mechanical injury. Damage results when the body strikes or is struck by another mass. Either or both may be in motion prior to impact.

absorb it without damage. If the duration is short, there is more chance of overwhelming the organ's energy absorption capabilities. In other words, it is the rate of change rather than the amount of change that is significant in wound production. For example, if the total mechanical energy in the sound waves produced by a typical rock band in five minutes were delivered at the ear in half a second, the eardrum would rupture. Listening over the duration of five minutes, on the other hand, might produce only the awareness of uncomfortable loudness. (Note that chronic exposure to such sound intensity can cause permanent damage to internal ear structures.)

Surface Area

The third factor that has a bearing on wound production is the body surface area over which the force is applied. Generally, the greater the surface area, the less serious is the mechanical injury. When a force is spread over a large surface area, any single tissue will bear a smaller portion of the total. If the same force is applied over a small surface area, each of the smaller number of organs involved will be forced to absorb much more energy, with greater risk of its being overwhelmed. Generally, a blow of given force is more damaging when delivered with a pointed object than with a blunt object, because of the much smaller surface area across which the energy is transferred. It is on this principle that a football or other helmet offers protection. It offers a large surface area over which impact can be dissipated.

Tissue Characteristics

The resilience of an organ is its ability to absorb energy and recover with minimal effect. This property allows a tissue to resist mechanical trauma. When a force is applied, a less resilient organ is less able to dissipate it without damage. For example, when equal forces are applied to their surfaces, the less resilient liver is more likely to be damaged than the more flexible and elastic pancreas. Similarly, a tightly contracted muscle is less resilient than a relaxed one. This may explain why, in auto accidents and falls, those who are asleep, unconscious, or in an alcoholic stupor seem to receive less traumatic injury than those who are conscious and bracing to resist injury. Of course, if muscles were contracted to produce resistance to acceleration or deceleration in the precise direction required, injury would be reduced. Unfortunately, in situations involving mechanical injury, it is usually impossible to predict timing or the exact angle at which impact forces will be applied, so that appropriate contractions are seldom brought into play.

WOUND CLASSIFICATION

The following sections describe the various wound types caused by mechanical forces.

Abrasion

One type of wound is produced by friction, usually applied at a low angle or parallel to the body's surface. As an object scrapes over the surface of the skin, the epidermis is forcibly removed. The resulting wound is called an **abrasion** (fig. 24.2). Deeper layers of the skin may also be involved. In extreme cases, subcutaneous tissues might be abraded.

Abrasion wounds occur frequently and are usually minor. In fact, it would be unusual for a normally active schoolchild to go through a week's play without receiving several minor skin abrasions. More severe abrasion is typical in automobile accidents in which an occupant is thrown from the vehicle or when a pedestrian or a cyclist is struck by a car. The result is rapid body motion along pavement, gravel, or similarly rough surfaces. Deep and extensive abrasion in such cases is common.

Contusion

A **contusion** is a bruise. It is a wound in which damage to small blood vessels allows blood loss into the tissue spaces. Usually, a contusion is the result of a blow delivered over a large surface area, at the skin or an organ's surface. Falls and other whole-body collisions usually produce much contusion, because forces are distributed over an extensive

Figure 24.2 Abrasion. *Top:* Normal skin. *Bottom:* Abraded skin. The epidermis is lost, but residual accessory structures can provide islands of cells from which regeneration can proceed.

Figure 24.3 Contusion. *Top:* Skin is normal. *Bottom:* The epidermis is unbroken, but there is damage and hemorrhage beneath the surface.

surface. **1** Although tissue and vessel damage occurs, the surface remains unbroken (fig. 24.3). Blood loss from the vascular system is usually minimal because blood hydrostatic pressure (BHP) in small vessels is low. As blood leaks into the tissue spaces, tissue hydrostatic pressure soon rises to exceed BHP and stop further escape of blood. When vessel damage is more severe, focal pooling of blood within a tissue produces a **hematoma**. **2**

The characteristic discoloration of a skin contusion is caused by various pigmented substances that are derived from hemoglobin. At the skin's surface, blood in the tissue spaces first appears as a dark red-blue. Later, purple, brown, and yellow-green colors emerge as phagocytes continue the sequence of hemoglobin breakdown. When contusions occur at greater subcutaneous depth, longer periods may pass before blood is visible at the skin's surface. In some

1 38259   **2** 41235

cases, there is no surface discoloration, and only inflammatory swelling and pain give evidence of injury.

Contusion of internal organs may occur secondary to body surface trauma. The heart, for example, may suffer bruising following thoracic wall trauma, because the ventricles are immediately deep to the sternum. Contusion is even more severe if the force is applied during systole, when the contracted tissue is in a less resilient state. The brain's surface may also suffer contusion. An abrupt blow to the skull can produce a force that is transmitted through the bone to reach the brain. If the skull remains intact, it dissipates the force over a greater surface, producing contusion. **3** Because the brain is confined by the rigid walls of the skull, a blow to one part of it can produce a contusion in another part. A single blow may produce contusion at the brain's surface below the point of impact, but since the brain can move slightly within the skull, the force of the blow may also cause it to be abruptly forced against the skull at a point opposite. The result is a second contusion at the brain's surface, called a **contrecoup** injury, from the French word meaning counterblow (fig. 24.4).

Laceration

The wound that results from a tearing or splitting of the skin or an organ's surface is called a **laceration.** It should be distinguished from a cut, or **incision,** in which a sharp edge slices through the surface. A laceration is a surface split that results from forces that stretch the skin or an organ's surface until it tears apart. **4** Lacerations may have different configurations. They may be straight, curved, or star-shaped (**stellate**), **5** depending on the organ's physical characteristics and the direction in which force is applied. A laceration's edge may be regular or ragged. If especially deep, or when a hollow organ's wall tears completely through, the laceration is called a **rupture.**

Surface lacerations can be produced in several ways. A strong blow with a blunt instrument can cause a laceration of the skin. An irregular stellate tear, surrounded by an area of extensive contusion, is often produced by crushing injuries where high pressures are applied over larger body surfaces. The abrupt application of force involved in high-speed automobile collisions will often produce lacerations of internal organs. At impact, the vehicle's speed is immediately reduced while the occupants continue to move until they strike some obstacle such as the dashboard, roof, or floor. The rapid deceleration subjects internal organs to forces that can cause their laceration and rupture. The lung and liver can be damaged in this way. In the case of hollow organs, rapidly building forces are more likely to produce rupture when the organ is filled. This effect is seen most frequently following large meals, when the stomach is quite full, and in accidents that involve forces applied to a full

Figure 24.4   Contrecoup injury. Since the brain can move relative to the skull, trauma at one site may be accompanied by contusion at an opposite surface.

urinary bladder. An improperly worn lap seat belt, stretching across the abdomen instead of the bones of the hip, can produce a sharp pressure pulse in the abdominal cavity in head-on collisions. Laceration of the mesentery and intestinal rupture may be the result.

Explosions often produce extensive lacerations of internal organs. As a blast abruptly applies forces that are then just as abruptly released, it produces compression of organs, followed by their immediate decompression. The result is surface tearing and often rupture (fig. 24.5).

Penetrating Wounds

A **penetrating wound** does most of its damage below the surface. It is usually caused by a sharp, elongated object and is typically deep and narrow (fig. 24.6). Bleeding is often more serious in penetrating wounds, although damage to deep vessels may mean that the blood lost may not be visible at the surface. **6** Knife stab wounds are good

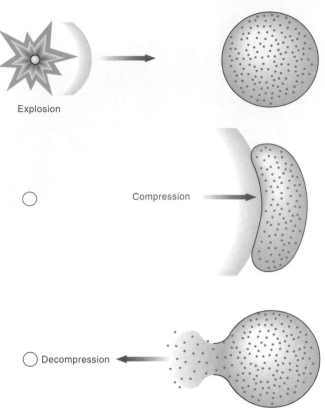

Figure 24.5   Laceration and rupture may result when an explosion produces an abrupt compression followed by an equally abrupt decompression.

Figure 24.6   Penetrating wounds. A sharp object, such as a knife, produces damage that is limited to its path through a tissue.

Figure 24.7   Bullet wound. This penetrating wound involves damage at some distance from the bullet's path because of the rotation of the bullet.

examples in that at the skin's surface they often appear less serious than they are later proven to be. If sufficiently long, the penetrating object may reach various vital organs, causing severe hemorrhage when major vessels or the heart are entered, or extensive peritonitis should gastric or bowel contents escape via a penetrating wound of the abdomen.

A gunshot wound is a special case of a penetrating injury (fig. 24.7). Damage from a bullet is produced by the large forces that derive from its high velocity. **7** (Recall the significance of the velocity in the kinetic energy equation.) For two penetrating wounds of equal depth, one produced by a knife and the other by a bullet, the bullet wound will produce more tissue destruction and more bleeding. In such cases, damage is produced not only by the bullet's tearing through organs, but also because it rapidly rotates around its long axis while in flight. This rotation releases energy into tissues at a right angle to its path, producing blood vessel rupture and other mechanical trauma, even though there is no direct contact with the bullet **8** (fig. 24.8a).

A bullet's passage through the body can also produce secondary effects. For example, in striking bone, the bullet may chip fragments from its surface. These are capable of producing lacerations in structures at an appreciable distance from the bullet's track. Bone fragments driven up near to the skin from deeper sites within can also produce

contusions at a surface that shows no other sign of injury (fig. 24.8b). Similarly, in striking the body, the bullet itself may fragment to disperse its destructive effects (fig. 24.8c).

Bone Fracture

When forces that overwhelm its substantial strength are applied to a bone, it breaks. Bone fractures take various forms (fig. 24.9). Some are **incomplete fractures,** in which the break does not produce complete separation of the two ends of the bone. For example, the break might appear only as a crack along a bone's surface (**fissure fracture**), or a

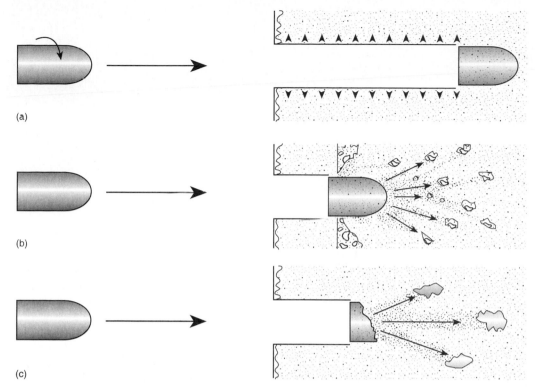

Figure 24.8   Factors in bullet wound damage. (*a*) Spinning of the bullet generates damaging forces at right angles to the bullet path. (*b*) Bone fragments act as secondary projectiles when shattered by the bullet. (*c*) The bullet itself has fragmented. Such fragments may lacerate or compress tissues, vessels, or nerves. They may also enter vessels to be transported as emboli.

bone might be punctured, by a bullet or other penetrating object, for example (**puncture fracture**). A third type of incomplete fracture is the **greenstick fracture,** which results from bending forces applied to a bone with breakage occurring at the convex surface of the bend. **9**

Simple fractures are breaks that form two quite separate bone fragments. **10** If three or more pieces are produced, the fracture is described as **comminuted. 11** In extreme cases, such as a bullet striking a bone, comminuted fractures may involve large numbers of separate small bone fragments. When a fracture causes a bone edge to pierce the skin's surface it is called a **compound fracture.** In a **depressed fracture** of the skull, a blunt instrument causes a portion of the skull to break and fall away from the intact portion **12** (fig. 24.10). If a disease process, such as neoplasia, **13** weakens a bone so that normal stresses cause breakage, the fracture is said to be a **pathological fracture.**

Fractures are common examples of trauma. They are frequently the result of falls, athletic injuries, and automobile accidents. Pedestrians struck by automobiles often first suffer lower leg fractures from the impact of the car's bumper. Other fractures may subsequently occur as they strike the pavement, often from some height. Skull fractures are common in such cases. **14** Occupants of a vehicle involved in a head-on collision frequently experience knee, hip, and shoulder fractures. The knees are often driven forward to strike rigid dashboard structures. Joint fractures occur as the arms and legs are braced in anticipation of impact. When collision follows, large forces are transmitted up the limb to cause fractures at the joint. **15**

Following bone fracture, the potential for damage to adjacent soft tissues is high. Ragged bone edges and small fragments can move against nearby vessels or other organs to disrupt their surfaces. Rib, hip, and skull fractures are all associated with secondary damage to the more vulnerable soft tissues they protect.

Because cartilage also has a certain rigidity, it is also subject to fracture. The cartilage of the tip of the nose is often broken. The cartilage segments of the larynx and trachea may also fracture in cases of neck or thoracic trauma. Such an injury is serious if collapsed airways block air flow to the lungs.

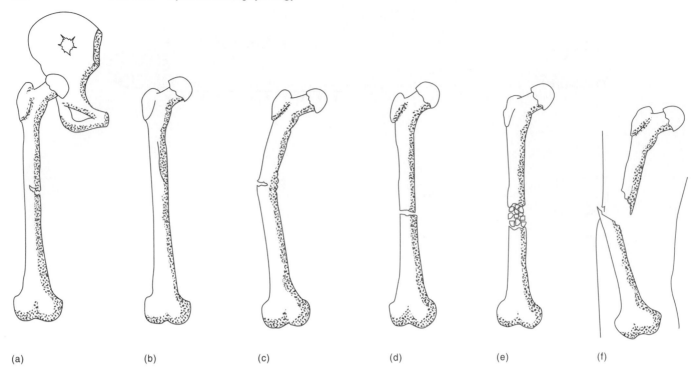

(a)   (b)   (c)   (d)   (e)   (f)

Figure 24.9 Bone fracture types. (*a*) Puncture fracture of pelvis and incomplete femoral fracture. (*b*) Fissure fracture. (*c*) Greenstick fracture. (*d*) Simple fracture. (*e*) Comminuted fracture. (*f*) Compound fracture; the sharp edge of an oblique fracture has penetrated the skin overlying the fracture site.

SYSTEMIC RESPONSES TO TRAUMA

Severe trauma of any kind produces not only local damage, but also an integrated series of systemic coping responses. These promote blood pressure maintenance and the metabolic responses that make adequate fuel and repair molecules available for distribution to traumatized tissues and the body generally.

The threat of circulatory shock is often present when trauma is severe. Its key elements, and the cardiovascular reflexes that counter it, were described in chapter 11. It is worth recalling that when the heart or the brain stem's cardiovascular regulatory centers are damaged, the threat of a progressive and irreversible decline in blood pressure is high. In cases where trauma involves the kidney, its sodium and water retention capacity may be compromised. The resultant loss of ability to support plasma volume, and therefore blood pressure, may allow shock to develop more rapidly and severely.

An array of coping responses mediated by the endocrine system is a valuable resource in confronting severe trauma. The general adaptation syndrome (GAS) was described more fully in chapter 17. Essentially, it promotes widespread metabolic responses that provide increased supplies of cellular energy sources and the amino acids needed for healing. As part of the GAS, hepatic glycogenolysis and gluconeogenesis are both increased to produce a characteristic posttrauma hyperglycemia. The GAS also produces a period of weight loss following trauma, as body proteins are

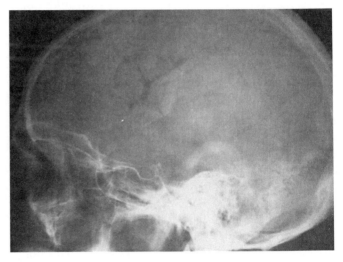

Figure 24.10 Depressed skull fracture. The fragments produced by a blow to the skull have been driven below the level of the cranial surface.

A 24-year-old male was drinking with friends in a hotel bar. He was pushed sideways in a scuffle, struck his temple on the corner of a metal chair, and briefly lost consciousness. Bleeding was minor but a lump rapidly developed at the site. En route to the hospital, his consciousness became clouded. This radiograph confirmed a depressed fracture of the skull. CT indicated an expanding extradural hematoma developing from laceration of the anterior meningeal artery. Immediate surgical evacuation of the hematoma and cauterization of the artery restored intracranial pressure and consciousness, with no neurological sequelae.

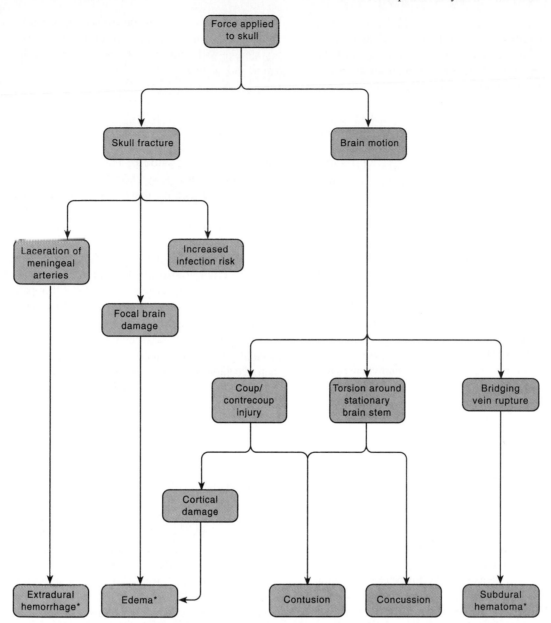

Figure 24.11   Elements of craniocerebral trauma. Asterisks indicate conditions involving increased cranial mass.

expended to sustain the elevated rates of gluconeogenesis. Subcutaneous adipose tissue is also reduced as fat is metabolized in many tissues as an alternative to glucose. A characteristic hyperlipidemia results. Protein and fat lost in this way are replaced after recovery.

PATTERNS OF REGIONAL TRAUMA

With basic concepts and terminology established, we can now turn to the principal body regions and give a more detailed treatment of their major patterns of trauma. In considering these, note that whereas the protection of the skeleton is an important factor in preventing injury, when mechanical forces are extreme, fragmented skeletal elements can themselves become injurious or even lethal.

Craniocerebral Trauma

Figure 24.11 illustrates the destructive mechanisms operating in head injury. The skull is struck by or strikes an object. Such direct trauma can fracture the skull, possibly lacerating meningeal arteries, which hemorrhage, or causing the brain tissue at the site to be contused or lacerated. The rapid linear or rotational acceleration of the skull can cause loss of consciousness and further vascular or neural damage. These effects are all considered **primary brain injury.** They can set the stage, singly or collectively, for a variety of delayed complications that can cause secondary brain injury. The one emphasized in the chart is the increase in brain mass that can develop from hemorrhage (hematoma) and cerebral edema. Other serious complications associated with craniocerebral trauma may be CSF leakage (with possible infection), locally introduced infection, the scarring of brain tissue, and the hypoxia due to vascular disruption. Together they can cause **secondary brain injury** such as local infarction and loss of function, epilepsy, diffuse encephalopathy, posttraumatic hydrocephalus, and psychiatric disorders. Thus a person may survive the primary injury only to succumb to the secondary complications.

In studying craniocerebral trauma, you should be aware that, despite the alarming nature of the material presented here, only about 20% of cases of craniocerebral trauma require referral to a neurologist.

Concussion

Concussion, the jarring of the brain or spinal cord, is a common though not inevitable accompaniment of craniocerebral trauma. It is characterized by the abrupt transfer of energy to the brain, producing an immediate, usually reversible paralysis of nervous function. The effects of concussion can range in severity from altered consciousness to deep coma but always involves a period of amnesia. Severe skull and brain trauma can occur without concussion if the force is delivered very rapidly and in such a focused way that the mass of brain tissue is not significantly moved. The classic documentation of this possibility goes back to 1868 in the case of Phineas Gage. He was engaged in tamping explosives with an iron rod when an accidental detonation drove the rod through his cheek, frontal lobe, and skull cap. He covered the wounds with his hands, got on a horse-drawn wagon, and was driven back to town, being fully capable of conversation. Conversely, concussion can occur with absolutely no evidence of brain trauma.

The mechanism of concussion is currently seen as torsional brain movement, focused at the juncture of the midbrain and subthalamic region, that disrupts the function of the reticular activating system of the brain stem (see chapter 22). The resulting amnesia is experienced as both retrograde (loss of memories extending back in time from the point of injury) and anterograde (impaired production of memories until some point after the injury). From the patient's perspective, loss of consciousness extends from the beginning of the retrograde memory loss to the end of the anterograde impairment. The length of this period of amnesia is the most reliable indicator of the extent of injury, with longer duration reflecting more severe injury.

In a concussive injury that results in coma, there is an immediate loss of consciousness and suppression of reflexes. The person falls to the ground and there is a transitory (seconds) arrest of breathing and fall in blood pressure. Immediate reflex testing would elicit a positive Babinski. The return to normal consciousness is gradual.

Reflexes return, as do responses to pain, simple commands and questions, and then conversation. Finally, normal memory storage will return and the person will recollect conversation and events.

Coup and Contrecoup Injuries

Even minor concussion demonstrates the principle of coup/contrecoup injury. If the impact causing the concussion is to the *right* side of the head, the greater deficit in function (even if very short-lived) will arise because of functional changes on the *left* side of the brain. Typical signs to look for are weakness in right hand grip (contralateral), perhaps slurring of speech and difficulty finding words (left localized), and the sensation of "pins and needles" on the right of the body. More severe injury, where there is actual contusion **16** (demonstrable bruising of particularly cortical tissue), will follow this pattern. Some contusion will be at the point of impact (coup) but more will tend to concentrate opposite the blow (contrecoup). The explanation for this phenomenon is that much of the force of the blow is transferred to the scalp and skull, which then accelerates brain tissue in its protective pool of CSF. At the end of its arc of movement, the motion of the brain is arrested against the cranial vault. The brain tissue then absorbs this compressive force and rebounds off the skull, setting up a second negative pressure that may do further damage (figure 24.4). These forces can produce edema, tiny petechial hemorrhages, laceration, and larger scale hemorrhage; if combined with rotational forces, they can also produce shearing of structures as large as the corpus callosum. In fact, in 20–30% of fatal head injuries, the skull remains completely intact. In circumstances where the moving head is suddenly stopped, for example in a car crash, the same explanation holds.

In this context, figure 24.12c presents the accumulated evidence of the brain areas that suffered contusion in a series of brain trauma cases, mostly motor vehicle accidents. The superimposed tracings show that the frontal and temporal poles received extensive injury (coup, presumably) as did the occipital pole (contrecoup). The medial frontal damage may be attributable to collision with the falx or crista gall.

Basal Skull Fracture

When picking up a watermelon, have you ever dropped it onto the table or floor? If this accident has happened you have probably observed the mechanics behind basal skull fracture. At the point of collision the skull experiences compressive forces that it is well designed to withstand. It is the opposite side of the skull (the equivalent of the split top of the watermelon) that is subjected to expansive forces, where the fracture occurs.

(a)   (b)

(c)

Figure 24.12   Mechanisms of brain injury. (*a,b*) Damage occurs from violent rotation of the brain, in which shearing forces cause injury to the centrally located corpus callosum. (*c*) Shading indicates the sites where contusions were found in a study of 40 brain trauma cases.

!! ***Babies, Boxers, and Brain Damage***

Because of combined torsional forces, coup/contrecoup injury, and the limited development of the falx and tentorium in young children, a baby or young child can receive sometimes fatal brain injuries when shaken violently. The child's head tends to swing more extensively than would an adult's because the neck is relatively weak.

At the other extreme of physical development, strong, healthy boxers can experience a variety of brain/brain stem injuries in response to repeated high-energy blows. Sometimes boxers are referred to specialists by the licensing commission or their doctors because of questionable neurological or CT scan findings. In a group of boxers who were studied using both CT and MRI, MRI proved better at imaging abnormalities, at least after 24 – 48 hours posttrauma. Findings included frontal lobe atrophy, small cysts in the cerebrum and brain stem, subtle changes in periventricular white matter, subdural hematomas, and evidence, in a retired 66-year-old boxer, of several areas of contusion or hemorrhage. MRI also ruled out some suspicious findings from CT. So babies, because of delicacy of structures, and boxers, because of the intensity and repetition of blows, are both at risk of brain damage.

Table 24.1   Effects and Evidence of Basal Skull Fracture

CSF Leaks	Complication	Characteristics of CSF	Other Signs
Basal skull fracture of the petrous portion of temporal bone can tear delicate membranes that line the bony labyrinth: CSF (with or without blood) may pass into the middle ear, where it is evident behind the eardrum. If the eardrum also perforates, CSF can leak out of ear canal (otorrhea). If dura in the vicinity of the cribriform plate (ethmoid bone) or the paranasal sinuses in the frontal or maxillary bones tears, CSF (and perhaps blood) can leak from nose or as postnasal drip (rhinorrhea).	Port of entry for microorganisms via ear, nose, paranasal sinuses, potential intracranial infection.	**"Halo sign"** (on dressing or bed linen). Blood is encircled with yellowish stain. **Fluid is watery,** versus viscous nasal mucous secretions. **Glucose content** (keto diastix). Mucous secretions do not contain glucose. If blood is mixed with the nasal discharge, presence of glucose is not confirmatory of CSF leak.	**Battle's sign.** A swollen hematoma over the mastoid process of the temporal bone (posterior and inferior to the ear), seen in cases of skull fracture. **Periorbital ecchymosis** (also called "raccoon eyes"). A hematoma surrounding (usually) both eyes, seen in cases of skull fracture affecting facial bones or base of skull; often associated with conjunctival hemorrhage.

In this way a blow to the forehead (like that produced by the head hitting the windshield) may cause a fracture of bones in the base of the skull somewhat distant from the impact. The strong bones of the skull can absorb the forces without fracturing and conduct the force of blows to the face or the back of the skull so that they are expressed at a distance. Table 24.1 provides some of the effects and evidence of basal skull fracture. The consequences of comminuted and depressed fractures and the need for routine X-rays were discussed in the section on bony protection in chapter 20.

Closed head injuries are fractures in which there is no breach of vascular and meningeal protection of the brain. The term **open head injuries** implies only that there has been some break in this protection, not that there are gaping wounds. Prophylactic antibiotic treatment is routine when an open head injury is suspected.

Hematomas

One of the consequences of craniocerebral trauma may be hemorrhage. The nature and location of hematomas were described in chapter 20. The **extradural hematoma** 17 is an extreme medical emergency because the usual source of blood is arterial (usually the middle meningeal) 18 and

therefore at great pressure (fig. 24.13). Treatment includes emergency evacuation of the hematoma and usually requires ligation of the torn artery. This can be done with no permanent disablement. Pathology can result from the increased intracranial pressure and herniation.

Subdural hematomas 19 can have a more varied presentation. The usual source is a ruptured bridging vein. These are carrying venous blood through the arachnoid to a venous sinus or from the dura through the arachnoid to join a vein traveling in the subarachnoid space (figs. 24.14, 24.15). Because of this "bridging," a subdural hematoma is often accompanied by a subarachnoid hemorrhage. An **acute subdural hematoma,** which often occurs bilaterally, evolves quite quickly (24–48 hours). This is slow compared to an extradural hemorrhage, which typically plunges the victim into a coma shortly after recovery from the original concussion. Routine instruction after any head injury thought to be serious enough to have possibly caused a hemorrhage, whether or not concussion occurred, is to have a friend stand by for the first 24 hours and waken the patient at least a few times during the night. This precaution is taken to monitor the possible evolution of an acute subdural bleed. The treatment is identical to that for extradural hematomas, as is the pathology of the expanding mass (see the sections on edema, increased intracranial

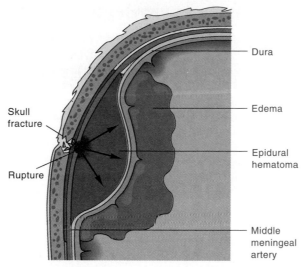

Figure 24.13   Extradural hematoma. Laceration of the middle meningeal artery by skull fragments has allowed arterial blood to separate the dura from the skull. The resulting pressure is expressed at various brain sites, producing local injury and distant herniation and hemorrhage.

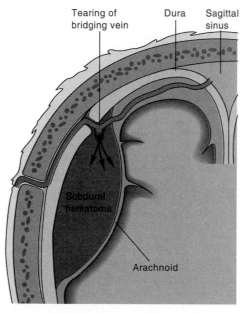

Figure 24.14   Subdural hematoma. Abrupt rotational forces or a blow to the skull can produce tearing of the bridging veins which cross from dura to arachnoid. The resulting bleeding produces a subdural hematoma and the threat of herniation.

pressure, and herniation syndromes in chapter 20). Even with appropriate care, both extradural and subdural hematomas are grave conditions.

Subacute subdural hematoma is the term applied to a slowly evolving (more than 48 hours, less than two weeks) subdural. Typically the person has experienced concussion but recovered normally. Then symptoms associated with a growing mass lesion gradually appear. Again, bilateral hematomas are common, and their surgical evacuation, with ligation as necessary, can restore normal function.

Figure 24.15   Subdural hematoma. The mass of coagulated blood is trapped within the meninges.
This subdural hematoma was confined within the meninges of an older woman. The compression of the brain that resulted caused left-sided paralysis which was misinterpreted as being due to a stroke. Because of her hemiplegia, she was confined for many years to a nursing home, where she died at age 86 of a severe attack of gastroenteritis, unrelated to her neurological dysfunction. At autopsy, no indications of infarction were found. Perhaps, then her last years might have been much different had the subdural bleeding not been allowed to become chronic. Regions of the hematoma appeared fresh, indicating that some further recent bleeding had occurred. It seems likely that some supposedly trivial trauma was initially responsible for the bleeding.

Blowout Fractures of the Orbit

Head trauma may be associated with injuries determined by the peculiarities of the orbits' structure. Although the orbit protects the eye on all but its anterior surface, its protective bony plates are quite thin. A direct blow to the eye, such as is increasingly common in squash and racketball, can generate very high orbital pressures. Such pressures can force the inferior orbital wall to fracture, driving orbital fat and parts of the inferior rectus and oblique muscles through it into the maxillary sinus below. In extreme cases, the entire eye has been forced into the maxilla. This injury is called a **blowout fracture of the orbit.** Even at such extremes, with prompt attention there is a high likelihood of completely restoring vision.

The prognosis is less favorable when a sharp object is driven superiorly through the orbit. Although thicker than the inferior wall, the superior wall is nevertheless quite thin and can be easily penetrated, allowing access to the brain.

The **chronic subdural hematoma** presents a diagnostic puzzle. This is usually found in older patients or debilitated people like chronic alcoholics. The initiating trauma may have been minor (the patient may not even recollect the head-banging incident). The development of a chronic subdural is more complex than that of the other subdurals described. A slow leak from a bridging vein produces a small hematoma that is then surrounded with a thin fibrous membrane produced by the surrounding connective tissue and the fibrin in the clot. Enzymatic activity within the clot breaks down larger molecules, thereby increasing the osmolarity of the solution and causing water to enter from the surrounding tissues (CSF and blood being adjacent). The water expands the hematoma, causing secondary trauma to bridging veins, causing further bleeding and expansion of the hematoma. This stepwise process can continue for months. Chronic subdural hematoma is often called the great imitator because the symptoms produced mimic epilepsy, stroke, demyelinating disease, etc. CT scan is often essential for diagnosis. Treatment involves craniotomy and evacuation of the hematoma. Because of its chronic evolution, permanent deficits are likely.

Acute Spinal Cord Trauma

Acute spinal cord trauma will affect the lives of approximately 10,000 North Americans in the coming year. These will have been the result of a variety of injuries: motor vehicle accidents, industrial and sports injuries, domestic accidents, military battle, and criminal assault.

Characteristics of the vertebral column protection and the agent of injury combine to produce different patterns of injury. The vertebral column is most vulnerable at its points of greatest natural mobility: at the first and second and fourth to sixth cervical vertebrae and at the eleventh thoracic to second lumbar vertebrae. The odontoid process (dens) is susceptible to fracture and displacement into the cord. Further, in the area of the cervical and lumbar enlargements there is less spare room in the dural canal to accommodate splinters from fractured vertebrae, the movement of dislocation, or vascular or edematous complications of injury. The velocity and force of the impact will be a factor. A sudden blow to the head may shatter C1 and the dens, whereas slower impact (a fall, whiplash injury) will tend to result in vertebral dislocation. Gunshots may drive bony fragments into the cord, or if near the cord itself, reduce it to a pulp. Extreme flexion/extension may cause diffuse contusion over a wide area, while a knife may sever cleanly. The nature of the activity is a further factor. For example, diving accidents commonly injure the cervical region of the cord. Industrial accidents commonly damage dorso-lumbar vertebrae. Figure 24.16 presents some of the common mechanisms of injury.

The care delivered immediately after the injury and in the weeks that follow is crucial. Effective emergency and acute care can limit the secondary injury that might otherwise occur. It is important to stabilize the vertebral column with minimal movement in the process, to limit further extension of the cord injury from dislocated vertebrae or bone splinters. Surgical intervention to remove bone fragments, clear a hematoma, or relieve compression may be necessary. Because of the cord's extreme susceptibility to edema and the secondary complications that edema can produce, aggressive control of inflammation, by means of corticosteroids, is routine.

Traction is commonly used to stabilize the vertebral column and avoid compression. With high cord lesions, which may be ultimately more disabling, the patient's vertebral column can engage in weight-bearing with the assistance of a halo brace much sooner than is the case with a trauma lower in the vertebral column. This is because the lower vertebrae must bear greater loads.

The characteristic response to trauma to the cord that results in a wide disruption of information flow, whether permanent or temporary, is a profound loss of cord function below the injury, called **spinal shock.** Not only are conscious movement and sensation lost, but reflex behaviors like deep tendon jerks and autonomic function (e.g., temperature regulation and vascular tone) are lost as well.

(a)

(b)

(c)

(d)

Figure 24.16   Mechanisms of spinal cord trauma. (*a*) Hyperextension of cervical spine causing central and intradural hemorrhage with edematous swelling of spinal cord above and below compression. (*b*) Crush fracture with fragmentation of vertebral body and projection of bone spicules into spinal canal. (*c*) Vertebral dislocation compromising the spinal canal. (*d*) Anterior dislocation of cervical vertebra with compression of spinal cord.

Spinal shock is apparently the response to a sudden cessation of descending motor/sensory input to the cord from the cortex and brain stem motor nuclei. The loss of the excitatory component of these descending inputs leaves inhibitory influences in the cord unopposed. It is not due to edema or other responses to the injury itself, and its extent is not predictive of eventual cord function. If the disruption was purely functional, movement, sensation, and reflex/autonomic function will return as spinal shock resolves, along with reversible conditions like inflammation and edema (within a few weeks for most people, much longer on occasion). Regular assessment of voluntary movement and the dermatomal distribution of sensation loss (see chapter 23) is an integral part of clinical care during this acute phase. The return of reflex behavior (i.e., resolution of spinal shock) *before* the return of sensation or voluntary movement is an indication of more extensive cord damage and less hopeful prognosis.

The most usual pattern of cord damage is diffuse, scattered injury, although very focal injury can occur. The nature of the permanent deficits depends on the location of areas of infarct. Localization of cord function was considered in chapter 21, as were the long-term changes that follow cord trauma.

Thoracic Trauma

Because the vital functions of the lungs and heart may be compromised by thoracic trauma, it is a major cause of trauma-related death in North America. It is frequently accompanied by some degree of spinal cord injury. This section describes the principal patterns of traumatic injury to the thoracic cage, lungs, and heart.

Whiplash Injury

A special case of a hyperextension injury is an acceleration stress to the neck, commonly called a **whiplash injury.** These typically arise when an automobile is struck from behind. The head is snapped posteriorly as the body is given an abrupt anterior acceleration. The head is then snapped forward in a recoil, which adds to the damage. Direct injury to the spinal cord is unusual in such accidents, although some brain injury may be involved. Most symptoms seem related to local spinal ligament damage, stretching of nerve roots, and stretching damage to anterior neck muscles and other throat structures. Headache, dizziness, and ear and eye disorders in whiplash injuries are thought to be caused by irritation of adjacent sympathetic ganglia or by altered cerebral blood flow through the affected neck.

Thoracic Cage Trauma

Most commonly, thoracic trauma produces rib fractures and raises the threat that jagged rib edges may tear through the soft underlying lungs and their richly supplied vasculature. Such injury is most likely to occur directly deep to the point of impact, as rib edges or fragments are forced into the pleura and lung. Less serious trauma may be resisted at the point of impact, with forces then transmitted to the weaker posterior ribs, where an outwardly directed break occurs. These are less likely to damage underlying structures.

Most often, the fifth through ninth ribs are fractured, probably because the more superior ribs are guarded by the shoulder girdle and the lower ribs are more heavily protected by muscle. For this reason, fractures of the upper ribs and the strong sternum are uncommon. When they do occur, they indicate greater impact forces and the potential for greater secondary soft tissue damage.

When several adjacent ribs are fractured, so that a section of the thoracic cage can move independently, the result is the condition of **flail chest,** which was described in chapter 13. Hypoxemia and hypercapnia can then arise because of hypoventilation of the lung underlying the detached wall section, the **flail segment.** Figure 24.17 illustrates the mechanism by which hypoventilation develops in flail chest.

Lung Trauma

Pneumothorax, whose pathophysiology was also described in chapter 13, commonly results because fractured rib surfaces cut through the pleura and lung and allow air to enter the pleural space. This condition is called a **closed**

Neck-Cracker Neuropathy

Voluntary and habitual "cracking" of the cervical spine can be annoying to those within hearing distance. The motivation for this activity is unclear, but participants relate a vague sense of discomfort in the neck that is relieved by forceful lateral flexion. We recently evaluated a patient whose case illustrates that such neck cracking may be injurious.

A 20-year-old college student recalled making an unusually vigorous cracking maneuver of forcing his neck to the left. He immediately experienced right-neck pain, which subsided over a week. A month later he noted winging of his scapula and limited abduction of the arm. Neurologic examination revealed depression of the right shoulder. The upper and middle fibers of the trapezius were weak and atrophic. Spinal accessory-nerve conduction studies and electromyographic examination confirmed a spinal accessory neuropathy. It seemed likely that the right spinal accessory nerve had been stretched by extreme neck flexion to the left.

Habitual neck crackers should be advised of the possible consequences.

A cautionary letter to the New England Journal of Medicine. K. R. Nelson, MD and P. Tibbs, MD.

pneumothorax, since the chest wall is not directly open to atmospheric air. Instead the air enters the pleural space through the lung airways and the lung's severed surface (fig. 12.32). Blunt trauma to the thoracic wall may also produce a closed pneumothorax when it induces abrupt pressure peaks that burst alveolar walls and the visceral pleura, providing air access to the pleural space.

An **open pneumothorax** exists when atmospheric air can directly enter the pleural space via an opening in the chest wall. If the defect that allows air entry remains open during both inspiration and expiration, the air flow through it may often be heard, hence the descriptive term **sucking chest wound.** If the defect is forced closed during expiration, a valvelike action is produced. That is, air can be drawn in to the pleural space but can't be exhaled. The result is a continually increasing pressure in one pleural cavity, which relentlessly forces the collapsed lung, heart, and other mediastinal structures into the opposite pleural cavity. This is the condition of **tension pneumothorax** (fig. 24.18). It is potentially lethal, in that its high pressures can collapse airways to restrict pulmonary air flow and collapse pulmonary vessels. Not only does this produce inadequate oxygenation of the blood, but vascular compression can severely limit venous return to the heart, thereby compromising cardiac output and posing the threat of circulatory shock.

(a)

(b)

Figure 24.17   The paradoxical motion of the flail segment (FS) in flail chest. (*a*) On inspiration, the lowered thoracic pressure draws the detached flail segment inward. (*b*) During expiration, higher pressures move the flail segment outward.

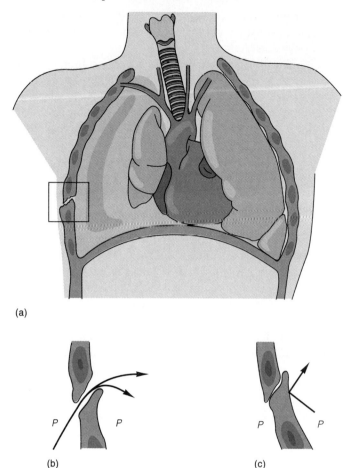

(a)

(b)   (c)

Figure 24.18   Tension pneumothorax. (*a*) Injury to thoracic wall allows air to enter pleural space and lung collapses. Trapped air causes displacement of thorax contents to the left. (*b*) On inhalation, pressure gradient draws air into thorax. (*c*) Checked valve action of wall defect on exhalation prevents relief of pressure.

Penetrating or blunt trauma to the thorax may produce contusions that are often of little clinical significance. Lacerations of the lung, however, may affect both airways and blood vessels, raising the possibility that blood will enter an airway, flow to its distal extremities, and interfere with respiration. Alternatively, blood may form a hematoma at the site of the injury. **20** If the laceration also involves the visceral pleura, blood may enter the pleural space to produce the condition of **hemothorax.**

Ruptures of the Diaphragm

Penetrating wounds or blunt trauma can rupture the diaphragm, disrupting its function of isolating the thoracic and abdominal cavities. If sufficiently large, the opening in the diaphragm can allow herniation of the spleen, stomach, or bowel into the thoracic cavity. The driving force for this displacement is the pressure gradient across the diaphragm between the higher-pressure abdomen and the lower-pressure thoracic cavity. Herniation usually involves the left portion of the diaphragm, since the liver is too large to herniate and it presents an obstacle to smaller organs on the right side of the abdomen.

Cardiac and Great Vessel Trauma

Automobile steering wheels present a threat to the anterior thoracic wall and the heart, which lies just deep to it. Particularly in those without a restraining seat belt, the heart is often subjected to blunt trauma in head-on automobile collisions. Contusions of the myocardium are a common result. They have the potential to cause cardiac dysrhythmias or reduced cardiac output due to a lowered stroke volume. As in myocardial infarction, a contused myocardium releases enzymes that may be of diagnostic value. Contusions may be severe enough to produce a ventricular aneurysm or complete myocardial rupture, but these are rare events.

Penetrating cardiac wounds are much more serious because they may lead to more severe damage and a rapidly progressive cardiogenic shock. If the myocardial defect allows ventricular pressures to force blood through it, the condition may be promptly fatal. In some cases, the torn pericardial sac may not allow blood to escape as rapidly as it fills. Cardiac tamponade follows, with trapped blood raising pericardial pressures and providing an external compression of the heart. This compression limits the heart's filling during diastole and can be fatal if it is not promptly treated.

In some cases, penetration of the heart may be achieved by a small bullet or bone fragment to cause only a minor myocardial wound. However, once within the heart, the object may lodge in a position that interferes with a valve's function, blocks a coronary vessel, or interferes with a component of the cardiac conduction system. In such cases, the immediate threat may be reduced, but only in exchange for the longer-term prospects of congestive heart failure.

Penetrating thoracic wounds that sever or lacerate the aorta or vena cavae are usually immediately fatal. Massive blood loss into the chest cavity is typical, or if the wound is at the base of the aorta, cardiac tamponade develops.

Nonpenetrating thoracic trauma commonly causes rupture of the aorta. Most often, high-speed automobile collisions are involved, but any source of high-impact forces to the thorax, such as falling from a height, airplane accidents, etc., can produce the same result. Most often the site of the aorta's rupture is in its arch, near the point where it is supported by the ligamentum arteriosum. (You may recall that this ligament is derived from the ductus arteriosus, which directly connects the pulmonary trunk to the aorta, bypassing the lungs in the fetal circulation; see chapter 10.) The ligament provides a line of support between the aorta and the base of the subclavian artery, and in so doing, seems to restrict the aorta's free motion (fig. 24.19). When an impact at the thoracic wall causes abrupt displacement of the aortic arch, the ligament's attachment point acts as a restraint to motion. When severe impact is involved, the aorta can tear near the point where the ligament is attached. **21** Surviving such an event is unlikely, as loss of pressure is pronounced and immediate. In some patients, survival may be prolonged if the inner wall layers tear but the tougher tunica adventitia remains intact. In these cases, the vessel may withstand the high aortic blood pressure long enough to allow therapeutic intervention, but without such intervention, complete rupture at some point is inevitable.

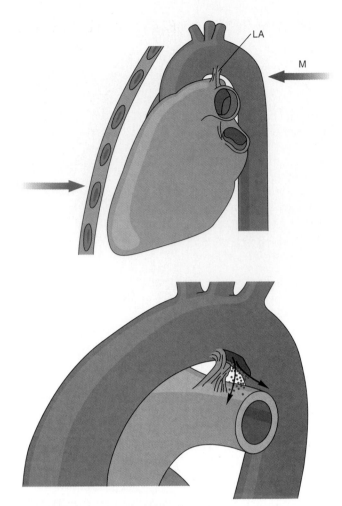

Figure 24.19   This lateral view of the thorax shows the ligamentum arteriosum (LA) fixing the aorta to the pulmonary artery. Below it, the aorta is free to tolerate displacement. Abrupt impact to the thorax (I) when the body is moving in the direction M can tear the vessel wall near the ligamentum arteriosum.

Abdominal Trauma

Nonpenetrating abdominal trauma can produce contusion, laceration, or rupture of the abdominal viscera. Factors affecting such injuries are the organ's structural resilience, whether it is hollow (and more likely to rupture) or solid, like the liver, and more likely to be lacerated. Also relevant is its position in the abdominal cavity with respect to overlying protective bones, i.e., the ribs, pelvis, and spinal column, although it should be noted that nonpenetrating trauma can damage an organ by crushing it against the vertebral column. Also, because of their size, fractured pelvic bone edges can produce large-scale tearing of the pelvic viscera where trauma is severe.

Seat Belt Trauma

Nonpenetrating trauma to the abdomen from improperly positioned automobile lap safety belts can cause contusions to the abdomen's wall and laceration and rupture of the intestine. Lap seat belts must be positioned so that restraining forces are spread over the iliac crests. When they are, the risk of abdominal trauma is very low.

Better protection against injury is provided by a three-point restraining system that supports with both lap and shoulder straps. Even when impact is high enough for the shoulder strap to cause rib fractures, such an outcome is far better than the results of ejection through the windshield onto pavement, and perhaps into the paths of other vehicles.

The spleen is particularly vulnerable **22** and is the most frequently damaged organ in cases of nonpenetrating abdominal trauma. Its rich vascular supply makes intra-abdominal hemorrhage and hypovolemic shock the major risks in splenic rupture. The large blood flow through the kidney and liver **23** make them similarly vulnerable.

In breaching the abdominal wall, penetrating wounds raise the threat of abdominal infection. In cases where a large wall defect allows abdominal organs to escape from the abdomen, an **evisceration,** the risk of infection is greatly increased.

The bowel, because of its length and its coiling within the cavity, can sustain multiple injuries from a single penetrating wound. When accompanied by damage to the high-volume abdominal blood vessels, such wounds present the risk of serious hemorrhage. As well, the spilling of bile, pancreatic or gastric juice, and intestinal contents onto peritoneal surfaces may cause widespread peritonitis and more extensive organ involvement.

Trauma in Athletics

Trauma in athletics can include any of the injuries described in the previous sections, such as when falls, racket injuries, ice skate blade severing injuries, etc., produce blunt or penetrating trauma to the head, chest, and abdomen. Most athletic injuries, however, affect the bones, ligaments, muscles, and tendons of the peripheral limbs when acute stresses overwhelm these structures.

The incidence of traumatic injuries in athletics is increasing because of the large numbers of individuals engaged in fitness or recreational activities who may not be

Overuse Syndromes

In athletics, it is helpful to distinguish acute traumatic injuries from the long-term, low-level injuries categorized as **overuse syndromes.** These typically produce inflammatory symptoms of pain and swelling, and most resolve with rest, which allows for healing to occur. In many cases, the risk of reinjury can be significantly reduced by adjusting training loads, improving technique, and supporting critical stress points. An example is **tennis elbow** or **lateral epicondylitis,** which involves inflammation of the region where forearm muscles join to the distal humerus near the elbow. This injury responds well if the forearm is supported with tape or elastic sleeving, but if playing technique is faulty, the condition may continue to interfere with play.

The variety of overuse disorders is indicated by the layman's terminology that describes them: handlebar palsy, tennis leg, bowler's thumb, runner's knee, golfer's elbow.

---

adequately trained or outfitted, or whose assessment of their abilities or capacities is unrealistic. Among those more skilled, advanced training and technical developments, together with the increasing height and weight of athletes, combine to produce greater risks of athletic trauma. For example, downhill skiing previously involved long, graceful, more horizontal arcs that took the skier to the bottom of a slope in a leisurely fashion. In recent years, much more aggressive skiing has become popular as a result of improvements in equipment and technique, which allow more abrupt and frequent turns in steep high-speed descents. These place much more stress on the legs and this pattern of skiing greatly increases the risks of knee injuries and bone fractures in falls. To add to the risk, higher-speed falls onto ski edges or ski pole points are likely to be more damaging.

Another example related to improved equipment can also be taken from downhill skiing. Previously, ski boots were worn to ankle height, where normal joint flexion could absorb shock. More recently, ski boot design has featured rigid, much taller boots, which, while supporting the ankle well, transmit stresses to higher, less yielding sites. As a result there has been a significant increase in fractures of the tibia at the level to which the rigid boot extends, the so-called **boot top fracture.**

The principal athletic injuries encountered can most conveniently be described on the basis of the structures involved.

---

22 |||| ||| | ||| | | ||| | || || || ||| |
        15769

23 |||| ||| | | ||| | ||| | || | ||| |
        15778

Bone Trauma

Essential patterns of bone fracture were considered earlier in this chapter. In this section, we will note only that particular athletic activities often produce typical patterns of injury as a result of their characteristic limb and joint loading.

A special case of the overuse syndrome is the **stress fracture,** sometimes known as a **fatigue fracture.** It most commonly arises in the tibia, femur, distal fibula, or the foot's second and third metatarsals as a result of repeated long-term application of stress. In such cases, the level of loading is insufficient to produce an acute fracture, but just exceeds the level that the bone can absorb without damage.

With a stress fracture, pain may arise during exercise, but is relieved during rest between activity sessions. Initially, X-rays may show no signs of damage, but later, callus formed in healing bone may verify the presence of the stress fracture.

Ligament and Joint Trauma

Ligaments are bands or sheets of dense, fibrous connective tissue whose collagen provides the high tensile strength needed to stabilize and strengthen joints. When impact or excessive joint stresses stretch or twist ligaments beyond their limits, they will tear. A **partial tear** leaves a portion of the ligament intact, usually enough to provide some degree of stability. In a **complete tear** or **rupture,** the ligament is completely separated and joint strength and stability are compromised. In cases where a pulling force is applied to a tendon or ligament, it may remain intact but pull off a section from bone at its attachment site. **24** This special case of a bone fracture is called an **avulsion fracture** (fig. 24.20).

Bleeding and sometimes bruising will accompany most ligament tears. When the damaged ligament lies within the joint capsule, e.g., the knee's cruciate ligaments, bleeding into the synovial fluid can delay healing. Restoration of a ruptured ligament may require surgery. More often, the tear is partial, and resting the joint can be expected to promote healing, although the process may take anywhere from six weeks to several months.

When forces applied to a joint are sufficient to displace the bone ends, the joint is said to be **dislocated.** A dislocation may be total—a **luxation,** where articular surfaces are no longer apposed, **25** —or it may be a **partial dislocation** or **subluxation.** In this case, the articular cartilages may be in partial contact but are usually misaligned. Some degree of ligament and joint capsule tearing always accompanies a

Figure 24.20   Avulsion fracture. The bone defect (arrow) was caused by an abrupt and forceful tension exerted by the attached tendon.

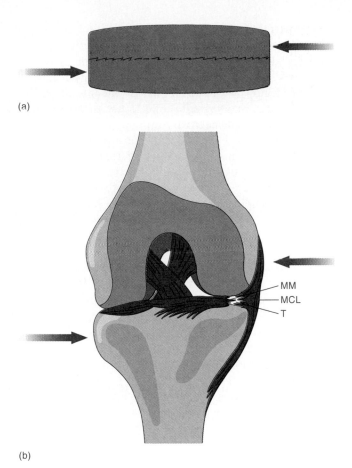

(a)

(b)

Figure 24.21   (*a*) Shear forces applied to a structure, with the jagged line representing the plane in which tears are likely to develop. (*b*) Shear forces applied to the knee can produce tears (T) in the medial meniscus (MM) because the medial collateral ligament (MCL) is firmly joined to it.

removal may be necessary. In such cases, knee loading may traumatize the articular cartilages and promote the development of degenerative joint disease (see chapter 18).

Tendon Trauma

The high tensile strength of tendon is adapted to its function of transmitting a muscle's contractile force to bone. Tendons are more susceptible to damage from shear forces and compression than to damage from tension, but abrupt or severe stretching can cause them to tear or completely rupture. Aging and disuse contribute to a tendon's loss of resiliency and strength, so those no longer young need to build tendon strength before applying the heavy loads of a new activity.

As with ligaments, a long healing time is required when tendon damage occurs, in particular because injuries often occur at poorly vascularized sites such as the insertion of the Achilles tendon on the calcaneus or the insertion of the supraspinatus muscle's tendon on the humerus.

Muscle Trauma

A muscle can suffer structural damage when it generates high intrinsic contractile loads or is excessively stretched. Such injuries are known as **distraction ruptures.** By contrast, **compression rupture** is trauma that results from a direct impact to the muscle, which often forces it against an underlying bone. In either type the rupture may be partial or complete.

Distraction ruptures typically result from abrupt loading beyond the muscle's resistance capacity. Actions that involve quick acceleration or deceleration can provide such overloading. Tearing the muscle will usually involve tearing blood vessels, as well, and bleeding into the area of damage is common (fig. 24.22*a*). In trauma to exercising muscle, bleeding is more severe because very high blood flow is required to meet the demands of vigorously active muscles. Bleeding is limited in trauma to resting muscle, e.g., in auto accidents, since blood flow rates are much lower. Scar tissue usually forms after the coagulated blood has been cleared because, when torn, the muscle's connective tissue architecture allows fiber ends to draw back from the wound site, making regeneration difficult.

In muscle compression ruptures, an underlying bone provides a rigid resistance that prevents dissipation of impact force. The impact can therefore cause deep contusions or hematomas in the muscle tissue adjacent to the bone (fig. 24.22*b*). Because compressive trauma leaves more of the muscle's connective tissue framework intact,

dislocation, but healing proceeds normally once the opposing bone ends have been **reduced,** i.e., maneuvered into their original articular relationships.

Twisting at the knee joint may impart shear forces to the lateral and medial meniscus. These are incomplete rings of fibrocartilage that promote joint stability. Shear involves the application of two forces at 180° to each other in the same plane (fig. 24.21*a*). In the knee joint, the result is a tearing apart of the meniscus, sometimes with fragments being freed to move about in the joint space. Because the medial collateral ligament of the knee is attached to the medial meniscus, tears in the ligament are often associated with tears in the meniscus (fig. 24.21*b*). Surgical removal of torn cartilage segments may be necessary to restore function. If damage to the menisci is severe, their complete

(a)

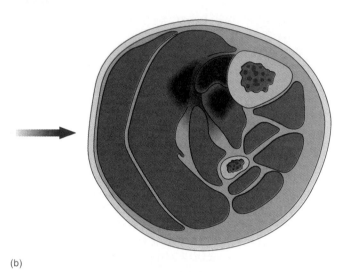

(b)

Figure 24.22 (*a*) Distraction rupture near tendinous muscle attachment with bleeding into torn area. (*b*) Transverse section through leg. Impact from left has driven muscle against bone to produce a deep compression rupture and hematoma.

there is more likelihood of muscle fiber regeneration, if bleeding is not too severe. Excessive bleeding between fiber ends that need to grow together can delay or prevent regeneration and may necessitate repair by fibrosis. After the injury, an appropriate program of rehabilitation can induce hypertrophy in the remaining tissue so that the muscle's original strength is restored.

BURN TRAUMA

The wound produced by thermal injury to the skin is called a burn. It arises when thermal energy is applied to the skin at a rate greater than that at which the energy can be dissipated. Several factors affect the skin's ability to absorb and dissipate thermal energy: its thickness (thin on eyelids and ventral forearms, thicker on soles and palms), blood supply, water content, the degree of pigmentation, and the presence of hair or extraneous surface matter, e.g., cosmetics, dirt, etc. Another factor is the time over which the energy is delivered. The same energy delivered to the skin over a

longer period produces less damage than if all must be dissipated in a brief interval. The combined effect of these variables determines the degree of skin damage.

Two systems of descriptive terminology are widely used in dealing with skin burns. In one system, a **first-degree burn** involves only mild injury to the epidermis without significant necrosis. Inflammatory vasodilation, swelling, and pain are present, but are usually limited. A typical sunburn is an example of first-degree burn. A **second-degree burn** involves destruction of the epidermis and part of the underlying dermis. Accumulating fluid between the epidermis and dermis may initially produce blisters, but subsequent loss of the necrotic epithelium exposes the deeper layers. In second-degree burns, intact sensory receptors can produce much pain as healing proceeds. However, residual hair follicles and other skin appendages provide sites from which newly formed epithelial cells can spread over the surface. **Third-degree burns** are most serious because they damage the epidermis, all of the dermis, and even some subcutaneous tissues. The lack of any functional remnants of the skin's follicles or glands as sources of epithelial regeneration usually means that skin grafting is needed to restore the surface.

The alternative system of burn classification ignores first-degree burns, since they heal readily without disruption of essential skin function. In this system, a skin burn that destroys the epidermis and some portion of the dermis is said to be a **partial-thickness burn** (essentially equivalent to a second-degree burn) while one that involves loss of all of the epidermis and dermis is said to be a **full-thickness burn** (essentially equivalent to a third-degree burn) (fig. 24.23).

In second- and third-degree burns, the surface regions are directly destroyed by heat effects that denature and coagulate protein, melt down lipids, and caramelize or "toast" carbohydrates. Adjacent regions may initially remain intact, but their energy absorption levels are high enough to damage heat-sensitive enzymes and they become necrotic after one or two days. Tissues beyond this region remain intact, and from them inflammatory and healing responses can develop.

There are three serious consequences of severe burns: shock, infection, and deformity. Hypovolemic shock can develop as a result of pronounced fluid loss from the circulating plasma. The inflammatory exudate that rapidly develops in response to burning is a major factor, but extensive necrosis also increases the osmotic pressure in the wound to draw water more rapidly from adjacent vessels. With loss of the skin's protective barrier, increased rate of evaporation contributes to fluid loss.

Infection is a second problem of burn wounds, also deriving from loss of the skin's barrier function and its antibacterial secretions. Exogenous organisms and those that normally colonize the skin and its appendages can both become established in a burn wound. Their proliferation is

Figure 24.23 Skin burn classification. A partial-thickness burn is essentially the same as a second-degree burn, while a full-thickness burn is the same as a third-degree burn.

particularly favored by the nutrient-rich exudate and tissue debris in the area of damage. Wound dressings also contribute by maintaining a warmer temperature within the exudate, which promotes bacterial growth. At the wound site, bacterial destruction of tissue can transform a partial-thickness burn to a full-thickness wound. A more serious consequence is **invasive burn wound sepsis,** in which bacteria enter the blood and are widely distributed. Secondary infection sites in the kidney, liver, and brain are responsible for the high mortality associated with invasive burn wound sepsis.

The third consequence often associated with burn trauma is the psychological and emotional impact of skin deformity and restricted mobility from extensive contracture. Even when surgical correction is possible, the prolonged period of healing that follows severe burns and the often multiple grafting and other restorative procedures can significantly delay ultimate resolution. Without continued psychological support, the loss of self-esteem in such cases can produce serious long-term psychological effects.

Although burns to the skin are most common, burns of the respiratory passages can occur when intensely heated air and combustion fumes are inhaled. The generally thinner respiratory epithelium is vulnerable, and burns at airway surfaces are usually more serious than skin burns. In such cases, apart from direct airway surface trauma, lung damage may be followed by large-scale fluid loss from pulmonary capillaries, raising the threat of adult respiratory distress syndrome (ARDS) and its potentially grave consequences. Pulmonary damage allows lung infections to arise, with bronchopneumonia offering yet another challenge to the already heavily burdened victim.

Case Study

Following a head-on motor vehicle accident in a rural area, three people were admitted to a small rural hospital. Two victims had immediately threatening injuries that demanded the attention of the limited staff. The other victim, a 45-year-old male, had been able to walk into the ER. A quick assessment showed that he had been wearing his seat belt and so was spared any facial or other head injury, although he did complain of chest pain on his right side and of difficulty in breathing.

On physical examination, there was pronounced local tenderness in his right thoracic wall, suggesting a possible rib fracture. His blood pressure was low, 100/50, but this and the patient's pallor were attributed to his localized chest pain and the emotional impact of the accident. He was left to rest quietly while the other victims' pressing needs were attended to.

When staff and the X-ray facilities became available, the patient was prepared for a chest X-ray. During these preparations, about 30 minutes after his arrival in the ER, it became evident that his dyspnea had worsened and that his trachea was deviated from the midline toward the left. Suspecting a tension pneumothorax, the doctor passed a needle through the right thoracic wall, expecting to release air trapped within the thoracic cavity. Instead, he obtained blood.

At this point the patient rapidly lost consciousness and collapsed. Resuscitation procedures were started immediately, IV lines were placed, ECG monitoring was established, blood volume expanders were administered, and a blood sample was sent for typing in the event that blood transfusions were necessary. The patient became increasingly pale and his skin cool and clammy.

His blood pressure was declining rapidly when the ECG indicated ventricular fibrillation and BP became undetectable. Vigorous resuscitation measures, including electrical defibrillation, were unsuccessful.

At autopsy, a rib fracture and lacerated internal mammary artery were found, in addition to a penetrating wound to the thoracic wall.

Commentary

It can be very difficult to cope when high demand arises without warning and facilities and personnel are limited. In this case, the staff had so much to do in so little time that they could not immediately and thoroughly assess the status of this patient and detect his hypovolemic shock. Only after someone noticed the trachea's deviation, indicating the likelihood of a tension pneumothorax, did the hemothorax and massive blood loss become evident. Unfortunately, by then it was too late to intervene successfully.

This is an example of the rapidity with which cardiovascular shock can produce grave consequences; recall that the patient had actually walked into the ER. The case also illustrates that in some circumstances very little can be done to interrupt a deteriorating condition and prevent a patient's death.

Key Concepts

1. Severe traumatic injury usually results from burns or mechanical injury, which typically produce wounds by disrupting organ surfaces (p. 631).

2. Wound production is influenced by the interplay of four variables: the amount of energy applied, the duration of impact, the surface area over which force is applied, and various factors related to the characteristics of the tissues involved (pp. 631–632).

3. Wounds are classified according to the surface features produced by the application of forces at body or organ surfaces (pp. 632–634).

4. An extensive terminology is employed to describe the various patterns of bone fractures that can result from motor vehicle accidents, falls, and many other sources of bone trauma (pp. 634–636).

5. Various systemic responses combine to maintain blood flow and metabolic support in the face of traumatic injury (pp. 636–637).

6. Craniocerebral trauma is particularly serious because the brain is especially delicate and is encased in a skull whose internal irregularities can damage the brain's surface (p. 637).

7. Torsion of the cerebrum around the brain stem may produce concussion, a reversible interruption of cerebral functions that is always accompanied by some degree of amnesia (p. 638).

8. Hematoma formation has varying effects, which are determined by the vessels involved, their relation to the meninges, and the time over which the bleeding occurs (p. 640).

9. Spinal cord trauma is closely linked to vertebral column trauma, because the cord is readily compressed in the narrow vertebral canal and because the column is vulnerable at its most mobile sections (pp. 642–643).

10. Trauma to the thoracic cage can disrupt respiratory movements or produce sharp bony edges capable of lacerating the lungs and heart (pp. 643–645).

11. The heart and great vessels are subject to traumatic injury that can produce contusions, dysrhythmias, or serious bleeding (pp. 645–646).

12. Nonpenetrating abdominal trauma may result in contusion, laceration, or rupture of the abdominal viscera, while penetrating wounds add the risk of infection (pp. 646–647).

13. Trauma is strongly associated with athletics, where forces are often focused at the peripheral limbs (pp. 647–650).

14. Thermal injuries to the skin result from the delivery of energy at rates faster than the skin can dissipate it, and are classified on the basis of the depth of skin damage (p. 650).

15. The most threatening sequelae of burns are related to fluid loss from burned surfaces and to infection, both aspects of the loss of the skin's barrier function (pp. 650–651).

REVIEW ACTIVITIES

1. Jot down the effects on wound production when a given force is applied: (a) over a shorter time, (b) over a larger area, (c) to an organ of lower resilience, (d) over a longer time, (e) to a highly resilient organ, (f) over a smaller area.

2. Think back to your youth and list the various traumatic injuries that were a part of your growing up. Assess each as to its type: laceration, contusion, burn, fracture, etc., and note any lingering effects.

3. Make two lists showing the consequences of different penetrating wounds to the same body region, one for effects caused by a sharp object, the other for effects caused by a bullet.

Photo Credits

Chapter 1

1.6b: Courtesy Kuang W. Jeon; **1.12a, 1.12b:** University of British Columbia, Department of Pathology; **1.21a–1:** © Larry Mulvehill/Photo Researchers, Inc.; **1.21a–2:** Courtesy Eastman Kodak;**1.21b–1:** © Larry Mulvehill/Photo Researchers, Inc.; **1.21b–2:** © Richard Anderson

Chapter 2

2.12: © Jean-Paul Revel; **2.19b:** University of British Columbia, Department of Pathology

Chapter 4

4.4: British Columbia Institute of Technology, Medical Laboratory Technology; **4.9:** Ken Kajiwara; **4.13a:** © Lester Bergman and Associates; **4.15:** University of British Columbia, Department of Pathology; **4.18:** University of British Columbia, Boyd Museum

Chapter 5

5.6b: © W. J. Johnson/Visuals Unlimited

Chapter 6

6.6: University of British Columbia, Department of Pathology; **6.7:** British Columbia Institute of Technology, Medical Laboratory Technology; **6.9, 6.11a:** British Columbia Institute of Technology, Medical Laboratory Technology; **6.11b, 6.12:** University of British Columbia, Department of Pathology; Box figs. **6.11–6.16, 6.24a, 6.24b:** University of British Columbia, Boyd Museum

Chapter 7

7.3b: © Manfred Kage/Peter Arnold, Inc.; **7.14:** University of British Columbia, Boyd Museum; **7.22a:** © Ed Reschke/Peter Arnold, Inc.; **7.22b, 7.23:** British Columbia Institute of Technology, Medical Laboratory Technology; **7.27a:** © Ed Reschke/Peter Arnold, Inc.; **7.27b:** © SIU/Peter Arnold, Inc.; **7.30:** British Columbia Institute of Technology, Medical Laboratory Technology

Chapter 8

8.1, 8.2: University of British Columbia, Boyd Museum; **8.8:** © Richard Anderson

Chapter 9

9.2: *Tissues and Organs: A Text-Atlas of Scanning Electron Microscopy,* by R. G. Kessel and R. H. Kardon. Copyright 1979 W. H. Freeman and Company; **9.4:** British Columbia Institute of Technology, Medical Laboratory Technology; **9.9, 9.10a, 9.10b, 9.11, 9.13:** University of British Columbia, Department of Pathology; **9.22:** British Columbia Institute of Technology, Medical Radiography Technology; **9.23:** University of British Columbia, Department of Pathology; **9.25:** University of British Columbia, Boyd Museum

Chapter 10

10.8: © WCB/Karl Rubin, Photographer; **10.9:** University of British Columbia, Department of Pathology; **10.12, 10.13, 10.14:** University of British Columbia, Boyd Museum; **10.16:** University of British Columbia, Boyd Museum; **10.26a, 10.26b:** British Columbia Institute of Technology, Medical Laboratory Technology; **10.37, 10.38a, 10.39a:** University of British Columbia, Boyd Museum

Chapter 12

12.16a, 12.16b: University of British Columbia, Department of Pathology; **12.17a, 12.17b:** University of British Columbia, Boyd Museum; **12.21a, 12.21b:** University of British Columbia, Department of Pathology; **12.28, 12.33:** University of British Columbia, Boyd Museum

Chapter 13

13.9: University of British Columbia, Department of Pathology; **13.10b, 13.11, 13.12, 13.17, 13.18, 13.21:** University of British Columbia, Boyd Museum

Chapter 14

14.11a, 14.11b: University of British Columbia, Department of Pathology; **14.12, 14.13:** University of British Columbia, Boyd Museum; **14.16:** University of British Columbia, Department of Pathology; **14.18, 14.19, 14.21:** University of British Columbia, Boyd Museum; **14.23, 14.24:** University of British Columbia, Boyd Museum

Chapter 15

15.7a, 15.7b, 15.7c, 15.7d: University of British Columbia, Department of Pathology; **15.14, 15.15, 15.18, 15.22:** University of British Columbia, Boyd Museum

Chapter 17

17.9b: © Martin Rotker; **17.10a, 17.10b, 17.10c, 17.10d:** University of British Columbia, Department of Pathology; **17.13, 17.14, 17.26:** © Lester Bergman & Associates; **17.29a, 17.29b, 17.29c, 17.29d:** Clinical Pathological Conference, "Acromegaly, Diabetes, Hypermetabolism, Proteinura and Heart Failure," *American Journal of Medicine,* 20 (1956): 133.

Chapter 18

18.1a, 18.1b: British Columbia Institute of Technology, Medical Radiography Technology; **18.4:** © Richard Anderson; **18.5:** University of British Columbia, Boyd Museum; **18.6a:** British Columbia Institute of Technology, Medical Radiography Technology; **18.6b–1, 18.6b–2:** Raisz, L. G., Dempster, D. W., et al, 1986. *J. Bone Miner Res* 1:15–21; **18.7:** © Biophoto Assoc./Photo Researchers, Inc.; **18.9:** British Columbia Institute of Technology, Medical Radiography Technology; **18.10:** University of British Columbia, Boyd Museum; **18.13a, 18.13b, 18.13c:** British Columbia Institute of Technology, Medical Radiography Technology; **18.15a:** © James Stevenson/SPL/Photo Researchers, Inc.;**18.15b:** © Richard Anderson; **18.16a, 18.16b:** British Columbia Institute of Technology, Medical Radiography Technology; **18.17:** University of British Columbia, Boyd Museum; **18.18:** © Biophoto Assoc./PhotoResearchers, Inc.

Chapter 19

19.2a: © BioPhoto Assoc./Photo Researchers, Inc.; **19.6,19.7a, 19.10, 19.11:** University of British Columbia, Boyd Museum; **19.13, 19.14:** University of British Columbia, Boyd Museum

Chapter 20

20.19, 20.21, 20.22b, 20.23a: University of British Columbia, Boyd Museum; **20.26:** © Biophoto Assoc./Photo Researchers, Inc.; **20.27b, 20.28, 20.31b, 20.31c–1, 20.31c–2, 20.32, 20.33, 20.34, 20.35, 20.36, 20.37:** University of British Columbia, Boyd Museum

Chapter 21

21.12b: © Per H. Kjeldsen; **21.14, 21.15:** University of British Columbia, Boyd Museum

Chapter 24

24.10: British Columbia Institute of Technology, Medical Radiography Technology; **24.15:** University of British Columbia, Boyd Museum; **24.20:** British Columbia Institute of Technology, Medical Radiography Technology

Index